COLLEGE BUILDING GUIDE

**College of Lake County
Main Building
1st Floor**
(over)

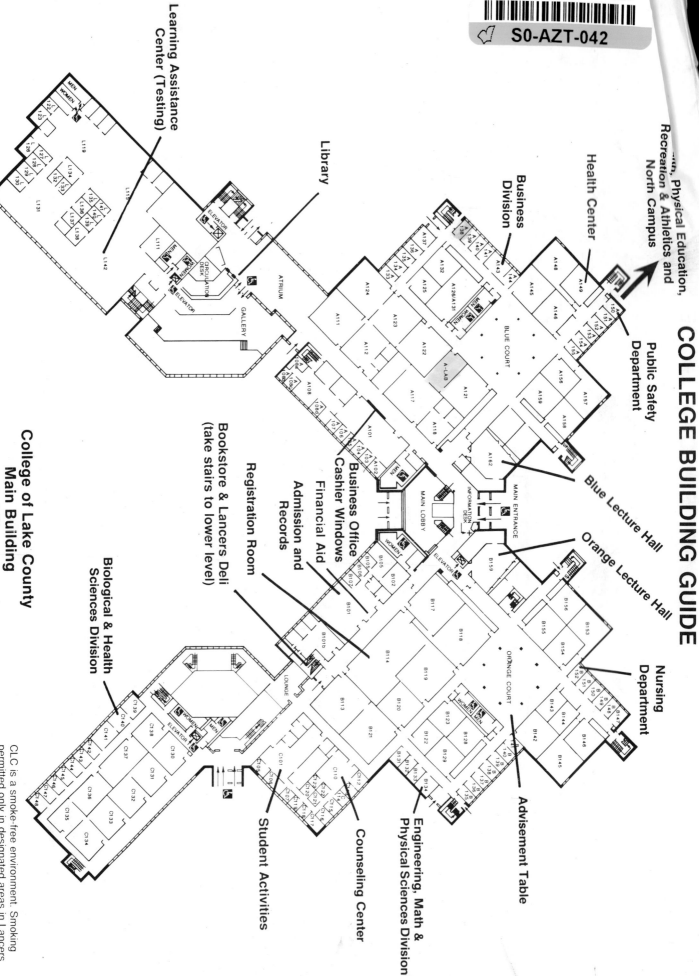

Recreation & Athletics and
North Campus

Health Center

Business
Division

Public Safety
Department

Blue Lecture Hall

Orange Lecture Hall

Nursing
Department

Advisement Table

Engineering, Math &
Physical Sciences Division

Counseling Center

Student Activities

Biological & Health
Sciences Division

Bookstore & Lancers Deli
(take stairs to lower level)

Registration Room

Business Office
Cashier Windows
Financial Aid
Admission and
Records

Library

Learning Assistance
Center (Testing)

CLC is a smoke-free environment. Smoking
permitted only in designated areas in Lancers
(lower level), Building One on north campus and
on the second floor as marked on the reverse of
this map.

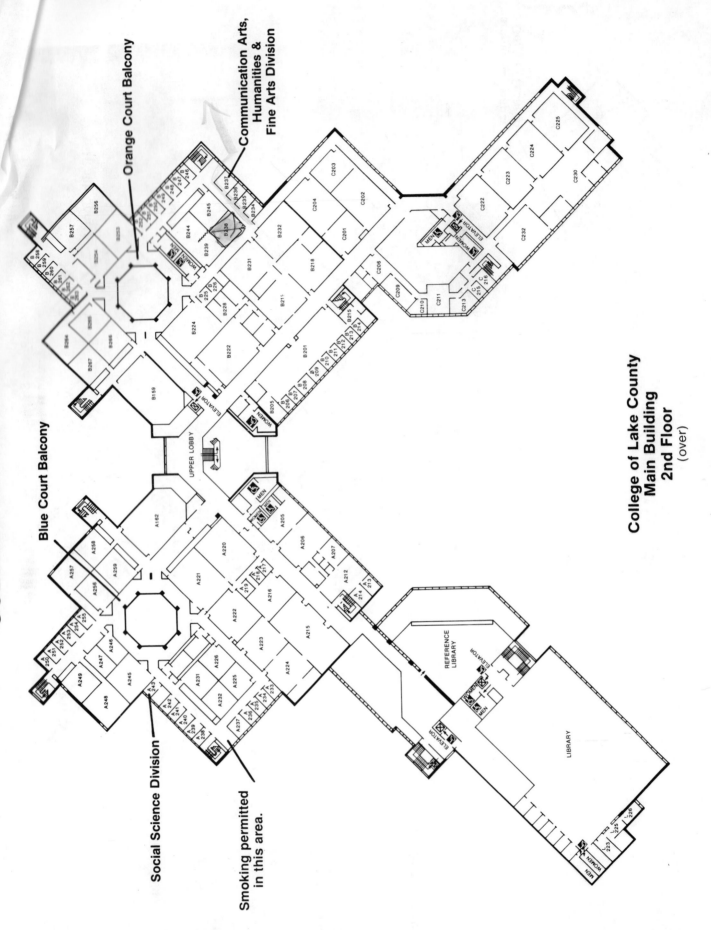

COLLEGE BUILDING GUIDE

Blue Court Balcony

Social Science Division

Smoking permitted in this area.

Orange Court Balcony

Communication Arts, Humanities & Fine Arts Division

UPPER LOBBY

ELEVATOR

ELEVATOR

ELEVATOR

WOMEN

MEN

REFERENCE LIBRARY

LIBRARY

College of Lake County
Main Building
2nd Floor
(over)

Comprehensive Structured COBOL

PWS-KENT Series in Computer Science

Comprehensive Structured COBOL

Third Edition

Gary S. Popkin, Ph.D.

New York City Technical College
of the City University of New York

PWS-KENT Publishing Company
Boston

PWS-KENT
Publishing Company

20 Park Plaza
Boston, Massachusetts 02116

PWS-KENT Publishing Company is a division of Wadsworth, Inc.

Library of Congress Cataloging-in-Publication Data

Popkin, Gary S.
  Comprehensive structured COBOL / Gary S. Popkin. — 3rd ed.
      p.   cm.
  Includes index.
  ISBN 0-534-91781-X
  1. COBOL (Computer program language) 2. Structured programming.
I. Title.
QA76.73.C25P668   1989   88-22563
005.13′3–dc19   CIP

Printed in the United States of America.
    90 91 92 93 — 10 9 8 7 6 5 4 3 2

Sponsoring Editor   J. Donald Childress, Jr.
Production Editor   Susan M. C. Caffey
Manufacturing Coordinator   Marcia A. Locke
Cover and Text Designer   Susan M. C. Caffey
Typesetter   Publication Services, Inc.
Printer and Binder   The Murray Printing Company

Cover photo courtesy of Michael Marks. Used with the permission of the artist.

Preface

COMPREHENSIVE STRUCTURED COBOL, Third Edition is a complete multi-purpose textbook. It can be used for a one-, two-, or three-term sequence in the COBOL programming language. The book is suitable for students with little or no knowledge of computer programming, as well as for those students who know one or more programming languages and wish to learn COBOL. Professional programmers who are working in a language other than COBOL and wish to learn COBOL will probably also find this book suitable.

The book starts with the most elementary material and covers all COBOL topics except the Communication Module (the CD entry and the RECEIVE and SEND verbs). Its modular design permits an instructor to teach only desired topics and to construct a course of any length. The treatment of very advanced topics is useful to advanced students and to programming professionals wishing just to study selected areas of the language or to use this volume for reference.

Comprehensive Structured COBOL, Third Edition provides well organized COBOL reference material for use during the course and later. Appendixes contain the complete reference summary of all elements of the 1974 ANSI standard COBOL language, a complete list of 1974 COBOL reserved words, and, new in the third edition, the complete reference summary of all elements of 1985 standard COBOL and a list of new reserved words added in the 1985 standard. The book also includes the 1974 ANSI COBOL glossary and the 1985 glossary.

Chapter 1 provides an elementary program and successive chapters introduce additional COBOL features of increasing logical complexity. Fifty-seven complete working COBOL programs are shown in facsimile, along with their inputs and outputs. Additional figures show the commands needed to create and use several different VSAM files. The figures in *Comprehensive Structured COBOL, Third Edition* constitute a valuable research tool, for they show what COBOL actually does in a variety of situations—not what the manual says it does, not what some author thinks it does, but what it does in actual performance.

Only those features needed for a particular program are discussed at each step, so that complications and details are postponed until needed. The programs comply with the highest level of the 1974 and 1985 ANSI COBOL standards and with IBM OS/VS COBOL and should therefore run on most compilers in use today. Where the ANSI standard and the IBM compiler are incompatible, as in a few minor instances in Report Writer, incompatibilities were resolved in favor of the compiler so that the programs shown in this book would run.

There is no discussion in this book of older COBOL systems that may not have all the capabilities of 1974 standard COBOL. Discussion of the 1985 standard is included where it provides some new feature that is likely to be of substantial importance when 1985 compilers come into widespread use. Formats shown in the body of the text are 1974 standard formats, for those are the formats students will be working with in real programs and real compilers for at least several years. If you are using a COBOL compiler that does not support the 1974 standard, you may find that some of the features used in some of the sample programs are not available to you. In such a case, you will have to develop alternative methods to code those features. For example, if your system does not allow the slash (/) as an editing character, you will have to modify some of the sample programs to avoid using it.

Program design techniques are used when suitable to particular programs. Flowcharts and hierarchy diagrams are used in appropriate circumstances, and pseudocode is discussed. The largest and most complicated programs use hierarchy diagrams to show the "big picture" in the most concise and practical way.

The book is organized into a Core part and a Modular part. In the Core, Chapters 1 through 6, all chapters must be covered in the order given in the book. In the Modular part—consisting of Chapters 7 through 19—any chapter may be covered at any time after its prerequisite chapters are covered. The chapters and their prerequisites follow.

Chapter	Prerequisite
7 Validity Checking	Chapters 1–5
8 Report Writer	Chapters 1–5
9 One-Dimensional Tables	Chapters 1–5
10 Two- and Three-Dimensional Tables	Chapter 9
11 Sorting and Merging	Chapters 1–5
12 Magnetic File Media	Chapter 11
13 Processing Sequential Master Files	Chapter 12
14 Indexed Files	Chapter 13
15 Relative Files	Chapter 13
16 Introduction to VSAM Processing	Chapter 12
17 String Processing	Chapters 1–5
18 Subprograms	Chapters 1–5
19 The Debugging Feature	Chapter 9

If your school has the facilities for doing so, I recommend that you cover Report Writer in sequence (after Chapter 7) and then use it in all subsequent chapters. Although the sample programs in Chapters 9–19 do not use Report Writer (in deference to those to whom it is not available), rewrites of five sample programs from those chapters, using Report Writer, appear in the Instructor's Manual accompanying this textbook.

The approach used to teach programming skills is practical and intuitive. Examples are used abundantly to illustrate every concept. Exercises are placed within the body of each chapter (except Chapter 16) to reinforce each topic where it is discussed. Each chapter contains a summary and fill-in exercises, and all but two of the chapters have review exercises that cover all the topics of the chapter.

Each chapter begins with a list of key points which the student should expect to learn from the chapter, followed by a list of key words contained in the chapter. At the first appearance of each key word in the body of the chapter, the word appears in boldface, where it is explained and used in context.

Appendix F of the book contains input data for selected programming exercises. An accompanying Instructor's Manual contains

1. Learning objectives for each chapter
2. Chapter highlights
3. Changes in the 1985 standard
4. Additional exercises for each chapter
5. Answers to all nonprogramming exercises and fill-in exercises
6. Solutions to the selected programming exercises
7. The output that is produced by the solutions when run with the data in Appendix F
8. Transparency masters for all the statement formats used in the book

9. Transparency masters for items 6 and 7 above
10. Sample examinations

I wish to thank the following people for providing many helpful suggestions: Robert J. Sandler of The Grand Union Company; Michael L. Trombetta of Queensborough Community College; and Louise Popkin.

I also wish to thank the following reviewers for their useful suggestions in the preparation of this edition and the previous editions: Charles W. Butler, *University of Arkansas*; Dennis Clarke, *Hillsborough Community College*; Bruce F. Crowley, *School of Computer Technology, Inc.*; William Eddins, *York College of Pennsylvania*; Bernadine Esposito, *University of Baltimore*; Arthur J. Geis, *College of Du Page*; Lawrence H. Gindler, *Southwest Texas State University*; Margaret Harrison, *State University of New York at Binghamton*; Joan E. Hoopes, *State University of New York at Binghamton*; Laurie E. MacDonald, *Bryant College*; Bahman Mirshab, *University of Detroit*; Malik M. Nazir, *Western Michigan University*; and Melanie Stopfer, *Dakota State College*.

COBOL is an industry language and is not the property of any company or group of companies, or of any organization or group of organizations.

No warranty, expressed or implied, is made by any contributor or by the CODASYL Programming Language Committee as to the accuracy and functioning of the programming system and language. Moreover, no responsibility is assumed by any contributor, or by the committee, in connection therewith.

The authors and copyright holders of the copyrighted material used herein

FLOW-MATIC (trademark of Sperry Rand Corporation), Programming for the UNIVAC® I and II, Data Automation Systems copyrighted 1958, 1959, by Sperry Rand Corporation; IBM commercial Translator Form No. F 28-8013, copyrighted 1959 by IBM; FACT, DSI 27A5260-2760, copyrighted 1960 by Minneapolis-Honeywell

have specifically authorized the use of this material in whole or in part, in the COBOL specifications. Such authorization extends to the reproduction and use of COBOL specifications in programming manuals or similar publications.

Gary S. Popkin

Contents

Comprehensive
Structured
COBOL

Computer Programming with COBOL

Here are the key points you should learn from this chapter:

1. The steps a person must follow to obtain useful results from a computer
2. What a computer program is, and what a programmer is
3. How to write an elementary program using COBOL
4. The complete format of the Identification Division

Key words to recognize and learn:

analysis	FILE-CONTROL
design	record
coding	FILE SECTION
COBOL	FD
program	file description
programmer	label record
memory	LABEL RECORDS ARE OMITTED
storage	level indicator
output	level number
input	record name
division	PICTURE
division header	reserved word
IDENTIFICATION DIVISION	user-defined word
ENVIRONMENT DIVISION	area A
DATA DIVISION	area B
PROCEDURE DIVISION	margin A
PROGRAM-ID	margin B
program name	paragraph name
section	OPEN
CONFIGURATION SECTION	statement
section header	MOVE
paragraph	WRITE
paragraph header	CLOSE
SOURCE-COMPUTER	STOP RUN
OBJECT-COMPUTER	format
compile	AUTHOR
INPUT-OUTPUT SECTION	comment-entry
file	DATE-COMPILED

A computer, by itself, cannot solve a problem or do anything useful. People can solve problems, using computers as tools. A person must do the following to obtain useful results from a computer:

1. Understand the problem to be solved. Only certain kinds of problems lend themselves to solution by computer. As we go through this book you will see what some of those problems are. A person must understand a problem thoroughly if a computer is to be used in its solution. This step is called **analysis** of the problem.

2. Plan how the computer can help to solve the problem. Since computers can do only certain things and not others, it is up to the human problem-solver to figure out exactly what the computer must do to contribute to the solution of the problem. This is called **designing** a solution. In this book you will study three design techniques now being used by computer professionals in industry.

3. Write instructions on a piece of paper, in a language the computer understands, that tell the computer what to do. This step is called **coding.**

    There are many languages in existence today that can be used to tell computers what to do. The language that you will study in this book is called **COBOL** (rhymes with snowball). COBOL stands for COmmon Business-Oriented Language. It is called common because the original designers of the COBOL language in 1959 envisioned a COBOL that all computers could understand. Since the 1960s, the growth of COBOL has been overseen by representatives of commerce, industry, education, and government acting through the American National Standards Institute, Inc. (ANSI) and publishing ANSI standards for the COBOL language. Three COBOL standards have been published, in 1968, 1974, and 1985. We will use 1974 standard COBOL in this book to the extent possible, because COBOL systems adhering to the 1985 standard are not yet widely available. You should write all of your programs in standard COBOL when possible, using the latest system available to you.

    Any complete set of instructions that a computer uses in solving a particular problem is called a **program.** The person who prepares the program is called a **programmer.** In this book there will be many opportunities for you to create programs. When you have completed all the exercises, you will be a COBOL programmer.

4. Get the program into the computer and have the computer carry out your instructions. The program must be placed into the computer's **memory,** or **storage,** to be executed. Then you wait while the computer does exactly what you told it to do.

In real life, errors can get into this process in any of the four steps. Errors in any of the steps will cause the programmer to have to redo some of the work. Depending on the severity of the error and the step where it occurs, more or less reworking may be required.

Some errors are so easy to find that even the computer can do it. In step 4, if you make some purely mechanical error in physically getting the program into the computer, the computer usually will object in one way or another and the error can be fixed in minutes. Or in step 3, if you write an instruction that does not follow COBOL's rules of grammar, the computer will point out the error to be corrected.

In most of the programs in this book, the computer presents the results of its processing by printing its **output** onto paper. You have probably seen computer-printed output. Most computers can print their output results onto continuous-form, fan-fold paper—the kind with sprocket holes along both sides.

However, computers can present their output in ways other than by printing. You have probably seen results come out of computers onto screens that look a lot like television screens. And computers can present their output in still other ways; in Chapters 12 through 16 we will study several COBOL programs that deal with some of the ways.

We also must have some way of getting programs and data into computer storage. We already know that a program, once written, must be put into the computer to be executed. One common way to get a program into a computer is to enter the program on a keyboard. An example of a COBOL instruction as it might appear on a screen is as follows:

```
SUBTRACT 40 FROM HOURS-WORKED GIVING OVERTIME-HOURS.
```

Another method of getting programs into storage is to punch the program into cards and have the computer read the cards.

You will study other **input** methods in Chapters 12 through 16.

A First COBOL Program

To lend concreteness to the ideas discussed so far, we will now do a complete working COBOL program. The techniques required will be presented without unnecessary details. In this program, and with all programs in this book, only as much detail will be presented as is needed at that stage to write the particular program being discussed. If some of the material seems incomplete at any time, just wait and it will be filled out later.

Let us now set to work on Program P01-01, which is a program that does nothing but print out the author's name and (fictitious) address. Figure 1.1 shows the output as it was produced by the program.

Figure 1.1 Output from Program P01-01.

```
G. S. POPKIN
1921 PRESIDENT ST.
BROOKLYN, NY  11221
```

The design for this program was done by the author and will not be shown here. We will save discussion of program design for more complicated programs.

Here is what the first few lines of Program P01-01 look like as they might appear on a screen:

```
00010   IDENTIFICATION DIVISION.
00020   PROGRAM-ID.  P01-01.
00030
00040 *  THIS PROGRAM PRINTS THE AUTHOR'S NAME AND
00050 *    (FICTITIOUS) ADDRESS, ON THREE LINES.   ZIP CODE IS
```

Each line contains a sequence number in character positions 1 through 5 on the screen. The sequence numbers are in intervals of 10 to allow for later insertions if necessary. Character position 6 can be used for sequence numbers also. Program P01-01 complete is shown in Figure 1.2.

Figure 1.2 Program P01-01.

```
CB1 RELEASE 2.4                                IBM OS/VS COBOL  JULY  1, 1982


                    22.04.38       MAR 27,1988


00010  IDENTIFICATION DIVISION.
00020  PROGRAM-ID.  P01-01.
00030
00040 *  THIS PROGRAM PRINTS THE AUTHOR'S NAME AND
00050 *    (FICTITIOUS) ADDRESS, ON THREE LINES.  ZIP CODE IS
00060 *    INCLUDED IN THE ADDRESS.
00070 *
00080 ****************************************************************************
```

(continued)

Figure 1.2 (continued)

```
00090
00100    ENVIRONMENT DIVISION.
00110    CONFIGURATION SECTION.
00120    SOURCE-COMPUTER.  IBM-370.
00130    OBJECT-COMPUTER.  IBM-370.
00140
00150    INPUT-OUTPUT SECTION.
00160    FILE-CONTROL.
00170        SELECT COMPLETE-ADDRESS ASSIGN TO PRINTER.
00180
00190    ***********************************************************
00200
00210    DATA DIVISION.
00220    FILE SECTION.
00230    FD  COMPLETE-ADDRESS
00240        LABEL RECORDS ARE OMITTED.
00250
00260    01  ADDRESS-LINE         PICTURE X(120).
00270
00280    ***********************************************************
00290
00300    PROCEDURE DIVISION.
00310    EXECUTABLE-PROGRAM-STEPS.
00320        OPEN OUTPUT COMPLETE-ADDRESS.
00330        MOVE "G. S. POPKIN"         TO ADDRESS-LINE.
00340        WRITE ADDRESS-LINE.
00350        MOVE "1921 PRESIDENT ST."  TO ADDRESS-LINE.
00360        WRITE ADDRESS-LINE.
00370        MOVE "BROOKLYN, NY  11221" TO ADDRESS-LINE.
00380        WRITE ADDRESS-LINE.
00390        CLOSE COMPLETE-ADDRESS.
00400        STOP RUN.
```

Program P01-01 consists of four **divisions,** as do all standard COBOL programs. Each division is identified by a **division header.** In the program shown each division header starts in position 8 but could have begun anywhere between positions 8 and 11. The four division headers are **IDENTIFICATION DIVISION** at line 00010, **ENVIRONMENT DIVISION** at line 00100, **DATA DIVISION** at line 00210, and **PROCEDURE DIVISION** at line 00300. You must use the exact spelling and punctuation shown for the four division headers.

In COBOL a dot (.) followed by a space is taken to be a period. A dot followed by anything else is taken to be a decimal point.

The Identification Division

The Identification Division is used to give the program a name and provide other descriptive information about the program. The **PROGRAM-ID** entry, at line 00020, is required and must include a **program name** made up by the programmer. In this program the made-up program name is P01-01. The rules for making up program names are given later in this chapter.

Following the PROGRAM-ID is a brief description of the program, in lines 00040 through 00060. Each line of description has an asterisk in position 7, identifying the line as descriptive comment.

PROGRAM-ID is the only required entry in the Identification Division. There are other, optional, entries. The complete form of the Identification Division is given later in this chapter.

The Environment Division

The Environment Division serves a number of purposes in COBOL. In this program the entries shown are used to indicate what kind of computer this program is being run on and that the output produced by the program is to be printed on the high-speed printer.

The Environment Division has one required **section** and one optional section. The required section is the **CONFIGURATION SECTION,** identified by the **section header** at line 00110. The Configuration Section must contain the two **paragraphs** shown at lines 00120 and 00130. The **paragraph headers SOURCE-COMPUTER** and **OBJECT-COMPUTER** are required. The SOURCE-COMPUTER paragraph specifies the computer on which the program is being **compiled,** or translated into machine language. The OBJECT-COMPUTER paragraph specifies the computer on which the translated program is to be executed. All the programs in this book were compiled using an IBM COBOL system. Your instructor will give you the exact entries you need for the Configuration Section in your programs.

The optional section in the Environment Division is the **INPUT-OUTPUT SECTION.** It is needed only if a program uses one or more **files,** as Program P01-01 does. It is identified by the section header at line 00150, and contains the required **FILE-CONTROL** paragraph, at line 00160.

It is in the Environment Division that the programmer must make up a name for every file used by the program. In Program P01-01 the output is to be three lines of name and address. Each line of printed output is considered to be one **record.** The complete printed output is a file, and its made-up name is COMPLETE-ADDRESS. The rules for making up file names are given later in this chapter.

Your instructor will give you the exact form of the Input-Output Section entries necessary for your particular computer. Later chapters contain further discussion of the Environment Division.

The Data Division

The Data Division also can be used for a number of purposes. In this program it is used to describe some details about the output to be printed. In the **FILE SECTION** of the Data Division we describe the output record and the output file. The section header for the File Section must appear exactly as shown at line 00220.

The letters **FD** stand for **file description.** There must be one FD entry for every file being used by a program. In this program there is only one file, so we need only one FD, at line 00230. The required letters FD must begin between positions 8 and 11 and be followed by the file name made up in the Environment Division. The file name and all other portions of the FD entry must begin in position 12 or to the right of position 12. In this program they begin in position 12. Each COBOL system has some rightmost position beyond which no statement may be written. In the system used to run the programs in this book, the rightmost position is position 72.

Since the file used in this program is a printer file, it contains no **label records.** Label records are special records discussed in Chapter 12. They are never present in printer files, files keyed at a terminal, or punched-card files. One correct way to indicate that label records are not present in a file is to include the clause **LABEL RECORDS ARE OMITTED** as part of the FD entry. Other ways will be shown later.

There must be only one period at the end of the entire FD entry. In this program the FD entry occupies two lines, but it could have been written on one line instead. It was written this way to make it easier to read.

FD is one of several **level indicators** in COBOL. Later in this book we will use two other level indicators.

The 01 at line 00260 indicates that we are now describing some characteristics of a single record of the output file. The 01 **level number** in position 8 must be followed by a record name made up by the programmer. Here the **record name** is ADDRESS-LINE. Rules for making up record names are given later in this chapter. The **PICTURE** clause shown tells the computer that the line of print may contain up to 120 characters. There must be at least one space between the record name and the word PICTURE, and there may be as many as you like. If your computer has a larger printer, such as a 132-character printer, you may use a larger number in the parentheses. Your instructor will give you the information you need for this.

Before going on to the next division, we can make some generalizations on the basis of what we have seen so far. First, in COBOL there are certain words that must be used exactly as given, and some that must be made up by the programmer. Those that must be used as given are called **reserved words,** and those made up by the programmer are called **user-defined words.** A reserved word must never be used where a user-defined word is required. Lists of COBOL reserved words are given in Appendices A and B.

Also, some entries must begin in positions 8 through 11, and some must begin in position 12 or beyond. The area in positions 8 through 11 is called **area A,** and that starting in position 12 is called **area B.** Figure 1.3 shows the four areas of a line in which a COBOL statement can be written. Areas A and B are sometimes incorrectly called **margin A** and **margin B.** Margins A and B are different from areas A and B. We will not refer to the margins any further in this book.

Area A is the place to begin division headers, section headers, paragraph headers, level indicators, 01 level numbers, and, as you will soon see, **paragraph names.** Later in this book you will see two other elements of COBOL that start in area A, and one that can begin in area A or area B. Everything else begins in area B. Lines that are entirely blank (except for their sequence numbers) and lines that contain an asterisk in position 7 may be included freely anywhere in the program to improve its appearance and readability.

Figure 1.3 Reference format for a line of COBOL coding.

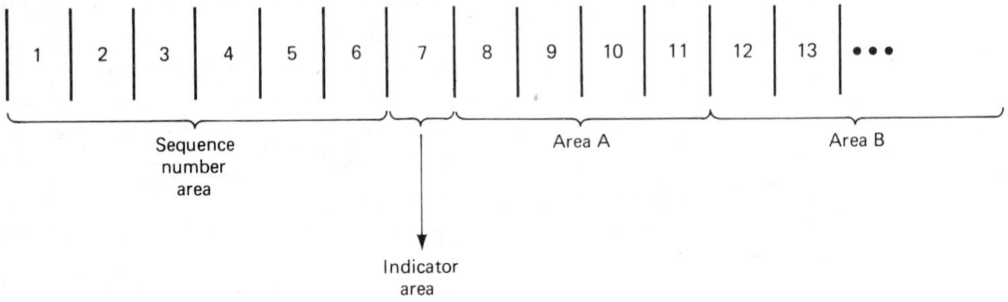

The Procedure Division

We come finally to the Procedure Division, which consists of the step-by-step procedure that the computer must follow to produce the desired output. The division header for the Procedure Division must begin in area A. There then must follow a paragraph name made up by the programmer. Whereas paragraph headers, in the Identification and Environment Divisions, must be written exactly as given, paragraph names, in the Procedure Division, must be made up. Here we have the made-up paragraph name EXECUTABLE-PROGRAM-STEPS, at line 00310. Of course it begins in area A. Rules for making up paragraph names are given later in the chapter.

We then have an instruction to **OPEN** the output file, at line 00320. All files must be OPENed before being used for an input or output operation, and the OPEN **statement** must say whether the file is going to be used for input or output or both. In our case the file will be used only for output to be printed upon. There then follow pairs of **MOVE** and **WRITE** statements, at lines 00330 through 00380. Each pair of statements causes a single line of output to be printed. There may be as many spaces as you like between words in COBOL statements. In COBOL multiple spaces are treated as one space, except when they appear inside quotation marks.

Following the instructions to print all three lines of output, we **CLOSE** the file, at line 00390. In standard COBOL all files must be CLOSEd when you are finished using them. The **STOP RUN** statement, line 00400, is the last executable statement in a program. Execution of the STOP RUN statement signals the computer to go on to its next job.

There are two important things to notice about this Procedure Division. First, in the OPEN and CLOSE statements we use the name of the file as we made it up in the Environment Division. The name of the file in the OPEN and CLOSE statements must be spelled exactly as it was made up. The computer does not understand English, and if even one letter is wrong in spelling the file name, the computer will not understand what we mean. So when you make up user-defined words, make them whatever you like (within the rules) and then use them exactly as you made them up.

Second, MOVE and WRITE statements use the record name that was made up in the Data Division. These usages are required by the rules of COBOL; that is, OPEN and CLOSE statements use file names, and MOVE and WRITE statements use record names. All these rules may be a bit confusing now, but as you begin to write programs they will become automatic and even reasonable.

Rules for Making Up Names

User-defined names in COBOL

1. Must contain between 1 and 30 characters
2. May contain any of the letters A through Z
3. May contain any of the digits 0 through 9
4. May contain one or more hyphens
5. Must not begin or end with a hyphen

File names and record names must contain at least one letter. Paragraph names need not contain a letter, and so may consist entirely of digits, or of digits and hyphens.

The ANSI standard directs that program names be made up according to the rules that apply to file names and record names. But each COBOL system has its own requirements for program names, which may or may not comply with the standard. Check with your instructor for the rules that apply to your system.

EXERCISE 1

Which of the following are valid as paragraph names, which are valid as file names and record names as well, and which are just invalid?

a. PROG-01
b. PROGRAM-ONE
c. PROG ONE
d. 001-050
e. 001-A50
f. -001A50

EXERCISE 2

Write and execute a COBOL program to print your own name and address. Your output file may be three or more lines as needed. Make up new user-defined words for the program name, the file name, the record name, and the paragraph name.

The Complete Identification Division

The **format** of the Identification Division is shown below. In any COBOL format words in capital letters are reserved words; items in lowercase are to be supplied by the programmer. Square brackets ([ ]) around an item indicate that it is optional. An ellipsis (...) following an item indicates that the item may be repeated as many times as desired.

```
IDENTIFICATION DIVISION.
PROGRAM-ID. program-name.
[AUTHOR. [comment-entry] ... ]
[INSTALLATION. [comment-entry] ... ]
[DATE-WRITTEN. [comment-entry] ... ]
[DATE-COMPILED. [comment-entry] ... ]
[SECURITY. [comment-entry] ... ]
```

The format shows that the division header and the PROGRAM-ID entry are required. The square brackets around the other entries show them to be optional. For example, the **AUTHOR** entry is optional. If you choose to include it in your program, you must write just the paragraph header AUTHOR starting in area A exactly as shown. Do not include the square brackets in the program. You then optionally follow the word AUTHOR with as many repetitions of **comment-entry** as you like, all in area B. A comment-entry consists of anything you would like to write, and is ignored by the COBOL system.

If you include the **DATE-COMPILED** entry in your program, when you submit your program for a run COBOL replaces any comment-entry you may have written with the current date.

All formats shown in the body of this textbook are from the 1974 standard. Appendix C contains formats of all elements of the COBOL language as specified in the 1974 standard; Appendix D has formats of all elements of the COBOL language from the 1985 standard.

Summary

Before a programmer can write a computer program, the problem to be solved must be completely understood. Then the programmer must plan how the computer can be used in the solution. The instructions that make up the program can be written first on a piece of paper. Then the instructions may be transferred to computer storage by being keyed on a terminal or by means of punched cards.

COBOL stands for COmmon Business-Oriented Language. Standard COBOL programs always consist of four divisions. The Identification Division can be used to give the program a name and to provide other identifying and/or descriptive information. The Configuration Section of the Environment Division describes the computer that the program is being run on. The Input-Output Section of the Environment Division relates input and output file names to the computer's input and output devices. The Data Division describes all the details of the files and records used by the program. The Procedure Division contains the steps the computer must execute to solve the given problem.

Files must be OPENed before being used for input or output, and CLOSEd after the last input or output operation on them. A WRITE statement may be used to place a record on an output file.

Area A is the region from position 8 through position 11. Area B starts in position 12. Division headers, section headers, paragraph headers, paragraph names, level indicators, and 01 level numbers must begin in area A.

Fill-in Exercises

1. The word COBOL stands for _____ _____ _____ _____ .

2. The set of instructions that a computer follows is called a(n) _____ .

3. The person who makes up the computer's instructions is called a(n) _____ .

4. The printed results of executing a program are called the program's _____ .

5. The four divisions of every standard COBOL program are the _____ Division, the _____ Division, the _____ Division, and the _____ Division.

6. The PROGRAM-ID entry is part of the _____ Division.

7. The FD entry is part of the _____ Division.

8. An OPEN statement would be found in the _____ Division.

9. The _____ and _____ statements have file names as their objects.

10. The level number used for defining a record name in the File Section is _____ .

11. The only required entry in the Identification Division is the _____ entry.

12. The required section in the Environment Division is the _____ Section.

13. The optional section in the Environment Division is the _____ Section.

14. In a COBOL format words in capital letters are _____ words.

15. In a COBOL format square brackets indicate that the item is _____ .

16. In a COBOL format an ellipsis indicates that the preceding item may be _____ .

Project

Obtain a copy of the COBOL manual for the compiler you will be using in this course. Find your compiler's reserved words. Make a list of all reserved words in your compiler that are not reserved words in the ANSI standard. Title your list "Additional reserved words in my COBOL compiler" and tape it onto the end of Appendix A.

Programs Using Input, Output, and Reformatting

Here are the key points you should learn from this chapter:

1. How to use the COBOL Coding Form
2. How to use a print chart
3. The rules of COBOL for reading input files
4. The general program structure for reading a variable number of input records
5. How to program column headings in COBOL
6. The format of the Environment Division

Key words to recognize and learn:

COBOL Coding Form	PERFORM
RECORD CONTAINS	UNTIL
field	EQUAL TO
data name	priming READ
FILLER	condition
READ	AFTER ADVANCING
AT END	SPACES
end-of-file	print chart
sending field	body line
source field	detail line
literal	FROM
nonnumeric	procedure name
numeric	SPECIAL-NAMES
assign	mnemonic name
WORKING-STORAGE SECTION	I-O-CONTROL
initialize	key word
VALUE	implementor name
PIC	

In this chapter we will write four programs which show more of the basic techniques of data handling. But first we will look at the **COBOL Coding Form.**

COBOL Coding Form

The COBOL Coding Form is helpful to a programmer writing COBOL programs. The forms are available in pads of about 50 at most college bookstores and wherever computer programming supplies are sold. Figure 2.1 shows a COBOL Coding Form.

Figure 2.1 A COBOL Coding Form.

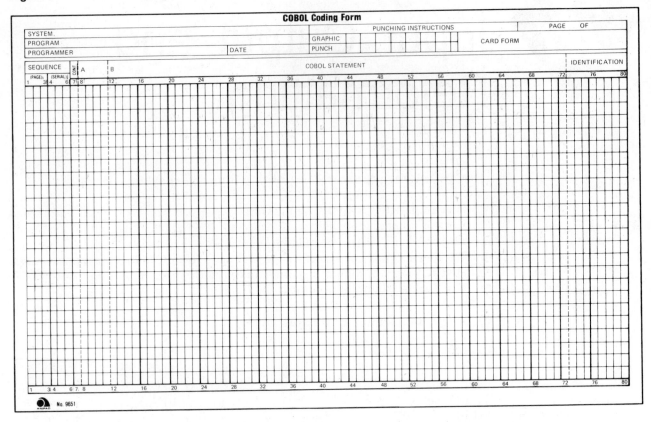

Figure 2.2 A COBOL Coding Form partially filled in with some of the coding from Program P01-01.

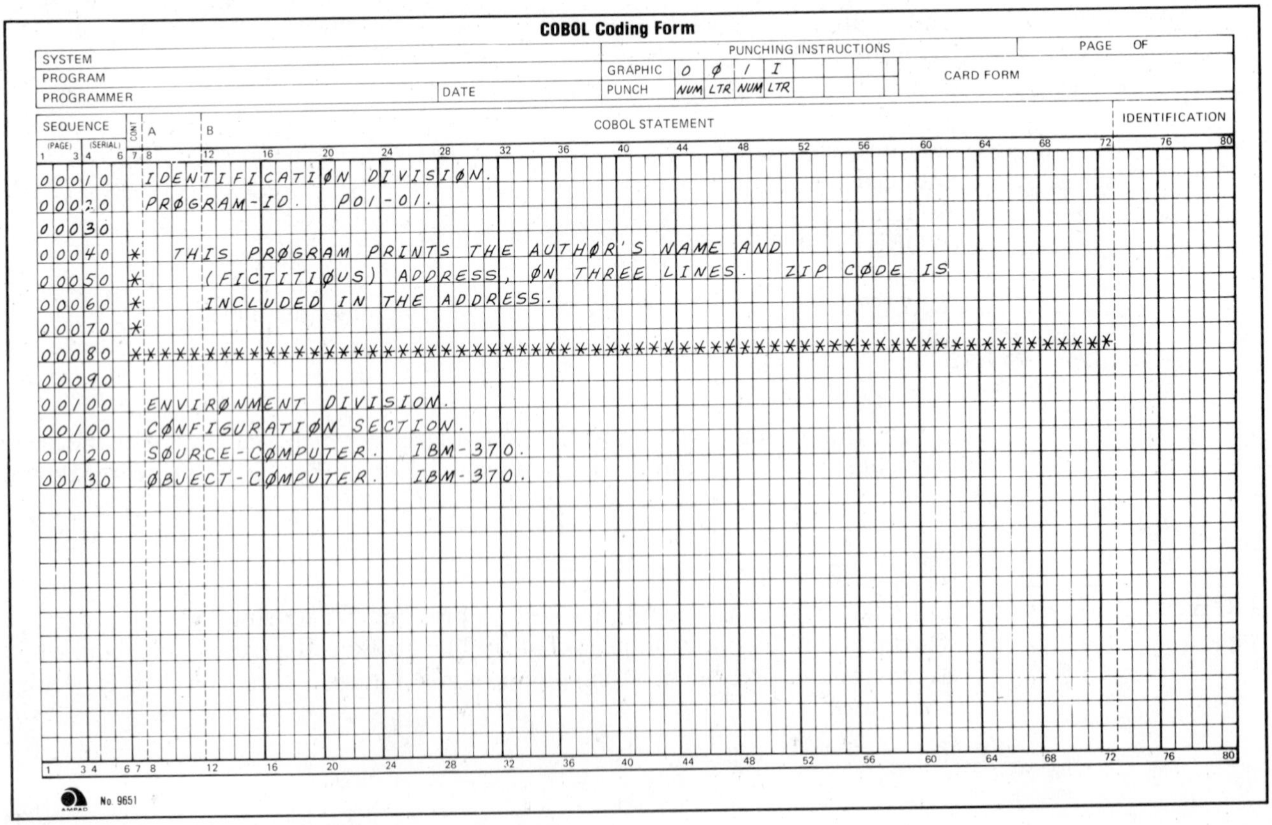

The form permits a programmer to write coding line for line exactly as it will be keyed. It has room at the top for identifying information, and space below for 24 lines of COBOL code. You can see that separate areas are marked off for the sequence number for each line, column 7 for the asterisk, and areas A and B. Columns 73-80, marked "Identification," can be used by the programmer for anything and are often used for the program name. Figure 2.2 shows a COBOL Coding Form partially filled in with some of the coding from Program P01-01.

A Program to Process One Input Data Record

We now try a program slightly more complicated than Program P01-01. This program, Program P02-01, prints a three-line name and address, but this time the program obtains the name and address to be printed by reading an input record containing them. Program P01-01 was able to print only the name and address that were written into the program in the MOVE statements, but Program P02-01 is now able to print any name and address merely by being provided with a data record containing the information to be printed. Depending on the equipment available at your school, the input record may be keyed in on a terminal, or it may be punched in a card, or it may be in some other form provided by your instructor. Let's assume that the input record to be read by Program P02-01 has the following format:

Positions	Field
1 – 20	Name
21 – 45	Street Address
46 – 70	City, State, ZIP
71 – 80	spaces

A typical input record in that format is shown in Figure 2.3.

Figure 2.3 Input to Program P02-01.

```
-------------------------------------------------------------------------------
          1         2         3         4         5         6         7         8
123456789012345678901234567890123456789012345678901234567890123456789012345678901234567890
-------------------------------------------------------------------------------
G. S. POPKIN       1921 PRESIDENT ST.      BROOKLYN, N. Y.  11220
```

Program P02-01 is shown in Figure 2.4. It differs from Program P01-01 in several ways. The input file, which consists of just one record, has been named INPUT-FILE. Since we now have two files, we must have two SELECT clauses, lines 00160 and 00170, and two FD entries. The FD entry for the output file, at line 00230, is the same as in Program P01-01, but the FD entry for the input file contains the clause **RECORD CONTAINS** 80 CHARACTERS. The RECORD CONTAINS clause is optional, but including it in the FD entry of all input files will help the programmer get the size of the input record correct. Incorrect input record size is one of the most common errors made by beginning programmers.

The computer system that I used to run the programs in this book is arranged so that the most convenient size for an input record is 80 characters. Standard COBOL accepts input records of any size, but for convenience all input records in this book are 80 characters long.

The 01 entry for the output record, at line 00260, is the same as in Program P01-01, but the 01 entry for the input record, at line 00330, introduces some new ideas. Since the input record is formatted in **fields,** we must describe those fields to the computer. The fields are described in this program by the level-05 entries, in lines 00340 through 00370. Each level-05 entry allows the programmer to make up a name for the field and indicate its length. Here the names of the three fields of input are NAME, STREET-ADDRESS, and CITY-STATE-ZIP. The names of the fields could have been any legal **data names,** of course, just as the names of files can be any legal made-up names, but it is always best to use meaningful names that describe the field contents well. The rules for data names are the same as for record names and file names. The name **FILLER** is a reserved word and may be used whenever a field is not referred to in a program. In this case the field of blanks

Figure 2.4 Program P02-01.

```
CB1 RELEASE 2.4                              IBM OS/VS COBOL  JULY  1, 1982


                           22.22.10      MAR 27,1988


00010   IDENTIFICATION.DIVISION.
00020   PROGRAM-ID.  P02-01.
00030
00040 *   THIS PROGRAM READS ONE INPUT RECORD AND PRINTS
00050 *      ITS CONTENTS ON THREE LINES.
00060 *
00070 ********************************************************************
00080
00090   ENVIRONMENT DIVISION.
00100   CONFIGURATION SECTION.
00110   SOURCE-COMPUTER.  IBM-370.
00120   OBJECT-COMPUTER.  IBM-370.
00130
00140   INPUT-OUTPUT SECTION.
00150   FILE-CONTROL.
00160       SELECT COMPLETE-ADDRESS      ASSIGN TO PRINTER.
00170       SELECT INPUT-FILE            ASSIGN TO INFILE.
00180
00190 ********************************************************************
00200
00210   DATA DIVISION.
00220   FILE SECTION.
00230   FD  COMPLETE-ADDRESS
00240       LABEL RECORDS ARE OMITTED.
00250
00260   01  ADDRESS-LINE             PICTURE X(120).
00270
00280
00290   FD  INPUT-FILE
00300       RECORD CONTAINS 80 CHARACTERS
00310       LABEL RECORDS ARE OMITTED.
00320
```

```
00330  01  INPUT-RECORD.
00340      05 NAME                PICTURE X(20).
00350      05 STREET-ADDRESS      PICTURE X(25).
00360      05 CITY-STATE-ZIP      PICTURE X(25).
00370      05 FILLER              PICTURE X(10).
00380
00390  ***************************************************************
00400
00410  PROCEDURE DIVISION.
00420  EXECUTABLE-PROGRAM-STEPS.
00430      OPEN INPUT   INPUT-FILE
00440           OUTPUT COMPLETE-ADDRESS.
00450      READ INPUT-FILE
00460          AT END
00470              CLOSE INPUT-FILE
00480                    COMPLETE-ADDRESS
00490              STOP RUN.
00500      MOVE NAME           TO ADDRESS-LINE.
00510      WRITE ADDRESS-LINE.
00520      MOVE STREET-ADDRESS TO ADDRESS-LINE.
00530      WRITE ADDRESS-LINE.
00540      MOVE CITY-STATE-ZIP TO ADDRESS-LINE.
00550      WRITE ADDRESS-LINE.
00560      CLOSE INPUT-FILE
00570            COMPLETE-ADDRESS.
00580      STOP RUN.
```

will not be used in the processing, and so can be given the name FILLER. The sizes of the fields must add up to the size of the input record, 80, and the total must agree with the RECORD CONTAINS clause.

If my computer allowed me to use records other than 80 characters in length conveniently, I would use a 70-character record in this program. I would leave out line 00370 so that the sizes of the fields added up to 70, and would change line 00300 to read RECORD CONTAINS 70 CHARACTERS.

In the File Section of the Data Division, the 01 level always describes a record. Fields within the record may use any level number from 02 through 49. Level numbers 02 through 49 may begin anywhere in area A or B.

Although the Procedure Division in this program differs but slightly from the Procedure Division in Program P01-01, it differs in significant ways. In this program we have both an input file and an output file. Both must be OPENed before they can be used and CLOSEd after we are through using them. The OPEN statement, line 00430, OPENs both files and indicates that INPUT-FILE is to be OPENed as an INPUT file and COMPLETE-ADDRESS is to be OPENed as an OUTPUT file. The **READ** statement at line 00450 causes the computer to READ one record from the file named in the READ statement and make that record available to the program under the record description entries associated with the file name. In this program the file being read by the READ statement is INPUT-FILE, and the record read from the file is made available to the program under the names INPUT-RECORD, NAME, STREET-ADDRESS, and CITY-STATE-ZIP.

An **AT END** phrase in a READ statement tells COBOL what to do if and when **end-of-file** is reached on a file being read. COBOL executes the AT END phrase when a READ is attempted and no more input records are found. It does not execute it when the last input record is read.

In this case, since we expect this file to contain only one record and this is the one and only READ statement to be executed on the file, the AT END phrase at line 00460 tells COBOL what to do if the file accidentally contains no input record. If our input file contains no data, the AT END phrase in this program just CLOSEs both files and executes a STOP RUN. Notice that there is only one period at the end of the entire READ statement.

Of course, if all is well, our file will contain the expected input record and the computer can go on to the MOVE and WRITE statements in lines 00500 through 00550. We give the MOVE statements in the order that we want the fields to print. Notice how the MOVE statements in this program differ from those in Program

P01-01. In Program P01-01 the **sending field** of the MOVE was some actual piece of data enclosed in quotation marks. Here the sending field, or **source field**, of the MOVE is a data name, so what will be MOVEd are the NAME, STREET-ADDRESS, and CITY-STATE-ZIP fields that were read from the input record, and not the words "NAME", "STREET-ADDRESS", or "CITY-STATE-ZIP". This very important difference between having a data name in a statement as distinguished from writing the actual data literally into the statement will be discussed further shortly.

After the three lines of output are MOVEd and written, we CLOSE the input and output files with a CLOSE statement, line 00560, and execute a STOP RUN in the usual way.

Program P02-01 was run with the input data shown in Figure 2.3 and produced the output shown in Figure 2.5.

Figure 2.5 Output from Program P02-01.

```
G. S. POPKIN
1921 PRESIDENT ST.
BROOKLYN, N. Y.  11220
```

Literals and Assignment

In Program P01-01, where the sending fields of the MOVE statements were pieces of data enclosed in quotation marks, the pieces of data are called **literals.** There are two categories of literals in COBOL. The ones we used in Program P01-01 are called **nonnumeric** literals. A nonnumeric literal is any string of characters, except the quotation mark, enclosed in quotation marks. Thus "G. S. POPKIN" is a valid nonnumeric literal, but " "MURDER," SHE SAID." is not. If you must have quotation marks inside a literal, they can be represented by two successive quotation marks, so " " "MURDER," " SHE SAID." is valid. When such a literal is printed as output, only one of the quotation marks from each pair prints, as "MURDER," SHE SAID. Nonnumeric literals may be up to 120 characters long. The enclosing quotation marks are not part of the literal.

The other category of literals is the **numeric** literal. We have not yet used any numeric literals in our programs. A numeric literal must contain at least one of the digits 0 through 9, and may contain up to 18 digits. It may have a plus or minus sign at its left end. It may contain a decimal point anywhere except at its right end, and it must not contain a comma. An unsigned numeric literal is assumed to be positive. A numeric literal is not enclosed in quotation marks. If a numeric quantity is enclosed in quotation marks, it is treated as a nonnumeric literal. The following are legal numeric literals:

```
145
+14500
-1541
13.06
13.0
.68
```

The following are not legal numeric literals:

```
100,000   (Numeric literal must not contain a comma.)
13.       (Decimal point, if present, must not be at right end.)
"145"     (Numeric literal must not be enclosed.)
```

In Program P02-01, Figure 2.4, the sending fields of the MOVE statements were not literals but data names. In such a case the data that are MOVEd are whatever data happen to be **assigned** to the data name at the time. In our program, data were assigned to the data names by the READ statement; that is, the READ statement brought in an input data record and assigned the first field in the record to the name NAME, the second field to the name STREET-ADDRESS, and the third field to the name CITY-STATE-ZIP. There are many ways in which data can be assigned to data names and they will be mentioned as needed. For now, the very important difference between

```
MOVE "DOG" TO OUTPUT-LINE
```

and

```
MOVE DOG TO OUTPUT-LINE
```

is that in the first case the word DOG will be MOVEd to the output line, but in the second what will be MOVEd to the output line is whatever data value happens to have been assigned to the data name DOG by some earlier part of the program. The MOVE does not change the value assigned to the sending field; that is, the value assigned to DOG after the MOVE is the same as the value it had before the MOVE.

EXERCISE 1

Write a program to process a single input record according to the following specifications:

Input

One record containing a name and address in the following format:

Positions	Field
1 – 15	Company Name
16 – 30	Street Address
31 – 45	City and State
46 – 65	Employee Name
66 – 80	Employee Title

Output

A five-line address containing, each on its own line, the Employee Name, Employee Title, Company Name, Street Address, and City and State.

A Program to Process Multiple Input Records

The usual situation in data processing is that a program will read many input records and process each one, but the number of input records to be processed is not known at the time the program is being written. In fact, it is usual for any program to be run many times, and in each running it can be expected to have to process different numbers of input records. So we must have some way to accommodate this variability in the number of input records to be read. We will do this by using the AT END phrase of the READ statement in a new way.

Program P02-02 uses data in the same format as does Program P02-01. Program P02-02 READs any number of input records whereas Program P02-01 READs only one. The contents of each input record are printed in the usual three-line format, single spaced as before, but Program P02-02 double-spaces between addresses.

Processing a Variable Number of Input Records

Program P02-02 is shown in Figure 2.6. The new things in this program are those needed to handle the unknown variable number of input records. First we need a new section in the Data Division, the **WORKING-STORAGE SECTION,** at line 00460. The Working Storage Section can be used for holding and naming any data that are neither read in nor written out; that is, any data that are not part of the File Section. In this program we use a single field called MORE-INPUT, at line 00470, to indicate to the program when there are no more input records to be processed. MORE-INPUT is a user-defined data name made up by the author. The

Figure 2.6 Program P02-02.

```
CB1 RELEASE 2.4                                    iBM OS/VS COBOL   JULY  1, 1982


                          22.35.24          MAR 27,1988


00010   IDENTIFICATION DIVISION.
00020   PROGRAM-ID.  P02-02.
00030
00040 *    INPUT - NAMES AND ADDRESSES IN THE FOLLOWING
00050 *    FORMAT:
00060 *
00070 *    POS.  1-20            NAME
00080 *    POS.  21-45           STREET ADDRESS
00090 *    POS.  46-65           CITY, STATE, ZIP
00100 *
00110 *    OUTPUT - THREE-LINE ADDRESSES, SINGLE SPACED, WITH A DOUBLE
00120 *    SPACE BETWEEN ADDRESSES.
00130 *
00140 ********************************************************************
00150
00160   ENVIRONMENT DIVISION.
00170   CONFIGURATION SECTION.
00180   SOURCE-COMPUTER.  IBM-370.
00190   OBJECT-COMPUTER.  IBM-370.
00200
00210   INPUT-OUTPUT SECTION.
00220   FILE-CONTROL.
00230      SELECT THREE-LINE-ADDRESSES ASSIGN TO PRINTER.
00240      SELECT ADDRESSES-IN         ASSIGN TO INFILE.
00250
00260 ********************************************************************
00270
00280   DATA DIVISION.
00290   FILE SECTION.
00300 FD  THREE-LINE-ADDRESSES
00310      LABEL RECORDS ARE OMITTED.
00320
00330 01  ADDRESS-LINE           PIC X(120).
00340
```

```
00350
00360  FD   ADDRESSES-IN
00370       RECORD CONTAINS 80 CHARACTERS
00380       LABEL RECORDS ARE OMITTED.
00390
00400  01   INPUT-RECORD.
00410       05 NAME                PIC X(20).
00420       05 STREET-ADDRESS      PIC X(25).
00430       05 CITY-STATE-ZIP      PIC X(20).
00440       05 FILLER              PIC X(15).
00450
00460  WORKING-STORAGE SECTION.
00470  01   MORE-INPUT             PIC X    VALUE "Y".
00480
00490  *********************************************************************
00500
00510  PROCEDURE DIVISION.
00520  CONTROL-PARAGRAPH.
00530       PERFORM INITIALIZATION.
00540       PERFORM MAIN-LOOP UNTIL MORE-INPUT IS EQUAL TO "N".
00550       PERFORM TERMINATION.
00560       STOP RUN.
00570
```

(continued)

field has been made one character long and is **initialized,** or started out, with a value of "Y", by use of the **VALUE** clause. This indicates that as the program begins execution we expect to find more input, since we have so far processed none at all. You will soon see how the coding in the program turns MORE-INPUT to "N" when there are no more input data to process.

This program also shows our first use of the abbreviation **PIC** for PICTURE. PIC is a reserved word specifically provided as an abbreviation for PICTURE. Only a few reserved words in COBOL have authorized abbreviations, and only those words for which abbreviations are given may be abbreviated. You cannot make up your own abbreviations for reserved words.

The Procedure Division in this program shows a conventional form that we will use whenever possible to process an unknown variable number of input records. The first paragraph of the program consists of three **PERFORM** statements, at lines 00530 through 00550, and a STOP RUN statement. A PERFORM statement directs the computer to carry out the paragraph named in the statement. Thus the PERFORM statement at line 00530 causes the paragraph called INITIALIZATION to be executed. Then the PERFORM statement at line 00540 causes the paragraph called MAIN-LOOP to be executed until all the input has been processed; that is, **UNTIL MORE-INPUT** has been made **EQUAL TO** "N". The last PERFORM statement, line 00550, causes the TERMINATION paragraph to execute, and then the STOP RUN statement ends the execution of the program. The names of all the paragraphs in the Procedure Division of this program (and of all COBOL programs) are user-defined words.

The INITIALIZATION Paragraph

The OPEN and READ statements in the INITIALIZATION paragraph, lines 00590 and 00610, are similar to those we saw in Program P02-01. In this program, however, the READ statement in this paragraph is used to READ only the first record from the file. This is called the **priming READ** statement. In this program all the other input records are read from the file by another READ statement elsewhere in the Procedure Division.

The AT END phrases in the READ statements in this program differ from the AT END phrase in Program P02-01. In that program, if the first (and only) READ statement discovered that there were accidentally no input data, the AT END phrase directed the computer to CLOSE the files and STOP RUN. We use here a more general procedure in both READ statements in this program. Each AT END phrase, if or when it discovers that there are no input data or no more input data, MOVEs the letter "N" to the working storage field MORE-INPUT.

The TERMINATION Paragraph

The function of the TERMINATION paragraph, line 00650, should be obvious. Notice that PERFORMed paragraphs can appear in any physical sequence in the program. The order in which the PERFORMed paragraphs are executed is determined by the PERFORM statements in the control paragraph. You thus can, and should, order your paragraphs in such a way that your program is easy to read and understand.

The Main Loop

The PERFORM statement at line 00540 causes the paragraph MAIN-LOOP to be executed as many times as necessary, UNTIL the specified **condition** has been met. MAIN-LOOP is first executed after the priming READ has been executed.

Figure 2.6 (continued)

```
00580    INITIALIZATION.
00590       OPEN INPUT   ADDRESSES-IN
00600            OUTPUT THREE-LINE-ADDRESSES.
00610       READ ADDRESSES-IN
00620          AT END
00630             MOVE "N" TO MORE-INPUT.
00640
00650    TERMINATION.
00660       CLOSE ADDRESSES-IN
00670             THREE-LINE-ADDRESSES.
00680
00690    MAIN-LOOP.
00700       MOVE NAME TO ADDRESS-LINE.
00710       WRITE ADDRESS-LINE AFTER ADVANCING 2 LINES.
00720       MOVE STREET-ADDRESS TO ADDRESS-LINE.
00730       WRITE ADDRESS-LINE.
00740       MOVE CITY-STATE-ZIP TO ADDRESS-LINE.
00750       WRITE ADDRESS-LINE.
00760       READ ADDRESSES-IN
00770          AT END
00780             MOVE "N" TO MORE-INPUT.
```

The loop processes the first record (already read) and READs the second record; then the loop executes again to process the second record and READ the third. MAIN-LOOP executes over and over, processing each record and READing the next, until finally there are no more data to be read, and MAIN-LOOP sets MORE-INPUT to "N".

The actions carried out by MAIN-LOOP are ones we have already seen, except for the double spacing of the first line of each address. The pairs of MOVE and WRITE statements, lines 00700 through 00750, print the input data, and the READ statement at line 00760 (to READ the second and subsequent records) is identical to the priming READ. Of course, whereas we expect the priming READ never to execute its AT END phrase, the READ statement at line 00760 eventually finds no more input data and carries out the instruction in its AT END phrase.

The WRITE statement that prints the first line of each address contains the phrase **AFTER ADVANCING** 2 LINES. This gives double spacing. When the ADVANCING option is omitted, as it is in the other two WRITE statements, COBOL gives single spacing, as if you had written AFTER ADVANCING 1 LINE.[1] There is no upper limit on the size of the integer that may appear in an ADVANCING phrase. You may use AFTER ADVANCING 0 LINES to suppress spacing.

Program P02-02 was run with the input data shown in Figure 2.7. It produced the output shown in Figure 2.8.

Figure 2.7 Input to Program P02-02.

```
--------------------------------------------------------------------------------------
         1         2         3         4         5         6         7         8
12345678901234567890123456789012345678901234567890123456789012345678901234567890
--------------------------------------------------------------------------------------
G. S. POPKIN          1921 PRESIDENT ST.        BROOKLYN, NY  11221
L. MORGAN             11 W. 42 ST.              NEW YORK, NY  10010
P. LIPPY              44 W. 10TH ST.            NEW YORK, NY  10036
S. O'MALLEY           121 5TH.AVE.              BROOKLYN, NY  11217
```

Figure 2.8 Output from Program P02-02.

```
G. S. POPKIN
1921 PRESIDENT ST.
BROOKLYN, NY  11221

L. MORGAN
11 W. 42 ST.
NEW YORK, NY  10010

P. LIPPY
44 W. 10TH ST.
NEW YORK, NY  10036

S. O'MALLEY
121 5TH AVE.
BROOKLYN, NY  11217
```

[1]Note to instructor: There is no need to reserve space for a carriage-control character. The ANSI standard does not call for such a space. In IBM OS/VS COBOL the compile-time option PARM.COB=ADV, which is the default in most installations, provides the space and satisfies the standard. In NCR VRX COBOL, the standard is always satisfied and no space is ever needed.

EXERCISE 2

Write a program to read and process input records according to the following specifications:

Input

Records in the following format:

Positions	Field
1 – 15	Company Name
16 – 30	Street Address
31 – 45	City and State
46 – 65	Employee Name
66 – 80	Employee Title

Output

For each input record, print a five-line address containing, each on its own line, an Employee Name, Employee Title, Company Name, Street Address, and City and State. The first line of each address is to be double spaced, and the address itself single spaced.

A Program with Output Line Formatting

In the programs we have done so far, only one field appeared on each output line of print. It is more usual to have several fields printed on a single line, and those fields must be properly spaced across the page to make the output easy to read. We will now consider a program to READ input records and print the entire contents of each record on one line. The format of the input records is:

Positions	Field
1 – 9	Social Security Number
10 – 34	Employee Name
35 – 39	Employee Number
40 – 46	Annual Salary (dollars and cents)
47 – 80	spaces

There are no blanks between fields. There may be blanks within the Employee Name field, however, as part of the name, as shown in the input data listing in Figure 2.9. We will now try to write a program that will READ an input record and print all four fields from it on one output line, then READ the next record and print the four fields from that record on a line, and so on. Since there are no blanks

Figure 2.9 Input to Program P02-03.

```
         1         2         3         4         5         6         7         8
12345678901234567890123456789012345678901234567890123456789012345678901234567890
----------------------------------------------------------------------------- 
100040002MORALES, LUIS           105035000000
101850005JACOBSON, MRS. NELLIE   108904651000
201110008GREENWOOD, JAMES        112774302000
209560011COSTELLO, JOSEPH S,     116643953000
301810014REITER, D.             120513604000
304870017MARRA, DITTA E.        124383255000
401710020LIPKE, VINCENT R.       128252906000
407390023KUGLER, CHARLES         132122557000
502070026JAVIER, CARLOS          135992208000
505680029GOODMAN, ISAAC          139861859000
604910032FELDSOTT, MS. SALLY     143731510000
608250035BUXBAUM, ROBERT         147601161000
703100038DUMAY, MRS. MARY        151470812000
708020041SMITH, R.              155340463000
803220044VINCENTE, MATTHEW J.    159210114000
901050047THOMAS, THOMAS T.       163084235000
901029857WONG, TIM              002361850000
```

between fields in the input record, if we print the record just as it is, the output will be difficult to read. Fortunately, in COBOL it is easy not only to insert spaces between the fields for printing, but also to rearrange the fields on the output line in any desired way. Let us say that we would like to print each line with the fields in the following print positions:

Print Positions	Field
5 – 9	Employee Number
12 – 20	Social Security Number
25 – 49	Employee Name
52 – 58	Annual Salary

Now not only have we specified spaces between the fields when printed, but also that the fields be in a different order on the output line from their order in the input record. Formatting output lines in this way is very easy in COBOL.

You can check that each output field has been made the same size as its corresponding input field. For example, the input Employee Number, positions 35 through 39, is five characters long. The Employee Number in the output, print positions 5 through 9, is also five characters. The way to compute the size of an input or output field is: Subtract the lower position number from the higher and add 1. Compute the sizes of the other three fields in the input and output before going on.

Program P02-03 is shown in Figure 2.10. In this program we can define the exact placement of the fields in the output line through the use of level-05 entries for the output record. We can arrange the fields in any desired order across the page, and by using FILLERs we can get any desired number of blank print positions between fields. If you now study the level-05 entries for EMPLOYEE-LINE-OUT, lines 00490 through 00560, you will see that the organization of the fields agrees with the requirements for the output line, as given in the statement of the problem.

Let us now examine the paragraph MAIN-LOOP, line 00810. It begins with a MOVE **SPACES** statement that assigns blanks to all the fields in EMPLOYEE-LINE-OUT; that is, it blanks out the entire output line area. This statement is needed mainly to blank out the FILLER areas in EMPLOYEE-LINE-OUT, as there is no other way to do it. SPACES is a reserved word, and stands for as many blank characters as are indicated by the context it is used in.

The MOVE SPACES statement is followed by four MOVE statements, lines 00830 through 00860, each moving a single field from the input area to the output area. Notice that there are no intervening WRITE statements as there were in the previous program. That is so because each WRITE statement causes a line of output to print, and in this program we don't want an output line until we have MOVEd all four fields of input to the output area. In this program the four fields can be MOVEd to the output area in any order; none of the MOVEs affects any of the others, and we don't WRITE a line until all four are MOVEd. In previous programs the fields had to be MOVEd to the output area in the order in which we wanted them to print, because we wrote a line after every MOVE.

Figure 2.10 Program P02-03.

```
CB1 RELEASE 2.4                                    IBM OS/VS COBOL   JULY  1, 1982


                        22.43.43        MAR 27,1988


00010    IDENTIFICATION DIVISION.
00020    PROGRAM-ID.  P02-03.
00030
00040 *      THIS PROGRAM READS INPUT RECORDS IN THE FOLLOWING FORMAT:
00050 *
00060 *      POS.  1-9          SOCIAL SECURITY NUMBER
00070 *      POS. 10-34         EMPLOYEE NAME
00080 *      POS. 35-39         EMPLOYEE NUMBER
00090 *      POS. 40-46         ANNUAL SALARY
00100 *
00110 *      FOR EACH RECORD, ONE LINE IS PRINTED IN THE FOLLOWING FORMAT:
00120 *
00130 *      PP  5-9            EMPLOYEE NUMBER
00140 *      PP 12-20           SOCIAL SECURITY NUMBER
00150 *      PP 25-49           EMPLOYEE NAME
00160 *      PP 52-58           ANNUAL SALARY
00170 *
00180 **********************************************************************
00190
```

```
00200   ENVIRONMENT DIVISION.
00210   CONFIGURATION SECTION.
00220   SOURCE-COMPUTER.  IBM-370.
00230   OBJECT-COMPUTER.  IBM-370.
00240
00250   INPUT-OUTPUT SECTION.
00260   FILE-CONTROL.
00270       SELECT EMPLOYEE-DATA-OUT ASSIGN TO PRINTER.
00280       SELECT EMPLOYEE-DATA-IN  ASSIGN TO INFILE.
00290
00300   **********************************************************************
00310
00320   DATA DIVISION.
00330   FILE SECTION.
00340   FD  EMPLOYEE-DATA-IN
00350       RECORD CONTAINS 80 CHARACTERS
00360       LABEL RECORDS ARE OMITTED.
00370
00380   01  EMPLOYEE-RECORD-IN.
00390       05 SOCIAL-SECURITY-NUMBER-IN     PIC X(9).
00400       05 EMPLOYEE-NAME-IN              PIC X(25).
00410       05 EMPLOYEE-NUMBER-IN            PIC X(5).
00420       05 ANNUAL-SALARY-IN              PIC X(7).
00430       05 FILLER                        PIC X(34).
00440
00450   FD  EMPLOYEE-DATA-OUT
00460       LABEL RECORDS ARE OMITTED.
00470
00480   01  EMPLOYEE-LINE-OUT.
00490       05 FILLER                        PIC X(4).
00500       05 EMPLOYEE-NUMBER-OUT           PIC X(5).
00510       05 FILLER                        PIC X(2).
00520       05 SOCIAL-SECURITY-NUMBER-OUT    PIC X(9).
00530       05 FILLER                        PIC X(4).
00540       05 EMPLOYEE-NAME-OUT             PIC X(25).
00550       05 FILLER                        PIC X(2).
00560       05 ANNUAL-SALARY-OUT             PIC X(7).
00570
00580   WORKING-STORAGE SECTION.
00590   01  MORE-INPUT                       PIC X     VALUE "Y".
00600
00610   **********************************************************************
00620
00630   PROCEDURE DIVISION.
00640   CONTROL-PARAGRAPH.
00650       PERFORM INITIALIZATION.
00660       PERFORM MAIN-LOOP UNTIL MORE-INPUT IS EQUAL TO "N".
00670       PERFORM TERMINATION.
00680       STOP RUN.
00690
00700   INITIALIZATION.
00710       OPEN INPUT  EMPLOYEE-DATA-IN
00720            OUTPUT EMPLOYEE-DATA-OUT.
00730       READ EMPLOYEE-DATA-IN
00740           AT END
00750               MOVE "N" TO MORE-INPUT.
00760
00770   TERMINATION.
00780       CLOSE EMPLOYEE-DATA-IN
00790             EMPLOYEE-DATA-OUT.
00800
00810   MAIN-LOOP.
00820       MOVE SPACES                      TO EMPLOYEE-LINE-OUT.
00830       MOVE SOCIAL-SECURITY-NUMBER-IN TO SOCIAL-SECURITY-NUMBER-OUT.
00840       MOVE EMPLOYEE-NUMBER-IN          TO EMPLOYEE-NUMBER-OUT.
00850       MOVE ANNUAL-SALARY-IN            TO ANNUAL-SALARY-OUT.
00860       MOVE EMPLOYEE-NAME-IN            TO EMPLOYEE-NAME-OUT.
00870       WRITE EMPLOYEE-LINE-OUT.
00880       READ EMPLOYEE-DATA-IN
00890           AT END
00900               MOVE "N" TO MORE-INPUT.
```

The output from Program P02-03 is shown in Figure 2.11.

Figure 2.11   Output from Program P02-03.

```
10503  100040002    MORALES, LUIS            5000000
10890  101850005    JACOBSON, MRS. NELLIE    4651000
11277  201110008    GREENWOOD, JAMES         4302000
11664  209560011    COSTELLO, JOSEPH S.      3953000
12051  301810014    REITER, D.               3604000
12438  304870017    MARRA, DITTA E.          3255000
12825  401710020    LIPKE, VINCENT R.        2906000
13212  407390023    KUGLER, CHARLES          2557000
13599  502070026    JAVIER, CARLOS           2208000
13986  505680029    GOODMAN, ISAAC           1859000
14373  604910032    FELDSOTT, MS. SALLY      1510000
14760  608250035    BUXBAUM, ROBERT          1161000
15147  703100038    DUMAY, MRS. MARY         0812000
15534  708020041    SMITH, R.                0463000
15921  803220044    VINCENTE, MATTHEW J.     0114000
16308  901050047    THOMAS, THOMAS T.        4235000
00236  901029857    WONG, TIM                1850000
```

EXERCISE 3

Write a program to read and process input records according to the following specifications:

Input

Records in the following format:

Positions	Field
1–15	Company Name
16–30	Street Address
31–45	City and State
46–65	Employee Name
66–80	Employee Title

Output

For each input record, print its contents on one line in the following format:

Print Positions	Field
6–20	Company Name
23–37	Street Address
40–54	City and State
60–74	Employee Title
76–95	Employee Name

The Print Chart

A second kind of form that is helpful when writing COBOL programs is the **print chart** as shown in Figure 2.12; it can usually be bought where you buy your coding forms. The chart can be used by the programmer to plan the format of an output report or listing before starting to code a program. You can see in Figure 2.12 the print positions numbered across the top of the chart. The print position numbers are in groups of 10 for ease of locating any particular position.

Figure 2.12 A print chart.

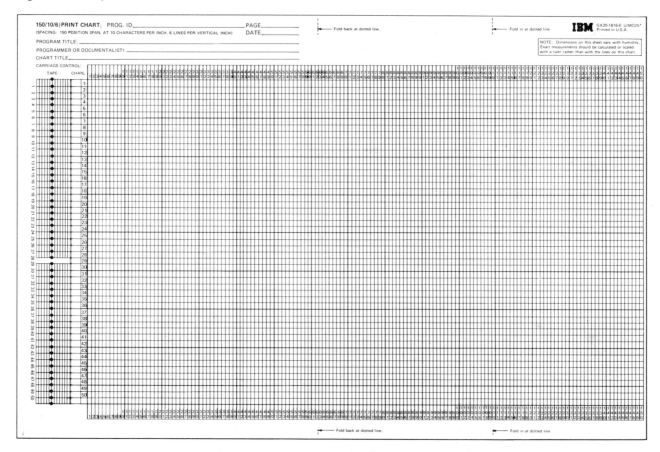

In planning an output report, the programmer determines the print positions in which the various fields of output are to appear and indicates those fields on the chart. The fields should be indicated on the chart with the same character that is used in a PICTURE for that field in a COBOL program. To give an example of the use of a print chart, we will use the output specifications of Program P02-03, page 24.

Since all the output fields in that program have PICTURE characters of X, we use Xs on the print chart. In Figure 2.13 you can see that several lines have been filled in in the print positions where the fields Employee Number, Social Security Number, Employee Name, and Annual Salary would appear. In Chapters 3 and 4 you will see all the other characters that may be used in PICTUREs in COBOL programs.

Figure 2.13   Print chart showing the output specifications of Program P02-03.

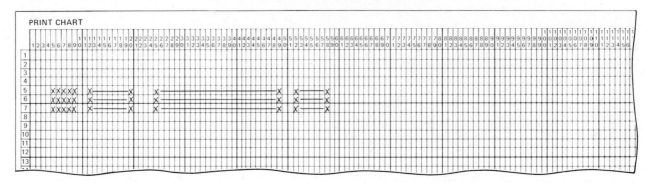

Ordinarily a print chart would not be used merely to visualize an output specification that already has been developed. Instead it is usually used to develop the output specification, that is, to plan what the output will look like. So for our next program you will be given the output requirements not in the form used previously, but in the form of a print chart. Later on you will be asked to develop your own output specifications using a print chart.

EXERCISE 4

Using a print chart, show the output specification from Exercise 3, page 26.

Column Headings

Sometimes it is useful to be able to print fixed heading information at the top of a page of output so that the reader can easily see what each column of output is supposed to contain. In the output of Program P02-03 it would have been useful to have the words EMP.NO., SOCIAL SECURITY NUMBER, EMPLOYEE NAME, and ANNUAL SALARY appear approximately over the corresponding columns of output. Figure 2.14 shows a modification of the print chart in Figure 2.13, which includes column headings.

Figure 2.14 Print chart showing column headings.

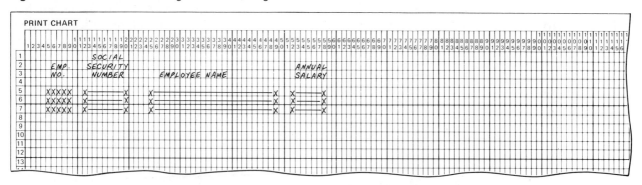

The three lines of column headings are constant information, and one place to set up such constants is in the Working Storage Section. The first heading line consists of 13 spaces and the word SOCIAL. The second heading line consists of five spaces, then the word EMP., then more spaces, then the word SECURITY, then a lot of spaces, and then the word ANNUAL. The third heading line consists of spaces and the words NO., NUMBER, EMPLOYEE NAME, and SALARY.

The first heading line can be set up in working storage as follows:

```
01  HEADING-LINE-1.
    05  FILLER              PIC X(13)    VALUE SPACES.
    05  FILLER              PIC X(6)     VALUE "SOCIAL".
```

The second heading line can be set up as follows:

```
01  HEADING-LINE-2.
    05  FILLER              PIC X(5)     VALUE SPACES.
    05  FILLER              PIC X(4)     VALUE "EMP.".
    05  FILLER              PIC X(3)     VALUE SPACES.
    05  FILLER              PIC X(8)     VALUE "SECURITY".
    05  FILLER              PIC X(32)    VALUE SPACES.
    05  FILLER              PIC X(6)     VALUE "ANNUAL".
```

You will see how to get a COBOL program to WRITE fields that have been defined in working storage when we look at Program P02-04.

EXERCISE 5

Write the working storage entries for the third heading line in Figure 2.14.

**A Program
with Column
Headings**

Program P02-04 is shown in Figure 2.15. The output records in this program have several different formats — the three heading lines and the **body line,** or **detail line,** of the report. Whenever you have more than one output-line format in a program, it is best to define all the fields of all the output lines in working storage. We have done that in this program, as you will see when we look at the Working Storage Section. You nonetheless must have some record definition in the File Section associated with the output file. Here we have OUTPUT-LINE, at line 00370. The size of OUTPUT-LINE has been made as long as the longest line that the program prints. You can see from the print chart that the longest line is 58 characters.

In the Working Storage Section you can find the definitions of the four types of lines that the program prints. EMPLOYEE-LINE-OUT, the detail line, is found at lines 00420 through 00500. The definition here is the same as in Program P02-03, except that VALUE SPACES clauses have been included in the definitions of the fields that are to be blank on the output. We did not use VALUE SPACES clauses to blank those output fields in Program P02-03 because COBOL does not permit the use of the VALUE clause to establish the value of a field in the File Section.

The definitions of HEADING-LINE-1, HEADING-LINE-2, and HEADING-LINE-3 are found in lines 00520 through 00720.

Figure 2.15 Program P02-04.

```
CB1 RELEASE 2.4                                 IBM OS/VS COBOL   JULY  1, 1982


                         22.52.29        MAR 27,1988


00010  IDENTIFICATION DIVISION.
00020  PROGRAM-ID.  P02-04.
00030
00040 *    THIS PROGRAM IS A MODIFICATION TO PROGRAM P02-03,
00050 *    WITH COLUMN HEADINGS.
00060 *
00070 **********************************************************************
00080
00090  ENVIRONMENT DIVISION.
00100  CONFIGURATION SECTION.
00110  SOURCE-COMPUTER.   IBM-370.
00120  OBJECT-COMPUTER.   IBM-370.
00130
00140  INPUT-OUTPUT SECTION.
00150  FILE-CONTROL.
00160      SELECT EMPLOYEE-DATA-OUT ASSIGN TO PRINTER.
00170      SELECT EMPLOYEE-DATA-IN  ASSIGN TO INFILE.
00180
00190 **********************************************************************
00200
```

```
00210  DATA DIVISION.
00220  FILE SECTION.
00230  FD  EMPLOYEE-DATA-IN
00240      RECORD CONTAINS 80 CHARACTERS
00250      LABEL RECORDS ARE OMITTED.
00260
00270  01  EMPLOYEE-RECORD-IN.
00390      05 SOCIAL-SECURITY-NUMBER-IN      PIC X(9).
00400      05 EMPLOYEE-NAME-IN               PIC X(25).
00410      05 EMPLOYEE-NUMBER-IN             PIC X(5).
00420      05 ANNUAL-SALARY-IN               PIC X(7).
00320      05 FILLER                         PIC X(34).
00330
00340  FD  EMPLOYEE-DATA-OUT
00350      LABEL RECORDS ARE OMITTED.
00360
00370  01  OUTPUT-LINE                       PIC X(58).
00380
00390  WORKING-STORAGE SECTION.
00400  01  MORE-INPUT                        PIC X(1)   VALUE "Y".
00410
00420  01  EMPLOYEE-LINE-OUT.
00430      05 FILLER                         PIC X(4)   VALUE SPACES.
00440      05 EMPLOYEE-NUMBER-OUT            PIC X(5).
00450      05 FILLER                         PIC X(2)   VALUE SPACES.
00460      05 SOCIAL-SECURITY-NUMBER-OUT     PIC X(9).
00470      05 FILLER                         PIC X(4)   VALUE SPACES.
00480      05 EMPLOYEE-NAME-OUT              PIC X(25).
00490      05 FILLER                         PIC X(2)   VALUE SPACES.
00500      05 ANNUAL-SALARY-OUT              PIC X(7).
00510
00520  01  HEADING-LINE-1.
00530      05 FILLER          PIC X(13)  VALUE SPACES.
00540      05 FILLER          PIC X(6)   VALUE "SOCIAL".
00550
00560  01  HEADING-LINE-2.
00570      05 FILLER          PIC X(5)   VALUE SPACES.
00580      05 FILLER          PIC X(4)   VALUE "EMP.".
00590      05 FILLER          PIC X(3)   VALUE SPACES.
00600      05 FILLER          PIC X(8)   VALUE "SECURITY".
00610      05 FILLER          PIC X(32)  VALUE SPACES.
00620      05 FILLER          PIC X(6)   VALUE "ANNUAL".
00630
00640  01  HEADING-LINE-3.
00650      05 FILLER          PIC X(5)   VALUE SPACES.
00660      05 FILLER          PIC X(3)   VALUE "NO.".
00670      05 FILLER          PIC X(5)   VALUE SPACES.
00680      05 FILLER          PIC X(6)   VALUE "NUMBER".
00690      05 FILLER          PIC X(7)   VALUE SPACES.
00700      05 FILLER          PIC X(13)  VALUE "EMPLOYEE NAME".
00710      05 FILLER          PIC X(13)  VALUE SPACES.
00720      05 FILLER          PIC X(6)   VALUE "SALARY".
00730
00740  ****************************************************************
00750
00760  PROCEDURE DIVISION.
00770  CONTROL-PARAGRAPH.
00780      PERFORM INITIALIZATION.
00790      PERFORM MAIN-LOOP UNTIL MORE-INPUT IS EQUAL TO "N".
00800      PERFORM TERMINATION.
00810      STOP RUN.
00820
```

(continued)

Figure 2.15 (continued)

```
00830   INITIALIZATION.
00840       OPEN INPUT  EMPLOYEE-DATA-IN,
00850            OUTPUT EMPLOYEE-DATA-OUT.
00860       WRITE OUTPUT-LINE FROM HEADING-LINE-1.
00870       WRITE OUTPUT-LINE FROM HEADING-LINE-2.
00880       WRITE OUTPUT-LINE FROM HEADING-LINE-3.
00890       MOVE SPACES TO OUTPUT-LINE.
00900       WRITE OUTPUT-LINE.
00910       READ EMPLOYEE-DATA-IN
00920           AT END
00930               MOVE "N" TO MORE-INPUT.
00940
00950   TERMINATION.
00960       CLOSE EMPLOYEE-DATA-IN,
00970             EMPLOYEE-DATA-OUT.
00980
00990   MAIN-LOOP.
01000       MOVE SOCIAL-SECURITY-NUMBER-IN TO SOCIAL-SECURITY-NUMBER-OUT.
01010       MOVE EMPLOYEE-NUMBER-IN       TO EMPLOYEE-NUMBER-OUT.
01020       MOVE ANNUAL-SALARY-IN         TO ANNUAL-SALARY-OUT.
01030       MOVE EMPLOYEE-NAME-IN         TO EMPLOYEE-NAME-OUT.
01040       WRITE OUTPUT-LINE FROM EMPLOYEE-LINE-OUT.
01050       READ EMPLOYEE-DATA-IN
01060           AT END
01070               MOVE "N" TO MORE-INPUT.
```

In the Procedure Division we have statements to WRITE the heading lines. But where should those statements be in the program to produce heading lines once and only once before the first detail line is printed? The answer suggests itself, if we remember that everything in the MAIN-LOOP paragraph is executed once for each detail line that is printed. Since we certainly don't want heading lines to print with each detail line, the statements that print the heading lines must be in INITIALIZATION, not in MAIN-LOOP. Statements placed in the INITIALIZATION paragraph are executed before the first detail line is printed, and statements in the TERMINATION paragraph are executed after the last detail line is printed. You can see the three WRITE . . . **FROM** statements that print the heading, at lines 00860 through 00880.

Notice the form of the WRITE . . . FROM statement. The word WRITE is followed by a record name, defined with 01 in the File Section. Following the reserved word FROM there must be a data name, which can refer to any record or field in the Working Storage Section or File Section except the output record or its component fields.

The WRITE . . . FROM statement works like a combined MOVE and WRITE. The statement

```
WRITE OUTPUT-LINE FROM HEADING-LINE-1.
```

works just as if we had written:

```
MOVE HEADING-LINE-1 TO OUTPUT-LINE.
WRITE OUTPUT-LINE.
```

Thus there is no need to blank out OUTPUT-LINE before giving the WRITE . . . FROM statement. The implied MOVE replaces any previous contents of OUTPUT-LINE with the value assigned to HEADING-LINE-1.

The statements at lines 00890 and 00900 print one blank line after the column headings and before the first detail line. In the paragraph MAIN-LOOP, notice that we do not need to MOVE SPACES to EMPLOYEE-LINE-OUT, for the VALUE SPACES clauses in the definition of the line provide the blanks we need.

Program P02-04 was run with the same input data as Program P02-03. Program P02-04 produced the output shown in Figure 2.16.

Figure 2.16 Output from Program P02-04.

```
        SOCIAL
EMP.    SECURITY                                   ANNUAL
NO.     NUMBER     EMPLOYEE NAME                   SALARY

10503   100040002  MORALES, LUIS                   5000000
10890   101850005  JACOBSON, MRS. NELLIE           4651000
11277   201110008  GREENWOOD, JAMES                4302000
11664   209560011  COSTELLO, JOSEPH S.             3953000
12051   301810014  REITER, D.                      3604000
12438   304870017  MARRA, DITTA E.                 3255000
12825   401710020  LIPKE, VINCENT R.               2906000
13212   407390023  KUGLER, CHARLES                 2557000
13599   502070026  JAVIER, CARLOS                  2208000
13986   505680029  GOODMAN, ISAAC                  1859000
14373   604910032  FELDSOTT, MS. SALLY             1510000
14760   608250035  BUXBAUM, ROBERT                 1161000
15147   703100038  DUMAY, MRS. MARY                0812000
15534   708020041  SMITH, R.                       0463000
15921   803220044  VINCENTE, MᴀTTHEW J.            0114000
16308   901050047  THOMAS, THOMAS T.               4235000
00236   901029857  WONG, TIM                       1850000
```

EXERCISE 6

Modify your solution to Exercise 3 so that it produces output in the format shown in Figure 2.E6.

Figure 2.E6 Output format for Exercise 6.

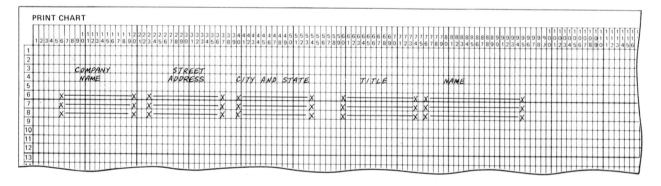

Two Formats of the PERFORM Statement

Four different formats of the PERFORM statement are given in the ANSI standard. Two of them are discussed here; the other two are discussed in Chapter 10. The simplest of the four is:

$$\underline{\text{PERFORM}} \text{ procedure-name-1} \quad \left[\left\{ \begin{array}{l} \underline{\text{THROUGH}} \\ \underline{\text{THRU}} \end{array} \right\} \text{ procedure-name-2} \right]$$

This format shows that the word PERFORM is required, and that it must be followed by a **procedure name** made up by the programmer. A procedure name is the name of a paragraph or section in the Procedure Division. We have not yet used any section names in our Procedure Divisions.

The square brackets show that the remainder of the statement is optional. Curly braces ({ }) in a COBOL format indicate that the programmer must choose exactly one of the items contained in the braces. In this format, if the programmer chooses to use the part of the statement inside the square brackets, then either THROUGH or THRU must be used, and a second procedure name must be used. THROUGH and THRU are identical in meaning.

If a program is properly designed, you should never have to use the THROUGH (or THRU) option in the Procedure Division, although some programmers may want to use it to make the meaning of a program clearer. But if your program is designed so that it needs a THROUGH option to carry out its logic, then your program is more likely to be error-prone and more difficult to maintain than programs that do not use the THROUGH option. We will not use it in any Procedure Division in this book.

Two PERFORM statements in this format that we have used so far are

```
PERFORM INITIALIZATION.
```

and:

```
PERFORM TERMINATION.
```

The format of the PERFORM . . . UNTIL statement is:

$$\underline{\text{PERFORM}} \text{ procedure-name-1} \quad \left[\left\{ \begin{array}{l} \underline{\text{THROUGH}} \\ \underline{\text{THRU}} \end{array} \right\} \text{procedure-name-2} \right]$$
$$\underline{\text{UNTIL}} \text{ condition-1}$$

This format shows that the words PERFORM and UNTIL are required, and a procedure name and a condition are also required. The only PERFORM . . . UNTIL statement we have used so far in this book is:

```
PERFORM MAIN-LOOP UNTIL MORE-INPUT IS EQUAL TO "N".
```

In this PERFORM statement MAIN-LOOP is procedure-name-1, and

```
MORE-INPUT IS EQUAL TO "N"
```

is condition-1. You will find the complete rules regarding conditions in Chapter 5.

In a PERFORM . . . UNTIL statement, condition-1 is evaluated each time before procedure-name-1 is executed. If the condition is false, the procedure is executed; if the condition is true, control passes to the statement after the PERFORM. If the condition is already true when control first passes to the PERFORM statement, procedure-name-1 is not executed and control passes to the next statement.

The Complete Environment Division

The ANSI standard format of the Environment Division is:

```
ENVIRONMENT DIVISION.
CONFIGURATION SECTION.
SOURCE-COMPUTER.  source-computer-entry
OBJECT-COMPUTER.  object-computer-entry
[SPECIAL-NAMES.  special-names-entry]
[INPUT-OUTPUT SECTION.
FILE-CONTROL.  file-control-entry  ...
[I-O-CONTROL.  input-output-control-entry] ]
```

The format shows that the Configuration Section is required and the Input-Output Section is optional. The Configuration Section has two required paragraphs, SOURCE-COMPUTER and OBJECT-COMPUTER, and one optional paragraph, **SPECIAL-NAMES.** The SPECIAL-NAMES paragraph is used to relate special user-defined words called **mnemonic names** to hardware and software features that are characteristic of the particular COBOL system being used. Thus the SPECIAL-NAMES paragraph is different in different COBOL systems. We will not need any SPECIAL-NAMES to do any of the programs in this book.

The Input-Output Section is considered optional because you use it only if your program has one or more input or output files. It has one required paragraph, FILE-CONTROL, and one optional paragraph, **I-O-CONTROL.** You already have seen examples of FILE-CONTROL paragraphs. There are four formats for the FILE-CONTROL entry. The one we have been using is Format 1:

```
SELECT [OPTIONAL] file-name
ASSIGN TO implementor-name-1 [, implementor-name-2] ...
                      ⎧ AREA  ⎫
[; RESERVE integer-1  ⎨       ⎬ ]
                      ⎩ AREAS ⎭
[; ORGANIZATION IS SEQUENTIAL]
[; ACCESS MODE IS SEQUENTIAL]
[; FILE STATUS IS data-name-1].
```

All the square brackets in the format show that there are several optional clauses and entries. We will not use any of the optional portions of this format in any programs in this book. Whenever commas or semicolons appear in a format, they may be included or omitted from the entry without changing the meaning.

The reserved words are, of course, in capital letters. But notice that some are not underlined. A reserved word that is not underlined is an optional word, and may be omitted without changing the meaning of the entry. That means that the ASSIGN clause

```
ASSIGN TO PRINTER
```

could just as well have been written:

```
ASSIGN PRINTER
```

An underlined reserved word is required, and is called a **key word.** The format shows that one **implementor name** is required, and that the programmer may use as many as desired. The implementor names that we have used so far are INFILE and PRINTER. Each COBOL system has its own form of implementor names.

You will see other formats of FILE-CONTROL entries when we need them, in Chapters 14 and 15.

The I-O-CONTROL paragraph defines special control techniques to be used in the program. We will not need such techniques in any of the programs in this book.

Summary

The COBOL Coding Form permits a programmer to write coding line for line as it will be keyed or punched.

Records may be described as being composed of fields. Level numbers are used to indicate the relationship between record names and field names.

The READ verb is used to obtain data from an input file and assign the data to the record name associated with the file. The AT END phrase in a READ statement tells the computer what to do when the file contains no more data. Reformatting of input data is accomplished easily by describing the output record in the desired format.

A nonnumeric literal consists of a string of characters, except for the quotation mark, enclosed in quotation marks.

A program to process an unknown number of input records can have a control paragraph consisting of three PERFORM statements and a STOP RUN statement. The three PERFORM statements execute the program's initialization, main loop, and termination in turn.

Fill-in Exercises

1. Area A extends from position _____ through position _____ .

2. Area B extends from position _____ to the right.

3. Fields may be described in the Data Division with level numbers in the range _____ through _____ .

4. The reserved word _____ may be used to name fields not referred to in the processing.

5. Two kinds of literals in COBOL are _____ literals and _____ literals.

6. The _____ Section is used to describe data that are not related to any input or output file.

7. A MOVE statement always leaves the value assigned to the _____ field unchanged.

8. The statement that obtains the first input record from an input file is called a _____ READ.

9. A nonnumeric literal must be enclosed in _____ _____ .

10. A _____ clause may be used to initialize data in the Working Storage Section.

11. The COBOL abbreviation for PICTURE is _____ .

12. A numeric literal may have a(n) _____ anywhere except at its right end.

13. In COBOL formats _____ are used to indicate that exactly one of the items contained within them must be chosen.

14. Two paragraphs that are required in the Configuration Section are _____ and _____ .

15. The required paragraph in the Input-Output Section is the _____ paragraph.

Review Exercises

1. Name the three paragraphs of the Configuration Section in the order in which they appear.
2. In which division of a COBOL program would each of the following be found?
   a. SPECIAL-NAMES
   b. The Working Storage Section
   c. A READ statement
   d. A PERFORM statement
   e. The I-O-CONTROL paragraph
3. Which of the following statement(s) must refer to a file name, and which must refer to a record name?
   a. OPEN
   b. CLOSE
   c. READ
   d. WRITE
4. If the input file to Program P02-03 contains five records, how many times will COBOL test the condition MORE-INPUT IS EQUAL TO "N", line 00660 in Figure 2.10, during execution of the program?
5. Write a COBOL program to the following specifications:

Input

Input records in the following format:

Positions	Field
1 – 8	Part Number
9 – 28	Part Description
35 – 37	Quantity on Hand
38 – 80	spaces

Output

Column headings and a listing of the contents of the records, one line per record, according to the format shown in Figure 2.RE5.

Figure 2.RE5   Output format for Review Exercise 5.

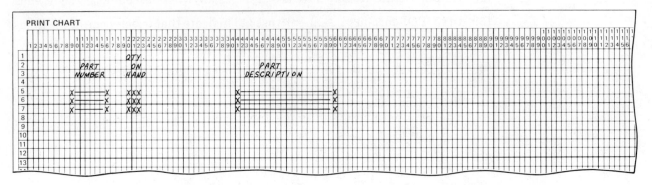

6.   Here is the format of the LABEL RECORDS clause:

Tell whether each of the following is or is not a legal form of the clause:
a.   LABEL RECORDS OMITTED
b.   LABELS ARE OMITTED
c.   LABEL ARE OMITTED
d.   LABEL RECORD IS STANDARD
e.   RECORDS ARE STANDARD
f.   LABEL RECORDS IS OMITTED
g.   LABEL RECORDS STANDARD

Project

Sometimes, input records contain so much data that the data cannot all fit conveniently on one output line when printed. In such a case, the data are printed on two or more lines as needed, with the columns offset horizontally for ease of reading. Column headings are correspondingly offset. The following exercise shows such an application.

Write a program to the following specifications:

Input

Records in the following format:

Positions	Field
1 – 8	Identification Number
9 – 11	Course Code 1
12	Grade 1
13 – 15	Course Code 2
16	Grade 2
17 – 19	Course Code 3
20	Grade 3
21 – 23	Course Code 4
24	Grade 4
25 – 27	Course Code 5
28	Grade 5
29 – 31	Course Code 6
32	Grade 6
33 – 35	Course Code 7
36	Grade 7
37 – 39	Course Code 8
40	Grade 8
41 – 43	Course Code 9
44	Grade 9
45 – 47	Course Code 10
48	Grade 10

Output

Column headings and a listing of the contents of the records, two lines per input record, according to the format shown in Figure 2.P1. Observe the single spacing within each record and the double spacing between records.

Figure 2.P1 Output format for Chapter 2 Project.

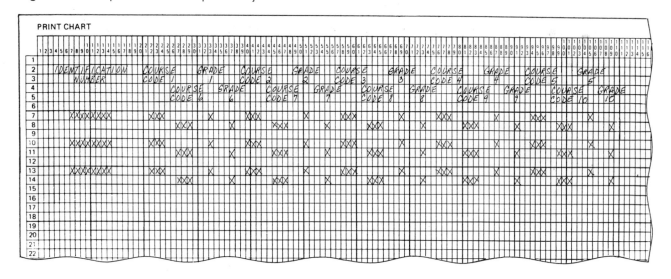

Arithmetic: Program Design I

Here are the key points you should learn from this chapter:

1. How to form PICTUREs for numeric fields
2. The formats of the verbs ADD, SUBTRACT, MULTIPLY, DIVIDE, and COMPUTE
3. The program-design technique called top-down design
4. How to develop and use hierarchy diagrams
5. How to use the arithmetic verbs in programs

Key words to recognize and learn:

ADD	GIVING
SUBTRACT	BY
MULTIPLY	INTO
DIVIDE	REMAINDER
COMPUTE	TO
category of data	top-down design
alphanumeric	subfunction
numeric edited	hierarchy diagram
SIGN	accumulate
default	ZERO
ROUNDED	arithmetic expression
identifier	unary
SIZE ERROR	

In this chapter we will study the arithmetic operations **ADD, SUBTRACT, MULTIPLY, DIVIDE, and COMPUTE,** and two sample programs using those operations. This chapter also contains the first of the three program-design techniques that we will cover in this book.

Numeric Fields

In this chapter we will be dealing, for the first time, with numeric fields in arithmetic operations. Up to now the only **category of data** we have used is **alphanumeric.** Alphanumeric data may consist of any of the computer's characters.

Numeric fields, like alphanumeric fields, may appear in input, output, or working storage. Whereas the PICTURE character X is used to describe alphanumeric fields, the PICTURE characters used to describe numeric fields are 9, S, V, and P. In this chapter we will discuss only 9, S, and V. The seldom used PICTURE character P is discussed in Chapter 10.

The only characters that legally may be assigned to numeric fields are the digits 0 through 9 and a plus or minus sign. A category of data closely related to numeric, called **numeric edited,** uses different PICTURE characters and is discussed in Chapter 4. Whereas a numeric field may not contain a decimal point, comma, or any character other than 0 through 9 and a sign, a numeric edited field may contain all those characters and more, as you will see.

Remember that a numeric literal, on the other hand, may contain digits, a plus or minus sign, and a decimal point (but not at the right end). The maximum size of a numeric field, as of a numeric literal, is 18 digits.

The PICTURE character for a single digit is 9, so to describe a three-digit integer you may use PICTURE 9(3), or PICTURE 999. To describe a number containing a decimal fractional portion, you use the PICTURE character V to show where the decimal point should be. A decimal point never appears explicitly in a numeric field, and a V is used to tell COBOL where to assume the decimal point to be. For example, a five-digit number consisting of three integer places and two decimal places could be described with PICTURE 999V99, or PICTURE 9(3)V99. Table 3-1 shows how different numeric values might be stored in working storage fields.

Table 3-1
How some numeric fields are stored under various PICTUREs.

Value	Field Description	Digits in Computer Storage
4561	05 SAMPLE-1 PIC 9(4)	4561
4561	05 SAMPLE-2 PIC 9(5)	04561
45.61	05 SAMPLE-3 PIC 99V99	4561
45.61	05 SAMPLE-4 PIC 99V9(3)	45610
.638	05 SAMPLE-5 PIC V9(3)	638
.638	05 SAMPLE-6 PIC 99V9(4)	006380

The numeric fields shown so far lack any explicit indication of a positive or negative sign, and are assumed by COBOL to be positive. The programmer can provide for a sign in a numeric field by affixing the character S at the left end of the PICTURE for the field. COBOL then recognizes that the field has the capability of having a plus or minus sign assigned to it. Table 3-2 shows three fields and the range of values that may be assigned to each.

Table 3-2
Three signed numeric fields and the range of values that may be assigned to each.

Field	Range of Values
05 SAMPLE-7 PIC S9(4)	− 9999 through +9999
05 SAMPLE-8 PIC S9(3)V99	− 999.99 through +999.99
05 SAMPLE-9 PIC SV99	− .99 through +.99

The programmer can designate where the sign is to appear in a numeric field in input, output, or working storage, or else can let COBOL store the sign wherever it likes. The sign may appear either immediately to the left or right of the number, or it may appear in the same computer storage location with the leftmost or rightmost digit of the number. The programmer tells COBOL where to locate the sign by using the **SIGN** clause. The SIGN clause can be included anywhere after the data name in the description of a data item.

Each COBOL system has its own **default** location where the sign is stored when the SIGN clause is omitted. In the system used to run the programs in this book, the sign is stored in the same storage location as the rightmost digit of the number unless the programmer uses a SIGN clause to say otherwise. In input and output fields, having the sign in the same position as the rightmost digit produces a mess that is difficult to interpret. It is not recommended. The possible locations of the sign and the corresponding SIGN clauses are:

Location of Sign	SIGN Clause
With leftmost digit	SIGN IS LEADING
With rightmost digit	SIGN IS TRAILING
Immediately to left of number	SIGN IS LEADING SEPARATE CHARACTER
Immediately to right of number	SIGN IS TRAILING SEPARATE CHARACTER

So if a signed, five-digit, dollars-and-cents field with its sign to the right of the number were being read, its description might be:

```
05  MONEY-IN  PIC S9(3)V99 SIGN IS TRAILING SEPARATE CHARACTER.
```

The SIGN clause may be used only with a numeric field whose PICTURE contains the character S. The character S, if used, always appears at the left end of the PICTURE regardless of the location of the sign in the field.

EXERCISE 1

Write level-05 entries for the following fields:

a. An unsigned six-digit dollars-and-cents field called COMMISSION-IN
b. A signed seven-digit field with three decimal places called GAMMA-W
c. A signed eight-digit integer, called DISTANCE-IN, with the sign immediately to the left of the number

SUBTRACT

An example of a subtract statement in COBOL is:

```
SUBTRACT 37.5 FROM HOURS-WORKED.
```

In this statement the difference which results from the subtraction is assigned to HOURS-WORKED and the original value of HOURS-WORKED is lost. Table 3-3 shows the results of this subtraction for different definitions and initial values of HOURS-WORKED.

Table 3-3
Results of the statement SUBTRACT 37.5 FROM HOURS-WORKED for different definitions and initial values of HOURS-WORKED.

Field	Value Before Subtraction	Value After Subtraction
05 HOURS-WORKED PIC 99V9	40.0	02.5
05 HOURS-WORKED PIC 99V99	50.00	12.50
05 HOURS-WORKED PIC 99V99	37.50	00.00
05 HOURS-WORKED PIC S99V9	+40.0	+02.5
05 HOURS-WORKED PIC S99V9	+10.0	−27.5
05 HOURS-WORKED PIC S99V9	−10.0	−47.5
05 HOURS-WORKED PIC 99V9	10.0	27.5

Note that in the numbers in Table 3-3, no decimal points are actually stored in HOURS-WORKED. The decimal points are shown in the table only for ease of understanding. The numeric literal 37.5 legally contains an explicit decimal point, however. Notice in the last entry in the table that an unsigned field can contain only positive numbers, even if the result of arithmetic is negative. Thus it is of the greatest importance that you use signed fields whenever there is the possibility that a result could be negative.

Another legal SUBTRACT statement is:

```
SUBTRACT PAYMENT FROM BALANCE-DUE.
```

In this statement the difference which results from the subtraction is assigned to BALANCE-DUE and the original value of BALANCE-DUE is lost. The value of PAYMENT is unchanged. Table 3-4 shows the results of this subtraction for different definitions and initial values of the fields PAYMENT and BALANCE-DUE.

Table 3-4

Results of the statement SUBTRACT PAYMENT FROM BALANCE-DUE with different definitions and initial values of the fields PAYMENT and BALANCE-DUE.

Field		Value Before Subtraction	Value After Subtraction
05 BALANCE-DUE	PIC 999V99	500.00	150.00
05 PAYMENT	PIC 999V99	350.00	350.00
05 BALANCE-DUE	PIC S999V999	+100.000	+049.200
05 PAYMENT	PIC S99V99	+50.80	+50.80
05 BALANCE-DUE	PIC S9(3)V99	+250.00	+239.14
05 PAYMENT	PIC S99V9(3)	+10.853	+10.853

Notice that in the last example in Table 3-4, the result assigned to BALANCE-DUE is incorrect (it should be 239.147, or 239.15 if rounded) because insufficient decimal places were provided for the answer. Such a situation may be corrected either by changing the PICTURE of BALANCE-DUE to S9(3)V9(3) to allow additional decimal places or by using the **ROUNDED** option.

The ROUNDED option is available with all the arithmetic verbs and directs COBOL to round the final result of arithmetic before assigning it to the result field. When rounding is requested, COBOL increases the least significant digit of the result by 1 whenever the most significant digit of the excess is 5 or greater. The statement

```
SUBTRACT PAYMENT FROM BALANCE-DUE ROUNDED.
```

would have produced the correct result, +239.15.

Format 1 of the SUBTRACT Statement

The format of the SUBTRACT statement that we have been using is:

```
SUBTRACT    {identifier-1}      [, identifier-2]
            {literal-1    }     [, literal-2   ]   . . .

    FROM identifier-m [ROUNDED]
        [, identifier-n [ROUNDED] ] . . .
    [; ON SIZE ERROR imperative-statement]
```

The braces following the word SUBTRACT show that either an **identifier** or a literal must follow SUBTRACT. So far in this book, the only kind of identifier we know is the data name, that is, the name of a field defined in the Data Division. You will see other kinds of identifiers later. The brackets around identifier-2 and literal-2 in the format show that a second identifier or literal optionally may appear before the word FROM. We did not have a second identifier or literal in either of the sample SUBTRACT statements. The ellipsis after the brackets indicates that the contents of the brackets may be repeated as many times as desired by the programmer; that is, optionally there could be a third, fourth, fifth, and so on identifier and/or literal if desired.

Following the required word FROM there is a required identifier. It is here called identifier-m because any number of identifiers might have appeared before the FROM. Following identifier-m is the optional word ROUNDED. The format then shows that there may be as many identifiers as desired following the word FROM, and that each may be accompanied by the optional word ROUNDED or not.

The format tells us that the following statement is legal:

```
SUBTRACT
    JUNE-PAYMENT,
    JULY-PAYMENT
        FROM BALANCE-DUE.
```

In that statement the values of JUNE-PAYMENT and JULY-PAYMENT would first be added, and then the sum would be subtracted from BALANCE-DUE and the difference assigned to BALANCE-DUE. The following statement is also legal:

```
SUBTRACT
    BASE-HOURS,
    2.5
        FROM HOURS-WORKED ROUNDED.
```

Here the value of BASE-HOURS would first be added to 2.5, and then the sum would be subtracted from HOURS-WORKED. If necessary, the difference would be ROUNDED to fit into HOURS-WORKED.

The format shows that several identifiers optionally may appear after the word FROM, so the following statement is legal:

```
SUBTRACT 10.00
    FROM
        TEACHER-PAY-RATE,
        JANITOR-PAY-RATE,
        SWEEPER-PAY-RATE,
```

In that statement 10.00 would be subtracted from the value in each of the result fields.

The **SIZE ERROR** phrase is discussed in Chapter 7.

SUBTRACT with the GIVING Option

To preserve the original values of the fields in a subtraction, the **GIVING** option may be used. For example, in the statement

```
SUBTRACT 40 FROM HOURS-WORKED GIVING OVERTIME-HOURS,
```

the original value assigned to HOURS-WORKED remains after the subtraction as it was before the subtraction, and the difference is assigned to OVERTIME-HOURS. Table 3-5 shows the results of the subtraction for different definitions and initial values of HOURS-WORKED and OVERTIME-HOURS.

Table 3-5
Results of the statement SUBTRACT 40 FROM HOURS-WORKED GIVING OVERTIME-HOURS with different definitions and initial values of the fields HOURS-WORKED and OVERTIME-HOURS.

Field		Value Before Subtraction	Value After Subtraction
05 HOURS-WORKED	PIC S999V99	+010.00	+010.00
05 OVERTIME-HOURS	PIC S99V99	+99.99	−30.00
05 HOURS-WORKED	PIC 999V99	010.00	010.00
05 OVERTIME-HOURS	PIC 99V99	99.99	30.00

Notice that the initial value of the result field, OVERTIME-HOURS, has no effect on the operation. The initial value of the field is replaced by the result.

In the statement

```
SUBTRACT PAYMENT FROM OLD-BALANCE GIVING NEW-BALANCE,
```

the original values assigned to PAYMENT and OLD-BALANCE remain as they were before the subtraction, and the difference is assigned to NEW-BALANCE. Table 3-6 shows the result of the subtraction for different definitions and initial values of the fields.

Table 3-6
Results of the statement SUBTRACT PAYMENT FROM OLD-BALANCE GIVING NEW-BALANCE with different definitions and initial values of the fields PAYMENT, OLD-BALANCE, and NEW-BALANCE.

Field		Value Before Subtraction	Value After Subtraction
05 OLD-BALANCE	PIC 999V999	568.463	568.463
05 PAYMENT	PIC 99V99	25.35	25.35
05 NEW-BALANCE	PIC 999V999	999.999	543.113
05 OLD-BALANCE	PIC 999V999	568.463	568.463
05 PAYMENT	PIC 999V999	25.355	25.355
05 NEW-BALANCE	PIC 999V99	999.99	543.10

Notice that in the last entry in Table 3-6, the result shown, 543.10, is incorrect. It should be 543.108, or 543.11 with rounding. By including the ROUNDED option, as in

```
SUBTRACT PAYMENT FROM OLD-BALANCE
    GIVING NEW-BALANCE ROUNDED.
```

the correct result would be obtained.

Format 2 of the SUBTRACT Statement

The format of the SUBTRACT statement with the GIVING option is:

```
SUBTRACT   {identifier-1}   [, identifier-2]   . . .
           {literal-1   }   [, literal-2   ]

    FROM   {identifier-m}
           {literal-m   }

    GIVING identifier-n [ROUNDED]
           [, identifier-o [ROUNDED] ] . . .
    [; ON SIZE ERROR imperative-statement]
```

The format shows that any number of identifiers are permitted after the word GIVING. If more than one identifier appears after GIVING, the difference from the subtraction is assigned to each of the identifiers. The sample SUBTRACT statements in this format have only one such identifier each.

EXERCISE 2

Write a COBOL statement that will subtract MARKDOWN from PRICE and assign the difference to PRICE.

EXERCISE 3

Write a COBOL statement that will subtract DEDUCTIONS from GROSS-PAY and assign the difference to NET-PAY.

EXERCISE 4

Write a COBOL statement that will subtract CREDITS-EARNED from 120 and assign the difference to CREDITS-REMAINING.

MULTIPLY

Multiplication, like subtraction, can be done with or without a GIVING option. The format for MULTIPLY without the GIVING option is:

```
MULTIPLY  {identifier-1}  BY identifier-2 [ROUNDED]
          {literal-1   }

          [, identifier-3 [ROUNDED] ] ...
          [; ON SIZE ERROR imperative-statement]
```

The multiplicand is given before the word **BY,** and the multiplier is given after the word BY. There may be more than one multiplier after the word BY if desired. COBOL multiplies the multiplicand BY each multiplier in turn and replaces each multiplier with the result of the multiplication, the product. A valid MULTIPLY under this format is:

```
MULTIPLY RATE-OF-PAY BY HOURS-WORKED.
```

Table 3-7 shows the results of the statement for different definitions and initial values of RATE-OF-PAY and HOURS-WORKED.

Table 3-7
Results of the statement MULTIPLY RATE-OF-PAY BY HOURS-WORKED with different definitions and initial values of the fields RATE-OF-PAY and HOURS-WORKED.

Field		Value Before Multiplication	Value After Multiplication
05 RATE-OF-PAY	PIC 99V99	02.85	02.85
05 HOURS-WORKED	PIC 9(3)V99	010.00	028.50
05 RATE-OF-PAY	PIC S99V9	−11.3	−11.3
05 HOURS-WORKED	PIC S9(3)V99	+021.10	−238.43
05 RATE-OF-PAY	PIC S9(3)V9(3)	−011.305	−011.305
05 HOURS-WORKED	PIC S9(3)V9	−010.0	+113.0

Notice that the sign of the product is determined by COBOL according to the rules of multiplication. The result in the last entry in Table 3-7 is incorrect because insufficient decimal places were allowed in the result field. The statement

```
MULTIPLY RATE-OF-PAY BY HOURS-WORKED ROUNDED.
```

would have produced the correct result, +113.1.

Another valid MULTIPLY in this format is:

```
MULTIPLY 1.5 BY OVERTIME-HOURS.
```

Table 3-8 shows the results of this multiplication for different definitions and initial values of the field OVERTIME-HOURS. As before, the product is assigned to the field given after the word BY.

Table 3-8
Results of the statement
MULTIPLY 1.5
BY OVERTIME-HOURS
with different
definitions and initial
values of the field
OVERTIME-HOURS.

Field		Value Before Multiplication	Value After Multiplication
05 OVERTIME-HOURS	PIC 99V99	10.50	15.75
05 OVERTIME-HOURS	PIC S99V9(3)	+10.500	+15.750
05 OVERTIME-HOURS	PIC S99V99	−10.50	−15.75
05 OVERTIME-HOURS	PIC 99V9	10.5	15.7

For the last entry in Table 3-8, the statement

```
MULTIPLY 1.5 BY OVERTIME-HOURS ROUNDED.
```

would have given the correct result, 15.8.

The format of the MULTIPLY statement shows that more than one identifier is permitted after the word BY, so the following statement is valid:

```
MULTIPLY 2 BY
    WHEEL-SPINS,
    PAYOFFS.
```

In this case the values assigned to both WHEEL-SPINS and PAYOFFS would be doubled.

Multiplication can also be written with the GIVING option, so that the product is assigned to a field specified by the programmer. The format of MULTIPLY with the GIVING option is:

```
MULTIPLY  {identifier-1}  BY  {identifier-2}
          {literal-1    }      {literal-2    }

    GIVING identifier-3 [ROUNDED]
            [, identifier-4 [ROUNDED] ] ...
    [; ON SIZE ERROR imperative-statement]
```

In this format COBOL carries out the indicated multiplication and assigns the product to each of the fields given after the word GIVING. A valid MULTIPLY in this format is:

```
MULTIPLY RATE-OF-PAY BY HOURS-WORKED GIVING GROSS-PAY.
```

Table 3-9 shows the results of this statement for different definitions and initial values of RATE-OF-PAY, HOURS-WORKED, and GROSS-PAY.

Table 3-9
Results of the statement
MULTIPLY RATE-OF-PAY
BY HOURS-WORKED
GIVING GROSS-PAY with
different definitions and
initial values of the fields
RATE-OF-PAY, HOURS-
WORKED, and GROSS-
PAY.

Field		Value Before Multiplication	Value After Multiplication
05 RATE-OF-PAY	PIC 99V99	02.85	02.85
05 HOURS-WORKED	PIC 9(3)V99	010.00	010.00
05 GROSS-PAY	PIC 9(3)V99	999.99	028.50
05 RATE-OF-PAY	PIC S99V9	−11.3	−11.3
05 HOURS-WORKED	PIC S9(3)V99	+021.10	+021.10
05 GROSS-PAY	PIC S9(3)V9(3)	+999.999	−238.430
05 RATE-OF-PAY	PIC S9(3)V9(3)	−011.305	−011.305
05 HOURS-WORKED	PIC S9(3)V9	−010.0	−010.0
05 GROSS-PAY	PIC S9(3)V9	+999.9	+113.0

Another legal MULTIPLY statement in this format is:

```
MULTIPLY 1.5 BY OVERTIME-HOURS
     GIVING OVERTIME-EQUIVALENT.
```

Table 3-10 shows the results of this statement for different definitions and initial values of OVERTIME-HOURS and OVERTIME-EQUIVALENT.

Table 3-10
Results of the statement
MULTIPLY 1.5 BY OVER-
TIME-HOURS GIVING
OVERTIME-EQUIVALENT
with different definitions
and initial values of the
fields OVERTIME-HOURS
and OVERTIME-
EQUIVALENT.

Field		Value Before Multiplication	Value After Multiplication
05 OVERTIME-HOURS	PIC 99V99	10.50	10.50
05 OVERTIME-EQUIVALENT	PIC 99V99	99.99	15.75
05 OVERTIME-HOURS	PIC S99V9(3)	+10.500	+10.500
05 OVERTIME-EQUIVALENT	PIC S99V99	+99.99	+15.75
05 OVERTIME-HOURS	PIC S99V99	−10.50	−10.50
05 OVERTIME-EQUIVALENT	PIC S99V9(3)	+99.999	−15.750
05 OVERTIME-HOURS	PIC 99V99	10.50	10.50
05 OVERTIME-EQUIVALENT	PIC 99V9	99.9	15.7

EXERCISE 5

Write a COBOL statement that will triple the value assigned to the field GROSS.

EXERCISE 6

Write a COBOL statement that will multiply together the values assigned to TOTAL-CREDITS and POINT-AVERAGE and assign the product to HONOR-POINTS.

DIVIDE

The DIVIDE verb is a little strange, because with the GIVING option come other options. First, DIVIDE without GIVING:

```
DIVIDE   {identifier-1}
         {literal-1   }

    INTO  identifier-2 [ROUNDED]
             [, identifier-3 [ROUNDED] ] ...
    [; ON SIZE ERROR imperative-statement]
```

The DIVIDE statement carries out the following division:

$$\text{divisor} \overline{)\begin{array}{c} \text{quotient} \\ \text{dividend} \end{array}}$$

Also:

$$\text{quotient} = \frac{\text{dividend}}{\text{divisor}}$$

In a DIVIDE statement the divisor is always given before the word **INTO,** and the dividend is always given after the word INTO. More than one dividend may be given after the word INTO if desired. COBOL divides the divisor INTO each of the dividends separately and replaces each dividend with the result of the division, the quotient. A sample DIVIDE statement in this format is:

```
DIVIDE NUMBER-OF-EXAMS INTO TOTAL-GRADE.
```

Table 3-11 shows the results of this division for different definitions and initial values of NUMBER-OF-EXAMS and TOTAL-GRADE.

Table 3-11
Results of the statement DIVIDE NUMBER-OF-EXAMS INTO TOTAL-GRADE with different definitions and initial values of the fields NUMBER-OF-EXAMS and TOTAL-GRADE.

Field		Value Before Division	Value After Division
05 TOTAL-GRADE	PIC 9(3)V9	366.0	091.5
05 NUMBER-OF-EXAMS	PIC 99	04	04
05 TOTAL-GRADE	PIC S9(3)V9	−247.0	−082.3
05 NUMBER-OF-EXAMS	PIC S99V9	+03.0	+03.0
05 TOTAL-GRADE	PIC S9(3)V9	+248.0	−082.6
05 NUMBER-OF-EXAMS	PIC S99	−03	−03

COBOL determines the sign of the result according to the rules of division. In the second entry in Table 3-11, notice that although the fractional portion of the answer should be .333 . . ., only .3 is stored because only one decimal place is given in the PICTURE for the result field.

In the last entry in the table, the fractional portion of the answer should be .666 . . ., but only .6 is stored. The statement

```
DIVIDE NUMBER-OF-EXAMS INTO TOTAL-GRADE ROUNDED.
```

would give the correct result, – 082.7.

In Chapter 7 we discuss methods for handling cases in which the divisor may be 0.

DIVIDE with GIVING and REMAINDER

With the GIVING option, the programmer also has a choice of writing the division in either direction (that is, DIVIDE A INTO B, or DIVIDE B BY A), and also the option of having the remainder from the division assigned to a separate field. There are two formats of the DIVIDE statement with the GIVING option. First, DIVIDE with GIVING and **REMAINDER:**

```
DIVIDE   {identifier-1}   {INTO}   {identifier-2 }
         {literal-1    }   {BY  }   {literal-2    }

    GIVING identifier-3 [ROUNDED]
    REMAINDER identifier-4
    [; ON SIZE ERROR imperative-statement]
```

In this format, if INTO is used, the divisor is given before the word INTO and the dividend is given after the word INTO. If BY is used, the dividend is given before the word BY and the divisor is given after the word BY. The quotient is assigned to the field given after the word GIVING and the remainder is assigned to the field given after the word REMAINDER. The remainder is computed by COBOL by multiplying the quotient by the divisor and subtracting that product from the dividend.

A sample DIVIDE statement in this format is:

```
DIVIDE TOTAL-SCORE BY 3
    GIVING HANDICAP
    REMAINDER H-REM.
```

Table 3-12 shows the results of this division for different definitions and initial values of the fields TOTAL-SCORE, HANDICAP, and H-REM.

Table 3-12
Results of the statement DIVIDE TOTAL-SCORE BY 3 GIVING HANDICAP REMAINDER H-REM with different definitions and initial values of the fields TOTAL-SCORE, HANDI-CAP, and H-REM.

Field		Value Before Division	Value After Division
05 TOTAL-SCORE	PIC 9(4)	0313	0313
05 HANDICAP	PIC 9(3)	999	104
05 H-REM	PIC 9	9	1
05 TOTAL-SCORE	PIC S9(4)	−0314	−0314
05 HANDICAP	PIC S9(3)	+999	−104
05 H-REM	PIC S9	+9	−2
05 TOTAL-SCORE	PIC 9(4)	0314	0314
05 HANDICAP	PIC 9(3)V9	999.9	104.6
05 H-REM	PIC V9(5)	.99999	.20000

In the second entry in Table 3-12, the REMAINDER is computed by multiplying the quotient, −104, by the divisor, 3, and subtracting that product, −312, from the dividend, −314. In the last entry in the table, the REMAINDER is computed by multiplying the quotient, 104.6, by the divisor and subtracting that product, 313.8, from the dividend, 314.

If the ROUNDED option is used in this format, the REMAINDER is computed before the quotient is ROUNDED, and then the quotient is ROUNDED. Thus for the statement

```
DIVIDE TOTAL-SCORE BY 3
    GIVING HANDICAP ROUNDED
    REMAINDER H-REM.
```

the REMAINDERs would be the same as in Table 3-12. The quotient for the second entry in the table would be −105, and the quotient for the last entry would be 104.7. Only the quotient field can use the ROUNDED option. The REMAINDER field has no ROUNDED option and is truncated on the right end, if necessary, to fit.

DIVIDE with GIVING and Multiple Result Fields

The final format of the DIVIDE statement provides for multiple result fields. It is:

```
DIVIDE   {identifier-1}  {INTO}  {identifier-2}
         {literal-1    }  {BY  }  {literal-2    }

    GIVING   identifier-3 [ROUNDED]
             [, identifier-4 [ROUNDED] ] ...
    [; ON SIZE ERROR imperative-statement]
```

In this format COBOL carries out the indicated division and assigns the result to each of the fields given after the word GIVING. The two statements

```
DIVIDE NUMBER-OF-EXAMS INTO TOTAL-GRADE
    GIVING AVERAGE-GRADE.
```

and

```
DIVIDE TOTAL-GRADE BY NUMBER-OF-EXAMS
    GIVING AVERAGE-GRADE.
```

give the same results. Table 3-13 shows the results of the two statements for different definitions and initial values of the fields TOTAL-GRADE, NUMBER-OF-EXAMS, and AVERAGE-GRADE.

Table 3-13

Results of the statements DIVIDE NUMBER-OF-EXAMS INTO TOTAL-GRADE GIVING AVERAGE-GRADE and DIVIDE TOTAL-GRADE BY NUMBER-OF-EXAMS GIVING AVERAGE-GRADE with different definitions and initial values of the fields NUMBER-OF-EXAMS, TOTAL-GRADE, and AVERAGE-GRADE.

Field		*Value Before Division*	*Value After Division*
05 TOTAL-GRADE	PIC 9(3)	366	366
05 NUMBER-OF-EXAMS	PIC 99	04	04
05 AVERAGE GRADE	PIC 9(3)V9	999.9	091.5
05 TOTAL-GRADE	PIC S9(3)	−247	−247
05 NUMBER-OF-EXAMS	PIC S99V9	+03.0	+03.0
05 AVERAGE-GRADE	PIC S99V9(3)	+99.999	−82.333
05 TOTAL-GRADE	PIC S9(3)V9	+248.0	+248.0
05 NUMBER-OF-EXAMS	PIC S99	−03	−03
05 AVERAGE-GRADE	PIC S99V99	+99.99	−82.66

For the last entry in Table 3-13, the statement

```
DIVIDE TOTAL-GRADE BY NUMBER-OF-EXAMS
    GIVING AVERAGE-GRADE ROUNDED.
```

would give the correct result, −82.67.

EXERCISE 7

Write a COBOL statement that will divide the value assigned to TOTAL-SALES by the value assigned to NUMBER-OF-STORES and assign the unrounded result to TOTAL-SALES.

EXERCISE 8

Write a COBOL statement that will divide the value assigned to TOTAL-SALES by the value assigned to NUMBER-OF-STORES and assign the rounded quotient to AVERAGE-SALES.

EXERCISE 9

Write a COBOL statement that will divide the value assigned to NUMBER-TEST by 2 and assign the unrounded quotient to a field called Q and the remainder to a field called ZERO-ONE.

EXERCISE 10

Write a COBOL statement that will divide the value assigned to NUMBER-TEST by 2 and assign the unrounded quotient to a field called QU and the rounded quotient to a field called QR.

ADD

Two formats of the ADD statement will be given. One of them contains the GIVING option. The other contains the required word **TO.** Whenever you write an ADD statement, it must contain either the word TO or the word GIVING. It must never contain both TO and GIVING. The format with TO is:

```
ADD    {identifier-1}    [, identifier-2]
       {literal-1    }    [, literal-2   ] ...

       TO identifier-m [ROUNDED]
          [, identifier-n [ROUNDED] ] ...
       [; on SIZE ERROR imperative-statement]
```

In this format only one identifier or literal is required before the word TO, although there may be as many as the programmer desires. After the word TO, one identifier is also required, and there may be as many as desired. A sample ADD statement in this format is:

```
ADD NEW-PURCHASES TO BALANCE.
```

In this statement COBOL ADDs the value assigned to NEW-PURCHASES to the value assigned to BALANCE and assigns the sum to BALANCE. Table 3-14 shows the results of that statement for different definitions and initial values of the fields NEW-PURCHASES and BALANCE.

Table 3-14

Results of the statement ADD NEW-PURCHASES TO BALANCE with different definitions and initial values of the fields NEW-PURCHASES and BALANCE.

Field		Value Before Addition	Value After Addition
05 NEW-PURCHASES	PIC 999	150	150
05 BALANCE	PIC 9999	0400	0550
05 NEW-PURCHASES	PIC S99V99	−25.15	−25.15
05 BALANCE	PIC 9(3)V9(3)	135.256	110.106
05 NEW-PURCHASES	PIC 99V99	10.43	10.43
05 BALANCE	PIC S99V9	−80.6	−70.1

For the last entry in Table 3-14, the statement

```
ADD NEW-PURCHASES TO BALANCE ROUNDED.
```

would give the correct result, −70.2.

Another legal ADD statement in this format is:

```
ADD SALESPERSON-NET, SALESPERSON-BONUS
     TO REGION-TOTAL.
```

Here COBOL ADDs together the values assigned to SALESPERSON-NET and SALESPERSON-BONUS, ADDs that sum to the value assigned to REGION-TOTAL, and assigns the final sum to REGION-TOTAL. Table 3-15 shows the results of that statement for different definitions and initial values of SALESPERSON-NET, SALESPERSON-BONUS, and REGION-TOTAL.

Table 3-15
Results of the statement ADD SALESPERSON-NET, SALESPERSON-BONUS TO REGION-TOTAL with different definitions and initial values of the fields SALESPERSON-NET, SALESPERSON-BONUS, and REGION-TOTAL.

Field		Value Before Addition	Value After Addition
05 SALESPERSON-NET	PIC 9(3)V99	100.75	100.75
05 SALESPERSON-BONUS	PIC 99V9(3)	50.665	50.665
05 REGION-TOTAL	PIC 9(3)V9(3)	510.675	662.090
05 SALESPERSON-NET	PIC S9(3)V99	+100.75	+100.75
05 SALESPERSON-BONUS	PIC S99V9(3)	−50.661	−50.661
05 REGION-TOTAL	PIC S9(3)V99	+510.50	+560.58

For the last entry in Table 3-15, the statement

```
ADD SALESPERSON-NET, SALESPERSON-BONUS
     TO REGION-TOTAL ROUNDED.
```

would give the correct result, +560.59.
Another legal ADD statement in this format is:

```
ADD OVERTIME-HOURS, 40
     TO DEPARTMENT-TOTAL,
        FACTORY-TOTAL.
```

In this statement COBOL first ADDs 40 to the value assigned to OVERTIME-HOURS, to form a temporary sum. It then ADDs the temporary sum to the value assigned to DEPARTMENT-TOTAL and assigns the final sum to DEPARTMENT-TOTAL. It then goes back and ADDs the temporary sum to the value assigned to FACTORY-TOTAL and assigns that final sum to FACTORY-TOTAL. Table 3-16 shows the results of this statement for different definitions and initial values of OVERTIME-HOURS, DEPARTMENT-TOTAL, and FACTORY-TOTAL.

Table 3-16
Results of the statement ADD OVERTIME-HOURS, 40 TO DEPARTMENT-TOTAL, FACTORY-TOTAL with different definitions and initial values of the fields OVERTIME-HOURS, DEPARTMENT-TOTAL, and FACTORY-TOTAL.

Field		Value Before Addition	Value After Addition
05 OVERTIME-HOURS	PIC 99V99	12.20	12.20
05 DEPARTMENT-TOTAL	PIC 999V99	350.00	402.20
05 FACTORY-TOTAL	PIC 999V99	600.50	652.70
05 OVERTIME-HOURS	PIC S99V9(3)	−10.002	−10.002
05 DEPARTMENT-TOTAL	PIC S9(3)V99	+300.00	+329.99
05 FACTORY-TOTAL	PIC S9(3)V99	+400.00	+429.99

In the last entry in Table 3-16, the result for DEPARTMENT-TOTAL should be +329.998, but insufficient decimal places are allowed in the PICTURE for DEPARTMENTAL-TOTAL. Similarly, FACTORY-TOTAL should be +429,998. The ROUNDED option may be used on either or both of the result fields, so the statement

```
ADD OVERTIME-HOURS, 40
        TO DEPARTMENT-TOTAL ROUNDED,
              FACTORY-TOTAL,
```

would give the same result for FACTORY-TOTAL as in Table 3-16, but would give the correct result for DEPARTMENT-TOTAL, +330.00.

The format of the ADD statement with the GIVING option is:

```
ADD  {identifier-1}  ,  {identifier-2}  [, identifier-3]...
     {literal-1   }     {literal-2   }  [, literal-3   ]

        GIVING identifier-m [ROUNDED]
             [, identifier-n [ROUNDED] ] ...
      [; ON SIZE ERROR imperative-statement]
```

In this form at least two identifiers and/or literals are required before the word GIVING, and there may be as many as desired. The format shows that any number of identifiers are allowed after the word GIVING. Notice that there is no TO in this form of the ADD. In ADD statements in this format, COBOL ADDs together the values assigned to the fields given before the word GIVING, and assigns the result to the fields given after the word GIVING. An ADD statement in this format is:

```
ADD FIELD-A, FIELD-B
       GIVING FIELD-C,
```

Here COBOL ADDs together the values assigned to FIELD-A and FIELD-B and assigns the sum to FIELD-C. Table 3-17 shows the results of this statement for different definitions and initial values of FIELD-A, FIELD-B, and FIELD-C.

Table 3-17
Results of the statement ADD FIELD-A, FIELD-B GIVING FIELD-C with different definitions and initial values of FIELD-A, FIELD-B, and FIELD-C.

Field		Value Before Addition	Value After Addition
05 FIELD-A	PIC 999	150	150
05 FIELD-B	PIC 9999	0400	0400
05 FIELD-C	PIC 9(5)	99999	00550
05 FIELD-A	PIC S99V99	−25.15	−25.15
05 FIELD-B	PIC 9(3)V99	135.25	135.25
05 FIELD-C	PIC 9(3)V9(3)	999.999	110.100
05 FIELD-A	PIC 99V99	80.57	80.57
05 FIELD-B	PIC S99V9	+10.3	+10.3
05 FIELD-C	PIC S9(3)V9	+999.9	+090.8

Another ADD statement in this format is:

```
ADD OVERTIME-HOURS,
    40
        GIVING TOTAL-HOURS,
                SCHEDULED-HOURS,
```

Here COBOL ADDs 40 to the value assigned to OVERTIME-HOURS and assigns the sum to TOTAL-HOURS and to SCHEDULED-HOURS. Table 3-18 shows the results of this statement for different definitions and initial values of OVERTIME-HOURS, TOTAL-HOURS, and SCHEDULED-HOURS,

Table 3-18
Results of the statement ADD OVERTIME-HOURS, 40 GIVING TOTAL-HOURS, SCHEDULED-HOURS with different definitions and initial values of the fields OVERTIME-HOURS, TOTAL-HOURS, and SCHEDULED-HOURS.

Field		Value Before Addition	Value After Addition
05 OVERTIME-HOURS	PIC 99V99	12.20	12.20
05 TOTAL-HOURS	PIC 999V99	999.99	052.20
05 SCHEDULED-HOURS	PIC 999V9	999.9	052.2
05 OVERTIME-HOURS	PIC S99V9(3)	−10.002	−10.002
05 TOTAL-HOURS	PIC S9(3)V9(3)	+999.999	+029.998
05 SCHEDULED-HOURS	PIC S9(3)V99	+999.99	+029.99

The following ADD statement is invalid because it contains both the words TO and GIVING:

```
ADD FIELD-1 TO FIELD-2 GIVING FIELD-3,
```

EXERCISE 11

Write a COBOL statement that will add together the values assigned to FIELD-1 and FIELD-2 and assign the sum to FIELD-3.

EXERCISE 12

Write a COBOL statement that will add the value of CASH-ADVANCES to the value of BALANCE-DUE and assign the sum to BALANCE-DUE.

A Program with Arithmetic

We will now study a program using addition and multiplication. Program P03-01 uses input data in the following format:

Positions	Field
1 – 7	Customer Number
8 – 15	Part Number
16 – 22	spaces
23 – 25	Quantity
26 – 31	Unit Price (in dollars and cents)
26 – 29	Unit Price dollars
30 – 31	Unit Price cents
32 – 35	Handling Charge (in dollars and cents)
32 – 33	Handling Charge dollars
34 – 35	Handling Charge cents
35 – 80	spaces

Each record represents a purchase of some parts by a customer. The record shows the quantity purchased, the price per unit, and a handling charge for the order. Notice that no positions have been allocated for decimal points in the numeric fields. Decimal points never appear explicitly in numeric fields in input.

The program is to read each record and compute the total cost of the merchandise (by multiplying the Quantity by the Unit Price) and a tax at 7 percent of the merchandise total. Then the program is to add together the merchandise total, the tax, and the Handling Charge to arrive at a total for the order. The information for each order is to be printed on one line as shown in Figure 3.1. Also shown in Figure 3.1 are column headings and a title for the report. At the end of the report, the program prints the total of all the merchandise amounts for all the orders and the totals of all the tax and Handling Charge amounts and a grand total of all the order totals, as shown in Figure 3.1.

Notice that no decimal points are indicated in the money fields in Figure 3.1. Instead there are little inverted Vs to show where the decimal points are to be assumed. We show Vs instead of decimal points because COBOL does not permit explicit decimal points in fields defined as numeric. In the next chapter you will see how to get COBOL to insert decimal points into printed output easily, by using numeric edited fields.

This program is much more difficult than any we have done so far, so we will have to design the program before we begin to code it. There are a variety of program design techniques in use in industry now. For any particular program, the choice of which design technique to use often depends on the complexity and/or size of the program, personal preference, and which technique your instructor tells you to use. In this book we discuss only three of the many techniques available; among the three, all of our design needs can be served. Here we study the technique called **top-down design.** In Chapter 5 we will look at the other two.

Figure 3.1 Output format for Program P03-01.

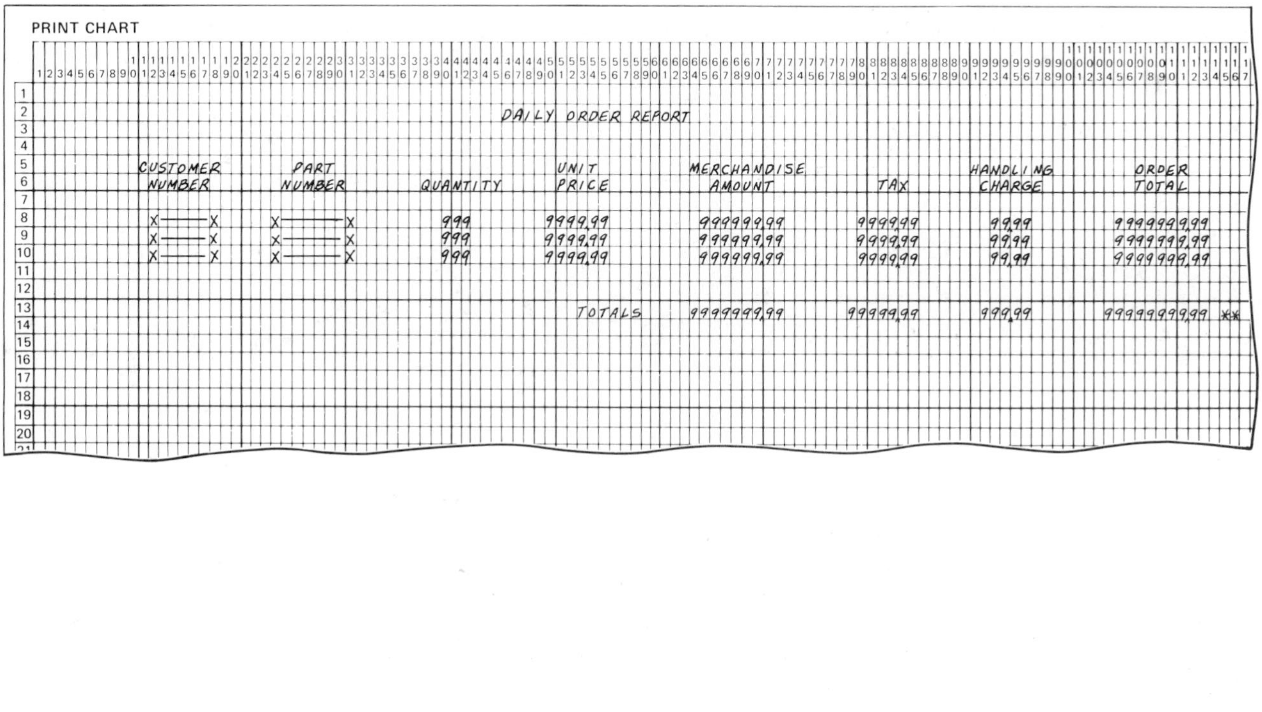

Top-Down Design

In top-down design the programmer avoids trying to think about the whole program at once and instead first decides what the major function of the program is. In our case we can say that the major function is "Produce daily order report." The programmer then decides what **subfunctions** the program must carry out to accomplish the main function. You have already seen from the programs in Chapter 2 that coding is straightforward if you divide a program into three subfunctions:

1. What the program has to do before entering the main loop (initialization)
2. The main loop
3. What the program has to do after end-of-file (termination)

These subfunctions are recorded in the form of a **hierarchy diagram.** In Program P03-01 we can call the three subfunctions "Initialization," "Produce report body," and "Termination." "Initialization" in this program will consist of all the functions it had in Program P02-04. "Termination" will now include printing the total line as well as closing the files. A hierarchy diagram for the program "Produce order report" is shown in Figure 3.2 as it reflects the main function and the subfunctions so far. Notice that the main function of the program is shown in a single box at the top, and the subfunctions are shown beneath it. If any of the subfunctions could be broken down further, we would show that breakdown on the hierarchy diagram also. The subfunction "Produce report body" can indeed be detailed a little more. Figure 3.3 shows the complete hierarchy diagram.

Figure 3.2 Hierarchy diagram with one level of subfunctions.

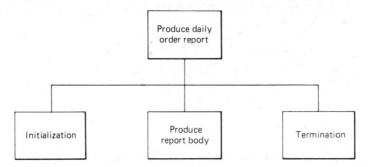

Figure 3.3 Complete hierarchy diagram for Program P03-01.

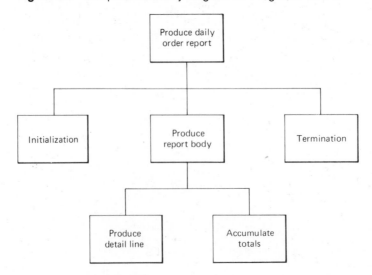

Let us examine the subfunction "Accumulate totals." Why is that shown under "Produce report body" instead of under "Termination," where the total line is printed? Remember that the program can work on only one input record at a time. It must do all required processing on each input record before READing in the next. So in this program, as we compute the several money amounts that we need for printing each line, we will also have to **accumulate** those amounts in some way as if we were adding them into a calculator. As each detail line is printed, therefore, we also add the money amounts into ever-growing subtotals, so that, after all the detail lines of the report have been printed, we will have the totals of the money amounts ready to be printed in the total line. COBOL provides an easy way for the programmer to do this, as you will soon see.

Using Arithmetic Statements in a Program

Program P03-01 is shown in Figure 3.4. There is nothing new in the Identification or Environment Divisions. In the Data Division the definition of ORDER-RECORD-IN, lines 00270 through 00340, shows how numeric fields in input are defined. You can see the definition of an integer, QUANTITY-IN, at line 00310, and the definitions of numbers with fractional parts at lines 00320 and 00330. The output record, REPORT-LINE, is as usual made as large as the longest line that the program is to print. You can see from the print chart in Figure 3.1 that the longest line is 116 characters.

Figure 3.4 Program P03-01.

```
CB1 RELEASE 2.4                            IBM OS/VS COBOL   JULY  1, 1982


                      23.08.48        MAR 27,1988


00010   IDENTIFICATION DIVISION.
00020   PROGRAM-ID.  P03-01.
00030 *
00040 *      THIS PROGRAM READS CUSTOMER ORDER RECORDS
00050 *      AND PRODUCES A DAILY ORDER REPORT.
00060 *
00070 *****************************************************************
00080
00090   ENVIRONMENT DIVISION.
00100   CONFIGURATION SECTION.
00110   SOURCE-COMPUTER.   IBM-370.
00120   OBJECT-COMPUTER.   IBM-370.
00130
00140   INPUT-OUTPUT SECTION.
00150   FILE-CONTROL.
00160       SELECT ORDER-FILE-IN ASSIGN TO INFILE.
00170       SELECT ORDER-REPORT  ASSIGN TO PRINTER.
00180
00190 *****************************************************************
00200
00210   DATA DIVISION.
00220   FILE SECTION.
00230   FD  ORDER-FILE-IN
00240       RECORD CONTAINS 80 CHARACTERS
00250       LABEL RECORDS ARE OMITTED.
00260
00270   01  ORDER-RECORD-IN.
00280       05 CUSTOMER-NUMBER-IN PIC X(7).
00290       05 PART-NUMBER-IN     PIC X(8).
00300       05 FILLER            PIC X(7).
00310       05 QUANTITY-IN        PIC 9(3).
00320       05 UNIT-PRICE-IN      PIC 9(4)V99.
00330       05 HANDLING-CHARGE-IN PIC 99V99.
00340       05 FILLER            PIC X(45).
00350
00360   FD  ORDER-REPORT
00370       LABEL RECORDS ARE OMITTED.
00380
00390   01  REPORT-LINE          PIC X(116).
00400
```

(continued)

In the Working Storage Section, we have the usual MORE-INPUT field at line 00420. We also have defined the constant .07 with the name TAX-RATE, at line 00430. It is good programming practice to define, in working storage, all constants used by a program. Notice that although the numeric literal .07 has an explicit decimal point, the PICTURE of the field contains a V and not a dot. This indicates to the system that the number is to be stored in purely numeric form, without an explicit decimal point, so that it can be used in arithmetic.

The report title line and the column heading lines are defined in lines 00450 through 00790. The detail line is defined at lines 00810 through 00970. You can see how the integer QUANTITY-OUT is defined for output, at line 00870, and how numbers with fractional parts are defined for output, at lines 00890, 00910, 00930, 00950, and 00970.

Figure 3.4 (continued)

```
00410    WORKING-STORAGE SECTION.
00420    01  MORE-INPUT              PIC X      VALUE "Y".
00430    01  TAX-RATE               PIC V99    VALUE .07.
00440
00450    01  REPORT-TITLE.
00460        05 FILLER              PIC X(45) VALUE SPACES.
00470        05 FILLER              PIC X(18) VALUE "DAILY ORDER REPORT".
00480
00490    01  COLUMN-HEADS-1.
00500        05 FILLER              PIC X(10) VALUE SPACES.
00510        05 FILLER              PIC X(8)  VALUE "CUSTOMER".
00520        05 FILLER              PIC X(7)  VALUE SPACES.
00530        05 FILLER              PIC X(4)  VALUE "PART".
00540        05 FILLER              PIC X(21) VALUE SPACES.
00550        05 FILLER              PIC X(4)  VALUE "UNIT".
00560        05 FILLER              PIC X(9)  VALUE SPACES.
00570        05 FILLER              PIC X(11) VALUE "MERCHANDISE".
00580        05 FILLER              PIC X(16) VALUE SPACES.
00590        05 FILLER              PIC X(8)  VALUE "HANDLING".
00600        05 FILLER              PIC X(8)  VALUE SPACES.
00610        05 FILLER              PIC X(5)  VALUE "ORDER".
00620
00630    01  COLUMN-HEADS-2.
00640        05 FILLER              PIC X(11) VALUE SPACES.
00650        05 FILLER              PIC X(6)  VALUE "NUMBER".
00660        05 FILLER              PIC X(7)  VALUE SPACES.
00670        05 FILLER              PIC X(6)  VALUE "NUMBER".
00680        05 FILLER              PIC X(7)  VALUE SPACES.
00690        05 FILLER              PIC X(8)  VALUE "QUANTITY".
00700        05 FILLER              PIC X(5)  VALUE SPACES.
00710        05 FILLER              PIC X(5)  VALUE "PRICE".
00720        05 FILLER              PIC X(10) VALUE SPACES.
00730        05 FILLER              PIC X(6)  VALUE "AMOUNT".
00740        05 FILLER              PIC X(10) VALUE SPACES.
00750        05 FILLER              PIC X(3)  VALUE "TAX".
00760        05 FILLER              PIC X(7)  VALUE SPACES.
00770        05 FILLER              PIC X(6)  VALUE "CHARGE".
00780        05 FILLER              PIC X(9)  VALUE SPACES.
00790        05 FILLER              PIC X(5)  VALUE "TOTAL".
00800
00810    01  DETAIL-LINE.
00820        05 FILLER                   PIC X(11)   VALUE SPACES.
00830        05 CUSTOMER-NUMBER-OUT      PIC X(7).
00840        05 FILLER                   PIC X(5)    VALUE SPACES.
00850        05 PART-NUMBER-OUT          PIC X(8).
00860        05 FILLER                   PIC X(8)    VALUE SPACES.
00870        05 QUANTITY-OUT             PIC 999.
00880        05 FILLER                   PIC X(7)    VALUE SPACES.
00890        05 UNIT-PRICE-OUT           PIC 9(4)V99.
00900        05 FILLER                   PIC X(9)    VALUE SPACES.
00910        05 MERCHANDISE-AMOUNT-OUT   PIC 9(6)V99.
00920        05 FILLER                   PIC X(7)    VALUE SPACES.
00930        05 TAX-OUT                  PIC 9(4)V99.
00940        05 FILLER                   PIC X(7)    VALUE SPACES.
00950        05 HANDLING-CHARGE-OUT      PIC 99V99.
00960        05 FILLER                   PIC X(8)    VALUE SPACES.
00970        05 ORDER-TOTAL-OUT          PIC 9(7)V99.
00980
```

```
00990  01   TOTAL-LINE.
01000       05  FILLER                        PIC X(52)    VALUE SPACES.
01010       05  FILLER                        PIC X(6)     VALUE "TOTALS".
01020       05  FILLER                        PIC X(5)     VALUE SPACES.
01030       05  MERCHANDISE-AMOUNT-TOT-OUT    PIC 9(7)V99  VALUE 0.
01040       05  FILLER                        PIC X(6)     VALUE SPACES.
01050       05  TAX-TOT-OUT                   PIC 9(5)V99  VALUE 0.
01060       05  FILLER                        PIC X(6)     VALUE SPACES.
01070       05  HANDLING-CHARGE-TOT-OUT       PIC 999V99   VALUE 0.
01080       05  FILLER                        PIC X(7)     VALUE SPACES.
01090       05  GRAND-TOT-OUT                 PIC 9(8)V99  VALUE 0.
01100       05  FILLER                        PIC X(3)     VALUE " **".
01110
01120  ********************************************************************
01130
01140  PROCEDURE DIVISION.
01150  PRODUCE-DAILY-ORDER-REPORT.
01160      PERFORM INITIALIZATION.
01170      PERFORM PRODUCE-REPORT-BODY UNTIL MORE-INPUT IS EQUAL TO "N".
01180      PERFORM TERMINATION.
01190      STOP RUN.
01200
01210  INITIALIZATION.
01220      OPEN INPUT  ORDER-FILE-IN,
01230           OUTPUT ORDER-REPORT.
01240      WRITE REPORT-LINE FROM REPORT-TITLE.
01250      WRITE REPORT-LINE FROM COLUMN-HEADS-1
01260          AFTER ADVANCING 3 LINES.
01270      WRITE REPORT-LINE FROM COLUMN-HEADS-2.
01280      MOVE SPACES TO REPORT-LINE.
01290      WRITE REPORT-LINE.
01300      READ ORDER-FILE-IN
01310          AT END
01320              MOVE "N" TO MORE-INPUT.
01330
01340  TERMINATION.
01350      WRITE REPORT-LINE FROM TOTAL-LINE AFTER ADVANCING 3 LINES.
01360      CLOSE ORDER-FILE-IN,
01370            ORDER-REPORT.
```

(continued)

The total line of the report is defined at lines 00990 through 01100. The numeric fields in that line serve as output fields for the four money-amount totals in the line. As you will see when we look at the Procedure Division, those numeric fields also serve as the working storage fields where the four totals are accumulated. Thus we initialize the four fields with VALUE 0, just as we would zero out a calculator before adding numbers into it. If you are inclined to mistake the letter O for the number 0, you can use VALUE **ZERO** instead. ZERO is a COBOL reserved word.

The Procedure Division begins at line 01140. Each paragraph in the Procedure Division corresponds to one box on the hierarchy diagram in Figure 3.3. For example, the main control paragraph, at line 01150, corresponds to the highest-level box on the diagram, and is given the name PRODUCE-DAILY-ORDER-REPORT. The three paragraphs at the first level of subfunctions are given the names INITIALIZATION, PRODUCE-REPORT-BODY, and TERMINATION to correspond to the hierarchy diagram. You can see in the INITIALIZATION paragraph, line 01210, how the report title and column headings are printed, and in the TERMINATION paragraph, line 01340, how the total line is printed. Remember that by the time the TERMINATION paragraph is executed, the totals have already been accumulated and there is nothing to do but print them.

The paragraph PRODUCE-REPORT-BODY, at line 01390, corresponds to the hierarchy diagram also. In the diagram the box "Produce report body" has two subfunctions; in the program the paragraph PRODUCE-REPORT-BODY has PERFORM statements to carry out the subfunctions. It also has a READ statement, even though such a statement is not shown on the hierarchy diagram. It is good practice for the main loop to obtain its input records either in the highest-level paragraph in the main loop, as we have done here, or directly under control of the highest-level paragraph, as we will do in later programs.

In the paragraph PRODUCE-DETAIL-LINE, you can see examples of arithmetic statements with the GIVING option, at lines 01470 through 01540. In the paragraph ACCUMULATE-TOTALS, you can see how the four money amounts are accumulated, in lines 01630 through 01660.

Program P03-01 was run with the input data shown in Figure 3.5 and produced the output shown in Figure 3.6.

Figure 3.4   (continued)

```
01380
01390    PRODUCE-REPORT-BODY.
01400        PERFORM PRODUCE-DETAIL-LINE.
01410        PERFORM ACCUMULATE-TOTALS.
01420        READ ORDER-FILE-IN
01430            AT END
01440                MOVE "N" TO MORE-INPUT.
01450
01460    PRODUCE-DETAIL-LINE.
01470        MULTIPLY QUANTITY-IN BY UNIT-PRICE-IN
01480            GIVING MERCHANDISE-AMOUNT-OUT.
01490        MULTIPLY MERCHANDISE-AMOUNT-OUT BY TAX-RATE
01500            GIVING TAX-OUT ROUNDED.
01510        ADD MERCHANDISE-AMOUNT-OUT,
01520            TAX-OUT,
01530            HANDLING-CHARGE-IN
01540                GIVING ORDER-TOTAL-OUT.
01550        MOVE CUSTOMER-NUMBER-IN    TO CUSTOMER-NUMBER-OUT.
01560        MOVE PART-NUMBER-IN        TO PART-NUMBER-OUT.
01570        MOVE QUANTITY-IN           TO QUANTITY-OUT.
01580        MOVE UNIT-PRICE-IN         TO UNIT-PRICE-OUT.
01590        MOVE HANDLING-CHARGE-IN    TO HANDLING-CHARGE-OUT.
01600        WRITE REPORT-LINE FROM DETAIL-LINE.
01610
01620    ACCUMULATE-TOTALS.
01630        ADD MERCHANDISE-AMOUNT-OUT TO MERCHANDISE-AMOUNT-TOT-OUT.
01640        ADD TAX-OUT                TO TAX-TOT-OUT.
01650        ADD HANDLING-CHARGE-OUT    TO HANDLING-CHARGE-TOT-OUT.
01660        ADD ORDER-TOTAL-OUT        TO GRAND-TOT-OUT.
```

Figure 3.5   Input to Program P03-01.

```
---------------------------------------------------------------------------
          1         2         3         4         5         6         7         8
12345678901234567890123456789012345678901234567890123456789012345678901234567890
---------------------------------------------------------------------------
ABC1234F2365-09        9000000100005
09G8239836-7YT7        8000010500050
ADGH784091AN-07        0500250000500
967547323S-1287        0067000295000
```

Figure 3.6 Output from Program P03-01.

DAILY ORDER REPORT

CUSTOMER NUMBER	PART NUMBER	QUANTITY	UNIT PRICE	MERCHANDISE AMOUNT	TAX	HANDLING CHARGE	ORDER TOTAL
ABC1234	F2365-09	900	000010	00009000	000630	0005	000009635
09G8239	836-7YT7	800	001050	00840000	058800	0050	000898850
ADGH784	091AN-07	050	025000	01250000	087500	0500	001338000
9675473	23S-1287	006	700029	04200174	294012	5000	004499186
			TOTALS	006299174	0440942	05555	0006745671 **

EXERCISE 13

Write a program to read and process input records in the following format:

Positions	Field
1	space
2 – 6	Account Number
7 – 9	spaces
10 – 16	Amount (in dollars and cents)
10 – 14	Amount dollars
15 – 16	Amount cents
17 – 80	spaces

For each record have your program compute a 2 percent discount on the Amount and a net amount (the original Amount minus the discount). For each record have your program print the Account Number, the Amount, the computed discount, and the computed net amount. At the end of the report have your program print the total of the input Amounts, the total of the computed discounts, and the total of the computed net amounts. Have your program produce output in the format shown in Figure 3.E13.

Figure 3.E13 Output format for Exercise 13.

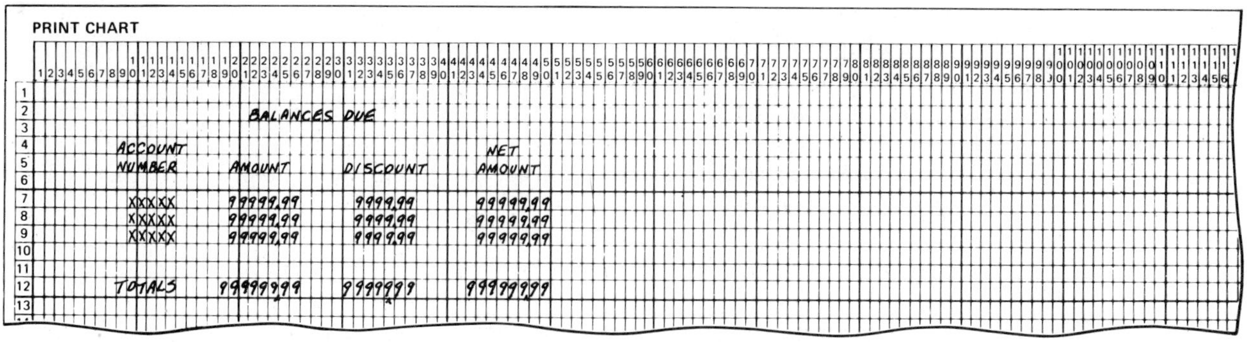

COMPUTE

The fifth and last arithmetic verb, COMPUTE, permits the programmer to carry out more than one arithmetic operation in a single statement. Here is an example of a COMPUTE statement:

```
COMPUTE AVERAGE-GRADE ROUNDED =
    (GRADE-1-IN +
     GRADE-2-IN +
     GRADE-3-IN +
     GRADE-4-IN) / NUMBER-OF-EXAMS.
```

In this statement COBOL would add the values of the four fields GRADE-1-IN, GRADE-2-IN, GRADE-3-IN, and GRADE-4-IN, and divide the sum by the value of NUMBER-OF-EXAMS. COBOL would then round the result and assign it to the field AVERAGE-GRADE. COBOL would set up its own field for the intermediate result, the sum.

The format of the COMPUTE statement is:

```
COMPUTE identifier-1 [ROUNDED]
        [, identifier-2 [ROUNDED] ] ...
        = arithmetic-expression
        [; ON SIZE ERROR imperative-statement]
```

In a COMPUTE statement COBOL carries out the computation indicated in the **arithmetic expression,** on the right side of the equal sign, and assigns the result of the computation to the field or fields given after the word COMPUTE, on the left side of the equal sign. The format shows that at least one identifier is required after the word COMPUTE, and that there may be as many as desired. Exactly one arithmetic expression is required to the right of the equal sign.

An arithmetic expression may consist of one numeric literal or one identifier defined as a numeric field or a combination of literals and/or identifiers connected by arithmetic operators. The arithmetic operators are:

+ addition
− subtraction
* multiplication
/ division
** exponentiation

Whenever arithmetic operators are used, they must be preceded and followed by a space. The expression

```
VOLTAGE ** 2
```

would compute the square of the value assigned to VOLTAGE.

A literal or identifier in an arithmetic expression may be optionally preceded by one of the **unary** operators, + or − . A unary operator of + has no effect; a unary operator of − has the effect of multiplying the value of the literal or identifier by − 1. A unary operator, if used, must be preceded and followed by a space. A unary operator may be used in addition to any + or − sign that may be part of a numeric literal. A + or − sign that is part of a numeric literal is always followed immediately by a digit.

Expressions may be enclosed in parentheses to indicate the order in which arithmetic is to be carried out. Arithmetic is carried out in the following order:

1. Contents of parentheses are evaluated first, and within nested parentheses the innermost level is evaluated first.
2. Unary plus or minus.
3. Exponentiation.
4. Multiplication and division.
5. Addition and subtraction.

If any ambiguity remains, the arithmetic is carried out from left to right.

For example, consider these three expressions:

1. A * B / C * D
2. A * (B / C) * D
3. (A * B) / (C * D)

Expression 1 is evaluated as follows: First A is multiplied by B, and then the product is divided by C. The quotient from the division is multiplied by D. Expression 2 is evaluated as follows: First B is divided by C, and A is multiplied by the quotient. The product of the multiplication is then multiplied by D. The arithmetic result is the same as in expression 1. Expression 3 in general gives a different arithmetic result from the other two. Here A is multiplied by B, and C is multiplied by D. The first product is then divided by the second. If $A = 5, B = 4, C = 2$, and $D = 10$, expressions 1 and 2 give the result 100 and expression 3 gives 1.

Do not use COMPUTE where one of the other arithmetic verbs will do. For example, if you want to ADD 1, use a statement such as

```
ADD 1 TO NUMBER-OF-STUDENTS
```

and not:

```
COMPUTE NUMBER-OF-STUDENTS = NUMBER-OF-STUDENTS + 1.
```

Be careful when using COMPUTE with very large or very small intermediate results. Significant digits may sometimes be lost. In some systems a statement such as:

```
COMPUTE ONE = (10 ** 18) * (10 ** 18) / (10 ** 18) / (10 ** 18)
```

may not produce the correct result, 1.

Using the COMPUTE Verb

Our next program, Program P03-02, uses input data in the following format:

Positions	Field
1 – 9	Student Number
18 – 20	Exam Grade 1
21 – 23	Exam Grade 2
24 – 26	Exam Grade 3
27 – 29	Exam Grade 4
30 – 80	spaces

Each record contains a Student Number and the grades that the student got on each of four exams. The program is to read the data and print a list showing each Student Number, the four grades, and the average of the four grades. At the end of the list, the program is to print the average of all the grades on exam 1, the average of all the grades on exams 2, 3, and 4, and the grand class average of all the individual student averages. The output format is shown in Figure 3.7. The little inverted Vs show that the averages are computed and printed to one decimal place. In Chapter 4 you will see how to insert real decimal points into printed numbers.

Figure 3.7   Output format for Program P03-02.

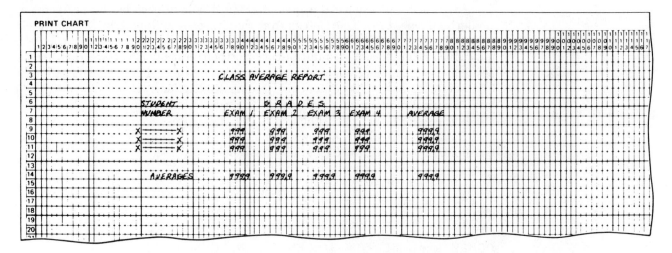

We first do the top-down design for Program P03-02. The main function of this program, "Produce class average report," and its main subfunctions are shown in Figure 3.8. Let us consider the subfunction "Termination" for a moment. What are the subfunctions of "Termination"? We know that all the subfunctions of "Termination" are things that are done after end-of-file is detected in the input, namely, producing the final print line on the list and closing the files. Producing the final print line, in turn, consists of two subfunctions. We place all of these subfunctions on the diagram as shown in Figure 3.9.

Figure 3.8 First-level hierarchy diagram for Program P03-02.

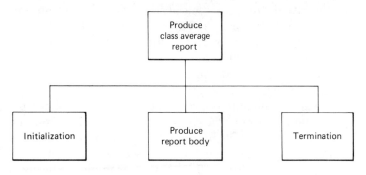

Figure 3.9 Hierarchy diagram for Program P03-02 showing the subfunctions of "Termination."

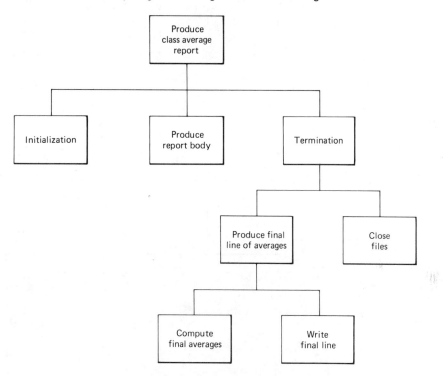

Now let us consider the subfunctions of "Produce report body." One of these subfunctions is "Produce detail line," which we already know how to do from Program P03-01. As part of "Produce report body" we will have to generate the data that will be needed at end-of-file for "Compute final averages" to do its work. What data will "Compute final averages" need to compute, let's say, the average grade on exam 1? It will need the sum of all the grades on exam 1 and also the number of students in the class. (For simplicity we will assume that all the students in the class took all the exams.) "Compute final averages" will have to have similar information about exams 2, 3, and 4. To provide this information, we show the subfunctions "Accumulate grades" and "Count number of students" as subfunctions of "Produce report body," as in Figure 3.10. These two new subfunctions are added under "Produce report body" instead of somewhere else in the diagram because this is the only place where they can be carried out. As each body line is written onto the report, the program will add the grades on the four exams into four accumulators and also the number 1 to another accumulator that will serve as a count of the number of students. When end-of-file is reached, we will have all the totals of grades that we need, as well as the number of students. The diagram in Figure 3.10 is then the complete hierarchy diagram.

Figure 3.10 Complete hierarchy diagram for Program P03-02.

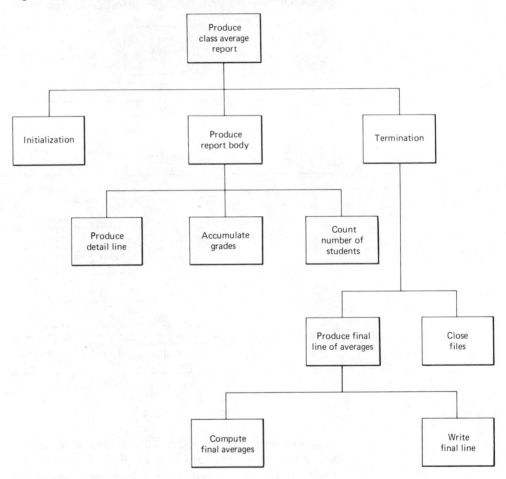

A Program Using the COMPUTE Verb

Program P03-02 is shown in Figure 3.11. Five accumulators have been set up in the Working Storage Section, at lines 00960 through 01000. EXAM-1-SUM is used for accumulating the sum of all the grades on exam 1, EXAM-2-SUM for accumulating the sum of all the grades on exam 2, and so on. NUMBER-OF-STUDENTS is used to count the number of students. Each of the accumulators is defined large enough to hold the largest possible expected sum.

Figure 3.11 Program P03-02.

```
CB1 RELEASE 2.4                                IBM OS/VS COBOL  JULY 1, 1982

                        8.36.42        MAR 28,1988

00010   IDENTIFICATION DIVISION.
00020   PROGRAM-ID.  P03-02.
00030 *
00040 *       THIS PROGRAM READS A FILE OF EXAM GRADES AND
00050 *       COMPUTES EACH STUDENT'S AVERAGE AND THE CLASS AVERAGE.
00060 *
00070 ****************************************************************************
00080
00090   ENVIRONMENT DIVISION.
00100   CONFIGURATION SECTION.
00110   SOURCE-COMPUTER.  IBM-370.
00120   OBJECT-COMPUTER.  IBM-370.
00130
00140   INPUT-OUTPUT SECTION.
00150   FILE-CONTROL.
00160       SELECT EXAM-GRADE-FILE-IN    ASSIGN TO INFILE.
00170       SELECT STUDENT-GRADE-REPORT  ASSIGN TO PRINTER.
00180
00190 ****************************************************************************
00200
00210   DATA DIVISION.
00220   FILE SECTION.
00230   FD  EXAM-GRADE-FILE-IN
00240       RECORD CONTAINS 80 CHARACTERS
00250       LABEL RECORDS ARE OMITTED.
00260
00270   01  EXAM-GRADE-RECORD.
00280       05 STUDENT-NUMBER-IN  PIC X(9).
00290       05 FILLER            PIC X(8).
00300       05 EXAM-GRADE-1-IN    PIC 9(3).
00310       05 EXAM-GRADE-2-IN    PIC 9(3).
00320       05 EXAM-GRADE-3-IN    PIC 9(3).
00330       05 EXAM-GRADE-4-IN    PIC 9(3).
00340       05 FILLER            PIC X(51).
00350
00360   FD  STUDENT-GRADE-REPORT
00370       LABEL RECORDS ARE OMITTED.
00380
00390   01  REPORT-LINE          PIC X(78).
00400
00410   WORKING-STORAGE SECTION.
00420   01  MORE-INPUT           PIC X     VALUE "Y".
00430
00440   01  REPORT-TITLE.
00450       05 FILLER            PIC X(35) VALUE SPACES.
00460       05 FILLER            PIC X(20) VALUE "CLASS AVERAGE REPORT".
00470
00480   01  COLUMN-HEADS-1.
00490       05 FILLER            PIC X(20) VALUE SPACES.
00500       05 FILLER            PIC X(7)  VALUE "STUDENT".
00510       05 FILLER            PIC X(17) VALUE SPACES.
00520       05 FILLER            PIC X(12) VALUE "G R A D E S ".
00530
```

(continued)

Figure 3.11   (continued)

```
00540   01   COLUMN-HEADS-2.
00550        05  FILLER                    PIC X(20) VALUE SPACES.
00560        05  FILLER                    PIC X(6)  VALUE "NUMBER".
00570        05  FILLER                    PIC X(10) VALUE SPACES.
00580        05  FILLER                    PIC X(6)  VALUE "EXAM 1".
00590        05  FILLER                    PIC X(2)  VALUE SPACES.
00600        05  FILLER                    PIC X(6)  VALUE "EXAM 2".
00610        05  FILLER                    PIC X(2)  VALUE SPACES.
00620        05  FILLER                    PIC X(6)  VALUE "EXAM 3".
00630        05  FILLER                    PIC X(2)  VALUE SPACES.
00640        05  FILLER                    PIC X(6)  VALUE "EXAM 4".
00650        05  FILLER                    PIC X(5)  VALUE SPACES.
00660        05  FILLER                    PIC X(7)  VALUE "AVERAGE".
00670
00680   01   DETAIL-LINE.
00690        05  FILLER                    PIC X(19) VALUE SPACES.
00700        05  STUDENT-NUMBER-OUT        PIC X(9).
00710        05  FILLER                    PIC X(9)  VALUE SPACES.
00720        05  EXAM-GRADE-1-OUT          PIC 999.
00730        05  FILLER                    PIC X(5)  VALUE SPACES.
00740        05  EXAM-GRADE-2-OUT          PIC 999.
00750        05  FILLER                    PIC X(5)  VALUE SPACES.
00760        05  EXAM-GRADE-3-OUT          PIC 999.
00770        05  FILLER                    PIC X(5)  VALUE SPACES.
00780        05  EXAM-GRADE-4-OUT          PIC 999.
00790        05  FILLER                    PIC X(9)  VALUE SPACES.
00800        05  AVERAGE-GRADE-OUT         PIC 999V9.
00810
00820   01   FINAL-AVERAGE-LINE.
00830        05  FILLER                    PIC X(22) VALUE SPACES.
00840        05  FILLER                    PIC X(15) VALUE "AVERAGES".
00850        05  EXAM-1-AVERAGE-OUT        PIC 999V9.
00860        05  FILLER                    PIC X(4)  VALUE SPACES.
00870        05  EXAM-2-AVERAGE-OUT        PIC 999V9.
00880        05  FILLER                    PIC X(4)  VALUE SPACES.
00890        05  EXAM-3-AVERAGE-OUT        PIC 999V9.
00900        05  FILLER                    PIC X(4)  VALUE SPACES.
00910        05  EXAM-4-AVERAGE-OUT        PIC 999V9.
00920        05  FILLER                    PIC X(8)  VALUE SPACES.
00930        05  CLASS-AVERAGE-OUT         PIC 999V9.
00940
00950   01   NUMBER-OF-EXAMS              PIC 9     VALUE 4.
00960   01   EXAM-1-SUM                   PIC 9(5)  VALUE 0.
00970   01   EXAM-2-SUM                   PIC 9(5)  VALUE 0.
00980   01   EXAM-3-SUM                   PIC 9(5)  VALUE 0.
00990   01   EXAM-4-SUM                   PIC 9(5)  VALUE 0.
01000   01   NUMBER-OF-STUDENTS          PIC 9(3)  VALUE 0.
01010
01020   **********************************************************************
01030
01040   PROCEDURE DIVISION.
01050   PRODUCE-CLASS-AVERAGE-REPORT.
01060        PERFORM INITIALIZATION.
01070        PERFORM PRODUCE-REPORT-BODY UNTIL MORE-INPUT IS EQUAL TO "N".
01080        PERFORM TERMINATION.
01090        STOP RUN.
01100
01110   INITIALIZATION.
01120        OPEN INPUT  EXAM-GRADE-FILE-IN,
01130             OUTPUT STUDENT-GRADE-REPORT.
01140        WRITE REPORT-LINE FROM REPORT-TITLE.
01150        WRITE REPORT-LINE FROM COLUMN-HEADS-1
01160             AFTER ADVANCING 3 LINES.
01170        WRITE REPORT-LINE FROM COLUMN-HEADS-2.
01180        MOVE SPACES TO REPORT-LINE.
01190        WRITE REPORT-LINE.
01200        READ EXAM-GRADE-FILE-IN
01210             AT END
01220                  MOVE "N" TO MORE-INPUT.
```

```
01230
01240    TERMINATION.
01250        PERFORM PRODUCE-FINAL-LINE-OF-AVERAGES.
01260        PERFORM CLOSE-FILES.
01270
01280    CLOSE-FILES.
0129,0       CLOSE EXAM-GRADE-FILE-IN,
01300            STUDENT-GRADE-REPORT.
01310
01320    PRODUCE-REPORT-BODY.
01330        PERFORM PRODUCE-DETAIL-LINE.
01340        PERFORM ACCUMULATE-GRADES.
01350        PERFORM COUNT-NUMBER-OF-STUDENTS.
01360        READ EXAM-GRADE-FILE-IN
01370            AT END
01380                MOVE "N" TO MORE-INPUT.
01390
01400    PRODUCE-FINAL-LINE-OF-AVERAGES.
01410        PERFORM COMPUTE-FINAL-AVERAGES.
01420        PERFORM WRITE-FINAL-LINE.
01430
01440    COMPUTE-FINAL-AVERAGES.
01450        DIVIDE EXAM-1-SUM BY NUMBER-OF-STUDENTS
01460                             GIVING EXAM-1-AVERAGE-OUT ROUNDED.
01470        DIVIDE EXAM-2-SUM BY NUMBER-OF-STUDENTS
01480                             GIVING EXAM-2-AVERAGE-OUT ROUNDED.
01490        DIVIDE EXAM-3-SUM BY NUMBER-OF-STUDENTS
01500                             GIVING EXAM-3-AVERAGE-OUT ROUNDED.
01510        DIVIDE EXAM-4-SUM BY NUMBER-OF-STUDENTS
01520                             GIVING EXAM-4-AVERAGE-OUT ROUNDED.
01530        COMPUTE CLASS-AVERAGE-OUT ROUNDED =
01540            (EXAM-1-SUM +
01550             EXAM-2-SUM +
01560             EXAM-3-SUM +
01570             EXAM-4-SUM) /
01580            (NUMBER-OF-EXAMS * NUMBER-OF-STUDENTS).
01590
01600    WRITE-FINAL-LINE.
01610        WRITE REPORT-LINE FROM FINAL-AVERAGE-LINE
01620            AFTER ADVANCING 3 LINES.
01630
01640    PRODUCE-DETAIL-LINE.
01650        MOVE STUDENT-NUMBER-IN TO STUDENT-NUMBER-OUT.
01660        MOVE EXAM-GRADE-1-IN    TO EXAM-GRADE-1-OUT.
01670        MOVE EXAM-GRADE-2-IN    TO EXAM-GRADE-2-OUT.
01680        MOVE EXAM-GRADE-3-IN    TO EXAM-GRADE-3-OUT.
01690        MOVE EXAM-GRADE-4-IN    TO EXAM-GRADE-4-OUT.
01700        COMPUTE AVERAGE-GRADE-OUT ROUNDED =
01710            (EXAM-GRADE-1-IN +
01720             EXAM-GRADE-2-IN +
01730             EXAM-GRADE-3-IN +
01740             EXAM-GRADE-4-IN) / NUMBER-OF-EXAMS.
01750        WRITE REPORT-LINE FROM DETAIL-LINE.
01760
01770    ACCUMULATE-GRADES.
01780        ADD EXAM-GRADE-1-IN TO EXAM-1-SUM.
01790        ADD EXAM-GRADE-2-IN TO EXAM-2-SUM.
01800        ADD EXAM-GRADE-3-IN TO EXAM-3-SUM.
01810        ADD EXAM-GRADE-4-IN TO EXAM-4-SUM.
01820
01830    COUNT-NUMBER-OF-STUDENTS.
01840        ADD 1 TO NUMBER-OF-STUDENTS.
```

The Procedure Division begins at line 01040. It follows the hierarchy diagram, with each box on the diagram being represented by one paragraph in the program. You can see examples of the DIVIDE statement with the GIVING option, at lines 01450 through 01520, and two COMPUTE statements, at lines 01530 and 01700.

Program P03-02 was run with the input data shown in Figure 3.12 and produced the output shown in Figure 3.13.

Figure 3.12 Input to Program P03-02.

```
------------------------------------------------------------------------------
         1         2         3         4         5         6         7         8
12345678901234567890123456789012345678901234567890123456789012345678901234567890
------------------------------------------------------------------------------
070543242      100078098084
091020222      090085098000
075655343      022067076057
513467845      076083082092
```

Figure 3.13 Output from Program P03-02.

```
                    CLASS  AVERAGE  REPORT


        STUDENT                  G R A D E S
        NUMBER         EXAM 1  EXAM 2  EXAM 3  EXAM 4    AVERAGE

        070543242       100     078     098     084       0900
        091020222       090     085     098     000       0683
        075655343       022     067     076     057       0555
        513467845       076     083     082     092       0833


        AVERAGES        0720    0783    0885    0583      0743
```

EXERCISE 14

Write a program to read and process input records in the following format:

Positions	Field
1 – 5	Salesperson Number
6 – 12	Commission 1 (in dollars and cents)
13 – 19	Commission 2 (in dollars and cents)
20 – 26	Commission 3 (in dollars and cents)
27 – 33	Commission 4 (in dollars and cents)
34 – 40	Commission 5 (in dollars and cents)
41 – 47	Commission 6 (in dollars and cents)
48 – 80	spaces

Each input record contains a Salesperson Number and six commission amounts. For each input record, have your program print the Salesperson Number, the six commission amounts, and the average commission amount, rounded to two decimal places. At the end of the report have your program print a single amount showing the average of all the commissions.

Design the output on a print chart before you begin coding. Provide for a report title, suitable column headings, and the final average line.

Summary

The arithmetic verbs in COBOL are ADD, SUBTRACT, MULTIPLY, DIVIDE, and COMPUTE. ADD, SUBTRACT, MULTIPLY, and DIVIDE can be written without the GIVING option, as ADD A TO B, SUBTRACT A FROM B, MULTIPLY A BY B, AND DIVIDE A INTO B. In each such form the result is assigned to one of the terms in the operation, destroying the original value of that term. The result of arithmetic optionally can be assigned to a particular field designated by the programmer through the use of the GIVING option, as SUBTRACT A FROM B GIVING C and MULTIPLY A BY B GIVING C. When the GIVING option is used with ADD, the word TO must not also be used, as in the correct statement ADD A, B GIVING C. When the GIVING option is used with DIVIDE, then INTO or BY may be used, as DIVIDE A INTO B GIVING C, or DIVIDE B BY A GIVING C. The DIVIDE statement also has the optional capability of assigning a REMAINDER to a field specified by the programmer.

The COMPUTE verb can be used to carry out more than one arithmetic operation in a single statement. A COMPUTE statement always contains an equal sign, and COBOL assigns the results of the computation to the field or fields named to the left of the sign. There must be an arithmetic expression to the right of the sign.

The order of arithmetic in an expression is unary operators first, then exponentiation, then multiplication and division, then addition and subtraction. Parentheses may be used to change the order of arithmetic. The arithmetic operators are $+$, $-$, $*$, $/$; for exponentiation, $**$. The unary operators $+$ and $-$ may appear before any expression.

In all arithmetic operations, COBOL can be directed to round the result if necessary.

In top-down design, a programmer produces a hierarchy diagram showing the major function of a program broken down into lower and lower levels of sub-functions. Top-down design enables the programmer to design the whole program by concentrating on only one small portion of it at a time.

Fill-in Exercises

1. An ADD statement must contain either the word _____ or the word _____, but not both.

2. In a top-down design the programmer draws a _____ diagram.

3. It is good programming practice to define and name all constants in _____ .

4. In a DIVIDE statement without the GIVING option, the quotient is assigned to the field given after the word _____ .

5. In a SUBTRACT statement without the GIVING option, the difference is assigned to the field given after the word _____ .

6. In a MULTIPLY statement without the GIVING option, the product is assigned to the field given after the word _____ .

7. In arithmetic statements with the GIVING option, the result is assigned to the field given after the word _____ .

8. The _____ verb permits more than one arithmetic operation to be carried out in a single statement.

9. The order of evaluation in an arithmetic expression is parentheses first, then _____ , then _____ , then _____ and _____ , then _____ and _____ .

10. When the signs + or − appear immediately before an arithmetic expression, they are called _____ .

11. The PICTURE character _____ is used to represent a digit.

12. The PICTURE character _____ is used to show the location of an assumed decimal point in a numeric field.

13. The PICTURE character _____ is used to show that COBOL may assign a plus or minus sign to a numeric field.

14. The REMAINDER in a division is found by multiplying the _____ by the _____ and subtracting the product from the _____ .

15. COBOL rounds a number by increasing the least significant digit of the result by _____ when the most significant digit of the excess is _____ or greater.

Review Exercises

1. Refer to the statement formats given in the chapter and explain why each of the following statements is illegal:
    a. ADD A, B TO C GIVING D.
    b. MULTIPLY RATE BY 2.
    c. DIVIDE A BY B.
    d. DIVIDE A INTO B REMAINDER C.
    e. COMPUTE A + B = C.

2. Write COBOL statements to accomplish the following:
    a. Add the value of DEPOSITS to the value of CURRENT-BALANCE and assign the sum to CURRENT-BALANCE.
    b. Subtract the value of WITHDRAWAL from the value of CURRENT-BALANCE and assign the difference to CURRENT-BALANCE.
    c. Multiply the value of INTEREST-RATE by the value of CURRENT-BALANCE and assign the result to CURRENT-INTEREST.

3. Write level-05 entries for the following working-storage fields:
    a. A signed nine-digit dollars-and-cents field called GROSS-REVENUES
    b. A signed six-digit integer called VELOCITY
    c. An unsigned seven-digit integer called BOXCARS

4. Show the digits that would appear in computer storage for each of the following fields:

Value	Field Description	Digits in Computer Storage
225	05 SAMPLE-1 PIC 9(3)	
225	05 SAMPLE-2 PIC 9(5)	
5.20	05 SAMPLE-3 PIC 9V99	
5.20	05 SAMPLE-4 PIC 99V9(3)	
.675	05 SAMPLE-5 PIC 9V9(3)	
.675	05 SAMPLE-6 PIC 99V9(4)	

5. Write a program to read and process input records in the following format:

Positions	Field
1 – 9	Social Security Number
10 – 12	Monday Hours Worked (to tenths of an hour)
13 – 15	Tuesday Hours Worked (to tenths of an hour)
16 – 18	Wednesday Hours Worked (to tenths of an hour)
19 – 21	Thursday Hours Worked (to tenths of an hour)
22 – 24	Friday Hours Worked (to tenths of an hour)
25 – 27	Saturday Hours Worked (to tenths of an hour)
28 – 80	spaces

Each input record contains the Hours Worked for one employee. For each employee have your program show the Hours Worked each day and the total hours worked during the week. Have your program show, at the end of the report, the total hours worked by all employees on Monday, the total hours worked on Tuesday, and so on, and the grand total of all hours worked during the week. Have your program produce its output in the format shown in Figure 3.RE5.

Figure 3.RE5 Output format for Review Exercise 5.

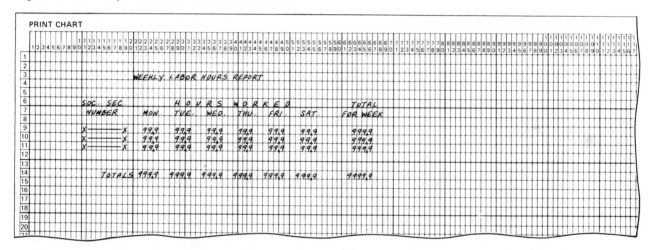

6. Write a program to read and process the input data for Program P02-03, described on page 23. Have your program print the contents of each record on one line. At the end of the report, have your program print the average salary of all employees, to the nearest cent. Plan the output format on a print chart before you begin coding. Provide a report title, suitable column headings, and a suitable final average line.

Project

Write a program that reads one record containing data about a single automobile loan and produces a repayment schedule in the format shown in Figure 3.P1. The input record is in the following format:

Positions	Field
1 – 7	Starting Loan Amount (dollars and cents)
8 – 9	Number of Monthly Payments
10 – 15	Monthly Payment (dollars and cents)
16 – 19	Annual Interest Rate
20 – 80	spaces

Define the Annual Interest Rate in the input with PICTURE V9(4). In Figure 3.P1, to print the Payment Number set up a two-digit numeric field and ADD 1 to it for each line printed. Use the following formulas for the other columns:

For Payment Number 1,
    Interest = Starting Loan Amount * Annual Interest Rate / 12
    Payment to Principal = Monthly Payment − Interest
    Principal Remaining = Starting Loan Amount − Payment to Principal
For all payments after Payment Number 1,
    Interest = Principal Remaining from previous payment
              * Annual Interest Rate / 12
    Payment to Principal = Monthly Payment − Interest
    Principal Remaining = Principal Remaining from previous payment −
                     Payment to Principal

The minus sign in the Payment to Principal and Principal Remaining columns in Figure 3.P1 indicate that a positive or negative sign is to print there. Define those output fields with SIGN IS TRAILING SEPARATE CHARACTER to get the printing sign.

Since only one record is read, you need not have an input data flag. Instead, you can PERFORM your main loop UNTIL PAYMENT-NUMBER IS EQUAL TO NUMBER-OF-PAYMENTS-IN.

Figure 3.P1   Output format for Chapter 3 Project.

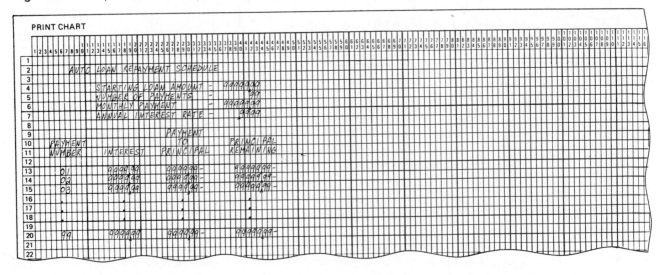

Editing

Here are the key points you should learn from this chapter:

1. How to insert today's date into an output report.
2. How to edit output data for printing.
3. The formats of the MOVE statement.

Key words to recognize and learn:

editing	data name qualification
validity checking	IN
alphanumeric edited	qualified
zero suppression	qualifier
insertion character	OF
check protection	CORRESPONDING
floating	CORR
ACCEPT	group item
DATE	elementary item
DAY	subordinate
TIME	

This chapter discusses the output **editing** features of COBOL which can be used to make output reports and listings easier to read. The word *editing* is sometimes incorrectly used to refer to automated checking and validation of input data. Validation of input is properly called **validity checking** and is discussed in Chapter 7. *Editing* refers to output.

Editing

COBOL provides facilities for rendering numeric and alphanumeric output more readable by making it easy for the programmer to do the following:

1. Insert a decimal point into numeric output
2. Insert commas into numeric output
3. Insert zeros, blanks, and/or slashes (/) into numeric or alphanumeric output
4. Suppress the printing of unwanted leading zeros in numeric output
5. Replace leading zeros with asterisks (*) in numeric output
6. Insert a dollar sign at the left end of numeric output
7. Insert one of the symbols + or − to indicate the sign of numeric output
8. Insert the characters CR or DB to indicate that numeric output is negative

To produce numeric edited or **alphanumeric edited** output, the programmer need only specify the desired editing in the PICTURE of the output field to be edited. Then, whenever data are assigned to that output field, COBOL carries out the desired editing with no further effort on the part of the programmer. Numeric edited fields may appear in arithmetic statements, but only immediately after the words REMAINDER or COMPUTE, or anywhere after the word GIVING.

Zero Suppression

The PICTURE character Z can be used to obtain suppression of insignificant leading zeros. For example, in Program P03-01 we could have printed the QUANTITY-OUT field with **zero suppression** to eliminate unwanted zeros when the quantity amount was small by using PICTURE ZZZ instead of PICTURE 999. The use of ZZZ instead of 999 in no way would affect the printing of three-digit quantities. Table 4-1 shows how different values of QUANTITY-OUT would print using the two PICTUREs 999 and ZZZ.

Table 4-1
How a three-digit integer would print using the two PICTUREs 999 and ZZZ.

999	*ZZZ*
800	800
395	395
035	35
006	6
000	

You can see a slight difficulty with the PICTURE ZZZ (or PICTURE Z(3), which means the same). When the quantity is zero, the entire field is zero suppressed, and nothing at all prints. Usually, in a listing where we are showing the quantity of each part, if the quantity on hand is zero we probably want a zero to print. We can obtain this result by telling COBOL to zero-suppress only the first two positions of the field and print the third regardless of what it is. We would use PICTURE ZZ9 to indicate only two positions of zero suppression in a three-digit field.

Inserting Commas and Decimal Points

The **insertion characters** comma and decimal point can be used in a PICTURE to show where commas and a decimal point should appear in printed output. Commas and decimal points are, as you know, never part of numeric input data, nor are they part of numeric data as COBOL is processing them. Since COBOL cannot do arithmetic on numeric edited fields, editing can be done on numbers only just before they are printed. Thus it is the PICTURE of the output field as it is to be printed that tells COBOL how to edit the field.

To use insertion characters, the programmer simply places them in the PIC-TURE as they are to appear in the printed output. For example, to print a four-digit number and insert a comma after the first digit, we can use PICTURE 9,999. To obtain zero suppression of the first three digits in case the number is small, and also to allow for the insertion of a comma in case the number has four digits, we can use PICTURE Z,ZZ9. Table 4-2 shows how several numbers would print under three different PICTUREs.

Table 4-2
How several four-digit numbers would print under three different edit PICTUREs.

Value	9,999	Z,ZZZ	Z,ZZ9
8000	8,000	8,000	8,000
3657	3,657	3,657	3,657
0657	0,657	657	657
0022	0,022	22	22
0000	0,000		0

You may have as many commas as you like in a PICTURE, and they may be anywhere you like, except that a comma must not be the last character in a PICTURE.

Decimal-point insertion may be obtained in a similar way. The programmer writes the PICTURE with a decimal point, showing where it should appear in the printed output. There must be no more than one decimal point in a PICTURE, and it must not be the last character. To print a five-digit number as a dollars-and-cents figure, we could use PICTURE 999.99; to obtain zero suppression up to the decimal point, we would use PICTURE ZZZ.99. Zero suppression can be stopped before it reaches the decimal point with the use of PICTURE ZZ9.99 or Z99.99. Table 4-3 shows how different money amounts would print under five different PICTUREs.

Table 4-3
How several different money amounts would print under five different PICTUREs.

Amount	999.99	ZZZ.ZZ	ZZZ.99	ZZ9.99	Z99.99
657.00	657.00	657.00	657.00	657.00	657.00
075.25	075.25	75.25	75.25	75.25	75.25
006.50	006.50	6.50	6.50	6.50	06.50
000.29	000.29	.29	.29	0.29	00.29
000.06	000.06	.06	.06	0.06	00.06
000.00	000.00		.00	0.00	00.00

If Z appears to the right of a decimal point in a PICTURE, then it must occupy every position to the right of the decimal point. In that case, if the value of the field is zero, the printed field will contain all blanks, as shown in the last line in Table 4-3. If the value of the field is not zero, then a PICTURE with Zs to the right of a decimal point acts as if the Zs stopped immediately to the left of the point, as shown in the fourth and fifth entries in Table 4-3.

EXERCISE 1

Write an edit PICTURE for each of the following output fields:

a. A five-digit integer, comma after the second digit, no zero suppression
b. A six-digit, dollars-and-cents money amount, comma after the first digit, zero suppression up to the decimal point
c. A seven-digit integer, comma after the first and fourth digits, entire field zero suppressed
d. A nine-digit, dollars-and-cents amount, comma after the first and fourth digits, zero suppression up to one place before the decimal point
e. A six-digit number with four decimal places, zero suppression up to one place before the decimal point

---

Printing a Sign Designation

When a numeric field is printed, the SIGN clause can be used to say where the sign should print. But with numeric editing, the programmer has much greater flexibility in printing a sign indication. Positive numbers may have a plus sign printed at or near the right or left end of a number, and negative numbers may have either a minus sign at or near the right or left end of a number or the letters CR or DB at or near the right end of a number. Here are some ways in which a positive number can be made to print:

```
 +675.28
+  675.28
   675.28+
   675.28 +
```

And here are some ways in which a negative number can be made to print:

```
   675.28 –
 – 675.28
–  675.28
   675.28CR
   675.28 DB
```

There can be as many blanks as desired between the number and its sign designation. Each digit, blank, and sign occupies one print position. The sign designations CR and DB each occupy two print positions. The programmer indicates the type of sign designation desired by placing the sign character in the edit PICTURE of the output field.

The following is a legal description:

```
05  FIELD-1-OUT              PIC -ZZZ.99.
```

This PICTURE tells COBOL to print a minus sign in the position shown if the printed value happens to be negative. If a positive value is edited under this PICTURE, a blank will print in the position allotted to the sign. Table 4-4 shows how several values would print under two edit PICTUREs.

Table 4-4
How several negative, positive, and zero values print under two different PICTUREs.

Value	− ZZZ.99	− ZZZ.ZZ
−675.28	−675.28	−675.28
−005.60	− 5.60	− 5.60
−000.05	− .05	− .05
+675.28	675.28	675.28
+000.07	.07	.07
000.00	.00	.00

Similarly, the PICTURE character − may be placed at the right end of the PICTURE, or the letters CR or DB may be placed at the right end of the PICTURE. You may not use the minus sign and the CR or DB designation in the same PICTURE. Table 4-5 shows how some values would print under four PICTUREs.

Table 4-5
How several negative, positive, and zero values print under four different PICTUREs.

Value	ZZZ.99−	ZZZ.99CR	Z99.99DB	ZZZ.ZZDB
−675.28	675.28−	675.28CR	675.28DB	675.28DB
−005.60	5.60−	5.60CR	05.60DB	5.60DB
−000.05	.05−	.05CR	00.05DB	.05DB
+675.28	675.28	675.28	675.28	675.28
000.00	.00	.00	00.00	

To obtain a printed plus sign, the PICTURE character + may be used. But the character + works a little differently from the other three sign designators, −, CR, and DB. When you use + you always get some printed sign indication, whether the printed value happens to be positive, negative, or zero, unless all the digits are zero suppressed, in which case the sign also disappears. The other three designators print only if the value happens to be negative, and they give no sign indication when the value is positive. When the PICTURE character + is used, a plus sign will print next to positive or zero values and a minus sign next to negative values. Table 4-6 shows how some values will print under four different PICTUREs.

Table 4-6
How several negative, positive, and zero values print under four different PICTUREs.

Value	+ZZZ	ZZZ+	+ZZ9	ZZ9+
+520	+520	520+	+520	520+
−520	−520	520−	−520	520−
+006	+ 6	6+	+ 6	6+
000			+ 0	0+

If a sign designation appears to the left of a number, there must be no PICTURE characters to the left of the sign. If a sign designation appears to the right of a number, there must be no PICTURE characters to the right of the sign.

The Insertion Characters B, /, and 0

To obtain insertion of spaces, slashes, and zeros in numeric or alphanumeric output, the PICTURE characters B, /, and 0 are used. These PICTURE characters may be used quite freely in combination with almost all other PICTURE characters. When any of these characters appears in a PICTURE, COBOL simply inserts the appropriate character into the edited result in the position indicated in the PICTURE.

For example, the PICTURE character B may be used to obtain one or more blank spaces between a sign designation and a number. Table 4-7 shows how some values will print under several edit PICTUREs.

Table 4-7
How several negative, positive, and zero values print under four different PICTUREs.

Value	-BZZZ,ZZ9	+BBZZZ,ZZ9	ZZZ,ZZ9BCR	ZZZ,ZZ9BBDB
-589000	- 589,000	- 589,000	589,000 CR	589,000 DB
-006890	- 6,890	- 6,890	6,890 CR	6,890 DB
-000055	- 55	- 55	55 CR	55 DB
+589000	589,000	+ 589,000	589,000	589,000
000000	0	+ 0	0	0

As an example of the use of the PICTURE character B in alphanumeric editing, assume we have the following two fields:

```
05   SOCIAL-SECURITY-NUMBER         PIC X(9),
05   SOCIAL-SECURITY-NUMBER-EDITED   PIC X(3)BXXBX(4),
```

If the value of SOCIAL-SECURITY-NUMBER is 023456789, the statement

```
MOVE SOCIAL-SECURITY-NUMBER TO SOCIAL-SECURITY-NUMBER-EDITED,
```

assigns the value 023 45 6789 to SOCIAL-SECURITY-NUMBER-EDITED. If instead SOCIAL-SECURITY-NUMBER-EDITED has the PICTURE X(3)/XX/X(4), then the statement

```
MOVE SOCIAL-SECURITY-NUMBER TO SOCIAL-SECURITY-NUMBER-EDITED,
```

assigns the value 023/45/6789 to SOCIAL-SECURITY-NUMBER-EDITED.

To see the use of / with a numeric field, assume we have:

```
05   MONTH-AND-DAY-IN    PIC 9(4),
05   MONTH-AND-DAY-OUT   PIC Z9/99,
```

If the value of MONTH-AND-DAY-IN is 0915, the statement

```
MOVE MONTH-AND-DAY-IN TO MONTH-AND-DAY-OUT,
```

assigns the value 9/15 to MONTH-AND-DAY-OUT.

Finally, to see how the insertion character 0 might be used, assume we have the following two fields:

```
05   MILLIONS-OF-DOLLARS          PIC 9(3).
05   DOLLARS-SPELLED-OUT          PIC ZZZ,000,000.
```

Table 4-8 shows what is assigned to DOLLARS-SPELLED-OUT for different initial values of MILLIONS-OF-DOLLARS and the statement:

```
MOVE MILLIONS-OF-DOLLARS TO DOLLARS-SPELLED-OUT.
```

Table 4-8
Values assigned to the field DOLLARS-SPELLED-OUT with different initial values of the field MILLIONS-OF-DOLLARS.

MILLIONS-OF-DOLLARS	DOLLARS-SPELLED-OUT
485	485,000,000
020	20,000,000
000	

The Dollar Sign

It is possible to have COBOL insert a dollar sign at the left end of a number. The PICTURE character $ is used to indicate the position of the sign. Table 4-9 shows how some money amounts print under two different PICTUREs.

Table 4–9
How some money amounts would print with dollar sign insertion.

Value	$ZZ,ZZZ.99	$ZZ,ZZZ.ZZ
58905.03	$58,905.03	$58,905.03
08905.03	$ 8,905.03	$ 8,905.03
00600.05	$ 600.05	$ 600.05
00005.29	$ 5.29	$ 5.29
00000.06	$ .06	$ .06
00000.00	$ .00	

If a single dollar sign appears to the left of a number, as in the PICTUREs in Table 4-9, the only character that may appear to the left of the dollar sign is + or −.

Asterisk Insertion

When COBOL programs are used to print checks, it is usually undesirable to leave any blank spaces in the place on the check where the money amount is printed. If the check has room for, let's say, a seven-digit number, and the particular check amount has only four or five digits, the blanks which result from suppression of the leading zeros are an invitation to forgery. The invitation is especially appealing if the check is for an amount less than $1 and only a decimal point and some pennies are printed. For this reason COBOL provides a form of zero suppression in which leading zeros are replaced not with blanks, but with asterisks (*). Replacing leading zeros with asterisks is sometimes called **check protection.** To obtain check protection, the programmer uses the PICTURE character * in the same way that the PICTURE character Z would be used. The characters * and Z may not appear in the same PICTURE. Table 4-10 shows how some money amounts print with and without check protection.

Table 4-10
How some money amounts would print with and without check protection.

Value	$Z,ZZZ.99CR	*,***.99-	$*,***.**DB
-8905.03	$8,905.03CR	8,905.03-	$8,905.03DB
+0600.05	$ 600.05	**600.05	$**600.05
-0005.29	$ 5.29CR	****5.29-	$****5.29DB
+0000.06	$ .06	*****.06	$*****.06
0000.00	$ .00	*****.00	******.****

When all the digit positions in a number are zero-suppressed by asterisks and the value of the field is zero, then the entire edited field is composed of asterisks except for the decimal point, as shown in the last entry in Table 4-10.

Floating Insertion

So far we have seen how a plus sign, a minus sign, or a dollar sign can be made to print in a fixed position to the left of a printed number. It is possible instead to have COBOL print those signs immediately to the left of the most significant digit in the number as printed. Such an operation is called **floating,** because the sign floats to the right until it finds the most significant digit and prints itself there. A floating sign is indicated by a string of two or more such signs in the edit PICTURE of the output field. A floating sign carries out zero suppression, so neither Z nor * may be used in any PICTURE that specifies a floating sign. Table 4-11 shows how some values would print with fixed signs and with floating signs.

Table 4-11
How some amounts would print with fixed and with floating sign insertion.

Value	-Z,ZZZ.99	--,---.99	$$,$$$.99CR	+$$,$$$.$$
-5890.00	-5,890.00	-5,890.00	$5,890.00CR	-$5,890.00
+0680.09	680.09	680.09	$680.09	+ $680.09
-0005.00	- 5.00	-5.00	$5.00CR	- $5.00
-0000.50	- .50	-.50	$.50CR	- $.50
0000.00	.00	.00	$.00	

When a floating plus or minus sign is used, there must be no PICTURE characters to the left of the leftmost sign. When a floating dollar sign is used, the only PICTURE character permitted to the left of the leftmost sign is a fixed + or −. When all the digit positions in a number are zero-suppressed by a floating sign and the value of the field is zero, then the entire edited field is made blank, as shown in the last entry in Table 4-11.

Notice that when a floating sign is used, there must be enough signs to allow for the largest possible number that might print and for the printing sign itself. So a three-digit number could have PICTURE − − − − to allow one sign to print even if digits occupied the other three places. Of course, a three-digit number could also have PICTURE − − − 9 if the programmer wanted zero suppression to stop before the rightmost digit. When a floating sign is used, there must always be at least two signs to the left of the leftmost comma. To see why, try to figure out what size number this illegal PICTURE is trying to represent: PICTURE −,−−−.

EXERCISE 2

Show how each of the following values would print under each of the edit PICTUREs shown:

Value	$ZZ9−	$ZZZ+	$$$$−	***CR	$***DB	$**9+
+590						
−590						
+060						
−060						
+005						
−005						
000						

Obtaining Today's Date from the COBOL System

One form of the **ACCEPT** statement can be used to obtain the date and time from the COBOL system at the moment the statement is executed. The ANSI standard format of that ACCEPT statement is:

```
ACCEPT identifier FROM {DATE}
                       {DAY }
                       {TIME}
```

This statement directs COBOL to move the **DATE, DAY,** or **TIME** into any desired field. The DATE is defined by COBOL as an unsigned six-digit field consisting of two digits for the year of century, two digits for the month, and two digits for the day. Thus July 1, 1990, would be expressed as 900701. DAY is defined as an unsigned five-digit field consisting of two digits for the year of century and three digits for the day of year. Thus July 1, 1990, would be expressed as 90183. TIME is defined as an unsigned eight-digit field consisting of two digits for hours, two digits for minutes, two digits for seconds, and two digits for hundredths of a second. TIME is expressed in so-called military time, on a 24-hour clock basis. Thus 2:41 PM would be expressed as 14410000.

As an example, if we have the following field

```
01  RUN-DATE.
    05  RUN-YEAR             PIC 99.
    05  RUN-MONTH-AND-DAY    PIC 9(4).
```

and the statement

```
ACCEPT RUN-DATE FROM DATE.
```

on July 1, 1990, COBOL will assign 90 to RUN-YEAR and 0701 to RUN-MONTH-AND-DAY.

Data Name Qualification

Data names in COBOL need not be unique. That is, the same name may be used for more than one field in the Data Division. But COBOL still requires that every field in some way be distinguishable from every other field. Distinguishing among two or more fields may be done on the basis of some larger field and is called **data name qualification.** For example, we might have the following fields in a program:

```
01    RUN-DATE.
      05  RUN-YEAR                    PIC 99.
      05  RUN-MONTH-AND-DAY           PIC 9(4).

01    DATE-LINE.
      05  RUN-MONTH-AND-DAY           PIC Z9/99/.
      05  RUN-YEAR                    PIC 99.
```

If it were necessary for us to distinguish one RUN-YEAR from another in the program, we could call one of the fields RUN-YEAR **IN** RUN-DATE and the other RUN-YEAR IN DATE-LINE. The name RUN-YEAR in each case would be said to be **qualified,** and the names of the larger fields, in this case RUN-DATE and DATE-LINE, would be said to be the **qualifiers.** A qualified data name is an identifier, and may be used in any statement where the format calls for an identifier. Now you know two kinds of identifiers: ordinary data names and qualified data names.

In data name qualification the word **OF** may be used interchangeably with IN. Other legal qualified data names thus are:

```
RUN-YEAR OF RUN-DATE
RUN-MONTH-AND-DAY OF DATE-LINE
```

More than one level of qualification may be used. Consider the following definitions:

```
01    RATES-LEVEL-A.
      05 RATES-LEVEL-1.
         10 RATE-I        PIC 99V99.
         10 RATE-II       PIC 99V99.
         10 RATE-III      PIC 99V99.
         10 RATE-VII      PIC 99V99.
      05 RATES-LEVEL-2.
         10 RATE-I        PIC 99V99.
         10 RATE-II       PIC 99V99.
         10 RATE-VI       PIC 99V99.

01    RATES-LEVEL-B.
      05 RATES-LEVEL-1.
         10 RATE-I        PIC 99V99.
         10 RATE-II       PIC 99V99.
         10 RATE-III      PIC 99V99.
      05 RATES-LEVEL-3.
         10 RATE-I        PIC 99V99.
         10 RATE-II       PIC 99V99.
         10 RATE-VI       PIC 99V99.
         10 RATE-VII      PIC 99V99.
```

Then the following are legal names:

```
RATES-LEVEL-1 IN RATES-LEVEL-A
RATES-LEVEL-1 IN RATES-LEVEL-B
```

To name any of the fields called RATE-I uniquely, you would have to use a name such as:

```
RATE-I IN RATES-LEVEL-1 IN RATES-LEVEL-A
```

Other legal names are:

```
RATE-VI  IN RATES-LEVEL-2
RATE-VI  IN RATES-LEVEL-3
RATE-VII IN RATES-LEVEL-A
RATE-VII IN RATES-LEVEL-B
```

Unnecessary qualification may be used and does no harm. The name

```
RATE-VII IN RATES-LEVEL-1 IN RATES-LEVEL-A
```

means the same as either of the following:

```
RATE-VII IN RATES-LEVEL-1
RATE-VII IN RATES-LEVEL-A
```

The MOVE Verb

There are two formats for MOVE statements. Format 1 is the one we have been using all along, and is:

```
MOVE   {identifier-1}   TO identifier-2 [, identifier-3] ...
       {literal     }
```

The format shows that the sending field of a MOVE may be any identifier or literal, and that there may be as many receiving fields as desired. The MOVE statement assigns the contents of the sending field to each of the receiving fields, and carries out any editing indicated by the PICTURE of each receiving field. The contents of the sending field remain unchanged.

Table 4-12 shows the types of MOVEs allowed under the 1974 ANSI standard. In the table an entry of YES indicates that the MOVE is allowed. The table refers to the definitions of the sending and receiving items, and not to their contents. For example, the table shows that it is legal to MOVE an item defined as numeric noninteger to an item defined as numeric edited. When such a MOVE is executed, though, the sending field actually must contain some numeric value. Since it is possible in COBOL for a field defined as numeric accidentally to get to contain some nonnumeric value, it is the programmer's responsibility to ensure that the fields used in any operation contain valid data. There is a full discussion of valid and invalid data in Chapter 7.

The 1985 standard permits a numeric edited field to be MOVEd to a field defined as numeric integer, numeric noninteger, or numeric edited. In such a MOVE, the contents of the sending field are de-edited before being placed in the receiving field.

Table 4-12
Valid and invalid MOVEs in the 1974 standard.

Sending Item Category	Receiving Item Category				
	Alphanumeric	Alphanumeric Edited	Numeric Integer	Numeric Noninteger	Numeric Edited
SPACE or SPACES	YES	YES	NO	NO	NO
Alphanumeric	YES	YES	YES	YES	YES
Alphanumeric Edited	YES	YES	NO	NO	NO
Numeric Integer	YES	YES	YES	YES	YES
Numeric Noninteger	NO	NO	YES	YES	YES
Numeric Edited	YES	YES	NO	NO	NO

Padding and Truncation

If a receiving field in a MOVE is longer or shorter than the sending field, COBOL either will fill the extra spaces in the receiving field or truncate characters as needed. The exact treatment depends on the category of the receiving field.

If the receiving field is alphanumeric or alphanumeric edited, data from the sending field are left-aligned in the receiving field and the right end of the receiving field is filled with spaces or truncated as needed. Table 4-13 shows the value assigned to a receiving field with PICTURE X(10) for different sending fields.

Table 4-13
Value assigned by MOVE statement to a receiving field with PICTURE X(10) for different sending fields.

PICTURE of Sending Field	Value of Sending Field	Value Assigned to Receiving Field
X(10)	TOTAL SETS	TOTAL SETS
X(12)	REGION TOTAL	REGION TOT
XXX	YES	YES
9(4)	8005	8005
9(13)	8574839574893	8574839574
ZZZ.999	5.300	5.300

If the receiving field is numeric or numeric edited, data are aligned on the decimal point, and the left and/or right end of the receiving field is filled with zeros or truncated as needed. Any filled-in zeros are subject to zero suppression if specified in the receiving field.

When an alphanumeric field is MOVEd to a numeric field, for purposes of alignment the sending field is considered to be an unsigned numeric integer. For such a MOVE to work properly and make sense, the alphanumeric source field must contain only numeric data. Table 4-14 shows the value assigned to a receiving field with PICTURE 9(4)V9(3) for different sending fields.

Table 4-14
Value assigned by MOVE statement to a receiving field with PICTURE 9(4)V9(3) for different sending fields.

PICTURE of Sending Field	Value of Sending Field	Value Assigned o Receiving Field
9(3)	685	0685.000
9(3)V99	68521	0685.210
9(6)	485621	5621.000
V9(4)	1279	0000.127
9(5)V9(5)	5463438732	4634.387
X(10)	5463438732	8732.000

Format 2 of the MOVE Statement

Format 2 of the MOVE statement is:

```
MOVE   {CORRESPONDING}   identifier-1 TO identifier-2
       {CORR         }
```

This form of the MOVE statement is sometimes called MOVE **CORRESPONDING.** The abbreviation **CORR** means exactly the same as CORRESPONDING. In this form COBOL MOVEs data from one or more sending fields to receiving fields that have names identical to the CORRESPONDING sending fields. As an example, consider the following fields:

```
01   RUN-DATE.
     05 RUN-YEAR              PIC 99.
     05 RUN-MONTH-AND-DAY     PIC 9(4).

01   DATE-LINE.
     05 RUN-MONTH-AND-DAY     PIC Z9/99/.
     05 RUN-YEAR             PIC 99.
```

The statement

```
MOVE CORRESPONDING RUN-DATE TO DATE-LINE.
```

will carry out the same steps as the following two statements:

```
MOVE RUN-YEAR IN RUN-DATE TO RUN-YEAR IN DATE-LINE.
MOVE RUN-MONTH-AND-DAY IN RUN-DATE
     TO RUN-MONTH-AND-DAY IN DATE-LINE.
```

For the fields RATES-LEVEL-A and RATES-LEVEL-B, defined on page 88, the following are legal statements:

1. MOVE CORRESPONDING RATES-LEVEL-1 IN RATES-LEVEL-A TO
   RATES-LEVEL-1 IN RATES-LEVEL-B.
2. MOVE CORRESPONDING RATES-LEVEL-1 IN RATES-LEVEL-A TO
   RATES-LEVEL-2.
3. MOVE CORRESPONDING RATES-LEVEL-2 TO RATES-LEVEL-3.
4. MOVE CORRESPONDING RATES-LEVEL-B TO RATES-LEVEL-A.

For statement 1 the fields RATE-I, RATE-II, and RATE-III will be MOVEd. For statement 2 the fields RATE-I, RATE-II will be MOVEd. For statement 3, fields RATE-I, RATE-II, and RATE-VI will be MOVEd.

For statement 4 only three fields will be MOVEd. The sending fields in the MOVE are as follows:

```
RATE-I IN RATES-LEVEL-1 IN RATES-LEVEL-B
RATE-II IN RATES-LEVEL-1 IN RATES-LEVEL-B
RATE-III IN RATES-LEVEL-1 IN RATES-LEVEL-B
```

The CORRESPONDING receiving fields are:

```
RATE-I IN RATES-LEVEL-1 IN RATES-LEVEL-A
RATE-II IN RATES-LEVEL-1 IN RATES-LEVEL-A
RATE-III IN RATES-LEVEL-1 IN RATES-LEVEL-A
```

The fields that make up RATES-LEVEL-2 and RATES-LEVEL-3 do not become involved in the MOVE. For purposes of the MOVE CORRESPONDING statement, fields are considered to be identically named only if all their qualifiers are identical also. This can sometimes give surprising results. Consider the following definitions:

```
01  HIGH-FIELD-1,
    05 MIDDLE-FIELD-1,
       10 LOW-FIELD-A   PIC X,
       10 LOW-FIELD-B   PIC X,

01  HIGH-FIELD-2,
    05 MIDDLE-FIELD-2,
       10 LOW-FIELD-A   PIC X,
       10 LOW-FIELD-B   PIC X,
```

Then the statement

```
MOVE CORRESPONDING HIGH-FIELD-1 TO HIGH-FIELD-2
```

will not MOVE any fields.

Both identifiers in a MOVE CORRESPONDING statement must be **group items.** A group item is any field that is broken down into smaller fields, as RUN-DATE and DATE-LINE are. Any field not broken down into smaller fields is called an **elementary item.** The elementary items into which a group item is broken down are said to be **subordinate** to the group item. The fields RUN-YEAR and RUN-MONTH-AND-DAY are elementary items. A group item never has a PICTURE clause; an elementary item always has a PICTURE clause.

Group-level MOVEs

If a sending or receiving field of a MOVE is a group item, the group item is considered to be defined with all Xs regardless of the category or categories of its elementary items. Under most conditions such treatment produces expected results. For example, consider the following definitions:

```
01   GROUP-1.
     05 FILLER            PIC X(3)   VALUE SPACES.
     05 NUMBER-1          PIC 9(5).
     05 FILLER            PIC X(5)   VALUE SPACES.
     05 NUMBER-2          PIC 9(4).

01   ITEM-2               PIC X(17).
```

Then the statement

```
MOVE GROUP-1 TO ITEM-2
```

will be treated as an alphanumeric-to-alphanumeric MOVE, and all 17 characters in GROUP-1 will be MOVEd to ITEM-2 with no change. But sometimes bizarre results develop. Consider the following definitions:

```
01   NUMBER-3             PIC 9(6).

01   GROUP-2.
     05 FILLER            PIC X(20) VALUE SPACES.
     05 FILLER            PIC ZZZ,ZZ9.
```

Then the statement

```
MOVE NUMBER-3 TO GROUP-2
```

will not give the desired results. The receiving field will be treated as a 27-character field defined with Xs. The short sending field (six characters) will be left-aligned in the long receiving field and the rightmost 21 positions filled with blanks. No editing will be done on the number.

A similar problem arises if we have the following definitions:

```
01   FIELD-4              PIC B(11)X(11).

01   GROUP-3.
     05 ELE-1             PIC X(5).
     05 ELE-2             PIC X(6).
```

Now the statement

```
MOVE GROUP-3 TO FIELD-4
```

will not give the desired results. The receiving field will be treated as a 22-character field defined with Xs. The short sending file will be left-aligned in the long receiving field and the rightmost 11 positions filled with blanks.

A Program Using Editing

Our next program, Program P04-01, shows the use of some of the features discussed in this chapter. Program P04-01 uses input in the same format as Program P03-01 and produces output in the format shown in Figure 4.1

The computations for merchandise amount, tax, order total, and the final totals line are the same in Program P04-01 as in Program P03-01, page 61. But there is one complication in this program that warrants construction of a new hierarchy diagram.

Figure 4.1   Output format for Program P04-01.

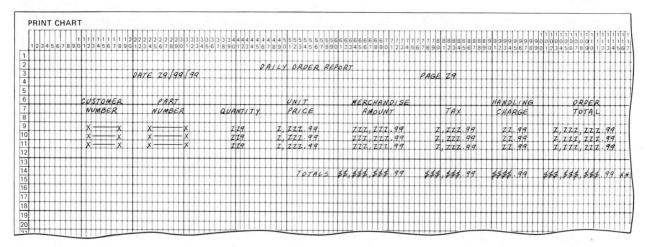

The complication in Program P04-01 derives from a restriction on the use of the arithmetic verbs. The restriction is this: All fields used in any ADD, SUBTRACT, MULTIPLY, or DIVIDE statement must be numeric except for fields appearing after the words GIVING or REMAINDER, which must be numeric or numeric edited. In a COMPUTE statement all fields must be numeric except the result field, on the left side of the equal sign, which must be numeric or numeric edited. When we look at Program P04-01, you will see the effects of this restriction.

We can create the hierarchy diagram for this program by starting with the hierarchy diagram for Program P03-01, which is repeated here as Figure 4.2. As

Figure 4.2   Hierarchy diagram for Program P03-01, repeated here as the starting diagram for Program P04-01.

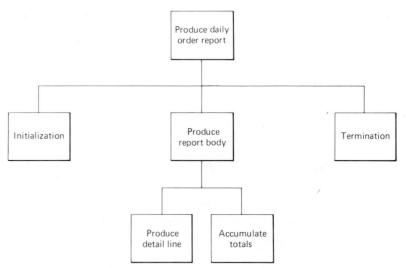

you will see when we look at Program P04-01, the restriction on the use of the arithmetic verbs prevents us from summing the merchandise amounts, tax amounts, handling charge amounts, and order total amounts in the total-line output area as we did in Program P03-01. Thus, producing the total line is complicated enough to warrant its own subfunction, so "Produce total line" is added in Figure 4.3. Figure 4.3 is the complete hierarchy diagram for Program P04-01.

Figure 4.3 Complete hierarchy diagram for Program P04-01.

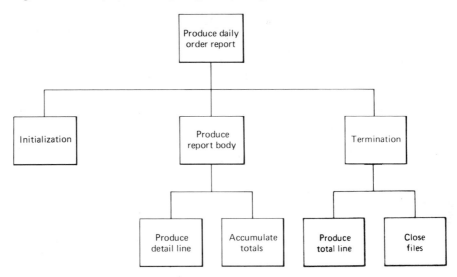

Program P04-01 is shown in Figure 4.4. The field RUN-DATE, line 00460, has been established to receive the date when it is extracted from the system by an ACCEPT statement.

Figure 4.4 Program P04-01.

```
CB1 RELEASE 2.4                                    IBM OS/VS COBOL  JULY  1, 1982


                        9.31.18         MAR 28,1988


00010   IDENTIFICATION DIVISION.
00020   PROGRAM-ID.  P04-01.
00030 *
00040 *      THIS PROGRAM IS A MODIFICATION OF PROGRAM P03-01.
00050 *      IT DEMONSTRATES OUTPUT EDITING AND INSERTING
00060 *      TODAY'S DATE INTO A REPORT.
00070 *
00080 ***********************************************************************
00090
00100   ENVIRONMENT DIVISION.
00110   CONFIGURATION SECTION.
00120   SOURCE-COMPUTER.  IBM-370.
00130   OBJECT-COMPUTER.  IBM-370.
00140
00150   INPUT-OUTPUT SECTION.
00160   FILE-CONTROL.
00170       SELECT ORDER-FILE-IN ASSIGN TO INFILE.
00180       SELECT ORDER-REPORT  ASSIGN TO PRINTER.
00190
00200   ***********************************************************************
00210
```

(continued)

This program shows a new way to enter constants such as report titles and column headings into working storage. Consider, for example, the field defined at line 00620. Although the constant, CUSTOMER, is only eight characters long, the field has a PICTURE of X(15). When the size of a constant disagrees with its PICTURE, COBOL stores the constant in the field in accordance with the rules given for the MOVE statement, as though the constant were being MOVEd to the field. In this case the word CUSTOMER is left-aligned in the field, and the remaining seven character positions are filled with spaces. This is just what we want, for you can see from the print chart in Figure 4.1 that the word CUSTOMER is followed by seven spaces. Similarly, the FILLER at line 00630 is defined as 25 characters, producing the word PART followed by 21 blanks. There is an easy way to figure out how large to make each FILLER without having to count spaces on the print chart. For example, to find out how big to make the FILLER for CUSTOMER, note from the print chart the print position where CUSTOMER begins (print position 11) and where the next word on the line, PART, begins (print position 26). Then subtract the smaller from the larger, and you have the size of the FILLER, 15. To compute the size of the FILLER for PART, subtract 26 from the starting position of the word UNIT (print position 51).

You can see some editing features in DETAIL-LINE and TOTAL-LINE, lines 00820 through 01070. The entries at lines 00830 through 00850 show the PIC-TURE character B used with alphanumeric and numeric edited fields. Other entries show zero suppression with replacement by blanks, insertion of commas and decimal points, and the floating dollar sign.

The INTERMEDIATE-NUMERIC-FIELDS are needed because of the restriction on the use of the arithmetic verbs. You will see exactly how the intermediate fields satisfy the restriction when we look at the Procedure Division.

Figure 4.4   (continued)

```
00220   DATA DIVISION.
00230   FILE SECTION.
00240   FD  ORDER-FILE-IN
00250       RECORD CONTAINS 80 CHARACTERS
00260       LABEL RECORDS ARE OMITTED.
00270
00280   01  ORDER-RECORD-IN.
00290       05 CUSTOMER-NUMBER-IN PIC X(7).
00300       05 PART-NUMBER-IN      PIC X(8).
00310       05 FILLER              PIC X(7).
00320       05 QUANTITY-IN         PIC 9(3).
00330       05 UNIT-PRICE-IN       PIC 9(4)V99.
00340       05 HANDLING-CHARGE-IN PIC 99V99.
00350       05 FILLER              PIC X(45).
00360
00370   FD  ORDER-REPORT
00380       LABEL RECORDS ARE OMITTED.
00390
00400   01  REPORT-LINE            PIC X(116).
00410
00420   WORKING-STORAGE SECTION.
00430   01  MORE-INPUT             PIC X      VALUE "Y".
00440   01  TAX-RATE               PIC V99    VALUE .07.
00450
00460   01  RUN-DATE.
00470       05 RUN-YEAR            PIC 99.
00480       05 RUN-MONTH-AND-DAY PIC 9(4).
00490
00500   01  REPORT-TITLE.
00510       05 FILLER              PIC X(45) VALUE SPACES.
00520       05 FILLER              PIC X(18) VALUE "DAILY ORDER REPORT".
00530
```

```
00540  01   DATE-LINE.
00550       05  FILLER                PIC X(20) VALUE SPACES.
00560       05  FILLER                PIC X(5)  VALUE "DATE".
00570       05  RUN-MONTH-AND-DAY     PIC Z9/99/.
00580       05  RUN-YEAR              PIC 99.
00590
00600  01   COLUMN-HEADS-1.
00610       05  FILLER                PIC X(10) VALUE SPACES.
00620       05  FILLER                PIC X(15) VALUE "CUSTOMER".
00630       05  FILLER                PIC X(25) VALUE "PART".
00640       05  FILLER                PIC X(13) VALUE "UNIT".
00650       05  FILLER                PIC X(27) VALUE "MERCHANDISE".
00660       05  FILLER                PIC X(16) VALUE "HANDLING".
00670       05  FILLER                PIC X(5)  VALUE "ORDER".
00680
00690  01   COLUMN-HEADS-2.
00700       05  FILLER                PIC X(11) VALUE SPACES.
00710       05  FILLER                PIC X(13) VALUE "NUMBER".
00720       05  FILLER                PIC X(13) VALUE "NUMBER".
00730       05  FILLER                PIC X(13) VALUE "QUANTITY".
00740       05  FILLER                PIC X(15) VALUE "PRICE".
00750       05  FILLER                PIC X(16) VALUE "AMOUNT".
00760       05  FILLER                PIC X(10) VALUE "TAX".
00770       05  FILLER                PIC X(15) VALUE "CHARGE".
00780       05  FILLER                PIC X(5)  VALUE "TOTAL".
00790
00800  01   BLANK-LINE                PIC X     VALUE SPACE.
00810
00820  01   DETAIL-LINE.
00830       05  CUSTOMER-NUMBER-OUT          PIC B(11)X(7).
00840       05  PART-NUMBER-OUT              PIC B(5)X(8).
00850       05  QUANTITY-OUT                 PIC B(8)ZZ9.
00860       05  FILLER                       PIC X(6)    VALUE SPACES.
00870       05  UNIT-PRICE-OUT               PIC Z,ZZZ.99.
00880       05  FILLER                       PIC X(7)    VALUE SPACES.
00890       05  MERCHANDISE-AMOUNT-OUT       PIC ZZZ,ZZZ.99.
00900       05  FILLER                       PIC X(6)    VALUE SPACES.
00910       05  TAX-OUT                      PIC Z,ZZZ.99.
00920       05  FILLER                       PIC X(5)    VALUE SPACES.
00930       05  HANDLING-CHARGE-OUT          PIC ZZ.99.
00940       05  FILLER                       PIC X(5)    VALUE SPACES.
00950       05  ORDER-TOTAL-OUT              PIC Z,ZZZ,ZZZ.99.
00960
00970  01   TOTAL-LINE.
00980       05  FILLER                       PIC X(52)    VALUE SPACES.
00990       05  FILLER                       PIC X(8)     VALUE "TOTALS".
01000       05  MERCHANDISE-AMOUNT-TOT-OUT   PIC $$,$$$,$$$.99.
01010       05  FILLER                       PIC X(4)     VALUE SPACES.
01020       05  TAX-TOT-OUT                  PIC $$$,$$$.99.
01030       05  FILLER                       PIC X(3)     VALUE SPACES.
01040       05  HANDLING-CHARGE-TOT-OUT      PIC $$$$.99.
01050       05  FILLER                       PIC X(3)     VALUE SPACES.
01060       05  GRAND-TOT-OUT                PIC $$$,$$$,$$$.99.
01070       05  FILLER                       PIC X(3)     VALUE " **".
01080
01090  01   INTERMEDIATE-NUMERIC-FIELDS.
01100       05  MERCHANDISE-AMOUNT-W         PIC 9(6)V99.
01110       05  TAX-W                        PIC 9(4)V99.
01120       05  ORDER-TOTAL-W                PIC 9(7)V99.
01130       05  MERCHANDISE-AMOUNT-TOT-W     PIC 9(7)V99 VALUE 0.
01140       05  TAX-TOT-W                    PIC 9(5)V99 VALUE 0.
01150       05  HANDLING-CHARGE-TOT-W        PIC 9(3)V99 VALUE 0.
01160       05  GRAND-TOT-W                  PIC 9(8)V99 VALUE 0.
01170
01180  ****************************************************************
01190
01200  PROCEDURE DIVISION.
01210  PRODUCE-DAILY-ORDER-REPORT.
01220       PERFORM INITIALIZATION.
01230       PERFORM PRODUCE-REPORT-BODY UNTIL MORE-INPUT IS EQUAL TO "N".
01240       PERFORM TERMINATION.
01250       STOP RUN.
01260
```

(continued)

Figure 4.4 (continued)

```
01270  INITIALIZATION.
01280      ACCEPT RUN-DATE FROM DATE.
01290      MOVE CORRESPONDING RUN-DATE TO DATE-LINE.
01300      OPEN INPUT  ORDER-FILE-IN,
01310          OUTPUT ORDER-REPORT.
01320      READ ORDER-FILE-IN
01330          AT END
01340              MOVE "N" TO MORE-INPUT.
01350      WRITE REPORT-LINE FROM REPORT-TITLE AFTER ADVANCING PAGE.
01360      WRITE REPORT-LINE FROM DATE-LINE.
01370      WRITE REPORT-LINE FROM COLUMN-HEADS-1 AFTER 3.
01380      WRITE REPORT-LINE FROM COLUMN-HEADS-2.
01390      WRITE REPORT-LINE FROM BLANK-LINE.
01400
01410  TERMINATION.
01420      PERFORM PRODUCE-TOTAL-LINE.
01430      PERFORM CLOSE-FILES.
01440
01450  CLOSE-FILES.
01460      CLOSE ORDER-FILE-IN,
01470          ORDER-REPORT.
01480
01490  PRODUCE-REPORT-BODY.
01500      PERFORM PRODUCE-DETAIL-LINE.
01510      PERFORM ACCUMULATE-TOTALS.
01520      READ ORDER-FILE-IN
01530          AT END
01540              MOVE "N" TO MORE-INPUT.
01550
01560  PRODUCE-DETAIL-LINE.
01570      MULTIPLY QUANTITY-IN BY UNIT-PRICE-IN
01580          GIVING MERCHANDISE-AMOUNT-OUT,
01590              MERCHANDISE-AMOUNT-W.
01600      MULTIPLY MERCHANDISE-AMOUNT-W BY TAX-RATE
01610          GIVING TAX-OUT ROUNDED,
01620              TAX-W ROUNDED.
01630      ADD MERCHANDISE-AMOUNT-W,
01640          TAX-W,
01650          HANDLING-CHARGE-IN
01660              GIVING ORDER-TOTAL-OUT,
01670                  ORDER-TOTAL-W.
01680      MOVE CUSTOMER-NUMBER-IN     TO CUSTOMER-NUMBER-OUT.
01690      MOVE PART-NUMBER-IN         TO PART-NUMBER-OUT.
01700      MOVE QUANTITY-IN            TO QUANTITY-OUT.
01710      MOVE UNIT-PRICE-IN          TO UNIT-PRICE-OUT.
01720      MOVE HANDLING-CHARGE-IN     TO HANDLING-CHARGE-OUT.
01730      WRITE REPORT-LINE FROM DETAIL-LINE.
01740
01750  ACCUMULATE-TOTALS.
01760      ADD MERCHANDISE-AMOUNT-W    TO MERCHANDISE-AMOUNT-TOT-W.
01770      ADD TAX-W                   TO TAX-TOT-W.
01780      ADD HANDLING-CHARGE-IN      TO HANDLING-CHARGE-TOT-W.
01790      ADD ORDER-TOTAL-W           TO GRAND-TOT-W.
01800
01810  PRODUCE-TOTAL-LINE.
01820      MOVE MERCHANDISE-AMOUNT-TOT-W TO MERCHANDISE-AMOUNT-TOT-OUT.
01830      MOVE TAX-TOT-W                TO TAX-TOT-OUT.
01840      MOVE HANDLING-CHARGE-TOT-W    TO HANDLING-CHARGE-TOT-OUT.
01850      MOVE GRAND-TOT-W              TO GRAND-TOT-OUT.
01860      WRITE REPORT-LINE FROM TOTAL-LINE AFTER 3.
```

The Procedure Division starts at line 01200. In the paragraph INITIALIZA-
TION you can see how the ACCEPT and MOVE CORRESPONDING statements
at lines 01280 and 01290 set up today's date in the output line DATE-LINE.
Arithmetic statements in the paragraph PRODUCE-DETAIL-LINE, line 01560,
show the use of multiple result fields. Why does the first MULTIPLY statement
assign its result to both MERCHANDISE-AMOUNT-OUT and MERCHANDISE-
AMOUNT-W? MERCHANDISE-AMOUNT-OUT is a numeric edited field, and
part of an output line. MERCHANDISE-AMOUNT-W is a numeric field, and is
used in the next MULTIPLY statement.

The paragraph ACCUMULATE-TOTALS, line 01750, uses more of the
INTERMEDIATE-NUMERIC-FIELDS. Why do we ADD the MERCHANDISE-

AMOUNT-W to MERCHANDISE-AMOUNT-TOT-W, instead of ADDing it directly to the output field, MERCHANDISE-AMOUNT-TOT-OUT? The answer is that MERCHANDISE-AMOUNT-TOT-OUT is an edited numeric field, and cannot be used in an ADD without the GIVING option.

Program P04-01 was run with the same input data as Program P03-01 and produced the output shown in Figure 4.5.

Figure 4.5 Output from Program P04-01.

```
                              DAILY  ORDER  REPORT
            DATE   3/28/88

CUSTOMER        PART                      UNIT         MERCHANDISE                    HANDLING          ORDER
 NUMBER        NUMBER      QUANTITY       PRICE          AMOUNT           TAX          CHARGE           TOTAL

 ABC1234      F2365-09       900           .10            90.00          6.30           .05             96.35
 09G8239      836-7YT7       800          10.50         8,400.00        588.00          .50           8,988.50
 ADGH784      091AN-07        50         250.00        12,500.00        875.00         5.00          13,380.00
 9675473      23S-1287         6       7,000.29        42,001.74      2,940.12        50.00          44,991.86

                                       TOTALS       $62,991.74     $4,409.42       $55.55         $67,456.71  *
```

EXERCISE 3

Modify your solution to Exercise 13, Chapter 3, page 65, so that it produces output in the format shown in Figure 4.E3.

Figure 4.E3 Output format for Exercise 3.

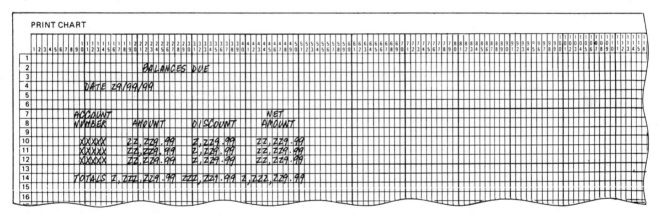

Summary

Edit PICTUREs may be used to prepare numeric and alphanumeric fields for printing. Commas and decimal points may be inserted into numeric fields, and leading zeros suppressed. Blanks, zeros, and/or slashes may be inserted into numeric or alphanumeric fields. A numeric field may have its sign designated by a fixed or floating plus or minus sign at the left end or by a fixed +, −, CR, or DB at the right end. A fixed or floating dollar sign may be printed with numeric output. Fixed positive and negative sign indications may appear to the left of a fixed or floating dollar sign.

COBOL provides a check-protection feature through the use of the PICTURE character *. In check protection, asterisks instead of blanks replace leading zeros to discourage forgery. The character * can be used in a PICTURE anywhere that a Z can be used.

The ACCEPT verb may be used to obtain the DATE, DAY, or TIME from the COBOL system at the time the program is run. The DATE comes into any field designated by the programmer in six-digit YYMMDD form.

Any item that is broken down into smaller fields is called a group item. Any item not broken down is called an elementary item.

The MOVE CORRESPONDING statement can be used to MOVE data from fields in one area to fields in another where the sending and receiving fields have duplicate names. Duplicate named fields can be distinguished from one another if necessary by data name qualification. They must be defined so that, through the use of IN or OF, every field is capable of being made unique. A qualified data name may be used in any COBOL statement whose format calls for an identifier.

Fill-in Exercises

1. When a fixed _____ sign is used in a PICTURE, the only PICTURE character that may appear to the left of it is a _____ or _____ sign.

2. When a floating _____ sign is used in a PICTURE, the only PICTURE character that may appear to the left of the leftmost sign is a fixed _____ or _____ sign.

3. The four ordinary insertion characters, which can be used as many times as you like in a PICTURE, are _____, _____, _____, and _____; the special insertion character _____ can appear no more than once in a PICTURE.

4. The PICTURE character for replacing leading zeros with blanks is _____ .

5. The PICTURE character for replacing leading zeros with asterisks is _____.

6. The PICTURE character _____ is used to obtain a printed decimal point.

7. When an alphanumeric constant is defined with a PICTURE having room for more characters than there are in the constant, COBOL inserts _____ to the right of the constant.

8. In ADD, SUBTRACT, MULTIPLY, and DIVIDE statements without the GIVING option, all identifiers must be defined as _____ .

9. In arithmetic statements with the GIVING option, fields given after the word GIVING must be defined as _____ or _____ .

10. A floating sign is designated by _____ or more such signs in a row.

11. The _____ verb can be used to obtain the date from the COBOL system on the day a program is run.

12. The _____ option can do several independent MOVEs in one MOVE statement.

13. Distinguishing among two or more fields having identical names by using the names of some larger fields is called _____ .

14. The PICTURE character _____ causes some sign to print whether the value of the output data item is positive, negative, or zero.

15. The sign designation DB prints only if the output data value is _____ .

Review Exercises

1. Show how the following numbers would print if edited by each of the PICTUREs 9,999.9, Z,ZZZ.9, and Z,ZZZ.Z:
   a. 4756.8
   b. 0005.0
   c. 0350.9
   d. 0000.0
   e. 0020.0

2. Modify your solution to Review Exercise 5, Chapter 3, page 77, to produce its output in the format shown in figure 4.RE2.

3. Modify your solution to Review Exercise 6, Chapter 3, page 77, to produce its output in the format shown in figure 4.RE3.

Figure 4.RE2 Output format for Review Exercise 2.

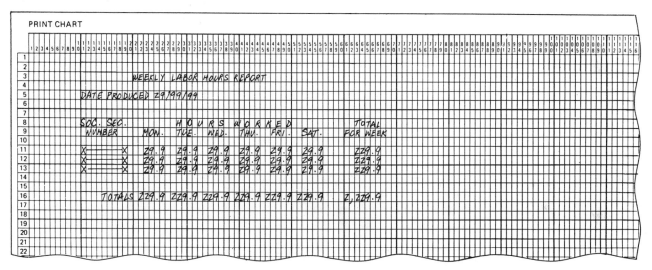

Figure 4.RE3 Output format for Review Exercise 3.

4. Given the following data definitions:

```
01   GROUP-1,
     05 FIELD-1              PIC X(5),
     05 FIELD-2              PIC X(8),
     05 FIELD-3              PIC X(6),

01   GROUP-2,
     05 FIELD-2              PIC X(8),
     05 FIELD-3              PIC X(6),
     05 FIELD-1              PIC X(5),
```

Which of the following are valid COBOL statements?
   a. MOVE FIELD-1 TO FIELD-1.
   b. MOVE FIELD-1 IN GROUP-2 TO FIELD-1 IN GROUP-1.
   c. MOVE CORRESPONDING FIELD-1 TO FIELD-1.
   d. MOVE CORRESPONDING GROUP-1 TO GROUP-2.
   e. MOVE CORRESPONDING FIELD-1 TO FIELD-2.

5. Write the PICTURE for each of the following output fields:
   a. An eight-digit dollars-and-cents number, fixed dollar sign to print at the left end of the number, comma after the third digit
   b. An eight-digit dollars-and-cents number, minus sign to print at the right end if the number is negative, no sign to print if the number is positive or zero, dollar sign to float to two places before the decimal point, no comma
   c. A six-digit integer, comma after the third digit, zero suppression up to but not including the rightmost digit, plus sign to float up to but not including the rightmost digit if the number is positive or zero, minus sign to float up to but not including the rightmost digit if the number is negative

Project

Modify your solution to the Project in Chapter 3, page 77. Have your program print its output in the format shown in Figure 4.P1. The minus signs in the format now indicate that you should use the PICTURE character − in that location. Multiply the Annual Interest Rate by 100 for the purpose of printing it in the page heading.

Figure 4.P1   Output format for Chapter 4 Project.

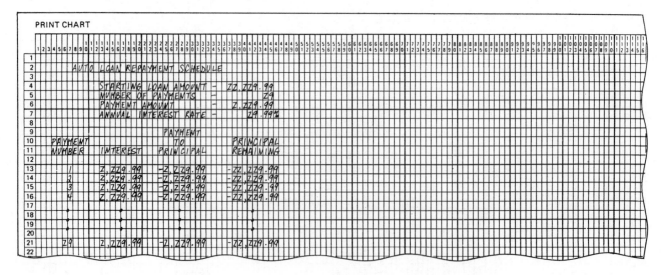

The IF Statement:
Program Design II

Here are the key points you should learn form this chapter:

1. How to program for page overflow and page numbering
2. How to use several forms of the IF statement
3. Flowcharts for the IF statement
4. The rules for forming nested IF statements
5. The kind of logic that cannot be coded using only nested IF statements, and how to code it
6. How to code IF statements with complex conditions
7. How to write abbreviated relation conditions
8. How to use condition names
9. The sign condition and the class condition
10. How to write pseudocode

Key words to recognize and learn:

conditional
PAGE
IF
ELSE
BEFORE
program flowchart
pseudocode
NEXT SENTENCE
sentence
simple condition
relation condition
class condition
condition-name condition
switch-status condition

sign condition
subject
object
NUMERIC
ALPHABETIC
level-88
nested
outer IF statement
inner IF statement
complex condition
negated simple condition
combined condition
negated combined condition
continuation indicator

In this chapter we will study COBOL statements that permit the computer to examine the data that it is working on and decide which one out of two or more processes should be executed. For example, the computer might examine an employee's number of hours worked and decide whether or not to compute overtime pay. Or, in an inventory application, the computer might examine the quantity on hand of a certain part and decide whether to reorder.

A Program Using IF Statements

Program P05-01 reads input records in the following format:

Positions	Field
1–8	Part Number
9–28	Part Description
29–31	Quantity on Hand
32–80	spaces

Each record is for a different part, and shows the Part Number, an English description of the part, and the Quantity on Hand. Program P05-01 lists the contents of each record on one line, and in addition examines the Quantity on Hand of each part and prints the word REORDER next to any part with fewer than 400 on hand. The output format is shown in the print chart in Figure 5.1. Notice that some of the lines have the word REORDER and some do not, indicating that the printing of the word is **conditional** on something in the data. Since the print chart shows only a sample of what the output might look like, we would not expect the actual output to correspond line for line with the chart. At the time the program is being written, we may not know what data values will be used, and the program must work correctly for any combination of inputs having more or fewer than 400 on hand, or even exactly 400 on hand. (Should the word REORDER print when there are exactly 400 on hand?)

Figure 5.1   Output format for Program P05-01.

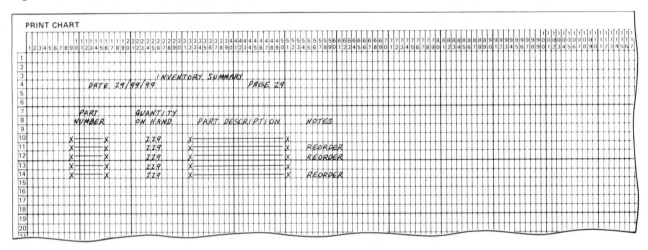

A hierarchy diagram for Program P05-01 is shown in Figure 5.2. The logic of this program is very straightforward. But, for the first time, we are going to have so much report output that it will occupy more than one page. As the program is printing detail lines, some detail line or another will find the page already full and there will be no room for it to print. The program will skip to a new page, print page headings, and then print the detail line on the new page. Thus the program will print new page headings only when it knows that it has a detail line to print on the new page. The subfunction "Produce page headings" is shown in the hierarchy diagram in Figure 5.3.

Figure 5.2 Hierarchy diagram for Program P05-01 showing one level of subfunctions.

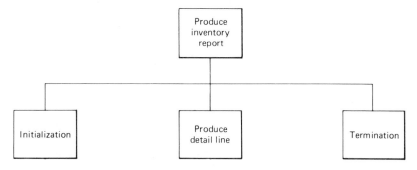

Figure 5.3 Hierarchy diagram for Program P05-01 showing three levels.

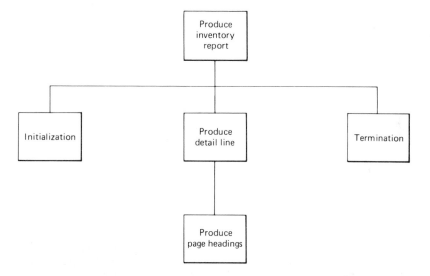

Now what does "Initialization" consist of in this program? We have the usual OPENing of the files, obtaining the DATE from the COBOL system, and the priming READ. It also turns out to be convenient to print the page headings for the first page of the report as part of "Initialization." We already have the subfunction "Produce page headings" in the diagram, so we can use that same subfunction as a subfunction of "Initialization." In Figure 5.4 we duplicate the box "Produce page headings" under the box "Initialization." The new box still represents the same coding as the original "Produce page headings." All the other functions of "Initialization" we lump together in a subfunction called "Housekeeping."

Program P05-01 is shown in Figure 5.5. In working storage the field PAGE-NUMBER-W, line 00480, is used by the program to count one page number each time it prints page headings. The field LINE-LIMIT, at line 00490, is a constant that is used to test for a full page. Its VALUE, 18, is 1 less than the last line on the page on which we want detail lines to print. The field LINE-COUNT-ER, line 00500, is used to count lines as they are printed. You will see how these fields are used to control page movement when we look at the Procedure Division.

The Procedure Division begins at line 00920. The paragraph PRODUCE-PAGE-HEADINGS, line 01120, shows a standard page-heading routine that you can use in any program with more than one page of output. First, at line 01130, we ADD 1 to the page number field in working storage. Remember that we initialized PAGE-NUMBER-W with VALUE 0, so PRODUCE-PAGE-HEADINGS works for

Figure 5.4 Complete hierarchy diagram for Program P05-01, showing the subfunctions of "Initialization."

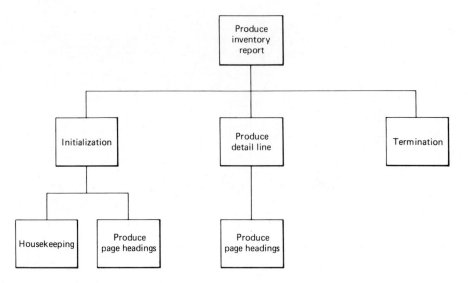

Figure 5.5 Program P05-01.

```
CB1 RELEASE 2.4                              IBM OS/VS COBOL   JULY  1, 1982


                        16.31.48          MAR 29,1988


   00010  IDENTIFICATION DIVISION.
   00020  PROGRAM-ID.  P05-01.
   00030 *
   00040 *     THIS PROGRAM READS RECORDS IN THE FOLLOWING FORMAT:
   00050 *
   00060 *     POS. 1-8         PART NUMBER
   00070 *     POS. 9-28        PART DESCRIPTION
   00080 *     POS. 29-31       QUANTITY ON HAND
   00090 *
   00100 *     THE PROGRAM PRINTS THE CONTENTS OF EACH RECORD ON ONE LINE.
   00110 *     IN ADDITION, THE WORD "REORDER" IS TO BE PRINTED
   00120 *     IN PRINT POSITIONS 55-61 NEXT TO ANY PART WHOSE
   00130 *     QUANTITY ON HAND IS LESS THAN 400.
   00140 *
   00150 ****************************************************************
   00160
   00170  ENVIRONMENT DIVISION.
   00180  CONFIGURATION SECTION.
   00190  SOURCE-COMPUTER.   IBM-370.
   00200  OBJECT-COMPUTER.   IBM-370.
   00210
   00220  INPUT-OUTPUT SECTION.
   00230  FILE-CONTROL.
   00240      SELECT INVENTORY-LIST     ASSIGN TO PRINTER.
   00250      SELECT INVENTORY-FILE-IN  ASSIGN TO INFILE.
   00260
   00270 ****************************************************************
   00280
   00290  DATA DIVISION.
   00300  FILE SECTION.
   00310  FD  INVENTORY-FILE-IN
   00320      RECORD CONTAINS 80 CHARACTERS
   00330      LABEL RECORDS ARE OMITTED.
   00340
   00350  01  INVENTORY-RECORD-IN.
   00360      05 PART-NUMBER-IN          PIC X(8).
   00370      05 PART-DESCRIPTION-IN     PIC X(20).
   00380      05 QUANTITY-ON-HAND-IN     PIC 9(3).
   00390      05 FILLER                  PIC X(49).
   00400
```

```
00410  FD   INVENTORY-LIST
00420       LABEL RECORDS ARE OMITTED.
00430
00440  01   OUTPUT-LINE              PIC X(61).
00450
00460  WORKING-STORAGE SECTION.
00470  01   MORE-INPUT               PIC X(1)  VALUE "Y".
00480  01   PAGE-NUMBER-W            PIC 99    VALUE 0.
00490  01   LINE-LIMIT               PIC 99    VALUE 18.
00500  01   LINE-COUNT-ER            PIC 99.
00510
00520  01   RUN-DATE.
00530       05 RUN-YEAR              PIC 99.
00540       05 RUN-MONTH-AND-DAY     PIC 9(4).
00550
00560  01   REPORT-TITLE.
00570       05 FILLER        PIC X(25) VALUE SPACES.
00580       05 FILLER        PIC X(17) VALUE "INVENTORY SUMMARY".
00590
00600  01   DATE-LINE.
00610       05 FILLER              PIC X(12) VALUE SPACES.
00620       05 FILLER              PIC X(5)  VALUE "DATE".
00630       05 RUN-MONTH-AND-DAY   PIC Z9/99/.
00640       05 RUN-YEAR            PIC 99B(18).
00650       05 FILLER              PIC X(5)  VALUE "PAGE".
00660       05 PAGE-NUMBER-OUT     PIC Z9.
00670
00680  01   COLUMN-HEADS-1.
00690       05 FILLER              PIC X(10) VALUE SPACES.
00700       05 FILLER              PIC X(11) VALUE "PART".
00710       05 FILLER              PIC X(8)  VALUE "QUANTITY".
00720
00730  01   COLUMN-HEADS-2.
00740       05 FILLER              PIC X(9)  VALUE SPACES.
00750       05 FILLER              PIC X(12) VALUE "NUMBER".
00760       05 FILLER              PIC X(12) VALUE "ON HAND".
00770       05 FILLER              PIC X(21) VALUE "PART DESCRIPTION".
00780       05 FILLER              PIC X(5)  VALUE "NOTES".
00790
00800  01   INVENTORY-LINE.
00810       05 FILLER              PIC X(8) VALUE SPACES.
00820       05 PART-NUMBER-OUT     PIC X(8).
00830       05 FILLER              PIC X(7) VALUE SPACES.
00840       05 QUANTITY-ON-HAND-OUT PIC ZZ9.
00850       05 FILLER              PIC X(5) VALUE SPACES.
00860       05 PART-DESCRIPTION-OUT PIC X(20).
00870       05 FILLER              PIC X(3) VALUE SPACES.
00880       05 MESSAGE-SPACE       PIC X(7).
00890
00900  ***********************************************************************
00910
00920  PROCEDURE DIVISION.
00930  PRODUCE-INVENTORY-REPORT.
00940       PERFORM INITIALIZATION.
00950       PERFORM PRODUCE-DETAIL-LINE UNTIL MORE-INPUT IS EQUAL TO "N".
00960       PERFORM TERMINATION.
00970       STOP RUN.
00980
00990  INITIALIZATION.
01000       PERFORM HOUSEKEEPING.
01010       PERFORM PRODUCE-PAGE-HEADINGS.
01020
01030  HOUSEKEEPING.
01040       OPEN INPUT  INVENTORY-FILE-IN,
01050            OUTPUT INVENTORY-LIST.
01060       ACCEPT RUN-DATE FROM DATE.
01070       MOVE CORRESPONDING RUN-DATE TO DATE-LINE.
01080       READ INVENTORY-FILE-IN
01090           AT END
01100               MOVE "N" TO MORE-INPUT.
01110
```

(continued)

Figure 5.5   (continued)

```
01120   PRODUCE-PAGE-HEADINGS.
01130       ADD 1 TO PAGE-NUMBER-W.
01140       MOVE PAGE-NUMBER-W TO PAGE-NUMBER-OUT.
01150       WRITE OUTPUT-LINE FROM REPORT-TITLE AFTER ADVANCING PAGE.
01160       WRITE OUTPUT-LINE FROM DATE-LINE.
01170       WRITE OUTPUT-LINE FROM COLUMN-HEADS-1
01180                           AFTER ADVANCING 3 LINES.
01190       WRITE OUTPUT-LINE FROM COLUMN-HEADS-2.
01200       MOVE SPACES TO OUTPUT-LINE.
01210       WRITE OUTPUT-LINE.
01220       MOVE 7 TO LINE-COUNT-ER.
01230
01240   TERMINATION.
01250       CLOSE INVENTORY-FILE-IN,
01260             INVENTORY-LIST.
01270
01280   PRODUCE-DETAIL-LINE.
01290       MOVE PART-NUMBER-IN       TO PART-NUMBER-OUT.
01300       MOVE PART-DESCRIPTION-IN TO PART-DESCRIPTION-OUT.
01310       MOVE QUANTITY-ON-HAND-IN TO QUANTITY-ON-HAND-OUT.
01320       IF QUANTITY-ON-HAND-IN IS LESS THAN 400
01330           MOVE "REORDER" TO MESSAGE-SPACE
01340       ELSE
01350           MOVE SPACES TO MESSAGE-SPACE.
01360       IF LINE-COUNT-ER IS GREATER THAN LINE-LIMIT
01370           PERFORM PRODUCE-PAGE-HEADINGS.
01380       WRITE OUTPUT-LINE FROM INVENTORY-LINE.
01390       ADD 1 TO LINE-COUNT-ER.
01400       READ INVENTORY-FILE-IN
01410           AT END
01420               MOVE "N" TO MORE-INPUT.
```

the first page as well as for all subsequent pages. Then we MOVE the page number to the output field PAGE-NUMBER-OUT, at line 01140. Why could we not just ADD 1 to PAGE-NUMBER-OUT and avoid the MOVE? The answer is that PAGE-NUMBER-OUT is a numeric edited field and must not appear in an ADD statement except after the word GIVING. Since we have no GIVING, we must use the numeric field PAGE-NUMBER-W in the ADD statement.

The WRITE statement at line 01150 uses the reserved word **PAGE** in the AFTER ADVANCING clause. This statement causes the printer to advance to the top of the next page and print the REPORT-TITLE. The program then prints the remaining lines of page headings, lines 01170 through 01210. Since the program has just printed seven lines of output, including lines of blanks, it MOVEs 7 to LINE-COUNTER-ER to keep track of how many lines have been printed on the page.

In the paragraph PRODUCE-DETAIL-LINE the three statements at lines 01290 through 01310 MOVE to the output area the three fields that are to appear unconditionally in the output line. The **IF** statement at lines 01320 through 01350 determines whether the word REORDER should be MOVEd to MESSAGE-SPACE, and if so, MOVEs it. If the value of QUANTITY-ON-HAND-IN IS LESS THAN 400, the MOVE statement at line 01330 executes. If the value of QUANTITY-ON-HAND-IN is not LESS THAN 400, the MOVE SPACES statement at line 01350 executes instead. Notice that there is only one period at the end of the entire IF statement, in line 01350.

The statement at lines 01360 and 01370 shows that an IF statement need not contain an **ELSE** clause. This IF statement tests whether there is any room on the page for the current detail line to print. The ADD statement at line 01390 ADDs 1 to LINE-COUNT-ER whenever a line is printed. IF the value of LINE-COUNT-ER IS GREATER THAN LINE-LIMIT, the PERFORM statement at line 01370 executes. If the value of LINE-COUNT-ER is not GREATER THAN LINE-LIMIT, the PERFORM statement is skipped. Then the WRITE statement at line 01380 executes unconditionally.

Program P05-01 was run with the input data shown in Figure 5.6 and produced the output shown in Figure 5.7. Notice that three pages of output are produced. Whenever you have a page heading routine in a program, you should test it with enough data to produce at least three pages of output.

Figure 5.6   Input to Program P05-01.

```
--------------------------------------------------------------------------------
          1         2         3         4         5         6         7         8
12345678901234567890123456789012345678901234567890123456789012345678901234567890
--------------------------------------------------------------------------------
100103341/8" WASHER        489
200335473/16" WASHER       301
300489291/4" WASHER        400
345543115/16" WASHER       259
555994326" HAMMER          999
000123498" HAMMER          557
0012343110" HAMMER         207
012567426' FOLDING LADDER  399
321098858' FOLDING LADDER  019
5667721210' FOLDING LADDER 456
0202340012' EXTENSION LADDER367
0473927416' EXTENSION LADDER000
4783926420' EXTENSION LADDER005
7462962224' EXTENSION LADDER500
7483613430' EXTENSION LADDER658
4738161935' EXTENSION LADDER400
2659172340' EXTENSION LADDER399
4738261225-GALLON TANK     401
8372040330-GALLON TANK     999
9164831235-GALLON TANK     000
2648103340-GALLON TANK     478
8371023850-GALLON TANK     582
6572650160-GALLON TANK     124
7583659275-GALLON TANK     231
732127431" PAINT BRUSH     238
829105241 1/4" PAINT BRUSH 145
375629111 1/2" PAINT BRUSH 563
748399212" PAINT BRUSH     123
```

Figure 5.7   Output from Program P05-01.

```
                        INVENTORY SUMMARY
          DATE   3/29/88                    PAGE   1


          PART        QUANTITY
          NUMBER      ON HAND      PART DESCRIPTION      NOTES

          10010334       489     1/8" WASHER
          20033547       301     3/16" WASHER            REORDER
          30048929       400     1/4" WASHER
          34554311       259     5/16" WASHER            REORDER
          55599432       999     6" HAMMER
          00012349       557     8" HAMMER
          00123431       207     10" HAMMER              REORDER
          01256742       399     6' FOLDING LADDER       REORDER
          32109885        19     8' FOLDING LADDER       REORDER
          56677212       456     10' FOLDING LADDER
          02023400       367     12' EXTENSION LADDER    REORDER
          04739274         0     16' EXTENSION LADDER    REORDER
```

(continued)

Figure 5.7   (continued)

```
                        INVENTORY  SUMMARY
           DATE    3/29/88                   PAGE    2


           PART        QUANTITY
           NUMBER      ON HAND      PART DESCRIPTION      NOTES

           47839264          5      20' EXTENSION LADDER   REORDER
           74629622        500      24' EXTENSION LADDER
           74836134        658      30' EXTENSION LADDER
           47381619        400      35' EXTENSION LADDER
           26591723        399      40' EXTENSION LADDER   REORDER
           47382612        401      25-GALLON TANK
           83720403        999      30-GALLON TANK
           91648312          0      35-GALLON TANK         REORDER
           26481033        478      40-GALLON TANK
           83710238        582      50-GALLON TANK
           65726501        124      60-GALLON TANK         REORDER
           75836592        231      75-GALLON TANK         REORDER


                        INVENTORY  SUMMARY
           DATE    3/29/88                   PAGE    3


           PART        QUANTITY
           NUMBER      ON HAND      PART DESCRIPTION      NOTES

           73212743        238      1" PAINT BRUSH         REORDER
           82910524        145      1 1/4" PAINT BRUSH     REORDER
           37562911        563      1 1/2" PAINT BRUSH
           74839921        123      2" PAINT BRUSH         REORDER
```

Format 1 of the WRITE Statement

The format of the WRITE statement that we have been using is:

```
WRITE record-name [FROM identifier-1]

 [ {BEFORE}  ADVANCING { {{identifier-2}   [LINE ]}}
   {AFTER }              { {integer    }    [LINES]}}              ]
                         {                           }
                         { {mnemonic-name}           }
                         { {PAGE         }           }

 [; AT {END-OF-PAGE}  imperative-statement]
       {EOP        }
```

You can see that a line can be written **BEFORE** the paper is advanced, as well as AFTER. We will use only AFTER in this book. Also, ADVANCING, LINE, and LINES are optional words, so the statement

```
WRITE REPORT-LINE FROM COLUMN-HEADS-1 AFTER 3.
```

means the same as:

```
WRITE REPORT-LINE FROM COLUMN-HEADS-1
    AFTER ADVANCING 3 LINES.
```

An identifier may be used instead of an integer to indicate the line spacing desired. The identifier must be defined as an integer. For example, if the value of LINE-SPACING is 2, the following statement

```
WRITE REPORT-LINE FROM DETAIL-LINE AFTER LINE-SPACING.
```

will execute just as:

```
WRITE REPORT-LINE FROM DETAIL-LINE AFTER 2.
```

We will not use mnemonic-name for paper control in this book.

Program Design with Conditions

We will now look at the other two design tools that we discuss in this book. They are the **program flowchart** and **pseudocode**. Program flowcharts are most useful in designing the parts of programs where IF statements would be used. Pseudocode can be used both in the way that hierarchy diagrams are used, to design the overall structure of a program, or as flowcharts would be used, to design the detailed logic in a program. We look at the program flowchart first.

The Program Flowchart

The program flowchart is one of the oldest tools for program design. It has drawbacks which have caused it to fall into disrepute in recent years, but it is still the most useful design tool for the decision-making portions of programs. A flowchart may show in diagram form a condition that the program has to test, the processes that the program carries out if the condition is True, and the processes that it carries out if the condition is False. For example, the first IF statement in Program P05-01 can be flowcharted as shown in Figure 5.8.

Figure 5.8 Flowchart of the statement

```
IF QUANTITY-ON-HAND IS LESS THAN 400
    MOVE "REORDER" TO MESSAGE-SPACE
ELSE
    MOVE SPACES TO MESSAGE-SPACE.
```

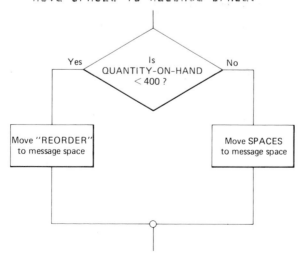

In a flowchart of a decision, either the True path or the False path, or both, may contain any amount of processing. In Figure 5.8 the True path and the False path each contain one processing step. The two paths of a decision must rejoin before the flowchart can continue. The period at the end of an IF statement is what tells COBOL that the IF is done and that the True and False paths are rejoined. Although it is good programming practice to indent IF statements the way we have done in Program P05-01, COBOL pays no attention to the indenting. Indenting is used only to make it easy for the programmer to see where the paths rejoin.

Figure 5.9 shows a flowchart for the second IF statement in Program P05-01. Here there is no processing in the False path.

Figure 5.9   Flowchart of the statement

```
IF LINE-COUNT-ER IS GREATER THAN LINE-LIMIT
    PERFORM PRODUCE-PAGE-HEADINGS.
```

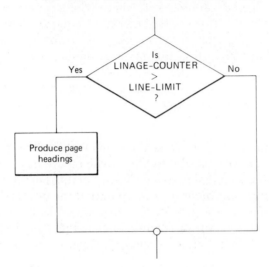

Another form of the IF statement is one where there is no processing in the True path but one or more steps in the False path. An example of such a situation is shown in the flowchart in Figure 5.10. The IF statement for that logic uses the reserved words **NEXT SENTENCE,** as follows:

```
IF RESPONSE-1 IS EQUAL TO RESPONSE-2
    NEXT SENTENCE
ELSE
    PERFORM RESPONSES-DIFFER.
```

In COBOL a **sentence** in the Procedure Division ends with a period, so the phrase NEXT SENTENCE sends the processing beyond the next period. The desired processing is thus obtained.

A flowchart with more than one processing step in a path is shown in Figure 5.11. That flowchart might be coded in this way:

```
IF QUANTITY-IN IS LESS THAN 400
    MOVE SPACES              TO OUTPUT-LINE
    MOVE PART-NUMBER-IN      TO PART-NUMBER-OUT
    MOVE PART-DESCRIPTION-IN TO PART-DESCRIPTION-OUT
    MOVE QUANTITY-IN         TO QUANTITY-OUT
    WRITE REPORT-LINE FROM OUTPUT-LINE.
```

This IF statement will execute all the MOVE statements and the WRITE statement when QUANTITY-IN IS LESS THAN 400, and skip all the statements when it is not. Notice that there is only one period at the end of the entire IF statement, for it is the period that indicates that the IF statement is done.

Figure 5.10 Flowchart of logic requiring processing in the False path only.

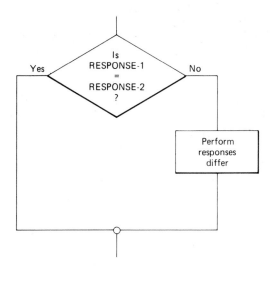

Figure 5.11 Flowchart with more than one processing step in a path.

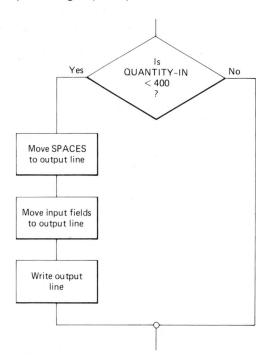

Pseudocode

Pseudocode has some of the advantages of hierarchy diagrams and some of the advantages of flowcharts. One of the advantages of pseudocode over all other methods of program design is that it can be written in plain English and does not require drawing any diagrams or charts. Pseudocode is written in a form that resembles COBOL code, but since pseudocode is English it has none of the language rules of COBOL (or any programming language). As an example, here is the pseudocode for the HOUSEKEEPING paragraph in Program P05-01:

Open files
Accept Run-date
Move corresponding Run-date to Date-line
Read Inventory-file-in at end move "N" to More-input

There are some important differences between pseudocode and COBOL. In pseudocode, only procedural steps are written; there is no reference in pseudocode to data descriptions or identification or environment details. Pseudocode may be written in as much or as little detail as desired. In the example given, the Move and Read operations are given in complete detail but the Open and Accept operations are not.

Pseudocode may be used to design a program in the same manner that top-down design is used. That is, we may first write pseudocode at a summary level, showing only the major subfunctions of the program, and fill in the details later. For example, if we were to use pseudocode to design Program P05-01, we could first write only as much detail as is shown in Figure 5.4. The pseudocode might look like this:

```
Perform initialization module
        Perform housekeeping module
        Perform produce page headings module
End-perform
Perform produce detail line module until More-input is equal to "N"
Perform termination module
Stop run
```

Notice that in pseudocode a performed procedure can be written directly under the Perform statement that controls it instead of in a paragraph by itself as in COBOL. The scope of the Perform statement is shown by indenting the performed procedure and ending it with the statement End-perform.

Pseudocode for the paragraph PRODUCE-DETAIL-LINE shows how decision logic is written:

```
Move Part-number-in to Part-number-out
Move Part-description-in to Part-description-out
Move Quantity-on-hand-in to Quantity-on-hand-out
If Quantity-on-hand-in is less than 400
        Move "REORDER" to Message-space
else
        Move spaces to Message-space
End-if
If Line-count-er is greater than Line-limit
        Perform Produce-page-headings-module
End-if
Write output line
Read Inventory-file-in at end move "N" to More-input
```

Each End-if statement matches the previous If and rejoins the True and False paths.

In actual practice, a programmer would probably not use both hierarchy diagrams and pseudocode to design a program. The one very big advantage of pseudocode is that performed procedures can be written right where they are performed. In COBOL, PERFORMed paragraphs are written elsewhere in the program, where they may be difficult to find. This difference sometimes makes pseudocode easier and faster to read than COBOL code. Of course, a hierarchy diagram also locates performed procedures conveniently.

EXERCISE 1

Write a program to read input records in the following format:

Positions	Field
1–5	Employee Number
6–14	Social Security Number
15–16	Hours Worked (whole hours)
17–80	spaces

Have your program print one line for each record in the format shown in Figure 5.E1. Have your program print the word OVERTIME next to each employee who worked more than 37.5 hours.

EXERCISE 2

Using the same input and output formats as in Exercise 1, write a program that reads all the input records and prints only those employees who worked fewer than 30 hours. Do not print the word OVERTIME for any employee.

Figure 5.E1 Output format for Exercise 1.

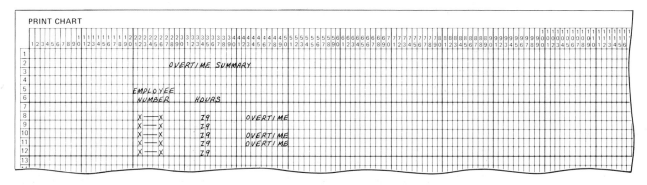

The Format of the IF Statement

The format of the IF statement is:

$$\text{IF condition; } \begin{Bmatrix} \text{statement-1} \\ \text{NEXT SENTENCE} \end{Bmatrix} \begin{Bmatrix} \text{; ELSE statement-2} \\ \text{; ELSE NEXT SENTENCE} \end{Bmatrix}$$

The format shows that the word IF must be followed by a condition supplied by the programmer. In Chapter 2 we saw a condition but it was used in a PERFORM statement, not an IF statement. It was as follows:

```
MORE-INPUT IS EQUAL TO "N"
```

In Program P05-01 we use two conditions in IF statements:

```
QUANTITY-ON-HAND-IN IS LESS THAN 400
```

and

```
LINE-COUNT-ER IS GREATER THAN LINE-LIMIT
```

You will find a complete discussion of conditions in the next section.

Following the condition we see braces, which mean that one of the items within must be chosen to follow the condition. We have used both forms, for in most of our IF statements we have had some processing statement following the condition, and in one of the IF statements in this chapter we had the reserved words NEXT SENTENCE. The format shows that if NEXT SENTENCE is chosen to be included in the IF statement, it must be spelled as shown. The next set of braces indicates that an ELSE clause is always required. The braces show that the word ELSE must always appear, followed by either a statement or the words NEXT SENTENCE. However, the words ELSE NEXT SENTENCE may be omitted if they immediately precede a period. That means that the statement

```
IF LINE-COUNT-ER IS GREATER THAN LINE-LIMIT
    PERFORM PRODUCE-PAGE-HEADINGS.
```

is the same as:

```
IF LINE-COUNT-ER IS GREATER THAN LINE-LIMIT
    PERFORM PRODUCE-PAGE-HEADINGS
ELSE
    NEXT SENTENCE.
```

The format says nothing about indenting in the IF statement because COBOL does not examine the indenting. Indenting is only for the programmer's convenience and should be used to improve the readability of programs.

Conditions

The **simple conditions** in COBOL are the **relation condition,** the **class condition,** the **condition-name condition,** the **switch-status condition,** and the **sign condition.** The relation condition is the only kind we have used so far in this book.

The Relation Condition

The format of the relation condition is:

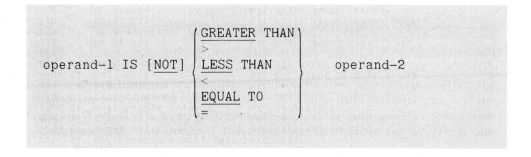

Operand-1 is called the **subject** of the relation condition. Operand-2 is called the **object** of the relation condition. Operand-1 and operand-2 may each be an identifier, a literal, or an arithmetic expression. The relation condition must contain at least one reference to an identifier.

Note the optional words in this format. In

```
IF QUANTITY-ON-HAND-IN IS LESS THAN 400 ...
```

both IS and THAN are optional, and the statement could have begun with

```
IF QUANTITY-ON-HAND-IN LESS THAN 400 ...
```

or

```
IF QUANTITY-ON-HAND-IN IS LESS 400 ...
```

or

```
IF QUANTITY-ON-HAND-IN LESS 400 ...
```

but the optional words were used to improve the readability. The signs >, <, and = may be used instead of the corresponding words. The signs, if used, are required, and we refrain from underlining them here because underlining might make them confusing. In the condition

```
MORE-INPUT IS EQUAL TO "N"
```

we could have used the equal sign instead:

```
MORE-INPUT = "N"
```

The brackets around the word NOT in the format show that the programmer may choose to use NOT or omit it. The underlining shows that if the programmer chooses to use the contents of the brackets, the word NOT must be used and spelled exactly as shown.

The Class Condition

The class condition allows a program to check whether a particular field does or does not contain only numbers, or whether it does or does not contain only the characters A through Z and the character space. The format of the class condition is:

```
identifier IS [NOT]    {NUMERIC  }
                       {ALPHABETIC}
```

To see how the class test works, assume we have the following fields:

```
05 MONEY-AMOUNT-IN      PIC 9(5)V99,
05 MONEY-AMOUNT-W       PIC S9(5)V99,
05 ALPHA-FIELD          PIC X(8),
```

The test

```
IF MONEY-AMOUNT-IN IS NOT NUMERIC ,,,
```

will execute the True path if any of the characters in MONEY-AMOUNT-IN are other than the digits 0 through 9. The field MONEY-AMOUNT-W, however, will be considered **NUMERIC** if it contains the digits 0 through 9 and a valid plus or minus sign. MONEY-AMOUNT-IN, which contains no S in its PICTURE, would be considered NOT NUMERIC if it were found to contain a sign.

The **ALPHABETIC** class condition permits a program to test whether all the characters in a field are the alphabetic characters, which are defined in COBOL as the letters A through Z and the character space. So the test

```
IF ALPHA-FIELD IS ALPHABETIC ,,,
```

would execute the False path if any of the characters in ALPHA-FIELD were not the letters A through Z or space.

It is legal and sometimes useful to be able to determine whether a field described with Xs contains all numbers. The test

```
IF ALPHA-FIELD IS NUMERIC ,,,
```

would execute the True path only if all the characters in ALPHA-FIELD were the digits 0 through 9. The ALPHABETIC class test may not be executed on a field defined as numeric.

The Condition-Name Condition

To use a condition-name test, the programmer must first define one or more condition names. A condition name is a name given to one or more values that might be assigned to a field. A condition name is defined by using a **level-88** entry in the Data Division. When a level-88 entry is used with a field, the field must still be described in the usual way. That is, the field must have an ordinary level number (from 01 to 49) and, if it is an elementary field, must have a PICTURE, and may have other optional clauses, such as SIGN and/or VALUE.

As an example, assume we have the following input field:

```
05 CODE-IN           PIC 9.
```

Let us say that valid values of CODE-IN are 1, 2, and 3. We can use a level-88 entry with this field to give a condition name to the valid codes. A level-88 entry, when used, must follow immediately the description of the field it applies to. If we want to give the condition name VALID-CODE to the values 1, 2, and 3, we can write

```
05 CODE-IN           PIC 9.
   88 VALID-CODE      VALUES ARE 1 THROUGH 3.
```

or:

```
05 CODE-IN           PIC 9.
   88 VALID-CODE      VALUES 1, 2, 3.
```

When you use a level-88 entry with a field defined as numeric, the literals in the VALUE clause in the level-88 entry must all be numeric. When the field is defined as alphanumeric, alphanumeric edited, or numeric edited, the literals must all be nonnumeric.

The format of the level-88 entry is:

```
88 condition-name;    {VALUE  IS }
                      {VALUES ARE}

    literal-1    [ {THROUGH}  literal-2]
                   {THRU   }

        [, literal-3 [{THROUGH} literal-4]]...
                      {THRU   }
```

The words THROUGH and THRU are equivalent. Although there is never any need to use the word THROUGH in the Procedure Division, it is quite proper to use it in the Data Division. The rules for making up condition names are the same as for making up data names. You can see from the format that exactly one VALUE clause is required in a level-88 entry and that no other clauses are permitted. Note especially that the PICTURE clause is not permitted in a level-88 entry. Level-88 entries must begin anywhere in area B.

In the Procedure Division a condition name may be tested in an IF statement. For example, the statement

```
IF VALID-CODE
    NEXT SENTENCE
ELSE
    PERFORM ERROR-ROUTINE.
```

will skip to the NEXT SENTENCE if CODE-IN is equal to 1 or 2 or 3 and will PERFORM the paragraph ERROR-ROUTINE otherwise. It is legal to use the word NOT before a condition name, so the following statement will do the same as the previous:

```
IF NOT VALID-CODE
    PERFORM ERROR-ROUTINE.
```

Notice that there is no relational operator in these IF statements. The condition name alone constitutes the entire condition in the IF statement.

The use of a level-88 entry in connection with coded fields such as CODE-IN makes it very convenient to see at a glance what all the valid codes are. The program is also very easy to change if the set of valid codes should change, and the Procedure Division coding is clearer when condition names are properly used.

EXERCISE 3

Write a level-05 entry and a level-88 entry for the following field: a three digit, unsigned integer called WORK-STATION. Give the condition name VALID-WORK-STATION to the valid work stations, whose numbers lie in the range 100 to 999 inclusive.

Condition names are most useful when used with input data fields. Many programmers use them with intermediate-result fields in working storage, but their use in such cases must be carefully examined to see whether they make the program easier or more difficult to understand. An unsuitable use of condition names is often found in connection with the input data flag in some programs. Consider this definition of the flag:

```
01 MORE-INPUT      PIC X      VALUE "Y".
   88 THERE-IS-MORE-INPUT                VALUE "Y".
   88 THERE-IS-NO-MORE-INPUT             VALUE "N".
```

This is a legal definition, and it shows that the VALUE clause may be used both to establish the initial VALUE of a field and to give names to particular VALUEs that might appear in the field. Now the following is a legal statement:

```
PERFORM MAIN-LOOP UNTIL THERE-IS-NO-MORE-INPUT.
```

This statement reads very nicely and is clear English. Any valid condition is legal following the word UNTIL in a PERFORM statement, whether relation condition, condition-name condition, or any of the others. But now look at the READ statement:

```
READ INPUT-FILE
    AT END
        MOVE "N" TO MORE-INPUT.
```

Now, in the Procedure Division, it is not clear that the field MORE-INPUT has any connection with the name THERE-IS-NO-MORE-INPUT. In order to understand these statements, the reader must look back at the Data Division to see the connection between moving "N" to MORE-INPUT and the condition name THERE-IS-NO-MORE-INPUT. In our programs we have the statements

```
PERFORM MAIN-LOOP UNTIL MORE-INPUT = "N".
```

and

```
READ-INPUT-FILE
    AT END
        MOVE "N" TO MORE-INPUT.
```

The connection between the two statements is evident, without any need for the reader to refer to the Data Division.

The Sign Condition

The sign condition determines whether the algebraic value of a numeric operand is less than, greater than, or equal to zero. The format of the sign condition is:

$$\text{operand IS [\underline{NOT}]} \begin{Bmatrix} \underline{\text{POSITIVE}} \\ \underline{\text{NEGATIVE}} \\ \underline{\text{ZERO}} \end{Bmatrix}$$

The operand being tested must be a field defined as numeric or it must be an arithmetic expression that contains at least one reference to an identifier. An operand greater than zero is considered POSITIVE, less than zero NEGATIVE. An operand of zero value is considered ZERO regardless of whether it is signed or unsigned.

An example of the use of the sign condition is:

```
IF BALANCE-DUE IS POSITIVE
    PERFORM BALANCE-DUE-ROUTINE.
```

The Switch-Status Condition

The switch-status condition permits the programmer to give names to switches which can be set on or off by the programmer or the computer operator at the time a COBOL program is executed. Entries in the SPECIAL-NAMES paragraph of the Environment Division are used to assign the names, and the names may then be used as conditions in the Procedure Division to determine whether a particular switch is on or off. The switches are set on or off externally to the COBOL program. In IBM COBOL systems, the switches are set through the use of the UPSI parameter in an EXEC statement. In NCR VRX COBOL, the switches are set by use of the OPTS parameter in the JOB statement.

Nested IF Statements

A **nested** IF statement is one where one or more IF statements appear in the True path or the False path, or both, of an IF statement. Figure 5.12 shows logic that may be coded with a nested IF statement. The coding is:

```
IF QUANTITY-IN LESS THAN 400
      MOVE SPACES              TO OUTPUT-LINE
      MOVE PART-NUMBER-IN      TO PART-NUMBER-OUT
      MOVE PART-DESCRIPTION-IN TO PART-DESCRIPTION-OUT
      MOVE QUANTITY-IN         TO QUANTITY-OUT
      IF LINE-COUNT-ER GREATER THAN LINE-LIMIT
          PERFORM PRODUCE-PAGE-HEADINGS
          WRITE REPORT-LINE FROM OUTPUT-LINE
      ELSE
          WRITE REPORT-LINE FROM OUTPUT-LINE.
```

Figure 5.12   Flowchart of logic that may be coded using a nested IF statement.

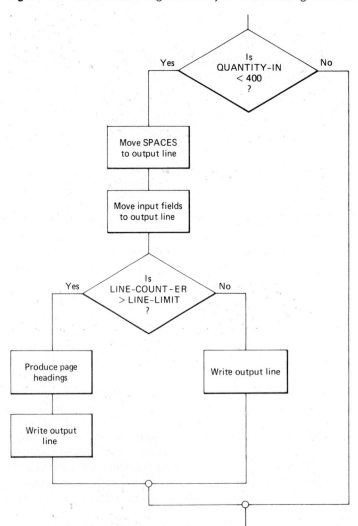

This nested IF staement consists of an **outer IF statement** containing an **inner IF statement** in its True path. Figure 5.13 shows a flowchart for a slightly more complex nested IF statement. In Figure 5.13 both the True and False paths of the outer IF contain an IF. Figure 5.13 may be coded as follows:

```
IF C1
     PERFORM P1
     IF C2
          NEXT SENTENCE
     ELSE
          PERFORM P2
          PERFORM P3
ELSE
     IF C3
          PERFORM P4
     ELSE
          PERFORM P5.
```

Figure 5.13 Flowchart of logic in which each path of the outer decision contains a decision.

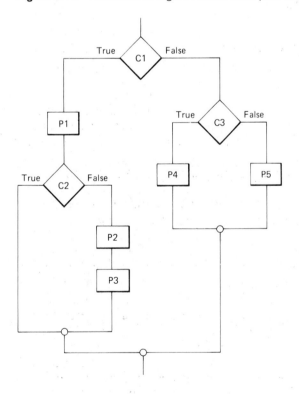

Nested IF statements should always be written with proper indentation so that the programmer can see which ELSE belongs to which IF and where the True and False paths of each of the IF tests are. In the IF statement above, the first IF tests the condition C1 and starts the True path for that condition. The ELSE aligned with the first IF starts the False path for that same condition, C1. Indented further are other IFs and ELSEs, each ELSE aligned with its corresponding IF. Each ELSE ends the True path for its corresponding IF and starts the False path.

Most important, there is only one period at the end of the whole thing. Remember that the period rejoins True and False paths in IF statements. In flowcharts of IF statements the rejoining of True and False paths is shown by a little circle. You can see in Figure 5.13 that there are three places where True and False paths rejoin, and in the IF statement the single period rejoins all three pairs of paths.

It has already been mentioned that COBOL does not examine indenting in IF statements (or in any others) and that indenting is only for the programmer's convenience. Here the programmer would use indenting to keep track of which ELSE belongs to which IF. But since COBOL does not examine indenting, it uses the following rule to determine for itself which ELSE belongs to which IF: Any ELSE encountered in the statement is considered to apply to the immediately preceding IF that has not already been paired with an ELSE.

Figure 5.14 shows a flowchart where there are two paths with no processing. The coding for the flowchart in Figure 5.14 is as follows:

```
IF  C1
    IF  C2
        PERFORM  P1
        PERFORM  P2
        PERFORM  P3
    ELSE
        NEXT  SENTENCE
ELSE
    IF  C3
        NEXT  SENTENCE
    ELSE
        PERFORM  P4.
```

Notice that in this statement the reserved words NEXT SENTENCE must be used whenever there is no processing in a path, and of course the single period at the end of the sentence rejoins all three pairs of True and False paths.

Figure 5.14   Flowchart of logic in which two paths contain no processing.

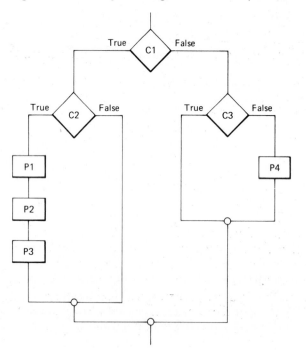

Figure 5.15 shows another flowchart with no processing in two paths. One way of coding Figure 5.15 is:

```
IF C1
    IF C2
        PERFORM P1
    ELSE
        NEXT SENTENCE
ELSE
    IF C3
        PERFORM P2
    ELSE
        NEXT SENTENCE.
```

But the rules of COBOL say that the words ELSE NEXT SENTENCE may be omitted if they appear immediately before a period, so Figure 5.15 may be coded equally well as:

```
IF C1
    IF C2
        PERFORM P1
    ELSE
        NEXT SENTENCE
ELSE
    IF C3
        PERFORM P2.
```

The remaining ELSE NEXT SENTENCE clause cannot be removed since it does not immediately precede the period.

Figure 5.15   Another flowchart in which two paths contain no processing.

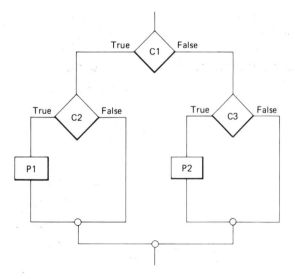

Figure 5.16 shows a flowchart of nested logic which cannot be implemented in 1974 COBOL by using just a nested IF statement. Although 1985 COBOL contains a language element that makes it possible to code the logic of Figure 5.16 with just one nested IF statement, what is it about the logic that makes it impossible to code

using only a 1974 nested IF statement? It is the paths from the condition C2; they rejoin before the end of the logic. In 1974 COBOL the only way to join True and False paths is with a period. There can be only one period in a 1974 IF statement, and so the only kind of logic that can be implemented with just a nested IF construction is that in which all the True and False pairs join at the end. An attempt to write the logic of Figure 5.16 might look like this:

```
IF  C1
     IF  C2
          PERFORM  P1
     ELSE
          PERFORM  P2
PERFORM  P3
ELSE
     IF  C3
          PERFORM  P4
     ELSE
          PERFORM  P5.
```

Figure 5.16 Flowchart of logic that cannot be implemented in 1974 COBOL using only a nested IF statement. The joining of a True path with a False path before box P3 cannot be coded.

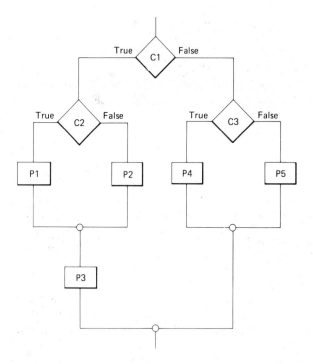

But aligning the statement PERFORM P3 with the first IF doesn't fool anyone but the programmer. It certainly doesn't fool COBOL, which does not examine the indenting and interprets the IF statement as if it were written:

```
IF C1
    IF C2
        PERFORM P1
    ELSE
        PERFORM P2
        PERFORM P3
ELSE
    IF C3
        PERFORM P4
    ELSE
        PERFORM P5.
```

Figure 5.17 Logic implied by an IF statement trying to implement the logic shown in Figure 5.16.

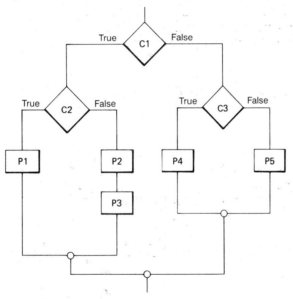

The logic implied by the IF statement above is given in Figure 5.17.

The correct way to handle a situation such as the logic in Figure 5.16 is to remove from the flowchart the entire portion that is causing the trouble and put it in a separate paragraph. The exact portion of the flowchart that must be removed in such cases can be located as follows: Find a little circle that appears anywhere before the end of the logic. In this case it's the circle before the box P3. Then trace back from that circle to its corresponding condition. In this case the condition that corresponds to the troublesome circle is C2. Now remove everything between the condition and the circle from this flowchart, including the condition and the circle, and place them all in a separate paragraph. Let's call that new paragraph C2-CONDITION-TEST, and redraw Figure 5.16 as Figure 5.18.

Now there are no little circles except at the end of the logic, and Figure 5.18 can be coded as:

```
IF C1
    PERFORM C2-CONDITION-TEST
    PERFORM P3
ELSE
    IF C3
        PERFORM P4
    ELSE
        PERFORM P5.
```

The paragraph C2-CONDITION-TEST, which could be placed anywhere in the Procedure Division, would be:

```
C2-CONDITION-TEST.
    IF C2
        PERFORM P1
    ELSE
        PERFORM P2.
```

Figure 5.18   Figure 5.16 redrawn so that it can be coded in 1974 COBOL.

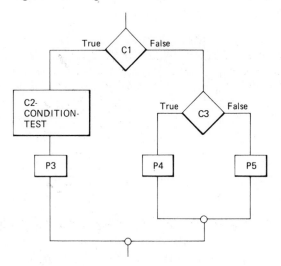

It is natural for students to consider it a challenge to try to code the logic of Figure 5.16 with just one nested IF statement. If you do, remember that P3 must be executed regardless of the outcome of the C2 condition. Also, check the format of the IF statement on page 115 to make sure you do not use any creative but illegal forms of the statement.

IF statements may be nested to any level within the limits of the size of the computer. That is, an IF statement in one of the paths of an outer IF statement may itself have an IF statement in one of its own paths. The logic shown in Figure 5.19 may be coded as:

```
IF C1
    PERFORM P1
    IF C2
        NEXT SENTENCE
    ELSE
        PERFORM P2
        IF C3
            PERFORM P3
            PERFORM P4
        ELSE
            NEXT SENTENCE
ELSE
    NEXT SENTENCE.
```

Or, by removing the unneeded ELSE NEXT SENTENCE clauses,

```
IF C1
    PERFORM P1
    IF C2
        NEXT SENTENCE
    ELSE
        PERFORM P2
        IF C3
            PERFORM P3
            PERFORM P4.
```

Figure 5.19 Logic requiring three levels of nesting in an IF statement.

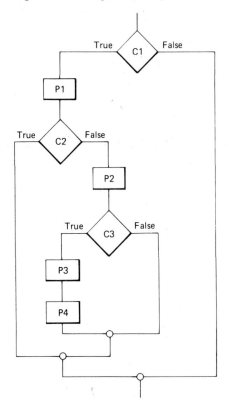

EXERCISE 4

Code the logic shown in Figure 5.E4 using only nested IF statements.

EXERCISE 5

Code the logic shown in Figure 5.E5 by first removing from each flowchart any segments whose True and False paths rejoin before the end of the flow and placing them into separate paragraphs. Code also the logic of the paragraphs removed.

Figure 5.E4   Flowcharts for Exercise 4.

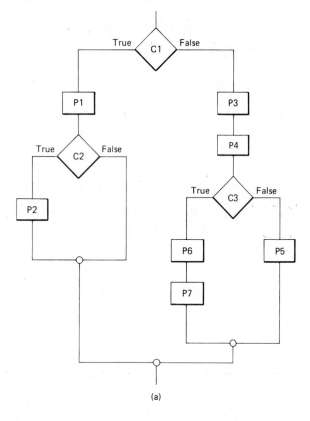

(a)

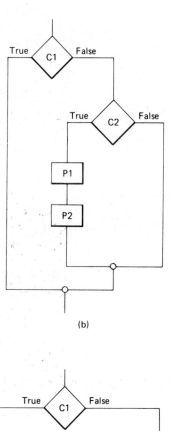

(b)

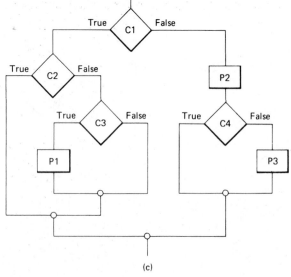

(c)

Figure 5.E5 Flowcharts for Exercise 5.

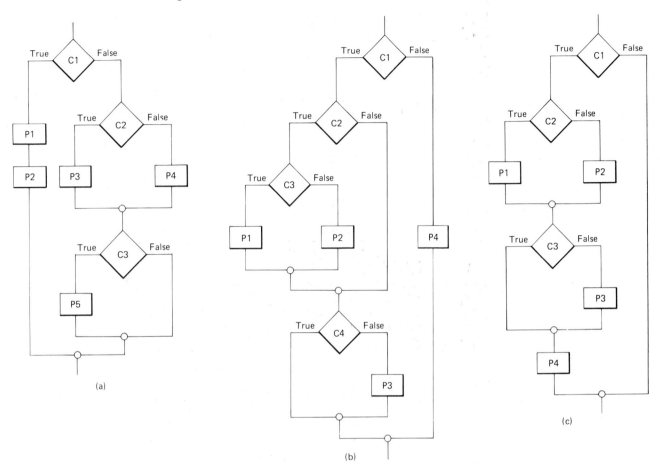

(a)

(b)

(c)

EXERCISE 6

Draw a flowchart showing the logic of each of the following statements:

a.
```
    IF C1
        PERFORM P1
        IF C2
            NEXT SENTENCE
        ELSE
            PERFORM P2
    ELSE
        IF C3
            PERFORM P3.
```

```
b.    IF C1
          IF C2
              PERFORM P1
              PERFORM P2
          ELSE
              NEXT SENTENCE
      ELSE
          IF C3
              NEXT SENTENCE
          ELSE
              PERFORM P3
              PERFORM P4.
c.    IF C1
          IF C2
              IF C3
                  PERFORM P1.
```

Complex Conditions

There are three kinds of **complex conditions** in COBOL. They are the **negated simple condition,** the **combined condition,** and the **negated combined condition.** A negated simple condition is formed by placing the word NOT before any simple condition. Earlier we saw a negated simple condition, in the section on condition-name conditions:

```
IF NOT VALID-CODE
    PERFORM ERROR-ROUTINE.
```

The word NOT can be placed before any simple condition, so the following is legal:

```
IF NOT A IS EQUAL TO B ...
```

The simple condition may be placed in parentheses without changing the meaning, so

```
IF NOT (A IS EQUAL TO B) ...
```

has the same effect. Both negated conditions have the same meaning as:

```
IF A IS NOT EQUAL TO B ...
```

A combined condition is one that uses the words AND and/or OR. An example of a combined condition used in an IF statement is:

```
IF QUANTITY-ON-HAND-IN IS LESS THAN 400 AND
    UNIT-PRICE IS GREATER THAN 10.00
      PERFORM REORDER-HIGH-PRICE
ELSE
      PERFORM TEST-2.
```

In the preceding IF statement both simple conditions would have to be true for the True path of the IF statement to be executed. In the statement

```
IF A = B OR
   C = D
     PERFORM FOUND-A-MATCH
ELSE
     PERFORM NO-MATCH.
```

if either A equals B or C equals D, the True path will be executed.

ANDs and ORs may be used together in a combined condition. Ordinarily, ANDs are evaluated first, followed by ORs. So the condition

```
IF A = B OR C = D AND E NOT = F ...
```

would be evaluated as if it were written:

```
IF A = B OR (C = D AND E NOT = F) ...
```

This statement would execute the True path if either:

1. A is equal to B, OR
2. C is equal to D and E is not equal to F.

In general a different result would be obtained from the statement:

```
IF (A = B OR C = D) AND E NOT = F ...
```

This statement would execute the True path only if:

1. Either A is equal to B or C is equal to D, AND
2. E is not equal to F.

A negated combined condition consists of the word NOT followed by a combined condition in parentheses, as in:

```
IF NOT (A = B AND C = D)
     PERFORM NOT-BOTH-EQUAL
ELSE
     PERFORM BOTH-EQUAL.
```

In this statement the False path would be executed if A is equal to B and C is equal to D.

Complex conditions can become extremely complicated. You should use them only when their use makes the meaning of the program clearer than it would be without the complex condition.

EXERCISE 7

Given the following statement:

```
IF AMOUNT IS LESS THAN 1000000
    PERFORM ERROR-ROUTINE
ELSE
    IF CHARGE-CODE NOT = "H"
        NEXT SENTENCE
    ELSE
        PERFORM ERROR-ROUTINE.
```

Rewrite this statement using a combined condition so that the logic is made clearer.

Abbreviated Combined Relation Conditions

In a combined condition having two or more relation conditions in a row, more than one of the relation conditions sometimes have the same subject and/or the same relational operator. For example, in the condition

```
IF A = B OR A IS GREATER THAN C ...
```

there are two relation conditions and they both have A as their subject. Such a condition can be abbreviated by leaving out the repetition of the subject, so the following would be legal:

```
IF A = B OR IS GREATER THAN C
    PERFORM IN-RANGE.
```

If the simple conditions in a complex condition have the same subject and the same relational operator, repetition of the subject and the operator may be omitted. So the condition

```
IF A NOT = B AND A NOT = C ...
```

can be abbreviated to the following:

```
IF A NOT = B AND C
    PERFORM EQUALS-NEITHER.
```

You may mix omitting just the subject with omitting the subject and the operator. In the condition

```
IF A IS NOT GREATER THAN B AND
   A IS LESS THAN C          OR
   A IS LESS THAN D ...
```

you can first omit the repetitious subject A, and then later omit the operator LESS THAN when it becomes repetitious, as:

```
IF A IS NOT GREATER THAN B AND LESS THAN C OR D
    PERFORM IN-RANGE.
```

Parentheses are not permitted within an abbreviated condition, even to improve readability.

A word of warning about a common error made by even experienced programmers. In testing whether the value of some data name is not equal to any of several values, the incorrect connective is sometimes used, and the abbreviation masks the error. For example, with the field CODE-IN, described earlier, where the legal values of CODE-IN are 1, 2, and 3, we might want to use an abbreviated relation condition to test for the legal values. Unfortunately COBOL does not permit us to say:

```
IF CODE-IN IS NEITHER 1 NOR 2 NOR 3
    PERFORM ERROR-ROUTINE.
```

Whenever you find this NEITHER . . . NOR situation, there are three correct ways to code it and one commonly used incorrect way (which, of course, eventually must be corrected by the programmer if the program is to work). You may write it as an OR and negate the whole condition, as in:

```
IF NOT (CODE-IN = 1 OR 2 OR 3)
    PERFORM ERROR-ROUTINE.
```

You may reverse the True and False paths, as:

```
IF CODE-IN = 1 OR 2 OR 3
    NEXT SENTENCE
ELSE
    PERFORM ERROR-ROUTINE.
```

Or in the form that is closest to the original wording:

```
IF CODE-IN NOT = 1 AND 2 AND 3
    PERFORM ERROR-ROUTINE.
```

This last form may look a little strange but it makes sense when you realize that in its fully expanded, unabbreviated form, the statement would be:

```
IF CODE-IN NOT = 1 AND
   CODE-IN NOT = 2 AND
   CODE-IN NOT = 3
    PERFORM ERROR-ROUTINE.
```

For the common wrong way of coding this situation, see Exercise 8. Of course, a better way to handle a situation like this is to use a condition name, as described earlier in the chapter.

EXERCISE 8

Expand the following statement into its unabbreviated form. Then answer the questions below.

```
IF CODE-IN NOT = 1 OR 2 OR 3
    PERFORM ERROR-ROUTINE.
```

How would the statement execute if CODE-IN is equal to:
a. 1
b. 2
c. 4

EXERCISE 9

Rewrite the following conditions using abbreviated subjects and/or operators, as appropriate:
a. IF FIELD-1 GREATER THAN FIELD-2 AND FIELD-1 LESS THAN FIELD 3 . . .
b. IF FIELD-1 NOT GREATER THAN FIELD-2 AND FIELD-1 NOT GREATER THAN FIELD-3 . . .
c. IF FIELD-1 LESS THAN FIELD-2 OR FIELD-1 GREATER THAN FIELD-3 AND FIELD-1 EQUAL TO FIELD-4 AND FIELD-1 EQUAL TO FIELD-5 . . .

A Program with Complicated Condition Testing

We now do a program for computing commissions on sales, using a somewhat involved schedule of commission rates. This program shows the use of a nested IF statement, a negated simple condition, a combined condition, and level-88 entries in context.

In this problem salespeople are each assigned to some class. The salespeople classes are A through H. All salespeople assigned to classes A through F are considered junior salespeople; salespeople in class G are associate salespeople; and class H salespeople are senior. Salespeople in different titles have different annual quotas, and their commission rates on current sales depend on whether or not they met their quota last year. The quotas are as follows: for junior salespeople, none; for associates, $150,000; for seniors, $250,000. The commission rates for each of the salespeople titles are shown in Table 5-1.

Table 5-1

Commission schedules for three salespeople titles for Program P05-02.

Title	Commission Schedule If Quota Was Not Met	Commission Schedule If Quota Was Met
Junior	10% of sale amount on all sales	10% of sale amount on all sales
Associate	5% of first $10,000 of sale amount; 20% of sale amount in excess of $10,000	20% of first $10,000 of sale amount; 30% of sale amount in excess of $10,000
Senior	20% of first $50,000 of sale amount; 30% of sale amount in excess of $50,000	30% of first $50,000 of sale amount; 40% of sale amount in excess of $50,000

For example, suppose that an associate salesperson met the quota last year and has just made a sale of $25,000. The commission on that sale would be 20 percent of $10,000 plus 30 percent of the excess. Now suppose that a senior salesperson did not meet the quota last year and has just made a sale of $40,000. The commission on that sale would be 20 percent of $40,000.

The input format for Program P05-02 is:

Positions	Field
1−5	Salesperson Number
6	Class
7−12	Last Year's Sales (in whole dollars)
13−20	Current Sale (in dollars and cents)
21−80	spaces

The output format is shown in Figure 5.20. Two types of error lines are shown. This program checks the salesperson Class in each input record before processing it, and if the Class is missing or invalid, the program prints an appropriate error message.

Figure 5.20 Output format for Program P05-02.

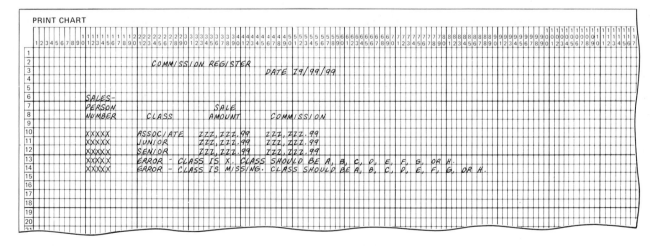

A hierarchy diagram for Program P05-02 is shown in Figure 5.21. Under "Produce detail line" there is shown one way to handle error checking in programs. We first separate the good records from the bad, and then execute either "Process erroneous record" or "Process good record," but not both. "Process erroneous record" determines whether the Class is missing or invalid and writes an appropriate error line.

"Process good record" is divided into three subfunctions. The first, "Select commission rates," determines which commission schedule to use on the basis of the salesperson's class and whether the salesperson met last year's quota. The remaining two subfunctions compute the commission on the Current Sale and write a detail line.

Program P05-02 is shown in Figure 5.22. Level-88 entries for the field CLASS-IN are shown in lines 00310 through 00350. Notice that it is legal to have as many level-88 entries as desired, and they may have any VALUEs or combinations of VALUEs that you like.

Figure 5.21   Hierarchy diagram for Program P05-02.

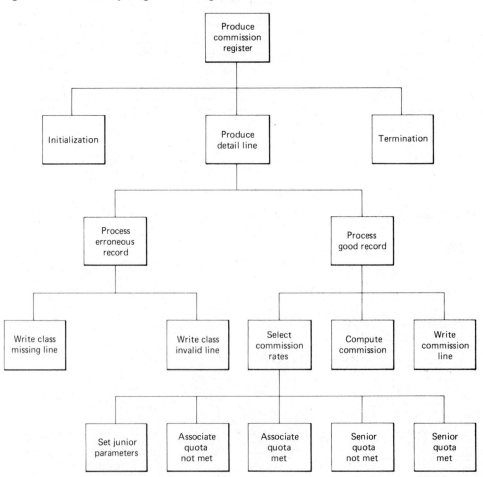

Figure 5.22 Program P05-02.

CB1 RELEASE 2.4   IBM OS/VS COBOL   JULY 1, 1982

18.34.00   MAR 29,1988

```
00010  IDENTIFICATION DIVISION.
00020  PROGRAM-ID.  P05-02.
00030 *
00040 *    AUTHOR. WENDEL KELLER.
00050 *    THIS PROGRAM COMPUTES SALESPERSON COMMISSIONS FOR JUNIOR
00060 *    SALESPERSONS, ASSOCIATE SALESPERSONS, AND SENIOR SALESPERSONS
00070 *
00080 **************************************************************
00090
00100  ENVIRONMENT DIVISION.
00110  CONFIGURATION SECTION.
00120  SOURCE-COMPUTER.  IBM-370.
00130  OBJECT-COMPUTER.  IBM-370.
00140
00150  INPUT-OUTPUT SECTION.
00160  FILE-CONTROL.
00170      SELECT COMMISSION-REPORT ASSIGN TO PRINTER.
00180      SELECT SALES-FILE-IN     ASSIGN TO INFILE.
00190
00200  **************************************************************
00210
00220  DATA DIVISION.
00230  FILE SECTION.
00240  FD  SALES-FILE-IN
00250      RECORD CONTAINS 80 CHARACTERS
00260      LABEL RECORDS ARE OMITTED.
00270
00280  01  SALES-RECORD-IN.
00290      05 SALESPERSON-NUMBER-IN    PIC X(5).
00300      05 CLASS-IN                 PIC X.
00310         88 SALESPERSON-IS-JUNIOR     VALUES "A" THRU "F".
00320         88 SALESPERSON-IS-ASSOCIATE VALUE "G".
00330         88 SALESPERSON-IS-SENIOR    VALUE "H".
00340         88 VALID-CLASS-CODE         VALUES "A" THRU "H".
00350         88 CLASS-CODE-IS-MISSING    VALUE SPACE.
00360      05 LAST-YEARS-SALES-IN      PIC 9(6).
00370      05 CURRENT-SALE-IN          PIC 9(6)V99.
00380      05 FILLER.                  PIC X(60).
00390
00400  FD  COMMISSION-REPORT
00410      LABEL RECORDS ARE OMITTED.
00420
00430  01  REPORT-LINE               PIC X(88).
00440
00450  WORKING-STORAGE SECTION.
00460  01  MORE-INPUT         PIC X      VALUE "Y".
00470  01  NO-INPUT-DATA      PIC X(15) VALUE " NO INPUT DATA".
00480
00490  01  PAGE-HEAD-1.
00500      05 FILLER             PIC X(23) VALUE SPACES.
00510      05 FILLER             PIC X(19) VALUE "COMMISSION REGISTER".
00520
00530  01  PAGE-HEAD-2.
00540      05 FILLER             PIC X(45) VALUE SPACES.
00550      05 FILLER             PIC X(5)  VALUE "DATE".
00560      05 RUN-MONTH-AND-DAY  PIC Z9/99/.
00570      05 RUN-YEAR           PIC 99.
00580
00590  01  PAGE-HEAD-3.
00600      05 FILLER             PIC X(10) VALUE SPACES.
00610      05 FILLER             PIC X(6)  VALUE "SALES-".
```

(continued)

A constant called NO-INPUT-DATA appears at line 00470. In this and nearly all subsequent programs, the program will check whether the input file contains no data and, if it does, will print out this constant.

At lines 00920 and 00930 we see for the first time a nonnumeric literal that is too long to fit on one line. The complete literal is supposed to be:

```
ERROR - CLASS IS MISSING. CLASS SHOULD BE A, B, C, D, E, F, G, OR H.
```

Whenever a nonnumeric literal cannot fit on a line, you must write as much of it as you can all the way up through the rightmost position of area B of the line, even if it means breaking a word in the middle. All spaces and punctuation that you write up through the rightmost position of area B also count as part of the literal. Then in position 7 of the next line you must use a hyphen to indicate that this line is a continuation. Then you must write a quotation mark in area B to indicate that a nonnumeric literal is being continued, and then the rest of the literal followed by its closing quotation mark. Remember that we use the **continuation indicator** in position 7 only for continuing a literal from one line to the next and not to continue ordinary statements and entries. Also remember that we have gotten this far without previously using the continuation indicator.

The COMMISSION-RATES used by this program are written in lines 01110 through 01320. These entries show a hierarchy of fields. The field COMMISSION-RATES is defined as consisting of the three fields: ASSOCIATE-RATES, SENIOR-RATES, and JUNIOR-RATES. In turn, each of those fields consists of two fields called QUOTA-NOT-MET and QUOTA-MET. And each of those consists of the elementary items LOW-RATE and HIGH-RATE. In this way all the commission rates from the problem are written into the program. Even though junior sales-people have only one commission rate, 10 percent, it was entered in a form consistent with the rates for associate and senior salespeople.

Figure 5.22   (continued)

```
00620
00630   01   PAGE-HEAD-4.
00640        05  FILLER              PIC X(10) VALUE SPACES.
00650        05  FILLER              PIC X(25) VALUE "PERSON".
00660        05  FILLER              PIC X(4)  VALUE "SALE".
00670
00680   01   PAGE-HEAD-5.
00690        05  FILLER              PIC X(10) VALUE SPACES.
00700        05  FILLER              PIC X(12) VALUE "NUMBER".
00710        05  FILLER              PIC X(12) VALUE "CLASS".
00720        05  FILLER              PIC X(12) VALUE "AMOUNT".
00730        05  FILLER              PIC X(10) VALUE "COMMISSION".
00740
00750   01   DETAIL-LINE.
00760        05  SALESPERSON-NUMBER-OUT    PIC B(10)X(5).
00770        05  CLASS-TITLE-OUT           PIC B(5)X(9)BBB.
00780        05  CURRENT-SALE-OUT          PIC ZZZ,ZZZ.99BBB.
00790        05  COMMISSION-OUT            PIC ZZZ,ZZZ.99.
00800
00810   01   CLASS-INVALID-LINE.
00820        05  SALESPERSON-NUMBER        PIC B(10)X(5)B(5).
00830        05  FILLER                    PIC X(17)
00840                                      VALUE "ERROR - CLASS IS".
00850        05  INVALID-CLASS             PIC X.
00860        05  FILLER                    PIC X(44)
00870            VALUE ". CLASS SHOULD BE A, B, C, D, E, F, G, OR H.".
00880
00890   01   CLASS-MISSING-LINE.
00900        05  SALESPERSON-NUMBER        PIC B(10)X(5)B(5).
00910        05  FILLER                    PIC X(68)
00920            VALUE "ERROR - CLASS IS MISSING. CLASS SHOULD BE A, B, C,
00930   -        "D, E, F, G, OR H.".
00940
00950   01   COMMISSION-BREAK-POINTS.
00960        05  JUNIOR-BREAK-POINT        PIC 9     VALUE 0.
00970        05  ASSOCIATE-BREAK-POINT     PIC 9(5)  VALUE 10000.
00980        05  SENIOR-BREAK-POINT        PIC 9(5)  VALUE 50000.
00990
```

```
01000  01   SELECTED-COMMISSION-RATES.
01010       05 LOW-COMMISSION-RATE        PIC V99.
01020       05 HIGH-COMMISSION-RATE       PIC V99.
01030
01040  01   SELECTED-BREAK-POINT          PIC 9(5).
01050
01060  01   SALE-QUOTAS.
01070       05 JUNIOR-SALE-QUOTA          PIC 9      VALUE 0.
01080       05 ASSOCIATE-SALE-QUOTA       PIC 9(6)   VALUE 150000.
01090       05 SENIOR-SALE-QUOTA          PIC 9(6)   VALUE 250000.
01100
01110  01   COMMISSION-RATES.
01120       05 ASSOCIATE-RATES.
01130          10 QUOTA-NOT-MET.
01140             15 LOW-RATE             PIC V99    VALUE .05.
01150             15 HIGH-RATE            PIC V99    VALUE .20.
01160          10 QUOTA-MET.
01170             15 LOW-RATE             PIC V99    VALUE .20.
01180             15 HIGH-RATE            PIC V99    VALUE .30.
01190       05 SENIOR-RATES.
01200          10 QUOTA-NOT-MET.
01210             15 LOW-RATE             PIC V99    VALUE .20.
01220             15 HIGH-RATE            PIC V99    VALUE .30.
01230          10 QUOTA-MET.
01240             15 LOW-RATE             PIC V99    VALUE .30.
01250             15 HIGH-RATE            PIC V99    VALUE .40.
01260       05 JUNIOR-RATES.
01270          10 QUOTA-NOT-MET.
01280             15 LOW-RATE             PIC V99    VALUE .10.
01290             15 HIGH-RATE            PIC V99    VALUE .10.
01300          10 QUOTA-MET.
01310             15 LOW-RATE             PIC V99    VALUE .10.
01320             15 HIGH-RATE            PIC V99    VALUE .10.
01330
01340  01   TODAYS-DATE.
01350       05 RUN-YEAR                   PIC 99.
01360       05 RUN-MONTH-AND-DAY          PIC 9(4).
01370
01380  ***********************************************************************
01390
01400  PROCEDURE DIVISION.
01410  PRODUCE-COMMISSION-REGISTER.
01420       PERFORM INITIALIZATION.
01430       PERFORM PRODUCE-DETAIL-LINE UNTIL MORE-INPUT = "N".
01440       PERFORM TERMINATION.
01450       STOP RUN.
01460
01470  INITIALIZATION.
01480       OPEN INPUT  SALES-FILE-IN,
01490           OUTPUT COMMISSION-REPORT.
01500       ACCEPT TODAYS-DATE FROM DATE.
01510       MOVE CORR TODAYS-DATE TO PAGE-HEAD-2.
01520       WRITE REPORT-LINE FROM PAGE-HEAD-1 AFTER PAGE.
01530       WRITE REPORT-LINE FROM PAGE-HEAD-2.
01540       WRITE REPORT-LINE FROM PAGE-HEAD-3 AFTER 3.
01550       WRITE REPORT-LINE FROM PAGE-HEAD-4.
01560       WRITE REPORT-LINE FROM PAGE-HEAD-5.
01570       MOVE SPACES TO REPORT-LINE.
01580       WRITE REPORT-LINE.
01590       READ SALES-FILE-IN
01600           AT END
01610               MOVE "N" TO MORE-INPUT.
01620       IF MORE-INPUT = "N"
01630           WRITE REPORT-LINE FROM NO-INPUT-DATA AFTER 2.
01640
01650  TERMINATION.
01660       CLOSE SALES-FILE-IN,
01670             COMMISSION-REPORT.
01680
01690  PRODUCE-DETAIL-LINE.
01700       IF NOT VALID-CLASS-CODE
01710           PERFORM PROCESS-ERRONEOUS-RECORD
01720       ELSE
01730           PERFORM PROCESS-GOOD-RECORD.
01740       READ SALES-FILE-IN
01750           AT END
01760               MOVE "N" TO MORE-INPUT.
01770
```

(continued)

Figure 5.22 (continued)

```
01780    PROCESS-ERRONEOUS-RECORD.
01790        IF CLASS-CODE-IS-MISSING
01800            PERFORM WRITE-CLASS-MISSING-LINE
01810        ELSE
01820            PERFORM WRITE-CLASS-INVALID-LINE.
01830
01840    PROCESS-GOOD-RECORD.
01850        PERFORM SELECT-COMMISSION-RATES.
01860        PERFORM COMPUTE-COMMISSION.
01870        PERFORM WRITE-COMMISSION-LINE.
01880
01890    SELECT-COMMISSION-RATES.
01900        IF SALESPERSON-IS-JUNIOR
01910            PERFORM SET-JUNIOR-PARAMETERS
01920        ELSE
01930            IF SALESPERSON-IS-ASSOCIATE AND
01940                LAST-YEARS-SALES-IN LESS THAN ASSOCIATE-SALE-QUOTA
01950                PERFORM ASSOCIATE-QUOTA-NOT-MET
01960            ELSE
01970                IF SALESPERSON-IS-ASSOCIATE
01980                    PERFORM ASSOCIATE-QUOTA-MET
01990                ELSE
02000                    IF LAST-YEARS-SALES-IN LESS THAN
02010                                            SENIOR-SALE-QUOTA
02020                        PERFORM SENIOR-QUOTA-NOT-MET
02030                    ELSE
02040                        PERFORM SENIOR-QUOTA-MET.
02050
02060    WRITE-CLASS-MISSING-LINE.
02070        MOVE SALESPERSON-NUMBER-IN TO
02080            SALESPERSON-NUMBER IN CLASS-MISSING-LINE.
02090        WRITE REPORT-LINE FROM CLASS-MISSING-LINE.
02100
02110    WRITE-CLASS-INVALID-LINE.
02120        MOVE CLASS-IN TO INVALID-CLASS.
02130        MOVE SALESPERSON-NUMBER-IN TO
02140            SALESPERSON-NUMBER IN CLASS-INVALID-LINE.
02150        WRITE REPORT-LINE FROM CLASS-INVALID-LINE.
02160
02170    SET-JUNIOR-PARAMETERS.
02180        MOVE JUNIOR-BREAK-POINT TO SELECTED-BREAK-POINT.
02190        MOVE "JUNIOR"          TO CLASS-TITLE-OUT.
02200        MOVE HIGH-RATE IN QUOTA-MET IN JUNIOR-RATES TO
02210            HIGH-COMMISSION-RATE.
02220        MOVE LOW-RATE  IN QUOTA-MET IN JUNIOR-RATES TO
02230            LOW-COMMISSION-RATE.
02240
02250    ASSOCIATE-QUOTA-NOT-MET.
02260        MOVE ASSOCIATE-BREAK-POINT TO SELECTED-BREAK-POINT.
02270        MOVE "ASSOCIATE"           TO CLASS-TITLE-OUT.
02280        MOVE HIGH-RATE IN QUOTA-NOT-MET IN ASSOCIATE-RATES TO
02290            HIGH-COMMISSION-RATE.
02300        MOVE LOW-RATE  IN QUOTA-NOT-MET IN ASSOCIATE-RATES TO
02310            LOW-COMMISSION-RATE.
02320
02330    ASSOCIATE-QUOTA-MET.
02340        MOVE ASSOCIATE-BREAK-POINT TO SELECTED-BREAK-POINT.
02350        MOVE "ASSOCIATE"           TO CLASS-TITLE-OUT.
02360        MOVE HIGH-RATE IN QUOTA-MET IN ASSOCIATE-RATES TO
02370            HIGH-COMMISSION-RATE.
02380        MOVE LOW-RATE  IN QUOTA-MET IN ASSOCIATE-RATES TO
02390            LOW-COMMISSION-RATE.
02400
02410    SENIOR-QUOTA-NOT-MET.
02420        MOVE SENIOR-BREAK-POINT TO SELECTED-BREAK-POINT.
02430        MOVE "SENIOR"          TO CLASS-TITLE-OUT.
02440        MOVE HIGH-RATE IN QUOTA-NOT-MET IN SENIOR-RATES TO
02450            HIGH-COMMISSION-RATE.
02460        MOVE LOW-RATE  IN QUOTA-NOT-MET IN SENIOR-RATES TO
02470            LOW-COMMISSION-RATE.
02480
02490    SENIOR-QUOTA-MET.
02500        MOVE SENIOR-BREAK-POINT TO SELECTED-BREAK-POINT.
02510        MOVE "SENIOR"          TO CLASS-TITLE-OUT.
02520        MOVE HIGH-RATE IN QUOTA-MET IN SENIOR-RATES TO
02530            HIGH-COMMISSION-RATE.
02540        MOVE LOW-RATE  IN QUOTA-MET IN SENIOR-RATES TO
02550            LOW-COMMISSION-RATE.
```

```
02560
02570    COMPUTE-COMMISSION.
02580       IF CURRENT-SALE-IN GREATER THAN SELECTED-BREAK-POINT
02590          COMPUTE COMMISSION-OUT ROUNDED =
02600             LOW-COMMISSION-RATE * SELECTED-BREAK-POINT +
02610             HIGH-COMMISSION-RATE *
02620                (CURRENT-SALE-IN - SELECTED-BREAK-POINT)
02630       ELSE
02640          COMPUTE COMMISSION-OUT ROUNDED =
02650             LOW-COMMISSION-RATE * CURRENT-SALE-IN.
02660
02670    WRITE-COMMISSION-LINE.
02680       MOVE SALESPERSON-NUMBER-IN TO SALESPERSON-NUMBER-OUT.
02690       MOVE CURRENT-SALE-IN       TO CURRENT-SALE-OUT.
02700       WRITE REPORT-LINE FROM DETAIL-LINE.
```

At line 01700 there is a negated simple condition, formed by placing the word NOT before the condition name VALID-CLASS-CODE. Lines 01900 through 02040 show a nested IF statement which contains a combined condition at lines 01930 and 01940.

There are many examples of data-name qualification. Many of them show that more than one level of qualification may sometimes be needed to identify a field uniquely. The name

```
HIGH-RATE IN QUOTA-MET IN JUNIOR-RATES
```

at line 02200 could not be made unique except with the two levels of qualification shown.

Program P05-02 was run with the input data shown in Figure 5.23 and produced the output shown in Figure 5.24. Then it was run with an empty input file and produced the output shown in Figure 5.25.

Figure 5.23 Input to Program P05-02.

```
-------------------------------------------------------------------------------
          1         2         3         4         5         6         7        8
12345678901234567890123456789012345678901234567890123456789012345678901234567890
-------------------------------------------------------------------------------
14756G08994307059243
14758G22342101000000
15008H07076399804299
19123H17036705376542
14689 16900001245968
10089G08054604307865
17665G15000008870099
15699A00000003000099
15003H06576305000000
12231B19630024367921
14769G21991219445399
15013H06920000782135
15014H42310003596299
14770G17630008235643
14771G29342100936951
15000Z24936204345621
15002H03421601934526
15004H02632105732123
12352G16030000698234
15006H07962303922431
14757G10009900198499
15010H25192304736554
13834F12989604598799
15011H25743205078654
14764115054320909324
15015H28996507987523
14759G02980004783965
15016H48990008535942
14761G06597600643912
15012H25000009368342
```

Figure 5.24   Output from Program P05-02.

```
                    COMMISSION REGISTER
                                    DATE   3/29/88


SALES-
PERSON                    SALE
NUMBER     CLASS          AMOUNT      COMMISSION

14756      ASSOCIATE      70,592.43    12,618.49
14758      ASSOCIATE      10,000.00     2,000.00
15008      SENIOR        998,042.99   294,412.90
19123      SENIOR         53,765.42    11,129.63
14689      ERROR - CLASS IS MISSING. CLASS SHOULD BE A, B, C, D, E, F, G, OR H.
10089      ASSOCIATE      43,078.65     7,115.73
17665      ASSOCIATE      88,700.99    25,610.30
15699      JUNIOR         30,000.99     3,000.10
15003      SENIOR         50,000.00    10,000.00
12231      JUNIOR        243,679.21    24,367.92
14769      ASSOCIATE     194,453.99    57,336.20
15013      SENIOR          7,821.35     1,564.27
15014      SENIOR         35,962.99    10,788.90
14770      ASSOCIATE      82,356.43    23,706.93
14771      ASSOCIATE       9,369.51     1,873.90
15000      ERROR - CLASS IS Z. CLASS SHOULD BE A, B, C, D, E, F, G, OR H.
15002      SENIOR         19,345.26     3,869.05
15004      SENIOR         57,321.23    12,196.37
12352      ASSOCIATE       6,982.34     1,396.47
15006      SENIOR         39,224.31     7,844.86
14757      ASSOCIATE       1,984.99        99.25
15010      SENIOR         47,365.54    14,209.66
13834      JUNIOR         45,987.99     4,598.80
15011      SENIOR         50,786.54    15,314.62
14764      ERROR - CLASS IS 1. CLASS SHOULD BE A, B, C, D, E, F, G, OR H.
15015      SENIOR         79,875.23    26,950.09
14759      ASSOCIATE      47,839.65     8,067.93
15016      SENIOR         85,359.42    29,143.77
14761      ASSOCIATE       6,439.12       321.96
15012      SENIOR         93,683.42    32,473.37
```

Figure 5.25   Output produced when Program P05-02 was run with an empty input file.

```
                    COMMISSION REGISTER
                                 DATE   3/29/88


SALES-
PERSON                    SALE
NUMBER     CLASS          AMOUNT      COMMISSION


NO INPUT DATA
```

A Special Kind of IF Statement

The nested IF statement in Program P05-02 is of a special type, in that the words IF and ELSE alternate. In this kind of IF statement, it is very easy to see which ELSE belongs to which IF since there are no unrelated IFs and ELSEs in the way. In such a statement only one, or none, of the True paths is executed each time the statement is executed. Since it is easy to know which ELSE belongs to which IF, it is not important to indent the levels of the nest as we have done. In fact, some programmers feel that since one of the True paths at most will be executed, it is clearer to write it this way:

```
IF SALESPERSON-IS-JUNIOR
    PERFORM SET-JUNIOR-PARAMETERS
ELSE
IF SALESPERSON-IS-ASSOCIATE AND
    LAST-YEARS-SALES-IN-LESS THAN ASSOCIATE-SALE-QUOTA
    PERFORM ASSOCIATE-QUOTA-NOT-MET
ELSE
IF SALESPERSON-IS-ASSOCIATE
    PERFORM ASSOCIATE-QUOTA-MET
ELSE
IF LAST-YEARS-SALES-IN LESS THAN SENIOR-SALE-QUOTA
    PERFORM SENIOR-QUOTA-NOT-MET
ELSE
    PERFORM SENIOR-QUOTA-MET.
```

EXERCISE 10

Rewrite the IF statement in lines 01900 through 02040 of Program P05-02 without using a combined condition. The resulting IF statement no longer will have alternating IFs and ELSEs. Which of the two forms of the IF statement do you think is easier to understand? What are the good and bad features of each form of the statement?

Summary

The IF statement enables a COBOL program to make decisions on the basis of data. The decision determines which of two paths will be executed. Either or both of the paths may contain as many processing steps as needed. When the True path contains no processing, the reserved words NEXT SENTENCE must be used. If the False path contains processing, the reserved word ELSE must be used to show where the False path begins. A single period terminates the IF statement and shows where the True and False paths rejoin. The coding of the True and False paths is indented to improve program readability. Indenting is not examined by the COBOL system.

A nested IF statement consists of one or more IF statements in the True and/or False paths of another IF statement. An IF statement may be nested to essentially any level, and there is only one period at the end of the entire nest of IFs. For the programmer to keep track of which ELSE belongs to which IF, conventional indenting should be adhered to. There may be as many processing steps as desired in any of the paths at any level of the nest, and any path containing no processing must use the words NEXT SENTENCE. The clause ELSE NEXT SENTENCE may be omitted if it appears immediately before the period.

Some nested logic cannot be implemented in 1974 COBOL using just a nested IF statement. This occurs whenever the True and False paths of one of the inner IFs rejoin before the end of the outer IF. In such a case a portion of the logic must be written as a separate paragraph and PERFORMed from the proper place in the IF statement.

The five simple conditions are the relation condition, the condition-name condition, the class condition, the sign condition, and the switch-status condition. Condition-name conditions depend on level-88 entries.

A level-88 entry may be used to give a condition name to particular values of fields. When a level-88 entry is used, the field must still be defined in the usual way. Condition names are most useful in the File Section, but many programmers use them also in the Working Storage Section. When a level-88 entry is used, it must immediately follow the description of the field to which it applies. A level-88 entry must contain exactly one VALUE clause and no other clauses, especially no PICTURE clause.

The complex conditions are the negated simple condition, as IF NOT VALID-CODE, the combined condition, as IF A = B AND C = D, and the negated combined condition, as IF NOT (A = B AND C = D). Care should be taken to avoid writing IF statements whose meaning is not clear to the human reader.

A special kind of nested IF statement is one in which the IFs and ELSEs alternate and there are no intervening IFs or ELSEs. Special indenting conventions different from the indenting used for regular nested IF statements are often used in writing such a statement.

Fill-in Exercises

1. The _____ phrase must be used whenever an IF statement contains processing in the False path but no processing in the True path.

2. The clause _____ may be omitted from an IF statement if it appears immediately before the period.

3. In a nested IF statement the _____ appearance of the word IF begins the outer IF.

4. Use of proper _____ enables the programmer to see which ELSE belongs to which IF.

5. IF statements may be _____ to any level.

6. Simple conditions may be connected by the words _____ and _____ to form combined conditions.

7. Placing the word NOT before a simple condition forms a _____ _____ _____ .

8. Placing the word NOT before a combined condition in parentheses forms a _____ _____ _____ .

9. The order of evaluation in a combined condition is _____ first and then _____ .

10. If the same _____ and/or _____ appears in more than one relation condition in a combined condition, the repetitions may be omitted.

11. A level-88 entry can be used to give a _____ to one or more values that might be assigned to a field.

12. Exactly one _____ clause is required in a level-88 entry.

13. In a flowchart of a decision the True path and the False path must _____ before the flowchart can continue.

14. The five simple conditions in COBOL are the relation condition, the _____ condition, the _____ condition, the _____ condition, and the _____ condition.

15. The continuation indicator is the character _____ in position _____ of the continuation line.

Review Exercises

1. Write a program to the following specifications:

Input

Records in the following format:

Positions	Field
1–5	Employee Number
6	Overtime Eligibility Indicator
	E - Exempt (not eligible for overtime pay)
	N - Nonexempt (eligible for overtime pay)
7–9	Hours Worked (to one decimal place)
10–80	spaces

Output

Use the output format shown in Figure 5.RE1.

Figure 5.RE1 Output format for Review Exercise 1.

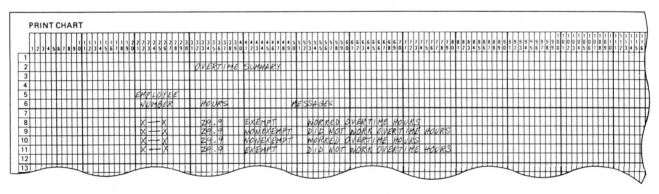

Processing

For each employee print the Employee Number and the Hours Worked. If the employee is not exempt from overtime pay, print the word EXEMPT. If the employee is nonexempt, print the word NONEXEMPT. If the Hours Worked are more than 40, print WORKED OVERTIME HOURS. If the Hours Worked are not more than 40, print DID NOT WORK OVERTIME HOURS.

2. Write a program using the same input format as in Review Exercise 1, and produce output in the format shown in Figure 5.RE2. For each input record, have your program print the Employee Number and the Hours Worked. Also, if the employee is eligible for overtime pay and the Hours Worked are more than 40, have your program print the words OVERTIME PAY.

Figure 5.RE2   Output format for Review Exercise 2.

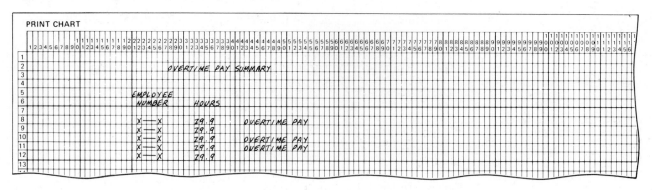

3. Write a program to process input data in the following format:

Positions	Field
1−9	Social Security Number
10	Job Grade
11−18	Annual Salary (to two decimal places)
19−80	spaces

Each input record is for one employee and shows the employee's Job Grade and current Annual Salary. The Job Grades are L through P and 1 through 6. The titles for each grade are:

Z   Smelter apprentice
Y   Junior smelter
X   Smelter
W   Gang chief
V   Foreman
6   Superintendent
5 – 1 Plant manager

The program is required to compute a cost-of-living raise for each employee on the basis of the employee's Job Grade and current Annual Salary and to print the results in the format shown in Figure 5.RE3. The schedule for cost-of-living increases is as follows:

Job Grade	Annual Salary	Increase
Any	Less than $15,000	15% of current salary
Z	Any	15% of current salary
V – Y	$15,000 – $19,999.99	7% of current salary, plus $1200
V – Y	$20,000 and over	5% of current salary, plus $1600
4 – 6	$15,000 – $19,999.99	15% of current salary
4 – 6	$20,000 and over	$3,000
1 – 3	$15,000 and over	$2,250

Figure 5.RE3 Output format for Review Exercise 3.

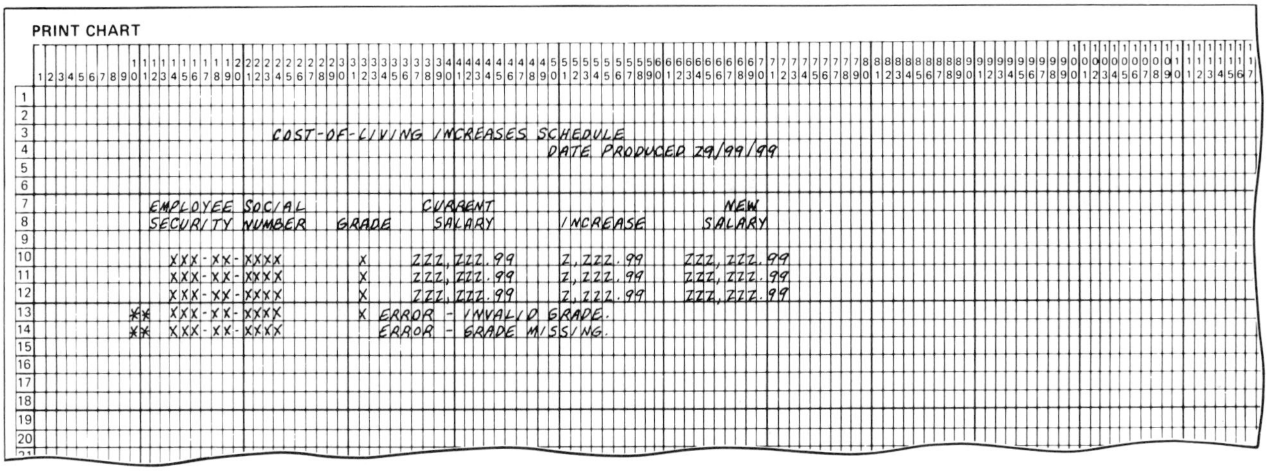

PRINT CHART

```
                    COST-OF-LIVING INCREASES SCHEDULE
                              DATE PRODUCED Z9/99/99

        EMPLOYEE SOCIAL           CURRENT                    NEW
        SECURITY NUMBER    GRADE  SALARY        INCREASE     SALARY

           XXX-XX-XXXX       X    ZZZ,ZZZ.99    Z,ZZZ.99    ZZZ,ZZZ.99
           XXX-XX-XXXX       X    ZZZ,ZZZ.99    Z,ZZZ.99    ZZZ,ZZZ.99
           XXX-XX-XXXX       X    ZZZ,ZZZ.99    Z,ZZZ.99    ZZZ,ZZZ.99
        **  XXX-XX-XXXX      X ERROR - INVALID GRADE.
        **  XXX-XX-XXXX        ERROR - GRADE MISSING.
```

4. Modify your solution to Review Exercise 3 to count the number of employees in each Job Grade and also to compute the total current salaries, the total increases, and the total salaries after the increase. The program should produce output in the format shown in Figure 5.RE4.

Figure 5.RE4 Output format for Review Exercise 4.

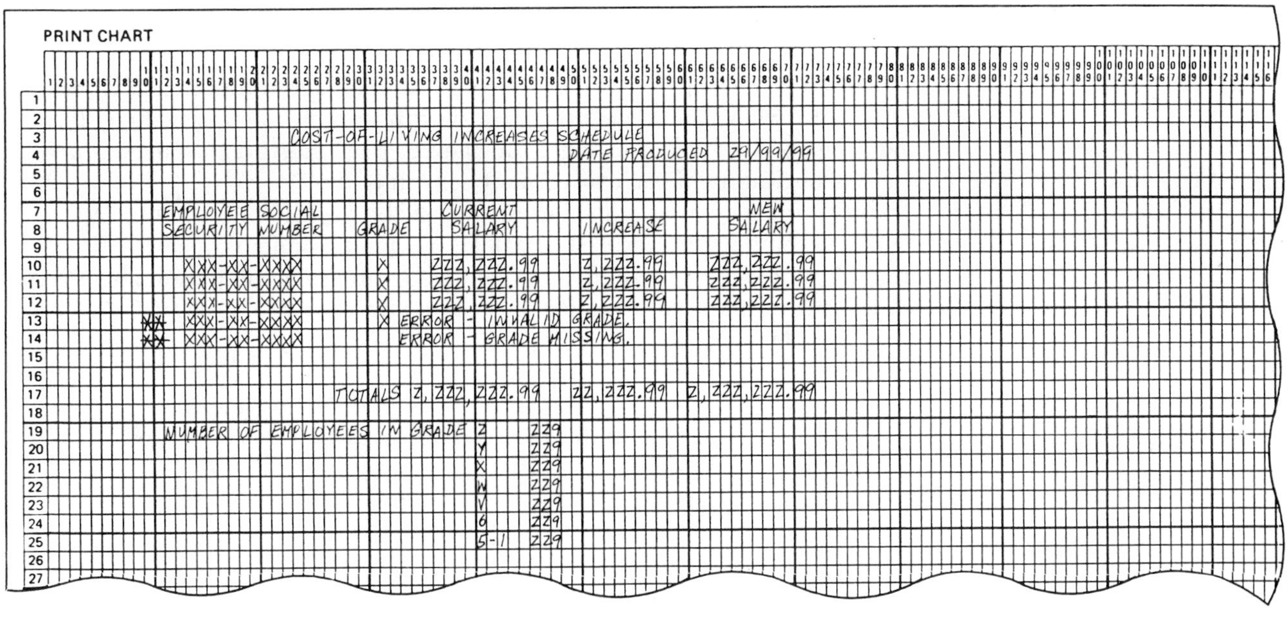

PRINT CHART

```
                    COST-OF-LIVING INCREASES SCHEDULE
                              DATE PRODUCED Z9/99/99

        EMPLOYEE SOCIAL           CURRENT                    NEW
        SECURITY NUMBER    GRADE  SALARY        INCREASE     SALARY

           XXX-XX-XXXX       X    ZZZ,ZZZ.99    Z,ZZZ.99    ZZZ,ZZZ.99
           XXX-XX-XXXX       X    ZZZ,ZZZ.99    Z,ZZZ.99    ZZZ,ZZZ.99
           XXX-XX-XXXX       X    ZZZ,ZZZ.99    Z,ZZZ.99    ZZZ,ZZZ.99
        **  XXX-XX-XXXX      X ERROR - INVALID GRADE.
        **  XXX-XX-XXXX        ERROR - GRADE MISSING.

                    TOTALS Z,ZZZ,ZZZ.99    ZZ,ZZZ.99   Z,ZZZ,ZZZ.99

        NUMBER OF EMPLOYEES IN GRADE Z     ZZ9
                                     Y     ZZ9
                                     X     ZZ9
                                     W     ZZ9
                                     G     ZZ9
                                     5-11  ZZ9
```

5. Draw a flowchart showing the logic of the following statement:

```
IF C1
    NEXT SENTENCE
ELSE
    PERFORM P1
    IF C2
        PERFORM P2
        PERFORM P3
        IF C3
            IF C4
                PERFORM P4
            ELSE
                NEXT SENTENCE
        ELSE
            NEXT SENTENCE
    ELSE
        PERFORM P5.
```

6. Rewrite the statement in Review Exercise 5 by combining C3 and C4 into a combined condition. Reduce the depth of nesting by one level.

Project

Modify your solution to the Project in Chapter 4, page 102. Have your program READ any number of input records, each relating to a different automobile loan, and produce a separate repayment schedule for each loan in the format shown in Figure 5.P1. Have your program read input records in the following format:

Positions	Field
1 – 7	Starting Loan Amount (dollars and cents)
8 – 13	Monthly Payment (dollars and cents)
14 – 17	Annual Interest Rate
18 – 80	spaces

Have your program skip to a new page at the beginning of each repayment schedule and when the page overflows within a repayment schedule. Put the complete heading information at the top of every page. Restart the page-numbering at 1 at the beginning of each repayment schedule.

Have your repayment schedules print just the payments needed to reduce the Principal Remaining to zero. If the last payment would reduce the Principal Remaining to a value less than zero, have your program compute instead a final payment that would reduce the Principal Remaining to zero exactly. The formula for the final payment is:

$$\text{Final Payment} = \text{Principal Remaining from previous payment} * (1 + \text{Annual Interest Rate} / 12)$$

You will need two PERFORM loops in this program, one inside the other. You will need an ordinary main loop, controlled by a PERFORM statement and executed until there is no more input. Somewhere within the main loop, you will need a PERFORM statement to generate one repayment schedule (PERFORM...UNTIL PRINCIPAL-REMAINING = ZERO). Each PERFORM statement will need its own kind of initialization immediately preceding it, similar to the initialization each has had in previous programs.

Design this program carefully and draw a hierarchy diagram before you begin coding. When you make up your input data, be sure your monthly payments are large enough to reduce the Principal Remaining each month; else the Principal Remaining will never get to zero and your program will be in an endless loop.

Figure 5.P1 Output format for Chapter 5 Project.

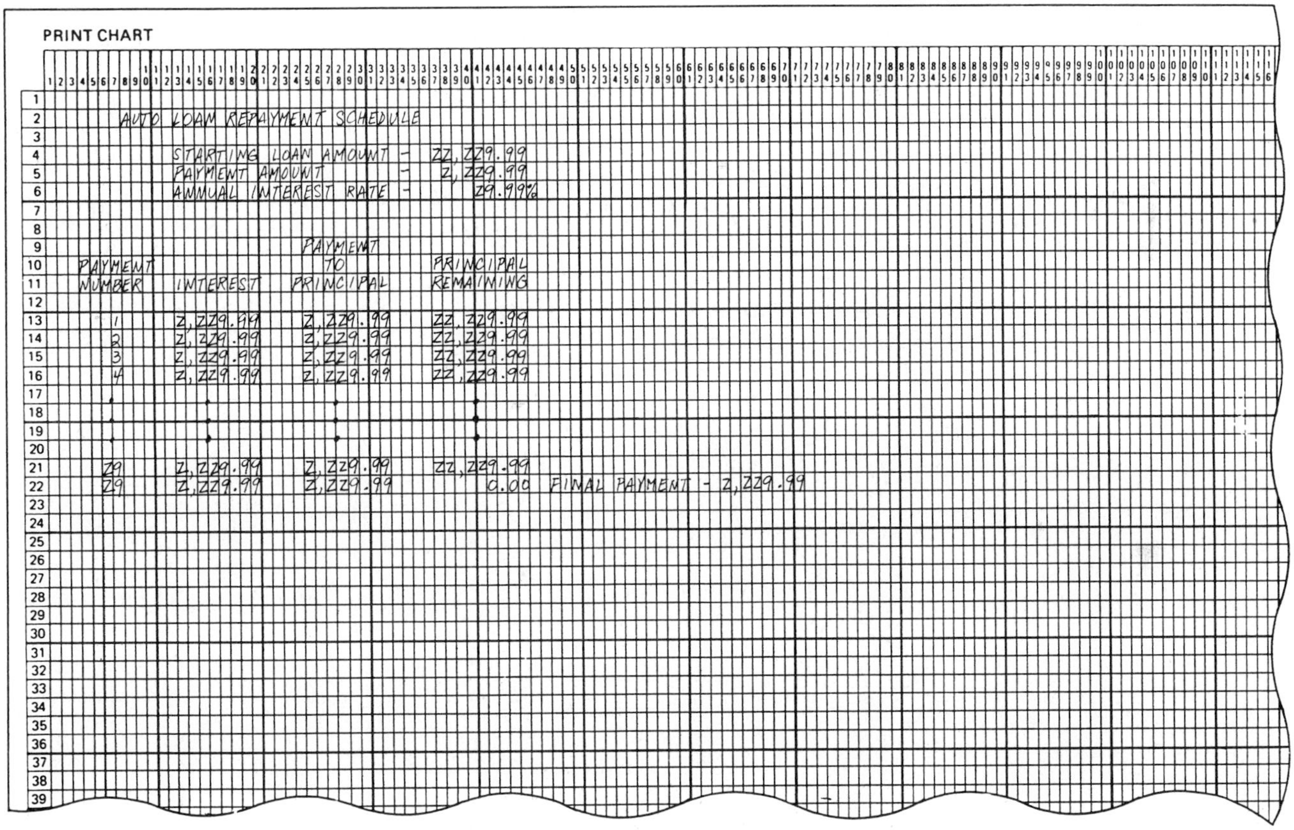

6 Control Breaks: Program Design III

Here are the key points you should learn from this chapter:

1. What control breaks are and why they are important in data processing
2. A generalized approach to developing hierarchy diagrams for programs with control breaks
3. How to program control breaks in COBOL

Key words to recognize and learn:

control break	QUOTE
control field	QUOTES
COMPUTATIONAL	READ . . . INTO
SYNCHRONIZED	rolling
COMP	forward
SYNC	group indicating
USAGE	ADD CORRESPONDING
DISPLAY	sort
figurative constant	major sort field
ZEROS	minor sort field
ZEROES	intermediate sort field
SPACE	minor control field
HIGH-VALUE	major control field
HIGH-VALUES	group printing
LOW-VALUE	summary reporting
LOW-VALUES	

In this chapter we will study techniques for printing totals throughout a report as well as at its end. This kind of processing is carried out in almost every COBOL installation in the world and can become quite complicated. By starting at the beginning and using top-down design, we will be able to keep the difficulties under control. In the course of studying these totaling techniques we will also see some other useful COBOL features.

A Report with One Control Break

The first program in this chapter uses input in the following format:

Positions	Field
1	Indicator
2–6	Account Number
7–9	spaces
10–16	Amount (to two decimal places)
17–80	spaces

Each record contains an Indicator to say whether the Amount is a credit or a debit. If there is a dash in the Indicator field, the Amount is a debit; if the Indicator is anything else, the Amount is a credit. There may be any number of input records for a single Account Number, and there may be any number of credits and/or debits for a single Account Number. The records for each Account Number will be grouped together in the input. The program is to READ the input file, print the contents of each record, and also print the total debits and the total credits for each Account Number. The totals for each Account Number are to be printed immediately following the printing of the group of lines for that Account Number. The output from Program P06-01 is to look like Figure 6.1, from the input shown in Figure 6.2.

Figure 6.1 Output from Program P06-01.

```
                            ACCOUNT ACTIVITY REPORT                   PAGE   1

         DATE   3/29/88


                      ACCT. NO.        DEBITS         CREDITS

                       02005            30.34
                       02005                              .00
                       02005                         98,762.01
                       02005              .06
                       02005          89,235.51
                       02005                         34,859.10

      TOTALS FOR ACCOUNT NUMBER 02005  $89,265.91   $133,621.11

                       04502                         99,999.99
                       04502            83.99
                       04502          45,672.12

      TOTALS FOR ACCOUNT NUMBER 04502  $45,756.11   $99,999.99

                       12121          75,499.00
                       12121              .02
                       12121              .00
                       12121                         23,411.11
                       12121                             66.67
                       12121          66,662.22

      TOTALS FOR ACCOUNT NUMBER 12121  $142,161.24  $23,477.78

                       19596                         92,929.29
                       19596          12,547.20
                       19596          23,487.64
```

ACCOUNT ACTIVITY REPORT

ACCT. NO.	DEBITS	CREDITS
19596	.20	
19596		2.39
19596		213.45

TOTALS FOR ACCOUNT NUMBER 19596 $36,035.04 $93,145.13

20023	99,999.99	
20023	87,654.99	
20023	86,868.68	
20023		88,888.80
20023		88,553.32
20023		56,789.23

TOTALS FOR ACCOUNT NUMBER 20023 $274,523.66 $234,231.35

23456	2.11	
23456	4.53	
23456	12.00	
23456		.12
23456		18.00
23456		.54

TOTALS FOR ACCOUNT NUMBER 23456 $18.64 $18.66

30721	1.01	
30721		99.12
30721	98.44	

TOTALS FOR ACCOUNT NUMBER 30721 $99.45 $99.12

ACCOUNT ACTIVITY REPORT

ACCT. NO.	DEBITS	CREDITS
40101	342.87	
40101		212.45
40101	60,002.01	
40101		67.00
40101	32,343.23	
40101		90,023.41

TOTALS FOR ACCOUNT NUMBER 40101 $92,688.11 $90,302.86

67689	11.14	
67689		1,010.10
67689	33.35	
67689		2,203.30
67689	3,040.20	
67689		10,000.00

TOTALS FOR ACCOUNT NUMBER 67689 $3,084.69 $13,213.40

72332	.04	
72332		44.44
72332	444.44	
72332		4.44
72332	.44	
72332		4,040.40

TOTALS FOR ACCOUNT NUMBER 72332 $444.92 $4,089.28

Figure 6.2 Input to Program P06-01.

```
                 1         2         3         4         5         6         7         8
        12345678901234567890123456789012345678901234567890123456789012345678901234567890
-------------------------------------------------------------------------------------------
        -02005    0003034
         02005    0000000
         02005    9876201
        -02005    0000006
        -02005    8923551
         02005    3485910
         04502    9999999
        -04502    0008399
        -04502    4567212
        -12121    7549900
        -12121    0000002
        -12121    0000000
         12121    2341111
         12121    0006667
        -12121    6666222
         19596    9292929
        -19596    1254720
        -19596    2348764
        -19596    0000020
         19596    0000239
         19596    0021345
        -20023    9999999
        -20023    8765499
        -20023    8686868
         20023    8888880
         20023    8855332
         20023    5678923
        -23456    0000211
        -23456    0000453
        -23456    0001200
         23456    0000012
         23456    0001800
         23456    0000054
        -30721    0000101
         30721    0009912
        -30721    0009844
        -40101    0034287
         40101    0021245
        -40101    6000201
         40101    0006700
        -40101    3234323
         40101    9002341
        -67689    0001114
         67689    0101010
        -67689    0003335
         67689    0220330
        -67689    0304020
         67689    1000000
        -72332    0000004
         72332    0004444
        -72332    0044444
         72332    0000444
        -72332    0000044
         72332    0404040
```

You can see that for a single Account Number there may be several debits and/or credits. All the lines for an Account Number print consecutively, and at the end of the group of lines there is a line showing the total of the debits and the total of the credits for the Account Number. At the end of the next Account Number are its totals, and so on for all the Account Numbers. The input to this program is in Account Number order, that is, each Account Number in the input is higher than the Account Number before it, and all records for a single Account Number are together in the input. This program would have worked as well even if the Account Numbers were not in order, just as long as all records for a single account come in one after the other in the input. The Account Numbers were ordered so that it would be easy to find them on the output.

Before doing a hierarchy diagram for this program, let's try to think about how this program can be done. We already know how to accumulate totals, so there is no problem in accumulating the total of the debits and the total of the credits for the first Account Number as we print each line. But how will the program know when all the records have been read for the first Account Number and that it is time to print the totals for that account? The program will know that all of the first account is processed when it READs the first record of the second Account Number. As the program READs records, it compares the Account Number in each record to the Account Number in the previous record, until it detects a change in Account Number. The change in the Account Number is called a **control break**, and the Account Number field itself is called a **control field.**

Once a control break is detected, the program will print the total line for the first Account Number and prepare to process the second Account Number. The preparation consists mainly of zeroing out the accumulator fields that were used to total the debits and credits for the first Account Number, so that the same fields may be used to total the debits and credits for the second. When the second control break is detected, the total line for the second Account Number can be printed, and the accumulators zeroed again in preparation for processing the third Account Number. In this way we can process an indefinite number of Account Numbers without having to provide endless numbers of accumulator fields.

Printing the very last total line sometimes presents a problem to programmers. Since a total line is printed only after the first record of the next group is detected, what will be printed when there is no next group? When end-of-file is detected on the input file, we still have not printed the totals of the debits and credits for the last Account Number, for the program has not detected a control break, a change in Account Number. So when doing the hierarchy diagram, we need only remember that, after end-of-file is detected, one more total line has to be written, and that is the total line for the last Account Number.

A Hierarchy Diagram for a Program with One Control Break

We can now begin to create the hierarchy diagram for this program. The first level of main subfunctions, as shown in Figure 6.3, is of the same form as in other first-level diagrams. We have an initialization box, a main loop, and termination. In this program, what is carried out in "Termination," after end-of-file is detected on the input, aside from closing the files, is only printing the last total line on the report — just the total line for the last group. All the other total lines on the report are printed by the main loop as we go along.

Figure 6.3 First-level hierarchy diagram for Program P06-01.

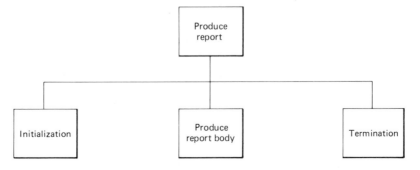

We next add to the hierarchy diagram two boxes showing that the main loop produces both detail lines and total lines. The hierarchy diagram showing "Produce a detail line" and "Account number break" is in Figure 6.4. The box "Account number break" will produce all total lines except the last one on the report, and the "Termination" box will produce the final line. We now add to the diagram the boxes "Print a detail line" and "Accumulate debits and credits," as shown in Figure 6.5. The relationship between printing a detail line and accumulating sums is similar here to what we have seen in earlier programs.

Figure 6.4 Partial hierarchy diagram for Program P06-01 showing "Produce a detail line" and "Account number break."

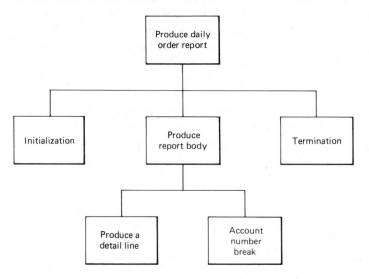

Figure 6.5 Partial hierarchy diagram for Program P06-01 showing subfunctions of "Produce a detail line."

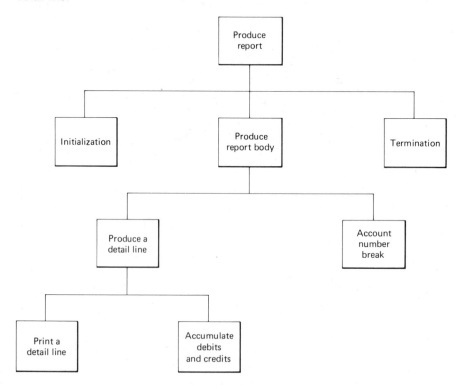

The customary subfunctions of "Initialization" are added to the diagram, and "Print page headings" has been added as a subfunction of "Print a detail line," in Figure 6.6.

Finally, what are the subfunctions of "Termination"? The box "Account number break" is all that is needed to produce the last total line, and so we add that as shown in Figure 6.7.

Notice that we have not shown "Print page headings" as a subfunction of "Account number break," for if a control break occurs when a page is already full, we don't want to skip to a new page, print page headings, and then print the total line at the top of the page without the detail group that it belongs to. In fact, in this kind of processing it is customary never to have total lines print at the top of a new page away from their corresponding detail lines. Sufficient space must be left at the bottom of each page of report output to accommodate any total lines that might appear. Figure 6.7 is the complete hierarchy diagram.

Figure 6.6 Partial hierarchy diagram for Program P06-01 showing subfunctions of "Initialization" and "Print a detail line."

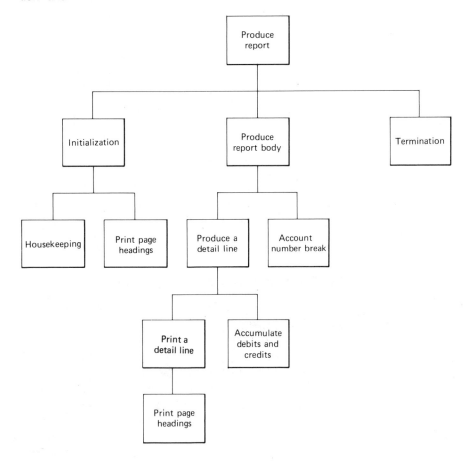

Figure 6.7 Complete hierarchy diagram for Program P06-01.

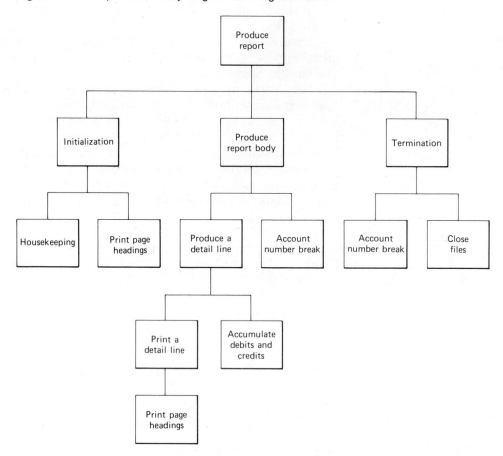

The First Control Break Program

The output format for Program P06-01 is shown in Figure 6.8. Program P06-01 is shown in Figure 6.9.

Notice the definition of the input file and input record at lines 00230 through 00270. In this and all subsequent control-break programs in this book, the input record is defined in the File Section as just one 80-character field. Each input record, after being read, is transferred to an area in working storage, in this program ACCOUNT-RECORD-W, line 00380, where it is worked on. Whenever you use the kind of control-break logic we have in this program, you must work on your input records in working storage and not in the File Section. The reason we set up our input area in working storage is that the logic of this program requires access to the input area after end-of-file has been read on the input file, and the rules of COBOL prohibit any reference to an input area in the File Section after end-of-file has been read on the input file associated with that area. All areas in the Working Storage Section, however, can be accessed at any time. Notice that the work area in working storage does not have to be 80 character positions long, but only as long as you need to handle all the input fields.

Figure 6.8 Output format for Program P06-01.

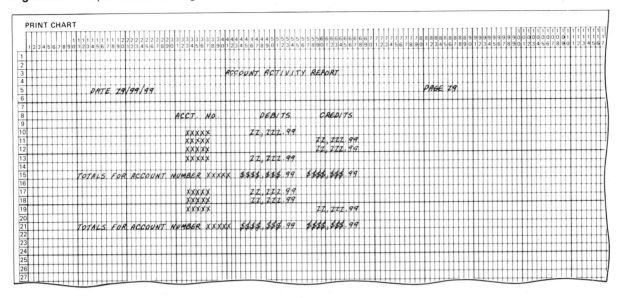

Figure 6.9 Program P06-01.

```
CB1 RELEASE 2.4                              IBM OS/VS COBOL   JULY  1, 1982

                        22.14.37        MAR 29,1988


00010   IDENTIFICATION DIVISION.
00020   PROGRAM-ID.  P06-01.
00030 *
00040 *    THIS PROGRAM PRODUCES AN ACCOUNT ACTIVITY REPORT
00050 *    WITH TOTALS OF DEBITS AND CREDITS FOR EACH ACCOUNT.
00060 *
00070 ************************************************************************
00080
00090   ENVIRONMENT DIVISION.
00100   CONFIGURATION SECTION.
00110   SOURCE-COMPUTER.  IBM-370.
00120   OBJECT-COMPUTER.  IBM-370.
00130
00140   INPUT-OUTPUT SECTION.
00150   FILE-CONTROL.
00160       SELECT ACCOUNT-ACTIVITY-REPORT  ASSIGN TO PRINTER.
00170       SELECT ACCOUNT-FILE-IN          ASSIGN TO INFILE.
00180
00190 ************************************************************************
00200
00210   DATA DIVISION.
00220   FILE SECTION.
00230   FD  ACCOUNT-FILE-IN
00240       RECORD CONTAINS 80 CHARACTERS
00250       LABEL RECORDS ARE OMITTED.
00260
00270   01  ACCOUNT-RECORD-IN        PIC X(80).
00280
00290   FD  ACCOUNT-ACTIVITY-REPORT
00300       LABEL RECORDS ARE OMITTED.
00310
00320   01  REPORT-LINE              PIC X(87).
00330
00340   WORKING-STORAGE SECTION.
00350   01  MORE-INPUT               PIC X     VALUE "Y".
00360   01  NO-INPUT-DATA            PIC X(15) VALUE "  NO INPUT DATA".
00370
```

(continued)

Figure 6.9   (continued)

```
00380    01    ACCOUNT-RECORD-W.
00390          05 INDICATOR              PIC X.
00400          05 ACCOUNT-NUMBER-IN      PIC X(5)  VALUE SPACES.
00410          05 FILLER                 PIC X(3).
00420          05 AMOUNT                 PIC 9(5)V99.
00430
00440    01    PAGE-HEAD-1.
00450          05 FILLER           PIC X(40) VALUE SPACES.
00460          05 FILLER           PIC X(23) VALUE "ACCOUNT ACTIVITY REPORT".
00470
00480    01    PAGE-HEAD-2.
00490          05 FILLER                 PIC X(13) VALUE SPACES.
00500          05 FILLER                 PIC X(5)  VALUE "DATE".
00510          05 RUN-MONTH-AND-DAY      PIC Z9/99/.
00520          05 RUN-YEAR               PIC 99.
00530          05 FILLER                 PIC X(54) VALUE SPACES.
00540          05 FILLER                 PIC X(5)  VALUE "PAGE".
00550          05 PAGE-NUMBER-OUT        PIC Z9.
00560
00570    01    PAGE-HEAD-3.
00580          05 FILLER                 PIC X(30) VALUE SPACES.
00590          05 FILLER                 PIC X(17) VALUE "ACCT. NO.".
00600          05 FILLER                 PIC X(12) VALUE "DEBITS".
00610          05 FILLER                 PIC X(7)  VALUE "CREDITS".
00620
00630    01    DETAIL-LINE.
00640          05 ACCOUNT-NUMBER-OUT     PIC B(32)X(5).
00650          05 DEBITS                 PIC B(8)ZZ,ZZZ.99.
00660          05 CREDITS                PIC B(4)ZZ,ZZZ.99.
00670
00680    01    CONTROL-BREAK-LINE.
00690          05 FILLER                 PIC X(10) VALUE SPACES.
00700          05 FILLER          PIC X(26) VALUE "TOTALS FOR ACCOUNT NUMBER".
00710          05 ACCOUNT-NUMBER-SAVE    PIC X(5)BB.
00720          05 DEBITS-TOTAL           PIC $$$$,$$$.99BB.
00730          05 CREDITS-TOTAL          PIC $$$$,$$$.99.
00740
00750    01    ACCUMULATORS-W.
00760          05 DEBITS-TOTAL   PIC S9(6)V99 VALUE 0.
00770          05 CREDITS-TOTAL  PIC S9(6)V99 VALUE 0.
00780
00790    01    LINE-LIMIT       PIC S99 VALUE 34 COMP SYNC.
00800    01    LINE-SPACING     PIC S9             COMP SYNC.
00810    01    PAGE-NUMBER-W     PIC S99 VALUE ZERO.
00820    01    LINE-COUNT-ER    PIC S99            COMP SYNC.
00830
00840    01    TODAYS-DATE.
00850          05 RUN-YEAR       PIC 99.
00860          05 RUN-MONTH-AND-DAY      PIC 9(4).
00870
00880    ****************************************************************
00890
```

(continued)

All fields being used for intermediate working storage results, such as the two accumulator fields at lines 00760 and 00770, are described with the PICTURE character S even though we expect all values to be positive. In many COBOL systems if you use the character S on numeric fields in working storage you will get programs that run faster and occupy less computer storage space. In addition three fields are described as being **COMPUTATIONAL** and **SYNCHRONIZED,** at lines 00790, 00800, and 00820. These designations may obtain more efficient processing for fields used solely for operations that are wholly internal to the program. That is, COMPUTATIONAL and SYNCHRONIZED should always be used on numeric fields that are neither read in nor written out and that have no operations performed on them with fields that are read in or written out. An example of such a field is LINE-LIMIT. LINE-LIMIT is used to compare against

LINE-COUNT-ER to determine whether a report page is full. No input or output ever interacts with this field, and so it should be designated COMPUTATIONAL and SYNCHRONIZED. The other COMPUTATIONAL SYNCHRONIZED field also does not interact with input or output. Mercifully, COMPUTATIONAL and SYNCHRONIZED have authorized abbreviations. They are the reserved words **COMP** and **SYNC.**

It is permissible to use COMPUTATIONAL and SYNCHRONIZED on fields that do interact with input and/or output, but improved efficiency is then no longer always likely.[1] When COMPUTATIONAL and SYNCHRONIZED are used, as we have done here, on wholly internal fields, they can never do harm — and they may do some good. But when they are used on fields that interact with input and/or output, they can result, in certain cases, in loss of efficiency. The only way to be certain is to run the program with and without the COMPUTATIONAL and SYNCHRONIZED designations and see which version takes less computer time.

COMPUTATIONAL is referred to as a **USAGE** of a field. A field whose USAGE is not specified as COMPUTATIONAL is said to have the USAGE **DISPLAY.**

The field called LINE-SPACING, at line 00800, is used to control the spacing of detail lines as they are printed. The print chart shows that a detail line should be double-spaced if it appears immediately after the column headings or after a total line and should be single-spaced if it appears after another detail line. When we look at the Procedure Division, you will see how LINE-SPACING controls the variable spacing. LINE-SPACING has been made COMPUTATIONAL and SYNCHRONIZED because it is used only internally to the program.

The word ZERO, as in line 00810, is a **figurative constant.** It can be used wherever a numeric or nonnumeric literal of zero would be legal. COBOL interprets ZERO as being numeric or nonnumeric depending on its context. The figurative constants **ZEROS** and **ZEROES** have exactly the same meaning as ZERO. They are provided only for the programmer's convenience.

Another figurative constant that we have been using all along is SPACES. It may be used interchangeably with the word **SPACE,** whose meaning in COBOL is identical to SPACES. SPACE and SPACES are always interpreted as nonnumeric literals consisting of as many blank characters as are required by the context in which they are used.

There is no great advantage in using the word ZERO instead of the numeral 0 when a numeric literal is desired, except perhaps to avoid confusion between O and 0. But when a nonnumeric literal consisting of a string of zeros is desired, then ZERO (or ZEROS or ZEROES) will be interpreted by COBOL to give the exact number of characters needed.

Other figurative constants are **HIGH-VALUE** and **HIGH-VALUES,** which both stand for the highest character that can be stored in the computer, **LOW-VALUE** and **LOW-VALUES,** which both stand for the lowest character that can be stored in the computer, and **QUOTE** and **QUOTES,** which both stand for the character ''.

---

[1]Some COBOL systems have COMPUTATIONAL-like options which can often improve program efficiency considerably under conditions where COMPUTATIONAL would be unsuitable. We refrain from using any pseudo-COMPUTATIONAL options in this book since they are not part of the ANSI standard.

Figure 6.9 (continued)

```
00900    PROCEDURE DIVISION.
00910    PRODUCE-REPORT.
00920        PERFORM INITIALIZATION.
00930        PERFORM PRODUCE-REPORT-BODY UNTIL MORE-INPUT = "N".
00940        PERFORM TERMINATION.
00950        STOP RUN.
00960
00970    INITIALIZATION.
00980        PERFORM HOUSEKEEPING.
00990        PERFORM PRINT-PAGE-HEADINGS.
01000        IF MORE-INPUT = "N"
01010            WRITE REPORT-LINE FROM NO-INPUT-DATA AFTER 2.
01020
01030    PRINT-PAGE-HEADINGS.
01040        ADD 1              TO PAGE-NUMBER-W.
01050        MOVE PAGE-NUMBER-W TO PAGE-NUMBER-OUT.
01060        WRITE REPORT-LINE FROM PAGE-HEAD-1 AFTER PAGE.
01070        WRITE REPORT-LINE FROM PAGE-HEAD-2 AFTER 2.
01080        WRITE REPORT-LINE FROM PAGE-HEAD-3 AFTER 3.
01090        MOVE 6 TO LINE-COUNT-ER.
01100        MOVE 2 TO LINE-SPACING.
01110
01120    HOUSEKEEPING.
01130        OPEN INPUT   ACCOUNT-FILE-IN,
01140             OUTPUT ACCOUNT-ACTIVITY-REPORT.
01150        ACCEPT TODAYS-DATE FROM DATE.
01160        MOVE CORRESPONDING TODAYS-DATE TO PAGE-HEAD-2.
01170        READ ACCOUNT-FILE-IN INTO ACCOUNT-RECORD-W
01180            AT END
01190                MOVE "N" TO MORE-INPUT.
01200        MOVE ACCOUNT-NUMBER-IN TO ACCOUNT-NUMBER-SAVE.
01210
01220    PRODUCE-REPORT-BODY.
01230        IF ACCOUNT-NUMBER-IN NOT = ACCOUNT-NUMBER-SAVE
01240            PERFORM ACCOUNT-NUMBER-BREAK.
01250        PERFORM PRODUCE-A-DETAIL-LINE.
01260        READ ACCOUNT-FILE-IN INTO ACCOUNT-RECORD-W
01270            AT END
01280                MOVE "N" TO MORE-INPUT.
01290
01300    ACCOUNT-NUMBER-BREAK.
01310        MOVE CORRESPONDING ACCUMULATORS-W TO CONTROL-BREAK-LINE.
01320        WRITE REPORT-LINE FROM CONTROL-BREAK-LINE AFTER ADVANCING 2.
01330        ADD 2               TO LINE-COUNT-ER.
01340        MOVE 2              TO LINE-SPACING.
01350        MOVE ZEROS          TO ACCUMULATORS-W.
01360        MOVE ACCOUNT-NUMBER-IN TO ACCOUNT-NUMBER-SAVE.
01370
01380    PRODUCE-A-DETAIL-LINE.
01390        PERFORM PRINT-A-DETAIL-LINE.
01400        PERFORM ACCUMULATE-DEBITS-AND-CREDITS.
```

The Procedure Division begins at line 00900. The paragraph PRINT-PAGE-HEADINGS, at line 01030, carries out the usual page heading functions, and it also sets LINE-SPACING to 2. This will mean, as you will see, that the first detail line following the printing of page headings is to be double-spaced. In fact, throughout the execution of the program, the field LINE-SPACING will always contain either 2 or 1, and you will see how the 2 and 1 are used to control the spacing of the detail lines.

The **READ...INTO** statement at line 01170 shows how a record can be read from an input file and transferred to working storage with a single statement. The READ ... INTO works like a combined READ and MOVE, so

```
READ ACCOUNT-FILE-IN INTO ACCOUNT-RECORD-W ...
```

does exactly the same thing as:

```
READ ACCOUNT-FILE-IN
MOVE ACCOUNT-RECORD-IN TO ACCOUNT-RECORD-W
```

The receiving field of the MOVE need not be the same size as the record defined in the File Section. The receiving field may be any field in working storage or in an output area in the File Section. If a READ . . . INTO statement finds an end-of-file condition, no MOVE is carried out and the contents of the receiving field remain unchanged.

The statement at line 01200 MOVEs the Account Number from the first input record to a field called ACCOUNT-NUMBER-SAVE, which happens to be part of CONTROL-BREAK-LINE but could have been described anywhere in working storage. ACCOUNT-NUMBER-SAVE is the field to which we assign the Account Number currently being worked on by the program. As the program READs each input record, it compares the Account Number in the record to the value of ACCOUNT-NUMBER-SAVE to see whether a control break has occurred. If the Account Number in the just-read record is the same as ACCOUNT-NUMBER-SAVE, that means that the program is still working on the same Account Number. If the two are different, it means that all the records for the previous account have been read and that a control break has occurred.

Let us now look at PRODUCE-REPORT-BODY, line 01220. The program always enters PRODUCE-REPORT-BODY with a newly read record waiting to be processed. The IF statement at line 01230 checks to see whether this new record is the first record of a group. If it is, a control break has occurred, so the program PERFORMs the paragraph ACCOUNT-NUMBER-BREAK and then goes to PRODUCE-A-DETAIL-LINE for the first record of the new group. If not, it goes directly to PRODUCE-A-DETAIL-LINE for the record.

In the paragraph ACCOUNT-NUMBER-BREAK, line 01300, the program formats and prints a total line. The totals it needs are already accumulated in the two ACCUMULATORS-W fields, and those merely have to be MOVEd to the total line, which in this program is called CONTROL-BREAK-LINE. The only other variable field in CONTROL-BREAK-LINE, ACCOUNT-NUMBER-SAVE, had the Account Number MOVEd to it when the program first started processing the group; so there is no further formatting needed in this line, and it is written with double spacing.

In line 01340, 2 is MOVEd to LINE-SPACING. This indicates, as you will see, that a detail line following an Account Number break is to be double-spaced. The field ACCUMULATORS-W is then zeroed, and the new ACCOUNT-NUMBER-IN is MOVEd to ACCOUNT-NUMBER-SAVE in preparation for processing the new Account Number.

The statement that zeros out the two accumulators, line 01350, looks harmless enough but could easily have not worked correctly if we had not been careful. ACCUMULATORS-W is a group item, and group items are always considered to be alphanumeric items of USAGE DISPLAY. Whenever you treat a group of accumulators as a single group item, the accumulators must also be defined as having USAGE DISPLAY. Remember that when a USAGE is not specified for a field, it is assumed to be DISPLAY, so the accumulators DEBITS-TOTAL and CREDITS-TOTAL are DISPLAY fields, as required. The only restriction on the programmer is that if you wish to handle accumulators using group-level operations, the accumulators cannot be COMPUTATIONAL. If you want to make the accumulators COMPUTATIONAL, then they must be processed one at a time by elementary operations.

Figure 6.9 (continued)

```
01410
01420   PRINT-A-DETAIL-LINE.
01430       MOVE SPACES TO DETAIL-LINE.
01440       MOVE ACCOUNT-NUMBER-IN TO ACCOUNT-NUMBER-OUT.
01450       IF INDICATOR IS EQUAL TO "-"
01460           MOVE AMOUNT TO DEBITS
01470       ELSE
01480           MOVE AMOUNT TO CREDITS.
01490       IF LINE-COUNT-ER + LINE-SPACING > LINE-LIMIT
01500           PERFORM PRINT-PAGE-HEADINGS.
01510       WRITE REPORT-LINE FROM DETAIL-LINE AFTER LINE-SPACING.
01520       ADD LINE-SPACING TO LINE-COUNT-ER.
01530       MOVE 1 TO LINE-SPACING.
01540
01550   ACCUMULATE-DEBITS-AND-CREDITS.
01560       IF INDICATOR IS EQUAL TO "-"
01570           ADD AMOUNT TO DEBITS-TOTAL IN ACCUMULATORS-W
01580       ELSE
01590           ADD AMOUNT TO CREDITS-TOTAL IN ACCUMULATORS-W.
01600
01610   TERMINATION.
01620       PERFORM ACCOUNT-NUMBER-BREAK.
01630       PERFORM CLOSE-FILES.
01640
01650   CLOSE-FILES.
01660       CLOSE ACCOUNT-FILE-IN,
01670             ACCOUNT-ACTIVITY-REPORT.
```

Let us look at PRINT-A-DETAIL-LINE, line 01420, to see how it handles page overflow and how it uses LINE-SPACING to get most detail lines single-spaced, but double-spaced after page headings and total lines.

Line 01510 shows how to use an identifier in an AFTER phrase to get variable line spacing. If the field LINE-SPACING has a value of 2 at the time the WRITE statement is executed, COBOL gives double spacing. If LINE-SPACING has a 1 at that time, the paper will be single-spaced. Both paragraphs PRINT-PAGE-HEADINGS and ACCOUNT-NUMBER-BREAK set LINE-SPACING to 2, and so the first detail line printed after the page headings or at the beginning of a new group will have double spacing. PRINT-A-DETAIL-LINE itself turns LINE-SPACING to 1, at line 01530, so that subsequent detail lines will be single-spaced.

The IF statement at line 01490 shows how page overflow can be detected when variable line spacing is in use. The IF statement determines whether the next detail line to be printed will fall beyond the LINE-LIMIT and, if so, PERFORMs PRINT-PAGE-HEADINGS.

EXERCISE 1

Explain why some working storage fields in Program P06-01 need a VALUE clause and some do not. These are fields with a VALUE clause:

```
PAGE-NUMBER-W
LINE-LIMIT
```

These fields do not have a VALUE clause:

```
PAGE-NUMBER-OUT
LINE-SPACING
LINE-COUNT-ER
```

EXERCISE 2

Write a program to read and process data in the following format:

Positions	Field
1–7	Customer Number
8–15	Part Number
16–22	spaces
23–25	Quantity
26–31	Unit Price (in dollars and cents)
26–29	Unit Price dollars
30–31	Unit Price cents
32–35	Handling Charge (in dollars and cents)
32–33	Handling Charge dollars
34–35	Handling Charge cents
36–80	spaces

Assume that there are several input records for each customer, each record containing a different Part Number. For each record have your program print a line showing the Customer Number, Part Number, Quantity, Unit Price, Handling Charge, and merchandise amount (compute the merchandise amount by multiplying the Unit Price by the Quantity). For each customer have your program print a total line showing the total Handling Charge and the total merchandise amount. Design your output on a print chart before you begin coding.

One Control Break and a Final Total

Our next program uses the same input as Program P06-01 and produces all of the same output. But in addition, Program P06-02 prints, at the end of the report, a final total of the debits for all the Account Numbers and of the credits for all the Account Numbers. To do this, we will use a technique called **rolling** the accumulators **forward.** Program P06-02 will contain a final total accumulator for the debits and a final total accumulator for the credits in addition to the accumulators we had in Program P06-01. Then, whenever a total line for an Account Number prints, the debits total for the Account Number will be added into the final debits accumulator and the credits total for the Account Number will be added into the final credits accumulator before the Account Number accumulators are zeroed.

Program P06-02 also introduces **group indicating.** Group indicating means that control fields are printed only the first time they appear on a page or the first time they appear after a control break. You will see in the output from Program P06-02 that the Account Number field prints only in the first detail line on each page and the first detail line after every control break, instead of printing in every detail line. In Program P06-01 we did not have group indicating; we printed the control field, Account Number, in every detail line.

Figure 6.10 Output format for Program P06-02.

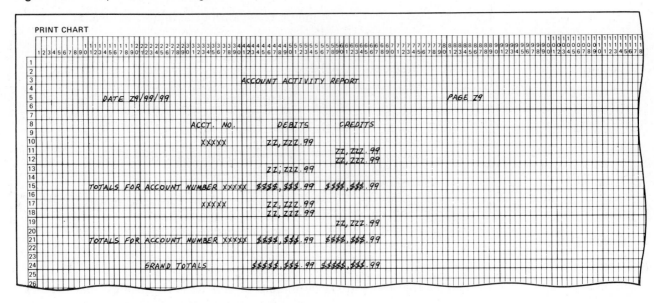

Figure 6.11 Hierarchy diagram for Program P06-02.

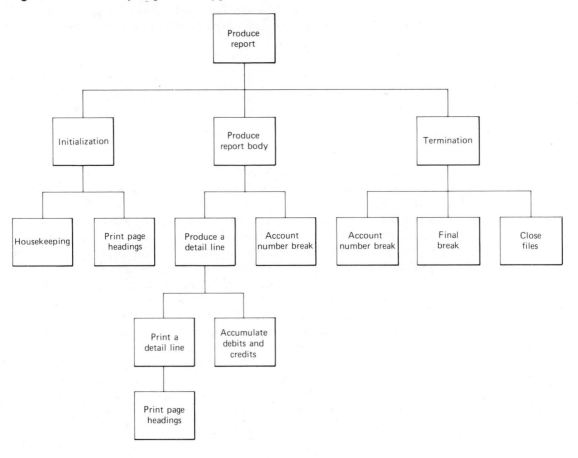

The output format for Program P06-02 is shown in Figure 6.10. You can see there the format of the final total line. Also you can see the Account Numbers shown with group indicating.

To produce a hierarchy diagram for this program, we can modify the final hierarchy diagram for Program P06-01, shown in Figure 6.7. To produce the hierarchy diagram for Program P06-02, we need to change only the "Termination" procedure. When Program P06-02 comes to end-of-file on the input file, we have to print the total line for the last Account Number, and then produce the final total line. Thus the box "Final break" is added as a subfunction of "Termination," as shown in Figure 6.11.

Program P06-02 is shown in Figure 6.12. The definition of the FINAL-TOTAL-LINE begins at line 00780. The two final total accumulators are defined starting at line 00880.

Figure 6.12 Program P06-02.

```
CB1 RELEASE 2.4                          IBM OS/VS COBOL   JULY  1, 1982


                      23.27.01       MAR 29,1988


00010  IDENTIFICATION DIVISION.
00020  PROGRAM-ID.  P06-02.
00030 *
00040 *     THIS PROGRAM PRODUCES AN ACCOUNT ACTIVITY REPORT
00050 *     WITH TOTALS OF DEBITS AND CREDITS FOR EACH ACCOUNT.
00060 *     IT ALSO PRODUCES A FINAL TOTAL LINE SHOWING THE
00070 *     TOTALS OF ALL THE DEBITS AND OF ALL THE CREDITS.
00080 *     THE ACCOUNT NUMBERS ARE GROUP INDICATED.
00090 *
00100 ********************************************************************
00110
00120  ENVIRONMENT DIVISION.
00130  CONFIGURATION SECTION.
00140  SOURCE-COMPUTER.  IBM-370.
00150  OBJECT-COMPUTER.  IBM-370.
00160
00170  INPUT-OUTPUT SECTION.
00180  FILE-CONTROL.
00190      SELECT ACCOUNT-ACTIVITY-REPORT  ASSIGN TO PRINTER.
00200      SELECT ACCOUNT-FILE-IN          ASSIGN TO INFILE.
00210
00220 ********************************************************************
00230
00240  DATA DIVISION.
00250  FILE SECTION.
00260  FD  ACCOUNT-FILE-IN
00270      RECORD CONTAINS 80 CHARACTERS
00280      LABEL RECORDS ARE OMITTED.
00290
00300  01  ACCOUNT-RECORD-IN        PIC X(80).
00310
00320  FD  ACCOUNT-ACTIVITY-REPORT
00330      LABEL RECORDS ARE OMITTED.
00340
00350  01  REPORT-LINE              PIC X(87).
00360
00370  WORKING-STORAGE SECTION.
00380  01  MORE-INPUT               PIC X      VALUE "Y".
00390  01  NO-INPUT-DATA            PIC X(15) VALUE "  NO INPUT DATA".
00400
00410  01  ACCOUNT-RECORD-W.
00420      05 INDICATOR             PIC X.
00430      05 ACCOUNT-NUMBER-IN     PIC X(5)  VALUE SPACES.
00440      05 FILLER                PIC X(3).
00450      05 AMOUNT                PIC 9(5)V99.
00460
```

(continued)

Four statements are needed in this program to accomplish group indication of the Account Number. Remember that group indication means that the Account Number will print in the first detail line after page headings and the first detail line after a control break. Thus, the statements at lines 01240 and 01250 MOVE the Account Number to the detail line output area after page headings are printed, and the statement at line 01520 MOVEs the Account Number to the detail line output area after a control break. At line 01690, SPACES are MOVEd to the detail line to blank out the Account Number so that it does not print on subsequent detail lines.

The **ADD CORRESPONDING** statement, at line 01500, shows how the two ACCUMULATORS-W are rolled forward into the FINAL-ACCUMULATORS-W, just before the ACCUMULATORS-W are zeroed during an ACCOUNT-NUMBER-BREAK. The CORRESPONDING option is available with the SUB-TRACT verb, also.

Figure 6.12   (continued)

```
00470    01  PAGE-HEAD-1.
00480        05 FILLER                    PIC X(40) VALUE SPACES.
00490        05 FILLER        PIC X(23) VALUE "ACCOUNT ACTIVITY REPORT".
00500
00510    01  PAGE-HEAD-2.
00520        05 FILLER                    PIC X(13) VALUE SPACES.
00530        05 FILLER                    PIC X(5)  VALUE "DATE".
00540        05 RUN-MONTH-AND-DAY         PIC Z9/99/.
00550        05 RUN-YEAR                  PIC 99.
00560        05 FILLER                    PIC X(54) VALUE SPACES.
00570        05 FILLER                    PIC X(5)  VALUE "PAGE".
00580        05 PAGE-NUMBER-OUT           PIC Z9.
00590
00600    01  PAGE-HEAD-3.
00610        05 FILLER                    PIC X(30) VALUE SPACES.
00620        05 FILLER                    PIC X(17) VALUE "ACCT. NO.".
00630        05 FILLER                    PIC X(12) VALUE "DEBITS".
00640        05 FILLER                    PIC X(7)  VALUE "CREDITS".
00650
00660    01  DETAIL-LINE.
00670        05 ACCOUNT-NUMBER-OUT        PIC B(32)X(5).
00680        05 DEBITS                    PIC B(8)ZZ,ZZZ.99.
00690        05 CREDITS                   PIC B(4)ZZ,ZZZ.99.
00700
00710    01  CONTROL-BREAK-LINE.
00720        05 FILLER                    PIC X(10) VALUE SPACES.
00730        05 FILLER        PIC X(26) VALUE "TOTALS FOR ACCOUNT NUMBER".
00740        05 ACCOUNT-NUMBER-SAVE       PIC X(5)BB.
00750        05 DEBITS-TOTAL              PIC $$$$,$$$.99BB.
00760        05 CREDITS-TOTAL             PIC $$$$,$$$.99.
00770
00780    01  FINAL-TOTAL-LINE.
00790        05 FILLER                    PIC X(21) VALUE SPACES.
00800        05 FILLER                    PIC X(21) VALUE "GRAND TOTALS".
00810        05 DEBITS-TOTAL              PIC $$$$$,$$$.99B.
00820        05 CREDITS-TOTAL             PIC $$$$$,$$$.99.
00830
00840    01  ACCUMULATORS-W.
00850        05 DEBITS-TOTAL              PIC S9(6)V99 VALUE 0.
00860        05 CREDITS-TOTAL             PIC S9(6)V99 VALUE 0.
00870
00880    01  FINAL-ACCUMULATORS-W.
00890        05 DEBITS-TOTAL              PIC S9(7)V99 VALUE 0.
00900        05 CREDITS-TOTAL             PIC S9(7)V99 VALUE 0.
00910
00920    01  LINE-LIMIT     PIC S99 VALUE 34 COMP SYNC.
00930    01  LINE-SPACING   PIC S9             COMP SYNC.
00940    01  PAGE-NUMBER-W  PIC S99 VALUE ZERO.
00950    01  LINE-COUNT-ER  PIC S99            COMP SYNC.
00960
```

```
00970  01   TODAYS-DATE.
00980       05  RUN-YEAR              PIC 99.
00990       05  RUN-MONTH-AND-DAY     PIC 9(4).
01000
01010  *********************************************************************
01020
01030  PROCEDURE DIVISION.
01040  PRODUCE-REPORT.
01050       PERFORM INITIALIZATION.
01060       PERFORM PRODUCE-REPORT-BODY UNTIL MORE-INPUT = "N".
01070       PERFORM TERMINATION.
01080       STOP RUN.
01090
01100  INITIALIZATION.
01110       PERFORM HOUSEKEEPING.
01120       PERFORM PRINT-PAGE-HEADINGS.
01130       IF MORE-INPUT = "N"
01140           WRITE REPORT-LINE FROM NO-INPUT-DATA AFTER 2.
01150
01160  PRINT-PAGE-HEADINGS.
01170       ADD 1              TO PAGE-NUMBER-W.
01180       MOVE PAGE-NUMBER-W TO PAGE-NUMBER-OUT.
01190       WRITE REPORT-LINE FROM PAGE-HEAD-1 AFTER PAGE.
01200       WRITE REPORT-LINE FROM PAGE-HEAD-2 AFTER 2.
01210       WRITE REPORT-LINE FROM PAGE-HEAD-3 AFTER 3.
01220       MOVE 6 TO LINE-COUNT-ER.
01230       MOVE 2 TO LINE-SPACING.
01240       MOVE SPACES TO DETAIL-LINE.
01250       MOVE ACCOUNT-NUMBER-SAVE TO ACCOUNT-NUMBER-OUT.
01260
01270  HOUSEKEEPING.
01280       OPEN INPUT  ACCOUNT-FILE-IN,
01290            OUTPUT ACCOUNT-ACTIVITY-REPORT.
01300       ACCEPT TODAYS-DATE FROM DATE.
01310       MOVE CORRESPONDING TODAYS-DATE TO PAGE-HEAD-2.
01320       READ ACCOUNT-FILE-IN INTO ACCOUNT-RECORD-W
01330           AT END
01340               MOVE "N" TO MORE-INPUT.
01350       MOVE ACCOUNT-NUMBER-IN TO ACCOUNT-NUMBER-SAVE.
01360
01370  PRODUCE-REPORT-BODY.
01380       IF ACCOUNT-NUMBER-IN NOT = ACCOUNT-NUMBER-SAVE
01390           PERFORM ACCOUNT-NUMBER-BREAK.
01400       PERFORM PRODUCE-A-DETAIL-LINE.
01410       READ ACCOUNT-FILE-IN INTO ACCOUNT-RECORD-W
01420           AT END
01430               MOVE "N" TO MORE-INPUT.
01440
01450  ACCOUNT-NUMBER-BREAK.
01460       MOVE CORRESPONDING ACCUMULATORS-W TO CONTROL-BREAK-LINE.
01470       WRITE REPORT-LINE FROM CONTROL-BREAK-LINE AFTER ADVANCING 2.
01480       ADD 2               TO LINE-COUNT-ER.
01490       MOVE 2              TO LINE-SPACING.
01500       ADD CORRESPONDING ACCUMULATORS-W TO FINAL-ACCUMULATORS-W.
01510       MOVE ZEROS          TO ACCUMULATORS-W.
01520       MOVE ACCOUNT-NUMBER-IN TO ACCOUNT-NUMBER-SAVE,
01530                              ACCOUNT-NUMBER-OUT.
01540
01550  PRODUCE-A-DETAIL-LINE.
01560       PERFORM PRINT-A-DETAIL-LINE.
01570       PERFORM ACCUMULATE-DEBITS-AND-CREDITS.
01580
01590  PRINT-A-DETAIL-LINE.
01600       IF INDICATOR IS EQUAL TO "-"
01610           MOVE AMOUNT TO DEBITS
01620       ELSE
01630           MOVE AMOUNT TO CREDITS.
01640       IF LINE-COUNT-ER + LINE-SPACING > LINE-LIMIT
01650           PERFORM PRINT-PAGE-HEADINGS.
01660       WRITE REPORT-LINE FROM DETAIL-LINE AFTER LINE-SPACING.
01670       ADD LINE-SPACING TO LINE-COUNT-ER.
01680       MOVE 1 TO LINE-SPACING.
01690       MOVE SPACES TO DETAIL-LINE.
01700
```

(continued)

Figure 6.12   (continued)

```
01710   ACCUMULATE-DEBITS-AND-CREDITS.
01720       IF INDICATOR IS EQUAL TO "-"
01730           ADD AMOUNT TO DEBITS-TOTAL IN ACCUMULATORS-W
01740       ELSE
01750           ADD AMOUNT TO CREDITS-TOTAL IN ACCUMULATORS-W.
01760
01770   TERMINATION.
01780       PERFORM ACCOUNT-NUMBER-BREAK.
01790       PERFORM FINAL-BREAK.
01800       PERFORM CLOSE-FILES.
01810
01820   FINAL-BREAK.
01830       MOVE CORRESPONDING FINAL-ACCUMULATORS-W TO FINAL-TOTAL-LINE.
01840       WRITE REPORT-LINE FROM FINAL-TOTAL-LINE AFTER 3.
01850
01860   CLOSE-FILES.
01870       CLOSE ACCOUNT-FILE-IN,
01880             ACCOUNT-ACTIVITY-REPORT.
```

Program P06-02 was run with the same input as Program P06-01. Program P06-02 produced the output shown in Figure 6.13.

Figure 6.13   Output from Program P06-02.

```
                              ACCOUNT ACTIVITY REPORT

        DATE   3/29/88                                                      PAGE   1


                          ACCT. NO.        DEBITS        CREDITS

                           02005            30.34
                                                              .00
                                                        98,762.01
                                              .06
                                        89,235.51
                                                        34,859.10

    TOTALS FOR ACCOUNT NUMBER 02005     $89,265.91    $133,621.11

                           04502                         99,999.99
                                           83.99
                                        45,672.12

    TOTALS FOR ACCOUNT NUMBER 04502     $45,756.11     $99,999.99

                           12121         75,499.00
                                              .02
                                              .00
                                                        23,411.11
                                                            66.67
                                        66,662.22

    TOTALS FOR ACCOUNT NUMBER 12121    $142,161.24     $23,477.78

                           19596                         92,929.29
                                        12,547.20
                                        23,487.64
```

```
                        ACCOUNT ACTIVITY REPORT

        DATE  3/29/88                                         PAGE  2


                    ACCT. NO.        DEBITS       CREDITS

                     19596
                                                     2.39
                                                   213.45

        TOTALS FOR ACCOUNT NUMBER 19596   $36,035.04   $93,145.13

                     20023          99,999.99
                                    87,654.99
                                    86,868.68
                                                 88,888.80
                                                 88,553.32
                                                 56,789.23

        TOTALS FOR ACCOUNT NUMBER 20023  $274,523.66  $234,231.35

                     23456              2.11
                                        4.53
                                       12.00
                                                       .12
                                                     18.00
                                                       .54

        TOTALS FOR ACCOUNT NUMBER 23456      $18.64       $18.66

                     30721              1.01
                                                     99.12
                                       98.44

        TOTALS FOR ACCOUNT NUMBER 30721      $99.45       $99.12



                        ACCOUNT ACTIVITY REPORT

        DATE  3/29/88                                         PAGE  3


                    ACCT. NO.        DEBITS       CREDITS

                     40101
                                                   212.45
                                    60,002.01
                                                    67.00
                                    32,343.23
                                                 90,023.41

        TOTALS FOR ACCOUNT NUMBER 40101   $92,688.11   $90,302.86

                     67689             11.14
                                                  1,010.10
                                       33.35
                                                  2,203.30
                                     3,040.20
                                                 10,000.00

        TOTALS FOR ACCOUNT NUMBER 67689    $3,084.69   $13,213.40

                     72332               .04
                                                     44.44
                                      444.44
                                                      4.44
                                         .44
                                                  4,040.40

        TOTALS FOR ACCOUNT NUMBER 72332     $444.92    $4,089.28

             GRAND TOTALS            $684,077.77  $692,198.68
```

Multiple Control Breaks

It is not uncommon for input data to have more than one control field and for reports to have several different kinds of total lines, each kind showing totals for a different control field. For example, consider input records in the following format:

Positions	Field
1-3	Store Number
4-6	Salesperson Number
7-12	Customer Number
13-19	Sale Amount (to two decimal places)
20-80	spaces

Each input record shows the dollars-and-cents amount of a purchase made by a customer. The record also shows the number of the salesperson who serviced the customer and the store number where the sale took place. Program P06-03 will produce a list of all these sales and show the total amount of sales made by each salesperson, the total amount of sales in each store, and the total amount of all sales. The output should look like Figure 6.14, from the input in Figure 6.15. The output format is shown in Figure 6.16.

Obviously, many of the ideas from Program P06-02 can be used in Program P06-03. The new ideas that we will need in order to create a report with three levels of totals are general enough that you will be able to apply them to reports of four or more levels.

Figure 6.14 Output from Program P06-03.

```
                    SALES REPORT
DATE   3/31/88                              PAGE   1

        STORE    SALES-    CUSTOMER    SALE
        NO.      PERSON    NUMBER      AMOUNT

        010      101       003001      1,234.56
                           007002          2.24
                           011003      6,665.70
                           039004      8,439.20
                           046005      8,448.48
                           053006         12.34
                           060006      9,494.93
                           067007      4,000.03

                                      38,297.48 *

        010      102       074212      5,454.99
                           081012           .33
                           088013      5,849.58
                           095015        393.90

                                      11,698.80 *

        010      103       003234        303.03

                                         303.03 *

        TOTAL FOR STORE NO. 010   $ 50,299.31 **

        020      011       007567      9,999.99
                           011454        456.00
                           015231      8,484.39
                           019345      8,459.44
                           023345      8,333.33

                                      35,733.15 *
```

```
                    SALES  REPORT
DATE   3/31/88                           PAGE   2

        STORE    SALES-    CUSTOMER    SALE
        NO.      PERSON    NUMBER      AMOUNT

        020      222       027345      4,343.43
                           031567      9,903.30
                           035001         34.21

                                      14,280.94 *

        020      266       039903      4,539.87
                           043854      5,858.30

                                      10,398.17 *

        TOTAL FOR STORE NO. 020  $ 60,412.26 **


        030      193       047231      9,391.93
                           051342      5,937.43
                           055034      9,383.22
                           059932      5,858.54
                           063419      3,949.49

                                      34,520.61 *

        TOTAL FOR STORE NO. 030  $ 34,520.61 **


        040      045       067333          .00
                           071323      5,959.50

                                       5,959.50 *

        040      403       048399      3,921.47


                    SALES  REPORT
DATE   3/31/88                           PAGE   3

        STORE    SALES-    CUSTOMER    SALE
        NO.      PERSON    NUMBER      AMOUNT

        040      403       054392          .00

                                       3,921.47 *

        040      412       060111      9,999.99

                                       9,999.99 *

        TOTAL FOR STORE NO. 040  $ 19,880.96 **

        046      012       013538          .00
                           017521        690.78
                           021504      1,381.56
                           025487      2,072.34
                           029470      2,763.12

                                       6,907.80 *

        046      028       033453      3,453.90
                           037436      4,144.68
                           041419      4,835.46

                                      12,434.04 *

        TOTAL FOR STORE NO. 046  $ 19,341.84 **

             GRAND TOTAL    $   184,454.98 ***
```

Figure 6.15 Input to Program P06-03.

```
-----------------------------------------------------------------------------------
         1         2         3         4         5         6         7         8
12345678901234567890123456789012345678901234567890123456789012345678901234567890
-----------------------------------------------------------------------------------
010101003001123456
010101007002000224
010101011003666570
010101039004843920
010101046005844848
010101053006001234
010101060006949493
010101067007400003
010102074212545499
010102081012000033
010102088013584958
010102095015039390
010103003234030303
020011007567999999
020011011454045600
020011015231848439
020011019345845944
020011023345833333
020222027345434343
020222031567990330
020222035001003421
020266039903453987
020266043854585830
030193047231939193
030193051342593743
030193055034938322
030193059932585854
030193063419394949
040045067333000000
040045071323595950
040403048399392147
040403054392000000
040412060111999999
046012013538000000
046012017521069078
046012021504138156
046012025487207234
046012029470276312
046028033453345390
046028037436414468
046028041419483546
```

The input data for Program P06-03 are grouped so that the printed output will be in the correct order for the totals to print. All sales for each store are grouped together in the input. Within each group of sales for a store, all sales made by one salesperson are grouped together; within each group of sales made by one salesperson, the customer numbers are in order. The input is thus **sorted** on the three fields: Store Number, Salesperson Number, and Customer Number. The Store Number is the most significant field and is called the **major sort field.** The Customer Number is the least significant field and is called the **minor sort field.** The Salesperson Number, whose significance falls between that of the Store Number and the Customer Number, is called the **intermediate sort field.** If there had been more than three fields used for ordering the data, the most significant would be the major, the least significant the minor, and all those between major and minor would be called intermediate. This input is said to be sorted by Store Number by Salesperson Number by Customer Number. Alternatively, the input can be described as being sorted by Customer Number within Salesperson Number within Store Number.

In this program control breaks will be taken only on Salesperson Number and Store Number and totals printed for those breaks. Salesperson Number will be the **minor control field,** and Store Number will be the **major control field.** There will also be a final total line.

Figure 6.16 Output format for Program P06-03.

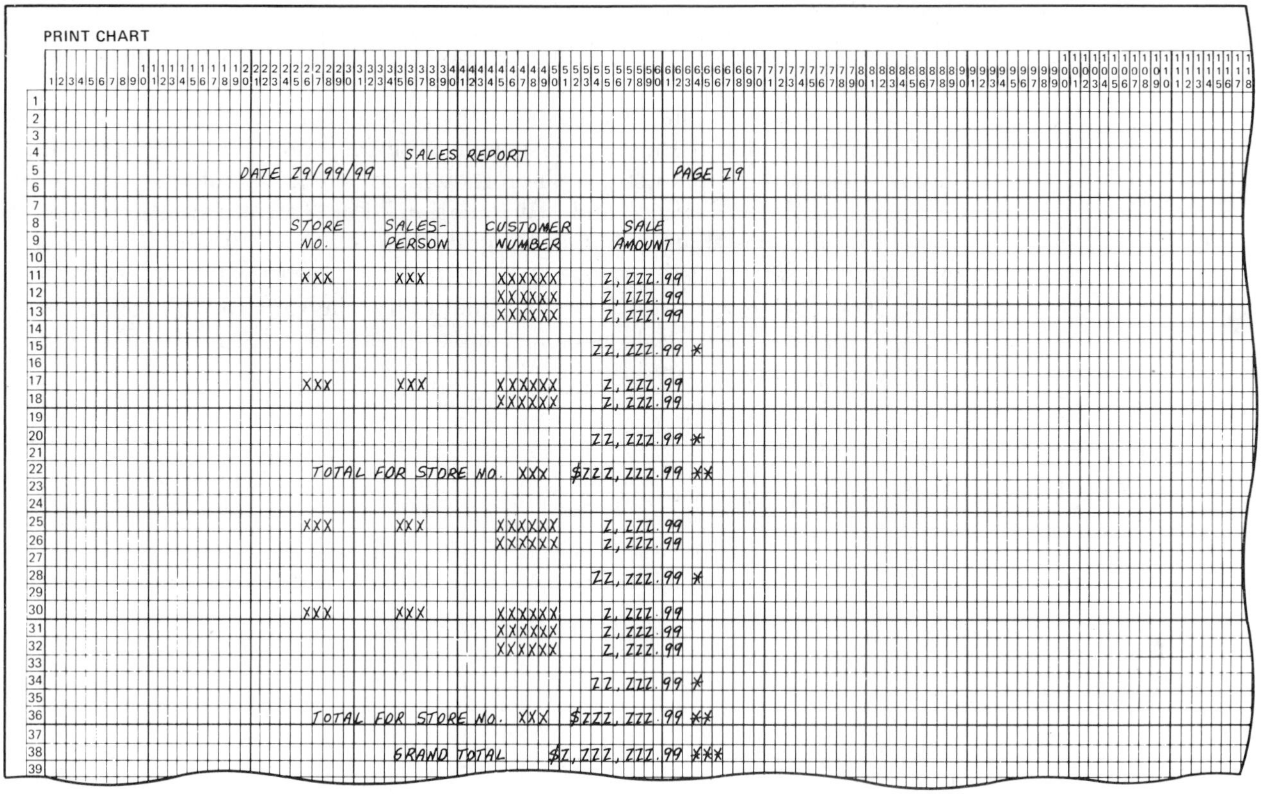

In this program there are three accumulators: one to accumulate the total of all sales for a salesperson, one for the total of all the sales in a store, and one for the total of all the sales. As each input record is read, the program prints it and adds the Sale Amount to the salesperson accumulator. When a salesperson break occurs, the total in the salesperson accumulator is printed, added into the store accumulator, and zeroed. When a break occurs on Store Number, the total in the store accumulator is printed, added into the final accumulator, and zeroed. Thus the accumulators are rolled forward from the most minor level to the most major.

The program will have to check each input record to see whether there is a control break on Salesperson Number and/or on Store Number. If there is a break on Salesperson Number, the program will print a total for the previous salesperson, roll the salesperson accumulator into the store accumulator, zero the salesperson accumulator, and prepare to process the next salesperson group. But if there is a break on Store Number, that means that all the data have been read not only for the previous store but also for the last salesperson of the previous store. So a break on Store Number first requires carrying out all the steps of a salesperson break for the last salesperson of the previous store and then carrying out the Store Number break for the previous store: printing the store total line, rolling the store accumulator into the final accumulator, and preparing to process the next Store Number. When end-of-file is reached on the input, there still remain to be printed the total line for the last salesperson in the last store, the total line for the last store, and the grand total line.

Hierarchy Diagram for Program P06-03

Using the ideas and rationale from the hierarchy diagram for Program P06-02, we can start with the diagram for Program P06-03 shown in Figure 6.17. Here the box "Produce report body" has three subfunctions instead of two. Now its subfunctions are "Produce a detail line," "Salesperson Number break," and "Store Number break." The diagram is not complete, though, for we have not filled in the subfunctions of "Initialization" and "Termination." For "Initialization" we need the same subfunctions that we had in Program P06-02. For "Termination" we must print the total line for the last salesperson in the last store, the total line for the last store, and the grand total line. The hierarchy diagram can be completed by duplicating the boxes "Salesperson Number break" and "Store Number break," and adding the box "Final break." This is done in Figure 6.18.

Figure 6.17 Partial hierarchy diagram for Program P06-03.

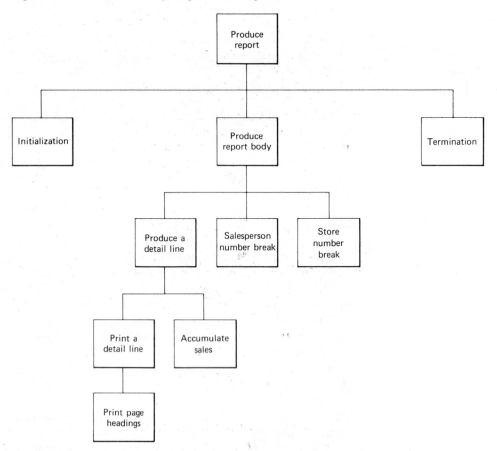

A Program with Three Levels of Totals

Program P06-03 is shown in Figure 6.19. You can follow the Procedure Division easily if you refer to the hierarchy diagram in Figure 6.18.

Figure 6.18 Complete hierarchy diagram for Program P06-03.

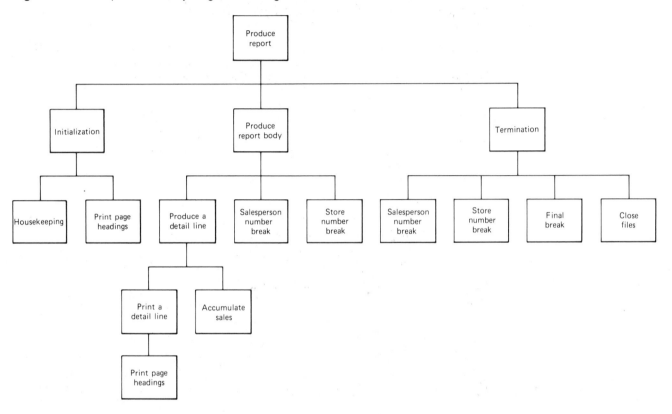

Figure 6.19 Program P06-03.

```
CB1 RELEASE 2.4                                    IBM OS/VS COBOL   JULY  1, 1982


                         18.19.37        MAR 31,1988


00010   IDENTIFICATION DIVISION.
00020   PROGRAM-ID.  P06-03.
00030 *
00040 *    THIS PROGRAM PRODUCES A SALES REPORT
00050 *    WITH THREE LEVELS OF TOTALS.
00060 *
00070 *************************************************************************
```

Figure 6.19 (continued)

```
00080
00090  ENVIRONMENT DIVISION.
00100  CONFIGURATION SECTION.
00110  SOURCE-COMPUTER.  IBM-370.
00120  OBJECT-COMPUTER.  IBM-370.
00130
00140  INPUT-OUTPUT SECTION.
00150  FILE-CONTROL.
00160      SELECT SALES-REPORT  ASSIGN TO PRINTER.
00170      SELECT SALES-FILE-IN ASSIGN TO INFILE.
00180
00190  ******************************************************************
00200
00210  DATA DIVISION.
00220  FILE SECTION.
00230  FD  SALES-FILE-IN
00240      RECORD CONTAINS 80 CHARACTERS
00250      LABEL RECORDS ARE OMITTED.
00260
00270  01  SALES-RECORD-IN          PIC X(80).
00280
00290  FD  SALES-REPORT
00300      LABEL RECORDS ARE OMITTED.
00310
00320  01  REPORT-LINE              PIC X(69).
00330
00340  WORKING-STORAGE SECTION.
00350  01  MORE-INPUT               PIC X     VALUE "Y".
00360  01  NO-INPUT-DATA            PIC X(15) VALUE "  NO INPUT DATA".
00370
00380  01  SALES-RECORD-W.
00390      05 STORE-NUMBER-IN        PIC 9(3)   VALUE 0.
00400      05 SALESPERSON-NUMBER-IN PIC 9(3)   VALUE 0.
00410      05 CUSTOMER-NUMBER       PIC 9(6).
00420      05 SALE-AMOUNT           PIC 9(4)V99.
00430
00440  01  PAGE-HEAD-1.
00450      05 FILLER                PIC X(35) VALUE SPACES.
00460      05 FILLER                PIC X(12) VALUE "SALES REPORT".
00470
00480  01  PAGE-HEAD-2.
00490      05 FILLER                PIC X(19) VALUE SPACES.
00500      05 FILLER                PIC X(5)  VALUE "DATE".
00510      05 RUN-MONTH-AND-DAY     PIC Z9/99/.
00520      05 RUN-YEAR              PIC 99.
00530      05 FILLER                PIC X(29) VALUE SPACES.
00540      05 FILLER                PIC X(5)  VALUE "PAGE".
00550      05 PAGE-NUMBER-OUT       PIC Z9.
00560
00570  01  PAGE-HEAD-3.
00580      05 FILLER                PIC X(24) VALUE SPACES.
00590      05 FILLER                PIC X(9)  VALUE "STORE".
00600      05 FILLER                PIC X(10) VALUE "SALES-".
00610      05 FILLER                PIC X(13) VALUE "CUSTOMER".
00620      05 FILLER                PIC X(4)  VALUE "SALE".
00630
00640  01  PAGE-HEAD-4.
00650      05 FILLER                PIC X(25) VALUE SPACES.
00660      05 FILLER                PIC X(8)  VALUE "NO.".
00670      05 FILLER                PIC X(11) VALUE "PERSON".
00680      05 FILLER                PIC X(11) VALUE "NUMBER".
00690      05 FILLER                PIC X(6)  VALUE "AMOUNT".
00700
00710  01  DETAIL-LINE.
00720      05 STORE-NUMBER-OUT       PIC B(25)9(3).
00730      05 SALESPERSON-NUMBER-OUT  PIC B(6)9(3).
00740      05 CUSTOMER-NUMBER       PIC B(7)9(6).
00750      05 SALE-AMOUNT           PIC B(4)Z,ZZZ.99.
00760
00770  01  SALESPERSON-TOTAL-LINE.
00780      05 SALESPERSON-TOTAL-OUT PIC B(53)ZZ,ZZZ.99B.
00790      05 FILLER                PIC X     VALUE "*".
00800
```

```
00810   01   STORE-TOTAL-LINE.
00820        05 FILLER                   PIC X(26) VALUE SPACES.
00830        05 FILLER       PIC X(20) VALUE "TOTAL FOR STORE NO.".
00840        05 STORE-NUMBER-SAVE        PIC 9(3).
00850        05 FILLER                   PIC X(2)  VALUE SPACES.
00860        05 STORE-TOTAL-OUT          PIC $ZZZ,ZZZ.99B.
00870        05 FILLER                   PIC X(2)  VALUE "**".
00880
00890   01   GRAND-TOTAL-LINE.
00900        05 FILLER                   PIC X(34) VALUE SPACES.
00910        05 FILLER                   PIC X(15) VALUE "GRAND TOTAL".
00920        05 GRAND-TOTAL-OUT          PIC $Z,ZZZ,ZZZ.99B.
00930        05 FILLER                   PIC X(3)  VALUE "***".
00940
00950   01   PAGE-NUMBER-W               PIC S99 VALUE 0.
00960   01   PAGE-LIMIT                  PIC S99 VALUE 38 COMP SYNC.
00970   01   LINE-SPACING                PIC S9          COMP SYNC.
00980   01   LINE-COUNT-ER               PIC S99         COMP SYNC.
00990   01   SALESPERSON-TOTAL-W         PIC S9(5)V99 VALUE 0.
01000   01   STORE-TOTAL-W               PIC S9(6)V99 VALUE 0.
01010   01   GRAND-TOTAL-W               PIC S9(7)V99 VALUE 0.
01020   01   SALESPERSON-NUMBER-SAVE PIC 9(3).
01030
01040   01   TODAYS-DATE.
01050        05 RUN-YEAR                 PIC 99.
01060        05 RUN-MONTH-AND-DAY        PIC 9(4).
01070
01080   **********************************************************************
01090
01100   PROCEDURE DIVISION.
01110   PRODUCE-REPORT.
01120        PERFORM INITIALIZATION.
01130        PERFORM PRODUCE-REPORT-BODY UNTIL MORE-INPUT = "N".
01140        PERFORM TERMINATION.
01150        STOP RUN.
01160
01170   INITIALIZATION.
01180        PERFORM HOUSEKEEPING.
01190        PERFORM PRINT-PAGE-HEADING.
01200        IF MORE-INPUT = "N"
01210            WRITE REPORT-LINE FROM NO-INPUT-DATA AFTER 2.
01220
01230   HOUSEKEEPING.
01240        OPEN INPUT  SALES-FILE-IN,
01250             OUTPUT SALES-REPORT.
01260        ACCEPT TODAYS-DATE FROM DATE.
01270        MOVE CORRESPONDING TODAYS-DATE TO PAGE-HEAD-2.
01280        READ SALES-FILE-IN INTO SALES-RECORD-W
01290            AT END
01300                MOVE "N" TO MORE-INPUT.
01310        MOVE SALESPERSON-NUMBER-IN TO SALESPERSON-NUMBER-SAVE.
01320        MOVE STORE-NUMBER-IN       TO STORE-NUMBER-SAVE.
01330
01340   PRODUCE-REPORT-BODY.
01350        IF STORE-NUMBER-IN NOT = STORE-NUMBER-SAVE
01360            PERFORM SALESPERSON-NUMBER-BREAK
01370            PERFORM STORE-NUMBER-BREAK
01380        ELSE
01390            IF SALESPERSON-NUMBER-IN NOT = SALESPERSON-NUMBER-SAVE
01400                PERFORM SALESPERSON-NUMBER-BREAK.
01410        PERFORM PRODUCE-A-DETAIL-LINE.
01420        READ SALES-FILE-IN INTO SALES-RECORD-W
01430            AT END
01440                MOVE "N" TO MORE-INPUT.
01450
```

(continued)

The IF statement at line 01350 carries out the logic shown in Figure 6.20. As each input record is read, it is tested first to see whether a major control break has occurred. If so, the minor control break routine and the major control break routine are PERFORMed; if not, it is then necessary to see whether the lower-level break has occurred. So we have in the False path of this nested IF statement another IF statement.

Figure 6.19   (continued)

```
01460    STORE-NUMBER-BREAK.
01470        MOVE STORE-TOTAL-W TO STORE-TOTAL-OUT.
01480        WRITE REPORT-LINE FROM STORE-TOTAL-LINE AFTER 2.
01490        ADD 2 TO LINE-COUNT-ER.
01500        ADD STORE-TOTAL-W TO GRAND-TOTAL-W.
01510        MOVE STORE-NUMBER-IN TO STORE-NUMBER-SAVE.
01520        MOVE 0 TO STORE-TOTAL-W.
01530        MOVE 3 TO LINE-SPACING.
01540
01550    SALESPERSON-NUMBER-BREAK.
01560        MOVE SALESPERSON-TOTAL-W TO SALESPERSON-TOTAL-OUT.
01570        WRITE REPORT-LINE FROM SALESPERSON-TOTAL-LINE AFTER 2.
01580        ADD 2                TO LINE-COUNT-ER.
01590        ADD SALESPERSON-TOTAL-W    TO STORE-TOTAL-W.
01600        MOVE SALESPERSON-NUMBER-IN TO SALESPERSON-NUMBER-OUT,
01610                                   SALESPERSON-NUMBER-SAVE.
01620        MOVE STORE-NUMBER-IN       TO STORE-NUMBER-OUT.
01630        MOVE 0                     TO SALESPERSON-TOTAL-W.
01640        MOVE 2                     TO LINE-SPACING.
01650
01660    PRODUCE-A-DETAIL-LINE.
01670        PERFORM PRINT-A-DETAIL-LINE.
01680        PERFORM ACCUMULATE-SALES.
01690
01700    PRINT-A-DETAIL-LINE.
01710        MOVE CORRESPONDING SALES-RECORD-W TO DETAIL-LINE.
01720        IF LINE-COUNT-ER + LINE-SPACING > PAGE-LIMIT
01730            PERFORM PRINT-PAGE-HEADING.
01740        WRITE REPORT-LINE FROM DETAIL-LINE AFTER LINE-SPACING.
01750        ADD LINE-SPACING TO LINE-COUNT-ER.
01760        MOVE 1          TO LINE-SPACING.
01770        MOVE SPACES     TO DETAIL-LINE.
01780
01790    ACCUMULATE-SALES.
01800        ADD SALE-AMOUNT IN SALES-RECORD-W TO SALESPERSON-TOTAL-W.
01810
01820    PRINT-PAGE-HEADING.
01830        ADD 1 TO PAGE-NUMBER-W.
01840        MOVE PAGE-NUMBER-W TO PAGE-NUMBER-OUT.
01850        WRITE REPORT-LINE FROM PAGE-HEAD-1 AFTER PAGE.
01860        WRITE REPORT-LINE FROM PAGE-HEAD-2.
01870        WRITE REPORT-LINE FROM PAGE-HEAD-3 AFTER 3.
01880        WRITE REPORT-LINE FROM PAGE-HEAD-4.
01890        MOVE 6                      TO LINE-COUNT-ER.
01900        MOVE 2                      TO LINE-SPACING.
01910        MOVE STORE-NUMBER-SAVE      TO STORE-NUMBER-OUT.
01920        MOVE SALESPERSON-NUMBER-SAVE TO SALESPERSON-NUMBER-OUT.
01930
01940    FINAL-BREAK.
01950        MOVE GRAND-TOTAL-W TO GRAND-TOTAL-OUT.
01960        WRITE REPORT-LINE FROM GRAND-TOTAL-LINE AFTER 2.
01970
01980    TERMINATION.
01990        PERFORM SALESPERSON-NUMBER-BREAK.
02000        PERFORM STORE-NUMBER-BREAK.
02010        PERFORM FINAL-BREAK.
02020        PERFORM CLOSE-FILES.
02030
02040    CLOSE-FILES.
02050        CLOSE SALES-FILE-IN,
02060              SALES-REPORT.
```

Group indication of the Salesperson Number and Store Number is carried out by five statements in the program. The two statements at lines 01600 and 01620 MOVE the Salesperson Number and Store Number to the output line after every control break. The two statements at lines 01910 and 01920 MOVE the Salesperson Number and Store Number to the output line at the beginning of each new page. And the MOVE statement at line 01770 blanks the output line so that the control fields do not print on subsequent detail lines.

Figure 6.20 Flowchart of the control–break testing logic.

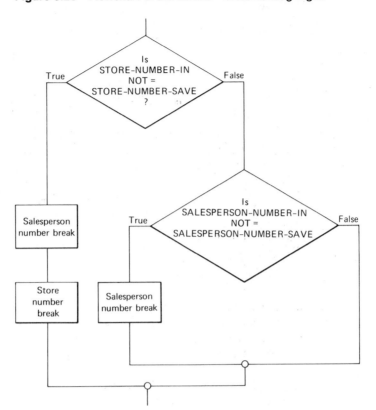

EXERCISE 3

Rewrite the program in Exercise 2 with group indication of the Customer Number. That is, have each Customer Number print on only the first detail line after a control break and on the first detail line of a page.

EXERCISE 4

Using the input of Program P06-03, write a program that will print a line for each input record showing the Customer Number, the Sale Amount, a tax amount on the sale (at 8 percent), and the total of the Sale amount and the tax. On each total line for salesperson, store, and grand total, show the total of all the appropriate Sale Amounts, tax amounts, and the totals of the Sale Amounts and the tax amounts. Group indicate the Store Numbers and Salesperson Numbers.

EXERCISE 5

Modify your solution to Exercise 4 so that no detail lines print; have your program print only the various levels of total lines. This is called **group printing** or **summary reporting.** On salesperson total lines, show the Store Number and the Salesperson Number. On store total lines, show the Store Number. Arrange the page overflow logic so that a salesperson total line may be the first line on a page (after the page headings) but so that a store total line will never print at the top of a page right after the headings.

EXERCISE 6

Modify your solution to Exercise 5 so that on each total line there also prints the number of sale amounts that make up the total.

Any Number of Control Breaks

You can see now how to plan and write a program having any number of control breaks. Let's say we have an application with five levels of breaks, called Level-A through Level-E, with Level-A being the lowest-level break and Level-E being the highest. You would of course need a save field for each control field A through E. One possible flowchart for the control-break logic is shown in Figure 6.21. The IF statement corresponding to the flowchart is as follows:

```
IF LEVEL-E-FIELD-IN NOT = LEVEL-E-FIELD-SAVE
    PERFORM LEVEL-A-BREAK
    PERFORM LEVEL-B-BREAK
    PERFORM LEVEL-C-BREAK
    PERFORM LEVEL-D-BREAK
    PERFORM LEVEL-E-BREAK
ELSE
IF LEVEL-D-FIELD-IN NOT = LEVEL-D-FIELD-SAVE
    PERFORM LEVEL-A-BREAK
    PERFORM LEVEL-B-BREAK
    PERFORM LEVEL-C-BREAK
    PERFORM LEVEL-D-BREAK
ELSE
IF LEVEL-C-FIELD-IN NOT = LEVEL-C-FIELD-SAVE
    PERFORM LEVEL-A-BREAK
    PERFORM LEVEL-B-BREAK
    PERFORM LEVEL-C-BREAK
ELSE
IF LEVEL-B-FIELD-IN NOT = LEVEL-B-FIELD-SAVE
    PERFORM LEVEL-A-BREAK
    PERFORM LEVEL-B-BREAK
ELSE
IF LEVEL-A-FIELD-IN NOT = LEVEL-A-FIELD-SAVE
    PERFORM LEVEL-A-BREAK.
```

The TERMINATION paragraph could include the following statements:

```
PERFORM LEVEL-A-BREAK.
PERFORM LEVEL-B-BREAK.
PERFORM LEVEL-C-BREAK.
PERFORM LEVEL-D-BREAK.
PERFORM LEVEL-E-BREAK.
PERFORM FINAL-BREAK.
```

There are methods for handling multiple levels of control breaks other than the ones shown in this chapter. These methods were chosen for ease of learning, understanding, and application.

Figure 6.21 Flowchart of control-break testing logic for five levels of breaks.

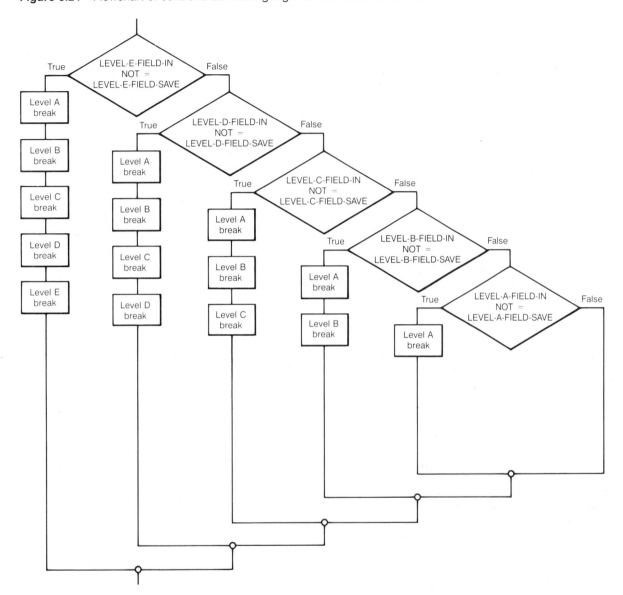

Summary

COBOL programs must often produce reports that have total lines throughout, as well as at the end. There may also be one or more levels of totals. There must be at least one accumulator for each level of total, including one accumulator for a final total if desired. Programs with any number of levels of control breaks can be organized in this same way. The input data are added into the minor accumulator. When a minor total line is printed, the contents of the minor accumulator are added into the next higher-level accumulator. When a total line for that accumulator is printed, its contents are added into the next higher-level accumulator, and so on.

COMPUTATIONAL may be designated as a USAGE of a field. Designating as COMPUTATIONAL those fields used entirely for operations internal to the program can improve program efficiency. When COMPUTATIONAL is designated for other fields, it may improve program efficiency or it may make it worse. Any field designated as COMPUTATIONAL should also be SYNCHRONIZED. The abbreviations for COMPUTATIONAL and SYNCHRONIZED are COMP and SYNC. Fields whose USAGE is not COMPUTATIONAL are DISPLAY fields.

The figurative constants ZERO, ZEROS, and ZEROES may be used whenever a numeric or nonnumeric constant of zero would otherwise be legal. COBOL interprets the figurative constant as numeric or nonnumeric, depending on the context. If a nonnumeric literal of zeros is called for, COBOL provides as many zeros as are needed, depending on the context.

SPACE and SPACES are equivalent, and both are treated as nonnumeric constants. When SPACE or SPACES is used, COBOL provides a string of blanks, the exact number of blank characters being determined by the context.

Other figurative constants are HIGH-VALUE, HIGH-VALUES, LOW-VALUE, LOW-VALUES, QUOTE, and QUOTES.

Group items are always treated as though they were of USAGE DISPLAY, even if their component fields are defined as COMPUTATIONAL.

Group indicating is printing each control field only the first time it appears on a page or the first time it appears after a control break. Group printing, also called summary reporting, is printing total lines only but not any detail lines.

Fill-in Exercises

1. A change in the value of a control _____ is called a control _____ .

2. When end-of-file is detected on the input file, the last _____ line(s) still remain to be printed.

3. Designating fields which do not interact with input or output fields as _____ can improve program efficiency.

4. Using the PICTURE character _____ on numeric fields in working storage can improve program efficiency.

5. The two field USAGEs we have studied so far are _____ and _____ .

6. SPACE and ZERO are _____ constants.

7. _____ and _____ stand for the highest character that can be stored in the computer.

8. A field that is broken down into smaller fields is called a(n) _____ _____ .

9. A field that is not broken down into smaller fields is called a(n) _____ _____ .

10. Printing only total lines and not printing any detail lines is called _____ _____ .

11. _____ and _____ stand for the lowest character that can be stored in the computer.

12. _____ and _____ stand for the character ”.

13. The most significant field used for sequencing data is called the _____ sort field.

14. Two COBOL words with the same meaning as ZERO are _____ and

_____ .

15. Group items are always treated as _____ items.

Review Exercises

1. Modify your solution to Exercise 3, page 183, to provide a grand total line in addition to the customer total lines.
2. Using the input for Program P06-01, write a program that will print and accumulate only the debits. Have your program print one line for each input record containing a debit. Have your program print a total line for each account, showing the total of only the debits for that account. Also show a final total line. Group indicate the Account Number.
3. Modify your solution to Exercise 4, page 183, so that on each salesperson total line there also prints the average Sale Amount (before tax) and, if the average Sale Amount is equal to or greater than $200, the words ABOVE QUOTA.
4. Modify your solution to Exercise 4, page 183, so that only Sale Amounts of $200 or less are printed and added into the totals. Sale Amounts greater than $200 should be ignored by the program.
5. Modify your solution to Exercise 4, page 183, so that on each total line there prints the number of sales less than $200 included in the total and the number of sales of $200 included in the total.

Project

Modify your solution to the Project in Chapter 5, page 150. Use input records in the following format:

Positions	Field
1 – 7	Starting Loan Amount (dollars and cents)
8 – 13	Monthly Payment (dollars and cents)
14 – 15	Month of First Payment
16 – 19	Year of First Payment
20 – 23	Annual Interest Rate
24 – 80	spaces

Have your program produce output in the format shown in Figure 6.P1. Use control-break logic to print the field Total Interest For Year, in the following way:

1. Set up an accumulator for the total interest for the year.
2. Every time you print an interest amount, add it to the accumulator.
3. At the end of each calendar year, print the accumulator and zero it out. Add 1 to the Year of Payment.

Group indicate the Year of Payment as shown in Figure 6.P1. Don't forget to print the Total Interest For Year in the last year of the loan.

Figure 6.P1   Output format for Chapter 6 Project.

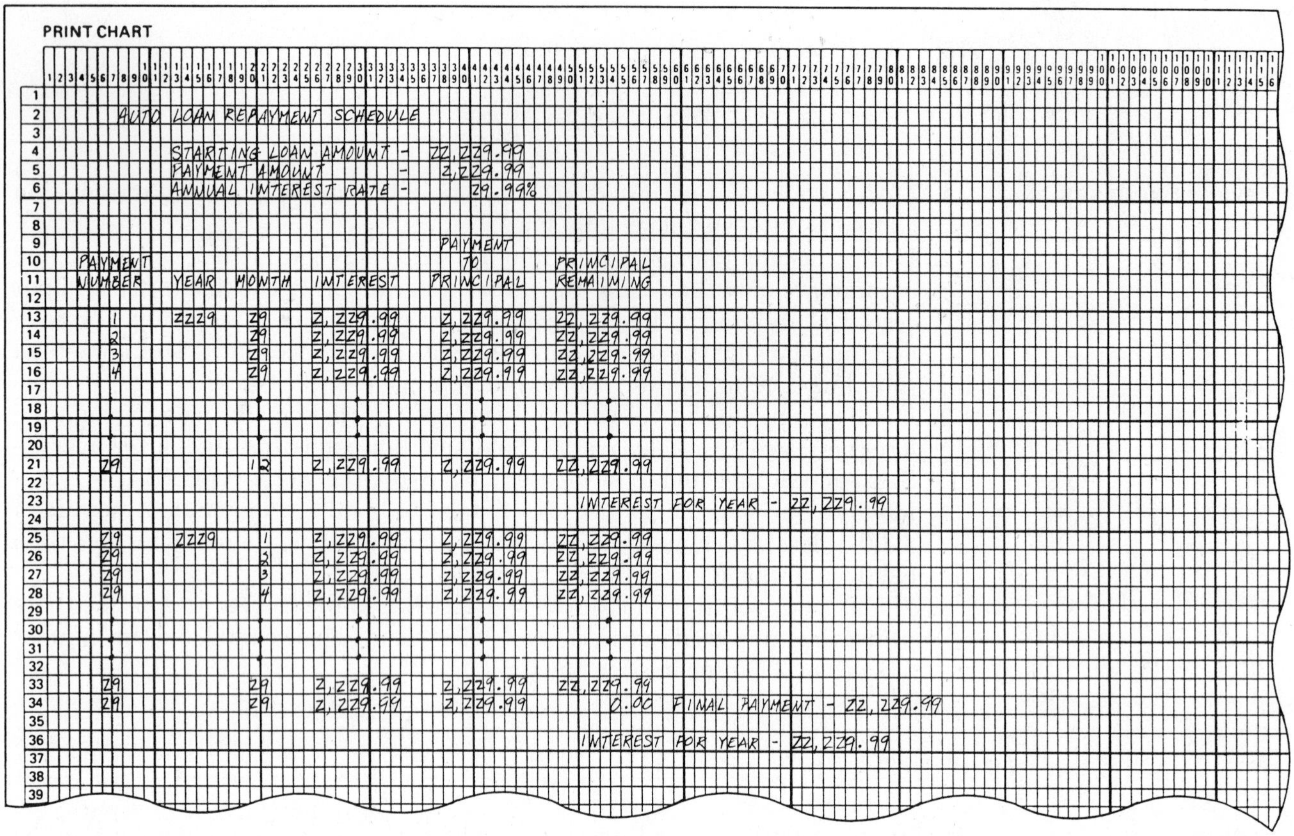

PRINT CHART

```
AUTO LOAN REPAYMENT SCHEDULE

    STARTING LOAN AMOUNT -  ZZ,ZZ9.99
    PAYMENT AMOUNT       -   Z,ZZ9.99
    ANNUAL INTEREST RATE -      Z9.99%


                          PAYMENT
PAYMENT                      TO        PRINCIPAL
NUMBER    YEAR   MONTH  INTEREST    PRINCIPAL   REMAINING

   1      ZZZ9    Z9    Z,ZZ9.99    Z,ZZ9.99   ZZ,ZZ9.99
   2              Z9    Z,ZZ9.99    Z,ZZ9.99   ZZ,ZZ9.99
   3              Z9    Z,ZZ9.99    Z,ZZ9.99   ZZ,ZZ9.99
   4              Z9    Z,ZZ9.99    Z,ZZ9.99   ZZ,ZZ9.99




  Z9             12     Z,ZZ9.99    Z,ZZ9.99   ZZ,ZZ9.99

                               INTEREST FOR YEAR - ZZ,ZZ9.99

  Z9     ZZZ9     1     Z,ZZ9.99    Z,ZZ9.99   ZZ,ZZ9.99
  Z9              2     Z,ZZ9.99    Z,ZZ9.99   ZZ,ZZ9.99
  Z9              3     Z,ZZ9.99    Z,ZZ9.99   ZZ,ZZ9.99
  Z9              4     Z,ZZ9.99    Z,ZZ9.99   ZZ,ZZ9.99




  Z9             Z9     Z,ZZ9.99    Z,ZZ9.99   ZZ,ZZ9.99
  Z9             Z9     Z,ZZ9.99    Z,ZZ9.99       0.00   FINAL PAYMENT - ZZ,ZZ9.99

                               INTEREST FOR YEAR - ZZ,ZZ9.99
```

Validity Checking

Here are the key points you should learn from this chapter:

1. The importance of checking the validity of input data
2. How to check for presence of data, class of data, valid codes, and reasonableness
3. How to program for arithmetic overflow

Key words to recognize and learn:

REDEFINES
overflow
imperative statement

COBOL has several features that permit a program to check the validity of the data it is working on. Invalid data can arise in essentially two ways, the more common of which is invalid data in program input. Most input data are prepared by people, usually on key machines such as a keypunch or a terminal. Even though such data are proofread and verified in other ways before being processed by the program, it is usual to expect that the input data still will contain errors, and the variety of errors will be literally impossible to imagine. After you think you have seen all the possible kinds of input errors, "you ain't seen nothing yet."

Obviously, programs should not execute on incorrect or invalid data. The worst thing that can happen if a program processes incorrect data is that the output will be incorrect and no one will notice the error until it is too late. Another is that incorrect data will cause the program to behave in such an obviously nonsensical way that the error becomes apparent to all. The best thing, though, is for the program itself to be able to detect errors and to handle them in a rational, planned way.

Aside from program input, the other source of invalid data is the program itself. It sometimes happens that in the course of execution the program generates unexpected intermediate results that cannot be further processed properly. COBOL provides ways for a program to protect itself against certain kinds of invalid input data and certain kinds of internally generated invalid data.

Validity Check of Input Data

Since the variety of possible invalid inputs is infinite, it is customary for COBOL programs to make just a few kinds of checks on the data before proceeding. The program can check that fields that are required in the input are in fact present; that fields that are supposed to contain only numbers are in fact purely numeric (and that fields that are supposed to contain only letters are in fact alphabetic); and that the contents of fields are reasonable values. We now look at these in order.

Checking for Presence of Data

In all the programs we have done so far, every field of input data was required to be present. For example, in Program P05-02 each input record had to contain some Salesperson Number, some Class, a figure for Last Year's Sales, and a figure for Current Sale. If any of those fields accidentally had been left blank in any record, the program would not have been able to process the record. Program P05-02 did check that the Class field was present, but the absence of any of the other fields also would have been a fatal error.

In real data processing in industry, not all input records always need to have all their fields present, but when the presence of a field is required, there are ways that COBOL can check that the field is filled in. One technique may be used for fields defined as alphanumeric and other techniques used for numeric fields.

Checking for the presence of data in alphanumeric fields. As in Program P05-02, the programmer may attach a level-88 entry to the field. A suitable condition name may be given and the VALUE SPACE or VALUE SPACES clause used, as in:

```
05  CLASS-IN                PIC X.
    88  CLASS-CODE-IS-MISSING    VALUE SPACE.
```

Then in the Procedure Division, the test

```
IF CLASS-CODE-IS-MISSING ...
```

may be used. The following relation test would work as well:

```
IF CLASS-IN = SPACE ...
```

The choice of which form to use is a matter of programmer preference.

Checking for the presence of unsigned integers. It is illegal in COBOL to use a VALUE SPACES clause with an item described as numeric. Thus a level-88 entry cannot be used to test for a missing integer. (Level-88 entries may be used with numeric fields in other contexts, however; see, for example, Exercise 3, Chapter 5.) The easiest way to check for the absence of an unsigned integer is with a relation condition in an IF statement, as for example:

```
IF STORE-NUMBER-IN = SPACES ...
```

Notice that it is legal to use SPACES in an IF statement with an unsigned integer field.

Checking for the presence of signed fields and noninteger fields. It is illegal to use SPACES in an IF statement with a noninteger field. And if you use SPACES in an IF statement with a signed field, the IF test may not work properly. So the best way to test for the presence of a signed or noninteger field is to take advantage of the COBOL feature that permits a single field to have more than one PICTURE and more than one name if necessary.

The **REDEFINES** clause permits the programmer to give as many different PICTUREs as desired to a single field, and so for purposes of testing the field, the programmer can assign an alphanumeric PICTURE to the field and use the techniques given earlier for testing for the presence of data in an alphanumeric field. For example, the entries

```
05  MONEY-AMOUNT-IN                PIC 9(6)V99.
05  MONEY-AMOUNT-IN-X
    REDEFINES MONEY-AMOUNT-IN      PIC X(8).
```

will let the programmer refer to the same field by either of two names — MONEY-AMOUNT-IN or MONEY-AMOUNT-IN-X. The choice of which name the programmer will use in any particular place in the Procedure Division depends on how the field is used: If the program were to do arithmetic with the field, the name MONEY-AMOUNT-IN would be used. But if the program were to use the field in some context where only alphanumeric fields are allowed, the name MONEY-AMOUNT-IN-X would be used. So to test MONEY-AMOUNT-IN for absence of data, the following would be legal:

```
IF MONEY-AMOUNT-IN-X = SPACES ...
```

But it is permissible to attach a level-88 entry to a field defined with a REDEFINES clause, so the following would be legal:

```
05  MONEY-AMOUNT-IN                PIC 9(6)V99.
05  MONEY-AMOUNT-IN-X
    REDEFINES MONEY-AMOUNT-IN      PIC X(8).
    88 MONEY-AMOUNT-IS-MISSING  VALUE SPACES.
```

Then in the Procedure Division, the programmer may write:

```
IF MONEY-AMOUNT-IS-MISSING ...
```

The presence of the REDEFINES clause does not interfere with other uses of the field MONEY-AMOUNT-IN. For example, MONEY-AMOUNT-IN still could have its own numeric level-88 entries if desired, as follows:

```
05  MONEY-AMOUNT-IN                PIC 9(6)V99.
    88 MONEY-AMOUNT-IS-LOW   VALUES 0 THRU 4999.99.
    88 MONEY-AMOUNT-IS-HIGH  VALUES 700000 THRU 999999.99.
05  MONEY-AMOUNT-IN-X
    REDEFINES MONEY-AMOUNT-IN   PIC X(8).
    88 MONEY-AMOUNT-IS-MISSING  VALUE SPACES.
```

This REDEFINES technique also can be used, of course, with unsigned integer fields as well. Names used to redefine fields are ignored by the CORRESPONDING option. In Chapter 9 we will see an entirely different use of the REDEFINES clause.

EXERCISE 1

Given the following COBOL statement:

```
05  PART-DESCRIPTION-IN            PIC X(20).
```

a. Without using a level-88 entry, write an IF statement to check for the absence of data in the field.
b. Write a level-88 entry using a VALUE SPACES clause and write an IF statement to check for the absence of data in the field.

EXERCISE 2

Given the following COBOL statement:

```
05  NUMBER-OF-SHEEP-IN              PIC 9(5).
```

a. Without using a REDEFINES entry or a level-88 entry, write an IF statement to check for the absence of data in the field.
b. Using a REDEFINES entry and a level-88 entry with a VALUE SPACES clause, write an IF statement to check for the absence of data in the field.

Checking the Class of Data

The class condition should be used to check whether input fields do or do not contain only numbers, or do or do not contain only alphabetic characters. The format of the class condition is given in Chapter 5.

These types of test are needed because the READ statement does not check that data being read agree with the PICTUREs of the fields the data are being read into. That is, if nonnumeric data are read into a field defined as numeric, the READ statement will not detect the error.

The results of not testing a numeric field for absence or invalidity of data can range from insignificant to disastrous. If the field is merely printed on a report, then its absence or invalidity will appear in the report and cause just that one item to be unreadable. If, instead, the missing or invalid field is a control field, then the control breaks for that group will not operate properly and a whole section of the output may be useless. The remainder of the output may be usable, however.

If a field used for numeric comparisons, numeric editing, or arithmetic is missing or invalid, any of several very unpleasant things can happen. Depending on the nature of the error in the numeric field and on the COBOL system being used, the program just might make up its own number and go merrily along using that number in processing. Of course, the output will be totally wrong and the error might not be noticed until too late. Another thing that might happen is that the program will terminate execution. At least that way everyone will know that an error has occurred, but none of the input records following the bad one will be processed. It is best to have the program check all numeric input fields and take care of the erroneous ones before they take care of you.

Checking Data for Reasonableness

Incorrect input data can often slip past tests for presence and tests of class. For example, a field described as

```
05  HOURS-WORKED                    PIC 99V9.
```

with room for three digits accidentally might contain 93.0 instead of the correct value of 39.0. This kind of error, which would not be detected by a class test or a presence test, can be detected by the program because it is so much larger than one would expect. The test could be coded as

```
05 HOURS-WORKED                     PIC 99V9.
   88 HOURS-WORKED-IS-VERY-HIGH VALUES 60.1 THRU 99.9.
```

and:

```
IF HOURS-WORKED-IS-VERY-HIGH ...
```

Fields that are supposed to contain only certain valid codes can be checked to see that one of the valid codes is present:

```
05 MARITAL-STATUS                   PIC X.
   88 SINGLE                     VALUE "S".
   88 MARRIED                    VALUE "M".
   88 LEGALLY-SEPARATED          VALUE "L".
   88 LIVING-APART               VALUE "V".
   88 LIVING-TOGETHER            VALUE "T".
   88 MENAGE-A-TROIS             VALUE "3".
   88 DONT-KNOW-MARITAL-STATUS VALUE "U".
   88 WIDOW-OR-WIDOWER           VALUE "W".
   88 DIVORCED                   VALUE "D".
   88 MARITAL-CODE-IS-MISSING  VALUE SPACE.
   88 VALID-MARITAL-STATUS     VALUE   "3"
                                       "S" "M" "L"
                                       "T" THRU "W"
                                       "D".
```

Then for processing the field the program may refer to any of the level-88 names, and for checking the field we can have

```
IF MARITAL-CODE-IS-MISSING ...
```

and:

```
IF NOT VALID-MARITAL-STATUS ...
```

Sometimes individual fields cannot be tested for reasonableness in cases where data can be detected as invalid only because of an unlikely combination of fields in the input. For example, in a certain payroll application it may be reasonable to have annual salaries in the range $5,000 to $200,000, because everyone from janitor to vice-president is processed by the one program. Combined conditions sometimes can be used to detect unlikely combinations of data, as in:

```
IF WORK-CODE-IS-JANITOR AND
   SALARY GREATER THAN JANITOR-SALARY-LIMIT ...
```

It usually is not wise to go to great lengths to include complicated and extensive reasonableness testing in a program. No matter how thorough the validity checking might be, some creative input clerk will make a keying error that gets through it. The easiest tests to make, like those for presence, class, and valid codes, and some straightforward reasonableness tests, are the ones that catch the greatest number of errors.

EXERCISE 3

Given the following field:

```
05 HOURS-WORKED                          PIC 99V9.
```

Write a level-88 entry and an IF statement to determine whether the contents of the field are outside the reasonable range. Fewer than 8 hours worked, or more than 65, is outside the reasonable range. Write the IF statement so that the True path will be executed if the field contents are found unreasonable.

EXERCISE 4

Given the following field:

```
05 TYPE-OF-SALE                          PIC X.
```

Write level-88 entries giving suitable names to the following codes for the different types of sales: wholesale, W; retail, R; return, N; preferred customer, P. Also write a level-88 entry giving a name to a missing code and a level-88 entry giving a name to the valid codes. Write IF statements to check for the absence of data in the field and for an invalid code.

A Program with Validity Checking of Input Data

In Program P07-01 you will see how to program validity checking of input data. In Program P07-01 each input record is supposed to contain a numeric Salesperson Number, a valid salesperson Class, a numeric value for Last Year's Sales, and a numeric value for Current Sale. The valid salesperson Classes are the letters A through H as before. The program is to check each input record for validity. If a record contains no validity errors, the program is to compute the ratio of the Current Sale to Last Year's Sales and print a line of output as shown in Figure 7.1.

Figure 7.1 also shows the different kinds of error messages that the program might produce and thus implies the kinds of errors the program is supposed to check for. The error message about the Current Sale amount being suspiciously large refers to Current Sales of more than $500,000. In this sales application it is assumed that so large a Current Sale amount is probably an error.

The program is to check for all possible errors in each input record. If there is more than one error in a single record, the program is to print an error line for each error found. A line is to be printed showing the ratio of the Current Sale to Last Year's Sales only if the input record contains no errors. If any errors are found in an input record, only the error lines are to print for that record.

A hierarchy diagram for Program P07-01 is shown in Figure 7.2. The subfunctions of "Check for errors" are the different validity checks that the program makes on each input record. For each type of error that may be found, the program will set up an appropriate error line and PERFORM a common routine called "Write an error line." If no errors are found in an input record, the program will carry out the step "Set up to write a good line." The error-line flag referred to in the hierarchy diagram is used to indicate to the program whether any errors have been found in the input record being processed. Its use will become clear when we look at the coding for Program P07-01, shown in Figure 7.3.

Figure 7.1 Output format for Program P07-01.

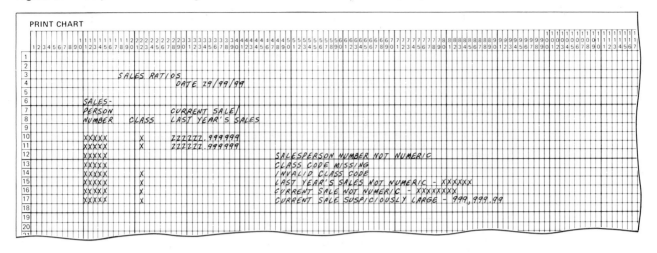

Figure 7.2 Hierarchy diagram for Program P07-01.

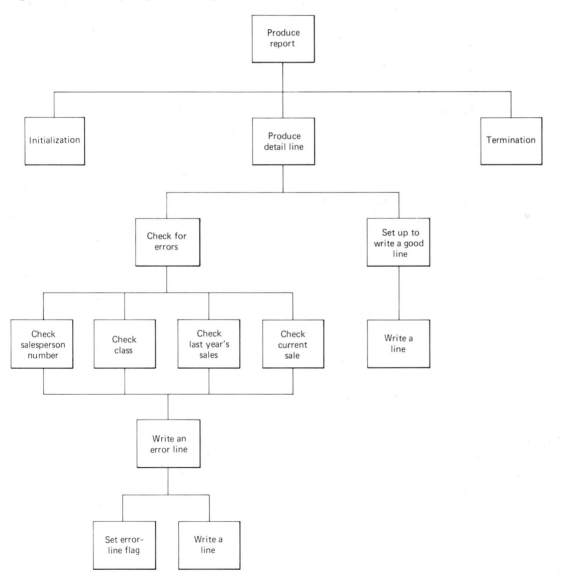

Figure 7.3 Program P07-01.

```
CB1 RELEASE 2.4                                    IBM OS/VS COBOL  JULY  1, 1982


                        19.12.27        MAR 31,1988


00010   IDENTIFICATION DIVISION.
00020   PROGRAM-ID.  P07-01.
00030
00040 *  AUTHOR. WENDEL KELLER.
00050 *  THIS PROGRAM CHECKS THE VALIDITY OF EACH FIELD
00060 *  IN EACH INPUT RECORD AND WRITES A LINE FOR EACH
00070 *  ERROR FOUND.
00080 *
00090 ****************************************************************
00100
00110   ENVIRONMENT DIVISION.
00120   CONFIGURATION SECTION.
00130   SOURCE-COMPUTER.  IBM-370.
00140   OBJECT-COMPUTER.  IBM-370.
00150
00160   INPUT-OUTPUT SECTION.
00170   FILE-CONTROL.
00180       SELECT SALES-RATIO-REPORT ASSIGN TO PRINTER.
00190       SELECT SALES-FILE-IN       ASSIGN TO INFILE.
00200
00210 ****************************************************************
00220
00230   DATA DIVISION.
00240   FILE SECTION.
00250   FD  SALES-FILE-IN
00260       RECORD CONTAINS 80 CHARACTERS
00270       LABEL RECORDS ARE OMITTED.
00280
00290   01  SALES-RECORD-IN.
00300       05 SALESPERSON-NUMBER-IN           PIC X(5).
00310       05 CLASS-IN                        PIC X.
00320          88 CLASS-CODE-IS-MISSING        VALUE SPACE.
00330          88 VALID-CLASS-CODE             VALUES "A" THRU "H".
00340       05 LAST-YEARS-SALES-IN             PIC 9(6).
00350       05 CURRENT-SALE-IN                 PIC 9(6)V99.
00360          88 CURRENT-SALE-VERY-LARGE  VALUES 500000 THRU 999999.99.
00370       05 CURRENT-SALE-IN-X
00380          REDEFINES CURRENT-SALE-IN       PIC X(8).
00390       05 FILLER                          PIC X(60).
00400
00410   FD  SALES-RATIO-REPORT
00420       LABEL RECORDS ARE OMITTED.
00430
00440   01  REPORT-LINE                        PIC X(91).
00450
00460   WORKING-STORAGE SECTION.
00470   01  MORE-INPUT        VALUE "Y"        PIC X.
00480   01  ERROR-LINE-FLAG                    PIC X.
00490
00500   01  PAGE-HEAD-1.
00510       05 FILLER          PIC X(17) VALUE SPACES.
00520       05 FILLER          PIC X(12) VALUE "SALES RATIOS".
00530
00540   01  PAGE-HEAD-2.
00550       05 FILLER          PIC X(28) VALUE SPACES.
00560       05 FILLER          PIC X(5)  VALUE "DATE".
00570       05 RUN-MONTH-AND-DAY PIC Z9/99/.
00580       05 RUN-YEAR        PIC 99.
00590
00600   01  PAGE-HEAD-3.
00610       05 FILLER          PIC X(10) VALUE SPACES.
00620       05 FILLER          PIC X(6)  VALUE "SALES-".
00630
00640   01  PAGE-HEAD-4.
00650       05 FILLER          PIC X(10) VALUE SPACES.
00660       05 FILLER          PIC X(17) VALUE "PERSON".
00670       05 FILLER          PIC X(13) VALUE "CURRENT SALE/".
00680
```

(continued)

In the description of SALES-RECORD-IN, a level-88 entry has been assigned to suspiciously large sale amounts, at line 00360. The ERROR-LINE-FLAG is shown at line 00480. You will see how it is used when we look at the Procedure Division.

The formatting of the error lines in this program is handled a little differently from Program P05-02. Here all lines on the report, whether they contain an error message or the sale ratio, are written from the same area in working storage, BODY-LINE, at line 00750. BODY-LINE has space for both the sale ratio and the longest possible error message, in fields called SALE-RATIO-OUT, line 00780, and ERROR-MESSAGE-OUT, line 00790. For any single printed line, of course, either the sale ratio or an error message will print, but never both. Some of the different kinds of error messages that may be MOVEd to ERROR-MESSAGE-OUT in the course of processing are defined in the level-01 entry ERROR-MESSAGES, line 00810. Within ERROR-MESSAGES we have, for example, the message called LAST-YEARS-SALES-NOT-NUMERIC, at line 00820. This message will be printed if the field LAST-YEARS-SALES-IN is found to be not numeric. Part of this message is the field NONNUMERIC-LAST-YEARS-SALES, at line 00850. To this field will be assigned the actual nonnumeric value found in LAST-YEARS-SALES-IN. As a general rule, whenever you are printing an erroneous field, the output PICTURE should be all Xs. In this way you will be able to see on the output exactly what the field looked like in the input, with no editing or other modifications.

CURRENT-SALE-IN, at line 00350, was redefined with Xs for error processing because it is illegal to MOVE a noninteger field to an alphanumeric field. If there had been any signed integer fields in the input, they too would have been redefined with Xs for it is unwise, though legal, to MOVE a signed integer to an alphanumeric field.

Figure 7.3 (continued)

```
00690   01   PAGE-HEAD-5.
00700        05 FILLER               PIC X(10) VALUE SPACES.
00710        05 FILLER               PIC X(9)  VALUE "NUMBER".
00720        05 FILLER               PIC X(8)  VALUE "CLASS".
00730        05 FILLER               PIC X(17) VALUE "LAST YEAR'S SALES".
00740
00750   01   BODY-LINE.
00760        05 SALESPERSON-NUMBER-OUT       PIC B(10)X(5).
00770        05 CLASS-OUT                    PIC B(6)X.
00780        05 SALE-RATIO-OUT               PIC B(5)Z(6).9(6)B(7).
00790        05 ERROR-MESSAGE-OUT            PIC X(44).
00800
00810   01   ERROR-MESSAGES.
00820        05 LAST-YEARS-SALES-NOT-NUMERIC.
00830           10 FILLER PIC X(32)
00840                   VALUE "LAST YEAR'S SALES NOT NUMERIC -".
00850           10 NONNUMERIC-LAST-YEARS-SALES PIC X(6).
00860        05 CURRENT-SALE-NOT-NUMERIC.
00870           10 FILLER PIC X(27) VALUE "CURRENT SALE NOT NUMERIC - ".
00880           10 NONNUMERIC-CURRENT-SALE    PIC X(8).
00890        05 LARGE-SALE-MESSAGE.
00900           10 FILLER PIC X(34)
00910                   VALUE "CURRENT SALE SUSPICIOUSLY LARGE - ".
00920           10 LARGE-CURRENT-SALE         PIC 999,999.99.
00930
00940   01   RUN-DATE.
00950        05 RUN-YEAR          PIC 99.
00960        05 RUN-MONTH-AND-DAY PIC 9(4).
00970
```

(continued)

Figure 7.3   (continued)

```
00980    01  NO-INPUT-DATA         PIC X(15) VALUE "  NO INPUT DATA".
00990
01000    *************************************************************************
01010
01020    PROCEDURE DIVISION.
01030    PRODUCE-REPORT.
01040        PERFORM INITIALIZATION.
01050        PERFORM PRODUCE-DETAIL-LINE UNTIL MORE-INPUT = "N".
01060        PERFORM TERMINATION.
01070        STOP RUN.
01080
01090    INITIALIZATION.
01100        OPEN INPUT  SALES-FILE-IN,
01110             OUTPUT SALES-RATIO-REPORT.
01120        ACCEPT RUN-DATE FROM DATE.
01130        MOVE CORRESPONDING RUN-DATE TO PAGE-HEAD-2.
01140        WRITE REPORT-LINE FROM PAGE-HEAD-1 AFTER PAGE.
01150        WRITE REPORT-LINE FROM PAGE-HEAD-2.
01160        WRITE REPORT-LINE FROM PAGE-HEAD-3 AFTER 2.
01170        WRITE REPORT-LINE FROM PAGE-HEAD-4.
01180        WRITE REPORT-LINE FROM PAGE-HEAD-5.
01190        MOVE SPACES TO REPORT-LINE.
01200        WRITE REPORT-LINE.
01210        READ SALES-FILE-IN
01220            AT END
01230                MOVE "N" TO MORE-INPUT.
01240        IF MORE-INPUT = "N"
01250            WRITE REPORT-LINE FROM NO-INPUT-DATA AFTER 2.
01260
01270    TERMINATION.
01280        CLOSE SALES-FILE-IN,
01290              SALES-RATIO-REPORT.
01300
01310    PRODUCE-DETAIL-LINE.
01320        MOVE "N" TO ERROR-LINE-FLAG.
01330        MOVE SPACES TO BODY-LINE.
01340        MOVE SALESPERSON-NUMBER-IN TO SALESPERSON-NUMBER-OUT.
01350        PERFORM CHECK-FOR-ERRORS.
01360        IF ERROR-LINE-FLAG = "N"
01370            PERFORM SET-UP-TO-WRITE-A-GOOD-LINE.
01380        READ SALES-FILE-IN
01390            AT END
01400                MOVE "N" TO MORE-INPUT.
01410
01420    WRITE-AN-ERROR-LINE.
01430        PERFORM SET-ERROR-LINE-FLAG.
01440        PERFORM WRITE-A-LINE.
01450
01460    CHECK-FOR-ERRORS.
01470        PERFORM CHECK-SALESPERSON-NUMBER.
01480        PERFORM CHECK-CLASS.
01490        PERFORM CHECK-LAST-YEARS-SALES.
01500        PERFORM CHECK-CURRENT-SALE.
01510
01520    CHECK-SALESPERSON-NUMBER.
01530        IF SALESPERSON-NUMBER-IN NOT NUMERIC
01540            MOVE "SALESPERSON NUMBER NOT NUMERIC"
01550                TO ERROR-MESSAGE-OUT
01560            PERFORM WRITE-AN-ERROR-LINE.
01570
01580    CHECK-CLASS.
01590        MOVE CLASS-IN TO CLASS-OUT.
```

```
01600        IF CLASS-CODE-IS-MISSING
01610            MOVE "CLASS CODE MISSING" TO ERROR-MESSAGE-OUT
01620            PERFORM WRITE-AN-ERROR-LINE
01630        ELSE
01640        IF NOT VALID-CLASS-CODE
01650            MOVE "INVALID CLASS CODE" TO ERROR-MESSAGE-OUT
01660            PERFORM WRITE-AN-ERROR-LINE.
01670
01680    CHECK-LAST-YEARS-SALES.
01690        IF LAST-YEARS-SALES-IN NOT NUMERIC
01700            MOVE LAST-YEARS-SALES-IN TO NONNUMERIC-LAST-YEARS-SALES
01710            MOVE LAST-YEARS-SALES-NOT-NUMERIC TO ERROR-MESSAGE-OUT
01720            PERFORM WRITE-AN-ERROR-LINE.
01730
01740    CHECK-CURRENT-SALE.
01750        IF CURRENT-SALE-IN NOT NUMERIC
01760            MOVE CURRENT-SALE-IN-X TO NONNUMERIC-CURRENT-SALE
01770            MOVE CURRENT-SALE-NOT-NUMERIC TO ERROR-MESSAGE-OUT
01780            PERFORM WRITE-AN-ERROR-LINE
01790        ELSE
01800        IF CURRENT-SALE-VERY-LARGE
01810            MOVE CURRENT-SALE-IN TO LARGE-CURRENT-SALE
01820            MOVE LARGE-SALE-MESSAGE TO ERROR-MESSAGE-OUT
01830            PERFORM WRITE-AN-ERROR-LINE.
01840
01850    SET-ERROR-LINE-FLAG.
01860        MOVE "Y" TO ERROR-LINE-FLAG.
01870
01880    SET-UP-TO-WRITE-A-GOOD-LINE.
01890        DIVIDE CURRENT-SALE-IN BY LAST-YEARS-SALES-IN
01900            GIVING SALE-RATIO-OUT.
01910        PERFORM WRITE-A-LINE.
01920
01930    WRITE-A-LINE.
01940        WRITE REPORT-LINE FROM BODY-LINE.
```

The Procedure Division begins at line 01020. The Paragraph PRODUCE-DETAIL-LINE, line 01310, starts by setting the ERROR-LINE-FLAG to "N" to indicate that no error lines have been printed for the input record being processed. SALESPERSON-NUMBER-IN is MOVEd to SALESPERSON-NUMBER-OUT because the Salesperson Number is to print regardless of whether or not the line is an error line and regardless of whether or not the Salesperson Number is valid.

The PERFORM statement at line 01350 checks for all errors. Whenever an error is found, an appropriate error message is set up and the paragraph WRITE-AN-ERROR-LINE, line 01420, is PERFORMed. When WRITE-AN-ERROR-LINE executes, it sets the ERROR-LINE-FLAG to "Y" to indicate that at least one error has been found in the input record. The IF statement at line 01360 tests to see whether any errors were found in the input record. If no errors are found even after all the error checks have been made, normal processing may be done and the sales ratio computed and printed.

The paragraph CHECK-CURRENT-SALE, line 01740, shows a field being checked for numeric before being used in a numeric comparison. Whenever a field must be checked for numeric and also used in a numeric comparison, the NUMERIC test must be done first.

Program P07-01 was run with the input data shown in Figure 7.4 and produced the output shown in Figure 7.5.

Figure 7.4 Input for Program P07-01.

```
-----------------------------------------------------------------------------
         1         2         3         4         5         6         7         8
12345678901234567890123456789012345678901234567890123456789012345678901234567890
-----------------------------------------------------------------------------
34ABA 06543X843961V9
78121H10000038745231
00000ACDEFGHIJKLMNOP
14758H22342101000000
45 4150 79218 542165
9#121H19087055089733
91A00A08749002384009
99121H19087045089733
82423 17142109865022
733151043960019250355
64876D099 4201000042
6745HA0953Z1043942)9
55252E054320043#0066
46701F21005054365281
374  317329907279823
00322A00000149999999
28421B06923Z50000000
14756A08994307059243
89  6 9"942117642972
78932ZA9324167632075
569$2 00943259239651
15008B07076306804299
05))6L0*923570092151
03442A03500004808989
19123G17036705376542
```

EXERCISE 5

Write a program to process input records in the following format:

Positions	Field
1−9	Social Security Number
10	Job Grade
11−18	Annual Salary (to two decimal places)
19−80	spaces

Have your program make the following validity checks on each input record:

a. Social Security Number numeric
b. Grade present
c. Grade valid (V through Z or 1 through 6)
d. Annual Salary numeric
e. Annual Salary not greater than $400,000

Have your program check each input record for all possible types of errors. Print an error line for each error found. If a record is completely free of errors, print its contents on one line (formatted so that it can be read easily). At the end of the report, have your program print a total of all the salaries printed, that is, the total of all the salaries in the error-free records.

Design a report format with a suitable title and suitable column headings. Include the date in the heading.

Figure 7.5 Output from Program P07-01.

```
                         SALES RATIOS
                              DATE   3/31/88

SALES-
PERSON              CURRENT SALE/
NUMBER    CLASS     LAST YEAR'S SALES

34ABA                                        SALESPERSON NUMBER NOT NUMERIC
34ABA                                        CLASS CODE MISSING
34ABA                                        LAST YEAR'S SALES NOT NUMERIC - 06543X
34ABA                                        CURRENT SALE NOT NUMERIC - 843961V9
78121     H         3.874523
00000     A                                  LAST YEAR'S SALES NOT NUMERIC - CDEFGH
00000     A                                  CURRENT SALE NOT NUMERIC - IJKLMNOP
14758     H          .044758
45 41                                        SALESPERSON NUMBER NOT NUMERIC
45 41     5                                  INVALID CLASS CODE
45 41     5                                  LAST YEAR'S SALES NOT NUMERIC - O 7921
45 41     5                                  CURRENT SALE NOT NUMERIC - 8 542165
9#121                                        SALESPERSON NUMBER NOT NUMERIC
9#121     H                                  CURRENT SALE SUSPICIOUSLY LARGE - 550,897.33
91A00                                        SALESPERSON NUMBER NOT NUMERIC
99121     H         2.362326
82423                                        CLASS CODE MISSING
73315     I                                  INVALID CLASS CODE
64876     D                                  LAST YEAR'S SALES NOT NUMERIC - 099 42
6745H                                        SALESPERSON NUMBER NOT NUMERIC
6745H     A                                  LAST YEAR'S SALES NOT NUMERIC - 0953Z1
6745H     A                                  CURRENT SALE NOT NUMERIC - 043942)9
55252     E                                  CURRENT SALE NOT NUMERIC - 043#0066
46701     F                                  CURRENT SALE SUSPICIOUSLY LARGE - 543,652.81
374                                          SALESPERSON NUMBER NOT NUMERIC
374       3                                  INVALID CLASS CODE
00322     A         499999.990000
28421     B                                  LAST YEAR'S SALES NOT NUMERIC - 06923Z
28421     B                                  CURRENT SALE SUSPICIOUSLY LARGE - 500,000.00
14756     A          .784857
89  6                                        SALESPERSON NUMBER NOT NUMERIC
89  6                                        CLASS CODE MISSING
89  6                                        LAST YEAR'S SALES NOT NUMERIC - 9"9421
78932     Z                                  INVALID CLASS CODE
78932     Z                                  LAST YEAR'S SALES NOT NUMERIC - A93241
78932     Z                                  CURRENT SALE SUSPICIOUSLY LARGE - 676,320.75
569$2                                        SALESPERSON NUMBER NOT NUMERIC
569$2                                        CLASS CODE MISSING
569$2                                        LAST YEAR'S SALES NOT NUMERIC - 009432
569$2                                        CURRENT SALE SUSPICIOUSLY LARGE - 592,396.51
15008     B          .961561
05))6                                        SALESPERSON NUMBER NOT NUMERIC
05))6     L                                  INVALID CLASS CODE
05))6     L                                  LAST YEAR'S SALES NOT NUMERIC - 0*9235
05))6     L                                  CURRENT SALE SUSPICIOUSLY LARGE - 700,921.51
03442     A         1.373996
19123     G          .315585
```

Arithmetic Overflow

Sometimes invalid data in the form of arithmetic **overflow** can be generated during execution of a program. An arithmetic result is considered to overflow if there are more places to the left of the decimal point in the answer than to the left of the point in the field provided by the programmer. Excess places to the right of the decimal point are never considered an overflow condition. Excess places to the right of the point are either truncated or rounded, depending on whether the ROUNDED option is present in the arithmetic statement.

The programmer can test for arithmetic overflow by using the SIZE ERROR phrase. The SIZE ERROR phrase is optional with all five arithmetic verbs—ADD, SUBTRACT, MULTIPLY, DIVIDE, and COMPUTE. The format of the SIZE ERROR phrase was given in Chapter 3:

```
ON SIZE ERROR imperative-statement
```

Following the words SIZE ERROR in an arithmetic statement, there must be one or more **imperative statements.** An imperative statement is a COBOL statement that begins with an imperative verb and specifies some unconditional action to be taken. Some typical imperative statements are

```
MOVE HANDLING-CHARGE-IN TO HANDLING-CHARGE-OUT.
```

and:

```
PERFORM INITIALIZATION.
```

Complete lists of imperative verbs are given on page 669.

Here are two examples of the SIZE ERROR condition in ADD statements:

```
ADD A TO B
    SIZE ERROR
        MOVE "Y" TO SIZE-ERROR-FLAG.

ADD A TO B ROUNDED
    SIZE ERROR
        MOVE SIZE-ERROR-MESSAGE TO ERROR-MESSAGE-OUT
        WRITE ERROR-LINE
        MOVE 0 TO B.
```

In these examples there is only one period at the end of the complete SIZE ERROR processing. In the next section we will see that when arithmetic is done inside an IF statement, the SIZE ERROR processing steps can be terminated with an ELSE. The period or the ELSE ends the last of the steps that are to be carried out in case of arithmetic overflow. Indenting is, of course, only for the programmer's convenience and is not examined by COBOL.

No conditional statements may follow the words SIZE ERROR up to the place where the SIZE ERROR processing ends (at the period or the ELSE). This means that no IF statements may appear, no READ statements (for READ statements contain the conditional AT END), and no arithmetic statements containing a SIZE ERROR phrase. If any such statements are needed for the program to process a SIZE ERROR properly, the statements can be placed in a separate paragraph. Then the SIZE ERROR phrase can be written as something like:

```
ADD A TO B
    SIZE ERROR
        PERFORM SIZE-ERROR-ROUTINE.
```

If the ROUNDED option is specified in an arithmetic operation, rounding is carried out before the field is tested for SIZE ERROR. Division by zero always causes a SIZE ERROR condition. If more than one result field is given in an arithmetic statement, a SIZE ERROR on one of the fields will not interfere with normal execution of arithmetic on the others. If a size error occurs during execution of a statement that contains a SIZE ERROR phrase, the result field is left unchanged from before the operation. If a size error occurs in a statement where the SIZE ERROR phrase is not specified, the results may be unpredictable.

SIZE ERROR Processing Terminated by ELSE

Figure 7.6 shows a flowchart of a situation where the steps of the SIZE ERROR processing are terminated not by a period, but by ELSE. The flowchart can be coded in COBOL as follows:

```
IF CURRENT-SALE-IN GREATER THAN SELECTED-BREAK-POINT
    COMPUTE COMMISSION-OUT ROUNDED =
        LOW-COMMISSION-RATE * SELECTED-BREAK-POINT +
        HIGH-COMMISSION-RATE *
            (CURRENT-SALE-IN - SELECTED-BREAK-POINT)
    SIZE ERROR PERFORM SIZE-ERROR-ROUTINE
ELSE
    COMPUTE COMMISSION-OUT ROUNDED =
        LOW-COMMISSION-RATE * CURRENT-SALE-IN.
```

Here the SIZE ERROR processing is contained between the words SIZE ERROR and ELSE. As before, no conditional statements may appear among the SIZE ERROR processing steps. Of course, the paragraph SIZE-ERROR-ROUTINE may contain any legal statements.

There never can be processing steps in the False path of a SIZE ERROR test in the 1974 standard. If the logic of a problem demands that certain steps be carried out only if there is no size error, then a size-error flag must be used. The 1985 standard contains a NOT SIZE ERROR phrase which can simplify program logic.

A Program with a SIZE ERROR

We now do a program that shows the SIZE ERROR phrase in context. Program P07-02 is a modification to Program P05-02, which computes commissions for junior, associate, and senior salespeople. In Program P07-02 a commission is limited to a maximum of $99,999.99. If any commission computation comes out larger than that, Program P07-02 will print a message so indicating. Program P07-02 is shown in Figure 7.7.

Figure 7.6 Flowchart showing SIZE ERROR processing within an IF statement where the SIZE ERROR steps are terminated by ELSE.

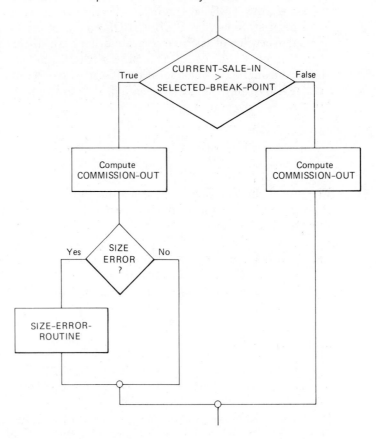

Figure 7.7 Program P07-02.

```
CB1 RELEASE 2.4                              IBM OS/VS COBOL  JULY  1, 1982


                        22.16.36        MAR 31,1988


00010   IDENTIFICATION DIVISION.
00020   PROGRAM-ID.  P07-02.
00030 *
00040 *     AUTHOR. WENDEL KELLER.
00050 *     THIS PROGRAM COMPUTES SALESPERSON COMMISSIONS FOR JUNIOR
00060 *     SALESPERSONS, ASSOCIATE SALESPERSONS, AND SENIOR SALESPERSONS
00070 *     ANY COMMISSION AMOUNT OVER $99,999.99 IS CONSIDERED A
00080 *     SIZE ERROR.
00090 *
00100 *****************************************************************
00110
00120   ENVIRONMENT DIVISION.
00130   CONFIGURATION SECTION.
00140   SOURCE-COMPUTER.  IBM-370.
00150   OBJECT-COMPUTER.  IBM-370.
00160
00170   INPUT-OUTPUT SECTION.
00180   FILE-CONTROL.
00190       SELECT COMMISSION-REPORT ASSIGN TO PRINTER.
00200       SELECT SALES-FILE-IN     ASSIGN TO INFILE.
00210
00220 *****************************************************************
00230
```

```
00240  DATA DIVISION.
00250  FILE SECTION.
00260  FD  SALES-FILE-IN
00270      RECORD CONTAINS 80 CHARACTERS
00280      LABEL RECORDS ARE OMITTED.
00290
00300  01  SALES-RECORD-IN.
00310      05 SALESPERSON-NUMBER-IN    PIC X(5).
00320      05 CLASS-IN                 PIC X.
00330         88 SALESPERSON-IS-JUNIOR    VALUES "A" THRU "F".
00340         88 SALESPERSON-IS-ASSOCIATE VALUE "G".
00350         88 SALESPERSON-IS-SENIOR    VALUE "H".
00360         88 CLASS-CODE-IS-VALID      VALUES "A" THRU "H".
00370         88 CLASS-CODE-IS-MISSING    VALUE SPACE.
00380      05 LAST-YEARS-SALES-IN      PIC 9(6).
00390      05 CURRENT-SALE-IN          PIC 9(6)V99.
00400      05 FILLER                   PIC X(60).
00410
00420  FD  COMMISSION-REPORT
00430      LABEL RECORDS ARE OMITTED.
00440
00450  01  REPORT-LINE                 PIC X(88).
00460
00470  WORKING-STORAGE SECTION.
00480  01  MORE-INPUT          PIC X     VALUE "Y".
00490  01  NO-INPUT-DATA       PIC X(15) VALUE " NO INPUT DATA".
00500
00510  01  PAGE-HEAD-1.
00520      05 FILLER           PIC X(23) VALUE SPACES.
00530      05 FILLER           PIC X(19) VALUE "COMMISSION REGISTER".
00540
00550  01  PAGE-HEAD-2.
00560      05 FILLER               PIC X(45) VALUE SPACES.
00570      05 FILLER               PIC X(5)  VALUE "DATE".
00580      05 RUN-MONTH-AND-DAY    PIC Z9/99/.
00590      05 RUN-YEAR             PIC 99.
00600
00610  01  PAGE-HEAD-3.
00620      05 FILLER           PIC X(10) VALUE SPACES.
00630      05 FILLER           PIC X(6)  VALUE "SALES-".
00640
00650  01  PAGE-HEAD-4.
00660      05 FILLER           PIC X(10) VALUE SPACES.
00670      05 FILLER           PIC X(25) VALUE "PERSON".
00680      05 FILLER           PIC X(4)  VALUE "SALE".
00690
00700  01  PAGE-HEAD-5.
00710      05 FILLER           PIC X(10) VALUE SPACES.
00720      05 FILLER           PIC X(12) VALUE "NUMBER".
00730      05 FILLER           PIC X(12) VALUE "CLASS".
00740      05 FILLER           PIC X(12) VALUE "AMOUNT".
00750      05 FILLER           PIC X(10) VALUE "COMMISSION".
00760
00770  01  DETAIL-LINE.
00780      05 SALESPERSON-NUMBER-OUT   PIC B(10)X(5).
00790      05 CLASS-TITLE-OUT          PIC B(5)X(9)BBB.
00800      05 CURRENT-SALE-OUT         PIC ZZZ,ZZZ.99BBB.
00810      05 COMMISSION-OUT           PIC ZZ,ZZZ.99B(18).
00820      05 DETAIL-ERROR REDEFINES COMMISSION-OUT
00830                                  PIC X(27).
00840
00850  01  CLASS-INVALID-LINE.
00860      05 SALESPERSON-NUMBER       PIC B(10)X(5)B(5).
00870      05 FILLER                   PIC X(17)
00880                                  VALUE "ERROR - CLASS IS".
00890      05 INVALID-CLASS            PIC X.
00900      05 FILLER                   PIC X(44)
00910         VALUE ". CLASS SHOULD BE A, B, C, D, E, F, G, OR H.".
00920
00930  01  CLASS-MISSING-LINE.
00940      05 SALESPERSON-NUMBER       PIC B(10)X(5)B(5).
00950      05 FILLER                   PIC X(68)
00960         VALUE "ERROR - CLASS IS MISSING. CLASS SHOULD BE A, B, C,
00970         "D, E, F, G, OR H.".
00980
```

(continued)

Figure 7.7   (continued)

```
00990  01   COMMISSION-BREAK-POINTS.
01000       05 JUNIOR-BREAK-POINT       PIC S9     VALUE 0.
01010       05 ASSOCIATE-BREAK-POINT    PIC S9(5) VALUE 10000.
01020       05 SENIOR-BREAK-POINT       PIC S9(5) VALUE 50000.
01030
01040  01   SELECTED-COMMISSION-RATES.
01050       05 LOW-COMMISSION-RATE      PIC SV99.
01060       05 HIGH-COMMISSION-RATE     PIC SV99.
01070
01080  01   SELECTED-BREAK-POINT        PIC S9(5).
01090
01100  01   SALE-QUOTAS.
01110       05 JUNIOR-SALE-QUOTA        PIC S9     VALUE 0.
01120       05 ASSOCIATE-SALE-QUOTA     PIC S9(6) VALUE 150000.
01130       05 SENIOR-SALE-QUOTA        PIC S9(6) VALUE 250000.
01140
01150  01   COMMISSION-RATES.
01160       05 ASSOCIATE-RATES.
01170          10 QUOTA-NOT-MET.
01180             15 LOW-RATE           PIC SV99   VALUE .05.
01190             15 HIGH-RATE          PIC SV99   VALUE .20.
01200          10 QUOTA-MET.
01210             15 LOW-RATE           PIC SV99   VALUE .20.
01220             15 HIGH-RATE          PIC SV99   VALUE .30.
01230       05 SENIOR-RATES.
01240          10 QUOTA-NOT-MET.
01250             15 LOW-RATE           PIC SV99   VALUE .20.
01260             15 HIGH-RATE          PIC SV99   VALUE .30.
01270          10 QUOTA-MET.
01280             15 LOW-RATE           PIC SV99   VALUE .30.
01290             15 HIGH-RATE          PIC SV99   VALUE .40.
01300       05 JUNIOR-RATES.
01310          10 QUOTA-NOT-MET.
01320             15 LOW-RATE           PIC SV99   VALUE .10.
01330             15 HIGH-RATE          PIC SV99   VALUE .10.
01340          10 QUOTA-MET.
01350             15 LOW-RATE           PIC SV99   VALUE .10.
01360             15 HIGH-RATE          PIC SV99   VALUE .10.
01370
01380  01   TODAYS-DATE.
01390       05 RUN-YEAR                 PIC 99.
01400       05 RUN-MONTH-AND-DAY        PIC 9(4).
01410
01420  ********************************************************************
01430
01440  PROCEDURE DIVISION.
01450  PRODUCE-COMMISSION-REPORT.
01460       PERFORM INITIALIZATION.
01470       PERFORM PRODUCE-DETAIL-LINE UNTIL MORE-INPUT = "N".
01480       PERFORM TERMINATION.
01490       STOP RUN.
01500
01510  INITIALIZATION.
01520       OPEN INPUT  SALES-FILE-IN,
01530            OUTPUT COMMISSION-REPORT.
01540       ACCEPT TODAYS-DATE FROM DATE.
01550       MOVE CORR TODAYS-DATE TO PAGE-HEAD-2.
01560       WRITE REPORT-LINE FROM PAGE-HEAD-1 AFTER PAGE.
01570       WRITE REPORT-LINE FROM PAGE-HEAD-2.
01580       WRITE REPORT-LINE FROM PAGE-HEAD-3 AFTER 3.
01590       WRITE REPORT-LINE FROM PAGE-HEAD-4.
01600       WRITE REPORT-LINE FROM PAGE-HEAD-5.
01610       MOVE SPACES TO REPORT-LINE.
01620       WRITE REPORT-LINE.
01630       READ SALES-FILE-IN
01640           AT END
01650               MOVE "N" TO MORE-INPUT.
01660       IF MORE-INPUT = "N"
01670           WRITE REPORT-LINE FROM NO-INPUT-DATA AFTER 2.
01680
01690  TERMINATION.
01700       CLOSE SALES-FILE-IN,
01710             COMMISSION-REPORT.
01720
```

```
01730    PRODUCE-DETAIL-LINE.
01740        IF NOT CLASS-CODE-IS-VALID
01750            PERFORM PROCESS-ERRONEOUS-RECORD
01760        ELSE
01770            PERFORM PROCESS-GOOD-RECORD.
01780        READ SALES-FILE-IN
01790            AT END
01800                MOVE "N" TO MORE-INPUT.
01810
01820    PROCESS-ERRONEOUS-RECORD.
01830        IF CLASS-CODE-IS-MISSING
01840            PERFORM WRITE-CLASS-MISSING-LINE
01850        ELSE
01860            PERFORM WRITE-CLASS-INVALID-LINE.
01870
01880    PROCESS-GOOD-RECORD.
01890        PERFORM SELECT-COMMISSION-RATES.
01900        PERFORM COMPUTE-COMMISSION.
01910        PERFORM WRITE-COMMISSION-LINE.
01920
01930    SELECT-COMMISSION-RATES.
01940        IF SALESPERSON-IS-JUNIOR
01950            PERFORM SET-JUNIOR-PARAMETERS
01960        ELSE
01970            IF SALESPERSON-IS-ASSOCIATE AND
01980            LAST-YEARS-SALES-IN LESS THAN ASSOCIATE-SALE-QUOTA
01990                PERFORM ASSOCIATE-QUOTA-NOT-MET
02000            ELSE
02010                IF SALESPERSON-IS-ASSOCIATE
02020                    PERFORM ASSOCIATE-QUOTA-MET
02030                ELSE
02040                    IF LAST-YEARS-SALES-IN LESS THAN
02050                                            SENIOR-SALE-QUOTA
02060                        PERFORM SENIOR-QUOTA-NOT-MET
02070                    ELSE
02080                        PERFORM SENIOR-QUOTA-MET.
02090
02100    WRITE-CLASS-MISSING-LINE.
02110        MOVE SALESPERSON-NUMBER-IN TO
02120            SALESPERSON-NUMBER IN CLASS-MISSING-LINE.
02130        WRITE REPORT-LINE FROM CLASS-MISSING-LINE.
02140
02150    WRITE-CLASS-INVALID-LINE.
02160        MOVE CLASS-IN TO INVALID-CLASS.
02170        MOVE SALESPERSON-NUMBER-IN TO
02180            SALESPERSON-NUMBER IN CLASS-INVALID-LINE.
02190        WRITE REPORT-LINE FROM CLASS-INVALID-LINE.
02200
02210    SET-JUNIOR-PARAMETERS.
02220        MOVE JUNIOR-BREAK-POINT TO SELECTED-BREAK-POINT.
02230        MOVE "JUNIOR"           TO CLASS-TITLE-OUT.
02240        MOVE HIGH-RATE IN QUOTA-MET IN JUNIOR-RATES TO
02250            HIGH-COMMISSION-RATE.
02260        MOVE LOW-RATE  IN QUOTA-MET IN JUNIOR-RATES TO
02270            LOW-COMMISSION-RATE.
02280
02290    ASSOCIATE-QUOTA-NOT-MET.
02300        MOVE ASSOCIATE-BREAK-POINT TO SELECTED-BREAK-POINT.
02310        MOVE "ASSOCIATE"            TO CLASS-TITLE-OUT.
02320        MOVE HIGH-RATE IN QUOTA-NOT-MET IN ASSOCIATE-RATES TO
02330            HIGH-COMMISSION-RATE.
02340        MOVE LOW-RATE  IN QUOTA-NOT-MET IN ASSOCIATE-RATES TO
02350            LOW-COMMISSION-RATE.
02360
02370    ASSOCIATE-QUOTA-MET.
02380        MOVE ASSOCIATE-BREAK-POINT TO SELECTED-BREAK-POINT.
02390        MOVE "ASSOCIATE"            TO CLASS-TITLE-OUT.
02400        MOVE HIGH-RATE IN QUOTA-MET IN ASSOCIATE-RATES TO
02410            HIGH-COMMISSION-RATE.
02420        MOVE LOW-RATE  IN QUOTA-MET IN ASSOCIATE-RATES TO
02430            LOW-COMMISSION-RATE.
02440
02450    SENIOR-QUOTA-NOT-MET.
02460        MOVE SENIOR-BREAK-POINT TO SELECTED-BREAK-POINT.
02470        MOVE "SENIOR"           TO CLASS-TITLE-OUT.
02480        MOVE HIGH-RATE IN QUOTA-NOT-MET IN SENIOR-RATES TO
02490            HIGH-COMMISSION-RATE.
02500        MOVE LOW-RATE  IN QUOTA-NOT-MET IN SENIOR-RATES TO
02510            LOW-COMMISSION-RATE.
```

(continued)

Figure 7.7   (continued)

```
02520
02530   SENIOR-QUOTA-MET.
02540       MOVE SENIOR-BREAK-POINT TO SELECTED-BREAK-POINT.
02550       MOVE "SENIOR"          TO CLASS-TITLE-OUT.
02560       MOVE HIGH-RATE IN QUOTA-MET IN SENIOR-RATES TO
02570           HIGH-COMMISSION-RATE.
02580       MOVE LOW-RATE  IN QUOTA-MET IN SENIOR-RATES TO
02590           LOW-COMMISSION-RATE.
02600
02610   COMPUTE-COMMISSION.
02620       IF CURRENT-SALE-IN GREATER THAN SELECTED-BREAK-POINT
02630           COMPUTE COMMISSION-OUT ROUNDED =
02640               LOW-COMMISSION-RATE * SELECTED-BREAK-POINT +
02650               HIGH-COMMISSION-RATE *
02660                   (CURRENT-SALE-IN - SELECTED-BREAK-POINT)
02670           SIZE ERROR PERFORM SIZE-ERROR-ROUTINE
02680       ELSE
02690           COMPUTE COMMISSION-OUT ROUNDED =
02700               LOW-COMMISSION-RATE * CURRENT-SALE-IN
02710           SIZE ERROR PERFORM SIZE-ERROR-ROUTINE.
02720
02730   SIZE-ERROR-ROUTINE.
02740       MOVE "COMMISSION AMOUNT TOO LARGE" TO DETAIL-ERROR.
02750
02760   WRITE-COMMISSION-LINE.
02770       MOVE SALESPERSON-NUMBER-IN TO SALESPERSON-NUMBER-OUT.
02780       MOVE CURRENT-SALE-IN       TO CURRENT-SALE-OUT.
02790       WRITE REPORT-LINE FROM DETAIL-LINE.
```

You can see the two SIZE ERROR phrases, at lines 02670 and 02710, which have been inserted into COMPUTE statements. If a size error occurs, the paragraph SIZE-ERROR-ROUTINE, at line 02730, is executed.

Program P07-02 was run on the same input data as Program P05-02. Program P07-02 produced the output shown in Figure 7.8.

EXERCISE 6

Write a program to read the same input data used in Exercise 5. The program is to compute a 20 percent Christmas bonus based on the employee's Annual Salary. For each record read, have your program print the employee's Social Security Number, Annual Salary, and computed bonus amount, except if the bonus amount exceeds $99,999.99. If the bonus amount exceeds $99,999.99, print no bonus amount, but instead print the message BONUS AMOUNT SUSPICIOUSLY LARGE. Accumulate the total of the bonus amounts printed and print the total at the end of the report.

Summary

Whenever a program reads input data that have been prepared by people, the program should check the validity of the data before proceeding to process them. The program should check that required data fields are in fact filled in. Different techniques may be used to check for the presence of alphanumeric data and for signed and unsigned integers and fractions. Among the COBOL features that can be used to check one or another kind of field are a level-88 entry with a VALUE SPACES clause, a relation condition where the field is compared with SPACES, and a REDEFINES clause.

The REDEFINES clause permits the programmer to assign more than one name and one PICTURE to a single field. Then the programmer may use any of the names of the field in the Procedure Division, depending on the requirements of each context.

Figure 7.8 Output from Program P07-02.

```
                    COMMISSION REGISTER
                                     DATE   3/31/88


SALES-
PERSON                    SALE
NUMBER      CLASS        AMOUNT      COMMISSION

14756     ASSOCIATE    70,592.43    12,618.49
14758     ASSOCIATE    10,000.00     2,000.00
15008     SENIOR      998,042.99    COMMISSION AMOUNT TOO LARGE
19123     SENIOR       53,765.42    11,129.63
14689     ERROR - CLASS IS MISSING. CLASS SHOULD BE A, B, C, D, E, F, G, OR H.
10089     ASSOCIATE    43,078.65     7,115.73
17665     ASSOCIATE    88,700.99    25,610.30
15699     JUNIOR       30,000.99     3,000.10
15003     SENIOR       50,000.00    10,000.00
12231     JUNIOR      243,679.21    24,367.92
14769     ASSOCIATE   194,453.99    57,336.20
15013     SENIOR        7,821.35     1,564.27
15014     SENIOR       35,962.99    10,788.90
14770     ASSOCIATE    82,356.43    23,706.93
14771     ASSOCIATE     9,369.51     1,873.90
15000     ERROR - CLASS IS Z. CLASS SHOULD BE A, B, C, D, E, F, G, OR H.
15002     SENIOR       19,345.26     3,869.05
15004     SENIOR       57,321.23    12,196.37
12352     ASSOCIATE     6,982.34     1,396.47
15006     SENIOR       39,224.31     7,844.86
14757     ASSOCIATE     1,984.99        99.25
15010     SENIOR       47,365.54    14,209.66
13834     JUNIOR       45,987.99     4,598.80
15011     SENIOR       50,786.54    15,314.62
14764     ERROR - CLASS IS 1. CLASS SHOULD BE A, B, C, D, E, F, G, OR H.
15015     SENIOR       79,875.23    26,950.09
14759     ASSOCIATE    47,839.65     8,067.93
15016     SENIOR       85,359.42    29,143.77
14761     ASSOCIATE     6,439.12       321.96
15012     SENIOR       93,683.42    32,473.37
```

If a program reads a coded field as input data, the program should check that the field contains one of the valid codes. If numeric fields are being read, the program should use the class test to check that the numeric fields contain only numbers. Sometimes there can be disastrous results if a program tries to do numeric comparisons, numeric editing, or arithmetic with fields containing characters other than numbers. Alphabetic fields can be checked for all letters and spaces.

Input data should be checked for reasonableness. That is, the program should check to the extent possible that the values present in input data fields are values that reasonably could be expected to be there. Sometimes it is possible to test individual fields for reasonable values, and sometimes fields must be tested in combinations to see whether their contents are reasonable.

The SIZE ERROR phrase may be used with arithmetic verbs to check for arithmetic overflow. Overflow is considered to occur when a result of arithmetic has more places to the left of the decimal point than the programmer has allowed for in the result field. The COBOL statements following the words SIZE ERROR may include any number of steps but no conditional statements, such as IF, READ, or arithmetic with a SIZE ERROR phrase. The SIZE ERROR processing is terminated with a period or an ELSE. If a size error occurs during execution of an arithmetic statement where the SIZE ERROR phrase is specified, the result field remains unchanged from what it was before the operation. If a size error occurs in a statement where the SIZE ERROR phrase is not specified, the results may be unpredictable.

Fill-in Exercises

1. A VALUE SPACES clause may appear in a level-88 entry only if the field is defined as _____ .

2. To use a VALUE SPACES clause with a numeric field, the field must be _____ .

3. The two classes of data that may be tested for with a class condition test are _____ and _____ .

4. Testing the contents of fields to determine whether the fields contain valid codes or values within an expected range of values is called checking data for _____ .

5. Arithmetic overflow can be tested for with the _____ phrase.

6. Arithmetic overflow occurs if there are too many places in the answer to the _____ of the decimal point.

7. Overflow processing is terminated by a(n) _____ or a(n) _____ .

8. _____ statements are prohibited in a SIZE ERROR phrase.

9. If the ROUNDED option is specified in an arithmetic operation, rounding takes place _____ the field is tested for size error.

10. There must be no processing in the _____ path of a SIZE ERROR test in 1974 standard COBOL.

11. Under certain conditions nonnumeric data in numeric fields will cause a program to _____ execution.

12. Excess places to the right of the decimal point in arithmetic results are _____ if the ROUNDED option is not used.

13. The SIZE ERROR phrase may be used with the verbs _____ , _____ , _____ , _____ , and _____ .

14. Only _____ statements may appear in a SIZE ERROR phrase.

15. Division by _____ always causes a size error.

Review Exercises

1. For each of the three fields defined below, write IF statements to test for the absence of data:
   a. Without using any level-88 entries or REDEFINES clauses, if possible
   b. Using level-88 entries but no REDEFINES clause, if possible
   c. Using level-88 entries and/or REDEFINES clauses

   ```
   I.   05 OFFICE-NAME-IN        PIC X(25).
   II.  05 NUMBER-OF-DAYS-IN     PIC 999.
   III. 05 PURCHASE-IN           PIC 9(4)V99.
   ```

2. Write an IF statement that will determine whether the field PURCHASE-IN, described in Review Exercise 1, contains all numbers, and execute the True path if it does not.

3. Given the following field:

```
05 SALE-AMOUNT-IN          PIC 999V99,
```

Write a level-88 entry and an IF statement that will execute the True path if the contents of the field SALE-AMOUNT-IN are outside the reasonable range of $5 through $750.

4. Given the following field:

```
05 SKILL-CODE              PIC X,
```

Write level-88 entries giving suitable names to the following codes for the different skills: machinist, M; carpenter, C; press operator, P; riveter, R. Also write a level-88 entry giving a name to a missing code. Write IF statements to check for the absence of data in the field and for an invalid code.

5. Write a program to read data in the following format:

Positions	Field
1−3	Customer Number
4−6	Store Number
7−12	Salesperson Number
13−19	Sale Amount (to two decimal places)
20−80	spaces

Have the program check the validity of the input as follows:

a. Store Number numeric
b. Salesperson Number numeric
c. Customer Number present
d. Customer Number numeric
e. Sale Amount numeric
f. Sale Amount not less than $10 nor greater than $50,000

Have your program list the contents of each error-free record. Have your program accumulate the Sale Amounts from the error-free records and print the total at the end of the report. Have your program check for all five types of errors in each record. If more than one error is found in a record, have your program print an error line for each error.

6. Write a program to read input data in the following format:

Positions	Field
1−7	Customer Number
8−15	Part Number
16−22	spaces
23−25	Quantity
26−31	Unit Price (in dollars and cents)
26−29	Unit Price dollars
30−31	Unit Price cents
32−35	Handling Charge (in dollars and cents)
32−33	Handling Charge dollars
34−35	Handling Charge cents
35−80	spaces

Have your program check that all Quantity and all Unit Price fields contain only numbers. If a field is found not to contain only numbers, a suitable error line is to be printed. For each valid record have your program print the Customer Number, Part Number, Quantity, Unit Price, and a merchandise amount (the Quantity times the Unit Price), except if the merchandise amount is greater than 999,999.99. If the merchandise amount is greater than 999,999.99, have your program print only the Customer Number, Part Number, Quantity, Unit Price, and a message MERCHANDISE AMOUNT SUSPICIOUSLY LARGE. At the end of the report, have your program print the total of the valid merchandise amounts.

Project

Modify your solution to the project in Chapter 6, page 187, to include checking the input data for validity before processing. Make the following checks on each input record:

a.   Starting Loan Amount numeric
b.   Monthly Payment numeric
c.   Month of First Payment numeric
d.   Month of First Payment within the range 1 through 12
e.   Year of First Payment numeric
f.   Year of First Payment within the range 1960 through 2011
g.   Annual Interest Rate numeric
h.   Annual Interest Rate within the range .04 through .23

Have your program check each input record for all possible errors. If one error is found in an input record, have your program print an error message and the entire input record on a page by themselves. If more than one error is found in the record, print an additional error message for each error on the same page as the first. Design your error messages before you begin coding.

Report Writer

Here are the key points you should learn from this chapter:

1. The concept of automatic generation of coding for report output
2. The features of the COBOL Report Writer
3. How to use Report Writer to produce a variety of reports
4. How to use declaratives in connection with Report Writer

Key words to recognize and learn:

Report Writer	PAGE
declarative	FIRST DETAIL
Report Section	absolute LINE NUMBER clause
REPORT IS	relative LINE NUMBER clause
report name	SUM
RD	sum counter
report description entry	LAST DETAIL
report group	FOOTING
TYPE	PAGE-COUNTER
DETAIL	LINE-COUNTER
REPORT HEADING	GROUP INDICATE
PAGE HEADING	NEXT GROUP
CONTROL FOOTING	ALL
PAGE FOOTING	declarative section
REPORT FOOTING	NEXT PAGE
LINE	DECLARATIVES
PLUS	USE
COLUMN	BEFORE REPORTING
SOURCE	SUPPRESS
INITIATE	PRINT-SWITCH
GENERATE	END
TERMINATE	CONTROL HEADING
CONTROL	UPON
FINAL	RESET ON

The **Report Writer** feature of COBOL makes programming for report output easier. The Report Writer provides, automatically, coding that otherwise would have to be written step by step by the programmer. With Report Writer, the programmer can describe certain characteristics that the output report is to have, and Report Writer generates the coding needed to make the report look that way. For example, Report Writer can provide all the page overflow coding needed in a program. The programmer need only tell Report Writer how big the page is, and Report Writer provides coding that will count lines as they print, test for page overflow, and skip to a new page and print headings when necessary. Report Writer can also provide coding that will take totals. If a total line is to print at the end of a report, the programmer need not code any of the totaling logic but just tell Report Writer which fields are to be totaled, and all the necessary coding will be provided automatically.

Report Writer also contains control break logic. If control breaks are needed on a report, the programmer need only say what the control fields are, and Report Writer provides coding to test for control breaks and print the appropriate total lines.

Another feature of Report Writer that makes programming easier is the way that output line formats are specified in Report Writer. Just tell Report Writer in which print positions each field is to print, and it provides all the necessary coding. There is no need to count FILLER spaces.

There have been many schemes to produce automatically programs that print reports. But Report Writer is more than a means of producing reports. Report Writer is the printing component of the whole powerful COBOL language. In using Report Writer, the programmer does not give up any of the capabilities of COBOL; the programmer still has command over all the output editing features, the nested IF, and complex conditions. Thus Report Writer should be used in any COBOL program that produces printed output. No matter what else the program might be doing, no matter how large the program is or how involved the logic, and no matter what volume of printed output is produced by the program, Report Writer should handle the formatting and printing of all lines. We refrain from using Report Writer in subsequent chapters of this book because it is not always available in the COBOL systems in use at some schools.

Even though Report Writer is extremely flexible and powerful, it sometimes happens that the programmer needs one or more features that Report Writer does not contain. Such features can be hand-coded using a **declarative** section, as will be shown later in the chapter.

The Report Section and Report Groups

The first program we will write using Report Writer reads input records and prints the contents of each one, reformatted, on one line. There are no page or column headings. Program P08-01 uses input records in the following format:

Positions	Field
1 – 9	Social Security Number
10 – 14	Employee Number
15 – 21	Annual Salary (in dollars and cents)
22 – 46	Employee Name
47 – 80	spaces

Figure 8.1   Output format for Program P08-01.

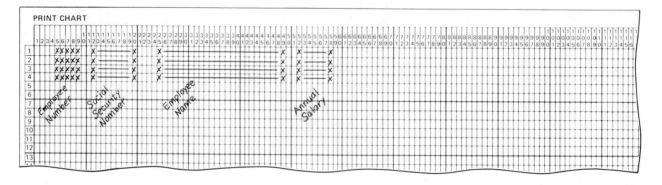

Figure 8.2 Program P08-01.

```
CB1 RELEASE 2.4                              IBM OS/VS COBOL   JULY  1, 1982

                    22.50.53        MAR 31,1988

00010  IDENTIFICATION DIVISION.
00020  PROGRAM-ID.  P08-01.
00030 *AUTHOR.  WENDEL KELLER.
00040 *
00050 *    THIS PROGRAM READS INPUT RECORDS
00060 *    PRINTS THE CONTENTS OF EACH RECORD ON ONE LINE.
00070 *
00080 *********************************************************************
00090
00100  ENVIRONMENT DIVISION.
00110  CONFIGURATION SECTION.
00120  SOURCE-COMPUTER.  IBM-370.
00130  OBJECT-COMPUTER.  IBM-370.
00140
00150  INPUT-OUTPUT SECTION.
00160  FILE-CONTROL.
00170      SELECT EMPLOYEE-DATA-FILE-IN    ASSIGN TO INFILE.
00180      SELECT EMPLOYEE-DATA-FILE-OUT   ASSIGN TO PRINTER.
00190
00200 *********************************************************************
00210
00220  DATA DIVISION.
00230  FILE SECTION.
00240  FD  EMPLOYEE-DATA-FILE-IN
00250      LABEL RECORDS ARE OMITTED
00260      RECORD CONTAINS 80 CHARACTERS.
00270
00280  01  EMPLOYEE-DATA-RECORD-IN.
00290      05   SOCIAL-SECURITY-NUMBER-IN   PIC X(9).
00300      05   EMPLOYEE-NUMBER-IN          PIC X(5).
00310      05   ANNUAL-SALARY-IN            PIC X(7).
00320      05   EMPLOYEE-NAME-IN            PIC X(25).
00330      05   FILLER                      PIC X(34).
00340
00350  FD  EMPLOYEE-DATA-FILE-OUT
00360      LABEL RECORDS ARE OMITTED
00370      REPORT IS EMPLOYEE-REPORT.
00380
00390  WORKING-STORAGE SECTION.
00400  01  MORE-INPUT                       PIC X        VALUE "Y".
00410
00420  REPORT SECTION.
00430  RD  EMPLOYEE-REPORT.
00440
```

(continued)

Program P08-01 produces output in the format shown in Figure 8.1. The program is shown in Figure 8.2.

In the Data Division we see the **Report Section,** beginning at line 00420. The Report Section must appear whenever Report Writer is used, and it must be the last section in the Data Division. In the File Section the output file FD entry, line 00350, has no level-01 entry associated with it. Instead, the **REPORT IS** clause in the FD entry tells COBOL that Report Writer will be writing out a report on this file. The REPORT IS clause gives a name to the report that is being produced. In this program the **report name** is EMPLOYEE-REPORT. The rules for making up report names are the same as for making up file names.

Every report name given in the File Section must appear in the Report Section as part of an **RD** entry **(report description entry).** Within the RD entry and the level numbers that follow it, many characteristics of the report are described. Report Writer uses these descriptions of the report to create the necessary coding.

Each level-01 entry following the RD entry describes a different type of line, or group of related lines, that may appear on the report. The line or lines appearing under a level-01 entry is called a **report group.** In Program P08-01 the level-01

Figure 8.2 (continued)

```
00450  01  REPORT-LINE
00460      TYPE DETAIL
00470      LINE PLUS 1.
00480      05  COLUMN 5     PIC X(5)     SOURCE EMPLOYEE-NUMBER-IN.
00490      05  COLUMN 12    PIC X(9)     SOURCE SOCIAL-SECURITY-NUMBER-IN.
00500      05  COLUMN 25    PIC X(25)    SOURCE EMPLOYEE-NAME-IN.
00510      05  COLUMN 52    PIC X(7)     SOURCE ANNUAL-SALARY-IN.
00520
00530  *****/*****************************************************************
00540
00550  PROCEDURE DIVISION.
00560  CONTROL-PARAGRAPH.
00570      PERFORM INITIALIZATION.
00580      PERFORM MAIN-PROCESS UNTIL MORE-INPUT IS EQUAL TO "N".
00590      PERFORM TERMINATION.
00600      STOP RUN.
00610
00620  INITIALIZATION.
00630      OPEN INPUT   EMPLOYEE-DATA-FILE-IN,
00640           OUTPUT  EMPLOYEE-DATA-FILE-OUT.
00650      INITIATE EMPLOYEE-REPORT.
00660      PERFORM READ-A-RECORD.
00670
00680  MAIN-PROCESS.
00690      GENERATE REPORT-LINE.
00700      PERFORM READ-A-RECORD.
00710
00720  TERMINATION.
00730      TERMINATE EMPLOYEE-REPORT.
00740      CLOSE EMPLOYEE-DATA-FILE-IN,
00750            EMPLOYEE-DATA-FILE-OUT.
00760
00770  READ-A-RECORD.
00780      READ EMPLOYEE-DATA-FILE-IN
00790          AT END
00800              MOVE "N" TO MORE-INPUT.
```

entry, shown in line 00450, describes a report group called REPORT-LINE. In this case the report group consists of only one line. The rules for making up report group names are the same as for making up data names.

The report group REPORT-LINE is shown as **TYPE DETAIL,** meaning that this is a detail line on the report. Some other TYPEs of report groups that may be described are

1. **REPORT HEADING,** one or more lines to print only once on the report at the beginning
2. **PAGE HEADING,** one or more lines to print at the top of every page
3. **CONTROL FOOTING,** one or more lines to print after a control break has been detected
4. **PAGE FOOTING,** one or more lines to print at the bottom of each page before skipping to a new page
5. **REPORT FOOTING,** one or more lines to print at the end of the report

The clause **LINE PLUS** 1, at line 00470, tells Report Writer that the detail lines on this report are to be single-spaced. The clause LINE PLUS 1 means that each detail line is to be printed on whatever LINE the previous one was printed, PLUS 1. By one means or another, you always must tell Report Writer explicitly where to put every line it prints.

We come now to the level-05 entries, beginning with line 00480, where we describe the individual fields that make up REPORT-LINE. Using the **COLUMN** clause, we tell Report Writer the print position where each field on the line begins. The column numbers shown in these COLUMN clauses were taken directly from the print chart in Figure 8.1. There is no need for FILLER entries or for counting the number of blanks between fields.

The **SOURCE** clause tells Report Writer where the data come from in the Data Division to fill each field. The SOURCE of a print field may be any identifier anywhere in the File Section or Working Storage Section or certain fields in the Report Section.

The Procedure Division introduces three new verbs. The **INITIATE** statement, line 00650, must be issued to initialize the report file. It must be issued after the output file has been OPENed in the usual way and before a **GENERATE** verb is issued for that report. The INITIATE statement must include the report name as it appears in the RD entry. The GENERATE verb may be used to print a report group. In this case we have only the one report group, REPORT-LINE. The statement GENERATE REPORT-LINE, at line 00690, does everything: It blanks the output areas that should be blank, moves data from the input area to the print line, single-spaces the paper, and writes a line.

After the complete report is written, a **TERMINATE** statement must be issued for the report name, as shown in line 00730. This must be done before the file is CLOSEd. Program P08-01 was run with the input data shown in Figure 8.3 and produced the output shown in Figure 8.4.

Figure 8.3 Input to Program P08-01.

```
--------------------------------------------------------------------------------
          1         2         3         4         5         6         7         8
12345678901234567890123456789012345678901234567890123456789012345678901234567890
--------------------------------------------------------------------------------
10004000210503 5000000MORALES, LUIS
101850005108904651000JACOBSON, MRS. NELLIE
201110008112774302000GREENWOOD, JAMES
209560011116643953000COSTELLO, JOSEPH S.
301810014120513604000REITER, D.
304870017124383255000MARRA, DITTA E.
401710020128252906000LIPKE, VINCENT R.
407390023132122557000KUGLER, CHARLES
502070026135992208000JAVIER, CARLOS
505680029139861859000GOODMAN, ISAAC
604910032143731510000FELDSOTT, MS. SALLY
608250035147601161000BUXBAUM, ROBERT
703100038151470812000DUMAY, MRS. MARY
708020041155340463000SMITH, R.
803220044159210114000VINCENTE, MATTHEW J.
901050047163084235000THOMAS, THOMAS T.
```

Figure 8.4 Output from Program P08-01.

```
10503   100040002   MORALES, LUIS          5000000
10890   101850005   JACOBSON, MRS. NELLIE  4651000
11277   201110008   GREENWOOD, JAMES       4302000
11664   209560011   COSTELLO, JOSEPH S.    3953000
12051   301810014   REITER, D.             3604000
12438   304870017   MARRA, DITTA E.        3255000
12825   401710020   LIPKE, VINCENT R.      2906000
13212   407390023   KUGLER, CHARLES        2557000
13599   502070026   JAVIER, CARLOS         2208000
13986   505680029   GOODMAN, ISAAC         1859000
14373   604910032   FELDSOTT, MS. SALLY    1510000
14760   608250035   BUXBAUM, ROBERT        1161000
15147   703100038   DUMAY, MRS. MARY       0812000
15534   708020041   SMITH, R.              0463000
15921   803220044   VINCENTE, MATTHEW J.   0114000
16308   901050047   THOMAS, THOMAS T.      4235000
```

EXERCISE 1

Using Report Writer, write a program to read and process input records in the following format:

Positions	Field
1 – 20	Company Name
21 – 35	Street Address
36 – 50	City and State
51 – 65	Employee Name
66 – 80	Employee Title

Have your program print the contents of each record on one line in the format shown in Figure 8.E1.

Figure 8.E1   Output format for Exercise 1.

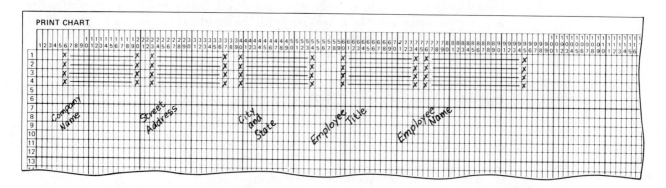

A Final Total Using Report Writer

We will now do a program that shows how Report Writer handles page and column headings, arithmetic manipulation of data before they are printed on a detail line, and totaling. Program P08-02 reads input records in the following format:

Positions	Field
1 – 7	Customer Number
8 – 15	Part Number
16 – 22	spaces
23 – 25	Quantity
26 – 31	Unit Price (in dollars and cents)
26 – 29	Unit Price dollars
30 – 31	Unit Price cents
32 – 35	Handling Charge (in dollars and cents)
32 – 33	Handling Charge dollars
34 – 35	Handling Charge cents
35 – 80	spaces

Each input record represents the purchase of some parts by a customer. The record shows the quantity purchased, the price per unit, and a handling charge for the order. The program is to read each record and compute the cost of the merchandise (by multiplying the Quantity by the Unit Price) and a tax at 7 percent of the merchandise amount. Then the program is to add together the merchandise amount, the tax, and the handling charge to arrive at a total for the order. The information for each order is to be printed on one line as shown in Figure 8.5. At the end of the report, the program is to print the total of all the merchandise amounts for all the orders, the totals of all the tax and handling charge amounts, and a grand total of all the order totals, as shown in Figure 8.5. The program is also to print a report title and column headings as shown in Figure 8.5.

Program P08-02 will handle an empty input file by printing the report title, the column headings, the words "No input data," and a total line with all zero totals. Later you will see how to suppress the printing of column headings and total lines by using declarative sections. Program P08-02 is shown in Figure 8.6.

Figure 8.5 Output format for Program P08-02.

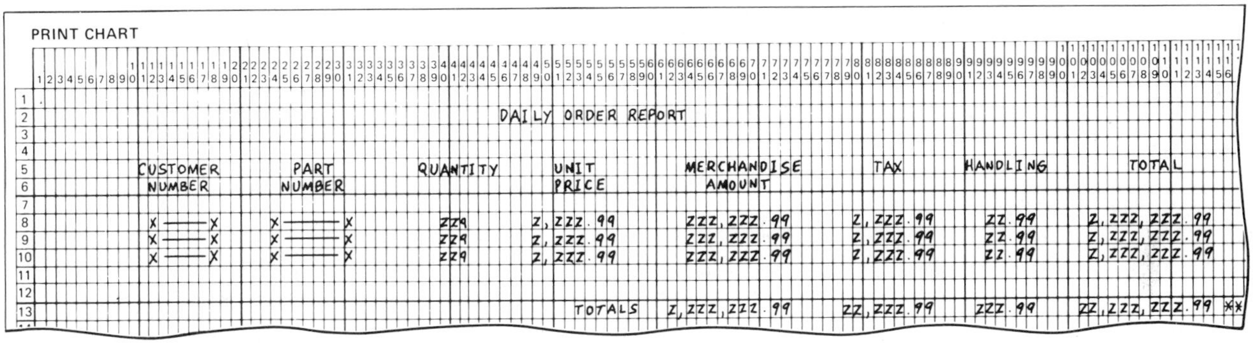

Figure 8.6 Program P08-02.

```
CB1 RELEASE 2.4                              IBM OS/VS COBOL  JULY  1, 1982


                       22.58.40        MAR 31,1988


     00010   IDENTIFICATION DIVISION.
     00020   PROGRAM-ID.  P08-02.
     00030  *AUTHOR.  WENDEL KELLER.
     00040  *
     00050  *    THIS PROGRAM PRINTS A REPORT TITLE, COLUMN HEADINGS,
     00060  *    DETAIL LINES, AND A FINAL TOTAL LINE.
     00070  *
     00080  ******************************************************************
     00090
     00100   ENVIRONMENT DIVISION.
     00110   CONFIGURATION SECTION.
     00120   SOURCE-COMPUTER.  IBM-370.
     00130   OBJECT-COMPUTER.  IBM-370.
     00140
     00150   INPUT-OUTPUT SECTION.
     00160   FILE-CONTROL.
     00170       SELECT ORDER-FILE-IN          ASSIGN TO INFILE.
     00180       SELECT ORDER-REPORT-FILE-OUT  ASSIGN TO PRINTER.
     00190
     00200  ******************************************************************
     00210
     00220   DATA DIVISION.
     00230   FILE SECTION.
     00240   FD  ORDER-FILE-IN
     00250       LABEL RECORDS ARE OMITTED.
     00260
```

(continued)

Figure 8.6   (continued)

```
00270    01    ORDER-RECORD-IN.
00280          05    CUSTOMER-NUMBER-IN       PIC  X(7).
00290          05    PART-NUMBER-IN           PIC  X(8).
00300          05    FILLER                   PIC  X(7).
00310          05    QUANTITY-IN              PIC  999.
00320          05    UNIT-PRICE-IN            PIC  9(4)V99.
00330          05    HANDLING-IN              PIC  99V99.
00340          05    FILLER                   PIC  X(45).
00350
00360    FD   ORDER-REPORT-FILE-OUT
00370         LABEL RECORDS ARE OMITTED
00380         REPORT IS DAILY-ORDER-REPORT.
00390
00400    WORKING-STORAGE SECTION.
00410    01   MORE-INPUT                      PIC  X           VALUE "Y".
00420    01   TAX-RATE                        PIC  V99         VALUE .07.
00430    01   MERCHANDISE-AMOUNT-W            PIC  9(6)V99.
00440    01   TAX-W                           PIC  9(4)V99.
00450    01   ORDER-TOTAL-W                   PIC  9(7)V99.
00460
00470    REPORT SECTION.
00480    RD   DAILY-ORDER-REPORT
00490         CONTROL FINAL
00500         PAGE 50 LINES
00510         FIRST DETAIL 8.
00520
00530    01   TYPE REPORT HEADING
00540         LINE 2.
00550         05    COLUMN 46        PIC X(18)    VALUE "DAILY ORDER REPORT".
00560
00570    01   TYPE PAGE HEADING.
00580         05    LINE 5.
00590               10    COLUMN 11    PIC X(8)       VALUE "CUSTOMER".
00600               10    COLUMN 26    PIC X(4)       VALUE "PART".
00610               10    COLUMN 38    PIC X(8)       VALUE "QUANTITY".
00620               10    COLUMN 51    PIC X(4)       VALUE "UNIT".
00630               10    COLUMN 64    PIC X(11)      VALUE "MERCHANDISE".
00640               10    COLUMN 82    PIC XXX        VALUE "TAX".
00650               10    COLUMN 91    PIC X(8)       VALUE "HANDLING".
00660               10    COLUMN 107   PIC X(5)       VALUE "TOTAL".
00670         05    LINE 6.
00680               10    COLUMN 12    PIC X(6)       VALUE "NUMBER".
00690               10    COLUMN 25    PIC X(6)       VALUE "NUMBER".
00700               10    COLUMN 51    PIC X(5)       VALUE "PRICE".
00710               10    COLUMN 66    PIC X(6)       VALUE "AMOUNT".
00720
```

The Working Storage Section, beginning on line 00400, contains fields that we will need for the results of arithmetic. The RD entry, line 00480, has a few clauses that we are seeing for the first time. The **CONTROL** clause tells Report Writer that **FINAL** totals are to be printed. In a later program we will see how totals for minor, intermediate, and major control breaks are indicated in the CONTROL clause. The **PAGE** clause is required if you want to control the vertical spacing of lines on the page. From the print chart in Figure 8.5, you can see that the first detail line of the report is to print on line 8 of the page, and we indicate this to Report Writer by saying **FIRST DETAIL** 8. We are also required to tell Report Writer how many lines can fit on a page, and here we arbitrarily said 50.

For this report we have five report groups: a REPORT HEADING group that consists of one line (the report title); a PAGE HEADING group that consists of two lines (the column headings); a DETAIL group of one line to handle the normal detail printing shown on the print chart; a DETAIL group consisting of one line containing the words "No input data"; and a FINAL total line. So we need five level-01 entries, one for each report group. The first level-01 entry is for the REPORT HEADING group and is indicated by the clause TYPE REPORT HEADING, line 00530. The print chart shows that the REPORT HEADING is to print on line 2 of the page, so that line number is indicated in the clause LINE 2. You can see that a VALUE clause is used in the level-05 entry when constant information is to print. Whenever you have the word LINE followed by an integer, you are using

```
00730  01   DETAIL-LINE
00740       TYPE DETAIL
00750       LINE PLUS 1.
00760       05   COLUMN 12     PIC X(7)         SOURCE CUSTOMER-NUMBER-IN.
00770       05   COLUMN 24     PIC X(8)         SOURCE PART-NUMBER-IN.
00780       05   COLUMN 40     PIC ZZ9          SOURCE QUANTITY-IN.
00790       05   COLUMN 49     PIC Z,ZZZ.99     SOURCE UNIT-PRICE-IN.
00800       05   COLUMN 64     PIC ZZZ,ZZZ.99
00810                          SOURCE MERCHANDISE-AMOUNT-W.
00820       05   COLUMN 80     PIC Z,ZZZ.99     SOURCE TAX-W.
00830       05   COLUMN 93     PIC ZZ.99        SOURCE HANDLING-IN.
00840       05   COLUMN 103    PIC Z,ZZZ,ZZZ.99
00850                          SOURCE ORDER-TOTAL-W.
00860
00870  01   NO-INPUT-DATA
00880       TYPE DETAIL
00890       LINE 8.
00900       05   COLUMN 49     PIC X(13)        VALUE "NO INPUT DATA".
00910
00920  01   TYPE CONTROL FOOTING FINAL
00930       LINE PLUS 3.
00940       05   COLUMN 53     PIC X(6)         VALUE "TOTALS".
00950       05   COLUMN 62     PIC Z,ZZZ,ZZZ.99
00960                          SUM MERCHANDISE-AMOUNT-W.
00970       05   COLUMN 79     PIC ZZ,ZZZ.99    SUM TAX-W.
00980       05   COLUMN 92     PIC ZZZ.99       SUM HANDLING-IN.
00990       05   COLUMN 102    PIC ZZ,ZZZ,ZZZ.99 SUM ORDER-TOTAL-W.
01000       05   COLUMN 116    PIC XX           VALUE "**".
01010
```

(continued)

what is called an **absolute LINE NUMBER clause.** When you use the words LINE PLUS followed by an integer, you are using a **relative LINE NUMBER clause.**

The next level-01 entry is for the column headings, and is indicated by the clause TYPE PAGE HEADING, line 00570. The print chart shows that the two lines that make up the PAGE HEADING are to print on lines 5 and 6 of the page, and so those line numbers are indicated in the level-05 entries, lines 00580 and 00670. The level-10 entries describe the individual fields that make up the two column-heading lines.

Whenever there is only one line in a report group, the entries that describe the fields on the line may have any level number in the range 02 – 49. When there is more than one line in a group and some line has only one field, that line and its field may be described in a single entry that has a level number in the range 02 – 49. Otherwise the level number of an entry immediately following a level-01 entry can be any number in the range 02 – 48; in our program it is 05. Then the entries that describe the fields in each line can have level numbers in the range 03 – 49; in our program they have level number 10.

The normal detail line in the program, called DETAIL-LINE and described in line 00730, is similar to the one in Program P08-01. But here we have some output editing. Note that the PICTUREs included in these descriptions are PICTUREs of the output fields as they are to print. Any PICTURE features may be used in the Report Section, including floating signs, check protection, and insertion, to obtain any kind of output editing.

The next level-01 entry, at line 00870, describes the DETAIL line that is to print when there are no input data. The clause LINE 8 says that this line is to print on LINE 8 of the page. You will see how this DETAIL line is used when we look at the Procedure Division.

The last level-01 entry, at line 00920, describes the final total line. Since Report Writer considers final total a control break, the final total line must be described as CONTROL FOOTING FINAL. The clause LINE PLUS 3 will cause the final total line to be triple-spaced down from the last detail line on the report.

In the FINAL total line we see the use of the **SUM** clause, as in line 00960, which tells Report Writer that a particular field is to be printed as the SUM of the

Figure 8.6   (continued)

```
01020  ********************************************************************
01030
01040  PROCEDURE DIVISION.
01050  CONTROL-PARAGRAPH.
01060      PERFORM INITIALIZATION.
01070      PERFORM MAIN-PROCESS UNTIL MORE-INPUT IS EQUAL TO "N".
01080      PERFORM TERMINATION.
01090      STOP RUN.
01100
01110  INITIALIZATION.
01120      OPEN INPUT  ORDER-FILE-IN,
01130          OUTPUT ORDER-REPORT-FILE-OUT.
01140      INITIATE DAILY-ORDER-REPORT.
01150      PERFORM READ-A-RECORD.
01160      IF MORE-INPUT IS EQUAL TO "N"
01170          GENERATE NO-INPUT-DATA.
01180
01190  MAIN-PROCESS.
01200      MULTIPLY QUANTITY-IN BY UNIT-PRICE-IN
01210              GIVING MERCHANDISE-AMOUNT-W.
01220      MULTIPLY MERCHANDISE-AMOUNT-W BY TAX-RATE
01230              GIVING TAX-W ROUNDED.
01240      ADD MERCHANDISE-AMOUNT-W,
01250          TAX-W,
01260          HANDLING-IN
01270              GIVING ORDER-TOTAL-W.
01280      GENERATE DETAIL-LINE.
01290      PERFORM READ-A-RECORD.
01300
01310  TERMINATION.
01320      TERMINATE DAILY-ORDER-REPORT.
01330      CLOSE ORDER-FILE-IN,
01340          ORDER-REPORT-FILE-OUT.
01350
01360  READ-A-RECORD.
01370      READ ORDER-FILE-IN
01380          AT END
01390              MOVE "N" TO MORE-INPUT.
```

values of the field named. For example, the clause SUM MERCHANDISE-AMOUNT-W will cause Report Writer to set up a field called a **sum counter** to accumulate the total of the MERCHANDISE-AMOUNT-W amounts. Whenever a GENERATE DETAIL-LINE statement is executed, Report Writer adds the value of MERCHANDISE-AMOUNT-W into the sum counter. The sum counter is defined by Report Writer as purely numeric. The PICTURE given in the level-05 entry with the clause SUM MERCHANDISE-AMOUNT-W is the PICTURE that Report Writer uses to edit the sum when it is finally printed. The SUM clause may appear only in a CONTROL FOOTING report group.

The Procedure Division of this program has very little that is new. The INITIALIZATION paragraph, starting at line 01110, contains the usual initialization, and also the processing needed to handle an empty input file. The IF statement at line 01160 does it. The MAIN-PROCESS routine, starting at line 01190, shows that any regular COBOL processing may be done on an input record. In this case some arithmetic is done, and the results are assigned to working storage fields, which are then used as SOURCE fields in the Report Section.

Notice that nowhere in the Procedure Division do we tell Report Writer when to print the REPORT HEADING group, the PAGE HEADING group, or the FINAL total line, nor do we code any of the logic for accumulating the sums or printing them. Report Writer automatically prints the REPORT HEADING and the PAGE HEADING when we give the first GENERATE statement. It accumulates SUMs with the execution of each GENERATE statement. And it automatically prints the FINAL total line when we give the TERMINATE statement.

Since we never had to refer to the REPORT HEADING, PAGE HEADING, or FINAL total line groups by name, their level-01 entries were written without names. The only groups that needed names were the DETAIL groups, so that they could be referred to in GENERATE statements. A level-01 entry needs a name only if the name is referred to in a GENERATE statement, in a declarative section, or in an entry elsewhere in the Report Section.

Program P08-02 was run first on the input data shown in Figure 8.7 and produced the output shown in Figure 8.8. Then it was run with an empty input file and produced the output shown in Figure 8.9.

Figure 8.7 Input to Program P08-02.

```
-----------------------------------------------------------------------
         1         2         3         4         5         6         7         8
12345678901234567890123456789012345678901234567890123456789012345678901234567890
-----------------------------------------------------------------------
ABC1234F2365-09        9000000100005
09G8239836-7YT7        8000010500050
ADGH784091AN-07        0500250000500
967547323S-1287        0067000295000
```

Figure 8.8 Output from Program P08-02.

DAILY ORDER REPORT

CUSTOMER NUMBER	PART NUMBER	QUANTITY	UNIT PRICE	MERCHANDISE AMOUNT	TAX	HANDLING	TOTAL
ABC1234	F2365-09	900	.10	90.00	6.30	.05	96.35
09G8239	836-7YT7	800	10.50	8,400.00	588.00	.50	8,988.50
ADGH784	091AN-07	50	250.00	12,500.00	875.00	5.00	13,380.00
9675473	23S-1287	6	7,000.29	42,001.74	2,940.12	50.00	44,991.86
			TOTALS	62,991.74	4,409.42	55.55	67,456.71 **

Figure 8.9 Output produced when Program P08-02 was run with an empty input file.

DAILY ORDER REPORT

CUSTOMER NUMBER	PART NUMBER	QUANTITY	UNIT PRICE	MERCHANDISE AMOUNT	TAX	HANDLING	TOTAL
			NO INPUT DATA				
			TOTALS	.00	.00	.00	.00 **

EXERCISE 2

Write a program to read input records in the following format:

Positions	Field
1 – 5	Account Number
6 – 10	spaces
11 – 17	Amount (to two decimal places)
11 – 15	Amount dollars
16 – 17	Amount cents
18 – 80	spaces

Have your program compute a 4 percent discount on the amount shown in each record and a net amount (the original amount minus the discount). For each record read, have your program print the Account Number, the Amount, the computed discount, and the computed net amount. At the end of the report, have your program print a total line showing the sum of all the input Amounts, the sum of all the discount amounts, and the sum of the net amounts.

Have your program print a report title "Discount Report" and column headings "Account Number," "Amount," "Discount," and "Net Amount." Use a print chart to plan the spacing of the output; the placement of decimal points and commas; zero suppression; the alignment of the report title, the column headings, and the columns of data; and the format of the total line.

Multiple Control Breaks Using Report Writer

Program P08-03 has a report title, column headings, three levels of control breaks, the date, page overflow, page numbering, and group indication of the control fields. Program P08-03 uses input data in the following format:

Positions	Field
1 – 3	Store Number
4 – 6	Salesperson Number
7 – 12	Customer Number
13 – 19	Sale Amount (to two decimal places)
20 – 80	spaces

The program produces output in the format shown in Figure 8.10. The program was run using the input data shown in Figure 8.11, and produced the output shown in Figure 8.12.

Figure 8.10 Output format for Program P08-03.

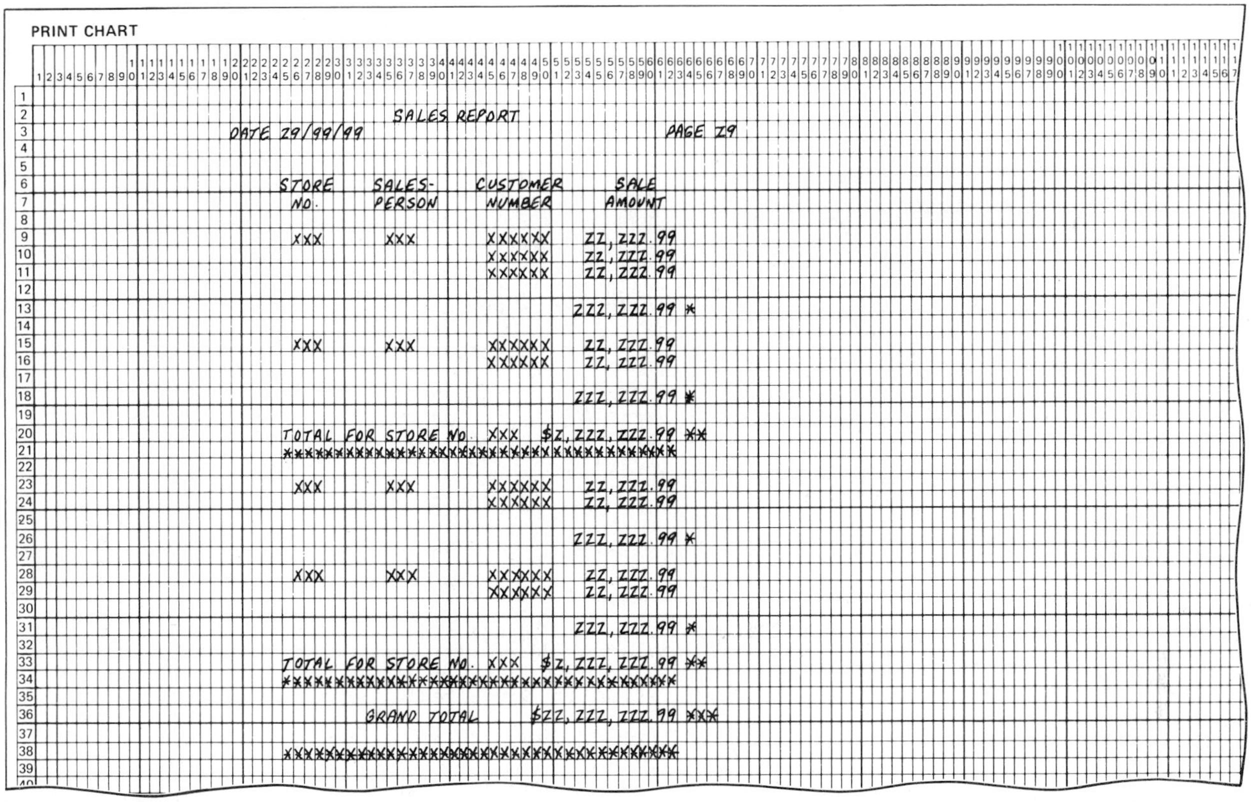

Figure 8.11 Input to Program P08-03.

```
          1         2         3         4         5         6         7         8
 1234567890123456789012345678901234567890123456789012345678901234567890123456789 0
-------------------------------------------------------------------------------
0101010030011234 56
0101010070020002 24
0101010390048439 20
0101010460058448 48
0101010530060012 34
0101010600069494 93
0101010670074000 03
0101020742125454 99
0101020810120000 33
0101020880135849 58
0101020950150393 90
0101030032340303 03
0200110075679999 99
0200110114540456 00
0200110233458333 33
0202220273454343 43
0202220315679903 30
0202220350010034 21
0202660399034539 87
0202660438545858 30
0301930599325858 54
0301930634193949 49
0400450673330000 00
0400450713235959 50
0404030483993921 47
0404030543920000 00
0404120601119999 99
0460120135380000 00
0460120175210690 78
0460120215041381 56
0460120254872072 34
0460120294702763 12
0460280334533453 90
0460280374364144 68
0460280414194835 46
```

Figure 8.12   Output from Program P08-03.

```
                          SALES REPORT
DATE   4/03/88                                        PAGE   1


          STORE      SALES-      CUSTOMER      SALE
          NO.        PERSON      NUMBER        AMOUNT

          010        101         003001        1,234.56
                                 007002             2.24
                                 039004        8,439.20
                                 046005        8,448.48
                                 053006            12.34
                                 060006        9,494.93
                                 067007        4,000.03

                                              31,631.78 *

          010        102         074212        5,454.99
                                 081012             .33
                                 088013        5,849.58
                                 095015          393.90

                                              11,698.80 *

          010        103         003234          303.03

                                                 303.03 *

          TOTAL FOR STORE NO. 010   $   43,633.61 **
          ************************************

          020        011         007567        9,999.99
                                 011454          456.00
                                 023345        8,333.33

                                              18,789.32 *

          020        222         027345        4,343.43


DATE   4/03/88                                        PAGE   2


          STORE      SALES-      CUSTOMER      SALE
          NO.        PERSON      NUMBER        AMOUNT

          020        222         031567        9,903.30
                                 035001            34.21

                                              14,280.94 *

          020        266         039903        4,539.87
                                 043854        5,858.30

                                              10,398.17 *

          TOTAL FOR STORE NO. 020   $   43,468.43 **
          ************************************

          030        193         059932        5,858.54
                                 063419        3,949.49

                                               9,808.03 *

          TOTAL FOR STORE NO. 030   $    9,808.03 **
          ************************************

          040        045         067333             .00
                                 071323        5,959.50

                                               5,959.50 *

          040        403         048399        3,921.47
                                 054392             .00

                                               3,921.47 *
```

```
DATE   4/03/88                              PAGE   3


        STORE     SALES-      CUSTOMER       SALE
        NO.       PERSON      NUMBER        AMOUNT

        040        412        060111        9,999.99

                                            9,999.99 *

   TOTAL FOR STORE NO. 040  $    19,880.96 **
   ************************************

        046        012        013538             .00
                              017521          690.78
                              021504        1,381.56
                              025487        2,072.34
                              029470        2,763.12

                                            6,907.80 *

        046        028        033453        3,453.90
                              037436        4,144.68
                              041419        4,835.46

                                           12,434.04 *

   TOTAL FOR STORE NO. 046  $    19,341.84 **
   ************************************

             GRAND TOTAL     $   136,132.87 ***

   ************************************
```

Program P08-03 is shown in Figure 8.13. In the Working Storage Section the field TODAYS-DATE, at line 00410, is set up to be used with the Procedure Division statement ACCEPT TODAYS-DATE FROM DATE. The fields TODAYS-YEAR and TODAYS-MONTH-AND-DAY will be used as SOURCE fields in the Report Section for printing the date on the report.

Figure 8.13   Program P08-03.

```
CB1 RELEASE 2.4                             IBM OS/VS COBOL   JULY  1, 1982


                    17.45.01        APR  3,1988


00010   IDENTIFICATION DIVISION.
00020   PROGRAM-ID.  P08-03.
00030  *AUTHOR.  WENDEL KELLER.
00040  *
00050  *    THIS PROGRAM PRINTS A REPORT TITLE, COLUMN HEADINGS,
00060  *    DETAIL LINES, AND THREE LEVELS OF TOTALS.
00070  *
00080  ****************************************************************
00090
00100   ENVIRONMENT DIVISION.
00110   CONFIGURATION SECTION.
00120   SOURCE-COMPUTER.  IBM-370.
00130   OBJECT-COMPUTER.  IBM-370.
00140
00150   INPUT-OUTPUT SECTION.
00160   FILE-CONTROL.
00170       SELECT SALES-FILE-IN          ASSIGN TO INFILE.
00180       SELECT SALES-REPORT-FILE-OUT  ASSIGN TO PRINTER.
00190
00200  ****************************************************************
00210
```

(continued)

In the RD entry, line 00460, we now must provide Report Writer with more information than in earlier programs. The CONTROL clause now must name all the levels of control breaks from the highest level to the most minor, in that order. Since a FINAL total is considered a control break, it must be named along with the two control fields STORE-NUMBER-IN and SALESPERSON-NUMBER-IN.

Since we have page overflow in this program, the PAGE clause must be more elaborate than before. The size of the overall page is still arbitrarily given as 50. From the print chart you can see that the FIRST DETAIL line is on line 9, so the PAGE clause includes FIRST DETAIL 9. We now include the **LAST DETAIL**

Figure 8.13   (continued)

```
00220   DATA DIVISION.
00230   FILE SECTION.
00240   FD  SALES-FILE-IN
00250       LABEL RECORDS ARE OMITTED
00260       RECORD CONTAINS 80 CHARACTERS.
00270
00280   01  SALES-RECORD-IN.
00290       05   STORE-NUMBER-IN          PIC XXX.
00300       05   SALESPERSON-NUMBER-IN    PIC XXX.
00310       05   CUSTOMER-NUMBER-IN       PIC X(6).
00320       05   SALE-AMOUNT-IN           PIC 9(4)V99.
00330       05   FILLER                   PIC X(62).
00340
00350   FD  SALES-REPORT-FILE-OUT
00360       LABEL RECORDS ARE OMITTED
00370       REPORT IS SALES-REPORT-OUT.
00380
00390   WORKING-STORAGE SECTION.
00400   01  MORE-INPUT                    PIC X         VALUE "Y".
00410   01  TODAYS-DATE.
00420       05   TODAYS-YEAR              PIC 99.
00430       05   TODAYS-MONTH-AND-DAY     PIC 9(4).
00440
00450   REPORT SECTION.
00460   RD  SALES-REPORT-OUT
00470       CONTROLS FINAL, STORE-NUMBER-IN, SALESPERSON-NUMBER-IN
00480       PAGE 50 LINES, FIRST DETAIL 9, LAST DETAIL 39, FOOTING 48.
00490
00500   01  TYPE REPORT HEADING
00510       LINE 2.
00520       05   COLUMN 36     PIC X(12)     VALUE "SALES REPORT".
00530
00540   01  TYPE PAGE HEADING.
00550       05   LINE 3.
00560            10   COLUMN 20     PIC X(4)      VALUE "DATE".
00570            10   COLUMN 25     PIC Z9/99/
00580                               SOURCE TODAYS-MONTH-AND-DAY.
00590            10   COLUMN 31     PIC 99        SOURCE TODAYS-YEAR.
00600            10   COLUMN 62     PIC X(4)      VALUE "PAGE".
00610            10   COLUMN 67     PIC Z9        SOURCE PAGE-COUNTER.
00620       05   LINE 6.
00630            10   COLUMN 25     PIC X(5)      VALUE "STORE".
00640            10   COLUMN 34     PIC X(6)      VALUE "SALES-".
00650            10   COLUMN 44     PIC X(8)      VALUE "CUSTOMER".
00660            10   COLUMN 57     PIC X(4)      VALUE "SALE".
00670       05   LINE 7.
00680            10   COLUMN 26     PIC XXX       VALUE "NO.".
00690            10   COLUMN 34     PIC X(6)      VALUE "PERSON".
00700            10   COLUMN 45     PIC X(6)      VALUE "NUMBER".
00710            10   COLUMN 56     PIC X(6)      VALUE "AMOUNT".
00720
00730   01  DETAIL-LINE
00740       TYPE DETAIL
00750       LINE PLUS 1.
00760       05   COLUMN 26     PIC XXX       GROUP INDICATE
00770                          SOURCE STORE-NUMBER-IN.
00780       05   COLUMN 35     PIC XXX       GROUP INDICATE
00790                          SOURCE SALESPERSON-NUMBER-IN.
00800       05   COLUMN 45     PIC X(6)      SOURCE CUSTOMER-NUMBER-IN.
00810       05   COLUMN 54     PIC ZZ,ZZZ.99 SOURCE SALE-AMOUNT-IN.
00820
```

(continued)

clause to tell Report Writer on which line of the page it may print the last detail line. Here LAST DETAIL 39 will permit Report Writer to print DETAIL lines up through line 39 of the page. Any DETAIL line that would print past line 39 will instead cause Report Writer to skip to a new page automatically and print the PAGE HEADING report group.

Report Writer recognizes that programmers usually will want to leave extra space at the bottom of each page for the printing of totals. That is, even though DETAIL lines may print up through line 39 of the page, we want to allow total lines to print beyond line 39 so that they will not appear on the next page separated from the control group being totaled. The **FOOTING** clause allows for this. With the FOOTING clause we can specify the last line of the page on which total lines (CONTROL FOOTING lines) may print. From the print chart you can see that we can have a maximum of nine lines of totals on this report (the last set of totals: three total lines, two lines of asterisks, and four blank lines). Since DETAIL lines can print up through line 39 of the page, we must permit the total lines to print up through line 48 to ensure that there will be room for them all. Thus we make the FOOTING limit 48. The depth of the full page, which we here made 50, could have been used to allow space beyond the limit of the total lines for PAGE FOOTINGs and a REPORT FOOTING. We have neither PAGE FOOTING nor REPORT FOOTING, so the depth of page could have been any number 48 or larger and the program would work the same way.

In the PAGE HEADING report group, which begins on line 00540, LINE 3 is the most interesting. You can see how the fields TODAYS-MONTH-AND-DAY and TODAYS-YEAR are used to print the date. The SOURCE field used for printing the page number is a special register called **PAGE-COUNTER.** Report Writer sets up a PAGE-COUNTER, with PICTURE 9(6), for every RD entry. The INITIATE statement for a report sets the PAGE-COUNTER to 1, and then Report Writer adds 1 to PAGE-COUNTER each time just before printing the PAGE HEADING report group (except the first PAGE HEADING). PAGE-COUNTER may be referred to and changed by ordinary Procedure Division statements. In this way the programmer may begin page-numbering a report with any desired page number. If a program contains more than one PAGE-COUNTER (because there is more than one RD entry in the program), then PAGE-COUNTER must be qualified by the RD name whenever it is referred to in the Procedure Division or in a report description other than the one it was set up for. Our program has only one PAGE-COUNTER, so it need not be qualified.

Report Writer also sets up a special register called **LINE-COUNTER** for every RD entry. The LINE-COUNTER is used by Report Writer to position print lines on the page and to detect page overflow. LINE-COUNTER may be referred to in the Procedure Division. An INITIATE statement for a report sets LINE-COUNTER to 0. If there is more than one LINE-COUNTER in a program, the name LINE-COUNTER must be qualified by the RD name whenever it is referred to in the Procedure Division or outside its own report description.[1]

In the description of the DETAIL line we see for the first time the **GROUP INDICATE** clause, at lines 00760 and 00780. These will cause the STORE-NUMBER-IN and SALESPERSON-NUMBER-IN fields to be group indicated, that is, to be printed only the first time this DETAIL line is printed after a control break or the first time it is printed on a page. The GROUP INDICATE clause may be used only in a TYPE DETAIL report group.

---

[1]In some COBOL systems, if a program contains more than one PAGE-COUNTER and LINE-COUNTER, all references to them must be qualified by the RD name.

In this report description we have three different CONTROL FOOTING report groups, one each for a control break on SALESPERSON-NUMBER-IN and STORE-NUMBER-IN and for a FINAL total. Each report group is defined with its own level-01 entry.

The Salesperson Total Line

This is the minor total line, the lowest level of totals, at line 00880. The clause LINE PLUS 2 that appears in the description of the salesperson total line causes the total line to be double-spaced from the last detail line before it. In the description of the salesperson total line, we see for the first time the use of the **NEXT GROUP** clause. The NEXT GROUP clause is used for spacing or skipping the report output after printing a report group. Here we use NEXT GROUP PLUS 1 to give one blank line after a salesperson total line. When a NEXT GROUP clause appears in a CONTROL FOOTING group, as this one does, it is effective only for a control break at the same level as the CONTROL FOOTING line; that is, the NEXT GROUP PLUS 1 is effective only when a salesperson total line is being printed because of a salesperson break. The clause is ignored when a salesperson total line is printed as a result of a break on store number or on the FINAL break. This is an extremely useful feature and allows the programmer great flexibility in spacing output lines of the report.

Figure 8.13   (continued)

```
00830  01  NO-INPUT-DATA
00840      TYPE DETAIL
00850      LINE 9.
00860      05  COLUMN 36      PIC X(13)      VALUE "NO INPUT DATA".
00870
00880  01  TYPE CONTROL FOOTING SALESPERSON-NUMBER-IN
00890      LINE PLUS 2
00900      NEXT GROUP PLUS 1.
00910      05  SALESPERSON-TOTAL
00920          COLUMN 53      PIC ZZZ,ZZZ.99
00930                         SUM SALE-AMOUNT-IN.
00940      05  COLUMN 64      PIC X          VALUE "*".
00950
00960  01  TYPE CONTROL FOOTING STORE-NUMBER-IN
00970      NEXT GROUP PLUS 1.
00980      05  LINE PLUS 2.
00990          10  COLUMN 25  PIC X(19)
01000                         VALUE "TOTAL FOR STORE NO.".
01010          10  COLUMN 45  PIC XXX        SOURCE STORE-NUMBER-IN.
01020          10  STORE-TOTAL
01030              COLUMN 50  PIC $Z,ZZZ,ZZZ.99
01040                         SUM SALESPERSON-TOTAL.
01050          10  COLUMN 64  PIC XX         VALUE "**".
01060      05  LINE PLUS 1
01070          COLUMN 25      PIC X(38)      VALUE ALL "*".
01080
01090  01  TYPE CONTROL FOOTING FINAL.
01100      05  LINE PLUS 2.
01110          10  COLUMN 33  PIC X(11)      VALUE "GRAND TOTAL".
01120          10  COLUMN 49  PIC $ZZ,ZZZ,ZZZ.99
01130                         SUM STORE-TOTAL.
01140          10  COLUMN 64  PIC XXX        VALUE "***".
01150      05  LINE PLUS 2
01160          COLUMN 25      PIC X(38)      VALUE ALL "*".
01170
01180  *****************************************************************
01190
01200  PROCEDURE DIVISION.
01210  CONTROL-PARAGRAPH.
01220      PERFORM INITIALIZATION.
01230      PERFORM MAIN-PROCESS UNTIL MORE-INPUT IS EQUAL TO "N".
01240      PERFORM TERMINATION.
01250      STOP RUN.
```

(continued)

The total field itself is described as being the SUM of all the SALE-AMOUNT-IN fields. The total field is given the name SALESPERSON-TOTAL. A SUMmed field has to be given a name only if it is referred to somewhere in the Procedure Division or elsewhere in the Report Section. In earlier programs our SUMmed fields were not referred to, and so they were not given names.

The Store Total Line

The CONTROL FOOTING group for the store total consists of two lines, one containing the total of all the SALESPERSON-TOTALs for that store, and the other a line of asterisks, as shown on the print chart in Figure 8.10. The clause NEXT GROUP PLUS 1 on line 00970 will give one blank line following the printing of the line of asterisks, but only if the line is printed as a result of a break on store number. When the store total report group is printed as part of the FINAL break, the NEXT GROUP clause is ignored. The NEXT GROUP clause, when used, must appear only in a level-01 entry, and it must not be used in a TYPE PAGE HEADING description or in TYPE REPORT FOOTING.

The clause LINE PLUS 2 in line 00980 will give double spacing for the total line. When a break on store number occurs, both a salesperson total line and a store total line print. First the salesperson total line prints, and the clause LINE PLUS 2 in the description of the salesperson total line causes it to be double spaced from the last detail line. The clause NEXT GROUP PLUS 1 is ignored. The store total line is printed, and the clause LINE PLUS 2 in the description of the store total line causes it to be double-spaced from the salesperson total report group.

In the store total line, the total field is described as being the SUM of all the SALESPERSON-TOTAL values. It could have been defined as the SUM of all the SALE-AMOUNT-IN values but the processing would have been slower. SALESPERSON-TOTAL is a SUMmed field and is defined in the Report Section. Whenever a SUMmed field such as SALESPERSON-TOTAL is itself used as the operand in some other SUM clause, it must be defined either at a level lower than where it is used in the control break hierarchy or at the same level. Our SUM fields meet that condition: SALESPERSON-TOTAL is defined in the salesperson line, which is at a lower level than the store total line, where it is used. The field that is the SUM of all the SALESPERSON-TOTAL amounts is given the name STORE-TOTAL. This name is used elsewhere in the Report Section.

The field whose SOURCE is STORE-NUMBER-IN shows that when a control break occurs, the previous value of the control field is used in producing total lines. That is, even though some new value of STORE-NUMBER-IN caused the break and is already assigned to the input area, Report Writer has saved and uses the correct, previous value.

The description of the line of asterisks, line 01070, shows the use of the figurative constant **ALL**. Whenever the word ALL is used, it must be followed by a nonnumeric literal or a figurative constant other than ALL. When a figurative constant follows the word ALL, the word ALL is redundant and is used for readability only.

The Final Total Line

The FINAL total report group is described in the CONTROL FOOTING FINAL entry beginning on line 01090. It consists of one line showing the SUM of all the STORE-TOTAL values and one line of asterisks. The grand total field itself needs no name, for it is not referred to anywhere.

Figure 8.13   (continued)

```
01260
01270   INITIALIZATION.
01280       OPEN INPUT  SALES-FILE-IN,
01290           OUTPUT SALES-REPORT-FILE-OUT.
01300       ACCEPT TODAYS-DATE FROM DATE.
01310       INITIATE SALES-REPORT-OUT.
01320       PERFORM READ-A-RECORD.
01330       IF MORE-INPUT IS EQUAL TO "N"
01340           GENERATE NO-INPUT-DATA.
01350
01360   MAIN-PROCESS.
01370       GENERATE DETAIL-LINE.
01380       PERFORM READ-A-RECORD.
01390
01400   TERMINATION.
01410       TERMINATE SALES-REPORT-OUT.
01420       CLOSE SALES-FILE-IN,
01430           SALES-REPORT-FILE-OUT.
01440
01450   READ-A-RECORD.
01460       READ SALES-FILE-IN
01470           AT END
01480               MOVE "N" TO MORE-INPUT.
```

The Procedure Division

The single GENERATE statement in MAIN-PROCESS, line 01370, creates nearly the entire report. When the first GENERATE is issued, Report Writer prints the page and column headings and then the first DETAIL line. After that, for every GENERATE statement that is issued, Report Writer checks for control breaks and page overflow, and takes the action indicated in the Report Section. Execution of the TERMINATE statement produces the last set of total lines on the report.

It is illegal to try to issue a GENERATE statement for a PAGE HEADING group or a CONTROL FOOTING group, or for any group other than TYPE DETAIL. There is no need to tell Report Writer when to print page headings or total lines, for all the necessary logic is built in and tested.

EXERCISE 3

Write a program to read and process data in the following format:

Positions	Field
1 – 7	Customer Number
8 – 9	spaces
10 – 15	Part Number
16 – 22	spaces
23 – 25	Quantity
26 – 31	Unit Price (in dollars and cents)
26 – 29	Unit Price dollars
30 – 31	Unit Price cents
32 – 35	Handling Charge (in dollars and cents)
32 – 33	Handling Charge dollars
34 – 35	Handling Charge cents
35 – 80	spaces

Assume that there are several input records for each customer, each record containing a different part number. For each record, print a line showing the Customer Number, Part Number, Quantity, Unit Price, Handling Charge, and merchandise amount (compute the merchandise amount by multiplying the Unit Price by the Quantity). For each customer, print a total line showing the total Handling Charge and the total merchandise amount. Design the output on a print chart before you begin coding.

EXERCISE 4

Using the input of Program P08-03, write a program that will print a line for each record showing the Customer Number, the Sale Amount, a tax amount on the sale (at 8¼ percent), and the total of the sale amount and the tax. On each total line for salesperson, store, and grand total, show the total of all the appropriate sale amounts, tax amounts, and the totals of the sale amounts and the tax amounts. Group indicate the store numbers and salesperson numbers.

Declaratives

Sometimes it happens that Report Writer does not contain some feature needed to produce exactly the report that is wanted. In that case the programmer may use a **declarative section** to insert the needed coding into the program. Declaratives may be used for other purposes as well, and we will discuss them in Chapters 14, 15, and 19.

Using a Declarative Section to Suppress Printing

Sometimes a programmer may want to prevent Report Writer from printing certain lines that otherwise would be printed in the course of Report Writer's normal processing. For example, we might want the final total line in Program P08-03 to print on a separate page of the report, with no detail lines present. In that case we would not want the PAGE HEADING group, which consists of column headings, to appear on the page with the final total, for the column headings refer to fields that do not appear in the final total line. In the normal course of processing, Report Writer prints the PAGE HEADING group at the top of every page, whether it is wanted or not. Declarative sections can be used to prevent the printing of unwanted lines. Program P08-04, in Figure 8.14, shows how.

Figure 8.14 Program P08-04.

```
CB1 RELEASE 2.4                          IBM OS/VS COBOL   JULY  1, 1982


                       14.47.16      APR  4,1988


00010   IDENTIFICATION DIVISION.
00020   PROGRAM-ID.  P08-04.
00030  *AUTHOR.  WENDEL KELLER.
00040  *
00050  *    THIS PROGRAM PRINTS A REPORT TITLE, COLUMN HEADINGS,
00060  *    DETAIL LINES, AND THREE LEVELS OF TOTALS.
00070  *
00080  ***************************************************************
00090
```

(continued)

Figure 8.14   (continued)

```
00100    ENVIRONMENT DIVISION.
00110    CONFIGURATION SECTION.
00120    SOURCE-COMPUTER.  IBM-370.
00130    OBJECT-COMPUTER.  IBM-370.
00140
00150    INPUT-OUTPUT SECTION.
00160    FILE-CONTROL.
00170        SELECT SALES-FILE-IN            ASSIGN TO INFILE.
00180        SELECT SALES-REPORT-FILE-OUT    ASSIGN TO PRINTER.
00190
00200    **********************************************************************
00210
00220    DATA DIVISION.
00230    FILE SECTION.
00240    FD  SALES-FILE-IN
00250        LABEL RECORDS ARE OMITTED
00260        RECORD CONTAINS 80 CHARACTERS.
00270
00280    01  SALES-RECORD-IN.
00290        05   STORE-NUMBER-IN          PIC XXX.
00300        05   SALESPERSON-NUMBER-IN    PIC XXX.
00310        05   CUSTOMER-NUMBER-IN       PIC X(6).
00320        05   SALE-AMOUNT-IN           PIC 9(4)V99.
00330        05   FILLER                   PIC X(62).
00340
00350    FD  SALES-REPORT-FILE-OUT
00360        LABEL RECORDS ARE OMITTED
00370        REPORT IS SALES-REPORT-OUT.
00380
00390    WORKING-STORAGE SECTION.
00400    01  MORE-INPUT                    PIC X             VALUE "Y".
00410    01  TODAYS-DATE.
00420        05   TODAYS-YEAR              PIC 99.
00430        05   TODAYS-MONTH-AND-DAY     PIC 9(4).
00440
00450    REPORT SECTION.
00460    RD  SALES-REPORT-OUT
00470        CONTROLS FINAL, STORE-NUMBER-IN, SALESPERSON-NUMBER-IN
00480        PAGE 50 LINES, FIRST DETAIL 9, LAST DETAIL 39, FOOTING 48.
00490
00500    01  TYPE REPORT HEADING
00510        LINE 2.
00520        05  COLUMN 36      PIC X(12)      VALUE "SALES REPORT".
00530
00540    01  COLUMN-HEADINGS
00550        TYPE PAGE HEADING.
00560        05  LINE 3.
00570            10  COLUMN 20  PIC X(4)       VALUE "DATE".
00580            10  COLUMN 25  PIC Z9/99/
00590                           SOURCE TODAYS-MONTH-AND-DAY.
00600            10  COLUMN 31  PIC 99         SOURCE TODAYS-YEAR.
00610            10  COLUMN 62  PIC X(4)       VALUE "PAGE".
00620            10  COLUMN 67  PIC Z9         SOURCE PAGE-COUNTER.
00630        05  LINE 6.
00640            10  COLUMN 25  PIC X(5)       VALUE "STORE".
00650            10  COLUMN 34  PIC X(6)       VALUE "SALES-".
00660            10  COLUMN 44  PIC X(8)       VALUE "CUSTOMER".
00670            10  COLUMN 57  PIC X(4)       VALUE "SALE".
00680        05  LINE 7.
00690            10  COLUMN 26  PIC XXX        VALUE "NO.".
00700            10  COLUMN 34  PIC X(6)       VALUE "PERSON".
00710            10  COLUMN 45  PIC X(6)       VALUE "NUMBER".
00720            10  COLUMN 56  PIC X(6)       VALUE "AMOUNT".
00730
00740    01  DETAIL-LINE
00750        TYPE DETAIL
00760        LINE PLUS 1.
00770        05  COLUMN 26      PIC XXX        GROUP INDICATE
00780                           SOURCE STORE-NUMBER-IN.
00790        05  COLUMN 35      PIC XXX        GROUP INDICATE
00800                           SOURCE SALESPERSON-NUMBER-IN.
00810        05  COLUMN 45      PIC X(6)       SOURCE CUSTOMER-NUMBER-IN.
00820        05  COLUMN 54      PIC ZZ,ZZZ.99 SOURCE SALE-AMOUNT-IN.
00830
00840    01  NO-INPUT-DATA
00850        TYPE DETAIL
00860        LINE 9.
00870        05  COLUMN 36      PIC X(13)      VALUE "NO INPUT DATA".
```

```
00880
00890  01  TYPE CONTROL FOOTING SALESPERSON-NUMBER-IN
00900      LINE PLUS 2
00910      NEXT GROUP PLUS 1.
00920      05  SALESPERSON-TOTAL
00930          COLUMN 53        PIC ZZZ,ZZZ.99
00940                           SUM SALE-AMOUNT-IN.
00950      05  COLUMN 64        PIC X          VALUE "*".
00960
00970  01  TYPE CONTROL FOOTING STORE-NUMBER-IN
00980      NEXT GROUP PLUS 1.
00990      05  LINE PLUS 2.
01000          10  COLUMN 25    PIC X(19)
01010                           VALUE "TOTAL FOR STORE NO.".
01020          10  COLUMN 45    PIC XXX        SOURCE STORE-NUMBER-IN.
01030          10  STORE-TOTAL
01040              COLUMN 50    PIC $Z,ZZZ,ZZZ.99
01050                           SUM SALESPERSON-TOTAL.
01060          10  COLUMN 64    PIC XX         VALUE "**".
01070      05  LINE PLUS 1.
01080          COLUMN 25        PIC X(38)      VALUE ALL "*".
01090
01100  01  TYPE CONTROL FOOTING FINAL.
01110      05  LINE NEXT PAGE.
01120          10  COLUMN 62    PIC X(4)       VALUE "PAGE".
01130          10  COLUMN 67    PIC Z9         SOURCE PAGE-COUNTER.
01140      05  LINE PLUS 2.
01150          10  COLUMN 33    PIC X(11)      VALUE "GRAND TOTAL".
01160          10  COLUMN 49    PIC $ZZ,ZZZ,ZZZ.99
01170                           SUM STORE-TOTAL.
01180          10  COLUMN 64    PIC XXX        VALUE "***".
01190      05  LINE PLUS 2
01200          COLUMN 25        PIC X(38)      VALUE ALL "*".
01210
01220  ************************************************************************
01230
01240  PROCEDURE DIVISION.
01250
01260  DECLARATIVES.
01270  SUPRESS-COLUMN-HEADINGS SECTION.
01280      USE BEFORE REPORTING COLUMN-HEADINGS.
01290  COLUMN-HEADINGS-PARAGRAPH.
01300      IF MORE-INPUT IS EQUAL TO "N"
01310          MOVE 1 TO PRINT-SWITCH.
01320  END DECLARATIVES.
01330
```

(continued)

In the Report Section we have now given a name to the PAGE HEADING group, at line 00540. Any group that is referred to in a declarative section must be given a name. We have also specified LINE **NEXT PAGE** for the final total, at line 01110. This clause causes Report Writer to skip to a new page before printing this report group. It also would be legal to use the clause NEXT GROUP NEXT PAGE if the context of a problem were to require it. Some COBOL systems require an integer immediately before the words NEXT PAGE to indicate the line number on which the report group is to print. The system used to run the programs in this book takes the line number from the PAGE clause in the RD entry instead.

In the Procedure Division, line 01240, we see that to use a declarative section you must have the reserved word **DECLARATIVES,** followed by a period, right after the division header and starting in area A. That must be followed by a section header. This is the first time we have seen a section in the Procedure Division. We have been using sections in the Environment Division and Data Division all along. In those two divisions the names of sections are always reserved words, such as INPUT-OUTPUT SECTION or REPORT SECTION. But when you use a section in the Procedure Division, its name must be made up by the programmer. Here the made-up section name is SUPPRESS-COLUMN-HEADINGS. The section header is shown in line 01270. The rules for making up section names are the same as for making up paragraph names.

Figure 8.14   (continued)

```
01340   NONDECLARATIVE SECTION.
01350   CONTROL-PARAGRAPH.
01360       PERFORM INITIALIZATION.
01370       PERFORM MAIN-PROCESS UNTIL MORE-INPUT IS EQUAL TO "N".
01380       PERFORM TERMINATION.
01390       STOP RUN.
01400
01410   INITIALIZATION.
01420       OPEN INPUT   SALES-FILE-IN,
01430            OUTPUT SALES-REPORT-FILE-OUT.
01440       ACCEPT TODAYS-DATE FROM DATE.
01450       INITIATE SALES-REPORT-OUT.
01460       PERFORM READ-A-RECORD.
01470       IF MORE-INPUT IS EQUAL TO "N"
01480           GENERATE NO-INPUT-DATA.
01490
01500   MAIN-PROCESS.
01510       GENERATE DETAIL-LINE.
01520       PERFORM READ-A-RECORD.
01530
01540   TERMINATION.
01550       TERMINATE SALES-REPORT-OUT.
01560       CLOSE SALES-FILE-IN,
01570             SALES-REPORT-FILE-OUT.
01580
01590   READ-A-RECORD.
01600       READ SALES-FILE-IN
01610           AT END
01620               MOVE "N" TO MORE-INPUT.
```

The section header must be followed by a **USE** sentence. When a declarative section is being used in connection with Report Writer, the USE sentence must consist of the reserved words USE **BEFORE REPORTING,** followed by the name of the report group related to this declarative section, followed by a period. In this case we wish to suppress the printing of the report group called COLUMN-HEADINGS, so we have the USE sentence shown in line 01280.

Following the USE sentence you may have one or more paragraphs containing the processing you want for the report group. Each paragraph must have its own made-up paragraph name. In this case the processing is very simple and can fit into one paragraph. When more than one paragraph is needed in a declarative section, the following rule must be followed: A PERFORM statement in a declarative section may refer only to a paragraph that is among the DECLARATIVES. The PERFORMed paragraph need not be in the same section as the PERFORM statement, however.

Here we want only to determine whether we should suppress the printing of the COLUMN-HEADINGS group or let Report Writer print it. If MORE-INPUT is equal to "N", then we want to suppress the printing of COLUMN-HEADINGS, for we know we are at end-of-file and doing the final total. If MORE-INPUT is equal to "Y", then we should do nothing and Report Writer will print the column headings as part of its normal processing. Many COBOL systems have the **SUPPRESS** verb which may be used to suppress printing, but in the system used to run the programs in this book, the special MOVE statement

```
MOVE 1 TO PRINT-SWITCH
```

is used instead. **PRINT-SWITCH** is a reserved word set up especially for the purpose of suppressing printing. Whenever the program sets PRINT-SWITCH to 1, Report Writer refrains from printing the indicated report group. PRINT-SWITCH is originally set to zero by the INITIATE statement for the report, and is reset to zero by Report Writer each time it is used. You can see how the IF statement at line 01300 controls the printing of COLUMN-HEADINGS.

If more than one declarative section is to appear in a program, the additional sections follow immediately after the first. Each declarative section must have a section header, a USE sentence, and zero, one, or more paragraphs. The last declarative section in a program must be followed by the reserved words **END DECLARATIVES** followed by a period, as shown in line 01320. The end of a USE BEFORE REPORTING section is indicated by the beginning of another section or the words END DECLARATIVES.

The regular Procedure Division statements then follow the declarative sections, in a section of their own. Whenever declarative sections are used, the remainder of the Procedure Division must be organized into sections. Here the section header for the remainder of the Procedure Division is shown in line 01340. The name of the section at line 01340 could have been any made-up name. The SECTION did not have to be called NONDECLARATIVE.

When a program containing DECLARATIVES is executed, the computer begins execution at the beginning of the first paragraph after the END DE-CLARATIVES statement. In this program execution begins at the beginning of CONTROL-PARAGRAPH. The procedures written in the declarative sections are executed only at the specified times, in this case just BEFORE REPORTING the report group COLUMN-HEADINGS.

Program P08-04 was run with the same input data as Program P08-03 and produced the results shown in Figure 8.15.

Figure 8.15 Output from Program P08-04.

```
                 SALES REPORT
DATE   4/04/88                                PAGE   1


      STORE      SALES-     CUSTOMER      SALE
       NO.       PERSON      NUMBER      AMOUNT

       010        101        003001     1,234.56
                             007002         2.24
                             039004     8,439.20
                             046005     8,448.48
                             053006        12.34
                             060006     9,494.93
                             067007     4,000.03

                                       31,631.78 *

       010        102        074212     5,454.99
                             081012          .33
                             088013     5,849.58
                             095015       393.90

                                       11,698.80 *

       010        103        003234       303.03

                                          303.03 *

     TOTAL FOR STORE NO. 010  $    43,633.61 **
     **********************************

       020        011        007567     9,999.99
                             011454       456.00
                             023345     8,333.33

                                       18,789.32 *

       020        222        027345     4,343.43
```

(continued)

Figure 8.15   (continued)

```
DATE   4/04/88                                    PAGE   2


              STORE      SALES-    CUSTOMER     SALE
              NO.        PERSON    NUMBER       AMOUNT

              020        222       031567       9,903.30
                                   035001          34.21

                                                14,280.94 *

              020        266       039903       4,539.87
                                   043854       5,858.30

                                                10,398.17 *

         TOTAL FOR STORE NO. 020  $   43,468.43 **
         ****************************************

              030        193       059932       5,858.54
                                   063419       3,949.49

                                                 9,808.03 *

         TOTAL FOR STORE NO. 030  $    9,808.03 **
         ****************************************

              040        045       067333          .00
                                   071323       5,959.50

                                                 5,959.50 *

              040        403       048399       3,921.47
                                   054392          .00

                                                 3,921.47 *


DATE   4/04/88                                    PAGE   3


              STORE      SALES-    CUSTOMER     SALE
              NO.        PERSON    NUMBER       AMOUNT

              040        412       060111       9,999.99

                                                 9,999.99 *

         TOTAL FOR STORE NO. 040  $   19,880.96 **
         ****************************************

              046        012       013538          .00
                                   017521        690.78
                                   021504       1,381.56
                                   025487       2,072.34
                                   029470       2,763.12

                                                 6,907.80 *

              046        028       033453       3,453.90
                                   037436       4,144.68
                                   041419       4,835.46

                                                12,434.04 *

         TOTAL FOR STORE NO. 046  $   19,341.84 **
         ****************************************

                                                 PAGE   4

         GRAND TOTAL     $    136,132.87 ***

         ****************************************
```

The SUPPRESS Statement

The format of the SUPPRESS statement is

```
SUPPRESS PRINTING
```

The SUPPRESS statement may appear only in a USE BEFORE REPORTING section. Its execution causes the associated report group not to be printed, and any LINE or NEXT GROUP clauses that appear in the description of the report group to be ignored.

Report Writer Entries in the Data Division

The ANSI standard format of the RD entry is

```
RD report-name

[; CODE literal-1]
   ⎧ CONTROL IS  ⎫ ⎧ data-name-1 [, data-name-2] ...                      ⎫
[; ⎨            ⎬ ⎨                                                        ⎬]
   ⎩ CONTROLS ARE⎭ ⎩ FINAL [, data-name-1 [, data-name-2] ...]]           ⎭


[; PAGE ⎡LIMIT IS ⎤ integer-1 ⎡LINE ⎤
        ⎣LIMITS ARE⎦          ⎣LINES⎦

      [, HEADING integer-2]
      [, FIRST DETAIL integer-3]
      [, LAST DETAIL integer-4]
      [, FOOTING integer-5]]
```

The clauses that follow the report name are optional, and may appear in any order. The CODE clause is used to distinguish reports when more than one report is written on a file. We do not use the CODE clause in this book.

Integer-2 is the first line on the page in which anything may print. If the HEADING option is omitted, integer-2 is assumed to be 1. If all report groups in the report use absolute line spacing, all the options in the PAGE clause may be omitted.

If any relative line spacing is used in a report, then it is illegal to provide conflicting or nonsensical information in the PAGE clause. For example, you cannot have a HEADING option here that conflicts with any LINE clauses that may appear in the definitions of any TYPE REPORT HEADING or TYPE PAGE HEADING report group. You cannot specify a line number for the FIRST DETAIL line that conflicts with the actual number of lines occupied by the REPORT HEADING or the PAGE HEADING. That is, if a REPORT HEADING and/or PAGE HEADING is to appear on the same page with DETAIL lines, then the headings must not run over into the line reserved for the FIRST DETAIL. If a REPORT HEADING or a REPORT FOOTING is to appear on a page by itself, then it may appear anywhere on the page.

The overall depth of the page, given by integer-1, must not be less than any of the other integers in the clause. Integer-5 must not be less than integer-4. Integer-4 must not be less than integer-3. And integer-3 must not be less than integer-2. All integers in the clause must be positive.

As mentioned earlier in this chapter, the line number given in the FOOTING option specifies the last line on which CONTROL FOOTING lines may print. Any additional space provided by the overall depth of the page can be used for PAGE FOOTING and REPORT FOOTING groups.

The TYPE Clause

The TYPE clause is the only required clause in a level-01 entry in the Report Section. The format of the TYPE clause is

```
         ⎧ ⎧REPORT HEADING⎫                      ⎫
         ⎪ ⎩RH            ⎭                      ⎪
         ⎪ ⎧PAGE HEADING⎫                        ⎪
         ⎪ ⎩PH          ⎭                        ⎪
         ⎪ ⎧CONTROL HEADING⎫   ⎧data-name-1⎫     ⎪
         ⎪ ⎩CH             ⎭   ⎩FINAL      ⎭     ⎪
TYPE IS  ⎨ ⎧DETAIL⎫                              ⎬
         ⎪ ⎩DE    ⎭                              ⎪
         ⎪ ⎧CONTROL FOOTING⎫   ⎧data-name-2⎫     ⎪
         ⎪ ⎩CF             ⎭   ⎩FINAL      ⎭     ⎪
         ⎪ ⎧PAGE FOOTING⎫                        ⎪
         ⎪ ⎩PF          ⎭                        ⎪
         ⎪ ⎧REPORT FOOTING⎫                      ⎪
         ⎩ ⎩RF            ⎭                      ⎭
```

RH is the abbreviation for REPORT HEADING; PH is the abbreviation for PAGE HEADING; DE is the abbreviation for DETAIL; CF is the abbreviation for CONTROL FOOTING; PF is the abbreviation for PAGE FOOTING; and RF is the abbreviation for REPORT FOOTING. Data-name-1 and data-name-2 must be names that are given in the CONTROL clause of the RD entry, that is, they must be fields that control breaks are taken on. We refrained from using abbreviations in the sample programs because their meanings are not at all obvious, as are PIC, COMP, and SYNC.

A **CONTROL HEADING** report group is one or more lines to be printed before the detail lines of a control group. It usually serves as a title for the control group. For example, consider the following entry:

```
RD SAMPLE-REPORT
   CONTROLS FINAL, YEAR, MONTH
   PAGE 50 LINES.
```

Then if there were entries of

```
01   TYPE CONTROL HEADING FINAL
01   TYPE CONTROL HEADING  YEAR
01   TYPE CONTROL HEADING   MONTH
01   TYPE CONTROL FOOTING   MONTH
01   TYPE CONTROL FOOTING  YEAR
01   TYPE CONTROL FOOTING FINAL
```

the report groups would print as follows:

```
final control heading (once on the report)
   year control heading
      month control heading
         first detail line on the report
         detail lines
                 .
                 .
                 .
      month control footing
      month control heading (for the next month)
         detail lines
                 .
                 .
                 .
      month control footing
   year control footing
   year control heading (for the next year)
      month control heading
         detail lines
                 .
                 .
                 .
         last detail line on the report
      month control footing
   year control footing
final control footing (once on the report)
```

   CONTROL HEADING lines may appear in the same areas of a report page as DETAIL lines, that is, from the FIRST DETAIL line number through the LAST DETAIL line number as given in the PAGE clause.

The SUM Clause

The format of the SUM clause is

```
{SUM  identifier-1  [, identifier-2] ...
   [UPON  data-name-1  [, data-name-2 ... ]} ...

      [RESET ON    {data-name-3}  ]
                   {FINAL      }
```

The ellipsis after the brace shows that there may be as many SUM clauses as desired in a single entry, except that some COBOL systems permit only one SUM clause in an entry. If there is more than one SUM clause in an entry, all the identifiers named in all the SUM clauses are added into the sum counter.

The **UPON** phrase, when used, causes the SUM clause to be executed only when a GENERATE statement is issued for one of the DETAIL report groups given as data-name-1 and data-name-2. The data name(s) given in the UPON phrase must be the names of DETAIL report groups in the same report as the SUM clause. Some COBOL systems permit only one data name in an UPON clause.

The **RESET ON** phrase gives the programmer the ability to delay resetting sum counters until after their normal time. Normally a sum counter is reset to zero automatically by Report Writer when a control break occurs and after the contents of the counter are printed. With the RESET phrase, the programmer can direct Report Writer not to reset the counter until some specified higher-level break occurs. This provides for printing ever-growing lower-level subtotals. The RESET ON phrase really should be called the DON'T RESET UNTIL phrase. Using RESET ON FINAL delays resetting the counter for the entire report, and so the report output shows only ever-growing subtotals for that SUM field.

Summary

Report Writer is a COBOL feature that permits the programmer to describe characteristics of a report rather than write the step-by-step coding needed to produce the report. Report Writer automatically provides the coding needed to format output lines, sum into accumulators, print report headings, test for page overflow, skip to a new page, print page headings, test for control breaks, print total lines, reset accumulators, and print page footings and report footings. At the same time, the programmer has complete command over all the logical capabilities of COBOL.

Before giving a GENERATE statement to print a DETAIL line, the program may carry out any desired processing on the input data. Before any other TYPEs of report groups are printed, any processing may be carried out in a declarative section with a USE BEFORE REPORTING sentence.

The characteristics of all the reports produced by a program may be described in the Report Section. There, each report has an RD entry with a report name. Within the RD entry, report groups are described. Report groups may be of TYPE REPORT HEADING, PAGE HEADING, CONTROL HEADING, DETAIL, CONTROL FOOTING, PAGE FOOTING, and REPORT FOOTING.

The LINE clause directs Report Writer to space or skip before printing a single line or a report group. The NEXT GROUP clause directs Report Writer to space or skip after printing a report group. The LINE clause can be written as an absolute LINE NUMBER clause or a relative LINE NUMBER clause. The NEXT GROUP clause can be written as an absolute NEXT GROUP clause or a relative NEXT GROUP clause. The NEXT PAGE option may be used in a LINE clause or a NEXT GROUP clause. When a NEXT GROUP clause appears in a CONTROL FOOTING report group, the clause is executed only when a control break occurs at the exact level of the CONTROL FOOTING. The NEXT GROUP clause is always effective when it appears in report groups other than TYPE CONTROL FOOTING.

Within each report group definition, fields to be printed may be defined. A printable item is recognized by the appearance of a COLUMN clause, a PICTURE clause, and one of the clauses SOURCE, SUM, or VALUE. It also must have a LINE clause properly related to it in order to tell Report Writer where it is to be printed.

The CONTROL clause in the RD entry indicates the fields on which control breaks are to be taken. The PAGE clause in the RD entry indicates the areas of the report output page where different TYPEs of report groups may print.

The INITIATE, GENERATE, and TERMINATE statements are used in the Procedure Division to control the printing of the report. The INITIATE statement must be given for each report after the report output file is OPENed and before any GENERATE statements are given. The GENERATE statement directs Report Writer to produce a DETAIL report group and at the same time to test whether any other report groups should be printed. For each DETAIL group printed, Report Writer tests for page overflow and control breaks. If any conditions are found that require printing lines in addition to the DETAIL line, Report Writer automatically prints them with no further effort on the part of the programmer. The programmer may suppress the printing of any report group by using a SUPPRESS statement or the special MOVE statement MOVE 1 TO PRINT-SWITCH.

The TERMINATE statement is given after the last GENERATE statement and before the report output file is CLOSEd. The TERMINATE statement signals the production of the last CONTROL FOOTING groups, the last PAGE FOOTING group, and any REPORT FOOTING group.

Fill-in Exercises

1. In the FD entry for a report file, the __*report is*__ clause must be used to name the report.

2. In the Report Section each report name must have a(n) __*RD*__ entry.

3. The TYPEs of report groups that Report Writer can process are __*detail*__, __*page head, ctr. H. Rpt. H. Ctr. F. Rpt. F.*__ , and __*page f.*__ .

4. The beginning print position of each printable item is given by a(n) __*Column*__ clause.

5. Vertical spacing of the paper is controlled by the __*line*__ and __*next group*__ clauses.

6. The words USE __*before reporty*__ indicate that a declarative section is to be used with Report Writer.

7. The statement that is used to begin processing a report is the __*initiate*__ statement.

8. The statement that causes a DETAIL report group to print is the __*generate*__ statement.

9. The areas on the page where different TYPEs of report groups may print are described by the _page_ clause.

10. The control fields of a report are listed in the _Control_ clause in the RD entry.

11. The control fields of a report are listed in order from _major_ to _minor_.

12. The clause LINE _plus 1_ may be used to obtain single spacing.

13. The _source_ clause indicates to Report Writer where data are to be obtained to fill an output field.

14. The _terminate_ statement is used to end the processing of a report.

15. The _reset_ clause is used to delay zeroing a sum counter until a specified control break has been executed.

Review Exercises

1. Write a program to read input records in the following format:

Positions	Field
1 – 8	Part Number
9 – 28	Part Description
29 – 31	Quantity on Hand
32 – 80	spaces

Have your program print the contents of each record on one line in the format shown in Figure 8.RE1.

Figure 8.RE1   Output format for Review Exercise 1.

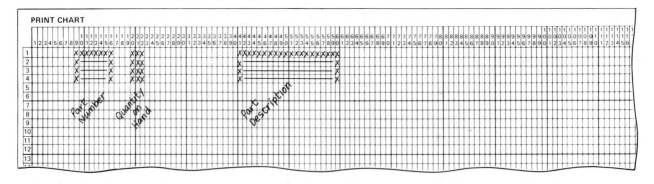

2. Write a program to read input records in the following format:

Positions	Field
1 – 5	Employee Number
6	Code
7 – 9	Hours Worked (to one decimal place)
10 – 80	spaces

Each record contains an Employee Number, a Code indicating whether the employee is eligible for overtime pay or is exempt from overtime pay, and the Hours Worked. The Code field contains an E if the employee is exempt from overtime pay and an N if the employee is eligible for overtime pay (nonexempt).

Have your program print one line for each employee in the format shown in Figure 8.RE2. If an employee worked more than 40 hours and is eligible for overtime pay, print the words OVERTIME PAY as shown in the print chart. Otherwise print only the Employee Number and the Hours Worked.

Figure 8.RE2 Output format for Review Exercise 2.

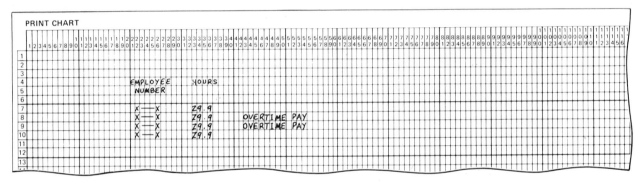

3. Write a program to read input records in the following format:

Positions	Field
1 – 9	Social Security Number
10 – 12	Monday Hours (to one decimal place)
13 – 15	Tuesday Hours (to one decimal place)
16 – 18	Wednesday Hours (to one decimal place)
19 – 21	Thursday Hours (to one decimal place)
22 – 24	Friday Hours (to one decimal place)
25 – 80	spaces

Have your program produce a report in the format shown in Figure 8.RE3. On the report list only those employees who worked more than 37.5 hours during the week. Compute each employee's number of overtime hours (hours worked during the week minus 37.5).

Figure 8.RE3 Output format for Review Exercise 3.

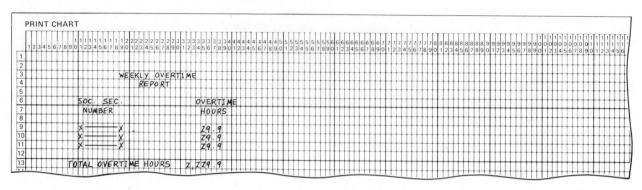

4. Write a program to read input records in the following format:

Positions	Field
1 – 5	Department Number
6 – 11	Employee Number
12 – 19	Annual Salary (to two decimal places)
20 – 44	Employee Name
45 – 80	spaces

Have your program produce a report in the format shown in Figure 8.RE4. Use a DECLARATIVES section to compute the averages in the CONTROL FOOTING lines.

Figure 8.RE4 Output format for Review Exercise 4.

5. Modify your solution to Review Exercise 4 so that, at the end of the report your program prints a final total of the number of employees and the average salary of all the employees. Design suitable final lines.

6. Write a program to read input records in the following format:

Positions	Field
1 – 7	Customer Number
8 – 9	spaces
10 – 15	Part Number
16 – 22	spaces
23 – 25	Quantity
26 – 31	Unit Price (to two decimal places)
32 – 80	spaces

The program is to check that all Quantity and all Unit Price fields contain only numbers. If a field is found not to contain only numbers, a suitable error line is to be printed. For each valid record have your program print the Customer Number, Part Number, Quantity, Unit Price, and a merchandise amount (the Quantity times the Unit Price), except if the merchandise amount is greater than 999,999.99. If the merchandise amount is greater than 999,999.99, print only the Customer Number, Part Number, Quantity, Unit Price, and a message MERCHANDISE AMOUNT SUSPICIOUSLY LARGE.

Project

Rewrite your solution to the Project in Chapter 7, page 212, using Report Writer.

One-Dimensional Tables

Here are the key points you should learn from this chapter:

1. The need for tables in computer programs
2. How to set up one-dimensional tables in COBOL
3. How to program for one-dimensional tables
4. How to load a table from an external file

Key words to recognize and learn:

table	argument
OCCURS	function
subscript	INDEXED BY
index	index name
SEARCH	direct indexing
VARYING	relative indexing
one-dimensional	SET
two-dimensional	WHEN
three-dimensional	SEARCH ALL
array	ASCENDING KEY
direct-reference table	DESCENDING KEY
search table	binary search
element	

It often happens that computer programs must operate on related fields of data that all have the same description. In many such cases the data can be arranged in a COBOL program in the form of a **table** and processed conveniently using the table-handling features of COBOL. The first program in this chapter shows how some of the table-handling features operate, and later programs show additional features. Also, later in the chapter you will see the exact definition of a table.

A Program Using Subscripting

Program P09-01 reads and processes input data in the following format:

Positions	Field
1 – 7	Salesperson Number
8 – 13	Sale Amount 1 (in dollars and cents)
14 – 19	Sale Amount 2 (in dollars and cents)
20 – 25	Sale Amount 3 (in dollars and cents)
26 – 31	Sale Amount 4 (in dollars and cents)
32 – 37	Sale Amount 5 (in dollars and cents)
38 – 43	Sale Amount 6 (in dollars and cents)
44 – 49	Sale Amount 7 (in dollars and cents)
50 – 55	Sale Amount 8 (in dollars and cents)
56 – 61	Sale Amount 9 (in dollars and cents)
62 – 67	Sale Amount 10 (in dollars and cents)
68 – 80	spaces

Each input record contains a salesperson number and 10 sale amounts. The program is to compute a commission on each sale according to the following schedule:

Sale Amount	Commission
0 – 100.00	5% of the sale amount
Over 100.00	5% of the first $100 of the sale amount plus 10% of the sale amount in excess of $100

The paragraph needed to test each sale amount and compute the commission obviously will be at least a little complicated. It would be a nuisance to have to write the paragraph 10 times in the program in order to compute each of the 10 commission amounts. Worse, even if we did get it correct in one place in the program, we might make a keying error and get it wrong somewhere else. So the program might compute the commission for sale 1 correctly but not for sale 2. Fortunately, we can use the table-handling features of COBOL to avoid having to write anything in the program 10 times.

The output format for Program P09-01 is shown in Figure 9.1. Program P09-01 is shown in Figure 9.2. The input record description, which begins at line 00300, does not name 10 different sale amount fields but instead uses an **OCCURS** clause. An OCCURS clause may be used whenever several fields have identical descriptions, as our 10 sale amount fields do. The OCCURS clause permits the programmer to describe the field once and tell COBOL how many such fields there are. Our OCCURS clause at line 00320 tells COBOL that there are 10 sale amount fields, one right after the other in the input record, and that each has PICTURE 9(4)V99. The OCCURS clause may appear before or after the PICTURE clause, so either of the following is legal:

```
05 SALE-AMOUNT-IN   PIC 9(4)V99   OCCURS 10 TIMES.
05 SALE-AMOUNT-IN   OCCURS 10 TIMES   PIC 9(4)V99.
```

Figure 9.1 Output format for Program P09-01.

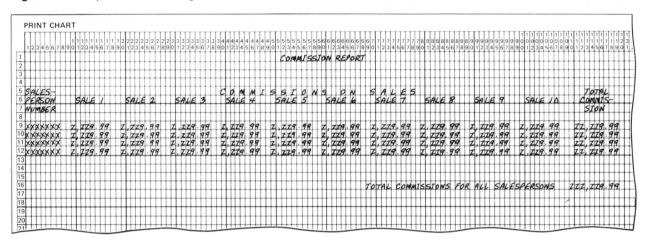

Figure 9.2 Program P09-01.

```
CB1 RELEASE 2.4                              IBM OS/VS COBOL  JULY 1, 1982


                         23.02.20          APR  5,1988


       00010    IDENTIFICATION DIVISION.
       00020    PROGRAM-ID.  P09-01.
       00030   *AUTHOR. DEBORAH ANN SENIOR.
       00040   *
       00050   *    THIS PROGRAM PRODUCES A SALESPERSON COMMISSION
       00060   *    REPORT SHOWING TEN COMMISSION AMOUNTS
       00070   *    AND THE TOTAL FOR EACH SALESPERSON.
       00080   *
       00090   *
       00100   ************************************************************
       00110
       00120    ENVIRONMENT DIVISION.
       00130    CONFIGURATION SECTION.
       00140    SOURCE-COMPUTER.   IBM-370.
       00150    OBJECT-COMPUTER.   IBM-370.
       00160
       00170    INPUT-OUTPUT SECTION.
       00180    FILE-CONTROL.
       00190        SELECT SALES-FILE-IN             ASSIGN TO INFILE.
       00200        SELECT COMMISSION-REPORT-FILE-OUT  ASSIGN TO PRINTER.
       00210
       00220   ************************************************************
       00230
       00240    DATA DIVISION.
       00250    FILE SECTION.
       00260    FD  SALES-FILE-IN
       00270        LABEL RECORDS ARE OMITTED
       00280        RECORD CONTAINS 80 CHARACTERS.
       00290
       00300    01  SALES-RECORD-IN.
       00310        05  SALESPERSON-NUMBER-IN    PIC X(7).
       00320        05  SALE-AMOUNT-IN           PIC 9(4)V99     OCCURS 10 TIMES.
       00330        05  FILLER                   PIC X(13).
       00340
       00350    FD  COMMISSION-REPORT-FILE-OUT
       00360        LABEL RECORDS ARE OMITTED.
       00370
       00380    01  REPORT-LINE              PIC X(119).
       00390
```

(continued)

All 10 SALE-AMOUNT-IN fields have, in a sense, the same name now. They are all called SALE-AMOUNT-IN, and COBOL must have some way of distinguishing one from the other. This is accomplished by means of a **subscript.** In COBOL a subscript is a positive or unsigned integer (or a field defined as an integer) that is written in parentheses following the data name being subscripted. The 10 SALE-AMOUNT-IN fields can be referred to in the Procedure Division as

```
SALE-AMOUNT-IN (1)   (pronounced "SALE-AMOUNT-IN sub one")
SALE-AMOUNT-IN (2)   (pronounced "SALE-AMOUNT-IN sub two")
SALE-AMOUNT-IN (3)   (pronounced "SALE-AMOUNT-IN sub three")
```

and so on. So the following would be a legal statement:

```
MOVE SALE-AMOUNT-IN (1) TO SALE-OUT.
```

It would be read as "MOVE SALE-AMOUNT-IN sub one TO SALE-OUT." Here are other legal statements:

```
IF SALE-AMOUNT-IN (2) GREATER THAN 50.00
    PERFORM 50-DOLLAR-ROUTINE.
ADD SALE-AMOUNT-IN (3) TO SALE-ACCUMULATOR ROUNDED.
```

Try reading the IF and ADD statements aloud before going on.

The subscript following the data name SALE-AMOUNT-IN in each statement tells COBOL which of the 10 SALE-AMOUNT-IN fields is being referred to in the statement.

Whenever a field is defined with an OCCURS clause, you must use a subscript (or an **index,** discussed later in this chapter) whenever you refer to that field (except with the **SEARCH** verb, also to be discussed later in this chapter). Also, whenever you want to use a subscript on a field, the field must be defined with an OCCURS clause. An OCCURS clause may not be used at the 01 level.

A subscript doesn't have to be just an integer; a subscript can be given in the form of a data name or a qualified data name. Any data name or qualified data name can be used as a subscript provided it is defined as an integer. So we could make up the following field to serve as a subscript:

```
05 SALE-SUBSCRIPT   PIC S99.
```

The field SALE-SUBSCRIPT looks like an ordinary field and it is. It could be used wherever a numeric variable would be legal. But, because it is defined as an integer, it could also be used as a subscript. So it would be legal to refer to the 10 fields called SALE-AMOUNT-IN this way:

```
SALE-AMOUNT-IN (SALE-SUBSCRIPT)
```

(pronounced "SALE-AMOUNT-IN subscripted by SALE-SUBSCRIPT").

The field SALE-SUBSCRIPT could be assigned any value 1 through 10, so that a statement such as

```
MOVE SALE-AMOUNT-IN (SALE-SUBSCRIPT) TO SALE-OUT.
```

would execute in a way that depends on the value assigned to SALE-SUBSCRIPT at the time the statement executes. If SALE-SUBSCRIPT happened to have the integer 4 assigned to it, the MOVE statement would execute as though it were written:

```
MOVE SALE-AMOUNT-IN (4) TO SALE-OUT.
```

If SALE-SUBSCRIPT has a 5 assigned when the MOVE executes, it will execute as:

```
MOVE SALE-AMOUNT-IN (5) TO SALE-OUT.
```

It would be illegal for SALE-SUBSCRIPT to have a value larger than 10 when the MOVE statement executes, since the OCCURS clause in the definition of SALE-AMOUNT-IN says that there are only 10 such fields. You can see that, by using a data name as a subscript, it is possible to get a statement such as

```
MOVE SALE-AMOUNT-IN (SALE-SUBSCRIPT) TO SALE-OUT.
```

to refer to all 10 of the fields SALE-AMOUNT-IN merely by changing the value assigned to SALE-SUBSCRIPT.

You will see in Program P09-01 that the field we use to subscript SALE-AMOUNT-IN is not called SALE-SUBSCRIPT. The name of a subscript need not have any special form; for a field to be used as a subscript, it need only be defined as an integer. A subscript in a COBOL program may be used on any field in the program that is defined with an OCCURS clause.

EXERCISE 1

Which of the following would be valid as a subscript?

```
a.  05 DOG            PIC S999.
b.  05 SUBSCRIPT-1    PIC S99V99.
c.  05 SUBSCRIPT-2    PIC X(3).
```

EXERCISE 2

Given the following fields:

```
05 PURCHASES    PIC 9(4)V99   OCCURS 5 TIMES.
05 RETURNS      PIC 9(3)V99   OCCURS 4 TIMES.
05 SUBSC-1      PIC S9.
05 SUBSC-2      PIC S99.
```

a. Which of the following statements could be legal in a COBOL program?
   1. ADD PURCHASES (SUBSC-1) TO ACCUMULATOR.
   2. ADD PURCHASES (SUBSC-2) TO ACCUMULATOR.
   3. ADD SUBSC-1 (PURCHASES) TO ACCUMULATOR.
   4. ADD RETURNS (SUBSC-1)   TO ACCUMULATOR.
   5. ADD 1 TO SUBSC-1.
b. What is the highest value that may legally be assigned to SUBSC-1 at the time statement 1 above executes?
c. What is the highest value that may legally be assigned to SUBSC-2 at the time statement 2 above executes?

Figure 9.2   (continued)

```
00400    WORKING-STORAGE SECTION.
00410    01   MORE-INPUT                PIC X          VALUE "Y".
00420    01   COMMISSION-RATE-1         PIC V99        VALUE .05.
00430    01   COMMISSION-RATE-2         PIC V99        VALUE .10.
00440    01   BRACKET-MAXIMUM           PIC 999V99     VALUE 100.00.
00450    01   NUMBER-OF-SALES           PIC S99        VALUE 10
00460                                   COMP           SYNC.
00470    01   GRAND-TOTAL-COMMISSIONS-W PIC S9(6)V99   VALUE 0.
00480    01   COMMISSIONS.
00490         05   COMMISSION-AMOUNT-W    PIC S9(4)V99 OCCURS 10 TIMES.
00500    01   COMMISSION-FOR-SALESPERSON  PIC S9(5)V99.
00510    01   COMPUTATION-SUBSCRIPT       PIC S99         COMP SYNC.
00520    01   LINE-SPACING   VALUE 1      PIC S9          COMP SYNC.
00530
00540    01   PAGE-HEADING-1.
00550         05   FILLER  PIC X(51)      VALUE SPACES.
00560         05   FILLER  PIC X(17)      VALUE "COMMISSION REPORT".
00570
00580    01   PAGE-HEADING-2.
00590         05   FILLER  PIC X(39)      VALUE "SALES-".
00600         05   FILLER  PIC X(73)
00610              VALUE "C O M M I S S I O N S   O N   S A L E S".
00620         05   FILLER  PIC X(5)       VALUE "TOTAL".
00630
00640    01   PAGE-HEADING-3.
00650         05   FILLER  PIC X(10)      VALUE "PERSON".
00660         05   FILLER  PIC X(10)      VALUE "SALE 1".
00670         05   FILLER  PIC X(10)      VALUE "SALE 2".
00680         05   FILLER  PIC X(10)      VALUE "SALE 3".
00690         05   FILLER  PIC X(10)      VALUE "SALE 4".
00700         05   FILLER  PIC X(10)      VALUE "SALE 5".
00710         05   FILLER  PIC X(10)      VALUE "SALE 6".
00720         05   FILLER  PIC X(10)      VALUE "SALE 7".
00730         05   FILLER  PIC X(10)      VALUE "SALE 8".
00740         05   FILLER  PIC X(10)      VALUE "SALE 9".
00750         05   FILLER  PIC X(11)      VALUE "SALE 10".
00760         05   FILLER  PIC X(7)       VALUE "COMMIS-".
00770
00780    01   PAGE-HEADING-4.
00790         05   FILLER  PIC X(112)     VALUE "NUMBER".
00800         05   FILLER  PIC X(4)       VALUE "SION".
00810
00820    01   DETAIL-LINE.
00830         05   SALESPERSON-NUMBER-OUT  PIC X(9).
00840         05   COMMISSION-AMOUNT-OUT   PIC Z,ZZ9.99BB
00850                                      OCCURS 10 TIMES.
00860         05   COMMISSION-FOR-SALESPERSON-OUT
00870                                      PIC BZZ,ZZ9.99.
00880
00890    01   NO-INPUT-DATA.
00900         05   FILLER                  PIC X(53) VALUE SPACES.
00910         05   FILLER                  PIC X(13) VALUE "NO INPUT DATA".
00920
00930    01   TOTAL-LINE.
00940         05   FILLER                  PIC X(68) VALUE SPACES.
00950         05   FILLER                  PIC X(41)
00960              VALUE "TOTAL COMMISSION FOR ALL SALESPERSONS".
00970         05   GRAND-TOTAL-COMMISSIONS PIC ZZZ,ZZ9.99.
00980
00990    ***********************************************************************
01000
```

```
01010    PROCEDURE DIVISION.
01020    CONTROL-PARAGRAPH.
01030        PERFORM INITIALIZATION.
01040        PERFORM MAIN-PROCESS UNTIL MORE-INPUT IS EQUAL TO "N".
01050        PERFORM TERMINATION.
01060        STOP RUN.
01070
```

(continued)

The Working Storage Section begins at line 00400. The commission rates for this problem have been written into working storage as constants, lines 00420 and 00430. This is better programming practice than writing the commission rates into the Procedure Division. First, all the commission rates for the problem can easily be seen since they are all written in one place. If the commission rates should change while this program is still being used, the program can be changed more easily than if the rates were written into the Procedure Division. Also, the use of the names COMMISSION-RATE-1 and COMMISSION-RATE-2 will make the Procedure Division clearer than if we just had the numbers .05 and .10 in it. Similar reasoning applies to the sale amount at which the commission rate changes. It too is written into working storage, instead of the number 100 being written into the Procedure Division.

Similarly, the NUMBER-OF-SALES is defined as a constant in working storage. Furthermore, it has been designated COMPUTATIONAL and SYN-CHRONIZED. Since the field is used only internally to the program and does not interact with input or output, it should be COMPUTATIONAL.

Ten COMMISSION-AMOUNT-W fields have been defined with an OCCURS clause, at line 00490. The OCCURS clause is not permitted at the 01 level, so the dummy name COMMISSIONS was included in the program just to give COM-MISSION-AMOUNT-W something to be subordinate to. The COMMISSION-AMOUNT-W fields will be used to store the 10 computed commission amounts for each salesperson before they are printed.

The field COMMISSION-FOR-SALESPERSON is used to accumulate the sum of the 10 commission amounts for each salesperson, for printing on the report. You will see how it is used when we look at the Procedure Division.

Also in working storage, a subscript has been defined, at line 00510. It is called COMPUTATION-SUBSCRIPT, but of course it could have had any legal data name. It will be used to permit the program to refer to all 10 of the SALE-AMOUNT-IN fields, all 10 of the COMMISSION-AMOUNT-W fields, and all 10 of the COMMISSION-AMOUNT-OUT fields, defined at line 00840. It was made large enough to accommodate the highest value that the subscript can take on. Since it often happens in COBOL that a subscript gets to take on a value that is one larger than the number of fields being subscripted, COMPUTATION-SUBSCRIPT should be big enough to hold the value 11. A two-digit field does it, and COM-PUTATION-SUBSCRIPT was given the PICTURE S99. You will see exactly how COMPUTATION-SUBSCRIPT is used when we look at the Procedure Division.

COMPUTATION-SUBSCRIPT has been designated COMPUTATIONAL and SYNCHRONIZED. Fields used as subscripts don't have to be COMPUTATIONAL, and the decision whether to make them COMPUTATIONAL is the same as with any other field: If a subscript is used only internally to the program, it should certainly be made COMPUTATIONAL; if, on the other hand, a field is used as a subscript and also interacts with input and/or output, then a COMPUTATIONAL designation may improve or worsen program efficiency.

Figure 9.2   (continued)

```
01080    INITIALIZATION.
01090        OPEN INPUT  SALES-FILE-IN,
01100            OUTPUT COMMISSION-REPORT-FILE-OUT.
01110        WRITE REPORT-LINE FROM PAGE-HEADING-1 AFTER PAGE.
01120        WRITE REPORT-LINE FROM PAGE-HEADING-2 AFTER 4.
01130        WRITE REPORT-LINE FROM PAGE-HEADING-3.
01140        WRITE REPORT-LINE FROM PAGE-HEADING-4.
01150        MOVE 2 TO LINE-SPACING.
01160        PERFORM READ-A-RECO1220        PERFORM COMMISSION-CALCULATION
01170        IF MORE-INPUT IS EQUAL TO "N"
01180            WRITE REPORT-LINE FROM NO-INPUT-DATA AFTER 2.
01190
01200    MAIN-PROCESS.
01210        MOVE ZERO TO COMMISSION-FOR-SALESPERSON.
01220        PERFORM COMMISSION-CALCULATION
01230            VARYING COMPUTATION-SUBSCRIPT FROM 1 BY 1 UNTIL
01240            COMPUTATION-SUBSCRIPT IS GREATER THAN NUMBER-OF-SALES.
01250        PERFORM PRODUCE-THE-REPORT.
01260        PERFORM READ-A-RECORD.
01270
01280    TERMINATION.
01290        PERFORM PRODUCE-FINAL-TOTAL-LINE.
01300        CLOSE SALES-FILE-IN,
01310            COMMISSION-REPORT-FILE-OUT.
01320
01330    READ-A-RECORD.
01340        READ SALES-FILE-IN
01350            AT END
01360                MOVE "N" TO MORE-INPUT.
01370
01380    COMMISSION-CALCULATION.
01390        IF SALE-AMOUNT-IN (COMPUTATION-SUBSCRIPT) IS NOT GREATER THAN
01400            BRACKET-MAXIMUM
01410            COMPUTE
01420            COMMISSION-AMOUNT-W (COMPUTATION-SUBSCRIPT) ROUNDED
01430            COMMISSION-AMOUNT-OUT (COMPUTATION-SUBSCRIPT) ROUNDED
01440                = SALE-AMOUNT-IN (COMPUTATION-SUBSCRIPT) *
01450                COMMISSION-RATE-1
01460        ELSE
01470            COMPUTE
01480            COMMISSION-AMOUNT-W (COMPUTATION-SUBSCRIPT) ROUNDED
01490            COMMISSION-AMOUNT-OUT (COMPUTATION-SUBSCRIPT) ROUNDED
01500                = BRACKET-MAXIMUM * COMMISSION-RATE-1 +
01510                (SALE-AMOUNT-IN (COMPUTATION-SUBSCRIPT) -
01520                BRACKET-MAXIMUM) * COMMISSION-RATE-2.
01530        ADD COMMISSION-AMOUNT-W (COMPUTATION-SUBSCRIPT) TO
01540            COMMISSION-FOR-SALESPERSON.
01550
01560    PRODUCE-THE-REPORT.
01570        MOVE SALESPERSON-NUMBER-IN TO SALESPERSON-NUMBER-OUT.
01580        MOVE COMMISSION-FOR-SALESPERSON TO
01590            COMMISSION-FOR-SALESPERSON-OUT.01630
01600        ADD COMMISSION-FOR-SALESPERSON TO GRAND-TOTAL-COMMISSIONS-W.
01610        WRITE REPORT-LINE FROM DETAIL-LINE AFTER LINE-SPACING.
01620        MOVE 1 TO LINE-SPACING.
01630
01640    PRODUCE-FINAL-TOTAL-LINE.
01650        MOVE GRAND-TOTAL-COMMISSIONS-W TO GRAND-TOTAL-COMMISSIONS.
01660        WRITE REPORT-LINE FROM TOTAL-LINE AFTER 4.
```

Controlling the Value of a Subscript with a PERFORM Statement

In the MAIN-PROCESS paragraph of the Procedure Division, we see a new form of the PERFORM statement, at line 01220. This is the PERFORM statement with the **VARYING** option. When you use the VARYING option, you must also use the required words FROM, BY, and UNTIL. The format of this PERFORM statement is given in the next chapter.

The VARYING option is often used when one or more subscripted fields are involved in the processing, but it can also be used in certain circumstances where there are no subscripted fields. The meaning of the PERFORM . . . VARYING statement in Program P09-01 is almost self-evident. The paragraph COMMISSION-CALCULATION is to be PERFORMed over and over. The first time the COMMISSION-CALCULATION is PERFORMed, COMPUTATION-SUBSCRIPT will be set to 1 by the PERFORM statement. Then each time COMMISSION-CALCULATION is PERFORMed again, the value of COMPUTATION-SUBSCRIPT will be increased by 1. This will go on until the value of COMPUTATION-SUBSCRIPT IS GREATER THAN the NUMBER-OF-SALES. So the PERFORM statement causes COMMISSION-CALCULATION to be executed with COMPUTATION-SUBSCRIPT set to 1, 2, 3, and so on to 10. When COMPUTATION-SUBSCRIPT finally gets to assume the value of 11, the PERFORM statement notices that COMPUTATION-SUBSCRIPT IS GREATER THAN the NUMBER-OF-SALES and does not execute the paragraph COMMISSION-CALCULATION.

In the paragraph COMMISSION-CALCULATION, which begins at line 01380, all references to SALE-AMOUNT-IN, COMMISSION-AMOUNT-W, and COMMISSION-AMOUNT-OUT are subscripted. All such references must be subscripted, since SALE-AMOUNT-IN, COMMISSION-AMOUNT-W, and COMMISSION-AMOUNT-OUT are all defined with OCCURS clauses. But the subscripting permits the entire paragraph to refer to all 10 SALE-AMOUNT-IN fields, all 10 COMMISSION-AMOUNT-W fields, and all 10 COMMISSION-AMOUNT-OUT fields, even though the coding is written only once. You can see how each of the 10 COMMISSION-AMOUNT-W values is computed and how the 10 amounts are accumulated to obtain the COMMISSION-FOR-SALESPERSON.

Program P09-01 was run using the input data shown in Figure 9.3 and produced the output shown in Figure 9.4.

Figure 9.3 Input to Program P09-01.

```
--------------------------------------------------------------------------------
         1         2         3         4         5         6         7         8
12345678901234567890123456789012345678901234567890123456789012345678901234567890
--------------------------------------------------------------------------------
000128950075000125680010004871218149200060001100000480001050008759 3
094238601000020000005192700955000279502000001250004122500600003615 0
368442002000001216500749501000000000000000000000000000000000000000 0
523671400841200451907236800685002951800000000000000000000000000000 0
661236400100002235800187309950000651502451201036800899501736006028 7
774711900520001650011950000735004489501250000687500142500999900000 0
```

Figure 9.4 Output from Program P09-01.

COMMISSION REPORT

SALES-PERSON NUMBER	SALE 1	SALE 2	SALE 3	COMMISSIONS ON SALES SALE 4	SALE 5	SALE 6	SALE 7	SALE 8	SALE 9	SALE 10	TOTAL COMMIS-SION
0001289	495.75	0.63	795.10	43.71	176.49	0.30	6.00	2.40	5.50	82.59	1,608.47
0942386	5.00	195.00	46.93	4.78	1.40	15.00	7.50	36.23	3.00	31.15	345.99
3684420	15.00	7.17	3.75	5.00	0.00	0.00	0.00	0.00	0.00	0.00	30.92
5236714	4.21	2.26	67.37	3.43	24.52	0.00	0.00	0.00	0.00	0.00	101.79
6612364	0.50	17.36	0.94	94.50	3.26	19.51	5.37	4.50	12.36	55.29	213.59
7747119	2.60	11.50	114.50	3.68	39.90	7.50	3.44	0.71	5.00	0.00	188.83

TOTAL COMMISSION FOR ALL SALESPERSONS 2,489.59

EXERCISE 3

Write a program to read input records in the following format:

Positions	Field
1 – 9	Social Security Number
10 – 12	Monday Hours (to one decimal place)
13 – 15	Tuesday Hours (to one decimal place)
16 – 18	Wednesday Hours (to one decimal place)
19 – 21	Thursday Hours (to one decimal place)
22 – 24	Friday Hours (to one decimal place)
25 – 80	spaces

For each record have your program print the number of hours worked each day, unless the number of hours worked in any day is greater than 7.5. If the number of hours worked in a day is greater than 7.5, have your program compute and print the number of effective hours worked that day according to the following formula:

$$\text{Effective hours} = \text{hours worked} + \frac{\text{hours worked} - 7.5}{2}$$

Have your program print its output in the format shown in Figure 9.E3.

Figure 9.E3 Output format for Exercise 3.

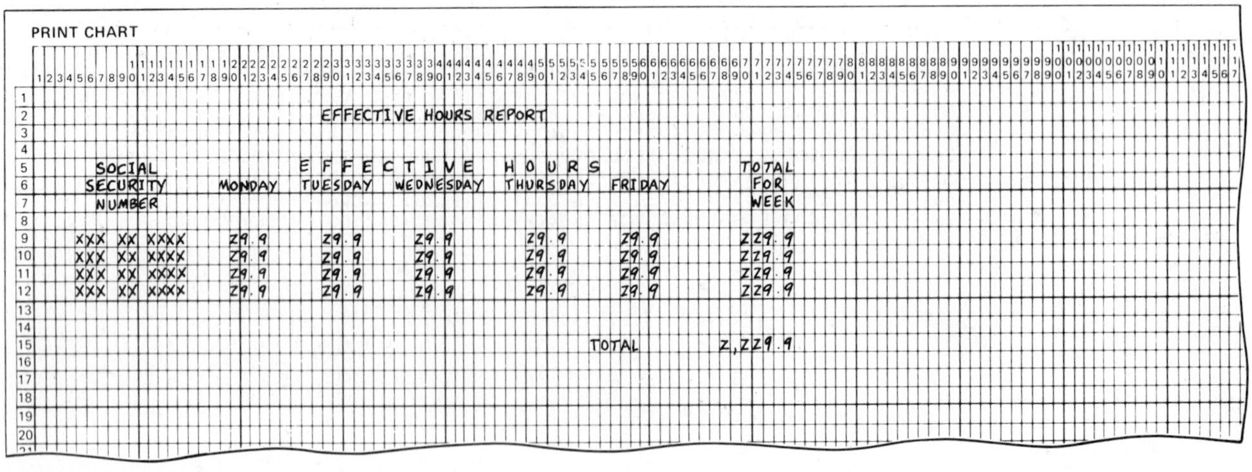

Tables

In COBOL, a table is a group of fields defined with an OCCURS clause. 1974 COBOL is capable of handling **one-dimensional** tables, as well as **two-dimensional** and **three-dimensional** ones. 1985 COBOL handles tables of up to seven dimensions. In this chapter, we will discuss only one-dimensional tables. Tables of higher dimension will be discussed in Chapter 10.

In computer terminology, tables are often referred to as **arrays.** Whereas in mathematics the words "table" and "array" may mean different things (as in an array of coefficients, but a table of trigonometric functions), in computer terminology they mean exactly the same thing. We will use only the word "table."

For our purposes, there are only two kinds of tables: **direct-reference tables** and **search tables.** Program P09-01 used direct-reference tables. The next section shows another way that a program can use a direct-reference table.

Direct-Reference Tables

A direct-reference table is one whose fields are referred to by their numerical position in the table; for example, a list of the names of the 12 months January, February, March, and so on. If we had such a list, and wanted to know the name of month 8, we would only have to look at the eighth entry in the table to find our answer, August. Actually it is easier for a COBOL program to find any particular item in such a list than it would be for you or me. We would have to count, either from the beginning or the end of the list, to find the item wanted. A COBOL program can go directly to the desired item without having to count. That is why such a table is called a direct-reference table.

Program P09-02 shows how such a table can be written into a COBOL program and how it might be used. Program P09-02 reads input records in the following format:

Positions	Field
1 – 2	Month Number (01 through 12)
3 – 4	Day Number (01 through 31)
5 – 6	Year of Century (01 through 99)
7 – 80	spaces

Each record contains a date in the usual American format MMDDYY. For each record read, Program P09-02 expands the date and prints the input and the expanded date on one line, as shown in Figure 9.5. Notice that the dates are formatted rather crudely; the short names such as May and June have a lot of space after them. COBOL provides a method of eliminating those unwanted spaces, which we will cover in Chapter 17.

For Program P09-02 to print out the names of months, it must have the names of the months in it somewhere. Tables that are written into COBOL programs are always written in the Working Storage Section. Most tables can be written into a program in more than one way, but in this book you will not see all the possible ways in which tables can be written. The ways shown here were selected for ease of use and clarity of meaning.

Figure 9.5 Output format for Program P09-02.

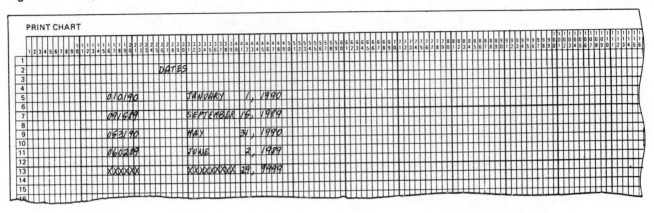

Program P09-02 is shown in Figure 9.6, and the table of month names begins at line 00440. A direct-reference table can be written into a program in several ways. The method used here is convenient for most applications. It consists of a series of FILLER entries preceded by a group-level name. Here the group-level name is MONTH-NAME-TABLE-ENTRIES. The FILLER entries must all be the same size, and so they were all made as large as the largest, SEPTEMBER.

Following the series of FILLER entries containing the **elements** of the direct-reference table, there must be an entry in the form shown in line 00570. The entry must contain the name of the table, a REDEFINES clause, a PICTURE clause, and an OCCURS clause. Names of tables are user-defined words made up according to the rules for making up any ordinary data names. The PICTURE clause and the OCCURS clause may be in either order, but the REDEFINES clause must immediately follow the data name, in this case MONTH-NAME. The entry containing the REDEFINES clause must have the same level number as the group name that appears before the FILLER entries immediately above it, in this case 05. A REDEFINES clause may be used in a level-01 entry in the Working Storage Section; remember that an OCCURS clause must not be used in a level-01 entry anywhere.

The dummy entry, line 00430, is needed to prevent the OCCURS clause in line 00580 from ending up at the 01 level. Remember that the entry in line 00570 must be at the same level as the group name in line 00440. Line 00430 was included in the program so that 00440 could be written at some level other than 01. If you have more than one table in a program, they may all be written under the same dummy level-01 entry.

Figure 9.6 Program P09-02.

```
CB1 RELEASE 2.4                              IBM OS/VS COBOL  JULY  1, 1982


                        23.27.08        APR  5,1988


      00010   IDENTIFICATION DIVISION.
      00020   PROGRAM-ID.  P09-02.
      00030  *AUTHOR.   DEBORAH ANN SENIOR.
      00040  *
      00050  *    THIS PROGRAM READS DATES IN MMDDYY FORM AND PRINTS THEM
      00060  *    WITH THE MONTH NAME SPELLED OUT
      00070  *
```

Figure 9.6

```
00080  *****************************************************************
00090
00100  ENVIRONMENT DIVISION.
00110  CONFIGURATION SECTION.
00120  SOURCE-COMPUTER.  IBM-370.
00130  OBJECT-COMPUTER.  IBM-370.
00140
00150  INPUT-OUTPUT SECTION.
00160  FILE-CONTROL.
00170      SELECT DATE-FILE-IN          ASSIGN TO INFILE.
00180      SELECT DATE-REPORT-FILE-OUT  ASSIGN TO PRINTER.
00190
00200  *****************************************************************
00210
00220  DATA DIVISION.
00230  FILE SECTION.
00240  FD  DATE-FILE-IN
00250      LABEL RECORDS ARE OMITTED
00260      RECORD CONTAINS 80 CHARACTERS.
00270
00280  01  DATE-RECORD-IN.
00290      05  DATE-IN.
00300          10  MONTH-IN    PIC 99.
00310          10  DAY-IN      PIC 99.
00320          10  YEAR-IN     PIC 99.
00330      05  FILLER          PIC X(74).
00340
00350  FD  DATE-REPORT-FILE-OUT
00360      LABEL RECORDS ARE OMITTED.
00370
00380  01  REPORT-LINE         PIC X(48).
00390
00400  WORKING-STORAGE SECTION.
00410  01  MORE-INPUT          PIC X           VALUE "Y".
00420  01  LINE-SPACING        PIC S9          COMP SYNC.
00430  01  MONTH-NAME-TABLE.
00440      05  MONTH-NAME-TABLE-ENTRIES.
00450          10  FILLER      PIC X(9)        VALUE "JANUARY".
00460          10  FILLER      PIC X(9)        VALUE "FEBRUARY".
00470          10  FILLER      PIC X(9)        VALUE "MARCH".
00480          10  FILLER      PIC X(9)        VALUE "APRIL".
00490          10  FILLER      PIC X(9)        VALUE "MAY".
00500          10  FILLER      PIC X(9)        VALUE "JUNE".
00510          10  FILLER      PIC X(9)        VALUE "JULY".
00520          10  FILLER      PIC X(9)        VALUE "AUGUST".
00530          10  FILLER      PIC X(9)        VALUE "SEPTEMBER".
00540          10  FILLER      PIC X(9)        VALUE "OCTOBER".
00550          10  FILLER      PIC X(9)        VALUE "NOVEMBER".
00560          10  FILLER      PIC X(9)        VALUE "DECEMBER".
00570      05  MONTH-NAME      REDEFINES MONTH-NAME-TABLE-ENTRIES
00580                          PIC X(9)        OCCURS 12 TIMES.
00590
00600  01  PAGE-HEADING.
00610      05  FILLER          PIC X(25)       VALUE SPACES.
00620      05  FILLER          PIC X(5)        VALUE "DATES".
00630
00640  01  DETAIL-LINE.
00650      05  FILLER          PIC X(16)       VALUE SPACES.
00660      05  DATE-OUT        PIC X(6).
00670      05  MONTH-OUT       PIC B(8)X(9).
00680      05  DAY-OUT         PIC BZ9.
00690      05  FILLER          PIC X(4)        VALUE ", 19".
00700      05  YEAR-OUT        PIC 99.
00710
00720  01  NO-INPUT-DATA.
00730      05  FILLER          PIC X(21)       VALUE SPACES.
00740      05  FILLER          PIC X(13)       VALUE "NO INPUT DATA".
00750
00760  *****************************************************************
00770
00780  PROCEDURE DIVISION.
00790  CONTROL-PARAGRAPH.
00800      PERFORM INITIALIZATION.
00810      PERFORM MAIN-PROCESS UNTIL MORE-INPUT IS EQUAL TO "N".
00820      PERFORM TERMINATION.
00830      STOP RUN.
```

(continued)

Figure 9.6 (continued)

```
00840
00850    INITIALIZATION.
00860        OPEN INPUT  DATE-FILE-IN,
00870                 OUTPUT DATE-REPORT-FILE-OUT.
00880        WRITE REPORT-LINE FROM PAGE-HEADING AFTER PAGE.
00890        MOVE 3 TO LINE-SPACING.
00900        PERFORM READ-A-RECORD.
00910        IF MORE-INPUT IS EQUAL TO "N"
00920            WRITE REPORT-LINE FROM NO-INPUT-DATA AFTER 3.
00930
00940    MAIN-PROCESS.
00950        MOVE DATE-IN                      TO DATE-OUT.
00960        MOVE MONTH-NAME (MONTH-IN)        TO MONTH-OUT.
00970        MOVE DAY-IN                       TO DAY-OUT.
00980        MOVE YEAR-IN                      TO YEAR-OUT.
00990        WRITE REPORT-LINE FROM DETAIL-LINE AFTER LINE-SPACING.
01000        MOVE 2 TO LINE-SPACING.
01010        PERFORM READ-A-RECORD.
01020
01030    TERMINATION.
01040        CLOSE DATE-FILE-IN,
01050                 DATE-REPORT-FILE-OUT.
```

We have already used a REDEFINES clause to give a single field more than one PICTURE in connection with validity checking, but here REDEFINES is used for an entirely different purpose. In this entry the PICTURE is the same as the PICTURE in the FILLER entries that were used for writing the table values, X(9). The OCCURS clause, of course, tells how many entries there are in the table. This whole set of entries — the 12 FILLER entries, their group-level name, and the REDEFINES entry — now permits us to refer to the 12 different names of the months by the names

```
MONTH-NAME (1)
MONTH-NAME (2)
MONTH-NAME (3)
```

and so on up to:

```
MONTH-NAME (12)
```

Better yet, we can have a data name be the subscript, let's say MONTH-SUBSCRIPT, and then we can refer to any of the month names as

```
MONTH-NAME (MONTH-SUBSCRIPT)
```

with MONTH-SUBSCRIPT assigned some value from 1 through 12. Of course, the field used for subscripting MONTH-NAME doesn't have to be called MONTH-SUBSCRIPT; it can be any field defined as an integer.

The MOVE statement at line 00960 shows how we can use subscripting to get the desired month name directly. Line 00960 has as its sending field MONTH-NAME (MONTH-IN). MONTH-IN is defined as an integer and so can be used as a subscript. Furthermore, it is defined in the File Section as part of the input area, and so the month number as it appears in the input record can be used as the subscript in the MOVE statement.

Program P09-02 was run with the input data shown in Figure 9.7 and produced the output shown in Figure 9.8.

Figure 9.7 Input to Program P09-02.

```
----------------------------------------------------------------------------------
            1         2         3         4         5         6         7         8
   12345678901234567890123456789012345678901234567890123456789012345678901234567890
----------------------------------------------------------------------------------
   010190
   091589
   053190
   060290
   071490
   112789
   050790
   090389
   063090
   021490
```

Figure 9.8 Output from Program P09-02.

```
       DATES

   010190       JANUARY     1, 1990

   091589       SEPTEMBER  15, 1989

   053190       MAY        31, 1990

   060290       JUNE        2, 1990

   071490       JULY       14, 1990

   112789       NOVEMBER   27, 1989

   050790       MAY         7, 1990

   090389       SEPTEMBER   3, 1989

   063090       JUNE       30, 1990

   021490       FEBRUARY   14, 1990
```

A Direct-Reference Table in Storage

Figure 9.9 shows how the month-name table in Program P09-02 is arranged in computer storage. The 12 FILLER entries in lines 00450 through 00560 establish 12 fields, containing the words JANUARY, FEBRUARY, and so on, in adjacent areas of storage. The REDEFINES entry with its OCCURS clause, line 00570, then establishes the 12 occurrences of MONTH-NAME, with each being assigned to one of the 12 fields.

Figure 9.9 How the MONTH-NAME-TABLE-ENTRIES of Program P09-02 are arranged in computer storage.

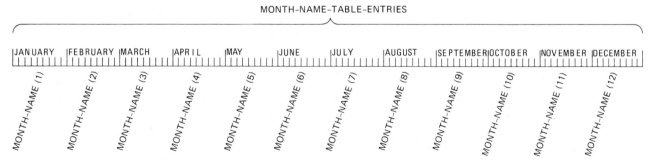

EXERCISE 4

Write a program to read and process input records in the following format:

Positions	Field
1 – 2	State Code
3 – 22	City Name
23 – 80	spaces

Each record contains a two-digit state code and the name of a city spelled out. For each record read, print the input data in their original form, and also print the city name and state name in the format shown in Figure 9.E4. Use the 16 state names listed in Table 9-E4. Include in your test data for this program at least one record with a state code of 01, at least one record with a state code of 16, and some with state codes in between.

Figure 9.E4 Output format for Exercise 4.

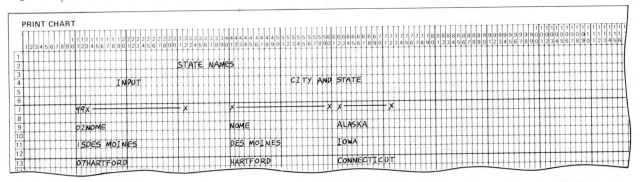

Table 9-E4
Sixteen state names in alphabetic order.

Alabama
Alaska
Arizona
Arkansas
California
Colorado
Connecticut
Delaware
Florida
Georgia
Hawaii
Idaho
Illinois
Indiana
Iowa
Kansas

A Search Table with Indexing

A search table is one whose contents must be examined in some way before any data can be extracted from the table. An example of such a table is Table 9-1, which might be used by the U.S. Postal Service.

Table 9-1

Sixteen state codes and their corresponding state names.

State Code	State Name
AL	Alabama
AK	Alaska
AZ	Arizona
AR	Arkansas
CA	California
CO	Colorado
CT	Connecticut
DE	Delaware
FL	Florida
GA	Georgia
HI	Hawaii
ID	Idaho
IL	Illinois
IN	Indiana
IA	Iowa
KS	Kansas

This table can be used two ways. If you know a state code, you can get the corresponding state name out of the table. Or you can enter the table knowing a state name and find the code. The entry keys to a table are called the **arguments,** and the pieces of data we want to extract are called **functions.** If we have the state code GA, for example, and want to find the state name, GA is the argument. The name we are looking for, Georgia, is the function. If we want to find the state code for California, then California is the argument. The code CA is the function.

With a table such as this, neither you nor I nor COBOL can find what we want without searching through the table arguments. Whenever you have to search a table in a COBOL program, it is best to use indexing with it, because the SEARCH verb can be used only with an indexed table and not with a subscripted one. Although using the SEARCH verb is not the only way to search a table, it is the best because it makes the program coding most easily understandable.

Indexes work essentially differently from subscripts. Subscripts are stored in the computer as the numbers 1, 2, 3, and so on, referring to the first, second, third, and so forth, entry in the table. Every time a subscript is used, COBOL must compute, using the subscript, the storage location of the corresponding table entry. Indexes, on the other hand, are stored in a form that reflects the actual storage locations of table entries, and so such computations are unnecessary when they are used. The programmer need never be concerned with storage locations, however, and can always think of an index simply as referring to the first, second, third, and so on, entry in a table.

To set up a table for indexing, you merely include an **INDEXED BY** phrase in the OCCURS clause that defines the table. For example, if we were to use indexing on the table in Program P09-02, then instead of the entry

```
05 MONTH-NAME REDEFINES MONTH-NAME-TABLE-ENTRIES
            PIC X(9)  OCCURS 12 TIMES.
```

we would have

```
05 MONTH-NAME REDEFINES MONTH-NAME-TABLE-ENTRIES
            PIC X(9)
            OCCURS 12 TIMES INDEXED BY MONTH-INDEX.
```

The made-up name referred to in the INDEXED BY phrase is called an **index name.** The rules for making up index names are the same as for making up ordinary data names. Once a name is given as an index name in an INDEXED BY phrase, it must not be defined further. COBOL will set up the index name field in its most efficient form. Unlike a subscript, which can be used to subscript any field in a program that is defined with an OCCURS clause, an index name can be used to index only the one OCCURS clause that it is defined with.

Once an index name is established, we can refer to fields by using **direct indexing.** Direct indexing looks just like subscripting. Here's how we could refer to some of the MONTH-NAME fields with direct indexing:

```
MONTH-NAME (1)
MONTH-NAME (2)
MONTH-NAME (12)
```

and

```
MONTH-NAME (MONTH-INDEX)
```

(pronounced "MONTH-NAME indexed by MONTH-INDEX"). It is also possible to refer to indexed fields by using **relative indexing,** which will be discussed in the next chapter, and by subscripting, in which we use an ordinary identifier defined as an integer.

We now will do a program using the Postal Service table of state names and two-letter state codes. The input to Program P09-03 is similar to the input for Exercise 4 (page 264) except that the State Code, in positions 1 and 2 of the input, is two letters instead of two digits. The City Name field remains the same as in Exercise 4, and the output is to be the same (Figure 9.E4).

In this program we have to write both the state names and the two-letter state codes into the program. We already know how to write a table of state names from Exercise 4. In Program P09-03 we will also have to write a table of two-letter state codes. The state codes will have to be in the same order as their corresponding state names. The state names are in alphabetic order, but the program would work regardless of the order of the state names as long as the codes were in the same order as the names. Then, for each input record the program reads, it will take the two-letter state code from the input and search the table of state codes looking for a match. Once a match is found between the input state code and a state code in the table, the program will be able to find the corresponding state name to print on the output report.

Program P09-03 is shown in Figure 9.10. In the Working Storage Section you can see the table of state names, set up for indexing, beginning at line 00430. The entries for this table should resemble very strongly the entries you wrote for the state-names table in Exercise 4, except that now we have an INDEXED BY phrase in the OCCURS clause at line 00610. Of course, once we establish the index name

Figure 9.10 Program P09-03.

```
CB1 RELEASE 2.4                              IBM CS/VS COBOL  JULY 1, 1982

                        23.53.43        APR 5,1988

00010  IDENTIFICATION DIVISION.
00020  PROGRAM-ID. P09-03.
00030 *AUTHOR. DEBORAH ANN SENIOR.
00040 *
00050 *    THIS PROGRAM PERFORMS A SEARCH OF STATE CODES AND PRINTS
00060 *    STATE NAMES.
00070 *
00080 *********************************************************************
00090
00100  ENVIRONMENT DIVISION.
00110  CONFIGURATION SECTION.
00120  SOURCE-COMPUTER. IBM-370.
00130  OBJECT-COMPUTER. IBM-370.
00140
00150  INPUT-OUTPUT SECTION.
00160  FILE-CONTROL.
00170      SELECT ADDRESS-FILE-IN        ASSIGN TO INFILE.
00180      SELECT ADDRESS-REPORT-FILE-OUT  ASSIGN TO PRINTER.
00190
00200 *********************************************************************
00210
00220  DATA DIVISION.
00230  FILE SECTION.
00240  FD  ADDRESS-FILE-IN
00250      LABEL RECORDS ARE OMITTED
00260      RECORD CONTAINS 80 CHARACTERS.
00270
00280  01  ADDRESS-RECORD-IN.
00290      05  STATE-AND-CITY-IN.
00300          10  STATE-CODE-IN        PIC XX.
00310          10  CITY-NAME-IN         PIC X(20).
00320      05  FILLER                   PIC X(58).
00330
00340  FD  ADDRESS-REPORT-FILE-OUT
00350      LABEL RECORDS ARE OMITTED.
00360
00370  01  REPORT-LINE      PIC X(72).
00380
00390  WORKING-STORAGE SECTION.
00400  01  LINE-SPACING     PIC S9        COMP SYNC.
00410  01  MORE-INPUT       PIC X         VALUE "Y".
00420  01  STATE-TABLES.
00430      05  STATE-NAME-TABLE-ENTRIES.
00440          10  FILLER   PIC X(11)     VALUE "ALABAMA".
00450          10  FILLER   PIC X(11)     VALUE "ALASKA".
00460          10  FILLER   PIC X(11)     VALUE "ARIZONA".
00470          10  FILLER   PIC X(11)     VALUE "ARKANSAS".
00480          10  FILLER   PIC X(11)     VALUE "CALIFORNIA".
00490          10  FILLER   PIC X(11)     VALUE "COLORADO".
00500          10  FILLER   PIC X(11)     VALUE "CONNECTICUT".
00510          10  FILLER   PIC X(11)     VALUE "DELAWARE".
00520          10  FILLER   PIC X(11)     VALUE "FLORIDA".
00530          10  FILLER   PIC X(11)     VALUE "GEORGIA".
00540          10  FILLER   PIC X(11)     VALUE "HAWAII".
00550          10  FILLER   PIC X(11)     VALUE "IDAHO".
00560          10  FILLER   PIC X(11)     VALUE "ILLINOIS".
00570          10  FILLER   PIC X(11)     VALUE "INDIANA".
00580          10  FILLER   PIC X(11)     VALUE "IOWA".
00590          10  FILLER   PIC X(11)     VALUE "KANSAS".
```

(continued)

Figure 9.10   (continued)

```
00600          05   STATE-NAME        REDEFINES STATE-NAME-TABLE-ENTRIES
00610               OCCURS 16 TIMES INDEXED BY STATE-NAME-INDEX
00620                                 PIC X(11).
00630          05   STATE-CODE-TABLE-ENTRIES.
00640               10  FILLER        PIC XX           VALUE "AL".
00650               10  FILLER        PIC XX           VALUE "AK".
00660               10  FILLER        PIC XX           VALUE "AZ".
00670               10  FILLER        PIC XX           VALUE "AR".
00680               10  FILLER        PIC XX           VALUE "CA".
00690               10  FILLER        PIC XX           VALUE "CO".
00700               10  FILLER        PIC XX           VALUE "CT".
00710               10  FILLER        PIC XX           VALUE "DE".
00720               10  FILLER        PIC XX           VALUE "FL".
00730               10  FILLER        PIC XX           VALUE "GA".
00740               10  FILLER        PIC XX           VALUE "HI".
00750               10  FILLER        PIC XX           VALUE "ID".
00760               10  FILLER        PIC XX           VALUE "IL".
00770               10  FILLER        PIC XX           VALUE "IN".
00780               10  FILLER        PIC XX           VALUE "IA".
00790               10  FILLERL       PIC XX           VALUE "KS".
00800          05   STATE-CODE        REDEFINES STATE-CODE-TABLE-ENTRIES
00810               OCCURS 16 TIMES INDEXED BY STATE-CCDE-INDEX
00820                                 PIC XX.
00830
00840   01   PAGE-HEADING-1.
00850        05 FILLER               PIC X(30)        VALUE SPACE.
00860        05 FILLER               PIC X(11)        VALUE "STATE NAMES".
00870
00880   01   PAGE-HEADING-2.
00890        05 FILLER               PIC X(18)        VALUE SPACES.
00900        05 FILLER               PIC X(5)         VALUE "INPUT".
00910        05 FILLER               PIC X(29)        VALUE SPACES.
00920        05 FILLER               PIC X(14)        VALUE "CITY AND STATE".
00930
00940   01   DETAIL-LINE.
00950        05 FILLER                          PIC X(10) VALUE SPACES.
00960        05 STATE-AND-CITY-OUT              PIC X(22).
00970        05 CITY-NAME-OUT                   PIC B(8)X(20).
00980        05 STATE-NAME-OUT                  PIC BX(11).
00990
01000   01   NO-INPUT-DATA.
01010        05 FILLER               PIC X(29)        VALUE SPACES.
01020        05 FILLER               PIC X(13)        VALUE "NO INPUT DATA".
01030
01040   **************************************************************
01050
01060   PROCEDURE DIVISION.
01070   CONTROL-PARAGRAPH.
01080        PERFORM INITIALIZATION.
01090        PERFORM MAIN-PROCESS UNTIL MORE-INPUT IS EQUAL TO "N".
01100        PERFORM TERMINATION.
01110        STOP RUN.
01120
01130   INITIALIZATION.
01140        OPEN INPUT  ADDRESS-FILE-IN,
01150             OUTPUT ADDRESS-REPORT-FILE-OUT.
01160        WRITE REPORT-LINE FROM PAGE-HEADING-1 AFTER PAGE.
01170        WRITE REPORT-LINE FROM PAGE-HEADING-2 AFTER 2.
01180        MOVE 3 TO LINE-SPACING.
01190        PERFORM READ-A-RECORD.
01200        IF MORE-INPUT IS EQUAL TO "N"
01210            WRITE REPORT-LINE FROM NO-INPUT-DATA AFTER 3.
01220
01230   MAIN-PROCESS.
01240        SET STATE-CODE-INDEX,
01250            STATE-NAME-INDEX TO 1.
01260        SEARCH STATE-CODE
01270            VARYING STATE-NAME-INDEX
01280            WHEN STATE-CODE-IN = STATE-CODE (STATE-CODE-INDEX)
01290                MOVE STATE-AND-CITY-IN     TO STATE-AND-CITY-OUT
01300                MOVE CITY-NAME-IN          TO CITY-NAME-OUT
01310                MOVE STATE-NAME (STATE-NAME-INDEX) TO STATE-NAME-OUT
01320                WRITE REPORT-LINE FROM DETAIL-LINE
01330                        AFTER LINE-SPACING
01340                MOVE 2 TO LINE-SPACING.
01350        PERFORM READ-A-RECORD.
01360
```

```
01370   TERMINATION.
01380      CLOSE ADDRESS-FILE-IN,
01390            ADDRESS-REPORT-FILE-OUT.
01400
01410   READ-A-RECORD.
01420      READ ADDRESS-FILE-IN
01430         AT END
01440            MOVE "N" TO MORE-INPUT.
```

STATE-NAME-INDEX, we must not define it elsewhere. You can see that the table of state codes is set up just below, starting at line 00630. It gets its own index, STATE-CODE-INDEX, in line 00810.

The statement at line 01310 will MOVE a STATE-NAME to the report output area. In that statement, STATE-NAME is indexed by its table index, STATE-NAME-INDEX. How will STATE-NAME-INDEX get the correct value assigned to it so that the correct STATE-NAME will print? In Program P09-02 and Exercise 4 we were able to subscript our output fields directly by using input data as the subscript because in those programs we were dealing with direct-reference tables. Here we have a search table, and for the program to get the value it needs for STATE-NAME-INDEX, it will have to search the STATE-CODE-TABLE-ENTRIES. You will soon see how.

In the MAIN-PROCESS paragraph in the Procedure Division are the two statements needed to search the STATE-CODE-TABLE-ENTRIES and assign the correct value to STATE-NAME-INDEX so that the MOVE statement in line 01310 will work correctly. The first is the **SET** statement in line 01240. Whenever you SEARCH a table sequentially as we are doing here, that is, whenever you examine the table entries one after another in order, you must tell COBOL where the SEARCH should begin. Here we want to begin the SEARCH at the beginning of the table, so we SET both table indexes to point to the first element in their respective tables. Then we give a SEARCH statement.

In a SEARCH statement the word SEARCH must be followed by the name of the field to be SEARCHed. The field to be SEARCHed must be defined with an OCCURS clause having an INDEXED BY phrase. In this case the field to be SEARCHed is STATE-CODE. This directs COBOL to step through the STATE-CODEs, stepping up the STATE-CODE-INDEX to point to successive elements of the state code table until the SEARCH finds what it is looking for.

Following the name of the field to be SEARCHed, you may have a VARYING phrase. The VARYING phrase is used when you are SEARCHing through a table and you want one index name to keep pace with another, as when there are two tables in a program. In our case, we want the STATE-NAME-INDEX to keep pace with the STATE-CODE-INDEX as the STATE-CODEs are SEARCHed. That is, when STATE-CODE-INDEX is pointing to the second STATE-CODE in the state code table, we want STATE-NAME-INDEX to be pointing to the second STATE-NAME in the state name table. If STATE-CODE-INDEX should get to point to the third STATE-CODE, we would want STATE-NAME-INDEX to point to the third STATE-NAME at the same time. Then when a match is found between STATE-CODE-IN and a STATE-CODE in the table, STATE-NAME-INDEX will be pointing to the corresponding STATE-NAME in the state name table.

The **WHEN** clause in a SEARCH statement tells COBOL under what conditions the SEARCH is to stop, and what to do then. Here we want the SEARCH to end WHEN STATE-CODE-IN is equal to one of the table STATE-CODEs. At that time, the STATE-NAME-INDEX has been set to its proper value by the VARYING phrase. We then give statements to format and print the output line. You may have as many imperative statements as you like in a WHEN clause. Alternatively, you may have the words NEXT SENTENCE if you want COBOL to skip to the next sentence when the SEARCH is completed.

Program P09-3 was run with the input data shown in Figure 9.11 and produced the output shown in Figure 9.12.

Figure 9.11 Input to Program P09-03.

```
         ----------------------------------------------------------------------------
              1         2         3         4         5         6         7         8
         12345678901234567890123456789012345678901234567890123456789012345678901234567890
         ----------------------------------------------------------------------------
         AKNOME
         IADES MOINES
         CTHARTFORD
         KSWICHITA
         CASAN FRANCISCO
         FLMIAMI
         HIHONOLULU
```

Figure 9.12 Output from Program P09-03.

```
                              STATE NAMES

                   INPUT                        CITY AND STATE


           AKNOME                       NOME              ALASKA

           IADES MOINES                 DES MOINES        IOWA

           CTHARTFORD                   HARTFORD          CONNECTICUT

           KSWICHITA                    WICHITA           KANSAS

           CASAN FRANCISCO              SAN FRANCISCO     CALIFORNIA

           FLMIAMI                      MIAMI             FLORIDA

           HIHONOLULU                   HONOLULU          HAWAII
```

The SET Statement

The SET statement can be used for several purposes and has two formats. Format 2 will be given later in this chapter. The SET statement in Program P09-03 has the following format:

```
SET  {index-name-1 [, index-name-2]...}  TO  {index-name-3 }
     {identifier-1 [, identifier-2]...}       {identifier-3 }
                                              {literal-1    }
```

The first set of braces, before the word TO, shows that index names and identifiers may have values assigned to them by the SET statement. An identifier is a data name followed by any legal combination of qualifiers, subscripts, and/or indexes. The square brackets within the braces show that more than one index name or more than one identifier may have a value assigned to them with a single SET statement. The second set of braces, after the word TO, shows that the sending field of the SET statement may be either an index name, an identifier, or a literal. If a literal is used, it must be an integer numeric literal.

In Program P09-03, the receiving fields of the SET statement were the index names STATE-CODE-INDEX and STATE-NAME-INDEX. The sending field was the numeric literal 1. Execution of the SET statement caused the literal 1 to be converted to a number that reflected the storage location of the first STATE-CODE, and to store that number in STATE-CODE-INDEX. It also caused the literal 1 to be converted to a number that reflected the storage location of the first STATE-NAME, and to store that number in STATE-NAME-INDEX.

If a SET statement of the form

```
SET index-name-1 TO identifier-3
```

is used, identifier-3 must be defined as an integer. The SET statement takes the number in identifier-3 (a 1, 2, or 3, and so on) and converts it to point to the first, second, or third (and so on) entry in the table related to index-name-1.

If a SET statement of the form

```
SET identifier-1 TO index-name-3
```

is used, the SET statement determines which entry in its table index-name-3 is pointing to (the first, second, or third, and so on) and converts it to the number 1, 2, or 3, and so on, and stores the number in identifier-1.

If a SET statement of the form

```
SET index-name-1 TO index-name-3
```

is used, the SET statement determines which entry in its table index-name-3 is pointing to and stores in index-name-1, a number that points to the corresponding entry in its table. Remember that in a SET statement, the sending field appears after the word TO, and the receiving field before.

Any other combination of sending and receiving fields is illegal. You cannot use

```
SET identifier-1 TO identifier-3
```

Use instead:

```
MOVE identifier-3 TO identifier-1
```

You cannot use

```
SET identifier-1 TO literal-1
```

Use instead:

```
MOVE literal-1 TO identifier-1
```

The only statements that can change the value of an index name are SET, SEARCH, and PERFORM . . . VARYING. An index name can be used in a relation condition anywhere that a condition is legal. Its value in the relation condition is taken to be 1, 2, or 3, and so on, depending on whether the index name is pointing to the first, second, or third, and so on, entry in its table. An index name by itself cannot be used as the sending or receiving field in any statement other than SET.

The SEARCH Statement

The format of the SEARCH statement is:

```
SEARCH identifier-1 [VARYING {identifier-2  } ]
                            {index-name-1}

    [; AT END imperative-statement-1]
     ;WHEN condition-1 {imperative-statement-2}
                       {NEXT SENTENCE        }
       [; WHEN condition-2 {imperative-statement-3} ]...
                           {NEXT SENTENCE        }
```

The first set of square brackets shows that the VARYING phrase is optional. The braces accompanying the VARYING phrase show that the SEARCH statement can vary either an index name or an identifier. In Program P09-03 we used it to vary the index name STATE-NAME-INDEX. When the VARYING phrase is used to vary an identifier, the identifier is assigned the value 1, 2, 3, and so on, as the SEARCH points to the first, second, third, and so on, entry of the table being SEARCHed. The AT END phrase is optional and is used when there is the possibility that the SEARCH may run off the end of the table. We will use an AT END phrase in our next program.

Any legal COBOL condition may be used in a WHEN clause to terminate a SEARCH (such as GREATER THAN, LESS THAN, and so on, and complex conditions). The square brackets and the ellipsis accompanying the second WHEN clause show that any number of WHEN clauses may be written into a SEARCH statement, and that each may have its own imperative statement or statements. If a SEARCH statement contains more than one WHEN clause, then for each setting of the search index the WHEN conditions are tested in the order in which they are written in the SEARCH statement. The first WHEN condition that is satisfied terminates the SEARCH, and the appropriate imperative statement or statements are carried out.

EXERCISE 5

Write a program to read input records in the following format:

Positions	Field
1 – 2	Branch Office Number
3 – 32	Agent Name
33 – 80	spaces

Each record contains an Agent Name and a Branch Office Number. For each record read, have your program print on one line the Agent Name, the Branch Office Number, and the branch office name. Use the following table for the branch office names:

Branch Office Number	Branch Office Name
02	Allentown
05	Bethlehem
07	Blue Ball
11	Delaware Water Gap
13	Dingmans Ferry
15	Harrisburg
20	King of Prussia
21	Philadelphia
37	Pittsburgh
39	Scranton
44	Wilkes-Barre

Design the output for this program before you begin coding. Provide a suitable report title and column headings. Include in your input data at least one record with Branch Office Number 44, at least one record with Branch Office Number 02, and at least two records with Branch Office Number 11.

A Program Using an Argument-Function Table

In Program P09-03 we wrote the table arguments into the program separately from the table functions. That is, the state names and the state codes were written into working storage as two separate tables. It is possible instead to arrange each argument and its corresponding function in a single working-storage entry. This approach is most convenient when all the arguments and functions are alphanumeric or can be treated as alphanumeric. If the arguments or functions, or both, are numeric, it is still possible to arrange each argument with its function in one entry, but less conveniently than if they are all alphanumeric. In Program P10-02, Chapter 10, you will see the inconvenience connected with having each argument in the same entry with its functions when the arguments and functions are not all alphanumeric.

In Program P09-03, we had tables in which all the arguments and functions were alphanumeric. In Exercise 5, although the arguments are branch office numbers, they can easily be treated as alphanumeric without affecting the working of the program (Did you define the branch office numbers with 9s or did you define them with Xs?).

There are several advantages to having each argument and its function in one entry. It takes less coding — often much less — to enter the table into the program. It usually makes the meaning of the table clearer. And it permits the whole table and all its entries to be referred to by a single index, without the need for two indexes as in Program P09-03 and Exercise 5.

In Program P09-04 we will rewrite Program P09-03 to show how each argument of a table and its function can be arranged in a single working-storage entry. We will also show how table entries can be read in from a file instead of being written as FILLERs, and we will introduce the **SEARCH ALL** statement.

Program P09-04 uses two input files. One is a file of state codes and city names similar to the input to Program P09-03. The other is read by Program P09-04 and placed into working storage to serve as the table of state codes and state names.

The table file is shown in Figure 9.13. Each input record contains one entire row of the table. The first record shows both AK and ALASKA, one right after the other. The second record similarly shows the argument and function for ALABAMA. In this way all the arguments and functions are written into the file. When we look at Program P09-04, you will see how this file is read and stored in working storage as a table. One of the advantages of having each argument with its function is that you can see at a glance which argument belongs to which function. In the tables of Program P09-03 it was necessary to count down the entries of both tables to find that AR belongs to ARKANSAS.

Figure 9.13   Table-file input for Program P09-04.

```
--------------------------------------------------------------------------------
          1         2         3         4         5         6         7         8
12345678901234567890123456789012345678901234567890123456789012345678901234567890
--------------------------------------------------------------------------------
AKALASKA
ALALABAMA
ARARKANSAS
AZARIZONA
CACALIFORNIA
COCOLORADO
CTCONNECTICUT
DEDELAWARE
FLFLORIDA
GAGEORGIA
HIHAWAII
IAIOWA
IDIDAHO
ILILLINOIS
ININDIANA
KSKANSAS
```

You may notice that the states are not in the same order in this table as they were in Program P09-03. The order has been changed so that we can use a SEARCH ALL statement in this program. SEARCH ALL provides a faster search than an ordinary SEARCH statement (except with very small tables), but SEARCH ALL can be used only when the SEARCH arguments are in alphabetic or numeric order. In Program P09-04 we want to use a SEARCH ALL on the state codes, and so the table was arranged so that the state codes are in alphabetic order.

Program P09-04 is shown in Figure 9.14. There are now three FILE-CONTROL entries, lines 00170 through 00190, for the two input files and the print file. The table of state codes and names, lines 00530 through 00580, is now defined without FILLERs, VALUE clauses, or a REDEFINES clause, in the manner of the table of commission amounts in Program P09-01. In Program P09-04 the table is initialized by READ and MOVE statements, as you will see. Each input record will be assigned to one of the 16 STATE-ENTRY fields, with the first two characters of each input record being assigned to a STATE-CODE field and characters 3 through 13 of the input record assigned to a STATE-NAME field.

Figure 9.14   Program P09-04.

```
CB1 RELEASE 2.4                          IBM OS/VS COBOL   JULY  1, 1982


                    15.01.48       APR  6,1988


00010   IDENTIFICATION DIVISION.
00020   PROGRAM-ID.  P09-04.
00030  *AUTHOR.  DEBORAH ANN SENIOR.
00040  *
00050  *    THIS PROGRAM SHOWS HOW AN ARGUMENT AND A FUNCTION MAY
00060  *    APPEAR AS A SINGLE TABLE ENTRY
```

```
00070 *
00080 ****************************************************************
00090
00100  ENVIRONMENT DIVISION.
00110  CONFIGURATION SECTION.
00120  SOURCE-COMPUTER.   IBM-370.
00130  OBJECT-COMPUTER.   IBM-370.
00140
00150  INPUT-OUTPUT SECTION.
00160  FILE-CONTROL.
00170      SELECT TABLE-FILE-IN          ASSIGN TO TABLEIN.
00180      SELECT ADDRESS-FILE-IN        ASSIGN TO INFILE.
00190      SELECT ADDRESS-REPORT-FILE-OUT  ASSIGN TO PRINTER.
00200
00210  ****************************************************************
00220
00230  DATA DIVISION.
00240  FILE SECTION.
00250  FD  ADDRESS-FILE-IN
00260      LABEL RECORDS ARE OMITTED
00270      RECORD CONTAINS 80 CHARACTERS.
00280
00290  01  ADDRESS-RECORD-IN.
00300      05   STATE-AND-CITY-IN.
00310           10   STATE-CODE-IN         PIC XX.
00320           10   CITY-NAME-IN          PIC X(20).
00330      05   FILLER                     PIC X(58).
00340
00350  FD  ADDRESS-REPORT-FILE-OUT
00360      LABEL RECORDS ARE OMITTED.
00370
00380  01  REPORT-LINE                     PIC X(79).
00390
00400  FD  TABLE-FILE-IN
00410      LABEL RECORDS ARE OMITTED
00420      RECORD CONTAINS 80 CHARACTERS.
00430
00440  01  TABLE-RECORD-IN                 PIC X(80).
00450
00460  WORKING-STORAGE SECTION.
00470  01  MORE-INPUT        PIC X         VALUE "Y".
00480  01  MORE-TABLE-INPUT  PIC X         VALUE "Y".
00490  01  NUMBER-OF-TABLE-ENTRIES
00500          COMP SYNC     PIC S99       VALUE 16.
00510  01  LINE-SPACING      PIC S9        COMP SYNC.
00520
00530  01  STATE-TABLE.
00540      05   STATE-ENTRY
00550           OCCURS 16 TIMES ASCENDING KEY STATE-CODE
00560           INDEXED BY STATE-INDEX.
00570           10   STATE-CODE  PIC XX.
00580           10   STATE-NAME  PIC X(11).
00590
```

(continued)

The OCCURS clause, line 00550, now contains an **ASCENDING KEY** phrase. The ASCENDING KEY phrase tells COBOL the field that the table is ordered on. In this case our table is in order on STATE-CODE. A table may also be stored in descending order, and then the programmer would specify a **DESCENDING KEY.** Whenever a SEARCH ALL is to be used on a table, the table must be defined with an ASCENDING KEY or DESCENDING KEY phrase. It is the programmer's responsibility to ensure that each and every entry in the table is in the order indicated by the ASCENDING KEY or DESCENDING KEY phrase. If an ASCENDING KEY or DESCENDING KEY phrase is used, it must appear before the INDEXED BY phrase in the OCCURS clause.

The INDEXED BY phrase names a single index name for the whole table. The single index name STATE-INDEX can now be used to refer to all the state codes and all the state names. One index does the job instead of two.

Since each input record in the table file contains two fields, both a state code and a state name, two PICTUREs are needed to describe them. The two PICTUREs are shown in the level-10 entries in lines 00570 and 00580. These level-10 entries also permit us to give the names STATE-CODE and STATE-NAME to the appropriate parts of each input record.

This table could have been written into working storage using FILLERs, VALUE clauses, and a REDEFINES clause. In that case the table would have been written this way:

```
01  STATE-TABLE.
    05  STATE-TABLE-ENTRIES.
        10  FILLER PIC X(13) VALUE "AKALASKA".
        10  FILLER PIC X(13) VALUE "ALALABAMA".
        10  FILLER PIC X(13) VALUE "ARARKANSAS".
        10  FILLER PIC X(13) VALUE "AZARIZONA".
        10  FILLER PIC X(13) VALUE "CACALIFORNIA".
        10  FILLER PIC X(13) VALUE "COCOLORADO".
        10  FILLER PIC X(13) VALUE "CTCONNECTICUT".
        10  FILLER PIC X(13) VALUE "DEDELAWARE".
        10  FILLER PIC X(13) VALUE "FLFLORIDA".
        10  FILLER PIC X(13) VALUE "GAGEORGIA".
        10  FILLER PIC X(13) VALUE "HIHAWAII".
        10  FILLER PIC X(13) VALUE "IAIOWA".
        10  FILLER PIC X(13) VALUE "IDIDAHO".
        10  FILLER PIC X(13) VALUE "ILILLINOIS".
        10  FILLER PIC X(13) VALUE "ININDIANA".
        10  FILLER PIC X(13) VALUE "KSKANSAS".
    05  STATE-ENTRY REDEFINES STATE-TABLE-ENTRIES
        OCCURS 16 TIMES ASCENDING KEY STATE-CODE
        INDEXED BY STATE-INDEX.
        10  STATE-CODE PIC XX.
        10  STATE-NAME PIC X(11).
```

The level-10 entries for STATE-CODE and STATE-NAME are subordinate to the level-05 entry called STATE-ENTRY. Items subordinate to an entry that contains an OCCURS clause must be subscripted or indexed whenever they appear in the program. In this case both STATE-CODE and STATE-NAME would be indexed by STATE-INDEX. You will see how when we look at the Procedure Division.

Figure 9.14   (continued)

```
00600  01  PAGE-HEADING-1.
00610      05  FILLER              PIC X(30)      VALUE SPACES.
00620      05  FILLER              PIC X(11)      VALUE "STATE NAMES".
00630
00640  01  PAGE-HEADING-2.
00650      05  FILLER              PIC X(18)      VALUE SPACES.
00660      05  FILLER              PIC X(5)       VALUE "INPUT".
00670      05  FILLER              PIC X(29)      VALUE SPACES.
00680      05  FILLER              PIC X(14)      VALUE "CITY AND STATE".
00690
00700
```

```
00710   01   IN-TABLE-DETAIL-LINE.
00720        05 FILLER                    PIC X(10) VALUE SPACES.
00730        05 STATE-AND-CITY-OUT        PIC X(22).
00740        05 FILLER                    PIC X(8)  VALUE SPACES.
00750        05 CITY-NAME-OUT             PIC X(20)B.
00760        05 STATE-NAME-OUT            PIC X(11).
00770
00780   01   NOT-IN-TABLE-DETAIL-LINE.
00790        05 FILLER                    PIC X(10) VALUE SPACES.
00800        05 STATE-AND-CITY-ERR        PIC X(22).
00810        05 CITY-NAME-ERR             PIC B(8)X(20)B.
00820        05 FILLER                    PIC X(18)
00830           VALUE "STATE CODE INVALID".
00840
00850   01   NO-INPUT-DATA.
00860        05 FILLER          PIC X(29)     VALUE SPACES.
00870        05 FILLER          PIC X(13)     VALUE "NO INPUT DATA".
00880
00890 ************************************************************************
00900
00910   PROCEDURE DIVISION.
00920   CONTROL-PARAGRAPH.
00930        PERFORM LOAD-STATE-TABLE.
00940        PERFORM INITIALIZATION.
00950        PERFORM MAIN-PROCESS UNTIL MORE-INPUT IS EQUAL TO "N".
00960        PERFORM TERMINATION.
00970        STOP RUN.
00980
00990   LOAD-STATE-TABLE.
01000       OPEN INPUT TABLE-FILE-IN.
01010       PERFORM LOAD-ONE-TABLE-ENTRY VARYING STATE-INDEX
01020           FROM 1 BY 1 UNTIL
01030           STATE-INDEX GREATER THAN NUMBER-OF-TABLE-ENTRIES.
01040       CLOSE TABLE-FILE-IN.
01050
01060   LOAD-ONE-TABLE-ENTRY.
01070       READ TABLE-FILE-IN
01080           AT END
01090               MOVE "N" TO MORE-TABLE-INPUT.
01100       MOVE TABLE-RECORD-IN TO STATE-ENTRY (STATE-INDEX).
01110
01120   INITIALIZATION.
01130       OPEN INPUT  ADDRESS-FILE-IN,
01140           OUTPUT ADDRESS-REPORT-FILE-OUT.
01150       WRITE REPORT-LINE FROM PAGE-HEADING-1 AFTER PAGE.
01160       WRITE REPORT-LINE FROM PAGE-HEADING-2 AFTER 2.
01170       MOVE 3 TO LINE-SPACING.
01180       PERFORM READ-A-CARD.
01190       IF MORE-INPUT IS EQUAL TO "N"
01200           WRITE REPORT-LINE FROM NO-INPUT-DATA AFTER 3.
01210
```

(continued)

At line 00780 there is a level-01 entry for an output line called NOT-IN-TABLE-DETAIL-LINE. This will be used if an invalid state code should appear in the input and no match can be found in the table. In earlier programs in this chapter we made no provision for invalid input data, but in Program P09-04 we will print the words "State code invalid" if no match can be found between the STATE-CODE-IN and the STATE-CODEs in the table. Notice that the error message "State code invalid" is superior to an error message such as "State code not in table." The latter message is clear to the programmer but would not be clear to users of the report. Users are unaware of any table; on seeing a message such as "State code not in table" they would not know what to do — whether to fix the state code, fix the table, or do nothing. The message "State code invalid," on the other hand, alerts users to an error and implies action on their part.

The CONTROL-PARAGRAPH of the Procedure Division begins at line 00920. Before any of the usual processing is done, we first PERFORM the steps needed to load the table of state codes and names from the external table file. Those steps are shown in lines 00990 through 01100. Here we are assuming that the table file contains exactly the number of records needed to fill the table, 16. In that case end-of-file would never be read because the statement at line 01010 would execute the paragraph LOAD-ONE-TABLE-ENTRY only 16 times.

In MAIN-PROCESS, beginning at line 01220, there is a SEARCH ALL statement, but no SET statement. The SEARCH ALL statement searches the entire table, unlike the ordinary SEARCH statement, which starts its sequential search from wherever we SET the index initially. Different COBOL systems may carry out a SEARCH ALL in different ways. Usually SEARCH ALL will not search sequentially but will hop around the table in some way.[1] Remember that SEARCH ALL will usually search a table faster than an ordinary SEARCH statement will. The improvement in speed becomes more noticeable with very large tables. Of course, to use SEARCH ALL the tables arguments must be in ASCENDING or DESCENDING order. To use an ordinary SEARCH, the table arguments may be in any order.

Following the words SEARCH ALL is the data name STATE-ENTRY. Even though it's the STATE-CODE fields that we want to examine during the search, the data name following the words SEARCH or SEARCH ALL must always be the name that has attached to it an OCCURS clause with an INDEXED BY phrase.

This SEARCH ALL statement shows the use of the optional AT END phrase. The AT END phrase may be used to tell COBOL what to do if the SEARCH examines the whole table without satisfying the WHEN conditions. In our case we will print a line containing the words "State code invalid" if the SEARCH ALL finds no match. The AT END phrase may be used in a SEARCH statement as well as in a SEARCH ALL statement.

The WHEN condition, line 01260, is written slightly differently in this program than in Program P09-03. In standard COBOL the index name being used for the SEARCH ALL must appear as an index on the left side of the equal sign. This requirement applies only to the SEARCH ALL statement and not to an ordinary SEARCH. Another requirement of the SEARCH ALL is that the only condition allowed in a WHEN clause is an equal condition. In SEARCH any condition may appear in a WHEN clause.

Figure 9.14   (continued)

```
01220    MAIN-PROCESS.
01230        SEARCH ALL STATE-ENTRY
01240            AT END
01250                PERFORM PRODUCE-NOT-IN-TABLE-DETAIL
01260            WHEN STATE-CODE (STATE-INDEX) = STATE-CODE-IN
01270                PERFORM PRODUCE-IN-TABLE-DETAIL.
01280        PERFORM READ-A-CARD.
01290
01300    TERMINATION.
01310        CLOSE ADDRESS-FILE-IN,
01320            ADDRESS-REPORT-FILE-OUT.
01330
01340    READ-A-CARD.
01350        READ ADDRESS-FILE-IN
01360            AT END
01370                MOVE "N" TO MORE-INPUT.
01380
01390    PRODUCE-IN-TABLE-DETAIL.
01400        MOVE STATE-AND-CITY-IN          TO STATE-AND-CITY-OUT.
01410        MOVE CITY-NAME-IN               TO CITY-NAME-OUT.
01420        MOVE STATE-NAME (STATE-INDEX)   TO STATE-NAME-OUT.
01430        WRITE REPORT-LINE FROM IN-TABLE-DETAIL-LINE
01440                          AFTER LINE-SPACING.
01450        MOVE 2                          TO LINE-SPACING.
01460
01470    PRODUCE-NOT-IN-TABLE-DETAIL.
01480        MOVE STATE-AND-CITY-IN          TO STATE-AND-CITY-ERR.
01490        MOVE CITY-NAME-IN               TO CITY-NAME-ERR.
01500        WRITE REPORT-LINE FROM NOT-IN-TABLE-DETAIL-LINE
01510                          AFTER LINE-SPACING.
01520        MOVE 2                          TO LINE-SPACING.
```

[1]In the system used to run the programs in this book, SEARCH ALL is implemented with a **binary search.** Binary search is not specified in the ANSI standard.

You can see how the STATE-NAME is printed on the output report, in the MOVE statement at line 01420. The SEARCH statement, line 01230, assigns the correct value to STATE-INDEX, so the correct STATE-NAME is MOVEd to the output area.

Program P09-04 was run with the state code and city name input data shown in Figure 9.15 and produced the output shown in Figure 9.16.

Figure 9.15 State code and city input to Program P09-04.

```
-----------------------------------------------------------------------------------
         1         2         3         4         5         6         7         8
12345678901234567890123456789012345678901234567890123456789012345678901234567890
-----------------------------------------------------------------------------------
AKNOME
IADES MOINES
PQMONTREAL
KSWICHITA
CTHARTFORD
CASAN FRANCISCO
NYBROOKLYN
FLMIAMI
HIHONOLULU
```

Figure 9.16 Output from Program P09-04.

```
                    STATE NAMES

          INPUT                              CITY AND STATE

     AKNOME                        NOME            ALASKA

     IADES MOINES                  DES MOINES      IOWA

     PQMONTREAL                    MONTREAL        STATE CODE INVALID

     KSWICHITA                     WICHITA         KANSAS

     CTHARTFORD                    HARTFORD        CONNECTICUT

     CASAN FRANCISCO               SAN FRANCISCO   CALIFORNIA

     NYBROOKLYN                    BROOKLYN        STATE CODE INVALID

     FLMIAMI                       MIAMI           FLORIDA

     HIHONOLULU                    HONOLULU        HAWAII
```

The SEARCH ALL Statement

The format of the SEARCH ALL statement is

```
SEARCH ALL identifier-1
     [; AT END imperative-statement-1]
  ; WHEN {relation-condition-1}
         {condition-name-1    }
     [AND {relation-condition-2}  ] ...
          {condition-name-2    }
         {imperative-statement-2}
         {NEXT SENTENCE         }
```

If one or more relation conditions are used, they must be of the form:

$$\text{data-name} \begin{Bmatrix} \text{IS} \underline{\text{EQUAL}} \text{ TO} \\ \text{IS} = \end{Bmatrix} \begin{Bmatrix} \text{identifier-2} \\ \text{literal} \\ \text{arithmetic-expression} \end{Bmatrix}$$

If one or more condition-names are used, each condition-name specified must have only a single value.

The format shows that a SEARCH ALL statement must contain exactly one WHEN clause, but the clause may contain as many conditions as desired, connected by AND. A SEARCH ALL terminates WHEN all conditions are satisfied. An ordinary SEARCH, on the other hand, may contain as many WHEN conditions as desired, and the SEARCH terminates when any of them is satisfied.

In a relation condition in the SEARCH ALL, the only relational operator allowed is EQUAL. The index name associated with the table being searched must appear on the left side of the condition and must not appear on the right side.

EXERCISE 6

Write a program to read input and produce output in the same formats as in Exercise 5. Have your program read in the branch office table from an external file containing records in the following format:

Positions	Field
1 – 2	Branch Office Number
3 – 25	Branch Office Name
26 – 80	spaces

Arrange the table in working storage so that you need only one index.

Include in your test data several records with invalid Branch Office Numbers. For each such input record, have your program print on one line the Agent Name, the Branch Office Number, and the words "Branch office number invalid."

The OCCURS Clause

There are two formats of the OCCURS clause. The one we have been using is

```
OCCURS integer-2 TIMES
    [ {ASCENDING }
      {DESCENDING} KEY IS data-name-2
    [, data-name-3]...]...
    [INDEXED BY index-name-1 [, index-name-2]...]
```

The format shows that an OCCURS clause may have more than one index associated with it. Any given index, though, can be associated with only one OCCURS clause.

The format also shows that the table elements may be ordered on more than one ASCENDING KEY or DESCENDING KEY. If so, the keys must be listed in the OCCURS clause from major to minor.

The other format of the OCCURS clause, used for variable-length tables, is:

```
OCCURS integer-1 TO integer-2 TIMES
DEPENDING ON data-name-1
    ⎧ASCENDING ⎫
  [ ⎨         ⎬ KEY IS data-name-2
    ⎩DESCENDING⎭
[, data-name-3]...]...
[INDEXED BY index-name-1 [, index-name-2]...]
```

In this format, the table always contains a number of elements equal to the value assigned to data-name-1. Data-name-1 must be a positive integer within the range of integer-1 through integer-2.

Format 2 of the SET Statement

Format 2 of the SET statement may be used to increase or decrease the setting of one or more indexes. It is

```
SET index-name-4 [, index-name-5]...
    ⎧UP BY  ⎫ ⎧identifier-4⎫
    ⎨       ⎬ ⎨           ⎬
    ⎩DOWN BY⎭ ⎩literal-2   ⎭
```

The receiving fields in this format are index-name-4, index-name-5, etc. After the SET statement is executed, the receiving field indexes must be within the range of their tables.

The sending fields are identifier-4 and literal-2. They must be integers. They refer to the number of table elements (1, 2, 3, and so on) that the indexes are to be increased or decreased by.

Identifier-4, if used, may be a subscripted or indexed data name and may be indexed by one of the receiving fields. Receiving fields are acted upon in the order in which they appear in the SET statement. The value of the sending field at the beginning of execution of the SET statement is used for all receiving fields.

Summary

If a program has to process several related fields all having the same description, the fields may be defined with an OCCURS clause and then subscripted or indexed. A subscript may be an integer literal or an identifier defined as an integer. An index may be an integer literal or an index name.

If a field is to be indexed, its OCCURS clause must contain an INDEXED BY phrase. An index name, given in an INDEXED BY phrase, must not be otherwise defined in the program.

Any table can be written into working storage with VALUE clauses or be read in from an external file.

A direct-reference table can be written in working storage as a series of FILLER entries preceded by a group-level name. Any field defined as an integer may be used as a subscript to refer to any item in the table directly.

A search table may be entered into a COBOL program with each argument and each function a separate entry. Alternatively, each argument and its corresponding function may appear together as a single entry.

The SET statement may be used to assign a value to an index. The SEARCH statement may be used to step through a table until one or more specified conditions are met. The SEARCH ALL statement will usually search a table faster than an ordinary SEARCH statement. If SEARCH ALL is used, the OCCURS clause that defines the table must contain either the ASCENDING KEY or DESCENDING KEY phrase, and the table items must be ordered on the key or keys named in the phrase.

Fill-in Exercises

1. In order for a field to be subscripted or indexed, it must be defined with a(n) _____ clause.

2. For a field to be indexed, its OCCURS clause must include a(n) _____ phrase.

3. If a SEARCH ALL statement is used on a table, its OCCURS clause must include a(n) _____ phrase or a(n) _____ phrase.

4. The field "TAX-AMOUNT subscripted by TAX-SUBSCRIPT" would be written in COBOL as _____ .

5. A subscript may be a positive or unsigned integer numeric literal or a field defined as a(n) _____ .

6. The value of a subscript may be controlled by a PERFORM statement with the _____ option.

7. A table that can be used without being searched is called a(n) _____ table.

8. The 1974 COBOL can process tables of up to _____ dimensions.

9. A name given in an INDEXED BY phrase is called a(n) _____ _____ .

10. The _____ clause can be used to specify the conditions under which a SEARCH or SEARCH ALL should terminate.

11. A table in COBOL is any group of fields defined with a(n) _____ clause.

12. A REDEFINES clause may be used in a level-01 entry in the _____ Section.

13. If an ASCENDING KEY phrase in an OCCURS clause contains the names of more than one field, the fields must be listed in order from _____ to _____ .

14. The only relational operator allowed in a relation condition in a SEARCH ALL statement is _____ .

15. The _____ phrase may be used in a SEARCH statement when one index name is to keep pace with another.

Review Exercises

1. Given the following fields:

```
05 AGE-RANGE         PIC 9(3)  OCCURS 15 TIMES,
05 OCCUPATION-CLASS PIC X     OCCURS 10 TIMES,
05 A-SUBSCRIPT       PIC S99,
05 B-SUBSCRIPT       PIC S99,
```

    a. Which of the following statements could be legal in a COBOL program?

        1. MOVE A-SUBSCRIPT (OCCUPATION-CLASS) TO LINE-OUT.
        2. MOVE OCCUPATION-CLASS (B-SUBSCRIPT) TO LINE-OUT.
        3. SUBTRACT 1 FROM A-SUBSCRIPT.

    b. What is the highest value that may legally be assigned to B-SUBSCRIPT at the time statement 2 executes?

2. Given the following table:

```
01 CITY-TABLE,
   05 CITY-TABLE-ENTRIES,
      10 FILLER PIC X(12) VALUE "PEEKSKILL",
      10 FILLER PIC X(12) VALUE "PLATTSBURGH",
      10 FILLER PIC X(12) VALUE "PORT JERVIS",
      10 FILLER PIC X(12) VALUE "POUGHKEEPSIE",
   05 CITY REDEFINES CITY-TABLE-ENTRIES
                   PIC X(12) OCCURS 4 TIMES,
```

What will be MOVEd to LINE-OUT by the following pair of statements?

```
MOVE 2 TO CITY-SUBSCRIPT,
MOVE CITY (CITY-SUBSCRIPT) TO LINE-OUT,
```

3. Write a program to read input records in the following format:

Positions	Field
1 – 6	Store Number
7 – 12	January Sales (in whole dollars)
13 – 18	February Sales (in whole dollars)
19 – 24	March Sales (in whole dollars)
25 – 30	April Sales (in whole dollars)
31 – 36	May Sales (in whole dollars)
37 – 42	June Sales (in whole dollars)
43 – 48	July Sales (in whole dollars)
49 – 54	August Sales (in whole dollars)
55 – 60	September Sales (in whole dollars)
61 – 66	October Sales (in whole dollars)
67 – 72	November Sales (in whole dollars)
73 – 78	December Sales (in whole dollars)
79 – 80	spaces

Each record contains a Store Number and a sales amount for each month of the year. For each record, have your program compute the sales tax for each month (at 4 percent of the sales amount) and print on one line the Store Number, the sales tax for each month, and the total sales tax for the year. At the end of the report print the total sales tax for the year for all stores.

4. A program can determine the day of the week that a particular date falls on if it is given the date (as a number from 1 to 365 or 366) and the day of the week that the year begins on. Assign each day of the week a number 1 through 7 in order from Sunday through Saturday. 1989 began on day 1 (a Sunday). 1990 begins on day 2 (a Monday).

Write a program to read input data in the following format:

Positions	Field
1 – 3	Day Number of Year
4	Day Number of the Day on which the year begins (1 through 7)
5 – 80	spaces

Each input record contains a date as a number from 1 to 366 and the day number that the year begins on.

For each input record, have your program print on one line the original input and the name of the day of the week that the date falls on.

5. Write a program to read input records in the following format:

Positions	Field
1 – 5	Employee Number
6	Job Classification Code
7 – 14	Annual Salary (to two decimal places)
15 – 80	spaces

There is one record for each employee. Each record contains a Job Classification Code and an Annual Salary. For each input record, print on one line the Employee Number, the employee's Job Classification Code, the employee's job title and the employee's Annual Salary. At the end of the report print a total of all the salaries.

Use the table below for Job Classification Codes and job titles. In your program, enter each argument and each function as a separate FILLER entry. Use two indexes. Use an ordinary SEARCH statement.

Include in your test data several records with invalid Job Classification Codes. For each such input record print on one line the employee number, the words "Job classification code invalid," and the employee's Annual Salary. Use the following Job Classification Codes and job titles in your program:

Job Classification Code	Job Title
Z	Smelter apprentice
Y	Junior smelter
X	Smelter
W	Gang chief
V	Foreman
6	Superintendent
5	Section manager
4	Division manager
3	Plant manager
2	Assistant vice-president
1	Vice-president
0	President

6. Write a program to read input and produce output in the same formats as in Review Exercise 5. Write each row of the job table as a single FILLER entry in your program. Arrange the entries so that the Job Classification Codes are in ascending order on your computer. Use a SEARCH ALL statement.

7. Modify your solution to Review Exercise 6 so that the job table entries are read in from an external file.

Project

Write a program to read records in the following format:

Positions	Field
1 – 9	Employee Number
10 – 15	Gross Pay
16 – 80	spaces

Each record contains an Employee Number and a Gross Pay amount for the employee. Have your program compute a tax on the gross Pay according to the following table:

If Gross Pay is:	Tax is:
less than $100	3% of Gross Pay
at least $100 but less than $200	$3 plus 4% of the excess over $100
at least $200 but less than $500	$7 plus 5% of the excess over $200
at least $500 but less than $1000	$22 plus 6% of the excess over $500
at least $1000 but less than $2000	$52 plus 7% of the excess over $1000
at least $2000 but less than $5000	$122 plus 8% of the excess over $2000
at least $5000	$362 plus 9% of the excess over $5000

Write the tax rates and the ranges of Gross Pay into one or more tables in your program with FILLER entries. Use a SEARCH statement to find the tax rates for each input record. For each record read, have your program print the Employee Number, the Gross Pay, and the tax amount computed by the program. Design a report with suitable headings before you begin coding.

Tables of Higher Dimension

Here are the key points you should learn from this chapter:

1. The need for tables of higher dimension
2. How to set up two- and three-dimensional tables in COBOL programs
3. How to program for two- and three-dimensional tables
4. How to load a table of more than three dimensions.

Key words to recognize and learn:

row
column
caption
procedure name
AFTER

A two-dimensional table is one in which two arguments are needed to find a function. One example of a two-dimensional table is a table showing the monthly payment per $1 of loan amount for loans of various interest rates and numbers of payments. If we wanted to find the monthly payment per $1 of principal for a 20-year home-mortgage loan (240 payments) at 12.5 percent, we could do so in such a table. A three-dimensional table needs three arguments to find a function. An example of a three-dimensional table is a table of insurance premiums for 5-year renewable term insurance where a person's age and sex and the face amount of the policy are needed to find a particular premium amount.

The first program in this chapter deals with a sales application. The program uses accumulators arranged as a two-dimensional table to compute the total sales in each of five stores in each of 6 months. Each accumulator is one element of the table and is identified by two arguments — a store number and a month number.

A Program with a Two-Dimensional Table

Program P10-01 processes input data in the following format:

Positions	Field
1	Store Number
2 – 6	Customer Number
7 – 12	January Sales (to two decimal places)
13 – 18	February Sales (to two decimal places)
19 – 24	March Sales (to two decimal places)
25 – 30	April Sales (to two decimal places)
31 – 36	May Sales (to two decimal places)
37 – 42	June Sales (to two decimal places)
43 – 80	spaces

Each record contains a Store Number, a Customer Number, and Sales for 6 months, January through June. Naturally, each store services many customers, and so the input will contain many records for each store. The stores are numbered 1 through 5. The input data might be in any random order, that is, we cannot assume that all records for a store are grouped together in the input.

Program P10-01 is to accumulate the total sales for each store for each month and produce a report in the format shown in Figure 10.1. The body of the report has the appearance of a typical two-dimensional table. It has **rows,** going across the page from left to right, and **columns,** going from top to bottom. The rows and columns have **captions,** saying what the rows and columns stand for. In our case each row represents a different store number and each column a different month. At the intersection of each row and column is a sales amount for that store and month.

Since the input data are in no particular order, this report cannot be produced in the same way that our earlier reports were produced. That is, we cannot accumulate all the data for store 1, print them, and then go on to process store 2, because we cannot be sure that all the records for store 1 precede the records for store 2. Thus we must set up 30 accumulators in storage, one for each store for each month. Then, as the program reads each input record, it can determine which accumulators to add the various sales amounts into. After all the data have been read and accumulated, the report can be printed.

Figure 10.1 Output format for Program P10-01.

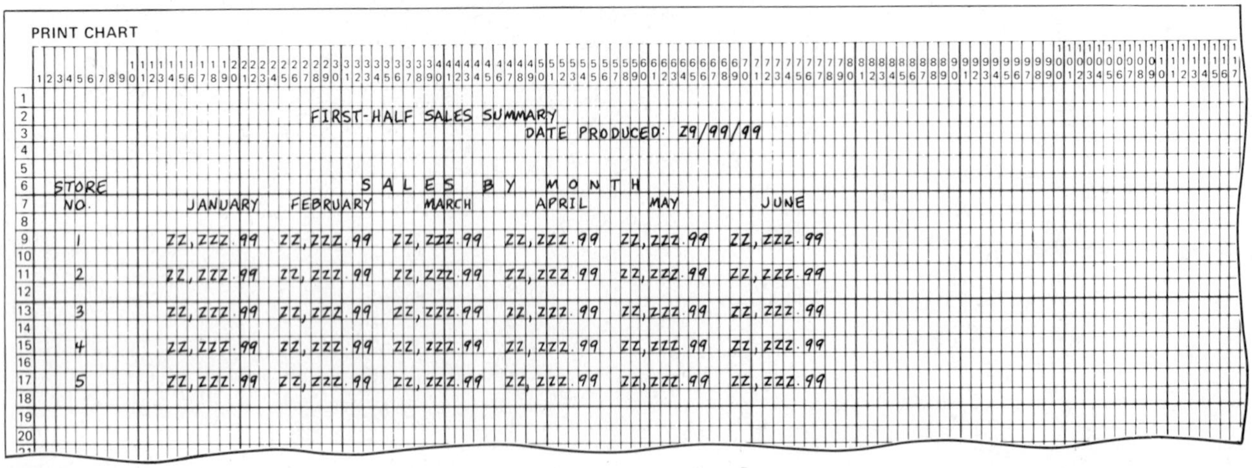

Top-Down Design for Program P10-01

This program is sufficiently difficult that we should do a top-down design before we begin coding. As we do the design, we must remember that for each input record we can do no more than add the sales amounts to the appropriate accumulators. We cannot print anything until after all the input records have been read and processed.

The first stage of the design is shown in the hierarchy diagram in Figure 10.2. There we have broken the main function of the program into the usual three subfunctions:

a. What we have to do before entering the main loop of the program
b. The main loop
c. What we do after end-of-file

Figure 10.2 The first stage of a hierarchy diagram for Program P10-01.

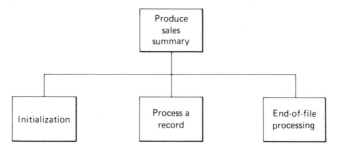

Now we can elaborate on the three subfunctions as necessary. The "Initialization" procedure contains nothing except the usual initializing steps that we have in earlier programs. The box "Process a record" needs a lower-level subfunction to show that each input record has its sales fields added to the appropriate six accumulators in storage. No printing is done.

The box "End-of-file processing" needs subfunctions to show exactly what processes are executed after end-of-file is reached on the input. Figure 10.3 shows that after end-of-file we can "Print the report" and then "Close files." The subfunction of "Print the report" shows that the report can be printed line after line with no further processing of input data. The subfunction of "Print a line" shows that we will need a separate paragraph to format each line of the report. You will see why when we look at the program. The hierarchy diagram in Figure 10.3 thus shows the complete design.

Program P10-01

Program P10-01 is shown in Figure 10.4. The definition of the input record starts at line 00280. You can see that the six SALE-AMOUNT-IN fields in the input record have been defined with an OCCURS clause, at line 00310. The value of STORE-NUMBER-IN, line 00290, used together with the month numbers 1 through 6, enables the program to refer to the six accumulators that the SALE-AMOUNT-IN amounts are to be added into.

Figure 10.3 Complete hierarchy diagram for Program P10-01.

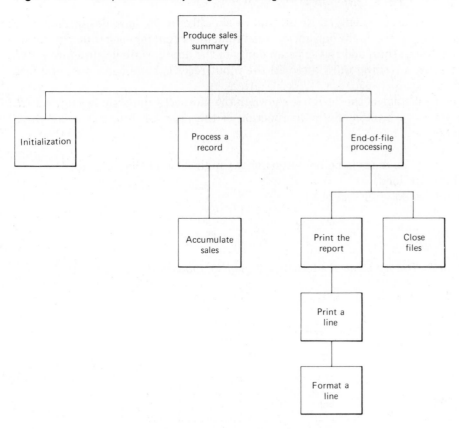

Figure 10.4 Program P10-01.

```
CB1 RELEASE 2.4                          IBM OS/VS COBOL  JULY  1, 1982


                       0.47.53        APR  6,1988


00010   IDENTIFICATION DIVISION.
00020   PROGRAM-ID.  P10-01.
00030  *AUTHOR.   DEBORAH ANN SENIOR.
00040  *
00050  *     THIS PROGRAM ACCUMULATES AND PRINTS SALES TOTALS
00060  *     FOR 5 STORES FOR 6 MONTHS
00070  *
00080  *****************************************************************
00090
00100   ENVIRONMENT DIVISION.
00110   CONFIGURATION SECTION.
00120   SOURCE-COMPUTER.  IBM-370.
00130   OBJECT-COMPUTER.  IBM-370.
00140
00150   INPUT-OUTPUT SECTION.
00160   FILE-CONTROL.
00170      SELECT SALES-FILE-IN           ASSIGN TO INFILE.
00180      SELECT SALES-REPORT-FILE-OUT   ASSIGN TO PRINTER.
00190
00200  *****************************************************************
00210
00220   DATA DIVISION.
00230   FILE SECTION.
00240   FD  SALES-FILE-IN
00250      LABEL RECORDS ARE OMITTED
00260      RECORD CONTAINS 80 CHARACTERS.
00270
```

```
00280  01   SALES-RECORD-IN.
00290       05   STORE-NUMBER-IN        PIC 9.
00300       05   CUSTOMER-NUMBER-IN     PIC X(5).
00310       05   SALE-AMOUNT-IN         PIC 9(4)V?9      OCCURS 6 TIMES.
00320       05   FILLER                 PIC X(38).
00330
00340  FD   SALES-REPORT-FILE-OUT
00350       LABEL RECORDS ARE OMITTED
00360
00370  01   REPORT-LINE                 PIC X(77).
00380
00390  WORKING-STORAGE SECTION.
00400  01   MORE-INPUT             PIC X            VALUE "Y".
00410  01   NUMBER-OF-STORES       PIC S99          VALUE 5
00420                              COMP             SYNC.
00430  01   NUMBER-OF-MONTHS       PIC S99          VALUE 6
00440                              COMP             SYNC.
00450  01   LINE-SPACING           PIC S9           COMP SYNC.
00460  01   SALES-ACCUMULATOR-TABLE                 VALUE ZEROS.
00470       05   STORE          OCCURS 5 TIMES.
00480         10   MONTH        OCCURS 6 TIMES.
00490           15   SALES-ACCUMULATOR        PIC S9(5)V99.
00500  01   MONTH-SUBSCRIPT        PIC S99          COMP SYNC.
00510  01   STORE-SUBSCRIPT        PIC S99          COMP SYNC.
00520
00530  01   PAGE-HEAD-1.
00540       05 FILLER             PIC X(27)         VALUE SPACES.
00550       05 FILLER             PIC X(24)
00560                             VALUE "FIRST-HALF SALES SUMMARY".
00570
00580  01   PAGE-HEAD-2.
00590       05 FILLER             PIC X(48)         VALUE SPACES.
00600       05 FILLER             PIC X(15)         VALUE "DATE PRODUCED:".
00610       05 RUN-MONTH-DAY      PIC Z9/99/.
00620       05 RUN-YEAR           PIC 99.
00630
```

(continued)

The Working Storage Section begins at line 00390. The fields NUMBER-OF-STORES and NUMBER-OF-MONTHS have been established. The reasons for having these fields are the usual: If the number of stores changes or the number of months covered by the report changes, the program will be easier to modify than if we had the numbers 5 or 6 appear in the Procedure Division. Also, the Procedure Division is made more readable by the use of the names NUMBER-OF-STORES and NUMBER-OF-MONTHS rather than the numbers 5 and 6.

You can see how the 30 sales accumulators have been set up, at SALES-ACCUMULATOR-TABLE in line 00460. The level-05 entry names the row caption and says how many rows there are. The level-10 entry names the column caption and says how many columns there are. Finally the level-15 entry names the table item itself, SALES-ACCUMULATOR, and gives its PICTURE. The VALUE clause in line 00460 initializes all 30 accumulators to ZEROS. A VALUE clause is not permitted in an entry that contains an OCCURS clause nor in an entry subordinate to one that contains an OCCURS clause. Thus we cannot initialize these accumulators at the elementary level, but we can zero them at the group level. Remember that group items are always treated as alphanumeric items of USAGE DISPLAY; so SALES-ACCUMULATOR must be of USAGE DISPLAY also. If we had wanted to define SALES-ACCUMULATOR with USAGE COMPUTATIONAL, we would have had to initialize them to zero individually with statements in the Procedure Division. The OCCURS clauses at lines 00470 and 00480 contain no INDEXED BY phrases because it turns out to be more convenient to use subscripting in this program than indexing.

You should consider using subscripting instead of indexing on a table whenever an input field is used as a subscript to refer to elements of the table and/or whenever the subscript value itself is to be used as an output field. Both situations are present in this program. The input field STORE-NUMBER-IN is used to refer to elements in the SALES-ACCUMULATOR-TABLE, and the subscript STORE-SUBSCRIPT is printed as part of the output.

Whenever we refer to one of the 30 SALES-ACCUMULATORS, we must use two subscripts to say which row and which column we are referring to. The subscripts must appear in parentheses in the order in which the OCCURS clauses are written. In Program P10-01 a reference to SALES-ACCUMULATOR could be

```
SALES-ACCUMULATOR (STORE-SUBSCRIPT, MONTH-SUBSCRIPT)
```

Either or both of the subscripts could be given as integer literals, if desired. For example, SALES-ACCUMULATOR (3, 2) refers to the sales in store 3 for February. Also

```
SALES-ACCUMULATOR (STORE-SUBSCRIPT, 4)
```

could refer to any of the April accumulators, depending on the value of STORE-SUBSCRIPT.

Figure 10.4 (continued)

```
00640   01   PAGE-HEAD-3.
00650        05 FILLER            PIC XX           VALUE SPACES.
00660        05 FILLER            PIC X(30)        VALUE "STORE".
00670        05 FILLER            PIC X(27)
00680                             VALUE "S A L E S   B Y   M O N T H".
00690
00700   01   PAGE-HEAD-4.
00710        05 FILLER            PIC X(3)         VALUE SPACES.
00720        05 FILLER            PIC X(12)        VALUE "NO.".
00730        05 FILLER            PIC X(10)        VALUE "JANUARY".
00740        05 FILLER            PIC X(13)        VALUE "FEBRUARY".
00750        05 FILLER            PIC X(11)        VALUE "MARCH".
00760        05 FILLER            PIC X(11)        VALUE "APRIL".
00770        05 FILLER            PIC X(11)        VALUE "MAY".
00780        05 FILLER            PIC X(4)         VALUE "JUNE".
00790
00800   01   STORE-LINE.
00810        05 STORE-NUMBER-OUT  PIC B(4)9B(6).
00820        05 SALES-TOTAL-OUT   PIC BBZZ,ZZZ.99 OCCURS 6 TIMES.
00830
00840   01   NO-INPUT-DATA.
00850        05 FILLER            PIC X(33)        VALUE SPACES.
00860        05 FILLER            PIC X(13)        VALUE "NO INPUT DATA".
00870
00880   01   TODAYS-DATE.
00890        05 RUN-YEAR          PIC 99.
00900        05 RUN-MONTH-DAY     PIC 9(4).
00910
00920   ************************************************************************
00930
00940   PROCEDURE DIVISION.
00950   PRODUCE-SALES-SUMMARY.
00960        PERFORM INITIALIZATION.
00970        PERFORM PROCESS-A-RECORD UNTIL MORE-INPUT IS EQUAL TO "N".
00980        PERFORM END-OF-FILE-PROCESSING.
00990        STOP RUN.
01000
01010   INITIALIZATION.
01020        ACCEPT TODAYS-DATE FROM DATE.
01030        MOVE CORR TODAYS-DATE TO PAGE-HEAD-2.
01040        OPEN INPUT  SALES-FILE-IN,
01050             OUTPUT SALES-REPORT-FILE-OUT.
01060        WRITE REPORT-LINE FROM PAGE-HEAD-1 AFTER PAGE.
01070        WRITE REPORT-LINE FROM PAGE-HEAD-2.
01080        WRITE REPORT-LINE FROM PAGE-HEAD-3 AFTER 3.
01090        WRITE REPORT-LINE FROM PAGE-HEAD-4.
01100        MOVE 2 TO LINE-SPACING.
01110        PERFORM READ-A-RECORD.
01120        IF MORE-INPUT IS EQUAL TO "N"
01130            WRITE REPORT-LINE FROM NO-INPUT-DATA AFTER 2.
01140
```

```
01150   PROCESS-A-RECORD.
01160       PERFORM ACCUMULATE-SALES
01170           VARYING MONTH-SUBSCRIPT FROM 1 BY 1 UNTIL
01180               MONTH-SUBSCRIPT IS GREATER THAN NUMBER-OF-MONTHS.
01190       PERFORM READ-A-RECORD.
01200
01210   END-OF-FILE-PROCESSING.
01220       PERFORM PRINT-THE-REPORT.
01230       PERFORM CLOSE-FILES.
01240
01250   READ-A-RECORD.
01260       READ SALES-FILE-IN
01270           AT END
01280               MOVE "N" TO MORE-INPUT.
01290
01300   ACCUMULATE-SALES.
01310       ADD SALE-AMOUNT-IN (MONTH-SUBSCRIPT) TO
01320           SALES-ACCUMULATOR (STORE-NUMBER-IN, MONTH-SUBSCRIPT).
01330
01340   PRINT-THE-REPORT.
01350       PERFORM PRINT-A-LINE
01360           VARYING STORE-SUBSCRIPT FROM 1 BY 1 UNTIL
01370               STORE-SUBSCRIPT IS GREATER THAN NUMBER-OF-STORES.
01380
```

(continued)

There is another way in which this table could have been set up. The columns could have been named at the 05 level and the rows at the 10 level. That is, we could have had

```
05 MONTH       OCCURS 6 TIMES.
   10 STORE    OCCURS 5 TIMES.
```

In either case, the individual table entry would be given at the 15 level.

If the table had been set up as shown above, with the MONTHs (the columns) named at the 05 level, then references to SALES-ACCUMULATOR would have to be of the form

```
SALES-ACCUMULATOR (MONTH-SUBSCRIPT, STORE-SUBSCRIPT)
```

and SALES-ACCUMULATOR (3, 2) would refer to the March sales in store 2.

Two detail lines have been defined, at lines 00800 and 00840. One of them is used only when there are no input data, and the other is used to print all five lines of accumulators. When the detail line at line 00800 is to be printed the first time, STORE-SUBSCRIPT will be assigned the value 1 and all the accumulators for store 1 will print. Then STORE-SUBSCRIPT will be assigned the value 2, and the accumulators for store 2 will print, and so on. You will see exactly how it all happens when we look at the Procedure Division.

The Procedure Division begins at line 00940. In the paragraph PROCESS-A-RECORD there is a PERFORM . . . VARYING statement, at line 01160. Each time the program enters PROCESS-A-RECORD, it has in its input area a record containing sales for 6 months and a store number. We want to add, from the input record, January's sales into the January accumulator for that store, and then add, from the input record, February's sales into the February accumulator for that store, and so on. That is, we want to vary the MONTH-SUBSCRIPT through all the months. The PERFORM statement at line 01160 does it. The paragraph ACCUMULATE-SALES begins at line 01300. You can see how, each time it executes, it fetches the correct SALE-AMOUNT-IN from the input area and adds it to the correct SALES-ACCUMULATOR. Notice that SALES-ACCUMULATOR is subscripted by the input field STORE-NUMBER-IN in the ADD statement at line 01310.

We enter the paragraph PRINT-THE-REPORT, line 01340, ready to print the entire report with no further reading of input data. We have five lines of data to print, one for each store. The PERFORM statement at line 01350 steps through all

Figure 10.4   (continued)

```
01390    CLOSE-FILES.
01400        CLOSE SALES-FILE-IN,
01410            SALES-REPORT-FILE-OUT.
01420
01430    PRINT-A-LINE.
01440        PERFORM FORMAT-A-LINE
01450            VARYING MONTH-SUBSCRIPT FROM 1 BY 1 UNTIL
01460                MONTH-SUBSCRIPT IS GREATER THAN NUMBER-OF-MONTHS.
01470        MOVE STORE-SUBSCRIPT TO STORE-NUMBER-OUT.
01480        WRITE REPORT-LINE FROM STORE-LINE AFTER 2.
01490
01500    FORMAT-A-LINE.
01510        MOVE SALES-ACCUMULATOR (STORE-SUBSCRIPT, MONTH-SUBSCRIPT)
01520            TO SALES-TOTAL-OUT (MONTH-SUBSCRIPT).
```

five stores. To build a print line for one store, we must step through the 6 months. The PERFORM statement at line 01440 does it.

Program P10-01 was run using the input shown in Figure 10.5 and produced the output shown in Figure 10.6.

Figure 10.5   Input to Program P10-01.

```
-----------------------------------------------------------------------------
        1         2         3         4         5         6         7         8
1234567890123456789012345678901234567890123456789012345678901234567890
-----------------------------------------------------------------------------
162947029438105368000000010647374398001618
527394000000000000000000275302406947293014
340268701268050275006453168927687941502000
345192942000627413000000801000000000712423
280628000000000000000000294508000000000000
514771231056289473962710643859711372969821
525168612943712900001124500295314000000000
171439091973050743063039081809013106090370
262437295368000000666804293000002937428536
327142000000680187000000000000000000000000
198104000000000000000000000000006400000000
472168302946095381673893847290399388274308
478527000295300042693937427290000138793814
172965039384293984893388392649030000188827
440463844392849683837939211682773904400055
```

Figure 10.6   Output from Program P10-01.

```
                        FIRST-HALF SALES SUMMARY
                                    DATE PRODUCED:  4/06/88


STORE                        S A L E S   B Y   M O N T H
NO.        JANUARY    FEBRUARY     MARCH      APRIL       MAY        JUNE

  1       1,607.95    4,500.95   9,564.27   4,851.05   4,175.10   6,808.15

  2       2,953.68         .00   6,668.04   5,875.08      29.37   4,285.36

  3      16,432.68   13,578.75      64.53   9,699.27   6,879.41  12,144.23

  4      11,476.33   12,451.06  22,057.69  14,862.62  11,734.30  14,681.77

  5       8,439.99   10,023.73   9,638.34  14,194.56  14,323.19  12,628.35
```

Two More Formats of the PERFORM Statement

There are four formats of the PERFORM statement. Two of them were given in Chapter 2. Here are the other two.

The format of the PERFORM statement that can vary the values of fields is

$$
\begin{aligned}
&\underline{\text{PERFORM}}\text{ procedure-name-1 }\left[\ \left\{ \begin{array}{l} \underline{\text{THROUGH}} \\ \underline{\text{THRU}} \end{array} \right\}\text{ procedure-name-2}\right] \\[4pt]
&\qquad \underline{\text{VARYING}}\ \left\{ \begin{array}{l} \text{index-name-1} \\ \text{identifier-1} \end{array} \right\}\quad \underline{\text{FROM}}\ \left\{ \begin{array}{l} \text{index-name-2} \\ \text{literal-2} \\ \text{identifier-2} \end{array} \right\} \\[4pt]
&\qquad \underline{\text{BY}}\ \left\{ \begin{array}{l} \text{literal-3} \\ \text{identifier-3} \end{array} \right\}\quad \underline{\text{UNTIL}}\text{ condition-1} \\[4pt]
&\qquad \left[\underline{\text{AFTER}}\ \left\{ \begin{array}{l} \text{index-name-4} \\ \text{identifier-4} \end{array} \right\}\quad \underline{\text{FROM}}\ \left\{ \begin{array}{l} \text{index-name-5} \\ \text{literal-5} \\ \text{identifier-5} \end{array} \right\} \right. \\[4pt]
&\qquad \underline{\text{BY}}\ \left\{ \begin{array}{l} \text{literal-6} \\ \text{identifier-6} \end{array} \right\}\quad \underline{\text{UNTIL}}\text{ condition-2} \\[4pt]
&\qquad \left[\underline{\text{AFTER}}\ \left\{ \begin{array}{l} \text{index-name-7} \\ \text{identifier-7} \end{array} \right\}\quad \underline{\text{FROM}}\ \left\{ \begin{array}{l} \text{index-name-8} \\ \text{literal-8} \\ \text{identifier-8} \end{array} \right\} \right. \\[4pt]
&\qquad \underline{\text{BY}}\ \left\{ \begin{array}{l} \text{literal-9} \\ \text{identifier-9} \end{array} \right\}\quad \underline{\text{UNTIL}}\text{ condition-3}]\ ]
\end{aligned}
$$

This is the form of the PERFORM statement that we used to vary the subscripts in Program P10-01. Whenever an identifier is used in a PERFORM . . . VARYING statement, the identifier must be described as a numeric elementary item. (Remember that an identifier can be a data name itself or a data name followed by any legal combination of qualifiers, subscripts, and indexes.) A PERFORM . . . VARYING statement can vary the value of any numeric field; it is not limited to VARYING only subscripts and indexes. When it is used to vary a field other than a subscript or index, the field being varied need not be described as an integer. Subscripts and indexes, of course, must always be integers.

In Program P10-01 the phrases FROM 1 and BY 1 use literal-2 and literal-3 in the format. Any literal used in a PERFORM . . . VARYING statement must be a numeric literal. If the literal is used in connection with a subscript or an index, it must be an integer as well.

Condition-1 in the PERFORM statement at line 01350 in Program P10-01 is

```
STORE-SUBSCRIPT IS GREATER THAN NUMBER-OF-STORES
```

You can see from the format that two or three fields can be varied by a single PERFORM . . . VARYING statement, through use of the reserved word AFTER. But no matter how many fields are being varied, the word VARYING appears only once in the statement.

A PERFORM . . . VARYING statement having one condition executes in the following manner:

It sets identifier-1 equal to its current FROM value.
It repeats the following steps 1 and 2 until condition-1 is true:

1. It executes procedure-name-1 [THRU procedure-name-2].
2. It augments identifier-1 with its current BY value.

A PERFORM . . . VARYING statement having two conditions executes in the following manner:

It sets identifier-1 and identifier-4 to their current FROM values.
It repeats steps 1, 2, and 3 until condition-1 is true:

1. It repeats steps a and b until condition-2 is true:
    a. It executes procedure-name-1 [THRU procedure-name-2].
    b. It augments identifier-4 with its current BY value.
2. It sets identifier-4 to its current FROM value.
3. It augments identifier-1 with its current BY value.

A PERFORM . . . VARYING statement having three conditions executes in the following manner:

It sets identifier-1, identifier-4, identifier-7 to their current FROM values.
It repeats steps 1, 2, and 3 until condition-1 is true:

1. It repeats steps a, b, and c until condition-2 is true:
    a. It repeats steps I and II until condition-3 is true:
        I.   It executes procedure-name-1 [THRU procedure-name-2].
        II. It augments identifier-7 with its current BY value.
    b. It sets identifier-7 to its current FROM value.
    c. It augments identifier-4 with its current BY value.
2. It sets identifier-4 to its current FROM value.
3. It augments identifier-2 with its current BY value.

Notice that in each case the value of the field being varied is changed after the procedure-name is executed and before the corresponding condition is evaluated.

An example of a PERFORM . . . VARYING statement with an AFTER phrase could arise if we wanted to carry out some operation on every accumulator in Program P10-01, such as zeroing each one individually. We might have a statement such as:

```
PERFORM PROCESS-ONE-ACCUMULATOR
    VARYING STORE-SUBSCRIPT FROM 1 BY 1 UNTIL
        STORE-SUBSCRIPT IS GREATER THAN
        NUMBER-OF-STORES
    AFTER MONTH-SUBSCRIPT FROM 1 BY 1 UNTIL
        MONTH-SUBSCRIPT IS GREATER THAN
        NUMBER-OF-MONTHS.
```

The paragraph PROCESS-ONE-ACCUMULATOR would contain some processing on just one of the 30 accumulators, and the PERFORM statement would control the subscripts so that each time PROCESS-ONE-ACCUMULATOR executes, the subscripts would be pointing to a different one of the 30 accumulators. When more than one field is being varied in a PERFORM . . . VARYING statement, the last named varies most rapidly and the first named varies least rapidly. In the PER-FORM . . . VARYING statement given, the subscripts would be set in the order shown in Table 10-1. Thus the paragraph PROCESS-ONE-ACCUMULATOR is PERFORMed 30 times, with the subscripts pointing to a different one of the accumulators each time.

Table 10-1
The settings of the subscripts STORE-SUBSCRIPT and MONTH-SUBSCRIPT for the 30 executions of the paragraph PROCESS-ONE-ACCUMULATOR.

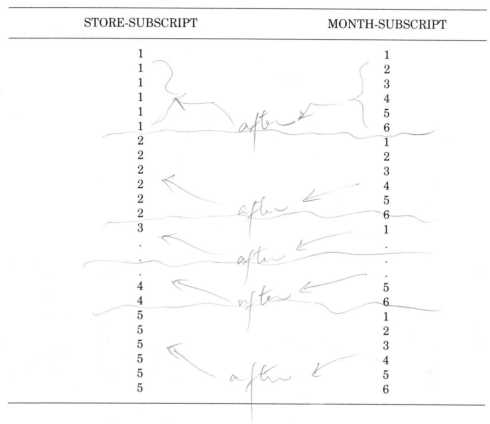

STORE-SUBSCRIPT	MONTH-SUBSCRIPT
1	1
1	2
1	3
1	4
1	5
1	6
2	1
2	2
2	3
2	4
2	5
2	6
3	1
.	.
.	.
.	.
4	5
4	6
5	1
5	2
5	3
5	4
5	5
5	6

The fourth format of the PERFORM statement is

```
PERFORM procedure-name-1 [ {THROUGH}  procedure-name-2]
                           {THRU    }
 {identifier-1}  TIMES
 {integer-1   }
```

This format permits the program to execute a paragraph a specific number of times. The number of times may be given as identifier-1 or integer-1. If identifier-1 is used, it must be defined as an integer. We use this kind of PERFORM statement in Chapter 18.

EXERCISE 1

Rewrite Program P10-01, defining the table with its columns (MONTHs) at the 05 level and the rows (STORE-NUMBERs) at the 10 level. Rearrange whatever subscripting needs rearranging. Change any of the PERFORM statements that need changing.

A Two-Dimensional Table with VALUE Clauses

In Program P10-01 you saw how to write a two-dimensional table in working storage and how to initialize all the elements of the table to zero with one VALUE clause. In Program P10-02 we see how to initialize the elements of a table to different values.

Program P10-02 reads input records in the following format:

Positions	Field
1 – 6	Loan Number
7 – 14	Principal (to two decimal places)
15 – 17	Number of Payments
18 – 20	Annual Interest Rate (to tenths of 1%)
21 – 80	spaces

Each record contains information about a home-mortgage loan — the Loan Number, the original Principal amount, the Number of monthly Payments, and the Annual Interest Rate. The program is to determine the monthly payment on the loan and print one line for each loan in the format shown in Figure 10.7.

The program uses Table 10-2. For each input record, the program looks up in the table the interest rate and number of payments for that particular loan to find the payment per $1 of loan. Then the program multiplies the table function by the full loan amount to arrive at the monthly payment for the loan.

Table 10-2

Monthly payments required per $1 of loan amount on loans of different interest rates and numbers of payments.

Annual Interest Rate, %	Number of Monthly Payments					
	60	120	180	240	300	360
10	.0212471	.0132151	.0107461	.0096503	.0090871	.0087758
10.5	.0214940	.0134935	.0110540	.0099838	.0094419	.0091474
11	.0217425	.0137751	.0113660	.0103219	.0098012	.0095233
11.5	.0219927	.0140596	.0116819	.0106643	.0101647	.0099030
12	.0222445	.0143471	.0120017	.0110109	.0105323	.0102862
12.5	.0224980	.0146377	.0123253	.0113615	.0109036	.0106726
13	.0227531	.0149311	.0126525	.0117158	.0112784	.0110620
13.5	.0230099	.0152275	.0129832	.0120738	.0116565	.0114542
14	.0232683	.0155267	.0133175	.0124353	.0120377	.0118488
14.5	.0235283	.0158287	.0136551	.0128000	.0124217	.0122456
15	.0237900	.0161335	.0139959	.0131679	.0128084	.0126445
15.5	.0240532	.0164411	.0143400	.0135389	.0131975	.0130452
16	.0243181	.0167514	.0146871	.0139126	.0135889	.0134476
16.5	.0245846	.0170643	.0150371	.0142891	.0139825	.0138515
17	.0248526	.0173798	.0153901	.0146681	.0143780	.0142568

Figure 10.7 Output format for Program P10-02.

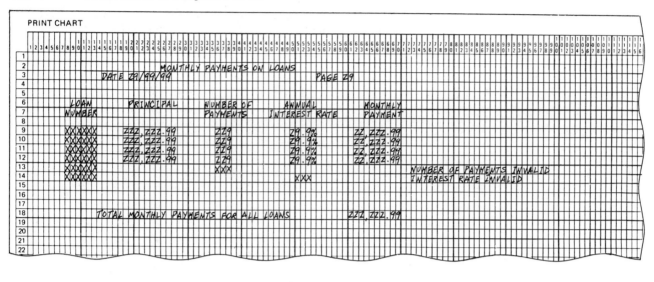

Figure 10.8 Program P10-02.

CB1 RELEASE 2.4   IBM OS/VS COBOL JULY 1, 1982

                        15.51.52   APR 6,1988

```
00010   IDENTIFICATION DIVISION.
00020   PROGRAM-ID.  P10-02.
00030  *AUTHOR.  DEBORAH ANN SENIOR.
00040  *
00050  *    THIS PROGRAM COMPUTES THE MONTHLY PAYMENT NEEDED
00060  *    TO REPAY A LOAN
00070  *
00080  *******************************************************************
00090
00100   ENVIRONMENT DIVISION.
00110   CONFIGURATION SECTION.
00120   SOURCE-COMPUTER.  IBM-370.
00130   OBJECT-COMPUTER.  IBM-370.
00140
00150   INPUT-OUTPUT SECTION.
00160   FILE-CONTROL.
00170       SELECT LOAN-FILE-IN           ASSIGN TO INFILE.
00180       SELECT PAYMENT-REPORT-FILE-OUT  ASSIGN TO PRINTER.
00190
00200  *******************************************************************
00210
00220   DATA DIVISION.
00230   FILE SECTION.
00240   FD  LOAN-FILE-IN
00250       LABEL RECORDS ARE OMITTED
00260       RECORD CONTAINS 80 CHARACTERS.
00270
00280   01  LOAN-RECORD-IN.
00290       05  LOAN-NUMBER-IN           PIC X(6).
00300       05  PRINCIPAL-IN             PIC 9(6)V99.
00310       05  NUMBER-OF-PAYMENTS-IN    PIC 999.
00320       05  NUMBER-OF-PAYMENTS-XXX-IN
00330           REDEFINES NUMBER-OF-PAYMENTS-IN    PIC XXX.
00340       05  ANNUAL-INTEREST-RATE-IN PIC 99V9.
00350       05  ANNUAL-INTEREST-RATE-XXX-IN
00360           REDEFINES ANNUAL-INTEREST-RATE-IN  PIC XXX.
00370       05  FILLER                   PIC X(60).
00380
00390   FD  PAYMENT-REPORT-FILE-OUT
00400       LABEL RECORDS ARE OMITTED.
00410
```

(continued)

If an input record contains an Annual Interest Rate or a Number of Payments that has no match in the table, an error line is to be printed as shown in Figure 10.7. The program is to check for valid Annual Interest Rate and valid Number of Payments and print two error lines if both fields are invalid. At the end of the report, the program is to print a total of the monthly payments for all the loans.

Program P10-02 is shown in Figure 10.8. In the File Section, the fields NUMBER-OF-PAYMENTS-IN and ANNUAL-INTEREST-RATE-IN have been REDEFINED with Xs. The reason for this is that either or both of these fields might be invalid and might contain nonnumeric values. We will use the alphanumeric redefinitions of the fields in the program up to the point where the program knows that the fields are numeric and valid.

The Working Storage Section begins at line 00440. In it there is a field called ANY-INPUT-ERRORS, at line 00460. This field is used to signal the program if either the ANNUAL-INTEREST-RATE-IN or the NUMBER-OF-PAYMENTS-IN, or both, is invalid.

The tables that we need for this program start at line 00620. First the ROW-ENTRIES are written, each complete row as a single FILLER entry. Whenever you write more than one numeric field into a single entry, as we are doing here, you may use a PICTURE of 9s and write all the numbers one after another (only the digits, no decimal points) as one big numeric literal. If you do that, you must write all the leading and trailing zeros of all the numbers, except the leftmost zeros of the leftmost number, to make the fields come out the right size. But numeric literals are limited to 18 digits. Our rows are longer than 18 digits, so we must make them alphanumeric. We must define them with Xs, put quotation marks around the numbers, and write all the leading and trailing zeros (including the leftmost zeros).

Following the entries for all the rows, we have a REDEFINES entry. Whenever you write a two-dimensional table into a program row by row, as we have done here, you must write the OCCURS clause for the rows as part of the REDEFINES entry and take care of the OCCURS clause for the columns later. Our REDEFINES entry in line 00940 says that there are 15 rows, and also sets up the rows with an ASCENDING KEY phrase and an INDEXED BY phrase so that we can use SEARCH ALL to find the row of the table that we want. You will see how we find the correct row for any particular loan when we look at the Procedure Division.

Since each row consists of two different types of data, two entries are needed to describe them. The level-10 entries at lines 00970 and 00980 do it. The first level-10 entry defines the first field in the row, TABLE-INTEREST-RATE. The second level-10 entry, line 00980, defines the remaining six fields in the row, using the name MONTHLY-PAYMENT-PER-DOLLAR and an OCCURS clause. MONTHLY-PAYMENT-PER-DOLLAR has an OCCURS clause in its description and is subordinate to an entry that has an OCCURS clause. Thus, whenever the name MONTHLY-PAYMENT-PER-DOLLAR is referred to, it must be followed by two subscripts or two indexes in parentheses, in the order in which the OCCURS clauses are written. Since the field to which MONTHLY-PAYMENT-PER-DOLLAR is subordinate, ROW, is defined to be indexed, not subscripted, MONTH-LY-PAYMENT-PER-DOLLAR must also be indexed, not subscripted. You cannot mix subscripting and indexing in a reference to a field in 1974 COBOL. Such mixing is permitted in the 1985 standard, however.

This is all jolly good as far as it goes, but we still have not entered into the program anywhere the different numbers of months of payments, the constants 60, 120, 180, and so on. We have entered the rows and their captions, but not the column captions. These must be entered as a separate one-dimensional table, as shown starting at line 01010. This table has been set up for SEARCH ALL, as you can see by the ASCENDING KEY and INDEXED BY phrases in lines 01100 and 01110.

Figure 10.8 (continued)

```
00420   01   REPORT-LINE            PIC X(98).
00430
00440   WORKING-STORAGE SECTION.
00450   01   MORE-INPUT             PIC X            VALUE "Y".
00460   01   ANY-INPUT-ERRORS      PIC X.
00470   01   TODAYS-DATE.
00480        05   TODAYS-YEAR       PIC 99.
00490        05   TODAYS-MONTH-AND-DAY         PIC 9(4).
00500   01   MONTHLY-PAYMENT-W     PIC S9(5)V99.
00510   01   TOTAL-MONTHLY-PAYMENTS-W
00520                              PIC S9(6)V99     VALUE ZERO.
00530   01   LINE-LIMIT            PIC S99          VALUE 40 COMP SYNC.
00540   01   LINE-COUNT-ER         PIC S99                   COMP SYNC.
00550   01   LINE-SPACING          PIC S9                    COMP SYNC.
00560   01   PAGE-NUMBER-W         PIC S99          VALUE 0.
00570   01   ERROR-MESSAGE-RATE                     PIC X(21)
00580                      VALUE "INTEREST RATE INVALID".
00590   01   ERROR-MESSAGE-PAYMENT                  PIC X(26)
00600                      VALUE "NUMBER OF PAYMENTS INVALID".
00610
00620   01   PAYMENT-TABLES.
00630        05   ROW-ENTRIES.
00640             10   FILLER      PIC X(45)
00650               VALUE "1000212471013215101074610096503009087100877758".
00660             10   FILLER      PIC X(45)
00670               VALUE "1050214940013493501105400099838009441900914742".
00680             10   FILLER      PIC X(45)
00690               VALUE "1100217425013775101136600103219009801200952333".
00700             10   FILLER      PIC X(45)
00710               VALUE "1150219927014059601168190106643010164700990303".
00720             10   FILLER      PIC X(45)
00730               VALUE "1200222445014347101200170110109010532301028623".
00740             10   FILLER      PIC X(45)
00750               VALUE "1250224980014637701232530113615010903601067263".
00760             10   FILLER      PIC X(45)
00770               VALUE "1300227531014931101265250117158011278401106203".
00780             10   FILLER      PIC X(45)
00790               VALUE "1350230099015227501298320120738011656501145423".
00800             10   FILLER      PIC X(45)
00810               VALUE "1400232683015526701331750124353012037701184883".
00820             10   FILLER      PIC X(45)
00830               VALUE "1450235283015828701365510128000012421701224563".
00840             10   FILLER      PIC X(45)
00850               VALUE "1500237900016133501399590131679012808401264453".
00860             10   FILLER      PIC X(45)
00870               VALUE "1550240532016441101434000135389013197501304523".
00880             10   FILLER      PIC X(45)
00890               VALUE "1600243181016751401468710139126013588901344763".
00900             10   FILLER      PIC X(45)
00910               VALUE "1650245846017064301503710142891013982501385153".
00920             10   FILLER      PIC X(45)
00930               VALUE "1700248526017379801539010146681014378001425683".
00940        05   ROW           REDEFINES ROW-ENTRIES
00950             OCCURS 15 TIMES ASCENDING KEY TABLE-INTEREST-RATE
00960             INDEXED BY ROW-INDEX.
00970             10   TABLE-INTEREST-RATE          PIC XXX.
00980             10   MONTHLY-PAYMENT-PER-DOLLAR   PIC V9(7)
00990                  OCCURS 6 TIMES INDEXED BY COLUMN-INDEX.
01000
01010        05   NUMBER-OF-PAYMENTS-ENTRIES.
01020             10   FILLER      PIC 999          VALUE 60.
01030             10   FILLER      PIC 999          VALUE 120.
01040             10   FILLER      PIC 999          VALUE 180.
01050             10   FILLER      PIC 999          VALUE 240.
01060             10   FILLER      PIC 999          VALUE 300.
01070             10   FILLER      PIC 999          VALUE 360.
01080        05   TABLE-NUMBER-OF-PAYMENTS
01090             REDEFINES NUMBER-OF-PAYMENTS-ENTRIES
01100             OCCURS 6 TIMES ASCENDING KEY TABLE-NUMBER-OF-PAYMENTS
01110             INDEXED BY NUMBER-OF-PAYMENTS-INDEX
01120                              PIC XXX.
01130
01140   01   PAGE-HEAD-1.
01150        05   FILLER           PIC X(25)        VALUE SPACES.
01160        05   FILLER           PIC X(25)
01170                              VALUE "MONTHLY PAYMENTS ON LOANS".
```

(continued)

Figure 10.8 (continued)

```
01180
01190    01    PAGE-HEAD-2.
01200          05 FILLER              PIC X(14)         VALUE SPACES.
01210          05 FILLER              PIC X(5)          VALUE "DATE".
01220          05 TODAYS-MONTH-AND-DAY                  PIC Z9/99/.
01230          05 TODAYS-YEAR         PIC 99B(27).
01240          05 FILLER              PIC X(5)          VALUE "PAGE".
01250          05 PAGE-NUMBER-OUT     PIC Z9.
01260
01270    01    PAGE-HEAD-3.
01280          05 FILLER              PIC X(8)          VALUE SPACES.
01290          05 FILLER              PIC X(11)         VALUE "LOAN".
01300          05 FILLER              PIC X(14)         VALUE "PRINCIPAL".
01310          05 FILLER              PIC X(15)         VALUE "NUMBER OF".
01320          05 FILLER              PIC X(15)         VALUE "ANNUAL".
01330          05 FILLER              PIC X(7)          VALUE "MONTHLY".
01340
01350    01    PAGE-HEAD-4.
01360          05 FILLER              PIC X(7)          VALUE SPACES.
01370          05 FILLER              PIC X(26)         VALUE "NUMBER".
01380          05 FILLER              PIC X(12)         VALUE "PAYMENTS".
01390          05 FILLER              PIC X(18)         VALUE "INTEREST RATE".
01400          05 FILLER              PIC X(7)          VALUE "PAYMENT".
01410
01420    01    GOOD-DETAIL-LINE.
01430          05 LOAN-NUMBER-OUT            PIC B(7)X(6).
01440          05 PRINCIPAL-OUT             PIC B(5)ZZZ,ZZZ.99.
01450          05 NUMBER-OF-PAYMENTS-OUT    PIC B(7)ZZ9.
01460          05 ANNUAL-INTEREST-RATE-OUT  PIC B(11)Z9.9.
01470          05 FILLER                    PIC X          VALUE "%".
01480          05 MONTHLY-PAYMENT-OUT       PIC B(7)ZZ,ZZZ.99.
01490
01500    01    TOTAL-LINE.
01510          05 FILLER              PIC X(13)          VALUE SPACES.
01520          05 FILLER              PIC X(47)
01530             VALUE "TOTAL MONTHLY PAYMENTS FOR ALL LOANS".
01540          05 TOTAL-PAYMENT-OUT        PIC ZZZ,ZZZ.99.
01550
01560    01    RATE-ERROR-DETAIL-LINE.
01570          05 LOAN-NUMBER-R-ERROR       PIC B(7)X(6).
01580          05 ANNUAL-INTEREST-RATE-XXX-OUT
01590                                       PIC B(37)X(3)B(19).
01600          05 RATE-ERROR-MESSAGE        PIC X(21).
01610
01620    01    PAYMENTS-ERROR-DETAIL-LINE.
01630          05 LOAN-NUMBER-P-ERROR       PIC B(7)X(6).
01640          05 NUMBER-OF-PAYMENTS-XXX-OUT
01650                                       PIC B(22)X(3)B(34).
01660          05 PAYMENT-ERROR-MESSAGE     PIC X(26).
01670
01680    01    NO-INPUT-DATA.
01690          05 FILLER              PIC X(31)          VALUE SPACES.
01700          05 FILLER              PIC X(13)          VALUE "NO INPUT DATA".
01710
01720    **********************************************************************
01730
01740    PROCEDURE DIVISION.
01750    CONTROL-PARAGRAPH.
01760          PERFORM INITIALIZATION.
01770          PERFORM MAIN-PROCESS UNTIL MORE-INPUT IS EQUAL TO "N".
01780          PERFORM TERMINATION.
01790          STOP RUN.
01800
01810    INITIALIZATION.
01820          ACCEPT TODAYS-DATE FROM DATE.
01830          MOVE CORR TODAYS-DATE TO PAGE-HEAD-2.
01840          OPEN INPUT  LOAN-FILE-IN,
01850              OUTPUT PAYMENT-REPORT-FILE-OUT.
01860          PERFORM PRINT-PAGE-HEADING-LINES.
01870          PERFORM READ-A-RECORD.
01880          IF MORE-INPUT IS EQUAL TO "N"
01890              WRITE REPORT-LINE FROM NO-INPUT-DATA AFTER 2.
01900
```

```
01910   MAIN-PROCESS.
01920       MOVE "N" TO ANY-INPUT-ERRORS.
01930       SEARCH ALL ROW
01940           AT END
01950               PERFORM INTEREST-RATE-INVALID
01960           WHEN TABLE-INTEREST-RATE (ROW-INDEX) IS EQUAL TO
01970               ANNUAL-INTEREST-RATE-XXX-IN
01980               NEXT SENTENCE.
01990       SEARCH ALL TABLE-NUMBER-OF-PAYMENTS
02000           AT END
02010               PERFORM NUMBER-OF-PAYMENTS-INVALID
02020           WHEN TABLE-NUMBER-OF-PAYMENTS (NUMBER-OF-PAYMENTS-INDEX)
02030               IS EQUAL TO NUMBER-OF-PAYMENTS-XXX-IN
02040               NEXT SENTENCE.
02050       IF ANY-INPUT-ERRORS IS EQUAL TO "N"
02060           SET COLUMN-INDEX TO NUMBER-OF-PAYMENTS-INDEX
02070           MULTIPLY PRINCIPAL-IN BY
02080               MONTHLY-PAYMENT-PER-DOLLAR (ROW-INDEX, COLUMN-INDEX)
02090               GIVING MONTHLY-PAYMENT-W ROUNDED
02100           PERFORM PRINT-A-GOOD-LINE.
02110       PERFORM READ-A-RECORD.
02120
02130   INTEREST-RATE-INVALID.
02140       MOVE LOAN-NUMBER-IN              TO LOAN-NUMBER-R-ERROR.
02150       MOVE ANNUAL-INTEREST-RATE-XXX-IN
02160                       TO ANNUAL-INTEREST-RATE-XXX-OUT
02170       MOVE ERROR-MESSAGE-RATE         TO RATE-ERROR-MESSAGE.
02180       IF LINE-COUNT-ER + LINE-SPACING > LINE-LIMIT
02190           PERFORM PRINT-PAGE-HEADING-LINES.
02200       WRITE REPORT-LINE FROM RATE-ERROR-DETAIL-LINE
02210               AFTER LINE-SPACING.
02220       ADD LINE-SPACING TO LINE-COUNT-ER.
02230       MOVE 1                          TO LINE-SPACING.
02240       MOVE "Y" TO ANY-INPUT-ERRORS.
02250
```

(continued)

For each input record the program can SEARCH ALL of the rows looking for a TABLE-INTEREST-RATE that matches the ANNUAL-INTEREST-RATE-IN, and SEARCH ALL of the column captions looking for a TABLE-NUMBER-OF-PAYMENTS equal to the NUMBER-OF-PAYMENTS-IN. The program will then have two index values it needs to do its further processing. The SEARCH ALL statements have suitable AT END clauses to take care of situations in which no match(es) is (are) found.

Four types of detail lines are defined. GOOD-DETAIL-LINE, line 01420, is the ordinary line that prints when the input record is error-free. Two other definitions, lines 01560 through 01660, describe the two types of error lines.

In the Procedure Division MAIN-PROCESS begins at line 01910. As we enter MAIN-PROCESS each time with an input record, the flag ANY-INPUT-ERRORS is first set to indicate that no errors have yet been found in this record. The program then SEARCHes ALL the ROWs looking for the condition given in the WHEN clause at line 01960:

```
TABLE-INTEREST-RATE (ROW-INDEX) IS EQUAL TO
    ANNUAL-INTEREST-RATE-XXX-IN
```

Notice that TABLE-INTEREST-RATE is indexed by ROW-INDEX even though TABLE-INTEREST-RATE has no OCCURS clause. That is because TABLE-INTEREST-RATE is subordinate to an entry that has an OCCURS clause with the phrase INDEXED BY ROW-INDEX.

If this SEARCH ALL fails to satisfy the WHEN condition, the AT END clause, line 01940, is executed. The paragraph INTEREST-RATE-INVALID, line 02130,

Figure 10.8   (continued)

```
02260    TERMINATION.
02270        PERFORM PRODUCE-TOTAL-LINE.
02280        CLOSE LOAN-FILE-IN,
02290              PAYMENT-REPORT-FILE-OUT.
02300
02310    READ-A-RECORD.
02320        READ LOAN-FILE-IN
02330            AT END
02340                MOVE "N" TO MORE-INPUT.
02350
02360    PRINT-PAGE-HEADING-LINES.
02370        ADD 1                           TO PAGE-NUMBER-W.
02380        MOVE PAGE-NUMBER-W              TO PAGE-NUMBER-OUT.
02390        WRITE REPORT-LINE FROM PAGE-HEAD-1 AFTER PAGE.
02400        WRITE REPORT-LINE FROM PAGE-HEAD-2.
02410        WRITE REPORT-LINE FROM PAGE-HEAD-3 AFTER 3.
02420        WRITE REPORT-LINE FROM PAGE-HEAD-4.
02430        MOVE 6                          TO LINE-COUNT-ER.
02440        MOVE 2                          TO LINE-SPACING.
02450
02460    PRODUCE-TOTAL-LINE.
02470        MOVE TOTAL-MONTHLY-PAYMENTS-W  TO TOTAL-PAYMENT-OUT.
02480        WRITE REPORT-LINE FROM TOTAL-LINE AFTER 4.
02490
02500    NUMBER-OF-PAYMENTS-INVALID.
02510        MOVE LOAN-NUMBER-IN             TO LOAN-NUMBER-P-ERROR.
02520        MOVE NUMBER-OF-PAYMENTS-XXX-IN TO NUMBER-OF-PAYMENTS-XXX-OUT.
02530        MOVE ERROR-MESSAGE-PAYMENT      TO PAYMENT-ERROR-MESSAGE.
02540        IF LINE-COUNT-ER + LINE-SPACING > LINE-LIMIT
02550            PERFORM PRINT-PAGE-HEADING-LINES.
02560        WRITE REPORT-LINE FROM PAYMENTS-ERROR-DETAIL-LINE
02570            AFTER LINE-SPACING.
02580        ADD LINE-SPACING                TO LINE-COUNT-ER.
02590        MOVE 1                          TO LINE-SPACING.
02600        MOVE "Y" TO ANY-INPUT-ERRORS.
02610
02620    PRINT-A-GOOD-LINE.
02630        MOVE LOAN-NUMBER-IN             TO LOAN-NUMBER-OUT.
02640        MOVE PRINCIPAL-IN               TO PRINCIPAL-OUT.
02650        MOVE NUMBER-OF-PAYMENTS-IN      TO NUMBER-OF-PAYMENTS-OUT.
02660        MOVE ANNUAL-INTEREST-RATE-IN    TO ANNUAL-INTEREST-RATE-OUT.
02670        MOVE MONTHLY-PAYMENT-W          TO MONTHLY-PAYMENT-OUT.
02680        IF LINE-COUNT-ER + LINE-SPACING > LINE-LIMIT
02690            PERFORM PRINT-PAGE-HEADING-LINES.
02700        WRITE REPORT-LINE FROM GOOD-DETAIL-LINE
02710            AFTER LINE-SPACING.
02720        ADD LINE-SPACING                TO LINE-COUNT-ER.
02730        MOVE 1                          TO LINE-SPACING.
02740        ADD MONTHLY-PAYMENT-W           TO TOTAL-MONTHLY-PAYMENTS-W.
```

prints an error line and sets ANY-INPUT-ERRORS to "Y" to indicate that at least one error was found in this input record.

Regardless of whether or not the row search was successful, the SEARCH ALL statement at line 01990 executes next. This SEARCH ALL examines the one-dimensional table TABLE-NUMBER-OF-PAYMENTS looking for the condition:

```
TABLE-NUMBER-OF-PAYMENTS (NUMBER-OF-PAYMENTS-INDEX)
        IS EQUAL TO NUMBER-OF-PAYMENTS-XXX-IN
```

If this SEARCH ALL fails to satisfy the condition, the AT END clause at line 02000 is executed. The paragraph NUMBER-OF-PAYMENTS-INVALID writes an error line and sets ANY-INPUT-ERRORS to "Y" to indicate that the input record contains at least one error.

Together the two SEARCH ALLs leave ROW-INDEX pointing to the row containing the desired interest rate, and NUMBER-OF-PAYMENTS-INDEX pointing to the entry in the NUMBER-OF-PAYMENTS-ENTRIES that represents the desired number of payments. Now we are ready to try to fetch the correct MONTHLY-PAYMENT-PER-DOLLAR and multiply it by the loan amount, PRINCIPAL-IN.

MONTHLY-PAYMENT-PER-DOLLAR is defined with the phrase IN-DEXED BY COLUMN-INDEX and is subordinate to an entry that is defined with the phrase INDEXED BY ROW-INDEX. That means that whenever MONTHLY-PAYMENT-PER-DOLLAR is referred to, it must be referred to either this way:

```
MONTHLY-PAYMENT-PER-DOLLAR (ROW-INDEX, COLUMN-INDEX)
```

or with integer literals or integer identifiers in place of the words ROW-INDEX and/or COLUMN-INDEX. It is not possible to use any other index names to refer to MONTHLY-PAYMENT-PER-DOLLAR. Unlike subscripting, where any field defined as an integer may be used to subscript any field defined with an OCCURS clause, indexing requires that if a field is referred to by index names, they must be the index names given in the INDEXED BY phrases that the field is defined with or is subordinate to.

When the IF statement at line 02050 executes, COLUMN-INDEX has not yet been assigned any value. The column we want to refer to corresponds to the setting of the NUMBER-OF-PAYMENTS-INDEX resulting from the SEARCH ALL at line 01990. We can use the SET statement at line 02060 to SET COLUMN-INDEX to point to the column we want. Remember that the sending field of a SET statement comes after the word TO, and the receiving field before. Notice that the SET, MULTIPLY, and PERFORM statements at lines 02060 through 02100 are executed only if ANY-INPUT-ERRORS indicates that the record is free of errors.

Program P10-02 was run with the input data shown in Figure 10.9 and produced the output shown in Figure 10.10.

Figure 10.9 Input to Program P10-02.

```
-------------------------------------------------------------------------------
         1         2         3         4         5         6         7         8
12345678901234567890123456789012345678901234567890123456789012345678901234567890
-------------------------------------------------------------------------------
00268310000000060100
07143901000000360100
17829400050000060170
24837100500000360170
57282901682788360125
66271468461121230115
72860520000000240115
74461800100500120135
82227700400000120180
90002600080000400175
95364100100000060140
```

Figure 10.10 Output from Program P10-02.

```
                        MONTHLY PAYMENTS ON LOANS
              DATE  4/06/88                              PAGE  1


      LOAN        PRINCIPAL      NUMBER OF      ANNUAL        MONTHLY
      NUMBER                     PAYMENTS    INTEREST RATE    PAYMENT

      002683     100,000.00         60          10.0%       2,124.71
      071439      10,000.00        360          10.0%          87.76
      178294         500.00         60          17.0%          12.43
      248371       5,000.00        360          17.0%          71.28
      572829      16,827.88        360          12.5%         179.60
      662714                       230                                   NUMBER OF PAYMENTS INVALID
      728605     200,000.00        240          11.5%       2,132.86
      744618       1,005.00        120          13.5%          15.30
      822277                                     180                     INTEREST RATE INVALID
      900026                                     175                     INTEREST RATE INVALID
      900026                       400                                   NUMBER OF PAYMENTS INVALID
      953641       1,000.00         60          14.0%          23.27


          TOTAL MONTHLY PAYMENTS FOR ALL LOANS            4,647.21
```

The PICTURE Character P

The character P is useful in PICTUREs that describe very large or very small numeric quantities. In this context "very large" numbers are those that have one or more zeros at the right end of the number; "very small" numbers have one or more zeros immediately to the right of the decimal point. In Table 10-2 all the entries in the body of the table have one zero just to the right of the decimal point. By using the PICTURE character P in one place in the program, we can indicate to COBOL the presence of all those zeros and not have to write them. Here's how we would change Program P10-02 to take advantage of P.

First we would write the ROW-ENTRIES without those leading zeros. For example, the first FILLER, line 00640, instead of having the VALUE

```
1000212471013215101074610096503009087100877758
```

would have the VALUE:

```
100212471132151107461096503090871087758
```

Of course, the PICTURE for that FILLER and all the other ROW-ENTRIES would be X(39) now instead of X(45).

Then the PICTURE for MONTHLY-PAYMENT-PER-DOLLAR, line 00980, would be changed to indicate that the zeros are missing. Instead of PIC V9(7), we would use:

```
10 MONTHLY-PAYMENT-PER-DOLLAR PIC P9(6)
   OCCURS 6 TIMES INDEXED BY COLUMN-INDEX.
```

The 9(6) in the PICTURE indicates that six digits were actually written into the ROW-ENTRIES. The P in the PICTURE tells COBOL to assume a zero at the left end of the number whenever the field is used for arithmetic or printing or anything. You may have one or more Ps at the left or right end of a PICTURE, but not both in the same PICTURE. P may be followed by an integer inside parentheses to indicate repetitions of P. For example, PIC PPPPPP9(5) is the same as PIC P(6)9(5). One or more Ps at the left end of a PICTURE tell COBOL that a decimal point is assumed to the left of the Ps. You may use a V to the left of one or more Ps, but it would be redundant. P is not counted in the size of a field. You may use an S to the left of one or more Ps.

One or more Ps at the right end of a PICTURE tell COBOL that a decimal point is assumed to the right of the Ps. You wouldn't be using V at the right end of an integer anyway.

We have been using P here in a purely numeric field in working storage. P may also be used in PICTUREs for numeric fields in input records, and in PICTUREs for numeric and edited numeric fields in output records. As an example of its use in an input record, let's say that an input record contains fields in the form .000000nnn, where the ns stand for digits in the number. The field may be defined with PICTURE P(6)9(3) and only the three digits indicated by n need to be keyed in the input.

P may be used in an edited numeric field in a print line when you don't want the digits at the right or left end of a number to print. For example, you might have a field in working storage that contains hundreds of millions of dollars and is defined with PICTURE 9(9). When you print this field, you may want only the three high-order digits to print, in millions of dollars. Then you could define the output field with PICTURE $ZZ9P(6).

EXERCISE 2

Write a program to read input records in the following format:

Positions	Field
1 – 5	Employee Number
6	Job Classification Code
7	Education Code
8 – 80	spaces

There is one input record for each employee. Each record contains an Employee Number, the employee's Job Classification Code, and the employee's Education Code.

Table 10-E2 shows the minimum annual salary for employees as a function of their Job Classification Code and their Education Code. For each employee, have your program compute the minimum weekly salary (annual salary divided by 52) and the minimum monthly salary (annual salary divided by 12) and print on one line the Employee Number, Job Classification Code, Education Code, minimum weekly salary, and minimum monthly salary. If any input record contains an invalid Job Classification Code or Education Code, or both, have your program print an error line showing the Employee Number and a suitable error message. At the end of the report have your program print totals of the minimum weekly salaries and the minimum monthly salaries.

Set up the salary figures in the table in your program without their two low-order zeros. Use two Ps in the description of the salary amount to tell COBOL that the zeros are missing.

Table 10-E2
Minimum annual salary for employees as a function of Job Classification Code and Education Code.

Job Classification Code	Education Code			
	A	B	C	D
Z	7,200	8,000	9,100	10,500
Y	7,800	8,500	9,800	11,100
X	8,800	9,600	10,800	12,600
W	10,400	11,300	12,700	14,900
V	13,800	16,000	19,200	21,100
6	15,600	18,900	23,000	25,400
5	20,200	24,100	27,600	31,000

Searching a Table for a Range of Values

In all our search tables so far we have always been SEARCHing for a specific value of a table argument. We have SEARCHed for state codes and interest rates and numbers of months of payment, always looking for an equal match between a table argument and a search argument. Our WHEN conditions have always been tests for equal. We will now write a program in which a condition other than EQUAL TO is used.

Program P10-03 reads input data in the following format:

Positions	Field
1 – 5	Salesperson Number
6	Grade
7 – 13	Sale Amount (to two decimal places)
14 – 80	spaces

Each record represents a sale made by a salesperson. The record contains a Salesperson Number, a Salesperson Grade, and a Sale Amount. The commission rate on the sale depends on the Sale Amount and the Salesperson Grade as shown in Table 10-3. Assume that there are several sales for each salesperson, grouped together in the input. For each record, the program is to look up the commission rate in the table, compute the commission by multiplying the commission rate by the Sale Amount, and print a line of output as shown in Figure 10.11. For each salesperson, the total sales and the total commission are to be shown.

Table 10-3
Commission rates on sales as a function of Sale Amount and Salesperson Grade.

Sale Amount	Salesperson Grade				
	1	2	3	4	5
1 – 1,000.00	5%	5%	10%	10%	15%
1,000.01 – 10,000.00	10%	15%	15%	20%	25%
10,000.01 – 50,000.00	15%	20%	25%	30%	35%
over 50,000	25%	30%	35%	45%	50%

Figure 10.11 Output format for Program P10-03.

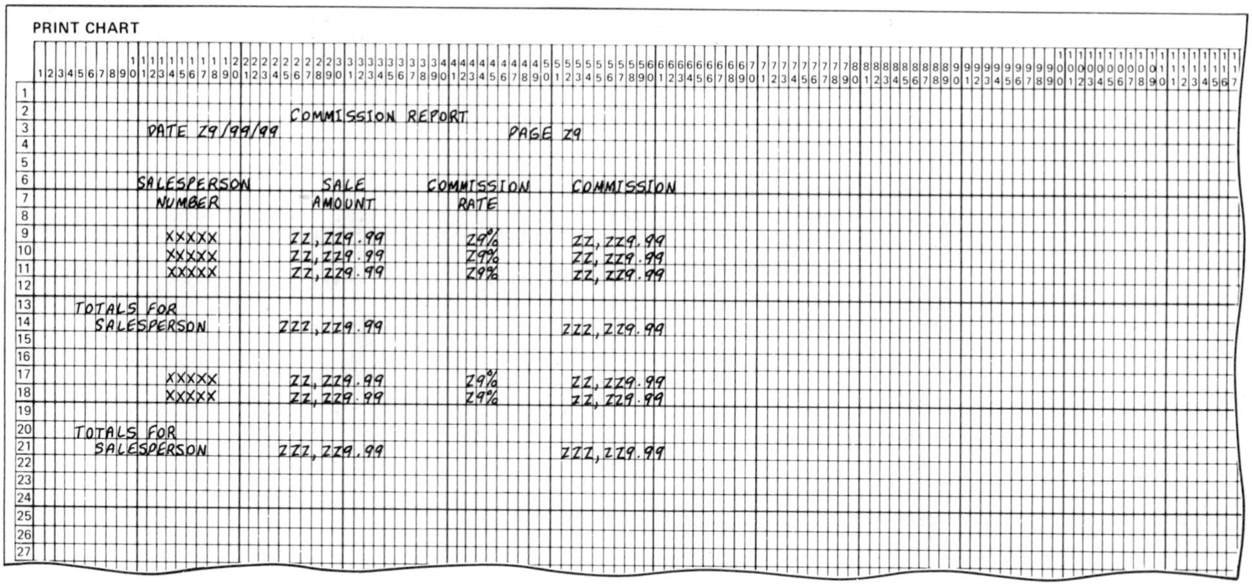

In Program P10-03 we have to write the rows of Table 10-3 into working storage. Whenever table captions involve contiguous ranges of values, or brackets, as our row captions do, it is best to write into the program only the high end of each bracket. In Program P10-03 we can determine into which bracket each input Sale Amount falls by comparing the Sale Amount to the table bracket amounts and using some sort of GREATER THAN or LESS THAN test to determine when the correct bracket is found. You will see how when we look at the Procedure Division.

There is no need to write both the high and low ends of the brackets, since each bracket begins where another leaves off. Experience has shown that writing the high end of each bracket into a program leads to far simpler coding than writing the low end. If the brackets were not contiguous, both the high and low ends of each would have to be written into the program. The fourth row of Table 10-3 doesn't seem at first glance to have a high end, but it really does. The largest possible Sale Amount allowed by the size of the input field is $99,999.99, so we use that as the high end of row 4.

Program P10-03 is shown in Figure 10.12. In the Working Storage Section

Figure 10.12 Program P10-03.

```
CB1 RELEASE 2.4                          IBM OS/VS COBOL  JULY  1, 1982


                      18.12.45        APR  6,1988


     00010   IDENTIFICATION DIVISION.
     00020   PROGRAM-ID.  P10-03.
     00030 *
     00040 *   THIS PROGRAM DEMONSTRATES SEARCHING A TABLE FOR A RANGE
     00050 *   OF VALUES TO CALCULATE COMMISSIONS
     00060 *
```

(continued)

Figure 10.12   (continued)

```
00070 ******************************************************************
00080
00090 ENVIRONMENT DIVISION.
00100 CONFIGURATION SECTION.
00110 SOURCE-COMPUTER.  IBM-370.
00120 OBJECT-COMPUTER.  IBM-370.
00130
00140 INPUT-OUTPUT SECTION.
00150 FILE-CONTROL.
00160     SELECT SALES-FILE-IN               ASSIGN TO INFILE.
00170     SELECT COMMISSION-REPORT-FILE-OUT  ASSIGN TO PRINTER.
00180
00190 ******************************************************************
00200
00210 DATA DIVISION.
00220 FILE SECTION.
00230 FD  SALES-FILE-IN
00240     LABEL RECORDS ARE OMITTED
00250     RECORD CONTAINS 80 CHARACTERS.
00260
00270 01  SALES-RECORD-IN            PIC X(80).
00280
00290 FD  COMMISSION-REPORT-FILE-OUT
00300     LABEL RECORDS ARE OMITTED.
00310
00320 01  COMMISSION-REPORT-RECORD-OUT       PIC X(62).
00330
00340 WORKING-STORAGE SECTION.
00350 01  MORE-INPUT          PIC X            VALUE "Y".
00360
00370 01  SALES-RECORD-W.
00380     05  SALESPERSON-NUMBER-IN  PIC X(5).
00390     05  SALESPERSON-GRADE-IN   PIC 9.
00400     05  SALE-AMOUNT-IN         PIC 9(5)V99.
00410     05  FILLER                 PIC X(67).
00420
00430 01  TODAYS-DATE.
00440     05  TODAYS-YEAR     PIC 99.
00450     05  TODAYS-MONTH-AND-DAY            PIC 9(4).
00460 01  COMMISSION-W        PIC S9(5)V99.
00470 01  PAGE-NUMBER-W       PIC S99           VALUE 0.
00480 01  LINE-LIMIT          PIC S99 COMP SYNC VALUE 40.
00490 01  LINE-COUNT-ER       PIC S99 COMP SYNC.
00500 01  LINE-SPACING        PIC S9  COMP SYNC.
00510 01  SALESPERSON-NUMBER-SAVE           PIC X(5).
00520
00530 01  ACCUMULATORS.
00540     05 SALES-TOTAL-W       PIC S9(6)V99    VALUE 0.
00550     05 COMMISSION-TOTAL-W PIC S9(6)V99    VALUE 0.
00560
00570 01  COMMISSION-TABLE.
00580     05  ROW-ENTRIES.
00590         10  FILLER      PIC 9(17)     VALUE  1000000505101015.
00600         10  FILLER      PIC 9(17)     VALUE 10000001015152025.
00610         10  FILLER      PIC 9(17)     VALUE 50000001520253035.
00620         10  FILLER      PIC 9(17)     VALUE 99999992530354550.
00630     05  ROW                 REDEFINES ROW-ENTRIES
00640         OCCURS 4 TIMES  INDEXED BY SALES-BRACKET-INDEX.
00650         10  TOP-OF-SALES-BRACKET       PIC 9(5)V99.
00660         10  COMMISSION-RATE
00670                       OCCURS 5 TIMES  INDEXED BY GRADE-INDEX.
00680             15  COMMISSION-RATE-F      PIC V99.
00690             15  COMMISSION-RATE-I
00700                       REDEFINES COMMISSION-RATE-F
00710                       PIC 99.
00720
00730 01  HEADING-LINE-2.
00740     05  FILLER          PIC X(25)     VALUE SPACES.
00750     05  FILLER          PIC X(17) VALUE "COMMISSION REPORT".
00760
00770 01  HEADING-LINE-3.
00780     05  FILLER          PIC X(11)     VALUE SPACES.
00790     05  FILLER          PIC X(5)      VALUE "DATE".
00800     05  TODAYS-MONTH-AND-DAY          PIC Z9/99/.
00810     05  TODAYS-YEAR                   PIC 99B(22).
00820     05  FILLER          PIC X(5)      VALUE "PAGE".
00830     05  PAGE-NUMBER-OUT PIC Z9.
00840
```

```
00850   01   HEADING-LINE-6.
00860        05   FILLER         PIC X(10)       VALUE SPACES.
00870        05   FILLER         PIC X(18)       VALUE "SALESPERSON".
00880        05   FILLER         PIC X(10)       VALUE "SALE".
00890        05   FILLER         PIC X(14)       VALUE "COMMISSION".
00900        05   FILLER         PIC X(10)       VALUE "COMMISSION".
00910
00920   01   HEADING-LINE-7.
00930        05   FILLER         PIC X(12)       VALUE SPACES.
00940        05   FILLER         PIC X(15)       VALUE "NUMBER".
00950        05   FILLER         PIC X(14)       VALUE "AMOUNT".
00960        05   FILLER         PIC X(4)        VALUE "RATE".
00970
00980   01   DETAIL-LINE.
00990        05   SALESPERSON-NUMBER-OUT         PIC B(13)X(5).
01000        05   SALE-AMOUNT-OUT                PIC B(7)ZZ,ZZ9.99.
01010        05   COMMISSION-RATE-OUT            PIC B(8)Z9.
01020        05   FILLER         PIC X           VALUE "%".
01030        05   COMMISSION-OUT                 PIC B(7)ZZ,ZZ9.99.
01040
01050   01   TOTAL-LINE-1.
01060        05   FILLER         PIC X(4)        VALUE SPACES.
01070        05   FILLER         PIC X(10)       VALUE "TOTALS FOR".
01080
01090   01   TOTAL-LINE-2.
01100        05   FILLER         PIC X(6)        VALUE SPACES.
01110        05   FILLER         PIC X(18)       VALUE "SALESPERSON".
01120        05   SALES-TOTAL-OUT                PIC ZZZ,ZZ9.99B(17).
01130        05   COMMISSION-TOTAL-OUT           PIC ZZZ,ZZ9.99.
01140
01150   01   NO-INPUT-DATA.
01160        05   FILLER         PIC X(27)       VALUE SPACES.
01170        05   FILLER         PIC X(13)       VALUE "NO INPUT DATA".
01180
01190   *************************************************************
01200
01210   PROCEDURE DIVISION.
01220   CONTROL-PARAGRAPH.
01230        PERFORM INITIALIZATION.
01240        PERFORM MAIN-PROCESS UNTIL MORE-INPUT IS EQUAL TO "N".
01250        PERFORM TERMINATION.
01260        STOP RUN.
01270
```

(continued)

there is a field called COMMISSION-W, at line 00460. This is used to hold the product of the Sale Amount by the commission rate found in the table.

Table 10-3 starts at line 00570. Here the rows are less than 18 digits long, so they are defined with 9s. There is no big advantage in defining the FILLERs with 9s instead of Xs, except that the leftmost zeros of the leftmost number can be omitted when the field is defined with 9s. It was done here mainly to show the idea.

In the redefinition of the ROW-ENTRIES there is no ASCENDING KEY clause, just an INDEXED BY clause. This table is set up for use of the SEARCH statement but not for the SEARCH ALL. Remember that the only condition permitted in a SEARCH ALL statement is the EQUAL TO condition, and in Program P10-03 we are going to have to use some form of a GREATER THAN or LESS THAN condition.

The COMMISSION-RATE, line 00660, is defined both as a fraction (line 00680) and as an integer (line 00690). Each definition has a different name. We use the name COMMISSION-RATE-F when we want to treat the percentage COMMISSION-RATE as a fraction, and we use COMMISSION-RATE-I when we want to treat it as an integer. This coding shows that an entry containing a REDEFINES clause may be subordinate to one containing an OCCURS clause.

We won't need a separate one-dimensional table for the column captions in this program, for the columns in Table 10-3 are numbered 1 through 5. The program will be able to use the value of SALESPERSON-GRADE-IN, a number from 1 through 5, to refer to the columns directly, without having to SEARCH.

Lines 00540 and 00550 show that level numbers other than 01 can begin anywhere in area A or B.

Figure 10.12   (continued)

```
01280    INITIALIZATION.
01290        ACCEPT TODAYS-DATE FROM DATE.
01300        MOVE CORR TODAYS-DATE TO HEADING-LINE-3.
01310        OPEN INPUT   SALES-FILE-IN,
01320            OUTPUT COMMISSION-REPORT-FILE-OUT.
01330        PERFORM PRINT-PAGE-HEADINGS.
01340        PERFORM READ-A-RECORD.
01350        MOVE SALESPERSON-NUMBER-IN TO SALESPERSON-NUMBER-SAVE.
01360        IF MORE-INPUT IS EQUAL TO "N"
01370            WRITE COMMISSION-REPORT-RECORD-OUT FROM NO-INPUT-DATA
01380                AFTER 2.
01390
01400    PRINT-PAGE-HEADINGS.
01410        ADD 1 TO PAGE-NUMBER-W.
01420        MOVE PAGE-NUMBER-W TO PAGE-NUMBER-OUT.
01430        WRITE COMMISSION-REPORT-RECORD-OUT FROM HEADING-LINE-2
01440            AFTER PAGE.
01450        WRITE COMMISSION-REPORT-RECORD-OUT FROM HEADING-LINE-3.
01460        WRITE COMMISSION-REPORT-RECORD-OUT FROM HEADING-LINE-6
01470            AFTER 3.
01480        WRITE COMMISSION-REPORT-RECORD-OUT FROM HEADING-LINE-7.
01490        MOVE 6 TO LINE-COUNT-ER.
01500        MOVE 2 TO LINE-SPACING.
01510
01520    MAIN-PROCESS.
01530        IF SALESPERSON-NUMBER-IN NOT = SALESPERSON-NUMBER-SAVE
01540            PERFORM CONTROL-BREAK.
01550        PERFORM PRODUCE-DETAIL-LINE.
01560        PERFORM READ-A-RECORD.
01570
01580    PRODUCE-DETAIL-LINE.
01590        SET SALES-BRACKET-INDEX TO 1.
01600        SEARCH ROW
01610            WHEN SALE-AMOUNT-IN IS NOT GREATER THAN
01620                TOP-OF-SALES-BRACKET (SALES-BRACKET-INDEX)
01630                NEXT SENTENCE.
01640        SET GRADE-INDEX TO SALESPERSON-GRADE-IN.
01650        MULTIPLY SALE-AMOUNT-IN BY
01660            COMMISSION-RATE-F (SALES-BRACKET-INDEX, GRADE-INDEX)
01670                GIVING COMMISSION-W   ROUNDED,
01680                    COMMISSION-OUT ROUNDED.
01690        ADD SALE-AMOUNT-IN TO SALES-TOTAL-W.
01700        ADD COMMISSION-W   TO COMMISSION-TOTAL-W.
01710        IF LINE-COUNT-ER + LINE-SPACING > LINE-LIMIT
01720            PERFORM PRINT-PAGE-HEADINGS.
01730        MOVE SALESPERSON-NUMBER-IN TO SALESPERSON-NUMBER-OUT.
01740        MOVE SALE-AMOUNT-IN      TO SALE-AMOUNT-OUT.
01750        MOVE COMMISSION-RATE-I (SALES-BRACKET-INDEX, GRADE-INDEX)
01760            TO COMMISSION-RATE-OUT.
01770        WRITE COMMISSION-REPORT-RECORD-OUT FROM DETAIL-LINE
01780            AFTER LINE-SPACING.
01790        ADD LINE-SPACING TO LINE-COUNT-ER.
01800        MOVE 1           TO LINE-SPACING.
01810
01820    CONTROL-BREAK.
01830        MOVE COMMISSION-TOTAL-W   TO COMMISSION-TOTAL-OUT.
01840        MOVE SALES-TOTAL-W        TO SALES-TOTAL-OUT.
01850        WRITE COMMISSION-REPORT-RECORD-OUT FROM TOTAL-LINE-1
01860            AFTER 2.
01870        WRITE COMMISSION-REPORT-RECORD-OUT FROM TOTAL-LINE-2.
01880        ADD 3                     TO LINE-COUNT-ER.
01890        MOVE ZEROS                TO ACCUMULATORS.
01900        MOVE SALESPERSON-NUMBER-IN TO SALESPERSON-NUMBER-SAVE.
01910        MOVE 3                    TO LINE-SPACING.
01920
01930    TERMINATION.
01940        PERFORM CONTROL-BREAK.
01950        CLOSE SALES-FILE-IN,
01960            COMMISSION-REPORT-FILE-OUT.
01970
01980    READ-A-RECORD.
01990        READ SALES-FILE-IN INTO SALES-RECORD-W
02000            AT END
02010                MOVE "N" TO MORE-INPUT.
```

PRODUCE-DETAIL-LINE begins at line 01580. In it, the program does a serial SEARCH of the ROWs looking for the correct sales bracket. First, SALES-BRACKET-INDEX must be SET to 1 to start the SEARCH at the first ROW of the table. Then, as the SEARCH statement steps through the ROWs, it tests the condition given in the WHEN clause in line 01610. SALE-AMOUNT-IN is compared with each of the different TOP-OF-SALES-BRACKET figures until the condition is met. You can see that IS NOT GREATER THAN is the relational operator we need to terminate the SEARCH, for as long as SALE-AMOUNT-IN is greater than the top of some sales bracket, we want the SEARCH to continue and try another, higher, bracket. Table 10-4 shows how three different values of SALE-AMOUNT-IN would cause the SEARCH to end.

Table 10-4

The value of TOP-OF-SALES-BRACKET (SALES-BRACKET-INDEX) that causes the SEARCH statement in line 01600 of Program P10-03 to terminate, for three different values of SALE-AMOUNT-IN.

SALE-AMOUNT-IN	TOP-OF-SALES-BRACKET (SALES-BRACKET-INDEX)
$15,000.00	$50,000.00
950.00	1,000.00
10,000.00	10,000.00

EXERCISE 3

What value of TOP-OF-SALES-BRACKET (SALES-BRACKET-INDEX) would cause the SEARCH statement in line 01600 of Program P10-03 to terminate, for each of the following values of SALE-AMOUNT-IN?

a. $500.00
b. $75,000.00
c. $50,000.00

In Program P10-03 we make no checks on the validity of the input data. We are assuming that it will all be correct. If we were to check for validity, we would check that SALE-AMOUNT-IN is numeric and that SALESPERSON-GRADE-IN is a number within the range 1 through 5. There would be no need to check that SALE-AMOUNT-IN is within a correct range, for any of its possible values 0 through 99,999.99 is valid. No AT END clause would be needed in the SEARCH statement, for the SEARCH cannot run off the end of the table if SALE-AMOUNT-IN is numeric.

WHEN the SEARCH in line 01600 terminates, the program goes to the NEXT SENTENCE. The SET statement at line 01640 SETs the GRADE-INDEX to point to the correct COMMISSION-RATE-F. We use the input value of SALESPERSON-GRADE-IN to SET the value of GRADE-INDEX.

Program P10-03 was run with the input data shown in Figure 10.13 and produced the output shown in Figure 10.14.

Figure 10.13 Input to Program P10-03.

```
--------------------------------------------------------------------------------
        1         2         3         4         5         6         7         8
12345678901234567890123456789012345678901234567890123456789012345678901234567890
--------------------------------------------------------------------------------
1072820012500
6530742500000
6530740012500
6530745000000
6530741000000
6530746000000
7143950012500
7143951200000
7143955432198
7143950200000
9037010010000
9037010020000
9037011100000
```

EXERCISE 4

Write a program to process input records in the following format:

Positions	Field
1 – 5	Employee Number
6 – 7	Years Employed
8	Job Code
9 – 15	Annual Salary (to two decimal places)
16 – 80	spaces

Each record is for one employee and contains an Employee Number, the number of Years Employed, a Job Code, and the employee's current Annual Salary. Each employee is to receive a percentage salary increase based on the Job Code and the number of Years Employed. Table 10-E4 shows the percentage increase for the different Job Codes and Years Employed.

Table 10-E4
Percentage salary increases as a function of Job Code and Years Employed.

Years Employed	Job Code			
	1	2	3	4
0 – 1	5%	5%	10%	10%
2 – 5	15%	20%	22%	25%
6 – 10	20%	22%	28%	30%
11 – 20	20%	25%	30%	35%
21 – 99	25%	28%	32%	36%

The program is to determine for each employee the dollar amount of the increase and print on one line the Employee Number, the increase, and the new salary after the increase. At the end of the report, have your program print the total of all the increases and the total of all the new salaries. Assume that all input data are valid.

Figure 10.14 Output from Program P10-03.

```
                        COMMISSION REPORT
        DATE   4/06/88                        PAGE   1


              SALESPERSON        SALE       COMMISSION    COMMISSION
                NUMBER          AMOUNT          RATE

                10728          125.00          5%             6.25
TOTALS FOR
  SALESPERSON                  125.00                        6.25


                65307       25,000.00         30%         7,500.00
                65307          125.00         10%            12.50
                65307       50,000.00         30%        15,000.00
                65307       10,000.00         20%         2,000.00
                65307       60,000.00         45%        27,000.00
TOTALS FOR
  SALESPERSON              145,125.00                    51,512.50


                71439          125.00         15%            18.75
                71439       12,000.00         35%         4,200.00
                71439       54,321.98         50%        27,160.99
                71439        2,000.00         25%           500.00
TOTALS FOR
  SALESPERSON               68,446.98                    31,879.74


                90370          100.00          5%             5.00
                90370          200.00          5%            10.00
                90370       11,000.00         15%         1,650.00
TOTALS FOR
  SALESPERSON               11,300.00                     1,665.00
```

Relative Indexing

It is sometimes convenient to be able to refer to a certain item in a table even when the table index is not pointing to it. It is especially useful during table SEARCHes to be able to examine neighboring items in a table. For example, if a table index is pointing to the sixth item in a table, it might be useful to be able to refer to the fifth item or the seventh. With relative indexing, it is possible to do so easily.

Even though we had no use for relative indexing in Program P10-03, we can use some fields from that program to give an example of relative indexing. Let's say that sometime during the SEARCH in Program P10-03 SALES-BRACKET-INDEX was pointing to the third ROW of Table 10-3. Then it would have been legal to refer to

```
TOP-OF-SALES-BRACKET (SALES-BRACKET-INDEX)
```

and that, of course, would have been the third TOP-OF-SALES-BRACKET figure, $50,000.00. Using relative indexing, it also would have been legal to refer to

```
TOP-OF-SALES-BRACKET (SALES-BRACKET-INDEX + 1)
```

and that would have been the fourth TOP-OF-SALES-BRACKET figure, $99,999.99. Subtraction as well as addition may be used in relative indexing, and so this would be legal:

```
TOP-OF-SALES-BRACKET (SALES-BRACKET-INDEX - 1)
```

and that would refer to the second TOP-OF-SALES-BRACKET figure.

The general form of a relative index is an index name followed by a space, followed by a plus or minus sign, followed by another space, followed by an integer literal. Note that after the plus or minus sign you may have only an unsigned numeric literal, never an identifier. Relative indexing may be used wherever direct indexing is allowed. It is the programmer's responsibility to ensure that a relative index always comes out within the range of the table being indexed. Note also that there is no relative subscripting in 1974 COBOL. The 1985 standard allows relative subscripting, in the same form as relative indexing.

Programming for a Three-Dimensional Table

A three-dimensional table can be visualized most easily as a book full of two-dimensional tables. In the example given at the beginning of the chapter, for 5-year renewable term insurance, a person's age and sex and the face amount of the policy were needed to find a particular premium amount. We will arrange our three-dimensional table as tables of age versus face amount, with each sex being on a different page of the book. Table 10-5 shows the first page of the book, the annual premium for different ages and face amounts for males, and Table 10-6 shows the second page of the book, the annual premium for different ages and face amounts for females.

Table 10-5

Annual premium for 5-year renewable term life insurance for males.

Age	$10,000 Policy	$25,000 Policy	$30,000 Policy
18	$30.30	$55.75	$66.90
19	30.70	56.75	68.10
20	31.00	57.50	69.00
21	31.30	58.25	69.90
22	31.50	58.75	70.50
23	31.90	59.75	71.70
24	32.20	60.50	72.60
25	32.50	61.25	73.50
26	32.90	62.25	74.70
27	33.30	63.25	75.90
28	33.80	64.50	77.40
29	34.50	66.25	79.50

Table 10-6

Annual premium for 5-year renewable term life insurance for females.

Age	$10,000 Policy	$25,000 Policy	$30,000 Policy
18	$28.40	$51.00	$61.20
19	29.10	52.75	63.30
20	29.80	54.50	65.40
21	30.30	55.75	66.90
22	30.70	56.75	68.10
23	31.00	57.50	69.00
24	31.30	58.25	69.90
25	31.50	58.75	70.50
26	31.90	59.75	71.70
27	32.20	60.50	72.60
28	32.50	61.25	73.50
29	32.90	62.25	74.70

Program P10-04 reads input records in the following format:

Positions	Field
1 – 25	Customer Name
26 – 27	Age
28	Sex
29 – 33	Face Amount (in whole dollars)
34 – 80	spaces

Each record represents a potential customer for life insurance, and contains the Customer Name, Age, Sex (M or F), and the Face Amount of the policy that the customer is interested in. For each error-free input record, Program P10-04 produces a page of output in the format shown in Figure 10.15.

Program P10-04 checks all input for valid Age, Sex, and Face Amount. Each input record is checked for all possible errors. For each error found, a line is printed on a separate error report in the format shown in Figure 10.16.

Figure 10.15 Output format for error-free records in Program P10-04.

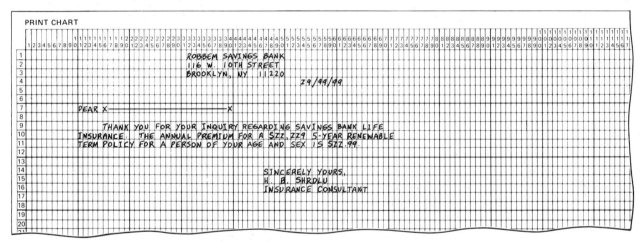

Figure 10.16 Output format for error report in Program P10-04.

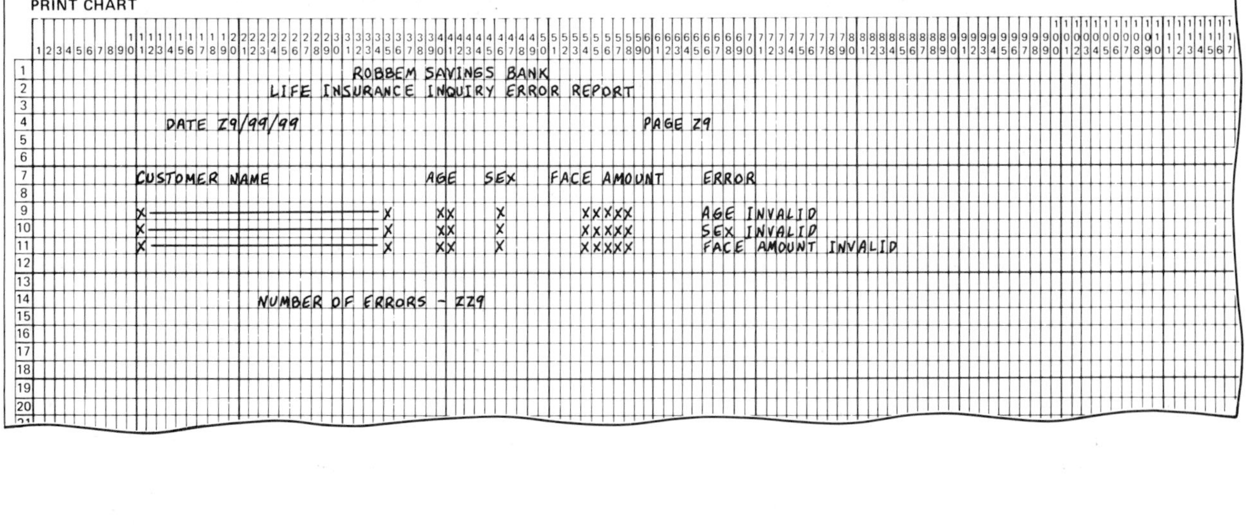

A hierarchy diagram for Program P10-04 is shown in Figure 10.17. The box "Process a record" consists of two subfunctions. The first, "Assign index values," does all the SEARCHing and validity checking needed to determine the values of all the indexes that are needed for the box "Print an inquiry letter." Any or all of three types of errors might be found by "Assign index values"—an invalid Sex code, an invalid Age, and/or an invalid Face Amount. The separate routines that handle each type of error are shown in the hierarchy diagram. The diagram also shows that all three error routines can use a common print routine to create the error report. For each input record, the box "Print an inquiry letter" executes only if the record is error-free.

Program P10-04 is shown in Figure 10.18. This program has one input file and two output files. Each of the two reports prints as a separate file. Both files may be assigned to the same printer, or they may be assigned to different printers.[1] Each file name has its own FD entry (lines 00410 and 00460).

In the description of the input record there is a good use of the 88 level. Level-88 entries are very useful in connection with input fields that contain coded values, as our SEX-IN field at line 00330 does. The use of level-88 entries here to give the names MALE and FEMALE to the coded input values M and F makes the Procedure Division coding clearer.

Figure 10.17   Hierarchy diagram for Program P10-04.

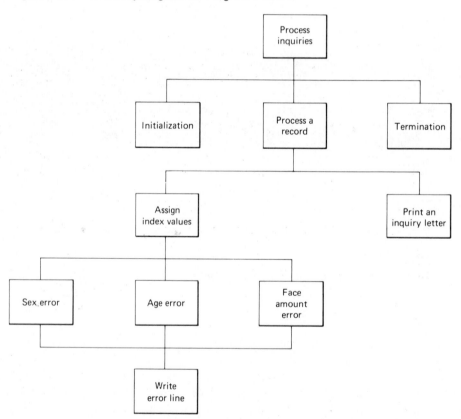

---

[1]If both files are assigned to the same printer, the reports will print one after the other only if the printer is not directly controlled by your program, as is the case with all modern large-scale operating systems. If your printer is directly controlled by your program, the two reports will print with their print lines interleaved.

Figure 10.18 Program P10-04.

CB1 RELEASE 2.4   IBM OS/VS COBOL   JULY 1, 1982

                    21.42.02   APR 6,1988


```
00010  IDENTIFICATION DIVISION.
00020  PROGRAM-ID.  P10-04.
00030 *
00040 *    THIS PROGRAM USES A THREE-DIMENSIONAL TABLE TO FIND
00050 *    INSURANCE PREMIUMS AS A FUNCTION OF AGE, SEX, AND
00060 *    FACE AMOUNT OF POLICY, AND PRODUCES INQUIRY-RESPONSE
00070 *    LETTERS AND AN ERROR REPORT
00080 *
00090 ****************************************************************
00100
00110  ENVIRONMENT DIVISION.
00120  CONFIGURATION SECTION.
00130  SOURCE-COMPUTER.  IBM-370.
00140  OBJECT-COMPUTER.  IBM-370.
00150
00160  INPUT-OUTPUT SECTION.
00170  FILE-CONTROL.
00180      SELECT INQUIRY-FILE-IN          ASSIGN TO INFILE.
00190      SELECT INQUIRY-LETTERS-FILE-OUT ASSIGN TO PRINTER1.
00200      SELECT ERROR-REPORT-FILE-OUT    ASSIGN TO PRINTER2.
00210
00220 ****************************************************************
00230
00240  DATA DIVISION.
00250  FILE SECTION.
00260  FD  INQUIRY-FILE-IN
00270      LABEL RECORDS ARE OMITTED
00280      RECORD CONTAINS 80 CHARACTERS.
00290
00300  01  INQUIRY-RECORD-IN.
00310      05  CUSTOMER-NAME-IN       PIC X(25).
00320      05  AGE-IN                 PIC XX.
00330      05  SEX-IN                 PIC X.
00340          88  MALE               VALUE "M".
00350          88  FEMALE             VALUE "F".
00360      05  FACE-AMOUNT-IN         PIC 9(5).
00370      05  FACE-AMOUNT-X5-IN      REDEFINES FACE-AMOUNT-IN
00380                                 PIC X(5).
00390      05  FILLER                 PIC X(47).
00400
00410  FD  INQUIRY-LETTERS-FILE-OUT
00420      LABEL RECORDS ARE OMITTED.
00430
00440  01  INQUIRY-LETTER-RECORD-OUT  PIC X(71).
00450
00460  FD  ERROR-REPORT-FILE-OUT
00470      LABEL RECORDS ARE OMITTED.
00480
00490  01  ERROR-REPORT-RECORD-OUT    PIC X(84).
00500
00510  WORKING-STORAGE SECTION.
00520  01  MORE-INPUT      PIC X           VALUE "Y".
00530  01  ANY-INPUT-ERRORS   PIC X.
00540  01  ERROR-REPORT-LINE-SPACING      PIC S9  COMP SYNC.
00550  01  ERROR-REPORT-LINE-COUNT        PIC S99 COMP SYNC.
00560  01  ERROR-REPORT-LINE-LIMIT        PIC S99 COMP SYNC
00570                                     VALUE 40.
00580  01  PAGE-NUMBER-W    PIC S99        VALUE 0.
00590  01  NUMBER-OF-ERRORS-W             PIC S99 VALUE 0.
00600  01  TODAYS-DATE.
00610      05  TODAYS-YEAR                PIC 99.
00620      05  TODAYS-MONTH-AND-DAY       PIC 9(4).
00630
```

(continued)

In the Working Storage Section the table of insurance premiums begins at line 00650. When you write a three-dimensional table into a COBOL program, it is best to write the row captions and the column captions into separate one-dimensional tables, and to write just the table functions in FILLER entries of their own. By this method you can avoid having to write the row captions more than once. Write each row of table functions as a single FILLER entry, starting with the first page of the "book" of tables. First, write all the rows from the first page of the book, and then continue right on with the rows from the second page and so on until all the rows are written.

Whenever you write a three-dimensional table into a program in this way, you must write the OCCURS clause for the pages of the book as part of the REDE-FINES entry. The next OCCURS clause after that must refer to the rows, and the last OCCURS clause must refer to the columns. You can see the REDEFINES entry in Program P10-04 at line 00900 and the three OCCURS clauses in lines 00910, 00920, and 00940. The one-dimensional table for the ages begins at line 00950, and the table for the face amounts begins at line 01120.

Figure 10.18 (continued)

```
00640  01  ALL-THE-TABLES.
00650      05  PREMIUM-ROW-ENTRIES.
00660          10  FILLER     PIC 9(12)     VALUE 303055756690.
00670          10  FILLER     PIC 9(12)     VALUE 307056756810.
00680          10  FILLER     PIC 9(12)     VALUE 310057506900.
00690          10  FILLER     PIC 9(12)     VALUE 313058256990.
00700          10  FILLER     PIC 9(12)     VALUE 315058757050.
00710          10  FILLER     PIC 9(12)     VALUE 319059757170.
00720          10  FILLER     PIC 9(12)     VALUE 322060507260.
00730          10  FILLER     PIC 9(12)     VALUE 325061257350.
00740          10  FILLER     PIC 9(12)     VALUE 329062257470.
00750          10  FILLER     PIC 9(12)     VALUE 333063257590.
00760          10  FILLER     PIC 9(12)     VALUE 338064507740.
00770          10  FILLER     PIC 9(12)     VALUE 345066257950.
00780          10  FILLER     PIC 9(12)     VALUE 284051006120.
00790          10  FILLER     PIC 9(12)     VALUE 291052756330.
00800          10  FILLER     PIC 9(12)     VALUE 298054506540.
00810          10  FILLER     PIC 9(12)     VALUE 303055756690.
00820          10  FILLER     PIC 9(12)     VALUE 307056756810.
00830          10  FILLER     PIC 9(12)     VALUE 310057506900.
00840          10  FILLER     PIC 9(12)     VALUE 313058256990.
00850          10  FILLER     PIC 9(12)     VALUE 315058757050.
00860          10  FILLER     PIC 9(12)     VALUE 319059757170.
00870          10  FILLER     PIC 9(12)     VALUE 322060507260.
00880          10  FILLER     PIC 9(12)     VALUE 325061257350.
00890          10  FILLER     PIC 9(12)     VALUE 329062257470.
00900      05  SEX            REDEFINES PREMIUM-ROW-ENTRIES
00910                         OCCURS 2 TIMES  INDEXED BY SEX-INDEX.
00920          10  ROW        OCCURS 12 TIMES INDEXED BY ROW-INDEX.
00930              15  ANNUAL-PREMIUM         PIC 99V99
00940                         OCCURS 3 TIMES  INDEXED BY COLUMN-INDEX.
00950      05  AGE-TABLE-ENTRIES.
00960          10  FILLER     PIC XX         VALUE "18".
00970          10  FILLER     PIC XX         VALUE "19".
00980          10  FILLER     PIC XX         VALUE "20".
00990          10  FILLER     PIC XX         VALUE "21".
01000          10  FILLER     PIC XX         VALUE "22".
01010          10  FILLER     PIC XX         VALUE "23".
01020          10  FILLER     PIC XX         VALUE "24".
01030          10  FILLER     PIC XX         VALUE "25".
01040          10  FILLER     PIC XX         VALUE "26".
01050          10  FILLER     PIC XX         VALUE "27".
01060          10  FILLER     PIC XX         VALUE "28".
01070          10  FILLER     PIC XX         VALUE "29".
01080      05  TABLE-AGE      REDEFINES AGE-TABLE-ENTRIES
01090                         PIC XX         OCCURS 12 TIMES
01100          ASCENDING KEY TABLE-AGE INDEXED BY AGE-INDEX.
01110
```

```
01120        05    FACE-AMOUNT-TABLE-ENTRIES.
01130              10    FILLER        PIC X(5)        VALUE "10000".
01140              10    FILLER        PIC X(5)        VALUE "25000".
01150              10    FILLER        PIC X(5)        VALUE "30000".
01160        05    TABLE-FACE-AMOUNT
01170                    REDEFINES FACE-AMOUNT-TABLE-ENTRIES
01180              OCCURS 3 TIMES   ASCENDING KEY TABLE-FACE-AMOUNT
01190              INDEXED BY FACE-AMOUNT-INDEX    PIC X(5).
01200
01210        05    ERROR-TABLE.
01220              10    FILLER        PIC X(19)       VALUE "SEX INVALID".
01230              10    FILLER        PIC X(19)       VALUE "AGE INVALID".
01240              10    FILLER        PIC X(19)
01250                    VALUE "FACE AMOUNT INVALID".
01260        05    ERROR-MESSAGE       REDEFINES ERROR-TABLE
01270                    OCCURS 3 TIMES   INDEXED BY ERROR-INDEX
01280                    PIC X(19).
01290
01300  01    PAGE-HEAD-1.
01310        05    FILLER           PIC X(31) VALUE SPACES.
01320        05    FILLER           PIC X(19) VALUE "ROBBEM SAVINGS BANK".
01330
01340  01    ERROR-REPORT-PAGE-HEAD-2.
01350        05    FILLER           PIC X(23) VALUE SPACES.
01360        05    FILLER           PIC X(35)
01370              VALUE "LIFE INSURANCE INQUIRY ERROR REPORT".
01380
01390  01    ERROR-REPORT-PAGE-HEAD-3.
01400        05    FILLER           PIC X(13) VALUE SPACES.
01410        05    FILLER           PIC X(5)  VALUE "DATE".
01420        05    TODAYS-MONTH-AND-DAY    PIC Z9/99/.
01430        05    TODAYS-YEAR             PIC 99B(33).
01440        05    FILLER           PIC X(5)  VALUE "PAGE".
01450        05    PAGE-NUMBER-OUT         PIC Z9.
01460
01470  01    ERROR-REPORT-PAGE-HEAD-4.
01480        05    FILLER                  PIC X(10) VALUE SPACES.
01490        05    FILLER           PIC X(28) VALUE "CUSTOMER NAME".
01500        05    FILLER           PIC X(6)  VALUE "AGE".
01510        05    FILLER           PIC X(6)  VALUE "SEX".
01520        05    FILLER           PIC X(15) VALUE "FACE AMOUNT".
01530        05    FILLER           PIC X(5)  VALUE "ERROR".
01540
01550  01    NO-INPUT-DATA.
01560        05    FILLER           PIC X(34) VALUE SPACES.
01570        05    FILLER           PIC X(13) VALUE "NO INPUT DATA".
01580
01590  01    ERROR-LINE.
01600        05    FILLER           PIC X(10) VALUE SPACES.
01610        05    CUSTOMER-NAME-E         PIC X(25)B(4).
01620        05    AGE-E                   PIC XXB(4).
01630        05    SEX-E                   PIC XB(7).
01640        05    FACE-AMOUNT-X5-OUT      PIC X(5)B(7).
01650        05    ERROR-MESSAGE-OUT       PIC X(19).
01660
01670  01    ERROR-REPORT-TOTAL-LINE.
01680        05    FILLER                  PIC X(22).
01690        05    FILLER           PIC X(19) VALUE "NUMBER OF ERRORS -".
01700        05    NUMBER-OF-ERRORS-OUT    PIC ZZ9.
01710
01720  01    LETTER-LINE-2.
01730        05    FILLER           PIC X(31) VALUE SPACES.
01740        05    FILLER           PIC X(18) VALUE "116 W. 10TH STREET".
01750
01760  01    LETTER-LINE-3.
01770        05    FILLER           PIC X(31) VALUE SPACES.
01780        05    FILLER           PIC X(19) VALUE "BROOKLYN, NY  11220".
01790
```

(continued)

The three different error messages that this program can produce are shown starting at line 01220. When the program discovers an error in an input field, it SETs ERROR-INDEX to point to the appropriate ERROR-MESSAGE. ERROR-MESSAGE (ERROR-INDEX) is used as the sending field of a MOVE statement to MOVE the correct error message to the output area.

Figure 10.18   (continued)

```
01800   01   LETTER-LINE-4.
01810        05   FILLER             PIC X(53) VALUE SPACES.
01820        05   TODAYS-MONTH-AND-DAY     PIC ZZ/99/.
01830        05   TODAYS-YEAR              PIC 99.
01840
01850   01   LETTER-LINE-7.
01860        05   FILLER             PIC X(10) VALUE SPACES.
01870        05   FILLER             PIC X(5)  VALUE "DEAR".
01880        05   CUSTOMER-NAME-OUT        PIC X(25).
01890
01900   01   LETTER-LINE-9.
01910        05   FILLER             PIC X(15) VALUE SPACES.
01920        05   FILLER             PIC X(27)
01930             VALUE "THANK YOU FOR YOUR INQUIRY".
01940        05   FILLER             PIC X(27)
01950             VALUE "REGARDING SAVINGS BANK LIFE".
01960
01970   01   LETTER-LINE-10.
01980        05   FILLER             PIC X(10) VALUE SPACES.
01990        05   FILLER             PIC X(37)
02000             VALUE "INSURANCE.  THE ANNUAL PREMIUM FOR A".
02010        05   FACE-AMOUNT-OUT PIC $ZZ,ZZ9B.
02020        05   FILLER             PIC X(16) VALUE "5-YEAR RENEWABLE".
02030
02040   01   LETTER-LINE-11.
02050        05   FILLER             PIC X(10) VALUE SPACES.
02060        05   FILLER             PIC X(28)
02070             VALUE "TERM POLICY FOR A PERSON OF".
02080        05   FILLER             PIC X(20)
02090             VALUE "YOUR AGE AND SEX IS".
02100        05   ANNUAL-PREMIUM-OUT       PIC $ZZ.99.
02110        05   FILLER             PIC X     VALUE ".".
02120
02130   01   LETTER-LINE-14.
02140        05   FILLER             PIC X(46) VALUE SPACES.
02150        05   FILLER             PIC X(16) VALUE "SINCERELY YOURS,".
02160
02170   01   LETTER-LINE-15.
02180        05   FILLER             PIC X(46) VALUE SPACES.
02190        05   FILLER             PIC X(12) VALUE "H. B. SHRDLU".
02200
02210   01   LETTER-LINE-16.
02220        05   FILLER             PIC X(46) VALUE SPACES.
02230        05   FILLER             PIC X(20) VALUE "INSURANCE CONSULTANT".
02240
02250   ***********************************************************************
02260
02270   PROCEDURE DIVISION.
02280   PROCESS-INQUIRIES.
02290       PERFORM INITIALIZATION.
02300       PERFORM PROCESS-A-RECORD UNTIL MORE-INPUT IS EQUAL TO "N".
02310       PERFORM TERMINATION.
02320       STOP RUN.
02330
02340   INITIALIZATION.
02350       ACCEPT TODAYS-DATE FROM DATE.
02360       MOVE CORR TODAYS-DATE TO LETTER-LINE-4.
02370       MOVE CORR TODAYS-DATE TO ERROR-REPORT-PAGE-HEAD-3.
02380       OPEN INPUT  INQUIRY-FILE-IN,
02390            OUTPUT INQUIRY-LETTERS-FILE-OUT,
02400                   ERROR-REPORT-FILE-OUT.
02410       PERFORM PRINT-PAGE-HEADINGS.
02420       PERFORM READ-A-RECORD.
02430       IF MORE-INPUT IS EQUAL TO "N"
02440           WRITE ERROR-REPORT-RECORD-OUT FROM NO-INPUT-DATA AFTER 2.
02450
02460   PRINT-PAGE-HEADINGS.
02470       ADD 1 TO PAGE-NUMBER-W.
02480       MOVE PAGE-NUMBER-W TO PAGE-NUMBER-OUT.
02490       WRITE ERROR-REPORT-RECORD-OUT FROM PAGE-HEAD-1
02500               AFTER ADVANCING PAGE.
02510       WRITE ERROR-REPORT-RECORD-OUT FROM ERROR-REPORT-PAGE-HEAD-2.
02520       WRITE ERROR-REPORT-RECORD-OUT FROM ERROR-REPORT-PAGE-HEAD-3
02530               AFTER ADVANCING 2.
02540       WRITE ERROR-REPORT-RECORD-OUT FROM ERROR-REPORT-PAGE-HEAD-4
02550               AFTER ADVANCING 3.
02560       MOVE 2 TO ERROR-REPORT-LINE-SPACING.
02570       MOVE 7 TO ERROR-REPORT-LINE-COUNT.
```

```
02580
02590    PROCESS-A-RECORD.
02600        MOVE "N" TO ANY-INPUT-ERRORS.
02610        PERFORM ASSIGN-INDEX-VALUES.
02620        IF ANY-INPUT-ERRORS IS EQUAL TO "N"
02630            PERFORM PRINT-AN-INQUIRY-LETTER.
02640        PERFORM READ-A-RECORD.
02650
02660    TERMINATION.
02670        MOVE NUMBER-OF-ERRORS-W TO NUMBER-OF-ERRORS-OUT.
02680        WRITE ERROR-REPORT-RECORD-OUT FROM ERROR-REPORT-TOTAL-LINE
02690                AFTER ADVANCING 3.
02700        CLOSE INQUIRY-FILE-IN,
02710            INQUIRY-LETTERS-FILE-OUT,
02720            ERROR-REPORT-FILE-OUT.
02730
02740    READ-A-RECORD.
02750        READ INQUIRY-FILE-IN
02760            AT END
02770                MOVE "N" TO MORE-INPUT.
02780
02790    ASSIGN-INDEX-VALUES.
02800        IF MALE
02810            SET SEX-INDEX TO 1
02820        ELSE
02830            IF FEMALE
02840                SET SEX-INDEX TO 2
02850            ELSE
02860                PERFORM SEX-ERROR.
02870        SEARCH ALL TABLE-AGE
02880            AT END
02890                PERFORM AGE-ERROR
02900            WHEN TABLE-AGE (AGE-INDEX) IS EQUAL TO AGE-IN
02910                SET ROW-INDEX TO AGE-INDEX.
02920        SEARCH ALL TABLE-FACE-AMOUNT
02930            AT END
02940                PERFORM FACE-AMOUNT-ERROR
02950            WHEN TABLE-FACE-AMOUNT (FACE-AMOUNT-INDEX) IS EQUAL TO
02960                FACE-AMOUNT-X5-IN
02970                SET COLUMN-INDEX TO FACE-AMOUNT-INDEX.
02980
02990    PRINT-AN-INQUIRY-LETTER.
03000        WRITE INQUIRY-LETTER-RECORD-OUT FROM PAGE-HEAD-1
03010                    AFTER ADVANCING PAGE.
03020        WRITE INQUIRY-LETTER-RECORD-OUT FROM LETTER-LINE-2.
03030        WRITE INQUIRY-LETTER-RECORD-OUT FROM LETTER-LINE-3.
03040        WRITE INQUIRY-LETTER-RECORD-OUT FROM LETTER-LINE-4.
03050        MOVE CUSTOMER-NAME-IN TO CUSTOMER-NAME-OUT.
03060        WRITE INQUIRY-LETTER-RECORD-OUT FROM LETTER-LINE-7 AFTER 3.
03070        WRITE INQUIRY-LETTER-RECORD-OUT FROM LETTER-LINE-9 AFTER 2.
03080        MOVE FACE-AMOUNT-IN TO FACE-AMOUNT-OUT.
03090        WRITE INQUIRY-LETTER-RECORD-OUT FROM LETTER-LINE-10.
03100        MOVE ANNUAL-PREMIUM (SEX-INDEX, ROW-INDEX, COLUMN-INDEX)
03110            TO ANNUAL-PREMIUM-OUT.
03120        WRITE INQUIRY-LETTER-RECORD-OUT FROM LETTER-LINE-11.
03130        WRITE INQUIRY-LETTER-RECORD-OUT FROM LETTER-LINE-14 AFTER 3.
03140        WRITE INQUIRY-LETTER-RECORD-OUT FROM LETTER-LINE-15.
03150        WRITE INQUIRY-LETTER-RECORD-OUT FROM LETTER-LINE-16.
03160
03170    SEX-ERROR.
03180        SET ERROR-INDEX TO 1.
03190        PERFORM WRITE-ERROR-LINE.
03200
03210    AGE-ERROR.
03220        SET ERROR-INDEX TO 2.
03230        PERFORM WRITE-ERROR-LINE.
03240
03250    FACE-AMOUNT-ERROR.
03260        SET ERROR-INDEX TO 3.
03270        PERFORM WRITE-ERROR-LINE.
03280
```

(continued)

The Procedure Division, which begins at line 02270, follows the hierarchy diagram. Program P10-04 was run with the input data shown in Figure 10.19 and produced the output shown in Figure 10.20.

Figure 10.18   (continued)

```
03290    WRITE-ERROR-LINE.
03300        MOVE "Y" TO ANY-INPUT-ERRORS.
03310        ADD 1 TO NUMBER-OF-ERRORS-W.
03320        MOVE CUSTOMER-NAME-IN  TO CUSTOMER-NAME-E.
03330        MOVE AGE-IN              TO AGE-E.
03340        MOVE SEX-IN              TO SEX-E.
03350        MOVE FACE-AMOUNT-X5-IN TO FACE-AMOUNT-X5-OUT.
03360        MOVE ERROR-MESSAGE (ERROR-INDEX) TO ERROR-MESSAGE-OUT.
03370        IF ERROR-REPORT-LINE-COUNT + ERROR-REPORT-LINE-SPACING >
03380            ERROR-REPORT-LINE-LIMIT
03390            PERFORM PRINT-PAGE-HEADINGS.
03400        WRITE ERROR-REPORT-RECORD-OUT FROM ERROR-LINE
03410                        AFTER ERROR-REPORT-LINE-SPACING.
03420        ADD ERROR-REPORT-LINE-SPACING TO ERROR-REPORT-LINE-COUNT.
03430        MOVE 1 TO ERROR-REPORT-LINE-SPACING.
```

Figure 10.19   Input to Program P10-04.

```
-----------------------------------------------------------------------------------
          1         2         3         4         5         6         7         8
12345678901234567890123456789012345678901234567890123456789012345678901234567890
-----------------------------------------------------------------------------------
MARY WILLIAMS            18F10000
DEBORAH THOMPSON         25F25000
MARTIN JONES             16Z18000
GEORGE JOHN O'SHAUGHNESSY29M30000
AMY SUSAN RICHARDS       20F15000
LAURA JANE BROWN         30F30000
ELLEN JOY SMITH          29Q10000
HENRY ANDREWS            19M25000
THOMAS CARTER            18Z11000
MARY BETH LINCOLN        33F40000
CARL JACKSON             16R25000
```

Figure 10.20   Output from Program P10-04.

```
                    ROBBEM SAVINGS BANK
                    116 W. 10TH STREET
                    BROOKLYN, NY  11220
                                        4/06/88


DEAR MARY WILLIAMS

     THANK YOU FOR YOUR INQUIRY REGARDING SAVINGS BANK LIFE
INSURANCE.  THE ANNUAL PREMIUM FOR A $10,000 5-YEAR RENEWABLE
TERM POLICY FOR A PERSON OF YOUR AGE AND SEX IS $28.40.


                              SINCERELY YOURS,
                              H. B. SHRDLU
                              INSURANCE CONSULTANT




                    ROBBEM SAVINGS BANK
                    116 W. 10TH STREET
                    BROOKLYN, NY  11220
                                        4/06/88


DEAR DEBORAH THOMPSON

     THANK YOU FOR YOUR INQUIRY REGARDING SAVINGS BANK LIFE
INSURANCE.  THE ANNUAL PREMIUM FOR A $25,000 5-YEAR RENEWABLE
TERM POLICY FOR A PERSON OF YOUR AGE AND SEX IS $58.75.


                              SINCERELY YOURS,
                              H. B. SHRDLU
                              INSURANCE CONSULTANT
```

```
              ROBBEM SAVINGS BANK
              116 W. 10TH STREET
              BROOKLYN, NY  11220
                                       4/06/88


DEAR GEORGE JOHN O'SHAUGHNESSY

     THANK YOU FOR YOUR INQUIRY REGARDING SAVINGS BANK LIFE
INSURANCE.  THE ANNUAL PREMIUM FOR A $30,000 5-YEAR RENEWABLE
TERM POLICY FOR A PERSON OF YOUR AGE AND SEX IS $79.50.


                            SINCERELY YOURS,
                            H. B. SHRDLU
                            INSURANCE CONSULTANT




              ROBBEM SAVINGS BANK
              116 W. 10TH STREET
              BROOKLYN, NY  11220
                                       4/06/88


DEAR HENRY ANDREWS

     THANK YOU FOR YOUR INQUIRY REGARDING SAVINGS BANK LIFE
INSURANCE.  THE ANNUAL PREMIUM FOR A $25,000 5-YEAR RENEWABLE
TERM POLICY FOR A PERSON OF YOUR AGE AND SEX IS $56.75.


                            SINCERELY YOURS,
                            H. B. SHRDLU
                            INSURANCE CONSULTANT




                   ROBBEM SAVINGS BANK
            LIFE INSURANCE INQUIRY ERROR REPORT

        DATE  4/06/88                          PAGE   1


   CUSTOMER NAME              AGE   SEX   FACE AMOUNT    ERROR

   MARTIN JONES               16    Z      18000        SEX INVALID
   MARTIN JONES               16    Z      18000        AGE INVALID
   MARTIN JONES               16    Z      18000        FACE AMOUNT INVALID
   AMY SUSAN RICHARDS         20    F      15000        FACE AMOUNT INVALID
   LAURA JANE BROWN           30    F      30000        AGE INVALID
   ELLEN JOY SMITH            29    Q      10000        SEX INVALID
   THOMAS CARTER              18    Z      11000        SEX INVALID
   THOMAS CARTER              18    Z      11000        FACE AMOUNT INVALID
   MARY BETH LINCOLN          33    F      40000        AGE INVALID
   MARY BETH LINCOLN          33    F      40000        FACE AMOUNT INVALID
   CARL JACKSON               16    R      25000        SEX INVALID
   CARL JACKSON               16    R      25000        AGE INVALID


        NUMBER OF ERRORS -  12
```

EXERCISE 5

Write a program to read input records in the following format:

Positions	Field
1 – 3	Country Code
4	Time-of-Day Code
5	Type of Call
6 – 80	spaces

Each record relates to an overseas telephone call and contains a code indicating the Country Called, a Time-of-Day Code indicating whether the call was made during peak hours (P) or during off-peak hours (O), and a code indicating the Type of Call — whether the call was direct-dialed (D), operator-assisted station-to-station (S), or person-to-person (P). For each record, the program is to print on one line the name of the country called and the cost of the first 3 minutes of the call.

Check each input record for all possible invalid codes. For each error print on one line the field in error and a suitable message.

Tables 10-E5.1 and 10-E5.2 show the cost of the first 3 minutes of certain overseas calls.

Table 10-E5.1
Cost of the first 3 minutes for calls to certain countries made during peak hours.

| | Country Called | Type of Call | | |
		D	S	P
55	Brazil	$4.95	$9.45	$12.60
49	West Germany	4.05	7.05	12.60
353	Ireland	3.00	5.70	10.10
972	Israel	4.95	9.45	12.60
39	Italy	4.05	7.05	12.60
886	Taiwan	4.95	9.45	12.60
44	United Kingdom	3.00	5.70	10.10

Table 10-E5.2
Cost of the first 3 minutes for calls to certain countries made during off-peak hours.

| | Country Called | Type of Call | | |
		D	S	P
55	Brazil	$3.75	$7.05	$9.45
49	West Germany	3.15	5.40	9.45
353	Ireland	2.40	4.25	7.50
972	Israel	3.75	7.05	9.45
39	Italy	3.15	5.40	9.45
886	Taiwan	3.75	7.05	9.45
44	United Kingdom	2.40	4.25	7.50

Tables of Four and More Dimensions

COBOL systems adhering to the 1985 standard can process tables of at least seven dimensions. We give here an example of a 4-dimensional table.

Let us say that we want to construct a table showing the cost of the initial period of certain telephone calls, and the cost of each additional minute of those calls. To find a function in this table, one would have to know the location of the calling number, the location of the called number, the time of day (day, evening, or night), and the type of call (direct-dialed, operator-assisted, or pay phone). We could define a table for the three types of calls, three different times of day, two calling locations, and 15 called locations as follows:

```
01 TABLES.
   02 TYPE-OF-CALL OCCURS 3 TIMES.
      03 TIME-OF-DAY OCCURS 3 TIMES.
         04 CALLING-LOCATION OCCURS 2 TIMES.
            05 CALLED-LOCATION OCCURS 15 TIMES.
               06 COST-OF-INITIAL-PERIOD      PIC V999.
               06 COST-PER-ADDITIONAL-MINUTE  PIC V999.
```

The number of computer storage locations occupied by a single element of this table is six—the sum of the sizes of COST-OF-INITIAL-PERIOD and COST-PER-ADDITIONAL-MINUTE. The number of elements in the table is found by multiplying together the integers in all the OCCURS clauses, 3 by 3 by 2 by 15, to give 270 elements. The number of computer storage locations occupied by the entire table is found by multiplying the number of elements by the size of one element, in this case 270 by 6, or 1,620. If you wanted to write this table into a program with FILLER entries, you would have to write 1,620 digits in many lines of FILLERs.

This table could be loaded easily from an external file. Let us assume that the external file contains 270 records, with each record containing one value for COST-OF-INITIAL-PERIOD and one for COST-PER-ADDITIONAL-MINUTE. Then the following routine will load the table:

```
PERFORM LOAD-TABLE
    VARYING TYPE-OF-CALL-SUBSCRIPT FROM 1 BY 1 UNTIL
            TYPE-OF-CALL-SUBSCRIPT GREATER THAN 3
    AFTER TIME-OF-DAY-SUBSCRIPT FROM 1 BY 1 UNTIL
          TIME-OF-DAY-SUBSCRIPT GREATER THAN 3
    AFTER CALLING-LOCATION-SUBSCRIPT FROM 1 BY 1 UNTIL
          CALLING-LOCATION-SUBSCRIPT GREATER THAN 2
    AFTER CALLED-LOCATION-SUBSCRIPT FROM 1 BY 1 UNTIL
          CALLED-LOCATION-SUBSCRIPT GREATER THAN 15.
```

The paragraph LOAD-TABLE, which could be anywhere in the Procedure Division, could be:

```
LOAD-TABLE.
    READ TABLE-FILE AT END MOVE "N" TO END-TABLE-FILE.
    MOVE COST-OF-INITIAL-PERIOD-IN TO
         COST-OF-INITIAL-PERIOD (TYPE-OF-CALL-SUBSCRIPT,
                                 TIME-OF-DAY-SUBSCRIPT,
                                 CALLING-LOCATION-SUBSCRIPT,
                                 CALLED-LOCATION-SUBSCRIPT).
    MOVE COST-PER-ADDITIONAL-MINUTE-IN TO
         COST-PER-ADDITIONAL-MINUTE (TYPE-OF-CALL-SUBSCRIPT,
                                     TIME-OF-DAY-SUBSCRIPT,
                                     CALLING-LOCATION-SUBSCRIPT,
                                     CALLED-LOCATION-SUBSCRIPT).
```

Summary

1974 standard COBOL can process two- and three-dimensional tables. Two-dimensional tables may be written in the Working Storage Section row by row. The OCCURS clause appearing in the REDEFINES entry must refer to the rows, and the OCCURS clause subordinate to it must refer to the columns.

A three-dimensional table may be thought of as a book full of two-dimensional tables. A three-dimensional table may be written into working storage row by row starting with the first row of the first page of the book. The OCCURS clause in the REDEFINES entry for such a table must refer to the pages of the book, the next subordinate OCCURS clause to the rows, and the last OCCURS clause to the columns.

A PERFORM . . . VARYING statement may be used to vary one, two, or three fields. Any identifiers used in a PERFORM . . . VARYING must be defined as numeric items. Any literals used in a PERFORM . . . VARYING must be numeric. In 1985 COBOL, tables may have up to seven dimensions and a PERFORM . . . VARYING statement can vary up to seven fields.

The PICTURE character P may be used in definitions of fields in input, working storage, or output. In input and working storage the use of the character P can eliminate writing or keying low-order zeros, or zeros immediately to the right of a decimal point. In output P can eliminate the printing of unwanted high- or low-order digits.

Relative indexing permits a program to refer to an entry in a table even though the table index is not pointing to it. A relative index consists of an index name followed by a space, followed by a plus or minus sign, followed by another space, followed by an integer.

Fill-In Exercises

1. The columns in a table run from _____ to _____ , and the rows run from _____ to _____ .

2. The labels that say what the rows and columns of a table stand for are called _____ .

3. If a field is referred to with two indexes, either or both of the indexes may be given as a(n) _____ , a(n) _____ , or a(n) _____ .

4. When a PERFORM . . . VARYING statement is used to vary more than one field, the reserved word _____ must be used.

5. In a three-dimensional table, _____ arguments are needed to locate a function.

6. The maximum number of fields that can be varied by a PERFORM . . . VARYING statement is _____ .

7. The maximum size of a numeric literal is _____ digits.

8. When a two-dimensional table is written in the Working Storage Section row by row, only the _____ captions can be written into the table; the _____ captions must be written into a separate one-dimensional table.

9. When a three-dimensional table is written in the Working Storage Section row by row, it is best to write the _____ _____ and the _____ _____ in separate one-dimensional tables.

10. The PICTURE character _____ may be used to eliminate the printing of unwanted low-order zeros.

11. It is sometimes convenient to initialize a table by using statements in the Procedure Division because the _____ clause is not permitted in an entry containing an OCCURS clause.

12. Fields subordinate to an OCCURS clause may have more than one PICTURE because the _____ clause is permitted in an entry that is subordinate to an entry containing an OCCURS clause.

13. When one dimension of a two-dimensional table is subscripted, not indexed, then the other dimension must be _____ , not _____ .

14. When an input field is used to refer to any dimension of a table, the table should be _____ rather than _____ .

15. In a PERFORM statement that is varying more than one field, the first-named field varies _____ rapidly; the last-named field varies _____ rapidly.

Review Exercises

1. Given the following statement:

```
PERFORM PARAGRAPH-1
    VARYING SUBSCRIPT-1 FROM 1 BY 1 UNTIL
            SUBSCRIPT-1 IS GREATER THAN 5
    AFTER   SUBSCRIPT-2 FROM 1 BY 1 UNTIL
            SUBSCRIPT-2 IS GREATER THAN 6.
```

   a. How many times will PARAGRAPH-1 execute?
   b. What will be the values of SUBSCRIPT-1 and SUBSCRIPT-2 the second time that PARAGRAPH-1 executes?
   c. Make a list showing the values of SUBSCRIPT-1 and SUBSCRIPT-2 for each execution of PARAGRAPH-1.

2. Write a program to read input records in the following format:

Positions	Field
1 – 2	County Code
3 – 7	Ranch Number
8 – 13	1983 Slaughter
14 – 19	1984 Slaughter
20 – 25	1985 Slaughter
26 – 31	1986 Slaughter
32 – 37	1987 Slaughter
38 – 43	1988 Slaughter
44 – 80	spaces

Each record contains data relating to the slaughter of cattle in seven counties in Wyoming in the years 1983 through 1988. There is one record for each cattle ranch in the seven counties, showing the Ranch Number, a County Code telling the location of the ranch, and six fields showing the number of head of cattle sent to slaughter in each of the six years 1983 through 1988.

Have your program sum the figures for each county for each year and produce a report in the format shown in Figure 10.RE2. Assume that the input data may be in any random order.

Figure 10.RE2 Output format for Review Exercise 2.

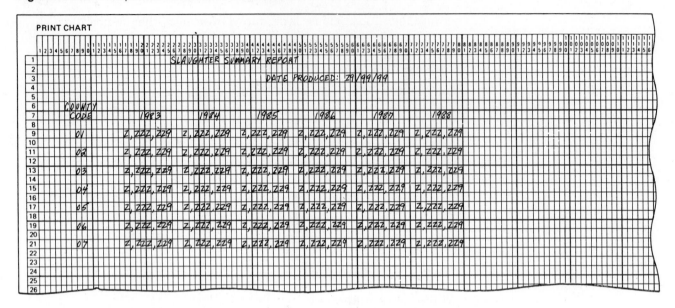

3. Write a program to read data in the following format:

Positions	Field
1 – 6	Policy Number
7 – 8	Age
9 – 10	Years to Run
11 – 18	Amount (to two decimal places)
19 – 80	spaces

Each record relates to a mortgage-protection life insurance policy and shows the Policy Number, the Age of the policy holder, the number of Years to Run on the mortgage, and the Amount of the mortgage. The program is to look up the monthly premium per $1 of mortgage amount in Table 10-RE3 and compute the monthly premium on the policy by multiplying the table function by the Amount of the mortgage. For each input record have your program print on one line the Policy Number, the Amount of the mortgage, and the computed premium. Check each input record for valid Age and valid Years to Run and print suitable error lines if any errors are found.

Table 10-RE3
Monthly premium per $1 of mortgage protection life insurance as a function of Age of policyholder and number of Years to Run on Mortgage.

Age of Policyholder	Years to Run on Mortgage		
	Over 15 but not over 20	Over 20 but not over 25	Over 25 but not over 30
26	.17	.19	.22
27	.17	.20	.22
28	.18	.21	.23
29	.19	.22	.24
30	.20	.23	.25
31	.21	.24	.26
32	.22	.25	.27
33	.23	.26	.29
34	.25	.28	.31
35	.26	.29	.32

Project

Rewrite your solution to the Project in Chapter 9. Use the following format for your input records instead of the one you used in Chapter 9:

Positions	Field
1 – 9	Employee Number
10 – 15	Gross Pay
16 – 17	Number of Exemptions
18 – 80	spaces

Write the following tax tables into your program as a two-dimensional table, and use it instead of the table you used in the Project in Chapter 9:

For 1 exemption:

If Gross Pay is:	Tax is:
less than $100	3% of Gross Pay
at least $100 but less than $200	$3 plus 4% of the excess over $100
at least $200 but less than $500	$7 plus 5% of the excess over $200
at least $500 but less than $1000	$22 plus 6% of the excess over $500
at least $1000 but less than $2000	$52 plus 7% of the excess over $1000
at least $2000 but less than $5000	$122 plus 8% of the excess over $2000
at least $5000	$362 plus 9% of the excess over $5000

For 2 exemptions:

If Gross Pay is:	Tax is:
less than $100	2% of Gross Pay
at least $100 but less than $200	$2 plus 3% of the excess over $100
at least $200 but less than $500	$5 plus 4% of the excess over $200
at least $500 but less than $1000	$17 plus 5% of the excess over $500
at least $1000 but less than $2000	$32 plus 6% of the excess over $1000
at least $2000 but less than $5000	$92 plus 7% of the excess over $2000
at least $5000	$302 plus 8% of the excess over $5000

For 3 exemptions:

If Gross Pay is:	Tax is:
less than $100	1% of Gross Pay
at least $100 but less than $200	$1 plus 2% of the excess over $100
at least $200 but less than $500	$3 plus 3% of the excess over $200
at least $500 but less than $1000	$12 plus 4% of the excess over $500
at least $1000 but less than $2000	$32 plus 5% of the excess over $1000
at least $2000 but less than $5000	$82 plus 6% of the excess over $2000
at least $5000	$262 plus 7% of the excess over $5000

For 4 or more exemptions:

If Gross Pay is:	Tax is:
less than $100	0
at least $100 but less than $200	1% of the excess over $100
at least $200 but less than $500	$1 plus 2% of the excess over $200
at least $500 but less than $1000	$4 plus 3% of the excess over $500
at least $1000 but less than $2000	$19 plus 4% of the excess over $1000
at least $2000 but less than $5000	$59 plus 5% of the excess over $2000
at least $5000	$209 plus 6% of the excess over $5000

Sorting and Merging

Here are the key points you should learn from this chapter:

1. What sorting and merging are
2. How to use the SORT verb
3. How to use the MERGE verb
4. How to write procedures that process data before or after they are sorted
5. How to write procedures that process data after they are merged

Key words to recognize and learn:

SORT	COLLATING SEQUENCE
MERGE	alphabet-name
SD	RELEASE
sort-merge file description entry	master file
key field	transaction file
USING	NATIVE
OUTPUT PROCEDURE	alphabet-name clause
GO TO statement	STANDARD-1
EXIT	ALSO
RETURN	BCD
INPUT PROCEDURE	binary-coded decimal

Arranging records in a particular order or sequence is a common requirement in data processing. Such record ordering can be accomplished using sorting or merging operations. A **SORT** produces an ordered file from one or more files that may be completely unordered. A **MERGE** produces an ordered file from two or more input files, each of which is already in sequence.

Sorting and merging have always constituted a large percentage of the workload in business data processing. COBOL has special language features that assist in sort and merge operations so that the user need not program these operations in detail. The COBOL sort and merge feature makes these operations easy to specify and to modify.

Using the SORT Verb

Our first program using the SORT verb, Program P11-01, reads input records in the following format:

Positions	Field
1 – 9	Social Security Number
10 – 14	Employee Number
15 – 21	Annual Salary (to two decimal places)
22 – 46	Employee Name
47 – 80	spaces

The program uses a SORT statement to SORT the input records into alphabetic order on Employee Name. The program then prints the SORTed records, and shows that the SORT process does not change the format of the records but only reorders them.

Program P11-01 is shown in Figure 11.1. The Environment Division shows a new FILE-CONTROL entry, one for a SORT-WORK-FILE, line 00180. SORTing and merging operations require a work file, which must be provided by the programmer. Here we provide SORT-WORK-FILE. SORT-WORK-FILE is a user-defined name. The name of the work file for a SORT or MERGE operation can be any legal name made up in accordance with the rules for making up file names.

Figure 11.1   Program P11-01.

```
CB1 RELEASE 2.4                              IBM OS/VS COBOL  JULY  1, 1982


                        22.19.05        APR  6,1988


00010  IDENTIFICATION DIVISION.
00020  PROGRAM-ID.  P11-01.
00030 *
00040 *     THIS PROGRAM SORTS A FILE OF EMPLOYEE RECORDS AND
00050 *     PRINTS EACH RECORD ON ONE LINE.
00060 *
00070 *******************************************************************
00080
00090  ENVIRONMENT DIVISION.
00100  CONFIGURATION SECTION.
00110  SOURCE-COMPUTER.  IBM-370.
00120  OBJECT-COMPUTER.  IBM-370.
00130
00140  INPUT-OUTPUT SECTION.
00150  FILE-CONTROL.
00160      SELECT EMPLOYEE-DATA-FILE-IN    ASSIGN TO INFILE.
00170      SELECT EMPLOYEE-DATA-FILE-OUT   ASSIGN TO PRINTER.
00180      SELECT SORT-WORK-FILE           ASSIGN TO SORTWK.
00190
00200 *******************************************************************
00210
00220  DATA DIVISION.
00230  FILE SECTION.
00240  FD  EMPLOYEE-DATA-FILE-IN
00250      LABEL RECORDS ARE OMITTED
00260      RECORD CONTAINS 80 CHARACTERS.
00270
00280  01  FILLER                          PIC X(80).
00290
00300  SD  SORT-WORK-FILE
00310      RECORD CONTAINS 80 CHARACTERS.
00320
00330  01  SORT-RECORD.
00340      05  SOCIAL-SECURITY-NUMBER-S    PIC X(9).
00350      05  EMPLOYEE-NUMBER-S           PIC X(5).
00360      05  ANNUAL-SALARY-S             PIC 9(5)V99.
00370      05  EMPLOYEE-NAME-S             PIC X(25).
00380      05  FILLER                      PIC X(34).
00390
00400  FD  EMPLOYEE-DATA-FILE-OUT
00410      RECORD CONTAINS 80 CHARACTERS
00420      LABEL RECORDS ARE OMITTED.
00430
00440  01  FILLER                          PIC X(80).
00450
00460 *******************************************************************
00470
00480  PROCEDURE DIVISION.
00490  ONLY-PARAGRAPH.
00500      SORT SORT-WORK-FILE
00510          ASCENDING KEY EMPLOYEE-NAME-S
00520          USING  EMPLOYEE-DATA-FILE-IN
00530          GIVING EMPLOYEE-DATA-FILE-OUT.
00540      STOP RUN.
```

In the Data Division there is a description of the input file and input record, lines 00240 through 00280. It turns out that we don't have to refer to any fields in the input record area, so we can use FILLER to define it.

Then, at line 00300, there is an **SD** entry (**sort-merge file description entry**) for the SORT-WORK-FILE. An SD entry must contain the file name made up in the SELECT clause and must not contain a LABEL RECORDS clause. The SD entry must have associated with it at least one level-01 entry. The level-01 entry for a SORT or MERGE file must be the same size as the records being SORTed or MERGEd. In this program we are SORTing 80-character records, but you will see in later programs that the size of the records being SORTed need not be the same as the size of the input records. Ordinarily, the level-01 entry is broken down into fields, at least one of which must be a **key field,** which the records are to be SORTed or MERGEd on. Other fields in the level-01 entry may serve other uses in the program, and in later programs you will see what those uses are.

In lines 00340 through 00380 you can see how the format of SORT-RECORD corresponds to the format of the input records being SORTed. It turns out that some of the fields defined here are not referred to in the program. Only EMPLOYEE-NAME-S is referred to, so SORT-RECORD could just as well have been defined as

```
01  SORT-RECORD.
    05   FILLER              PIC X(21).
    05   EMPLOYEE-NAME-S     PIC X(25).
    05   FILLER              PIC X(34).
```

with EMPLOYEE-NAME-S positioned properly in the 80-character record.

The Procedure Division begins at line 00480. The ONLY-PARAGRAPH in this program consists of just a SORT statement and a STOP RUN statement. Ordinarily you would not write a COBOL program just to do a SORT in this manner if you have a sort utility program available on your computer to do the job. Here you see just how to use a SORT statement. Later you will see how to incorporate a SORT statement into a useful COBOL program.

Following the word SORT must be the name of the file as given in the SD entry. Then we must say whether the records are to be SORTed in ASCENDING or DESCENDING order on their KEY field, and we must say what that field is. In this case we want to SORT the records into alphabetic order on Employee Name, so we say ASCENDING KEY EMPLOYEE-NAME-S. The field named in the ASCENDING KEY or DESCENDING KEY phrase must be defined within a level-01 entry associated with the file named after the word SORT, or as the level-01 entry itself. More than one key field may be given in this phrase. We will use more than one key field later, in Program P11-02.

The third entry in our SORT statement names the input file to be SORTed, after the reserved word **USING.** And the last entry in the statement uses the reserved word GIVING to tell the SORT where to put the SORTed records when done. In this program we put the SORTed records directly onto the printer file, EMPLOYEE-DATA-FILE-OUT.

You can now follow how the program works. First, the contents of EM-PLOYEE-DATA-FILE-IN are read in, SORTed, and written onto EMPLOYEE-DATA-FILE-OUT. Then the STOP RUN statement executes. The original input records, in EMPLOYEE-DATA-FILE-IN, remain in that file in their original order.

Program P11-01 was run with the input data shown in Figure 11.2 and produced the output shown in Figure 11.3.

Figure 11.2 Input to Program P11-01.

```
----------------------------------------------------------------------------
        1         2         3         4         5         6         7         8
12345678901234567890123456789012345678901234567890123456789012345678901234567890
----------------------------------------------------------------------------
100040002105035000000MORALES, LUIS
209560011116643953000COSTELLO, JOSEPH S.
502070026135992208000JAVIER, CARLOS
703100038151470812000DUMAY, MRS. MARY
401710020128252906000LIPKE, VINCENT R.
608250035147601161000BUXBAUM, ROBERT
708020041155340463000SMITH, R.
604910032143731510000FELDSOTT, MS. SALLY
101850005108904651000JACOBSON, MRS. NELLIE
201110008112774302000GREENWOOD, JAMES
301810014120513604000REITER, D.
304870017124383255000MARRA, DITTA E.
407390023132122557000KUGLER, CHARLES
046302813714393604000MILLER, D.
505680029139861859000GOODMAN, ISAAC
987654321917735000000JANES, LAURA M.
803220044159210114000VINCENTE, MATTHEW J.
901050047163084235000THOMAS, THOMAS T.
007360661626394651000LAMBERT, GEORGE
```

Figure 11.3 Output from Program P11-01.

```
608250035147601161000BUXBAUM, ROBERT
209560011116643953000COSTELLO, JOSEPH S.
703100038151470812000DUMAY, MRS. MARY
604910032143731510000FELDSOTT, MS. SALLY
505680029139861859000GOODMAN, ISAAC
201110008112774302000GREENWOOD, JAMES
101850005108904651000JACOBSON, MRS. NELLIE
987654321917735000000JANES, LAURA M.
502070026135992208000JAVIER, CARLOS
407390023132122557000KUGLER, CHARLES
007360661626394651000LAMBERT, GEORGE
401710020128252906000LIPKE, VINCENT R.
304870017124383255000MARRA, DITTA E.
046302813714393604000MILLER, D.
100040002105035000000MORALES, LUIS
301810014120513604000REITER, D.
708020041155340463000SMITH, R.
901050047163084235000THOMAS, THOMAS T.
803220044159210114000VINCENTE, MATTHEW J.
```

EXERCISE 1

Write a program to read input records in the following format

Positions	Field
1 – 15	Company Name
16 – 30	Street Address
31 – 45	City and State
46 – 65	Employee Name
66 – 80	Employee Title

SORT them, and list them. Use a SORT statement to SORT the input data into alphabetic order on Company Name.

The SORT Verb with USING and GIVING

In Program P11-01 we had a SORT statement with a USING phrase and a GIVING phrase. The USING phrase told the SORT from which file to get the records to be SORTed, and the GIVING phrase told the SORT on which file to put the SORTed records when done. Not all SORT statements have USING or GIVING phrases. Later we will see some that don't.

A SORT statement with a USING and a GIVING phrase goes through the following steps to complete the SORT:

1. It OPENs the USING file as INPUT.
2. It READs each record in the file and releases it to the sorting process.
3. It CLOSEs the USING file.
4. It SORTs the records.
5. It OPENs the GIVING file as OUTPUT.
6. It returns each record from the sorting process and WRITEs it onto the GIVING file.
7. It CLOSEs the GIVING file.

Figure 11.4 shows the flow of records in a program having a SORT statement with USING and GIVING. Remember that the sorting takes place only after all the input records have been released to the sort system.

Since the SORT statement OPENs and CLOSEs both the USING file and the GIVING file, the files must not already be OPENed when the SORT statement is executed, and you must not try to CLOSE them when the SORT is done. You may OPEN the USING and GIVING files yourself outside of the SORT in order to use them for your own purposes, and then you must CLOSE them when you are through with them.

You must not issue an OPEN, CLOSE, READ, or WRITE statement to a SORT or MERGE work file itself.

Figure 11.4   Flow of records in a program having a SORT statement with USING and GIVING.

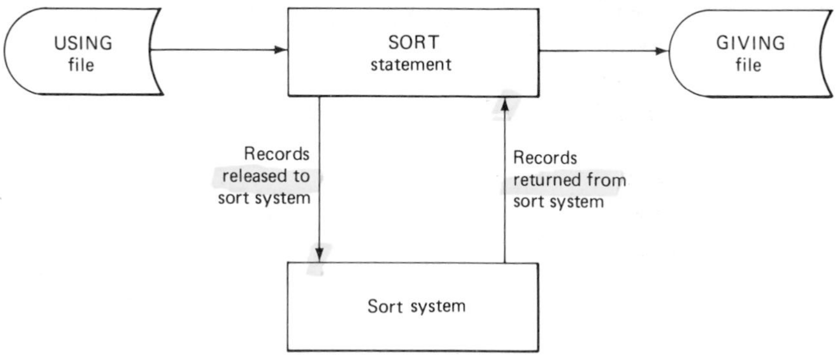

Using an OUTPUT PROCEDURE

Now let us say that we would like to be able to process the input records after they are SORTed, rather than having the SORT just dump the records out onto some GIVING file. As it happens, we can easily get the SORT to hold onto the records after SORTing them and return them one at a time, in SORTed order, to the processing portion of a program as they are needed. We do this by using an **OUTPUT PROCEDURE** phrase instead of a GIVING phrase in the SORT statement. This tells the SORT that there is no GIVING file, no place for it to put its SORTed results.

Program P11-02 shows how an OUTPUT PROCEDURE is used and also some other features of SORTing. Program P11-02 uses the same input data as Program P11-01 and produces output in the format shown in Figure 11.5. This time the data are SORTed in a different order. This time the output prints so that all the employees who have the highest salary are first, followed by all the employees with the second-highest salary, and so on down to the employees with the lowest salary. If there is more than one employee with the same salary, such employees are printed one right after the other in order on Employee Number.

Figure 11.5 Output format for Program P11-02.

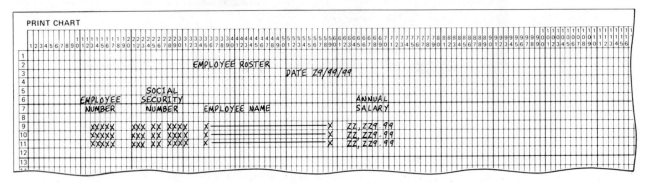

The output from Program P11-02 may be said to be sorted on Annual Salary as a descending key and Employee Number as an ascending key. Alternatively it can be said to be sorted on Employee Number as an ascending key within Annual Salary as a descending key. Annual Salary is the major sort field and Employee Number the minor sort field.

A Program with an OUTPUT PROCEDURE

Program P11-02 is shown in Figure 11.6. In the File Section, the input file is defined in the usual way, at line 00240, and the input record, at line 00280, once again is not broken down into fields. As a general rule, if you don't OPEN an input file in a program, you need not break down the input record into fields. You will soon see how we avoid OPENing the input file in this program.

Figure 11.6 Program P11-02.

```
CB1 RELEASE 2.4                          IBM OS/VS COBOL   JULY  1, 1982


                       22.47.28      APR  6,1988


00010   IDENTIFICATION DIVISION.
00020   PROGRAM-ID.  P11-02.
00030 *
00040 *    THIS PROGRAM SORTS A FILE OF EMPLOYEE RECORDS AND
00050 *    PRINTS THE CONTENTS OF EACH RECORD ON ONE LINE.
00060 *
00070 *****************************************************************
00080
00090   ENVIRONMENT DIVISION.
00100   CONFIGURATION SECTION.
00110   SOURCE-COMPUTER.  IBM-370.
00120   OBJECT-COMPUTER.  IBM-370.
00130
00140   INPUT-OUTPUT SECTION.
00150   FILE-CONTROL.
```

```
00160        SELECT EMPLOYEE-DATA-FILE-IN     ASSIGN TO INFILE.
00170        SELECT EMPLOYEE-DATA-FILE-OUT    ASSIGN TO PRINTER.
00180        SELECT SORT-WORK-FILE            ASSIGN TO SORTWK.
00190
00200 ***********************************************************
00210
00220 DATA DIVISION.
00230 FILE SECTION.
00240 FD  EMPLOYEE-DATA-FILE-IN
00250     LABEL RECORDS ARE OMITTED
00260     RECORD CONTAINS 80 CHARACTERS.
00270
00280 01  FILLER                          PIC X(80).
00290
00300 SD  SORT-WORK-FILE
00310     RECORD CONTAINS 80 CHARACTERS.
00320
00330 01  SORT-RECORD.
00340     05  SOCIAL-SECURITY-NUMBER-S    PIC X(9).
00350     05  EMPLOYEE-NUMBER-S           PIC X(5).
00360     05  ANNUAL-SALARY-S             PIC 9(5)V99.
00370     05  EMPLOYEE-NAME-S             PIC X(25).
00380     05  FILLER                      PIC X(34).
00390
00400 FD  EMPLOYEE-DATA-FILE-OUT
00410     LABEL RECORDS ARE OMITTED.
00420
00430 01  REPORT-LINE                     PIC X(71).
00440
00450 WORKING-STORAGE SECTION.
00460 01  MORE-INPUT                      PIC X        VALUE "Y".
00470 01  TODAYS-DATE.
00480     05  TODAYS-YEAR                 PIC 99.
00490     05  TODAYS-MONTH-AND-DAY        PIC 9(4).
00500
00510 01  HEADING-LINE-1.
00520     05  FILLER          PIC X(32) VALUE SPACES.
00530     05  FILLER          PIC X(15) VALUE "EMPLOYEE ROSTER".
00540
00550 01  HEADING-LINE-2.
00560     05  FILLER          PIC X(50) VALUE SPACES.
00570     05  FILLER          PIC X(5)  VALUE "DATE".
00580     05  TODAYS-MONTH-AND-DAY        PIC Z9/99/.
00590     05  TODAYS-YEAR                 PIC 99.
00600
00610 01  COLUMN-HEADS-1.
00620     05  FILLER          PIC X(23) VALUE SPACES.
00630     05  FILLER          PIC X(6)  VALUE "SOCIAL".
00640
00650 01  COLUMN-HEADS-2.
00660     05  FILLER          PIC X(10) VALUE SPACES.
00670     05  FILLER          PIC X(12) VALUE "EMPLOYEE".
00680     05  FILLER          PIC X(42) VALUE "SECURITY".
00690     05  FILLER          PIC X(6)  VALUE "ANNUAL".
00700
00710 01  COLUMN-HEADS-3.
00720     05  FILLER          PIC X(11) VALUE SPACES.
00730     05  FILLER          PIC X(12) VALUE "NUMBER".
00740     05  FILLER          PIC X(11) VALUE "NUMBER".
00750     05  FILLER          PIC X(30) VALUE "EMPLOYEE NAME".
00760     05  FILLER          PIC X(6)  VALUE "SALARY".
00770
00780 01  DETAIL-LINE.
00790     05  FILLER                      PIC X(12) VALUE SPACES.
00800     05  EMPLOYEE-NUMBER-OUT         PIC X(5)B(3).
00810     05  SOCIAL-SECURITY-NUMBER-OUT
00820                                     PIC X(3)BXXBX(4)B(3).
00830     05  EMPLOYEE-NAME-OUT           PIC X(25)B(3).
00840     05  ANNUAL-SALARY-OUT           PIC ZZ,ZZ9.99.
```

(continued)

The SD and level-01 entries for SORT-WORK-FILE and SORT-RECORD follow, at lines 00300 through 00380. This time we need all the level-05 entries in SORT-RECORD.

Figure 11.6　(continued)

```
00850
00860   01  NO-INPUT-DATA.
00870       05  FILLER              PIC X(33) VALUE SPACES.
00880       05  FILLER              PIC X(13) VALUE "NO INPUT DATA".
00890
00900   **************************************************************************
00910
00920   PROCEDURE DIVISION.
00930   CONTROL-SECTION SECTION.
00940   CONTROL-PARAGRAPH.
00950       SORT SORT-WORK-FILE
00960           DESCENDING KEY ANNUAL-SALARY-S
00970           ASCENDING  KEY EMPLOYEE-NUMBER-S
00980           USING EMPLOYEE-DATA-FILE-IN
00990           OUTPUT PROCEDURE IS PRODUCE-REPORT.
01000       STOP RUN.
01010
01020   PRODUCE-REPORT SECTION.
01030   PRODUCE-REPORT-PARAGRAPH.
01040       PERFORM INITIALIZATION.
01050       PERFORM MAIN-PROCESS UNTIL MORE-INPUT IS EQUAL TO "N".
01060       PERFORM TERMINATION.
01070       GO TO END-OF-THIS-SECTION.
01080
01090   INITIALIZATION.
01100       OPEN OUTPUT EMPLOYEE-DATA-FILE-OUT.
01110       ACCEPT TODAYS-DATE FROM DATE.
01120       MOVE CORRESPONDING TODAYS-DATE TO HEADING-LINE-2.
01130       WRITE REPORT-LINE FROM HEADING-LINE-1 AFTER PAGE.
01140       WRITE REPORT-LINE FROM HEADING-LINE-2.
01150       WRITE REPORT-LINE FROM COLUMN-HEADS-1 AFTER 2.
01160       WRITE REPORT-LINE FROM COLUMN-HEADS-2.
01170       WRITE REPORT-LINE FROM COLUMN-HEADS-3.
01180       MOVE SPACES TO REPORT-LINE.
01190       WRITE REPORT-LINE.
01200       PERFORM READ-A-RECORD.
01210       IF MORE-INPUT IS EQUAL TO "N"
01220           WRITE REPORT-LINE FROM NO-INPUT-DATA.
01230
01240   MAIN-PROCESS.
01250       MOVE EMPLOYEE-NUMBER-S TO EMPLOYEE-NUMBER-OUT.
01260       MOVE SOCIAL-SECURITY-NUMBER-S
01270                           TO SOCIAL-SECURITY-NUMBER-OUT.
01280       MOVE EMPLOYEE-NAME-S    TO EMPLOYEE-NAME-OUT.
01290       MOVE ANNUAL-SALARY-S    TO ANNUAL-SALARY-OUT.
01300       WRITE REPORT-LINE FROM DETAIL-LINE.
01310       PERFORM READ-A-RECORD.
01320
01330   TERMINATION.
01340       CLOSE EMPLOYEE-DATA-FILE-OUT.
01350
01360   READ-A-RECORD.
01370       RETURN SORT-WORK-FILE
01380           AT END
01390               MOVE "N" TO MORE-INPUT.
01400
01410   END-OF-THIS-SECTION.
01420       EXIT.
```

The Procedure Division begins at line 00920. The SORT statement at line 00950 contains a DESCENDING KEY phrase and an ASCENDING KEY phrase, to describe the desired SORT sequence fully. Whenever there is more than one KEY field in a SORT, they must be listed in order from major to minor. Although each KEY field must be indicated as ASCENDING or DESCENDING, you will see when we look at the format of the SORT statement that it is sometimes not necessary to repeat the words ASCENDING KEY or DESCENDING KEY for each KEY field.

At line 00990 there is an OUTPUT PROCEDURE phrase instead of a GIVING phrase. An OUTPUT PROCEDURE is a SECTION in the Procedure Division that contains processing steps to be carried out after the SORT is complete. The OUTPUT PROCEDURE phrase gives the name of the SECTION. In this program the

OUTPUT PROCEDURE has been given the name PRODUCE-REPORT. PRO-DUCE-REPORT is shown as the name of a SECTION at line 01020. Notice that the word SECTION does not appear in the SORT statement.

Program P11-02 shows the best way to organize the Procedure Division in a program containing an OUTPUT PROCEDURE. In standard COBOL, if there is even one SECTION in the Procedure Division, the entire division must be organized into SECTIONs. Each SECTION may contain zero, one, or more paragraphs.

The control paragraph in PRODUCE-REPORT SECTION, called PRODUCE-REPORT-PARAGRAPH, contains three familiar-looking PERFORM statements. It also contains a new statement, the **GO TO statement.** 1974 standard COBOL requires that PERFORM statements in an OUTPUT PROCEDURE refer only to paragraphs that are within the PROCEDURE. That restriction effectively requires the last executable statement in an OUTPUT PROCEDURE to be also physically the last statement in the PROCEDURE. There is no logical need for such a restriction, and it has been removed in the 1985 standard. While the restriction is with us, though, we need the GO TO statement. A GO TO statement transfers control to any paragraph or section name in the Procedure Division.

The least disruptive way to handle this useless restriction is as shown in Program P11-02. Set up a dummy paragraph at the end of the SECTION, containing only the one verb **EXIT.** An EXIT statement allows the programmer to establish a paragraph name or section name anywhere in the Procedure Division. It has no other effect on the execution of the program. EXIT is a reserved word, and when used it must be the only word in its paragraph. In Program P11-02 we have set up the paragraph END-OF-THIS-SECTION, at line 01410. Then use a GO TO statement to transfer control to the dummy paragraph, as shown in line 01070.

The SORT and STOP RUN statements must be in a SECTION, since in this program the entire Procedure Division must be organized in SECTIONs. The section header is shown at line 00930. And since each paragraph must have a name, we have line 00940.

Our read routine, at line 01360, now contains a **RETURN** statement where we would ordinarily expect a READ. A RETURN statement, like a READ statement, brings records into a program one at a time for processing. But whereas a READ statement brings a record into the program from an external file, a RE-TURN statement brings in a SORTed or MERGEd record from the SORT or MERGE process. Notice that the file name given in the SD entry is the one that must be used in the RETURN statement. A RETURN statement makes the next SORTed or MERGEd record available to the program in the level-01 entry associated with the work file.

The MOVE statements at lines 01250 through 01290 show that fields that are part of a level-01 entry associated with a work file can be operated on just like any other fields. You can now see why we don't have to OPEN the input file in this program. The SORT statement OPENs the input file originally to READ the records for SORTing and then RETURNs the SORTed records to the level-01 area associated with the SD entry.

When this program executes, the SORT statement first brings in and SORTs all the records in the file EMPLOYEE-DATA-FILE-IN. The program then executes the OUTPUT PROCEDURE. When a RETURN statement is encountered in the OUTPUT PROCEDURE, the SORT provides the next SORTed record for processing. When execution of the OUTPUT PROCEDURE is complete, the program executes the STOP RUN statement. Figure 11.7 shows the flow of records in a program having a SORT statement with USING and an OUTPUT PROCEDURE.

Program P11-02 was run with the same input data as Program P11-01 and produced the output shown in Figure 11.8.

Figure 11.7 Flow of records in a program having a SORT statement with USING and an OUTPUT PROCEDURE.

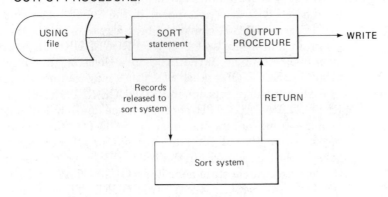

Figure 11.8 Output from Program P11-02.

```
                        EMPLOYEE ROSTER
                                      DATE   4/06/88

                 SOCIAL
 EMPLOYEE      SECURITY                                  ANNUAL
  NUMBER        NUMBER      EMPLOYEE NAME               SALARY
   10503     100 04 0002    MORALES, LUIS             50,000.00
   91773     987 65 4321    JANES, LAURA M.           50,000.00
   10890     101 85 0005    JACOBSON, MRS. NELLIE     46,510.00
   62639     007 36 0661    LAMBERT, GEORGE           46,510.00
   11277     201 11 0008    GREENWOOD, JAMES          43,020.00
   16308     901 05 0047    THOMAS, THOMAS T.         42,350.00
   11664     209 56 0011    COSTELLO, JOSEPH S.       39,530.00
   12051     301 81 0014    REITER, D.                36,040.00
   71439     046 30 2813    MILLER, D.                36,040.00
   12438     304 87 0017    MARRA, DITTA E.           32,550.00
   12825     401 71 0020    LIPKE, VINCENT R.         29,060.00
   13212     407 39 0023    KUGLER, CHARLES           25,570.00
   13599     502 07 0026    JAVIER, CARLOS            22,080.00
   13986     505 68 0029    GOODMAN, ISAAC            18,590.00
   14373     604 91 0032    FELDSOTT, MS. SALLY       15,100.00
   14760     608 25 0035    BUXBAUM, ROBERT           11,610.00
   15147     703 10 0038    DUMAY, MRS. MARY           8,120.00
   15534     708 02 0041    SMITH, R.                  4,630.00
   15921     803 22 0044    VINCENTE, MATTHEW J.       1,140.00
```

The SORT Statement

The format of the SORT statement is:

```
SORT file-name-1
   ON  {ASCENDING }  KEY data-name-1 [, data-name-2]...
       {DESCENDING}
   [ON {ASCENDING }  KEY data-name-3 [, data-name-4]...]...
       {DESCENDING}
   [COLLATING SEQUENCE IS alphabetic-name]
   ⎧ USING file-name-2 [, file-name-3]...                    ⎫
   ⎪ INPUT PROCEDURE                                         ⎪
   ⎪                                                         ⎪
   ⎪     IS section-name-1 [{THROUGH} section-name-2]        ⎪
or ⎨                        {THRU   }                        ⎬
   ⎪ GIVING file-name-4                                      ⎪
   ⎪ OUTPUT PROCEDURE                                        ⎪
   ⎪                                                         ⎪
   ⎩     IS section-name-3 [{THROUGH} section-name-4]        ⎭
                            {THRU   }
```

The format shows that the programmer may specify as many KEY fields as desired to control the SORT. The fields must be specified in order from major to minor. There may be as many ASCENDING KEY and DESCENDING KEY phrases as desired, and each phrase may contain as many data names as desired.

For input to the SORT the programmer must choose either USING or **INPUT PROCEDURE.** Then, regardless of which choice was made for input, the programmer must choose either GIVING or OUTPUT PROCEDURE for the output from the SORT.

COLLATING SEQUENCE and **alphabet-name** will be discussed later in this chapter.

The RETURN Statement

The format of the RETURN statement is:

```
RETURN file-name RECORD [INTO identifier]
     ; AT END imperative-statement
```

The RETURN statement may be used only within an OUTPUT PROCEDURE, and every OUTPUT PROCEDURE must contain at least one RETURN statement. After all SORTed records have been RETURNed, the AT END phrase is executed, and no more RETURN statements may be executed.

The INTO option in a RETURN statement works the same way that it does in a READ statement. You will see it used in a RETURN statement later in this chapter.

EXERCISE 2

Explain why the paragraph name PRODUCE-REPORT-PARAGRAPH in Program P11-02 has hyphens throughout, but the section header PRODUCE-REPORT SECTION has no hyphen before the word SECTION.

EXERCISE 3

Write a program that uses the same input format as Exercise 1, page 336, and produces output in the format shown in Figure 11.E3. Use a SORT statement to SORT the input data into alphabetic order on Employee Name within Company Name. Use an OUTPUT PROCEDURE to print the output.

Figure 11.E3 Output format for Exercise 3.

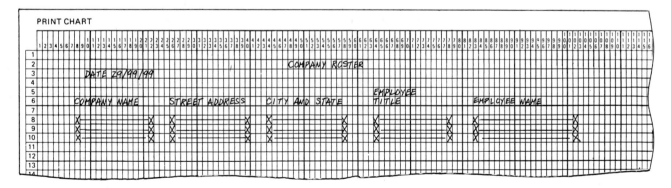

Using an INPUT PROCEDURE

An INPUT PROCEDURE is a SECTION in the Procedure Division that contains processing steps to be carried out before SORTing begins. In Program P11-03 we will use an INPUT PROCEDURE to select certain input records for SORTing. An INPUT PROCEDURE may also be used to modify input records before they are SORTed.

Program P11-03 reads input records in the following format:

Positions	Field
1 – 6	Part Number
7 – 26	Description
27 – 31	Reorder Quantity
32 – 36	Reorder Point
37 – 41	Quantity on Hand
42 – 80	spaces

Each record contains a Part Number, a Description of the part, a Reorder Quantity, a Reorder Point, and a Quantity on Hand. The program is to print a reorder report showing the parts that have a Quantity on Hand less than their Reorder Point. The output is to be in Part Number order and is to have the format shown in Figure 11.9.

In Program P11-03 we want to SORT only the records that are going to be printed, namely, the ones whose Quantity on Hand is less than their Reorder Point. We will use an INPUT PROCEDURE to select out only those records and release them to the SORT process.

Figure 11.9   Output format for Program P11-03.

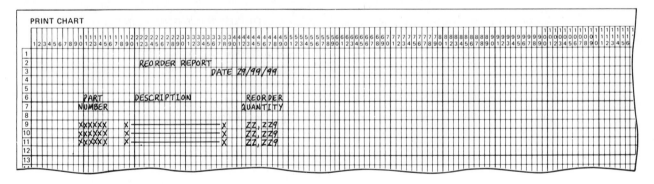

A Program with an INPUT PROCEDURE

Program P11-03 is shown in Figure 11.10. The input file is defined starting at line 00250. The input record is broken down into fields in this program because the field names are needed for processing in the INPUT PROCEDURE. The description of SORT-RECORD, starting at line 00400, includes only the fields that are needed for the SORT and for processing after the SORT is complete. As a general rule you should arrange a SORT so that you SORT as few and as small records as possible.

Figure 11.10 Program P11-03.

```
CB1 RELEASE 2.4                           IBM OS/VS COBOL  JULY  1, 1982


                        22.57.46      APR  6,1988


00010  IDENTIFICATION DIVISION.
00020  PROGRAM-ID.  P11-03.
00030 *
00040 *    THIS PROGRAM SORTS SOME FIELDS OF SELECTED INVENTORY RECORDS
00050 *    AND THEN PRINTS THE SELECTED FIELDS OF EACH SELECTED RECORD
00060 *    ON ONE LINE.
00070 *
00080 **********************************************************************
00090
00100  ENVIRONMENT DIVISION.
00110  CONFIGURATION SECTION.
00120  SOURCE-COMPUTER.  IBM-370.
00130  OBJECT-COMPUTER.  IBM-370.
00140
00150  INPUT-OUTPUT SECTION.
00160  FILE-CONTROL.
00170       SELECT INVENTORY-FILE-IN        ASSIGN TO INFILE.
00180       SELECT REORDER-REPORT-FILE-OUT  ASSIGN TO PRINTER.
00190       SELECT SORT-WORK-FILE           ASSIGN TO SORTWK.
00200
00210 **********************************************************************
00220
00230  DATA DIVISION.
00240  FILE SECTION.
00250  FD  INVENTORY-FILE-IN
00260       LABEL RECORDS ARE OMITTED
00270       RECORD CONTAINS 80 CHARACTERS.
00280
00290  01  INVENTORY-RECORD-IN.
00300       05  PART-NUMBER-IN           PIC X(6).
00310       05  DESCRIPTION-IN           PIC X(20).
00320       05  REORDER-QUANTITY-IN      PIC 9(5).
00330       05  REORDER-POINT-IN         PIC 9(5).
00340       05  QUANTITY-ON-HAND-IN      PIC 9(5).
00350       05  FILLER                   PIC X(39).
00360
00370  SD  SORT-WORK-FILE
00380       RECORD CONTAINS 31 CHARACTERS.
00390
00400  01  SORT-RECORD.
00410       05  PART-NUMBER-S            PIC X(6).
00420       05  DESCRIPTION-S            PIC X(20).
00430       05  REORDER-QUANTITY-S       PIC 9(5).
00440
00450  FD  REORDER-REPORT-FILE-OUT
00460       LABEL RECORDS ARE OMITTED.
00470
00480  01  REPORT-LINE                   PIC X(49).
00490
```

(continued)

SORTing is one of the most time-consuming operations in data processing, and if you can make your records small and few, you can save a lot of computer time. Also, the capacity of the COBOL SORT is limited. For any given record size and work-file size, only a certain maximum number of records can be SORTed. The smaller the records, the more that can be SORTed. If you have more records to SORT than the SORT can handle, you must SORT the records in groups of manageable size and then MERGE the results (more about MERGE later in this chapter).

Figure 11.10   (continued)

```
00500   WORKING-STORAGE SECTION.
00510   01   MORE-INPUT                          PIC X        VALUE "Y".
00520   01   MORE-SORTED-RECORDS                 PIC X        VALUE "Y".
00530   01   TODAYS-DATE.
00540        05   TODAYS-YEAR                PIC 99.
00550        05   TODAYS-MONTH-AND-DAY       PIC 9(4).
00560
00570   01   HEADING-LINE-1.
00580        05   FILLER        PIC X(21) VALUE SPACES.
00590        05   FILLER        PIC X(14) VALUE "REORDER REPORT".
00600
00610   01   HEADING-LINE-2.
00620        05   FILLER        PIC X(35) VALUE SPACES.
00630        05   FILLER        PIC X(5)  VALUE "DATE".
00640        05   TODAYS-MONTH-AND-DAY
00650                           PIC Z9/99/.
00660        05   TODAYS-YEAR   PIC 99.
00670
00680   01   COLUMN-HEADS-1.
00690        05   FILLER        PIC X(10) VALUE SPACES.
00700        05   FILLER        PIC X(10) VALUE "PART".
00710        05   FILLER        PIC X(22) VALUE "DESCRIPTION".
00720        05   FILLER        PIC X(7)  VALUE "REORDER".
00730
00740   01   COLUMN-HEADS-2.
00750        05   FILLER        PIC X(9)  VALUE SPACES.
00760        05   FILLER        PIC X(32) VALUE "NUMBER".
00770        05   FILLER        PIC X(8)  VALUE "QUANTITY".
00780
00790   01   DETAIL-LINE.
00800        05   FILLER             PIC X(9)  VALUE SPACES.
00810        05   PART-NUMBER-OUT    PIC X(6)B(3).
00820        05   DESCRIPTION-OUT    PIC X(20)B(4).
00830        05   REORDER-QUANTITY-OUT PIC ZZ,ZZ9.
00840
00850   01   NO-INPUT-DATA.
00860        05   FILLER        PIC X(21) VALUE SPACES.
00870        05   FILLER        PIC X(13) VALUE "NO INPUT DATA".
00880
00890   ***************************************************************
00900
00910   PROCEDURE DIVISION.
00920   CONTROL-SECTION SECTION.
00930   CONTROL-PARAGRAPH.
00940        SORT SORT-WORK-FILE
00950             ASCENDING KEY PART-NUMBER-S
00960             INPUT  PROCEDURE IS SELECT-RECORDS
00970             OUTPUT PROCEDURE IS PRODUCE-REPORT.
00980        STOP RUN.
00990
```

The Working Storage Section begins at line 00500. In this program we use two flags to signal end-of-file, MORE-INPUT at line 00510 and MORE-SORTED-RECORDS at line 00520. The first is used during the original input and selection process to signal that there are no more input records. The other is used during the printing of the report to signal that the SORT has no more records to RETURN to the program. You will see how both are used when we look at the Procedure Division.

The Procedure Division of Program P11-03 starts at line 00910. The SORT and STOP RUN statements are of course in their own SECTION. The SORT statement names SELECT-RECORDS as its INPUT PROCEDURE and PRODUCE-REPORT as its OUTPUT PROCEDURE. SELECT-RECORDS and PRODUCE-REPORT must be defined as SECTIONs in the Procedure Division, and they are. You can find the section headers at lines 01000 and 01300. When this program executes, it first carries out the INPUT PROCEDURE, then SORTs the records that have been released to it by the INPUT PROCEDURE, then carries out the OUTPUT PROCEDURE, and then executes the STOP RUN.

```
01000    SELECT-RECORDS SECTION.
01010    SELECT-RECORDS-PARAGRAPH.
01020        PERFORM INITIALIZATION.
01030        PERFORM SELECTION UNTIL MORE-INPUT IS EQUAL TO "N".
01040        PERFORM TERMINATION.
01050        GO TO END-OF-THIS-SECTION.
01060
01070    INITIALIZATION.
01080        OPEN INPUT INVENTORY-FILE-IN.
01090        PERFORM READ-A-RECORD.
01100
01110    SELECTION.
01120        IF QUANTITY-ON-HAND-IN IS LESS THAN REORDER-POINT-IN
01130            MOVE PART-NUMBER-IN      TO PART-NUMBER-S
01140            MOVE DESCRIPTION-IN       TO DESCRIPTION-S
01150            MOVE REORDER-QUANTITY-IN TO REORDER-QUANTITY-S
01160            RELEASE SORT-RECORD.
01170        PERFORM READ-A-RECORD.
01180
01190    TERMINATION.
01200        CLOSE INVENTORY-FILE-IN.
01210
01220    READ-A-RECORD.
01230        READ INVENTORY-FILE-IN
01240            AT END
01250                MOVE "N" TO MORE-INPUT.
01260
01270    END-OF-THIS-SECTION.
01280        EXIT.
01290
```

(continued)

The INPUT PROCEDURE

The control paragraph in the SELECT-RECORDS SECTION, called SELECT-RECORDS-PARAGRAPH, is organized like the OUTPUT PROCEDURE in Program P11-03, with three PERFORM statements and a GO TO statement. As with that OUTPUT PROCEDURE, a dummy paragraph is set up at the end of the SECTION, at line 01270. The GO TO statement at line 01050 transfers control to END-OF-THIS-SECTION.

The INITIALIZATION paragraph, at line 01070, OPENs only the INPUT file. This INPUT PROCEDURE deals only with the INPUT file and the SORT-WORK-FILE. Later, the OUTPUT PROCEDURE will operate on the SORT-WORK-FILE and the OUTPUT file. So we need to OPEN only the INPUT file now. The OUTPUT PROCEDURE will later OPEN only the OUTPUT file. After the priming READ, there is no need to test for an empty INPUT file. That test will be made later, in the OUTPUT PROCEDURE.

In the SELECTION paragraph, line 01110, each input record is tested to see whether it meets the condition for being printed on the output report. If it does, the three MOVE statements set up the record that is to be SORTed, and the **RE-LEASE** statement RELEASEs the record to the sorting process. Whereas a WRITE statement transfers a record from the program to an external file, a RELEASE statement transfers a record from the program to the SORT process. Notice that the object of the RELEASE verb is the record name in the level-01 entry associated with the sort work file. The format of the RELEASE statement will be given shortly.

Any source fields may be used to build the record that is RELEASEd to the SORT system. In this program the three source fields used were PART-NUMBER-IN, DESCRIPTION-IN, and REORDER-QUANTITY-IN. But the fields used to build the SORT record need not all come from input areas. They can come from fields in working storage as well, or they can be the result of computation. There is no limit to the amount or complexity of coding that may be contained in an INPUT PROCEDURE and executed before any records are SORTed.

Figure 11.10   (continued)

```
01300    PRODUCE-REPORT SECTION.
01310    PRODUCE-REPORT-PARAGRAPH.
01320        PERFORM INITIALIZATION.
01330        PERFORM PRINT-REPORT UNTIL MORE-SORTED-RECORDS = "N".
01340        PERFORM TERMINATION.
01350        GO TO END-OF-THIS-SECTION.
01360
01370    INITIALIZATION.
01380        OPEN OUTPUT REORDER-REPORT-FILE-OUT.
01390        ACCEPT TODAYS-DATE FROM DATE.
01400        MOVE CORRESPONDING TODAYS-DATE TO HEADING-LINE-2.
01410        WRITE REPORT-LINE FROM HEADING-LINE-1 AFTER PAGE.
01420        WRITE REPORT-LINE FROM HEADING-LINE-2.
01430        WRITE REPORT-LINE FROM COLUMN-HEADS-1 AFTER 3.
01440        WRITE REPORT-LINE FROM COLUMN-HEADS-2.
01450        MOVE SPACES TO REPORT-LINE.
01460        WRITE REPORT-LINE.
01470        PERFORM READ-A-RECORD.
01480        IF MORE-SORTED-RECORDS IS EQUAL TO "N"
01490            WRITE REPORT-LINE FROM NO-INPUT-DATA.
01500
01510    PRINT-REPORT.
01520        MOVE PART-NUMBER-S TO PART-NUMBER-OUT.
01530        MOVE DESCRIPTION-S TO DESCRIPTION-OUT.
01540        MOVE REORDER-QUANTITY-S TO REORDER-QUANTITY-OUT.
01550        WRITE REPORT-LINE FROM DETAIL-LINE.
01560        PERFORM READ-A-RECORD.
01570
01580    TERMINATION.
01590        CLOSE REORDER-REPORT-FILE-OUT.
01600
01610    READ-A-RECORD.
01620        RETURN SORT-WORK-FILE
01630            AT END
01640                MOVE "N" TO MORE-SORTED-RECORDS.
01650
01660    END-OF-THIS-SECTION.
01670        EXIT.
```

The OUTPUT PROCEDURE

PRODUCE-REPORT SECTION begins at line 01300. The control paragraph, PRODUCE-REPORT-PARAGRAPH, contains the usual three PERFORM statements and a GO TO statement. Notice that the names INITIALIZATION, TERMINATION, and END-OF-THIS-SECTION may be reused in this SECTION. Paragraph names in COBOL need not be unique in the Procedure Division. They must be unique in the SECTION in which they appear. A paragraph name referred to in its own SECTION can be referred to in the ordinary way as in lines 01320, 01330, and 01340. A paragraph name referred to in a statement outside of its SECTION must be qualified by the SECTION name; for example,

```
PERFORM PARAGRAPH-NAME-1 IN SECTION-NAME-2.
```

or

```
PERFORM PARAGRAPH-NAME-1 OF SECTION-NAME-2.
```

If you are inclined to spell paragraph names incorrectly, you should not attempt to duplicate such names in different sections. Incorrect spelling of supposedly duplicate names leads to programming errors that are difficult to detect. You should use instead unique names such as

```
INITIALIZATION-I
INITIALIZATION-O
TERMINATION-I
TERMINATION-O
END-OF-INPUT-PROCEDURE
```

and

```
END-OF-OUTPUT-PROCEDURE
```

In the INITIALIZATION paragraph in this SECTION, the OPEN statement OPENs only the OUTPUT file. After the priming RETURN, the usual test is made to see if there are any data. The RETURN statement at line 01620 signals the program when there are no more records to be RETURNed by moving "N" to MORE-SORTED-RECORDS.

Figure 11.11 shows the flow of records in a program having a SORT statement with an INPUT PROCEDURE and OUTPUT PROCEDURE. Remember that sorting takes place only after execution of the INPUT PROCEDURE is completed.

Program P11-03 was run with the input data shown in Figure 11.12 and produced the output shown in Figure 11.13.

Figure 11.11 Flow of records in a program having a SORT statement with an INPUT PROCEDURE and an OUTPUT PROCEDURE.

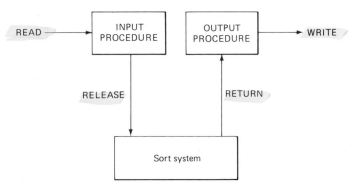

Figure 11.12 Input to Program P11-03.

```
--------------------------------------------------------------------------------
         1         2         3         4         5         6         7         8
12345678901234567890123456789012345678901234567890123456789012345678901234567890
--------------------------------------------------------------------------------
071439BALL-PEEN HAMMER      000250001000009
8028371/2 IN. FLAT WASHER   020000050000400
2836419/16 IN. STOVE BOLT   001000005000110
002363CROSS-CUT SAW         000100000800006
001042RIP SAW               000100000800007
8028389/16 IN. FLAT WASHER025000120001100
283741DRAWER HANDLE         000300001000009
58374350 FT. GARDEN HOSE   001800012000110
583744100 FT. GARDEN HOSE 001250008000100
```

Figure 11.13 Output from Program P11-03.

```
                     REORDER REPORT
                              DATE   4/06/88


         PART        DESCRIPTION              REORDER
         NUMBER                               QUANTITY

         001042      RIP SAW                       10
         002363      CROSS-CUT SAW                 10
         071439      BALL-PEEN HAMMER              25
         283741      DRAWER HANDLE                 30
         583743      50 FT. GARDEN HOSE           180
         802837      1/2 IN. FLAT WASHER        2,000
         802838      9/16 IN. FLAT WASHER       2,500
```

The RELEASE Statement

The format of the RELEASE statement is:

```
RELEASE record-name [FROM identifier]
```

A RELEASE statement may be given only within an INPUT PROCEDURE, and every INPUT PROCEDURE must contain at least one RELEASE statement. The FROM option serves the same purpose in a RELEASE statement as it does in a WRITE statement.

EXERCISE 4

Write a program to read input records in the following format:

Positions	Field
1 – 3	Department Number
4 – 8	Employee Number
9 – 11	Monday Hours (to one decimal place)
12 – 14	Tuesday Hours (to one decimal place)
15 – 17	Wednesday Hours (to one decimal place)
18 – 20	Thursday Hours (to one decimal place)
21 – 23	Friday Hours (to one decimal place)
24 – 26	Saturday Hours (to one decimal place)
27 – 80	spaces

Have your program select for printing only those employees who worked more than 30 hours in the week. For each such employee, have your program print on one line the Employee Number, the number of hours worked in the week, and the difference between 30 and the number of hours worked.

Have your program produce its output in ascending order by Employee Number within Department Number.

The MERGE Statement

The MERGE statement may be used to combine two or more files into one such that the resulting file is in ASCENDING or DESCENDING order on one or more KEY fields. The files used as input to a MERGE must already be in the same order that the resulting file is to be.

The format of the MERGE statement is

```
MERGE  file-name-1
    ON  {ASCENDING }  KEY data-name-1 [, data-name-2]...
        {DESCENDING}
   [ON  {ASCENDING }  KEY data-name-3 [. data-name-4]...]...
        {DESCENDING}
   [COLLATING SEQUENCE IS alphabet-name]
    USING file-name-2, file-name-3 [, file-name-4]...
  { GIVING file-name-5                                     }
  { OUTPUT PROCEDURE                                       }
  {     IS section-name-1 [ {THROUGH} section-name-2]      }
  {                         {THRU   }                      }
```

The file name given after the word MERGE must be a name defined in an SD entry. The MERGE statement has an optional OUTPUT PROCEDURE, as the SORT statement does, but no INPUT PROCEDURE capability.

The USING clause names the files to be used as input, and, of course, there must be at least two of them. It makes no sense to try to MERGE only one file.

Using the MERGE Statement

Program P11-04 shows a typical use of a MERGE capability. The program produces customer invoices in the format shown in Figure 11.14. The customer's name and address may occupy as many as five lines and are printed on lines 6 through 10 of the invoice. If the name and address of any particular customer occupy fewer than five lines, the unneeded lines are left blank. The column headings are printed on lines 13 and 14 regardless of the number of lines in the name and address. The detail lines, showing the items being billed on this invoice, print on lines 16 through 25. The invoice total always prints on line 26 regardless of the number of detail lines. If there are more than 10 detail lines, the excess lines print on successive pages, and the invoice total prints on line 26 of the last page for that customer.

These invoices are prepared from two input files. One file is a more or less permanent one containing the names and addresses of all of Northwestern Hard-Pressed Hardware Company's customers. This file is changed only when a customer's name or address changes, when a new customer opens an account, or when an inactive customer is removed from the file. This is a typical **master file.** In this application the master file might be called the "customer name and address master." Its records are in the following format:

Positions	Field
1	Code
2 – 6	Customer Number
7 – 26	Name and Address Line
27 – 80	spaces

The Code in position 1, which can be a number from 1 through 5, tells which line of the name and address this record represents.

Figure 11.14 Output format for Program P11-04.

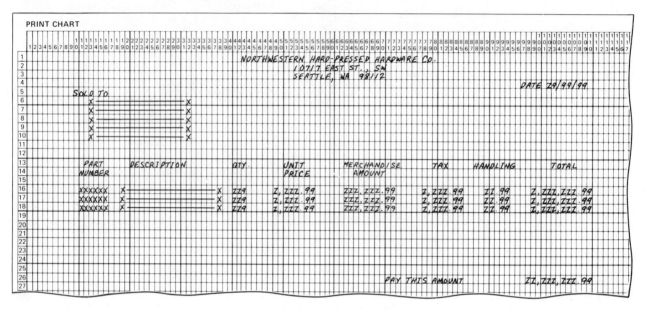

The second input file contains records relating to purchases by customers, for which they will now be billed. The records in this file contain the data the program needs to make up the line items which are to appear on the invoices. The record format is

Positions	Field
1	Code
2 – 6	Customer Number
7 – 12	Part Number
13 – 32	Description
33 – 35	Quantity
36 – 41	Unit Price (to two decimal places)
42 – 45	Handling (to two decimal places)
46 – 80	spaces

This is a typical **transaction file.** Position 1 of each transaction contains the number 6.

The program also produces a separate error report, whose format is not shown. The error report lists erroneous transactions or or indicates that there are no input data. A transaction is in error if it does not contain a 6 in position 1 or if the Customer Number in the transaction does not match any Customer Number on the master file.

A Hierarchy Diagram for a MERGE Program

The hierarchy diagram in Figure 11.15 shows the approach taken in Program P11-04. First the transaction file is SORTed so that the transactions are in order on Customer Number, and the SORTed transactions are stored on a temporary file. The master file must be in order on Customer Number also, but we do not SORT it in this program. Since the master file is used over and over, it pays to sort it once, by hand if necessary, and leave it that way. Presumably that has already been done.

Then the master file and the SORTed transaction file are MERGEd on Customer Number. The MERGE statement has an OUTPUT PROCEDURE phrase, and the OUTPUT PROCEDURE is the entire remainder of the hierarchy diagram, "Produce invoices" and its subfunctions. The MERGE feeds records one at a time to "Produce invoices" from the master file and the transaction file such that for any

Figure 11.15 Hierarchy diagram for Program P11-04.

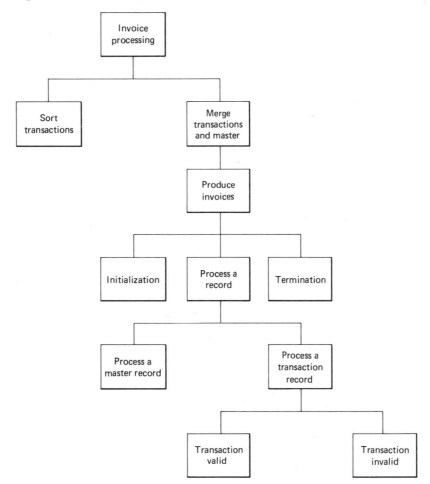

customer the master name and address records are RETURNed from the MERGE first, followed by the transactions for that customer. If there are no transactions for a particular customer, only the master name and address records are RETURNed from the MERGE. If there are no name and address records to match a particular transaction, the transaction is in error.

"Produce invoices" is organized like any ordinary program. You will see what the "Initialization" and "Termination" consist of when we look at the program. The box "Process a record" is entered with each record RETURNed from the MERGE. "Process a record" first determines whether a master record or a transaction record has been RETURNed, and handles it accordingly. If it is a transaction record, the box "Process a transaction record" determines whether the transaction is valid or invalid, and processes it accordingly.

A Program with a MERGE Statement

Program P11-04 is shown in Figure 11.16. The SD entry has now been given the name SORT-MERGE-WORK-FILE, for in this program it is used for both SORT-ing and merging. Although two different types of records are being MERGEd in this program, only the transaction record is described under the SD entry for the SORT-MERGE-WORK-FILE, at line 00310. The format of the master record is described in the Working Storage Section, as you will see. The program uses control-break logic to determine when the first master record for each customer is RETURNed from the MERGE, and so master records are worked on in working storage in the manner discussed in Chapter 6. Transaction records are worked on in the File Section.

When a record is RETURNed or read from a file that contains records in more than one format, your program must have some way of determining which type of record it is. In Program P11-04 we can tell the master records from the transactions, for each master record has some number 1 through 5 in position 1, whereas the transactions have the number 6.

CUSTOMER-MASTER-FILE-IN is defined starting at line 00430, and TRANSACTION-FILE-IN is defined starting at line 00490. The level-01 entries in those files have not been broken down into fields because neither of the files is OPENed by us. In this program, they are OPENed and CLOSEd only by the SORT and MERGE statements. The file TRANSACTION-FILE-SRT, at line 00550, is used by the SORT statement as a place to put the SORTed transactions temporarily before they are MERGEd. It too is not OPENed by us.

Figure 11.16 Program P11-04.

```
CB1 RELEASE 2.4                              IBM OS/VS COBOL   JULY  1, 1982


                  17.28.07        APR  7,1988


00010   IDENTIFICATION DIVISION.
00020   PROGRAM-ID.  P11-04.
00030 *
00040 *    THIS PROGRAM SORTS TRANSACTION RECORDS AND THEN MERGES THEM
00050 *    WITH THE MASTER FILE WHICH IS ALREADY IN SEQUENCE.  IT THEN
00060 *    PRODUCES INVOICES AND AN ERROR REPORT.
00070 *
00080 ************************************************************************
00090
00100   ENVIRONMENT DIVISION.
00110   CONFIGURATION SECTION.
```

```
00120   SOURCE-COMPUTER.  IBM-370.
00130   OBJECT-COMPUTER.  IBM-370.
00140
00150   INPUT-OUTPUT SECTION.
00160   FILE-CONTROL.
00170       SELECT SORT-MERGE-WORK-FILE    ASSIGN TO SORTWK.
00180       SELECT CUSTOMER-MASTER-FILE-IN  ASSIGN TO INFILE1.
00190       SELECT TRANSACTION-FILE-IN     ASSIGN TO INFILE2.
00200       SELECT TRANSACTION-FILE-SRT    ASSIGN TO TEMPFILE.
00210       SELECT INVOICE-FILE-OUT        ASSIGN TO PRINTER1.
00220       SELECT ERROR-FILE-OUT          ASSIGN TO PRINTER2.
00230
00240   ********************************************************************
00250
00260   DATA DIVISION.
00270   FILE SECTION.
00280   SD  SORT-MERGE-WORK-FILE
00290       RECORD CONTAINS 80 CHARACTERS.
00300
00310   01  TRANSACTION-WORK-RECORD.
00320       05  CODE-T                     PIC 9.
00330       05  CODE-T-X REDEFINES CODE-T  PIC X.
00340           88  CODE-T-VALID           VALUE "6".
00350       05  CUSTOMER-NUMBER-T          PIC X(5).
00360       05  PART-NUMBER-T              PIC X(6).
00370       05  DESCRIPTION-T              PIC X(20).
00380       05  QUANTITY-T                 PIC 999.
00390       05  UNIT-PRICE-T               PIC 9(4)V99.
00400       05  HANDLING-T                 PIC 99V99.
00410       05  FILLER                     PIC X(35).
00420
00430   FD  CUSTOMER-MASTER-FILE-IN
00440       LABEL RECORDS ARE OMITTED
00450       RECORD CONTAINS 80 CHARACTERS.
00460
00470   01  CUSTOMER-MASTER-RECORD-IN      PIC X(80).
00480
00490   FD  TRANSACTION-FILE-IN
00500       LABEL RECORDS ARE OMITTED
00510       RECORD CONTAINS 80 CHARACTERS.
00520
00530   01  TRANSACTION-RECORD-IN          PIC X(80).
00540
00550   FD  TRANSACTION-FILE-SRT
00560       LABEL RECORDS ARE OMITTED
00570       RECORD CONTAINS 80 CHARACTERS.
00580
00590   01  TRANSACTION-RECORD-SRT         PIC X(80).
00600
00610   FD  INVOICE-FILE-OUT
00620       LABEL RECORDS ARE OMITTED.
00630
00640   01  INVOICE-RECORD-OUT             PIC X(110).
00650
00660   FD  ERROR-FILE-OUT
00670       LABEL RECORDS ARE OMITTED.
00680
00690   01  ERROR-RECORD-OUT               PIC X(120).
00700
00710   WORKING-STORAGE SECTION.
00720   01  CUSTOMER-MASTER-WORK-RECORD.
00730       05  CODE-M                     PIC 9.
00740       05  CODE-M-X REDEFINES CODE-M  PIC X.
00750           88  CODE-M-VALID           VALUES "1" THRU "5".
00760       05  CUSTOMER-NUMBER-M          PIC X(5).
00770       05  NAME-AND-ADDRESS-LINE-M    PIC X(20).
00780       05  FILLER                     PIC X(54).
00790
00800   01  LINE-SPACING                   PIC S9  COMP SYNC.
00810   01  CUSTOMER-NUMBER-SAVE           PIC X(5).
00820   01  LINE-LIMIT                     PIC S99 COMP SYNC VALUE 24.
00830   01  INVOICE-LINE-COUNTER           PIC S99 COMP SYNC VALUE 0.
00840   01  INVOICE-TOTAL-W                PIC S9(7)V99      VALUE 0.
00850   01  MORE-INPUT                     PIC X       VALUE "Y".
```

(continued)

The Working Storage Section begins at line 00710. There we have defined five fields to hold the customer names and addresses in preparation for printing on

Figure 11.16 (continued)

```
00860   01  MASTERS-EXIST                        PIC X       VALUE "N".
00870   01  TRANSACTIONS-EXIST                   PIC X       VALUE "N".
00880   01  TODAYS-DATE.
00890       05  TODAYS-YEAR                      PIC 99.
00900       05  TODAYS-MONTH-AND-DAY             PIC 9(4).
00910   01  TAX-RATE                             PIC V999    VALUE .085.
00920   01  MERCHANDISE-AMOUNT-W                 PIC S9(6)V99.
00930   01  TAX-AMOUNT-W                         PIC S9(4)V99.
00940   01  LINE-ITEM-TOTAL-W                    PIC S9(7)V99.
00950   01  NAME-AND-ADDRESS-TABLE.
00960       05  NAME-AND-ADDRESS                 PIC X(20)   OCCURS 5 TIMES.
00970   01  CUSTOMER-NUMBER-W                    PIC X(5)    VALUE SPACES.
00980
00990   01  INVOICE-REPORT-HEAD-1.
01000       05  FILLER          PIC X(42) VALUE SPACES.
01010       05  FILLER          PIC X(48)
01020           VALUE "NORTHWESTERN HARD-PRESSED HARDWARE CO.".
01030
01040   01  INVOICE-REPORT-HEAD-2.
01050       05  FILLER          PIC X(52)   VALUE SPACES.
01060       05  FILLER          PIC X(18)   VALUE "10717 EAST ST., SW".
01070
01080   01  INVOICE-REPORT-HEAD-3.
01090       05  FILLER          PIC X(52)   VALUE SPACES.
01100       05  FILLER          PIC X(18)   VALUE "SEATTLE, WA  98112".
01110
01120   01  INVOICE-REPORT-HEAD-4.
01130       05  FILLER          PIC X(96)   VALUE SPACES.
01140       05  FILLER          PIC X(5)    VALUE "DATE".
01150       05  TODAYS-MONTH-AND-DAY         PIC Z9/99/.
01160       05  TODAYS-YEAR                  PIC 99.
01170
01180   01  INVOICE-REPORT-HEAD-5.
01190       05  FILLER          PIC X(9)    VALUE SPACES.
01200       05  FILLER          PIC X(7)    VALUE "SOLD TO".
01210
01220   01  NAME-AND-ADDRESS-LINE.
01230       05  FILLER          PIC X(12)   VALUE SPACES.
01240       05  NAME-AND-ADDRESS-OUT         PIC X(20).
01250
01260   01  INVOICE-COLUMN-HEAD-1.
01270       05  FILLER          PIC X(11)   VALUE SPACES.
01280       05  FILLER          PIC X(9)    VALUE "PART".
01290       05  FILLER          PIC X(20)   VALUE "DESCRIPTION".
01300       05  FILLER          PIC X(10)   VALUE "QTY.".
01310       05  FILLER          PIC X(12)   VALUE "UNIT".
01320       05  FILLER          PIC X(17)   VALUE "MERCHANDISE".
01330       05  FILLER          PIC X(8)    VALUE "TAX".
01340       05  FILLER          PIC X(15)   VALUE "HANDLING".
01350       05  FILLER          PIC X(5)    VALUE "TOTAL".
01360
01370   01  INVOICE-COLUMN-HEAD-2.
01380       05  FILLER          PIC X(10)   VALUE SPACES.
01390       05  FILLER          PIC X(40)   VALUE "NUMBER".
01400       05  FILLER          PIC X(14)   VALUE "PRICE".
01410       05  FILLER          PIC X(6)    VALUE "AMOUNT".
01420
01430   01  LINE-ITEM.
01440       05  FILLER                       PIC X(10) VALUE SPACES.
01450       05  PART-NUMBER-OUT              PIC X(6)BB.
01460       05  DESCRIPTION-OUT              PIC X(20)BB.
01470       05  QUANTITY-OUT                 PIC ZZ9B(5).
01480       05  UNIT-PRICE-OUT               PIC Z,ZZZ.99B(6).
01490       05  MERCHANDISE-AMOUNT-OUT       PIC ZZZ,ZZZ.99B(5).
01500       05  TAX-OUT                      PIC Z,ZZZ.99B(4).
01510       05  HANDLING-OUT                 PIC ZZ.99B(4).
01520       05  LINE-ITEM-TOTAL-OUT          PIC Z,ZZZ,ZZZ.99.
01530
```

the invoices, at line 00960. We also have defined CUSTOMER-NUMBER-W, at line 00970, and CUSTOMER-NUMBER-SAVE, at line 00810. CUSTOMER-NUMBER-W is used to hold the Customer Number of the master records being worked on, and CUSTOMER-NUMBER-SAVE is used to hold the Customer Number of the transaction records being worked on. You will see how both fields are

```
01540  01   INVOICE-TOTAL-LINE.
01550       05   FILLER              PIC X(70)   VALUE SPACES.
01560       05   FILLER              PIC X(27)   VALUE "PAY THIS AMOUNT".
01570       05   INVOICE-TOTAL-OUT               PIC ZZ,ZZZ,ZZZ.99.
01580
01590  01   ERROR-REPORT-HEADING-1.
01600       05   FILLER              PIC X(96)
01610            VALUE "INVOICE PROGRAM ERROR REPORT".
01620       05   FILLER              PIC X(5)    VALUE "DATE".
01630       05   TODAYS-MONTH-AND-DAY            PIC Z9/99/.
01640       05   TODAYS-YEAR                     PIC 99.
01650
01660  01   ERROR-REPORT-HEADING-2.
01670       05   FILLER              PIC X(6)    VALUE "TRANS".
01680       05   FILLER              PIC X(9)    VALUE "CUSTOMER".
01690       05   FILLER              PIC X(81)   VALUE "INPUT RECORD".
01700       05   FILLER              PIC X(5)    VALUE "ERROR".
01710
01720  01   ERROR-REPORT-HEADING-3.
01730       05   FILLER              PIC X(7)    VALUE " CODE".
01740       05   FILLER              PIC X(8)    VALUE "NUMBER".
01750       05   FILLER              PIC X(40)
01760            VALUE "....+....1....+....2....+....3....+....4".
01770       05   FILLER              PIC X(41)
01780            VALUE "....+....5....+....6....+....7....+....8".
01790       05   FILLER              PIC X(7)    VALUE "MESSAGE".
01800
01810  01   NO-MASTER-DATA.
01820       05   FILLER              PIC X(96)   VALUE SPACES.
01830       05   FILLER              PIC X(14)   VALUE "NO MASTER DATA".
01840
01850  01   NO-TRANSACTION-DATA.
01860       05   FILLER              PIC X(96)   VALUE SPACES.
01870       05   FILLER              PIC X(19)   VALUE "NO TRANSACTION DATA".
01880
01890  01   ERROR-LINE.
01900       05   FILLER                          PIC XX VALUE SPACES.
01910       05   CODE-T-E                        PIC XB(5).
01920       05   CUSTOMER-NUMBER-E               PIC X(5)BB.
01930       05   TRANSACTION-WORK-RECORD-E       PIC X(80)B.
01940       05   ERROR-MESSAGE-E                 PIC X(24).
01950
01960  ***********************************************************************
01970
01980  PROCEDURE DIVISION.
01990  CONTROL-SECTION SECTION.
02000  INVOICE-PROCESSING.
02010      PERFORM SORT-TRANSACTIONS.
02020      PERFORM MERGE-TRANSACTIONS-AND-MASTER.
02030      STOP RUN.
02040
```

(continued)

used when we look at the Procedure Division. Also in working storage are fields
that we need to hold the results of arithmetic.

ERROR-LINE, line 01890, defines an output area that is used for printing
error messages. This program detects invalid transaction codes in transaction
input records and also transaction records that have no matching master records.
Error messages are printed in ERROR-FILE-OUT, separate from the invoices,
which are printed in INVOICE-FILE-OUT. When you have more than one printer
output file in a COBOL program, the outputs may be assigned to different printers
if your installation has more than one, or the outputs can be made to print one after
the other on a single printer if the operating system provides such capability.
Otherwise, the print lines of the several output files will be interleaved in an
unpredictable manner.

The Procedure Division starts at line 01980 and consists of two SECTIONs.
You can see the two section headers at lines 01990 and 02200. CONTROL-
SECTION represents the three boxes highest on the hierarchy diagram of Figure
11.15, and PRODUCE-INVOICES represents the rest of the diagram. In the SORT

Figure 11.16 (continued)

```
02050    SORT-TRANSACTIONS.
02060        SORT SORT-MERGE-WORK-FILE
02070            ASCENDING KEY CUSTOMER-NUMBER-T,
02080                        PART-NUMBER-T
02090            USING   TRANSACTION-FILE-IN
02100            GIVING  TRANSACTION-FILE-SRT.
02110
02120    MERGE-TRANSACTIONS-AND-MASTER.
02130        MERGE SORT-MERGE-WORK-FILE
02140            ASCENDING KEY CUSTOMER-NUMBER-T,
02150                        CODE-T-X
02160            USING CUSTOMER-MASTER-FILE-IN,
02170                  TRANSACTION-FILE-SRT
02180            OUTPUT PROCEDURE IS PRODUCE-INVOICES.
02190
02200    PRODUCE-INVOICES SECTION.
02210    PRODUCE-INVOICES-PARAGRAPH.
02220        PERFORM INITIALIZATION.
02230        PERFORM PROCESS-A-RECORD UNTIL MORE-INPUT IS EQUAL TO "N".
02240        PERFORM TERMINATION.
02250        GO TO END-OF-THIS-SECTION.
02260
02270    INITIALIZATION.
02280        OPEN OUTPUT INVOICE-FILE-OUT,
02290                    ERROR-FILE-OUT.
02300        ACCEPT TODAYS-DATE FROM DATE.
02310        MOVE CORRESPONDING TODAYS-DATE TO INVOICE-REPORT-HEAD-4.
02320        MOVE CORRESPONDING TODAYS-DATE TO ERROR-REPORT-HEADING-1.
02330        WRITE ERROR-RECORD-OUT FROM ERROR-REPORT-HEADING-1
02340                            AFTER PAGE.
02350        WRITE ERROR-RECORD-OUT FROM ERROR-REPORT-HEADING-2 AFTER 3.
02360        WRITE ERROR-RECORD-OUT FROM ERROR-REPORT-HEADING-3.
02370        MOVE SPACES TO ERROR-RECORD-OUT.
02380        WRITE ERROR-RECORD-OUT.
02390        PERFORM READ-A-RECORD.
02400        MOVE CUSTOMER-NUMBER-M TO CUSTOMER-NUMBER-SAVE.
02410
02420    PROCESS-A-RECORD.
02430        IF CODE-M-VALID
02440            PERFORM PROCESS-A-MASTER-RECORD
02450        ELSE
02460            PERFORM PROCESS-A-TRANSACTION-RECORD.
02470        PERFORM READ-A-RECORD.
02480
02490    INVOICE-TOTAL-BREAK.
02500        MOVE INVOICE-TOTAL-W TO INVOICE-TOTAL-OUT.
02510        MOVE 0 TO INVOICE-TOTAL-W.
02520        MOVE CUSTOMER-NUMBER-M TO CUSTOMER-NUMBER-SAVE.
02530        COMPUTE LINE-SPACING = LINE-LIMIT + 2 - INVOICE-LINE-COUNTER.
02540        WRITE INVOICE-RECORD-OUT FROM INVOICE-TOTAL-LINE
02550                                AFTER LINE-SPACING.
02560        ADD LINE-SPACING TO INVOICE-LINE-COUNTER.
02570
02580    TERMINATION.
02590        PERFORM INVOICE-TOTAL-BREAK.
02600        IF MASTERS-EXIST IS EQUAL TO "N"
02610            WRITE ERROR-RECORD-OUT FROM NO-MASTER-DATA.
02620        IF TRANSACTIONS-EXIST IS EQUAL TO "N"
02630            WRITE ERROR-RECORD-OUT FROM NO-TRANSACTION-DATA.
02640        CLOSE INVOICE-FILE-OUT,
02650              ERROR-FILE-OUT.
02660
02670    READ-A-RECORD.
02680        RETURN SORT-MERGE-WORK-FILE INTO CUSTOMER-MASTER-WORK-RECORD
02690            AT END
02700                MOVE "N" TO MORE-INPUT.
02710
```

statement, at line 02060, you can see that the transactions are SORTed on Customer Number and Part Number (or, alternatively, on Part Number within Customer Number). This causes each customer's invoice to print in Part Number order. The MERGE statement, at line 02130, MERGEs on CUSTOMER-NUMBER-T and CODE-T-X. This assures that each customer's name and address records, with Codes 1 through 5, will MERGE in before its transactions, with Code 6.

```
02720    PROCESS-A-MASTER-RECORD.
02730        MOVE "Y" TO MASTERS-EXIST.
02740        IF CUSTOMER-NUMBER-M IS NOT EQUAL TO CUSTOMER-NUMBER-W
02750            MOVE CUSTOMER-NUMBER-M TO CUSTOMER-NUMBER-W
02760            MOVE SPACES              TO NAME-AND-ADDRESS-TABLE.
02770        MOVE NAME-AND-ADDRESS-LINE-M
02780            TO NAME-AND-ADDRESS (CODE-M).
02790
02800    PROCESS-A-TRANSACTION-RECORD.
02810        MOVE "Y" TO TRANSACTIONS-EXIST.
02820        IF CODE-T-VALID
02830            AND CUSTOMER-NUMBER-T IS EQUAL TO CUSTOMER-NUMBER-W
02840                PERFORM TRANSACTION-VALID
02850        ELSE
02860            PERFORM TRANSACTION-INVALID.
02870
02880    TRANSACTION-VALID.
02890        IF CUSTOMER-NUMBER-M NOT = CUSTOMER-NUMBER-SAVE
02900            PERFORM INVOICE-TOTAL-BREAK.
02910        MULTIPLY QUANTITY-T BY UNIT-PRICE-T
02920            GIVING MERCHANDISE-AMOUNT-W.
02930        MULTIPLY MERCHANDISE-AMOUNT-W BY TAX-RATE
02940            GIVING TAX-AMOUNT-W ROUNDED.
02950        ADD MERCHANDISE-AMOUNT-W,
02960            TAX-AMOUNT-W,
02970            HANDLING-T GIVING LINE-ITEM-TOTAL-W.
02980        PERFORM PRODUCE-INVOICE-LINE.
02990
03000    TRANSACTION-INVALID.
03010        IF NOT CODE-T-VALID
03020            PERFORM PRODUCE-INVALID-TRANS-CODE.
03030        IF CUSTOMER-NUMBER-T IS NOT EQUAL TO CUSTOMER-NUMBER-W
03040            PERFORM PRODUCE-INVALID-CUST-NUMB.
03050
```

(continued)

The Procedure Division follows the hierarchy diagram exactly. The paragraph PROCESS-A-MASTER-RECORD, line 02720, saves each customer's number, name, and address in working storage. The name and address are used for printing on the invoice, and the customer number is used to determine whether there are any valid transactions for this customer.

The statement at line 02680 shows the use of the INTO option in a RETURN statement. You saw the INTO option used with a READ statement in Chapter 6. RETURN . . . INTO acts like a combined RETURN and MOVE. The RETURN . . . INTO statement at line 02680 works just like the following two statements:

```
RETURN SORT-MERGE-WORK-FILE
MOVE TRANSACTION-WORK-RECORD TO CUSTOMER-MASTER-WORK-RECORD
```

After the RETURN . . . INTO executes, the RETURNed record is available both in the level-01 area associated with the file — in this case TRANSACTION-WORK-RECORD, and the working-storage area that the record was MOVEd INTO — in this case CUSTOMER-MASTER-WORK-RECORD.

In PROCESS-A-TRANSACTION-RECORD, line 02800, the program determines whether each transaction is valid or invalid. For a transaction to be valid it must have a 6 in position 1 and its Customer Number must match a Customer Number from the name and address file.

Program P11-04 was run with the customer name-and-address master file shown in Figure 11.17 and the transactions shown in Figure 11.18. It produced the invoices shown in Figure 11.19 and the error report shown in Figure 11.20.

Figure 11.16   (continued)

```
03060    PRODUCE-INVOICE-LINE.
03070        IF INVOICE-LINE-COUNTER IS LESS THAN 2 OR
03080            GREATER THAN LINE-LIMIT
03090            WRITE INVOICE-RECORD-OUT FROM INVOICE-REPORT-HEAD-1
03100                                     AFTER PAGE
03110            WRITE INVOICE-RECORD-OUT FROM INVOICE-REPORT-HEAD-2
03120            WRITE INVOICE-RECORD-OUT FROM INVOICE-REPORT-HEAD-3
03130            WRITE INVOICE-RECORD-OUT FROM INVOICE-REPORT-HEAD-4
03140            WRITE INVOICE-RECORD-OUT FROM INVOICE-REPORT-HEAD-5
03150            PERFORM WRITE-CUSTMER-NAME-AND-ADDRESS
03160                VARYING CODE-M FROM 1 BY 1 UNTIL CODE-M > 5
03170            WRITE INVOICE-RECORD-OUT FROM INVOICE-COLUMN-HEAD-1
03180                                     AFTER 3
03190            WRITE INVOICE-RECORD-OUT FROM INVOICE-COLUMN-HEAD-2
03200            MOVE 14 TO INVOICE-LINE-COUNTER
03210            MOVE 2 TO LINE-SPACING.
03220        MOVE PART-NUMBER-T        TO PART-NUMBER-OUT.
03230        MOVE DESCRIPTION-T        TO DESCRIPTION-OUT.
03240        MOVE QUANTITY-T           TO QUANTITY-OUT.
03250        MOVE UNIT-PRICE-T         TO UNIT-PRICE-OUT.
03260        MOVE MERCHANDISE-AMOUNT-W TO MERCHANDISE-AMOUNT-OUT.
03270        MOVE TAX-AMOUNT-W         TO TAX-OUT.
03280        MOVE HANDLING-T           TO HANDLING-OUT.
03290        MOVE LINE-ITEM-TOTAL-W    TO LINE-ITEM-TOTAL-OUT.
03300        ADD LINE-ITEM-TOTAL-W TO INVOICE-TOTAL-W.
03310        WRITE INVOICE-RECORD-OUT FROM LINE-ITEM AFTER LINE-SPACING.
03320        ADD LINE-SPACING          TO INVOICE-LINE-COUNTER.
03330        MOVE 1                    TO LINE-SPACING.
03340
03350    PRODUCE-INVALID-TRANS-CODE.
03360        MOVE "INVALID TRANSACTION CODE" TO ERROR-MESSAGE-E.
03370        PERFORM PRODUCE-ERROR-LINE.
03380
03390    WRITE-CUSTMER-NAME-AND-ADDRESS.
03400        MOVE NAME-AND-ADDRESS (CODE-M) TO NAME-AND-ADDRESS-OUT.
03410        WRITE INVOICE-RECORD-OUT FROM NAME-AND-ADDRESS-LINE.
03420
03430    PRODUCE-ERROR-LINE.
03440        MOVE CODE-T-X             TO CODE-T-E.
03450        MOVE CUSTOMER-NUMBER-T TO CUSTOMER-NUMBER-E.
03460        MOVE TRANSACTION-WORK-RECORD
03470                                 TO TRANSACTION-WORK-RECORD-E
03480        WRITE ERROR-RECORD-OUT FROM ERROR-LINE.
03490
03500    PRODUCE-INVALID-CUST-NUMB.
03510        MOVE "INVALID CUSTOMER NUMBER" TO ERROR-MESSAGE-E.
03520        PERFORM PRODUCE-ERROR-LINE.
03530
03540    END-OF-THIS-SECTION.
03550        EXIT.
```

EXERCISE 5

Write a program to produce the gross pay computation report shown in Figure 11.E5. Have your program use two input files. One file is an employee master file, with records in the following format:

Positions	Field
1	Code
2 – 4	Department Number
5 – 9	Employee Number
10 – 12	Monday Hours (to one decimal place)
13 – 15	Tuesday Hours (to one decimal place)
16 – 18	Wednesday Hours (to one decimal place)
19 – 21	Thursday Hours (to one decimal place)
22 – 24	Friday Hours (to one decimal place)
25 – 27	Saturday Hours (to one decimal place)
28 – 80	spaces

Have your program SORT the transactions in order by Employee Number within Department Number. Make sure your master file is in that order. Then have your program MERGE the two files and compute the gross pay for each employee who worked that week by multiplying the total hours worked during the week by the employee's Hourly Rate of Pay.

Produce a separate error report showing each transaction that has no matching master record.

Figure 11.E5 Output format for Exercise 5.

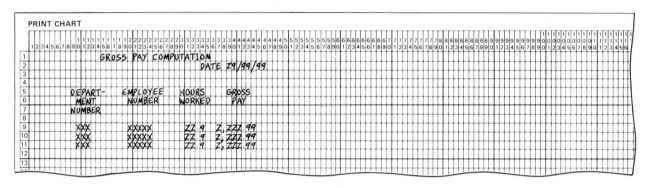

Figure 11.17 Customer name-and-address master file input to Program P11-04.

```
           1         2         3         4         5         6         7         8
  12345678901234567890123456789012345678901234567890123456789012345678901234567890
  -----------------------------------------------------------------------------
  100112JERRY PARKS
  200112106 WEST 10TH ST.
  300112BROOKLYN NY 11221
  100189ROBERT S. BAUXBAUM
  200189BOND EXTERMINATORS
  300189458 LITTLE NECK PKWY
  400189NORTHERN BLVD.
  500189LITTLE NECK NY 11261
  100217W & W HOUSEWARES INC
  200217127-91 ELLIOT AV.
  300217FLUSHING NY 11423
  100513FILONE NICHOLAS
  20051364-21 SMITH ST.
  300513FOREST DRIVE NY
  100561PARKER BROS. INC.
  20056146 BEACH PKWY BLVD.
  300561SPRINGFIELD GARDENS
  400561NEWPORT NJ 11468
  100579JUAN ALVAREZ
  200579SUNNYSIDE SUPPLIES
  3005791375 EARLE COPIAG ST
  400579FRESH MEADOW PARK
  500579QUEENS VILLAGE NY
```

Figure 11.18 Transaction input to Program P11-04.

```
-----------------------------------------------------------------------------------
         1         2         3         4         5         6         7         8
1234567890123456789012345678901234567890123456789012345678901234567890123456789 0
-----------------------------------------------------------------------------------
600579234110HAND SAWS           0640034590131
900513096310LIGHT BULB          0090001490014
600561100241CIRCULAR SAW        0010129160967
600579712346LEVEL               0290015790102
600561146312LAWNMOWER           0050106310512
600579641139RUBBER WASHERS      2160000120089
600112241321HAMMER              0020029190106
600579413821MEASURING TAPE      1090003990084
600561846329WORK BENCH          0090094670413
601421246317SANDER              0010094890431
600561004267LATHE               0010219631315
600579817390TEN FOOT LADDER     0080064990812
600561091426BAND SAW            0010640901519
600579041210PAINT               0710021160143
600195631789CLAMPS              0030016990431
600579114316PAINT BRUSH         1350011990091
600579121613SCREWDRIVER         0870009470110
```

Figure 11.19 Invoices produced by Program P11-04.

```
              NORTHWESTERN HARD-PRESSED HARDWARE CO.
                      10717 EAST ST., SW
                      SEATTLE, WA  98112
                                                          DATE   4/07/88
SOLD TO
   JERRY PARKS
   106 WEST 10TH ST.
   BROOKLYN NY 11221

   PART      DESCRIPTION      QTY.     UNIT      MERCHANDISE    TAX     HANDLING      TOTAL
   NUMBER                              PRICE       AMOUNT

   241321    HAMMER            2       29.19       58.38       4.96      1.06         64.40

                                                 PAY THIS AMOUNT                      64.40
```

```
              NORTHWESTERN HARD-PRESSED HARDWARE CO.
                      10717 EAST ST., SW
                      SEATTLE, WA  98112
                                                          DATE   4/07/88
SOLD TO
   PARKER BROS. INC.
   46 BEACH PKWY BLVD.
   SPRINGFIELD GARDENS
   NEWPORT NJ 11468

   PART      DESCRIPTION      QTY.     UNIT      MERCHANDISE    TAX     HANDLING      TOTAL
   NUMBER                              PRICE       AMOUNT

   004267    LATHE             1      219.63      219.63      18.67     13.15        251.45
   091426    BAND SAW          1      640.90      640.90      54.48     15.19        710.57
   100241    CIRCULAR SAW      1      129.16      129.16      10.98      9.67        149.81
   146312    LAWNMOWER         5      106.31      531.55      45.18      5.12        581.85
   846329    WORK BENCH        9       94.67      852.03      72.42      4.13        928.58

                                                 PAY THIS AMOUNT                   2,622.26
```

```
                    NORTHWESTERN HARD-PRESSED HARDWARE CO.
                              10717 EAST ST., SW
                              SEATTLE, WA  98112
                                                              DATE  4/07/88

    SOLD TO
       JUAN ALVAREZ
       SUNNYSIDE SUPPLIES
       1375 EARLE COPIAG ST
       FRESH MEADOW PARK
       QUEENS VILLAGE NY


    PART      DESCRIPTION        QTY.    UNIT     MERCHANDISE    TAX    HANDLING      TOTAL
    NUMBER                               PRICE      AMOUNT

    041210   PAINT                71     21.16     1,502.36    127.70     1.43      1,631.49
    114316   PAINT BRUSH         135     11.99     1,618.65    137.59      .91      1,757.15
    121613   SCREWDRIVER          87      9.47       823.89     70.03     1.10        895.02
    234110   HAND SAWS            64     34.59     2,213.76    188.17     1.31      2,403.24
    413821   MEASURING TAPE      109      3.99       434.91     36.97      .84        472.72
    641139   RUBBER WASHERS      216       .12        25.92      2.20      .89         29.01
    712346   LEVEL                29     15.79       457.91     38.92     1.02        497.85
    817390   TEN FOOT LADDER       8     64.99       519.92     44.19     8.12        572.23


                                              PAY THIS AMOUNT             8,258.71
```

Figure 11.20 Error report produced by Program P11-04.

```
INVOICE PROGRAM ERROR REPORT                                      DATE  4/07/88


TRANS CUSTOMER INPUT RECORD                                       ERROR
CODE  NUMBER   ....+....1....+....2....+....3....+....4....+....5....+....6....+....7....+....8 MESSAGE

   6   00195   600195631789CLAMPS           0030016990431        INVALID CUSTOMER NUMBER
   9   00513   900513096310LIGHT BULB        0090001490014        INVALID TRANSACTION CODE
   6   01421   601421246317SANDER           0010094890431        INVALID CUSTOMER NUMBER
```

COLLATING SEQUENCE and Alphabet Name

Every computer has its own sequence for ordering characters, from the lowest character to the highest. That is, whenever a computer compares two unequal characters, one of the characters must be the lower and one must be the higher. This holds true whether the two characters being compared are both numbers, both letters, or one a number and one a letter, or even if special characters like $, %, the comma, and the decimal point are being compared. The order of the characters from lowest to highest is called the COLLATING SEQUENCE.

On the computer used to run the programs in this book, the COLLATING SEQUENCE is:

Blank
Special characters
Lowercase letters a through z
Uppercase letters A through Z
Digits 0 through 9

The ASCII (American National Standard Code for Information Interchange) COLLATING SEQUENCE is:

Blank
Some special characters
Digits 0 through 9
A few more special characters
Uppercase letters A through Z
A few more special characters
Lowercase letters a through z
A few more special characters

Sometimes a programmer would like to use a COLLATING SEQUENCE different from the one that is **NATIVE** to the computer that the program is being run on. For example, if I wanted to use the SORT verb to help prepare the index for this book I would want lowercase "a" and uppercase "A" both to fall before lowercase "b" and uppercase "B." Furthermore, I would want "a" and "A" both to have the same position in the COLLATING SEQUENCE. That is, I would not want "a" to be considered lower or higher than "A."

A COLLATING SEQUENCE other than the NATIVE one may be defined by including an **alphabet-name clause** in the SPECIAL-NAMES paragraph of the Environment Division. The format of the alphabet-name clause is:

```
[, alphabet-name IS
    ⎧ STANDARD-1                                              ⎫
    ⎪ NATIVE                                                  ⎪
    ⎪ implementor-name                                        ⎪
    ⎪            ⎡ ⎧THROUGH⎫ literal-2            ⎤            ⎪
    ⎨ literal-1  ⎢ ⎩THRU   ⎭                      ⎥           ⎬ ]...
    ⎪            ⎢ ALSO literal-3                 ⎥            ⎪
    ⎪            ⎣      [, ALSO literal-4] ...    ⎦            ⎪
    ⎪                      ⎡ ⎧THROUGH⎫ literal-6          ⎤   ⎪
    ⎪            [literal-5 ⎢ ⎩THRU   ⎭                    ⎥ ]...⎪
    ⎩                      ⎢ ALSO literal-7                ⎥   ⎭
                          ⎣      [, ALSO literal-8] ...   ⎦
```

If **STANDARD-1** is specified, the ASCII COLLATING SEQUENCE is used. In some COBOL systems, implementor names define COLLATING SEQUENCEs used in those systems other than the NATIVE sequence. In the system used in this book, there are no implementor names associated with the alphabet-name clause.

Literals used in the alphabet-name clause may be nonnumeric or numeric. If nonnumeric, the literals specify the desired COLLATING SEQUENCE of the characters. If numeric, the literals specify the desired COLLATING SEQUENCE of the characters that occupy the ordinal positions of the literals in the computer's NATIVE character set. For example, in the COLLATING SEQUENCE that is NATIVE to this computer the character blank is in ordinal position 65 and the character zero is in ordinal position 241. A numeric literal in an alphabet-name clause cannot be larger than the number of characters in the computer's character set, in this computer 256.

To use the SORT verb to help prepare the index for this book we could use an alphabet-name clause such as the following, with the made-up alphabet name INDEX-SEQUENCE and the reserved word **ALSO**:

```
INDEX-SEQUENCE IS
  "a" ALSO "A"
  "b" ALSO "B"
  "c" ALSO 196
  "d" ALSO 197
  "e" ALSO "E"
  "f" ALSO "F"
  "g" ALSO "G"
  "h" ALSO "H"
  "i" ALSO 202
  "j" ALSO 210
  "k" ALSO 211
  "l" ALSO "L"
  "m" ALSO "M"
  "n" ALSO "N"
  "o" ALSO "O"
  "p" ALSO "P"
  "q" ALSO "Q"
  "r" ALSO "R"
  "s" ALSO "S"
  "t" ALSO "T"
  "u" ALSO "U"
  "v" ALSO "V"
  "w" ALSO "W"
  "x" ALSO "X"
  "y" ALSO "Y"
  "z" ALSO "Z"
```

Characters not specified in the alphabet-name clause are placed at the end of the COLLATING SEQUENCE, in their NATIVE order.

You may define as many COLLATING SEQUENCEs as you like in a COBOL program, each with a different alphabet name. Then in any SORT or MERGE statement in the program, you may indicate which COLLATING SEQUENCE is to be used by including the COLLATING SEQUENCE IS clause in the SORT or MERGE statement.

Summary

The SORT/MERGE feature of COBOL permits programs to rearrange the order of records and to combine two or more files in order.

Records may be SORTed directly from an input file, or else an INPUT PROCEDURE may be carried out before the records are SORTed. After the records are SORTed they may be placed directly onto an output file, or else an OUTPUT PROCEDURE may be carried out on the records in their new sequence.

Records may be MERGEd from two or more files in order on one or more specified KEY fields. The input files must be in the same order as the final MERGEd result. An OUTPUT PROCEDURE may be used, but no INPUT PROCEDURE.

An SD entry must be used to describe the file that the SORT and/or MERGE is to use for a work area. INPUT and OUTPUT PROCEDUREs must be defined as SECTIONs in the Procedure Division, and the last executable instruction in an INPUT or OUTPUT PROCEDURE must be the last physical instruction in the PROCEDURE. The GO TO statement can be used to skip to the last paragraph of the PROCEDURE, which should consist of only the verb EXIT.

The RELEASE verb can be used only in an INPUT PROCEDURE. It is executed after all the necessary input processing has been carried out on an input record and the record is ready for SORTing. The RETURN verb is used in an OUTPUT PROCEDURE to fetch SORTed and MERGEd records for processing.

An alphabet-name may be defined in the SPECIAL-NAMES paragraph to establish a COLLATING SEQUENCE different from the NATIVE one. The COLLATING SEQUENCE phrase may be used in a SORT or MERGE statement to indicate that the sequence defined in the alphabet-name clause is to be used for ordering the records.

Fill-in Exercises

1. The work file for a SORT or MERGE statement must be defined in a(n) _____ entry.

2. One or more _____ _____ or _____ _____ phrases must be used in each SORT or MERGE statement to indicate which field(s) is (are) to be used for ordering the records.

3. The _____ phrase may be used to name the file or files that contain the records to be used as input to a SORT or MERGE.

4. The _____ phrase may be used to name the file where the output records from a SORT or MERGE are to be placed.

5. If records are to be SORTed or MERGEd before being processed, the programmer must specify a(n) _____ PROCEDURE.

6. If records are to be processed before being SORTed, the programmer must specify a(n) _____ PROCEDURE.

7. In a SORT or MERGE statement, the KEY fields must be listed in order from _____ to _____ .

8. INPUT PROCEDUREs and OUTPUT PROCEDUREs must be defined as _____ in the Procedure Division.

9. The _____ statement may be used to transfer control to the end of an INPUT or OUTPUT PROCEDURE.

10. The last paragraph in an INPUT or OUTPUT PROCEDURE contains only a(n) _____ statement.

11. The _____ clause may be used to define a COLLATING SEQUENCE other than the NATIVE one.

12. The RETURN verb may be used only in a(n) _____ PROCEDURE.

13. The RELEASE verb may be used only in a(n) _____ PROCEDURE.

14. The use of STANDARD-1 in an alphabet-name clause causes the _____ COLLATING SEQUENCE to be used.

15. You need not define the fields of a record if you do not _____ the file that the record is associated with.

16. The last executable statement in an INPUT or OUTPUT PROCEDURE must be the last _____ statement in the section.

Review Exercises

1. Write a program to SORT the input data you used in Review Exercise 1, Chapter 8, page 244, into alphabetic order on Part Description. Use GIVING in the SORT statement, and ASSIGN a printer as the GIVING file.

2. Write a program to read the same input data you used in Review Exercise 1 above. Have your program SORT the input data into alphabetical order on Part Description and produce a report in the format shown in Figure 11.RE2. Use an OUTPUT PROCEDURE to produce the report.

Figure 11.RE2 Output format for Review Exercise 2.

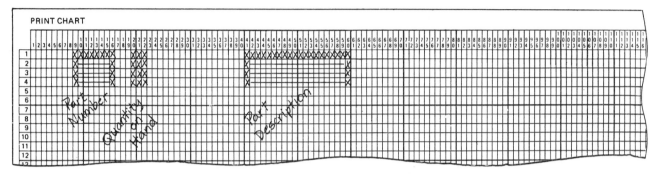

3. Write a program to read input records in the following format:

Positions	Field
1 – 5	Employee Number
6	Code
7 – 9	Hours Worked (to one decimal place)
10 – 80	spaces

Each record contains an Employee Number, a Code indicating whether the employee is eligible for overtime pay or is exempt from overtime pay, and the Hours Worked. The Code field contains an E if the employee is exempt from overtime pay and an N if the employee is eligible for overtime pay (nonexempt).

Use an INPUT PROCEDURE to select for SORTing only those employees who are eligible for overtime pay and who worked more than 40 hours. Have your program SORT the selected records into order on Employee Number and produce a list of the SORTed records showing each Employee Number and the Hours Worked.

4. Write the ASCENDING KEY and DESCENDING KEY phrases that would be needed to SORT the records in the employee master file in Exercise 5, page 360, into ascending order on Department Number. Within each Department Number, employees with the highest Hourly Rate of Pay should fall together first, followed by employees with the second-highest hourly rate, down to employees with the lowest hourly rate. If, within a department, there is more than one employee with the same hourly rate, they should fall together SORTed on Employee Number.

5. Write an alphabet-name clause to establish the following COLLATING SEQUENCE: the digits 0 through 9, the uppercase letters A through R, the character /, and the uppercase letters S through Z. This is part of the COLLATING SEQUENCE of the Hollerith card code and the **BCD** code (**binary-coded decimal** code). There are no lowercase letters in the Hollerith or BCD codes.

Project

Write a program to read records in the following format:

Positions	Field
1 – 6	Course Code
7 – 15	Student Number
16 – 18	Exam Grade 1
19 – 21	Exam Grade 2
22 – 24	Exam Grade 3
25 – 27	Exam Grade 4
28 – 80	spaces

Each record contains a Course Code, a Student Number, and the grades that the student got on each of four exams. The program is to READ the data and select for SORTing those records where the average grade on the four exams is less than 75. The selected records are to be SORTed in ascending order on Student Number within descending order on average grade within ascending order on Course Code.

Have your program print a report from the SORTed records in the format shown in Figure 11.P1. Group indicate the Course Code. Double-space between courses, single-space within courses.

Figure 11.P1   Output format for Chapter 11 Project.

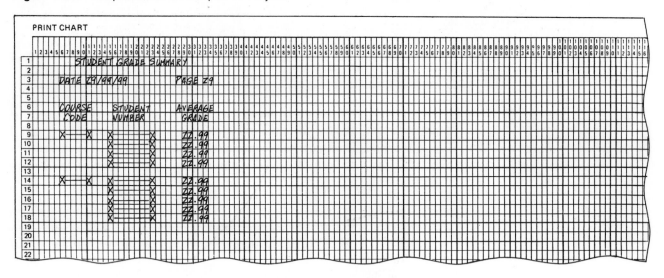

Magnetic File Media

Here are the key points you should learn from this chapter:

1. The nature of files stored on magnetic media
2. Types of master files and their uses
3. How to create a sequential file
4. How to delete records from a sequential file

Key words to recognize and learn:

magnetic file media	direct-access storage device
magnetic tape	DASD
magnetic disk	mass storage device
magnetic drum	block
data cell	physical record
mass storage system	logical record
tape deck	update
tape transport	record key
tape drive	file activity
read-write head	file volatility
sequential	LABEL RECORDS ARE STANDARD
access	BLOCK CONTAINS
direct-access	balance line algorithm
random access	

Up to this point all of our programs have written their output files onto paper, producing what is usually called a list, a listing, or a report. Your input files may have been entered on a keyboard or punched in cards. There are other kinds of materials, though, that computers can read input data from and write output onto. In this chapter we will discuss one such material, **magnetic file media.** There are a number of forms of magnetic media commonly processed by COBOL programs, such as **magnetic tape, magnetic disk, magnetic drum, data cell,** and **mass storage system.**

Magnetic computer tape is very much like regular recording tape, except that computer tape is wider, thicker, and stronger. It is available on reels or cassettes just as recording tape is, and just as music can be stored on recording tape as magnetic patterns, computer tape can store characters as a series of magnetic impulses. The characters are stored one after another along the length of the tape, forming fields and records. Fields and records on tape can be thousands of characters long.

A computer installation that uses magnetic tape files will usually have one or more **tape decks** attached to the computer. The tape deck, or **tape transport** or **tape drive** as it is sometimes called, works just like a tape deck for recording tape. It moves the tape from one reel to the other and back, so that the computer can read data from the tape and write data onto it. Computer tapes can be removed from the transport when not in use and stored in a cabinet or on a rack.

A magnetic disk looks like a large phonograph record coated on both sides with a thin layer of magnetizable material. Characters, fields, and records can be stored one after another in circular tracks on both sides of the disk. Data can be written onto and read from the disk by a device called a **read-write head.** The read-write head can be directed by the computer to any location on the disk surface to read any particular desired record or to write a record into any particular location.

You can now see the fundamental difference between files on tape and files on disk. Tape is a **sequential** medium; records on tape can be **accessed** only sequentially, which means that they can be read and written on tape only one after another, in order. Disk is a **direct-access** medium, which means that the computer can go to any location on the disk directly for reading or writing. So a file on disk can enjoy **random access.** A file on disk can also be accessed sequentially, just as a phonograph record can be played through from beginning to end.

All other magnetic media, aside from magnetic tape, can be thought of as operating the same way that disk does. Even though the actual principles of operation may be quite different, for our purposes we need differentiate only between magnetic tape and magnetic disk. Disk and all the other media that work the same way are called **direct-access storage devices (DASD).**[1]

On both sequential and direct-access media, records are often grouped into larger units called **blocks.** Blocks have no logical meaning for a program; our tape and disk programs will still READ and WRITE one record at a time. The programmer has no responsibility regarding blocks except to decide how many records should be grouped into each one. Grouping a large number of records into a block saves storage space on tape or disk and increases the amount of primary storage space needed to run the program. Having large blocks in a sequential file usually reduces execution time of the program; having large blocks in a random-access file usually increases it A block is sometimes called a **physical record.** What we have been calling a record is sometimes called a **logical record.** At this point in your study of COBOL it is best to have your instructor decide how many records you should have in your blocks.

Advantages of Magnetic Media

Keyed input files and printed output are good for computers to use to receive data from the outside world and to communicate results back. They are easy for people to handle, and their contents can be read fairly easily. They have their role in data processing.

The big advantage of magnetic media is that the computer can write data onto them and then, at a later time, read the same data in again; the later time may be seconds later, weeks later, or, due to the extremely stable nature of magnetic media, years later. Other advantages of magnetic media over paper ones are:

1. Magnetic media are reusable; obsolete data can be erased and new data written in their place.
2. Computers can read and write magnetic media much faster than paper media.
3. Huge volumes of data can be stored more compactly on magnetic media than on paper.

[1]COBOL literature refers to direct-access storage devices as **mass storage devices.** We prefer the term "direct-access storage device" to avoid confusion with IBM's Model 3850 Mass Storage System.

Uses of Magnetic Media

The characteristics of magnetic media just given make them ideally suited for storing master files of data. In Chapter 11 we had a customer name-and-address master file. In the file we had up to five records for each customer, each record containing one line of the customer's name and address. If the file were to be stored on tape or disk, the records could be made as big as we like, and all five lines of name and address data for a single customer could fit into one record. When a master file is stored on magnetic media, changes to the file cannot be made by hand, but instead by a computer program. Such a program is called an **update** program.

A master file quite different from our name-and-address master might be found in a sales application. The file could be a catalog master file with one record for every part number. Each record would contain a part number, a description of the part, a price, a shipping weight, and perhaps other data. In this application the entire file would be used for reference and would be changed only when a new catalog was issued, perhaps every 6 months. Then the old master file could be thrown out (erased would be better) and a complete new catalog master created.

A catalog master could be used daily by a program that prints invoices. The program would read the day's orders and look in the master file to see that the part numbers in the orders were valid. Then it would get the description of the part for printing on the invoice and the price for computing the merchandise amount.

EXERCISE 1

Think of another application of a master file. Tell the following about the file:

a. What does each record on the file represent? That is, is there one record for each customer or one record for each part number or one record for each what?

b. What are some of the fields that would be in the record?

c. Under what circumstances would each of the fields in the master file have to be changed?

d. In what ways would the file be used?

A Master File

In this and the next three chapters we will be discussing master files and how to handle them. Many of the programming examples deal with the same master file, a bank savings-account master. There is one record on the file for each savings account in the bank. Each record contains a unique account number. The account number is used to order and locate records in the file, and is the **record key.** Each record also contains the depositor's name, the date of the last transaction to the account (either the date the account was opened or the date of the last deposit or withdrawal), and the current balance. When a new account is opened it must be accompanied by an initial deposit; when an account is closed, the former balance is assumed to be the final withdrawal.

You will see how to create and maintain the savings-account master file first as a sequential file on tape or disk and then as a random-access file on disk. In industry practice, several criteria may be used to decide whether a file should be sequential or random-access.

1. The use to which the file will be put. A master file is maintained in an up-to-date condition so that the information on it can be used for some data processing purpose. The uses made of a file, aside from updating it, are often

the most important considerations in determining whether the file will be sequential or random-access.

2. **File activity.** Activity refers to the average number of master records changed in an update run. For example, if on the average 15 percent of the records in a master file are changed in an update run, the file activity would be said to be 15 percent. Files with high activity tend to be stored as sequential files; those with low activity, as random-access files.

3. **File volatility.** Volatility refers to the number of additions and deletions from a file. Files with high volatility tend to be stored as sequential files, those with low volatility as random-access files.

4. File size. File size can sometimes be a determining factor. Sequential files can often be of any size. If necessary, sequential files may extend over several reels of tape or over several disks. When the file is used, only one reel or disk need be mounted at any one time. Since the file is processed sequentially, when a reel or disk is read completely it can be removed and the next one mounted. With random-access files, the entire file must be mounted during a processing run since any portion of the file may be needed at any time during the run. Random-access files are thus limited in size by the available equipment.

Validity of Data on a Master File

It is very important to ensure that data on a master file are valid. Erroneous data on a master file can cause much more trouble than erroneous input to a program that merely produces a report. There are three general kinds of difficulty that can be caused by invalid data on a master file, each one worse than the previous.

Master Records Out of Sequence

As you will see, much of the program logic dealing with master file updating requires that the records be in sequence on the record key and that there be no duplicate keys. In our master file it means that the records must be in order on account number and that there not be two records with the same account number. A duplicate or out-of-sequence condition in a master file will ruin the execution of any update program that uses the file as input. The master file would have to be recreated correctly and the update program tried again.

Invalid Numeric Field

If a numeric field on a master file somehow gets to contain something other than numbers, the field may cause abnormal termination of any program that tries to use it in arithmetic, numeric editing, or numeric comparison. Since the field might not be used until months or years after it is put on the master file, it sits there like a time bomb waiting to cause an abnormal termination when one is least expected.

Erroneous Data

Worst of all is a field whose contents are simply wrong. It doesn't do anything dramatic, such as cause a program to terminate suddenly. It just comes out wrong week after week, month after month, and maybe no one notices the error until it is too late.

Creating a Sequential Master File

Program P12-01 shows one way to create a savings-account master file on magnetic tape or disk. The input to Program P12-01 is a batch of new accounts to create the file. The new account data are in the following format:

Positions	Field
1	Code 1
2–6	Account Number
7–26	Depositor Name
27–32	Date of Transaction
33–40	Amount (to two decimal places)
41–80	spaces

The 1 in position 1 of the input record is a Code that identifies this as a new account. The Amount field is the initial deposit, which becomes the account's current balance on the master file. To create this master file, the input records must be in order on the key field, which in this application is the Account Number. Program P12-01 SORTs the input into order on Account Number and then, in the OUTPUT PROCEDURE of the SORT, checks the input for validity, creates a master file out of the good input records, and produces two reports. One report lists the good records, which were placed on the master file, and the other shows the erroneous transactions. The two report formats are shown in Figures 12.1 and 12.2.

Figure 12.1 Output format for good records for Program P12-01.

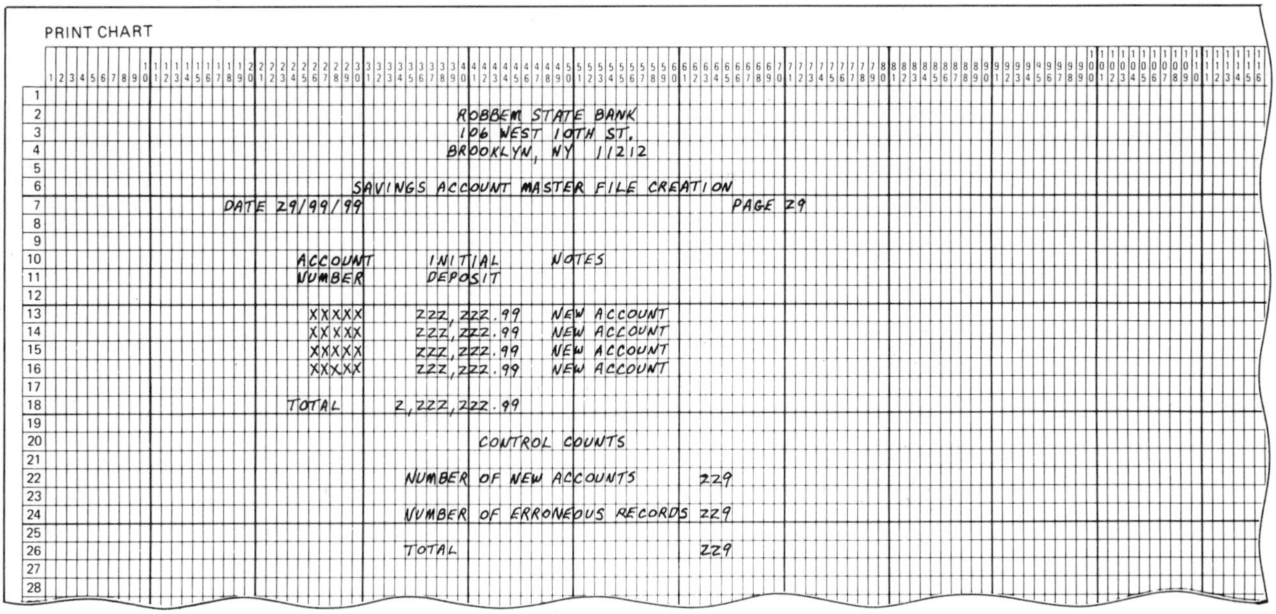

Figure 12.2 Output format for error report for Program P12-01.

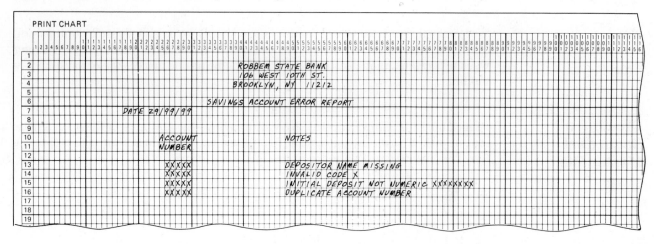

A Hierarchy Diagram for Creating a Master File

The hierarchy diagram for Program P12-01 is shown in Figure 12.3. The OUTPUT PROCEDURE consists of the box "Produce master file" and its subfunctions. The box "Process a record" is entered with each input record. Each record is checked to see that all its fields are valid. For each field found invalid, the program prints an error message onto the error report. If an input record is found to be error-free, the program writes it onto the output master file and prints a NEW ACCOUNT line, as shown in Figure 12.1.

Figure 12.3 Hierarchy diagram for Program P12-01.

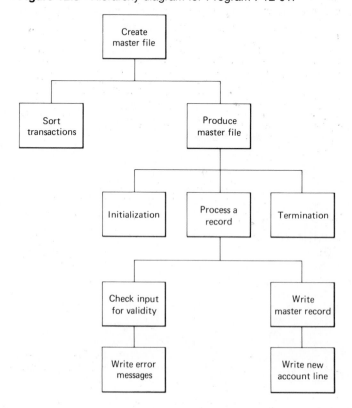

A Program to Create a Sequential Master File

Program P12-01 is shown in Figure 12.4. In the File Section you can find the FD entry for the master file that is to be created on tape or disk, at line 00470. We have the clause **LABEL RECORDS ARE STANDARD.** Label records are special records written onto tape and disk files by the COBOL system and used by the system to identify the file. You should always use STANDARD labels on all your tape and disk files unless there is some compelling reason to do otherwise.

In the **BLOCK CONTAINS** clause we have indicated that the system should process 100 records as a single block. We need do nothing else regarding BLOCKs.

Figure 12.4 Program P12-01.

```
CB1 RELEASE 2.4                           IBM OS/VS COBOL  JULY  1, 1982


                       18.56.08        APR  7,1988


00010  IDENTIFICATION DIVISION.
00020  PROGRAM-ID. P12-01.
00030 * AUTHOR. SHAMEZE SULTAN
00040 *         REVISED BY GAETANO MURATORE
00050 *
00060 *     THIS PROGRAM CREATES A SEQUENTIAL MASTER FILE.
00070 *
00080 ****************************************************************
00090
00100  ENVIRONMENT DIVISION.
00110  CONFIGURATION SECTION.
00120  SOURCE-COMPUTER. IBM-370.
00130  OBJECT-COMPUTER. IBM-370.
00140
00150  INPUT-OUTPUT SECTION.
00160  FILE-CONTROL.
00170      SELECT SAVINGS-ACCOUNT-DATA-FILE-IN      ASSIGN TO INFILE.
00180      SELECT SORT-WORK-FILE                    ASSIGN TO SORTWK.
00190      SELECT SAVINGS-ACCOUNT-MASTER-FLE-OUT    ASSIGN TO MASTER.
00200      SELECT TRANSACTION-REGISTER-FILE-OUT     ASSIGN TO PRINTER1.
00210      SELECT ERROR-FILE-OUT                    ASSIGN TO PRINTER2.
00220
00230  ****************************************************************
00240
00250  DATA DIVISION.
00260  FILE SECTION.
00270  FD  SAVINGS-ACCOUNT-DATA-FILE-IN
00280      LABEL RECORDS ARE OMITTED
00290      RECORD CONTAINS 80 CHARACTERS.
00300
00310  01  SAVINGS-ACCOUNT-DATA-RECORD-IN          PIC X(80).
00320
00330  SD  SORT-WORK-FILE
00340      RECORD CONTAINS 80 CHARACTERS.
00350
00360  01  SORT-WORK-RECORD.
00370      05  CODE-IN                      PIC X.
00380          88  VALID-CODE               VALUE "1".
00390      05  ACCOUNT-NUMBER-IN            PIC X(5).
00400      05  DEPOSITOR-NAME-IN            PIC X(20).
00410          88  DEPOSITOR-NAME-MISSING   VALUE SPACES.
00420      05  DATE-OF-LAST-TRANSACTION-IN  PIC 9(6).
00430      05  AMOUNT-IN                    PIC 9(6)V99.
00440      05  AMOUNT-IN-X REDEFINES AMOUNT-IN  PIC X(8).
00450      05  FILLER                       PIC X(40).
00460
00470  FD  SAVINGS-ACCOUNT-MASTER-FLE-OUT
00480      LABEL RECORDS ARE STANDARD
00490      RECORD CONTAINS 80 CHARACTERS
00500      BLOCK CONTAINS 100 RECORDS.
00510
```

(continued)

Figure 12.4   (continued)

```
00520   01   SAVINGS-ACCOUNT-MASTER-REC-OUT        PIC X(80).
00530
00540   FD   TRANSACTION-REGISTER-FILE-OUT
00550        LABEL RECORDS ARE OMITTED.
00560
00570   01   TRANSACTION-REGISTER-RECORD          PIC X(72).
00580
00590   FD   ERROR-FILE-OUT
00600        LABEL RECORDS ARE OMITTED.
00610
00620   01   ERROR-RECORD-OUT                     PIC X(84).
00630
00640   WORKING-STORAGE SECTION.
00650   01   MORE-INPUT                           PIC X VALUE "Y".
00660   01   ANY-ERRORS                           PIC X.
00670   01   NUMBER-OF-INPUT-RECORDS-W            PIC S9(3)    VALUE ZERO.
00680   01   NUMBER-OF-ERRONEOUS-RECORDS-W        PIC S9(3)    VALUE ZERO.
00690   01   NUMBER-OF-NEW-ACCOUNTS-W             PIC S9(3)    VALUE ZERO.
00700   01   ACCOUNT-NUMBER-SAVE       PIC X(5) VALUE HIGH-VALUES.
00710   01   TODAYS-DATE.
00720        05 TODAYS-YEAR                       PIC 99.
00730        05 TODAYS-MONTH-AND-DAY              PIC 9(4).
00740   01   AMOUNT-IN-COUNTER                    PIC 9(7)V99 VALUE 0.
00750   01   PAGE-NUMBER-W                        PIC S9 VALUE 0.
00760   01   ERROR-PAGE-NUMBER-W                  PIC S9 VALUE 0.
00770   01   BLANK-LINE                           PIC X   VALUE SPACE.
00780   01   LINE-LIMIT                           PIC S99 COMP SYNC VALUE 34.
00790   01   LINE-COUNT-ER                        PIC S99 COMP SYNC.
00800   01   ERROR-LINE-LIMIT                     PIC S99 COMP SYNC VALUE 54.
00810   01   ERROR-LINE-COUNTER                   PIC S99 COMP SYNC.
00820
00830   01   REPORT-HEADING-1.
00840        05 FILLER                            PIC X(39) VALUE SPACES.
00850        05 FILLER           PIC X(17) VALUE "ROBBEM STATE BANK".
00860
00870   01   REPORT-HEADING-2.
00880        05 FILLER                            PIC X(39) VALUE SPACES.
00890        05 FILLER           PIC X(17) VALUE "106 WEST 10TH ST.".
00900
00910   01   REPORT-HEADING-3.
00920        05 FILLER                            PIC X(38) VALUE SPACES.
00930        05 FILLER           PIC X(19) VALUE "BROOKLYN, NY  11212".
00940
00950   01   PAGE-HEADING-1.
00960        05 FILLER                            PIC X(29) VALUE SPACES.
00970        05 FILLER                            PIC X(36)
00980                     VALUE "SAVINGS ACCOUNT MASTER FILE CREATION".
00990
01000   01   ERROR-HEADING-1.
01010        05 FILLER                            PIC X(33) VALUE SPACES.
01020        05 FILLER                            PIC X(29)
01030                             VALUE "SAVINGS ACCOUNT ERROR REPORT".
01040
01050   01   PAGE-HEADING-2.
01060        05 FILLER                            PIC X(17) VALUE SPACES.
01070        05 FILLER                            PIC X(5) VALUE "DATE".
01080        05 TODAYS-MONTH-AND-DAY              PIC Z9/99/.
01090        05 TODAYS-YEAR                       PIC 99.
01100        05 FILLER                            PIC X(35) VALUE SPACES.
01110        05 FILLER                            PIC X(4)  VALUE "PAGE".
01120        05 PAGE-NUMBER-OUT                   PIC Z9.
01130
01140   01   PAGE-HEADING-3.
01150        05 FILLER                            PIC X(24) VALUE SPACES.
01160        05 FILLER                            PIC X(7)  VALUE "ACCOUNT".
01170        05 FILLER                            PIC X(5)  VALUE SPACES.
01180        05 FILLER                            PIC X(7)  VALUE "INITIAL".
01190        05 FILLER                            PIC X(5)  VALUE SPACES.
01200        05 FILLER                            PIC X(5)  VALUE "NOTES".
01210
01220   01   ERROR-PAGE-HEADING-3.
01230        05 FILLER                            PIC X(24) VALUE SPACES.
01240        05 FILLER                            PIC X(7)  VALUE "ACCOUNT".
01250        05 FILLER                            PIC X(17) VALUE SPACES.
01260        05 FILLER                            PIC X(5)  VALUE "NOTES".
01270
```

```
01280   01   PAGE-HEADING-4.
01290        05 FILLER                            PIC X(24) VALUE SPACES.
01300        05 FILLER                            PIC X(6)  VALUE "NUMBER".
01310        05 FILLER                            PIC X(6)  VALUE SPACES.
01320        05 FILLER                            PIC X(7) VALUE  "DEPOSIT".
01330
01340   01   ERROR-PAGE-HEADING-4.
01350        05 FILLER                            PIC X(24) VALUE SPACES.
01360        05 FILLER                            PIC X(6)  VALUE "NUMBER".
01370
01380   01   REPORT-LINE.
01390        05 ACCOUNT-NUMBER-OUT                PIC B(25)X(5).
01400        05 AMOUNT-OUT                        PIC B(5)ZZZ,ZZZ.99B(3).
01410        05 FILLER                      PIC X(11) VALUE "NEW ACCOUNT".
01420
01430   01   ERROR-LINE.
01440        05 ACCOUNT-NUMBER-E                  PIC B(25)X(5).
01450        05 LONG-MESSAGES.
01460           10 MSG                            PIC B(18)X(27).
01470           10 AMOUNT-E                       PIC BX(9).
01480        05 SHORT-MESSAGES REDEFINES LONG-MESSAGES.
01490           10 SHORT-MESSAGE                  PIC B(18)X(12).
01500           10 CODE-E                         PIC BXB(23).
01510
01520   01   TOTAL-LINE-1.
01530        05 FILLER                            PIC X(23) VALUE SPACES.
01540        05 FILLER                      PIC X(5)B(5) VALUE "TOTAL".
01550        05 AMOUNT-OUT-TOTAL                  PIC Z,ZZZ,ZZZ.99.
01560
01570   01   TOTAL-LINE-2.
01580        05 FILLER                            PIC X(41) VALUE SPACES.
01590        05 FILLER                      PIC X(14) VALUE "CONTROL COUNTS".
01600
01610   01   TOTAL-LINE-3.
01620        05 FILLER                            PIC X(34) VALUE SPACES.
01630        05 FILLER                            PIC X(22)
01640                          VALUE "NUMBER OF NEW ACCOUNTS".
01650        05 NUMBER-OF-NEW-ACCOUNTS            PIC B(6)ZZ9.
01660
01670   01   TOTAL-LINE-4.
01680        05 FILLER                            PIC X(34) VALUE SPACES.
01690        05 FILLER                            PIC X(27)
01700                          VALUE "NUMBER OF ERRONEOUS RECORDS".
01710        05 NUMBER-OF-ERRONEOUS-RECORDS       PIC BZZ9.
01720
01730   01   TOTAL-LINE-5.
01740        05 FILLER                            PIC X(34) VALUE SPACES.
01750        05 FILLER                            PIC X(5)  VALUE "TOTAL".
01760        05 NUMBER-OF-INPUT-RECORDS           PIC B(23)ZZ9.
01770
```

(continued)

In working storage we have three fields that are used for counting records: NUMBER-OF-INPUT-RECORDS-W, NUMBER-OF-ERRONEOUS-RECORDS-W, and NUMBER-OF-NEW-ACCOUNTS-W. We use the field NUMBER-OF-NEW-ACCOUNTS-W to count the number of good records as they are written onto the master file. We use NUMBER-OF-ERRONEOUS-RECORDS-W to count the number of input records that contain one or more errors and were not written onto the master. The sum of NUMBER-OF-NEW-ACCOUNTS-W and NUMBER-OF-ERRONEOUS-RECORDS-W should equal NUMBER-OF-INPUT-RECORDS-W.

Also we have a field called ACCOUNT-NUMBER-SAVE, at line 00700. This field is used to check that every input record contains a different Account Number. As mentioned earlier, it is of the greatest importance that records on a master file be in sequence on their key and that there be no duplicate keys. The SORT in Program P12-01 will assure that the input records are in nondescending order on Account Number, but the SORT does not check for duplicates. We will have to do that with coding in the Data Division and the Procedure Division.

The Data Division coding connected with checking for duplicate Account Numbers is in line 00700. There ACCOUNT-NUMBER-SAVE was given a

VALUE that could not be a legal Account Number in the COBOL system used to run the programs in this book, the figurative constant HIGH-VALUES. In your own COBOL system you would use an initial VALUE for ACCOUNT-NUMBER-SAVE that could not be a legal Account Number in that system. If there is no VALUE in your COBOL system that could not be a legal Account Number, the cleanest way to handle the matter is to define ACCOUNT-NUMBER-SAVE to be one character longer than the Account Number and initialize ACCOUNT-NUMBER-SAVE to any VALUE that is neither blanks nor zeros.

The Procedure Division, which starts at line 01840, follows the hierarchy diagram. Upon entering PROCESS-A-RECORD each time, we ADD 1 to the count of the number of input records. Later, as we find each record to be either free of errors or erroneous, we will ADD 1 to either the number of good records written onto the master or the count of the number of erroneous records.

In WRITE-MASTER-RECORD we MOVE the KEY field to ACCOUNT-NUMBER-SAVE, at line 02210. This is part of the processing to check for duplicate Account Numbers. The rest of that processing is in the paragraph CHECK-INPUT-FOR-VALIDITY, at line 02250. You can now see why we gave ACCOUNT-NUMBER-SAVE an initial VALUE of HIGH-VALUES—to cause the first input record to have an Account Number different from ACCOUNT-NUMBER-SAVE.

Figure 12.4   (continued)

```
01780   01  NO-INPUT-DATA.
01790       05  FILLER                                   PIC X(21) VALUE SPACES.
01800       05  FILLER           VALUE "NO INPUT DATA" PIC X(13).
01810
01820   ************************************************************************
01830
01840   PROCEDURE DIVISION.
01850   CONTROL-SECTION SECTION.
01860   CREATE-MASTER-FILE.
01870       SORT SORT-WORK-FILE
01880           ASCENDING KEY ACCOUNT-NUMBER-IN
01890           USING SAVINGS-ACCOUNT-DATA-FILE-IN
01900           OUTPUT PROCEDURE IS PRODUCE-MASTER-FILE.
01910       STOP RUN.
01920
01930   PRODUCE-MASTER-FILE SECTION.
01940   PRODUCE-MASTER-FILE-PARAGRAPH.
01950       PERFORM INITIALIZATION.
01960       PERFORM PROCESS-A-RECORD UNTIL MORE-INPUT = "N".
01970       PERFORM TERMINATION.
01980       GO TO END-OF-THIS-SECTION.
01990
02000   INITIALIZATION.
02010       OPEN OUTPUT SAVINGS-ACCOUNT-MASTER-FLE-OUT
02020                   ERROR-FILE-OUT
02030                   TRANSACTION-REGISTER-FILE-OUT.
02040       ACCEPT TODAYS-DATE FROM DATE.
02050       MOVE CORR TODAYS-DATE TO PAGE-HEADING-2.
02060       PERFORM PRINT-REPORT-HEADINGS.
02070       PERFORM READ-A-RECORD.
02080       IF MORE-INPUT = "N"
02090           WRITE TRANSACTION-REGISTER-RECORD FROM NO-INPUT-DATA.
02100
02110   PROCESS-A-RECORD.
02120       ADD 1 TO NUMBER-OF-INPUT-RECORDS-W.
02130       MOVE "N" TO ANY-ERRORS.
02140       PERFORM CHECK-INPUT-FOR-VALIDITY.
02150       IF ANY-ERRORS = "N"
02160           PERFORM WRITE-MASTER-RECORD.
02170       PERFORM READ-A-RECORD.
02180
02190   WRITE-MASTER-RECORD.
02200       WRITE SAVINGS-ACCOUNT-MASTER-REC-OUT FROM SORT-WORK-RECORD.
02210       MOVE ACCOUNT-NUMBER-IN TO ACCOUNT-NUMBER-SAVE.
02220       ADD 1 TO NUMBER-OF-NEW-ACCOUNTS-W.
02230       PERFORM WRITE-NEW-ACCOUNT-LINE.
02240
```

```
02250    CHECK-INPUT-FOR-VALIDITY.
02260        MOVE SPACES TO ERROR-LINE.
02270        IF NOT VALID-CODE
02280            MOVE "Y" TO ANY-ERRORS
02290            MOVE CODE-IN TO CODE-E
02300            MOVE "INVALID CODE" TO SHORT-MESSAGE
02310            PERFORM WRITE-ERROR-MESSAGE.
02320        IF ACCOUNT-NUMBER-IN = ACCOUNT-NUMBER-SAVE
02330            MOVE "Y" TO ANY-ERRORS
02340            MOVE "DUPLICATE ACCOUNT NUMBER" TO MSG
02350            PERFORM WRITE-ERROR-MESSAGE.
02360        IF DEPOSITOR-NAME-MISSING
02370            MOVE "Y" TO ANY-ERRORS
02380            MOVE "DEPOSITOR NAME MISSING" TO MSG
02390            PERFORM WRITE-ERROR-MESSAGE.
02400        IF AMOUNT-IN NOT NUMERIC
02410            MOVE "Y" TO ANY-ERRORS
02420            MOVE AMOUNT-IN-X TO AMOUNT-E
02430            MOVE "INITIAL DEPOSIT NOT NUMERIC" TO MSG
02440            PERFORM WRITE-ERROR-MESSAGE.
02450        IF ANY-ERRORS = "Y"
02460            ADD 1 TO NUMBER-OF-ERRONEOUS-RECORDS-W.
02470
02480    WRITE-ERROR-MESSAGE.
02490        MOVE ACCOUNT-NUMBER-IN TO ACCOUNT-NUMBER-E.
02500        PERFORM ERROR-LINE-COUNT-CHECK.
02510        WRITE ERROR-RECORD-OUT FROM ERROR-LINE.
02520        ADD 1 TO ERROR-LINE-COUNTER.
02530
02540    ERROR-LINE-COUNT-CHECK.
02550        IF 1 + ERROR-LINE-COUNTER > ERROR-LINE-LIMIT
02560            PERFORM PRINT-ERROR-REPORT-HEAD.
02570
02580    TERMINATION.
02590        PERFORM WRITE-TOTALS.
02600        CLOSE SAVINGS-ACCOUNT-MASTER-FLE-OUT
02610              ERROR-FILE-OUT
02620              TRANSACTION-REGISTER-FILE-OUT.
02630
02640    READ-A-RECORD.
02650        RETURN SORT-WORK-FILE
02660            AT END
02670                MOVE "N" TO MORE-INPUT.
02680
02690    LINE-COUNT-CHECK.
02700        IF 1 + LINE-COUNT-ER
02710            GREATER THAN LINE-LIMIT
02720                PERFORM PRINT-REGISTER-HEAD.
02730
02740    WRITE-TOTALS.
02750        MOVE AMOUNT-IN-COUNTER TO AMOUNT-OUT-TOTAL.
02760        WRITE TRANSACTION-REGISTER-RECORD FROM TOTAL-LINE-1 AFTER 2.
02770        WRITE TRANSACTION-REGISTER-RECORD FROM TOTAL-LINE-2 AFTER 2.
02780        MOVE NUMBER-OF-NEW-ACCOUNTS-W TO NUMBER-OF-NEW-ACCOUNTS.
02790        WRITE TRANSACTION-REGISTER-RECORD FROM TOTAL-LINE-3 AFTER 2.
02800        MOVE NUMBER-OF-ERRONEOUS-RECORDS-W TO
02810                                NUMBER-OF-ERRONEOUS-RECORDS.
02820        WRITE TRANSACTION-REGISTER-RECORD FROM TOTAL-LINE-4 AFTER 2.
02830        MOVE NUMBER-OF-INPUT-RECORDS-W TO
02840                                NUMBER-OF-INPUT-RECORDS.
02850        WRITE TRANSACTION-REGISTER-RECORD FROM TOTAL-LINE-5 AFTER 2.
02860
02870    PRINT-REPORT-HEADINGS.
02880        PERFORM PRINT-REGISTER-HEAD.
02890        PERFORM PRINT-ERROR-REPORT-HEAD.
02900
02910    PRINT-ERROR-REPORT-HEAD.
02920        ADD 1 TO ERROR-PAGE-NUMBER-W.
02930        MOVE ERROR-PAGE-NUMBER-W TO PAGE-NUMBER-OUT.
02940        WRITE ERROR-RECORD-OUT FROM REPORT-HEADING-1
02950                                AFTER ADVANCING PAGE.
02960        WRITE ERROR-RECORD-OUT FROM REPORT-HEADING-2.
02970        WRITE ERROR-RECORD-OUT FROM REPORT-HEADING-3.
02980        WRITE ERROR-RECORD-OUT FROM ERROR-HEADING-1 AFTER 2.
02990        WRITE ERROR-RECORD-OUT FROM PAGE-HEADING-2.
03000        WRITE ERROR-RECORD-OUT FROM ERROR-PAGE-HEADING-3
03010                                AFTER ADVANCING 3.
03020        WRITE ERROR-RECORD-OUT FROM ERROR-PAGE-HEADING-4
03030        WRITE ERROR-RECORD-OUT FROM BLANK-LINE.
03040        MOVE 11 TO ERROR-LINE-COUNTER.
```

(continued)

Figure 12.4   (continued)

```
03050
03060  PRINT-REGISTER-HEAD.
03070      ADD 1 TO PAGE-NUMBER-W.
03080      MOVE PAGE-NUMBER-W TO PAGE-NUMBER-OUT.
03090      WRITE TRANSACTION-REGISTER-RECORD FROM REPORT-HEADING-1
03100                          AFTER ADVANCING PAGE.
03110      WRITE TRANSACTION-REGISTER-RECORD FROM REPORT-HEADING-2.
03120      WRITE TRANSACTION-REGISTER-RECORD FROM REPORT-HEADING-3.
03130      WRITE TRANSACTION-REGISTER-RECORD FROM PAGE-HEADING-1
03140                          AFTER ADVANCING 2.
03150      WRITE TRANSACTION-REGISTER-RECORD FRCM PAGE-HEADING-2.
03160      WRITE TRANSACTION-REGISTER-RECORD FROM PAGE-HEADING-3
03170                          AFTER ADVANCING 3.
03180      WRITE TRANSACTION-REGISTER-RECORD FROM PAGE-HEADING-4.
03190      WRITE TRANSACTION-REGISTER-RECORD FROM BLANK-LINE.
03200      MOVE 11 TO LINE-COUNT-ER.
03210
03220  WRITE-NEW-ACCOUNT-LINE.
03230      MOVE ACCOUNT-NUMBER-IN TO ACCOUNT-NUMBER-OUT.
03240      MOVE AMOUNT-IN TO AMOUNT-OUT.
03250      PERFORM LINE-COUNT-CHECK.
03260      WRITE TRANSACTION-REGISTER-RECORD FROM REPORT-LINE.
03270      ADD 1 TO LINE-COUNT-ER.
03280      ADD AMOUNT-IN TO AMOUNT-IN-COUNTER.
03290
03300  END-OF-THIS-SECTION.
03310      EXIT.
```

Program P12-01 was run with the input data shown in Figure 12.5 and produced the report output shown in Figure 12.6. The output that was written onto the master file is shown in Figure 12.7. In the installation where this program was run, both the error report and the transaction register were printed on the same printer, one report after the other.

EXERCISE 2

Write a program to create a sequential inventory master file. Use the following input format:

Positions	Field
1 – 5	Part Number
6 – 25	Part Description
26	Units
	E – each
	L – pound
	G – gross
	D – dozen
27 – 29	Quantity on Hand
30 – 35	Unit Cost (dollars and cents)
36 – 41	Date of Last Withdrawal from Inventory (yymmdd)
42 – 47	Date of Last Receipt into Inventory (yymmdd)
48 – 80	spaces

Make the following validity checks on the input records:

Part Number	—numeric
Part Description	—present
Units	—valid code
Quantity on Hand	—numeric
Unit Cost	—numeric
Date of Last Withdrawal	—numeric
Date of Last Receipt	—numeric

Design appropriate reports for your program to show the error messages and the good records that were placed on the file. Create your master file on tape if your computer has facilities for doing so. Otherwise, create the sequential file on disk.

Figure 12.5 Input to Program P12-01.

```
------------------------------------------------------------------------------
         1         2         3         4         5         6         7         8
12345678901234567890123456789012345678901234567890123456789012345678901234567890
------------------------------------------------------------------------------
100063                      10268500007500
100070PATRICK J. LEE        11248500050000
100077LESLIE MINSKY         10268500001037
100084JOHN DAPRINO          10148500150000
100091JOE'S DELI            10158500010000
100098GEORGE CULHANE        10168500050000
100105LENORE MILLER         10038500005000
100112ROSEMARY LANE         10018500025000
300007MICHELE CAPUANO       1020850CA00000
100126JAMES BUDD            11048500075000
100133PAUL LERNER, D.D.S.   11018500100000
100035JOHN J. LEHMAN        11298500015000
100032JOSEPH CAMILLO        11138500002500
100049JAY GREENE            10168500015000
100056EVELYN SLATER         10178500000100
200182BOB LANIGAN           11068500007500
100189J. & L. CAIN          11068500003500
100196IMPERIAL FLORIST      10308500015000
100203JOYCE MITCHELL        10278500000500
100210JERRY PARKS           10288500025000
100217CARL CALDERON         11078500005000
100224JOHN WILLIAMS         11188500017550
100231BILL WILLIAMS         11278500055500
100238KEVIN PARKER          11198500001000
100245FRANK CAPUTO          11148500003500
100252GENE GALLI            12088500001500
100259                      11208500002937
100266MARTIN LANG           11288500009957
100140BETH FALLON           11038500002575
100098JANE HALEY            11058500002000
100105ONE DAY CLEANERS      11058500005000
100161ROBERT RYAN           11058500002450
100168KELLY HEDERMAN        11058500012550
100175MARY KEATING          11068500001000
100007ROSEBUCCI             10258500100784
100014ROBERT DAVIS M.D.     10268500001000
100021LORICE MONTI          10278500012500
100028MICHAEL SMITH         11048500700159
100273VITO CACACI           12048500027500
100280COMMUNITY DRUGS       11168500002000
100287SOLOMON CHAPELS       11238500001500
100294JOHN BURKE            12198500150000
100301PAT P. POWERS         1212850FG15750
100308JOE GARCIA            11278500200000
100315GRACE MICELI          11298500025000
100322                      11248500002000
100329GUY VOLPONE           12288500001000
100336SALVATORE CALI        121885))))!%))
100343JOE & MARY SESSA      12138500100000
100350ROGER SHAW            12318500250000
```

Figure 12.6   Report output from Program P12-01.

```
                          ROBBEM STATE BANK
                          106 WEST 10TH ST.
                          BROOKLYN, NY  11212

                     SAVINGS ACCOUNT ERROR REPORT
     DATE   4/07/88                                      PAGE 1


            ACCOUNT                     NOTES
            NUMBER

             00007                      INVALID CODE 3
             00007                      INITIAL DEPOSIT NOT NUMERIC 0CA00000
             00063                      DEPOSITOR NAME MISSING
             00098                      DUPLICATE ACCOUNT NUMBER
             00105                      DUPLICATE ACCOUNT NUMBER
             00182                      INVALID CODE 2
             00259                      DEPOSITOR NAME MISSING
             00301                      INITIAL DEPOSIT NOT NUMERIC 0FG15750
             00322                      DEPOSITOR NAME MISSING
             00336                      INITIAL DEPOSIT NOT NUMERIC ))))!%))
```

```
                          ROBBEM STATE BANK
                          106 WEST 10TH ST.
                          BROOKLYN, NY  11212

                  SAVINGS ACCOUNT MASTER FILE CREATION
     DATE   4/07/88                                      PAGE 1


            ACCOUNT     INITIAL     NOTES
            NUMBER      DEPOSIT

             00007     1,007.84     NEW ACCOUNT
             00014        10.00     NEW ACCOUNT
             00021       125.00     NEW ACCOUNT
             00028     7,001.59     NEW ACCOUNT
             00032        25.00     NEW ACCOUNT
             00035       150.00     NEW ACCOUNT
             00049       150.00     NEW ACCOUNT
             00056         1.00     NEW ACCOUNT
             00070       500.00     NEW ACCOUNT
             00077        10.37     NEW ACCOUNT
             00084     1,500.00     NEW ACCOUNT
             00091       100.00     NEW ACCOUNT
             00098       500.00     NEW ACCOUNT
             00105        50.00     NEW ACCOUNT
             00112       250.00     NEW ACCOUNT
             00126       750.00     NEW ACCOUNT
             00133     1,000.00     NEW ACCOUNT
             00140        25.75     NEW ACCOUNT
             00161        24.50     NEW ACCOUNT
             00168       125.50     NEW ACCOUNT
             00175        10.00     NEW ACCOUNT
             00189        35.00     NEW ACCOUNT
             00196       150.00     NEW ACCOUNT
```

```
                    ROBBEM STATE BANK
                     106 WEST 10TH ST.
                    BROOKLYN, NY  11212

                 SAVINGS ACCOUNT MASTER FILE CREATION
    DATE  4/07/88                                    PAGE 2


        ACCOUNT      INITIAL      NOTES
        NUMBER       DEPOSIT

        00203           5.00      NEW ACCOUNT
        00210         250.00      NEW ACCOUNT
        00217          50.00      NEW ACCOUNT
        00224         175.50      NEW ACCOUNT
        00231         555.00      NEW ACCOUNT
        00238          10.00      NEW ACCOUNT
        00245          35.00      NEW ACCOUNT
        00252          15.00      NEW ACCOUNT
        00266          99.57      NEW ACCOUNT
        00273         275.00      NEW ACCOUNT
        00280          20.00      NEW ACCOUNT
        00287          15.00      NEW ACCOUNT
        00294       1,500.00      NEW ACCOUNT
        00308       2,000.00      NEW ACCOUNT
        00315         250.00      NEW ACCOUNT
        00329          10.00      NEW ACCOUNT
        00343       1,000.00      NEW ACCOUNT
        00350       2,500.00      NEW ACCOUNT

    TOTAL          22,266.62

                      CONTROL COUNTS

        NUMBER OF NEW ACCOUNTS         41

        NUMBER OF ERRONEOUS RECORDS     9

        TOTAL                          50
```

Building a Master Record in Storage

In Program P12-01 we wrote a master file containing no small amount of garbage. For example, positions 41 through 80 of the input records contained blanks or perhaps random useless characters. We wrote those characters as part of the master records. Also, the 1 in position 1 of the input records was written onto the master file even though it was not needed there. It was needed only in the input record for validity checking.

Program P12-02 shows how to build master records from input records so that only the fields worth saving get onto the master file. Program P12-02 and the programs following also introduce some general techniques relating to file creation and updating. Some of these techniques may not seem extremely useful at the time they are presented, but their usefulness will become evident as we get into more complex file-handling situations.

Program P12-02 uses input data in the following format:

Positions	Field
1	Code 1
2–6	Account Number
7–14	Amount (to two decimal places)
15–34	Depositor Name
35–80	spaces

Figure 12.7   Master file produced by Program P12-01.

```
-------------------------------------------------------------------------------
          1         2         3         4         5         6         7         8
12345678901234567890123456789012345678901234567890123456789012345678901234567890
-------------------------------------------------------------------------------
100007ROSEBUCCI           10258500100784
100014ROBERT DAVIS M.D.   10268500001000
100021LORICE MONTI        10278500012500
100028MICHAEL SMITH       11048500700159
100032JOSEPH CAMILLO      11138500002500
100035JOHN J. LEHMAN      11298500015000
100049JAY GREENE          10168500015000
100056EVELYN SLATER       10178500000100
100070PATRICK J. LEE      11248500050000
100077LESLIE MINSKY       10268500001037
100084JOHN DAPRINO        10148500150000
100091JOE'S DELI          10158500010000
100098GEORGE CULHANE      10168500050000
100105ONE DAY CLEANERS    11058500005000
100112ROSEMARY LANE       10018500025000
100126JAMES BUDD          11048500075000
100133PAUL LERNER, D.D.S. 11018500100000
100140BETH FALLON         11038500002575
100161ROBERT RYAN         11058500002450
100168KELLY HEDERMAN      11058500012550
100175MARY KEATING        11068500001000
100189J. & L. CAIN        11068500003500
100196IMPERIAL FLORIST    10308500015000
100203JOYCE MITCHELL      10278500000500
100210JERRY PARKS         10288500025000
100217CARL CALDERON       11078500005000
100224JOHN WILLIAMS       11188500017550
100231BILL WILLIAMS       11278500055500
100238KEVIN PARKER        11198500001000
100245FRANK CAPUTO        11148500003500
100252GENE GALLI          12088500001500
100266MARTIN LANG         11288500009957
100273VITO CACACI         12048500027500
100280COMMUNITY DRUGS     11168500002000
100287SOLOMON CHAPELS     11238500001500
100294JOHN BURKE          12198500150000
100308JOE GARCIA          11278500200000
100315GRACE MICELI        11298500025000
100329GUY VOLPONE         12288500001000
100343JOE & MARY SESSA    12138500100000
100350ROGER SHAW          12318500250000
```

You will soon see why there is no need to key the Date of Transaction into the input records. Program P12-02 produces report output in the same formats as Program P12-01.

The master records produced by Program P12-02 will contain only the following fields:

Account Number — 5 characters
Depositor Name — 20 characters
Date of Last Transaction — 6 characters
Current Balance — 8 characters

The master records will contain no Code field nor any useless character positions. Each master record will be only 39 characters long.

Program P12-02 is shown in Figure 12.8. It is very similar to Program P12-01. In the File Section, the output record is now defined as containing 39 characters, at line 00500. The master record is broken down into fields in the Working Storage

Figure 12.8 Program P12-02.

CB1 RELEASE 2.4   IBM OS/VS COBOL   JULY 1, 1982

                         21.17.05   APR 7,1988

```
00010  IDENTIFICATION DIVISION.
00020  PROGRAM-ID. P12-02.
00030 * AUTHOR. SHAMEZE SULTAN
00040 *         REVISED BY GAETANO MURATORE
00050 *
00060 *    THIS PROGRAM CREATES A SEQUENTIAL MASTER FILE.
00070 *
00080 *********************************************************************
00090
00100  ENVIRONMENT DIVISION.
00110  CONFIGURATION SECTION.
00120  SOURCE-COMPUTER. IBM-370.
00130  OBJECT-COMPUTER. IBM-370.
00140
00150  INPUT-OUTPUT SECTION.
00160  FILE-CONTROL.
00170      SELECT SAVINGS-ACCOUNT-DATA-FILE-IN    ASSIGN TO INFILE.
00180      SELECT SORT-WORK-FILE                  ASSIGN TO SORTWK.
00190      SELECT SAVINGS-ACCOUNT-MASTER-FLE-OUT  ASSIGN TO MASTER.
00200      SELECT TRANSACTION-REGISTER-FILE-OUT   ASSIGN TO PRINTER1.
00210      SELECT ERROR-FILE-OUT                  ASSIGN TO PRINTER2.
00220
00230 *********************************************************************
00240
00250  DATA DIVISION.
00260  FILE SECTION.
00270  FD  SAVINGS-ACCOUNT-DATA-FILE-IN
00280      LABEL RECORDS ARE OMITTED
00290      RECORD CONTAINS 80 CHARACTERS.
00300
00310  01  SAVINGS-ACCOUNT-DATA-RECORD-IN       PIC X(80).
00320
00330  SD  SORT-WORK-FILE
00340      RECORD CONTAINS 34 CHARACTERS.
00350
00360  01  SORT-WORK-RECORD.
00370      05 CODE-IN                           PIC X.
00380          88  VALID-CODE                   VALUE "1".
00390      05 ACCOUNT-NUMBER-IN                 PIC X(5).
00400      05 AMOUNT-IN                         PIC 9(6)V99.
00410      05 AMOUNT-IN-X REDEFINES AMOUNT-IN   PIC X(8).
00420      05 DEPOSITOR-NAME-IN                 PIC X(20).
00430          88  DEPOSITOR-NAME-MISSING       VALUE SPACES.
00440
00450  FD  SAVINGS-ACCOUNT-MASTER-FLE-OUT
00460      LABEL RECORDS ARE STANDARD
00470      RECORD CONTAINS 39 CHARACTERS
00480      BLOCK CONTAINS 100 RECORDS.
00490
00500  01  SAVINGS-ACCOUNT-MASTER-REC-OUT       PIC X(39).
00510
00520  FD  TRANSACTION-REGISTER-FILE-OUT
00530      LABEL RECORDS ARE OMITTED.
00540
00550  01  TRANSACTION-REGISTER-RECORD          PIC X(72).
00560
00570  FD  ERROR-FILE-OUT
00580      LABEL RECORDS ARE OMITTED.
00590
00600  01  ERROR-RECORD-OUT                     PIC X(84).
00610
00620  WORKING-STORAGE SECTION.
00630  01  MORE-INPUT                           PIC X VALUE "Y".
00640  01  ANY-ERRORS                           PIC X.
00650  01  NUMBER-OF-INPUT-RECORDS-W            PIC S9(3)    VALUE ZERO.
00660  01  NUMBER-OF-ERRONEOUS-RECORDS-W        PIC S9(3)    VALUE ZERO.
00670  01  NUMBER-OF-NEW-ACCOUNTS-W             PIC S9(3)    VALUE ZERO.
00680  01  ACCOUNT-NUMBER-SAVE            PIC X(5) VALUE HIGH-VALUES.
```

                                                              (continued)

Section, at line 00810. Although this program would have worked if the master record had been broken down into fields in the File Section instead, it is better programming practice to have the breakdown in working storage. Having the fields defined in working storage allows for greater complexity of master-file organization and results in a more general program.

Figure 12.8   (continued)

```
00690  01  TODAYS-DATE.
00700      05  TODAYS-YEAR                    PIC 99.
00710      05  TODAYS-MONTH-AND-DAY           PIC 9(4).
00720  01  AMOUNT-IN-COUNTER                  PIC 9(7)V99 VALUE 0.
00730  01  PAGE-NUMBER-W                      PIC S9 VALUE 0.
00740  01  ERROR-PAGE-NUMBER-W                PIC S9 VALUE 0.
00750  01  BLANK-LINE                         PIC X   VALUE SPACE.
00760  01  LINE-LIMIT               PIC S99 COMP SYNC VALUE 34.
00770  01  LINE-COUNT-ER            PIC S99 COMP SYNC.
00780  01  ERROR-LINE-LIMIT         PIC S99 COMP SYNC VALUE 54.
00790  01  ERROR-LINE-COUNTER       PIC S99 COMP SYNC.
00800
00810  01  MASTER-RECORD-W.
00820      05  ACCOUNT-NUMBER                 PIC X(5).
00830      05  DEPOSITOR-NAME                 PIC X(20).
00840      05  DATE-OF-LAST-TRANSACTION       PIC 9(6).
00850      05  CURRENT-BALANCE                PIC 9(6)V99.
00860
00870  01  REPORT-HEADING-1.
00880      05  FILLER                         PIC X(39) VALUE SPACES.
00890      05  FILLER        PIC X(17) VALUE "ROBBEM STATE BANK".
00900
00910  01  REPORT-HEADING-2.
00920      05  FILLER                         PIC X(39) VALUE SPACES.
00930      05  FILLER        PIC X(17) VALUE "106 WEST 10TH ST.".
00940
00950  01  REPORT-HEADING-3.
00960      05  FILLER                         PIC X(38) VALUE SPACES.
00970      05  FILLER        PIC X(19) VALUE "BROOKLYN, NY  11212".
00980
00990  01  PAGE-HEADING-1.
01000      05  FILLER                         PIC X(29) VALUE SPACES.
01010      05  FILLER                         PIC X(36)
01020              VALUE "SAVINGS ACCOUNT MASTER FILE CREATION".
01030
01040  01  ERROR-HEADING-1.
01050      05  FILLER                         PIC X(33) VALUE SPACES.
01060      05  FILLER                         PIC X(29)
01070                      VALUE "SAVINGS ACCOUNT ERROR REPORT".
01080
01090  01  PAGE-HEADING-2.
01100      05  FILLER                         PIC X(17) VALUE SPACES.
01110      05  FILLER                         PIC X(5) VALUE "DATE".
01120      05  TODAYS-MONTH-AND-DAY           PIC Z9/99/.
01130      05  TODAYS-YEAR                    PIC 99.
01140      05  FILLER                         PIC X(35) VALUE SPACES.
01150      05  FILLER                         PIC X(4)  VALUE "PAGE".
01160      05  PAGE-NUMBER-OUT                PIC Z9.
01170
01180  01  PAGE-HEADING-3.
01190      05  FILLER                         PIC X(24) VALUE SPACES.
01200      05  FILLER                         PIC X(7)  VALUE "ACCOUNT".
01210      05  FILLER                         PIC X(5)  VALUE SPACES.
01220      05  FILLER                         PIC X(7)  VALUE "INITIAL".
01230      05  FILLER                         PIC X(5)  VALUE SPACES.
01240      05  FILLER                         PIC X(5)  VALUE "NOTES".
01250
01260  01  ERROR-PAGE-HEADING-3.
01270      05  FILLER                         PIC X(24) VALUE SPACES.
01280      05  FILLER                         PIC X(7)  VALUE "ACCOUNT".
01290      05  FILLER                         PIC X(17) VALUE SPACES.
01300      05  FILLER                         PIC X(5)  VALUE "NOTES".
01310
01320  01  PAGE-HEADING-4.
01330      05  FILLER                         PIC X(24) VALUE SPACES.
01340      05  FILLER                         PIC X(6)  VALUE "NUMBER".
01350      05  FILLER                         PIC X(6)  VALUE SPACES.
01360      05  FILLER                         PIC X(7)  VALUE  "DEPOSIT".
01370
```

```
01380   01   ERROR-PAGE-HEADING-4.
01390        05 FILLER                          PIC X(24) VALUE SPACES.
01400        05 FILLER                          PIC X(6)  VALUE "NUMBER".
01410
01420   01   REPORT-LINE.
01430        05 ACCOUNT-NUMBER-OUT                PIC B(25)X(5).
01440        05 AMOUNT-OUT                        PIC B(5)ZZZ,ZZZ.99B(3).
01450        05 FILLER                       PIC X(11) VALUE "NEW ACCOUNT".
01460
01470   01   ERROR-LINE.
01480        05 ACCOUNT-NUMBER-E                  PIC B(25)X(5).
01490        05 LONG-MESSAGES.
01500           10 MSG                            PIC B(18)X(27).
01510           10 AMOUNT-E                       PIC BX(9).
01520        05 SHORT-MESSAGES REDEFINES LONG-MESSAGES.
01530           10 SHORT-MESSAGE                  PIC B(18)X(12).
01540           10 CODE-E                         PIC BXB(23).
01550
01560   01   TOTAL-LINE-1.
01570        05 FILLER                            PIC X(23) VALUE SPACES.
01580        05 FILLER                       PIC X(5)B(5) VALUE "TOTAL".
01590        05 AMOUNT-OUT-TOTAL                  PIC Z,ZZZ,ZZZ.99.
01600
01610   01   TOTAL-LINE-2.
01620        05 FILLER                            PIC X(41) VALUE SPACES.
01630        05 FILLER                      PIC X(14) VALUE "CONTROL COUNTS".
01640
01650   01   TOTAL-LINE-3.
01660        05 FILLER                            PIC X(34) VALUE SPACES.
01670        05 FILLER                            PIC X(22)
01680                           VALUE "NUMBER OF NEW ACCOUNTS".
01690        05 NUMBER-OF-NEW-ACCOUNTS            PIC B(6)ZZ9.
01700
01710   01   TOTAL-LINE-4.
01720        05 FILLER                            PIC X(34) VALUE SPACES.
01730        05 FILLER                            PIC X(27)
01740                           VALUE "NUMBER OF ERRONEOUS RECORDS".
01750        05 NUMBER-OF-ERRONEOUS-RECORDS       PIC BZZ9.
01760
01770   01   TOTAL-LINE-5.
01780        05 FILLER                            PIC X(34) VALUE SPACES.
01790        05 FILLER                            PIC X(5)  VALUE "TOTAL".
01800        05 NUMBER-OF-INPUT-RECORDS           PIC B(23)ZZ9.
01810
01820   01   NO-INPUT-DATA.
01830        05 FILLER                            PIC X(21) VALUE SPACES.
01840        05 FILLER           VALUE "NO INPUT DATA" PIC X(13).
01850
01860   ************************************************************************
01870
01880   PROCEDURE DIVISION.
01890   CONTROL-SECTION SECTION.
01900   CREATE-MASTER-FILE.
01910        SORT SORT-WORK-FILE
01920             ASCENDING KEY ACCOUNT-NUMBER-IN
01930             USING SAVINGS-ACCOUNT-DATA-FILE-IN
01940             OUTPUT PROCEDURE IS PRODUCE-MASTER-FILE.
01950        STOP RUN.
01960
01970   PRODUCE-MASTER-FILE SECTION.
01980   PRODUCE-MASTER-FILE-PARAGRAPH.
01990        PERFORM INITIALIZATION.
02000        PERFORM PROCESS-A-RECORD UNTIL MORE-INPUT = "N".
02010        PERFORM TERMINATION.
02020        GO TO END-OF-THIS-SECTION.
02030
02040   INITIALIZATION.
02050        OPEN OUTPUT SAVINGS-ACCOUNT-MASTER-FLE-OUT
02060                    ERROR-FILE-OUT
02070                    TRANSACTION-REGISTER-FILE-OUT.
02080        ACCEPT TODAYS-DATE FROM DATE.
02090        MOVE CORR TODAYS-DATE TO PAGE-HEADING-2.
02100        PERFORM PRINT-REPORT-HEADINGS.
02110        PERFORM READ-A-RECORD.
02120        IF MORE-INPUT = "N"
02130           WRITE TRANSACTION-REGISTER-RECORD FROM NO-INPUT-DATA.
02140
```

(continued)

Figure 12.8   (continued)

```
02150    PROCESS-A-RECORD.
02160        ADD 1 TO NUMBER-OF-INPUT-RECORDS-W.
02170        MOVE "N" TO ANY-ERRORS.
02180        PERFORM CHECK-INPUT-FOR-VALIDITY.
02190        IF ANY-ERRORS = "N"
02200            PERFORM BUILD-MASTER-RECORD
02210            PERFORM WRITE-MASTER-RECORD.
02220        PERFORM READ-A-RECORD.
02230
02240    BUILD-MASTER-RECORD.
02250        MOVE ACCOUNT-NUMBER-IN TO ACCOUNT-NUMBER.
02260        MOVE DEPOSITOR-NAME-IN TO DEPOSITOR-NAME.
02270        MOVE AMOUNT-IN         TO CURRENT-BALANCE.
02280        MOVE TODAYS-DATE       TO DATE-OF-LAST-TRANSACTION.
02290
02300    WRITE-MASTER-RECORD.
02310        WRITE SAVINGS-ACCOUNT-MASTER-REC-OUT FROM MASTER-RECORD-W.
02320        MOVE ACCOUNT-NUMBER-IN TO ACCOUNT-NUMBER-SAVE.
02330        ADD 1 TO NUMBER-OF-NEW-ACCOUNTS-W.
02340        PERFORM WRITE-NEW-ACCOUNT-LINE.
02350
02360    CHECK-INPUT-FOR-VALIDITY.
02370        MOVE SPACES TO ERROR-LINE.
02380        IF NOT VALID-CODE
02390            MOVE "Y" TO ANY-ERRORS
02400            MOVE CODE-IN TO CODE-E
02410            MOVE "INVALID CODE" TO SHORT-MESSAGE
02420            PERFORM WRITE-ERROR-MESSAGE.
02430        IF ACCOUNT-NUMBER-IN = ACCOUNT-NUMBER-SAVE
02440            MOVE "Y" TO ANY-ERRORS
02450            MOVE "DUPLICATE ACCOUNT NUMBER" TO MSG
02460            PERFORM WRITE-ERROR-MESSAGE.
02470        IF DEPOSITOR-NAME-MISSING
02480            MOVE "Y" TO ANY-ERRORS
02490            MOVE "DEPOSITOR NAME MISSING" TO MSG
02500            PERFORM WRITE-ERROR-MESSAGE.
02510        IF AMOUNT-IN NOT NUMERIC
02520            MOVE "Y" TO ANY-ERRORS
02530            MOVE AMOUNT-IN-X TO AMOUNT-E
02540            MOVE "INITIAL DEPOSIT NOT NUMERIC" TO MSG
02550            PERFORM WRITE-ERROR-MESSAGE.
02560        IF ANY-ERRORS = "Y"
02570            ADD 1 TO NUMBER-OF-ERRONEOUS-RECORDS-W.
02580
02590    WRITE-ERROR-MESSAGE.
02600        MOVE ACCOUNT-NUMBER-IN TO ACCOUNT-NUMBER-E.
02610        PERFORM ERROR-LINE-COUNT-CHECK.
02620        WRITE ERROR-RECORD-OUT FROM ERROR-LINE.
02630        ADD 1 TO ERROR-LINE-COUNTER.
02640
02650    ERROR-LINE-COUNT-CHECK.
02660        IF 1 + ERROR-LINE-COUNTER > ERROR-LINE-LIMIT
02670            PERFORM PRINT-ERROR-REPORT-HEAD.
```

In the paragraph PROCESS-A-RECORD we now have a new PERFORM statement, at line 02200. The paragraph BUILD-MASTER-RECORD, at line 02240, constructs the master record in working storage in preparation for writing it onto the master file. It is good practice to have separate paragraphs for building the master record and for writing it, even though in this program the functions of the two paragraphs could easily have been combined in one. Program P12-02 was run with the input data shown in Figure 12.9 and produced the report output shown in Figure 12.10. The master file produced by the program is shown in Figure 12.11.

```
02680
02690    TERMINATION.
02700        PERFORM WRITE-TOTALS.
02710        CLOSE SAVINGS-ACCOUNT-MASTER-FLE-OUT
02720            ERROR-FILE-OUT
02730            TRANSACTION-REGISTER-FILE-OUT.
02740
02750    READ-A-RECORD.
02760        RETURN SORT-WORK-FILE
02770            AT END
02780                MOVE "N" TO MORE-INPUT.
02790
02800    LINE-COUNT-CHECK.
02810        IF 1 + LINE-COUNT-ER GREATER THAN LINE-LIMIT
02820            PERFORM PRINT-REGISTER-HEAD.
02830
02840    WRITE-TOTALS.
02850        MOVE AMOUNT-IN-COUNTER TO AMOUNT-OUT-TOTAL.
02860        WRITE TRANSACTION-REGISTER-RECORD FROM TOTAL-LINE-1 AFTER 2.
02870        WRITE TRANSACTION-REGISTER-RECORD FROM TOTAL-LINE-2 AFTER 2.
02880        MOVE NUMBER-OF-NEW-ACCOUNTS-W TO NUMBER-OF-NEW-ACCOUNTS.
02890        WRITE TRANSACTION-REGISTER-RECORD FROM TOTAL-LINE-3 AFTER 2.
02900        MOVE NUMBER-OF-ERRONEOUS-RECORDS-W TO
02910                                    NUMBER-OF-ERRONEOUS-RECORDS.
02920        WRITE TRANSACTION-REGISTER-RECORD FROM TOTAL-LINE-4 AFTER 2.
02930        MOVE NUMBER-OF-INPUT-RECORDS-W TO
02940                                    NUMBER-OF-INPUT-RECORDS.
02950        WRITE TRANSACTION-REGISTER-RECORD FROM TOTAL-LINE-5 AFTER 2.
02960
02970    PRINT-REPORT-HEADINGS.
02980        PERFORM PRINT-REGISTER-HEAD.
02990        PERFORM PRINT-ERROR-REPORT-HEAD.
03000
03010    PRINT-ERROR-REPORT-HEAD.
03020        ADD 1 TO ERROR-PAGE-NUMBER-W.
03030        MOVE ERROR-PAGE-NUMBER-W TO PAGE-NUMBER-OUT.
03040        WRITE ERROR-RECORD-OUT FROM REPORT-HEADING-1
03050                                    AFTER ADVANCING PAGE.
03060        WRITE ERROR-RECORD-OUT FROM REPORT-HEADING-2.
03070        WRITE ERROR-RECORD-OUT FROM REPORT-HEADING-3.
03080        WRITE ERROR-RECORD-OUT FROM ERROR-HEADING-1 AFTER 2.
03090        WRITE ERROR-RECORD-OUT FROM PAGE-HEADING-2.
03100        WRITE ERROR-RECORD-OUT FROM ERROR-PAGE-HEADING-3
03110                                    AFTER ADVANCING 3.
03120        WRITE ERROR-RECORD-OUT FROM ERROR-PAGE-HEADING-4.
03130        WRITE ERROR-RECORD-OUT FROM BLANK-LINE.
03140        MOVE 11 TO ERROR-LINE-COUNTER.
03150
03160    PRINT-REGISTER-HEAD.
03170        ADD 1 TO PAGE-NUMBER-W.
03180        MOVE PAGE-NUMBER-W TO PAGE-NUMBER-OUT.
03190        WRITE TRANSACTION-REGISTER-RECORD FROM REPORT-HEADING-1
03200                                    AFTER ADVANCING PAGE.
03210        WRITE TRANSACTION-REGISTER-RECORD FROM REPORT-HEADING-2.
03220        WRITE TRANSACTION-REGISTER-RECORD FROM REPORT-HEADING-3.
03230        WRITE TRANSACTION-REGISTER-RECORD FROM PAGE-HEADING-1
03240                                    AFTER ADVANCING 2.
03250        WRITE TRANSACTION-REGISTER-RECORD FROM PAGE-HEADING-2.
03260        WRITE TRANSACTION-REGISTER-RECORD FROM PAGE-HEADING-3
03270                                    AFTER ADVANCING 3.
03280        WRITE TRANSACTION-REGISTER-RECORD FROM PAGE-HEADING-4.
03290        WRITE TRANSACTION-REGISTER-RECORD FROM BLANK-LINE.
03300        MOVE 11 TO LINE-COUNT-ER.
03310
03320    WRITE-NEW-ACCOUNT-LINE.
03330        MOVE ACCOUNT-NUMBER-IN TO ACCOUNT-NUMBER-OUT.
03340        MOVE AMOUNT-IN TO AMOUNT-OUT.
03350        PERFORM LINE-COUNT-CHECK.
03360        WRITE TRANSACTION-REGISTER-RECORD FROM REPORT-LINE.
03370        ADD 1 TO LINE-COUNT-ER.
03380        ADD AMOUNT-IN TO AMOUNT-IN-COUNTER.
03390
03400    END-OF-THIS-SECTION.
03410        EXIT.
```

Figure 12.9 Input to Program P12-02.

```
--------------------------------------------------------------------
          1         2         3         4         5         6         7         8
12345678901234567890123456789012345678901234567890123456789012345678901234567890
--------------------------------------------------------------------
10010500005000LENORE MILLER
10011200025000ROSEMARY LANE
3000070CA00000MICHELE CAPUANO
10012600075000JAMES BUDD
10013300100000PAUL LERNER, D.D.S.
10014000002575BETH FALLON
10009800002000JANE HALEY
100105000050000NE DAY CLEANERS
10016100002450ROBERT RYAN
10016800012550KELLY HEDERMAN
10017500001000MARY KEATING
20018200007500BOB LANIGAN
10018900003500J. & L. CAIN
10019600015000IMPERIAL FLORIST
10020300000500JOYCE MITCHELL
10021000025000JERRY PARKS
10021700005000CARL CALDERON
10022400017550JOHN WILLIAMS
10003500015000JOHN J. LEHMAN
10003200002500JOSEPH CAMILLO
10004900015000JAY GREENE
10005600000100EVELYN SLATER
10006300007500
10007000050000PATRICK J. LEE
10007700001037LESLIE MINSKY
10008400150000JOHN DAPRINO
10009100010000JOE'S DELI
10009800050000GEORGE CULHANE
10026600009957MARTIN LANG
10027300027500VITO CACACI
10028000002000COMMUNITY DRUGS
10028700001500SOLOMON CHAPELS
10029400150000JOHN BURKE
1003010FG15750PAT P. POWERS
10030800200000JOE GARCIA
10031500025000GRACE MICELI
10032200002000
10032900001000GUY VOLPONE
100336))))!%))SALVATORE CALI
10023100055500BILL WILLIAMS
10023800001000KEVIN PARKER
10024500003500FRANK CAPUTO
10025200001500GENE GALLI
10025900002937
10000700100784ROSEBUCCI
10001400001000ROBERT DAVIS M.D.
10002100012500LORICE MONTI
10002800700159MICHAEL SMITH
10034300100000JOE & MARY SESSA
10035000250000ROGER SHAW
```

Figure 12.10 Report output from Program P12-02.

```
                        ROBBEM STATE BANK
                        106 WEST 10TH ST.
                      BROOKLYN, NY  11212

                 SAVINGS ACCOUNT ERROR REPORT
   DATE   4/07/88                               PAGE 1


         ACCOUNT                      NOTES
         NUMBER

          00007              INVALID CODE 3
          00007              INITIAL DEPOSIT NOT NUMERIC OCAOOOOO
          00063              DEPOSITOR NAME MISSING
          00098              DUPLICATE ACCOUNT NUMBER
          00105              DUPLICATE ACCOUNT NUMBER
          00182              INVALID CODE 2
          00259              DEPOSITOR NAME MISSING
          00301              INITIAL DEPOSIT NOT NUMERIC OFG15750
          00322              DEPOSITOR NAME MISSING
          00336              INITIAL DEPOSIT NOT NUMERIC ))))!%))


                        ROBBEM STATE BANK
                        106 WEST 10TH ST.
                      BROOKLYN, NY  11212

              SAVINGS ACCOUNT MASTER FILE CREATION
   DATE   4/07/88                               PAGE 1


         ACCOUNT     INITIAL      NOTES
         NUMBER      DEPOSIT

          00007      1,007.84     NEW ACCOUNT
          00014         10.00     NEW ACCOUNT
          00021        125.00     NEW ACCOUNT
          00028      7,001.59     NEW ACCOUNT
          00032         25.00     NEW ACCOUNT
          00035        150.00     NEW ACCOUNT
          00049        150.00     NEW ACCOUNT
          00056          1.00     NEW ACCOUNT
          00070        500.00     NEW ACCOUNT
          00077         10.37     NEW ACCOUNT
          00084      1,500.00     NEW ACCOUNT
          00091        100.00     NEW ACCOUNT
          00098        500.00     NEW ACCOUNT
          00105         50.00     NEW ACCOUNT
          00112        250.00     NEW ACCOUNT
          00126        750.00     NEW ACCOUNT
          00133      1,000.00     NEW ACCOUNT
          00140         25.75     NEW ACCOUNT
          00161         24.50     NEW ACCOUNT
          00168        125.50     NEW ACCOUNT
          00175         10.00     NEW ACCOUNT
          00189         35.00     NEW ACCOUNT
          00196        150.00     NEW ACCOUNT
```

(continued)

Figure 12.10   (continued)

```
                        ROBBEM STATE BANK
                        106 WEST 10TH ST.
                        BROOKLYN, NY  11212

                   SAVINGS ACCOUNT MASTER FILE CREATION
        DATE  4/07/88                                    PAGE  2


            ACCOUNT        INITIAL       NOTES
            NUMBER         DEPOSIT

             00203            5.00       NEW ACCOUNT
             00210          250.00       NEW ACCOUNT
             00217           50.00       NEW ACCOUNT
             00224          175.50       NEW ACCOUNT
             00231          555.00       NEW ACCOUNT
             00238           10.00       NEW ACCOUNT
             00245           35.00       NEW ACCOUNT
             00252           15.00       NEW ACCOUNT
             00266           99.57       NEW ACCOUNT
             00273          275.00       NEW ACCOUNT
             00280           20.00       NEW ACCOUNT
             00287           15.00       NEW ACCOUNT
             00294        1,500.00       NEW ACCOUNT
             00308        2,000.00       NEW ACCOUNT
             00315          250.00       NEW ACCOUNT
             00329           10.00       NEW ACCOUNT
             00343        1,000.00       NEW ACCOUNT
             00350        2,500.00       NEW ACCOUNT

        TOTAL            22,266.62

                          CONTROL COUNTS

            NUMBER OF NEW ACCOUNTS          41

            NUMBER OF ERRONEOUS RECORDS      9

            TOTAL                          50
```

EXERCISE 3

Write a program to create a sequential inventory master file using input in the following format:

Positions	Field
1 – 5	Part Number
6 – 25	Part Description
26	Units
	E – each
	L – pound
	G – gross
	D – dozen
27 – 32	Unit Cost (dollars and cents)
33 – 36	Supplier Code
37 – 41	Storage Location
42 – 44	Reorder Point
45 – 47	Reorder Quantity
48 – 80	spaces

Figure 12.11 Master file produced by Program P12-02.

```
-------------------------------------------------------------------------------
         1         2         3         4         5         6         7         8
12345678901234567890123456789012345678901234567890123456789012345678901234567890
-------------------------------------------------------------------------------
00007ROSEBUCCI            88040700100784
00014ROBERT DAVIS M.D.    88040700001000
00021LORICE MONTI         88040700012500
00028MICHAEL SMITH        88040700700159
00032JOSEPH CAMILLO       88040700002500
00035JOHN J. LEHMAN       88040700015000
00049JAY GREENE           88040700015000
00056EVELYN SLATER        88040700000100
00070PATRICK J. LEE       88040700050000
00077LESLIE MINSKY        88040700001037
00084JOHN DAPRINO         88040700150000
00091JOE'S DELI           88040700010000
00098GEORGE CULHANE       88040700050000
00105ONE DAY CLEANERS     88040700005000
00112ROSEMARY LANE        88040700025000
00126JAMES BUDD           88040700075000
00133PAUL LERNER, D.D.S.  88040700100000
00140BETH FALLON          88040700002575
00161ROBERT RYAN          88040700002450
00168KELLY HEDERMAN       88040700012550
00175MARY KEATING         88040700001000
00189J. & L. CAIN         88040700003500
00196IMPERIAL FLORIST     88040700015000
00203JOYCE MITCHELL       88040700000500
00210JERRY PARKS          88040700025000
00217CARL CALDERON        88040700005000
00224JOHN WILLIAMS        88040700017550
00231BILL WILLIAMS        88040700055500
00238KEVIN PARKER         88040700001000
00245FRANK CAPUTO         88040700003500
00252GENE GALLI           88040700001500
00266MARTIN LANG          88040700009957
00273VITO CACACI          88040700027500
00280COMMUNITY DRUGS      88040700002000
00287SOLOMON CHAPELS      88040700001500
00294JOHN BURKE           88040700150000
00308JOE GARCIA           88040700200000
00315GRACE MICELI         88040700025000
00329GUY VOLPONE          88040700001000
00343JOE & MARY SESSA     88040700100000
00350ROGER SHAW           88040700250000
```

Have your program build the master records in working storage. Have each master record contain the following fields:

Part Number — 5 characters
Part Description — 20 characters
Units — 1 character
Quantity on Hand — 3 characters
Unit Cost (dollars and cents) — 6 characters
Supplier Code — 4 characters
Storage Location — 5 characters
Reorder Point — 3 characters
Reorder Quantity — 3 characters
Date of Last Withdrawal from Inventory (yymmdd) — 8 characters
Date of Last Receipt into Inventory (yymmdd) — 8 characters
Date Created (yymmdd) — 8 characters
Date of Last Access (yymmdd) — 8 characters

Create the Quantity on Hand field and the Dates of Last Withdrawal and Last Receipt with values of zero. Have your program insert today's date into the Date Created and Date of Last Access fields in each master record. Use 15 records per block. Have your program make the following validity checks on the input records:

Part Number   — numeric
Part Description — present
Units   — valid code
Unit Cost   — numeric
Supplier Code   — first character alphabetic, second through fourth
                    characters numeric
Storage Location — first two characters alphabetic, third through fifth
                    characters numeric
Reorder Point   — numeric
Reorder Quantity — numeric

Have your program produce a report showing the good records and a report showing the errors.

Save the file that you create in this exercise for use in later exercises in this chapter and the next.

Deleting Records from a Sequential File

We will now study the first of the several file-update programs in this book, one that deletes records from a master file. You will see other update programs, which change existing records and add new ones, in the following chapters.

A master file needs to have records deleted from it when they become obsolete. In our savings-account master file a record would be deleted when a depositor closes an account. Any balance remaining in the account would be paid to the depositor as a final withdrawal. The format of the transaction input to Program P12-03 is:

Positions	Field
1	Code 5
2–6	Account Number
7–80	spaces

There is one transaction for each record that is to be removed from the master file. The transaction contains only the Code 5, identifying the transaction as a deletion, and the Account Number of the master record to be deleted.

If a deletion transaction contains an Account Number that is not on the master file, the transaction is in error. If there is more than one transaction with the same Account Number, only one of them could be valid. If one were valid and successfully deleted a master record, the other transaction records with the same Account Number would be invalid because there would no longer be a master record with that Account Number. Program P12-03 produces a report in the format shown in Figure 12.12 showing the records deleted. The erroneous transactions are shown in the format given in Figure 12.13. Notice that neither report shows the complete contents of the master file.

When records are to be deleted from a tape file, we cannot remove them with scissors. Nor can we erase the obsolete records and somehow move the remaining ones up along the tape to fill the gaps. Even if COBOL permitted that kind of processing, which it does not, it would involve too much time-consuming movement of tape back and forth. The way that records are deleted from a tape file is

Figure 12.12 Output format for deletion report for Program P12-03.

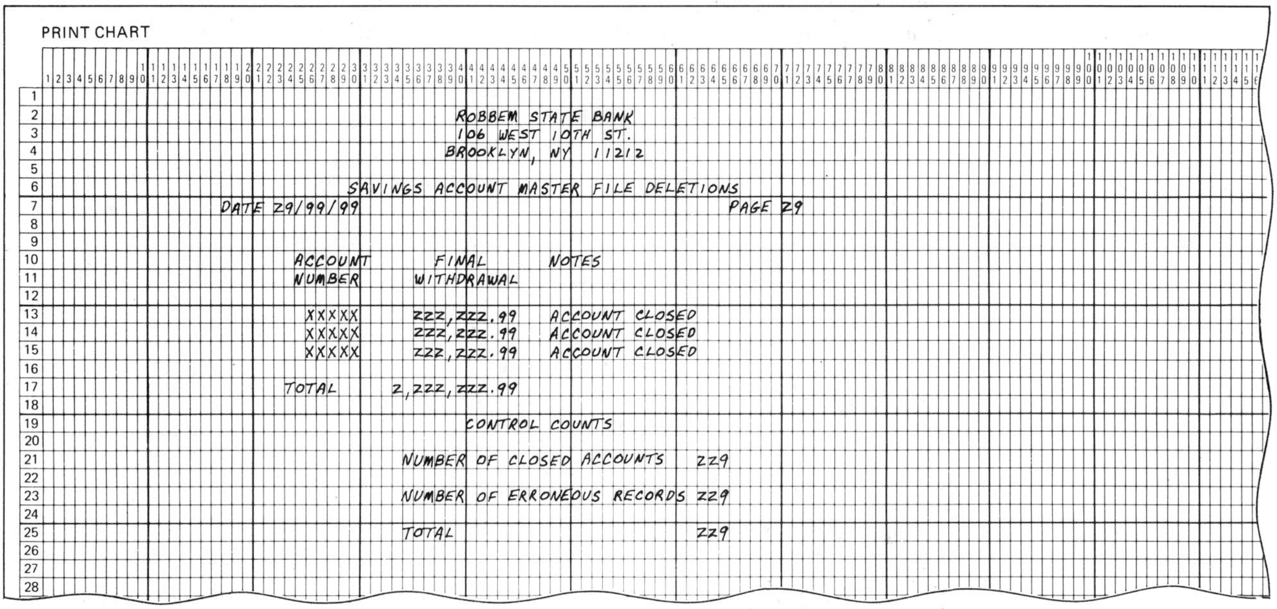

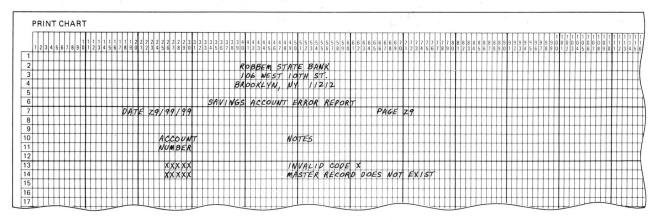

Figure 12.13 Output format for error report for Program P12-03.

this: The update program reads the existing master file and, by referring to the deletion transactions, copies the master onto a new tape, omitting the deleted records. The transactions must be in sequence on the same key field as the master file — in this case, Account Number. The same procedure is followed for deleting records from a sequential file on disk.

All the update programs in this book use the well-known **balance line algorithm.** This is a widely published and widely accepted algorithm, and is known to be correct.[2] Its use is certain to become more widespread as programmers recognize

[2]See, for example, Dwyer, Barry. January 1981. One more time — How to update a master file, *Communications of the ACM* 24:1, pp. 3–8; Grauer, Robert T. 1983. *Structured Methods Through COBOL.* Englewood Cliffs, NJ: Prentice-Hall, pp. 140–167.

that it can easily accommodate update logic of any imaginable complexity. The algorithm uses a transaction input area in working storage with space for one transaction record, a master input area with space for one incoming master record, and a master work area for working on each master record. There is a field in working storage called CURRENT-KEY, to which is assigned the key of the record being worked on.

A Hierarchy Diagram for Deleting Records from a Sequential File

The hierarchy diagram for Program P12-03 is shown in Figure 12.14. The diagram is more complex than is absolutely necessary for doing deletions. The logic contained in the diagram is very general, though, and will be able easily to accommodate all the additional features of all the update programs to come. You will see that if you learn the logic of this hierarchy diagram, there will be very little more to learn. The diagram is not easy to follow, but the effort expended in learning it is extremely worthwhile.

The boxes of the hierarchy diagram are described briefly in this section. In the next section, we will step through the diagram with sample data to see how it would handle some deletions and some error conditions.

In the diagram, the program SORTs the transactions into order on their key, in this case Account Number, and the OUTPUT PROCEDURE of the SORT is the rest of the hierarchy diagram. As part of the "Initialization" the program reads the first master record and the first transaction record, in the boxes "Read a master record" and "Read a transaction record." These two records are assigned to their respective input areas in working storage. Later in the program, whenever we get done with either a master record or a transaction record in its input area, we immediately replace it with the next incoming master or transaction record. In that way we always have in the input areas in working storage the next master record and the next transaction record.

The box "Choose current key" determines the key of the next record to be worked on and assigns it to the field CURRENT-KEY. In a sequential update, you must always work on the record in storage with the lowest key. If the record in the master input area has a lower key than the record in the transaction input area, the program assigns the key of the master record to CURRENT-KEY; if the transaction has a lower key than the master record, the program assigns the key of the transaction to CURRENT-KEY. If the two keys are equal, the program assigns their common key to CURRENT-KEY. Master records are worked on in the master work area, and transaction records are worked on in the transaction input area. In the course of execution of the hierarchy diagram, every key on the master and transaction files is assigned to CURRENT-KEY, in ascending order.

"Process one key" is the main loop of the program. It executes once for each different value of CURRENT-KEY. Each time CURRENT-KEY is assigned a new value, the four subfunctions of "Process one key" execute left to right. In so doing, they process any master record whose key is equal to CURRENT-KEY (if there is one), and all the transactions whose keys are equal to CURRENT-KEY (if there are any). The subfunctions "Process master record," "Process transaction record," "Check to write master," and "Choose current key" thus keep executing over and over until all the keys on the master and transaction files have been processed.

The box "Process master record" determines whether the record in the master input area should be moved to the master work area. It does this by comparing the key of the record in the master input area to CURRENT-KEY. If they are equal, then "Process master record"

Figure 12.14 Hierarchy diagram for Program P12-03.

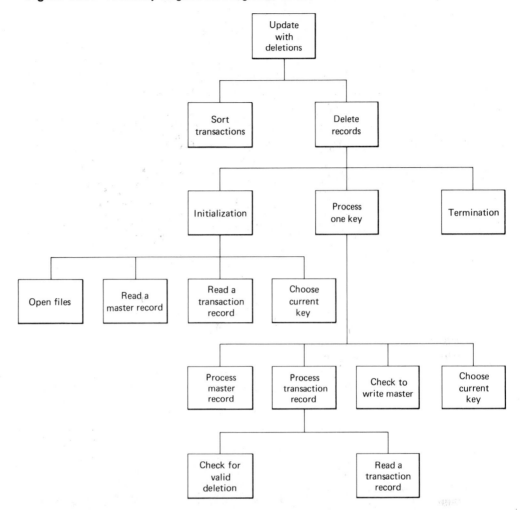

a. moves the contents of the master input area to the master work area

b. reads the next incoming master record and assigns it to the master input area

c. moves "Y" to a flag to indicate that a record was moved to the master work area

If the key of the record in the master input area is not equal to CURRENT-KEY, "Process master record" moves "N" to the flag to indicate that no record was moved to the master work area.

"Process transaction record" executes only if the key of the record in the transaction input area is equal to CURRENT-KEY. If there is more than one transaction whose key is equal to CURRENT-KEY, "Process transaction record" processes all of them. In our deletion program there can be no more than one valid transaction for any key.

"Check to write master" looks to see if there is a master record in the work area, by checking whether the flag is "Y" or "N." If the flag is "Y," "Check to write master" writes the contents of the master work area onto the new master output tape. If the flag is "N," "Check to write master" does nothing.

This hierarchy diagram allows for erroneous transactions of both types mentioned earlier, that is, a deletion transaction whose key does not match the key of any master record, and more than one deletion transaction against a single master record.

How the Hierarchy Diagram Works

Let us look at a few master records and a few deletion transactions to see how the hierarchy diagram would execute. For this example we will assume that we have the master file that was created by Program P12-02. The Account Numbers of the first eight records in that file are listed here:

```
00007
00014
00021
00028
00032
00035
00049
00056
```

Now let us assume that we have the following four deletion transactions, two of which are in error:

```
5 00021
5 00021
5 00029
5 00035
```

One of the transactions is in error because it has no match on the master file; one of the others is in error because it is a duplicate and will be trying to delete a record that will have already been deleted. Now let us follow the hierarchy diagram as it processes the master records and deletion transactions shown.

First, "Initialization" reads the first master record, 00007, into the master input area in working storage. It then reads the first transaction, 00021, into the transaction input area in working storage. "Choose current key" assigns the lower of the two keys, 00007, to CURRENT-KEY.

Now we enter the main loop. First, "Process master record" compares the key of the master record in the master input area to CURRENT-KEY. Since they are equal, "Process master record" moves the master record to the work area and reads the next master record, 00014, into the master input area. It also sets a flag to "Y" to indicate that a master record was moved. Then the program goes on to "Process transaction record." Since there are no transactions whose key is equal to the CURRENT-KEY, 00007, the program goes to "Check to write master." "Check to write master" looks to see whether there is a master record in the work area, and since there is one, writes it onto the new output master file. "Choose current key" now executes, and chooses between the master key in the master input area, 00014, and the transaction key, which is still 00021. The master key is again lower, so 00014 is assigned to CURRENT-KEY.

We now go around the main loop again. "Process master record" determines that the key of the master record in the master input area is equal to CURRENT-KEY, and so moves master record 00014 to the work area, reads master record 00021 into the master input area, and sets the flag to "Y" to indicate that the move was made. Once again there are no transactions for the CURRENT-KEY, so we go directly to "Check to write master." "Check to write master" finds that the work area contains a master record, and so writes it onto the new output master file. Now "Choose current key" finds the keys of the master record and the transaction the same, 00021. It assigns 00021 to CURRENT-KEY.

As we go around the main loop again, "Process master record" moves master record 00021 to the work area, reads master record 00028 into the master input area, and sets the flag to "Y" to reflect the move. Now we have a transaction in the transaction input area whose key is equal to CURRENT-KEY, so "Process transaction record" executes. Since there is more than one transaction with this same key, "Process transaction record" will execute over and over until they are all processed. "Check for valid deletion" checks that the transaction contains a Code of 5 and that the flag is "Y," indicating that there is a master record in the work area that can be deleted. It then processes the deletion as follows: It takes the Current Balance in master record 00021 to be the final withdrawal and prints a line on the transaction report showing the amount. Then it sets the flag to "N" to indicate that master record 00021 is no longer present. Of course, the record is still sitting in the work area, but as far as the program cares, the record has disappeared. The transaction is thus processed, and "Read a transaction record" reads in the next transaction, the second of the 00021s.

Since this transaction has the same key as the previous one, "Process transaction record" executes again. This time the transaction is found invalid because there is no longer a master record with a key of 00021. The program writes an error message saying that there is no such master record. The next transaction, 00029, is then read into the transaction input area.

Since all transactions with a key of 00021 have been processed, "Check to write master" executes. Now "Check to write master" finds no master record in the work area, because the processing of the valid deletion transaction made it disappear. So the program goes on to "Choose current key." The lower of the two keys, 00028, is assigned to CURRENT-KEY.

You can now trace the execution of the main loop and see that master record 00028 gets written onto the output master tape. "Choose current key" then chooses between the master key, 00032, and the transaction key, 00029. It assigns the lower, 00029, to CURRENT-KEY.

As we go around the loop again, "Process master record" notes that the key of the master record in the input area is not equal to CURRENT-KEY, so it does not move anything to the work area. It sets the flag to "N" to indicate that no master record was moved. In "Process transaction record" the program checks that the transaction contains a Code of 5 and whether there is a master record in the work area. Since the flag is "N," indicating that there is no master record in the work area, the program knows that this transaction is in error. Indeed, the transaction is trying to delete master record 00029, and no such master record exists. The program writes an error message, and "Read a transaction record" reads transaction 00035. "Check to write master" of course finds the flag "N," indicating that there is no master record in the work area, and so the program goes on to "Choose current key."

EXERCISE 4

Step through the hierarchy diagram in Figure 12.14 and show how the master records 00032, 00035, 00049, and 00056 are processed. Answer the following questions:

a. Which of the three master records 00032, 00035, and 00049 get written onto the new output master tape?

b. What is the value assigned to CURRENT-KEY at the time the last transaction is processed?

c. What is the value assigned to CURRENT-KEY at the time master record 00056 is written onto the new master tape?

How the Hierarchy Diagram Handles End-of-file

We now discuss how the hierarchy diagram handles end-of-file on the transaction file and the master file. In an update program such as this, there is no field such as MORE-INPUT, for there are two input files, and both must reach end-of-file before the program can proceed to the termination routine. In the sample data that we were using to step through the hierarchy diagram, an end-of-file would be detected on the transaction file after transaction 00035 was processed. At that time, master records 00049 and 00056 still need to be copied from the incoming master file to the new output master file.

The simplest way to handle transaction end-of-file is this: When end-of-file is detected on the transaction file, move HIGH-VALUES to the transaction input area. That way, "Choose current key" will keep choosing master keys as lower, and the remaining master records will be copied.

When end-of-file is detected on the incoming master file, HIGH-VALUES is moved to the master input area. When CURRENT-KEY finally gets HIGH-VALUES assigned to it, that means that both the master and transaction files have been completely processed, and then the "Termination" box is executed.

A Program to Delete Records from a Sequential File

Program P12-03 is shown in Figure 12.15. The definition of the SORT-WORK-FILE, line 00430, shows that only the first six characters of each record from the transaction file will be processed by the SORT. Those are the only characters needed for later processing.

In the Working Storage Section you can find CURRENT-KEY, at line 00670. The field IS-MASTER-RECORD-IN-WORK-AREA is the flag that is used to record whether or not there is a master record in the work area. You will see how the flag is set to "Y" and "N" as needed when we look at the Procedure Division.

The three areas in working storage that are used to store master and transaction records are shown in lines 00800 through 00940. Remember that a master record is worked on only when it is in the WORK-AREA.

Figure 12.15   Program P12-03.

```
CB1 RELEASE 2.4                                    IBM OS/VS COBOL   JULY  1, 1982


                              23.00.56        APR  7,1988


00010   IDENTIFICATION DIVISION.
00020   PROGRAM-ID. P12-03.
00030 * AUTHOR. SHAMEZE SULTAN
00040 *         REVISED BY GAETANO MURATORE
00050 *
00060 *    THIS PROGRAM DELETES RECORDS FROM A SEQUENTIAL MASTER
00070 *    FILE.
00080 *
00090 *************************************************************************
00100
00110   ENVIRONMENT DIVISION.
00120   CONFIGURATION SECTION.
00130   SOURCE-COMPUTER. IBM-370.
00140   OBJECT-COMPUTER. IBM-370.
00150
```

```
00160    INPUT-OUTPUT SECTION.
00170    FILE-CONTROL.
00180        SELECT ACCOUNT-MASTER-FILE-IN            ASSIGN TO MASTIN.
00190        SELECT ACCOUNT-MASTER-FILE-OUT           ASSIGN TO MASTOUT.
00200        SELECT TRANSACTION-FILE-IN               ASSIGN TO INFILE.
00210        SELECT TRANSACTION-REGISTER-FILE-OUT     ASSIGN TO PRINTER1.
00220        SELECT ERROR-FILE-OUT                    ASSIGN TO PRINTER2.
00230        SELECT SORT-WORK-FILE                    ASSIGN TO SORTWK.
00240
00250    *********************************************************************
00260
00270    DATA DIVISION.
00280    FILE SECTION.
00290    FD  ACCOUNT-MASTER-FILE-IN
00300        LABEL RECORDS ARE STANDARD
00310        RECORD CONTAINS 39 CHARACTERS
00320        BLOCK CONTAINS 100 RECORDS.
00330
00340    01  ACCOUNT-MASTER-RECORD-IN        PIC X(39).
00350
00360    FD  ACCOUNT-MASTER-FILE-OUT
00370        LABEL RECORDS ARE STANDARD
00380        RECORD CONTAINS 39 CHARACTERS
00390        BLOCK CONTAINS 100 RECORDS.
00400
00410    01  ACCOUNT-MASTER-RECORD-OUT       PIC X(39).
00420
00430    SD  SORT-WORK-FILE
00440        RECORD CONTAINS 6 CHARACTERS.
00450
00460    01  SORT-WORK-RECORD.
00470        05  TRANSACTION-CODE-S          PIC X.
00480        05  ACCOUNT-NUMBER-S            PIC X(5).
00490
00500    FD  TRANSACTION-FILE-IN
00510        LABEL RECORDS ARE OMITTED
00520        RECORD CONTAINS 80 CHARACTERS.
00530
00540    01  TRANSACTION-RECORD-IN           PIC X(80).
00550
00560    FD  TRANSACTION-REGISTER-FILE-OUT
00570        LABEL RECORDS ARE OMITTED.
00580
00590    01  TRANSACTION-REGISTER-RECORD     PIC X(72).
00600
00610    FD  ERROR-FILE-OUT
00620        LABEL RECORDS ARE OMITTED.
00630
00640    01  ERROR-RECORD-OUT                PIC X(76).
00650
00660    WORKING-STORAGE SECTION.
00670    01  CURRENT-KEY                     PIC X(5).
00680    01  IS-MASTER-RECORD-IN-WORK-AREA   PIC X.
00690    01  NUMBER-OF-INPUT-RECORDS-W       PIC S9(3) VALUE ZERO.
00700    01  NUMBER-OF-DELETIONS-W           PIC S9(3) VALUE ZERO.
00710    01  PAGE-NUMBER-W                   PIC S9(3) VALUE ZERO.
00720    01  ERROR-PAGE-NUMBER-W             PIC S9(3) VALUE ZERO.
00730    01  NUMBER-OF-ERRONEOUS-RECORDS-W   PIC S9(3) VALUE ZERO.
00740    01  CURRENT-BALANCE-TOTAL           PIC 9(7)V99 VALUE ZERO.
00750    01  BLANK-LINE                      PIC X     VALUE SPACE.
00760    01  TODAYS-DATE.
00770        05  TODAYS-YEAR                 PIC 99.
00780        05  TODAYS-MONTH-AND-DAY        PIC 9(4).
00790
00800    01  MASTER-INPUT-AREA.
00810        05  ACCOUNT-NUMBER              PIC X(5).
00820        05  FILLER                      PIC X(34).
00830
00840    01  TRANSACTION-INPUT-AREA.
00850        05  TRANSACTION-CODE            PIC X.
00860            88  DELETION                VALUE "5".
00870        05  ACCOUNT-NUMBER              PIC X(5).
00880        05  FILLER                      PIC X(74).
00890
00900    01  WORK-AREA.
00910        05  ACCOUNT-NUMBER-W            PIC X(5).
00920        05  DEPOSITOR-NAME-W            PIC X(20).
00930        05  DATE-OF-LAST-TRANSACTION-W  PIC 9(6).
00940        05  CURRENT-BALANCE-W           PIC 9(6)V99.
00950
```

(continued)

Figure 12.15   (continued)

```
00960   01   REPORT-HEADING-1.
00970        05 FILLER                              PIC X(39) VALUE SPACES.
00980        05 FILLER          PIC X(17) VALUE "ROBBEM STATE BANK".
00990
01000   01   REPORT-HEADING-2.
01010        05 FILLER                              PIC X(39) VALUE SPACES.
01020        05 FILLER          PIC X(17) VALUE "106 WEST 10TH ST.".
01030
01040   01   REPORT-HEADING-3.
01050        05 FILLER                              PIC X(38) VALUE SPACES.
01060        05 FILLER          PIC X(19) VALUE "BROOKLYN, NY  11212".
01070
01080   01   PAGE-HEADING-1.
01090        05 FILLER                              PIC X(29) VALUE SPACES.
01100        05 FILLER                              PIC X(37)
01110                 VALUE "SAVINGS ACCOUNT MASTER FILE DELETIONS".
01120
01130   01   ERROR-PAGE-HEADING-1.
01140        05  FILLER                             PIC X(33) VALUE SPACES.
01150        05  FILLER                             PIC X(28)
01160                 VALUE     "SAVINGS ACCOUNT ERROR REPORT".
01170
01180   01   PAGE-HEADING-2.
01190        05 FILLER                              PIC X(17) VALUE SPACES.
01200        05 FILLER                              PIC X(5) VALUE "DATE".
01210        05 TODAYS-MONTH-AND-DAY                PIC Z9/99/.
01220        05 TODAYS-YEAR                         PIC 99.
01230        05 FILLER                              PIC X(35) VALUE SPACES.
01240        05 FILLER                              PIC X(4)  VALUE "PAGE".
01250        05 PAGE-NUMBER-OUT                     PIC Z9.
01260
01270   01   PAGE-HEADING-3.
01280        05 FILLER                              PIC X(24) VALUE SPACES.
01290        05 FILLER                         PIC X(7)  VALUE "ACCOUNT".
01300        05 FILLER                              PIC X(6) VALUE SPACES.
01310        05 FILLER                         PIC X(5)  VALUE "FINAL".
01320        05 FILLER                              PIC X(6) VALUE SPACES.
01330        05 FILLER                              PIC X(5)  VALUE "NOTES".
01340
01350   01   ERROR-PAGE-HEADING-3.
01360        05 FILLER                              PIC X(24) VALUE SPACES.
01370        05 FILLER                         PIC X(7)  VALUE "ACCOUNT".
01380        05 FILLER                              PIC X(17) VALUE SPACES.
01390        05 FILLER                              PIC X(5)  VALUE "NOTES".
01400
01410   01   PAGE-HEADING-4.
01420        05 FILLER                              PIC X(24) VALUE SPACES.
01430        05 FILLER                         PIC X(6)  VALUE "NUMBER".
01440        05 FILLER                              PIC X(5) VALUE SPACES.
01450        05 FILLER                              PIC X(10)
01460                 VALUE "WITHDRAWAL".
01470
01480   01   ERROR-PAGE-HEADING-4.
01490        05 FILLER                              PIC X(24) VALUE SPACES.
01500        05 FILLER                         PIC X(6)  VALUE "NUMBER".
01510
01520   01   REPORT-LINE.
01530        05 ACCOUNT-NUMBER-OUT                  PIC B(25)X(5).
01540        05 CURRENT-BALANCE-OUT                 PIC B(5)ZZZ,ZZZ.99B(3).
01550        05 FILLER                              PIC X(14)
01560                 VALUE "ACCOUNT CLOSED".
01570
01580   01   INVALID-CODE-LINE.
01590        05 ACCOUNT-NUMBER-E                    PIC B(25)X(5)B(18).
01600        05 MSG                                 PIC X(12)
01610                 VALUE "INVALID CODE".
01620        05 TRANSACTION-CODE-OUT                PIC BX.
01630
01640   01   MASTER-MISSING-LINE.
01650        05 ACCOUNT-NUMBER-MISSING              PIC B(25)X(5)B(18).
01660        05 FILLER                              PIC X(28)
01670            VALUE "MASTER RECORD DOES NOT EXIST".
01680
01690   01   TOTAL-LINE-1.
01700        05 FILLER                              PIC X(23) VALUE SPACES.
01710        05 FILLER                         PIC X(5)B(5) VALUE "TOTAL".
01720        05 CURRENT-BALANCE-TOTAL-OUT           PIC Z,ZZZ,ZZZ.99.
```

```
01730
01740   01   TOTAL-LINE-2.
01750        05 FILLER                              PIC X(41) VALUE SPACES.
01760        05 FILLER                    PIC X(14) VALUE "CONTROL COUNTS".
01770
01780   01   TOTAL-LINE-3.
01790        05 FILLER                              PIC X(34) VALUE SPACES.
01800        05 FILLER                              PIC X(25)
01810                             VALUE "NUMBER OF CLOSED ACCOUNTS".
01820        05 NUMBER-OF-DELETIONS                 PIC B(3)ZZ9.
01830
01840   01   TOTAL-LINE-4.
01850        05 FILLER                              PIC X(34) VALUE SPACES.
01860        05 FILLER                              PIC X(27)
01870                          VALUE "NUMBER OF ERRONEOUS RECORDS".
01880        05 NUMBER-OF-ERRONEOUS-RECORDS         PIC BZZ9.
01890
01900   01   TOTAL-LINE-5.
01910        05 FILLER                              PIC X(34) VALUE SPACES.
01920        05 FILLER                              PIC X(5)   VALUE "TOTAL".
01930        05 NUMBER-OF-INPUT-RECORDS             PIC B(23)ZZ9.
01940
01950   01   NO-INPUT-DATA.
01960        05 FILLER                              PIC X(21) VALUE SPACES.
01970        05 FILLER                    PIC X(13) VALUE "NO INPUT DATA".
01980
01990   *****************************************************************
02000
02010   PROCEDURE DIVISION.
02020   CONTROL-SECTION SECTION.
02030   UPDATE-WITH-DELETIONS.
02040       SORT SORT-WORK-FILE
02050            ASCENDING KEY ACCOUNT-NUMBER-S
02060            USING TRANSACTION-FILE-IN
02070            OUTPUT PROCEDURE IS DELETE-RECORDS.
02080       STOP RUN.
02090
02100   DELETE-RECORDS SECTION.
02110   DELETE-RECORDS-PARAGRAPH.
02120       PERFORM INITIALIZATION.
02130       PERFORM PROCESS-ONE-KEY UNTIL
02140           CURRENT-KEY = HIGH-VALUES.
02150       PERFORM TERMINATION.
02160       GO TO END-OF-THIS-SECTION.
02170
02180   INITIALIZATION.
02190       OPEN INPUT  ACCOUNT-MASTER-FILE-IN
02200            OUTPUT ACCOUNT-MASTER-FILE-OUT
02210                   ERROR-FILE-OUT
02220                   TRANSACTION-REGISTER-FILE-OUT.
02230       ACCEPT TODAYS-DATE FROM DATE.
02240       MOVE CORR TODAYS-DATE TO PAGE-HEADING-2.
02250       PERFORM PRINT-REPORT-HEADINGS.
02260       PERFORM READ-A-MASTER-RECORD.
02270       PERFORM READ-A-TRANSACTION-RECORD.
02280       PERFORM CHOOSE-CURRENT-KEY.
02290       IF CURRENT-KEY = HIGH-VALUES
02300           WRITE TRANSACTION-REGISTER-RECORD FROM NO-INPUT-DATA.
```

(continued)

The Procedure Division begins at line 02010. The main control paragraph of the OUTPUT PROCEDURE begins at line 02110. The PERFORM statement that controls the main loop is at line 02130. You can see that in this program the main loop, PROCESS-ONE-KEY, continues to execute UNTIL CURRENT-KEY IS EQUAL TO HIGH-VALUES, signaling the end of both the master and transaction files. If there are no input data on either the master or transaction files, the IF statement at line 02290 prints the words "No input data."

Figure 12.15   (continued)

```
02310
02320   PROCESS-ONE-KEY.
02330       PERFORM PROCESS-MASTER-RECORD.
02340       PERFORM PROCESS-TRANSACTION-RECORD UNTIL
02350           ACCOUNT-NUMBER IN TRANSACTION-INPUT-AREA
02360           IS NOT EQUAL TO CURRENT-KEY.
02370       PERFORM CHECK-TO-WRITE-MASTER.
02380       PERFORM CHOOSE-CURRENT-KEY.
02390
02400   PROCESS-TRANSACTION-RECORD.
02410       PERFORM CHECK-FOR-VALID-DELETION.
02420       PERFORM READ-A-TRANSACTION-RECORD.
02430
02440   CHECK-TO-WRITE-MASTER.
02450       IF IS-MASTER-RECORD-IN-WORK-AREA = "Y"
02460           WRITE ACCOUNT-MASTER-RECORD-OUT FROM WORK-AREA.
02470
02480   CHOOSE-CURRENT-KEY.
02490       IF ACCOUNT-NUMBER IN TRANSACTION-INPUT-AREA IS LESS THAN
02500           ACCOUNT-NUMBER IN MASTER-INPUT-AREA
02510           MOVE ACCOUNT-NUMBER IN TRANSACTION-INPUT-AREA TO
02520               CURRENT-KEY
02530       ELSE
02540           MOVE ACCOUNT-NUMBER IN MASTER-INPUT-AREA TO
02550               CURRENT-KEY.
02560
02570   PROCESS-MASTER-RECORD.
02580       IF ACCOUNT-NUMBER IN MASTER-INPUT-AREA IS EQUAL TO
02590           CURRENT-KEY
02600           MOVE MASTER-INPUT-AREA TO WORK-AREA
02610           PERFORM READ-A-MASTER-RECORD
02620           MOVE "Y" TO IS-MASTER-RECORD-IN-WORK-AREA
02630       ELSE
02640           MOVE "N" TO IS-MASTER-RECORD-IN-WORK-AREA.
02650
02660   READ-A-TRANSACTION-RECORD.
02670       RETURN SORT-WORK-FILE INTO TRANSACTION-INPUT-AREA
02680           AT END
02690               MOVE HIGH-VALUES TO TRANSACTION-INPUT-AREA.
02700       IF TRANSACTION-INPUT-AREA NOT EQUAL TO HIGH-VALUES
02710           ADD 1 TO NUMBER-OF-INPUT-RECORDS-W.
02720
02730   READ-A-MASTER-RECORD.
02740       READ ACCOUNT-MASTER-FILE-IN INTO MASTER-INPUT-AREA
02750           AT END
02760               MOVE HIGH-VALUES TO MASTER-INPUT-AREA.
02770
02780   CHECK-FOR-VALID-DELETION.
02790       IF NOT DELETION
02800           PERFORM WRITE-INVALID-CODE-LINE
02810           ADD 1 TO NUMBER-OF-ERRONEOUS-RECORDS-W
02820       ELSE
02830       IF IS-MASTER-RECORD-IN-WORK-AREA = "N"
02840           PERFORM WRITE-MASTER-MISSING-LINE
02850           ADD 1 TO NUMBER-OF-ERRONEOUS-RECORDS-W
02860       ELSE
02870           PERFORM WRITE-REPORT-LINE
02880           MOVE "N" TO IS-MASTER-RECORD-IN-WORK-AREA
02890           ADD 1 TO NUMBER-OF-DELETIONS-W.
02900
02910   WRITE-REPORT-LINE.
02920       MOVE ACCOUNT-NUMBER-W TO ACCOUNT-NUMBER-OUT.
02930       MOVE CURRENT-BALANCE-W TO CURRENT-BALANCE-OUT.
02940       WRITE TRANSACTION-REGISTER-RECORD FROM REPORT-LINE.
02950       ADD CURRENT-BALANCE-W TO CURRENT-BALANCE-TOTAL.
02960
02970   WRITE-INVALID-CODE-LINE.
02980       MOVE ACCOUNT-NUMBER IN TRANSACTION-INPUT-AREA TO
02990                               ACCOUNT-NUMBER-E.
03000       MOVE TRANSACTION-CODE TO TRANSACTION-CODE-OUT.
03010       WRITE ERROR-RECORD-OUT FROM INVALID-CODE-LINE.
03020
03030   WRITE-MASTER-MISSING-LINE.
03040       MOVE ACCOUNT-NUMBER IN TRANSACTION-INPUT-AREA TO
03050                                   ACCOUNT-NUMBER-MISSING.
03060       WRITE ERROR-RECORD-OUT FROM MASTER-MISSING-LINE.
03070
```

```
03080    TERMINATION.
03090        PERFORM WRITE-TOTALS.
03100        CLOSE ACCOUNT-MASTER-FILE-IN
03110              ACCOUNT-MASTER-FILE-OUT
03120              ERROR-FILE-OUT
03130              TRANSACTION-REGISTER-FILE-OUT.
03140
03150    WRITE-TOTALS.
03160        MOVE CURRENT-BALANCE-TOTAL TO CURRENT-BALANCE-TOTAL-OUT.
03170        WRITE TRANSACTION-REGISTER-RECORD FROM TOTAL-LINE-1 AFTER 2.
03180        WRITE TRANSACTION-REGISTER-RECORD FROM TOTAL-LINE-2 AFTER 2.
03190        MOVE NUMBER-OF-DELETIONS-W TO NUMBER-OF-DELETIONS.
03200        WRITE TRANSACTION-REGISTER-RECORD FROM TOTAL-LINE-3 AFTER 2
03210        MOVE NUMBER-OF-ERRONEOUS-RECORDS-W TO
03220                                   NUMBER-OF-ERRONEOUS-RECORDS.
03230        WRITE TRANSACTION-REGISTER-RECORD FROM TOTAL-LINE-4 AFTER 2.
03240        MOVE NUMBER-OF-INPUT-RECORDS-W TO
03250                                   NUMBER-OF-INPUT-RECORDS.
03260        WRITE TRANSACTION-REGISTER-RECORD FROM TOTAL-LINE-5 AFTER 2.
03270
03280    PRINT-REPORT-HEADINGS.
03290        PERFORM PRINT-REGISTER-HEADINGS.
03300        PERFORM PRINT-ERROR-HEADINGS.
03310
03320    PRINT-REGISTER-HEADINGS.
03330        ADD 1 TO PAGE-NUMBER-W.
03340        MOVE PAGE-NUMBER-W TO PAGE-NUMBER-OUT.
03350        WRITE TRANSACTION-REGISTER-RECORD FROM REPORT-HEADING-1
03360                                   AFTER ADVANCING PAGE.
03370        WRITE TRANSACTION-REGISTER-RECORD FROM REPORT-HEADING-2.
03380        WRITE TRANSACTION-REGISTER-RECORD FROM REPORT-HEADING-3.
03390        WRITE TRANSACTION-REGISTER-RECORD FROM PAGE-HEADING-1
03400                                   AFTER 2.
03410        WRITE TRANSACTION-REGISTER-RECORD FROM PAGE-HEADING-2.
03420        WRITE TRANSACTION-REGISTER-T-ERROR-HEADINGS.
03480        ADD 1 TO ERROR-PAGE-NUMBER-W.
03490        MOVE ERROR-PAGE-NUMBER-W TO PAGE-NUMBER-OUT.
03500        WRITE ERROR-RECORD-OUT FROM REPORT-HEADING-1 AFTER PAGE.
03510        WRITE ERROR-RECORD-OUT FROM REPORT-HEADING-2.
03520        WRITE ERROR-RECORD-OUT FROM REPORT-HEADING-3.
03530        WRITE ERROR-RECORD-OUT FROM ERROR-PAGE-HEADING-1 AFTER 2.
03540        WRITE ERROR-RECORD-OUT FROM PAGE-HEADING-2.
03550        WRITE ERROR-RECORD-OUT FROM ERROR-PAGE-HEADING-3 AFTER 3.
03560        WRITE ERROR-RECORD-OUT FROM ERROR-PAGE-HEADING-4.
03570        WRITE ERROR-RECORD-OUT FROM BLANK-LINE.
03580
03590    END-OF-THIS-SECTION.
03600        EXIT.
```

The paragraph PROCESS-ONE-KEY, line 02320, executes exactly once for each different value of CURRENT-KEY. The PERFORM statement at line 02330 causes a master record to be moved to the master work area if the Account Number in the master record is equal to CURRENT-KEY, and the PERFORM statement at line 02340 executes PROCESS-TRANSACTION-RECORD over and over as long as the transaction Account Number is equal to CURRENT-KEY.

In CHOOSE-CURRENT-KEY, line 02480, the program chooses the lower of two keys. CHECK-FOR-VALID-DELETION, line 02780, checks each transaction for validity. The successful deletion of a master record is shown in lines 02870 through 02890.

The paragraphs at lines 02660 and 02730 show the use of the INTO option in RETURN and READ statements. The INTO option permits a record to be read from a file and placed in working storage, just as the FROM option permits a record to be written FROM working storage. When the INTO option is used with a READ statement, a record is first transferred from the external file to the File Section and then moved to working storage as we have seen earlier, in Chapter 6. When the INTO option is used with a RETURN statement, a record is first RETURNed from the SORT into the File Section and then moved to working storage.

Program P12-03 was run with the transaction input shown in Figure 12.16 and the master file that was created in Program P12-02. The report output produced by Program P12-03 is shown in Figure 12.17. The contents of the new output master file are shown in Figure 12.18.

Figure 12.16   Transaction input to Program P12-03.

```
------------------------------------------------------------------------------
        1         2         3         4         5         6         7         8
1234567890123456789012345678901234567890123456789012345678901234567890123456789 0
------------------------------------------------------------------------------
500350
500245
100299
500077
500003
500508
500168
500350
500599
700320
500280
500609
```

Figure 12.17   Report output from Program P12-03.

```
                         ROBBEM STATE BANK
                         106 WEST 10TH ST.
                         BROOKLYN, NY  11212

                    SAVINGS ACCOUNT ERROR REPORT
      DATE   4/07/88                                    PAGE 1


            ACCOUNT                 NOTES
            NUMBER

             00003                  MASTER RECORD DOES NOT EXIST
             00299                  INVALID CODE 1
             00320                  INVALID CODE 7
             00350                  MASTER RECORD DOES NOT EXIST
             00508                  MASTER RECORD DOES NOT EXIST
             00599                  MASTER RECORD DOES NOT EXIST
             00609                  MASTER RECORD DOES NOT EXIST




                         ROBBEM STATE BANK
                         106 WEST 10TH ST.
                         BROOKLYN, NY  11212

                 SAVINGS ACCOUNT MASTER FILE DELETIONS
      DATE   4/07/88                               PAGE 1


            ACCOUNT       FINAL      NOTES
            NUMBER     WITHDRAWAL

             00077         10.37     ACCOUNT CLOSED
             00168        125.50     ACCOUNT CLOSED
             00245         35.00     ACCOUNT CLOSED
             00280         20.00     ACCOUNT CLOSED
             00350      2,500.00     ACCOUNT CLOSED

          TOTAL        2,690.87


                       CONTROL COUNTS

              NUMBER OF CLOSED ACCOUNTS      5

              NUMBER OF ERRONEOUS RECORDS    7

              TOTAL                         12
```

Figure 12.18 Master file produced by Program P12-03.

```
--------------------------------------------------------------------------------
         1         2         3         4         5         6         7         8
12345678901234567890123456789012345678901234567890123456789012345678901234567890
--------------------------------------------------------------------------------
00007ROSEBUCCI            88040700100784
00014ROBERT DAVIS M.D.    88040700001000
00021LORICE MONTI         88040700012500
00028MICHAEL SMITH        88040700700159
00032JOSEPH CAMILLO       88040700002500
00035JOHN J. LEHMAN       88040700015000
00049JAY GREENE           88040700015000
00056EVELYN SLATER        88040700000100
00070PATRICK J. LEE       8804070005000C
00084JOHN DAPRINO         8804070015000C
00091JOE'S DELI           88040700010000
00098GEORGE CULHANE       88040700050000
00105ONE DAY CLEANERS     88040700005000
00112ROSEMARY LANE        88040700025000
00126JAMES BUDD           88040700075000
00133PAUL LERNER, D.D.S.  88040700100000
00140BETH FALLON          88040700002575
00161ROBERT RYAN          88040700002450
00175MARY KEATING         88040700001000
00189J. & L. CAIN         88040700003500
00196IMPERIAL FLORIST     88040700015000
00203JOYCE MITCHELL       88040700000500
00210JERRY PARKS          88040700025000
00217CARL CALDERON        88040700005000
00224JOHN WILLIAMS        88040700017550
00231BILL WILLIAMS        88040700055500
00238KEVIN PARKER         88040700001000
00252GENE GALLI           88040700001500
00266MARTIN LANG          88040700009957
00273VITO CACACI          88040700027500
00287SOLOMON CHAPELS      88040700001500
00294JOHN BURKE           88040700150000
00308JOE GARCIA           88040700200000
00315GRACE MICELI         88040700025000
00329GUY VOLPONE          88040700001000
00343JOE & MARY SESSA     88040700100000
```

EXERCISE 5

Write a program to update the master file you created in Exercise 3 with deletion transactions in the following format:

Positions	Field
1	Code 12
2–6	Part Number
7–80	spaces

Design reports to show the records deleted and the erroneous transactions. Have your program check all transactions for validity. If an attempt is made to delete a Part Number having a nonzero Quantity on Hand, have your program count the transaction as erroneous and print the Part Number, the Quantity on Hand, and a message NONZERO QUANTITY ON HAND on the error report. Save the updated file for use in Chapter 13.

Summary

Magnetic storage media include magnetic tape, magnetic disk, magnetic drum, data cell, and mass storage system. Magnetic tape is a sequential medium, and disk is a direct-access medium. Records on tape may be accessed only sequentially, whereas records on disk may be accessed sequentially or randomly.

Master files of data may be stored on magnetic media. A computer can write data onto the files, and then later read or change the data. Huge volumes of data can be stored on modern magnetic media.

It is especially important that data on a master file be correct. Much of the program logic dealing with master files relies on the sequence of the records in the file.

A sequential master file may be created from data entered on a keyboard or punched in cards. A program may read the data, check them for validity, and write a master file. The file so created may later be used as input to an update program.

Records may be deleted from a master file. A program to delete records reads the master file and, by referring to a file of deletion transactions, copies the old file onto a new one, omitting the deleted records.

Fill-in Exercises

1. Five kinds of magnetic storage media that computers can read input data from and write output onto are _____ , _____ , _____ , _____ , and _____ .

2. The only access method available for tape files is _____ access.

3. Three advantages of magnetic media over paper media are:

    a. _____

    b. _____

    c. _____

4. The _____ clause tells the system how many records are in a block.

5. Special records written onto magnetic files for identification are called _____ records.

6. Magnetic media that can enjoy sequential or random access are called _____ - _____ storage devices.

7. A block of records is sometimes called a(n) _____ record.

8. In a program that deletes records from a master file, there can be no more than _____ valid transaction(s) for a single master record.

9. In a sequential update, the program must always work on the record in storage with the _____ key.

10. The best way to handle end-of-file in a sequential update is to move _____ to the file input areas in working storage.

11. The average number of records on a master file changed during an update run is referred to as file _____ .

12. The average number of records added to or deleted from a master file during an update run is referred to as file _____ .

13. A numeric field containing nonnumeric data may cause abnormal termination of a run if the field is used for _____ , _____ _____ , or _____ _____ .

14. In a program to delete records from a sequential file, the field _____ gets assigned in turn every key on the master and transaction files.

15. In the hierarchy diagram for a program to delete records from a master file, the box "Process one key" executes once for every different _____ on the master file and the transaction file.

Review Exercises

1. A school wishes to maintain a file of alumni names and addresses. Write a program to create a sequential master file on tape or disk using transaction input in the following format:

Positions	Field
1	Code 1
2–10	Social Security Number
11–30	Student Name
31–50	Street Address
51–70	City State Zip
71–72	Major Department
73–74	Year of Graduation
75–80	spaces

Have your program check for the presence of all fields in each input record.
For each error-free input record, have your program write the entire 80-character record onto the master file. Have your program print a report showing the good records written onto the master file and a report showing the erroneous transactions. Create your master file with 50 records per block.

2. Using the same input data as in Review Exercise 1, write a program to create a sequential master file on tape or disk. Have your program build the master records in working storage. Each master record should contain the following fields:

Social Security Number
Student Name
Street Address
City, State, Zip
Major Department
Year of Graduation

Create your master file with 25 records per block. Have your program check for the presence of all fields in each input record. Have your program print a report showing the records written onto the master file and a report showing the erroneous transactions. Save the master file for use in Chapter 13.

3. Write a program to update the master file you created in Review Exercise 2. Use deletion transactions in the following format:

Positions	Field
1	Code 7
2–10	Social Security Number
11–80	spaces

Have your program print a report showing the complete contents of the records deleted from the file, and a report showing the erroneous transactions. Save the updated file for use in Review Exercises in Chapter 13.

4. Step through the hierarchy diagram in Figure 12.14 and show what would happen if the very first transaction had an Account Number lower than the Account Number of the first incoming master record. Would the hierarchy diagram work in such a situation?

Project

Write a program to create a sequential customer-name-and-address master file using input in the format described on page 352. Each master record should have room for up to five lines of name and address data, and should be in the following format:

Positions	Field
1–5	Customer Number
6–25	First line of name and address
26–45	Second line of name and address
46–65	Third line of name and address
66–85	Fourth line of name and address, if any
86–105	Fifth line of name and address, if any

Master records should contains blanks in any unused fields not needed for names-and-address lines. Have your program SORT the input transactions on the Code in position 1 within Customer Number, and check each input record to see that the Code it contains is valid. Have your program produce reports showing any errors found in the input and showing, for each good record written onto the master tape, the Customer Number and the first line of the name and address. Save the master file for use in Chapter 13.

Processing Sequential Master Files

Here are the key points you should learn from this chapter:

1. How to develop a hierarchy diagram for any program that reads a master file and a transaction file
2. How to list selected records from a master file
3. How to update a master file with additions, changes, and deletions
4. How to list the complete contents of a master file

There are no new key words in this chapter.

In this chapter we develop four programs. Three of them read a master file and a transaction file, and one reads only a master file. You will see that the hierarchy diagrams for the three programs that read a master and a transaction file differ from one another only at the lowest level. The upper portions of the three hierarchy diagrams will be identical, and also identical to the upper portion of the hierarchy diagram we used for the update program in Chapter 12. Thus you will see that the balance line algorithm can be used for reading the master and transaction files in any program that reads such files. About the only things that change from one program to the next are the details of the box "Process transaction record."

Listing Selected Records from a Master File

To return to our savings-account master file, let us assume that the bank would like to list the complete contents of certain master records each evening. That is, the bank would like to see printed, for certain accounts, the Account Number, the Current Balance, the Depositor Name, and the Date of Last Transaction.

Program P13-01 lists selected records from a master file. The program uses two input files. One is the master file itself, and the other is a transaction file indicating which master records are to be listed. The format of the transactions is:

Positions	Field
1	Code 6
2–6	Account Number
7–80	spaces

Each record contains the Account Number of the master record to be listed, and a transaction Code of 6 designating this transaction as a request to list a master record. Nothing else is needed in the transaction, since all of the information to be listed comes from the master record. The listing of the selected master records has the format shown in Figure 13.1. The program also lists erroneous transactions, in the format shown in Figure 13.2.

Figure 13.1 Output format for selected records in Program P13-01.

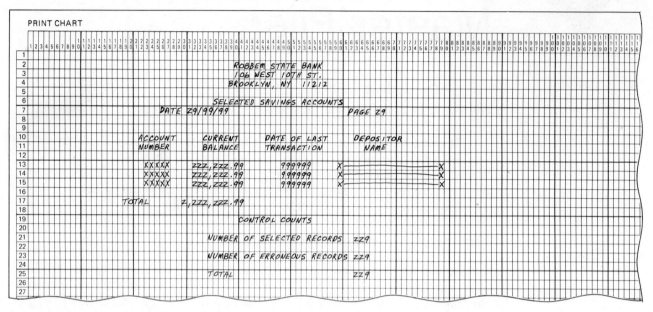

Figure 13.2 Output format for error report for Program P13-01.

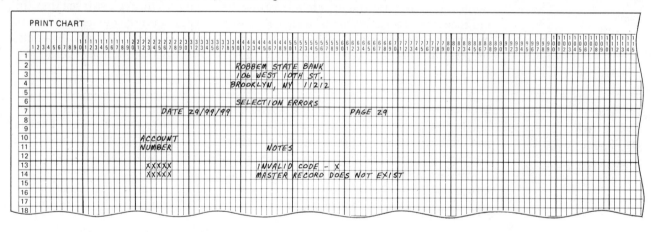

A Hierarchy Diagram for Listing Selected Records from a Master File

The hierarchy diagram for Program P13-01 is shown in Figure 13.3. Almost all of the boxes are the same as in the hierarchy diagram for Program P12-03, in Figure 12.14, page 397. One difference is in the box "Process transaction record." In Program P12-03 processing a transaction involved deleting a master record from the file. In Program P13-01 processing a transaction means listing a master record on a report.

Also, in Program P13-01 we will not be writing a new output master file. Program P13-01 is not an update program and does not create a new file. It merely reads the old master file and lists some of its records. So in the hierarchy diagram of Figure 13.3, we have simply omitted the box "Check to write master" and left a gap to remind you where it once was.

Figure 13.3 Hierarchy diagram for Program P13-01.

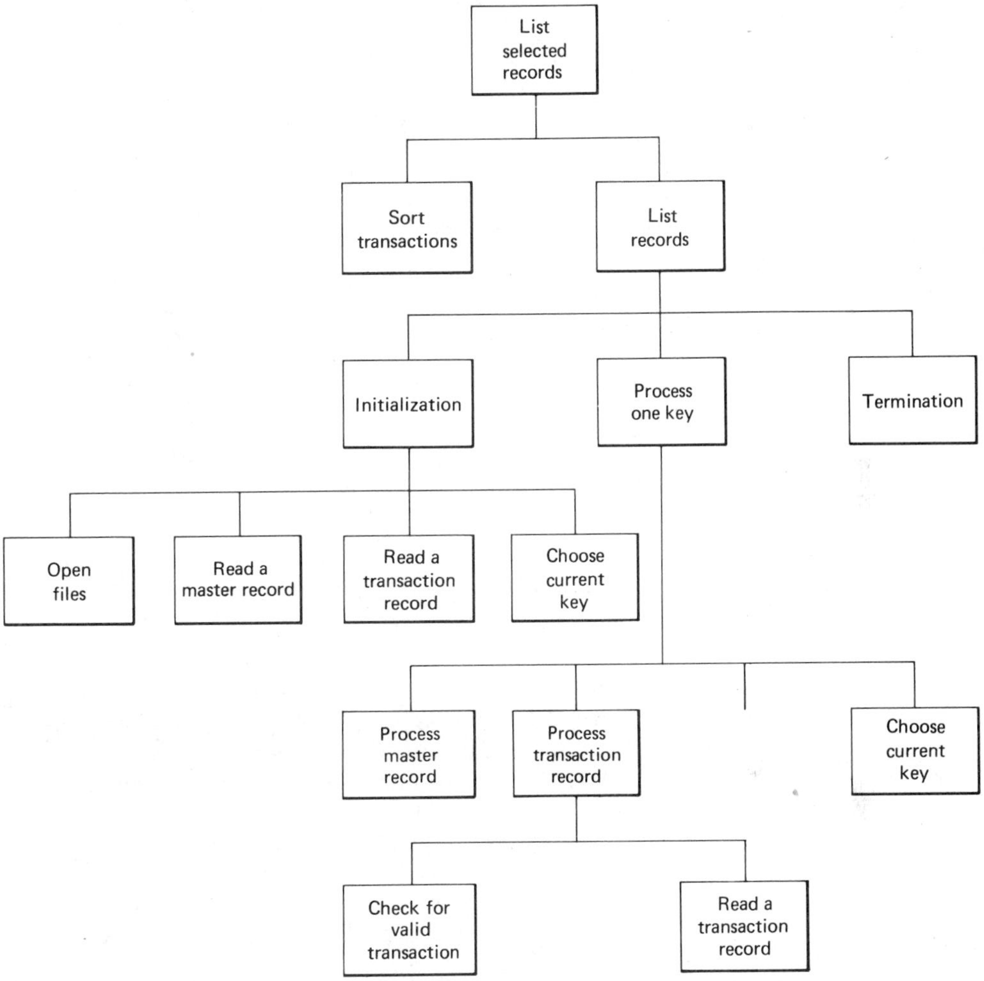

Listing selected records from a master file is really not a very complicated operation, and this hierarchy diagram is much more elaborate than is needed to do the job. We have included it here to show how the hierarchy diagram introduced in Chapter 12 can easily be modified to handle any kind of program that reads a master file and a transaction file.

This hierarchy diagram will handle erroneous transactions. In this program errors could include an invalid transaction Code, or a transaction to list a master record that does not exist. We will also consider duplicate transactions an error. That is, we will not list a master record more than once, even if there is more than one transaction with a Account Number that matches the Account Number of a master record. We will treat duplicate transactions as errors and print a message saying that no master record exists for them.

Stepping Through the Hierarchy Diagram

As before, we will use a few master records and transactions to step through the execution of the hierarchy diagram and see that it does its job of listing only those master records having matching transactions. We will also see that it handles erroneous transactions properly.

We can use the same savings-account master file as before. The Account Numbers of the first seven records of that file are:

```
00007
00014
00021
00028
00032
00035
00049
```

Assume we have the following transactions:

```
6 00006
6 00021
6 00021
6 00035
6 00064
```

Of these transactions, three are in error. Two are asking us to list master records that don't exist, and one is a duplicate. As we step through the hierarchy diagram you will see what happens when the first input transaction has a key lower than the key of the first incoming master record, and the last transaction a key higher than the key of the last master record.

"Initialization" brings master record 00007 and transaction 00006 into their respective areas in working storage. "Choose current key" assigns 00006 to CURRENT-KEY, and we enter the main loop of the program with CURRENT-KEY equal to 00006.

Now "Process master record" executes. Since the key of the master record in the master input area is not equal to CURRENT-KEY, "Process master record" sets the flag to "N" to indicate that no master record was moved to the work area. "Process transaction record" executes, since the key of the transaction in the transaction input area is equal to CURRENT-KEY. For transaction 00006 to be valid it must have a Code of 6 and there must be a master record in the work area waiting to be listed. Since the flag is "N," the program knows that there is no master record to match this transaction. The program writes an error message and "Read a transaction record" reads transaction 00021 into the transaction input area.

"Choose current key" assigns 00007 to CURRENT-KEY. "Process master record" moves master record 00007 to the work area, reads master record 00014 into the master input area, and sets the flag to "Y." Since there are no transactions whose key is equal to CURRENT-KEY, "Process transaction record" does not execute. "Choose current key" next assigns 00014 to CURRENT-KEY.

"Process master record" moves master record 00014 to the work area, reads master record 00021 into the master input area, and sets the flag to "Y." "Process transaction record" is skipped, and "Choose current key" assigns 00021 to CURRENT-KEY. "Process master record" moves master record 00021 to the work area, reads master record 00028 into the master input area, and sets the flag to "Y." Since there now is a transaction whose key is equal to CURRENT-KEY, "Process transaction record" executes. Of course, "Process transaction record" will execute over and over until all transactions whose key is equal to CURRENT-KEY are processed. For the present transaction to be valid, its Code must be 6 and the flag must indicate that there is a master record in the work area. The flag is "Y," so the contents of master record 00021 are listed out from the work area. The program now sets the flag to "N" to indicate that the record in the work area is not available for any further processing. It is as if the record were not there. Note that if we wanted to allow duplicate transactions to list the contents of a record more than once, we would simply omit the step that turns the flag to "N."

"Read a transaction record" reads the second of the transactions with a key of 00021. Since this is still equal to CURRENT-KEY, "Process transaction record" executes again. This time it finds no master record in the work area waiting to be listed. An error message is printed for this transaction, and "Read a transaction record" reads transaction 00035 into the transaction input area. "Choose current key" assigns 00028 to CURRENT-KEY.

"Process master record" moves master record 00028 to the work area, reads master record 00032 into the master input area, and sets the flag to "Y." "Choose current key" now executes, and assigns 00032 to CURRENT-KEY. "Process master record" moves master record 00032 to the work area, reads master record 00035 into the master input area, and sets the flag to "Y." "Choose current key" then assigns 00035 to CURRENT-KEY. "Process master record" moves master record 00035 to the work area, reads master record 00049 into the master input area, and sets the flag to "Y." "Process transaction record" processes transaction 00035 by printing out the contents of master record 00035 from the work area and reading transaction 00064 into the transaction input area. "Choose current key" assigns 00049 to CURRENT-KEY.

"Process master record" moves master record 00049 to the work area. In attempting to read the next master record, the program encounters end-of-file on the master file and so moves HIGH-VALUES to the master input area. It sets the flag to "Y" to indicate that master record 00049 was moved to the work area.

Since there is no transaction whose key is equal to CURRENT-KEY, "Process transaction record" does not execute. "Choose current key" assigns 00064 to CUR-RENT-KEY, since 00064 is lower than HIGH-VALUES. "Process master record" finds that the key of the master record in the master input area is not equal to CURRENT-KEY, and so sets the flag to "N."

Since there is a transaction whose key is equal to CURRENT-KEY, "Process transaction record" executes. Since the flag is set to "N," the program knows that there is no matching master record for this transaction. An error line is printed, and "Read a transaction record" reads end-of-file on the transaction file. The program moves HIGH-VALUES to the transaction input area. "Choose current key" assigns HIGH-VALUES to CURRENT-KEY, and the program goes to "Termination."

You can now review how the five transactions were processed. The three erroneous transactions caused error messages to be printed, and the two valid transactions caused the contents of master records 00021 and 00035 to be printed.

A Program to List Selected Records from a Master File

Program P13-01 is shown in Figure 13.4. It is very similar to Program P12-03. There is no output master file in this program, nor a FILE-CONTROL entry or an FD for such a file. There is no paragraph CHECK-TO-WRITE-MASTER, since

Figure 13.4 Program P13-01.

```
CB1 RELEASE 2.4                                IBM OS/VS COBOL   JULY 1, 1982


                          23.52.16        APR 7,1988


00010  IDENTIFICATION DIVISION.
00020   PROGRAM-ID. P13-01.
00030  * AUTHOR. SHAMEZE SULTAN
00040  *          REVISED BY GAETANO MURATORE
00050  *
00060  *    THIS PROGRAM LISTS SELECTED RECORDS FROM A SEQUENTIAL
00070  *    MASTER FILE.
00080  *
00090  *******************************************************************
00100
00110   ENVIRONMENT DIVISION.
00120   CONFIGURATION SECTION.
00130   SOURCE-COMPUTER. IBM-370.
00140   OBJECT-COMPUTER. IBM-370.
00150
00160   INPUT-OUTPUT SECTION.
00170   FILE-CONTROL.
00180       SELECT ACCOUNT-MASTER-FILE-IN     ASSIGN TO MASTER.
00190       SELECT TRANSACTION-FILE-IN        ASSIGN TO INFILE.
00200       SELECT LISTING-FILE-OUT           ASSIGN TO PRINTER1.
00210       SELECT ERROR-FILE-OUT             ASSIGN TO PRINTER2.
00220       SELECT SORT-WORK-FILE             ASSIGN TO SORTWK.
00230
00240  *******************************************************************
00250
00260   DATA DIVISION.
00270   FILE SECTION.
00280   FD  ACCOUNT-MASTER-FILE-IN
00290       LABEL RECORDS ARE STANDARD
00300       RECORD CONTAINS 39 CHARACTERS
00310       BLOCK CONTAINS 100 RECORDS.
00320
00330   01  ACCOUNT-MASTER-RECORD-IN          PIC X(39).
00340
00350   SD  SORT-WORK-FILE
00360       RECORD CONTAINS 6 CHARACTERS.
00370
00380   01  SORT-WORK-RECORD.
00390       05  TRANSACTION-CODE-S            PIC X.
00400       05  ACCOUNT-NUMBER-S              PIC X(5).
00410
00420   FD  TRANSACTION-FILE-IN
00430       LABEL RECORDS ARE OMITTED
00440       RECORD CONTAINS 80 CHARACTERS.
00450
00460   01  TRANSACTION-RECORD-IN             PIC X(80).
00470
00480   FD  LISTING-FILE-OUT
00490       LABEL RECORDS ARE OMITTED.
00500
00510   01  LISTING-RECORD                    PIC X(79).
00520
00530   FD  ERROR-FILE-OUT
00540       LABEL RECORDS ARE OMITTED.
00550
00560   01  ERROR-RECORD-OUT                  PIC X(71).
00570
00580   WORKING-STORAGE SECTION.
00590   01  CURRENT-KEY                       PIC X(5).
00600   01  IS-MASTER-RECORD-IN-WORK-AREA     PIC X.
00610   01  NUMBER-OF-INPUT-RECORDS-W         PIC S9(3) VALUE ZERO.
00620   01  NUMBER-OF-SELECTED-RECORDS-W      PIC S9(3) VALUE ZERO.
00630   01  PAGE-NUMBER-W                     PIC S9(2) VALUE ZERO.
00640   01  ERROR-PAGE-NUMBER-W               PIC S9(2) VALUE ZERO.
00650   01  NUMBER-OF-ERRONEOUS-RECORDS-W     PIC S9(3) VALUE ZERO.
00660   01  CURRENT-BALANCE-TOTAL             PIC 9(7)V99 VALUE ZERO.
00670   01  BLANK-LINE                        PIC X     VALUE SPACE.
00680   01  TODAYS-DATE.
00690       05  TODAYS-YEAR                   PIC 99.
00700       05  TODAYS-MONTH-AND-DAY          PIC 9(4).
```

```
00710
00720    01  MASTER-INPUT-AREA.
00730        05  ACCOUNT-NUMBER                   PIC X(5).
00740        05  FILLER                           PIC X(34).
00750
00760    01  TRANSACTION-INPUT-AREA.
00770        05  TRANSACTION-CODE                 PIC X.
00780            88  LISTING-REQUEST              VALUE "6".
00790        05  ACCOUNT-NUMBER                   PIC X(5).
00800
00810    01  WORK-AREA.
00820        05  ACCOUNT-NUMBER-W                 PIC X(5).
00830        05  DEPOSITOR-NAME-W                 PIC X(20).
00840        05  DATE-OF-LAST-TRANSACTION-W       PIC 9(6).
00850        05  CURRENT-BALANCE-W                PIC 9(6)V99.
00860
00870    01  REPORT-HEADING-1.
00880        05  FILLER                           PIC X(39) VALUE SPACES.
00890        05  FILLER          PIC X(17) VALUE "ROBBEM STATE BANK".
00900
00910    01  REPORT-HEADING-2.
00920        05  FILLER                           PIC X(39) VALUE SPACES.
00930        05  FILLER          PIC X(17) VALUE "106 WEST 10TH ST.".
00940
00950    01  REPORT-HEADING-3.
00960        05  FILLER                           PIC X(38) VALUE SPACES.
00970        05  FILLER          PIC X(19) VALUE "BROOKLYN, NY  11212".
00980
00990    01  PAGE-HEADING-1.
01000        05  FILLER                           PIC X(35) VALUE SPACES.
01010        05  FILLER                           PIC X(25)
01020                VALUE "SELECTED SAVINGS ACCOUNTS".
01030
01040    01  ERROR-PAGE-HEADING-1.
01050        05  FILLER                           PIC X(39) VALUE SPACES.
01060        05  FILLER                           PIC X(16)
01070                VALUE      "SELECTION ERRORS".
01080
01090    01  PAGE-HEADING-2.
01100        05  FILLER                           PIC X(25) VALUE SPACES.
01110        05  FILLER                           PIC X(5) VALUE "DATE".
01120        05  TODAYS-MONTH-AND-DAY             PIC Z9/99/.
01130        05  TODAYS-YEAR                      PIC 99.
01140        05  FILLER                           PIC X(23) VALUE SPACES.
01150        05  FILLER                           PIC X(5)  VALUE "PAGE".
01160        05  PAGE-NUMBER-OUT                  PIC Z9.
01170
01180    01  PAGE-HEADING-3.
01190        05  FILLER                           PIC X(21) VALUE SPACES.
01200        05  FILLER                           PIC X(7) VALUE "ACCOUNT".
01210        05  FILLER                           PIC X(5) VALUE SPACES.
01220        05  FILLER                           PIC X(7) VALUE "CURRENT".
01230        05  FILLER                           PIC X(5) VALUE SPACES.
01240        05  FILLER          VALUE "DATE OF LAST" PIC X(17).
01250        05  FILLER          VALUE "DEPOSITOR" PIC X(9).
01260
01270    01  ERROR-PAGE-HEADING-3.
01280        05  FILLER                           PIC X(21) VALUE SPACES.
01290        05  FILLER                           PIC X(7) VALUE "ACCOUNT".
01300
01310    01  PAGE-HEADING-4.
01320        05  FILLER                           PIC X(21) VALUE SPACES.
01330        05  FILLER                           PIC X(12) VALUE "NUMBER".
01340        05  FILLER                           PIC X(12) VALUE "BALANCE".
01350        05  FILLER                           PIC X(19)
01360                                             VALUE "TRANSACTION".
01370        05  FILLER                           PIC X(4)  VALUE "NAME".
01380
01390    01  ERROR-PAGE-HEADING-4.
01400        05  FILLER                           PIC X(21) VALUE SPACES.
01410        05  FILLER                           PIC X(24) VALUE "NUMBER".
01420        05  FILLER                           PIC X(5)  VALUE "NOTES".
01430
01440    01  REPORT-LINE.
01450        05  ACCOUNT-NUMBER-OUT               PIC B(22)X(5)B(4).
01460        05  CURRENT-BALANCE-OUT              PIC ZZZ,ZZZ.99B(7).
01470        05  DATE-OF-LAST-TRANSACTION         PIC 9(6)B(5).
01480        05  DEPOSITOR-NAME                   PIC X(20).
```

(continued)

Figure 13.4   (continued)

```
01490
01500   01   INVALID-CODE-LINE.
01510        05 ACCOUNT-NUMBER-E                    PIC B(22)X(5)B(16).
01520        05 FILLER                              PIC X(15)
01530                                               VALUE "INVALID CODE - ".
01540        05 TRANSACTION-CODE-OUT                PIC BX.
01550
01560   01   MASTER-MISSING-LINE.
01570        05 ACCOUNT-NUMBER-MISSING              PIC B(22)X(5)B(16).
01580        05 FILLER                              PIC X(28)
01590           VALUE "MASTER RECORD DOES NOT EXIST".
01600
01610   01   TOTAL-LINE-1.
01620        05 FILLER                              PIC X(18) VALUE SPACES.
01630        05 FILLER                              PIC X(11) VALUE "TOTAL".
01640        05 CURRENT-BALANCE-TOTAL-OUT           PIC Z,ZZZ,ZZZ.99.
01650
01660   01   TOTAL-LINE-2.
01670        05 FILLER                              PIC X(40) VALUE SPACES.
01680        05 FILLER                    PIC X(14) VALUE "CONTROL COUNTS".
01690
01700   01   TOTAL-LINE-3.
01710        05 FILLER                              PIC X(34) VALUE SPACES.
01720        05 FILLER                              PIC X(27)
01730                            VALUE "NUMBER OF SELECTED ACCOUNTS".
01740        05 NUMBER-OF-SELECTED-RECORDS          PIC BZZ9.
01750
01760   01   TOTAL-LINE-4.
01770        05 FILLER                              PIC X(34) VALUE SPACES.
01780        05 FILLER                              PIC X(27)
01790                            VALUE "NUMBER OF ERRONEOUS RECORDS".
01800        05 NUMBER-OF-ERRONEOUS-RECORDS         PIC BZZ9.
01810
01820   01   TOTAL-LINE-5.
01830        05 FILLER                              PIC X(34) VALUE SPACES.
01840        05 FILLER                              PIC X(5)  VALUE "TOTAL".
01850        05 NUMBER-OF-INPUT-RECORDS             PIC B(23)ZZ9.
01860
01870   01   NO-INPUT-DATA.
01880        05 FILLER                              PIC X(21) VALUE SPACES.
01890        05 FILLER                    PIC X(13) VALUE "NO INPUT DATA".
01900
01910   **************************************************************************
01920
01930   PROCEDURE DIVISION.
01940   CONTROL-SECTION SECTION.
01950   LIST-SELECTED-RECORDS.
01960        SORT SORT-WORK-FILE
01970             ASCENDING KEY ACCOUNT-NUMBER-S
01980             USING TRANSACTION-FILE-IN
01990             OUTPUT PROCEDURE IS LIST-RECORDS.
02000        STOP RUN.
02010
02020   LIST-RECORDS SECTION.
02030   LIST-RECORDS-PARAGRAPH.
02040        PERFORM INITIALIZATION.
02050        PERFORM PROCESS-ONE-KEY UNTIL
02060           TRANSACTION-INPUT-AREA IS EQUAL TO HIGH-VALUES.
02070        PERFORM TERMINATION.
02080        GO TO END-OF-THIS-SECTION.
02090
02100   INITIALIZATION.
02110        OPEN INPUT  ACCOUNT-MASTER-FILE-IN
02120             OUTPUT LISTING-FILE-OUT
02130                    ERROR-FILE-OUT.
02140        ACCEPT TODAYS-DATE FROM DATE.
02150        MOVE CORR TODAYS-DATE TO PAGE-HEADING-2.
02160        PERFORM PRINT-REPORT-HEADINGS.
02170        PERFORM READ-A-MASTER-RECORD.
02180        PERFORM READ-A-TRANSACTION-RECORD.
02190        PERFORM CHOOSE-CURRENT-KEY.
02200        IF CURRENT-KEY = HIGH-VALUES
02210           WRITE LISTING-RECORD FROM NO-INPUT-DATA.
02220
```

```
02230    PROCESS-ONE-KEY.
02240        PERFORM PROCESS-MASTER-RECORD.
02250        PERFORM PROCESS-TRANSACTION-RECORD UNTIL
02260            ACCOUNT-NUMBER IN TRANSACTION-INPUT-AREA
02270            IS NOT EQUAL TO CURRENT-KEY.
02280        PERFORM CHOOSE-CURRENT-KEY.
02290
02300    PROCESS-TRANSACTION-RECORD.
02310        PERFORM CHECK-FOR-VALID-LIST-REQUEST.
02320        PERFORM READ-A-TRANSACTION-RECORD.
02330
02340    CHOOSE-CURRENT-KEY.
02350        IF ACCOUNT-NUMBER IN TRANSACTION-INPUT-AREA IS LESS THAN
02360            ACCOUNT-NUMBER IN MASTER-INPUT-AREA
02370                MOVE ACCOUNT-NUMBER IN TRANSACTION-INPUT-AREA TO
02380                    CURRENT-KEY
02390        ELSE
02400                MOVE ACCOUNT-NUMBER IN MASTER-INPUT-AREA TO
02410                    CURRENT-KEY.
02420
02430    PROCESS-MASTER-RECORD.
02440        IF ACCOUNT-NUMBER IN MASTER-INPUT-AREA IS EQUAL TO
02450            CURRENT-KEY
02460            MOVE MASTER-INPUT-AREA TO WORK-AREA
02470            PERFORM READ-A-MASTER-RECORD
02480            MOVE "Y" TO IS-MASTER-RECORD-IN-WORK-AREA
02490        ELSE
02500            MOVE "N" TO IS-MASTER-RECORD-IN-WORK-AREA.
02510
02520    READ-A-TRANSACTION-RECORD.
02530        RETURN SORT-WORK-FILE INTO TRANSACTION-INPUT-AREA
02540            AT END
02550                MOVE HIGH-VALUES TO TRANSACTION-INPUT-AREA.
02560        IF TRANSACTION-INPUT-AREA NOT = HIGH-VALUES
02570            ADD 1 TO NUMBER-OF-INPUT-RECORDS-W.
02580
02590    READ-A-MASTER-RECORD.
02600        READ ACCOUNT-MASTER-FILE-IN INTO MASTER-INPUT-AREA
02610            AT END
02620                MOVE HIGH-VALUES TO MASTER-INPUT-AREA.
02630
02640    CHECK-FOR-VALID-LIST-REQUEST.
02650        IF NOT LISTING-REQUEST
02660            PERFORM WRITE-INVALID-CODE-LINE
02670            ADD 1 TO NUMBER-OF-ERRONEOUS-RECORDS-W
02680        ELSE
02690        IF IS-MASTER-RECORD-IN-WORK-AREA = "N"
02700            PERFORM WRITE-MASTER-MISSING-LINE
02710            ADD 1 TO NUMBER-OF-ERRONEOUS-RECORDS-W
02720        ELSE
02730            PERFORM WRITE-REPORT-LINE
02740            MOVE "N" TO IS-MASTER-RECORD-IN-WORK-AREA
02750            ADD 1 TO NUMBER-OF-SELECTED-RECORDS-W.
02760
02770    WRITE-REPORT-LINE.
02780        MOVE ACCOUNT-NUMBER-W TO ACCOUNT-NUMBER-OUT.
02790        MOVE CURRENT-BALANCE-W TO CURRENT-BALANCE-OUT.
02800        MOVE DATE-OF-LAST-TRANSACTION-W TO DATE-OF-LAST-TRANSACTION.
02810        MOVE DEPOSITOR-NAME-W TO DEPOSITOR-NAME.
02820        WRITE LISTING-RECORD FROM REPORT-LINE.
02830        ADD CURRENT-BALANCE-W TO CURRENT-BALANCE-TOTAL.
02840
02850    WRITE-INVALID-CODE-LINE.
02860        MOVE ACCOUNT-NUMBER IN TRANSACTION-INPUT-AREA TO
02870                                        ACCOUNT-NUMBER-E.
02880        MOVE TRANSACTION-CODE TO TRANSACTION-CODE-OUT.
```

(continued)

none is written. And of course the paragraph PROCESS-ONE-KEY, line 02230, does not have PERFORM CHECK-TO-WRITE-MASTER.

The main loop of this program terminates a little differently from the main loop in Program P12-03. In Program P13-01 the PERFORM statement at line 02050 ceases executing when there are no more transactions, that is, when the

Figure 13.4   (continued)

```
02890          WRITE ERROR-RECORD-OUT FROM INVALID-CODE-LINE.
02900
02910    WRITE-MASTER-MISSING-LINE.
02920          MOVE ACCOUNT-NUMBER IN TRANSACTION-INPUT-AREA TO
02930                               ACCOUNT-NUMBER-MISSING.
02940          WRITE ERROR-RECORD-OUT FROM MASTER-MISSING-LINE.
02950
02960    TERMINATION.
02970          PERFORM WRITE-TOTALS.
02980          CLOSE ACCOUNT-MASTER-FILE-IN
02990                LISTING-FILE-OUT
03000                ERROR-FILE-OUT.
03010
03020    WRITE-TOTALS.
03030          MOVE CURRENT-BALANCE-TOTAL TO CURRENT-BALANCE-TOTAL-OUT.
03040          WRITE LISTING-RECORD FROM TOTAL-LINE-1 AFTER 2.
03050          WRITE LISTING-RECORD FROM TOTAL-LINE-2 AFTER 2.
03060          MOVE NUMBER-OF-SELECTED-RECORDS-W
03070                       TO NUMBER-OF-SELECTED-RECORDS.
03080          WRITE LISTING-RECORD FROM TOTAL-LINE-3 AFTER 2.
03090          MOVE NUMBER-OF-ERRONEOUS-RECORDS-W TO
03100                               NUMBER-OF-ERRONEOUS-RECORDS.
03110          WRITE LISTING-RECORD FROM TOTAL-LINE-4 AFTER 2.
03120          MOVE NUMBER-OF-INPUT-RECORDS-W TO
03130                               NUMBER-OF-INPUT-RECORDS.
03140          WRITE LISTING-RECORD FROM TOTAL-LINE-5 AFTER 2.
03150
03160    PRINT-REPORT-HEADINGS.
03170          PERFORM PRINT-LISTING-HEADINGS.
03180          PERFORM PRINT-ERROR-REPORT-HEADINGS.
03190
03200    PRINT-LISTING-HEADINGS.
03210          ADD 1 TO PAGE-NUMBER-W.
03220          MOVE PAGE-NUMBER-W TO PAGE-NUMBER-OUT.
03230          WRITE LISTING-RECORD FROM REPORT-HEADING-1
03240                               AFTER ADVANCING PAGE.
03250          WRITE LISTING-RECORD FROM REPORT-HEADING-2.
03260          WRITE LISTING-RECORD FROM REPORT-HEADING-3.
03270          WRITE LISTING-RECORD FROM PAGE-HEADING-1
03280                               AFTER 2.
03290          WRITE LISTING-RECORD FROM PAGE-HEADING-2.
03300          WRITE LISTING-RECORD FROM PAGE-HEADING-3
03310                               AFTER 3.
03320          WRITE LISTING-RECORD FROM PAGE-HEADING-4.
03330          WRITE LISTING-RECORD FROM BLANK-LINE.
03340
03350    PRINT-ERROR-REPORT-HEADINGS.
03360          ADD 1 TO ERROR-PAGE-NUMBER-W.
03370          MOVE ERROR-PAGE-NUMBER-W TO PAGE-NUMBER-OUT.
03380          WRITE ERROR-RECORD-OUT FROM REPORT-HEADING-1
03390                               AFTER ADVANCING PAGE.
03400          WRITE ERROR-RECORD-OUT FROM REPORT-HEADING-2.
03410          WRITE ERROR-RECORD-OUT FROM REPORT-HEADING-3.
03420          WRITE ERROR-RECORD-OUT FROM ERROR-PAGE-HEADING-1
03430                               AFTER 2.
03440          WRITE ERROR-RECORD-OUT FROM PAGE-HEADING-2.
03450          WRITE ERROR-RECORD-OUT FROM ERROR-PAGE-HEADING-3
03460                               AFTER 3.
03470          WRITE ERROR-RECORD-OUT FROM ERROR-PAGE-HEADING-4.
03480          WRITE ERROR-RECORD-OUT FROM BLANK-LINE.
03490
03500    END-OF-THIS-SECTION.
03510          EXIT.
```

TRANSACTION-INPUT-AREA is equal to HIGH-VALUES. In Program P12-03 the main loop ceased executing only when CURRENT-KEY got to be equal to HIGH-VALUES, that is, after both the master and transaction files had reached end-of-file. The reason for the difference lies in the fact that Program P12-03 is an update program and creates a new output master file. Thus the entire input master file must be processed to ensure that all records from the incoming master file are copied onto the output master if they are not deleted. Program P13-01 is not an update program and does not create an output master file. The input master file is read and used, but remains unchanged. In Program P13-01, as soon as the transaction file reaches end-of-file, there is no reason to read the remainder of the input master file.

Program P13-01 was run with the transaction input shown in Figure 13.5 and the input master file created by Program P12-02, and produced the output shown in Figure 13.6.

Figure 13.5   Transaction input to Program P13-01.

```
--------------------------------------------------------------------------------
         1         2         3         4         5         6         7         8
12345678901234567890123456789012345678901234567890123456789012345678901234567890
--------------------------------------------------------------------------------
600350
600245
100299
600077
600003
600508
600168
600350
600599
700320
600280
600609
500390
```

Figure 13.6   Output from Program P13-01.

```
                         ROBBEM  STATE  BANK
                         106 WEST 10TH ST.
                         BROOKLYN,  NY   11212

                      SELECTED  SAVINGS  ACCOUNTS
           DATE  4/07/88                        PAGE   1

        ACCOUNT       CURRENT        DATE OF LAST      DEPOSITOR
        NUMBER        BALANCE        TRANSACTION         NAME

         00077          10.37          880407        LESLIE  MINSKY
         00168         125.50          880407        KELLY  HEDERMAN
         00245          35.00          880407        FRANK  CAPUTO
         00280          20.00          880407        COMMUNITY  DRUGS
         00350       2,500.00          880407        ROGER  SHAW

     TOTAL            2,690.87


                         CONTROL  COUNTS

              NUMBER  OF  SELECTED  ACCOUNTS     5

              NUMBER  OF  ERRONEOUS  RECORDS     8

              TOTAL                             13



                         ROBBEM  STATE  BANK
                         106 WEST 10TH ST.
                         BROOKLYN,  NY   11212

                         SELECTION  ERRORS
           DATE   4/07/88                        PAGE   1

     ACCOUNT
     NUMBER                      NOTES

         00003                   MASTER RECORD DOES NOT EXIST
         00299                   INVALID CODE -  1
         00320                   INVALID CODE -  7
         00350                   MASTER RECORD DOES NOT EXIST
         00390                   INVALID CODE -  5
         00508                   MASTER RECORD DOES NOT EXIST
         00599                   MASTER RECORD DOES NOT EXIST
         00609                   MASTER RECORD DOES NOT EXIST
```

EXERCISE 1

Write a program to list selected records from the inventory master file you created in Exercise 3, Chapter 12, page 392. List the following fields from each record selected:

Part Number
Part Description
Quantity on Hand
Reorder Point

The Quantity on Hand should show as zero in each record. Use input transactions in the following format:

Positions	Field
1	Code 13
2–6	Part Number
7–80	spaces

Design suitable reports for your program. Have your program check the input transactions for validity, and print error messages and the selected master records.

An Update Program with Changes and Deletions

We will now develop a program to handle four different kinds of transactions in a single run. Program P13-02 will be able to update a sequential master file using an input transaction file that may contain any combination of changes to existing master records and deletions of existing master records.

Records on our savings-account master file can be changed in the following ways: A depositor may make a deposit or withdrawal, or a depositor may change his or her name. If a deposit were made, we would want to add the deposit amount to the Current balance field in the master record for the account; if a withdrawal were made, we would want to subtract the withdrawal amount from the Current Balance field. If a depositor name change occurs, we would want to change the Depositor Name field in the master record. There may be any combination of these kinds of changes to a single master record in one run. A depositor may make one or more deposits and/or one or more withdrawals in a single day, and may change his or her name during the day. Each of these different events would be reflected in a single transaction record, and Program P13-02 would be able to process all transactions against any master record.

There may even be one or more changes and a deletion against a single master record in one run. A depositor may make a deposit and then close the account all in the same day. The transaction input would then contain one record for the deposit and one for the deletion. Of course, any change transactions to a master record must precede the deletion in the transaction input.

The formats of the four types of transactions that can be processed by Program P13-02 are:

Positions	Field
1	Code 2 (Deposit)
2-6	Account Number
7-14	Deposit Amount (to two decimal places)
15-80	spaces
1	Code 3 (Withdrawal)
2-6	Account Number
7-14	Withdrawal Amount (to two decimal places)
15-80	spaces
1	Code 4 (Depositor name change)
2-6	Account Number
7-26	Depositor Name
27-80	spaces
1	Code 5 (Close account)
2-6	Account Number
7-80	spaces

Even though the different types of transactions have different formats, they can all be processed in one transaction input area in working storage. When we look at Program P13-02, you will see how the transaction input area can be defined to accommodate the different formats.

The format of the transaction register produced by Program P13-02 is shown in Figure 13.7. The format shows the output that is printed for a valid deposit, a

Figure 13.7 Output format for transaction register for Program P13-02.

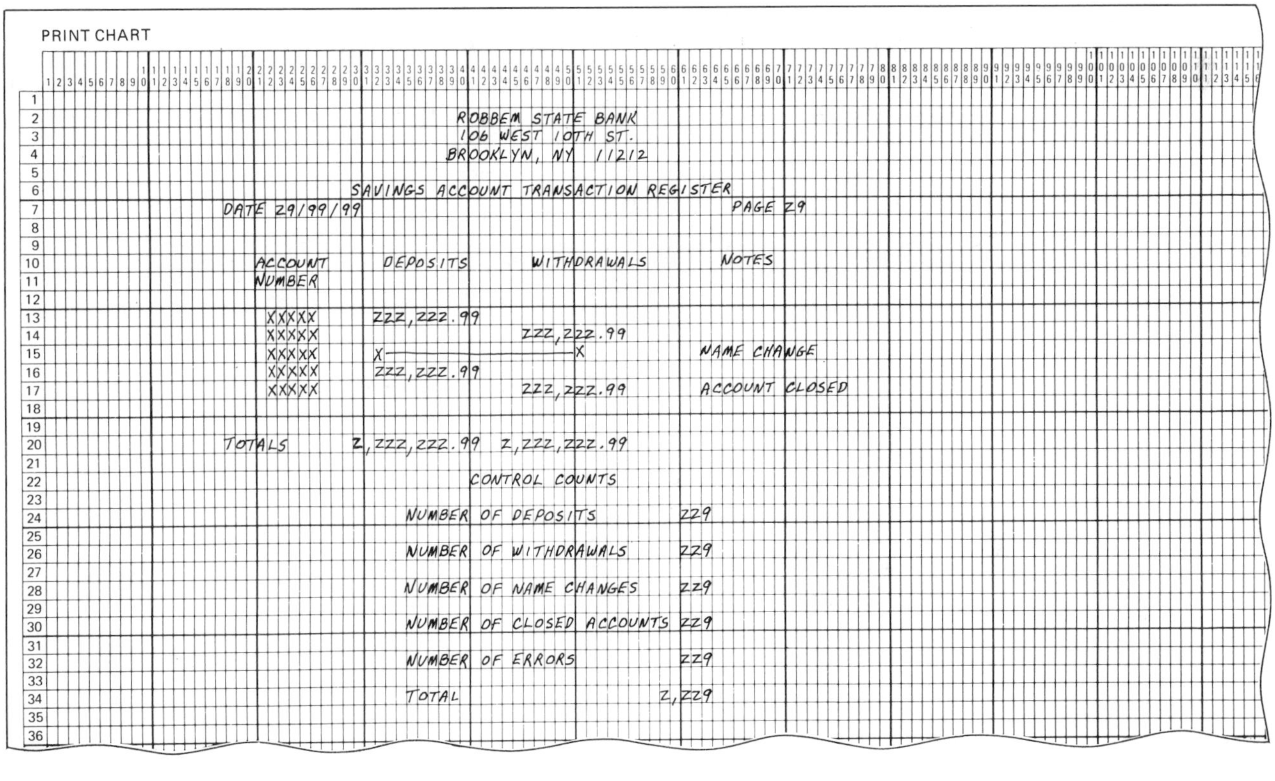

valid withdrawal, a valid name change, and a valid closing of an account. The format of the error report for this program, Figure 13.8, shows the types of errors that can be detected by the program.

In this update program it is legal for there to be more than one transaction against a master record in a single run. The several transactions may all have the same transaction Code (as when several deposits are being made to one account) or they may have different transaction Codes (as when a deposit and a withdrawal are being made). Thus the program must examine the transaction Code of each input transaction to determine how the transaction is to be processed.

Figure 13.8 Output format for error report for Program P13-02.

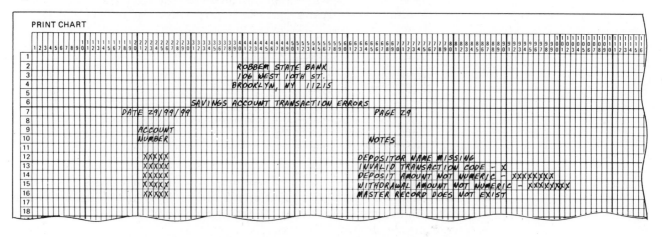

A Hierarchy Diagram for Making Changes and Deletions to a Master File

In a hierarchy diagram for Program P13-02, the box "Process transaction record" would be much more elaborate than in any program we have done so far. However, all of the boxes above "Process transaction record" would be identical to those in the hierarchy diagram for deleting records from a master file, Figure 12.14.

Figure 13.9 shows just the box "Process transaction record" and its subfunctions for Program P13-02. Here there is one subfunction, "Apply transaction,"

Figure 13.9 Hierarchy diagram for "Process transaction record" for Program P13-02.

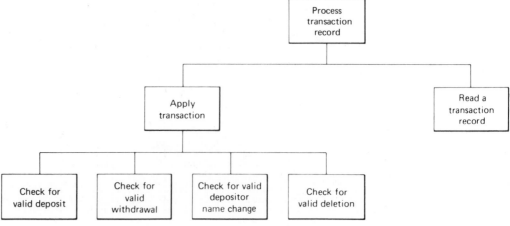

just to determine which of the several types of transactions is being processed. Then, at lower levels, the program coding carries out the validity checking and processing suitable to each type of transaction.

Figure 13.10 Program P13-02.

```
CB1 RELEASE 2.4                        IBM OS/VS COBOL  JULY  1, 1982

                    12.36.48        APR  8,1988
00010  IDENTIFICATION DIVISION.
00020  PROGRAM-ID. P13-02.
00030 *
00040 *     THIS PROGRAM UPDATES A SEQUENTIAL MASTER FILE
00050 *     WITH CHANGES AND DELETIONS.
00060 *
00070 ************************************************************************
00080
00090  ENVIRONMENT DIVISION.
00100  CONFIGURATION SECTION.
00110  SOURCE-COMPUTER. IBM-370.
00120  OBJECT-COMPUTER. IBM-370.
00130
00140  INPUT-OUTPUT SECTION.
00150  FILE-CONTROL.
00160      SELECT ACCOUNT-MASTER-FILE-IN        ASSIGN TO MASTIN.
00170      SELECT ACCOUNT-MASTER-FILE-OUT       ASSIGN TO MASTOUT.
00180      SELECT TRANSACTION-FILE-IN           ASSIGN TO INFILE.
00190      SELECT TRANSACTION-REGISTER-FILE-OUT ASSIGN TO PRINTER1.
00200      SELECT ERROR-FILE-OUT                ASSIGN TO PRINTER2.
0G210      SELECT SORT-WORK-FILE                ASSIGN TO SORTWK.
00220
00230 ************************************************************************
00240
00250  DATA DIVISION.
00260  FILE SECTION.
00270  FD  ACCOUNT-MASTER-FILE-IN
00280      LABEL RECORDS ARE STANDARD
00290      RECORD CONTAINS 39 CHARACTERS
00300      BLOCK CONTAINS 100 RECORDS.
00310
00320  01  ACCOUNT-MASTER-RECORD-IN          PIC X(39).
00330
00340  FD  ACCOUNT-MASTER-FILE-OUT
00350      LABEL RECORDS ARE STANDARD
00360      RECORD CONTAINS 39 CHARACTERS
00370      BLOCK CONTAINS 100 RECORDS.
00380
00390  01  ACCOUNT-MASTER-RECORD-OUT         PIC X(39).
00400
00410  SD  SORT-WORK-FILE
00420      RECORD CONTAINS 26 CHARACTERS.
00430
00440  01  SORT-WORK-RECORD.
00450      05   TRANSACTION-CODE-S           PIC X.
00460      05   ACCOUNT-NUMBER-S             PIC X(5).
00470      05   FILLER                       PIC X(20).
00480
00490  FD  TRANSACTION-FILE-IN
00500      LABEL RECORDS ARE OMITTED
00510      RECORD CONTAINS 80 CHARACTERS.
00520
00530  01  TRANSACTION-RECORD-IN             PIC X(80).
00540
00550  FD  TRANSACTION-REGISTER-FILE-OUT
00560      LABEL RECORDS ARE OMITTED.
00570
00580  01  TRANSACTION-REGISTER-RECRD-OUT    PIC X(76).
00590
00600  FD  ERROR-FILE-OUT
00610      LABEL RECORDS ARE OMITTED.
00620
00630  01  ERROR-RECORD-OUT                  PIC X(102).
00640
00650  WORKING-STORAGE SECTION.
00660  01  CURRENT-KEY                       PIC X(5).
00670  01  IS-MASTER-RECORD-IN-WORK-AREA     PIC X.
```

(continued)

A Program to Make Changes and Deletions to a Master File

Program P13-02 is shown in Figure 13.10. The TRANSACTION-INPUT-AREA, at line 00920, is defined so that it can accommodate the several transaction types with their different formats. The transaction Code and Account Number occupy positions 1 through 6 in all the transaction input, so those fields are defined at lines 00930 through 00980. The TRANSACTION-CODE has level-88 entries for the valid Codes.

The next fields in the transaction input are the deposit and withdrawal amount fields, and the name-change field. We first define the Amount fields, under the heading DEPOSIT-AND-WITHDRAWAL-AMTS at line 00990, and later we will define the Depositor Name field. Since the Deposit Amount and the Withdrawal Amount both occupy the same eight positions of the transaction input, the field WITHDRAWAL-AMOUNT is used to redefine the field DEPOSIT-AMOUNT. The two fields have also been redefined as alphanumeric in case it turns out that they contain one or more nonnumeric characters and must be printed without editing. Notice that when a field is redefined more than once, as DEPOSIT-AMOUNT is, all the redefinitions must refer to the original name of the field, DEPOSIT-AMOUNT. That is, you cannot redefine a field whose definition contains a REDEFINES clause.

The FILLER in line 01070 is needed so that we can process transactions of Code 4 properly. The Depositor Name field in those transactions presents a slight difficulty because part of it overlaps the Deposit and Withdrawal Amount fields in transactions of Codes 2 and 3. We accommodate type-4 transactions as shown in lines 01080 through 01110. We first redefine the entire TRANSACTION-INPUT-AREA. Then, by using the FILLER in line 01090, we can position the DEPOSITOR-NAME field to correspond to the position of the Depositor Name in the transaction record. Since a redefining entry must occupy the same number of character positions as the entry being redefined, the FILLER at line 01070 is included in the definition of TRANSACTION-INPUT-AREA to make it the same size as TRANSACTION-4-INPUT-AREA.

Figure 13.10   (continued)

```
00680  01  NUMBER-OF-INPUT-RECORDS-W        PIC S9(3) VALUE ZERO.
00690  01  NUMBER-OF-ERRONEOUS-RECORDS-W    PIC S9(3) VALUE ZERO.
00700  01  DEPOSIT-TOTAL-W                  PIC S9(7)V99 VALUE ZERO.
00710  01  WITHDRAWAL-TOTAL-W               PIC S9(7)V99 VALUE ZERO.
00720  01  NUMBER-OF-DEPOSITS-W             PIC S9(3) VALUE ZERO.
00730  01  NUMBER-OF-WITHDRAWALS-W          PIC S9(3) VALUE ZERO.
00740  01  NUMBER-OF-NAME-CHANGES-W         PIC S9(3) VALUE ZERO.
00750  01  NUMBER-OF-CLOSED-ACCOUNTS-W      PIC S9(3) VALUE ZERO.
00760  01  BLANK-LINE                       PIC X     VALUE SPACE.
00770  01  PAGE-NUMBER-W                    PIC S99   VALUE 0.
00780  01  ERROR-PAGE-NUMBER-W              PIC S99   VALUE 0.
00790  01  PAGE-LIMIT          COMP SYNC    PIC S99   VALUE 28.
00800  01  LINE-COUNT-ER       COMP SYNC    PIC S99.
00810  01  ERROR-PAGE-LIMIT    COMP SYNC    PIC S99   VALUE 45.
00820  01  ERROR-LINE-COUNTER  COMP SYNC    PIC S99.
00830
00840  01  TODAYS-DATE.
00850      05  TODAYS-YEAR                  PIC 99.
00860      05  TODAYS-MONTH-AND-DAY         PIC 9(4).
00870
00880  01  MASTER-INPUT-AREA.
00890      05  ACCOUNT-NUMBER               PIC X(5).
00900      05  FILLER                       PIC X(34).
00910
```

```
00920  01  TRANSACTION-INPUT-AREA.
00930      05   TRANSACTION-CODE              PIC X.
00940           88   DEPOSIT                  VALUE "2".
00950           88   WITHDRAWAL               VALUE "3".
00960           88   NAME-CHANGE              VALUE "4".
00970           88   DELETION                 VALUE "5".
00980      05   ACCOUNT-NUMBER               PIC X(5).
00990      05   DEPOSIT-AND-WITHDRAWAL-AMTS.
01000           10   DEPOSIT-AMOUNT           PIC 9(6)V99.
01010           10   DEPOSIT-AMOUNT-X   REDEFINES DEPOSIT-AMOUNT
01020                                         PIC X(8).
01030           10   WITHDRAWAL-AMOUNT   REDEFINES DEPOSIT-AMOUNT
01040                                         PIC 9(6)V99.
01050           10   WITHDRAWAL-AMOUNT-X REDEFINES DEPOSIT-AMOUNT
01060                                         PIC X(8).
01070      05   FILLER                       PIC X(12).
01080  01  TRANSACTION-4-INPUT-AREA REDEFINES TRANSACTION-INPUT-AREA.
01090      05   FILLER                       PIC X(6).
01100      05   DEPOSITOR-NAME               PIC X(20).
01110           88   DEPOSITOR-NAME-MISSING   VALUE SPACES.
01120
01130  01  WORK-AREA.
01140      05   ACCOUNT-NUMBER-W             PIC X(5).
01150      05   DEPOSITOR-NAME-W             PIC X(20).
01160      05   DATE-OF-LAST-TRANSACTION-W   PIC 9(6).
01170      05   CURRENT-BALANCE-W            PIC S9(6)V99.
01180
01190  01  REPORT-HEADING-1.
01200      05   FILLER    PIC X(39) VALUE SPACES.
01210      05   FILLER    PIC X(17) VALUE "ROBBEM STATE BANK".
01220
01230  01  REPORT-HEADING-2.
01240      05   FILLER    PIC X(39) VALUE SPACES.
01250      05   FILLER    PIC X(17) VALUE "106 WEST 10TH ST.".
01260
01270  01  REPORT-HEADING-3.
01280      05   FILLER    PIC X(38) VALUE SPACES.
01290      05   FILLER    PIC X(19) VALUE "BROOKLYN, NY  11212".
01300
01310  01  PAGE-HEADING-1.
01320      05   FILLER    PIC X(29) VALUE SPACES.
01330      05   FILLER    PIC X(36)
01340                     VALUE "SAVINGS ACCOUNT TRANSACTION REGISTER".
01350
01360  01  ERROR-PAGE-HEADING-1.
01370      05   FILLER    PIC X(30) VALUE SPACES.
01380      05   FILLER    PIC X(34)
01390                     VALUE  "SAVINGS ACCOUNT TRANSACTION ERRORS".
01400
01410  01  PAGE-HEADING-2.
01420      05   FILLER            PIC X(17) VALUE SPACES.
01430      05   FILLER            PIC X(5)  VALUE "DATE".
01440      05   TODAYS-MONTH-AND-DAY          PIC Z9/99/.
01450      05   TODAYS-YEAR                   PIC 99B(35).
01460      05   FILLER            PIC X(5)  VALUE "PAGE".
01470      05   PAGE-NUMBER-OUT               PIC Z9.
01480
01490  01  PAGE-HEADING-3.
01500      05   FILLER            PIC X(20) VALUE SPACES.
01510      05   FILLER            PIC X(12) VALUE "ACCOUNT".
01520      05   FILLER            PIC X(14) VALUE "DEPOSITS".
01530      05   FILLER            PIC X(18) VALUE "WITHDRAWALS".
01540      05   FILLER            PIC X(5)  VALUE "NOTES".
01550
01560  01  ERROR-PAGE-HEADING-3.
01570      05   FILLER            PIC X(20) VALUE SPACES.
01580      05   FILLER            PIC X(44) VALUE "ACCOUNT".
01590      05   FILLER            PIC X(5)  VALUE "NOTES".
01600
01610  01  PAGE-HEADING-4.
01620      05   FILLER            PIC X(20) VALUE SPACES.
01630      05   FILLER            PIC X(6)  VALUE "NUMBER".
01640
01650  01  DEPOSIT-LINE.
01660      05   FILLER            PIC X(21) VALUE SPACES.
01670      05   ACCOUNT-NUMBER-OUT           PIC X(5)B(5).
01680      05   DEPOSIT-AMOUNT-OUT           PIC ZZZ,ZZZ.99.
01690
```

(continued)

Figure 13.10   (continued)

```
01700   01   WITHDRAWAL-LINE.
01710        05   FILLER           PIC X(21) VALUE SPACES.
01720        05   ACCOUNT-NUMBER-OUT        PIC X(5)B(19).
01730        05   WITHDRAWAL-AMOUNT-OUT     PIC ZZZ,ZZZ.99.
01740
01750   01   NAME-CHANGE-LINE.
01760        05   FILLER           PIC X(21) VALUE SPACES.
01770        05   ACCOUNT-NUMBER-OUT        PIC X(5)B(5).
01780        05   DEPOSITOR-NAME-OUT        PIC X(20)B(11).
01790        05   FILLER           PIC X(11) VALUE "NAME CHANGE".
01800
01810   01   DELETION-LINE.
01820        05   FILLER           PIC X(21) VALUE SPACES.
01830        05   ACCOUNT-NUMBER-OUT        PIC X(5)B(19).
01840        05   CURRENT-BALANCE-OUT       PIC ZZZ,ZZZ.99B(7).
01850        05   FILLER           PIC X(14) VALUE "ACCOUNT CLOSED".
01860
01870   01   DEPOSIT-AMOUNT-INVALID-MSG.
01880        05   FILLER           PIC X(29)
01890                      VALUE "DEPOSIT AMOUNT NOT NUMERIC -".
01900        05   DEPOSIT-AMOUNT-OUT        PIC X(8).
01910
01920   01   WITHDRAWAL-AMOUNT-INVALID-MSG.
01930        05   FILLER           PIC X(32)
01940                      VALUE "WITHDRAWAL AMOUNT NOT NUMERIC -".
01950        05   WITHDRAWAL-AMOUNT-OUT     PIC X(8).
01960
01970   01   INVALID-CODE-MSG.
01980        05   FILLER     PIC X(27) VALUE "INVALID TRANSACTION CODE -".
01990        05   TRANSACTION-CODE-OUT      PIC X.
02000
02010   01   ERROR-LINE.
02020        05   ACCOUNT-NUMBER-E         PIC B(21)X(5)B(36).
02030        05   ERROR-MESSAGE            PIC X(40).
02040
02050   01   FINAL-LINE-1.
02060        05   FILLER           PIC X(17) VALUE SPACES.
02070        05   FILLER           PIC X(12) VALUE "TOTALS".
02080        05   DEPOSIT-TOTAL-OUT         PIC Z,ZZZ,ZZZ.99BB.
02090        05   WITHDRAWAL-TOTAL-OUT      PIC Z,ZZZ,ZZZ.99.
02100
02110   01   FINAL-LINE-2.
02120        05   FILLER           PIC X(40) VALUE SPACES.
02130        05   FILLER           PIC X(14) VALUE "CONTROL COUNTS".
02140
02150   01   FINAL-LINE-3.
02160        05   FILLER           PIC X(34) VALUE SPACES.
02170        05   FILLER           PIC X(26)
02180                      VALUE "NUMBER OF DEPOSITS".
02190        05   NUMBER-OF-DEPOSITS-OUT        PIC ZZ9.
02200
02210   01   FINAL-LINE-4.
02220        05   FILLER           PIC X(34) VALUE SPACES.
02230        05   FILLER           PIC X(26)
02240                      VALUE "NUMBER OF WITHDRAWALS".
02250        05   NUMBER-OF-WITHDRAWALS-OUT     PIC ZZ9.
02260
02270   01   FINAL-LINE-5.
02280        05   FILLER           PIC X(34) VALUE SPACES.
02290        05   FILLER           PIC X(26)
02300                      VALUE "NUMBER OF NAME CHANGES".
02310        05   NUMBER-OF-NAME-CHANGES-OUT    PIC ZZ9.
02320
02330   01   FINAL-LINE-6.
02340        05   FILLER           PIC X(34) VALUE SPACES.
02350        05   FILLER           PIC X(26)
02360                      VALUE "NUMBER OF CLOSED ACCOUNTS".
02370        05   NUMBER-OF-CLOSED-ACCOUNTS-OUT PIC ZZ9.
02380
02390   01   FINAL-LINE-7.
02400        05   FILLER           PIC X(34) VALUE SPACES.
02410        05   FILLER           PIC X(26)
02420                      VALUE "NUMBER OF ERRORS".
02430        05   NUMBER-OF-ERRONEOUS-RECRDS-OUT PIC ZZ9.
02440
```

```
02450   01   FINAL-LINE-8.
02460        05   FILLER          PIC X(34) VALUE SPACES.
02470        05   FILLER          PIC X(26) VALUE "TOTAL".
02480        05   NUMBER-OF-INPUT-RECORDS-OUT   PIC ZZ9.
02490
02500   01   NO-INPUT-DATA.
02510        05   FILLER          PIC X(21) VALUE SPACES.
02520        05   FILLER          PIC X(13) VALUE "NO INPUT DATA".
02530
02540   ********************************************************************
02550
02560   PROCEDURE DIVISION.
02570   CONTROL-SECTION SECTION.
02580   UPDATE-PARAGRAPH.
02590        SORT SORT-WORK-FILE
02600             ASCENDING KEY ACCOUNT-NUMBER-S
02610                           TRANSACTION-CODE-S
02620             USING TRANSACTION-FILE-IN
02630             OUTPUT PROCEDURE IS UPDATE-RECORDS.
02640        STOP RUN.
02650
02660   UPDATE-RECORDS SECTION.
02670   UPDATE-RECORDS-PARAGRAPH.
02680        PERFORM INITIALIZATION.
02690        PERFORM PROCESS-ONE-KEY UNTIL
02700             CURRENT-KEY = HIGH-VALUES.
02710        PERFORM TERMINATION.
02720        GO TO END-OF-THIS-SECTION.
02730
02740   INITIALIZATION.
02750        OPEN INPUT  ACCOUNT-MASTER-FILE-IN
02760             OUTPUT ACCOUNT-MASTER-FILE-OUT
02770                    ERROR-FILE-OUT
02780                    TRANSACTION-REGISTER-FILE-OUT.
02790        ACCEPT TODAYS-DATE FROM DATE.
02800        MOVE CORR TODAYS-DATE TO PAGE-HEADING-2.
02810        PERFORM PRODUCE-REPORT-HEADINGS.
02820        PERFORM READ-A-MASTER-RECORD.
02830        PERFORM READ-A-TRANSACTION-RECORD.
02840        PERFORM CHOOSE-CURRENT-KEY.
02850        IF CURRENT-KEY = HIGH-VALUES
02860             WRITE TRANSACTION-REGISTER-RECRD-OUT FROM NO-INPUT-DATA.
02870
02880   PRODUCE-REPORT-HEADINGS.
02890        PERFORM WRITE-REGISTER-HEADINGS.
02900        PERFORM WRITE-ERROR-REPORT-HEADINGS.
02910
02920   WRITE-REGISTER-HEADINGS.
02930        ADD 1 TO PAGE-NUMBER-W.
02940        MOVE PAGE-NUMBER-W TO PAGE-NUMBER-OUT.
02950        WRITE TRANSACTION-REGISTER-RECRD-OUT FROM
02960             REPORT-HEADING-1 AFTER ADVANCING PAGE.
02970        WRITE TRANSACTION-REGISTER-RECRD-OUT FROM REPORT-HEADING-2.
02980        WRITE TRANSACTION-REGISTER-RECRD-OUT FROM REPORT-HEADING-3.
02990        WRITE TRANSACTION-REGISTER-RECRD-OUT FROM PAGE-HEADING-1
03000                                                 AFTER 2.
03010        WRITE TRANSACTION-REGISTER-RECRD-OUT FROM PAGE-HEADING-2.
03020        WRITE TRANSACTION-REGISTER-RECRD-OUT FROM PAGE-HEADING-3
03030                                                 AFTER 3.
03040        WRITE TRANSACTION-REGISTER-RECRD-OUT FROM PAGE-HEADING-4.
03050        WRITE TRANSACTION-REGISTER-RECRD-OUT FROM BLANK-LINE.
03060        MOVE 11 TO LINE-COUNT-ER.
03070
```

(continued)

The Procedure Division, which follows the hierarchy diagram, begins at line 02560. It is nearly identical to the Procedure Division of Program P13-02 except at the lowest level. The SORT statement, at line 02590, SORTs the input transactions on their transaction Code as well as their Account Number. This assures that if there is more than one transaction against a single master record, a deletion transaction, if present, will fall after all other transactions.

Figure 13.10   (continued)

```
03080    WRITE-ERROR-REPORT-HEADINGS.
03090        ADD 1 TO ERROR-PAGE-NUMBER-W.
03100        MOVE ERROR-PAGE-NUMBER-W TO PAGE-NUMBER-OUT.
03110        WRITE ERROR-RECORD-OUT FROM REPORT-HEADING-1 AFTER PAGE.
03120        WRITE ERROR-RECORD-OUT FROM REPORT-HEADING-2.
03130        WRITE ERROR-RECORD-OUT FROM REPORT-HEADING-3.
03140        WRITE ERROR-RECORD-OUT FROM ERROR-PAGE-HEADING-1 AFTER 2.
03150        WRITE ERROR-RECORD-OUT FROM PAGE-HEADING-2.
03160        WRITE ERROR-RECORD-OUT FROM ERROR-PAGE-HEADING-3 AFTER 3.
03170        WRITE ERROR-RECORD-OUT FROM PAGE-HEADING-4.
03180        WRITE ERROR-RECORD-OUT FROM BLANK-LINE.
03190        MOVE 11 TO ERROR-LINE-COUNTER.
03200
03210    PROCESS-ONE-KEY.
03220        PERFORM PROCESS-MASTER-RECORD.
03230        PERFORM PROCESS-TRANSACTION-RECORD UNTIL
03240            ACCOUNT-NUMBER IN TRANSACTION-INPUT-AREA IS NOT EQUAL TO
03250            CURRENT-KEY.
03260        PERFORM CHECK-TO-WRITE-MASTER.
03270        PERFORM CHOOSE-CURRENT-KEY.
03280
03290    PROCESS-TRANSACTION-RECORD.
03300        PERFORM APPLY-TRANSACTION.
03310        PERFORM READ-A-TRANSACTION-RECORD.
03320
03330    CHECK-TO-WRITE-MASTER.
03340        IF IS-MASTER-RECORD-IN-WORK-AREA = "Y"
03350            WRITE ACCOUNT-MASTER-RECORD-OUT FROM WORK-AREA.
03360
03370    CHOOSE-CURRENT-KEY.
03380        IF ACCOUNT-NUMBER IN TRANSACTION-INPUT-AREA IS LESS THAN
03390            ACCOUNT-NUMBER IN MASTER-INPUT-AREA
03400            MOVE ACCOUNT-NUMBER IN TRANSACTION-INPUT-AREA TO
03410                CURRENT-KEY
03420        ELSE
03430            MOVE ACCOUNT-NUMBER IN MASTER-INPUT-AREA TO
03440                CURRENT-KEY.
03450
03460    PROCESS-MASTER-RECORD.
03470        IF ACCOUNT-NUMBER IN MASTER-INPUT-AREA
03480            IS EQUAL TO CURRENT-KEY
03490            MOVE MASTER-INPUT-AREA TO WORK-AREA
03500            PERFORM READ-A-MASTER-RECORD
03510            MOVE "Y" TO IS-MASTER-RECORD-IN-WORK-AREA
03520        ELSE
03530            MOVE "N" TO IS-MASTER-RECORD-IN-WORK-AREA.
03540
03550    READ-A-TRANSACTION-RECORD.
03560        RETURN SORT-WORK-FILE INTO TRANSACTION-INPUT-AREA
03570            AT END
03580                MOVE HIGH-VALUES TO TRANSACTION-INPUT-AREA.
03590        IF TRANSACTION-INPUT-AREA NOT = HIGH-VALUES
03600            ADD 1 TO NUMBER-OF-INPUT-RECORDS-W.
03610
03620    READ-A-MASTER-RECORD.
03630        READ ACCOUNT-MASTER-FILE-IN INTO MASTER-INPUT-AREA
03640            AT END
03650                MOVE HIGH-VALUES TO MASTER-INPUT-AREA.
03660
```

The paragraph APPLY-TRANSACTION, at line 03670, determines the TRANSACTION-CODE of the transaction, in the transaction input area, and PERFORMs the appropriate paragraph to apply the transaction to the master record in the work area. Each of the paragraphs CHECK-FOR-VALID-DEPOSIT, CHECK-FOR-VALID-WITHDRAWAL, CHECK-FOR-VALID-NAME-CHANGE, and CHECK-FOR-VALID-DELETION makes suitable validity checks

```
03670    APPLY-TRANSACTION.
03680        IF DEPOSIT
03690            PERFORM CHECK-FOR-VALID-DEPOSIT
03700        ELSE
03710        IF WITHDRAWAL
03720            PERFORM CHECK-FOR-VALID-WITHDRAWAL
03730        ELSE
03740        IF NAME-CHANGE
03750            PERFORM CHECK-FOR-VALID-NAME-CHANGE
03760        ELSE
03770        IF DELETION
03780            PERFORM CHECK-FOR-VALID-DELETION
03790        ELSE
03800            ADD 1 TO NUMBER-OF-ERRONEOUS-RECORDS-W
03810            PERFORM WRITE-INVALID-CODE-LINE.
03820
03830    CHECK-FOR-VALID-DEPOSIT.
03840        IF DEPOSIT-AMOUNT NOT NUMERIC
03850            ADD 1 TO NUMBER-OF-ERRONEOUS-RECORDS-W
03860            PERFORM WRITE-DEPOSIT-INVALID-LINE
03870        ELSE
03880        IF IS-MASTER-RECORD-IN-WORK-AREA = "N"
03890            ADD 1 TO NUMBER-OF-ERRONEOUS-RECORDS-W
03900            PERFORM WRITE-MASTER-MISSING-LINE
03910        ELSE
03920            ADD DEPOSIT-AMOUNT TO CURRENT-BALANCE-W
03930            MOVE TODAYS-DATE TO DATE-OF-LAST-TRANSACTION-W
03940            PERFORM WRITE-DEPOSIT-LINE.
03950
03960    CHECK-FOR-VALID-WITHDRAWAL.
03970        IF WITHDRAWAL-AMOUNT NOT NUMERIC
03980            ADD 1 TO NUMBER-OF-ERRONEOUS-RECORDS-W
03990            PERFORM WRITE-WITHDRAWAL-INVALID-LINE
04000        ELSE
04010        IF IS-MASTER-RECORD-IN-WORK-AREA = "N"
04020            ADD 1 TO NUMBER-OF-ERRONEOUS-RECORDS-W
04030            PERFORM WRITE-MASTER-MISSING-LINE
04040        ELSE
04050            SUBTRACT WITHDRAWAL-AMOUNT FROM CURRENT-BALANCE-W
04060            MOVE TODAYS-DATE TO DATE-OF-LAST-TRANSACTION-W
04070            PERFORM WRITE-WITHDRAWAL-LINE.
04080
04090    CHECK-FOR-VALID-NAME-CHANGE.
04100        IF DEPOSITOR-NAME-MISSING
04110            ADD 1 TO NUMBER-OF-ERRONEOUS-RECORDS-W
04120            PERFORM WRITE-NAME-MISSING-LINE
04130        ELSE
04140        IF IS-MASTER-RECORD-IN-WORK-AREA = "N"
04150            ADD 1 TO NUMBER-OF-ERRONEOUS-RECORDS-W
04160            PERFORM WRITE-MASTER-MISSING-LINE
04170        ELSE
04180            MOVE DEPOSITOR-NAME TO DEPOSITOR-NAME-W
04190            MOVE TODAYS-DATE TO DATE-OF-LAST-TRANSACTION-W
04200            PERFORM WRITE-NAME-CHANGE-LINE.
04210
04220    CHECK-FOR-VALID-DELETION.
04230        IF IS-MASTER-RECORD-IN-WORK-AREA = "N"
04240            ADD 1 TO NUMBER-OF-ERRONEOUS-RECORDS-W
04250            PERFORM WRITE-MASTER-MISSING-LINE
04260        ELSE
04270            PERFORM WRITE-DELETION-LINE
04280            MOVE "N" TO IS-MASTER-RECORD-IN-WORK-AREA.
04290
```

(continued)

before applying the transaction. Each of the four paragraphs checks that there is a master record in the work area whose key is equal to the transaction key. They do so by checking the flag IS-MASTER-RECORD-IN-WORK-AREA.

Lines 04270 and 04280 show the application of a valid deletion transaction to a master record. The flag is set to "N" to indicate that the master record is no longer

Figure 13.10   (continued)

```
04300   WRITE-DEPOSIT-LINE.
04310       MOVE CURRENT-KEY TO ACCOUNT-NUMBER-OUT     IN DEPOSIT-LINE.
04320       MOVE DEPOSIT-AMOUNT TO DEPOSIT-AMOUNT-OUT IN DEPOSIT-LINE.
04330       IF 1 + LINE-COUNT-ER GREATER THAN PAGE-LIMIT
04340           PERFORM WRITE-REGISTER-HEADINGS.
04350       WRITE TRANSACTION-REGISTER-RECRD-OUT FROM DEPOSIT-LINE.
04360       ADD 1 TO LINE-COUNT-ER.
04370       ADD DEPOSIT-AMOUNT TO DEPOSIT-TOTAL-W.
04380       ADD 1 TO NUMBER-OF-DEPOSITS-W.
04390
04400   WRITE-WITHDRAWAL-LINE.
04410       MOVE CURRENT-KEY TO ACCOUNT-NUMBER-OUT IN WITHDRAWAL-LINE.
04420       MOVE WITHDRAWAL-AMOUNT TO
04430           WITHDRAWAL-AMOUNT-OUT IN WITHDRAWAL-LINE.
04440       IF 1 + LINE-COUNT-ER GREATER THAN PAGE-LIMIT
04450           PERFORM WRITE-REGISTER-HEADINGS.
04460       WRITE TRANSACTION-REGISTER-RECRD-OUT FROM WITHDRAWAL-LINE.
04470       ADD 1 TO LINE-COUNT-ER.
04480       ADD WITHDRAWAL-AMOUNT TO WITHDRAWAL-TOTAL-W.
04490       ADD 1 TO NUMBER-OF-WITHDRAWALS-W.
04500
04510   WRITE-DEPOSIT-INVALID-LINE.
04520       MOVE DEPOSIT-AMOUNT-X TO
04530           DEPOSIT-AMOUNT-OUT IN DEPOSIT-AMOUNT-INVALID-MSG.
04540       MOVE DEPOSIT-AMOUNT-INVALID-MSG TO ERROR-MESSAGE.
04550       PERFORM WRITE-ERROR-LINE.
04560
04570    WRITE-WITHDRAWAL-INVALID-LINE.
04580       MOVE WITHDRAWAL-AMOUNT-X TO
04590           WITHDRAWAL-AMOUNT-OUT IN WITHDRAWAL-AMOUNT-INVALID-MSG.
04600       MOVE WITHDRAWAL-AMOUNT-INVALID-MSG TO ERROR-MESSAGE.
04610       PERFORM WRITE-ERROR-LINE.
04620
04630   WRITE-NAME-MISSING-LINE.
04640       MOVE "DEPOSITOR NAME MISSING" TO ERRORк-MESSAGE.
04650       PERFORM WRITE-ERROR-LINE.
04660
04670   WRITE-NAME-CHANGE-LINE.
04680       MOVE CURRENT-KEY TO ACCOUNT-NUMBER-OUT IN NAME-CHANGE-LINE.
04690       MOVE DEPOSITOR-NAME TO DEPOSITOR-NAME-OUT.
04700       IF 1 + LINE-COUNT-ER GREATER THAN PAGE-LIMIT
04710           PERFORM WRITE-REGISTER-HEADINGS.
04720       WRITE TRANSACTION-REGISTER-RECRD-OUT FROM NAME-CHANGE-LINE.
04730       ADD 1 TO LINE-COUNT-ER.
04740       ADD 1 TO NUMBER-OF-NAME-CHANGES-W.
04750
04760   WRITE-DELETION-LINE.
04770       MOVE CURRENT-KEY TO ACCOUNT-NUMBER-OUT IN DELETION-LINE.
04780       MOVE CURRENT-BALANCE-W TO CURRENT-BALANCE-OUT.
04790       IF 1 + LINE-COUNT-ER GREATER THAN PAGE-LIMIT
04800           PERFORM WRITE-REGISTER-HEADINGS.
04810       WRITE TRANSACTION-REGISTER-RECRD-OUT FROM DELETION-LINE.
04820       ADD 1 TO LINE-COUNT-ER.
04830       ADD CURRENT-BALANCE-W TO WITHDRAWAL-TOTAL-W.
04840       ADD 1 TO NUMBER-OF-CLOSED-ACCOUNTS-W.
04850
```

present in the work area. The other paragraphs that apply transactions to master records do not change the flag, because a deposit or withdrawal or name change does not make the master record disappear. The flag must remain set to "Y" to

```
04860   WRITE-INVALID-CODE-LINE.
04870       MOVE TRANSACTION-CODE TO TRANSACTION-CODE-OUT.
04880       MOVE INVALID-CODE-MSG TO ERROR-MESSAGE.
04890       PERFORM WRITE-ERROR-LINE.
04900
04910   WRITE-MASTER-MISSING-LINE.
04920       MOVE "MASTER RECORD DOES NOT EXIST" TO ERROR-MESSAGE.
04930       PERFORM WRITE-ERROR-LINE.
04940
04950   WRITE-ERROR-LINE.
04960       IF 1 + ERROR-LINE-COUNTER GREATER THAN
04970           ERROR-PAGE-LIMIT
04980            PERFORM WRITE-ERROR-REPORT-HEADINGS.
04990       MOVE CURRENT-KEY TO ACCOUNT-NUMBER-E.
05000       WRITE ERROR-RECORD-OUT FROM ERROR-LINE.
05010       ADD 1 TO ERROR-LINE-COUNTER.
05020
05030   TERMINATION.
05040       PERFORM PRODUCE-TOTAL-LINES.
05050       CLOSE ACCOUNT-MASTER-FILE-IN
05060             ACCOUNT-MASTER-FILE-OUT
05070             ERROR-FILE-OUT
05080             TRANSACTION-REGISTER-FILE-OUT.
05090
05100   PRODUCE-TOTAL-LINES.
05110       MOVE DEPOSIT-TOTAL-W    TO DEPOSIT-TOTAL-OUT.
05120       MOVE WITHDRAWAL-TOTAL-W TO WITHDRAWAL-TOTAL-OUT.
05130       WRITE TRANSACTION-REGISTER-RECRD-OUT FROM FINAL-LINE-1
05140                                    AFTER 3.
05150       WRITE TRANSACTION-REGISTER-RECRD-OUT FROM FINAL-LINE-2
05160                                    AFTER 2.
05170       MOVE NUMBER-OF-DEPOSITS-W TO NUMBER-OF-DEPOSITS-OUT.
05180       WRITE TRANSACTION-REGISTER-RECRD-OUT FROM FINAL-LINE-3
05190                                    AFTER 2.
05200       MOVE NUMBER-OF-WITHDRAWALS-W TO NUMBER-OF-WITHDRAWALS-OUT.
05210       WRITE TRANSACTION-REGISTER-RECRD-OUT FROM FINAL-LINE-4
05220                                    AFTER 2.
05230       MOVE NUMBER-OF-NAME-CHANGES-W TO NUMBER-OF-NAME-CHANGES-OUT.
05240       WRITE TRANSACTION-REGISTER-RECRD-OUT FROM FINAL-LINE-5
05250                                    AFTER 2.
05260       MOVE NUMBER-OF-CLOSED-ACCOUNTS-W
05270            TO NUMBER-OF-CLOSED-ACCOUNTS-OUT.
05280       WRITE TRANSACTION-REGISTER-RECRD-OUT FROM FINAL-LINE-6
05290                                    AFTER 2.
05300       MOVE NUMBER-OF-ERRONEOUS-RECORDS-W
05310            TO NUMBER-OF-ERRONEOUS-RECRDS-OUT.
05320       WRITE TRANSACTION-REGISTER-RECRD-OUT FROM FINAL-LINE-7
05330                                    AFTER 2.
05340       MOVE NUMBER-OF-INPUT-RECORDS-W
05350            TO NUMBER-OF-INPUT-RECORDS-OUT.
05360       WRITE TRANSACTION-REGISTER-RECRD-OUT FROM FINAL-LINE-8
05370                                    AFTER 2.
05380
05390   END-OF-THIS-SECTION.
05400       EXIT.
```

indicate that the master record is still present, in case there are more transactions against this master still to come, and so that CHECK-TO-WRITE-MASTER will write the updated master record out onto the new master file.

Program P13-02 was run with the transaction input shown in Figure 13.11 and the input master file created in Program P12-02. It produced the report output shown in Figure 13.12. The output master file produced is shown in Figure 13.13.

The rightmost position of the Current Balance field prints strangely because the sign of the field is in the same storage location as the rightmost digit.

Figure 13.11   Transaction input to Program P13-02.

```
--------------------------------------------------------------------------------
          1         2         3         4         5         6         7         8
12345678901234567890123456789012345678901234567890123456789012345678901234567890
--------------------------------------------------------------------------------
20007700015000
20037100015000
70038500007500JAMES WASHINGTON
10039200007500INEZ WASHINGTON
400084JOHN & SALLY DUPRINO
20016100125634
30002800150050
10042000150000JOHN RICE
20008400357429
20009100150000
400140BETH DENNY
100399000014Z00GARY NASTI
200007)))$%)))
30001400100000
20002100012750
30011900002735
70042700002500GREG PRUITT
20006300007500
20013300256300
20012600035000
30016800011000
400266
20002800015327
20009100120000
20021000025000
20021000025000
500232
30009100050000
30025929390000
20027300172500
400098GEORGE & ANN CULHANE
500168
20017500019202
500182
20021000025000
20028000231700
80031500013798
200182
20030100005763
5
10030800017000AL MARRELLA
20030800005000
10037100001000THOMAS HERR
20032200006875
10035700001000ROBIN RATANSKI
10036400150000JOSE TORRES
10037100015000ALISE MARKOVITZ
10040600120000
10041300010000BILL HAYES
10039800001000JUAN ALVAREZ
30010500015025
```

Figure 13.12 Report output from Program P13-02.

```
                    ROBBEM STATE BANK
                     106 WEST 10TH ST.
                    BROOKLYN, NY  11212

             SAVINGS ACCOUNT TRANSACTION ERRORS
DATE  4/08/88                              PAGE   1


    ACCOUNT                                    NOTES
    NUMBER

                                    MASTER RECORD DOES NOT EXIST
    00007                           DEPOSIT AMOUNT NOT NUMERIC - )))$%)))
    00063                           MASTER RECORD DOES NOT EXIST
    00105                           WITHDRAWAL AMOUNT NOT NUMERIC - 00015025
    00119                           MASTER RECORD DOES NOT EXIST
    00182                           DEPOSIT AMOUNT NOT NUMERIC -
    00182                           MASTER RECORD DOES NOT EXIST
    00232                           MASTER RECORD DOES NOT EXIST
    00259                           MASTER RECORD DOES NOT EXIST
    00266                           DEPOSITOR NAME MISSING
    00301                           MASTER RECORD DOES NOT EXIST
    00308                           INVALID TRANSACTION CODE - 1
    00315                           INVALID TRANSACTION CODE - 8
    00322                           MASTER RECORD DOES NOT EXIST
    00357                           INVALID TRANSACTION CODE - 1
    00364                           INVALID TRANSACTION CODE - 1
    00371                           INVALID TRANSACTION CODE - 1
    00371                           INVALID TRANSACTION CODE - 1
    00371                           MASTER RECORD DOES NOT EXIST
    00385                           INVALID TRANSACTION CODE - 7
    00392                           INVALID TRANSACTION CODE - 1
    00398                           INVALID TRANSACTION CODE - 1
    00399                           INVALID TRANSACTION CODE - 1
    00406                           INVALID TRANSACTION CODE - 1
    00413                           INVALID TRANSACTION CODE - 1
    00420                           INVALID TRANSACTION CODE - 1
    00427                           INVALID TRANSACTION CODE - 7


                    ROBBEM STATE BANK
                     106 WEST 10TH ST.
                    BROOKLYN, NY  11212

            SAVINGS ACCOUNT TRANSACTION REGISTER
DATE  4/08/88                              PAGE   1


    ACCOUNT     DEPOSITS      WITHDRAWALS      NOTES
    NUMBER

    00014                      1,000.00
    00021         127.50
    00028         153.27
    00028                      1,500.50
    00077         150.00
    00084       3,574.29
    00084     JOHN & SALLY DUPRINO           NAME CHANGE
    00091       1,500.00
    00091       1,200.00
    00091                        500.00
    00098     GEORGE & ANN CULHANE           NAME CHANGE
    00126         350.00
    00133       2,563.00
    00140     BETH DENNY                     NAME CHANGE
    00161       1,256.34
    00168                        110.00
    00168                         15.50     ACCOUNT CLOSED
```

```
                            ROBBEM STATE BANK
                             106 WEST 10TH ST.
                           BROOKLYN, NY  11212

                       SAVINGS ACCOUNT TRANSACTION REGISTER
        DATE  4/08/88                                    PAGE  2

              ACCOUNT      DEPOSITS      WITHDRAWALS       NOTES
              NUMBER

               00175        192.02
               00210        250.00
               00210        250.00
               00210        250.00
               00273      1,725.00
               00280      2,317.00
               00308         50.00

        TOTALS         15,908.42       3,126.00
                              CONTROL COUNTS

                       NUMBER OF DEPOSITS         16

                       NUMBER OF WITHDRAWALS       4

                       NUMBER OF NAME CHANGES      3

                       NUMBER OF CLOSED ACCOUNTS   1

                       NUMBER OF ERRORS           27

                       TOTAL                      51
```

Figure 13.13 Master file produced by Program P13-02.

```
-------------------------------------------------------------------------------
          1         2         3         4         5         6         7        8
12345678901234567890123456789012345678901234567890123456789012345678901234567890
-------------------------------------------------------------------------------
00007ROSEBUCCI              88040700100784
00014ROBERT DAVIS M.D.      88040800009900%
00021LORICE MONTI           8804080002525%
00028MICHAEL SMITH          8804080056543F
00032JOSEPH CAMILLO         88040700002500
00035JOHN J. LEHMAN         88040700015000
00049JAY GREENE             88040700015000
00056EVELYN SLATER          88040700000100
00070PATRICK J. LEE         88040700050000
00077LESLIE MINSKY          8804080001603G
00084JOHN & SALLY DUPRINO8804080005074 2I
00091JOE'S DELI             8804080023000%
00098GEORGE & ANN CULHANE88040800050000
00105ONE DAY CLEANERS       88040700005000
00112ROSEMARY LANE          88040700025000
00126JAMES BUDD             8804080011000%
00133PAUL LERNER, D.D.S.    8804080035630%
00140BETH DENNY             88040800002575
00161ROBERT RYAN            8804080012808D
00175MARY KEATING           8804080002020B
00189J. & L. CAIN           88040700003500
00196IMPERIAL FLORIST       88040700015000
00203JOYCE MITCHELL         88040700000500
00210JERRY PARKS            8804080010000%
00217CARL CALDERON          88040700005000
00224JOHN WILLIAMS          88040700017550
00231BILL WILLIAMS          88040700055500
00238KEVIN PARKER           88040700001000
00245FRANK CAPUTO           88040700003500
00252GENE GALLI             88040700001500
00266MARTIN LANG            88040700009957
00273VITO CACACI            8804080020000%
00280COMMUNITY DRUGS        8804080023370%
00287SOLOMON CHAPELS        88040700001500
00294JOHN BURKE             88040700150000
00308JOE GARCIA             8804080020500%
00315GRACE MICELI           88040700025000
00329GUY VOLPONE            88040700001000
00343JOE & MARY SESSA       88040700100000
00350ROGER SHAW             88040700250000
```

EXERCISE 2

Write a program to update the master file you created in Exercise 3, Chapter 12, page 392. Use transactions in the following formats:

Positions	Field
1	Code 2 (Receipt of goods into inventory)
2 – 6	Part Number
7 – 9	Quantity Received
10 – 80	spaces
1	Code 3 (Withdrawal of goods from inventory)
2 – 6	Part Number
7 – 9	Quantity Withdrawn
10 – 80	spaces
1	Code 4 (Part Description change)
2 – 6	Part Number
7 – 26	Part Description
27 – 80	spaces
1	Code 5 (Units change)
2 – 6	Part Number
7	Units
8 – 80	spaces
1	Code 6 (Quantity on Hand correction)
2 – 6	Part Number
7	Sign of correction (+ or −)
8 – 10	Quantity on Hand correction
11 – 80	spaces
1	Code 7 (Unit Cost change)
2 – 6	Part Number
7 – 12	Unit Cost (dollars and cents)
13 – 80	spaces
1	Code 8 (Supplier Code change)
2 – 6	Part Number
7 – 10	Supplier Code
11 – 80	spaces
1	Code 9 (Storage Location change)
2 – 6	Part Number
7 – 11	Storage Location
12 – 80	spaces
1	Code 10 (Reorder Point change)
2 – 6	Part Number
7 – 9	Reorder Point
10 – 80	spaces
1	Code 11 (Reorder Quantity change)
2 – 6	Part Number
7 – 9	Reorder Quantity
10 – 80	spaces

Design suitable reports for your program. Have your program check the input transactions for validity. Have your program print a line for each transaction processed. For each master record that is updated, have your program insert today's date in the Date of Last Access field. Also for each master record that is updated, have your program check whether the Quantity on Hand is equal to or less than the Reorder Point, and print a message showing the Reorder Quantity and the word REORDER if it is. If an attempt is made to delete a Part Number having a non-zero Quantity on Hand, do not delete it. Instead, count the transaction as erroneous and have your program print the Quantity on Hand and a message NONZERO QUANTITY ON HAND on the error report.

A Complete Update Program

We will now develop a program to process additions of new savings-account records to the master file in the same run as changes and deletions to existing records. We have only to make a few small changes to Program P13-02 and we will have our complete update program, Program P13-03. Program P13-03 will be able to create a new master record and process changes to it in the same run, just as Program P13-02 could change a record and delete it in one run. Program P13-03 will check for all kinds of errors. For example, if a transaction attempts to add to the master file a record whose key is already present on the file, the transaction will be detected as an error. If a valid transaction to add a record to the file is followed by another transaction to add a record with the same key, the second add will be detected as an error. And of course all of the error checking that is present in Program P13-02 will be used in Program P13-03.

For Program P13-03 the formats of input transactions having transaction Codes 2 through 5 are the same as for Program P13-02. In addition, Program P13-03 will accept transactions in the following format, to add new records to the master file:

Positions	Field
1	Code 1
2–6	Account Number
7–14	Amount (to two decimal places)
15–34	Depositor Name
35–80	spaces

Notice that the Depositor Name field in this transaction partially overlaps the Depositor Name field in the depositor name-change transaction described on page 423. Such overlapping presents no problem. All five transaction types can be defined in a single transaction input area by using redefinition, as you will see when we look at Program P13-03.

The format of the transaction register produced by Program P13-03 is shown in Figure 13.14. It is very similar to the transaction register produced by Program P13-02, except that provision is made for handling new accounts. The format of the error report, Figure 13.15, has provision for all the usual errors and for those dealing with new accounts.

Figure 13.14 Output format for transaction register for Program P13-03.

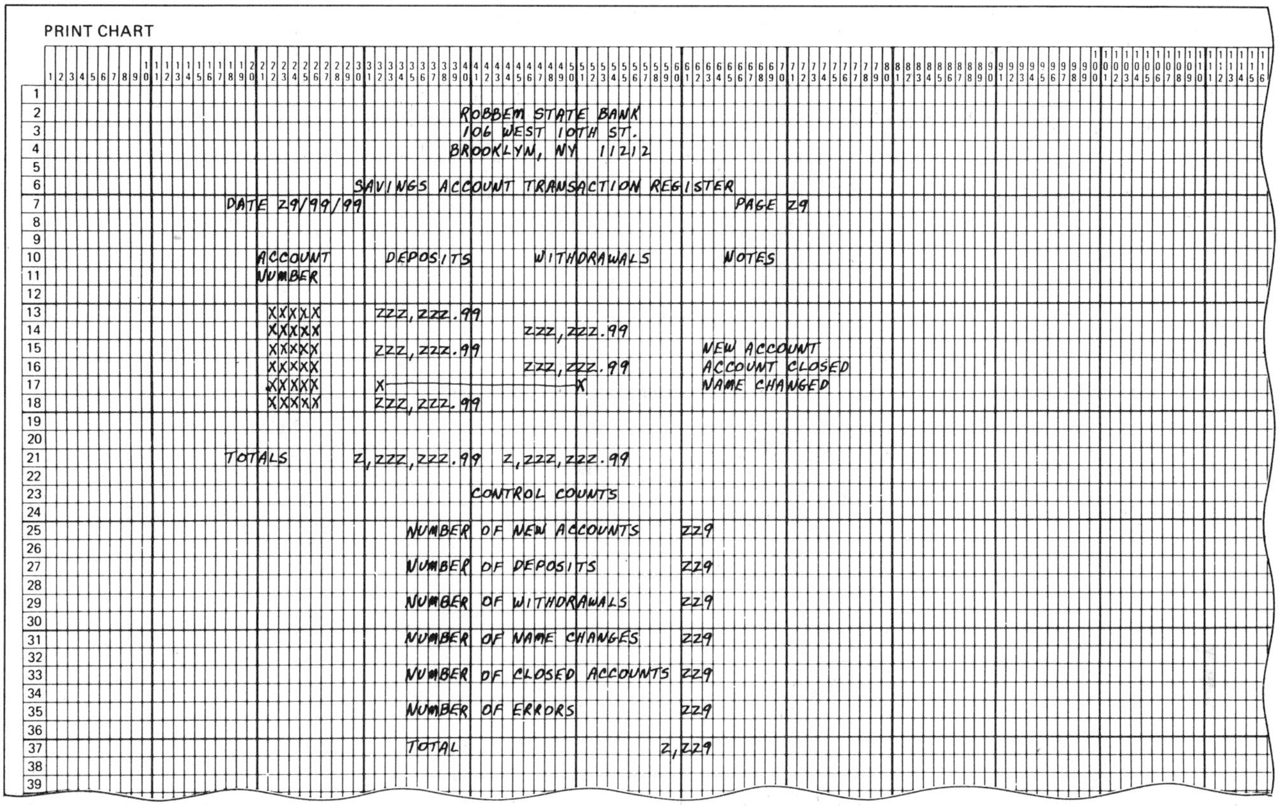

Figure 13.15 Output format for error report for Program P13-03.

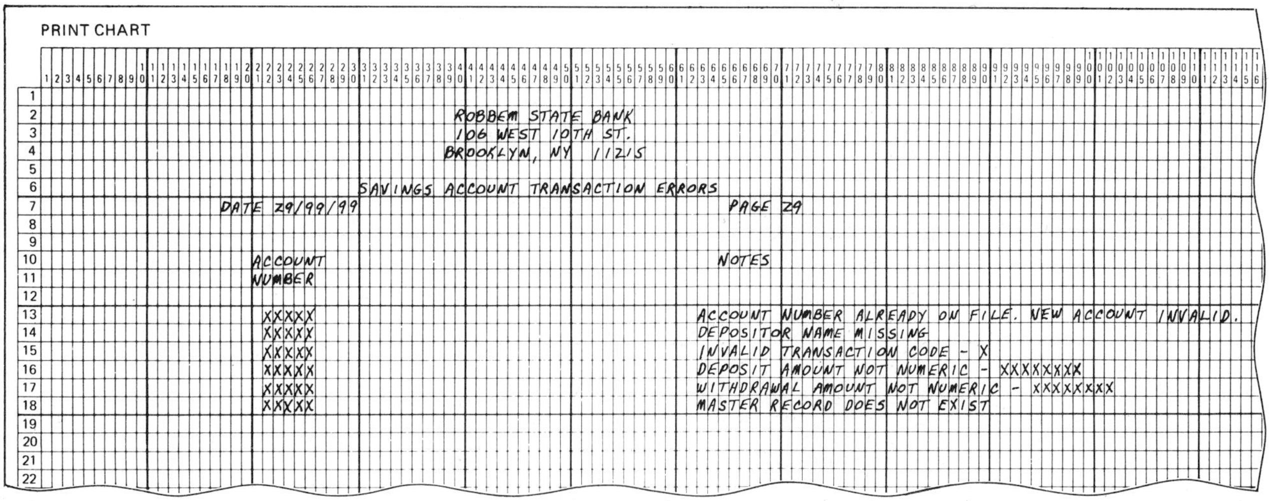

A Hierarchy Diagram for a Complete Update Program

The hierarchy diagram for "Process transaction record" for Program P13-03 is shown in Figure 13.16. It is the same as the hierarchy diagram for "Process transaction record" for Program P13-02 except that this diagram includes the ability to add new savings-account master records to the output master file. The box "Check for valid new account" is now included as one of the subfunctions of "Apply transaction."

Figure 13.16   Hierarchy diagram for "Process transaction record" for Program P13-03.

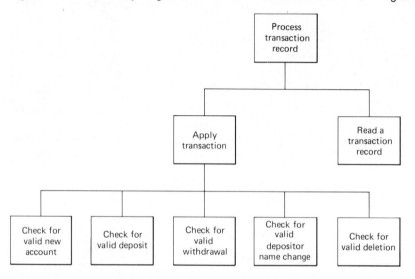

Stepping Through the Hierarchy Diagram

To see how this hierarchy diagram would add a record to the output master file, assume we have a master file containing records with the following Account Numbers:

```
00007
00014
00021
00028
```

Now assume that we have transactions with the following Codes and Account Numbers:

```
2 00007
1 00018
2 00018
3 00028
```

These transactions are all valid. The first transaction is a deposit to Account Number 00007. The second transaction is to create a new master record for Account Number 00018. The third transaction makes a deposit to the newly created master record, and the last transaction is a withdrawal from Account

Number 00028. Of course the program must write the new master record into its proper place on the output master file, that is, between master records 00014 and 00021.

When the program executes, 00007 is first assigned to CURRENT-KEY. Master record 00007 is updated with the deposit and the updated record written onto the output master file. Then 00014 is assigned to CURRENT-KEY, and master record 00014 is written onto the output master file unchanged. CHOOSE-CURRENT-KEY then chooses between 00018 and 00021. 00018 is assigned to CURRENT-KEY. Since the key of the master record in the master input area is not equal to CURRENT-KEY, PROCESS-MASTER-RECORD moves nothing to the work area and sets the flag to "N."

This is exactly the situation we need in order to create a new master record and insert it in the correct place in the output master file. There must be no master record in the work area, so that we can build the new master record there. The flag must be set to "N." Whereas in all of our other types of transactions there had to be a matching master record in the work area for the transaction to be applied to, when we are creating a new master record we want no matching master record in the work area. If there were one, it would mean that a transaction is trying to create a new master record having an Account Number that is already on the file. So in all our previous update programs a transaction could be immediately recognized as erroneous if the flag were set to "N"; when we are trying to create a new master record the transaction is erroneous if the flag is set to "Y."

The box "Check for valid new account" now makes the usual validity checks on the input transaction. If the transaction passes all the checks, a new master record with Account Number 00018 is created in the work area the same way that we created master records in Program P12-02 when we were first creating the master file.

Then, after the master record is created in the work area, the program must set the flag to "Y" to indicate that now there is in the work area a master record whose key matches CURRENT-KEY. The flag must be set to "Y" so that the deposit transaction to Account Number 00018, which is coming in next, finds a matching master record in the work area, and so that CHECK-TO-WRITE-MASTER, when its time comes to execute, recognizes that there is a master record, 00018, waiting in the work area to be written out.

A Program to Update a Sequential Master File with Additions, Changes, and Deletions

Program P13-03 is shown in Figure 13.17. It is of course very similar to Program P13-02. The TRANSACTION-INPUT-AREA now has a level-88 entry for the

Figure 13.17 Program P13-03.

```
CB1 RELEASE 2.4                          IBM OS/VS COBOL  JULY  1, 1982

              13.49.12        APR  8,1988

00010   IDENTIFICATION DIVISION.
00020   PROGRAM-ID. P13-03.
00030 *
00040 *     THIS PROGRAM UPDATES A SEQUENTIAL MASTER FILE
00050 *     WITH ADDITIONS, CHANGES, AND DELETIONS.
00060 *
```

(continued)

TRANSACTION-CODE for a NEW-ACCOUNT, at line 00950.

You can see how the transaction input area has been defined to accommodate the formats of all the transaction types. The level-05 entries at lines 00940 through 01090 provide for all the fields in transactions with Codes 1, 2, 3, and 5. the redefined transaction input area at lines 01110 through 01150 provides for the DEPOSITOR-NAME as it appears in transactions with Code 4.

Figure 13.17 (continued)

```
00070 ******************************************************************
00080
00090  ENVIRONMENT DIVISION.
00100  CONFIGURATION SECTION.
00110  SOURCE-COMPUTER. IBM-370.
00120  OBJECT-COMPUTER. IBM-370.
00130
00140  INPUT-OUTPUT SECTION.
00150  FILE-CONTROL.
00160      SELECT ACCOUNT-MASTER-FILE-IN          ASSIGN TO MFILEIN.
00170      SELECT ACCOUNT-MASTER-FILE-OUT         ASSIGN TO MFILEOUT.
00180      SELECT TRANSACTION-FILE-IN             ASSIGN TO INFILE.
00190      SELECT TRANSACTION-REGISTER-FILE-OUT   ASSIGN TO PRINTER1.
00200      SELECT ERROR-FILE-OUT                  ASSIGN TO PRINTER2.
00210      SELECT SORT-WORK-FILE                  ASSIGN TO SORTWK.
00220
00230 ******************************************************************
00240
00250  DATA DIVISION.
00260  FILE SECTION.
00270  FD  ACCOUNT-MASTER-FILE-IN
00280      LABEL RECORDS ARE STANDARD
00290      RECORD CONTAINS 39 CHARACTERS
00300      BLOCK CONTAINS 100 RECORDS.
00310
00320  01  ACCOUNT-MASTER-RECORD-IN        PIC X(39).
00330
00340  FD  ACCOUNT-MASTER-FILE-OUT
00350      LABEL RECORDS ARE STANDARD
00360      RECORD CONTAINS 39 CHARACTERS
00370      BLOCK CONTAINS 100 RECORDS.
00380
00390  01  ACCOUNT-MASTER-RECORD-OUT       PIC X(39).
00400
00410  SD  SORT-WORK-FILE
00420      RECORD CONTAINS 34 CHARACTERS.
00430
00440  01  SORT-WORK-RECORD.
00450      05  TRANSACTION-CODE-S          PIC X.
00460      05  ACCOUNT-NUMBER-S            PIC X(5).
00470      05  FILLER                      PIC X(28).
00480
00490  FD  TRANSACTION-FILE-IN
00500      LABEL RECORDS ARE OMITTED
00510      RECORD CONTAINS 80 CHARACTERS.
00520
00530  01  TRANSACTION-RECORD-IN           PIC X(80).
00540
00550  FD  TRANSACTION-REGISTER-FILE-OUT
00560      LABEL RECORDS ARE OMITTED.
00570
00580  01  REGISTER-RECORD-OUT             PIC X(76).
00590
00600  FD  ERROR-FILE-OUT
00610      LABEL RECORDS ARE OMITTED.
00620
00630  01  ERROR-RECORD-OUT                PIC X(114).
00640
```

```
00650     WORKING-STORAGE SECTION.
00660     01   CURRENT-KEY                          PIC X(5).
00670     01   IS-MASTER-RECORD-IN-WORK-AREA        PIC X.
00680     01   NUMBER-OF-INPUT-RECORDS-W            PIC S9(3) VALUE ZERO.
00690     01   NUMBER-OF-ERRONEOUS-RECORDS-W        PIC S9(3) VALUE ZERO.
00700     01   DEPOSIT-TOTAL-W                      PIC S9(7)V99 VALUE ZERO.
00710     01   WITHDRAWAL-TOTAL-W                   PIC S9(7)V99 VALUE ZERO.
00720     01   NUMBER-OF-NEW-ACCOUNTS-W             PIC S9(3) VALUE ZERO.
00730     01   NUMBER-OF-DEPOSITS-W                 PIC S9(3) VALUE ZERO.
00740     01   NUMBER-OF-WITHDRAWALS-W              PIC S9(3) VALUE ZERO.
00750     01   NUMBER-OF-NAME-CHANGES-W             PIC S9(3) VALUE ZERO.
00760     01   NUMBER-OF-CLOSED-ACCOUNTS-W          PIC S9(3) VALUE ZERO.
00770     01   BLANK-LINE                           PIC X     VALUE SPACE.
00780     01   PAGE-NUMBER-W                        PIC S99   VALUE 0.
00790     01   ERROR-PAGE-NUMBER-W                  PIC S99   VALUE 0.
00800     01   PAGE-LIMIT            COMP SYNC      PIC S99   VALUE 28.
00810     01   LINE-COUNT-ER        COMP SYNC      PIC S99.
00820     01   ERROR-PAGE-LIMIT     COMP SYNC      PIC S99   VALUE 45.
00830     01   ERROR-LINE-COUNTER   COMP SYNC      PIC S99.
00840
00850     01   TODAYS-DATE.
00860          05   TODAYS-YEAR                     PIC 99.
00870          05   TODAYS-MONTH-AND-DAY            PIC 9(4).
00880
00890     01   MASTER-INPUT-AREA.
00900          05   ACCOUNT-NUMBER                  PIC X(5).
00910          05   FILLER                          PIC X(34).
00920
00930     01   TRANSACTION-INPUT-AREA.
00940          05   TRANSACTION-CODE                PIC X.
00950               88   NEW-ACCOUNT                VALUE "1".
00960               88   DEPOSIT                    VALUE "2".
00970               88   WITHDRAWAL                 VALUE "3".
00980               88   NAME-CHANGE                VALUE "4".
00990               88   DELETION                   VALUE "5".
01000          05   ACCOUNT-NUMBER                  PIC X(5).
01010          05   DEPOSIT-AND-WITHDRAWAL-AMTS.
01020               10   DEPOSIT-AMOUNT             PIC 9(6)V99.
01030               10   DEPOSIT-AMOUNT-X     REDEFINES DEPOSIT-AMOUNT
01040                                               PIC X(8).
01050               10   WITHDRAWAL-AMOUNT    REDEFINES DEPOSIT-AMOUNT
01060                                               PIC 9(6)V99.
01070               10   WITHDRAWAL-AMOUNT-X  REDEFINES DEPOSIT-AMOUNT
01080                                               PIC X(8).
01090          05   DEPOSITOR-NAME-NEW-ACCOUNT      PIC X(20).
01100               88   DEPOSITOR-NAME-MISSING     VALUE SPACES.
01110     01   TRANSACTION-4-INPUT-AREA REDEFINES TRANSACTION-INPUT-AREA.
01120          05   FILLER                          PIC X(6).
01130          05   DEPOSITOR-NAME                  PIC X(20).
01140               88   REPLACEMENT-NAME-MISSING   VALUE SPACES.
01150          05   FILLER                          PIC X(8).
01160
01170     01   WORK-AREA.
01180          05   ACCOUNT-NUMBER-W                PIC X(5).
01190          05   DEPOSITOR-NAME-W                PIC X(20).
01200          05   DATE-OF-LAST-TRANSACTION-W      PIC 9(6).
01210          05   CURRENT-BALANCE-W               PIC S9(6)V99.
01220
01230     01   REPORT-HEADING-1.
01240          05   FILLER    PIC X(39) VALUE SPACES.
01250          05   FILLER    PIC X(17) VALUE "ROBBEM STATE BANK".
01260
01270     01   REPORT-HEADING-2.
01280          05   FILLER    PIC X(39) VALUE SPACES.
01290          05   FILLER    PIC X(17) VALUE "106 WEST 10TH ST.".
01300
01310     01   REPORT-HEADING-3.
01320          05   FILLER    PIC X(38) VALUE SPACES.
01330          05   FILLER    PIC X(19) VALUE "BROOKLYN, NY  11212".
01340
01350     01   PAGE-HEADING-1.
01360          05   FILLER    PIC X(29) VALUE SPACES.
01370          05   FILLER    PIC X(36)
01380                         VALUE "SAVINGS ACCOUNT TRANSACTION REGISTER".
01390
```

(continued)

Figure 13.17   (continued)

```
01400    01   ERROR-PAGE-HEADING-1.
01410         05   FILLER      PIC X(30) VALUE SPACES.
01420         05   FILLER      PIC X(34)
01430                          VALUE  "SAVINGS ACCOUNT TRANSACTION ERRORS".
01440
01450    01   PAGE-HEADING-2.
01460         05   FILLER          PIC X(17) VALUE SPACES.
01470         05   FILLER          PIC X(5)  VALUE "DATE".
01480         05   TODAYS-MONTH-AND-DAY             PIC Z9/99/.
01490         05   TODAYS-YEAR                      PIC 99B(35).
01500         05   FILLER          PIC X(5)  VALUE "PAGE".
01510         05   PAGE-NUMBER-OUT                  PIC Z9.
01520
01530    01   PAGE-HEADING-3.
01540         05   FILLER          PIC X(20) VALUE SPACES.
01550         05   FILLER          PIC X(12) VALUE "ACCOUNT".
01560         05   FILLER          PIC X(14) VALUE "DEPOSITS".
01570         05   FILLER          PIC X(18) VALUE "WITHDRAWALS".
01580         05   FILLER          PIC X(5)  VALUE "NOTES".
01590
01600    01   ERROR-PAGE-HEADING-3.
01610         05   FILLER          PIC X(20) VALUE SPACES.
01620         05   FILLER          PIC X(44) VALUE "ACCOUNT".
01630         05   FILLER          PIC X(5)  VALUE "NOTES".
01640
01650    01   PAGE-HEADING-4.
01660         05   FILLER          PIC X(20) VALUE SPACES.
01670         05   FILLER          PIC X(6)  VALUE "NUMBER".
01680
01690    01   NEW-ACCOUNT-LINE.
01700         05   FILLER          PIC X(21) VALUE SPACES.
01710         05   ACCOUNT-NUMBER-OUT    PIC X(5)B(5).
01720         05   DEPOSIT-AMOUNT-OUT    PIC ZZZ,ZZZ.99B(21).
01730         05   FILLER          PIC X(11) VALUE "NEW ACCOUNT".
01740
01750    01   DEPOSIT-LINE.
01760         05   FILLER          PIC X(21) VALUE SPACES.
01770         05   ACCOUNT-NUMBER-OUT    PIC X(5)B(5).
01780         05   DEPOSIT-AMOUNT-OUT    PIC ZZZ,ZZZ.99.
01790
01800    01   WITHDRAWAL-LINE.
01810         05   FILLER          PIC X(21) VALUE SPACES.
01820         05   ACCOUNT-NUMBER-OUT    PIC X(5)B(19).
01830         05   WITHDRAWAL-AMOUNT-OUT PIC ZZZ,ZZZ.99.
01840
01850    01   NAME-CHANGE-LINE.
01860         05   FILLER          PIC X(21) VALUE SPACES.
01870         05   ACCOUNT-NUMBER-OUT    PIC X(5)B(5).
01880         05   DEPOSITOR-NAME-OUT    PIC X(20)B(11).
01890         05   FILLER          PIC X(11) VALUE "NAME CHANGE".
01900
01910    01   DELETION-LINE.
01920         05   FILLER          PIC X(21) VALUE SPACES.
01930         05   ACCOUNT-NUMBER-OUT    PIC X(5)B(19).
01940         05   CURRENT-BALANCE-OUT   PIC ZZZ,ZZZ.99B(7).
01950         05   FILLER          PIC X(14) VALUE "ACCOUNT CLOSED".
01960
01970    01   DEPOSIT-AMOUNT-INVALID-MSG.
01980         05   FILLER          PIC X(29)
01990                          VALUE "DEPOSIT AMOUNT NOT NUMERIC -".
02000         05   DEPOSIT-AMOUNT-OUT    PIC X(8).
02010
02020    01   WITHDRAWAL-AMOUNT-INVALID-MSG.
02030         05   FILLER          PIC X(32)
02040                          VALUE "WITHDRAWAL AMOUNT NOT NUMERIC -".
02050         05   WITHDRAWAL-AMOUNT-OUT PIC X(8).
02060
02070    01   INVALID-CODE-MSG.
02080         05   FILLER      PIC X(27) VALUE "INVALID TRANSACTION CODE -".
02090         05   TRANSACTION-CODE-OUT  PIC X.
02100
02110    01   ERROR-LINE.
02120         05   ACCOUNT-NUMBER-E      PIC B(21)X(5)B(36).
02130         05   ERROR-MESSAGE         PIC X(52).
```

```
02140
02150   01  FINAL-LINE-1.
02160        05  FILLER           PIC X(17) VALUE SPACES.
02170        05  FILLER           PIC X(12) VALUE "TOTALS".
02180        05  DEPOSIT-TOTAL-OUT            PIC Z,ZZZ,ZZZ.99BB.
02190        05  WITHDRAWAL-TOTAL-OUT         PIC Z,ZZZ,ZZZ.99.
02200
02210   01  FINAL-LINE-2.
02220        05  FILLER           PIC X(40) VALUE SPACES.
02230        05  FILLER           PIC X(14) VALUE "CONTROL COUNTS".
02240
02250   01  FINAL-LINE-3.
02260        05  FILLER           PIC X(34) VALUE SPACES.
02270        05  FILLER           PIC X(26)
02280                             VALUE "NUMBER OF NEW ACCOUNTS".
02290        05  NUMBER-OF-NEW-ACCOUNTS-OUT   PIC ZZ9.
02300
02310   01  FINAL-LINE-4.
02320        05  FILLER           PIC X(34) VALUE SPACES.
02330        05  FILLER           PIC X(26)
02340                             VALUE "NUMBER OF DEPOSITS".
02350        05  NUMBER-OF-DEPOSITS-OUT       PIC ZZ9.
02360
02370   01  FINAL-LINE-5.
02380        05  FILLER           PIC X(34) VALUE SPACES.
02390        05  FILLER           PIC X(26)
02400                             VALUE "NUMBER OF WITHDRAWALS".
02410        05  NUMBER-OF-WITHDRAWALS-OUT    PIC ZZ9.
02420
02430   01  FINAL-LINE-6.
02440        05  FILLER           PIC X(34) VALUE SPACES.
02450        05  FILLER           PIC X(26)
02460                             VALUE "NUMBER OF NAME CHANGES".
02470        05  NUMBER-OF-NAME-CHANGES-OUT   PIC ZZ9.
02480
02490   01  FINAL-LINE-7.
02500        05  FILLER           PIC X(34) VALUE SPACES.
02510        05  FILLER           PIC X(26)
02520                             VALUE "NUMBER OF CLOSED ACCOUNTS".
02530        05  NUMBER-OF-CLOSED-ACCOUNTS-OUT  PIC ZZ9.
02540
02550   01  FINAL-LINE-8.
02560        05  FILLER           PIC X(34) VALUE SPACES.
02570        05  FILLER           PIC X(26)
02580                             VALUE "NUMBER OF ERRORS".
02590        05  NUMBER-OF-ERRONEOUS-RECRDS-OUT PIC ZZ9.
02600
02610   01  FINAL-LINE-9.
02620        05  FILLER           PIC X(34) VALUE SPACES.
02630        05  FILLER           PIC X(24) VALUE "TOTAL".
02640        05  NUMBER-OF-INPUT-RECORDS-OUT  PIC Z,ZZ9.
02650
02660   01  NO-INPUT-DATA.
02670        05  FILLER           PIC X(21) VALUE SPACES.
02680        05  FILLER           PIC X(13) VALUE "NO INPUT DATA".
02690
02700   **********************************************************************
02710
02720   PROCEDURE DIVISION.
02730   CONTROL-SECTION SECTION.
02740   UPDATE-PARAGRAPH.
02750        SORT SORT-WORK-FILE
02760             ASCENDING KEY ACCOUNT-NUMBER-S
02770                           TRANSACTION-CODE-S
02780             USING TRANSACTION-FILE-IN
02790             OUTPUT PROCEDURE IS UPDATE-RECORDS.
02800        STOP RUN.
02810
02820   UPDATE-RECORDS SECTION.
02830   UPDATE-RECORDS-PARAGRAPH.
02840        PERFORM INITIALIZATION.
02850        PERFORM PROCESS-ONE-KEY UNTIL
02860             CURRENT-KEY = HIGH-VALUES.
02870        PERFORM TERMINATION.
02880        GO TO END-OF-THIS-SECTION.
02890
```

(continued)

Figure 13.17   (continued)

```
02900    INITIALIZATION.
02910        OPEN INPUT   ACCOUNT-MASTER-FILE-IN
02920             OUTPUT ACCOUNT-MASTER-FILE-OUT
02930                    ERROR-FILE-OUT
02940                    TRANSACTION-REGISTER-FILE-OUT.
02950        ACCEPT TODAYS-DATE FROM DATE.
02960        MOVE CORR TODAYS-DATE TO PAGE-HEADING-2.
02970        PERFORM PRODUCE-REPORT-HEADINGS.
02980        PERFORM READ-A-MASTER-RECORD.
02990        PERFORM READ-A-TRANSACTION-RECORD.
03000        PERFORM CHOOSE-CURRENT-KEY.
03010        IF CURRENT-KEY = HIGH-VALUES
03020            WRITE REGISTER-RECORD-OUT FROM NO-INPUT-DATA.
03030
03040    PRODUCE-REPORT-HEADINGS.
03050        PERFORM WRITE-REGISTER-HEADINGS.
03060        PERFORM WRITE-ERROR-REPORT-HEADINGS.
03070
03080    WRITE-REGISTER-HEADINGS.
03090        ADD 1 TO PAGE-NUMBER-W.
03100        MOVE PAGE-NUMBER-W TO PAGE-NUMBER-OUT.
03110        WRITE REGISTER-RECORD-OUT FROM
03120            REPORT-HEADING-1 AFTER ADVANCING PAGE.
03130        WRITE REGISTER-RECORD-OUT FROM REPORT-HEADING-2.
03140        WRITE REGISTER-RECORD-OUT FROM REPORT-HEADING-3.
03150        WRITE REGISTER-RECORD-OUT FROM PAGE-HEADING-1 AFTER 2.
03160        WRITE REGISTER-RECORD-OUT FROM PAGE-HEADING-2.
03170        WRITE REGISTER-RECORD-OUT FROM PAGE-HEADING-3 AFTER 3.
03180        WRITE REGISTER-RECORD-OUT FROM PAGE-HEADING-4.
03190        WRITE REGISTER-RECORD-OUT FROM BLANK-LINE.
03200        MOVE 11 TO LINE-COUNT-ER.
03210
03220    WRITE-ERROR-REPORT-HEADINGS.
03230        ADD 1 TO ERROR-PAGE-NUMBER-W.
03240        MOVE ERROR-PAGE-NUMBER-W TO PAGE-NUMBER-OUT.
03250        WRITE ERROR-RECORD-OUT FROM REPORT-HEADING-1 AFTER PAGE.
03260        WRITE ERROR-RECORD-OUT FROM REPORT-HEADING-2.
03270        WRITE ERROR-RECORD-OUT FROM REPORT-HEADING-3.
03280        WRITE ERROR-RECORD-OUT FROM ERROR-PAGE-HEADING-1 AFTER 2.
03290        WRITE ERROR-RECORD-OUT FROM PAGE-HEADING-2.
03300        WRITE ERROR-RECORD-OUT FROM ERROR-PAGE-HEADING-3 AFTER 3.
03310        WRITE ERROR-RECORD-OUT FROM PAGE-HEADING-4.
03320        WRITE ERROR-RECORD-OUT FROM BLANK-LINE.
03330        MOVE 11 TO ERROR-LINE-COUNTER.
03340
03350    PROCESS-ONE-KEY.
03360        PERFORM PROCESS-MASTER-RECORD.
03370        PERFORM PROCESS-TRANSACTION-RECORD UNTIL
03380            ACCOUNT-NUMBER IN TRANSACTION-INPUT-AREA
03390            IS NOT EQUAL TO CURRENT-KEY.
03400        PERFORM CHECK-TO-WRITE-MASTER.
03410        PERFORM CHOOSE-CURRENT-KEY.
03420
03430    PROCESS-TRANSACTION-RECORD.
03440        PERFORM APPLY-TRANSACTION.
03450        PERFORM READ-A-TRANSACTION-RECORD.
03460
03470    CHECK-TO-WRITE-MASTER.
03480        IF IS-MASTER-RECORD-IN-WORK-AREA = "Y"
03490            WRITE ACCOUNT-MASTER-RECORD-OUT FROM WORK-AREA.
03500
03510    CHOOSE-CURRENT-KEY.
03520        IF ACCOUNT-NUMBER IN TRANSACTION-INPUT-AREA IS LESS THAN
03530            ACCOUNT-NUMBER IN MASTER-INPUT-AREA
03540            MOVE ACCOUNT-NUMBER IN TRANSACTION-INPUT-AREA TO
03550                CURRENT-KEY
03560        ELSE
03570            MOVE ACCOUNT-NUMBER IN MASTER-INPUT-AREA TO
03580                CURRENT-KEY.
03590
03600    PROCESS-MASTER-RECORD.
03610        IF ACCOUNT-NUMBER IN MASTER-INPUT-AREA
03620            IS EQUAL TO CURRENT-KEY
03630            MOVE MASTER-INPUT-AREA TO WORK-AREA
03640            PERFORM READ-A-MASTER-RECORD
03650            MOVE "Y" TO IS-MASTER-RECORD-IN-WORK-AREA
03660        ELSE
03670            MOVE "N" TO IS-MASTER-RECORD-IN-WORK-AREA.
```

```
03680
03690   READ-A-TRANSACTION-RECORD.
03700       RETURN SORT-WORK-FILE INTO TRANSACTION-INPUT-AREA
03710           AT END
03720               MOVE HIGH-VALUES TO TRANSACTION-INPUT-AREA.
03730       IF TRANSACTION-INPUT-AREA NOT EQUAL TO HIGH-VALUES
03740           ADD 1 TO NUMBER-OF-INPUT-RECORDS-W.
03750
03760   READ-A-MASTER-RECORD.
03770       READ ACCOUNT-MASTER-FILE-IN INTO MASTER-INPUT-AREA
03780           AT END
03790               MOVE HIGH-VALUES TO MASTER-INPUT-AREA.
03800
03810   APPLY-TRANSACTION.
03820       IF NEW-ACCOUNT
03830           PERFORM CHECK-FOR-VALID-NEW-ACCOUNT
03840       ELSE
03850       IF DEPOSIT
03860           PERFORM CHECK-FOR-VALID-DEPOSIT
03870       ELSE
03880       IF WITHDRAWAL
03890           PERFORM CHECK-FOR-VALID-WITHDRAWAL
03900       ELSE
03910       IF NAME-CHANGE
03920           PERFORM CHECK-FOR-VALID-NAME-CHANGE
03930       ELSE
03940       IF DELETION
03950           PERFORM CHECK-FOR-VALID-DELETION
03960       ELSE
03970           ADD 1 TO NUMBER-OF-ERRONEOUS-RECORDS-W
03980           PERFORM WRITE-INVALID-CODE-LINE.
03990
04000   CHECK-FOR-VALID-NEW-ACCOUNT.
04010       IF IS-MASTER-RECORD-IN-WORK-AREA = "Y"
04020           ADD 1 TO NUMBER-OF-ERRONEOUS-RECORDS-W
04030           PERFORM WRITE-NEW-ACCT-INVALID-LINE
04040       ELSE
04050       IF DEPOSIT-AMOUNT NOT NUMERIC
04060           ADD 1 TO NUMBER-OF-ERRONEOUS-RECORDS-W
04070           PERFORM WRITE-DEPOSIT-INVALID-LINE
04080       ELSE
04090       IF DEPOSITOR-NAME-MISSING
04100           ADD 1 TO NUMBER-OF-ERRONEOUS-RECORDS-W
04110           PERFORM WRITE-NAME-MISSING-LINE
04120       ELSE
04130           MOVE ACCOUNT-NUMBER IN TRANSACTION-INPUT-AREA
04140               TO ACCOUNT-NUMBER-W
04150           MOVE DEPOSITOR-NAME-NEW-ACCOUNT
04160               TO DEPOSITOR-NAME-W
04170           MOVE TODAYS-DATE TO DATE-OF-LAST-TRANSACTION-W
04180           MOVE DEPOSIT-AMOUNT TO CURRENT-BALANCE-W
04190           PERFORM WRITE-NEW-ACCOUNT-LINE
04200           MOVE "Y" TO IS-MASTER-RECORD-IN-WORK-AREA.
04210
04220   CHECK-FOR-VALID-DEPOSIT.
04230       IF DEPOSIT-AMOUNT NOT NUMERIC
04240           ADD 1 TO NUMBER-OF-ERRONEOUS-RECORDS-W
04250           PERFORM WRITE-DEPOSIT-INVALID-LINE
04260       ELSE
04270       IF IS-MASTER-RECORD-IN-WORK-AREA = "N"
04280           ADD 1 TO NUMBER-OF-ERRONEOUS-RECORDS-W
04290           PERFORM WRITE-MASTER-MISSING-LINE
04300       ELSE
04310           ADD DEPOSIT-AMOUNT TO CURRENT-BALANCE-W
04320           MOVE TODAYS-DATE TO DATE-OF-LAST-TRANSACTION-W
04330           PERFORM WRITE-DEPOSIT-LINE.
04340
```

(continued)

In the Procedure Division, the paragraph APPLY-TRANSACTION now has an additional IF test, at line 03820. We also have the paragraph CHECK-FOR-VALID-NEW-ACCOUNT, at line 04000, and the paragraphs that are PER-FORMed by CHECK-FOR-VALID-NEW-ACCOUNT. Program P13-03 was run

Figure 13.17 (continued)

```
04350   CHECK-FOR-VALID-WITHDRAWAL.
04360       IF WITHDRAWAL-AMOUNT NOT NUMERIC
04370           ADD 1 TO NUMBER-OF-ERRONEOUS-RECORDS-W
04380           PERFORM WRITE-WITHDRAWAL-INVALID-LINE
04390       ELSE
04400       IF IS-MASTER-RECORD-IN-WORK-AREA = "N"
04410           ADD 1 TO NUMBER-OF-ERRONEOUS-RECORDS-W
04420           PERFORM WRITE-MASTER-MISSING-LINE
04430       ELSE
04440           SUBTRACT WITHDRAWAL-AMOUNT FROM CURRENT-BALANCE-W
04450           MOVE TODAYS-DATE TO DATE-OF-LAST-TRANSACTION-W
04460           PERFORM WRITE-WITHDRAWAL-LINE.
04470
04480   CHECK-FOR-VALID-NAME-CHANGE.
04490       IF REPLACEMENT-NAME-MISSING
04500           ADD 1 TO NUMBER-OF-ERRONEOUS-RECORDS-W
04510           PERFORM WRITE-NAME-MISSING-LINE
04520       ELSE
04530       IF IS-MASTER-RECORD-IN-WORK-AREA = "N"
04540           ADD 1 TO NUMBER-OF-ERRONEOUS-RECORDS-W
04550           PERFORM WRITE-MASTER-MISSING-LINE
04560       ELSE
04570           MOVE DEPOSITOR-NAME TO DEPOSITOR-NAME-W
04580           MOVE TODAYS-DATE TO DATE-OF-LAST-TRANSACTION-W
04590           PERFORM WRITE-NAME-CHANGE-LINE.
04600
04610   CHECK-FOR-VALID-DELETION.
04620       IF IS-MASTER-RECORD-IN-WORK-AREA = "N"
04630           ADD 1 TO NUMBER-OF-ERRONEOUS-RECORDS-W
04640           PERFORM WRITE-MASTER-MISSING-LINE
04650       ELSE
04660           PERFORM WRITE-DELETION-LINE
04670           MOVE "N" TO IS-MASTER-RECORD-IN-WORK-AREA.
04680
04690   WRITE-NEW-ACCOUNT-LINE.
04700       MOVE CURRENT-KEY TO ACCOUNT-NUMBER-OUT IN NEW-ACCOUNT-LINE.
04710       MOVE DEPOSIT-AMOUNT
04720           TO DEPOSIT-AMOUNT-OUT IN NEW-ACCOUNT-LINE.
04730       IF 1 + LINE-COUNT-ER GREATER THAN PAGE-LIMIT
04740           PERFORM WRITE-REGISTER-HEADINGS.
04750       WRITE REGISTER-RECORD-OUT FROM NEW-ACCOUNT-LINE.
04760       ADD 1 TO LINE-COUNT-ER.
04770       ADD DEPOSIT-AMOUNT TO DEPOSIT-TOTAL-W.
04780       ADD 1 TO NUMBER-OF-NEW-ACCOUNTS-W.
04790
04800   WRITE-DEPOSIT-LINE.
04810       MOVE CURRENT-KEY TO ACCOUNT-NUMBER-OUT    IN DEPOSIT-LINE.
04820       MOVE DEPOSIT-AMOUNT TO DEPOSIT-AMOUNT-OUT IN DEPOSIT-LINE.
04830       IF 1 + LINE-COUNT-ER GREATER THAN PAGE-LIMIT
04840           PERFORM WRITE-REGISTER-HEADINGS.
04850       WRITE REGISTER-RECORD-OUT FROM DEPOSIT-LINE.
04860       ADD 1 TO LINE-COUNT-ER.
04870       ADD DEPOSIT-AMOUNT TO DEPOSIT-TOTAL-W.
04880       ADD 1 TO NUMBER-OF-DEPOSITS-W.
04890
04900   WRITE-WITHDRAWAL-LINE.
04910       MOVE CURRENT-KEY TO ACCOUNT-NUMBER-OUT IN WITHDRAWAL-LINE.
04920       MOVE WITHDRAWAL-AMOUNT TO
04930           WITHDRAWAL-AMOUNT-OUT IN WITHDRAWAL-LINE.
04940       IF 1 + LINE-COUNT-ER GREATER THAN PAGE-LIMIT
04950           PERFORM WRITE-REGISTER-HEADINGS.
04960       WRITE REGISTER-RECORD-OUT FROM WITHDRAWAL-LINE.
04970       ADD 1 TO LINE-COUNT-ER.
04980       ADD WITHDRAWAL-AMOUNT TO WITHDRAWAL-TOTAL-W.
04990       ADD 1 TO NUMBER-OF-WITHDRAWALS-W.
05000
05010   WRITE-DEPOSIT-INVALID-LINE.
05020       MOVE DEPOSIT-AMOUNT-X TO
05030           DEPOSIT-AMOUNT-OUT IN DEPOSIT-AMOUNT-INVALID-MSG.
05040       MOVE DEPOSIT-AMOUNT-INVALID-MSG TO ERROR-MESSAGE.
05050       PERFORM WRITE-ERROR-LINE.
05060
05070   WRITE-WITHDRAWAL-INVALID-LINE.
05080       MOVE WITHDRAWAL-AMOUNT-X TO
05090           WITHDRAWAL-AMOUNT-OUT IN WITHDRAWAL-AMOUNT-INVALID-MSG.
05100       MOVE WITHDRAWAL-AMOUNT-INVALID-MSG TO ERROR-MESSAGE.
05110       PERFORM WRITE-ERROR-LINE.
```

```
05120
05130    WRITE-NAME-MISSING-LINE.
05140        MOVE "DEPOSITOR NAME MISSING" TO ERROR-MESSAGE.
05150        PERFORM WRITE-ERROR-LINE.
05160
05170    WRITE-NAME-CHANGE-LINE.
05180        MOVE CURRENT-KEY TO ACCOUNT-NUMBER-OUT IN NAME-CHANGE-LINE.
05190        MOVE DEPOSITOR-NAME TO DEPOSITOR-NAME-OUT.
05200        IF 1 + LINE-COUNT-ER GREATER THAN PAGE-LIMIT
05210            PERFORM WRITE-REGISTER-HEADINGS.
05220        WRITE REGISTER-RECORD-OUT FROM NAME-CHANGE-LINE.
05230        ADD 1 TO LINE-COUNT-ER.
05240        ADD 1 TO NUMBER-OF-NAME-CHANGES-W.
05250
05260    WRITE-DELETION-LINE.
05270        MOVE CURRENT-KEY TO ACCOUNT-NUMBER-OUT IN DELETION-LINE.
05280        MOVE CURRENT-BALANCE-W TO CURRENT-BALANCE-OUT.
05290        IF 1 + LINE-COUNT-ER GREATER THAN PAGE-LIMIT
05300            PERFORM WRITE-REGISTER-HEADINGS.
05310        WRITE REGISTER-RECORD-OUT FROM DELETION-LINE.
05320        ADD 1 TO LINE-COUNT-ER.
05330        ADD CURRENT-BALANCE-W TO WITHDRAWAL-TOTAL-W.
05340        ADD 1 TO NUMBER-OF-CLOSED-ACCOUNTS-W.
05350
05360    WRITE-INVALID-CODE-LINE.
05370        MOVE TRANSACTION-CODE TO TRANSACTION-CODE-OUT.
05380        MOVE INVALID-CODE-MSG TO ERROR-MESSAGE.
05390        PERFORM WRITE-ERROR-LINE.
05400
05410    WRITE-MASTER-MISSING-LINE.
05420        MOVE "MASTER RECORD DOES NOT EXIST" TO ERROR-MESSAGE.
05430        PERFORM WRITE-ERROR-LINE.
05440
05450    WRITE-NEW-ACCT-INVALID-LINE.
05460        MOVE "ACCOUNT NUMBER ALREADY ON FILE. NEW ACCOUNT INVALID."
05470            TO ERROR-MESSAGE.
05480        PERFORM WRITE-ERROR-LINE.
05490
05500    WRITE-ERROR-LINE.
05510        IF 1 + ERROR-LINE-COUNTER GREATER THAN ERROR-PAGE-LIMIT
05520            PERFORM WRITE-ERROR-REPORT-HEADINGS.
05530        MOVE CURRENT-KEY TO ACCOUNT-NUMBER-E.
05540        WRITE ERROR-RECORD-OUT FROM ERROR-LINE.
05550        ADD 1 TO ERROR-LINE-COUNTER.
05560
05570    TERMINATION.
05580        PERFORM PRODUCE-TOTAL-LINES.
05590        CLOSE ACCOUNT-MASTER-FILE-IN
05600              ACCOUNT-MASTER-FILE-OUT
05610              ERROR-FILE-OUT
05620              TRANSACTION-REGISTER-FILE-OUT.
05630
05640    PRODUCE-TOTAL-LINES.
05650        MOVE DEPOSIT-TOTAL-W     TO DEPOSIT-TOTAL-OUT.
05660        MOVE WITHDRAWAL-TOTAL-W TO WITHDRAWAL-TOTAL-OUT.
05670        WRITE REGISTER-RECORD-OUT FROM FINAL-LINE-1 AFTER 3.
05680        WRITE REGISTER-RECORD-OUT FROM FINAL-LINE-2 AFTER 2.
05690        MOVE NUMBER-OF-NEW-ACCOUNTS-W TO NUMBER-OF-NEW-ACCOUNTS-OUT.
05700        WRITE REGISTER-RECORD-OUT FROM FINAL-LINE-3 AFTER 2.
05710        MOVE NUMBER-OF-DEPOSITS-W TO NUMBER-OF-DEPOSITS-OUT.
05720        WRITE REGISTER-RECORD-OUT FROM FINAL-LINE-4 AFTER 2.
05730        MOVE NUMBER-OF-WITHDRAWALS-W TO NUMBER-OF-WITHDRAWALS-OUT.
05740        WRITE REGISTER-RECORD-OUT FROM FINAL-LINE-5 AFTER 2.
05750        MOVE NUMBER-OF-NAME-CHANGES-W TO NUMBER-OF-NAME-CHANGES-OUT.
05760        WRITE REGISTER-RECORD-OUT FROM FINAL-LINE-6 AFTER 2.
05770        MOVE NUMBER-OF-CLOSED-ACCOUNTS-W
05780            TO NUMBER-OF-CLOSED-ACCOUNTS-OUT.
05790        WRITE REGISTER-RECORD-OUT FROM FINAL-LINE-7 AFTER 2.
05800        MOVE NUMBER-OF-ERRONEOUS-RECORDS-W
05810            TO NUMBER-OF-ERRONEOUS-RECRDS-OUT.
05820        WRITE REGISTER-RECORD-OUT FROM FINAL-LINE-8 AFTER 2.
05830        MOVE NUMBER-OF-INPUT-RECORDS-W
05840            TO NUMBER-OF-INPUT-RECORDS-OUT.
05850        WRITE REGISTER-RECORD-OUT FROM FINAL-LINE-9 AFTER 2.
05860
05870    END-OF-THIS-SECTION.
05880        EXIT.
```

using the same master file input and transaction input as Program P13-02 and produced the report output shown in Figure 13.18. The output master file produced is shown in Figure 13.19.

Figure 13.18   Report output from Program P13-03.

```
                        ROBBEM STATE BANK
                        106 WEST 10TH ST.
                        BROOKLYN, NY  11212

            SAVINGS ACCOUNT TRANSACTION ERRORS
  DATE   4/08/88                                PAGE   1


      ACCOUNT                              NOTES
      NUMBER

                              MASTER RECORD DOES NOT EXIST
      00007                   DEPOSIT AMOUNT NOT NUMERIC - )))$%)))
      00063                   MASTER RECORD DOES NOT EXIST
      00105                   WITHDRAWAL AMOUNT NOT NUMERIC - 00015025
      00119                   MASTER RECORD DOES NOT EXIST
      00182                   DEPOSIT AMOUNT NOT NUMERIC -
      00182                   MASTER RECORD DOES NOT EXIST
      00232                   MASTER RECORD DOES NOT EXIST
      00259                   MASTER RECORD DOES NOT EXIST
      00266                   DEPOSITOR NAME MISSING
      00301                   MASTER RECORD DOES NOT EXIST
      00308                   ACCOUNT NUMBER ALREADY ON FILE. NEW ACCOUNT INVALID.
      00315                   INVALID TRANSACTION CODE - 8
      00322                   MASTER RECORD DOES NOT EXIST
      00371                   ACCOUNT NUMBER ALREADY ON FILE. NEW ACCOUNT INVALID.
      00385                   INVALID TRANSACTION CODE - 7
      00399                   DEPOSIT AMOUNT NOT NUMERIC - 00014Z00
      00406                   DEPOSITOR NAME MISSING
      00427                   INVALID TRANSACTION CODE - 7
```

```
                        ROBBEM STATE BANK
                        106 WEST 10TH ST.
                        BROOKLYN, NY  11212

                SAVINGS ACCOUNT TRANSACTION REGISTER
        DATE   4/08/88                              PAGE   1


        ACCOUNT     DEPOSITS      WITHDRAWALS       NOTES
        NUMBER

        00014                      1,000.00
        00021        127.50
        00028        153.27
        00028                      1,500.50
        00077        150.00
        00084      3,574.29
        00084    JOHN & SALLY DUPRINO          NAME CHANGE
        00091      1,500.00
        00091      1,200.00
        00091                        500.00
        00098    GEORGE & ANN CULHANE          NAME CHANGE
        00126        350.00
        00133      2,563.00
        00140    BETH DENNY                    NAME CHANGE
        00161      1,256.34
        00168                        110.00
        00168                         15.50    ACCOUNT CLOSED
```

(continued)

Figure 13.18   (continued)

```
                        ROBBEM STATE BANK
                        106 WEST 10TH ST.
                        BROOKLYN, NY  11212

                 SAVINGS ACCOUNT TRANSACTION REGISTER
DATE  4/08/88                                    PAGE  2

       ACCOUNT     DEPOSITS     WITHDRAWALS        NOTES
       NUMBER
       00175         192.02
       00210         250.00
       00210         250.00
       00210         250.00
       00273       1,725.00
       00280       2,317.00
       00308          50.00
       00357          10.00                     NEW ACCOUNT
       00364       1,500.00                     NEW ACCOUNT
       00371          10.00                     NEW ACCOUNT
       00371         150.00
       00392          75.00                     NEW ACCOUNT
       00398          10.00                     NEW ACCOUNT
       00413         100.00                     NEW ACCOUNT
       00420       1,500.00                     NEW ACCOUNT
TOTALS           19,263.42       3,126.00

                       CONTROL COUNTS

          NUMBER OF NEW ACCOUNTS      7

          NUMBER OF DEPOSITS         17

          NUMBER OF WITHDRAWALS       4

          NUMBER OF NAME CHANGES      3

          NUMBER OF CLOSED ACCOUNTS   1

          NUMBER OF ERRORS           19

          TOTAL                      51
```

EXERCISE 3

Write a program to update the accounts-receivable master file you created in Exercise 3, Chapter 12, page 392. Have your program accept transactions in the formats described in Exercise 2, page 437, and also transactions to create new inventory records, in the following format:

Positions	Field
1	Code 1
2 – 6	Part Number
7 – 26	Part Description
27	Units
	E — each
	L — pound
	G — gross
	D — dozen
28 – 33	Unit Cost (dollars and cents)
34 – 37	Supplier Code
38 – 42	Storage Location
43 – 45	Reorder Point
46 – 48	Reorder Quantity
49 – 80	spaces

Have your program carry out all the processing required in Exercise 2, page 437. In addition, for a new inventory record created on the master file, set the Quantity on Hand field and the Dates of Last Withdrawal and Last Receipt to zero, and insert today's date into the Date Created and Date of Last Access fields.

Figure 13.19   Master file produced by Program P13-03.

```
-----------------------------------------------------------------------------------
         1         2         3         4         5         6         7         8
12345678901234567890123456789012345678901234567890123456789012345678901234567890
-----------------------------------------------------------------------------------
00007ROSEBUCCI           88040700100784
00014ROBERT DAVIS M.D.   8804080009900%
00021LORICE MONTI        8804080002525%
00028MICHAEL SMITH       8804080056543F
00032JOSEPH CAMILLO      88040700002500
00035JOHN J. LEHMAN      88040700015000
00049JAY GREENE          88040700015000
00056EVELYN SLATER       88040700000100
00070PATRICK J. LEE      88040700050000
00077LESLIE MINSKY       8804080001603G
00084JOHN & SALLY DUPRINO88040800050742I
00091JOE'S DELI          8804080023000%
00098GEORGE & ANN CULHANE88040800050000
00105ONE DAY CLEANERS    88040700005000
00112ROSEMARY LANE       88040700025000
00126JAMES BUDD          8804080011000%
00133PAUL LERNER, D.D.S. 8804080035630%
00140BETH DENNY          88040800002575
00161ROBERT RYAN         8804080012808D
00175MARY KEATING        8804080002020B
00189J. & L. CAIN        88040700003500
00196IMPERIAL FLORIST    88040700015000
00203JOYCE MITCHELL      88040700000500
00210JERRY PARKS         8804080010000%
00217CARL CALDERON       88040700005000
00224JOHN WILLIAMS       88040700017550
00231BILL WILLIAMS       88040700055500
00238KEVIN PARKER        88040700001000
00245FRANK CAPUTO        88040700003500
00252GENE GALLI          88040700001500
00266MARTIN LANG         88040700009957
00273VITO CACACI         8804080020000%
00280COMMUNITY DRUGS     8804080023370%
00287SOLOMON CHAPELS     88040700001500
00294JOHN BURKE          88040700150000
00308JOE GARCIA          8804080020500%
00315GRACE MICELI        88040700025000
00329GUY VOLPONE         88040700001000
00343JOE & MARY SESSA    88040700100000
00350ROGER SHAW          88040700250000
00357ROBIN RATANSKI      8804080000100%
00364JOSE TORRES         8804080015000%
00371THOMAS HERR         8804080001600%
00392INEZ WASHINGTON     8804080000750%
00398JUAN ALVAREZ        8804080000100%
00413BILL HAYES          8804080001000%
00420JOHN RICE           8804080015000%
```

Listing the Contents of a Sequential File on Tape

Listing the complete contents of a sequential tape file is no different in concept from listing the contents of a file entered on a keyboard or punched in cards. Program P13-04, to list the contents of the output master file created in Program P13-03, just reads in one record after another from the tape and lists its contents reformatted. Program P13-04 is shown in Figure 13.20. The output produced by the program is shown in Figure 13.21. In the output you can see that all the deposits, withdrawals, and name changes were made correctly, new records added, and the records for the closed accounts removed. Provision was made to show any negative Current Balance amount.

Figure 13.20 Program P13-04.

```
CB1 RELEASE 2.4                              IBM OS/VS COBOL  JULY  1, 1982


                       17.31.40          APR  8,1988


00010  IDENTIFICATION DIVISION.
00020  PROGRAM-ID. P13-04.
00030 *
00040 *    THIS PROGRAM LISTS A SEQUENTIAL FILE.
00050 *
00060 ************************************************************************
00070
00080  ENVIRONMENT DIVISION.
00090  CONFIGURATION SECTION.
00100  SOURCE-COMPUTER. IBM-370.
00110  OBJECT-COMPUTER. IBM-370.
00120
00130  INPUT-OUTPUT SECTION.
00140  FILE-CONTROL.
00150       SELECT LIST-FILE-OUT    ASSIGN TO PRINTER.
00160       SELECT MASTER-FILE-IN   ASSIGN TO MFILEIN.
00170
00180 ************************************************************************
00190
00200  DATA DIVISION.
00210  FILE SECTION.
00220  FD  MASTER-FILE-IN
00230      LABEL RECORDS ARE STANDARD
00240      RECORD CONTAINS 39 CHARACTERS
00250      BLOCK CONTAINS 100 RECORDS.
00260
00270  01  MASTER-RECORD-IN.
00280      05  ACCOUNT-NUMBER                     PIC X(5).
00290      05  DEPOSITOR-NAME                     PIC X(20).
00300      05  TRANSACTION-YEAR                   PIC 99.
00310      05  TRANSACTION-MONTH                  PIC 99.
00320      05  TRANSACTION-DAY                    PIC 99.
00330      05  CURRENT-BALANCE                    PIC S9(6)V99.
00340
00350  FD  LIST-FILE-OUT
00360      LABEL RECORDS ARE OMITTED.
00370
00380  01  LIST-RECORD-OUT                        PIC X(81).
00390
00400  WORKING-STORAGE SECTION.
00410  01  MORE-INPUT        VALUE  "Y"           PIC X.
00420  01  PAGE-NUMBER-W     VALUE 0              PIC S99.
00430  01  PAGE-LIMIT        VALUE 38 COMP SYNC   PIC S99.
00440  01  LINE-COUNT-ER              COMP SYNC   PIC S99.
00450  01  BLANK-LINE        VALUE SPACE          PIC X.
00460
00470  01  RUN-DATE.
00480      05  RUN-YEAR                           PIC 99.
00490      05  RUN-MONTH-AND-DAY                  PIC 9(4).
00500
00510  01  PAGE-HEADING-1.
00520      05  FILLER        VALUE SPACES         PIC X(40).
00530      05  FILLER        VALUE  "SAVINGS ACCOUNT MASTER"
00540                                             PIC X(22).
00550
00560  01  PAGE-HEADING-2.
00570      05  FILLER        VALUE SPACES         PIC X(28).
00580      05  FILLER        VALUE  "DATE"        PIC X(5).
00590      05  RUN-MONTH-AND-DAY                  PIC Z9/99/.
00600      05  RUN-YEAR                           PIC 99B(21).
00610      05  FILLER        VALUE  "PAGE"        PIC X(5).
00620      05  PAGE-NUMBER-OUT                    PIC Z9.
00630
00640  01  PAGE-HEADING-3.
00650      05  FILLER        VALUE SPACES         PIC X(46).
00660      05  FILLER        VALUE  "DATE OF LAST" PIC X(12).
00670
```

(continued)

Figure 13.20   (continued)

```
00680   01   PAGE-HEADING-4.
00690        05   FILLER        VALUE SPACES            PIC X(20).
00700        05   FILLER        VALUE  "ACCOUNT"         PIC X(13).
00710        05   FILLER        VALUE  "CURRENT"         PIC X(13).
00720        05   FILLER        VALUE  "TRANSACTION"     PIC X(15).
00730        05   FILLER        VALUE  "DEPOSITOR NAME"  PIC X(14).
00740
00750   01   PAGE-HEADING-5.
00760        05   FILLER        VALUE SPACES            PIC X(20).
00770        05   FILLER        VALUE  "NUMBER"          PIC X(13).
00780        05   FILLER        VALUE  "BALANCE"         PIC X(14).
00790        05   FILLER        VALUE  "YR  MO   DA"     PIC X(10).
00800
00810   01   DETAIL-LINE.
00820        05   FILLER            VALUE SPACES     PIC X(21).
00830        05   ACCOUNT-NUMBER                     PIC X(5)B(4).
00840        05   CURRENT-BALANCE                    PIC Z,ZZZ,ZZZ.99-.
00850        05   TRANSACTION-YEAR                   PIC B(4)99BB.
00860        05   TRANSACTION-MONTH                  PIC 99BB.
00870        05   TRANSACTION-DAY                    PIC 99B(4).
00880        05   DEPOSITOR-NAME                     PIC X(20).
00890
00900   01   NO-INPUT-DATA.
00910        05   FILLER      VALUE SPACES          PIC X(21).
00920        05   FILLER      VALUE "NO INPUT DATA" PIC X(13).
00930
00940   ***********************************************************************
00950
00960   PROCEDURE DIVISION.
00970   CONTROL-PARAGRAPH.
00980        PERFORM INITIALIZATION.
00990        PERFORM MAIN-PROCESS UNTIL MORE-INPUT = "N".
01000        PERFORM TERMINATION.
01010        STOP RUN.
01020
01030   INITIALIZATION.
01040        OPEN INPUT   MASTER-FILE-IN,
01050             OUTPUT LIST-FILE-OUT.
01060        ACCEPT RUN-DATE FROM DATE.
01070        MOVE CORR RUN-DATE TO PAGE-HEADING-2.
01080        PERFORM PRODUCE-PAGE-HEADINGS.
01090        READ MASTER-FILE-IN
01100             AT END
01110                 MOVE "N" TO MORE-INPUT.
01120        IF MORE-INPUT = "N"
01130             WRITE LIST-RECORD-OUT FROM NO-INPUT-DATA.
01140
01150   PRODUCE-PAGE-HEADINGS.
01160        ADD 1 TO PAGE-NUMBER-W.
01170        MOVE PAGE-NUMBER-W TO PAGE-NUMBER-OUT.
01180        WRITE LIST-RECORD-OUT FROM PAGE-HEADING-1 AFTER PAGE.
01190        WRITE LIST-RECORD-OUT FROM PAGE-HEADING-2.
01200        WRITE LIST-RECORD-OUT FROM PAGE-HEADING-3 AFTER 3.
01210        WRITE LIST-RECORD-OUT FROM PAGE-HEADING-4.
01220        WRITE LIST-RECORD-OUT FROM PAGE-HEADING-5.
01230        WRITE LIST-RECORD-OUT FROM BLANK-LINE.
01240        MOVE 8 TO LINE-COUNT-ER.
01250
01260   TERMINATION.
01270        CLOSE MASTER-FILE-IN,
01280              LIST-FILE-OUT.
01290
01300   MAIN-PROCESS.
01310        MOVE CORR MASTER-RECORD-IN TO DETAIL-LINE.
01320        IF 1 + LINE-COUNT-ER > PAGE-LIMIT
01330             PERFORM PRODUCE-PAGE-HEADINGS.
01340        WRITE LIST-RECORD-OUT FROM DETAIL-LINE.
01350        ADD 1 TO LINE-COUNT-ER.
01360        READ MASTER-FILE-IN
01370             AT END
01380                 MOVE "N" TO MORE-INPUT.
```

Figure 13.21 Output from Program P13-04.

```
                         SAVINGS ACCOUNT MASTER
           DATE   4/08/88                        PAGE   1


                         DATE OF LAST
     ACCOUNT   CURRENT   TRANSACTION       DEPOSITOR NAME
     NUMBER    BALANCE   YR  MO  DA

      00007    1,007.84  88  04  07    ROSEBUCCI
      00014      990.00- 88  04  08    ROBERT DAVIS M.D.
      00021      252.50  88  04  08    LORICE MONTI
      00028    5,654.36  88  04  08    MICHAEL SMITH
      00032       25.00  88  04  07    JOSEPH CAMILLO
      00035      150.00  88  04  07    JOHN J. LEHMAN
      00049      150.00  88  04  07    JAY GREENE
      00056        1.00  88  04  07    EVELYN SLATER
      00070      500.00  88  04  07    PATRICK J. LEE
      00077      160.37  88  04  08    LESLIE MINSKY
      00084    5,074.29  88  04  08    JOHN & SALLY DUPRINO
      00091    2,300.00  88  04  08    JOE'S DELI
      00098      500.00  88  04  08    GEORGE & ANN CULHANE
      00105       50.00  88  04  07    ONE DAY CLEANERS
      00112      250.00  88  04  07    ROSEMARY LANE
      00126    1,100.00  88  04  08    JAMES BUDD
      00133    3,563.00  88  04  08    PAUL LERNER, D.D.S.
      00140       25.75  88  04  08    BETH DENNY
      00161    1,280.84  88  04  08    ROBERT RYAN
      00175      202.02  88  04  08    MARY KEATING
      00189       35.00  88  04  07    J. & L. CAIN
      00196      150.00  88  04  07    IMPERIAL FLORIST
      00203        5.00  88  04  07    JOYCE MITCHELL
      00210    1,000.00  88  04  08    JERRY PARKS
      00217       50.00  88  04  07    CARL CALDERON
      00224      175.50  88  04  07    JOHN WILLIAMS
      00231      555.00  88  04  07    BILL WILLIAMS
      00238       10.00  88  04  07    KEVIN PARKER
      00245       35.00  88  04  07    FRANK CAPUTO
      00252       15.00  88  04  07    GENE GALLI
      00266       99.57  88  04  07    MARTIN LANG
      00273    2,000.00  88  04  08    VITO CACACI
      00280    2,337.00  88  04  08    COMMUNITY DRUGS
      00287       15.00  88  04  07    SOLOMON CHAPELS
      00294    1,500.00  88  04  07    JOHN BURKE
      00308    2,050.00  88  04  08    JOE GARCIA
      00315      250.00  88  04  07    GRACE MICELI
      00329       10.00  88  04  07    GUY VOLPONE
      00343    1,000.00  88  04  07    JOE & MARY SESSA
      00350    2,500.00  88  04  07    ROGER SHAW
      00357       10.00  88  04  08    ROBIN RATANSKI
      00364    1,500.00  88  04  08    JOSE TORRES
      00371      160.00  88  04  08    THOMAS HERR
      00392       75.00  88  04  08    INEZ WASHINGTON
      00398       10.00  88  04  08    JUAN ALVAREZ
      00413      100.00  88  04  08    BILL HAYES
      00420    1,500.00  88  04  08    JOHN RICE
```

EXERCISE 4

Write a program to list the contents of the master files produced by the programs in Chapter 12, Exercise 3, page 392 and Exercise 5, page 407; and Exercises 2 and 3 in this chapter. Show whether any of the Quantity on Hand fields on the master file are negative. For any record whose Quantity on Hand is equal to or less than the Reorder Point, print a message showing the Reorder Quantity and the word REORDER.

Summary

The balance line algorithm can be used to design all programs that read a sequential master file and a transaction file. The algorithm was first used in Chapter 12 to design a program to delete records from a master file. The same algorithm also can be used to design a program to list selected records from a master file and to design programs to add new master records, delete obsolete ones, and make all kinds of changes to master records in a single run.

For the algorithm to work, the input master file and the transaction file must both be in sequence on the record key. The master file must contain no duplicate values of any key. If the program is designed to process more than one kind of transaction, every transaction record must contain a code to say what kind of transaction it is. The algorithm contains in its main loop a comparison between the record key in the master input area and the record key in the transaction input area. The lower of the two keys is always processed first. Master records are processed in the master work area; transaction records are processed in the transaction input area.

The main difference among the different program designs lies in the box on the hierarchy diagram called "Process transaction record." By properly designing and coding the function "Process transaction record" it is possible to create a file-update program of any imaginable complexity.

An input area can be defined to process records with different formats by redefining the input area for as many formats as necessary. A redefining entry must specify exactly as many computer storage locations as the entry being redefined.

Listing the complete contents of a sequential tape file is conceptually identical to listing any ordinary sequential file. The input records are read one after another and their contents are printed.

Fill-in Exercises

1. In a program to list selected records from a master file, the keys of the master records to be listed are provided by way of a _____ file.

2. Five files needed in a sequential file update program are the _____ input file, the _____ input file, the transaction register file, the error report file, and the _____ output file.

3. Of the five files named in Fill-in Exercise 2, the one that is not used in a program to list selected records from a master file is the _____ .

4. Master records are always worked on in the master _____ area.

5. "Process transaction record" executes when there are one or more transactions whose key is equal to _____ .

6. "Choose current key" assigns to CURRENT-KEY the _____ of the two keys in the master _____ area and the transaction _____ area.

7. "Process master record" moves a master record from the master _____ area to the master _____ area when the key of the master record in the master _____ is equal to _____ .

8. "Check to write master" writes a master record onto the output master tape when the flag is set to _____ .

9. A deposit transaction is considered to have a matching master record in the master work area when the flag is set to _____ .

10. A master record for a new account may be built in the master work area when the flag is set to _____ .

11. In a program to list the contents of selected master records, only the Account Number is needed in the transaction record because all the other information listed comes from the _____ record.

12. The contents of a selected master record can be listed only when the flag is set to _____ .

13. In a program to list selected records from a master file, processing can cease when end-of-file is reached on the _____ file.

14. If a new master record is created, and changes are made to it in the same run, the transaction that creates the record must fall _____ any of the transactions that change it.

15. A redefining entry must specify the same number of _____ _____ _____ as the entry being redefined.

Review Exercises

1. Write a program to list the complete contents of records selected from the master file you created in Review Exercise 2, Chapter 12, page 409. Use transactions in the following format.

Positions	Field
1–9	Social Security Number
10–80	spaces

2. Write a program to list selected fields from records selected from the master file you created in Review Exercise 2, Chapter 12, page 409. Use transactions in the following format:

Positions	Field
1	Code (8 or 9)
2–10	Social Security Number
11–80	spaces

Do not treat duplicate transactions as erroneous.

For transactions with Code 8, have your program print the following fields from the records selected:

Social Security Number
Student Name
Major Department

For transactions with a Code of 9, have your program print the following fields from the records selected:

Social Security Number
Student Name
Year of Graduation

Design suitable reports for your program before you begin coding.

3. Write a program to update the master file you created in Review Exercise 2, Chapter 12, page 409, with changes and deletions. Use transactions in the following formats:

Positions	Field
1	Code 2 (Student Name change)
2–10	Social Security Number
11–30	Student Name
31–80	spaces
1	Code 3 (Street Address change)
2–10	Social Security Number
11–30	Street Address
31–80	spaces
1	Code 4 (City, State, Zip change)
2–10	Social Security Number
11–30	City, State, Zip
31–80	spaces
1	Code 5 (Major Department change)
2–10	Social Security Number
11–12	Major Department
13–80	spaces
1	Code 6 (Year of Graduation change)
2–10	Social Security Number
11–12	Year of Graduation
13–80	spaces
1	Code 7 (Delete record)
2–10	Social Security Number

Have your program make all suitable validity checks on each transaction, and print a line on one of the output reports for each transaction. For any change to an existing master record, have your program print the Social Security Number and the contents of the changed field from the master record. For a record deleted from the master file, have your program print the Social Security Number, the Student Name, and the Year of Graduation from the master file.

4. Write a program to update the master file you created in Review Exercise 2, Chapter 12, page 409, with transactions in the formats given in Review Exercise 3 above. Have your program accept also transactions in the following format, to add new records to the master file:

Positions	Field
1	Code 1
2–10	Social Security Number
11–30	Student Name
31–50	Street Address
51–70	City, State, Zip
71–72	Major Department
73–74	Year of Graduation
75–80	spaces

For a record added to the master file, print the Social Security Number and the Student Name.

5. Explain why each of the REDEFINES entries below is illegal:

a.
```
01   RECORD-NAME.
     05   FIELD-1.
          10   FIELD-2   PIC X(4).
          10   FIELD-3   PIC X(5).
01   NEW-FIELD REDEFINES RECORD-NAME   PIC X(80).
```
b.
```
01   RECORD-NAME.
     05   FIELD-1.
          10   FIELD-2   PIC X(4).
          10   FIELD-3   PIC X(5).
     05   FIELD-4 REDEFINES FIELD-1.
```

6. Write a program to produce customer invoices in the format shown in Figure 11.14, page 352. Use as inputs the customer-name-and-address master file you created in the Project in Chapter 12, page 410, and transactions in the format used for Program 11-04 and described on page 352. Have your program SORT the transactions into order on Customer Number. Have your program make all suitable validity checks on the transactions and produce an error report separate from the invoices.

Project

Write a program to update the sequential master file you created in the Project in Chapter 12, page 410. Use input transactions in the following formats:

Positions	Field
1	Transaction Code: 1 — Add customer to file 2 — Change a Name and Address Line
2	Line Number of Address — 1 through 5
3 – 7	Customer Number
8 – 27	Name and Address Line
28 – 80	spaces
1	Transaction Code: 3 — Delete customer from file
3 – 7	Customer Number
8 – 80	spaces

Have your program SORT the input transactions on Line Number of Address within Transaction Code within Customer Number. Have your program make all suitable validity checks on each transaction, and print a line on one of the output reports for each transaction. For any change to an existing master record, have your program print the Customer Number and the contents of the changed field from the master record. For a record deleted from the master file, have your program print the Customer Number and the first line of the Customer Name and Address from the master file. For a record added to the master file, have your program print the Customer Number and the first line of the Customer Name and Address.

Indexed Files

Here are the key points you should learn from this chapter:

1. What an indexed file is
2. Why indexed files are useful
3. How to get COBOL to create an indexed file
4. How to access an indexed file randomly
5. How to update an indexed file
6. How to access an indexed file sequentially and randomly in a single run
7. How to list the contents of an indexed file

Key words to recognize and learn:

organization	STATUS IS
indexed file	INVALID KEY
indexed organization	AFTER ERROR PROCEDURE
DELETE	DISPLAY
relative organization	ACCESS
standard sequential organization	RANDOM
indexed-sequential organization	I-O
dynamic access	OPEN mode
prime record key	EXTEND
alternate record key	REWRITE
ORGANIZATION	DYNAMIC
INDEXED	START
RECORD KEY IS	key of reference
ALTERNATE RECORD KEY IS	NEXT
WITH DUPLICATES	

In Chapters 12 and 13 we worked with sequential master files on tape. Our transaction files were sequential files also. Even our printed reports were sequential files. A sequential file is said to have sequential **organization.** A characteristic of sequential organization is that all the records in a file sit there in the order in which they were written. All files having sequential organization must be accessed sequentially. A characteristic of sequential access is that a program must read or write the first record of a file before it can read or write the second. When a program is reading a tape file, a card file, or a file entered on a keyboard, it must read the first record in the file before it can read the second; when a program is writing a tape file or a printer file, it must write the first record before it writes the second.

On the other hand, **indexed files,** or files having **indexed organization,** may be accessed randomly. An indexed file cannot be stored on magnetic tape. It must be stored on disk or some other direct-access storage device. An indexed file has its records stored more or less in sequence on some key field; also it has indexes, which tell COBOL where each record on the file is located. COBOL constructs and maintains the indexes automatically, with almost no effort on the part of the programmer.

The indexes permit COBOL to do some very remarkable things with an indexed file. Imagine that our savings-account master file was an indexed file on disk instead of a sequential file on tape. Then if we wanted to make a deposit to an account, COBOL could find on the disk just the master record we need, and READ it into the File Section. There we could update it by adding the deposit to the current balance. Then we could ask COBOL to put the updated record back onto the disk in the same place it came from, erasing the old record in that location on the disk and replacing it with the new. Thus there would be no need to READ the entire master file in order to change some of the records on it.

Random access of an indexed file also permits COBOL to add new records to the file without having to create a whole new file. If we have a record to add, we just WRITE it. COBOL automatically finds the place in the file where the new record should go, moves a few existing records around if necessary to make space for the new one, and slips it in.

Similarly, random access of an indexed file permits COBOL to delete a record without having to create a whole new file. The **DELETE** verb enables a program to remove a record from a file.

A Summary of File Terminology

Before discussing indexed files further, it is worthwhile to review all the terminology we have studied so far relating to file storage media, file organization, and file access methods. In doing so, we will also see some new related terminology.

File Storage Media

As mentioned in Chapter 12, for our purposes there are only two types of storage media — sequential media and direct-access media. Examples of sequential media are punched cards, magnetic tape, and printed output. Examples of direct-access media are magnetic disk and magnetic drum. Direct-access media are also sometimes called mass storage media.

File Organization

Three types of file organization are supported by modern COBOL systems — sequential organization, indexed organization, and **relative organization.** All of the files we have used up through Chapter 13 have had sequential organization. In this chapter we will study a file having indexed organization. In Chapter 15 we will study files with relative organization.

Sequential organization is also sometimes called **standard sequential organization.** Sequentially organized files can be stored on punched cards and on magnetic tape. Of course a printed file is sequential also, since the records appear in the file in the order in which they are written there. Sequential files can also be stored on direct-access storage devices.

An indexed file contains indexes as well as data records. Since most of the records in an indexed file are in sequence on the record key, indexed organization is also sometimes called **indexed-sequential organization.** An indexed file can be stored only on a direct-access storage device.

File Access

There are really only two ways to READ records from a file or WRITE records onto a file—sequentially and randomly. When a program READs a file sequentially, the first READ statement brings in the first record on the file; the second READ issued by the program brings in the second record on the file. When a program WRITEs a file sequentially, the first WRITE statement issued by the program puts the first record onto the file; the second WRITE statement puts the second record.

When a program READs a file randomly, however, any READ statement issued by the program can bring in any record from anywhere on the file. When a program WRITEs a file randomly, the program can insert a new record into any location in the file.

A sequential file may be accessed only sequentially. Indexed files and relative files may be accessed sequentially or randomly.

A third form of access, called **dynamic access,** is merely a combination of sequential access and random access. COBOL programs have the ability to switch back and forth between sequential access and random access in a single run. In this chapter we will use all three access methods on our indexed file.

Creating an Indexed File on Disk

We are now ready to write a program to create an indexed file. The program will create a savings-account master file on disk, using the same formats for transaction and master records that we had for Program P12-02, when we created a master file on tape. The input format for Program P12-02 (and Program P14-01) is repeated here:

Positions	Field
1	Code 1
2–6	Account Number
7–14	Amount (to two decimal places)
15–34	Depositor Name
35–80	spaces

Our indexed master file will have its records in order on Account Number, just as our sequential master file did on tape. But now our master file will be indexed so that COBOL can find the record for any Account Number in the file. In addition, we will have COBOL index the file on Depositor Name also, so that a program can find the record or records for any Depositor Name in the file. Since the master records are in order on Account Number, the Account Number field is called the **prime record key** of the file. The Depositor Name field is called an **alternate record key.** An indexed file may have more than one alternate key. The maximum number of alternate keys that an indexed file may have is different in different COBOL systems.

The input to Program P14-01 will be a batch of new accounts to create the master file, in the format just given. The input will be in order on the prime record key field, Account Number, so that the system can create the file and the indexes sequentially. It is possible for COBOL to create an indexed file randomly if the input records are not in order on the prime key field, but doing so usually uses much more computer time than if the input records are in order. After the file is created, we will be able to access the master records randomly with transactions in any order.

Program P14-01 is shown in Figure 14.1. It is, of course, very similar to Program P12-02. Some differences are found in the FILE-CONTROL entry for the output master file, at line 00200. Here we use the **ORGANIZATION** clause to tell COBOL that we would like it to create the output master file as an indexed file. Whenever you use ORGANIZATION **INDEXED,** you must use the **RECORD KEY IS** clause to tell COBOL the prime key on which the file is ordered. The prime key must be a field defined within a level-01 entry in the File Section associated with this file.

The **ALTERNATE RECORD KEY IS** clause, lines 00230 and 00240, tells COBOL that we would like to be able to access records in this file on the basis of the alternate record key. The ALTERNATE RECORD KEY field, like the prime key, must be defined within a level-01 entry in the File Section associated with this file. The **WITH DUPLICATES** phrase tells COBOL that any given value of the alternate key may appear more than once in the file. In this case it means that a depositor may have more than one account. Duplicate appearances of the prime record key in an indexed file are never allowed.

If an indexed file has more than one ALTERNATE RECORD KEY, the FILE-CONTROL entry for the file must contain a separate ALTERNATE RECORD KEY clause for each such KEY. The ALTERNATE RECORD KEY clauses must follow one immediately after the other in the FILE-CONTROL entry, and each clause may have a WITH DUPLICATES phrase or not as appropriate.

A **STATUS IS** clause, such as the one shown in line 00250, should always be used with any indexed or relative file and can be used with sequential files also. The STATUS IS clause is used to name a two-character alphanumeric field in working storage. The field is used by COBOL to record the STATUS of input and output operations on the file. Statements in the Procedure Division can use the contents of the STATUS field at any time.

After each input or output operation on a file, COBOL places two characters into the STATUS field for the file if such a field is specified. The 1974 ANSI standard meanings of the STATUS codes related to writing an indexed file sequentially are shown in Table 14-1.

Table 14-1
1974 ANSI standard STATUS codes related to writing an indexed file sequentially.

Status Code	Meaning
00	Successful completion
02	Successful completion, and the record just written created a duplicate key value for an ALTERNATE RECORD KEY for which DUPLICATES are allowed[a]
21	Invalid key — prime RECORD KEY out of order
22	Invalid key — an attempt has been made to WRITE a record that would create an invalid duplicate key value[a]
24	Invalid key — boundary violation (attempt to WRITE past the physical end of the file)
30	Permanent error (hardware malfunction)

[a] Under certain conditions some COBOL systems do not check for the presence of duplicate values of alternate keys during file creation. In such situations, the condition described for STATUS code 02 would return a STATUS code of 00, and an attempt to WRITE a record that would create an invalid duplicate value of an ALTERNATE RECORD KEY would also return a STATUS code of 00. An attempt to WRITE a record that would create a duplicate value of the prime RECORD KEY always returns a STATUS code of 22. Any error condition resulting from invalid duplicate values of alternate keys would be discovered in later processing. See Chapter 16 for a full discussion of this matter.

Your own COBOL system may have additional codes in the range 90 through 99. The sequence error, STATUS code 21, arises if an attempt is made to WRITE on the file a record whose prime key is less than a prime key already on the file. Our input records are SORTed on the prime key, Account Number, so Program P14-01 could not be writing a record with a key lower than one already on the file. It could be erroneously attempting to WRITE a record with a duplicate key, however, and such a situation would cause the STATUS field to be set to 22.

The STATUS code reflecting the successful execution of an OPEN statement is 00.

The description of SORT-WORK-RECORD, line 00400, is only 34 characters long. Only 34 characters from each input record are SORTed in this program. SORT time is reduced by not SORTing all 80 characters of each input record, since only 34 are needed for processing after the SORT is complete.

Figure 14.1 Program P14-01.

```
CB1 RELEASE 2.4                           IBM OS/VS COBOL   JULY  1, 1982


                        18.09.07        APR  8,1988


00010    IDENTIFICATION DIVISION.
00020    PROGRAM-ID. P14-01.
00030  *
00040  *     THIS PROGRAM CREATES AN INDEXED
00050  *     MASTER FILE OF SAVINGS ACCOUNT RECORDS.
00060  *
00070  ********************************************************************
00080
00090    ENVIRONMENT DIVISION.
00100    CONFIGURATION SECTION.
00110    SOURCE-COMPUTER. IBM-370.
00120    OBJECT-COMPUTER. IBM-370.
00130
00140    INPUT-OUTPUT SECTION.
00150    FILE-CONTROL.
00160        SELECT TRANSACTION-REGISTER-FILE-OUT ASSIGN TO PRINTER1.
00170        SELECT ERROR-FILE-OUT                ASSIGN TO PRINTER2.
00180        SELECT SAVINGS-ACCOUNT-DATA-FILE-IN  ASSIGN TO INFILE.
00190        SELECT SORT-WORK-FILE                ASSIGN TO SORTWK.
00200        SELECT ACCOUNT-MASTER-FILE-OUT       ASSIGN TO DISKOUT
00210            ORGANIZATION INDEXED
00220            RECORD KEY IS ACCOUNT-NUMBER-M
00230            ALTERNATE RECORD KEY IS DEPOSITOR-NAME-M
00240               WITH DUPLICATES
00250            STATUS IS FILE-CHECK.
00260
00270  ********************************************************************
00280
00290    DATA DIVISION.
00300    FILE SECTION.
00310    FD  SAVINGS-ACCOUNT-DATA-FILE-IN
00320        LABEL RECORDS ARE OMITTED
00330        RECORD CONTAINS 80 CHARACTERS.
00340
00350    01  SAVINGS-ACCOUNT-DATA-RECORD-IN            PIC X(80).
00360
00370    SD  SORT-WORK-FILE
00380        RECORD CONTAINS 34 CHARACTERS.
00390
00400    01  SORT-WORK-RECORD.
00410        05  CODE-IN                              PIC X.
00420            88  VALID-CODE                            VALUE "1".
00430        05  ACCOUNT-NUMBER-IN                    PIC X(5).
00440        05  AMOUNT-IN                            PIC 9(6)V99.
00450        05  AMOUNT-IN-X
00460            REDEFINES AMOUNT-IN                  PIC X(8).
00470        05  DEPOSITOR-NAME-IN                    PIC X(20).
00480            88  DEPOSITOR-NAME-IS-MISSING             VALUE SPACES.
00490
```

(continued)

Figure 14.1   (continued)

```
00500    FD    ACCOUNT-MASTER-FILE-OUT
00510          LABEL RECORDS ARE STANDARD
00520          RECORD CONTAINS 39 CHARACTERS.
00530
00540    01    ACCOUNT-MASTER-RECORD-OUT.
00550          05  ACCOUNT-NUMBER-M                       PIC X(5).
00560          05  DEPOSITOR-NAME-M                       PIC X(20).
00570          05  DATE-OF-LAST-TRANSACTION-M             PIC 9(6).
00580          05  CURRENT-BALANCE-M                      PIC S9(6)V99.
00590
00600    FD    TRANSACTION-REGISTER-FILE-OUT
00610          LABEL RECORDS ARE OMITTED.
00620
00630    01    REGISTER-RECORD-OUT                        PIC X(72).
00640
00650    FD    ERROR-FILE-OUT
00660          LABEL RECORDS ARE OMITTED.
00670
00680    01    ERROR-RECORD-OUT                  PIC X(84).
00690
00700    WORKING-STORAGE SECTION.
00710    01    BLANKS                            PIC X      VALUE SPACE.
00720    01    REGISTER-PAGE-NUMBER-W            PIC S99    VALUE 0.
00730    01    ERROR-PAGE-NUMBER-W               PIC S99    VALUE 0.
00740    01    REGISTER-PAGE-LIMIT   COMP SYNC   PIC S99    VALUE 35.
00750    01    LINE-COUNT-ER         COMP SYNC   PIC S99.
00760    01    ERROR-PAGE-LIMIT      COMP SYNC   PIC S99    VALUE 50.
00770    01    ERROR-LINE-COUNTER    COMP SYNC   PIC S99.
00780    01    DEPOSIT-TOTAL-W                   PIC S9(7)V99 VALUE 0.
00790    01    FILE-CHECK.
00800          05   STATUS-KEY-1                 PIC X      VALUE ZERO.
00810          05   STATUS-KEY-2                 PIC X      VALUE ZERO.
00820    01    MORE-INPUT                        PIC X      VALUE "Y".
00830    01    ANY-ERRORS                        PIC X.
00840    01    NUMBER-OF-INPUT-RECORDS-W         PIC S9(3)  VALUE ZERO.
00850    01    NUMBER-OF-ERRONEOUS-RECORDS-W     PIC S9(3)  VALUE ZERO.
00860    01    NUMBER-OF-NEW-ACCOUNTS-W          PIC S9(3)  VALUE ZERO.
00870    01    TODAYS-DATE.
00880          05   TODAYS-YEAR                  PIC 99.
00890          05   TODAYS-MONTH-AND-DAY         PIC 9(4).
00900
00910    01    REPORT-HEADING-1.
00920          05   FILLER     PIC X(39) VALUE SPACES.
00930          05   FILLER     PIC X(17) VALUE "ROBBEM STATE BANK".
00940
00950    01    REPORT-HEADING-2.
00960          05   FILLER     PIC X(39) VALUE SPACES.
00970          05   FILLER     PIC X(17) VALUE "106 WEST 10TH ST.".
00980
00990    01    REPORT-HEADING-3.
01000          05   FILLER     PIC X(38) VALUE SPACES.
01010          05   FILLER     PIC X(19) VALUE "BROOKLYN, NY  11212".
01020
01030    01    REGISTER-PAGE-HEADING-1.
01040          05   FILLER     PIC X(29) VALUE SPACES.
01050          05   FILLER     PIC X(36)
01060                          VALUE "SAVINGS ACCOUNT MASTER FILE CREATION".
01070
01080    01    ERROR-PAGE-HEADING-1.
01090          05   FILLER     PIC X(30) VALUE SPACES.
01100          05   FILLER     PIC X(34)
01110                          VALUE "SAVINGS ACCOUNT MASTER FILE ERRORS".
01120
01130    01    PAGE-HEADING-2.
01140          05   FILLER          PIC X(17) VALUE SPACES.
01150          05   FILLER          PIC X(5)  VALUE "DATE".
01160          05   TODAYS-MONTH-AND-DAY      PIC Z9/99/.
01170          05   TODAYS-YEAR    PIC 99B(35).
01180          05   FILLER          PIC X(5)  VALUE "PAGE".
01190          05   PAGE-NUMBER-OUT           PIC Z9.
01200
```

```
01210   01   REGISTER-PAGE-HEADING-3.
01220        05   FILLER          PIC X(24) VALUE SPACES.
01230        05   FILLER          PIC X(12) VALUE "ACCOUNT".
01240        05   FILLER          PIC X(12) VALUE "INITIAL".
01250        05   FILLER          PIC X(5)  VALUE "NOTES".
01260
01270   01   ERROR-PAGE-HEADING-3.
01280        05   FILLER          PIC X(24) VALUE SPACES.
01290        05   FILLER          PIC X(24) VALUE "ACCOUNT".
01300        05   FILLER          PIC X(5)  VALUE "NOTES".
01310
01320   01   REGISTER-PAGE-HEADING-4.
01330        05   FILLER          PIC X(24) VALUE SPACES.
01340        05   FILLER          PIC X(12) VALUE "NUMBER".
01350        05   FILLER          PIC X(7)  VALUE "DEPOSIT".
01360
01370   01   ERROR-PAGE-HEADING-4.
01380        05   FILLER          PIC X(24) VALUE SPACES.
01390        05   FILLER          PIC X(6)  VALUE "NUMBER".
01400
01410   01   NEW-ACCOUNT-LINE.
01420        05   FILLER     PIC X(25)        VALUE SPACES.
01430        05   ACCOUNT-NUMBER-OUT-G        PIC X(5)B(5).
01440        05   AMOUNT-OUT-G                PIC ZZZ,ZZZ.99B(3).
01450        05   FILLER     PIC X(11)        VALUE "NEW ACCOUNT".
01460
01470   01   ERROR-LINE.
01480        05   FILLER     PIC X(25) VALUE SPACES.
01490        05   ACCOUNT-NUMBER-OUT-E PIC X(5)B(18).
01500        05   MESSAGE-E            PIC X(36).
01510
01520   01   INVALID-CODE-MSG.
01530        05   FILLER     PIC X(13) VALUE "INVALID CODE".
01540        05   CODE-OUT   PIC X.
01550
01560   01   AMOUNT-NOT-NUMERIC-MSG.
01570        05   FILLER     PIC X(28) VALUE "INITIAL DEPOSIT NOT NUMERIC".
01580        05   AMOUNT-OUT-X         PIC X(9).
01590
01600   01   FINAL-LINE-1.
01610        05   FILLER          PIC X(23) VALUE SPACES.
01620        05   FILLER          PIC X(10) VALUE "TOTAL".
01630        05   AMOUNT-TOTAL-OUT          PIC Z,ZZZ,ZZZ.99.
01640
01650   01   FINAL-LINE-2.
01660        05   FILLER          PIC X(40) VALUE SPACES.
01670        05   FILLER          PIC X(14) VALUE "CONTROL COUNTS".
01680
01690   01   FINAL-LINE-3.
01700        05   FILLER          PIC X(34) VALUE SPACES.
01710        05   FILLER          PIC X(28) VALUE "NUMBER OF NEW ACCOUNTS".
01720        05   NUMBER-OF-NEW-ACCOUNTS-OUT PIC ZZ9.
01730
01740   01   FINAL-LINE-4.
01750        05   FILER           PIC X(34) VALUE SPACES.
01760        05   FILLER          PIC X(28)
01770                             VALUE "NUMBER OF ERRONEOUS RECORDS".
01780        05   NUMBER-OF-ERRONEOUS-RCDS-OUT PIC ZZ9.
01790
01800   01   FINAL-LINE-5.
01810        05   FILLER          PIC X(34) VALUE SPACES.
01820        05   FILLER          PIC X(28) VALUE "TOTAL".
01830        05   NUMBER-OF-INPUT-RECORDS-OUT PIC ZZ9.
01840
01850   01   NO-INPUT-DATA.
01860        05   FILLER          PIC X(21) VALUE SPACES.
01870        05   FILLER          PIC X(13) VALUE "NO INPUT DATA".
01880
01890   ***************************************************************
01900
```

(continued)

Figure 14.1   (continued)

```
01910    PROCEDURE DIVISION.
01920    DECLARATIVES.
01930    DUMMY-USE SECTION.
01940        USE AFTER ERROR PROCEDURE ACCOUNT-MASTER-FILE-OUT.
01950    END DECLARATIVES.
01960
01970    NONDECLARATIVE SECTION.
01980    CREATE-MASTER-FILE.
01990        SORT SORT-WORK-FILE
02000            ASCENDING KEY ACCOUNT-NUMBER-IN
02010            USING SAVINGS-ACCOUNT-DATA-FILE-IN
02020            OUTPUT PROCEDURE IS PRODUCE-MASTER-FILE.
02030        STOP RUN.
02040
02050    PRODUCE-MASTER-FILE SECTION.
02060    PRODUCE-MASTER-FILE-PARAGRAPH.
02070        PERFORM INITIALIZATION.
02080        PERFORM PROCESS-A-RECORD UNTIL MORE-INPUT = "N".
02090        PERFORM TERMINATION.
02100        GO TO END-OF-THIS-SECTION.
02110
02120    INITIALIZATION.
02130        OPEN OUTPUT ACCOUNT-MASTER-FILE-OUT
02140                    ERROR-FILE-OUT
02150                    TRANSACTION-REGISTER-FILE-OUT.
02160        IF FILE-CHECK NOT = ZEROS
02170            DISPLAY " MASTER FILE OPEN STATUS = ", FILE-CHECK
02180            CLOSE TRANSACTION-REGISTER-FILE-OUT,
02190                ERROR-FILE-OUT,
02200                ACCOUNT-MASTER-FILE-OUT
02210            STOP RUN.
02220        ACCEPT TODAYS-DATE FROM DATE.
02230        MOVE CORRESPONDING TODAYS-DATE TO PAGE-HEADING-2.
02240        PERFORM PRODUCE-REGISTER-HEAD.
02250        PERFORM PRODUCE-ERROR-HEAD.
02260        PERFORM READ-A-RECORD.
02270        IF MORE-INPUT = "N"
02280            WRITE ERROR-RECORD-OUT FROM NO-INPUT-DATA.
02290
02300    PRODUCE-REGISTER-HEAD.
02310        WRITE REGISTER-RECORD-OUT FROM REPORT-HEADING-1 AFTER PAGE.
02320        WRITE REGISTER-RECORD-OUT FROM REPORT-HEADING-2.
02330        WRITE REGISTER-RECORD-OUT FROM REPORT-HEADING-3.
02340        ADD 1 TO REGISTER-PAGE-NUMBER-W.
02350        MOVE REGISTER-PAGE-NUMBER-W TO PAGE-NUMBER-OUT.
02360        WRITE REGISTER-RECORD-OUT FROM REGISTER-PAGE-HEADING-1
02370                                      AFTER 2.
02380        WRITE REGISTER-RECORD-OUT FROM PAGE-HEADING-2.
02390        WRITE REGISTER-RECORD-OUT FROM REGISTER-PAGE-HEADING-3
02400                                      AFTER 3.
02410        WRITE REGISTER-RECORD-OUT FROM REGISTER-PAGE-HEADING-4.
02420        WRITE REGISTER-RECORD-OUT FROM BLANKS.
02430        MOVE 11 TO LINE-COUNT-ER.
02440
02450    PRODUCE-ERROR-HEAD.
02460        WRITE ERROR-RECORD-OUT FROM REPORT-HEADING-1 AFTER PAGE.
02470        WRITE ERROR-RECORD-OUT FROM REPORT-HEADING-2.
02480        WRITE ERROR-RECORD-OUT FROM REPORT-HEADING-3.
02490        ADD 1 TO ERROR-PAGE-NUMBER-W.
02500        MOVE ERROR-PAGE-NUMBER-W TO PAGE-NUMBER-OUT.
02510        WRITE ERROR-RECORD-OUT FROM ERROR-PAGE-HEADING-1 AFTER 2.
02520        WRITE ERROR-RECORD-OUT FROM PAGE-HEADING-2.
02530        WRITE ERROR-RECORD-OUT FROM ERROR-PAGE-HEADING-3 AFTER 3.
02540        WRITE ERROR-RECORD-OUT FROM ERROR-PAGE-HEADING-4.
02550        WRITE ERROR-RECORD-OUT FROM BLANKS.
02560        MOVE 11 TO ERROR-LINE-COUNTER.
02570
02580    PROCESS-A-RECORD.
02590        ADD 1 TO NUMBER-OF-INPUT-RECORDS-W.
02600        MOVE "N" TO ANY-ERRORS.
02610        PERFORM CHECK-INPUT-FOR-VALIDITY.
02620        IF ANY-ERRORS = "N"
02630            PERFORM BUILD-MASTER-RECORD
02640            PERFORM WRITE-MASTER-RECORD.
02650        PERFORM READ-A-RECORD.
02660
```

```
02670  BUILD-MASTER-RECORD.
02680      MOVE ACCOUNT-NUMBER-IN  TO ACCOUNT-NUMBER-M.
02690      MOVE DEPOSITOR-NAME-IN  TO DEPOSITOR-NAME-M.
02700      MOVE AMOUNT-IN          TO CURRENT-BALANCE-M.
02710      MOVE TODAYS-DATE        TO DATE-OF-LAST-TRANSACTION-M.
02720
```

(continued)

The Procedure Division of this program, which starts at line 01910, is very much like the Procedure Division of Program P12-02. One difference lies in the appearance of DECLARATIVES in the program, at line 01920. The DECLARATIVES are needed to satisfy one of the least useful requirements in the entire ANSI COBOL standard. The requirement is this: Every operation on an indexed or relative file that could cause an invalid key condition (sequence error, invalid duplicate key, no record found, or boundary violation) must have either an **INVALID KEY** clause or a USE **AFTER ERROR PROCEDURE** section.[1] The best way to satisfy the requirement is to include, in any program that uses indexed or relative files, lines 01920 through 01950 exactly as you see them here, except that you replace the name ACCOUNT-MASTER-FILE-OUT with the name of the file in your program. If your program has more than one indexed and/or relative file, just list the names of the files one after the other in the USE AFTER ERROR PROCEDURE sentence. If there are any USE BEFORE REPORTING sections in your program, they may appear before or after the USE AFTER ERROR PROCEDURE section. In any case, there must be only one DECLARATIVES header and only one END DECLARATIVES statement.

The IF statement at line 02160 shows how the STATUS field, FILE-CHECK, might be used. Here it is being used to check whether the indexed file was OPENed successfully by the statement at line 02130. If the OPEN was successful, FILE-CHECK will be equal to zeros and the program will proceed normally. If FILE-CHECK is anything other than zeros, the OPEN was not successful. We use a **DISPLAY** statement to print an error message, and then we terminate the run.

A DISPLAY statement may be used to print any kind of output and is not limited to printing error messages. The DISPLAY verb has severe limitations, however, and it should not be used for printing normal report output. It is convenient to use when precise formatting of the output is not needed. Output produced by a DISPLAY statement normally prints on a separate report from output produced by WRITE or GENERATE statements. The two reports can be printed on separate printers, or they can be printed one after the other on a single printer if the printer is not directly under the control of your program, as is the case with most modern operating systems. If only one printer directly under the control of your program is available, the report lines will be interleaved in an unpredictable manner.

A DISPLAY statement prints the values of the literals and/or data names listed in the statement, one right after the other from left to right on the print line. You must not have any entries in the File Section in connection with DISPLAY print output, and, of course, you cannot OPEN or CLOSE a DISPLAY file, since there is no such file defined. This is one of the advantages of using DISPLAY for printing error messages. You can print the message even if you are unable to OPEN any output print files.

[1]IBM OS/VS COBOL demonstrates the uselessness of the ANSI requirement by permitting such operations to lack both an INVALID KEY clause and a USE AFTER ERROR PROCEDURE section. The 1985 standard retains the requirement.

Figure 14.1   (continued)

```
02730    WRITE-MASTER-RECORD.
02740        WRITE ACCOUNT-MASTER-RECORD-OUT.
02750        IF STATUS-KEY-1 = ZERO
02760            ADD 1 TO NUMBER-OF-NEW-ACCOUNTS-W
02770            ADD AMOUNT-IN TO DEPOSIT-TOTAL-W
02780            PERFORM WRITE-NEW-ACCOUNT-LINE
02790        ELSE
02800        IF FILE-CHECK = "22"
02810            ADD 1 TO NUMBER-OF-ERRONEOUS-RECORDS-W
02820            PERFORM WRITE-DUPLICATE-ERROR-MESSAGE
02830        ELSE
02840            DISPLAY " MASTER FILE WRITE STATUS = ", FILE-CHECK
02850            PERFORM TERMINATION
02860            STOP RUN.
02870
02880    CHECK-INPUT-FOR-VALIDITY.
02890        IF NOT VALID-CODE
02900            MOVE "Y" TO ANY-ERRORS
02910            PERFORM WRITE-INVALID-CODE-LINE.
02920        IF DEPOSITOR-NAME-IS-MISSING
02930            MOVE "Y" TO ANY-ERRORS
02940            PERFORM WRITE-NAME-ERROR-MESSAGE.
02950        IF AMOUNT-IN NOT NUMERIC
02960            MOVE "Y" TO ANY-ERRORS
02970            PERFORM WRITE-AMOUNT-MESSAGE.
02980        IF ANY-ERRORS = "Y"
02990            ADD 1 TO NUMBER-OF-ERRONEOUS-RECORDS-W.
03000
03010    WRITE-NEW-ACCOUNT-LINE.
03020        MOVE ACCOUNT-NUMBER-IN TO ACCOUNT-NUMBER-OUT-G.
03030        MOVE AMOUNT-IN           TO AMOUNT-OUT-G.
03040        IF LINE-COUNT-ER + 1 > REGISTER-PAGE-LIMIT
03050            PERFORM PRODUCE-REGISTER-HEAD.
03060        WRITE REGISTER-RECORD-OUT FROM NEW-ACCOUNT-LINE.
03070        ADD 1 TO LINE-COUNT-ER.
03080
03090    WRITE-INVALID-CODE-LINE.
03100        MOVE ACCOUNT-NUMBER-IN TO ACCOUNT-NUMBER-OUT-E.
03110        MOVE CODE-IN           TO CODE-OUT.
03120        MOVE INVALID-CODE-MSG  TO MESSAGE-E.
03130        PERFORM WRITE-ERROR-LINE.
03140
03150    WRITE-ERROR-LINE.
03160        IF ERROR-LINE-COUNTER + 1 > ERROR-PAGE-LIMIT
03170            PERFORM PRODUCE-ERROR-HEAD.
03180        WRITE ERROR-RECORD-OUT FROM ERROR-LINE.
03190        ADD 1 TO ERROR-LINE-COUNTER.
03200
03210    WRITE-DUPLICATE-ERROR-MESSAGE.
03220        MOVE "DUPLICATE ACCOUNT NUMBER" TO MESSAGE-E.
03230        MOVE ACCOUNT-NUMBER-IN          TO ACCOUNT-NUMBER-OUT-E.
03240        PERFORM WRITE-ERROR-LINE.
03250
03260    WRITE-NAME-ERROR-MESSAGE.
03270        MOVE "DEPOSITOR NAME MISSING" TO MESSAGE-E.
03280        MOVE ACCOUNT-NUMBER-IN          TO ACCOUNT-NUMBER-OUT-E.
03290        PERFORM WRITE-ERROR-LINE.
03300
03310    WRITE-AMOUNT-MESSAGE.
03320        MOVE AMOUNT-IN-X                TO AMOUNT-OUT-X.
03330        MOVE AMOUNT-NOT-NUMERIC-MSG TO MESSAGE-E.
03340        MOVE ACCOUNT-NUMBER-IN          TO ACCOUNT-NUMBER-OUT-E.
03350        PERFORM WRITE-ERROR-LINE.
03360
03370    TERMINATION.
03380        PERFORM PRODUCE-TOTAL-LINES.
03390        CLOSE ACCOUNT-MASTER-FILE-OUT
03400              ERROR-FILE-OUT
03410              TRANSACTION-REGISTER-FILE-OUT.
03420
```

```
03430    PRODUCE-TOTAL-LINES.
03440        MOVE DEPOSIT-TOTAL-W TO AMOUNT-TOTAL-OUT.
03450        MOVE NUMBER-OF-NEW-ACCOUNTS-W TO NUMBER-OF-NEW-ACCOUNTS-OUT.
03460        MOVE NUMBER-OF-ERRONEOUS-RECORDS-W
03470            TO NUMBER-OF-ERRONEOUS-RCDS-OUT.
03480        MOVE NUMBER-OF-INPUT-RECORDS-W
03490            TO NUMBER-OF-INPUT-RECORDS-OUT.
03500        WRITE REGISTER-RECORD-OUT FROM FINAL-LINE-1 AFTER 2.
03510        WRITE REGISTER-RECORD-OUT FROM FINAL-LINE-2 AFTER 2.
03520        WRITE REGISTER-RECORD-OUT FROM FINAL-LINE-3 AFTER 2.
03530        WRITE REGISTER-RECORD-OUT FROM FINAL-LINE-4 AFTER 2.
03540        WRITE REGISTER-RECORD-OUT FROM FINAL-LINE-5 AFTER 2.
03550
03560    READ-A-RECORD.
03570        RETURN SORT-WORK-FILE
03580            AT END
03590                MOVE "N" TO MORE-INPUT.
03600
03610    END-OF-THIS-SECTION.
03620        EXIT.
```

The WRITE statement at line 02740 attempts to place each master record onto the output master file. When COBOL is writing an indexed file, it will not WRITE duplicate prime keys. That is, if we tell COBOL to WRITE a record sequentially on the file, and COBOL finds that there is already on the file a record with the same Account Number as the one we are trying to WRITE, COBOL will not WRITE the record but will instead set the STATUS code to 22. For this reason, we do not have to check for duplicate Account Numbers the way we did in Program P12-02. In Program P14-01 COBOL does it for us. COBOL checks for duplicate keys when it is working with indexed files, but not when it is working with sequential files.

And so, in the paragraph CHECK-INPUT-FOR-VALIDITY, line 02880, we don't have to check the ACCOUNT-NUMBER-IN against any ACCOUNT-NUMBER-SAVE field. Instead, in the paragraph WRITE-MASTER-RECORD, line 02730, we can detect a duplicate Account Number by testing the STATUS code for 22 after trying to WRITE each output record.

Program P14-01 was run with the input data shown in Figure 14.2 and produced the report output shown in Figure 14.3.

The DISPLAY Statement

The format of the DISPLAY statement is:

$$\underline{\text{DISPLAY}} \left\{ \begin{array}{l} \text{identifier-1} \\ \text{literal-1} \end{array} \right\} \left[\begin{array}{l} , \text{ identifier-2} \\ , \text{ literal-2} \end{array} \right] \dots$$
$$[\underline{\text{UPON}} \text{ mnemonic-name}]$$

Figure 14.2   Input to Program P14-01.

```
--------------------------------------------------------------------------------
          1         2         3         4         5         6         7         8
12345678901234567890123456789012345678901234567890123456789012345678901234567890
--------------------------------------------------------------------------------
10002300110000ROSEMARY LANE
10010500005000LENORE MILLER
10022000002460GENE GALLI
10017500001000MARY KEATING
20018200007500BOB LANIGAN
10018900003500J. & L. CAIN
10011200025000ROSEMARY LANE
3000070CA00000MICHELE CAPUANO
10012600075000JAMES BUDD
10041000031800GENE GALLI
10013300100000PAUL LERNER, D.D.S.
10014000002575BETH FALLON
10009800002000JANE HALEY
10010500005000ONE DAY CLEANERS
10016100002450ROBERT RYAN
10039100064200GENE GALLI
10016800012550KELLY HEDERMAN
10021000025000JERRY PARKS
10003500015000JOHN J. LEHMAN
10003200002500JOSEPH CAMILLO
10030600049300COMMUNITY DRUGS
10005600000100EVELYN SLATER
10006300007500
10007000050000PATRICK J. LEE
10027300027500VITO CACACI
10028000002000COMMUNITY DRUGS
10009600087100GENE GALLI
1003010FG15750PAT P. POWERS
10030800200000JOE GARCIA
10007700001037LESLIE MINSKY
10008400150000JOHN DAPRINO
10009100010000JOE'S DELI
10009800050000GEORGE CULHANE
10026600009957MARTIN LANG
10031500025000GRACE MICELI
10032200002000
10019900002100COMMUNITY DRUGS
10032900001000GUY VOLPONE
100336))))!%))SALVATORE CALI
10023100055500BILL WILLIAMS
10024500003500FRANK CAPUTO
10034900123400COMMUNITY DRUGS
10025200001500GENE GALLI
10025900002937
10000700100784ROSEBUCCI
10001400001000ROBERT DAVIS M.D.
10002100012500LORICE MONTI
10001500070000LENORE MILLER
10002000080000LENORE MILLER
10002100090000ROSEMARY LANE
10002200100000ROSEMARY LANE
10002800700159MICHAEL SMITH
10034300100000JOE & MARY SESSA
1000880021A000COMMUNITY DRUGS
10035000250000ROGER SHAW
```

Figure 14.3 Report output from Program P14-01.

```
                          ROBBEM STATE BANK
                          106 WEST 10TH ST.
                          BROOKLYN, NY  11212

                 SAVINGS ACCOUNT MASTER FILE ERRORS
DATE   4/08/88                                      PAGE   1


        ACCOUNT                     NOTES
        NUMBER

         00007                      INVALID CODE 3
         00007                      INITIAL DEPOSIT NOT NUMERIC OCA00000
         00021                      DUPLICATE ACCOUNT NUMBER
         00063                      DEPOSITOR NAME MISSING
         00088                      INITIAL DEPOSIT NOT NUMERIC 0021A000
         00098                      DUPLICATE ACCOUNT NUMBER
         00105                      DUPLICATE ACCOUNT NUMBER
         00182                      INVALID CODE 2
         00259                      DEPOSITOR NAME MISSING
         00301                      INITIAL DEPOSIT NOT NUMERIC OFG15750
         00322                      DEPOSITOR NAME MISSING
         00336                      INITIAL DEPOSIT NOT NUMERIC ))))!%))


                          ROBBEM STATE BANK
                          106 WEST 10TH ST.
                          BROOKLYN, NY  11212

                 SAVINGS ACCOUNT MASTER FILE CREATION
DATE   4/08/88                                      PAGE   1


        ACCOUNT     INITIAL     NOTES
        NUMBER      DEPOSIT

         00007     1,007.84    NEW ACCOUNT
         00014        10.00    NEW ACCOUNT
         00015       700.00    NEW ACCOUNT
         00020       800.00    NEW ACCOUNT
         00021       125.00    NEW ACCOUNT
         00022     1,000.00    NEW ACCOUNT
         00023     1,100.00    NEW ACCOUNT
         00028     7,001.59    NEW ACCOUNT
         00032        25.00    NEW ACCOUNT
         00035       150.00    NEW ACCOUNT
         00056         1.00    NEW ACCOUNT
         00070       500.00    NEW ACCOUNT
         00077        10.37    NEW ACCOUNT
         00084     1,500.00    NEW ACCOUNT
         00091       100.00    NEW ACCOUNT
         00096       871.00    NEW ACCOUNT
         00098        20.00    NEW ACCOUNT
         00105        50.00    NEW ACCOUNT
         00112       250.00    NEW ACCOUNT
         00126       750.00    NEW ACCOUNT
         00133     1,000.00    NEW ACCOUNT
         00140        25.75    NEW ACCOUNT
         00161        24.50    NEW ACCOUNT
         00168       125.50    NEW ACCOUNT
```

(continued)

Figure 14.3   (continued)

```
                         ROBBEM STATE BANK
                         106 WEST 10TH ST.
                         BROOKLYN, NY  11212

                    SAVINGS ACCOUNT MASTER FILE CREATION
         DATE   4/08/88                                    PAGE   2


              ACCOUNT       INITIAL      NOTES
              NUMBER        DEPOSIT

               00175          10.00      NEW ACCOUNT
               00189          35.00      NEW ACCOUNT
               00199          21.00      NEW ACCOUNT
               00210         250.00      NEW ACCOUNT
               00220          24.60      NEW ACCOUNT
               00231         555.00      NEW ACCOUNT
               00245          35.00      NEW ACCOUNT
               00252          15.00      NEW ACCOUNT
               00266          99.57      NEW ACCOUNT
               00273         275.00      NEW ACCOUNT
               00280          20.00      NEW ACCOUNT
               00306         493.00      NEW ACCOUNT
               00308       2,000.00      NEW ACCOUNT
               00315         250.00      NEW ACCOUNT
               00329          10.00      NEW ACCOUNT
               00343       1,000.00      NEW ACCOUNT
               00349       1,234.00      NEW ACCOUNT
               00350       2,500.00      NEW ACCOUNT
               00391         642.00      NEW ACCOUNT
               00410         318.00      NEW ACCOUNT

          TOTAL          26,934.72


                         CONTROL COUNTS

              NUMBER OF NEW ACCOUNTS          44

              NUMBER OF ERRONEOUS RECORDS     11

              TOTAL                           55
```

A DISPLAY statement can be used either to punch output or to print it on a high-speed printer or console typewriter. The DISPLAY statement prints or punches literal-1, literal-2, and so on and the values assigned to identifier-1, identifier-2, and so on from left to right in the output record in the order in which they appear in the DISPLAY statement, using as many output records as necessary to print or punch all the data items listed. A mnemonic-name can be used in the optional UPON clause to tell COBOL which output device the output data are to appear on. Each COBOL system has its own default output device in case the UPON clause is omitted.

The DISPLAY verb has very limited capabilities for line formatting, line skipping and spacing, and output editing. It is best used only for error output and for transmitting messages to the computer operator by way of the console typewriter. You will find a fuller discussion of the limitations of the DISPLAY verb in Chapter 19.

EXERCISE 1

Write a program to create an indexed inventory master file. Use the same formats for transaction and master records that you used when you created your sequential master file in Exercise 3, Chapter 12, page 392. Specify the Supplier Code and Storage Location as alternate keys. Decide for yourself whether either or both of the alternate keys should be specified WITH DUPLICATES. Save the master file for use later in this chapter.

Updating an Indexed File

The big difference between updating a sequential master file and updating an indexed master file is that when you are updating an indexed file there is no need to copy the old file in order to make the desired changes. COBOL can take advantage of its random-access capability to update existing master records in place on the file, add new records in their proper places, and delete existing master records from the file.

The hierarchy diagram for Program P14-02 is shown in Figure 14.4. The "Initialization" includes a priming read of the transaction file. The program READs each transaction and determines from the Account Number of the transaction which master record it should try to READ from the master file.

"Process master record" tries to READ into the master input area the master record whose key is equal to the transaction key, regardless of the type of transaction that is being processed. Even if the current transaction is to add a new record to the master file, "Process master record" nevertheless READs the master file in search of a record having the same key as the transaction. If there is such a record, "Process master record" sets a flag to "Y"; if not, it sets the flag to "N."

"Process transaction record" applies the transaction record to the master record in the master input area. For each of the five different types of transactions, suitable validity checks are carried out. If the transaction is valid, it is applied to the master record in the master input area. For a valid transaction of Code 1, to add a new record to the file, there will be no record in the master input area, and the new master record is built there.

"Check to write master" determines whether a master record should be written from the master input area to replace an existing master record on the file, whether a new master record should be written from the input area to the file, whether a master record should be deleted from the file, or whether none of those actions should be taken. "Check to write master" then carries out any action it finds necessary.

A Program to Update an Indexed File

The transaction input formats for Program P14-02 are the same as the ones we used when we updated a sequential master file on tape, in Program P13-03. The formats are described on pages 423 and 438.

Program P14-02 is shown in Figure 14.5. There is only one FILE-CONTROL

Figure 14.4   Hierarchy diagram for Program P14-02.

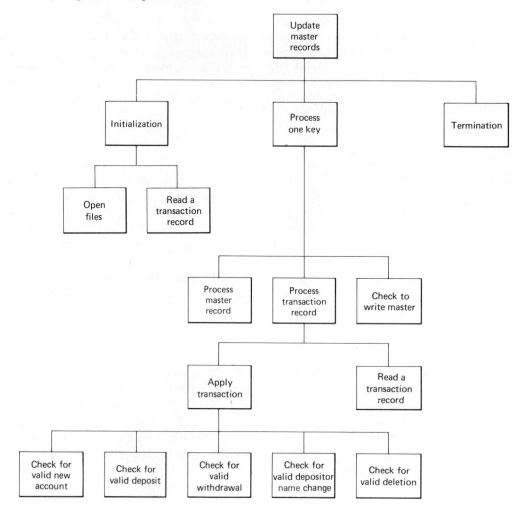

entry for the master file, at line 00160, because there is only one master file. The one master file serves as both the input and output file. It has its records read in, updated, and put back in the same place. The FILE-CONTROL entry includes the **ACCESS RANDOM** clause, line 00220, to tell COBOL that in this program the ACCOUNT-MASTER-FILE-I-O will be accessed randomly.

In the Data Division the TRANSACTION-FILE-IN and the TRANSACTION-INPUT-AREA are defined as in Program P13-03, at lines 00410 through 00450 and 00830 through 01000, respectively. The TRANSACTION-INPUT-AREA is redefined as in Program P13-03 to accommodate all the different transaction formats. Notice that the TRANSACTION-INPUT-AREA is only 34 characters long. This shows that an area in working storage INTO which an input record will be read need not be 80 characters long. In this case the first 34 of the 80 characters in each input record will be read INTO the TRANSACTION-INPUT-AREA.

The master area is defined a little differently from the way it was defined in Chapter 13. It turns out that we don't need a master input area separate from a master work area in this program, as we did in Program P13-03. So the master input area is defined in the File Section as ACCOUNT-MASTER-RECORD-I-O, at line 00350, and serves as both the master input area and the place where we work on master records.

Figure 14.5   Program P14-02.

CB1 RELEASE 2.4   IBM OS/VS COBOL   JULY 1, 1982

                         14.09.31   APR   9,1988


```
00010  IDENTIFICATION DIVISION.
00020  PROGRAM-ID. P14-02.
00030 *
00040 *    THIS PROGRAM UPDATES AN INDEXED MASTER FILE ON DISK
00050 *    WITH ADDITIONS, CHANGES, AND DELETIONS.
00060 *
00070 **********************************************************************
00080
00090  ENVIRONMENT DIVISION.
00100  CONFIGURATION SECTION.
00110  SOURCE-COMPUTER. IBM-370.
00120  OBJECT-COMPUTER. IBM-370.
00130
00140  INPUT-OUTPUT SECTION.
00150  FILE-CONTROL.
00160      SELECT ACCOUNT-MASTER-FILE-I-O           ASSIGN TO MSTRDISK
00170          ORGANIZATION INDEXED
00180          RECORD KEY IS ACCOUNT-NUMBER-M
00190          ALTERNATE RECORD KEY IS DEPOSITOR-NAME-M
00200              WITH DUPLICATES
00210          STATUS IS FILE-CHECK
00220          ACCESS RANDOM.
00230      SELECT TRANSACTION-FILE-IN              ASSIGN TO INFILE.
00240      SELECT TRANSACTION-REGISTER-FILE-OUT    ASSIGN TO PRINTER1.
00250      SELECT ERROR-FILE-OUT                   ASSIGN TO PRINTER2.
00260
00270 **********************************************************************
00280
00290  DATA DIVISION.
00300  FILE SECTION.
00310  FD  ACCOUNT-MASTER-FILE-I-O
00320      LABEL RECORDS ARE STANDARD
00330      RECORD CONTAINS 39 CHARACTERS.
00340
00350  01  ACCOUNT-MASTER-RECORD-I-O.
00360      05  ACCOUNT-NUMBER-M              PIC X(5).
00370      05  DEPOSITOR-NAME-M              PIC X(20).
00380      05  DATE-OF-LAST-TRANSACTION-M    PIC 9(6).
00390      05  CURRENT-BALANCE-M             PIC S9(6)V99.
00400
00410  FD  TRANSACTION-FILE-IN
00420      LABEL RECORDS ARE OMITTED
00430      RECORD CONTAINS 80 CHARACTERS.
00440
00450  01  TRANSACTION-RECORD-IN            PIC X(80).
00460
00470  FD  TRANSACTION-REGISTER-FILE-OUT
00480      LABEL RECORDS ARE OMITTED.
00490
00500  01  REGISTER-RECORD-OUT              PIC X(76).
00510
00520  FD  ERROR-FILE-OUT
00530      LABEL RECORDS ARE OMITTED.
00540
00550  01  ERROR-RECORD-OUT                 PIC X(114).
00560
```

(continued)

And of course we don't need any sort file. In this program the transactions can be processed in random order and do not need to be SORTed. Some programmers might want to SORT the transaction file so that the transaction register and the error report will print in Account Number sequence, but such SORTing is not needed for the update to take place correctly. The random-access capability of indexed files is used to advantage even if the transaction file is SORTed, for the program can still READ just the master records it needs and no others.

Figure 14.5   (continued)

```
00570   WORKING-STORAGE SECTION.
00580   01   FILE-CHECK.
00590        05   STATUS-KEY-1                        PIC X      VALUE ZERO.
00600        05   STATUS-KEY-2                        PIC X      VALUE ZERO.
00610   01   IS-MASTER-RECORD-IN-WORK-AREA            PIC X.
00620   01   IS-MASTER-RECORD-IN-THE-FILE             PIC X.
00630   01   NUMBER-OF-INPUT-RECORDS-W                PIC S9(3) VALUE ZERO.
00640   01   NUMBER-OF-ERRONEOUS-RECORDS-W            PIC S9(3) VALUE ZERO.
00650   01   DEPOSIT-TOTAL-W                          PIC S9(7)V99 VALUE ZERO.
00660   01   WITHDRAWAL-TOTAL-W                       PIC S9(7)V99 VALUE ZERO.
00670   01   NUMBER-OF-DEPOSITS-W                     PIC S9(3) VALUE 0.
00680   01   NUMBER-OF-WITHDRAWALS-W                  PIC S9(3) VALUE 0.
00690   01   NUMBER-OF-NAME-CHANGES-W                 PIC S9(3) VALUE 0.
00700   01   NUMBER-OF-CLOSED-ACCOUNTS-W              PIC S9(3) VALUE 0.
00710   01   NUMBER-OF-NEW-ACCOUNTS-W                 PIC S9(3) VALUE 0.
00720   01   BLANK-LINE                               PIC X      VALUE SPACE.
00730   01   PAGE-NUMBER-W                            PIC S99    VALUE 0.
00740   01   ERROR-PAGE-NUMBER-W                      PIC S99    VALUE 0.
00750   01   PAGE-LIMIT              COMP SYNC        PIC S99    VALUE 28.
00760   01   LINE-COUNT-ER          COMP SYNC        PIC S99.
00770   01   ERROR-PAGE-LIMIT       COMP SYNC        PIC S99    VALUE 45.
00780   01   ERROR-LINE-COUNTER     COMP SYNC        PIC S99.
00790   01   TODAYS-DATE.
00800        05   TODAYS-YEAR                         PIC 99.
00810        05   TODAYS-MONTH-AND-DAY                PIC 9(4).
00820
00830   01   TRANSACTION-INPUT-AREA.
00840        05   TRANSACTION-CODE                    PIC X.
00850             88   NEW-ACCOUNT                    VALUE "1".
00860             88   DEPOSIT                        VALUE "2".
00870             88   WITHDRAWAL                     VALUE "3".
00880             88   NAME-CHANGE                    VALUE "4".
00890             88   DELETION                       VALUE "5".
00900        05   ACCOUNT-NUMBER-T                    PIC X(5).
00910        05   DEPOSIT-AND-WITHDRAWAL-AMTS.
00920             10   DEPOSIT-AMOUNT                 PIC 9(6)V99.
00930             10   DEPOSIT-AMOUNT-X   REDEFINES DEPOSIT-AMOUNT
00940                                                 PIC X(8).
00950             10   WITHDRAWAL-AMOUNT  REDEFINES DEPOSIT-AMOUNT
00960                                                 PIC 9(6)V99.
00970             10   WITHDRAWAL-AMOUNT-X REDEFINES DEPOSIT-AMOUNT
00980                                                 PIC X(8).
00990        05   DEPOSITOR-NAME-NEW-ACCOUNT          PIC X(20).
01000             88 DEPOSITOR-NAME-MISSING           VALUE SPACES.
01010   01   TRANSACTION-4-INPUT-AREA REDEFINES TRANSACTION-INPUT-AREA.
01020        05   FILLER                              PIC X(6).
01030        05   DEPOSITOR-NAME                      PIC X(20).
01040             88   REPLACEMENT-NAME-MISSING VALUE SPACES.
01050        05   FILLER                              PIC X(8).
01060
01070   01   REPORT-HEADING-1.
01080        05   FILLER     PIC X(39) VALUE SPACES.
01090        05   FILLER     PIC X(17) VALUE "ROBBEM STATE BANK".
01100
01110   01   REPORT-HEADING-2.
01120        05   FILLER     PIC X(39) VALUE SPACES.
01130        05   FILLER     PIC X(17) VALUE "106 WEST 10TH ST.".
01140
01150   01   REPORT-HEADING-3.
01160        05   FILLER     PIC X(38) VALUE SPACES.
01170        05   FILLER     PIC X(19) VALUE "BROOKLYN, NY  11212".
01180
01190   01   PAGE-HEADING-1.
01200        05   FILLER     PIC X(29) VALUE SPACES.
01210        05   FILLER     PIC X(36)
01220                        VALUE "SAVINGS ACCOUNT TRANSACTION REGISTER".
01230
01240   01   PAGE-HEADING-2.
01250        05   FILLER     PIC X(17)      VALUE SPACES.
01260        05   FILLER     PIC X(5)       VALUE "DATE".
01270        05   TODAYS-MONTH-AND-DAY      PIC Z9/99/.
01280        05   TODAYS-YEAR               PIC 99B(35).
01290        05   FILLER     PIC X(5)       VALUE "PAGE".
01300        05   PAGE-NUMBER-OUT           PIC Z9.
01310
```

```
01320   01   PAGE-HEADING-3.
01330        05   FILLER         PIC X(20) VALUE SPACES.
01340        05   FILLER         PIC X(12) VALUE "ACCOUNT".
01350        05   FILLER         PIC X(14) VALUE "DEPOSITS".
01360        05   FILLER         PIC X(18) VALUE "WITHDRAWALS".
01370        05   FILLER         PIC X(5)  VALUE "NOTES".
01380
01390   01   PAGE-HEADING-4.
01400        05   FILLER         PIC X(20) VALUE SPACES.
01410        05   FILLER         PIC X(6)  VALUE "NUMBER".
01420
01430   01   ERROR-PAGE-HEADING-1.
01440        05   FILLER         PIC X(33) VALUE SPACES.
01450        05   FILLER         PIC X(28) VALUE
01460                            "SAVINGS ACCOUNT ERROR REPORT".
01470
01480   01   ERROR-PAGE-HEADING-3.
01490        05   FILLER         PIC X(20) VALUE SPACES.
01500        05   FILLER         PIC X(44) VALUE "ACCOUNT".
01510        05   FILLER         PIC X(5)  VALUE "NOTES".
01520
01530   01   NEW-ACCOUNT-LINE.
01540        05   FILLER         PIC X(21) VALUE SPACES.
01550        05   ACCOUNT-NUMBER-OUT      PIC 9(5)B(5).
01560        05   DEPOSIT-AMOUNT-OUT      PIC ZZZ,ZZZ.99B(21).
01570        05   FILLER         PIC X(11) VALUE "NEW ACCOUNT".
01580
01590   01   DEPOSIT-LINE.
01600        05   FILLER         PIC X(21) VALUE SPACES.
01610        05   ACCOUNT-NUMBER-OUT      PIC 9(5)B(5).
01620        05   DEPOSIT-AMOUNT-OUT      PIC ZZZ,ZZZ.99.
01630
01640   01   WITHDRAWAL-LINE.
01650        05   FILLER         PIC X(21) VALUE SPACES.
01660        05   ACCOUNT-NUMBER-OUT      PIC 9(5)B(19).
01670        05   WITHDRAWAL-AMOUNT-OUT   PIC ZZZ,ZZZ.99.
01680
01690   01   NAME-CHANGE-LINE.
01700        05   FILLER         PIC X(21) VALUE SPACES.
01710        05   ACCOUNT-NUMBER-OUT      PIC 9(5)B(5).
01720        05   DEPOSITOR-NAME-OUT      PIC X(20)B(11).
01730        05   FILLER         PIC X(11) VALUE "NAME CHANGE".
01740
01750   01   DELETION-LINE.
01760        05   FILLER         PIC X(21) VALUE SPACES.
01770        05   ACCOUNT-NUMBER-OUT      PIC 9(5)B(19).
01780        05   CURRENT-BALANCE-M-OUT   PIC ZZZ,ZZZ.99B(7).
01790        05   FILLER         PIC X(14) VALUE "ACCOUNT CLOSED".
01800
01810   01   ERROR-LINE.
01820        05   FILLER    PIC X(21) VALUE SPACES.
01830        05   ACCOUNT-NUMBER-E     PIC X(5)B(36).
01840        05   ERROR-MESSAGE        PIC X(52).
01850
01860   01   DEPOSIT-AMOUNT-INVALID-MSG.
01870        05   FILLER    PIC X(29) VALUE
01880                       "DEPOSIT AMOUNT NOT NUMERIC -".
01890        05   DEPOSIT-AMOUNT-OUT    PIC X(8).
01900
01910   01   WITHDRAWAL-AMOUNT-INVALID-MSG.
01920        05   FILLER    PIC X(32) VALUE
01930                       "WITHDRAWAL AMOUNT NOT NUMERIC -".
01940        05   WITHDRAWAL-AMOUNT-E   PIC X(8).
01950
01960   01   INVALID-CODE-MSG.
01970        05   FILLER    PIC X(27) VALUE "INVALID TRANSACTION CODE -".
01980        05   TRANSACTION-CODE-OUT PIC X.
01990
```

(continued)

A flag IS-MASTER-RECORD-IN-THE-FILE has been defined, at line 00620. This flag is needed in addition to the usual flag IS-MASTER-RECORD-IN-WORK-AREA, line 00610. You will see how the two flags are used when we look at the Procedure Division.

Figure 14.5 (continued)

```
02000   01   FINAL-LINE-1.
02010        05   FILLER            PIC X(17) VALUE SPACES.
02020        05   FILLER            PIC X(12) VALUE "TOTALS".
02030        05   DEPOSIT-TOTAL-OUT        PIC Z,ZZZ,ZZZ.99BB.
02040        05   WITHDRAWAL-TOTAL-OUT     PIC Z,ZZZ,ZZZ.99.
02050
02060   01   FINAL-LINE-2.
02070        05   FILLER            PIC X(40) VALUE SPACES.
02080        05   FILLER            PIC X(14) VALUE "CONTROL COUNTS".
02090
02100   01   FINAL-LINE-3.
02110        05   FILLER            PIC X(34) VALUE SPACES.
02120        05   FILLER            PIC X(26)
02130                               VALUE "NUMBER OF NEW ACCOUNTS".
02140        05   NUMBER-OF-NEW-ACCOUNTS-OUT PIC ZZ9.
02150
02160   01   FINAL-LINE-4.
02170        05   FILLER            PIC X(34) VALUE SPACES.
02180        05   FILLER            PIC X(26)
02190                               VALUE "NUMBER OF DEPOSITS".
02200        05   NUMBER-OF-DEPOSITS-OUT    PIC ZZ9.
02210
02220   01   FINAL-LINE-5.
02230        05   FILLER            PIC X(34) VALUE SPACES.
02240        05   FILLER            PIC X(26)
02250                               VALUE "NUMBER OF WITHDRAWALS".
02260        05   NUMBER-OF-WITHDRAWALS-OUT PIC ZZ9.
02270
02280   01   FINAL-LINE-6.
02290        05   FILLER            PIC X(34) VALUE SPACES.
02300        05   FILLER            PIC X(26)
02310                               VALUE "NUMBER OF NAME CHANGES".
02320        05   NUMBER-OF-NAME-CHANGES-OUT PIC ZZ9.
02330
02340   01   FINAL-LINE-7.
02350        05   FILLER            PIC X(34) VALUE SPACES.
02360        05   FILLER            PIC X(26)
02370                               VALUE "NUMBER OF CLOSED ACCOUNTS".
02380        05   NUMBER-OF-CLOSED-ACCOUNTS-OUT   PIC ZZ9.
02390
02400   01   FINAL-LINE-8.
02410        05   FILLER            PIC X(34) VALUE SPACES.
02420        05   FILLER            PIC X(26)
02430                               VALUE "NUMBER OF ERRORS".
02440        05   NUMBER-OF-ERRONEOUS-RECRDS-OUT
02450                               PIC ZZ9.
02460
02470   01   FINAL-LINE-9.
02480        05   FILLER            PIC X(34) VALUE SPACES.
02490        05   FILLER            PIC X(24) VALUE "TOTAL".
02500        05   NUMBER-OF-INPUT-RECORDS-OUT PIC Z,ZZ9.
02510
02520   01   NO-TRANSACTIONS.
02530        05   FILLER            PIC X(21) VALUE SPACES.
02540        05   FILLER            PIC X(15) VALUE "NO TRANSACTIONS".
02550
02560   ****************************************************************
02570
02580   PROCEDURE DIVISION.
02590   DECLARATIVES.
02600   DUMMY-USE SECTION.
02610        USE AFTER ERROR PROCEDURE ACCOUNT-MASTER-FILE-I-O.
02620   END DECLARATIVES.
02630
02640   NONDECLARATIVE SECTION.
02650   UPDATE-MASTER-RECORDS.
02660        PERFORM INITIALIZATION.
02670        PERFORM PROCESS-ONE-KEY UNTIL
02680            TRANSACTION-INPUT-AREA = HIGH-VALUES.
02690        PERFORM TERMINATION.
02700        STOP RUN.
02710
```

```
02720   INITIALIZATION.
02730       OPEN INPUT   TRANSACTION-FILE-IN
02740            OUTPUT  TRANSACTION-REGISTER-FILE-OUT
02750                    ERROR-FILE-OUT
02760            I-O     ACCOUNT-MASTER-FILE-I-O.
02770       IF FILE-CHECK NOT = ZEROS
02780           DISPLAY " MASTER FILE OPEN STATUS = ", FILE-CHECK
02790           CLOSE TRANSACTION-FILE-IN
02800                 TRANSACTION-REGISTER-FILE-OUT
02810                 ERROR-FILE-OUT
02820                 ACCOUNT-MASTER-FILE-I-O
02830           STOP RUN.
02840       ACCEPT TODAYS-DATE FROM DATE.
02850       MOVE CORR TODAYS-DATE TO PAGE-HEADING-2.
02860       PERFORM PRODUCE-REPORT-HEADINGS.
02870       PERFORM READ-A-TRANSACTION-RECORD.
02880       IF TRANSACTION-INPUT-AREA = HIGH-VALUES
02890           WRITE REGISTER-RECORD-OUT FROM NO-TRANSACTIONS.
02900
02910   PRODUCE-REPORT-HEADINGS.
02920       PERFORM WRITE-REGISTER-HEADINGS.
02930       PERFORM WRITE-ERROR-REPORT-HEADINGS.
02940
02950   WRITE-REGISTER-HEADINGS.
02960       ADD 1 TO PAGE-NUMBER-W.
02970       MOVE PAGE-NUMBER-W TO PAGE-NUMBER-OUT.
02980       WRITE REGISTER-RECORD-OUT FROM
02990           REPORT-HEADING-1 AFTER ADVANCING PAGE.
03000       WRITE REGISTER-RECORD-OUT FROM REPORT-HEADING-2.
03010       WRITE REGISTER-RECORD-OUT FROM REPORT-HEADING-3.
03020       WRITE REGISTER-RECORD-OUT FROM PAGE-HEADING-1 AFTER 2.
03030       WRITE REGISTER-RECORD-OUT FROM PAGE-HEADING-2.
03040       WRITE REGISTER-RECORD-OUT FROM PAGE-HEADING-3 AFTER 3.
03050       WRITE REGISTER-RECORD-OUT FROM PAGE-HEADING-4.
03060       WRITE REGISTER-RECORD-OUT FROM BLANK-LINE.
03070       MOVE 11 TO LINE-COUNT-ER.
03080
```

(continued)

The Procedure Division begins at line 02580. The USE section is included to satisfy the ANSI standard. We have no SORTing to do in this program, so the entire structure of the Procedure Division is simplified by the omission of the SORT statement.

Notice that ACCOUNT-MASTER-FILE-I-O is OPENed as both an input and output file, at line 02760. **I-O** is a third **OPEN mode**, in addition to the OPEN modes that you already know, INPUT and OUTPUT. Be careful how you spell I-O when you use it in an OPEN statement. You must not spell it INPUT-OUTPUT. INPUT-OUTPUT is the name of a section in the Environment Division, the INPUT-OUTPUT SECTION. And the section header INPUT-OUTPUT SECTION cannot be written I-O SECTION.

There is a fourth OPEN mode, **EXTEND**, that is used in the 1974 standard only to add records to the end of a sequential file.[2] We will not discuss the EXTEND mode in this book.

---

[2]Some COBOL systems adhering to the 1974 standard permit the EXTEND mode to be used to add records sequentially to the end of an indexed file. The 1985 standard permits the use of the EXTEND mode to add records sequentially to the end of a file of any ORGANIZATION.

The paragraph PROCESS-MASTER-RECORD shows how to READ an indexed file randomly on its prime key. First, the key of the desired record must be MOVEd to whatever field was named in the RECORD KEY clause in the FILE-CONTROL entry for the file. That is done by the MOVE statement at line 03320. Then a READ statement is given, naming the file to be read. A random READ statement of an indexed file sets the STATUS field if one is given for the file. The ANSI standard meanings of the STATUS codes related to READing an indexed file randomly on its prime key are given in Table 14-2.

Table 14-2
ANSI standard STATUS codes related to READing an indexed file randomly on its prime RECORD KEY.

Status Code	Meaning
00	Successful completion
23	Invalid key — no record found
30	Permanent error (hardware malfunction)

Your own COBOL system may have additional codes in the range 90 through 99. STATUS code 23 arises from an attempt to READ a master record not on the file. That is, if we give COBOL an Account Number and ask it to READ a master record from the file having that Account Number, and the record is not found on the file, COBOL sets the STATUS field to 23. As with the WRITE statement, an IF statement and the STATUS code are all we need to determine the outcome of the READ.

Figure 14.5   (continued)

```
03090   WRITE-ERROR-REPORT-HEADINGS.
03100       ADD 1 TO ERROR-PAGE-NUMBER-W.
03110       MOVE ERROR-PAGE-NUMBER-W TO PAGE-NUMBER-OUT.
03120       WRITE ERROR-RECORD-OUT FROM REPORT-HEADING-1 AFTER PAGE.
03130       WRITE ERROR-RECORD-OUT FROM REPORT-HEADING-2.
03140       WRITE ERROR-RECORD-OUT FROM REPORT-HEADING-3.
03150       WRITE ERROR-RECORD-OUT FROM ERROR-PAGE-HEADING-1 AFTER 2.
03160       WRITE ERROR-RECORD-OUT FROM PAGE-HEADING-2.
03170       WRITE ERROR-RECORD-OUT FROM ERROR-PAGE-HEADING-3 AFTER 3.
03180       WRITE ERROR-RECORD-OUT FROM PAGE-HEADING-4.
03190       WRITE ERROR-RECORD-OUT FROM BLANK-LINE.
03200       MOVE 11 TO ERROR-LINE-COUNTER.
03210
03220   PROCESS-ONE-KEY.
03230       PERFORM PROCESS-MASTER-RECORD.
03240       PERFORM PROCESS-TRANSACTION-RECORD.
03250       PERFORM CHECK-TO-WRITE-MASTER.
03260
03270   PROCESS-TRANSACTION-RECORD.
03280       PERFORM APPLY-TRANSACTION.
03290       PERFORM READ-A-TRANSACTION-RECORD.
03300
03310   PROCESS-MASTER-RECORD.
03320       MOVE ACCOUNT-NUMBER-T TO ACCOUNT-NUMBER-M.
03330       READ ACCOUNT-MASTER-FILE-I-O.
03340       IF FILE-CHECK = ZEROS
03350           MOVE "Y" TO IS-MASTER-RECORD-IN-THE-FILE,
03360                       IS-MASTER-RECORD-IN-WORK-AREA
03370       ELSE
03380       IF FILE-CHECK = "23"
03390           MOVE "N" TO IS-MASTER-RECORD-IN-THE-FILE,
03400                       IS-MASTER-RECORD-IN-WORK-AREA
03410       ELSE
03420           DISPLAY " MASTER FILE READ STATUS = ", FILE-CHECK
03430           PERFORM TERMINATION
03440           STOP RUN.
03450
```

```
03460    CHECK-TO-WRITE-MASTER.
03470        MOVE ZEROS TO FILE-CHECK.
03480        IF IS-MASTER-RECORD-IN-WORK-AREA = "Y" AND
03490            IS-MASTER-RECORD-IN-THE-FILE   = "N"
03500            WRITE ACCOUNT-MASTER-RECORD-I-O
03510        ELSE
03520        IF IS-MASTER-RECORD-IN-WORK-AREA = "Y" AND
03530            IS-MASTER-RECORD-IN-THE-FILE   = "Y"
03540            REWRITE ACCOUNT-MASTER-RECORD-I-O
03550        ELSE
03560        IF IS-MASTER-RECORD-IN-WORK-AREA = "N" AND
03570            IS-MASTER-RECORD-IN-THE-FILE   = "Y"
03580            DELETE ACCOUNT-MASTER-FILE-I-O.
03590        IF STATUS-KEY-1 NOT = ZERO
03600            DISPLAY " MASTER FILE WRITE STATUS = ", FILE-CHECK
03610            PERFORM TERMINATION
03620            STOP RUN.
03630
```

(continued)

If PROCESS-MASTER-RECORD finds a master record whose key is equal to the key of the current transaction, it READs the master record into the master area and sets both flags, IS-MASTER-RECORD-IN-WORK-AREA and IS-MASTER-RECORD-IN-THE-FILE, to "Y." If no master record is found with a key equal to the key of the current transaction, nothing is placed in the master area and both flags are set to "N."

After PROCESS-MASTER-RECORD executes, the paragraph PROCESS-TRANSACTION-RECORD executes APPLY-TRANSACTION. APPLY-TRANS-ACTION performs validity checks and carries out the actions implied by each particular transaction. Among the validity checks is one to see that a master record is in the master area if one is supposed to be there and that nothing is in the master area if nothing is supposed to be there. Remember that for most transactions, namely a deposit, a withdrawal, a name change, and a deletion, there must be in the master area a master record whose key is equal to the key of the transaction. But for adding a new account, there most definitely must not be a master record with the key of the transaction, for that would mean that the transaction was trying to create a record for an Account Number that is already in the file.

So in the course of its execution, APPLY-TRANSACTION might leave both flags alone (if it does a deposit, a withdrawal, or a name change), or it might set IS-MASTER-RECORD-IN-WORK-AREA to "N" (if it does a deletion), or it might set IS-MASTER-RECORD-IN-WORK-AREA to "Y" (if it builds a new master record in the master area). Notice that APPLY-TRANSACTION can never change the flag IS-MASTER-RECORD-IN-THE-FILE, for APPLY-TRANSACTION never acts directly upon the file on disk.

After APPLY-TRANSACTION has applied the transaction to the master record in the master area, CHECK-TO-WRITE-MASTER executes. CHECK-TO-WRITE-MASTER determines whether or not there is a master record in the master area and what to do about it. If there is a master record in the master area, CHECK-TO-WRITE-MASTER will want to put the record onto the master file. But what about this master record to be put onto the file — is it a new record being added to the file or is it replacing a record already on the file? CHECK-TO-WRITE-MASTER examines the flag IS-MASTER-RECORD-IN-THE-FILE to determine whether it should WRITE a new record onto the master file, as at line 03500, or **REWRITE** an existing master record, as at line 03540. Any successful WRITE statement to a file with any kind of organization always adds a record to the file. A random WRITE to an indexed file tells COBOL to find the place on the file where this new record should be slipped in and to move some existing records around if necessary to make space for it. A REWRITE statement tells COBOL to find the place on the file where this key is already located, and replace the existing record with a new one.

If CHECK-TO-WRITE-MASTER finds that there is no master record in the master area but that there is on the file a master record whose key is equal to the transaction key, it means that there was a successful deletion transaction to this record in the master area and that now the record must be physically DELETEd from the master file. CHECK-TO-WRITE-MASTER does this if necessary at line 03580. Notice that the object of the DELETE verb is a file name, whereas the object of the WRITE and REWRITE verbs is a record name.

Figure 14.5   (continued)

```
03640    READ-A-TRANSACTION-RECORD.
03650        READ TRANSACTION-FILE-IN INTO TRANSACTION-INPUT-AREA
03660            AT END
03670                MOVE HIGH-VALUES TO TRANSACTION-INPUT-AREA.
03680        IF TRANSACTION-INPUT-AREA NOT EQUAL TO HIGH-VALUES
03690            ADD 1 TO NUMBER-OF-INPUT-RECORDS-W.
03700
03710    APPLY-TRANSACTION.
03720        IF NEW-ACCOUNT
03730            PERFORM CHECK-FOR-VALID-NEW-ACCOUNT
03740        ELSE
03750        IF DEPOSIT
03760            PERFORM CHECK-FOR-VALID-DEPOSIT
03770        ELSE
03780        IF WITHDRAWAL
03790            PERFORM CHECK-FOR-VALID-WITHDRAWAL
03800        ELSE
03810        IF NAME-CHANGE
03820            PERFORM CHECK-FOR-VALID-NAME-CHANGE
03830        ELSE
03840        IF DELETION
03850            PERFORM CHECK-FOR-VALID-DELETION
03860        ELSE
03870            ADD 1 TO NUMBER-OF-ERRONEOUS-RECORDS-W
03880            PERFORM WRITE-INVALID-CODE-LINE.
03890
03900    CHECK-FOR-VALID-NEW-ACCOUNT.
03910        IF IS-MASTER-RECORD-IN-WORK-AREA = "Y"
03920            ADD 1 TO NUMBER-OF-ERRONEOUS-RECORDS-W
03930            PERFORM WRITE-NEW-ACCT-INVALID-LINE
03940        ELSE
03950        IF DEPOSIT-AMOUNT NOT NUMERIC
03960            ADD 1 TO NUMBER-OF-ERRONEOUS-RECORDS-W
03970            PERFORM WRITE-DEPOSIT-INVALID-LINE
03980        ELSE
03990        IF DEPOSITOR-NAME-MISSING
04000            ADD 1 TO NUMBER-OF-ERRONEOUS-RECORDS-W
04010            PERFORM WRITE-NAME-MISSING-LINE
04020        ELSE
04030            MOVE DEPOSITOR-NAME-NEW-ACCOUNT TO DEPOSITOR-NAME-M
04040            MOVE TODAYS-DATE TO DATE-OF-LAST-TRANSACTION-M
04050            MOVE DEPOSIT-AMOUNT TO CURRENT-BALANCE-M
04060            PERFORM WRITE-NEW-ACCOUNT-LINE
04070            MOVE "Y" TO IS-MASTER-RECORD-IN-WORK-AREA.
04080
04090    CHECK-FOR-VALID-DEPOSIT.
04100        IF DEPOSIT-AMOUNT NOT NUMERIC
04110            ADD 1 TO NUMBER-OF-ERRONEOUS-RECORDS-W
04120            PERFORM WRITE-DEPOSIT-INVALID-LINE
04130        ELSE
04140        IF IS-MASTER-RECORD-IN-WORK-AREA = "N"
04150            ADD 1 TO NUMBER-OF-ERRONEOUS-RECORDS-W
04160            PERFORM WRITE-MASTER-MISSING-LINE
04170        ELSE
04180            ADD DEPOSIT-AMOUNT TO CURRENT-BALANCE-M
04190            MOVE TODAYS-DATE TO DATE-OF-LAST-TRANSACTION-M
04200            PERFORM WRITE-DEPOSIT-LINE.
04210
```

```
04220    CHECK-FOR-VALID-WITHDRAWAL.
04230        IF WITHDRAWAL-AMOUNT NOT NUMERIC
04240            ADD 1 TO NUMBER-OF-ERRONEOUS-RECORDS-W
04250            PERFORM WRITE-WITHDRAWAL-INVALID-LINE
04260        ELSE
04270        IF IS-MASTER-RECORD-IN-WORK-AREA = "N"
04280            ADD 1 TO NUMBER-OF-ERRONEOUS-RECORDS-W
04290            PERFORM WRITE-MASTER-MISSING-LINE
04300        ELSE
04310            SUBTRACT WITHDRAWAL-AMOUNT FROM CURRENT-BALANCE-M
04320            MOVE TODAYS-DATE TO DATE-OF-LAST-TRANSACTION-M
04330            PERFORM WRITE-WITHDRAWAL-LINE.
04340
04350    CHECK-FOR-VALID-NAME-CHANGE.
04360        IF REPLACEMENT-NAME-MISSING
04370            ADD 1 TO NUMBER-OF-ERRONEOUS-RECORDS-W
04380            PERFORM WRITE-NAME-MISSING-LINE
04390        ELSE
04400        IF IS-MASTER-RECORD-IN-WORK-AREA = "N"
04410            ADD 1 TO NUMBER-OF-ERRONEOUS-RECORDS-W
04420            PERFORM WRITE-MASTER-MISSING-LINE
04430        ELSE
04440            MOVE DEPOSITOR-NAME TO DEPOSITOR-NAME-M
04450            MOVE TODAYS-DATE TO DATE-OF-LAST-TRANSACTION-M
04460            PERFORM WRITE-NAME-CHANGE-LINE.
04470
04480    CHECK-FOR-VALID-DELETION.
04490        IF IS-MASTER-RECORD-IN-WORK-AREA = "N"
04500            ADD 1 TO NUMBER-OF-ERRONEOUS-RECORDS-W
04510            PERFORM WRITE-MASTER-MISSING-LINE
04520        ELSE
04530            PERFORM WRITE-DELETION-LINE
04540            MOVE "N" TO IS-MASTER-RECORD-IN-WORK-AREA.
04550
04560    WRITE-NEW-ACCOUNT-LINE.
04570        MOVE ACCOUNT-NUMBER-T
04580            TO ACCOUNT-NUMBER-OUT IN NEW-ACCOUNT-LINE.
04590        MOVE DEPOSIT-AMOUNT
04600            TO DEPOSIT-AMOUNT-OUT IN NEW-ACCOUNT-LINE.
04610        IF 1 + LINE-COUNT-ER GREATER THAN PAGE-LIMIT
04620            PERFORM WRITE-REGISTER-HEADINGS.
04630        WRITE REGISTER-RECORD-OUT FROM NEW-ACCOUNT-LINE.
04640        ADD 1 TO LINE-COUNT-ER.
04650        ADD DEPOSIT-AMOUNT TO DEPOSIT-TOTAL-W.
04660        ADD 1 TO NUMBER-OF-NEW-ACCOUNTS-W.
04670
04680    WRITE-DEPOSIT-LINE.
04690        MOVE ACCOUNT-NUMBER-T TO ACCOUNT-NUMBER-OUT IN DEPOSIT-LINE.
04700        MOVE DEPOSIT-AMOUNT TO DEPOSIT-AMOUNT-OUT IN DEPOSIT-LINE.
04710        IF 1 + LINE-COUNT-ER GREATER THAN PAGE-LIMIT
04720            PERFORM WRITE-REGISTER-HEADINGS.
04730        WRITE REGISTER-RECORD-OUT FROM DEPOSIT-LINE.
04740        ADD 1 TO LINE-COUNT-ER.
04750        ADD DEPOSIT-AMOUNT TO DEPOSIT-TOTAL-W.
04760        ADD 1 TO NUMBER-OF-DEPOSITS-W.
04770
04780    WRITE-WITHDRAWAL-LINE.
04790        MOVE ACCOUNT-NUMBER-T
04800            TO ACCOUNT-NUMBER-OUT IN WITHDRAWAL-LINE.
04810        MOVE WITHDRAWAL-AMOUNT TO
04820            WITHDRAWAL-AMOUNT-OUT IN WITHDRAWAL-LINE.
04830        IF 1 + LINE-COUNT-ER GREATER THAN PAGE-LIMIT
04840            PERFORM WRITE-REGISTER-HEADINGS.
04850        WRITE REGISTER-RECORD-OUT FROM WITHDRAWAL-LINE.
04860        ADD 1 TO LINE-COUNT-ER.
04870        ADD WITHDRAWAL-AMOUNT TO WITHDRAWAL-TOTAL-W.
04880        ADD 1 TO NUMBER-OF-WITHDRAWALS-W.
04890
04900    WRITE-DEPOSIT-INVALID-LINE.
04910        MOVE DEPOSIT-AMOUNT-X TO
04920            DEPOSIT-AMOUNT-OUT IN DEPOSIT-AMOUNT-INVALID-MSG.
04930        MOVE DEPOSIT-AMOUNT-INVALID-MSG TO ERROR-MESSAGE.
04940        PERFORM WRITE-ERROR-LINE.
04950
```

(continued)

Figure 14.5   (continued)

```
04960    WRITE-WITHDRAWAL-INVALID-LINE.
04970        MOVE WITHDRAWAL-AMOUNT-X TO WITHDRAWAL-AMOUNT-E.
04980        MOVE WITHDRAWAL-AMOUNT-INVALID-MSG TO ERROR-MESSAGE.
04990        PERFORM WRITE-ERROR-LINE.
05000
05010    WRITE-NAME-MISSING-LINE.
05020        MOVE "DEPOSITOR NAME MISSING" TO ERROR-MESSAGE.
05030        PERFORM WRITE-ERROR-LINE.
05040
05050    WRITE-NAME-CHANGE-LINE.
05060        MOVE ACCOUNT-NUMBER-T
05070            TO ACCOUNT-NUMBER-OUT IN NAME-CHANGE-LINE.
05080        MOVE DEPOSITOR-NAME TO DEPOSITOR-NAME-OUT.
05090        IF 1 + LINE-COUNT-ER GREATER THAN PAGE-LIMIT
05100            PERFORM WRITE-REGISTER-HEADINGS.
05110        WRITE REGISTER-RECORD-OUT FROM NAME-CHANGE-LINE.
05120        ADD 1 TO LINE-COUNT-ER.
05130        ADD 1 TO NUMBER-OF-NAME-CHANGES-W.
05140
05150    WRITE-DELETION-LINE.
05160        MOVE ACCOUNT-NUMBER-T TO ACCOUNT-NUMBER-OUT IN DELETION-LINE.
05170        MOVE CURRENT-BALANCE-M TO CURRENT-BALANCE-M-OUT.
05180        IF 1 + LINE-COUNT-ER GREATER THAN PAGE-LIMIT
05190            PERFORM WRITE-REGISTER-HEADINGS.
05200        WRITE REGISTER-RECORD-OUT FROM DELETION-LINE.
05210        ADD 1 TO LINE-COUNT-ER.
05220        ADD CURRENT-BALANCE-M TO WITHDRAWAL-TOTAL-W.
05230        ADD 1 TO NUMBER-OF-CLOSED-ACCOUNTS-W.
05240
05250    WRITE-INVALID-CODE-LINE.
05260        MOVE TRANSACTION-CODE TO TRANSACTION-CODE-OUT.
05270        MOVE INVALID-CODE-MSG TO ERROR-MESSAGE.
05280        PERFORM WRITE-ERROR-LINE.
05290
05300    WRITE-MASTER-MISSING-LINE.
05310        MOVE "MASTER RECORD DOES NOT EXIST" TO ERROR-MESSAGE.
05320        PERFORM WRITE-ERROR-LINE.
05330
05340    WRITE-NEW-ACCT-INVALID-LINE.
05350        MOVE "ACCOUNT NUMBER ALREADY ON FILE. NEW ACCOUNT INVALID."
05360            TO ERROR-MESSAGE.
05370        PERFORM WRITE-ERROR-LINE.
05380
05390    WRITE-ERROR-LINE.
05400        IF 1 + ERROR-LINE-COUNTER GREATER THAN ERROR-PAGE-LIMIT
05410            PERFORM WRITE-ERROR-REPORT-HEADINGS.
05420        MOVE ACCOUNT-NUMBER-T TO ACCOUNT-NUMBER-E.
05430        WRITE ERROR-RECORD-OUT FROM ERROR-LINE.
05440        ADD 1 TO ERROR-LINE-COUNTER.
05450
05460    TERMINATION.
05470        PERFORM PRODUCE-TOTAL-LINES.
05480        CLOSE TRANSACTION-FILE-IN
05490            ACCOUNT-MASTER-FILE-I-O
05500            ERROR-FILE-OUT
05510            TRANSACTION-REGISTER-FILE-OUT.
05520
05530    PRODUCE-TOTAL-LINES.
05540        MOVE DEPOSIT-TOTAL-W      TO DEPOSIT-TOTAL-OUT.
05550        MOVE WITHDRAWAL-TOTAL-W TO WITHDRAWAL-TOTAL-OUT.
05560        WRITE REGISTER-RECORD-OUT FROM FINAL-LINE-1 AFTER 3.
05570        WRITE REGISTER-RECORD-OUT FROM FINAL-LINE-2 AFTER 2.
05580        MOVE NUMBER-OF-NEW-ACCOUNTS-W TO NUMBER-OF-NEW-ACCOUNTS-OUT.
05590        WRITE REGISTER-RECORD-OUT FROM FINAL-LINE-3 AFTER 2.
05600        MOVE NUMBER-OF-DEPOSITS-W TO NUMBER-OF-DEPOSITS-OUT.
05610        WRITE REGISTER-RECORD-OUT FROM FINAL-LINE-4 AFTER 2.
05620        MOVE NUMBER-OF-WITHDRAWALS-W TO NUMBER-OF-WITHDRAWALS-OUT.
05630        WRITE REGISTER-RECORD-OUT FROM FINAL-LINE-5 AFTER 2.
05640        MOVE NUMBER-OF-NAME-CHANGES-W TO NUMBER-OF-NAME-CHANGES-OUT.
05650        WRITE REGISTER-RECORD-OUT FROM FINAL-LINE-6 AFTER 2.
05660        MOVE NUMBER-OF-CLOSED-ACCOUNTS-W
05670            TO NUMBER-OF-CLOSED-ACCOUNTS-OUT.
05680        WRITE REGISTER-RECORD-OUT FROM FINAL-LINE-7 AFTER 2.
05690        MOVE NUMBER-OF-ERRONEOUS-RECORDS-W
05700            TO NUMBER-OF-ERRONEOUS-RECRDS-OUT.
05710        WRITE REGISTER-RECORD-OUT FROM FINAL-LINE-8 AFTER 2.
05720        MOVE NUMBER-OF-INPUT-RECORDS-W
05730            TO NUMBER-OF-INPUT-RECORDS-OUT.
05740        WRITE REGISTER-RECORD-OUT FROM FINAL-LINE-9 AFTER 2.
```

A random WRITE, REWRITE, or DELETE to an indexed file sets the STATUS code if one is specified for the file. The 1974 ANSI standard meanings of the STATUS codes for a random WRITE to an indexed file are given in Table 14-3.

Table 14-3

1974 ANSI standard STATUS codes related to writing an indexed file randomly.

Status Code	Meaning
00	Successful completion
02	Successful completion, and the record just written created a duplicate key value for an ALTERNATE RECORD KEY for which DUPLICATES are allowed
22	Invalid key — an attempt has been made to WRITE a record that would create an invalid duplicate key
24	Invalid key — boundary violation (attempt to WRITE past the physical end of the file)
30	Permanent error (hardware malfunction)

The 1974 meanings of the STATUS codes for a random REWRITE to an indexed file are given in Table 14-4.

Table 14-4

1974 ANSI standard STATUS codes related to rewriting an indexed file randomly.

Status Code	Meaning
00	Successful completion
02	Successful completion, and the record just written created a duplicate key value for an ALTERNATE RECORD KEY for which DUPLICATES are allowed
22	Invalid key — an attempt has been made to REWRITE a record that would create an invalid duplicate key
23	Invalid key — the record to be rewritten over is not on the file
30	Permanent error (hardware malfunction)

The 1974 meanings of the STATUS codes for a random DELETE to an indexed file are given in Table 14-5.

Table 14-5

1974 ANSI standard STATUS codes related to deleting records from an indexed file randomly.

Status Code	Meaning
00	Successful completion
23	Invalid key — the record to be DELETEd is not on the file
30	Permanent error (hardware malfunction)

In all cases, your own COBOL system may have additional codes in the range 90 through 99.

Program P14-02 was run with the transaction input data shown in Figure 14.6 and the master file created by Program P14-01. Program P14-02 produced the report output shown in Figure 14.7.

Figure 14.6   Transaction input to Program P14-02.

```
----------------------------------------------------------------------------
         1         2         3         4         5         6         7         8
12345678901234567890123456789012345678901234567890123456789012345678901234567890
----------------------------------------------------------------------------
200077000150000
200371000150000
70038500007500JAMES WASHINGTON
10039200007500INEZ WASHINGTON
400084JOHN & SALLY DUPRINO
20016100125634
30002800150050
10042000150000JOHN RICE
30022000002460
20008400357429
20009100150000
400140BETH DENNY
10039900014ZOOGARY NASTI
200007)))$%)))
20039100064200
30001400100000
20002100012750
30011900002735
70042700002500GREG PRUITT
20013300256300
400220GENE & THERESA GALLI
20012600035000
30016800011000
400266
20002800015327
20009100120000
20021000025000
20021000025000
10009200043200GENE GALLI
30009100050000
20027300172500
400098GEORGE & ANN CULHANE
500168
20017500019202
500182
20021000025000
20028000231700
80031500013798
200182
5
10030800017000AL MARRELLA
20030800005000
10037100001000THOMAS HERR
400032GENE GALLI
10037100015000ALISE MARKOVITZ
10040600120000
10041300010000BILL HAYES
10039800001000JUAN ALVAREZ
30010500015025
```

EXERCISE 2

Write a program to randomly update the indexed inventory master file you created in Exercise 1, page 475. Use the same transaction formats that you used when you updated your sequential inventory master file in Exercise 3, Chapter 13, page 451.

Use the same report formats you used in Exercise 3, Chapter 13. Have your program print a line for each transaction processed. For a new inventory record created on the master file, set the Quantity on Hand field and the Dates of Last Withdrawal and Last Receipt to zero, and insert today's date into the Date Created and Date of Last Access fields.

For each existing master record that is updated, have your program insert today's date into the Date of Last Access field. Also for each existing master record that is updated, have your program check whether the Quantity on Hand is equal to or less than the Reorder Point, and print a message showing the Reorder Quantity and the word REORDER if it is. If an attempt is made to delete a Part Number having a nonzero Quantity on Hand, do not delete it. Instead, count the transaction as erroneous and have your program print the Quantity on Hand and a message NONZERO QUANTITY ON HAND on the error report. Save the updated file for use later in this chapter.

Using Dynamic Access

Our next program demonstrates how an indexed file can be accessed sequentially and randomly in a single run. Program P14-03 lists selected records, and the records to be listed may be selected in either of two ways. We can ask Program P14-03 to list the contents of the master record for a particular Account Number, or we can ask it to list the contents of all the master records for all the Depositor Names that start with a particular letter of the alphabet. The requests may be in any order and the two types of requests may be mixed in any desired way.

To find a record on the master file for a particular Account Number, Program P14-03 does a random READ the way Program P14-02 did. But to find all the master records for all Depositor Names beginning with a given letter, Program P14-03 has to combine random access with sequential access. First it uses its random-access capability to find the first record for the given letter of the alphabet and then READs the file sequentially on Depositor Name, listing out the contents of all master records for that same letter. The formats of the two types of transactions accepted by Program P14-03 are:

Positions	Field
1	Code 6
2–6	Account Number
1	Code 7
2	First letter of Depositor Name

The meanings of the transaction Codes are:

6 — List the contents of the master record for this Account Number
7 — List the contents of all the master records for all Depositor Names that start with this letter

The hierarchy diagram for Program P14-03 is similar to the one for Program P13-01, which listed selected records from our sequential savings-account master file. Program P13-01 listed records only on their Account Number and so had only

Figure 14.17   Report output from Program P14-02.

```
                           ROBBEM STATE BANK
                           106 WEST 10TH ST.
                           BROOKLYN, NY  11212

                    SAVINGS ACCOUNT TRANSACTION REGISTER
        DATE  4/09/88                                    PAGE   1


            ACCOUNT      DEPOSITS       WITHDRAWALS        NOTES
            NUMBER


            00077         150.00
            00392          75.00                        NEW ACCOUNT
            00084      JOHN & SALLY DUPRINO             NAME CHANGE
            00161       1,256.34
            00028                        1,500.50
            00420       1,500.00                        NEW ACCOUNT
            00220                           24.60
            00084       3,574.29
            00091       1,500.00
            00140      BETH DENNY                       NAME CHANGE
            00391         642.00
            00014                        1,000.00
            00021         127.50
            00133       2,563.00
            00220      GENE & THERESA GALLI             NAME CHANGE
            00126         350.00
            00168                          110.00



                           ROBBEM STATE BANK
                           106 WEST 10TH ST.
                           BROOKLYN, NY  11212

                    SAVINGS ACCOUNT TRANSACTION REGISTER
        DATE  4/09/88                                    PAGE   2


            ACCOUNT      DEPOSITS       WITHDRAWALS        NOTES
            NUMBER


            00028         153.27
            00091       1,200.00
            00210         250.00
            00210         250.00
            00092         432.00                        NEW ACCOUNT
            00091                          500.00
            00273       1,725.00
            00098      GEORGE & ANN CULHANE             NAME CHANGE
            00168                           15.50       ACCOUNT CLOSED
            00175         192.02
            00210         250.00
            00280       2,317.00
            00308          50.00
            00371          10.00                        NEW ACCOUNT
            00032      GENE GALLI                       NAME CHANGE
            00413         100.00                        NEW ACCOUNT
            00398          10.00                        NEW ACCOUNT


        TOTALS        18,677.42        3,150.60

                           CONTROL COUNTS

                 NUMBER OF NEW ACCOUNTS          6

                 NUMBER OF DEPOSITS             17

                 NUMBER OF WITHDRAWALS           5

                 NUMBER OF NAME CHANGES          5

                 NUMBER OF CLOSED ACCOUNTS       1

                 NUMBER OF ERRORS               15

                 TOTAL                          49
```

```
                    ROBBEM STATE BANK
                    106 WEST 10TH ST.
                    BROOKLYN, NY   11212

                  SAVINGS ACCOUNT ERROR REPORT

DATE   4/09/88                             PAGE   1


    ACCOUNT                            NOTES
    NUMBER

     00371                    MASTER RECORD DOES NOT EXIST
     00385                    INVALID TRANSACTION CODE - 7
     00399                    DEPOSIT AMOUNT NOT NUMERIC - 00014Z00
     00007                    DEPOSIT AMOUNT NOT NUMERIC - )))$%)))
     00119                    MASTER RECORD DOES NOT EXIST
     00427                    INVALID TRANSACTION CODE - 7
     00266                    DEPOSITOR NAME MISSING
     00182                    MASTER RECORD DOES NOT EXIST
     00315                    INVALID TRANSACTION CODE - 8
     00182                    DEPOSIT AMOUNT NOT NUMERIC -
                              MASTER RECORD DOES NOT EXIST
     00308                    ACCOUNT NUMBER ALREADY ON FILE. NEW ACCOUNT INVALID.
     00371                    ACCOUNT NUMBER ALREADY ON FILE. NEW ACCOUNT INVALID.
     00406                    DEPOSITOR NAME MISSING
     00105                    WITHDRAWAL AMOUNT NOT NUMERIC - 00015025
```

one type of input transaction. In Program P14-03 we have two types of transactions, so the procedure for processing a transaction is more involved. The portion of the hierarchy diagram for "Process transaction record" and its subfunctions is shown in Figure 14.8. The box "Process one transaction" determines whether the transaction is asking for a listing of one master record by Account Number or for a listing of all the Depositor Names beginning with a certain letter and processes it accordingly.

Figure 14.8 Hierarchy diagram for "Process transaction record" and its subfunctions for Program P14-03.

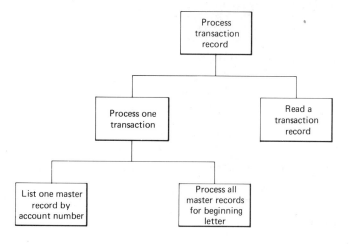

**A Program
Using
Dynamic
Access**

Program P14-03 is shown in Figure 14.9. The FILE-CONTROL entry at line 00180 shows the use of the ACCESS **DYNAMIC** clause. In ACCOUNT-MASTER-RECORD-IN, line 00350, the DEPOSITOR-NAME-M field is broken down into two elementary items. As you already know, COBOL can access an indexed file on its prime key and its alternate key(s). COBOL can also access an indexed file on any field that is a subordinate part of an alternate key field, provided that the subordinate field is at the left end of the alternate key field. Our field FIRST-LETTER-OF-DEPOSITOR-NAME is subordinate to and at the left end of the alternate key field DEPOSITOR-NAME-M, so Program P14-03 can access the master file on the basis of FIRST-LETTER-OF-DEPOSITOR-NAME. You will see how this feature is used when we look at the Procedure Division.

Figure 14.9 Program 14-03.

```
CB1 RELEASE 2.4                           IBM OS/VS COBOL  JULY  1, 1982


                              18.30.34       APR  9,1988


00010  IDENTIFICATION DIVISION.
00020   PROGRAM-ID. P14-03.
00030 *
00040 *     THIS PROGRAM LISTS SELECTED RECORDS FROM AN INDEXED
00050 *     MASTER FILE.
00060 *
00070 *************************************************************************
00080
00090  ENVIRONMENT DIVISION.
00100  CONFIGURATION SECTION.
00110  SOURCE-COMPUTER. IBM-370.
00120  OBJECT-COMPUTER. IBM-370.
00130
00140  INPUT-OUTPUT SECTION.
00150  FILE-CONTROL.
00160      SELECT ACCOUNT-MASTER-FILE-IN        ASSIGN TO DISKUNIT
00170          ORGANIZATION INDEXED
00180          ACCESS DYNAMIC
00190          RECORD KEY IS ACCOUNT-NUMBER-M
00200          ALTERNATE RECORD KEY IS DEPOSITOR-NAME-M
00210              WITH DUPLICATES
00220          STATUS IS MASTER-FILE-CHECK.
00230      SELECT TRANSACTION-FILE-IN           ASSIGN TO INFILE.
00240      SELECT LISTING-FILE-OUT              ASSIGN TO PRINTER1.
00250      SELECT ERROR-FILE-OUT                ASSIGN TO PRINTER2.
00260
00270 *************************************************************************
00280
00290  DATA DIVISION.
00300  FILE SECTION.
00310  FD  ACCOUNT-MASTER-FILE-IN
00320      LABEL RECORDS ARE STANDARD
00330      RECORD CONTAINS 39 CHARACTERS.
00340
00350  01  ACCOUNT-MASTER-RECORD-IN.
00360      05   ACCOUNT-NUMBER-M              PIC X(5).
00370      05   DEPOSITOR-NAME-M.
00380          10  FIRST-LETTER-OF-DEPOSITOR-NAME
00390                                         PIC X.
00400          10  FILLER                     PIC X(19).
00410      05   DATE-OF-LAST-TRANSACTION-M    PIC 9(6).
00420      05   CURRENT-BALANCE-M             PIC S9(6)V99.
00430
00440  FD  TRANSACTION-FILE-IN
00450      LABEL RECORDS ARE OMITTED
00460      RECORD CONTAINS 80 CHARACTERS.
00470
00480  01  TRANSACTION-RECORD-IN             PIC X(80).
00490
00500  FD  LISTING-FILE-OUT
00510      LABEL RECORDS ARE OMITTED.
```

```
00520
00530   01   LISTING-RECORD-OUT              PIC X(79).
00540
00550   FD   ERROR-FILE-OUT
00560        LABEL RECORDS ARE OMITTED.
00570
00580   01   ERROR-RECORD-OUT                PIC X(71).
00590
00600   WORKING-STORAGE SECTION.
00610   01   MASTER-FILE-CHECK.
00620        05   MASTER-STATUS-KEY-1        PIC X      VALUE ZERO.
00630        05   MASTER-STATUS-KEY-2        PIC X      VALUE ZERO.
00640   01   IS-THERE-A-MASTER-RECORD        PIC X.
00650   01   NUMBER-OF-INPUT-RECORDS-W       PIC S9(3) VALUE ZERO.
00660   01   NUMBER-OF-ERRONEOUS-RECORDS-W   PIC S9(3) VALUE ZERO.
00670   01   NUMBER-OF-SELECTED-RECORDS-W     PIC S9(3) VALUE ZERO.
00680   01   CURRENT-BALANCE-TOTAL-W         PIC S9(7)V99    VALUE 0.
00690   01   PAGE-NUMBER-W                   PIC S99    VALUE 0.
00700   01   ERROR-PAGE-NUMBER-W             PIC S99    VALUE 0.
00710   01   PAGE-LIMIT        COMP SYNC     PIC S99    VALUE 35.
00720   01   LINE-COUNT-ER     COMP SYNC     PIC S99.
00730   01   ERROR-PAGE-LIMIT COMP SYNC      PIC S99    VALUE 45.
00740   01   ERROR-LINE-COUNTER COMP SYNC    PIC S99.
00750   01   BLANK-LINE                      PIC X      VALUE SPACE.
00760   01   TODAYS-DATE.
00770        05   TODAYS-YEAR                PIC 99.
00780        05   TODAYS-MONTH-AND-DAY       PIC 9(4).
00790
00800   01   TRANSACTION-INPUT-AREA.
00810        05   TRANSACTION-CODE-T         PIC X.
00820             88   ACCOUNT-NUMBER-REQUEST   VALUE "6".
00830             88   DEPOSITOR-NAMES-REQUEST  VALUE "7".
00840             88   TRANSACTION-CODE-IS-VALID
00850                                         VALUES "6", "7".
00860        05   TRANSACTION-KEY            PIC X(5).
00870        05   ACCOUNT-NUMBER-T REDEFINES TRANSACTION-KEY
00880                                         PIC X(5).
00890        05   LETTER-KEY        REDEFINES TRANSACTION-KEY.
00900             10   STARTING-LETTER-T     PIC X.
00910             10   FILLER                PIC X(4).
```

(continued)

The TRANSACTION-INPUT-AREA, at line 00800, is defined a little differently from before. Since the two different kinds of transactions contain two different kinds of fields that will be used to access the master file, it is convenient to define the single field TRANSACTION-KEY, as at line 00860, and to redefine that field as both ACCOUNT-NUMBER-T and STARTING-LETTER-T. Thus Program P14-03 can use TRANSACTION-KEY to access the master file on the basis of either the Account Number or the Depositor Name. You will see how TRANSACTION-KEY is used when we look at the Procedure Division.

Program P14-03 has some complications that we have not seen in earlier programs. All of the complications stem from the fact that the two different types of transactions provide two different kinds of access keys to the master file. In all our earlier programs dealing with master files, only the Account Number was used to access the master file regardless of what kind of transaction the program was processing. In Program P14-03, on the other hand, we use a single field, TRANSACTION-KEY, to hold the key of the current transaction whether that key is a letter of the alphabet followed by four blanks or a five-character Account Number.

Nearly all the complications relating to the TRANSACTION-KEY can be confined to the portion of the program that READs transaction records. This shows a general principle of the logic we are using to process our master files: Any complications regarding the formats of the transaction or master records can usually be confined to the lowest levels of the hierarchy diagram, namely to the READing of the files. The logic expressed in the upper levels of the diagram remains unchanged, or nearly so.

Figure 14.9   (continued)

```
00920
00930    01    REPORT-HEADING-1.
00940          05   FILLER     PIC X(39) VALUE SPACES.
00950          05   FILLER     PIC X(17) VALUE "ROBBEM STATE BANK".
00960
00970    01    REPORT-HEADING-2.
00980          05   FILLER     PIC X(39) VALUE SPACES.
00990          05   FILLER     PIC X(17) VALUE "106 WEST 10TH ST.".
01000
01010    01    REPORT-HEADING-3.
01020          05   FILLER     PIC X(38) VALUE SPACES.
01030          05   FILLER     PIC X(19) VALUE "BROOKLYN, NY  11212".
01040
01050    01    PAGE-HEADING-1.
01060          05   FILLER     PIC X(35) VALUE SPACES.
01070          05   FILLER     PIC X(25) VALUE "SELECTED SAVINGS ACCOUNTS".
01080
01090    01    ERROR-HEADING-1.
01100          05   FILLER     PIC X(39) VALUE SPACES.
01110          05   FILLER     PIC X(16) VALUE "SELECTION ERRORS".
01120
01130    01    PAGE-HEADING-2.
01140          05   FILLER             PIC X(25) VALUE SPACES.
01150          05   FILLER             PIC X(5)  VALUE "DATE".
01160          05   TODAYS-MONTH-AND-DAY     PIC Z9/99/.
01170          05   TODAYS-YEAR  PIC 99B(23).
01180          05   FILLER             PIC X(5)  VALUE "PAGE".
01190          05   PAGE-NUMBER-OUT          PIC Z9.
01200
01210    01    PAGE-HEADING-3.
01220          05   FILLER             PIC X(21) VALUE SPACES.
01230          05   FILLER             PIC X(12) VALUE "ACCOUNT".
01240          05   FILLER             PIC X(12) VALUE "CURRENT".
01250          05   FILLER             PIC X(19) VALUE "DATE OF LAST".
01260          05   FILLER             PIC X(9)  VALUE "DEPOSITOR".
01270
01280    01    ERROR-HEADING-3.
01290          05   FILLER             PIC X(21) VALUE SPACES.
01300          05   FILLER             PIC X(12) VALUE "ACCOUNT".
01310
01320    01    PAGE-HEADING-4.
01330          05   FILLER             PIC X(21) VALUE SPACES.
01340          05   FILLER             PIC X(12) VALUE "NUMBER".
01350          05   FILLER             PIC X(12) VALUE "BALANCE".
01360          05   FILLER             PIC X(19) VALUE "TRANSACTION".
01370          05   FILLER             PIC X(4)  VALUE "NAME".
01380
01390    01    ERROR-HEADING-4.
01400          05   FILLER             PIC X(21) VALUE SPACES.
01410          05   FILLER             PIC X(12) VALUE "NUMBER".
01420
01430    01    REPORT-LINE.
01440          05   FILLER             PIC X(22)  VALUE SPACES.
01450          05   ACCOUNT-NUMBER-OUT          PIC X(5)B(4).
01460          05   CURRENT-BALANCE-OUT         PIC ZZZ,ZZZ.99B(7).
01470          05   DATE-OF-LAST-TRANSACTION-OUT PIC 9(6)B(5).
01480          05   DEPOSITOR-NAME-OUT          PIC X(20).
01490
01500    01    INVALID-CODE-LINE.
01510          05   FILLER     PIC X(22)  VALUE SPACES.
01520          05   TRANSACTION-KEY-OUT     PIC X(5)B(16).
01530          05   FILLER     PIC X(15)  VALUE "INVALID CODE - ".
01540          05   TRANSACTION-CODE-OUT    PIC X.
01550
01560    01    MASTER-MISSING-LINE.
01570          05   FILLER     PIC X(22)  VALUE SPACES.
01580          05   TRANSACTION-KEY-OUT     PIC X(5)B(16).
01590          05   FILLER     PIC X(28)
01600               VALUE "MASTER RECORD DOES NOT EXIST".
```

```
01610
01620   01  FINAL-LINE-1.
01630       05  FILLER              PIC X(23) VALUE SPACES.
01640       05  FILLER              PIC X(6)  VALUE "TOTAL".
01650       05  CURRENT-BALANCE-TOTAL-OUT PIC Z,ZZZ,ZZZ.99.
01660
01670   01  FINAL-LINE-2.
01680       05  FILLER              PIC X(40) VALUE SPACES.
01690       05  FILLER              PIC X(14) VALUE "CONTROL COUNTS".
01700
01710   01  FINAL-LINE-3.
01720       05  FILLER              PIC X(34) VALUE SPACES.
01730       05  FILLER              PIC X(28)
01740                               VALUE "NUMBER OF SELECTED RECORDS".
01750       05  NUMBER-OF-SELECTED-RECORDS-OUT  PIC ZZ9.
01760
01770   01  FINAL-LINE-4.
01780       05  FILLER              PIC X(34) VALUE SPACES.
01790       05  FILLER              PIC X(28)
01800                               VALUE "NUMBER OF ERRONEOUS RECORDS".
01810       05  NUMBER-OF-ERRONEOUS-RECRDS-OUT PIC ZZ9.
01820
01830   01  FINAL-LINE-5.
01840       05  FILLER              PIC X(34) VALUE SPACES.
01850       05  FILLER              PIC X(28)
01860                               VALUE "NUMBER OF INPUT RECORDS".
01870       05  NUMBER-OF-INPUT-RECORDS-OUT     PIC ZZ9.
01880
01890   01  NO-TRANSACTIONS.
01900       05  FILLER              PIC X(21) VALUE SPACES.
01910       05  FILLER              PIC X(20) VALUE "NO TRANSACTION INPUT".
01920
01930   ***********************************************************************
01940
01950   PROCEDURE DIVISION.
01960   DECLARATIVES.
01970   DUMMY-USE SECTION.
01980       USE AFTER ERROR PROCEDURE ACCOUNT-MASTER-FILE-IN.
01990   END DECLARATIVES.
02000
02010   NONDECLARATIVES SECTION.
02020   LIST-RECORDS.
02030       PERFORM INITIALIZATION.
02040       PERFORM PROCESS-ONE-KEY UNTIL
02050           TRANSACTION-INPUT-AREA IS EQUAL TO HIGH-VALUES.
02060       PERFORM TERMINATION.
02070       STOP RUN.
02080
02090   INITIALIZATION.
02100       OPEN INPUT   ACCOUNT-MASTER-FILE-IN
02110                    TRANSACTION-FILE-IN
02120            OUTPUT  LISTING-FILE-OUT
02130                    ERROR-FILE-OUT.
02140       IF MASTER-FILE-CHECK NOT = ZEROS
02150           DISPLAY " MASTER FILE OPEN STATUS = ", MASTER-FILE-CHECK
02160           CLOSE ACCOUNT-MASTER-FILE-IN
02170                 TRANSACTION-FILE-IN
02180                 LISTING-FILE-OUT
02190                 ERROR-FILE-OUT
02200           STOP RUN.
02210       ACCEPT TODAYS-DATE FROM DATE.
02220       MOVE CORR TODAYS-DATE TO PAGE-HEADING-2.
02230       PERFORM PRODUCE-REPORT-HEADINGS.
02240       PERFORM READ-A-TRANSACTION-RECORD.
02250       IF TRANSACTION-INPUT-AREA = HIGH-VALUES
02260           WRITE LISTING-RECORD-OUT FROM NO-TRANSACTIONS.
02270
02280   PROCESS-ONE-KEY.
02290       PERFORM PROCESS-MASTER-RECORD.
02300       PERFORM PROCESS-TRANSACTION-RECORD.
02310
```

(continued)

Figure 14.9   (continued)

```
02320    READ-A-TRANSACTION-RECORD.
02330        MOVE ZERO TO TRANSACTION-CODE-T.
02340        PERFORM READ-TRANSACTION-FILE UNTIL
02350            TRANSACTION-CODE-IS-VALID OR
02360            TRANSACTION-INPUT-AREA = HIGH-VALUES.
02370        IF DEPOSITOR-NAMES-REQUEST
02380            MOVE STARTING-LETTER-T TO TRANSACTION-KEY.
02390
02400    READ-TRANSACTION-FILE.
02410        READ TRANSACTION-FILE-IN INTO TRANSACTION-INPUT-AREA
02420            AT END
02430                MOVE HIGH-VALUES TO TRANSACTION-INPUT-AREA.
02440        IF TRANSACTION-INPUT-AREA NOT = HIGH-VALUES
02450            ADD 1 TO NUMBER-OF-INPUT-RECORDS-W
02460            IF NOT TRANSACTION-CODE-IS-VALID
02470                ADD 1 TO NUMBER-OF-ERRONEOUS-RECORDS-W
02480                PERFORM WRITE-INVALID-CODE-LINE.
02490
02500    PROCESS-MASTER-RECORD.
02510        IF ACCOUNT-NUMBER-REQUEST
02520            MOVE TRANSACTION-KEY TO ACCOUNT-NUMBER-M
02530            READ ACCOUNT-MASTER-FILE-IN
02540        ELSE
02550            MOVE TRANSACTION-KEY TO FIRST-LETTER-OF-DEPOSITOR-NAME
02560            START ACCOUNT-MASTER-FILE-IN
02570                KEY = FIRST-LETTER-OF-DEPOSITOR-NAME.
02580        IF MASTER-STATUS-KEY-1 = "0"
02590            MOVE "Y" TO IS-THERE-A-MASTER-RECORD
02600        ELSE
02610        IF MASTER-FILE-CHECK = "23"
02620            MOVE "N" TO IS-THERE-A-MASTER-RECORD
02630        ELSE
02640            DISPLAY " MASTER FILE RANDOM READ/START STATUS = ",
02650                MASTER-FILE-CHECK,
02660            PERFORM TERMINATION
02670            STOP RUN.
02680
02690    PROCESS-TRANSACTION-RECORD.
02700        PERFORM PROCESS-ONE-TRANSACTION.
02710        PERFORM READ-A-TRANSACTION-RECORD.
02720
02730    PROCESS-ONE-TRANSACTION.
02740        IF ACCOUNT-NUMBER-REQUEST
02750            PERFORM LIST-1-MASTR-REC-BY-ACCT-NUM
02760        ELSE
02770            PERFORM PROCESS-ALL-MSTR-RECS-FOR-LTR.
02780
02790    LIST-1-MASTR-REC-BY-ACCT-NUM.
02800        IF IS-THERE-A-MASTER-RECORD = "N"
02810            ADD 1 TO NUMBER-OF-ERRONEOUS-RECORDS-W
02820            PERFORM WRITE-MASTER-MISSING-LINE
02830        ELSE
02840            ADD 1 TO NUMBER-OF-SELECTED-RECORDS-W
02850            PERFORM WRITE-REPORT-LINE.
02860
```

(continued)

Consider the section of the program that READs transaction records. It consists of the two paragraphs: READ-A-TRANSACTION-RECORD and READ-TRANSACTION-FILE, at lines 02320 through 02480. READ-A-TRANSACTION-RECORD returns to the upper portions of the hierarchy diagram only records having a valid transaction code, 6 or 7. Furthermore, READ-A-TRANSACTION-RECORD makes sure that TRANSACTION-KEY is set properly regardless of what type of transaction is being processed. The upper portions of the diagram can then operate on TRANSACTION-KEY. The statement at line 02380 shows how the sending field of a MOVE can overlap the receiving field. Here a one-character sending field is MOVEd to a five-character receiving field. COBOL inserts four trailing blanks into the receiving field, giving us the exact value of TRANSACTION-KEY that we need for later processing.

The statement at line 02330 demonstrates a principle that is important to remember whenever you use a PERFORM . . . UNTIL statement, as we do at line 02340. A PERFORM . . . UNTIL evaluates its condition before executing the PERFORMed paragraph, so you must be sure before you enter the PERFORM that the condition is not true if you want to be sure that the PERFORMed paragraph will be executed at least once. In line 02330 we set TRANSACTION-CODE-T to a value that makes the condition in the PERFORM statement false, so that the PERFORMed paragraph will be executed at least once. Without the MOVE statement at line 02330, TRANSACTION-CODE-IS-VALID would be true from the previous transaction, and we would never PERFORM the paragraph READ-TRANSACTION-FILE after that.

Now examine the paragraph PROCESS-MASTER-RECORD, line 02500. If a transaction is asking for a master record to be retrieved on its Account Number, the program tries to do a random READ in the usual way, at lines 02520 and 02530. But if a transaction is asking for a listing of master records on the basis of the first letter of the Depositor Name, the program uses a **START** statement to locate the first record in the file (if any) whose Depositor Name begins with the desired letter of the alphabet, in lines 02550 through 02570. The START statement does not bring a record in from the file; it merely locates a particular record, if it exists, so that sequential READ statements issued later can bring in the records wanted. Successful execution of a START statement establishes a **key of reference** for later sequential READs. In our case, the START statement used a field subordinate to DEPOSITOR-NAME-M, so DEPOSITOR-NAME-M becomes the key of reference. Only the prime RECORD KEY or any ALTERNATE RECORD KEY may be the key of reference. The complete format of the START statement will be given shortly.

The START statement may be used on an indexed file in any program using ACCESS DYNAMIC, as we are doing here, or ACCESS SEQUENTIAL. It is not permitted in a program using ACCESS RANDOM. We will not use the START statement in any other programs in this book.

Execution of the START statement sets the STATUS field if one is specified for the file. The 1974 ANSI standard meanings of the STATUS codes related to executing a START statement on an indexed file are given in Table 14-6.

Table 14-6
1974 ANSI standard STATUS codes related to executing a START statement on an indexed file.

Status Code	Meaning
00	Successful completion
23	Invalid key — no record found
30	Permanent error (hardware malfunction)

As usual, your own system may have additional codes in the range 90 through 99. Since the STATUS codes for START are the same as for a random READ, the IF statement at line 02580 does its job regardless of whether the preceding IF statement executes the READ at line 02530 or the START at line 02560.

We now come to the portion of the program corresponding to the hierarchy diagram in Figure 14.8. The paragraphs PROCESS-TRANSACTION-RECORD, PROCESS-ONE-TRANSACTION, and LIST-1-MASTER-REC-BY-ACCT-NUM, at lines 02690, 02730, and 02790, respectively, are all straightforward. The paragraph PROCESS-ALL-MSTR-RECS-FOR-LTR shows how the program finds all the master records having a Depositor Name beginning with the letter given in the transaction. First, at line 02880, it tests whether the START statement found any such records at all. If so, it brings in the first such record by PERFORMing the paragraph READ-MASTER-FILE-SEQUENTIALLY.

The paragraph READ-MASTER-FILE-SEQUENTIALLY, at line 03030, shows how to READ an indexed file sequentially when ACCESS DYNAMIC is given. The reserved word **NEXT** must follow the file name, indicating to COBOL that records are to be read sequentially. A READ . . . NEXT statement may be given after a successful START, READ, or OPEN statement. If given after a START statement, the READ . . . NEXT brings in from the file the record that the START statement found. If given after an OPEN statement, a READ . . . NEXT brings in the first record in the file. If given after a READ or READ . . . NEXT, it brings in from the file the next record in sequence. In our case, the READ . . . NEXT brings into the master work area the record that the START statement found.

Subsequent READ . . . NEXT statements bring records in from the file in sequence on the key of reference. In our case, the key of reference is DEPOSITOR-NAME-M, so READ . . . NEXT statements will bring in records sequentially on Depositor Name. READ . . . NEXT statements given after an OPEN statement bring in records sequentially on the prime key of the file.

When an indexed file is read sequentially on an alternate key for which duplicate key values exist, the records are brought in from the file in the order in which they were placed on the file. If during an update operation the value of an alternate key in a record is changed to a value that already exists on the file, the updated record is considered to be the last of the records with that value of the alternate key placed on the file. If the file were to be accessed sequentially on that value of the alternate key, the newly updated record would be the last retrieved.

A READ . . . NEXT statement sets the STATUS field if one is specified for the file. The 1974 ANSI standard meanings of the STATUS codes related to READing an indexed file sequentially are given in Table 14-7.

Table 14-7
1974 ANSI standard STATUS codes related to READing an indexed file sequentially.

Status Code	Meaning
00	Successful completion
02	Successful completion, and the NEXT record on the file has the same key value as the record just read (this can happen only when an indexed file is being read on a key other than its prime key)
10	At end — end-of-file encountered
30	Permanent error (hardware malfunction)

In this application, a code of 02 will be returned if the next record in the file after the record just read has the same Depositor Name as the record just read. Your system may have additional codes in the range 90 – 99.

After a master record has been read sequentially, the PERFORM statement at line 02930 brings in records UNTIL the first letter of the depositor name changes or end-of-file is encountered in READing the master file sequentially.

Program P14-03 was run with the transaction input shown in Figure 14.10 and the updated master file created by Program P14-02. Program P14-03 produced the report output shown in Figure 14.11.

Figure 14.9 (continued)

```
02870   PROCESS-ALL-MSTR-RECS-FOR-LTR.
02880       IF IS-THERE-A-MASTER-RECORD = "N"
02890           ADD 1 TO NUMBER-OF-ERRONEOUS-RECORDS-W
02900           PERFORM WRITE-MASTER-MISSING-LINE
02910       ELSE
02920           PERFORM READ-MASTER-FILE-SEQUENTIALLY
02930           PERFORM LIST-ALL-MSTR-RECS-FOR-LTR UNTIL
02940               FIRST-LETTER-OF-DEPOSITOR-NAME
02950               NOT = STARTING-LETTER-T
02960               OR MASTER-FILE-CHECK = "10".
02970
02980   LIST-ALL-MSTR-RECS-FOR-LTR.
02990       ADD 1 TO NUMBER-OF-SELECTED-RECORDS-W.
03000       PERFORM WRITE-REPORT-LINE.
03010       PERFORM READ-MASTER-FILE-SEQUENTIALLY.
03020
03030   READ-MASTER-FILE-SEQUENTIALLY.
03040       READ ACCOUNT-MASTER-FILE-IN NEXT.
03050       IF MASTER-STATUS-KEY-1 = "0" OR
03060           MASTER-FILE-CHECK    = "10"
03070           NEXT SENTENCE
03080       ELSE
03090           DISPLAY " SEQUENTIAL MASTER READ STATUS = ",
03100                       MASTER-FILE-CHECK
03110           PERFORM TERMINATION
03120           STOP RUN.
03130
03140   WRITE-REPORT-LINE.
03150       MOVE ACCOUNT-NUMBER-M TO ACCOUNT-NUMBER-OUT.
03160       MOVE CURRENT-BALANCE-M TO CURRENT-BALANCE-OUT.
03170       MOVE DATE-OF-LAST-TRANSACTION-M
03180           TO DATE-OF-LAST-TRANSACTION-OUT.
03190       MOVE DEPOSITOR-NAME-M TO DEPOSITOR-NAME-OUT.
03200       IF 1 + LINE-COUNT-ER > PAGE-LIMIT
03210           PERFORM PRINT-LISTING-HEADINGS.
03220       WRITE LISTING-RECORD-OUT FROM REPORT-LINE.
03230       ADD 1 TO LINE-COUNT-ER.
03240       ADD CURRENT-BALANCE-M TO CURRENT-BALANCE-TOTAL-W.
03250
03260   WRITE-INVALID-CODE-LINE.
03270       MOVE TRANSACTION-KEY TO TRANSACTION-KEY-OUT IN
03280                                   INVALID-CODE-LINE.
03290       MOVE TRANSACTION-CODE-T TO TRANSACTION-CODE-OUT.
03300       IF 1 + ERROR-LINE-COUNTER > ERROR-PAGE-LIMIT
03310           PERFORM PRINT-ERROR-REPORT-HEADINGS.
03320       WRITE ERROR-RECORD-OUT FROM INVALID-CODE-LINE.
03330       ADD 1 TO ERROR-LINE-COUNTER.
03340
03350   WRITE-MASTER-MISSING-LINE.
03360       MOVE TRANSACTION-KEY TO TRANSACTION-KEY-OUT IN
03370                                   MASTER-MISSING-LINE.
03380       IF 1 + ERROR-LINE-COUNTER > ERROR-PAGE-LIMIT
03390           PERFORM PRINT-ERROR-REPORT-HEADINGS.
03400       WRITE ERROR-RECORD-OUT FROM MASTER-MISSING-LINE.
03410       ADD 1 TO ERROR-LINE-COUNTER.
03420
03430   TERMINATION.
03440       PERFORM PRODUCE-FINAL-LINES.
03450       CLOSE ACCOUNT-MASTER-FILE-IN
03460           TRANSACTION-FILE-IN
03470           LISTING-FILE-OUT
03480           ERROR-FILE-OUT.
03490
03500   PRODUCE-FINAL-LINES.
03510       MOVE CURRENT-BALANCE-TOTAL-W TO CURRENT-BALANCE-TOTAL-OUT.
03520       WRITE LISTING-RECORD-OUT FROM FINAL-LINE-1 AFTER 2.
03530       WRITE LISTING-RECORD-OUT FROM FINAL-LINE-2 AFTER 2.
03540       MOVE NUMBER-OF-SELECTED-RECORDS-W
03550                       TO NUMBER-OF-SELECTED-RECORDS-OUT.
03560       WRITE LISTING-RECORD-OUT FROM FINAL-LINE-3 AFTER 2.
03570       MOVE NUMBER-OF-ERRONEOUS-RECORDS-W TO
03580                       NUMBER-OF-ERRONEOUS-RECRDS-OUT.
03590       WRITE LISTING-RECORD-OUT FROM FINAL-LINE-4 AFTER 2.
03600       MOVE NUMBER-OF-INPUT-RECORDS-W TO
03610                       NUMBER-OF-INPUT-RECORDS-OUT.
03620       WRITE LISTING-RECORD-OUT FROM FINAL-LINE-5 AFTER 2.
```

(continued)

Figure 14.9   (continued)

```
03630
03640    PRODUCE-REPORT-HEADINGS.
03650        PERFORM PRINT-LISTING-HEADINGS.
03660        PERFORM PRINT-ERROR-REPORT-HEADINGS.
03670
03680    PRINT-LISTING-HEADINGS.
03690        ADD 1 TO PAGE-NUMBER-W.
03700        MOVE PAGE-NUMBER-W TO PAGE-NUMBER-OUT.
03710        WRITE LISTING-RECORD-OUT FROM REPORT-HEADING-1
03720                                     AFTER ADVANCING PAGE.
03730        WRITE LISTING-RECORD-OUT FROM REPORT-HEADING-2.
03740        WRITE LISTING-RECORD-OUT FROM REPORT-HEADING-3.
03750        WRITE LISTING-RECORD-OUT FROM PAGE-HEADING-1
03760                                     AFTER 2.
03770        WRITE LISTING-RECORD-OUT FROM PAGE-HEADING-2.
03780        WRITE LISTING-RECORD-OUT FROM PAGE-HEADING-3
03790                                     AFTER 3.
03800        WRITE LISTING-RECORD-OUT FROM PAGE-HEADING-4.
03810        WRITE LISTING-RECORD-OUT FROM BLANK-LINE.
03820        MOVE 11 TO LINE-COUNT-ER.
03830
03840    PRINT-ERROR-REPORT-HEADINGS.
03850        ADD 1 TO ERROR-PAGE-NUMBER-W.
03860        MOVE ERROR-PAGE-NUMBER-W TO PAGE-NUMBER-OUT.
03870        WRITE ERROR-RECORD-OUT FROM REPORT-HEADING-1
03880                                     AFTER ADVANCING PAGE.
03890        WRITE ERROR-RECORD-OUT FROM REPORT-HEADING-2.
03900        WRITE ERROR-RECORD-OUT FROM REPORT-HEADING-3.
03910        WRITE ERROR-RECORD-OUT FROM ERROR-HEADING-1
03920                                     AFTER 2.
03930        WRITE ERROR-RECORD-OUT FROM PAGE-HEADING-2.
03940        WRITE ERROR-RECORD-OUT FROM ERROR-HEADING-3
03950                                     AFTER 3.
03960        WRITE ERROR-RECORD-OUT FROM ERROR-HEADING-4.
03970        WRITE ERROR-RECORD-OUT FROM BLANK-LINE.
03980        MOVE 11 TO ERROR-LINE-COUNTER.
```

Figure 14.10   Transaction input to Program P14-03.

```
-----------------------------------------------------------------------------
        1         2         3         4         5         6         7         8
12345678901234567890123456789012345678901234567890123456789012345678901234567890
-----------------------------------------------------------------------------
600350
600245
100299
600077
600003
600508
600168
600350
600599
7G
600280
600609
7C0390
7D
```

Figure 14.11   Report output from Program P14-03.

```
                        ROBBEM STATE BANK
                        106 WEST 10TH ST.
                        BROOKLYN, NY  11212

                      SELECTED SAVINGS ACCOUNTS
            DATE   4/09/88                    PAGE   1


      ACCOUNT      CURRENT     DATE OF LAST       DEPOSITOR
      NUMBER       BALANCE     TRANSACTION        NAME

      00350       2,500.00       880408       ROGER SHAW
      00245          35.00       880408       FRANK CAPUTO
      00077         160.37       880409       LESLIE MINSKY
      00350       2,500.00       880408       ROGER SHAW
      00220            .00       880409       GENE & THERESA GALLI
      00096         871.00       880408       GENE GALLI
      00252          15.00       880408       GENE GALLI
      00391       1,284.00       880409       GENE GALLI
      00410         318.00       880408       GENE GALLI
      00092         432.00       880409       GENE GALLI
      00032          25.00       880409       GENE GALLI
      00098          20.00       880409       GEORGE & ANN CULHANE
      00315         250.00       880408       GRACE MICELI
      00329          10.00       880408       GUY VOLPONE
      00280       2,337.00       880409       COMMUNITY DRUGS
      00199          21.00       880408       COMMUNITY DRUGS
      00280       2,337.00       880409       COMMUNITY DRUGS
      00306         493.00       880408       COMMUNITY DRUGS
      00349       1,234.00       880408       COMMUNITY DRUGS

       TOTAL     14,842.37

                       CONTROL COUNTS

            NUMBER OF SELECTED RECORDS    19

            NUMBER OF ERRONEOUS RECORDS    7

            NUMBER OF INPUT RECORDS       14
```

```
                        ROBBEM STATE BANK
                        106 WEST 10TH ST.
                        BROOKLYN, NY  11212

                        SELECTION ERRORS
            DATE   4/09/88                    PAGE   1


      ACCOUNT
      NUMBER

      00299                    INVALID CODE - 1
      00003                    MASTER RECORD DOES NOT EXIST
      00508                    MASTER RECORD DOES NOT EXIST
      00168                    MASTER RECORD DOES NOT EXIST
      00599                    MASTER RECORD DOES NOT EXIST
      00609                    MASTER RECORD DOES NOT EXIST
      D                        MASTER RECORD DOES NOT EXIST
```

The START Statement

The format of the START statement is:

```
START file-name [KEY  ⎧ IS EQUAL TO         ⎫
                      ⎪ IS =                ⎪
                      ⎪ IS GREATER THAN     ⎪ data-name]
                      ⎨ IS >                ⎬
                      ⎪ IS NOT LESS THAN    ⎪
                      ⎩ IS NOT <            ⎭
     [; INVALID KEY imperative-statement]
```

The START statement locates the first record in an indexed file that satisfies the condition given in the KEY clause. If the KEY clause is omitted, the EQUAL condition is assumed and the comparison is made on the prime RECORD KEY of the file. If the KEY clause is given, data-name may be either the prime key, an alternate key, or an alphanumeric data item subordinate to an alternate key and at the left end of the alternate key.

If the condition in the KEY clause is satisfied, the START is considered successful, and the key field used for the START becomes the key of reference for subsequent READ . . . NEXT statements. If no record is found that satisfies the condition given in the KEY clause, the STATUS field is set to 23 and the imperative-statement in the INVALID KEY clause is executed. If the INVALID KEY clause is not present and if the condition in the KEY clause is not satisfied, the START statement sets the STATUS code to 23 and executes the USE AFTER ERROR PROCEDURE for the file.

If the symbols for equal, greater than, or less than are used, they are required. We refrain from underlining them here to avoid possible confusion with other mathematical symbols.

The Sequential READ Statement

A READ statement, when used for any kind of sequential retrieval of records from a file with any kind of organization, has the following format:

```
READ file-name [NEXT] RECORD [INTO identifier]
     [; AT END imperative-statement]
```

When this READ statement is used with a file in dynamic access mode, the word NEXT is required to obtain sequential retrieval of records. When used with a file in sequential access mode, the word NEXT may appear and has no effect.

If end-of-file is encountered, the STATUS code is set to 10 and the imperative statement in the AT END clause is executed. If the AT END clause is not present, and if end-of-file is encountered, the READ statement sets the STATUS code to 10 and executes the USE AFTER ERROR PROCEDURE for the file.

6

EXERCISE 3

Write a program to list selected records from the files you created in Exercises 1 and 2 in this chapter. Have your program accept transactions in the following formats:

Positions	Field
1	Code A
2–6	Account Number
7–80	spaces
1	Code B
2	First character of Supplier Code
3–80	spaces
1	Code C
2	First character of Storage Location
3–80	spaces

The meanings of the transaction Codes are as follows:

A — list the contents of the master record having this Account Number
B — list the contents of all master records whose Supplier Code begins with this character
C — list the contents of all master records whose Storage Location begins with this character

For each record listed, have your program determine whether the Quantity on Hand is equal to or less than the Reorder Point, and print the message REORDER if it is.

Listing the Complete Contents of an Indexed File

Listing an indexed file sequentially on its prime key is very much like doing any sequential listing. Program P14-04, shown in Figure 14.12, lists the contents of our savings-account master file.

Figure 14.12 Program P14-04.

```
CB1 RELEASE 2.4                              IBM OS/VS COBOL   JULY  1, 1982


                     22.34.33        APR  9,1988


00010  IDENTIFICATION DIVISION.
00020  PROGRAM-ID. P14-04.
00030 *
00040 *    THIS PROGRAM LISTS AN INDEXED FILE.
00050 *
00060 ************************************************************************
00070
00080  ENVIRONMENT DIVISION.
00090  CONFIGURATION SECTION.
00100  SOURCE-COMPUTER. IBM-370.
00110  OBJECT-COMPUTER. IBM-370.
00120
```

(continued)

Figure 14.12   (continued)

```
00130    INPUT-OUTPUT SECTION.
00140    FILE-CONTROL.
00150        SELECT LIST-FILE-OUT     ASSIGN TO PRINTER.
00160        SELECT MASTER-FILE-IN    ASSIGN TO DISKUNIT
00170            ORGANIZATION INDEXED
00180            RECORD KEY IS ACCOUNT-NUMBER IN MASTER-RECORD-IN
00190            STATUS IS FILE-CHECK.
00200
00210    ***********************************************************************
00220
00230    DATA DIVISION.
00240    FILE SECTION.
00250    FD  MASTER-FILE-IN
00260        LABEL RECORDS ARE STANDARD
00270        RECORD CONTAINS 39 CHARACTERS.
00280
00290    01  MASTER-RECORD-IN.
00300        05  ACCOUNT-NUMBER                         PIC X(5).
00310        05  DEPOSITOR-NAME                         PIC X(20).
00320        05  DATE-OF-LAST-TRANSACTION               PIC 9(6).
00330        05  CURRENT-BALANCE                        PIC S9(6)V99.
00340
00350    FD  LIST-FILE-OUT
00360        LABEL RECORDS ARE OMITTED.
00370
00380    01  LIST-RECORD-OUT                            PIC X(81).
00390
00400    WORKING-STORAGE SECTION.
00410    01  BLANK-LINE        VALUE SPACE              PIC X.
00420    01  FILE-CHECK        VALUE ZEROS              PIC XX.
00430    01  RUN-DATE.
00440        05  RUN-YEAR                               PIC 99.
00450        05  RUN-MONTH-AND-DAY                      PIC 9(4).
00460
00470    01  PAGE-NUMBER-W     VALUE 0                  PIC S99.
00480    01  PAGE-LIMIT        VALUE 38      COMP SYNC  PIC S99.
00490    01  LINE-COUNT-ER                   COMP SYNC  PIC S99.
00500
00510    01  PAGE-HEADING-1.
00520        05  FILLER            VALUE SPACES         PIC X(40).
00530        05  FILLER            VALUE  "SAVINGS ACCOUNT MASTER"
00540                                                   PIC X(22).
00550
00560    01  PAGE-HEADING-2.
00570        05  FILLER            VALUE  SPACES        PIC X(28).
00580        05  FILLER            VALUE  "DATE"        PIC X(5).
00590        05  RUN-MONTH-AND-DAY                      PIC Z9/99/.
00600        05  RUN-YEAR                               PIC 99B(21).
00610        05  FILLER            VALUE  "PAGE"        PIC X(5).
00620        05  PAGE-NUMBER-OUT                        PIC Z9.
00630
00640    01  PAGE-HEADING-3.
00650        05  FILLER            VALUE SPACES         PIC X(46).
00660        05  FILLER            VALUE  "DATE OF LAST" PIC X(12).
00670
00680    01  PAGE-HEADING-4.
00690        05  FILLER            VALUE SPACES         PIC X(20).
00700        05  FILLER            VALUE  "ACCOUNT"     PIC X(13).
00710        05  FILLER            VALUE  "CURRENT"     PIC X(13).
00720        05  FILLER            VALUE  "TRANSACTION" PIC X(15).
00730        05  FILLER            VALUE  "DEPOSITOR NAME" PIC X(14).
00740
00750    01  PAGE-HEADING-5.
00760        05  FILLER            VALUE  SPACES        PIC X(20).
00770        05  FILLER            VALUE  "NUMBER"      PIC X(13).
00780        05  FILLER            VALUE  "BALANCE"     PIC X(14).
00790        05  FILLER            VALUE  "YR  MO  DA"  PIC X(10).
00800
00810    01  DETAIL-LINE.
00820        05  FILLER            VALUE SPACES         PIC X(21).
00830        05  ACCOUNT-NUMBER                         PIC X(5)B(4).
00840        05  CURRENT-BALANCE                        PIC Z,ZZZ,ZZZ.99-.
00850        05  DATE-OF-LAST-TRANSACTION
00860                      PIC B(4)99BB99BB99B(4).
00870        05  DEPOSITOR-NAME                         PIC X(20).
00880
```

```
00890   01  NO-INPUT-DATA.
00900       05  FILLER      VALUE SPACES           PIC X(21).
00910       05  FILLER      VALUE "NO INPUT DATA"  PIC X(13).
00920
00930   ***********************************************************************
00940
00950   PROCEDURE DIVISION.
00960   DECLARATIVES.
00970   DUMMY-USE SECTION.
00980       USE AFTER ERROR PROCEDURE MASTER-FILE-IN.
00990   END DECLARATIVES.
01000
01010   NONDECLARATIVE SECTION.
01020   CONTROL-PARAGRAPH.
01030       PERFORM INITIALIZATION.
01040       PERFORM MAIN-PROCESS UNTIL FILE-CHECK = "10".
01050       PERFORM TERMINATION.
01060       STOP RUN.
01070
01080   INITIALIZATION.
01090       OPEN INPUT  MASTER-FILE-IN,
01100            OUTPUT LIST-FILE-OUT.
01110       IF FILE-CHECK NOT = ZEROS
01120           DISPLAY " MASTER FILE OPEN STATUS = ", FILE-CHECK
01130           CLOSE MASTER-FILE-IN,
01140                 LIST-FILE-OUT
01150           STOP RUN.
01160       ACCEPT RUN-DATE FROM DATE.
01170       MOVE CORR RUN-DATE TO PAGE-HEADING-2.
01180       PERFORM PRODUCE-PAGE-HEADINGS.
01190       READ MASTER-FILE-IN.
01200       IF FILE-CHECK = ZEROS
01210           NEXT SENTENCE
01220       ELSE
01230       IF FILE-CHECK = "10"
01240           WRITE LIST-RECORD-OUT FROM NO-INPUT-DATA
01250       ELSE
01260           DISPLAY " MASTER FILE READ STATUS = ", FILE-CHECK
01270           CLOSE MASTER-FILE-IN,
01280                 LIST-FILE-OUT
01290           STOP RUN.
01300
01310   PRODUCE-PAGE-HEADINGS.
01320       ADD 1 TO PAGE-NUMBER-W.
01330       MOVE PAGE-NUMBER-W TO PAGE-NUMBER-OUT.
01340       WRITE LIST-RECORD-OUT FROM PAGE-HEADING-1 AFTER PAGE.
01350       WRITE LIST-RECORD-OUT FROM PAGE-HEADING-2.
01360       WRITE LIST-RECORD-OUT FROM PAGE-HEADING-3 AFTER 3.
01370       WRITE LIST-RECORD-OUT FROM PAGE-HEADING-4.
01380       WRITE LIST-RECORD-OUT FROM PAGE-HEADING-5.
01390       WRITE LIST-RECORD-OUT FROM BLANK-LINE.
01400       MOVE 8 TO LINE-COUNT-ER.
01410
01420   TERMINATION.
01430       CLOSE MASTER-FILE-IN,
01440             LIST-FILE-OUT.
01450
01460   MAIN-PROCESS.
01470       MOVE CORR MASTER-RECORD-IN TO DETAIL-LINE.
01480       IF LINE-COUNT-ER + 1 > PAGE-LIMIT
01490           PERFORM PRODUCE-PAGE-HEADINGS.
01500       WRITE LIST-RECORD-OUT FROM DETAIL-LINE.
01510       ADD 1 TO LINE-COUNT-ER.
01520       READ MASTER-FILE-IN.
01530       IF FILE-CHECK = ZEROS OR "10"
01540           NEXT SENTENCE
01550       ELSE
01560           DISPLAY " MASTER FILE READ STATUS = ", FILE-CHECK
01570           CLOSE MASTER-FILE-IN,
01580                 LIST-FILE-OUT
01590           STOP RUN.
```

In the FILE-CONTROL entry for the master file, line 00160, we can omit the ALTERNATE RECORD KEY clause because this program makes no reference to the Depositor Name field as a key. In the Working Storage Section, we can use FILE-CHECK, line 00420, instead of MORE-INPUT to signal the end-of-file.

Program P14-04 was run using the updated master file created in Program P14-02. Program P14-04 produced the output shown in Figure 14.13.

Figure 14.13 Output from Program P14-04.

```
                         SAVINGS ACCOUNT MASTER
            DATE   4/09/88                          PAGE   1


                             DATE OF LAST
       ACCOUNT     CURRENT    TRANSACTION    DEPOSITOR NAME
       NUMBER      BALANCE    YR  MO  DA


        00007     1,007.84    88  04  08    ROSEBUCCI
        00014       990.00-   88  04  09    ROBERT DAVIS M.D.
        00015       700.00    88  04  08    LENORE MILLER
        00020       800.00    88  04  08    LENORE MILLER
        00021       252.50    88  04  09    LORICE MONTI
        00022     1,000.00    88  04  08    ROSEMARY LANE
        00023     1,100.00    88  04  08    ROSEMARY LANE
        00028     5,654.36    88  04  09    MICHAEL SMITH
        00032        25.00    88  04  09    GENE GALLI
        00035       150.00    88  04  08    JOHN J. LEHMAN
        00056         1.00    88  04  08    EVELYN SLATER
        00070       500.00    88  04  08    PATRICK J. LEE
        00077       160.37    88  04  09    LESLIE MINSKY
        00084     5,074.29    88  04  09    JOHN & SALLY DUPRINO
        00091     2,300.00    88  04  09    JOE'S DELI
        00092       432.00    88  04  09    GENE GALLI
        00096       871.00    88  04  08    GENE GALLI
        00098        20.00    88  04  09    GEORGE & ANN CULHANE
        00105        50.00    88  04  08    ONE DAY CLEANERS
        00112       250.00    88  04  08    ROSEMARY LANE
        00126     1,100.00    88  04  09    JAMES BUDD
        00133     3,563.00    88  04  09    PAUL LERNER, D.D.S.
        00140        25.75    88  04  09    BETH DENNY
        00161     1,280.84    88  04  09    ROBERT RYAN
        00175       202.02    88  04  09    MARY KEATING
        00189        35.00    88  04  08    J. & L. CAIN
        00199        21.00    88  04  08    COMMUNITY DRUGS
        00210     1,000.00    88  04  09    JERRY PARKS
        00220          .00    88  04  09    GENE & THERESA GALLI
        00231       555.00    88  04  08    BILL WILLIAMS
```

```
                         SAVINGS ACCOUNT MASTER
            DATE   4/09/88                          PAGE   2


                             DATE OF LAST
       ACCOUNT     CURRENT    TRANSACTION    DEPOSITOR NAME
       NUMBER      BALANCE    YR  MO  DA


        00245        35.00    88  04  08    FRANK CAPUTO
        00252        15.00    88  04  08    GENE GALLI
        00266        99.57    88  04  08    MARTIN LANG
        00273     2,000.00    88  04  09    VITO CACACI
        00280     2,337.00    88  04  09    COMMUNITY DRUGS
        00306       493.00    88  04  08    COMMUNITY DRUGS
        00308     2,050.00    88  04  09    JOE GARCIA
        00315       250.00    88  04  08    GRACE MICELI
        00329        10.00    88  04  08    GUY VOLPONE
        00343     1,000.00    88  04  08    JOE & MARY SESSA
        00349     1,234.00    88  04  08    COMMUNITY DRUGS
        00350     2,500.00    88  04  08    ROGER SHAW
        00371        10.00    88  04  09    THOMAS HERR
        00391     1,284.00    88  04  09    GENE GALLI
        00392        75.00    88  04  09    INEZ WASHINGTON
        00398        10.00    88  04  09    JUAN ALVAREZ
        00410       318.00    88  04  08    GENE GALLI
        00413       100.00    88  04  09    BILL HAYES
        00420     1,500.00    88  04  09    JOHN RICE
```

EXERCISE 4

Write a program to list the complete contents of the master files created in Exercises 1 and 2, this chapter. For each record listed, have your program determine whether the Quantity on Hand is equal to or less than the Reorder Point and print a message REORDER if it is.

Other Operations on Indexed Files

Several kinds of input and output operations on indexed files that are supported by COBOL have not been referred to in this chapter. They are:

a. READing a record randomly on an alternate key
b. Rewriting a record in sequential access mode
c. Deleting a record in sequential access mode

Each of these operations has its own STATUS code values. For details on these operations and their STATUS codes, see your COBOL manual.

Summary

Files with indexed organization have most of their records stored in order on their prime RECORD KEY. An indexed file is equipped with indexes, which permit COBOL to access the file sequentially or randomly. An indexed file may have one or more ALTERNATE RECORD KEYs. The ALTERNATE RECORD KEYs permit COBOL to access the file sequentially or randomly on those KEYs.

An indexed file may be created sequentially or randomly. If the file is created sequentially, the first WRITE statement issued by the program places the first record onto the file. The prime key of each record written after the first must be greater than the prime key of the previous record written. If the file is created randomly, records may be placed onto the file in any order, and COBOL will insert each record into its proper place in sequence. The prime key of each record written must not be a duplicate of a prime key already on the file.

An indexed file may be updated in place. To process a transaction to change an existing master record, COBOL brings the master record in from the file. The record may then be updated in the File Section or in working storage and rewritten onto the file, replacing the old record. To process a transaction to delete an existing master record, COBOL physically removes the record from the file.

To process a transaction to create a new master record, the program builds the new record in the File Section or in working storage. A WRITE statement then directs COBOL to find the place on the file where the new record should be slipped in and to move some existing records around, if necessary, to make room for it.

Some applications require that an indexed file be accessed dynamically. Then a random READ statement or a START statement can find any record on the file on the basis of the prime key or one of the alternate keys. READ . . . NEXT statements can then bring in records sequentially from that record.

All operations, OPEN, CLOSE, READ, READ . . . NEXT, WRITE, REWRITE, and DELETE, set the STATUS code if one is provided for the file. The meanings of the STATUS code depend on the operation being performed. The program may test the STATUS code at any time and take appropriate action.

Fill-in Exercises

1. The three types of file organization supported by COBOL are _Seq_ , _Index_ , and _Relative_

2. The three types of file access supported by COBOL are _Seq_ , _Random_, and _Dynamic_

3. The field on which the records in an indexed file are ordered is called the _Key_ .

4. A field that may be used to access records in an indexed file but is not used for ordering them is called a(n) _alternate record key_

5. The _Organization_ clause in the FILE-CONTROL entry for a file tells whether the file is indexed.

6. The _access_ clause in the FILE-CONTROL entry for a file tells whether records will be read and written randomly, sequentially, or dynamically.

7. The STATUS field is ___2___ characters long. _pic XX_

8. Every _read/write_ statement to a file attempts to place a new record onto the file.

9. Every _write_ statement to a file attempts to replace an existing record on the file.

10. A _start_ statement may be used to locate a record randomly on an indexed file but not bring the record in from the file.

11. The _Width_ _____ phrase is used to indicate that more than one record in an indexed file may contain the same value of an ALTERNATE RECORD KEY.

12. The OPEN mode used for updating records in an indexed file in place is _I/O_ .

13. The _Status_ _____ clause is used to indicate which field is the STATUS field for a file.

14. The OPEN mode used to add records sequentially to the end of a sequential file is _extend_.

15. The verb that can be used physically to remove a record from an indexed file is _delete_ .

Review Exercises

1. Write a program to create an indexed file of alumni records. Use the same formats for transaction and master records that you used when you created your sequential alumni file in Review Exercise 2, Chapter 12, page 409.

   Have your program check for the presence of all fields in each input record. Have your program print reports showing the records written onto the file and the erroneous transactions.

   In your program specify the Major Department field and the Year of Graduation field as ALTERNATE RECORD KEYs.

2. Write a program to update the indexed file you created in Review Exercise 1. Use the same transaction formats you used when you updated your sequential alumni file in Review Exercise 4, Chapter 13, page 458.

   Have your program make all suitable validity checks on each transaction. For any change to an existing master record, have your program print the Social Security Number and the contents of the changed field from the master record. For a record deleted from the master file, have your program print the Social Security Number, the Student Name, and the Year of Graduation from the master file.

   Include among your update transactions at least one that changes a Major Department field in an existing master record and at least one that changes a Year of Graduation field in an existing master record.

3. Write a program to list selected records from the alumni master files produced by the programs in Review Exercises 1 and 2. Have your program accept listing requests in the following formats:

Positions	Field
1	Code A
2–10	Social Security Number
11–80	spaces
1	Code B
2–3	Major Department
4–80	spaces
1	Code C
2–3	Year of Graduation
4–80	spaces

The meanings of the transaction codes are:

A — list the record for this Social Security Number
B — list all records having this Major Department Code
C — list all records having this Year of Graduation

Include among your transactions a request to list, by Year of Graduation, at least one of the records whose Year of Graduation field was changed in Review Exercise 2 and a request to list, by Major Department Code, at least one of the records whose Major Department Code was changed in Review Exercise 2.

4. Modify your solution to Review Exercise 3, so that the selected records are sorted into alphabetic order on Student Name before being listed.

5. Write a program to list, in sequence on Social Security Number, the complete contents of all records on the master files produced in Review Exercises 1 and 2 of this chapter.

6. Write a program to create an indexed inventory master file randomly. Use the same formats for transaction and master records that you used in Exercise 3, Chapter 12, page 392. Have your program accept transactions in random, unSORTed order. Specify the City-State-Zip field as an alternate key WITH DUPLICATES, and specify the Customer Name as an alternate key and do not include the WITH DUPLICATES phrase. Have your program test for erroneous duplicate values of Customer Name if your COBOL system has facilities for doing so.

Project

Rewrite your solution to the Project in Chapter 12, page 410, creating an indexed file instead of a sequential file. Specify the Customer Number as the prime RECORD KEY, and the third name-and-address line as the ALTERNATE RECORD KEY.

Relative Files

Here are the key points you should learn from this chapter:

1. What a relative file is
2. Why relative files are useful
3. How to get COBOL to create a relative file
4. How to access a relative file randomly
5. How to update a relative file
6. How to process a relative file sequentially

Key words to recognize and learn:

relative record number   division/remainder method
RELATIVE   prime number
RELATIVE KEY   home slot
SEQUENTIAL   synonym

A relative file may be thought of as consisting of a number of slots into which records may be placed. The slots are numbered from 1 to the last slot in the file. At any one time, any slot may contain a record or it may be empty. Once COBOL places a record into a slot, COBOL will not move the record to another slot unless directed to do so by a program. Relative files can be accessed sequentially, randomly, and dynamically. COBOL can randomly WRITE a record into any empty slot, REWRITE a record into a slot that already contains a record, DELETE an existing record from a slot and make that slot available for a new record, and READ a record from any slot in the file.

The sequential operations on a relative file are WRITE, REWRITE, START, DELETE, and READ. The dynamic access operations include all the sequential and random operations and also READ . . . NEXT. A relative file must be stored on a direct-access storage device.

A record in a relative file is referred to by its **relative record number,** not by any key field. The relative record number of a record is the number of the slot that the record is in. So if slots 1 and 2 of a relative file are empty, and the first record of the file is in slot number 3, the relative record number of that record is 3. The relative record number need not be stored as a field in the record.

The main advantage of relative files over indexed files is the speed with which records in a relative file may be accessed. In a relative file, there is no need for COBOL to refer to indexes to locate a record. Another difference between relative files and indexed files, which may be an advantage or a disadvantage, is that in a relative file the programmer is responsible for the location of each record. COBOL will not move a record from one slot to another automatically, or keep track of the locations of records.

Using a Relative File

In this first application of a relative file, we will assume that an instructor wants to be able to use a computer to compute students' grades at the end of each term. The instructor plans to accumulate and store each student's examination grades and homework grades in a master file during the term. The master file will have relative organization and one record for each student. The students in the class are numbered 1 through 21.

At the beginning of the term the instructor will establish a relative file containing one record for each student. Each record will have room for 5 exam grades, 12 homework grades, course or section identification, and a count field telling how many records there are in the file. At the start of the term all fields except the identification and count fields will contain zeros. During the term the instructor will update the file, inserting grades into the file when exams are given and when homework assignments are graded. If a student drops the course after a record has been established for that student, the instructor will remove the student's record from the file. Occasionally a grade in the file will have to be changed, as when the instructor makes a mistake entering a grade.

At the end of the term the instructor will run a program that examines the exam and homework grades for each student, gives each grade a weight as indicated by the instructor, and computes a letter grade.

Creating a Relative File Sequentially

Program P15-01 creates a relative file containing master records full of zero grades. Program P15-01 reads only one input record, whose format is as follows:

Positions	Field
1	Code "N"
2–4	Number of Students
5–10	Course or Section
11–80	spaces

The record contains the code "N" in column 1. Columns 2 through 4 say how many records Program P15-01 should create on the master file, and columns 5 through 10 give the course code or section number for identification purposes.

Figure 15.1 Report output format for Program P15-01.

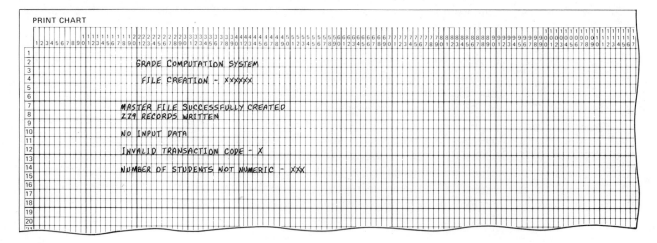

The report output produced by Program P15-01 consists of a report heading and one or two lines telling what happened. The format of the report output is shown in Figure 15.1. Only one of the messages shown is printed by Program P15-01 in any one run.

A hierarchy diagram for Program P15-01 is shown in Figure 15.2. It is very straightforward. The "Initialization" procedure reads and checks the one input record. If the record is valid, "Produce grades file" writes master records sequentially onto the master file and prints the appropriate message.

Figure 15.2 Hierarchy diagram for Program P15-01.

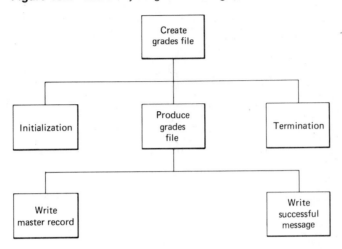

Program P15-01 is shown in Figure 15.3. The FILE-CONTROL entry at line 00170 shows the use of the ORGANIZATION **RELATIVE** clause. There is no RECORD KEY clause in the FILE-CONTROL entry because COBOL does not examine or process record key values in a RELATIVE file.

Figure 15.3 Program P15-01.

```
CB1 RELEASE 2.4                              IBM OS/VS COBOL   JULY  1, 1982


                           0.17.41        APR 10,1988


00010   IDENTIFICATION DIVISION.
00020   PROGRAM-ID.  P15-01.
00030 *
00040 *    THIS PROGRAM CREATES A RELATIVE FILE SEQUENTIALLY
00050 *
00060 ******************************************************************
00070
00080   ENVIRONMENT DIVISION.
00090   CONFIGURATION SECTION.
00100   SOURCE-COMPUTER.   IBM-370.
00110   OBJECT-COMPUTER.   IBM-370.
00120
00130   INPUT-OUTPUT SECTION.
00140   FILE-CONTROL.
00150       SELECT TRANSACTION-FILE-IN  ASSIGN TO INFILE.
00160       SELECT REPORT-FILE-OUT      ASSIGN TO PRINTER.
00170       SELECT GRADES-FILE-OUT      ASSIGN TO DISKUNIT
00180           ORGANIZATION RELATIVE
00190           STATUS IS MASTER-FILE-CHECK.
00200
00210 ******************************************************************
```

(continued)

Figure 15.3   (continued)

```
00220
00230  DATA DIVISION.
00240  FILE SECTION.
00250  FD  TRANSACTION-FILE-IN
00260      RECORD CONTAINS 80 CHARACTERS
00270      LABEL RECORDS ARE OMITTED.
00280
00290  01  TRANSACTION-RECORD-IN                    PIC X(80).
00300
00310  FD  GRADES-FILE-OUT
00320      LABEL RECORDS ARE STANDARD.
00330
00340  01  MASTER-RECORD-OUT                        PIC X(60).
00350
00360  FD  REPORT-FILE-OUT
00370      LABEL RECORDS ARE OMITTED.
00380
00390  01  REPORT-RECORD-OUT                        PIC X(51).
00400
00410  WORKING-STORAGE SECTION.
00420  01  MASTER-FILE-CHECK                        PIC XX.
00430
00440  01  CODE-N-RECORD-W.
00450      05  TRANSACTION-CODE-W                   PIC X.
00460          88  CODE-N            VALUE "N".
00470      05  NUMBER-OF-STUDENTS-W                 PIC 9(3).
00480      05  NUMBER-OF-STUDENTS-X REDEFINES NUMBER-OF-STUDENTS-W
00490                                               PIC X(3).
00500      05  COURSE-OR-SECTION-W                  PIC X(6).
00510
00520  01  GRADES-RECORD-OUT           VALUE ZEROS.
00530      05  COURSE-OR-SECTION                    PIC X(6).
00540      05  NUMBER-OF-STUDENTS                   PIC 9(3).
00550      05  EXAM-GRADE      OCCURS 5 TIMES       PIC 9(3).
00560      05  HOMEWORK-GRADE OCCURS 12 TIMES       PIC 9(3).
00570
00580  01  PAGE-HEADING-1.
00590      05  FILLER              VALUE SPACES     PIC X(20).
00600      05  FILLER
00610          VALUE "GRADE COMPUTATION SYSTEM"     PIC X(24).
00620
00630  01  PAGE-HEADING-2.
00640      05  FILLER              VALUE SPACES     PIC X(21).
00650      05  FILLER          VALUE "FILE CREATION -"
00660                                               PIC X(16).
00670      05  COURSE-OR-SECTION-OUT                PIC X(6).
00680
00690  01  SUCCESSFUL-MESSAGE-1.
00700      05  FILLER              VALUE SPACES     PIC X(17).
00710      05  FILLER
00720          VALUE "MASTER FILE SUCCESSFULLY CREATED"
00730                                               PIC X(32).
00740
00750  01  SUCCESSFUL-MESSAGE-2.
00760      05  FILLER              VALUE SPACES     PIC X(17).
00770      05  NUMBER-OF-STUDENTS-OUT               PIC ZZ9B.
00780      05  FILLER              VALUE "RECORDS WRITTEN"
00790                                               PIC X(15).
00800
00810  01  NO-INPUT-DATA.
00820      05  FILLER      VALUE SPACES             PIC X(17).
00830      05  FILLER      VALUE "NO INPUT DATA"    PIC X(13).
00840
00850  01  INVALID-CODE-LINE.
00860      05  FILLER      VALUE SPACES             PIC X(17).
00870      05  FILLER      VALUE "INVALID TRANSACTION CODE -"
00880                                               PIC X(27).
00890      05  TRANSACTION-CODE-OUT                 PIC X.
00900
00910  01  NUMBER-OF-STUDENTS-INVALID.
00920      05  FILLER      VALUE SPACES             PIC X(17).
00930      05  FILLER      VALUE "NUMBER OF STUDENTS NOT NUMERIC -"
00940                                               PIC X(33).
00950      05  NUMBER-OF-STUDENTS-X-OUT             PIC X(3).
00960
00970  ******************************************************************
00980
```

```
00990   PROCEDURE DIVISION.
01000   DECLARATIVES.
01010   DUMMY-USE SECTION.
01020       USE AFTER ERROR PROCEDURE GRADES-FILE-OUT.
01030   END DECLARATIVES.
01040
01050   NONDECLARATIVE SECTION.
01060   CREATE-GRADES-FILE.
01070       PERFORM INITIALIZATION.
01080       IF CODE-N-RECORD-W NOT = HIGH-VALUES
01090           PERFORM PRODUCE-GRADES-FILE.
01100       PERFORM TERMINATION.
01110       STOP RUN.
01120
01130   INITIALIZATION.
01140       OPEN INPUT   TRANSACTION-FILE-IN
01150            OUTPUT  REPORT-FILE-OUT
01160                    GRADES-FILE-OUT.
01170       IF MASTER-FILE-CHECK NOT = ZEROS
01180           DISPLAY " MASTER FILE OPEN STATUS = ", MASTER-FILE-CHECK
01190           CLOSE TRANSACTION-FILE-IN
01200                 REPORT-FILE-OUT
01210                 GRADES-FILE-OUT
01220           STOP RUN.
01230       WRITE REPORT-RECORD-OUT FROM PAGE-HEADING-1 AFTER PAGE.
01240       PERFORM READ-TRANSACTION-FILE.
01250       MOVE COURSE-OR-SECTION-W TO COURSE-OR-SECTION-OUT.
01260       WRITE REPORT-RECORD-OUT FROM PAGE-HEADING-2 AFTER 2.
01270
01280   READ-TRANSACTION-FILE.
01290       READ TRANSACTION-FILE-IN INTO CODE-N-RECORD-W
01300           AT END
01310               MOVE HIGH-VALUES TO CODE-N-RECORD-W.
01320       IF CODE-N-RECORD-W IS EQUAL TO HIGH-VALUES
01330           PERFORM WRITE-NO-INPUT-DATA
01340       ELSE
01350       IF NOT CODE-N
01360           PERFORM WRITE-INVALID-CODE-LINE
01370           MOVE HIGH-VALUES TO CODE-N-RECORD-W
01380       ELSE
01390       IF NUMBER-OF-STUDENTS-W NOT NUMERIC
01400           PERFORM WRITE-NO-OF-STUDENTS-INVALID
01410           MOVE HIGH-VALUES TO CODE-N-RECORD-W.
01420
01430   PRODUCE-GRADES-FILE.
01440       MOVE NUMBER-OF-STUDENTS-W TO NUMBER-OF-STUDENTS.
01450       MOVE COURSE-OR-SECTION-W TO COURSE-OR-SECTION.
01460       PERFORM WRITE-MASTER-RECORD NUMBER-OF-STUDENTS-W TIMES.
01470       PERFORM WRITE-SUCCESSFUL-MESSAGE.
01480
01490   WRITE-MASTER-RECORD.
01500       WRITE MASTER-RECORD-OUT FROM GRADES-RECORD-OUT.
01510       IF MASTER-FILE-CHECK NOT = ZEROS
01520           DISPLAY   " MASTER FILE WRITE STATUS = ",
01530                     MASTER-FILE-CHECK
01540           PERFORM TERMINATION
01550           STOP RUN.
```

(continued)

The master record, GRADES-RECORD-OUT, is defined at line 00520. The fields EXAM-GRADE and HOMEWORK-GRADE are included here only to show the format of the master record. They did not have to be defined in this program, for the field names are not referred to. Notice that the student number does not appear in the record, since the location of the record in the file tells which student the record belongs to.

The paragraph READ-TRANSACTION-FILE, line 01280, READs the one input record into CODE-N-RECORD-W and checks it for validity. If the record is found to be in error, READ-TRANSACTION-FILE prints an error message and sets CODE-N-RECORD-W to HIGH-VALUES to indicate that there is no valid input record.

The WRITE statement at line 01500 sets the STATUS field MASTER-FILE-CHECK. The 1974 ANSI standard meanings of the STATUS codes related to writing a relative file sequentially are given in Table 15-1.

Figure 15.3   (continued)

```
01560
01570     TERMINATION.
01580         CLOSE TRANSACTION-FILE-IN
01590               REPORT-FILE-OUT
01600               GRADES-FILE-OUT.
01610
01620     WRITE-NO-INPUT-DATA.
01630         WRITE REPORT-RECORD-OUT FROM NO-INPUT-DATA AFTER 2.
01640
01650     WRITE-INVALID-CODE-LINE.
01660         MOVE TRANSACTION-CODE-W TO TRANSACTION-CODE-OUT.
01670         WRITE REPORT-RECORD-OUT FROM INVALID-CODE-LINE AFTER 2.
01680
01690     WRITE-NO-OF-STUDENTS-INVALID.
01700         MOVE NUMBER-OF-STUDENTS-X TO NUMBER-OF-STUDENTS-X-OUT.
01710         WRITE REPORT-RECORD-OUT FROM NUMBER-OF-STUDENTS-INVALID.
01720
01730     WRITE-SUCCESSFUL-MESSAGE.
01740         MOVE NUMBER-OF-STUDENTS-W TO NUMBER-OF-STUDENTS-OUT.
01750         WRITE REPORT-RECORD-OUT FROM SUCCESSFUL-MESSAGE-1 AFTER 3.
01760         WRITE REPORT-RECORD-OUT FROM SUCCESSFUL-MESSAGE-2.
```

Table 15-1

1974 ANSI standard STATUS codes related to writing a relative file sequentially.

Status Code	Meaning
00	Successful completion
24	Invalid key — boundary violation (attempt to WRITE past the physical end of the file)
30	Permanent error (hardware malfunction)

Your COBOL system may have additional codes in the range 90 through 99.

Program P15-01 was run with the input data shown in Figure 15.4 and produced the report output shown in Figure 15.5.

Figure 15.4   Input to Program P15-01.

```
-------------------------------------------------------------------------------
          1         2         3         4         5         6         7         8
1234567890123456789012345678901234567890123456789012345678901234567890123456789 0
-------------------------------------------------------------------------------
N021DP407
```

Figure 15.5   Report output from Program P15-01.

```
GRADE COMPUTATION SYSTEM

  FILE CREATION - DP407


MASTER FILE SUCCESSFULLY CREATED
21 RECORDS WRITTEN
```

EXERCISE 1

Write a program to create a relative file of 135 master records, one record for each cash register in a chain of supermarkets. The format of the record is:

Starting cash balance — 9(4)V99
Sales
    Grocery — 9(4)V99
    Produce — 9(4)V99
    Meat — 9(4)V99
    Dairy — 9(4)V99
Tax — 9(3)V99
Bottle and can deposits — 9(3)V99
Coupons — 9(3)V99
Deposit returns — 9(3)V99
Adjustments — S9(3)V99
Ending cash balance — 9(4)V99

Create the file with all zero values in all fields. After the file is created, have your program print a message so indicating. Save the file for use later in this chapter.

Updating a Relative File Randomly

In Program P15-02, we will show how the file created by Program P15-01 can have grades inserted and changed, and how a student's record can be deleted. Program P15-02 accepts transactions in random order in the following formats:

Positions	Field
1	Code "E"
2–4	Student Number
5	Exam-Homework Type
6–7	Exam-Homework Number
8–10	Grade
11–80	spaces
1	Code "C"
2–4	Student Number
5	Exam-Homework Type
6–7	Exam-Homework Number
8–10	Grade
11–80	spaces
1	Code "D"
2–4	Student Number
5–80	spaces

The transaction codes are:

E — enter one exam or homework grade into the file
C — change an existing exam or homework grade in the file
D — delete this student's record from the file

All three types of transactions contain a Student Number in positions 2 through 4. Transaction types E and C contain, in positions 5 through 7, an indication of which exam or homework grade is being entered or changed. Position 5 contains the letter E or H to say whether the transaction relates to an exam grade or a homework grade, and positions 6 and 7 say to which exam number (1 through 5) or homework number (1 through 12) the transaction relates.

Program P15-02 produces a transaction register in the format shown in Figure 15.6. The first line in the body of the report shows the successful entering of an exam grade. The second line shows the entering of a homework grade. The next two lines show the changing of an exam grade and a homework grade. The program also produces an error report in the format shown in Figure 15.7. The body lines, containing error messages, show all the errors that can be detected by the program. The last line on the format shows an attempt to change a grade that is not in the file; the second from the last line shows an attempt to insert a grade for an exam or homework that already has a grade entered.

Figure 15.6   Output format for transaction register for Program P15-02.

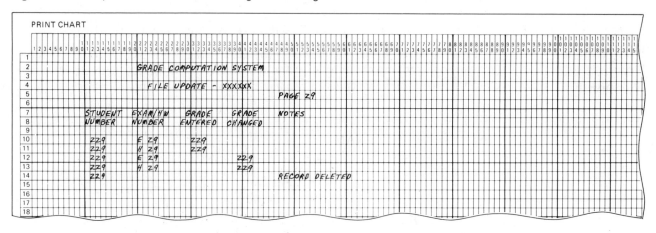

Figure 15.7   Output format for error report for Program P15-02.

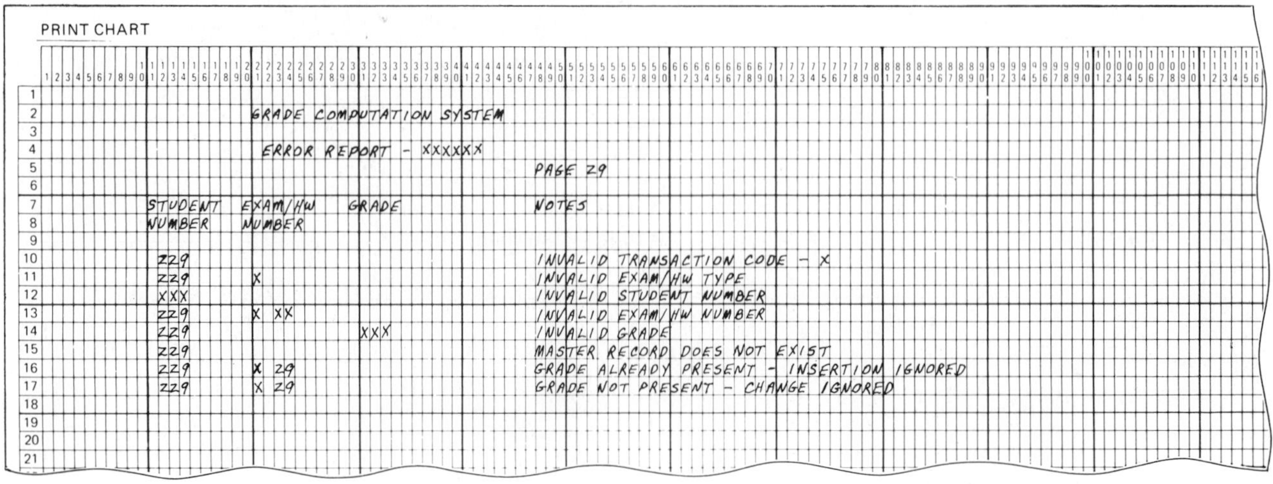

A hierarchy diagram for "Apply transaction" for Program P15-02 is shown in Figure 15.8. It resembles the other "Apply transaction" boxes in the hierarchy diagrams for previous update programs. A difference is in the procedure for checking the validity of the E- and C-type transactions. It turns out that certain validity checks on the two types of transactions are identical, so "Test for valid input" is used for both. If an input transaction is free of errors, the program then enters or changes an exam grade or a homework grade, as appropriate.

Figure 15.8 Hierarchy diagram for "Apply transaction" for Program P15-02.

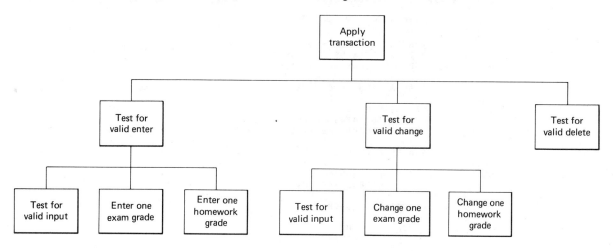

Program P15-02 is shown in Figure 15.9. The FILE-CONTROL entry at line 00210 shows the use of the **RELATIVE KEY** phrase. The RELATIVE KEY phrase is part of the ACCESS clause and must be used whenever ACCESS RANDOM or ACCESS DYNAMIC is specified. The RELATIVE KEY phrase must also be used in any program that uses a START statement on a relative file. The field named as the RELATIVE KEY, in this case RELATIVE-KEY, must be defined as an unsigned integer and must not be a field that is part of a level-01 entry associated with this file. When the file is accessed randomly, the value of the RELATIVE KEY indicates the record to be accessed.

Figure 15.9 Program P15-02.

```
CB1 RELEASE 2.4                              IBM OS/VS COBOL  JULY  1, 1982


                       0.17.47        APR 10,1988


        00010   IDENTIFICATION DIVISION.
        00020   PROGRAM-ID.  P15-02.
        00030 *
        00040 *    THIS PROGRAM UPDATES A RELATIVE FILE RANDOMLY
        00050 *
        00060 ***********************************************************
        00070
        00080   ENVIRONMENT DIVISION.
        00090   CONFIGURATION SECTION.
        00100   SOURCE-COMPUTER.  IBM-370.
        00110   OBJECT-COMPUTER.  IBM-370.
        00120
```

(continued)

Figure 15.9   (continued)

```
00130   INPUT-OUTPUT SECTION.
00140   FILE-CONTROL.
00150       SELECT TRANSACTION-FILE-IN   ASSIGN TO INFILE.
00160       SELECT REPORT-FILE-OUT       ASSIGN TO PRINTER1.
00170       SELECT ERROR-FILE-OUT        ASSIGN TO PRINTER2.
00180       SELECT GRADES-FILE-I-O       ASSIGN TO DISKUNIT
00190           ORGANIZATION RELATIVE
00200           ACCESS DYNAMIC
00210           RELATIVE KEY IS RELATIVE-KEY
00220           STATUS IS MASTER-FILE-CHECK.
00230
00240   ************************************************************************
00250
00260   DATA DIVISION.
00270   FILE SECTION.
00280   FD  TRANSACTION-FILE-IN
00290       RECORD CONTAINS 80 CHARACTERS
00300       LABEL RECORDS ARE OMITTED.
00310
00320   01  TRANSACTION-RECORD-IN                  PIC X(80).
00330
00340   FD  GRADES-FILE-I-O
00350       RECORD CONTAINS 60 CHARACTERS
00360       LABEL RECORDS ARE STANDARD.
00370
00380   01  GRADES-RECORD-I-O                      PIC X(60).
00390
00400   FD  REPORT-FILE-OUT
00410       LABEL RECORDS ARE OMITTED.
00420
00430   01  REPORT-RECORD-OUT                      PIC X(61).
00440
00450   FD  ERROR-FILE-OUT
00460       LABEL RECORDS ARE OMITTED.
00470
00480   01  ERROR-RECORD-OUT                       PIC X(88).
00490
00500   WORKING-STORAGE SECTION.
00510   01  PAGE-LIMIT              VALUE 50       PIC S99 COMP SYNC.
00520   01  RELATIVE-KEY                           PIC 9(3).
00530   01  REPORT-PAGE-COUNTER     VALUE 0        PIC S99.
00540   01  LINE-COUNT-ER                          PIC S99 COMP SYNC.
00550   01  ERROR-PAGE-COUNTER      VALUE 0        PIC S99.
00560   01  ERROR-LINE-COUNTER                     PIC S99 COMP SYNC.
00570   01  MASTER-FILE-CHECK                      PIC XX.
00580   01  IS-MASTER-RECORD-IN-THE-FILE           PIC X.
00590   01  IS-MASTER-RECORD-IN-WORK-AREA          PIC X.
00600   01  ANY-ERRORS-IN-INPUT                    PIC X.
00610
00620   01  TRANSACTION-INPUT-AREA.
00630       05  TRANSACTION-CODE-T                 PIC X.
00640           88  TRANSACTION-IS-ENTER    VALUE "E".
00650           88  TRANSACTION-IS-CHANGE   VALUE "C".
00660           88  TRANSACTION-IS-DELETE   VALUE "D".
00670       05  STUDENT-NUMBER-T                   PIC 9(3).
00680       05  STUDENT-NUMBER-X REDEFINES STUDENT-NUMBER-T
00690                                              PIC X(3).
```

In the TRANSACTION-INPUT-AREA, which starts at line 00620, the Student Number is defined as both numeric and alphanumeric, at lines 00670 through 00690. We use the numeric definition when we do arithmetic or numeric editing, and the alphanumeric definition when STUDENT-NUMBER-X might contain HIGH-VALUES or other nonnumeric data. The field EXAM-HW, line 00700 refers to positions 5 through 7 of the transaction. Position 5, EXAM-HW-TYPE, is to contain either an E or an H and tells whether the transaction refers to an exam grade or a homework grade. Positions 6 and 7, EXAM-HW-NUMBER, tell which exam or homework number the transaction refers to. If to an exam, EXAM-HW-

```
00700          05  EXAM-HW.
00710              10  EXAM-HW-TYPE                       PIC X.
00720                  88  EXAM                    VALUE "E".
00730                  88  HOMEWORK                VALUE "H".
00740                  88  EXAM-HW-TYPE-VALID      VALUES "E", "H".
00750              10  EXAM-HW-NUMBER                     PIC 99.
00760                  88  EXAM-NUMBER-VALID              VALUES 1 THRU 5.
00770                  88  HOMEWORK-NUMBER-VALID          VALUES 1 THRU 12.
00780              10  EXAM-HW-NUMBER-X REDEFINES EXAM-HW-NUMBER
00790                                                     PIC XX.
00800          05  GRADE-T                               PIC 9(3).
00810          05  GRADE-X REDEFINES GRADE-T             PIC X(3).
00820
00830      01  GRADES-RECORD-M.
00840          05  COURSE-OR-SECTION-M                   PIC X(6).
00850          05  NUMBER-OF-STUDENTS-M                  PIC 9(3).
00860          05  EXAM-GRADE      OCCURS 5 TIMES        PIC 9(3).
00870          05  HOMEWORK-GRADE OCCURS 12 TIMES        PIC 9(3).
00880
00890      01  PAGE-HEADING-1.
00900          05  FILLER          VALUE SPACES          PIC X(20).
00910          05  FILLER
00920              VALUE "GRADE COMPUTATION SYSTEM"      PIC X(24).
00930
00940      01  REPORT-PAGE-HEADING-2.
00950          05  FILLER          VALUE SPACES          PIC X(22).
00960          05  FILLER          VALUE "FILE UPDATE -" PIC X(14).
00970          05  COURSE-OR-SECTION-M-OUT               PIC X(6).
00980
00990      01  ERROR-PAGE-HEADING-2.
01000          05  FILLER          VALUE SPACES          PIC X(21).
01010          05  FILLER          VALUE "ERROR REPORT - "
01020                                                    PIC X(15).
01030          05  COURSE-OR-SECTION-M-OUT               PIC X(6).
01040
01050      01  PAGE-HEADING-3.
01060          05  FILLER          VALUE SPACES          PIC X(47).
01070          05  FILLER          VALUE "PAGE"          PIC X(5).
01080          05  PAGE-NUMBER-OUT                       PIC Z9.
01090
01100      01  REPORT-PAGE-HEADING-4.
01110          05  FILLER          VALUE SPACES          PIC X(10).
01120          05  FILLER          VALUE "STUDENT"       PIC X(9).
01130          05  FILLER          VALUE "EXAM/HW"       PIC X(10).
01140          05  FILLER          VALUE "GRADE"         PIC X(9).
01150          05  FILLER          VALUE "GRADE"         PIC X(9).
01160          05  FILLER          VALUE "NOTES"         PIC X(5).
01170
01180      01  ERROR-PAGE-HEADING-4.
01190          05  FILLER          VALUE SPACES          PIC X(10).
01200          05  FILLER          VALUE "STUDENT"       PIC X(9).
01210          05  FILLER          VALUE "EXAM/HW"       PIC X(10).
01220          05  FILLER          VALUE "GRADE"         PIC X(18).
01230          05  FILLER          VALUE "NOTES"         PIC X(5).
01240
01250      01  REPORT-PAGE-HEADING-5.
01260          05  FILLER          VALUE SPACES          PIC X(10).
01270          05  FILLER          VALUE "NUMBER"        PIC X(9).
01280          05  FILLER          VALUE "NUMBER"        PIC X(9).
01290          05  FILLER          VALUE "ENTERED"       PIC X(9).
01300          05  FILLER          VALUE "CHANGED"       PIC X(7).
01310
01320      01  ERROR-PAGE-HEADING-5.
01330          05  FILLER          VALUE SPACES          PIC X(10).
01340          05  FILLER          VALUE "NUMBER"        PIC X(9).
01350          05  FILLER          VALUE "NUMBER"        PIC X(9).
01360
01370      01  NO-TRANSACTIONS.
01380          05  FILLER      VALUE SPACES              PIC X(17).
01390          05  FILLER      VALUE "NO TRANSACTIONS"   PIC X(15).
01400
01410      01  ERROR-LINE.
01420          05  FILLER      VALUE SPACES              PIC X(11).
01430          05  STUDENT-NUMBER-E                      PIC ZZ9B(6).
01440          05  STUDENT-NUMBER-E-X REDEFINES STUDENT-NUMBER-E
01450                                                    PIC X(3)B(6).
```

(continued)

Figure 15.9   (continued)

```
01460        05   EXAM-HW-TYPE-E                        PIC XB.
01470        05   EXAM-HW-NUMBER-E                      PIC Z9B(6).
01480        05   GRADE-E                               PIC ZZ9B(14).
01490        05   GRADE-X-E REDEFINES GRADE-E           PIC X(3)B(14).
01500        05   MESSAGE-E                             PIC X(41).
01510
01520   01   INVALID-CODE-MESSAGE.
01530        05   FILLER      VALUE "INVALID TRANSACTION CODE -"
01540                                                   PIC X(27).
01550        05   TRANSACTION-CODE-E                    PIC X.
01560
01570   01   GRADE-ENTERED-LINE.
01580        05   FILLER      VALUE SPACES              PIC X(11).
01590        05   STUDENT-NUMBER-T                      PIC ZZ9B(6).
01600        05   EXAM-HW-TYPE                          PIC XB.
01610        05   EXAM-HW-NUMBER                        PIC Z9B(6).
01620        05   GRADE-T                               PIC ZZ9.
01630
01640   01   GRADE-CHANGED-LINE.
01650        05   FILLER      VALUE SPACES              PIC X(11).
01660        05   STUDENT-NUMBER-T                      PIC ZZ9B(6).
01670        05   EXAM-HW-TYPE                          PIC XB.
01680        05   EXAM-HW-NUMBER                        PIC Z9B(15).
01690        05   GRADE-T                               PIC ZZ9.
01700
01710   ************************************************************************
01720
01730   PROCEDURE DIVISION.
01740   DECLARATIVES.
01750   DUMMY-USE SECTION.
01760        USE AFTER ERROR PROCEDURE GRADES-FILE-I-O.
01770   END DECLARATIVES.
01780
01790   NONDECLARATIVE SECTION.
01800   UPDATE-GRADES-FILE.
01810        PERFORM INITIALIZATION.
01820        PERFORM PROCESS-ONE-KEY UNTIL TRANSACTION-INPUT-AREA
01830            IS EQUAL TO HIGH-VALUES.
01840        PERFORM TERMINATION.
01850        STOP RUN.
01860
01870   INITIALIZATION.
01880        OPEN INPUT   TRANSACTION-FILE-IN
01890             OUTPUT  REPORT-FILE-OUT
01900                     ERROR-FILE-OUT
01910             I-O     GRADES-FILE-I-O.
01920        IF MASTER-FILE-CHECK NOT = ZEROS
01930            DISPLAY " MASTER FILE OPEN STATUS = ", MASTER-FILE-CHECK
01940            PERFORM TERMINATION
01950            STOP RUN.
01960        READ GRADES-FILE-I-O NEXT INTO GRADES-RECORD-M.
01970        IF MASTER-FILE-CHECK NOT = ZEROS
01980            DISPLAY " NO MASTER RECORDS "
01990            PERFORM TERMINATION
02000            STOP RUN.
02010        MOVE COURSE-OR-SECTION-M
02020            TO COURSE-OR-SECTION-M-OUT OF REPORT-PAGE-HEADING-2
02030               COURSE-OR-SECTION-M-OUT OF ERROR-PAGE-HEADING-2.
02040        PERFORM PRODUCE-ERROR-HEADINGS.
02050        PERFORM PRODUCE-REPORT-HEADINGS.
02060        PERFORM READ-A-TRANSACTION-RECORD.
02070        IF TRANSACTION-INPUT-AREA IS EQUAL TO HIGH-VALUES
02080            PERFORM WRITE-NO-TRANSACTIONS.
02090
02100   PRODUCE-REPORT-HEADINGS.
02110        WRITE REPORT-RECORD-OUT FROM PAGE-HEADING-1 AFTER PAGE.
02120        ADD 1 TO REPORT-PAGE-COUNTER.
02130        MOVE REPORT-PAGE-COUNTER TO PAGE-NUMBER-OUT.
02140        WRITE REPORT-RECORD-OUT FROM REPORT-PAGE-HEADING-2 AFTER 2.
02150        WRITE REPORT-RECORD-OUT FROM PAGE-HEADING-3.
02160        WRITE REPORT-RECORD-OUT FROM REPORT-PAGE-HEADING-4 AFTER 2.
02170        WRITE REPORT-RECORD-OUT FROM REPORT-PAGE-HEADING-5.
02180        MOVE SPACES TO REPORT-RECORD-OUT.
02190        WRITE REPORT-RECORD-OUT.
02200        MOVE 8 TO LINE-COUNT-ER.
02210
```

```
02220   PRODUCE-ERROR-HEADINGS.
02230       WRITE ERROR-RECORD-OUT FROM PAGE-HEADING-1 AFTER PAGE.
02240       ADD 1 TO ERROR-PAGE-COUNTER.
02250       MOVE ERROR-PAGE-COUNTER TO PAGE-NUMBER-OUT.
02260       WRITE ERROR-RECORD-OUT FROM ERROR-PAGE-HEADING-2 AFTER 2.
02270       WRITE ERROR-RECORD-OUT FROM PAGE-HEADING-3.
02280       WRITE ERROR-RECORD-OUT FROM ERROR-PAGE-HEADING-4 AFTER 3.
02290       WRITE ERROR-RECORD-OUT FROM ERROR-PAGE-HEADING-5.
02300       MOVE SPACES TO ERROR-RECORD-OUT.
02310       WRITE ERROR-RECORD-OUT.
02320       MOVE 9 TO ERROR-LINE-COUNTER.
02330
02340   READ-A-TRANSACTION-RECORD.
02350       MOVE SPACES TO STUDENT-NUMBER-X.
02360       PERFORM READ-TRANSACTION-FILE UNTIL
02370           STUDENT-NUMBER-T IN TRANSACTION-INPUT-AREA IS NUMERIC OR
02380           TRANSACTION-INPUT-AREA IS EQUAL TO HIGH-VALUES.
02390
02400   READ-TRANSACTION-FILE.
02410       READ TRANSACTION-FILE-IN INTO TRANSACTION-INPUT-AREA
02420           AT END
02430               MOVE HIGH-VALUES TO TRANSACTION-INPUT-AREA.
02440       IF TRANSACTION-INPUT-AREA NOT EQUAL TO HIGH-VALUES
02450           IF STUDENT-NUMBER-T IN TRANSACTION-INPUT-AREA NOT NUMERIC
02460               PERFORM WRITE-INVALID-STUDENT-NO-LINE.
02470
02480   PROCESS-ONE-KEY.
02490       PERFORM PROCESS-MASTER.
02500       PERFORM PROCESS-TRANSACTION.
02510       PERFORM CHECK-TO-WRITE-MASTER.
02520
02530   PROCESS-MASTER.
02540       MOVE STUDENT-NUMBER-T IN TRANSACTION-INPUT-AREA
02550           TO RELATIVE-KEY.
02560       READ GRADES-FILE-I-O INTO GRADES-RECORD-M.
02570       IF MASTER-FILE-CHECK = ZEROS
02580           MOVE "Y" TO IS-MASTER-RECORD-IN-THE-FILE,
02590                       IS-MASTER-RECORD-IN-WORK-AREA
02600       ELSE
02610       IF MASTER-FILE-CHECK = "23"
02620           MOVE "N" TO IS-MASTER-RECORD-IN-THE-FILE,
02630                       IS-MASTER-RECORD-IN-WORK-AREA
02640       ELSE
02650           DISPLAY " MASTER FILE READ STATUS = ", MASTER-FILE-CHECK
02660           PERFORM TERMINATION
02670           STOP RUN.
```

(continued)

NUMBER must be a number 1 through 5; if to homework, EXAM-HW-NUMBER must be a number 1 through 12.

The Procedure Division, which starts at line 01730, follows the hierarchy diagram. The paragraph READ-A-TRANSACTION-RECORD, line 02340, uses a validity-checking technique similar to the one used in Program P14-03. READ-A-TRANSACTION-RECORD does not simply READ the next record on the input transaction file and return it to the higher-level paragraph in the program. Instead, READ-A-TRANSACTION-RECORD returns only transaction records having a numeric Student Number. READ-TRANSACTION-FILE, line 02400, checks the Student Number in each transaction after it has been read. If the Student Number is not numeric, READ-TRANSACTION-FILE prints an error message and READs another transaction.

The READ statement at line 02560 is a random READ. When a relative file is read randomly, COBOL uses the value of the RELATIVE KEY field to know which

Figure 15.9   (continued)

```
02680
02690   CHECK-TO-WRITE-MASTER.
02700       MOVE ZEROS TO MASTER-FILE-CHECK.
02710       IF IS-MASTER-RECORD-IN-WORK-AREA = "Y"
02720           REWRITE GRADES-RECORD-I-O FROM GRADES-RECORD-M
02730       ELSE
02740       IF IS-MASTER-RECORD-IN-WORK-AREA = "N" AND
02750           IS-MASTER-RECORD-IN-THE-FILE  = "Y"
02760           DELETE GRADES-FILE-I-O.
02770       IF MASTER-FILE-CHECK NOT = ZEROS
02780           DISPLAY " MASTER FILE WRITE STATUS = ", MASTER-FILE-CHECK
02790           PERFORM TERMINATION
02800           STOP RUN.
02810
02820   PROCESS-TRANSACTION.
02830       PERFORM APPLY-TRANSACTION.
02840       PERFORM READ-A-TRANSACTION-RECORD.
02850
02860   APPLY-TRANSACTION.
02870       IF TRANSACTION-IS-ENTER
02880           PERFORM TEST-FOR-VALID-ENTER
02890       ELSE
02900       IF TRANSACTION-IS-CHANGE
02910           PERFORM TEST-FOR-VALID-CHANGE
02920       ELSE
02930       IF TRANSACTION-IS-DELETE
02940           PERFORM TEST-FOR-VALID-DELETE
02950       ELSE
02960           PERFORM WRITE-INVALID-CODE-LINE.
02970
02980   TEST-FOR-VALID-ENTER.
02990       MOVE "N" TO ANY-ERRORS-IN-INPUT.
03000       PERFORM TEST-FOR-VALID-INPUT.
03010       IF ANY-ERRORS-IN-INPUT = "N"
03020           IF EXAM
03030               PERFORM ENTER-ONE-EXAM-GRADE
03040           ELSE
03050               PERFORM ENTER-ONE-HOMEWORK-GRADE.
03060
03070   ENTER-ONE-EXAM-GRADE.
03080       IF EXAM-GRADE (EXAM-HW-NUMBER IN TRANSACTION-INPUT-AREA) = 0
03090           MOVE GRADE-T IN TRANSACTION-INPUT-AREA TO
03100               EXAM-GRADE (EXAM-HW-NUMBER IN TRANSACTION-INPUT-AREA)
03110           PERFORM WRITE-GRADE-ENTERED-LINE
03120       ELSE
03130           PERFORM WRITE-GRADE-PRESENT-LINE.
03140
03150   ENTER-ONE-HOMEWORK-GRADE.
03160       IF HOMEWORK-GRADE (EXAM-HW-NUMBER IN TRANSACTION-INPUT-AREA)
03170       = 0
03180           MOVE GRADE-T IN TRANSACTION-INPUT-AREA TO
03190           HOMEWORK-GRADE (EXAM-HW-NUMBER IN TRANSACTION-INPUT-AREA)
03200           PERFORM WRITE-GRADE-ENTERED-LINE
03210       ELSE
03220           PERFORM WRITE-GRADE-PRESENT-LINE.
03230
03240   TEST-FOR-VALID-CHANGE.
03250       MOVE "N" TO ANY-ERRORS-IN-INPUT.
03260       PERFORM TEST-FOR-VALID-INPUT.
03270       IF ANY-ERRORS-IN-INPUT = "N"
03280           IF EXAM
03290               PERFORM CHANGE-ONE-EXAM-GRADE
03300           ELSE
03310               PERFORM CHANGE-ONE-HOMEWORK-GRADE.
```

record in the file to READ. Similarly, the REWRITE statement at line 02720 and the DELETE statement at line 02760 are random operations. COBOL uses the value of the RELATIVE KEY field to know which record to REWRITE or DELETE. READ, REWRITE, and DELETE all set the STATUS field if one is specified for the file. The 1974 ANSI standard meanings of the STATUS codes for random READ, REWRITE, and DELETE statements on a relative file are given in Table 15-2. Your COBOL system may have additional codes in the range 90 through 99.

```
03320
03330    CHANGE-ONE-EXAM-GRADE.
03340        IF EXAM-GRADE (EXAM-HW-NUMBER IN TRANSACTION-INPUT-AREA) NOT
03350        = 0
03360            MOVE GRADE-T IN TRANSACTION-INPUT-AREA TO
03370                EXAM-GRADE (EXAM-HW-NUMBER IN TRANSACTION-INPUT-AREA)
03380            PERFORM WRITE-GRADE-CHANGED-LINE
03390        ELSE
03400            PERFORM WRITE-GRADE-NOT-PRESENT-LINE.
03410
03420    CHANGE-ONE-HOMEWORK-GRADE.
03430        IF HOMEWORK-GRADE (EXAM-HW-NUMBER IN TRANSACTION-INPUT-AREA)
03440        NOT = 0
03450            MOVE GRADE-T IN TRANSACTION-INPUT-AREA TO
03460            HOMEWORK-GRADE (EXAM-HW-NUMBER IN TRANSACTION-INPUT-AREA)
03470            PERFORM WRITE-GRADE-CHANGED-LINE
03480        ELSE
03490            PERFORM WRITE-GRADE-NOT-PRESENT-LINE.
03500
03510    TEST-FOR-VALID-DELETE.
03520        IF IS-MASTER-RECORD-IN-WORK-AREA = "N"
03530            PERFORM WRITE-MASTER-MISSING-LINE
03540        ELSE
03550            MOVE "N" TO IS-MASTER-RECORD-IN-WORK-AREA
03560            PERFORM WRITE-RECORD-DELETED-LINE.
03570
03580    TEST-FOR-VALID-INPUT.
03590        IF IS-MASTER-RECORD-IN-WORK-AREA = "N"
03600            MOVE "Y" TO ANY-ERRORS-IN-INPUT
03610            PERFORM WRITE-MASTER-MISSING-LINE.
03620        IF NOT EXAM-HW-TYPE-VALID
03630            MOVE "Y" TO ANY-ERRORS-IN-INPUT
03640            PERFORM WRITE-INVALID-TYPE-LINE.
03650        IF EXAM-HW-NUMBER IN TRANSACTION-INPUT-AREA NOT NUMERIC
03660            MOVE "Y" TO ANY-ERRORS-IN-INPUT
03670            PERFORM WRITE-INVALID-EXAM-HW-NUMBER.
03680        IF GRADE-T IN TRANSACTION-INPUT-AREA NOT NUMERIC
03690            MOVE "Y" TO ANY-ERRORS-IN-INPUT
03700            PERFORM WRITE-INVALID-GRADE-LINE.
03710        IF EXAM AND NOT EXAM-NUMBER-VALID
03720            MOVE "Y" TO ANY-ERRORS-IN-INPUT
03730            PERFORM WRITE-INVALID-EXAM-HW-NUMBER.
03740        IF HOMEWORK AND NOT HOMEWORK-NUMBER-VALID
03750            MOVE "Y" TO ANY-ERRORS-IN-INPUT
03760            PERFORM WRITE-INVALID-EXAM-HW-NUMBER.
03770
03780    TERMINATION.
03790        CLOSE TRANSACTION-FILE-IN
03800              REPORT-FILE-OUT
03810              ERROR-FILE-OUT
03820              GRADES-FILE-I-O.
03830
```

(continued)

Table 15-2

1974 ANSI standard STATUS codes relating to random READ, REWRITE, and DELETE operations on a relative file.

Status Code	Meaning
00	Successful completion
23	Invalid key — no record found
30	Permanent error (hardware malfunction)

The paragraphs ENTER-ONE-EXAM-GRADE, line 03070, and ENTER-ONE-HOMEWORK-GRADE, line 03150, enter a grade into the file only if there is not already a grade there for that exam or homework number. The paragraphs CHANGE-ONE-EXAM-GRADE, line 03330, and CHANGE-ONE-HOMEWORK-GRADE, line 03420, change a grade in the file only if there is already a grade entered. Otherwise, the program prints an error message.

Figure 15.9   (continued)

```
03840    WRITE-INVALID-CODE-LINE.
03850        MOVE SPACES TO ERROR-LINE.
03860        MOVE TRANSACTION-CODE-T TO TRANSACTION-CODE-E.
03870        MOVE INVALID-CODE-MESSAGE TO MESSAGE-E.
03880        MOVE STUDENT-NUMBER-T IN TRANSACTION-INPUT-AREA
03890            TO STUDENT-NUMBER-E.
03900        PERFORM WRITE-ERROR-LINE.
03910
03920    WRITE-NO-TRANSACTIONS.
03930        WRITE ERROR-RECORD-OUT FROM NO-TRANSACTIONS.
03940
03950    WRITE-INVALID-STUDENT-NO-LINE.
03960        MOVE SPACES TO ERROR-LINE.
03970        MOVE STUDENT-NUMBER-X TO STUDENT-NUMBER-E-X.
03980        MOVE "INVALID STUDENT NUMBER" TO MESSAGE-E.
03990        PERFORM WRITE-ERROR-LINE.
04000
04010    WRITE-GRADE-PRESENT-LINE.
04020        MOVE SPACES TO ERROR-LINE.
04030        MOVE STUDENT-NUMBER-T IN TRANSACTION-INPUT-AREA
04040            TO STUDENT-NUMBER-E.
04050        MOVE EXAM-HW-TYPE IN TRANSACTION-INPUT-AREA
04060            TO EXAM-HW-TYPE-E.
04070        MOVE EXAM-HW-NUMBER IN TRANSACTION-INPUT-AREA
04080            TO EXAM-HW-NUMBER-E.
04090        MOVE "GRADE ALREADY PRESENT - INSERTION IGNORED"
04100                            TO MESSAGE-E.
04110        PERFORM WRITE-ERROR-LINE.
04120
04130    WRITE-ERROR-LINE.
04140        IF ERROR-LINE-COUNTER + 1 > PAGE-LIMIT
04150            PERFORM PRODUCE-ERROR-HEADINGS.
04160        WRITE ERROR-RECORD-OUT FROM ERROR-LINE.
04170        ADD 1 TO ERROR-LINE-COUNTER.
04180
04190    WRITE-GRADE-ENTERED-LINE.
04200        MOVE CORRESPONDING TRANSACTION-INPUT-AREA
04210            TO GRADE-ENTERED-LINE.
04220        MOVE CORRESPONDING EXAM-HW TO GRADE-ENTERED-LINE.
04230        IF LINE-COUNT-ER + 1 > PAGE-LIMIT
04240            PERFORM PRODUCE-REPORT-HEADINGS.
04250        WRITE REPORT-RECORD-OUT FROM GRADE-ENTERED-LINE.
04260        ADD 1 TO LINE-COUNT-ER.
04270
04280    WRITE-GRADE-NOT-PRESENT-LINE.
04290        MOVE SPACES TO ERROR-LINE.
04300        MOVE STUDENT-NUMBER-T IN TRANSACTION-INPUT-AREA
04310            TO STUDENT-NUMBER-E.
04320        MOVE EXAM-HW-TYPE IN TRANSACTION-INPUT-AREA
04330            TO EXAM-HW-TYPE-E.
04340        MOVE EXAM-HW-NUMBER IN TRANSACTION-INPUT-AREA
04350            TO EXAM-HW-NUMBER-E.
04360        MOVE "GRADE NOT PRESENT - CHANGE IGNORED"
04370            TO MESSAGE-E.
04380        PERFORM WRITE-ERROR-LINE.
04390
04400    WRITE-GRADE-CHANGED-LINE.
04410        MOVE CORRESPONDING TRANSACTION-INPUT-AREA
04420            TO GRADE-CHANGED-LINE.
04430        MOVE CORRESPONDING EXAM-HW TO GRADE-CHANGED-LINE.
04440        IF LINE-COUNT-ER + 1 > PAGE-LIMIT
04450            PERFORM PRODUCE-REPORT-HEADINGS.
04460        WRITE REPORT-RECORD-OUT FROM GRADE-CHANGED-LINE.
04470        ADD 1 TO LINE-COUNT-ER.
04480
04490    WRITE-MASTER-MISSING-LINE.
04500        MOVE SPACES TO ERROR-LINE.
04510        MOVE STUDENT-NUMBER-T IN TRANSACTION-INPUT-AREA
04520            TO STUDENT-NUMBER-E.
04530        MOVE "MASTER RECORD DOES NOT EXIST" TO MESSAGE-E.
04540        PERFORM WRITE-ERROR-LINE.
04550
```

```
04560  WRITE-RECORD-DELETED-LINE.
04570      MOVE SPACES TO ERROR-LINE.
04580      MOVE STUDENT-NUMBER-T IN TRANSACTION-INPUT-AREA
04590          TO STUDENT-NUMBER-E.
04600      MOVE "RECORD DELETED" TO MESSAGE-E.
04610      IF LINE-COUNT-ER + 1 > PAGE-LIMIT
04620          PERFORM PRODUCE-REPORT-HEADINGS.
04630      WRITE REPORT-RECORD-OUT FROM ERROR-LINE.
04640      ADD 1 TO LINE-COUNT-ER.
04650
04660  WRITE-INVALID-TYPE-LINE.
04670      MOVE SPACES TO ERROR-LINE.
04680      MOVE STUDENT-NUMBER-T IN TRANSACTION-INPUT-AREA
04690          TO STUDENT-NUMBER-E.
04700      MOVE EXAM-HW-TYPE IN TRANSACTION-INPUT-AREA
04710          TO EXAM-HW-TYPE-E.
04720      MOVE "INVALID EXAM/HW TYPE" TO MESSAGE-E.
04730      PERFORM WRITE-ERROR-LINE.
04740
04750  WRITE-INVALID-EXAM-HW-NUMBER.
04760      MOVE SPACES TO ERROR-LINE.
04770      MOVE STUDENT-NUMBER-T IN TRANSACTION-INPUT-AREA
04780          TO STUDENT-NUMBER-E.
04790      MOVE EXAM-HW-TYPE IN TRANSACTION-INPUT-AREA
04800          TO EXAM-HW-TYPE-E.
04810      MOVE EXAM-HW-NUMBER IN TRANSACTION-INPUT-AREA
04820          TO EXAM-HW-NUMBER-E.
04830      MOVE "INVALID EXAM/HW NUMBER" TO MESSAGE-E.
04840      PERFORM WRITE-ERROR-LINE.
04850
04860  WRITE-INVALID-GRADE-LINE.
04870      MOVE SPACES TO ERROR-LINE.
04880      MOVE STUDENT-NUMBER-T IN TRANSACTION-INPUT-AREA
04890          TO STUDENT-NUMBER-E.
04900      MOVE GRADE-X          TO GRADE-X-E.
04910      MOVE "INVALID GRADE"  TO MESSAGE-E.
04920      PERFORM WRITE-ERROR-LINE.
```

Program P15-02 was run with the transaction data shown in Figure 15.10 and the master file created by Program P15-01. Program P15-02 produced the report output shown in Figure 15.11.

Figure 15.10 Transaction input to Program P15-02.

```
-------------------------------------------------------------------------------
         1         2         3         4         5         6         7         8
1234567890123456789012345678901234567890123456789012345678901234567890123456789 0
-------------------------------------------------------------------------------
D002
E001E01090
E003E02065
E003E04066
E010H04090
E011E01079
E012H10099
E017E02078
E020H02070
E001E04081
E003H07071
E010H01078
E011H07083
E012E02088
E017H04089
E020E01060
D004
E001E05093
E003E03050
E010E01093
E011E03094
D005
```

(continued)

Figure 15.10   (continued)

```
E020H09067
D021
E017H07090
E011H09098
D014
E012E04061
E020H05080
E008E02081
E013H04090
D006
T016E02090
C008E02090
E0ABE02086
C016E03100
E008E01095
E008H11079
E003H16095
E019H07070
D018
E001H12088
E020E04089
E017E05080
C017E05090
E001H020A2
E013H09069
E019N05088
D009
E011E05091
E001H09079
D015
C013H09070
C010H01085
E071E05090
E010E03089
E017E03094
E003H06059
E012H11076
E020H09067
E010H05069
E012H12069
E016E01098
D007
E001E02100
E001H03100
E001H04097
E001H05065
E001H06075
E001H07088
E003E01075
E003E05075
E003H02065
E003H03075
E003H04088
E003H05073
E003H06075
E003H07085
E003H08089
E003H09095
E008E03075
E008E04085
E008H01065
E008H02075
E008H03088
E008H04073
E008H05075
E008H06085
E008H07089
E008H08095
E010E02088
E010E04075
E010E05085
E010H06075
E010H07088
E010H08073
E010H09075
E010H10085
E010H11089
E010H12095
```

```
E010H13090
E011H01073
E011H02075
E011H03085
E011H04089
E012E01073
E012E03075
E012E05085
E013E01075
E013E02085
E013E03089
E013E04095
E013E05090
E013H05065
E013H06075
E013H07088
E013H08073
E017E01089
E017E04095
E017H08085
E017H09089
E017H10095
E017H11090
E017H12095
E020E02073
E020E03075
E020E01085
E020H06065
E020H07075
E020H08088
E017H01100
E017H02100
E017H03100
```

Figure 15.11 Report output from Program P15-02.

```
              GRADE COMPUTATION SYSTEM

              FILE UPDATE - DP407
                                        PAGE   1

STUDENT   EXAM/HW    GRADE     GRADE     NOTES
NUMBER    NUMBER     ENTERED   CHANGED

   2                                     RECORD DELETED
   1      E   1       90
   3      E   2       65
   3      E   4       66
  10      H   4       90
  11      E   1       79
  12      H  10       99
  17      E   2       78
  20      H   2       70
   1      E   4       81
   3      H   7       71
  10      H   1       78
  11      H   7       83
  12      E   2       88
  17      H   4       89
  20      E   1       60
   4                                     RECORD DELETED
   1      E   5       93
   3      E   3       50
  10      E   1       93
  11      E   3       94
   5                                     RECORD DELETED
  20      H   9       67
  21                                     RECORD DELETED
  17      H   7       90
  11      H   9       98
  14                                     RECORD DELETED
  12      E   4       61
  20      H   5       80
   8      E   2       81
  13      H   4       90
```

(continued)

Figure 15.11   (continued)

STUDENT NUMBER	EXAM/HW NUMBER		GRADE ENTERED	GRADE CHANGED	NOTES
6					RECORD DELETED
8	E	2		90	
8	E	1	95		
8	H	11	79		
19	H	7	70		
18					RECORD DELETED
1	H	12	88		
20	E	4	89		
17	E	5	80		
17	E	5		90	
13	H	9	69		

GRADE COMPUTATION SYSTEM

FILE UPDATE - DP407

PAGE   2

STUDENT NUMBER	EXAM/HW NUMBER		GRADE ENTERED	GRADE CHANGED	NOTES
9					RECORD DELETED
11	E	5	91		
1	H	9	79		
15					RECORD DELETED
13	H	9		70	
10	H	1		85	
10	E	3	89		
17	E	3	94		
3	H	6	59		
12	H	11	76		
10	H	5	69		
12	H	12	69		
16	E	1	98		
7					RECORD DELETED
1	E	2	100		
1	H	3	100		
1	H	4	97		
1	H	5	65		
1	H	6	75		
1	H	7	88		
3	E	1	75		
3	E	5	75		
3	H	2	65		
3	H	3	75		
3	H	4	88		
3	H	5	73		
3	H	8	89		
3	H	9	95		
8	E	3	75		
8	E	4	85		
8	H	1	65		
8	H	2	75		
8	H	3	88		
8	H	4	73		
8	H	5	75		
8	H	6	85		
8	H	7	89		
8	H	8	95		
10	E	2	88		
10	E	4	75		
10	E	5	85		
10	H	6	75		

```
                GRADE COMPUTATION SYSTEM

                FILE UPDATE - DP407
                                          PAGE  3

    STUDENT   EXAM/HW    GRADE     GRADE      NOTES
    NUMBER    NUMBER    ENTERED   CHANGED

      10      H  7        88
      10      H  8        73
      10      H  9        75
      10      H 10        85
      10      H 11        89
      10      H 12        95
      11      H  1        73
      11      H  2        75
      11      H  3        85
      11      H  4        89
      12      E  1        73
      12      E  3        75
      12      E  5        85
      13      E  1        75
      13      E  2        85
      13      E  3        89
      13      E  4        95
      13      E  5        90
      13      H  5        65
      13      H  6        75
      13      H  7        88
      13      H  8        73
      17      E  1        89
      17      E  4        95
      17      H  8        85
      17      H  9        89
      17      H 10        95
      17      H 11        90
      17      H 12        95
      20      E  2        73
      20      E  3        75
      20      H  6        65
      20      H  7        75
      20      H  8        88
      17      H  1       100
      17      H  2       100
      17      H  3       100
```

```
                GRADE COMPUTATION SYSTEM

                ERROR REPORT - DP407
                                          PAGE  1

    STUDENT   EXAM/HW    GRADE              NOTES
    NUMBER    NUMBER

      16                            INVALID TRANSACTION CODE - T
      0AB                           INVALID STUDENT NUMBER
      16      E  3                  GRADE NOT PRESENT - CHANGE IGNORED
       3      H 16                  INVALID EXAM/HW NUMBER
       1                 0A2        INVALID GRADE
      19      N                     INVALID EXAM/HW TYPE
      71                            MASTER RECORD DOES NOT EXIST
      20      H  9                  GRADE ALREADY PRESENT - INSERTION IGNORED
       3      H  6                  GRADE ALREADY PRESENT - INSERTION IGNORED
       3      H  7                  GRADE ALREADY PRESENT - INSERTION IGNORED
      10      H 13                  INVALID EXAM/HW NUMBER
      20      E  1                  GRADE ALREADY PRESENT - INSERTION IGNORED
```

EXERCISE 2

Write a program to update the file you created in Exercise 1. Have your program accept transactions in the following formats:

Positions	Field
1 – 2	Transaction code
	01 — Starting cash balance
	02 — Ending cash balance
	03 — Grocery sale
	04 — Produce sale
	05 — Meat sale
	06 — Dairy sale
	07 — Tax
	08 — Bottle and can deposit
	09 — Coupon
	10 — Deposit return
	11 — Adjustment
3 – 5	Register Number
6 – 11	Amount (in dollars and cents)
6 – 9	Amount dollars
10 – 11	Amount cents
12 – 80	spaces

The format for a deletion transaction is:

Positions	Field
1 – 2	Code 12
3 – 5	Register Number

For transaction types 01 and 02, have your program replace the corresponding field in the master record with the Amount field in the transaction. For transaction types 03 through 10, have your program add the Amount field in the transaction to the corresponding field in the master record. In transactions of type 11, adjustments may be positive or negative; have your program add the Amount field in the transaction to the Adjustments field in the master record. For transaction type 12, have your program remove the master record from the file.

Have your program make all suitable validity checks on each transaction. Have your program print reports showing erroneous transactions and all changes made to the master file. Save the updated master file for use later in this chapter.

Processing a Relative File Sequentially

Program P15-03 computes student grades from the updated master file produced by Program P15-02. In many ways, processing a relative file sequentially is the same as processing any file sequentially. But there is one interesting characteristic of a relative file that gives the programmer an option when the file is processed sequentially. Remember that a relative file may have some of its slots empty. Sequential READs to a relative file bring in only records that are actually in the file. Empty slots are skipped over and ignored by the READ statements. At the option of the programmer, COBOL can be asked to provide the program with the relative record number (the slot number) of each record that is read. Program P15-03 will use that option, so that as each student's record is read the program can know the Student Number of the record.

Program P15-03 computes and prints a letter grade for each student. The letter grade depends one-third on the final exam (exam number 5), one-third on the average of the other four exams, and one-third on the homework. If a student missed an exam, the grade on that exam is taken as zero. Letter grades correspond to the following numeric ranges:

90 or higher	A
80 or higher and below 90	B
70 or higher and below 80	C
60 or higher and below 70	D
below 60	F

If a student dropped the course, the program assigns a grade of W. The grade listing has the format shown in Figure 15.12. It shows that every Student Number is assigned some grade, either W or a letter A through F. If a particular Student Number has no record in the file, that number is assigned a grade of W. If a Student Number has a record in the file, a grade A through F is computed and printed along with the numeric values that were used in the computation.

Figure 15.12 Output format for Program P15-03.

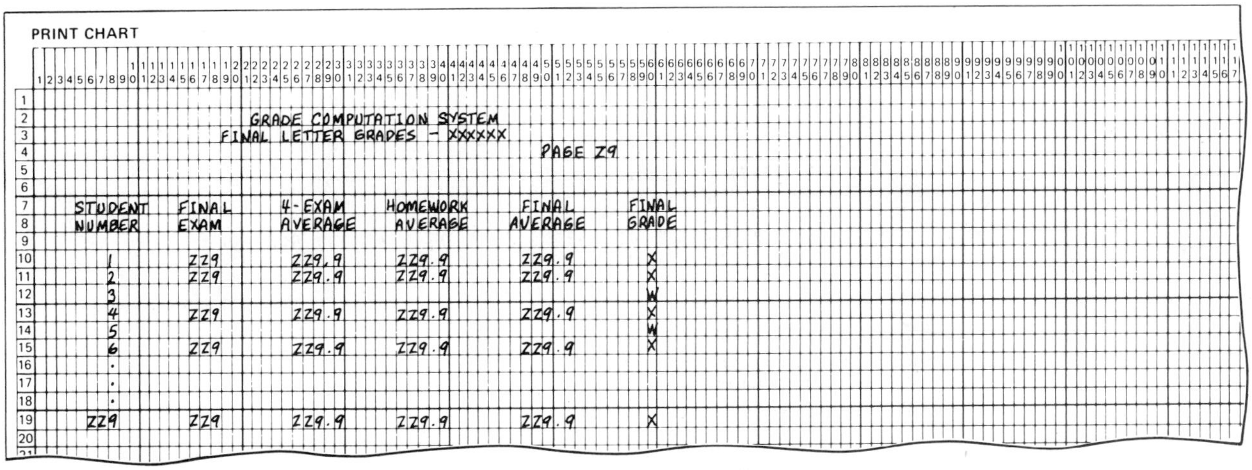

A hierarchy diagram for Program P15-03 is shown in Figure 15.13. For each Student Number, the box "Produce a final grade" determines whether a W grade or a letter grade A to F is to be assigned, depending on whether that Student Number has a record in the master file.

Figure 15.13   Hierarchy diagram for Program P15-03.

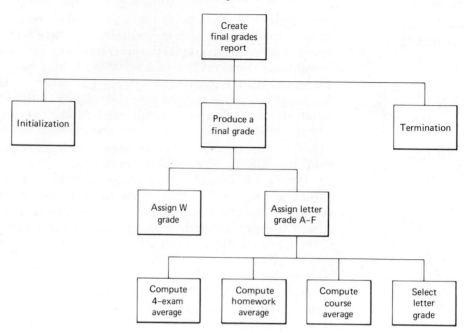

Program P15-03 is shown in Figure 15.14. The FILE-CONTROL entry for the master file contains the clause ACCESS **SEQUENTIAL,** at line 00190. In most programs, no ACCESS SEQUENTIAL clause is needed, for if ACCESS SEQUENTIAL is omitted, sequential access is assumed. But in this program we need a RELATIVE KEY, and the RELATIVE KEY phrase is part of the ACCESS clause. So in order to have a RELATIVE KEY you must include an ACCESS clause. The general rule is that whenever you have ACCESS RANDOM or ACCESS DYNAMIC you must have a RELATIVE KEY phrase, and whenever you need a RELA-

Figure 15.14   Program P15-03.

```
CB1 RELEASE 2.4                              IBM OS/VS COBOL  JULY  1, 1982


                    8.33.37          APR 10,1988


00010   IDENTIFICATION DIVISION.
00020   PROGRAM-ID.  P15-03.
00030 *
00040 *    THIS PROGRAM PROCESSES A FILE OF EXAM AND HOMEWORK
00050 *    GRADES AND PRODUCES A LETTER GRADE FOR EACH STUDENT.
00060 *
00070 ***************************************************************
00080
00090   ENVIRONMENT DIVISION.
00100   CONFIGURATION SECTION.
00110   SOURCE-COMPUTER.  IBM-370.
00120   OBJECT-COMPUTER.  IBM-370.
00130
00140   INPUT-OUTPUT SECTION.
00150   FILE-CONTROL.
00160      SELECT LETTER-GRADES-FILE-OUT ASSIGN TO PRINTER.
00170      SELECT GRADES-MASTER-FILE-IN  ASSIGN TO DISKUNIT
00180          ORGANIZATION RELATIVE
00190          ACCESS SEQUENTIAL
00200          RELATIVE KEY IS STUDENT-NUMBER-W
00210          STATUS IS MASTER-FILE-CHECK.
00220
```

```
00230    ******************************************************************
00240
00250    DATA DIVISION.
00260
00270    FILE SECTION.
00280    FD  GRADES-MASTER-FILE-IN
00290        RECORD CONTAINS 60 CHARACTERS
00300        LABEL RECORDS ARE STANDARD.
00310
00320    01  GRADES-RECORD-IN                         PIC X(60).
00330
00340    FD  LETTER-GRADES-FILE-OUT
00350        LABEL RECORDS ARE OMITTED.
00360
00370    01  GRADES-RECORD-OUT                        PIC X(62).
00380
00390    WORKING-STORAGE SECTION.
00400    01  PAGE-NUMBER-W           VALUE ZERO       PIC S99.
00410    01  PAGE-LIMIT             VALUE 50         PIC S99 COMP SYNC.
00420    01  LINE-COUNT-ER                           PIC S99 COMP SYNC.
00430    01  MASTER-FILE-CHECK                       PIC XX.
00440    01  STUDENT-COUNTER                         PIC S9(3).
00450    01  STUDENT-NUMBER-W                        PIC 9(3).
00460    01  NUMBER-OF-STUDENTS-W    VALUE ZERO       PIC S9(3).
00470    01  NUMBER-OF-HOMEWORKS     VALUE 12        PIC 99.
00480    01  HOMEWORK-SUBSCRIPT                      PIC S99 COMP SYNC.
00490    01  LETTER-GRADE                            PIC X.
00500
00510    01  GRADES-RECORD-M.
00520        05  COURSE-OR-SECTION-M                 PIC X(6).
00530        05  NUMBER-OF-STUDENTS-M                PIC 9(3).
00540        05  EXAM-GRADE       OCCURS 5 TIMES     PIC 9(3).
00550        05  HOMEWORK-GRADE OCCURS 12 TIMES      PIC 9(3).
00560
00570    01  ARITHMETIC-RESULTS.
00580        05  4-EXAM-AVERAGE                      PIC S9(3)V9.
00590        05  HOMEWORK-AVERAGE                    PIC S9(3)V9.
00600        05  HOMEWORK-TOTAL                      PIC S9(4).
00610        05  COURSE-AVERAGE                      PIC S9(3)V9.
00620            88  GRADE-IS-EXCELLENT      VALUES 90 THRU 999.9.
00630            88  GRADE-IS-GOOD           VALUES 80 THRU 89.9.
00640            88  GRADE-IS-AVERAGE        VALUES 70 THRU 79.9.
00650            88  GRADE-IS-LOWEST-PASSING VALUES 60 THRU 69.9.
00660
00670    01  PAGE-HEADING-1.
00680        05  FILLER            VALUE SPACES      PIC X(20).
00690        05  FILLER
00700            VALUE "GRADE COMPUTATION SYSTEM"    PIC X(24).
```

(continued)

TIVE KEY for any reason, you must have some form of ACCESS clause. You are permitted to have ACCESS SEQUENTIAL without a RELATIVE KEY phrase.

When a relative file is read sequentially, each READ statement brings in the next record that is actually in the file. In Program P15-03 we have a RELATIVE KEY, STUDENT-NUMBER-W. Each time a record is read from the master file, COBOL will place the relative record number of that record into STUDENT-NUMBER-W. You will see when we look at the Procedure Division how the program uses STUDENT-NUMBER-W to determine whether there are any Student Numbers to be given grades of W.

In the Working Storage Section the field STUDENT-COUNTER, line 00440, is used to ensure that every Student Number is assigned a grade. During execution of the program, STUDENT-COUNTER is varied from 1 on up in increments of 1, and some grade is printed for each different value of STUDENT-COUNTER, whether or not there is a record in the master file for that Student Number. The field NUMBER-OF-STUDENTS-W, line 00460, is used to show how many records the master file contained when it was created, that is, the number of students represented in the file before any withdrawals.

Figure 15.14   (continued)

```
00710
00720   01  PAGE-HEADING-2.
00730       05  FILLER           VALUE SPACES        PIC X(18).
00740       05  FILLER           VALUE "FINAL LETTER GRADES -"
00750                                                PIC X(22).
00760       05  COURSE-OR-SECTION-M-OUT             PIC X(6).
00770
00780   01  PAGE-HEADING-3.
00790       05  FILLER           VALUE SPACES        PIC X(49).
00800       05  FILLER           VALUE "PAGE"        PIC X(5).
00810       05  PAGE-NUMBER-OUT                      PIC Z9.
00820
00830   01  PAGE-HEADING-4.
00840       05  FILLER           VALUE SPACES        PIC X(4).
00850       05  FILLER           VALUE "STUDENT"     PIC X(10).
00860       05  FILLER           VALUE "FINAL"       PIC X(10).
00870       05  FILLER           VALUE "4-EXAM"      PIC X(10).
00880       05  FILLER           VALUE "HOMEWORK"    PIC X(13).
00890       05  FILLER           VALUE "FINAL"       PIC X(10).
00900       05  FILLER           VALUE "FINAL"       PIC X(5).
00910
00920   01  PAGE-HEADING-5.
00930       05  FILLER           VALUE SPACES        PIC X(4).
00940       05  FILLER           VALUE "NUMBER"      PIC X(10).
00950       05  FILLER           VALUE "EXAM"        PIC X(10).
00960       05  FILLER           VALUE "AVERAGE"     PIC X(11).
00970       05  FILLER           VALUE "AVERAGE"     PIC X(11).
00980       05  FILLER           VALUE "AVERAGE"     PIC X(11).
00990       05  FILLER           VALUE "GRADE"       PIC X(5).
01000
01010   01  LETTER-GRADE-LINE.
01020       05  FILLER       VALUE SPACES            PIC X(5).
01030       05  STUDENT-COUNTER-OUT                  PIC ZZ9B(7).
01040       05  EXAM-GRADE-5-OUT                     PIC ZZ9B(7).
01050       05  4-EXAM-AVERAGE-OUT                   PIC ZZ9.9B(5).
01060       05  HOMEWORK-AVERAGE-OUT                 PIC ZZ9.9B(7).
01070       05  COURSE-AVERAGE-OUT                   PIC ZZ9.9B(7).
01080       05  LETTER-GRADE-OUT                     PIC X.
01090
01100   01  NO-INPUT-DATA.
01110       05  FILLER           VALUE SPACES        PIC X(17).
01120       05  FILLER           VALUE "NO INPUT DATA"  PIC X(13).
01130
01140   ************************************************************
01150
01160   PROCEDURE DIVISION.
01170   DECLARATIVES.
01180   DUMMY-USE SECTION.
01190       USE AFTER ERROR PROCEDURE GRADES-MASTER-FILE-IN.
01200   END DECLARATIVES.
01210
01220   NONDECLARATIVE SECTION.
01230   CREATE-FINAL-GRADES-REPORT.
01240       PERFORM INITIALIZATION.
01250       PERFORM PRODUCE-A-FINAL-GRADE
01260           VARYING STUDENT-COUNTER FROM 1 BY 1 UNTIL
01270           STUDENT-COUNTER GREATER THAN NUMBER-OF-STUDENTS-W.
01280       PERFORM TERMINATION.
01290       STOP RUN.
01300
```

The Procedure Division begins at line 01160. The PERFORM statement at line 01250 causes a grade to be produced for every Student Number that was originally in the master file.

```
01310   INITIALIZATION.
01320       OPEN INPUT  GRADES-MASTER-FILE-IN
01330            OUTPUT LETTER-GRADES-FILE-OUT.
01340       IF MASTER-FILE-CHECK NOT = ZEROS
01350           DISPLAY " MASTER FILE OPEN STATUS = ", MASTER-FILE-CHECK
01360           CLOSE LETTER-GRADES-FILE-OUT,
01370                 GRADES-MASTER-FILE-IN
01380           STOP RUN.
01390       PERFORM READ-MASTER-FILE.
01400       IF MASTER-FILE-CHECK = "10"
01410           WRITE GRADES-RECORD-OUT FROM NO-INPUT-DATA AFTER PAGE
01420       ELSE
01430           MOVE COURSE-OR-SECTION-M  TO COURSE-OR-SECTION-M-OUT
01440           MOVE NUMBER-OF-STUDENTS-M TO NUMBER-OF-STUDENTS-W
01450           PERFORM PRODUCE-PAGE-HEADINGS.
01460
01470   PRODUCE-PAGE-HEADINGS.
01480       ADD 1 TO PAGE-NUMBER-W.
01490       MOVE PAGE-NUMBER-W TO PAGE-NUMBER-OUT.
01500       WRITE GRADES-RECORD-OUT FROM PAGE-HEADING-1 AFTER PAGE.
01510       WRITE GRADES-RECORD-OUT FROM PAGE-HEADING-2.
01520       WRITE GRADES-RECORD-OUT FROM PAGE-HEADING-3.
01530       WRITE GRADES-RECORD-OUT FROM PAGE-HEADING-4 AFTER 4.
01540       WRITE GRADES-RECORD-OUT FROM PAGE-HEADING-5.
01550       MOVE SPACES TO GRADES-RECORD-OUT.
01560       WRITE GRADES-RECORD-OUT.
01570       MOVE 9 TO LINE-COUNT-ER.
01580
01590   READ-MASTER-FILE.
01600       READ GRADES-MASTER-FILE-IN INTO GRADES-RECORD-M.
01610       IF MASTER-FILE-CHECK = ZEROS OR "10"
01620           NEXT SENTENCE
01630       ELSE
01640           DISPLAY " MASTER FILE READ STATUS = ",
01650                   MASTER-FILE-CHECK
01660           PERFORM TERMINATION
01670           STOP RUN.
01680
01690   PRODUCE-A-FINAL-GRADE.
01700       IF STUDENT-COUNTER NOT EQUAL TO STUDENT-NUMBER-W
01710           PERFORM ASSIGN-W-GRADE
01720       ELSE
01730           PERFORM ASSIGN-LETTER-GRADE-A-F
01740           PERFORM READ-MASTER-FILE.
```

(continued)

The READ statement at line 01600 is a sequential READ. Each time it executes, COBOL brings in from the file the next record actually in the file, skipping over and ignoring any empty slots. Since there is a RELATIVE KEY given for this file, the READ statement updates the RELATIVE KEY field by placing into it the relative record number of the record just read. A sequential READ statement to a relative file sets the STATUS field if one is specified for the file. The 1974 ANSI standard meanings of the STATUS codes related to READing a relative file sequentially are given in Table 15-3.

Table 15-3
1974 ANSI standard STATUS codes related to READing a relative file sequentially.

Status Code	Meaning
00	Successful completion
10	At end — end-of-file encountered
30	Permanent error (hardware malfunction)

Your own COBOL system may have other codes in the range 90 – 99.

The paragraph PRODUCE-A-FINAL-GRADE begins at line 01690. The IF statement at line 01700 determines whether the Student Number that is next to be assigned a grade has a record in the master file. It does this by comparing

Figure 15.14   (continued)

```
01750
01760  ASSIGN-LETTER-GRADE-A-F.
01770      PERFORM COMPUTE-4-EXAM-AVERAGE.
01780      PERFORM COMPUTE-HOMEWORK-AVERAGE.
01790      PERFORM COMPUTE-COURSE-AVERAGE.
01800      PERFORM SELECT-LETTER-GRADE.
01810
01820  COMPUTE-4-EXAM-AVERAGE.
01830      COMPUTE 4-EXAM-AVERAGE ROUNDED =
01840          (EXAM-GRADE (1) +
01850           EXAM-GRADE (2) +
01860           EXAM-GRADE (3) +
01870           EXAM-GRADE (4)) / 4.
01880
01890  COMPUTE-COURSE-AVERAGE.
01900      COMPUTE COURSE-AVERAGE ROUNDED =
01910          (EXAM-GRADE (5) +
01920           4-EXAM-AVERAGE +
01930           HOMEWORK-AVERAGE) / 3.
01940
01950  SELECT-LETTER-GRADE.
01960      IF GRADE-IS-EXCELLENT
01970          MOVE "A" TO LETTER-GRADE
01980      ELSE
01990      IF GRADE-IS-GOOD
02000          MOVE "B" TO LETTER-GRADE
02010      ELSE
02020      IF GRADE-IS-AVERAGE
02030          MOVE "C" TO LETTER-GRADE
02040      ELSE
02050      IF GRADE-IS-LOWEST-PASSING
02060          MOVE "D" TO LETTER-GRADE
02070      ELSE
02080          MOVE "F" TO LETTER-GRADE.
02090      PERFORM WRITE-LETTER-GRADE-LINE.
02100
02110  COMPUTE-HOMEWORK-AVERAGE.
02120      MOVE 0 TO HOMEWORK-TOTAL.
02130      PERFORM ACCUMULATE-HOMEWORK-GRADES
02140          VARYING HOMEWORK-SUBSCRIPT FROM 1 BY 1 UNTIL
02150          HOMEWORK-SUBSCRIPT GREATER THAN NUMBER-OF-HOMEWORKS.
02160      COMPUTE HOMEWORK-AVERAGE ROUNDED =
02170          HOMEWORK-TOTAL / NUMBER-OF-HOMEWORKS.
02180
02190  ACCUMULATE-HOMEWORK-GRADES.
02200      ADD HOMEWORK-GRADE (HOMEWORK-SUBSCRIPT) TO HOMEWORK-TOTAL.
02210
02220  ASSIGN-W-GRADE.
02230      MOVE SPACES TO LETTER-GRADE-LINE.
02240      MOVE STUDENT-COUNTER TO STUDENT-COUNTER-OUT.
02250      MOVE "W"              TO LETTER-GRADE-OUT.
02260      PERFORM WRITE-GRADE-LINE.
02270
02280  WRITE-GRADE-LINE.
02290      IF LINE-COUNT-ER + 1 > PAGE-LIMIT
02300          PERFORM PRODUCE-PAGE-HEADINGS.
02310      WRITE GRADES-RECORD-OUT FROM LETTER-GRADE-LINE.
02320      ADD 1 TO LINE-COUNT-ER.
02330
02340  WRITE-LETTER-GRADE-LINE.
02350      MOVE STUDENT-COUNTER TO STUDENT-COUNTER-OUT.
02360      MOVE EXAM-GRADE (5)   TO EXAM-GRADE-5-OUT.
02370      MOVE 4-EXAM-AVERAGE   TO 4-EXAM-AVERAGE-OUT.
02380      MOVE HOMEWORK-AVERAGE TO HOMEWORK-AVERAGE-OUT.
02390      MOVE COURSE-AVERAGE   TO COURSE-AVERAGE-OUT.
02400      MOVE LETTER-GRADE     TO LETTER-GRADE-OUT.
02410      PERFORM WRITE-GRADE-LINE.
02420
02430  TERMINATION.
02440      CLOSE GRADES-MASTER-FILE-IN
02450            LETTER-GRADES-FILE-OUT.
```

STUDENT-COUNTER (whose value is the Student Number next to be assigned a grade) to STUDENT-NUMBER-W (whose value is the Student Number of the master record now in GRADES-RECORD-M). If the Student Numbers are not EQUAL, it means that the student's record has been removed from the master file and the student should be assigned a grade of W.

Program P15-03 was run with the updated master file created by Program P15-02. Program P15-03 produced the output shown in Figure 15.15.

Figure 15.15 Output from Program P15-03.

```
                    GRADE COMPUTATION SYSTEM
                 FINAL LETTER GRADES - DP407
                                                PAGE   1


    STUDENT     FINAL      4-EXAM     HOMEWORK     FINAL      FINAL
    NUMBER      EXAM       AVERAGE    AVERAGE      AVERAGE    GRADE

       1         93         67.8       49.3         70.0        C
       2                                                        W
       3         75         64.0       51.3         63.4        D
       4                                                        W
       5                                                        W
       6                                                        W
       7                                                        W
       8          0         86.3       60.3         48.9        F
       9                                                        W
      10         85         86.3       68.7         80.0        B
      11         91         43.3       41.9         58.7        F
      12         85         74.3       20.3         59.9        F
      13         90         86.0       38.4         71.5        C
      14                                                        W
      15                                                        W
      16          0         24.5        0.0          8.2        F
      17         90         89.0       77.8         85.6        B
      18                                                        W
      19          0          0.0        5.8          1.9        F
      20          0         74.3       37.1         37.1        F
      21                                                        W
```

EXERCISE 3

Write a program to process the master file you updated in Exercise 2 and produce a report in the format shown in Figure 15.E3. Have your program print a line for every cash register number 1 through 135. If any register has no record in the master file, have your program print a message REGISTER OUT OF SERVICE for that register.

For each register having a record in the master file, have your program carry out the following processing:

1. Print the Starting Cash Balance, Adjustments, and Ending Cash Balance from the master record.
2. In the column headed CASH ADDITIONS, print the total of all Sales fields, Tax, and Bottle and Can Deposits from the master record.
3. In the column headed CASH REMOVALS, print the total of the Coupons field and the Deposit Returns field from the master record.
4. Compute a trial sum of the Starting Cash Balance, plus Cash Additions, minus Cash Removals, plus Adjustments.
5. If the trial sum is not equal to the Ending Cash Balance, subtract the trial sum from the Ending Cash Balance and print the difference in the column headed OUT OF BALANCE. If the trial sum is equal to the Ending Cash Balance, print nothing in the OUT OF BALANCE column.

Figure 15.E3   Output format for Exercise 3.

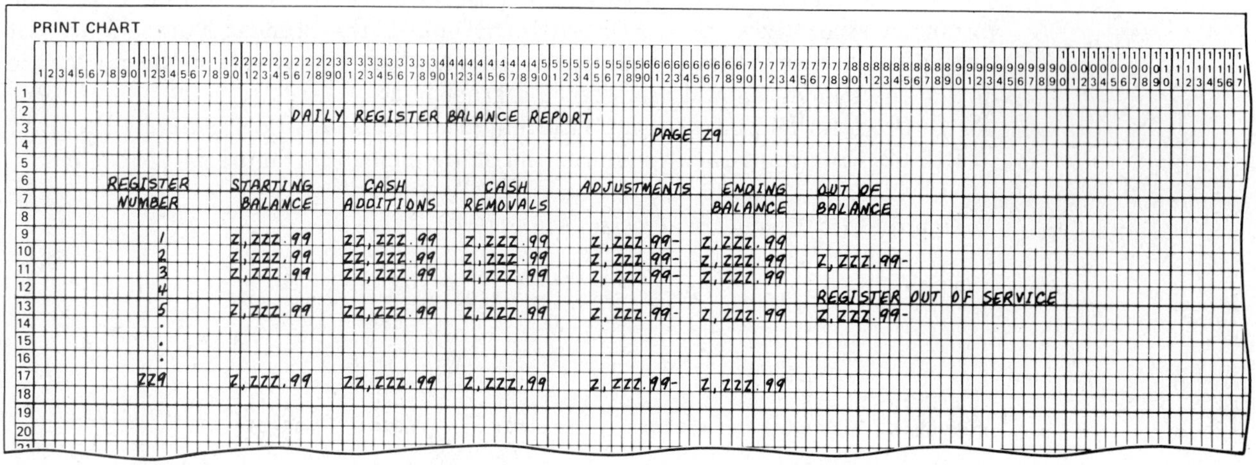

An Application Using Randomizing

In the grades file we have used so far, the students were numbered consecutively, from 1 through 21, with every number being used. Similarly, in Exercises 1 through 3, the cash registers were also numbered consecutively, from 1 through 135. In the real world it does not always happen that the objects to be described in a master file are numbered consecutively. More often there are gaps, sometimes quite large gaps, in the numbering.

Consider the savings account master file we used in Chapters 12 through 14. There we had a five-digit account number, but we did not use all the 100,000 different numbers from 00000 to 99999. We didn't even come close to using all of the numbers. In fact, we had at most not more than 55 accounts in the master file. If we wanted to store the savings account master as a relative file using only the techniques we have studied so far, we would have to set up a file with 100,000 slots (99,999 slots actually, because there cannot be any slot number 0), and put records into only about 55 of them.

Fortunately, well-known techniques exist that permit this kind of situation to be adapted for use in a relative file. One of the simplest of such techniques is called the **division/remainder method.** It proceeds as follows:

1. Determine the number of slots needed in the file. Often, a relative file using the division/remainder method should contain about 20 percent more slots than there are records in the file. If 20 percent turns out not to be a satisfactory figure for a particular file, it can be changed. You will see later why the extra slots are needed and how to tell whether 20 percent is enough. For our file of 55 savings account records, a file with 66 slots should be suitable to start with.

2. Select the nearest **prime number** that is less than the number of slots selected in step 1. A prime number is a number divisible only by itself and the integer 1. The nearest prime less than 66 is 61, so we select it.

3. Then, to find which slot any particular account record should go into, divide the account number by the prime number chosen in step 2, ignore the quotient, add 1 to the remainder, and use that as the slot number for the record. So if we wanted to determine into which slot to place the record for account number 00298, we divide 298 by 61 (which gives a quotient of 4 and a remainder of 54). Thus the record for account number 00298 should be stored in slot number 55. Table 15-4 shows some possible account numbers and the slots they would go into.

Table 15-4
Some Account Numbers and the relative record numbers of their records, using the division/ remainder method with a divisor of 61.

Account Number	Remainder After Dividing by 61	Slot Number
00001	1	2
00013	13	14
00060	60	61
00080	19	20
00122	0	1
00123	1	2
00202	19	20
00250	6	7

You can see that when the division/remainder method is used, different record keys can sometimes yield the same **home slot** number. Any two or more record keys that yield the same home slot number are called **synonyms.** There is no way to avoid synonyms when the division/remainder method is used, but you will see how the conflict for slots is resolved when we do a program using the division/ remainder technique.

The division/remainder method can be used even if a record key contains one or more nonnumeric characters. The procedures involved are beyond the scope of this book, but can be found in any complete book on systems design.

Creating a Relative File Randomly

Program P15-04 creates a savings-account master file as a relative file, using the file specifications developed in the preceding section. The logic in Program P15-04 is very similar to that in Program P12-02, which created a sequential savings-account master file on tape. The input to Program P15-04 is the same as to Program P12-02, records representing new accounts (The input format is described on page 383.). In Program P15-04, as in Program P12-02, the input transactions are SORTed on Account Number and checked for duplicate keys and other errors. If an input record is found to be error-free, the program constructs a master record and writes it to the output master file. In Program P12-02, master records were written sequentially onto an output tape. But in Program P15-04, each master record is instead written into a particular slot in a relative file, and the slot number is computed for each record by the division/remainder method described in the preceding section.

Program P15-04 is shown in Figure 15.16. The FILE-CONTROL entry for the

Figure 15.16 Program P15-04.

```
CB1 RELEASE 2.4                              IBM OS/VS COBOL  JULY  1, 1982

                    19.01.46        APR 10,1988

00010  IDENTIFICATION DIVISION.
00020  PROGRAM-ID.  P15-04.
00030 *
00040 *    THIS PROGRAM CREATES A RELATIVE
00050 *    MASTER FILE OF SAVINGS ACCOUNT RECORDS.
00060 *
00070 ****************************************************************
00080
00090  ENVIRONMENT DIVISION.
00100  CONFIGURATION SECTION.
00110  SOURCE-COMPUTER.  IBM-370.
00120  OBJECT-COMPUTER.  IBM-370.
```

Figure 15.16   (continued)

```
00130
00140    INPUT-OUTPUT SECTION.
00150    FILE-CONTROL.
00160        SELECT SAVINGS-ACCOUNT-DATA-FILE-IN   ASSIGN TO INFILE.
00170        SELECT SORT-WORK-FILE                 ASSIGN TO SORTWK.
00180        SELECT TRANSACTION-REGISTER-FILE-OUT  ASSIGN TO PRINTER1.
00190        SELECT ERROR-FILE-OUT                 ASSIGN TO PRINTER2.
00200        SELECT ACCOUNT-MASTER-FILE-OUT        ASSIGN TO DISKOUT
00210            ORGANIZATION RELATIVE
00220            ACCESS RANDOM
00230            RELATIVE KEY IS SLOT-NUMBER
00240            STATUS IS FILE-CHECK.
00250
00260    *****************************************************************
00270
00280    DATA DIVISION.
00290    FILE SECTION.
00300    FD  SAVINGS-ACCOUNT-DATA-FILE-IN
00310        LABEL RECORDS ARE OMITTED
00320        RECORD CONTAINS 80 CHARACTERS.
00330
00340    01  SAVINGS-ACCOUNT-DATA-RECORD-IN     PIC X(80).
00350
00360    SD  SORT-WORK-FILE
00370        RECORD CONTAINS 80 CHARACTERS.
00380
00390    01  SORT-WORK-RECORD.
00400        05  CODE-IN                        PIC X.
00410            88  CODE-VALID                  VALUE "1".
00420        05  ACCOUNT-NUMBER-IN              PIC 9(5).
00430        05  ACCOUNT-NUMBER-X  REDEFINES ACCOUNT-NUMBER-IN
00440                                           PIC X(5).
00450        05  AMOUNT-IN                      PIC 9(6)V99.
00460        05  AMOUNT-IN-X REDEFINES AMOUNT-IN PIC X(8).
00470        05  DEPOSITOR-NAME-IN              PIC X(20).
00480            88  DEPOSITOR-NAME-MISSING      VALUE SPACES.
00490        05  FILLER                         PIC X(46).
00500
00510    FD  ACCOUNT-MASTER-FILE-OUT
00520        LABEL RECORDS ARE STANDARD
00530        RECORD CONTAINS 39 CHARACTERS.
00540
00550    01  ACCOUNT-MASTER-RECORD-OUT          PIC X(39).
00560
00570    FD  TRANSACTION-REGISTER-FILE-OUT
00580        LABEL RECORDS ARE OMITTED.
00590
00600    01  REGISTER-RECORD-OUT                PIC X(72).
00610
00620    FD  ERROR-FILE-OUT
00630        LABEL RECORDS ARE OMITTED.
00640
00650    01  ERROR-RECORD-OUT                   PIC X(84).
00660
00670    WORKING-STORAGE SECTION.
00680    01  AMOUNT-TOTAL-W           VALUE 0    PIC S9(7)V99.
00690    01  REGISTER-PAGE-NUMBER-W   VALUE 0    PIC S99.
00700    01  ERROR-PAGE-NUMBER-W      VALUE 0    PIC S99.
00710    01  REGISTER-PAGE-LIMIT      VALUE 35   PIC S99 COMP SYNC.
00720    01  LINE-COUNT-ER                       PIC S99 COMP SYNC.
00730    01  ERROR-PAGE-LIMIT         VALUE 50   PIC S99 COMP SYNC.
00740    01  ERROR-LINE-COUNTER                  PIC S99 COMP SYNC.
00750    01  BLANK-LINE               VALUE " "  PIC X.
00760    01  SLOT-NUMBER                         PIC 99      COMP SYNC.
00770    01  INTEGER-QUOTIENT                    PIC S9(4) COMP SYNC.
00780    01  INTEGER-REMAINDER                   PIC S99     COMP SYNC.
00790    01  DIVISOR                  VALUE 61   PIC 99      COMP SYNC.
00800    01  EXTENDED-SEARCH-LIMIT               PIC S99     COMP SYNC.
00810    01  EXTENDED-SEARCH-STEPS    VALUE 10   PIC S99     COMP SYNC.
00820    01  NUMBER-OF-SLOTS-IN-FILE  VALUE 66   PIC S99     COMP SYNC.
00830    01  FILE-CHECK                          PIC XX.
00840    01  MORE-INPUT                          PIC X       VALUE "Y".
00850    01  ANY-ERRORS                          PIC X.
00860    01  NUMBER-OF-INPUT-RECORDS-W           PIC S9(3)   VALUE ZERO.
00870    01  NUMBER-OF-ERRONEOUS-RECORDS-W       PIC S9(3)   VALUE ZERO.
00880    01  NUMBER-OF-NEW-ACCOUNTS-W            PIC S9(3)   VALUE ZERO.
00890    01  ACCOUNT-NUMBER-SAVE        PIC 9(5) VALUE 99999.
```

```
00900    01   TODAYS-DATE.
00910         05   TODAYS-YEAR                      PIC 99.
00920         05   TODAYS-MONTH-AND-DAY             PIC 9(4).
00930
00940    01   MASTER-RECORD-W.
00950         05   ACCOUNT-NUMBER                   PIC 9(5).
00960         05   DEPOSITOR-NAME                   PIC X(20).
00970         05   DATE-OF-LAST-TRANSACTION         PIC 9(6).
00980         05   CURRENT-BALANCE                  PIC S9(6)V99.
00990
01000    01   REPORT-HEADING-1.
01010         05   FILLER     PIC X(39) VALUE SPACES.
01020         05   FILLER     PIC X(17) VALUE "ROBBEM STATE BANK".
01030
01040    01   REPORT-HEADING-2.
01050         05   FILLER     PIC X(39) VALUE SPACES.
01060         05   FILLER     PIC X(17) VALUE "106 WEST 10TH ST.".
01070
01080    01   REPORT-HEADING-3.
01090         05   FILLER     PIC X(38) VALUE SPACES.
01100         05   FILLER     PIC X(19) VALUE "BROOKLYN, NY  11212".
01110
01120    01   REGISTER-PAGE-HEADING-1.
01130         05   FILLER     PIC X(29) VALUE SPACES.
01140         05   FILLER     PIC X(36)
01150                         VALUE "SAVINGS ACCOUNT MASTER FILE CREATION".
01160
01170    01   ERROR-PAGE-HEADING-1.
01180         05   FILLER     PIC X(30) VALUE SPACES.
01190         05   FILLER     PIC X(34)
01200                         VALUE "SAVINGS ACCOUNT MASTER FILE ERRORS".
01210
01220    01   PAGE-HEADING-2.
01230         05   FILLER           PIC X(17) VALUE SPACES.
01240         05   FILLER           PIC X(5)  VALUE "DATE".
01250         05   TODAYS-MONTH-AND-DAY   PIC Z9/99/.
01260         05   TODAYS-YEAR      PIC 99B(35).
01270         05   FILLER           PIC X(5)  VALUE "PAGE".
01280         05   PAGE-NUMBER-OUT        PIC Z9.
01290
01300    01   REGISTER-PAGE-HEADING-3.
01310         05   FILLER     PIC X(24) VALUE SPACES.
01320         05   FILLER     PIC X(12) VALUE "ACCOUNT".
01330         05   FILLER     PIC X(12) VALUE "INITIAL".
01340         05   FILLER     PIC X(5)  VALUE "NOTES".
01350
01360    01   ERROR-PAGE-HEADING-3.
01370         05   FILLER     PIC X(24) VALUE SPACES.
01380         05   FILLER     PIC X(24) VALUE "ACCOUNT".
01390         05   FILLER     PIC X(5)  VALUE "NOTES".
01400
```

(continued)

master file, at line 00200, specifies ACCESS RANDOM. For even though the input records will be processed in ASCENDING Account Number sequence, in general the master records will not go into sequential slots in the master file.

ACCOUNT-NUMBER-IN is defined as a numeric field at line 00420 and redefined as alphanumeric at line 00430. We refer to the Account Number as numeric for purposes of arithmetic. We use the alphanumeric form in the SORT to insure that the SORT statement will operate on the Account Number fields exactly as they appear in the input, with no modifications of form for the purpose of performing numeric comparisons on them.

The COMPUTATIONAL SYNCHRONIZED fields in lines 00760 through 00820 are all used in connection with placing each master record into its correct slot in the file. SLOT-NUMBER is the RELATIVE KEY. INTEGER-QUOTIENT, INTEGER-REMAINDER, and DIVISOR are used for computing the home slot number of each master record before it is written.

EXTENDED-SEARCH-LIMIT and EXTENDED-SEARCH-STEPS are used to resolve space conflicts when more than one Account Number yields the same home slot number. Master records are of course written onto the file one at a time

Figure 15.16   (continued)

```
01410    01   REGISTER-PAGE-HEADING-4.
01420         05   FILLER          PIC X(24) VALUE SPACES.
01430         05   FILLER          PIC X(12) VALUE "NUMBER".
01440         05   FILLER          PIC X(7)  VALUE "DEPOSIT".
01450
01460    01   ERROR-PAGE-HEADING-4.
01470         05   FILLER          PIC X(24) VALUE SPACES.
01480         05   FILLER          PIC X(6)  VALUE "NUMBER".
01490
01500    01   NEW-ACCOUNT-LINE.
01510         05   FILLER     PIC X(25)      VALUE SPACES.
01520         05   ACCOUNT-NUMBER-OUT-G      PIC X(5)B(5).
01530         05   AMOUNT-OUT-G              PIC ZZZ,ZZZ.99B(3).
01540         05   FILLER     PIC X(11)      VALUE "NEW ACCOUNT".
01550
01560    01   ERROR-LINE.
01570         05   FILLER     PIC X(25) VALUE SPACES.
01580         05   ACCOUNT-NUMBER-OUT-E PIC X(5)B(18).
01590         05   MESSAGE-E            PIC X(36).
01600
01610    01   INVALID-CODE-MSG.
01620         05   FILLER     PIC X(13) VALUE "INVALID CODE".
01630         05   CODE-OUT   PIC X.
01640
01650    01   AMOUNT-NOT-NUMERIC-MSG.
01660         05   FILLER     PIC X(28) VALUE "INITIAL DEPOSIT NOT NUMERIC".
01670         05   AMOUNT-OUT-X         PIC X(9).
01680
01690    01   FINAL-LINE-1.
01700         05   FILLER          PIC X(23) VALUE SPACES.
01710         05   FILLER          PIC X(10) VALUE "TOTAL".
01720         05   AMOUNT-TOTAL-OUT          PIC Z,ZZZ,ZZZ.99.
01730
01740    01   FINAL-LINE-2.
01750         05   FILLER          PIC X(40) VALUE SPACES.
01760         05   FILLER          PIC X(14) VALUE "CONTROL COUNTS".
01770
01780    01   FINAL-LINE-3.
01790         05   FILLER          PIC X(34) VALUE SPACES.
01800         05   FILLER          PIC X(28) VALUE "NUMBER OF NEW ACCOUNTS".
01810         05   NUMBER-OF-NEW-ACCOUNTS-OUT PIC ZZ9.
01820
01830    01   FINAL-LINE-4.
01840         05   FILER           PIC X(34) VALUE SPACES.
01850         05   FILLER          PIC X(28)
01860                              VALUE "NUMBER OF ERRONEOUS RECORDS".
01870         05   NUMBER-OF-ERRONEOUS-RCDS-OUT PIC ZZ9.
01880
01890    01   FINAL-LINE-5.
01900         05   FILLER          PIC X(34) VALUE SPACES.
01910         05   FILLER          PIC X(28) VALUE "TOTAL".
01920         05   NUMBER-OF-INPUT-RECORDS-OUT PIC ZZ9.
01930
01940    01   NO-INPUT-DATA.
01950         05   FILLER          PIC X(21) VALUE SPACES.
01960         05   FILLER          PIC X(13) VALUE "NO INPUT DATA".
01970
01980    01   INSUFFICIENT-FILE-SPACE.
01990         05   FILLER          PIC X(21) VALUE SPACES.
02000         05   FILLER          PIC X(23) VALUE "INSUFFICIENT FILE SPACE".
02010
02020    ***********************************************************************
02030
02040    PROCEDURE DIVISION.
02050    DECLARATIVES.
02060    DUMMY-USE SECTION.
02070         USE AFTER ERROR PROCEDURE ACCOUNT-MASTER-FILE-OUT.
02080    END DECLARATIVES.
02090
02100    NONDECLARATIVE SECTION.
02110    CREATE-MASTER-FILE.
02120         SORT SORT-WORK-FILE
02130             ASCENDING KEY ACCOUNT-NUMBER-X
02140             USING SAVINGS-ACCOUNT-DATA-FILE-IN
02150             OUTPUT PROCEDURE IS PRODUCE-MASTER-FILE.
02160         STOP RUN.
02170
```

```
02180    PRODUCE-MASTER-FILE SECTION.
02190    PRODUCE-MASTER-FILE-PARAGRAPH.
02200        PERFORM INITIALIZATION.
02210        PERFORM PROCESS-A-RECORD UNTIL MORE-INPUT = "N".
02220        PERFORM TERMINATION.
02230        GO TO END-OF-THIS-SECTION.
02240
02250    INITIALIZATION.
02260        OPEN OUTPUT ACCOUNT-MASTER-FILE-OUT
02270                    ERROR-FILE-OUT
02280                    TRANSACTION-REGISTER-FILE-OUT.
02290        IF FILE-CHECK NOT = ZEROS
02300            DISPLAY " MASTER FILE OPEN STATUS = ", FILE-CHECK
02310            CLOSE TRANSACTION-REGISTER-FILE-OUT
02320                  ERROR-FILE-OUT
02330                  ACCOUNT-MASTER-FILE-OUT
02340            STOP RUN.
02350        ACCEPT TODAYS-DATE FROM DATE.
02360        MOVE CORRESPONDING TODAYS-DATE TO PAGE-HEADING-2.
02370        PERFORM PRODUCE-REPORT-HEADINGS.
02380        PERFORM READ-A-RECORD.
02390        IF MORE-INPUT = "N"
02400            WRITE ERROR-RECORD-OUT FROM NO-INPUT-DATA.
02410
02420    PRODUCE-REPORT-HEADINGS.
02430        PERFORM PRODUCE-REGISTER-HEADINGS.
02440        PERFORM PRODUCE-ERROR-HEADINGS.
02450
02460    PRODUCE-REGISTER-HEADINGS.
02470        WRITE REGISTER-RECORD-OUT FROM REPORT-HEADING-1 AFTER PAGE.
02480        WRITE REGISTER-RECORD-OUT FROM REPORT-HEADING-2.
02490        WRITE REGISTER-RECORD-OUT FROM REPORT-HEADING-3.
02500        ADD 1 TO REGISTER-PAGE-NUMBER-W.
02510        MOVE REGISTER-PAGE-NUMBER-W TO PAGE-NUMBER-OUT.
02520        WRITE REGISTER-RECORD-OUT FROM REGISTER-PAGE-HEADING-1
02530                                  AFTER 2.
02540        WRITE REGISTER-RECORD-OUT FROM PAGE-HEADING-2.
02550        WRITE REGISTER-RECORD-OUT FROM REGISTER-PAGE-HEADING-3
02560                                  AFTER 3.
02570        WRITE REGISTER-RECORD-OUT FROM REGISTER-PAGE-HEADING-4.
02580        WRITE REGISTER-RECORD-OUT FROM BLANK-LINE.
02590        MOVE 11 TO LINE-COUNT-ER.
02600
```

(continued)

as each input transaction is processed. If some Account Number yields a home slot that is already occupied by a master record, the program will examine slots in the master file immediately following the home slot, looking for an empty one. The number of such slots to be examined is given in the field EXTENDED-SEARCH-STEPS. The field EXTENDED-SEARCH-LIMIT is used to record the number of the last slot that would be examined in such a search. If no empty slot is found within the specified limit, the program terminates with a message that there is no room for this particular master record. There is nothing to do then but increase the size of the file (increase the VALUE of NUMBER-OF-SLOTS-IN-FILE), choose a new higher DIVISOR (a prime number less than the new NUMBER-OF-SLOTS-IN-FILE), and create the file from scratch all over again.

The choice of the number of slots to examine when looking for an empty one is a systems design problem and is beyond the scope of this book. In general, if the number of steps is made too small, the probability is increased that some master record will have no place to go and the program will terminate. If the number of steps is made too large, many master records might end up being stored far from their home slots; thus finding them later would take a lot of computer time.

The Prodecure Division starts at line 02040. This Procedure Division is divided into three sections—one each for DECLARATIVES, the SORT statement, and the OUTPUT PROCEDURE.

Figure 15.16   (continued)

```
02610    PRODUCE-ERROR-HEADINGS.
02620       WRITE ERROR-RECORD-OUT FROM REPORT-HEADING-1 AFTER PAGE.
02630       WRITE ERROR-RECORD-OUT FROM REPORT-HEADING-2.
02640       WRITE ERROR-RECORD-OUT FROM REPORT-HEADING-3.
02650       ADD 1 TO ERROR-PAGE-NUMBER-W.
02660       MOVE ERROR-PAGE-NUMBER-W TO PAGE-NUMBER-OUT.
02670       WRITE ERROR-RECORD-OUT FROM ERROR-PAGE-HEADING-1 AFTER 2.
02680       WRITE ERROR-RECORD-OUT FROM PAGE-HEADING-2.
02690       WRITE ERROR-RECORD-OUT FROM ERROR-PAGE-HEADING-3 AFTER 3.
02700       WRITE ERROR-RECORD-OUT FROM ERROR-PAGE-HEADING-4.
02710       WRITE ERROR-RECORD-OUT FROM BLANK-LINE.
02720       MOVE 11 TO ERROR-LINE-COUNTER.
02730
02740    PROCESS-A-RECORD.
02750       ADD 1 TO NUMBER-OF-INPUT-RECORDS-W.
02760       MOVE "N" TO ANY-ERRORS.
02770       PERFORM CHECK-INPUT-FOR-VALIDITY.
02780       IF ANY-ERRORS = "N"
02790          PERFORM BUILD-NEW-ACCOUNT-RECORD
02800          PERFORM WRITE-NEW-ACCOUNT-RECORD.
02810       MOVE ACCOUNT-NUMBER-IN TO ACCOUNT-NUMBER-SAVE.
02820       PERFORM READ-A-RECORD.
02830
02840    BUILD-NEW-ACCOUNT-RECORD.
02850       MOVE ACCOUNT-NUMBER-IN TO ACCOUNT-NUMBER.
02860       MOVE DEPOSITOR-NAME-IN TO DEPOSITOR-NAME.
02870       MOVE AMOUNT-IN        TO CURRENT-BALANCE.
02880       MOVE TODAYS-DATE       TO DATE-OF-LAST-TRANSACTION.
02890
02900    WRITE-NEW-ACCOUNT-RECORD.
02910       PERFORM COMPUTE-SLOT-NUMBER.
02920       PERFORM WRITE-A-MASTER-RECORD.
02930       IF FILE-CHECK = "22"
02940          PERFORM EXTENDED-WRITE-SEARCH.
02950       ADD 1 TO NUMBER-OF-NEW-ACCOUNTS-W.
02960       PERFORM WRITE-NEW-ACCOUNT-LINE.
02970
```

The WRITE statement at line 02990 is a random WRITE. Each time it executes, COBOL uses the current value of the RELATIVE KEY, SLOT-NUMBER, to know which slot to WRITE the record into. The value of SLOT-NUMBER is computed under control of the PERFORM statement at line 02910. A WRITE statement sets the STATUS field if one is specified for the file. The 1974 ANSI standard meanings of the STATUS codes for random WRITEs to a relative file are given in Table 15-5. Your system may have additional codes in the range 90–99.

Table 15-5
1974 ANSI standard STATUS codes related to writing a relative file randomly.

Status Code	Meaning
00	Successful completion
22	Invalid key — an attempt has been made to WRITE a record into an occupied slot
24	Invalid key — boundary violation (attempt to WRITE beyond the physical end of the file)
30	Permanent error (hardware malfunction)

The paragraph EXTENDED-WRITE-SEARCH, line 03070, executes if a WRITE statement returns a STATUS code of 22. EXTENDED-WRITE-SEARCH first computes EXTENDED-SEARCH-LIMIT, the highest slot number that it will examine while looking for an empty slot. It then PERFORMs the paragraph WRITE-A-MASTER-RECORD UNTIL an empty slot is found or all of the examined slots are found to be occupied.

```
02980    WRITE-A-MASTER-RECORD.
02990        WRITE ACCOUNT-MASTER-RECORD-OUT FROM MASTER-RECORD-W.
03000        IF FILE-CHECK = ZEROS OR "22"
03010            NEXT SENTENCE
03020        ELSE
03030            DISPLAY " MASTER FILE WRITE STATUS = ", FILE-CHECK
03040            PERFORM TERMINATION
03050            STOP RUN.
03060
03070    EXTENDED-WRITE-SEARCH.
03080        ADD SLOT-NUMBER, EXTENDED-SEARCH-STEPS
03090            GIVING EXTENDED-SEARCH-LIMIT.
03100        PERFORM WRITE-A-MASTER-RECORD
03110            VARYING SLOT-NUMBER FROM SLOT-NUMBER BY 1
03120                UNTIL
03130                    FILE-CHECK IS EQUAL TO ZEROS OR
03140                    SLOT-NUMBER GREATER THAN
03150                        EXTENDED-SEARCH-LIMIT OR
03160                        NUMBER-OF-SLOTS-IN-FILE.
03170        IF FILE-CHECK = ZEROS
03180            NEXT SENTENCE
03190        ELSE
03200            PERFORM WRITE-INSUFFICIENT-FILE-SPACE
03210            DISPLAY " MASTER FILE WRITE STATUS = ", FILE-CHECK
03220            PERFORM TERMINATION
03230            STOP RUN.
03240
03250    COMPUTE-SLOT-NUMBER.
03260        DIVIDE ACCOUNT-NUMBER-IN BY DIVISOR
03270            GIVING INTEGER-QUOTIENT
03280            REMAINDER INTEGER-REMAINDER.
03290        ADD 1, INTEGER-REMAINDER GIVING SLOT-NUMBER.
03300
03310    CHECK-INPUT-FOR-VALIDITY.
03320        IF ACCOUNT-NUMBER-IN NOT NUMERIC
03330            MOVE "Y" TO ANY-ERRORS
03340            PERFORM WRITE-INVALID-KEY-LINE.
03350        IF NOT CODE-VALID
03360            MOVE "Y" TO ANY-ERRORS
03370            PERFORM WRITE-INVALID-CODE-LINE.
03380        IF ACCOUNT-NUMBER-IN = ACCOUNT-NUMBER-SAVE
03390            MOVE "Y" TO ANY-ERRORS
03400            PERFORM WRITE-DUPLICATE-ERROR-MESSAGE.
03410        IF DEPOSITOR-NAME-MISSING
03420            MOVE "Y" TO ANY-ERRORS
03430            PERFORM WRITE-NAME-ERROR-MESSAGE.
03440        IF AMOUNT-IN NOT NUMERIC
03450            MOVE "Y" TO ANY-ERRORS
03460            PERFORM WRITE-AMOUNT-MESSAGE.
03470        IF ANY-ERRORS = "Y"
03480            ADD 1 TO NUMBER-OF-ERRONEOUS-RECORDS-W.
03490
03500    WRITE-NEW-ACCOUNT-LINE.
03510        MOVE ACCOUNT-NUMBER-IN TO ACCOUNT-NUMBER-OUT-G.
03520        MOVE AMOUNT-IN         TO AMOUNT-OUT-G.
03530        ADD AMOUNT-IN          TO AMOUNT-TOTAL-W.
03540        IF LINE-COUNT-ER + 1 > REGISTER-PAGE-LIMIT
03550            PERFORM PRODUCE-REGISTER-HEADINGS.
03560        WRITE REGISTER-RECORD-OUT FROM NEW-ACCOUNT-LINE.
03570        ADD 1 TO LINE-COUNT-ER.
03580
03590    WRITE-INVALID-CODE-LINE.
03600        MOVE ACCOUNT-NUMBER-IN     TO ACCOUNT-NUMBER-OUT-E.
03610        MOVE CODE-IN               TO CODE-OUT.
03620        MOVE INVALID-CODE-MSG TO MESSAGE-E.
03630        PERFORM WRITE-ERROR-LINE.
03640
03650    WRITE-ERROR-LINE.
03660        IF ERROR-LINE-COUNTER + 1 > ERROR-PAGE-LIMIT
03670            PERFORM PRODUCE-ERROR-HEADINGS.
03680        WRITE ERROR-RECORD-OUT FROM ERROR-LINE.
03690        ADD 1 TO ERROR-LINE-COUNTER.
03700
03710    WRITE-DUPLICATE-ERROR-MESSAGE.
03720        MOVE ACCOUNT-NUMBER-IN TO ACCOUNT-NUMBER-OUT-E.
03730        MOVE "DUPLICATE ACCOUNT NUMBER" TO MESSAGE-E.
03740        PERFORM WRITE-ERROR-LINE.
03750
```

(continued)

Figure 15.16   (continued)

```
03760   WRITE-NAME-ERROR-MESSAGE.
03770       MOVE ACCOUNT-NUMBER-IN TO ACCOUNT-NUMBER-OUT-E.
03780       MOVE "DEPOSITOR NAME MISSING" TO MESSAGE-E.
03790       PERFORM WRITE-ERROR-LINE.
03800
03810   WRITE-AMOUNT-MESSAGE.
03820       MOVE ACCOUNT-NUMBER-IN TO ACCOUNT-NUMBER-OUT-E.
03830       MOVE AMOUNT-IN-X        TO AMOUNT-OUT-X.
03840       MOVE AMOUNT-NOT-NUMERIC-MSG TO MESSAGE-E.
03850       PERFORM WRITE-ERROR-LINE.
03860
03870   WRITE-INVALID-KEY-LINE.
03880       MOVE ACCOUNT-NUMBER-X TO ACCOUNT-NUMBER-OUT-E.
03890       MOVE "ACCOUNT NUMBER NOT NUMERIC" TO MESSAGE-E.
03900       PERFORM WRITE-ERROR-LINE.
03910
03920   WRITE-INSUFFICIENT-FILE-SPACE.
03930       WRITE ERROR-RECORD-OUT FROM INSUFFICIENT-FILE-SPACE.
03940
03950   PRODUCE-FINAL-LINES.
03960       MOVE AMOUNT-TOTAL-W TO AMOUNT-TOTAL-OUT.
03970       MOVE NUMBER-OF-INPUT-RECORDS-W
03980           TO NUMBER-OF-INPUT-RECORDS-OUT.
03990       MOVE NUMBER-OF-ERRONEOUS-RECORDS-W
04000           TO NUMBER-OF-ERRONEOUS-RCDS-OUT.
04010       MOVE NUMBER-OF-NEW-ACCOUNTS-W TO NUMBER-OF-NEW-ACCOUNTS-OUT.
04020       WRITE REGISTER-RECORD-OUT FROM FINAL-LINE-1 AFTER 2.
04030       WRITE REGISTER-RECORD-OUT FROM FINAL-LINE-2 AFTER 2.
04040       WRITE REGISTER-RECORD-OUT FROM FINAL-LINE-3 AFTER 2.
04050       WRITE REGISTER-RECORD-OUT FROM FINAL-LINE-4 AFTER 2.
04060       WRITE REGISTER-RECORD-OUT FROM FINAL-LINE-5 AFTER 2.
04070
04080   TERMINATION.
04090       PERFORM PRODUCE-FINAL-LINES.
04100       CLOSE ACCOUNT-MASTER-FILE-OUT
04110             ERROR-FILE-OUT
04120             TRANSACTION-REGISTER-FILE-OUT.
04130
04140   READ-A-RECORD.
04150       RETURN SORT-WORK-FILE
04160           AT END
04170               MOVE "N" TO MORE-INPUT.
04180
04190   END-OF-THIS-SECTION.
04200       EXIT.
```

Program P15-04 was run with the input data shown in Figure 15.17 and produced the report output shown in Figure 15.18. Notice that several of the Account Numbers are synonyms, requiring extended search (for example 00080, 00202, and 06180).

EXERCISE 4

Write a program to create a relative inventory file. Use the same formats for input transactions and master records that you used when you created your sequential inventory master file in Exercise 3, Chapter 12, page 392.

Select a file size (number of slots) suitable to the largest number of records you expect your master file to contain. Select a divisor suitable to the number of slots in the file.

Have your program perform the same validity checks as did your program for Exercise 3, Chapter 12. In addition, have your program check that each Account Number is numeric before you divide it by the divisor. Have your program produce reports in the same format that you used in Exercise 3, Chapter 12.

Figure 15.17 Input to Program P15-04.

```
--------------------------------------------------------------------------
          1         2         3         4         5         6         7         8
1234567890123456789012345678901234567890123456789012345678901234567890123456789 0
--------------------------------------------------------------------------
10008000005000LENORE MILLER
10020200025000ROSEMARY LANE
3122960CA00000MICHELE CAPUANO
10618000075000JAMES BUDD
14674900100000PAUL LERNER, D.D.S.
17549500002575BETH FALLON
12701300002000JANE HALEY
15002700005000ONE DAY CLEANERS
13394600002450ROBERT RYAN
17054900012550KELLY HEDERMAN
19668100001000MARY KEATING
20293300007500BOB LANIGAN
17203200003500J. & L. CAIN
14396700015000IMPERIAL FLORIST
12505500000500JOYCE MITCHELL
13478000025000JERRY PARKS
16574500005000CARL CALDERON
13280900017550JOHN WILLIAMS
17688400015000JOHN J. LEHMAN
16416500002500JOSEPH CAMILLO
18829800015000JAY GREENE
16756600000100EVELYN SLATER
19675200007500
13091700050000PATRICK J. LEE
16695200001037LESLIE MINSKY
11962500150000JOHN DAPRINO
13612600010000JOE'S DELI
11886200050000GEORGE CULHANE
10016900009957MARTIN LANG
16871800027500VITO CACACI
10005400002000COMMUNITY DRUGS
13149000001500SOLOMON CHAPELS
16171400150000JOHN BURKE
100IEROFG15750PAT P. POWERS
15549600200000JOE GARCIA
13823400025000GRACE MICELI
11469700002000
19023000001000GUY VOLPONE
135101))))!%))SALVATORE CALI
19023000055500BILL WILLIAMS
13310000001000KEVIN PARKER
13510100003500FRANK CAPUTO
11510900001500GENE GALLI
13665000002937
11168200100784ROSEBUCCI
16683500001000ROBERT DAVIS M.D.
18191900012500LORICE MONTI
16017500700159MICHAEL SMITH
17666000100000JOE & MARY SESSA
14749100250000ROGER SHAW
```

Figure 15.18   Report output from Program P15-04.

```
                          ROBBEM STATE BANK
                          106 WEST 10TH ST.
                          BROOKLYN, NY  11212

                     SAVINGS ACCOUNT MASTER FILE ERRORS
        DATE   4/10/88                                    PAGE   1


               ACCOUNT                  NOTES
               NUMBER

               OOIER                    ACCOUNT NUMBER NOT NUMERIC
               OOIER                    INITIAL DEPOSIT NOT NUMERIC OFG15750
               02933                    INVALID CODE 2
               12296                    INVALID CODE 3
               12296                    INITIAL DEPOSIT NOT NUMERIC OCAOOOOO
               14697                    DEPOSITOR NAME MISSING
               35101                    INITIAL DEPOSIT NOT NUMERIC ))))!%))
               35101                    DUPLICATE ACCOUNT NUMBER
               36650                    DEPOSITOR NAME MISSING
               90230                    DUPLICATE ACCOUNT NUMBER
               96752                    DEPOSITOR NAME MISSING




                          ROBBEM STATE BANK
                          106 WEST 10TH ST.
                          BROOKLYN, NY  11212

                    SAVINGS ACCOUNT MASTER FILE CREATION
        DATE   4/10/88                                    PAGE   1


               ACCOUNT      INITIAL     NOTES
               NUMBER       DEPOSIT

               00054         20.00      NEW ACCOUNT
               00080         50.00      NEW ACCOUNT
               00169         99.57      NEW ACCOUNT
               00202        250.00      NEW ACCOUNT
               06180        750.00      NEW ACCOUNT
               11682      1,007.84      NEW ACCOUNT
               15109         15.00      NEW ACCOUNT
               18862        500.00      NEW ACCOUNT
               19625      1,500.00      NEW ACCOUNT
               25055          5.00      NEW ACCOUNT
               27013         20.00      NEW ACCOUNT
               30917        500.00      NEW ACCOUNT
               31490         15.00      NEW ACCOUNT
               32809        175.50      NEW ACCOUNT
               33100         10.00      NEW ACCOUNT
               33946         24.50      NEW ACCOUNT
               34780        250.00      NEW ACCOUNT
               36126        100.00      NEW ACCOUNT
               38234        250.00      NEW ACCOUNT
               43967        150.00      NEW ACCOUNT
               46749      1,000.00      NEW ACCOUNT
               47491      2,500.00      NEW ACCOUNT
               50027         50.00      NEW ACCOUNT
               55496      2,000.00      NEW ACCOUNT
```

```
                    ROBBEM STATE BANK
                    106 WEST 10TH ST.
                   BROOKLYN, NY  11212

              SAVINGS ACCOUNT MASTER FILE CREATION
DATE  4/10/88                                  PAGE  2


       ACCOUNT      INITIAL      NOTES
       NUMBER       DEPOSIT

        60175      7,001.59      NEW ACCOUNT
        61714      1,500.00      NEW ACCOUNT
        64165         25.00      NEW ACCOUNT
        65745         50.00      NEW ACCOUNT
        66835         10.00      NEW ACCOUNT
        66952         10.37      NEW ACCOUNT
        67566          1.00      NEW ACCOUNT
        68718        275.00      NEW ACCOUNT
        70549        125.50      NEW ACCOUNT
        72032         35.00      NEW ACCOUNT
        75495         25.75      NEW ACCOUNT
        76660      1,000.00      NEW ACCOUNT
        76884        150.00      NEW ACCOUNT
        81919        125.00      NEW ACCOUNT
        88298        150.00      NEW ACCOUNT
        90230        555.00      NEW ACCOUNT
        96681         10.00      NEW ACCOUNT

   TOTAL          22,291.62

                   CONTROL COUNTS

           NUMBER OF NEW ACCOUNTS         41

           NUMBER OF ERRONEOUS RECORDS     9

           TOTAL                          50
```

Updating a Randomized Relative File

Program P15-05 updates our relative savings-account master file with additions, changes, and deletions. The input transactions come in from the transaction file in random Account Number sequence, and master records are read from the master file randomly as needed.

To find the master record having a particular Account Number, Program P15-05 must do some of the same steps that Program P15-04 did when it originally put records onto the file. Given an Account Number, Program P15-05 computes the home slot number of the master record and then READs the contents of that slot. If the desired master record is not found in its home slot, the program must then carry out an extended search to determine whether the record is in a nearby slot or not in the file at all.

To add a new savings-account record to the master file, Program P15-05 must find space for it the same way that Program P15-04 found space for master records when it first created the file. Program P15-04 uses the same WRITE logic that Program P15-04 did. Given an Account Number, Program P15-05 computes the home slot number of the master record and then tries to WRITE it in that slot. If the slot is already occupied, Program P15-05 carries out an extended search to determine whether there is a vacant slot nearby. If not, it writes a message IN-SUFFICIENT FILE SPACE. In that case, the master file must be made larger and recreated.

Program P15-05 is shown in Figure 15.19. Its high-level logic is similar to that used in Program P14-02, a random update to an indexed file. In the Working

Figure 15.19   Program P15-05.

```
CB1 RELEASE 2.4                                      IBM OS/VS COBOL  JULY  1, 1982


                         12.48.27        APR 19,1988


00010  IDENTIFICATION DIVISION.
00020  PROGRAM-ID.  P15-05.
00030 *
00040 *    THIS PROGRAM UPDATES A RELATIVE MASTER FILE ON DISK
00050 *    WITH ADDITIONS, CHANGES, AND DELETIONS.
00060 *
00070 ********************************************************************
00080
00090  ENVIRONMENT DIVISION.
00100  CONFIGURATION SECTION.
00110  SOURCE-COMPUTER.  IBM-370.
00120  OBJECT-COMPUTER.  IBM-370.
00130
00140  INPUT-OUTPUT SECTION.
00150  FILE-CONTROL.
00160      SELECT ACCOUNT-MASTER-FILE-I-O         ASSIGN TO MSTRDISK
00170          ORGANIZATION RELATIVE
00180          STATUS IS FILE-CHECK
00190          ACCESS RANDOM
00200          RELATIVE KEY IS SLOT-NUMBER.
00210      SELECT TRANSACTION-FILE-IN             ASSIGN TO TFILEIN.
00220      SELECT TRANSACTION-REGISTER-FILE-OUT   ASSIGN TO PRINTER1.
00230      SELECT ERROR-REPORT-FILE-OUT           ASSIGN TO PRINTER2.
00240
00250 ********************************************************************
00260
00270  DATA DIVISION.
00280  FILE SECTION.
00290  FD  ACCOUNT-MASTER-FILE-I-O
00300      LABEL RECORDS ARE STANDARD
00310      RECORD CONTAINS 39 CHARACTERS.
00320
00330  01  ACCOUNT-MASTER-RECORD-I-O.
00340      05  ACCOUNT-NUMBER-M             PIC 9(5).
00350      05  ACCOUNT-NUMBER-MX REDEFINES ACCOUNT-NUMBER-M
00360                                       PIC X(5).
00370      05  DEPOSITOR-NAME-M             PIC X(20).
00380      05  DATE-OF-LAST-TRANSACTION-M   PIC 9(6).
00390      05  CURRENT-BALANCE-M            PIC S9(6)V99.
00400
00410  FD  TRANSACTION-FILE-IN
00420      LABEL RECORDS ARE OMITTED
00430      RECORD CONTAINS 80 CHARACTERS.
00440
00450  01  TRANSACTION-RECORD-IN            PIC X(80).
00460
00470  FD  TRANSACTION-REGISTER-FILE-OUT
00480      LABEL RECORDS ARE OMITTED.
00490
00500  01  TRANSACTION-REGISTER-REC-OUT     PIC X(76).
00510
```

Storage Section, you can find the usual flags and counters in lines 00580 through 00770. The fields needed for converting Account Numbers to slot numbers and for carrying out extended searches are found in lines 00580 through 00640.

Notice that ACCOUNT-NUMBER-M, line 00340, and ACCOUNT-NUMBER-T, line 00890, are both defined as numeric and redefined as alphanumeric. That is because they must sometimes be treated as numeric (for division) and sometimes as alphanumeric (such as when assigned HIGH-VALUES). In programs in previous chapters the key field was defined only as alphanumeric because it was never used for arithmetic.

```
00520  FD  ERROR-REPORT-FILE-OUT
00530      LABEL RECORDS ARE OMITTED.
00540
00550  01  ERROR-REPORT-RECORD-OUT            PIC X(102).
00560
00570  WORKING-STORAGE SECTION.
00580  01  SLOT-NUMBER                     PIC 99      COMP SYNC.
00590  01  INTEGER-QUOTIENT                PIC S9(4) COMP SYNC.
00600  01  INTEGER-REMAINDER               PIC S99   COMP SYNC.
00610  01  DIVISOR            VALUE 61     PIC 99    COMP SYNC.
00620  01  EXTENDED-SEARCH-LIMIT           PIC S99   COMP SYNC.
00630  01  EXTENDED-SEARCH-STEPS   VALUE 10 PIC S99  COMP SYNC.
00640  01  NUMBER-OF-SLOTS-IN-FILE VALUE 66 PIC S99  COMP SYNC.
00650  01  BLANKS                          PIC X      VALUE " ".
00660  01  FILE-CHECK                      PIC XX     VALUE ZEROS.
00670  01  IS-MASTER-RECORD-IN-WORK-AREA   PIC X.
00680  01  IS-MASTER-RECORD-IN-THE-FILE    PIC X.
00690  01  NUMBER-OF-INPUT-RECORDS-W       PIC S9(3) VALUE ZERO.
00700  01  NUMBER-OF-ERRONEOUS-RECORDS-W   PIC S9(3) VALUE ZERO.
00710  01  DEPOSIT-TOTAL-W      VALUE 0    PIC S9(7)V99.
00720  01  WITHDRAWAL-TOTAL-W   VALUE 0    PIC S9(7)V99.
00730  01  NUMBER-OF-DEPOSITS-W            PIC S9(3) VALUE 0.
00740  01  NUMBER-OF-WITHDRAWALS-W         PIC S9(3) VALUE 0.
00750  01  NUMBER-OF-NEW-ACCOUNTS-W        PIC S9(3) VALUE 0.
00760  01  NUMBER-OF-NAME-CHANGES-W        PIC S9(3) VALUE 0.
00770  01  NUMBER-OF-DELETIONS-W           PIC S9(3) VALUE 0.
00780  01  TODAYS-DATE.
00790      05  TODAYS-YEAR                 PIC 99.
00800      05  TODAYS-MONTH-AND-DAY        PIC 9(4).
00810
00820  01  TRANSACTION-INPUT-AREA.
00830      05  TRANSACTION-CODE            PIC X.
00840          88  NEW-ACCOUNT             VALUE "1".
00850          88  DEPOSIT                 VALUE "2".
00860          88  WITHDRAWAL              VALUE "3".
00870          88  NAME-CHANGE             VALUE "4".
00880          88  DELETION                VALUE "5".
00890      05  ACCOUNT-NUMBER-T            PIC 9(5).
00900      05  ACCOUNT-NUMBER-X REDEFINES ACCOUNT-NUMBER-T
00910                                      PIC X(5).
00920      05  DEPOSIT-AND-WITHDRAWAL-AMTS.
00930          10  DEPOSIT-AMOUNT              PIC 9(6)V99.
00940          10  DEPOSIT-AMOUNT-X   REDEFINES DEPOSIT-AMOUNT
00950                                      PIC X(8).
00960          10  WITHDRAWAL-AMOUNT  REDEFINES DEPOSIT-AMOUNT
00970                                      PIC 9(6)V99.
00980          10  WITHDRAWAL-AMOUNT-X REDEFINES DEPOSIT-AMOUNT
00990                                      PIC X(8).
01000      05  DEPOSITOR-NAME-NEW-ACCOUNT  PIC X(20).
01010          88  DEPOSITOR-NAME-MISSING  VALUE SPACES.
01020  01  TRANSACTION-4-INPUT-AREA REDEFINES TRANSACTION-INPUT-AREA.
01030      05  FILLER                      PIC X(6).
01040      05  DEPOSITOR-NAME              PIC X(20).
01050          88  REPLACEMENT-NAME-MISSING VALUE SPACES.
01060      05  FILLER                      PIC X(8).
01070
01080  01  REGISTER-LINE-LIMIT             PIC S99 VALUE 37 COMP SYNC.
01090  01  REGISTER-PAGE-COUNTER           PIC S99 VALUE 0.
01100  01  LINE-COUNT-ER                   PIC S99          COMP SYNC.
01110  01  ERROR-REPORT-LINE-LIMIT         PIC S99 VALUE 56 COMP SYNC.
01120  01  ERROR-REPORT-PAGE-COUNTER       PIC S99 VALUE 0.
01130  01  ERROR-LINE-COUNTER              PIC S99          COMP SYNC.
01140
01150  01  REPORT-HEADING-1.
01160      05  FILLER    PIC X(39) VALUE SPACES.
01170      05  FILLER    PIC X(17) VALUE "ROBBEM STATE BANK".
01180
01190  01  REPORT-HEADING-2.
01200      05  FILLER    PIC X(39) VALUE SPACES.
01210      05  FILLER    PIC X(17) VALUE "106 WEST 10TH ST.".
01220
01230  01  REPORT-HEADING-3.
01240      05  FILLER    PIC X(38) VALUE SPACES.
01250      05  FILLER    PIC X(19) VALUE "BROOKLYN, NY  11212".
01260
01270  01  REGISTER-PAGE-HEAD-1.
01280      05  FILLER    PIC X(29) VALUE SPACES.
01290      05  FILLER    PIC X(36)
01300                    VALUE "SAVINGS ACCOUNT TRANSACTION REGISTER".
```

(continued)

Figure 15.18   (continued)

```
01310
01320  01  PAGE-HEAD-2.
01330      05  FILLER         PIC X(17)        VALUE SPACES.
01340      05  FILLER         PIC X(5)         VALUE "DATE".
01350      05  TODAYS-MONTH-AND-DAY            PIC Z9/99/.
01360      05  TODAYS-YEAR                     PIC 99B(35).
01370      05  FILLER         PIC X(5)         VALUE "PAGE".
01380      05  PAGE-NUMBER-OUT                 PIC Z9.
01390
01400  01  REGISTER-PAGE-HEAD-3.
01410      05  FILLER         PIC X(20) VALUE SPACES.
01420      05  FILLER         PIC X(12) VALUE "ACCOUNT".
01430      05  FILLER         PIC X(14) VALUE "DEPOSITS".
01440      05  FILLER         PIC X(18) VALUE "WITHDRAWALS".
01450      05  FILLER         PIC X(5)  VALUE "NOTES".
01460
01470  01  PAGE-HEAD-4.
01480      05  FILLER         PIC X(20) VALUE SPACES.
01490      05  FILLER         PIC X(6)  VALUE "NUMBER".
01500
01510  01  ERROR-REPORT-PAGE-HEAD-1.
01520      05  FILLER         PIC X(33) VALUE SPACES.
01530      05  FILLER         PIC X(28) VALUE
01540                         "SAVINGS ACCOUNT ERROR REPORT".
01550
01560  01  ERROR-REPORT-PAGE-HEAD-3.
01570      05  FILLER         PIC X(20) VALUE SPACES.
01580      05  FILLER         PIC X(44) VALUE "ACCOUNT".
01590      05  FILLER         PIC X(5)  VALUE "NOTES".
01600
01610  01  NEW-ACCOUNT-LINE.
01620      05  FILLER          PIC X(21) VALUE SPACES.
01630      05  ACCOUNT-NUMBER-OUT        PIC 9(5)B(5).
01640      05  DEPOSIT-AMOUNT-OUT        PIC ZZZ,ZZZ.99B(21).
01650      05  FILLER          PIC X(11) VALUE "NEW ACCOUNT".
01660
01670  01  DEPOSIT-LINE.
01680      05  FILLER          PIC X(21) VALUE SPACES.
01690      05  ACCOUNT-NUMBER-M-OUT      PIC 9(5)B(5).
01700      05  DEPOSIT-AMOUNT-OUT        PIC ZZZ,ZZZ.99.
01710
01720  01  WITHDRAWAL-LINE.
01730      05  FILLER          PIC X(21) VALUE SPACES.
01740      05  ACCOUNT-NUMBER-M-OUT      PIC 9(5)B(19).
01750      05  WITHDRAWAL-AMOUNT-OUT     PIC ZZZ,ZZZ.99.
01760
01770  01  NAME-CHANGE-LINE.
01780      05  FILLER          PIC X(21) VALUE SPACES.
01790      05  ACCOUNT-NUMBER-M-OUT      PIC 9(5)B(5).
01800      05  DEPOSITOR-NAME-OUT        PIC X(20)B(11).
01810      05  FILLER          PIC X(11) VALUE "NAME CHANGE".
01820
01830  01  DELETION-LINE.
01840      05  FILLER          PIC X(21) VALUE SPACES.
01850      05  ACCOUNT-NUMBER-M-OUT      PIC 9(5)B(19).
01860      05  CURRENT-BALANCE-M-OUT     PIC ZZZ,ZZZ.99B(7).
01870      05  FILLER          PIC X(14) VALUE "ACCOUNT CLOSED".
01880
01890  01  ERROR-MESSAGE-LINE.
01900      05  FILLER          PIC X(21) VALUE SPACES.
01910      05  ACCOUNT-NUMBER-T-E        PIC X(5)B(36).
01920      05  ERROR-MESSAGE-OUT         PIC X(52).
01930
01940  01  DEPOSIT-AMOUNT-INVALID-MSG.
01950      05  FILLER          PIC X(29) VALUE
01960                         "DEPOSIT AMOUNT NOT NUMERIC -".
01970      05  DEPOSIT-AMOUNT-X-E        PIC X(8).
01980
01990  01  WITHDRAWAL-AMOUNT-INVALID-MSG.
02000      05  FILLER          PIC X(32) VALUE
02010                         "WITHDRAWAL AMOUNT NOT NUMERIC -".
02020      05  WITHDRAWAL-AMOUNT-X-E PIC X(8).
02030
02040  01  INVALID-CODE-MSG.
02050      05  FILLER          PIC X(27) VALUE "INVALID TRANSACTION CODE -".
02060      05  TRANSACTION-CODE-E        PIC X.
02070
```

```
02080  01   FINAL-LINE-1.
02090       05   FILLER        PIC X(17) VALUE SPACES.
02100       05   FILLER        PIC X(12) VALUE "TOTALS".
02110       05   DEPOSIT-TOTAL-OUT       PIC Z,ZZZ,ZZZ.99BB.
02120       05   WITHDRAWAL-TOTAL-OUT    PIC Z,ZZZ,ZZZ.99.
02130
02140  01   FINAL-LINE-2.
02150       05   FILLER        PIC X(40) VALUE SPACES.
02160       05   FILLER        PIC X(14) VALUE "CONTROL COUNTS".
02170
02180  01   FINAL-LINE-3.
02190       05   FILLER        PIC X(34) VALUE SPACES.
02200       05   FILLER        PIC X(26)
02210                          VALUE "NUMBER OF NEW ACCOUNTS".
02220       05   NUMBER-OF-NEW-ACCOUNTS-OUT PIC ZZ9.
02230
02240  01   FINAL-LINE-4.
02250       05   FILLER        PIC X(34) VALUE SPACES.
02260       05   FILLER        PIC X(26)
02270                          VALUE "NUMBER OF DEPOSITS".
02280       05   NUMBER-OF-DEPOSITS-OUT   PIC ZZ9.
02290
02300  01   FINAL-LINE-5.
02310       05   FILLER        PIC X(34) VALUE SPACES.
02320       05   FILLER        PIC X(26)
02330                          VALUE "NUMBER OF WITHDRAWALS".
02340       05   NUMBER-OF-WITHDRAWALS-OUT PIC ZZ9.
02350
02360  01   FINAL-LINE-6.
02370       05   FILLER        PIC X(34) VALUE SPACES.
02380       05   FILLER        PIC X(26)
02390                          VALUE "NUMBER OF NAME CHANGES".
02400       05   NUMBER-OF-NAME-CHANGES-OUT PIC ZZ9.
02410
02420  01   FINAL-LINE-7.
02430       05   FILLER        PIC X(34) VALUE SPACES.
02440       05   FILLER        PIC X(26)
02450                          VALUE "NUMBER OF CLOSED ACCOUNTS".
02460       05   NUMBER-OF-DELETIONS-OUT   PIC ZZ9.
02470
02480  01   FINAL-LINE-8.
02490       05   FILLER        PIC X(34) VALUE SPACES.
02500       05   FILLER        PIC X(26)
02510                          VALUE "NUMBER OF ERRORS".
02520       05   NUMBER-OF-ERRONEOUS-RCDS-OUT
02530                                    PIC ZZ9.
02540
02550  01   FINAL-LINE-9.
02560       05   FILLER        PIC X(34) VALUE SPACES.
02570       05   FILLER        PIC X(24) VALUE "TOTAL".
02580       05   NUMBER-OF-INPUT-RECORDS-OUT PIC Z,ZZ9.
02590
02600  01   NO-TRANSACTIONS.
02610       05   FILLER        PIC X(21) VALUE SPACES.
02620       05   FILLER        PIC X(15) VALUE "NO TRANSACTIONS".
02630
02640  01   INSUFFICIENT-FILE-SPACE.
02650       05   FILLER        PIC X(21) VALUE SPACES.
02660       05   FILLER        PIC X(23) VALUE "INSUFFICIENT FILE SPACE".
02670
02680  ******************************************************************
02690
02700  PROCEDURE DIVISION.
02710  DECLARATIVES.
02720  DUMMY-USE SECTION.
02730       USE AFTER ERROR PROCEDURE ACCOUNT-MASTER-FILE-I-O.
02740  END DECLARATIVES.
02750
02760  NONDECLARATIVE SECTION.
02770  UPDATE-MASTER-RECORDS.
02780       PERFORM INITIALIZATION.
02790       PERFORM PROCESS-ONE-KEY UNTIL
02800            ACCOUNT-NUMBER-X = HIGH-VALUES.
02810       PERFORM TERMINATION.
02820       STOP RUN.
```

(continued)

Figure 15.19 (continued)

```
02830
02840    INITIALIZATION.
02850        OPEN INPUT   TRANSACTION-FILE-IN
02860             OUTPUT  TRANSACTION-REGISTER-FILE-OUT
02870                     ERROR-REPORT-FILE-OUT
02880             I-O     ACCOUNT-MASTER-FILE-I-O.
02890        IF FILE-CHECK NOT = ZEROS
02900           DISPLAY " MASTER FILE OPEN STATUS = ", FILE-CHECK
02910           CLOSE TRANSACTION-FILE-IN,
02920                 TRANSACTION-REGISTER-FILE-OUT,
02930                 ACCOUNT-MASTER-FILE-I-O
02940           STOP RUN.
02950        ACCEPT TODAYS-DATE FROM DATE.
02960        MOVE CORRESPONDING TODAYS-DATE TO PAGE-HEAD-2.
02970        PERFORM WRITE-REGISTER-PAGE-HEAD.
02980        PERFORM WRITE-ERROR-REPORT-PAGE-HEAD.
02990        PERFORM READ-A-TRANSACTION-RECORD.
03000        IF ACCOUNT-NUMBER-X = HIGH-VALUES
03010           WRITE ERROR-REPORT-RECORD-OUT FROM NO-TRANSACTIONS.
03020
03030    WRITE-REGISTER-PAGE-HEAD.
03040        WRITE TRANSACTION-REGISTER-REC-OUT FROM REPORT-HEADING-1
03050                                            AFTER PAGE.
03060        WRITE TRANSACTION-REGISTER-REC-OUT FROM REPORT-HEADING-2.
03070        WRITE TRANSACTION-REGISTER-REC-OUT FROM REPORT-HEADING-3.
03080        ADD 1 TO REGISTER-PAGE-COUNTER.
03090        MOVE REGISTER-PAGE-COUNTER TO PAGE-NUMBER-OUT.
03100        WRITE TRANSACTION-REGISTER-REC-OUT
03110             FROM REGISTER-PAGE-HEAD-1 AFTER 2.
03120        WRITE TRANSACTION-REGISTER-REC-OUT FROM PAGE-HEAD-2.
03130        WRITE TRANSACTION-REGISTER-REC-OUT
03140             FROM REGISTER-PAGE-HEAD-3 AFTER 3.
03150        WRITE TRANSACTION-REGISTER-REC-OUT FROM PAGE-HEAD-4.
03160        WRITE TRANSACTION-REGISTER-REC-OUT FROM BLANKS.
03170        MOVE 11 TO LINE-COUNT-ER.
03180
03190    WRITE-ERROR-REPORT-PAGE-HEAD.
03200        WRITE ERROR-REPORT-RECORD-OUT FROM REPORT-HEADING-1
03210                                       AFTER PAGE.
03220        WRITE ERROR-REPORT-RECORD-OUT FROM REPORT-HEADING-2.
03230        WRITE ERROR-REPORT-RECORD-OUT FROM REPORT-HEADING-3.
03240        ADD 1 TO ERROR-REPORT-PAGE-COUNTER.
03250        MOVE ERROR-REPORT-PAGE-COUNTER TO PAGE-NUMBER-OUT.
03260        WRITE ERROR-REPORT-RECORD-OUT FROM ERROR-REPORT-PAGE-HEAD-1
03270             AFTER 2.
03280        WRITE ERROR-REPORT-RECORD-OUT FROM PAGE-HEAD-2.
03290        WRITE ERROR-REPORT-RECORD-OUT FROM ERROR-REPORT-PAGE-HEAD-3
03300             AFTER 3.
03310        WRITE ERROR-REPORT-RECORD-OUT FROM PAGE-HEAD-4.
03320        WRITE ERROR-REPORT-RECORD-OUT FROM BLANKS.
03330        MOVE 11 TO ERROR-LINE-COUNTER.
03340
03350    PROCESS-ONE-KEY.
03360        PERFORM PROCESS-MASTER-RECORD.
03370        PERFORM PROCESS-TRANSACTION-RECORD.
03380        PERFORM CHECK-TO-WRITE-MASTER.
03390
03400    PROCESS-TRANSACTION-RECORD.
03410        PERFORM APPLY-TRANSACTION.
03420        PERFORM READ-A-TRANSACTION-RECORD.
03430
03440    PROCESS-MASTER-RECORD.
03450        PERFORM COMPUTE-SLOT-NO-FOR-READ.
03460        PERFORM READ-A-MASTER-RECORD.
03470        IF ACCOUNT-NUMBER-MX IS EQUAL TO ACCOUNT-NUMBER-X
03480           MOVE "Y" TO IS-MASTER-RECORD-IN-THE-FILE,
03490                       IS-MASTER-RECORD-IN-WORK-AREA
03500        ELSE
03510           PERFORM EXTENDED-READ-SEARCH
03520           IF ACCOUNT-NUMBER-MX IS EQUAL TO ACCOUNT-NUMBER-X
03530              MOVE "Y" TO IS-MASTER-RECORD-IN-THE-FILE,
03540                          IS-MASTER-RECORD-IN-WORK-AREA
03550              SUBTRACT 1 FROM SLOT-NUMBER
03560           ELSE
03570              MOVE "N" TO IS-MASTER-RECORD-IN-THE-FILE,
03580                          IS-MASTER-RECORD-IN-WORK-AREA.
03590
```

```
03600   COMPUTE-SLOT-NO-FOR-READ.
03610       DIVIDE ACCOUNT-NUMBER-T BY DIVISOR
03620           GIVING INTEGER-QUOTIENT
03630           REMAINDER INTEGER-REMAINDER.
03640       ADD 1, INTEGER-REMAINDER GIVING SLOT-NUMBER.
03650
03660   COMPUTE-SLOT-NO-FOR-WRITE.
03670       DIVIDE ACCOUNT-NUMBER-M BY DIVISOR
03680           GIVING INTEGER-QUOTIENT
03690           REMAINDER INTEGER-REMAINDER.
03700       ADD 1, INTEGER-REMAINDER GIVING SLOT-NUMBER.
03710
03720   EXTENDED-READ-SEARCH.
03730       ADD SLOT-NUMBER, EXTENDED-SEARCH-STEPS
03740           GIVING EXTENDED-SEARCH-LIMIT.
03750       PERFORM READ-A-MASTER-RECORD
03760           VARYING SLOT-NUMBER FROM SLOT-NUMBER BY 1
03770               UNTIL
03780                   ACCOUNT-NUMBER-MX IS EQUAL TO ACCOUNT-NUMBER-X OR
03790                   SLOT-NUMBER GREATER THAN
03800                       EXTENDED-SEARCH-LIMIT OR
03810                       NUMBER-OF-SLOTS-IN-FILE.
03820
03830   READ-A-MASTER-RECORD.
03840       READ ACCOUNT-MASTER-FILE-I-O.
03850       IF FILE-CHECK = ZEROS OR "23"
03860           NEXT SENTENCE
03870       ELSE
03880           DISPLAY " MASTER FILE READ STATUS = ", FILE-CHECK
03890           PERFORM TERMINATION
03900           STOP RUN.
03910
03920   CHECK-TO-WRITE-MASTER.
03930       MOVE ZEROS TO FILE-CHECK.
03940       IF IS-MASTER-RECORD-IN-WORK-AREA = "Y" AND
03950           IS-MASTER-RECORD-IN-THE-FILE  = "N"
03960           PERFORM WRITE-NEW-ACCOUNT-RECORD
03970       ELSE
03980       IF IS-MASTER-RECORD-IN-WORK-AREA = "Y" AND
03990           IS-MASTER-RECORD-IN-THE-FILE  = "Y"
04000           REWRITE ACCOUNT-MASTER-RECORD-I-O
04010       ELSE
04020       IF IS-MASTER-RECORD-IN-WORK-AREA = "N" AND
04030           IS-MASTER-RECORD-IN-THE-FILE  = "Y"
04040           DELETE ACCOUNT-MASTER-FILE-I-O.
04050       IF FILE-CHECK NOT = ZERO
04060           DISPLAY " MASTER FILE WRITE STATUS = ", FILE-CHECK
04070           PERFORM TERMINATION
04080           STOP RUN.
04090
04100   WRITE-NEW-ACCOUNT-RECORD.
04110       PERFORM COMPUTE-SLOT-NO-FOR-WRITE.
04120       PERFORM WRITE-A-MASTER-RECORD.
04130       IF FILE-CHECK = "22"
04140           PERFORM EXTENDED-WRITE-SEARCH.
04150
```

(continued)

In PROCESS-MASTER-RECORD, line 03440, the program tries to READ a record from the master file. If it succeeds in finding a record key equal to the Account Number in the transaction on the first try, it sets the appropriate flags, in lines 03480 and 03490. Otherwise, it PERFORMs an extended search to try to find the desired master record. If the record is found, 1 is SUBTRACTed from SLOT-NUMBER because the extended search leaves the value of SLOT-NUMBER greater by 1 than the number of the slot that the record was found in. To see why, look at the PERFORM statement at line 03750.

A PERFORM . . . VARYING statement changes the value of its VARYING field after it carries out the PERFORMed paragraph and before it tests the UNTIL conditions. So if READ-A-MASTER-RECORD brings in a record whose Account Number IS EQUAL TO ACCOUNT-NUMBER-X, SLOT-NUMBER is nonetheless increased by 1 before the UNTIL tests are made.

Figure 15.19   (continued)

```
04160   WRITE-A-MASTER-RECORD.
04170       WRITE ACCOUNT-MASTER-RECORD-I-O.
04180       IF FILE-CHECK = ZEROS OR "22"
04190           NEXT SENTENCE
04200       ELSE
04210           DISPLAY " MASTER FILE WRITE STATUS = ", FILE-CHECK
04220           PERFORM TERMINATION
04230           STOP RUN.
04240
04250   EXTENDED-WRITE-SEARCH.
04260       ADD SLOT-NUMBER, EXTENDED-SEARCH-STEPS
04270           GIVING EXTENDED-SEARCH-LIMIT.
04280       PERFORM WRITE-A-MASTER-RECORD
04290           VARYING SLOT-NUMBER FROM SLOT-NUMBER BY 1
04300               UNTIL
04310                   FILE-CHECK IS EQUAL TO ZEROS OR
04320                   SLOT-NUMBER GREATER THAN
04330                       EXTENDED-SEARCH-LIMIT OR
04340                       NUMBER-OF-SLOTS-IN-FILE.
04350       IF FILE-CHECK = ZEROS
04360           NEXT SENTENCE
04370       ELSE
04380           PERFORM WRITE-INSUFFICIENT-FILE-SPACE
04390           DISPLAY " MASTER FILE WRITE STATUS = ", FILE-CHECK
04400           PERFORM TERMINATION
04410           STOP RUN.
04420
04430   READ-A-TRANSACTION-RECORD.
04440       MOVE SPACES TO ACCOUNT-NUMBER-X.
04450       PERFORM READ-TRANSACTION-FILE UNTIL
04460           ACCOUNT-NUMBER-T IS NUMERIC OR
04470           TRANSACTION-INPUT-AREA IS EQUAL TO HIGH-VALUES.
04480
04490   READ-TRANSACTION-FILE.
04500       READ TRANSACTION-FILE-IN INTO TRANSACTION-INPUT-AREA
04510           AT END
04520               MOVE HIGH-VALUES TO TRANSACTION-INPUT-AREA.
04530       IF TRANSACTION-INPUT-AREA NOT EQUAL TO HIGH-VALUES
04540           ADD  1 TO NUMBER-OF-INPUT-RECORDS-W
04550           IF ACCOUNT-NUMBER-T NOT NUMERIC
04560               ADD 1 TO NUMBER-OF-ERRONEOUS-RECORDS-W
04570               PERFORM WRITE-INVALID-KEY-LINE.
04580
04590   APPLY-TRANSACTION.
04600       IF NEW-ACCOUNT
04610           PERFORM CHECK-FOR-VALID-NEW-ACCOUNT
04620       ELSE
04630       IF DEPOSIT
04640           PERFORM CHECK-FOR-VALID-DEPOSIT
04650       ELSE
04660       IF WITHDRAWAL
04670           PERFORM CHECK-FOR-VALID-WITHDRAWAL
04680       ELSE
04690       IF NAME-CHANGE
04700           PERFORM CHECK-FOR-VALID-NAME-CHANGE
04710       ELSE
04720       IF DELETION
04730           PERFORM CHECK-FOR-VALID-DELETION
04740       ELSE
04750           ADD 1 TO NUMBER-OF-ERRONEOUS-RECORDS-W
04760           PERFORM WRITE-INVALID-CODE-LINE.
04770
```

```
04780    CHECK-FOR-VALID-NEW-ACCOUNT.
04790        IF IS-MASTER-RECORD-IN-WORK-AREA = "Y"
04800            ADD 1 TO NUMBER-OF-ERRONEOUS-RECORDS-W
04810            PERFORM WRITE-NEW-ACCT-INVALID-LINE
04820        ELSE
04830        IF DEPOSIT-AMOUNT NOT NUMERIC
04840            ADD 1 TO NUMBER-OF-ERRONEOUS-RECORDS-W
04850            PERFORM WRITE-DEPOSIT-INVALID-LINE
04860        ELSE
04870        IF DEPOSITOR-NAME-MISSING
04880            ADD 1 TO NUMBER-OF-ERRONEOUS-RECORDS-W
04890            PERFORM WRITE-NAME-MISSING-LINE
04900        ELSE
04910            MOVE ACCOUNT-NUMBER-T TO ACCOUNT-NUMBER-M
04920            MOVE DEPOSITOR-NAME-NEW-ACCOUNT
04930                TO DEPOSITOR-NAME-M
04940            MOVE TODAYS-DATE TO DATE-OF-LAST-TRANSACTION-M
04950            MOVE DEPOSIT-AMOUNT TO CURRENT-BALANCE-M
04960            PERFORM WRITE-NEW-ACCOUNT-LINE
04970            MOVE "Y" TO IS-MASTER-RECORD-IN-WORK-AREA.
04980
04990    CHECK-FOR-VALID-DEPOSIT.
05000        IF DEPOSIT-AMOUNT NOT NUMERIC
05010            ADD 1 TO NUMBER-OF-ERRONEOUS-RECORDS-W
05020            PERFORM WRITE-DEPOSIT-INVALID-LINE
05030        ELSE
05040        IF IS-MASTER-RECORD-IN-WORK-AREA = "N"
05050            ADD 1 TO NUMBER-OF-ERRONEOUS-RECORDS-W
05060            PERFORM WRITE-MASTER-MISSING-LINE
05070        ELSE
05080            ADD DEPOSIT-AMOUNT TO CURRENT-BALANCE-M
05090            MOVE TODAYS-DATE TO DATE-OF-LAST-TRANSACTION-M
05100            PERFORM WRITE-DEPOSIT-LINE.
05110
05120     CHECK-FOR-VALID-WITHDRAWAL.
05130        IF WITHDRAWAL-AMOUNT NOT NUMERIC
05140            ADD 1 TO NUMBER-OF-ERRONEOUS-RECORDS-W
05150            ·PERFORM WRITE-WITHDRAWAL-INVALID-LINE
05160        ELSE
05170        IF IS-MASTER-RECORD-IN-WORK-AREA = "N"
05180            ADD 1 TO NUMBER-OF-ERRONEOUS-RECORDS-W
05190            PERFORM WRITE-MASTER-MISSING-LINE
05200        ELSE
05210            SUBTRACT WITHDRAWAL-AMOUNT FROM CURRENT-BALANCE-M
05220            MOVE TODAYS-DATE TO DATE-OF-LAST-TRANSACTION-M
05230            PERFORM WRITE-WITHDRAWAL-LINE.
05240
05250    CHECK-FOR-VALID-NAME-CHANGE.
05260        IF REPLACEMENT-NAME-MISSING
05270            ADD 1 TO NUMBER-OF-ERRONEOUS-RECORDS-W
05280            PERFORM WRITE-NAME-MISSING-LINE
05290        ELSE
05300        IF IS-MASTER-RECORD-IN-WORK-AREA = "N"
05310            ADD 1 TO NUMBER-OF-ERRONEOUS-RECORDS-W
05320            PERFORM WRITE-MASTER-MISSING-LINE
05330        ELSE
05340            MOVE DEPOSITOR-NAME TO DEPOSITOR-NAME-M
05350            MOVE TODAYS-DATE TO DATE-OF-LAST-TRANSACTION-M
05360            PERFORM WRITE-NAME-CHANGE-LINE.
05370
```

(continued)

Figure 15.19   (continued)

```
05380    CHECK-FOR-VALID-DELETION.
05390        IF IS-MASTER-RECORD-IN-WORK-AREA = "N"
05400            ADD 1 TO NUMBER-OF-ERRONEOUS-RECORDS-W
05410                PERFORM WRITE-MASTER-MISSING-LINE
05420        ELSE
05430                PERFORM WRITE-DELETION-LINE
05440                MOVE "N" TO IS-MASTER-RECORD-IN-WORK-AREA.
05450
05460    WRITE-NEW-ACCOUNT-LINE.
05470        MOVE ACCOUNT-NUMBER-T TO ACCOUNT-NUMBER-OUT.
05480        MOVE DEPOSIT-AMOUNT
05490            TO DEPOSIT-AMOUNT-OUT OF NEW-ACCOUNT-LINE.
05500        ADD 1 TO NUMBER-OF-NEW-ACCOUNTS-W.
05510        ADD DEPOSIT-AMOUNT TO DEPOSIT-TOTAL-W.
05520        IF LINE-COUNT-ER + 1 > REGISTER-LINE-LIMIT
05530            PERFORM WRITE-REGISTER-PAGE-HEAD.
05540        WRITE TRANSACTION-REGISTER-REC-OUT FROM NEW-ACCOUNT-LINE.
05550        ADD 1 TO LINE-COUNT-ER.
05560
05570    WRITE-DEPOSIT-LINE.
05580        MOVE ACCOUNT-NUMBER-M
05590            TO ACCOUNT-NUMBER-M-OUT OF DEPOSIT-LINE.
05600        MOVE DEPOSIT-AMOUNT TO DEPOSIT-AMOUNT-OUT OF DEPOSIT-LINE.
05610        ADD 1 TO NUMBER-OF-DEPOSITS-W.
05620        ADD DEPOSIT-AMOUNT TO DEPOSIT-TOTAL-W.
05630        IF LINE-COUNT-ER + 1 > REGISTER-LINE-LIMIT
05640            PERFORM WRITE-REGISTER-PAGE-HEAD.
05650        WRITE TRANSACTION-REGISTER-REC-OUT FROM DEPOSIT-LINE.
05660        ADD 1 TO LINE-COUNT-ER.
05670
05680    WRITE-WITHDRAWAL-LINE.
05690        MOVE ACCOUNT-NUMBER-M
05700            TO ACCOUNT-NUMBER-M-OUT OF WITHDRAWAL-LINE.
05710        MOVE WITHDRAWAL-AMOUNT TO WITHDRAWAL-AMOUNT-OUT.
05720        ADD 1 TO NUMBER-OF-WITHDRAWALS-W.
05730        ADD WITHDRAWAL-AMOUNT TO WITHDRAWAL-TOTAL-W.
05740        IF LINE-COUNT-ER + 1 > REGISTER-LINE-LIMIT
05750            PERFORM WRITE-REGISTER-PAGE-HEAD.
05760        WRITE TRANSACTION-REGISTER-REC-OUT FROM WITHDRAWAL-LINE.
05770        ADD 1 TO LINE-COUNT-ER.
05780
05790    WRITE-DEPOSIT-INVALID-LINE.
05800        MOVE DEPOSIT-AMOUNT-X TO DEPOSIT-AMOUNT-X-E.
05810        MOVE ACCOUNT-NUMBER-T TO ACCOUNT-NUMBER-T-E.
05820        MOVE DEPOSIT-AMOUNT-INVALID-MSG TO ERROR-MESSAGE-OUT.
05830        PERFORM WRITE-ERROR-LINE.
05840
05850    WRITE-WITHDRAWAL-INVALID-LINE.
05860        MOVE WITHDRAWAL-AMOUNT-X TO WITHDRAWAL-AMOUNT-X-E.
05870        MOVE ACCOUNT-NUMBER-T TO ACCOUNT-NUMBER-T-E.
05880        MOVE WITHDRAWAL-AMOUNT-INVALID-MSG TO ERROR-MESSAGE-OUT.
05890        PERFORM WRITE-ERROR-LINE.
05900
05910    WRITE-NAME-MISSING-LINE.
05920        MOVE "DEPOSITOR NAME MISSING" TO ERROR-MESSAGE-OUT.
05930        MOVE ACCOUNT-NUMBER-T TO ACCOUNT-NUMBER-T-E.
05940        PERFORM WRITE-ERROR-LINE.
05950
05960    WRITE-NAME-CHANGE-LINE.
05970        MOVE ACCOUNT-NUMBER-M
05980            TO ACCOUNT-NUMBER-M-OUT IN NAME-CHANGE-LINE.
05990        MOVE DEPOSITOR-NAME    TO DEPOSITOR-NAME-OUT.
06000        ADD 1 TO NUMBER-OF-NAME-CHANGES-W.
06010        IF LINE-COUNT-ER + 1 > REGISTER-LINE-LIMIT
06020            PERFORM WRITE-REGISTER-PAGE-HEAD.
06030        WRITE TRANSACTION-REGISTER-REC-OUT FROM NAME-CHANGE-LINE.
06040        ADD 1 TO LINE-COUNT-ER.
06050
06060    WRITE-DELETION-LINE.
06070        MOVE ACCOUNT-NUMBER-M
06080            TO ACCOUNT-NUMBER-M-OUT IN DELETION-LINE.
06090        MOVE CURRENT-BALANCE-M TO CURRENT-BALANCE-M-OUT.
06100        ADD 1 TO NUMBER-OF-DELETIONS-W.
06110        ADD CURRENT-BALANCE-M TO WITHDRAWAL-TOTAL-W.
06120        IF LINE-COUNT-ER + 1 > REGISTER-LINE-LIMIT
06130            PERFORM WRITE-REGISTER-PAGE-HEAD.
06140        WRITE TRANSACTION-REGISTER-REC-OUT FROM DELETION-LINE.
06150        ADD 1 TO LINE-COUNT-ER.
```

```
06160
06170    WRITE-INVALID-CODE-LINE.
06180        MOVE TRANSACTION-CODE TO TRANSACTION-CODE-E.
06190        MOVE ACCOUNT-NUMBER-T TO ACCOUNT-NUMBER-T-E.
06200        MOVE INVALID-CODE-MSG TO ERROR-MESSAGE-OUT.
06210        PERFORM WRITE-ERROR-LINE.
06220
06230    WRITE-MASTER-MISSING-LINE.
06240        MOVE "MASTER RECORD DOES NOT EXIST" TO ERROR-MESSAGE-OUT.
06250        MOVE ACCOUNT-NUMBER-T TO ACCOUNT-NUMBER-T-E.
06260        PERFORM WRITE-ERROR-LINE.
06270
06280    WRITE-NEW-ACCT-INVALID-LINE.
06290        MOVE
06300        "ACCOUNT NUMBER ALREADY IN FILE. NEW ACCOUNT INVALID" TO
06310            ERROR-MESSAGE-OUT.
06320        MOVE ACCOUNT-NUMBER-T TO ACCOUNT-NUMBER-T-E.
06330        PERFORM WRITE-ERROR-LINE.
06340
06350    WRITE-ERROR-LINE.
06360        IF ERROR-LINE-COUNTER + 1 > ERROR-REPORT-LINE-LIMIT
06370            PERFORM WRITE-ERROR-REPORT-PAGE-HEAD.
06380        WRITE ERROR-REPORT-RECORD-OUT FROM ERROR-MESSAGE-LINE.
06390        ADD 1 TO ERROR-LINE-COUNTER.
06400
06410    WRITE-INSUFFICIENT-FILE-SPACE.
06420        MOVE "INSUFFICIENT FILE SPACE" TO ERROR-MESSAGE-OUT.
06430        MOVE ACCOUNT-NUMBER-T           TO ACCOUNT-NUMBER-T-E.
06440        PERFORM WRITE-ERROR-LINE.
06450
06460    WRITE-INVALID-KEY-LINE.
06470        MOVE ACCOUNT-NUMBER-X            TO ACCOUNT-NUMBER-T-E.
06480        MOVE "ACCOUNT NUMBER NOT NUMERIC" TO ERROR-MESSAGE-OUT.
06490        PERFORM WRITE-ERROR-LINE.
06500
06510    TERMINATION.
06520        PERFORM PRODUCE-FINAL-LINES.
06530        CLOSE TRANSACTION-FILE-IN
06540            ERROR-REPORT-FILE-OUT
06550            ACCOUNT-MASTER-FILE-I-O
06560            TRANSACTION-REGISTER-FILE-OUT.
06570
06580    PRODUCE-FINAL-LINES.
06590        MOVE   DEPOSIT-TOTAL-W TO DEPOSIT-TOTAL-OUT.
06600        MOVE WITHDRAWAL-TOTAL-W TO WITHDRAWAL-TOTAL-OUT.
06610        WRITE TRANSACTION-REGISTER-REC-OUT FROM FINAL-LINE-1 AFTER 3.
06620        WRITE TRANSACTION-REGISTER-REC-OUT FROM FINAL-LINE-2 AFTER 2.
06630        MOVE NUMBER-OF-NEW-ACCOUNTS-W TO NUMBER-OF-NEW-ACCOUNTS-OUT.
06640        WRITE TRANSACTION-REGISTER-REC-OUT FROM FINAL-LINE-3 AFTER 2.
06650        MOVE NUMBER-OF-DEPOSITS-W TO NUMBER-OF-DEPOSITS-OUT.
06660        WRITE TRANSACTION-REGISTER-REC-OUT FROM FINAL-LINE-4 AFTER 2.
06670        MOVE NUMBER-OF-WITHDRAWALS-W TO NUMBER-OF-WITHDRAWALS-OUT.
06680        WRITE TRANSACTION-REGISTER-REC-OUT FROM FINAL-LINE-5 AFTER 2.
06690        MOVE NUMBER-OF-NAME-CHANGES-W TO NUMBER-OF-NAME-CHANGES-OUT.
06700        WRITE TRANSACTION-REGISTER-REC-OUT FROM FINAL-LINE-6 AFTER 2.
06710        MOVE NUMBER-OF-DELETIONS-W TO NUMBER-OF-DELETIONS-OUT.
06720        WRITE TRANSACTION-REGISTER-REC-OUT FROM FINAL-LINE-7 AFTER 2.
06730        MOVE NUMBER-OF-ERRONEOUS-RECORDS-W
06740            TO NUMBER-OF-ERRONEOUS-RCDS-OUT.
06750        WRITE TRANSACTION-REGISTER-REC-OUT FROM FINAL-LINE-8 AFTER 2.
06760        MOVE NUMBER-OF-INPUT-RECORDS-W
06770            TO NUMBER-OF-INPUT-RECORDS-OUT.
06780        WRITE TRANSACTION-REGISTER-REC-OUT FROM FINAL-LINE-9 AFTER 2.
```

The MOVE statement at line 05810 demonstrates that it is legal to MOVE a numeric source, or sending, field (ACCOUNT-NUMBER-T) to an alphanumeric receiving field. If a numeric field is defined as an unsigned integer and is of USAGE DISPLAY, as ACCOUNT-NUMBER-T is, the value of the field will be transferred to the alphanumeric field exactly as it appears in the numeric field, with no change in its form, whether the contents of the sending field are actually numeric or nonnumeric.

Program P15-05 was run with the input transactions shown in Figure 15.20 and the master file created by Program P15-04. Program P15-05 produced the report output shown in Figure 15.21.

Figure 15.20 Transaction input to Program P15-05.

```
--------------------------------------------------------------------------------
          1         2         3         4         5         6         7         8
1234567890123456789012345678901234567890123456789012345678901234567890123456789012
--------------------------------------------------------------------------------
20042600015000
24749100015000
70038500007500JAMES WASHINGTON
10039200007500INEZ WASHINGTON
476660JOHN & SALLY DUPRINO
26017500125634
34749100150050
10042000150000JOHN RICE
38191900002460
26683500357429
28191900150000
436650BETH DENNY
10039900014ZOOGARY NASTI
200007)))$X)))
20039100064200
31510900100000
23310000012750
39023000002735
70042700002500GREG PRUITT
23510100256300
414697GENE & THERESA GALLI
23823400035000
35549600011000
461714
23149000015327
20005400120000
26871800025000
20016900025000
10009200043200GENE GALLI
30009200050000
20009200172500
418862GEORGE & ANN CULHANE
536126
21962500019202
536126
26695200025000
23612600231700
80031500013798
230917
5
20030800005000
400308GENE GALLI
10040600120000
37688400015025
23280900001006
10014100035075IRVING STURDUVAN
```

EXERCISE 5

Write a program to update the master file you created in Exercise 4, this chapter. Use transactions in the same format you used when you updated your sequential master file in Exercise 3, Chapter 13, page 451.

Have your program make all suitable validity checks on input transactions, and produce suitable reports.

Figure 15.21 Report output from Program P15-05.

```
                        ROBBEM STATE BANK
                        106 WEST 10TH ST.
                       BROOKLYN, NY  11212

                 SAVINGS ACCOUNT TRANSACTION REGISTER
      DATE   4/19/88                              PAGE   1


         ACCOUNT      DEPOSITS      WITHDRAWALS       NOTES
         NUMBER

          47491        150.00
          00392         75.00                       NEW ACCOUNT
          76660    JOHN & SALLY DUPRINO             NAME CHANGE
          60175      1,256.34
          47491                      1,500.50
          00420      1,500.00                       NEW ACCOUNT
          81919                         24.60
          66835      3,574.29
          81919      1,500.00
          15109                      1,000.00
          33100        127.50
          90230                         27.35
          38234        350.00
          55496                        110.00
          31490        153.27
          00054      1,200.00
          68718        250.00
          00169        250.00
          00092        432.00                       NEW ACCOUNT
          00092                        500.00
          00092      1,725.00
          18862    GEORGE & ANN CULHANE             NAME CHANGE
          36126                        100.00       ACCOUNT CLOSED
          19625        192.02
          66952        250.00
          32809         10.06




                        ROBBEM STATE BANK
                        106 WEST 10TH ST.
                       BROOKLYN, NY  11212

                 SAVINGS ACCOUNT TRANSACTION REGISTER
      DATE   4/19/88                              PAGE   2


         ACCOUNT      DEPOSITS      WITHDRAWALS       NOTES
         NUMBER

          00141        350.75                       NEW ACCOUNT


      TOTALS        13,346.23       3,262.45

                        CONTROL COUNTS

                  NUMBER OF NEW ACCOUNTS        4

                  NUMBER OF DEPOSITS           14

                  NUMBER OF WITHDRAWALS         6

                  NUMBER OF NAME CHANGES        2

                  NUMBER OF CLOSED ACCOUNTS     1

                  NUMBER OF ERRORS             19

                  TOTAL                        46
```

(continued)

Figure 15.21   (continued)

```
                         ROBBEM STATE BANK
                         106 WEST 10TH ST.
                         BROOKLYN, NY  11212

                      SAVINGS ACCOUNT ERROR REPORT
          DATE  4/19/88                            PAGE   1


             ACCOUNT                       NOTES
             NUMBER

              00426                MASTER RECORD DOES NOT EXIST
              00385                INVALID TRANSACTION CODE - 7
              36650                MASTER RECORD DOES NOT EXIST
              00399                DEPOSIT AMOUNT NOT NUMERIC - 00014ZOO
              00007                DEPOSIT AMOUNT NOT NUMERIC - )))$%)))
              00391                MASTER RECORD DOES NOT EXIST
              00427                INVALID TRANSACTION CODE - 7
              35101                MASTER RECORD DOES NOT EXIST
              14697                MASTER RECORD DOES NOT EXIST
              61714                DEPOSITOR NAME MISSING
              36126                MASTER RECORD DOES NOT EXIST
              36126                MASTER RECORD DOES NOT EXIST
              00315                INVALID TRANSACTION CODE - 8
              30917                DEPOSIT AMOUNT NOT NUMERIC -
                                   ACCOUNT NUMBER NOT NUMERIC
              00308                MASTER RECORD DOES NOT EXIST
              00308                MASTER RECORD DOES NOT EXIST
              00406                DEPOSITOR NAME MISSING
              76884                WITHDRAWAL AMOUNT NOT NUMERIC - 00015025
```

Listing the Contents of a Relative File

A relative file may be accessed sequentially, as we have seen in Program P15-03 when we produced a list of letter grades for students. But if we were to access our savings-account master file sequentially, we would get the records in slot number sequence rather than in sequence on Account Number. ACCESS SEQUENTIAL on a relative file means in sequence on slot number.

Program P15-06 lists our savings-account master records in sequence on Account Number. It does so by SORTing the entire master file on Account Number, using a SORT statement. The SORT then RETURNs the master records one at a time, sequenced on Account Number, to be printed.

Program P15-06 is shown in Figure 15.22. The FILE-CONTROL entry at line 00200 contains no RELATIVE KEY clause, because in this program we have no need to refer to the slot numbers of the records. We therefore need no ACCESS clause. Also, a STATUS field would be of no use, since the SORT is going to be OPENing and READing this file, and we would have no opportunity to test the STATUS field anyway.

In the Procedure Division, we need no DUMMY-USE SECTION as we had in Program P15-05 and earlier programs, since nowhere in Program P15-06 do we refer to the relative file with any input or output statements.

Figure 15.22 Program P15-06.

```
CB1 RELEASE 2.4                             IBM OS/VS COBOL   JULY  1, 1982


                    16.07.18          APR 22,1988


00010   IDENTIFICATION DIVISION.
00020   PROGRAM-ID.  P15-06.
00030
00040 *     THIS PROGRAM LISTS A RELATIVE FILE IN SEQUENCE ON
00050 *     ITS RECORD KEY.  THE PROGRAM FIRST SORTS THE FILE
00060 *     INTO SEQUENCE ON ITS KEY, AND THEN LISTS THE SORTED
00070 *     RECORDS.
00080 *
00090 ********************************************************************
00100
00110   ENVIRONMENT DIVISION.
00120   CONFIGURATION SECTION.
00130   SOURCE-COMPUTER.  IBM-370.
00140   OBJECT-COMPUTER.  IBM-370.
00150
00160   INPUT-OUTPUT SECTION.
00170   FILE-CONTROL.
00180       SELECT LIST-FILE-OUT     ASSIGN TO PRINTER.
00190       SELECT SORT-WORK-FILE    ASSIGN TO SORTWK.
00200       SELECT MASTER-FILE-IN    ASSIGN TO DISKUNIT
00210           ORGANIZATION RELATIVE.
00220
00230 ********************************************************************
00240
00250   DATA DIVISION.
00260   FILE SECTION.
00270   FD  MASTER-FILE-IN
00280       LABEL RECORDS ARE STANDARD
00290       RECORD CONTAINS 39 CHARACTERS.
00300
00310   01  MASTER-RECORD-IN                      PIC X(39).
00320
00330   SD  SORT-WORK-FILE
00340       RECORD CONTAINS 39 CHARACTERS.
00350
00360   01  SORT-WORK-RECORD.
00370       05  ACCOUNT-NUMBER-M                  PIC X(5).
00380       05  DEPOSITOR-NAME-M                  PIC X(20).
00390       05  DATE-OF-LAST-TRANSACTION-M.
00400           10  TRANSACTION-YEAR-M            PIC 99.
00410           10  TRANSACTION-MONTH-M           PIC 99.
00420           10  TRANSACTION-DAY-M             PIC 99.
00430       05  CURRENT-BALANCE-M                 PIC S9(6)V99.
00440
00450   FD  LIST-FILE-OUT
00460       LABEL RECORDS ARE OMITTED.
00470
00480   01  LIST-RECORD-OUT                       PIC X(81).
00490
00500   WORKING-STORAGE SECTION.
00510   01  PAGE-LIMIT        VALUE 38   COMP SYNC   PIC S99.
00520   01  LINE-COUNT-ER                COMP SYNC   PIC S99.
00530   01  PAGE-NUMBER-W     VALUE 0                PIC S99.
00540   01  MORE-INPUT        VALUE  "Y"            PIC X(3).
00550   01  FILE-CHECK        VALUE ZEROS           PIC XX.
00560
00570   01  RUN-DATE.
00580       05  RUN-YEAR                           PIC 99.
00590       05  RUN-MONTH-AND-DAY                  PIC 9(4).
00600
00610   01  HEADING-1.
00620       05  FILLER          VALUE SPACES       PIC X(40).
00630       05  FILLER          VALUE "SAVINGS ACCOUNT MASTER"
00640                                              PIC X(22).
```

(continued)

Figure 15.22   (continued)

```
00650
00660   01   HEADING-2.
00670        05   FILLER                 VALUE SPACES          PIC X(28).
00680        05   FILLER                 VALUE  "DATE"          PIC X(5).
00690        05   RUN-MONTH-AND-DAY                            PIC Z9/99/.
00700        05   RUN-YEAR                                     PIC 99B(21).
00710        05   FILLER                 VALUE  "PAGE"          PIC X(5).
00720        05   PAGE-NUMBER-OUT                              PIC Z9.
00730
00740   01   HEADING-3.
00750        05   FILLER                 VALUE SPACES          PIC X(46).
00760        05   FILLER                 VALUE  "DATE OF LAST" PIC X(12).
00770
00780   01   HEADING-4.
00790        05   FILLER                 VALUE SPACES          PIC X(20).
00800        05   FILLER                 VALUE  "ACCOUNT"       PIC X(13).
00810        05   FILLER                 VALUE  "CURRENT"       PIC X(13).
00820        05   FILLER                 VALUE  "TRANSACTION"   PIC X(15).
00830        05   FILLER                 VALUE  "DEPOSITOR NAME" PIC X(14).
00840
00850   01   HEADING-5.
00860        05   FILLER                 VALUE SPACES          PIC X(20).
00870        05   FILLER                 VALUE  "NUMBER"        PIC X(13).
00880        05   FILLER                 VALUE  "BALANCE"       PIC X(14).
00890        05   FILLER                 VALUE  "YR  MO  DA"    PIC X(10).
00900
00910   01   DETAIL-LINE.
00920        05   FILLER         VALUE SPACES          PIC X(21).
00930        05   ACCOUNT-NUMBER-OUT                   PIC X(5)B(4).
00940        05   CURRENT-BALANCE-OUT                  PIC Z,ZZZ,ZZZ.99-.
00950        05   FILLER         VALUE SPACES          PIC X(4).
00960        05   TRANSACTION-YEAR-OUT                 PIC 99BB.
00970        05   TRANSACTION-MONTH-OUT                PIC 99BB.
00980        05   TRANSACTION-DAY-OUT                  PIC 99B(4).
00990        05   DEPOSITOR-NAME-OUT                   PIC X(20).
01000
01010   01   NO-INPUT-DATA.
01020        05   FILLER         VALUE SPACES          PIC X(21).
01030        05   FILLER         VALUE "NO INPUT DATA" PIC X(13).
01040
01050   *******************************************************************
01060
01070   PROCEDURE DIVISION.
01080   SORT-STATEMENT SECTION.
01090   SORT-STATEMENT-PARAGRAPH.
01100        SORT SORT-WORK-FILE
01110             ASCENDING KEY ACCOUNT-NUMBER-M
01120             USING MASTER-FILE-IN
01130             OUTPUT PROCEDURE LIST-MASTER-FILE.
01140        STOP RUN.
01150
01160   LIST-MASTER-FILE SECTION.
01170   CONTROL-PARAGRAPH.
01180        PERFORM INITIALIZATION.
01190        PERFORM MAIN-PROCESS UNTIL MORE-INPUT = "N".
01200        PERFORM TERMINATION.
01210        GO TO END-OF-THIS-SECTION.
01220
01230   INITIALIZATION.
01240        OPEN OUTPUT LIST-FILE-OUT.
01250        ACCEPT RUN-DATE FROM DATE.
01260        MOVE CORRESPONDING RUN-DATE TO HEADING-2.
01270        PERFORM PRODUCE-PAGE-HEADINGS.
01280        RETURN SORT-WORK-FILE
01290             AT END
01300                  MOVE "N" TO MORE-INPUT.
01310        IF MORE-INPUT = "N"
01320             WRITE LIST-RECORD-OUT FROM NO-INPUT-DATA.
01330
```

```
01340   PRODUCE-PAGE-HEADINGS.
01350       ADD 1 TO PAGE-NUMBER-W.
01360       MOVE PAGE-NUMBER-W TO PAGE-NUMBER-OUT.
01370       WRITE LIST-RECORD-OUT FROM HEADING-1 AFTER PAGE.
01380       WRITE LIST-RECORD-OUT FROM HEADING-2.
01390       WRITE LIST-RECORD-OUT FROM HEADING-3 AFTER 3.
01400       WRITE LIST-RECORD-OUT FROM HEADING-4.
01410       WRITE LIST-RECORD-OUT FROM HEADING-5.
01420       MOVE SPACES TO LIST-RECORD-OUT.
01430       WRITE LIST-RECORD-OUT.
01440       MOVE 8 TO LINE-COUNT-ER.
01450
01460   TERMINATION.
01470       CLOSE LIST-FILE-OUT.
01480
01490   MAIN-PROCESS.
01500       MOVE ACCOUNT-NUMBER-M      TO ACCOUNT-NUMBER-OUT.
01510       MOVE CURRENT-BALANCE-M     TO CURRENT-BALANCE-OUT.
01520       MOVE TRANSACTION-YEAR-M    TO TRANSACTION-YEAR-OUT.
01530       MOVE TRANSACTION-MONTH-M TO TRANSACTION-MONTH-OUT.
01540       MOVE TRANSACTION-DAY-M     TO TRANSACTION-DAY-OUT.
01550       MOVE DEPOSITOR-NAME-M      TO DEPOSITOR-NAME-OUT.
01560       IF LINE-COUNT-ER + 1 > PAGE-LIMIT
01570           PERFORM PRODUCE-PAGE-HEADINGS.
01580       WRITE LIST-RECORD-OUT FROM DETAIL-LINE.
01590       ADD 1 TO LINE-COUNT-ER.
01600       RETURN SORT-WORK-FILE
01610           AT END
01620               MOVE "N" TO MORE-INPUT.
01630
01640   END-OF-THIS-SECTION.
01650       EXIT.
```

Program P15-06 was run with the updated master file produced by Program P15-05. Program P15-06 produced the output shown in Figure 15.23.

Figure 15.23 Output from Program P15-06.

```
                      SAVINGS ACCOUNT MASTER
          DATE   4/22/88                    PAGE   1


                          DATE OF LAST
    ACCOUNT     CURRENT   TRANSACTION   DEPOSITOR NAME
    NUMBER      BALANCE   YR  MO  DA

    00054       1,220.00  88  04  19    COMMUNITY DRUGS
    00080          50.00  88  04  10    LENORE MILLER
    00092       1,657.00  88  04  19    GENE GALLI
    00141         350.75  88  04  19    IRVING STURDUVAN
    00169         349.57  88  04  19    MARTIN LANG
    00202         250.00  88  04  10    ROSEMARY LANE
    00392          75.00  88  04  19    INEZ WASHINGTON
    00420       1,500.00  88  04  19    JOHN RICE
    06180         750.00  88  04  10    JAMES BUDD
    11682       1,007.84  88  04  10    ROSEBUCCI
    15109         985.00- 88  04  19    GENE GALLI
    18862         500.00  88  04  19    GEORGE & ANN CULHANE
    19625       1,692.02  88  04  19    JOHN DAPRINO
    25055           5.00  88  04  10    JOYCE MITCHELL
    27013          20.00  88  04  10    JANE HALEY
    30917         500.00  88  04  10    PATRICK J. LEE
    31490         168.27  88  04  19    SOLOMON CHAPELS
    32809         185.56  88  04  19    JOHN WILLIAMS
    33100         137.50  88  04  19    KEVIN PARKER
    33946          24.50  88  04  10    ROBERT RYAN
    34780         250.00  88  04  10    JERRY PARKS
    38234         600.00  88  04  19    GRACE MICELI
    43967         150.00  88  04  10    IMPERIAL FLORIST
    46749       1,000.00  88  04  10    PAUL LERNER, D.D.S.
    47491       1,149.50  88  04  19    ROGER SHAW
    50027          50.00  88  04  10    ONE DAY CLEANERS
    55496       1,890.00  88  04  19    JOE GARCIA
    60175       8,257.93  88  04  19    MICHAEL SMITH
    61714       1,500.00  88  04  10    JOHN BURKE
    64165          25.00  88  04  10    JOSEPH CAMILLO
```

(continued)

Figure 15.23   (continued)

```
                          SAVINGS ACCOUNT MASTER
             DATE   4/22/88                      PAGE   2


                              DATE OF LAST
            ACCOUNT    CURRENT   TRANSACTION      DEPOSITOR NAME
            NUMBER     BALANCE   YR  MO  DA

            65745         50.00  88  04  10       CARL CALDERON
            66835      3,584.29  88  04  19       ROBERT DAVIS M.D.
            66952        260.37  88  04  19       LESLIE MINSKY
            67566          1.00  88  04  10       EVELYN SLATER
            68718        525.00  88  04  19       VITO CACACI
            70549        125.50  88  04  10       KELLY HEDERMAN
            72032         35.00  88  04  10       J. & L. CAIN
            75495         25.75  88  04  10       BETH FALLON
            76660      1,000.00  88  04  19       JOHN & SALLY DUPRINO
            76884        150.00  88  04  10       JOHN J. LEHMAN
            81919      1,600.40  88  04  19       LORICE MONTI
            88298        150.00  88  04  10       JAY GREENE
            90230        527.65  88  04  19       BILL WILLIAMS
            96681         10.00  88  04  10       MARY KEATING
```

EXERCISE 6

Write a program to list the contents of your accounts-receivable master file. Have your program SORT the file into Account Number sequence before listing. Run the program using the files produced by your programs in Exercises 4 and 5, this chapter.

Other Operations on Relative Files

There are other operations that may be carried out on a relative file, which have not been discussed in this chapter. Among them are START, the sequential access uses of REWRITE and DELETE, and the dynamic access operations. Details of these may be found in the COBOL manual for your system.

Summary

A relative file may be thought of as consisting of a string of consecutively numbered slots in which records may be stored. A relative file may be accessed sequentially, randomly, and dynamically. Relative files must be stored on direct-access storage devices.

The sequential operations on a relative file are READ, WRITE, REWRITE, DELETE, and START. The random operations are READ, WRITE, REWRITE, and DELETE. The dynamic-access operations include all the sequential and random operations and also READ . . . NEXT.

A RELATIVE KEY field is used with certain operations. All random operations require a RELATIVE KEY to tell COBOL which record on the file to READ, WRITE, REWRITE, or DELETE. Whenever a START statement is used, a RELATIVE KEY field is required to tell COBOL where to START. When READing a relative file sequentially, if the programmer wants COBOL to provide the relative record number of each record as it is read, a RELATIVE KEY field must be used.

The RELATIVE KEY phrase is part of the ACCESS clause. Whenever a RELATIVE KEY phrase is used, an ACCESS clause must appear. Whenever ACCESS RANDOM or ACCESS DYNAMIC is used, a RELATIVE KEY phrase must appear. ACCESS SEQUENTIAL may appear without a RELATIVE KEY phrase. If the ACCESS clause is omitted, sequential access is assumed.

When items to be represented in a relative file are numbered nonconsecutively, a randomizing technique may be used to compute a home slot number for each record. If more than one record key randomizes to the same home slot number, an extended search is required to locate each record near its home slot.

When a relative file is processed sequentially, the records in the file are processed in slot-number order. If processing in record-key order is desired, the file can be SORTed.

Fill-In Exercises

1. A relative file can be thought of as consisting of a number of _____ into which records can be placed.

2. COBOL can _____ a record into any slot that already contains a record.

3. COBOL can _____ a record into any empty slot.

4. A record in a relative file is referred to by its _____ _____ _____ .

5. To process a relative file, the FILE-CONTROL entry for the file must contain a(n) _____ clause.

6. A RELATIVE KEY phrase must be used whenever ACCESS _____ or ACCESS _____ is used.

7. In any random operation on a relative file, the _____ _____ field contains the number of the slot to be operated upon.

8. When a relative file is read sequentially, COBOL can place the relative record number of each record into the _____ _____ field as each record is read.

9. If a random READ attempts to READ an empty slot, the STATUS field is set to _____ .

10. In the division/remainder method of randomizing, the divisor is a prime number _____ than the number of _____ in the file.

11. The RELATIVE KEY phrase is part of the _____ clause.

12. In the division/remainder method of randomizing, you ignore the _____ and add 1 to the _____ .

13. In the division/remainder method of randomizing, each record key yields a _____ _____ number.

14. Randomizing is needed only when the records in a file are _____ _____ .

15. The main advantage of relative files over indexed files is the _____ with which records in a relative file may be accessed.

Review Exercises

1. Write a program to list the relative record number and Account Number of each record in the accounts-receivable file of Exercises 4 and 5, this chapter, in relative record number order. Run your program using as input first the file you created in Exercise 4, and then the updated file you created in Exercise 5.

    Have your program READ the file sequentially, without SORTing it. Check whether your randomizing scheme worked and that each Account Number went into its intended slot. Did your file contain any synonyms? What slots did they go into?

2. Write a program to create an alumni file as a relative file. Use the same formats for input transactions and master records that you used when you created your sequential alumni file in Review Exercise 2, Chapter 12, page 409. Choose a file size suitable to the maximum number of alumni records that you expect to have in your file, and choose a divisor suitable to the file size.

    Have your program check for the presence of all fields in each input record and that the Social Security Number is numeric. Have your program print a report showing the records written onto the master file and the erroneous transactions.

3. Write a program to update randomly the alumni file you created in Review Exercise 2. Use the same transaction formats that you used when you updated your alumni file in Review Exercise 4, Chapter 13, page 458. Have your program check that the Social Security Number in each input record is numeric and also make all other suitable validity checks. Have your program print a suitable report.

4. Write a program to list the relative record number and the Social Security Number of each record in your alumni file, in relative record number order. Run your program using as input first the file you created in Review Exercise 2 and then the updated file you produced in Review Exercise 3.

5. Write a program to list the contents of your alumni file in Social Security Number order. Run your program using as input first the file you created in Review Exercise 2 and then the updated file you produced in Review Exercise 3.

Project

Rewrite your solution to the Project in Chapter 12, page 410, creating a relative file instead of a sequential file. Use Customer Numbers that are wholly numeric, and use the division/remainder method to compute a home slot number for each record.

16 Introduction to VSAM File Processing

Here are the key points you should learn from this chapter:

1. Why VSAM processing is used
2. How to use the Access Method Services program
3. What outputs to expect from Access Method Services
4. How to establish a key-sequenced data set
5. Two ways to establish an alternate index
6. How to establish a relative-record data set

Key words to recognize and learn:

VSAM
Virtual Storage Access Method
OS
VS
Operating System
Virtual Storage
DOS
Disk Operating System
physical sequential
entry-sequenced data set
key-sequenced data set
relative-record data set
VS1
VS2
Access Method Services
unloaded
command
DEFINE
master catalog
user catalog
JOBCAT
STEPCAT
alternate index
PATH
CYLINDER
data component
index component
BLDINDEX
ALTER
PRINT
LISTCAT
VERIFY
DATASET
CLUSTER

ALTERNATEINDEX
base cluster
NAME
VOLUME
primary amount
secondary amount
RECORDSIZE
FREESPACE
control interval
control area
INDEXED
data organization parameter
NUMBERED
NONINDEXED
KEYS
UNIQUE
SUBALLOCATION
RELATE
NONUNIQUEKEY
UNIQUEKEY
UPGRADE
PATHENTRY
UPDATE
NOUPDATE
INDATASET
OUTDATATSET
allocation status
condition code
AIXBLD
ENTRY
INFILE
OUTFILE
prefix

VSAM stands for **Virtual Storage Access Method.** It is an IBM system that can be used to organize files and carry out input and output functions for programs running under **OS/VS** (**Operating System/Virtual Storage**) and **DOS/VS** (**Disk Operating System**/Virtual Storage). VSAM provides high-speed retrieval and storage of data, several different ways to protect files by using passwords, and device independence. VSAM is used only with IBM systems. If your school has computing equipment of some other manufacturer, you can skip this chapter.

IBM OS/VS COBOL, which was used to run the programs in this book, has the ability to process files in seven different formats. The only file processing in OS/VS COBOL that adheres to the ANSI standard is that provided for the following four types of files:

1. VSAM indexed files
2. VSAM relative files
3. VSAM sequential files
4. **Physical sequential** files (ordinary OS files)

The other three types of files, whose processing does not adhere to the ANSI standard, are:

1. ISAM indexed files
2. BSAM and BDAM direct files
3. BSAM and BDAM relative files

All the sequential files used in this book are physical sequential. If you wish instead to use VSAM sequential files, you must include the letters AS before the ddname in the ASSIGN clause for the file. For example, you might have:

```
SELECT ACCOUNT-MASTER-FILE-IN ASSIGN TO AS-MSTRIN.
```

All VSAM files must be on direct-access storage devices. A VSAM sequential file is called an **entry-sequenced data set.** A VSAM indexed file is called a **key-sequenced data set.** And a VSAM relative file is called a **relative-record data set.**

References

To establish and use VSAM files you must have the proper reference materials. This chapter can serve only as an introduction to VSAM to help you understand the relevant IBM manuals. The following five manuals are absolutely essential if you wish to use VSAM files with OS/VS COBOL:

1. IBM VS COBOL for OS/VS, Order No. GC26-3857
2. IBM OS/VS COBOL Compiler and Library Programmer's Guide, Order No. SC28-6483
3. OS/VS1 Access Method Services, Order No. GC26-3840
   or
   OS/VS2 Access Method Services, Order No. GC26-3841
4. OS/VS Virtual Storage Access Method (VSAM) Programmer's Guide, Order No. GC26-3838
5. OS/VS Message Library: VS1 System Messages, Order No. GC38-1001
   or
   OS/VS Message Library: VS2 System Messages, Order No. GC38-1002

You will have to find out whether your school uses **VS1** or **VS2** in order to know which manuals are appropriate.

For DOS/VS, use the following manuals instead:

1. VS COBOL for DOS/VSE, Language Reference, Order No. GC26-3998
2. DOS/VS COBOL Compiler and Library Programmer's Guide, Order No. SC28-6478
3. DOS/VS Access Method Services User's Guide, Order No. GC33-5382
4. DOS/VSE Messages, Order No. GC33-5379

This chapter assumes that you have some experience with OS JCL, and that you have created, cataloged, and deleted at least one OS file at your school. If not, you may find that you are unable to understand some parts of this chapter. The programming examples given here are very complete, however, and may provide you with all the JCL you need to use VSAM files with COBOL.

These examples show what works at my school. Your school may have different requirements and conventions, and so the coding that worked for me may have to be modified slightly to work in your installation. Your instructor can provide you with the details you need.

Access Method Services

Access Method Services is the name of a big IBM utility program that creates VSAM files and carries out many useful functions in connection with them. Access Method Services is the only program that can create a VSAM file. This is a radical departure from file-handling techniques in existence before VSAM. In older systems, a new file could be created by a COBOL program and the proper JCL by simply OPENing the file as OUTPUT. With VSAM files, however, Access Method Services must first create a file with no records in it, called an **unloaded** file, and then a COBOL program can place records into the file by OPENing it as OUTPUT.

You get Access Method Services to do what you want by giving it one or more **commands.** You will see descriptions and examples of some important Access Method Services commands later in this chapter. The commands are described in complete detail in the OS and DOS references number 3 above.

The command you use to create a VSAM file is the **DEFINE** command. When a DEFINE command executes, Access Method Services reserves space for the file on a direct-access storage device and enters information about the file into the appropriate VSAM catalog. VSAM catalogs are separate from the OS catalogs. Every VSAM file must be cataloged in one of the VSAM catalogs. NonVSAM files may be cataloged in an OS catalog or a VSAM catalog, or not cataloged.

When a file is first DEFINEd, Access Method Services catalogs the file with no extra effort on the part of the programmer. Later, when the file is used, VSAM automatically keeps the catalog information current. One important piece of information contained in a VSAM catalog entry is the amount of space currently occupied by records in the file. Each time a file is CLOSEd, VSAM determines the amount of space occupied in the file and updates the catalog entry to reflect that information. So beware, if for any reason one of your VSAM files does not get CLOSEd, the catalog entry may not be correct and there will be trouble in store when you later try to use the file. You will soon see a simple way to remedy that difficulty.

VSAM Catalogs

An installation can have any number of VSAM catalogs. Each installation must have exactly one **master catalog,** and it may also have one or more **user catalogs.** In most installations the catalogs are established and named by the systems programmers, so a COBOL programmer (you) need not worry about creating one. A VSAM file may be cataloged in the master catalog or in one of the user catalogs.

All of my VSAM files were cataloged in a user catalog named USERCAT. If you are required to know the name of any user catalog you might be using, write it here:

_____

You will have to find out whether there are any rules for naming files in your installation. In the installation where I ran the programs in this book all of my file names had to be of the form:

```
VSAM.NY.GSP.xxxxxxx
```

where xxxxxxx stands for any legal name. When you see the programming examples later in this chapter, you will see the file names that I used. The file-naming rules that apply to me almost certainly will not apply to you. You will have to find what file-naming rules apply at your school and use them. You can use the following space to write in the required form of the names of your files, if any:

_____

_____

JCL with VSAM

The JCL used with VSAM is usually very simple. Since all VSAM files used by any COBOL program have already been created and cataloged, the JCL for most VSAM files has the form:

```
//ddname DD DSN=datasetname,DISP=OLD
```

You may instead specify DISP=SHR if sharing is allowed. No further information is needed in the JCL. A disposition of KEEP is implied for all VSAM files and need not be coded. If you should want to DELETE a file, there is no use putting DELETE in the DISP parameter. Only Access Method Services can delete a VSAM file. You must not specify DISP=NEW under any conditions, even if you are using a VSAM file for the first time. If you do, OS will allocate space for the file and the space will not be available to VSAM.

Sometimes it is necessary to include UNIT and VOL parameters in the JCL for a VSAM file. When we look at the programming examples, you will see when those parameters are needed. Of course, OS ordinarily would not examine any catalog entries when UNIT and VOL are given in the JCL, and would thus not know that the file being described is a VSAM file. So whenever you have to use UNIT and VOL in a DD statement, you must also include the parameter AMP='AMORG' to tell OS that this is a VSAM file. The form of the JCL for a VSAM file with the UNIT and VOL parameters is:

```
//ddname DD DSN=datasetname,DISP=OLD,UNIT=unit,VOL=volume,AMP='AMORG'
```

Whenever you use UNIT and VOL, if your file is cataloged in one of the user catalogs, you must tell the system which catalog. There are two statements you can use to tell the system which user catalog your file is cataloged in — the **JOBCAT** statement and the **STEPCAT** statement. An example of a JOBCAT statement specifying a user catalog named USERCAT is:

```
//JOBCAT DD DSN=USERCAT,DISP=SHR
```

An example of a STEPCAT statement is:

```
//STEPCAT DD DSN=USERCAT,DISP=SHR
```

The DISP parameter can also be specified as OLD if sharing is not wanted. The JOBCAT statement tells the system what user catalog is to be used for the entire job. A STEPCAT statement tells the system what user catalog is to be used for a single job step. When both JOBCAT and STEPCAT are specified, the catalog specified by STEPCAT is used for the job step. If your file is cataloged in the master catalog, you never have to indicate that explicitly to the system, and so you can omit JOBCAT and STEPCAT statements.

A JOBCAT statement, if used, is placed after the JOB statement and before the first EXEC statement. Each STEPCAT statement used is placed immediately after the EXEC statement of the step to which it applies.

The installation at my school does not permit the use of JOBCAT and STEPCAT statements because they interfere with the operation of other systems in use here. I can instead designate a user catalog for only a single procedure step by including the following kind of DD statement, with any legal ddname, among the DD statements for that procedure step:

```
//procstepname.anyname DD DSN=VSAM.CATALOG,DISP=SHR
```

To get Access Method Services to run, you must have an EXEC statement of the form:

```
//stepname EXEC PGM=IDCAMS
```

For its message output file Access Method Services needs the DD statement

```
//SYSPRINT DD SYSOUT=A
```

and a DD statement for its input file, which contains the commands to be executed. If the input file is in the input stream, the DD statement is:

```
//SYSIN DD *
```

Usually no other JCL is needed to run Access Method Services.

Access Method Services Commands

In this section we will briefly describe some of the important Access Method Services commands, most of which are used in the programming examples later in the chapter. When we look at the examples, each of the parameters used in each command will be fully explained.

Define

As mentioned earlier, the DEFINE command is used to create a file. The DEFINE command must also be used to reserve direct-access storage space for **alternate indexes,** in connection with ALTERNATE RECORD KEYs in indexed files. When an ALTERNATE RECORD KEY is used, it is also necessary to DEFINE something called a **PATH.** You will see what the PATH is used for when we look at the programming examples. Each ALTERNATE RECORD KEY in an indexed file requires its own alternate index file and at least one PATH.

In the DEFINE command you assign a name to the file or PATH being DEFINEd. You also say how much direct-access storage space is required for the file being DEFINEd (a PATH occupies no storage space). You may specify the space requirement as a certain number of RECORDS, TRACKS, or **CYLINDERS.** You must also say what VOLUME or VOLUMES the file is to reside on.

In the DEFINE command, you tell Access Method Services whether the file is to be sequential, indexed, or relative. If it is to be indexed, then you must provide Access Method Services with additional information, including the size of the prime RECORD KEY and its location in the record. You must also provide similar information about ALTERNATE RECORD KEYs when you DEFINE the alternate indexes.

The DEFINE command has many optional parameters that can be used to improve the speed efficiency of VSAM's record storage and retrieval. We refrain from using them in the programming examples in the interest of programming simplicity and because our files are so small.

The DEFINE command can be used to assign a password to a file and/or its index, and to assign names to the **data component** and **index component** of an indexed file if desired.

DELETE

The DELETE command is used to free direct-access storage space used for a file or an alternate index and to remove from the catalog the entries relating to those objects or to a PATH. Optionally you can have Access Method Services simply release storage space so that it can be used by another file, or actually erase the contents of the storage, presumably for security purposes.

BLDINDEX

The **BLDINDEX** command is used with indexed files to construct alternate indexes in connection with ALTERNATE RECORD KEYs. An alternate index for an indexed file can be built only after the indexed file has been loaded with records.

There are two ways to use the BLDINDEX command. One is more efficient in that it uses less virtual storage in its execution and generally runs faster. The other method complies with the ANSI standard. Both methods are shown in the programming examples dealing with the indexed file.

In the first method the programmer first DEFINEs the indexed file, then runs a COBOL program to load the file with records (such as Program P14-01), then DEFINEs the alternate index and its PATH, and then gives the BLDINDEX command to direct Access Method Services to build the alternate index using the data in the indexed file. It is during the building of the alternate index that Access Method Services can detect the presence of duplicate ALTERNATE RECORD KEY values, after the indexed file has already been completely loaded with records.

The ANSI standard, on the other hand, requires that duplicate values of ALTERNATE RECORD KEYs be detected during, not after, the loading of the indexed file. For this reason, the less efficient use of BLDINDEX has been provided for those who need such processing. In Program P14-01 we did not need to detect duplicate values of the ALTERNATE RECORD KEY and so were able to use the first method. Both will be shown shortly, however.

ALTER

It is possible, after a file has been DEFINEd, to change its description in the catalog. The particular descriptors that can be **ALTERed** depend on what kind of file has been DEFINEd and which attributes have been permitted to assume their default values.

PRINT

The **PRINT** command allows Access Method Services to list out the contents of all records in a file or just selected records. The records may be listed in character form, in hexadecimal, or in both character and hexadecimal.

LISTCAT

The **LISTCAT** command allows Access Method Services to print the catalog entries for VSAM files. You may request that the entire catalog entry for a certain file be printed, or you may request that only certain parts of the catalog entry be printed.

    The LISTCAT command also allows you to request catalog information for a whole group of files with similar names. For example, you could request that the catalog entries for all files whose names begin with VSAM.NY.GSP be printed.

VERIFY

The **VERIFY** command causes Access Method Services to check that the catalog entries for a file agree with the actual state of the file. Access Method Services does this by examining the file and then making any necessary corrections in the catalog. VERIFY then CLOSEs the file, if it is not already CLOSEd.

    You may use the VERIFY command if you suspect or know that a VSAM file was not CLOSEd after its last use. There is no harm in using VERIFY freely before any attempt to OPEN a VSAM file.

    An example of a VERIFY command, using the reserved word **DATASET**, is:

```
VERIFY DATASET(VSAM.NY.GSP.IMSTR)
```

Creating an Indexed File

This part of the chapter shows how to create the indexed file and the alternate index file and PATH for the programs in Chapter 14. Some of the conventions that are in force in my installation might be different from the ones in yours. Therefore, the Access Method Services commands that work for me might not be exactly what you need. I will explain each of the commands that I used and each parameter in each command, but if you need or want to use others (like passwords or the optional parameters that improve efficiency), see reference 3 on pages 572 and 573. First we will look at a typical input stream, which might be usable at most schools, and then at the input stream I used.

A typical input stream for Program P14-01 is shown in Figure 16.1. The JOBCAT statement indicates that all files created in this run are to be cataloged in the user catalog USERCAT. If your installation does not require you to specify the user catalog, or if your files are to be cataloged in the master catalog, you should omit the JOBCAT statement. The first EXEC statement, with stepname IDCAMS1, executes Access Method Services. You can see the use of the //SYSPRINT and //SYSIN statements for Access Method Services.

Figure 16.1 Typical input stream to create an indexed file and alternate index.

```
//GSPNY438 JOB 'P14X01',REGION=1120K
//JOBCAT DD DSN=USERCAT,DISP=SHR
//IDCAMS1 EXEC PGM=IDCAMS
//SYSPRINT DD SYSOUT=A
//SYSIN    DD *
    DEFINE CLUSTER -
           (NAME(VSAM.NY.GSP.IMSTR) -
           VOLUME(CNY005) -
           RECORDS(100 10) -
           RECORDSIZE(39 39) -
           FREESPACE(25 10) -
           INDEXED -
           KEYS(5 0))
/*
//COBOL1 EXEC COBUCG
//SYSIN DD *
00010  IDENTIFICATION DIVISION.
00020  PROGRAM-ID.  P14-01.
              .
              .
              .

       COBOL SOURCE PROGRAM
              .
              .
              .
//GO.PRINTER1 DD SYSOUT=A
//GO.PRINTER2 DD SYSOUT=A
//GO.DISKOUT DD DSN=VSAM.NY.GSP.IMSTR,DISP=OLD,
// UNIT=SYSDA,VOL=SER=CNY005,AMP='AMORG'
//GO.SORTWK01 DD UNIT=SYSDA,VOL=SER=SCR001,
//    SPACE=(TRK,(2),,CONTIG)
//GO.SORTWK02 DD UNIT=SYSDA,VOL=SER=SCR001,
//    SPACE=(TRK,(2),,CONTIG)
//GO.SORTWK03 DD UNIT=SYSDA,VOL=SER=SCR001,
//    SPACE=(TRK,(2),,CONTIG)
//GO.SORTLIB DD DSN=SYS1.SORTLIB,DISP=SHR
//GO.SYSOUT DD SYSOUT=A
//GO.INFILE DD *
              .
              .
              .

       INPUT DATA FOR PROGRAM P14-01
              .
              .
              .
//IDCAMS2 EXEC PGM=IDCAMS
//SYSPRINT DD SYSOUT=A
//SYSIN DD *
    DEFINE ALTERNATEINDEX -
           (NAME(VSAM.NY.GSP.IMSTR.ALTIX) -
           RELATE(VSAM.NY.GSP.IMSTR) -
           VOLUME(CNY008) -
           RECORDSIZE(35 75) -
           FREESPACE(25 10) -
           RECORDS(100 10) -
           KEYS(20 5) -
           NONUNIQUEKEY UPGRADE)
    DEFINE PATH -
           (NAME(VSAM.NY.GSP.IMSTR.ALTPATH) -
           PATHENTRY(VSAM.NY.GSP.IMSTR.ALTIX) -
           UPDATE)
    BLDINDEX INDATASET(VSAM.NY.GSP.IMSTR) -
             OUTDATASET(VSAM.NY.GSP.IMSTR.ALTIX)
/*
//
```

Defining the Indexed File

The first command to Access Method Services is DEFINE **CLUSTER.** Commands must be written in positions 2 through 72. For an indexed file a CLUSTER consists of the file and its index. Later I will DEFINE **ALTERNATE INDEX** and DEFINE PATH for this indexed file. Once an alternate index and a PATH are established, the original CLUSTER created with this DEFINE CLUSTER command is referred to as the **base cluster.**

This long DEFINE command shows the use of the continuation indicator, the dash. When used, the dash must be the last character on the line except for trailing blanks. Following the word CLUSTER are a number of parameters enclosed in one set of parentheses. You must give the **NAME** of the file and the **VOLUME** on which it is to reside. Just as you will have to make up a suitable name for your own file (my file name may not work in your installation), you will also have to provide a correct VOLUME (you probably don't have a VOLUME called CNY005 in your installation). You will have to find out what VOLUMEs are used for VSAM files in your installation. You can write them here:

_____

_____

The file size must be given, in numbers of RECORDS, TRACKS, or CYLINDERS. I used RECORDS. The file size can be specified as a **primary amount** and a **secondary amount.** The primary amount specifies the initial amount of space that is to be allocated to the CLUSTER. The secondary amount specifies the amount of space that is to be allocated each time the CLUSTER extends. Here I allowed for a primary amount of 100 Account Numbers.

The **RECORDSIZE** parameter specifies the average size of the records to be placed in the file and the maximum size, in bytes. In our indexed file, the records are fixed-length, 39-byte records, so the average and maximum size are both given as 39. If this parameter is omitted, Access Method Services assumes a RECORDSIZE of 4089 bytes.

The **FREESPACE** parameter tells Access Method Services how much unoccupied file space to provide and where in the file it should be. The empty file space is useful if records in the indexed file later have to be rearranged, as when new records are randomly inserted into the file. The FREESPACE parameter specifies the percentage of unused space that Access Method Services is to allocate in each **control interval** and each **control area** in the file. A control interval is the number of bytes that is read or written by VSAM at one time, and is always a multiple of 512. A control area is usually one cylinder, although under certain conditions it can be less than one cylinder. A control area can never be larger than one cylinder. Here we are asking that 25 percent of each control interval and 10 percent of each control area be left unoccupied when the file is initially loaded with records. If the FREESPACE parameter is omitted, Access Method Services allocates no free space.

The next parameter says that this is an **INDEXED** file. Other **data organization parameters** that may be specified are **NUMBERED** for a relative file and **NONINDEXED** for a sequential file. If no data organization parameter is given, INDEXED is assumed.

The **KEYS** parameter allows the programmer to specify the size of the prime RECORD KEY, in bytes, and its location in the record. In our case the prime RECORD KEY, Account Number, is 5 bytes long and starts in position 1 of the record. Position 1 is indicated with a KEYS parameter of 0. If KEYS is omitted, a 64-byte key starting at the beginning of the record is assumed.

The **UNIQUE** attribute is required in some installations, but not in mine. If UNIQUE is required in your installation, you can include it anywhere, as for example:

```
UNIQUE KEYS(5 0))
```

The opposite of UNIQUE is **SUBALLOCATION.** If this parameter is omitted, SUBALLOCATION is assumed. Notice the closing parenthesis that matches the parenthesis before the NAME parameter.

Thus the file VSAM.NY.GSP.IMSTR is established. Program P14-01 then places records into it.

JCL for Execution of Program P14-01

In the JCL for the GO step, you can find the usual statements for the output printer file and the input data file

```
//GO.PRINTER DD SYSOUT=A
```

and:

```
//GO.INFILE DD *
```

Notice the DD statement for the output VSAM master file:

```
//GO.DISKOUT DD DSN=VSAM.NY.GSP.IMSTR,DISP=OLD,
// UNIT=SYSDA,VOL=SER=CNY005,AMP='AMORG'
```

The DISP parameter must be OLD, for OLD is always required with VSAM files. But when this job is first run, there is no file with the name VSAM.NY.-GSP.IMSTR. It is not OLD. It does not exist.

To prevent the JCL interpreter from examining any catalogs at the very beginning of the run to see whether the file is OLD, we must include UNIT and VOL parameters. As mentioned earlier, whenever you have to include UNIT and VOL, you must also include AMP='AMORG' to tell the system that this is a VSAM file. By the time we get to execute this step, the file will be OLD. It already will have been created by Access Method Services.

Under no circumstances should you specify DISP=NEW. DISP=NEW will satisfy the JCL interpreter, but does not work with VSAM files.

The remaining JCL statements for the GO step are sometimes needed when a SORT statement is used in a COBOL program, as is done in Program P14-01. These are ordinary OS DD statements.

After the CLUSTER VSAM.NY.GSP.IMSTR is loaded, we can DEFINE the alternate index and its PATH, and build the alternate index. All of that is done with another execution of Access Method Services, in the step IDCAMS2.

Defining the Alternate Index

Here we reserve direct-access storage space for the alternate index by saying DEFINE ALTERNATEINDEX. Following the word ALTERNATEINDEX in the DEFINE command are a number of parameters enclosed in one set of parentheses. First, a NAME must be given for the alternate index. This can be any legal made-up NAME and need have no special relationship to the NAME of the base cluster. The **RELATE** parameter must name the base cluster of which this is an alternate index. The VOLUME parameter names the volume on which the alternate index file is to reside. Here I specified CNY008 as the VOLUME. This shows that the alternate index can be on a different VOLUME from the CLUSTER that it is related to. You would of course specify a VOLUME that is legal in your installation, instead of CNY008.

The UNIQUE attribute may be required for an alternate index in your installation. If so, you can include it anywhere, as for a CLUSTER. For example, you could have

```
UNIQUE VOLUME(CNY008) -
```

An alternate index file is itself organized as an indexed file. The programmer must DEFINE a separate alternate index for each ALTERNATE RECORD KEY in the indexed file. Remember that the DEFINE command only reserves file space. Access Method Services builds the alternate index(es) later, when we give the BLDINDEX command. Here is how Access Method Services would build one alternate index:

1. It goes through the base cluster, extracting from each record the prime RECORD KEY and the ALTERNATE RECORD KEY. In this case it would extract the Account Number and the Depositor Name. It builds a small record containing each Depositor Name and its corresponding Account Number.
2. It sorts the small records on the ALTERNATE RECORD KEY, in this case, Depositor Name. If there is not enough internal virtual storage for the sort, the programmer must provide work files. In our case the amount of data to be sorted was so small that it was sorted internally.
3. It builds an alternate index file in ascending order on the ALTERNATE RECORD KEY from the small sorted records. If duplicate values of the ALTERNATE RECORD KEY are not allowed and more than one record contains the same ALTERNATE RECORD KEY value, processing terminates with an error message.

If the ALTERNATE RECORD KEY is defined WITH DUPLICATES, as ours is, then Access Method Services may have to reformat some of the records. Access Methods Services finds whether there are any small records with duplicate values of the ALTERNATE RECORD KEY and if there are it puts them together into a single record. In our case, if there is more than one record with the same Depositor Name, it means that a depositor has more than one account. Access Method Services will construct an alternate index record consisting of the Depositor Name and all its Account Numbers. It then constructs the alternate index file. So the alternate index contains exactly one record for each Depositor Name, and each record contains all the Account Numbers for that Depositor Name. A record in the

582 · CHAPTER 16 ◆ INTRODUCTION TO VSAM FILE PROCESSING

alternate index is as large as the size of the Depositor Name, plus the size of all the Account Numbers for that Depositor Name, plus 5. The 5 is a constant that applies to all records in all alternate index files.

In the RECORDSIZE parameter we may tell Access Method Services what we guess the average and maximum sizes of the records in the alternate index file will be. If we guess that no depositor will have more than 10 accounts, the largest record in the alternate index file will be the size of the Depositor Name field (20 characters), plus 10 times the size of the Account Number field (10 times 5, or 50), plus 5, a total of 75. If any depositor has more than 10 accounts, only 10 Account Numbers would be entered in the alternate index for that depositor. BLDINDEX would continue to execute and would print a message giving the number of excess Account Numbers not entered in the alternate index. Subsequent processing of the erroneous index entry by a COBOL program may cause the COBOL program to execute incorrectly.

If we guess that the average number of accounts that a depositor may have is 2, the average record size will be 20 plus 10 plus 5, or 35. This guess need not be precise. VSAM can extend the alternate index file as necessary to absorb some of the inaccuracy in the guess. If the guess is much too small, however, VSAM will not be able to extend the file enough times to accommodate all the records needed. If the guess is much too large, Access Method Services will reserve an unnecessarily large amount of direct-access space when it first establishes the file, and you may run into trouble with the space limitations in your installation. Each program and programmer must operate within the space limitations established by the installation.

One way to avoid having to guess at the average and maximum number of prime record keys associated with a given value of an alternate key is to define the data record so that the alternate key field is immediately to the left of the prime key field. Then designate as the ALTERNATE KEY the combination of the alternate key and the prime key in the record. To implement this method in our savings-account master file, we would define the master record as follows:

```
01    ACCOUNT-MASTER-RECORD.
      05 ALTERNATE-KEY.
         10 DEPOSITOR-NAME-M             PIC X(20).
         10 ACCOUNT-NUMBER-M             PIC X(5).
      05 DATE-OF-LAST-TRANSACTION        PIC 9(6).
      05 CURRENT-BALANCE-M               PIC S9(6)V99.
```

Then in the Environment Division we would have:

```
      RECORD KEY IS ACCOUNT-NUMBER-M
      ALTERNATE RECORD KEY IS ALTERNATE-KEY
```

There would be no WITH DUPLICATES phrase, even if a depositor has more than one account, for the combination of Depositor Name and Account Number is unique. The size of every record in the alternate index file would be equal to the sum of the size of the ALTERNATE-KEY (now 25), the size of the prime key (5), and 5, or 35. This method can be used only when the record contains exactly one alternate key field.

In the DEFINE command, the FREESPACE parameter tells Access Method Services what percentage of unoccupied space to leave in each control interval and each control area when the alternate index is initially constructed. The free space will be needed if records must be moved around later when new Depositor Names are added to the file. The size of the alternate index file must be given in REC-

ORDS, TRACKS, or CYLINDERS. Here I allowed for a primary amount of 100 Depositor Names.

The KEYS parameter allows the programmer to give the size of the ALTER-NATE RECORD KEY and its lication in the data record in the base cluster. Our Depositor Name is 20 charactrs long and starts in position 6, so we have KEYS (20 5). The **NONUNIQUEKEY** attribute tells Access Method Services that the ALTERNATE RECORD KEY was defined WITH DUPLICATES in the COBOL program. If the ALTERNATE RECORD KEY had not been defined WITH DUPLI-CATES, I would have had to say **UNIQUEKEY** here instead. If this attribute is omitted, NONUNIQUEKEY is assumed.

The **UPGRADE** attribute tells Access Method Services that this alternate index is to be kept up-to-date with the base cluster VSAM.NY.GSP.IMSTR. When you use VSAM with COBOL, an alternate index must always be kept up-to-date with the CLUSTER to which it is RELATEd, although in VSAM with Assembler Language it need not be so. UPGRADE tells VSAM that if the base cluster is modified in any way, with additions, changes, or deletions, VSAM should change the alternate index to reflect the modifications. Notice the closing parenthesis following the word UPGRADE. It matches the opening parenthesis before the word NAME.

Defining the PATH

We now DEFINE a PATH for the alternate index. Following the word PATH we have only three parameters enclosed in a set of parentheses. First we give a name for the PATH. The NAME can be any legal name and need not have any relation-ship to the NAMEs of either the alternate index or the CLUSTER. In the param-eter **PATHENTRY** we give the name of the alternate index of which this is a PATH. We then give the **UPDATE** attribute. The UPDATE attribute tells Access Method Services that this PATH will be used with some program that UPDATEs the base cluster. To DEFINE a PATH for a program that does not update the base cluster, you would specify **NOUPDATE** instead. A PATH that is DEFINEd with UPDATE can also be used with a program that does not update the base cluster. You may DEFINE as many PATHs as you like with an alternate index.

We are now ready to build the alternate index.

Building the Alternate Index

As you can see, the BLDINDEX command is simplicity itself. You tell Access Method Services the name of the **INDATASET,** the name of the base cluster from which the alternate index is to be built. Then you tell it the name of the **OUT-DATASET,** the name of the alternate index file already DEFINEd. If the indexed file has been defined in the COBOL program with more than one ALTERNATE RECORD KEY, you may build all the required alternate indexes with a single BLDINDEX command by giving the names of all the alternate indexes in the OUTDATASET parameter. For example:

```
OUTDATASET(VSAM.NY.GSP.IMSTR.NAMEIX -
          VSAM.NY.GSP.IMSTR.BALIX -
          VSAM.NY.GSP.IMSTR.DATEIX)
```

Access Method Services Output

The output produced by Access Method Services for the step IDCAMS1 is shown in Figure 16.2. There you can see the original DEFINE CLUSTER command, and the messages from Access Method Services telling us what it did. First, the **allocation**

Figure 16.2 Output from step IDCAMS1.

```
IDCAMS  SYSTEM SERVICES                                           TIME: 18:09:05


      DEFINE CLUSTER -
            (NAME(VSAM.NY.GSP.IMSTR) -
            VOLUME(CNY005) -
            RECORDS(100 10) -
            RECORDSIZE(39 39) -
            FREESPACE(25 10) -
            INDEXED -
            KEYS(5 0))

IDC0508I DATA ALLOCATION STATUS FOR VOLUME CNY005 IS 0

IDC0509I INDEX ALLOCATION STATUS FOR VOLUME CNY005 IS 0

IDC0512I NAME GENERATED-(D) VSAM.TDA69836.VDD88099.T9E5693C

IDC0512I NAME GENERATED-(I) VSAM.TDA69B78.VID88099.T9E5693C

IDC0001I FUNCTION COMPLETED, HIGHEST CONDITION CODE WAS 0


IDC0002I IDCAMS PROCESSING COMPLETE. MAXIMUM CONDITION CODE WAS 0
```

status is given for the data component and the index component of the file. An allocation status of 0 indicates success.

Access Method Services then shows us the long and funny names it generated for the data component and the index component. The names contain the date and time that the CLUSTER was created. If you want to give your own names to data and index components, you can do so when you DEFINE them.

Following the messages about the names is the message FUNCTION COMPLETED. A **condition code** of 0 signals a perfect, clean execution of the command. The other possible condition codes you can get have the following meanings.

4   Warning message; successful execution is probable.
8   Serious error, but processing is completed.
12   Terminating error; processing of the command is terminated.

The Access Method Services output from step IDCAMS2 is shown in Figure 16.3. There you can see the original DEFINE ALTERNATEINDEX command and its results. The data component and index component both were allocated space on VOLUME CNY008 and had names made up for them.

The DEFINE PATH command allocates no storage space, for a PATH occupies none. The BUILDINDEX command is seen to have executed successfully.

Figure 16.3 Output from step IDCAMS2.

```
IDCAMS  SYSTEM SERVICES                                    TIME: 18:09:18


     DEFINE ALTERNATEINDEX -
          (NAME(VSAM.NY.GSP.IMSTR.ALTIX) -
          RELATE(VSAM.NY.GSP.IMSTR) -
          VOLUME(CNY008) -
          FREESPACE(25 10) -
          RECORDS(100 10) -
          KEYS(20 5) -
          RECORDSIZE(35 75) -
          NONUNIQUEKEY UPGRADE)

IDC0508I DATA ALLOCATION STATUS FOR VOLUME CNY008 IS 0

IDC0509I INDEX ALLOCATION STATUS FOR VOLUME CNY008 IS 0

IDC0512I NAME GENERATED-(D) VSAM.TAED82AA.VDD88099.T9E5693D

IDC0512I NAME GENERATED-(I) VSAM.TAED85F2.VID88099.T9E5693D

IDC0001I FUNCTION COMPLETED, HIGHEST CONDITION CODE WAS 0


     DEFINE PATH -
          (NAME(VSAM.NY.GSP.IMSTR.ALTPATH) -
          PATHENTRY(VSAM.NY.GSP.IMSTR.ALTIX) -
          UPDATE)

IDC0001I FUNCTION COMPLETED, HIGHEST CONDITION CODE WAS 0


     BLDINDEX INDATASET(VSAM.NY.GSP.IMSTR) -
          OUTDATASET(VSAM.NY.GSP.IMSTR.ALTIX)

IDC0652I VSAM.NY.GSP.IMSTR.ALTIX SUCCESSFULLY BUILT

IDC0001I FUNCTION COMPLETED, HIGHEST CONDITION CODE WAS 0


IDC0002I IDCAMS PROCESSING COMPLETE. MAXIMUM CONDITION CODE WAS 0
```

Creating an Indexed File at CUNY

Figure 16.4 shows the kind of input stream I used to create a VSAM indexed file at my school. It differs from the input stream shown in Figure 16.1 because the conventions here are different from those at other schools.

I have no job name in my JOB statement, for the remote job entry system I use creates and inserts the job name. I have no JOBCAT statement, for it is forbidden in my installation. Instead, I have the DD statement

```
//GO.ANYNAME DD VSAM.CATALOG,DISP=SHR
```

in the procedure step where it is needed. In my EXEC statement for the step COBOL1, I have PARM.COB=(QUOTE,ADV), which I need to get my system to accept the quote symbol as the delimiter surrounding nonnumeric literals and to handle my AFTER ADVANCING clauses properly. And finally, I have no need for any of the job control statements relating to the SORT, for the sort system in my installation provides its own work areas.

Figure 16.4 Input stream to create an indexed file and alternate index at CUNY.

```
// JOB 'P14X01',REGION=1120K
//IDCAMS1 EXEC PGM=IDCAMS
//SYSPRINT DD SYSOUT=A
//SYSIN    DD *
    DEFINE CLUSTER -
           (NAME(VSAM.NY.GSP.IMSTR) -
           VOLUME(CNY005) -
           RECORDS(100 10) -
           RECORDSIZE(39 39) -
           FREESPACE(25 10) -
           INDEXED -
           KEYS(5 0))
/*
//COBOL1 EXEC COBUCG,PARM.COB=(QUOTE,ADV)
//SYSIN DD *
00010  IDENTIFICATION DIVISION.
00020  PROGRAM-ID.  P14-01.
                    .
                    .
                    .

       COBOL SOURCE PROGRAM
                    .
                    .

//GO.ANYNAME DD DSN=VSAM.CATALOG,DISP=SHR
//GO.PRINTER1 DD SYSOUT=A
//GO.PRINTER2 DD SYSOUT=A
//GO.DISKOUT DD DSN=VSAM.NY.GSP.IMSTR,DISP=OLD,
// UNIT=SYSDA,VOL=SER=CNY005,AMP='AMORG'
//GO.INFILE DD *
                    .
                    .
                    .

       INPUT DATA FOR PROGRAM P14-01
                    .
                    .

//IDCAMS2 EXEC PGM=IDCAMS
//SYSPRINT DD SYSOUT=A
//SYSIN DD *
    DEFINE ALTERNATEINDEX -
           (NAME(VSAM.NY.GSP.IMSTR.ALTIX) -
           RELATE(VSAM.NY.GSP.IMSTR) -
           VOLUME(CNY008) -
           RECORDSIZE(35 75) -
           FREESPACE(25 10) -
           RECORDS(100 10) -
           KEYS(20 5) -
           NONUNIQUEKEY UPGRADE)
    DEFINE PATH -
           (NAME(VSAM.NY.GSP.IMSTR.ALTPATH) -
           PATHENTRY(VSAM.NY.GSP.IMSTR.ALTIX) -
           UPDATE)
    BLDINDEX INDATASET(VSAM.NY.GSP.IMSTR) -
             OUTDATASET(VSAM.NY.GSP.IMSTR.ALTIX)
/*
//
```

Using an Indexed File

A typical input stream for Program P14-02 is shown in Figure 16.5. This is the program that updates the indexed file created by Program P14-01. In the GO step you can find the usual DD statements for RECORDIN and the PRINTERs. There is also a DD statement for the master file:

```
//GO.MSTRDISK DD DSN=VSAM.NY.GSP.IMSTR,DISP=OLD
```

Now, if an indexed file is defined with one or more ALTERNATE RECORD KEYs, each alternate index PATH must have its own DD statement. If there is only one ALTERNATE RECORD KEY, as in this case, the ddname for the alternate PATH must be formed by attaching the number 1 onto the end of the ddname for the base cluster. So in our case, we would attach the number 1 on to the end of the ddname MSTRDISK. But if the combination of the ddname and the number exceeds eight characters, the ddname must be truncated on the right end so that the combination is just eight characters long. Thus the ddname for the alternate PATH is MSTRDIS1 as shown in the DD statement:

```
//GO.MSTRDIS1 DD DSN=VSAM.NY.GSP.IMSTR.ALTPATH,DISP=OLD
```

Notice that it is the name of the alternate PATH, not the alternate index file, that is given in the DSN parameter.

If there is more than one alternate index, the ddnames for their PATHs are formed by attaching 2, 3, and so on to the end of the base cluster's ddname, in the order in which the ALTERNATE RECORD KEY clauses appear in the COBOL program.

Figure 16.5 Typical input stream to update an indexed file having an alternate index.

```
//GSPNY452 JOB 'P14X02'
// EXEC COBUCG
//SYSIN DD *
00010   IDENTIFICATION DIVISION.
00020   PROGRAM-ID.  P14-02.
               .
               .
               .

        COBOL SOURCE PROGRAM

               .
               .
               .
//GO.PRINTER1 DD SYSOUT=A
//GO.PRINTER2 DD SYSOUT=A
//GO.MSTRDISK DD DSN=VSAM.NY.GSP.IMSTR,DISP=OLD
//GO.MSTRDIS1 DD DSN=VSAM.NY.GSP.IMSTR.ALTPATH,DISP=OLD
//GO.INFILE DD *
               .
               .
               .

        INPUT DATA FOR PROGRAM P14-02

               .
               .
               .
/*
//
```

Creating an Alternate Index with AIXBLD

As mentioned earlier, there is a way to arrange the alternate index so that VSAM can detect duplicate values of ALTERNATE RECORD KEYs while the base cluster is being initially loaded with records. To do this, the alternate index must be in existence at the time the base cluster is being loaded. But we have seen that an alternate index can be created only after its base cluster has been loaded. The remedy for this is provided by the COBOL execution-time option **AIXBLD**.

When AIXBLD is specified in the COBOL program that initially loads the base cluster, here is what COBOL does. Before executing your COBOL program, it loads the base cluster with dummy records, issues a BLDINDEX command to Access Method Services to build the alternate index with dummy entries, and then erases the dummy records from the base cluster, restoring it to its previously unloaded state.

Then the COBOL program executes and loads the base cluster. As each record is placed into the base cluster, VSAM makes an entry for it in the alternate index and can see when a duplicate value of an ALTERNATE RECORD KEY is processed.

AIXBLD provides one additional service free of charge. Before it loads the base cluster with dummy records, COBOL enters the RECORDSIZE and KEYS parameters into the catalog for the base cluster, and the KEYS parameter for the alternate index. It does this by issuing ALTER commands to Access Method Services to change the catalog entries for the base cluster and the alternate index to their correct values.

An Input Stream with AIXBLD

A typical input stream showing the use of AIXBLD is given in Figure 16.6. You can see that in one execution of Access Method Services we DEFINE the base cluster, the alternate index, and the PATH. We do not specify RECORDSIZE or KEYS parameters in the DEFINE CLUSTER command, or a KEYS parameter in the DEFINE ALTERNATEINDEX command, because AIXBLD will put them into the catalog with an ALTER command.

If the UNIQUE attribute is required at your school, you can include it anywhere, for example,

```
UNIQUE VOLUME(SCR002) -
```

in both the DEFINE CLUSTER and DEFINE ALTERNATEINDEX commands.

Preceding the DEFINE CLUSTER command is a DELETE command. This removes any copy of VSAM.NY.GSP.IMSTR2 that might be left over from a prior run of this program. If there is no such copy, the DELETE command does no harm. In our case, there was a VSAM.NY.GSP.IMSTR2 left over, and the **ENTRY** codes in Figure 16.7 tell us what type of object was DELETEd. Following the ENTRY code is the name of the DELETEd object. Some of the Access Method Services ENTRY codes are

C CLUSTER
D data component
G alternate index
I index component
R PATH
V VOLUME
U user catalog
M master catalog
A nonVSAM

The EXEC statement with stepname COBOL in Figure 16.6 shows how to use the AIXBLD option. It is included in the PARM.GO parameter, along with any other execution-time options you may be using. Here it is shown without any other execution-time options. The single quotation marks and the slash are required.

If other execution-time options are also used, such as DEBUG, they can be included along with AIXBLD. For example:

```
PARM.GO='/DEBUG,AIXBLD'
```

Figure 16.6 Typical input stream showing the use of AIXBLD.

```
//GSPNY503 JOB 'AIXJOB',REGION=1308K
//JOBCAT DD DSN=USERCAT,DISP=SHR
//IDCAMS EXEC PGM=IDCAMS
//SYSPRINT DD SYSOUT=A
//SYSIN    DD *
     DELETE VSAM.NY.GSP.IMSTR2 CLUSTER
     DEFINE CLUSTER -
            (NAME(VSAM.NY.GSP.IMSTR2) -
            VOLUME(SCR001) -
            RECORDS(100 10) -
            FREESPACE(25 10) -
            INDEXED)
     DEFINE ALTERNATEINDEX -
            (NAME(VSAM.NY.GSP.IMSTR2.ALTIX2) -
            RELATE(VSAM.NY.GSP.IMSTR2) -
            VOLUME(SCR001) -
            RECORDSIZE(35 75) -
            FREESPACE(25 10) -
            RECORDS(100 10) -
            NONUNIQUEKEY UPGRADE)
     DEFINE PATH -
            (NAME(VSAM.NY.GSP.IMSTR2.ALTPATH2) -
            PATHENTRY(VSAM.NY.GSP.IMSTR2.ALTIX2) -
            UPDATE)
/*
//COBOL EXEC COBUCLG,PARM.COB=STATE,PARM.GO='/AIXBLD'
//SYSIN DD *
00010  IDENTIFICATION DIVISION.
00020  PROGRAM-ID.  P14-01.
                .
                .
                .

       COBOL SOURCE PROGRAM
                .
                .
                .
//GO.PRINTER1 DD SYSOUT=A
//GO.PRINTER2 DD SYSOUT=A
//GO.SYSPRINT DD SYSOUT=A
//GO.DISKOUT DD DSN=VSAM.NY.GSP.IMSTR2,DISP=OLD,
//   VOL=SER=SCR001,UNIT=SYSDA,AMP='AMORG'
//GO.DISKOUT1 DD DSN=VSAM.NY.GSP.IMSTR2.ALTPATH2,DISP=OLD,
//   VOL=SER=SCR001,UNIT=SYSDA,AMP='AMORG'
//GO.SORTWK01 DD UNIT=SYSDA,VOL=SER=SCR001,
//     SPACE=(TRK,(2),,CONTIG)
//GO.SORTWK02 DD UNIT=SYSDA,VOL=SER=SCR001,
//     SPACE=(TRK,(2),,CONTIG)
//GO.SORTWK03 DD UNIT=SYSDA,VOL=SER=SCR001,
//     SPACE=(TRK,(2),,CONTIG)
//GO.SORTLIB DD DSN=SYS1.SORTLIB,DISP=SHR
//GO.SYSOUT DD SYSOUT=A
//GO.INFILE DD *
                .
                .
                .

       INPUT DATA FOR AIXJOB
                .
                .
                .
/*
//
```

Remember that if PARM.COB is also present in the EXEC statement, it must appear before PARM.GO.

In the GO step, we have DD statements GO.PRINTER1 and GO.PRINTER2. These are for the output from the COBOL program. We also have GO.SYSPRINT. This is for output from Access Method Services. Whenever you use AIXBLD, you must provide a SYSPRINT for the Access Method Services messages.

The DD statement for the base cluster has the ddname DISKOUT. You can see that UNIT and VOL are used, and so AMP='AMORG' is needed also. This DD statement works whether or not the base cluster VSAM.NY.GSP.IMSTR2 is in existence from a previous run. A DD statement for the alternate PATH must now be given as part of the GO step because AIXBLD needs it. You can see that the ddname for the alternate PATH VSAM.NY.GSP.IMSTR2.ALTPATH2 is made up by attaching a 1 to the end of the ddname of the base cluster. The result is DISKOUT1. Notice that DISKOUT did not have to be truncated.

Output from a Run Using AIXBLD

The output from Access Method Services for the step IDCAMS is shown in Figure 16.7. It is entirely routine and is identical in all material respects to output we have already seen.

The output from the step COBOL of course includes all the usual COBOL output, not shown here, and also includes the Access Method Services output resulting from the AIXBLD option. The Access Method Services output is shown in Figure 16.8.

In Figure 16.8 you can see the first ALTER command issued. This is to change the RECORDSIZE and KEYS parameters in the base cluster to their correct values, a RECORDSIZE of (39 39) and a KEYS parameter of (5 0). The second ALTER command corrects only the KEYS parameter of the alternate index, because Access Method Services has no way of knowing how big the records in the alternate index file will be. We guessed at that and used a RECORDSIZE parameter of (35 75) in the DEFINE ALTERNATEINDEX command. Notice that the name of the PATH, not of the alternate index file, is used in the second ALTER command.

Finally COBOL issues the BLDINDEX command. This command uses different parameters from the ones we used in the BLDINDEX command in Figure 16.1. There, we used the following:

```
INDATASET(VSAM.NY.GSP.IMSTR) -
OUTDATASET(VSAM.NY.GSP.IMSTR.ALTPATH)
```

Here, **INFILE** and **OUTFILE** are used instead of INDATASET and OUT-DATASET. When you use INFILE and OUTFILE, you then use ddnames inside the parentheses instead of using the names of clusters or PATHs.

Figure 16.7 Output from step IDCAMS with AIXBLD in use.

```
IDCAMS  SYSTEM SERVICES                                    TIME: 18:38:35

     DELETE VSAM.NY.GSP.IMSTR2 CLUSTER
IDC0550I ENTRY (R) VSAM.NY.GSP.IMSTR2.ALTPATH2 DELETED

IDC0550I ENTRY (D) VSAM.T384F060.VDD88103.T9E5B9D8 DELETED

IDC0550I ENTRY (I) VSAM.T384F3A0.VID88103.T9E5B9D8 DELETED

IDC0550I ENTRY (G) VSAM.NY.GSP.IMSTR2.ALTIX2 DELETED

IDC0550I ENTRY (D) VSAM.T1480542.VDD88103.T9E5B9D8 DELETED

IDC0550I ENTRY (I) VSAM.T1480894.VID88103.T9E5B9D8 DELETED

IDC0550I ENTRY (C) VSAM.NY.GSP.IMSTR2 DELETED

IDC0001I FUNCTION COMPLETED, HIGHEST CONDITION CODE WAS 0


     DEFINE CLUSTER -
          (NAME(VSAM.NY.GSP.IMSTR2) -
          VOLUME(SCR001) -
          RECORDS(100 10) -
          FREESPACE(25 10) -
          INDEXED)

IDC0508I DATA ALLOCATION STATUS FOR VOLUME SCR001 IS 0

IDC0509I INDEX ALLOCATION STATUS FOR VOLUME SCR001 IS 0

IDC0512I NAME GENERATED-(D) VSAM.TFB2FA70.VDD88103.T9E5BA1D

IDC0512I NAME GENERATED-(I) VSAM.TFB2FDDC.VID88103.T9E5BA1D

IDC0001I FUNCTION COMPLETED, HIGHEST CONDITION CODE WAS 0


     DEFINE ALTERNATEINDEX -
          (NAME(VSAM.NY.GSP.IMSTR2.ALTIX2) -
          RELATE(VSAM.NY.GSP.IMSTR2) -
          VOLUME(SCR001) -
          RECORDSIZE(35 75) -
          FREESPACE(25 10) -
          RECORDS(100 10) -
          NONUNIQUEKEY UPGRADE)

IDC0508I DATA ALLOCATION STATUS FOR VOLUME SCR001 IS 0

IDC0509I INDEX ALLOCATION STATUS FOR VOLUME SCR001 IS 0

IDC0512I NAME GENERATED-(D) VSAM.T1F97FE0.VDD88103.T9E5BA1E

IDC0512I NAME GENERATED-(I) VSAM.T1F98338.VID88103.T9E5BA1E

IDC0001I FUNCTION COMPLETED, HIGHEST CONDITION CODE WAS 0


     DEFINE PATH -
          (NAME(VSAM.NY.GSP.IMSTR2.ALTPATH2) -
          PATHENTRY(VSAM.NY.GSP.IMSTR2.ALTIX2) -
          UPDATE)

IDC0001I FUNCTION COMPLETED, HIGHEST CONDITION CODE WAS 0


IDC0002I IDCAMS PROCESSING COMPLETE. MAXIMUM CONDITION CODE WAS 0
```

Figure 16.8 Access Method Services output from procedure step GO with AIXBLD in use.

```
IDCAMS   SYSTEM SERVICES                                         TIME: 18:38:53


  ALTER VSAM.NY.GSP.IMSTR2                                    -
  FILE( DISKOUT  ) RECORDSIZE( 00039 00039 ) KEYS( 005 00000)
IDC0531I ENTRY VSAM.NY.GSP.IMSTR2 ALTERED

IDC0001I FUNCTION COMPLETED, HIGHEST CONDITION CODE WAS 0


IDC0002I IDCAMS PROCESSING COMPLETE. MAXIMUM CONDITION CODE WAS 0


IDCAMS   SYSTEM SERVICES                                         TIME: 18:38:55


  ALTER VSAM.NY.GSP.IMSTR2.ALTPATH2                           -
  FILE( DISKOUT1 )                          KEYS( 020 00005)
IDC0531I ENTRY VSAM.NY.GSP.IMSTR2.ALTPATH2 ALTERED

IDC0001I FUNCTION COMPLETED, HIGHEST CONDITION CODE WAS 0


IDC0002I IDCAMS PROCESSING COMPLETE. MAXIMUM CONDITION CODE WAS 0


IDCAMS   SYSTEM SERVICES                                         TIME: 18:39:01


  BLDINDEX INFILE( DISKOUT          ) OUTFILE( DISKOUT1         )
IDC0652I VSAM.NY.GSP.IMSTR2.ALTPATH2 SUCCESSFULLY BUILT

IDC0001I FUNCTION COMPLETED, HIGHEST CONDITION CODE WAS 0


IDC0002I IDCAMS PROCESSING COMPLETE. MAXIMUM CONDITION CODE WAS 0
```

Creating a Relative File

Using Access Method Services to create a relative file involves no new concepts. A typical input stream for Program P15-01, which creates a relative file, is shown in Figure 16.9. You can see the use of the NUMBERED attribute for a relative file. There is no KEYS parameter, for COBOL does not process keys in relative files. There is no FREESPACE parameter, for COBOL does not move records around in a relative file.

Notice that we have no JOBCAT or STEPCAT statements. Here we are taking advantage of a feature that permits Access Message Services to locate by itself the correct catalog in which to enter an object. The **prefix** part of a file name, the part before the first dot (in this case VSAM.), can be used to direct Access Method Services to the correct catalog. This feature is set up by the systems programmers at the time the catalogs are established. You can use this feature only if you are not using UNIT, VOL, and AMP='AMORG' in the DD statement for the file, as is the case here.

Figure 16.9 Typical input stream to create a relative file.

```
//GSPNY678 JOB 'P15X01',REGION=300K
//FILESTEP EXEC PGM=IDCAMS
//SYSPRINT DD SYSOUT=A
//SYSIN DD *
    DELETE VSAM.NY.GSP.RELMSTR CLUSTER
    DEFINE CLUSTER( -
           NAME(VSAM.NY.GSP.RELMSTR) -
           VOLUMES(CNY005) -
           RECORDS(30) -
           RECORDSIZE(60 60) -
           NUMBERED -
           )
/*
//COBSTEP EXEC COBUCG
//SYSIN DD *
00010  IDENTIFICATION DIVISION.
00020  PROGRAM-ID.  P15-01.
00030
                .
                .
                .

       COBOL SOURCE PROGRAM
                .
                .
                .
//GO.PRINTER DD SYSOUT=A
//GO.DISKUNIT DD DSN=VSAM.NY.GSP.RELMSTR,DISP=OLD
//GO.INFILE DD *
NO21DP407
/*
//
```

The JCL shown here works only if there is already a file called RELMSTR in existence from some previous run. If there is not, the techniques shown earlier in this chapter must be used instead.

The output from this execution of Access Method Services is shown in Figure 16.10.

Figure 16.10 Output from step FILESTEP.

```
IDCAMS  SYSTEM SERVICES                                    TIME: 00:17:39


    DELETE VSAM.NY.GSP.RELMSTR CLUSTER

IDC0550I ENTRY (D) VSAM.T8A611D0.VDD88101.T9E5826D DELETED

IDC0550I ENTRY (C) VSAM.NY.GSP.RELMSTR DELETED

IDC0001I FUNCTION COMPLETED, HIGHEST CONDITION CODE WAS 0


    DEFINE CLUSTER( -
           NAME(VSAM.NY.GSP.RELMSTR) -
           VOLUMES(CNY005) -
           RECORDS(400) -
           RECORDSIZE(60 60) -
           NUMBERED -
           )

IDC0508I DATA ALLOCATION STATUS FOR VOLUME CNY005 IS 0

IDC0512I NAME GENERATED-(D) VSAM.TD8A8306.VDD88101.T9E58280

IDC0001I FUNCTION COMPLETED, HIGHEST CONDITION CODE WAS 0



IDC0002I IDCAMS PROCESSING COMPLETE. MAXIMUM CONDITION CODE WAS 0
```

Summary

IBM's Virtual Storage Access Method (VSAM) is a high-speed access method for use with sequential, relative, or indexed files on direct-access storage devices. Management of VSAM files and the VSAM catalogs is carried out by a utility program called Access Method Services. With Access Method Services, you may DEFINE or DELETE a file, build an alternate index in connection with an ALTERNATE RECORD KEY defined in a COBOL program, ALTER a file's catalog entries, PRINT all or part of a file, list the catalog entry for a file, and VERIFY that a file's catalog entry agrees with the physical state of the file.

To run Access Method Services, you must use an EXEC statement specifying PGM=IDCAMS. You must also provide a SYSPRINT DD statement for Access Method Services output messages and a SYSIN DD statement for the input file of Access Method Services commands.

A VSAM file can be created only by Access Method Services. When the file is used in a program, its DD statement must specify DISP=OLD. If for any reason the DD statement must contain UNIT and VOL parameters, then it must also contain the parameter AMP='AMORG'.

Some installations have one or more user catalogs. If a file is to be cataloged in one of the user catalogs, the programmer can include a JOBCAT or STEPCAT statement. If a file is cataloged in a user catalog and AMP='AMORG' is used, then a JOBCAT or STEPCAT statement must be used also. If a file is cataloged in the master catalog, no catalog indication is ever needed.

There are two ways to create an indexed file having an alternate index. In one method the programmer first DEFINEs the base cluster, then loads it, then DEFINEs the alternate index and its PATH, and then builds the alternate index. The other method uses the COBOL execution-time option AIXBLD. With AIXBLD, the programmer DEFINEs the base cluster, the alternate index, and the PATH, and then gives the AIXBLD option as part of the COBOL program that is to load the file with records. With AIXBLD, COBOL first calls upon Access Method Services to ALTER the catalog entries of the base cluster and the alternate index, correcting the RECORDSIZE and KEYS parameters to agree with the record definition in the COBOL program. Then COBOL loads the base cluster with dummy records, builds the alternate index, erases the dummy records from the base cluster, and loads the file with data records.

A relative file may be created with the DEFINE command through the use of the NUMBERED parameter.

ESDS file

Fill-in Exercises

1. To use a VSAM sequential file you must include the letters AS before the _DD_ name in the _Assign_ clause for the file.

2. The name of the IBM utility program that can create a VSAM file is _Access Method Services_. = IDCAMS

3. A VSAM installation must have exactly one _Master_ catalog and may have any number of _user_ catalogs.

4. The data organization parameter used to DEFINE a VASM relative file is _numbered_

5. A _jobcat_ statement tells the system what user catalog to use for an entire job; a _stepcat_ statement tells the system what user catalog to use for a job step.

6. The command that can be used to build an alternate index is _bldindex_

7. The command that can be used to check that a file's catalog entries agree with the physical state of the file is _verify_ .

8. A VSAM indexed file is called a _key seq_ data set. KSDS

9. The data organization parameter used to DEFINE a VSAM sequential file is _Nonindexed_

10. An alternate index can be built only after its base cluster has been _loaded_

11. The command that is used to create a VSAM file is _Define_.

12. The command that is used to change catalog entries for a VSAM file is _Alter_.

13. The DISP parameter for a VSAM file may be _old_ or _share_ ; it must never be _new_ . SHR

14. The space requirement for a VSAM file may be given in terms of the number of _records_ , _Tracks_ , or _Cylinders_

15. The size and location of the record key in an indexed file is given in the _Key's_ parameter.

Project

Rewrite your solution to the Project in Chapter 14, page 510, using AIXBLD.

String Processing

Here are the key points you should learn from this chapter:

1. How to use the STRING verb
2. How to use the UNSTRING verb
3. How to use the INSPECT verb

Key words to recognize and learn:

string processing	TALLYING
STRING	span
OVERFLOW	DELIMITER
delimiter	INSPECT
DELIMITED BY	LEADING
SIZE	REPLACING
POINTER	CHARACTERS
UNSTRING	INITIAL
COUNT	FIRST

The **string processing** features of COBOL permit programs to operate on the individual characters contained in fields. Each field is treated as if it consisted of one or more characters strung together end-to-end — hence the name string processing.

The STRING Statement

The **STRING** verb enables COBOL to attach two or more fields or parts of fields end to end to form one large field. The sending fields, the fields to be strung together, must be defined as alphanumeric or unedited integer. The receiving field must be alphanumeric.

When you write a STRING statement, you write the sending fields in the order in which you want them to be strung together. COBOL sends the sending fields to the receiving field in the order in which they appear in the STRING statement, adding each sending field on to the right end of the ever-growing string in the receiving field.

The STRING statement has an optional **OVERFLOW** phrase to handle situations where the sending fields together are all too big to fit into the receiving field.

If only a part of a sending field is to be sent, COBOL must have some way of knowing which part it is. The STRING verb uses one or more **delimiters** to tell COBOL which parts of sending fields to send. A programmer may select any one or more alphanumeric characters or an unedited integer to use as a delimiter.

The format of the STRING statement is:

```
STRING  {identifier-1}  [, identifier-2]  ...
        {literal-1    }  [, literal-2   ]

          DELIMITED BY {identifier-3}
                       {literal-3   }
                       {SIZE        }

    [{, identifier-4} [, identifier-5]  ...
     {, literal-4   } [, literal-5   ]

          DELIMITED BY {identifier-6}
                       {literal-6   }  ]  ...
                       {SIZE        }

    INTO identifier-7
    [WITH POINTER identifier-8]
    [; ON OVERFLOW imperative-statement]
```

The sending fields in this format are identifier-1, identifier-2, literal-1, literal-2, identifier-4, identifier-5, literal-4, and literal-5. If a figurative constant is used as a sending-field literal, it stands for one character of data (for example, SPACE or HIGH-VALUE).

Each sending field or group of sending fields has its own **DELIMITED BY** phrase. The DELIMITED BY phrases tell whether all or part of each sending field is to be sent to the receiving field. If **SIZE** is used, the entire sending field is added to the right end of the string in the receiving field; if a delimiter is used (identifier-3, literal-3, identifier-6, or literal-6), only that portion of the sending field up to but not including the first appearance of the delimiter in the sending field is added to the string in the receiving field. If there are no appearances of the delimiter in a sending field, the entire sending field is added to the string in the receiving field.

Identifier-7 is the receiving field. The STRING statement does not blank out the receiving field before placing characters from sending fields into it. The only character positions in the receiving field that are changed by the STRING statement are the ones that have characters from sending fields placed into them.

The optional **POINTER** phrase will be discussed in the next section. All identifiers shown in the format of the STRING statement must be of USAGE DISPLAY except the POINTER, which must be DISPLAY or COMPUTATIONAL.

Using the STRING Verb

Our first application of the STRING verb uses input data in the following format:

Positions	Field
1−6	Date
1−2	MM
3−4	DD
5−6	YY
7−80	spaces

Each input record contains a date in the usual American form MMDDYY. For each record read, Program P17-01 converts the date to English and prints the input and the English date on one line, as shown in Figure 17.1. Notice that there is only one space between the name of the month and the day, regardless of the length of the name or whether the day is a one-digit number or two. The STRING verb allows us to place the output components exactly where we want them in the output field.

Program P17-01 is shown in Figure 17.2. The names of the 12 months are

Figure 17.1 Output format for Program P17-01.

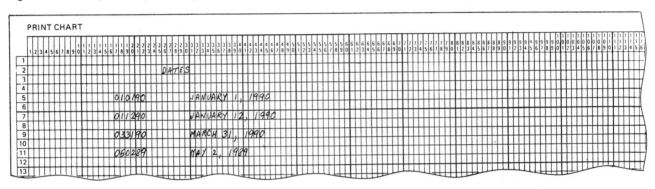

Figure 17.2 Program P17-01.

```
CB1 RELEASE 2.4                              IBM OS/VS COBOL   JULY  1, 1982

                          21.53.47        APR 12,1988

00010    IDENTIFICATION DIVISION.
00020    PROGRAM-ID.  P17-01.
00030 *
00040 *    THIS PROGRAM READS DATES IN MMDDYY FORM
00050 *    AND CONVERTS THEM TO ENGLISH.
00060 *
00070 ********************************************************************
00080
00090    ENVIRONMENT DIVISION.
00100    CONFIGURATION SECTION.
Z,<00110  SOURCE-COMPUTER.  IBM-370.
00120    OBJECT-COMPUTER.  IBM-370.
00130
00140    INPUT-OUTPUT SECTION.
00150    FILE-CONTROL.
00160       SELECT DATE-LIST-FILE  ASSIGN TO PRINTER.
00170       SELECT DATE-FILE-IN    ASSIGN TO INFILE.
00180
00190 ********************************************************************
00200
00210    DATA DIVISION.
00220    FILE SECTION.
00230 FD  DATE-FILE-IN
00240       RECORD CONTAINS 80 CHARACTERS
00250       LABEL RECORDS ARE OMITTED.
00260
00270  01  DATE-RECORD-IN.
00280      05 DATE-IN.
00290         10 MONTH-IN                         PIC 99.
00300         10 DAY-IN.
00310            15 TENS-PLACE                    PIC 9.
00320            15 UNITS-PLACE                   PIC 9.
00330         10 YEAR-IN                          PIC 99.
00340      05 FILLER                              PIC X(74).
00350
00360 FD  DATE-LIST-FILE
00370       LABEL RECORDS ARE OMITTED.
00380
```

(continued)

Figure 17.2   (continued)

```
00390    01    DATE-RECORD-OUT                          PIC X(48).
00400
00410    WORKING-STORAGE SECTION.
00420    01    MORE-INPUT      VALUE "Y"                PIC X.
00430
00440    01    MONTHS.
00450          05 FILLER       VALUE "JANUARY ."        PIC X(10).
00460          05 FILLER       VALUE "FEBRUARY ."       PIC X(10).
00470          05 FILLER       VALUE "MARCH ."          PIC X(10).
00480          05 FILLER       VALUE "APRIL ."          PIC X(10).
00490          05 FILLER       VALUE "MAY ."            PIC X(10).
00500          05 FILLER       VALUE "JUNE ."           PIC X(10).
00510          05 FILLER       VALUE "JULY ."           PIC X(10).
00520          05 FILLER       VALUE "AUGUST ."         PIC X(10).
00530          05 FILLER       VALUE "SEPTEMBER "       PIC X(10).
00540          05 FILLER       VALUE "OCTOBER ."        PIC X(10).
00550          05 FILLER       VALUE "NOVEMBER ."       PIC X(10).
00560          05 FILLER       VALUE "DECEMBER ."       PIC X(10).
00570    01    MONTHS-TABLE
00580          REDEFINES MONTHS.
00590          05 MONTH             OCCURS 12 TIMES     PIC X(10).
00600
00610    01    ENGLISH-DATE                             PIC X(18).
00620    01    ENGLISH-DATE-POINTER    COMP SYNC        PIC S99.
00630    01    COMMA-SPACE-CENTURY
00640                              VALUE ", 19"         PIC X(4).
00650
00660    01    REPORT-HEADING.
00670          05  FILLER          VALUE SPACES         PIC X(25).
00680          05  FILLER          VALUE "DATES"        PIC  X(5).
00690
00700    01    DETAIL-LINE.
00710          05  FILLER          VALUE SPACES         PIC X(16).
00720          05  DATE-OUT                             PIC 9(6)B(8).
00730          05  ENGLISH-DATE-OUT                     PIC X(18).
00740
00750     01 NO-INPUT-DATA.
00760          05  FILLER          VALUE SPACES         PIC X(21).
00770          05  FILLER          VALUE "NO INPUT DATA" PIC X(13).
00780
00790    ****************************************************************
00800
00810    PROCEDURE DIVISION.
00820    CONTROL-PARAGRAPH.
00830         PERFORM INITIALIZATION.
00840         PERFORM MAIN-PROCESS UNTIL MORE-INPUT = "N".
00850         PERFORM TERMINATION.
00860         STOP RUN.
00870
00880    INITIALIZATION.
00890         OPEN INPUT  DATE-FILE-IN,
00900              OUTPUT DATE-LIST-FILE.
00910         READ DATE-FILE-IN
00920            AT END
00930                 MOVE "N" TO MORE-INPUT.
00940         WRITE DATE-RECORD-OUT FROM REPORT-HEADING AFTER PAGE.
00950         MOVE SPACES TO DATE-RECORD-OUT.
00960         WRITE DATE-RECORD-OUT.
00970         IF MORE-INPUT = "N"
00980            WRITE DATE-RECORD-OUT FROM NO-INPUT-DATA AFTER 2.
00990
01000    MAIN-PROCESS.
01010         MOVE SPACES TO ENGLISH-DATE.
01020         PERFORM STRING-MONTH.
01030         PERFORM STRING-DAY.
01040         PERFORM STRING-YEAR.
01050         MOVE DATE-IN      TO DATE-OUT.
01060         MOVE ENGLISH-DATE TO ENGLISH-DATE-OUT.
01070         WRITE DATE-RECORD-OUT FROM dEaAIL-LINE AFTER 2.
01080         READ DATE-FILE-IN
01090            AT END
01100                 MOVE "N" TO MORE-INPUT.
01110
01120    STRING-MONTH.
01130         MOVE 1 TO ENGLISH-DATE-POINTER.
01140         STRING MONTH (MONTH-IN) DELIMITED BY "."
01150            INTO ENGLISH-DATE
01160            POINTER ENGLISH-DATE-POINTER.
```

```
01170
01180    STRING-DAY.
01190        IF TENS-PLACE IS EQUAL TO ZERO
01200            STRING UNITS-PLACE       DELIMITED BY SIZE
01210                INTO ENGLISH-DATE
01220                POINTER ENGLISH-DATE-POINTER
01230        ELSE
01240            STRING DAY-IN            DELIMITED BY SIZE
01250                INTO ENGLISH-DATE
01260                POINTER ENGLISH-DATE-POINTER.
01270
01280    STRING-YEAR.
01290        STRING  COMMA-SPACE-CENTURY,
01300                YEAR-IN              DELIMITED BY SIZE
01310            INTO ENGLISH-DATE
01320            POINTER ENGLISH-DATE-POINTER.
01330
01340    TERMINATION.
01350        CLOSE DATE-FILE-IN,
01360            DATE-LIST-FILE.
```

arranged in a MONTHS-TABLE, lines 00440 through 00590, so that the month number in the input can be used directly as a subscript to obtain the name of the month.

The field ENGLISH-DATE, line 00610, is used for assigning the date in English ready to be printed. ENGLISH-DATE-POINTER, line 00620, is the POINTER, which keeps track of character positions in ENGLISH-DATE as they are used. A POINTER field must be big enough to contain a number one larger than the number of character positions in the receiving field. In this case our receiving field, ENGLISH-DATE, is 18 characters long; so the POINTER field must be big enough to hold the number 19. Unless there is some reason to do otherwise, a POINTER field should always be made COMPUTATIONAL and SYNCHRONIZED, as we have done. You will see the exact function of ENGLISH-DATE-POINTER when we look at the Procedure Division.

The field COMMA-SPACE-CENTURY, line 00630, is a constant that is inserted into every date processed.

In the MAIN-PROCESS paragraph of the Procedure Division, line 01000, we first blank out ENGLISH-DATE. Then with a series of PERFORM statements, lines 01020 through 01040, we build up the complete date in English in the field ENGLISH-DATE.

In the paragraph STRING-MONTH, line 01120, we first set the POINTER field to 1. When used, the POINTER field always points to the next available character position in the receiving field. As we begin to build up the date in English, we want it to start at the left end (character position 1) of the receiving field, ENGLISH-DATE. The STRING statement at line 01140 first STRINGs all the characters in MONTH (MONTH-IN), up to but not including the first period, INTO the receiving field. If no period is found in the sending field, as in SEPTEMBER, the entire sending field is assigned to the receiving field.

When execution of the STRING statement is complete, COBOL sets the POINTER field to point to the next available unused character position in ENGLISH-DATE.

In the paragraph STRING-DAY, line 01180, one STRING statement or another is executed depending on whether the day of the month has a nonzero tens' place. The phrase DELIMITED BY SIZE causes all characters in the sending field to be added to the string in the receiving field.

The STRING statement at line 01290 shows that more than one sending field in a STRING statement can use the same DELIMITED BY phrase. You may have as many DELIMITED BY phrases as you like in a STRING statement, and each one may have as many fields as you like associated with it.

Program P17-01 was run with the input data shown in Figure 17.3 and produced the output shown in Figure 17.4.

Figure 17.3   Input to Program P17-01.

```
-------------------------------------------------------------------------------
          1         2         3         4         5         6         7         8
12345678901234567890123456789012345678901234567890123456789012345678901234567890
-------------------------------------------------------------------------------
091589
010291
010190
011290
033190
050290
121491
073191
112490
021491
```

Figure 17.4   Output from Program P17-01.

```
        DATES

091589          SEPTEMBER 15, 1989

010291          JANUARY 2, 1991

010190          JANUARY 1, 1990

011290          JANUARY 12, 1990

033190          MARCH 31, 1990

050290          MAY 2, 1990

121491          DECEMBER 14, 1991

073191          JULY 31, 1991

112490          NOVEMBER 24, 1990

021491          FEBRUARY 14, 1991
```

EXERCISE 1

Write a program to print a list of city names and state abbreviations. Your program should read data in the following format:

Positions	Field
1–20	City Name
21–30	spaces
31–32	State Abbreviation
33–80	spaces

Each input record contains a City Name, some blanks, and a State Abbreviation. For each input record, have your program print the City Name and State Abbreviation separated by a comma and one space, as shown in the format in Figure 17.E1.

Figure 17.E1 Output format for Exercise 1.

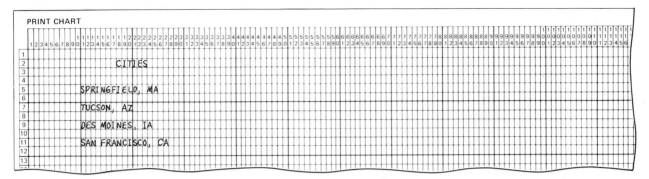

Another Application of the STRING Verb

We now develop a more elaborate application of the STRING verb. Program P17-02 reads input data in the following format:

Positions	Field
1−8	Dollars-and-cents amount
1−6	Dollar amount
7−8	Cents amount
9−80	spaces

Each input record contains an eight-digit dollars-and-cents amount, from $.00 up to $999,999.99. The program is to read each record and print the money amount, edited, and also print the six-digit dollar amount in words, as shown in Figure 17.5.

A number can sometimes be expressed in few words, like THREE or TWO HUNDRED or TWENTY-SIX, or sometimes in many words. There can be as many as 11 different pieces of data needed to write a six-digit number in English; six words for the digits, two hyphens, two appearances of the word HUNDRED, and one appearance of the word THOUSAND. An example of a number that uses all 11 pieces is SEVEN HUNDRED SEVENTY-SEVEN THOUSAND SEVEN HUN-

Figure 17.5 Output format for Program P17-02.

```
PRINT CHART

           MONEY

$900,000.00  NINE HUNDRED THOUSAND DOLLARS AND 00/XX

$ 87,017.06  EIGHTY-SEVEN THOUSAND SEVENTEEN DOLLARS AND 00/XX

$777,777.77  SEVEN HUNDRED SEVENTY-SEVEN THOUSAND SEVEN HUNDRED SEVENTY-SEVEN DOLLARS AND 77/XX

$      .05   ONLY 05/XX

$  1,119.19  ONE THOUSAND ONE HUNDRED NINETEEN DOLLARS AND 19/XX

$ 20,000.00  TWENTY THOUSAND DOLLARS AND 00/XX

$      .00   ONLY 00/XX

$     1.10   ONE DOLLAR AND 10/XX
```

DRED SEVENTY-SEVEN. The number THREE contains only one piece, the number TWO HUNDRED contains two, and the number TWENTY-SIX contains three.

Peculiarities in the way that numbers are written complicate Program P17-02. For example, the word THOUSAND appears in the number if there are any hundreds of thousands of dollars, tens of thousands of dollars, or thousands of dollars. Every word used in the expression of a number is always followed by a space, except words like TWENTY, THIRTY, FORTY, and so on. They may be followed by a space or a hyphen, depending on the word following. Values between 11 and 19 (and thousands between 11,000 and 19,000) have to be handled in a special way because they are irregular forms.

A hierarchy diagram for the main loop of Program P17-02, "Process a number," is shown in Figure 17.6. The step "String word fields and cent field together" determines which words are needed and STRINGs them INTO an output field for printing.

Figure 17.6   Hierarchy diagram for main loop of Program P17-02.

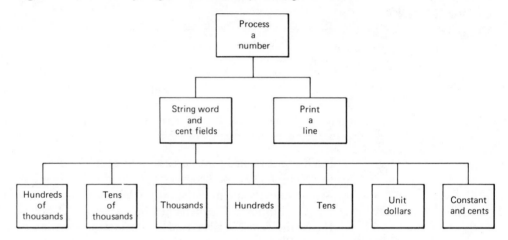

Program P17-02 is shown in Figure 17.7. The field MONEY-IN, line 00280, has been redefined as MONEY-BREAKDOWN, at line 00310. In this way the program can process each of the digits in MONEY-IN individually. Also, the units place and the tens place have been redefined as a single two-digit field so the program can handle the irregular numbers, 11 through 19. Similarly, the thousands place and the tens-of-thousands place have been redefined as a two-digit field so the program can handle thousands from 11 through 19.

A UNITS-PLACES-TABLE and a TENS-PLACES-TABLE have been set up at lines 00580 through 00940 to provide words to be used in the output. We need no

Figure 17.7   Program P17-02.

```
CB1 RELEASE 2.4                                    IBM OS/VS COBOL   JULY  1, 1982


                            22.35.29        APR 12,1988


00010   IDENTIFICATION DIVISION.
00020   PROGRAM-ID.  P17-02.
00030 *
00040 *    THIS PROGRAM READS IN MONEY AMOUNTS AND PRINTS
00050 *    THEM IN WORDS.
00060 *
00070 ***********************************************************************
00080
```

```
00090   ENVIRONMENT DIVISION.
00100   CONFIGURATION SECTION.
00110   SOURCE-COMPUTER.  IBM-370.
00120   OBJECT-COMPUTER.  IBM-370.
00130
00140   INPUT-OUTPUT SECTION.
00150   FILE-CONTROL.
00160       SELECT MONEY-FILE-IN  ASSIGN TO INFILE.
00170       SELECT MONEY-FILE-OUT ASSIGN TO PRINTER.
00180
00190   *******************************************************************
00200
00210   DATA DIVISION.
00220   FILE SECTION.
00230   FD  MONEY-FILE-IN
00240       RECORD CONTAINS 80 CHARACTERS
00250       LABEL RECORDS ARE OMITTED.
00260
00270   01  MASTER-RECORD-IN.
00280       05  MONEY-IN                           PIC 9(6)V99.
00290           88  LESS-THAN-A-DOLLAR     VALUES 0 THRU .99.
00300           88  ONE-DOLLAR             VALUES 1 THRU 1.99.
00310       05  MONEY-BREAKDOWN REDEFINES MONEY-IN.
00320           10  HUNDREDS-OF-THOUSANDS-W        PIC 9.
00330           10  TEENS-OF-THOUSANDS.
00340               15  TENS-OF-THOUSANDS-W        PIC 9.
00350               15  THOUSANDS-W                PIC 9.
00360           10  TEENS-OF-THOUSANDS-W REDEFINES TEENS-OF-THOUSANDS
00370                                              PIC 99.
00380           10  HUNDREDS-W                     PIC 9.
00390           10  TEENS.
00400               15  TENS-W                     PIC 9.
00410               15  UNIT-DOLLARS-W             PIC 9.
00420           10  TEENS-W REDEFINES TEENS        PIC 99.
00430           10  CENTS-UNEDITED-W               PIC V99.
00440           10  WHOLE-CENTS-W
00450               REDEFINES CENTS-UNEDITED-W     PIC  99.
00460       05 FILLER                              PIC X(72).
00470
00480   FD  MONEY-FILE-OUT
00490       LABEL RECORDS ARE OMITTED.
00500
00510   01  MONEY-RECORD-OUT                       PIC X(97).
00520
00530   WORKING-STORAGE SECTION.
00540   01  MORE-INPUT    VALUE "Y"                PIC X.
00550   01  MONEY-AMOUNT-IN-ENGLISH               PIC X(82).
00560   01  ENGLISH-FIELD-POINTER                 PIC S99.
00570
00580   01  UNITS-PLACES-TABLE-ENTRIES.
00590       05  FILLER      VALUE "ONE ."          PIC X(10).
00600       05  FILLER      VALUE "TWO ."          PIC X(10).
00610       05  FILLER      VALUE "THREE ."        PIC X(10).
00620       05  FILLER      VALUE "FOUR ."         PIC X(10).
00630       05  FILLER      VALUE "FIVE ."         PIC X(10).
00640       05  FILLER      VALUE "SIX ."          PIC X(10).
00650       05  FILLER      VALUE "SEVEN ."        PIC X(10).
00660       05  FILLER      VALUE "EIGHT ."        PIC X(10).
00670       05  FILLER      VALUE "NINE ."         PIC X(10).
00680       05  FILLER      VALUE "TEN ."          PIC X(10).
00690       05  FILLER      VALUE "ELEVEN ."       PIC X(10).
00700       05  FILLER      VALUE "TWELVE ."       PIC X(10).
00710       05  FILLER      VALUE "THIRTEEN ."     PIC X(10).
00720       05  FILLER      VALUE "FOURTEEN ."     PIC X(10).
00730       05  FILLER      VALUE "FIFTEEN ."      PIC X(10).
00740       05  FILLER      VALUE "SIXTEEN ."      PIC X(10).
00750       05  FILLER      VALUE "SEVENTEEN "     PIC X(10).
00760       05  FILLER      VALUE "EIGHTEEN ."     PIC X(10).
00770       05  FILLER      VALUE "NINETEEN ."     PIC X(10).
00780   01  UNITS-PLACES-TABLE
00790       REDEFINES UNITS-PLACES-TABLE-ENTRIES.
00800       05  UNITS-PLACE  OCCURS 19 TIMES       PIC X(10).
00810
```

(continued)

table for higher-place values because all the place values higher than tens use the
same words as either the units' place or the tens' place. All the numbers up through
19 are included in the UNITS-PLACES-TABLE to facilitate programming for the
numbers 11 through 19. In this program, all numbers below 20 are treated as units,
and programming for the tens' place handles numbers of 20 and larger. A space is
included after each word in the UNITS-PLACES-TABLE because the space is part
of the field. The units' words are always followed by a space whenever they appear
in the output. There is no such space in the entries in the TENS-PLACES-TABLE,
because the tens' words are not always followed by a space; they are sometimes
followed by a hyphen. An IF test in the Procedure Division determines whether

Figure 17.7   (continued)

```
00820   01   TENS-PLACES-TABLE-ENTRIES.
00830        05   FILLER       VALUE "TEN"          PIC X(7).
00840        05   FILLER       VALUE "TWENTY"       PIC X(7).
00850        05   FILLER       VALUE "THIRTY"       PIC X(7).
00860        05   FILLER       VALUE "FORTY"        PIC X(7).
00870        05   FILLER       VALUE "FIFTY"        PIC X(7).
00880        05   FILLER       VALUE "SIXTY"        PIC X(7).
00890        05   FILLER       VALUE "SEVENTY"      PIC X(7).
00900        05   FILLER       VALUE "EIGHTY"       PIC X(7).
00910        05   FILLER       VALUE "NINETY"       PIC X(7).
00920   01   TENS-PLACES-TABLE
00930        REDEFINES TENS-PLACES-TABLE-ENTRIES.
00940        05   TENS-PLACE OCCURS 9 TIMES         PIC X(7).
00950
00960   01   PAGE-HEADING.
00970        05   FILLER       VALUE SPACES         PIC X(15).
00980        05   FILLER       VALUE "MONEY"        PIC X(5).
00990
01000   01   DETAIL-LINE.
01010        05   FILLER       VALUE SPACES         PIC XX.
01020        05   MONEY-OUT                         PIC $ZZZ,ZZZ.99BB.
01030        05   MONEY-OUT-IN-ENGLISH              PIC X(82).
01040
01050   01   NO-INPUT-DATA.
01060        05   FILLER       VALUE SPACES         PIC X(15).
01070        05   FILLER       VALUE "NO INPUT DATA" PIC X(13).
01080
01090   ***********************************************************************
01100
01110   PROCEDURE DIVISION.
01120   CONTROL-PARAGRAPH.
01130       PERFORM INITIALIZATION.
01140       PERFORM PROCESS-A-NUMBER UNTIL MORE-INPUT = "N".
01150       PERFORM TERMINATION.
01160       STOP RUN.
01170
01180   INITIALIZATION.
01190       OPEN INPUT   MONEY-FILE-IN,
01200            OUTPUT  MONEY-FILE-OUT.
01210       WRITE MONEY-RECORD-OUT FROM PAGE-HEADING AFTER PAGE.
01220       READ MONEY-FILE-IN
01230           AT END
01240               MOVE "N" TO MORE-INPUT.
01250       IF MORE-INPUT = "N"
01260           WRITE MONEY-RECORD-OUT FROM NO-INPUT-DATA AFTER 2.
01270
01280   TERMINATION.
01290       CLOSE MONEY-FILE-IN,
01300             MONEY-FILE-OUT.
01310
01320   PROCESS-A-NUMBER.
01330       PERFORM STRING-WORD-AND-CENT-FIELDS.
01340       PERFORM PRINT-A-LINE.
01350       READ MONEY-FILE-IN
01360           AT END
01370               MOVE "N" TO MORE-INPUT.
01380
```

```
01390    PRINT-A-LINE.
01400        MOVE MONEY-IN                        TO MONEY-OUT.
01410        MOVE MONEY-AMOUNT-IN-ENGLISH TO MONEY-OUT-IN-ENGLISH.
01420        WRITE MONEY-RECORD-OUT FROM DETAIL-LINE AFTER 2.
01430
01440    STRING-WORD-AND-CENT-FIELDS.
01450        MOVE SPACES TO MONEY-AMOUNT-IN-ENGLISH.
01460        MOVE 1 TO ENGLISH-FIELD-POINTER.
01470        PERFORM HUNDREDS-OF-THOUSANDS.
01480        PERFORM TENS-OF-THOUSANDS.
01490        PERFORM THOUSANDS.
01500        PERFORM HUNDREDS.
01510        PERFORM TENS.
01520        PERFORM UNIT-DOLLARS.
01530        PERFORM CONSTANT-AND-CENTS.
01540
01550    HUNDREDS-OF-THOUSANDS.
01560        IF HUNDREDS-OF-THOUSANDS-W NOT = 0
01570            STRING UNITS-PLACE (HUNDREDS-OF-THOUSANDS-W)
01580                                             DELIMITED BY "."
01590                    "HUNDRED "               DELIMITED BY SIZE
01600                INTO MONEY-AMOUNT-IN-ENGLISH
01610                POINTER ENGLISH-FIELD-POINTER.
01620
01630    TENS-OF-THOUSANDS.
01640        IF TENS-OF-THOUSANDS-W NOT = 0 AND NOT = 1
01650            STRING TENS-PLACE (TENS-OF-THOUSANDS-W)
01660                                             DELIMITED BY SPACE
01670                INTO MONEY-AMOUNT-IN-ENGLISH
01680                POINTER ENGLISH-FIELD-POINTER
01690            IF THOUSANDS-W NOT = 0
01700                STRING "-"                   DELIMITED BY SIZE
01710                    INTO MONEY-AMOUNT-IN-ENGLISH
01720                    POINTER ENGLISH-FIELD-POINTER
01730            ELSE
01740                STRING SPACE                 DELIMITED BY SIZE
01750                    INTO MONEY-AMOUNT-IN-ENGLISH
01760                    POINTER ENGLISH-FIELD-POINTER.
01770        IF TENS-OF-THOUSANDS-W = 1
01780            STRING UNITS-PLACE (TEENS-OF-THOUSANDS-W)
01790                                             DELIMITED BY "."
01800                INTO MONEY-AMOUNT-IN-ENGLISH
01810                POINTER ENGLISH-FIELD-POINTER.
01820
```

(continued)

any particular tens' word is to be followed by a space or a hyphen and STRINGs the appropriate character.

In the Procedure Division, the paragraph PROCESS-A-NUMBER, line 01320, follows the hierarchy diagram. In STRING-WORD-AND-CENT-FIELDS, line 01440, the POINTER is set to 1 to point to the first character position of the output field. The PERFORM statements at lines 01470 through 01530 fill the output field with the appropriate words.

In the paragraph HUNDREDS-OF-THOUSANDS, for example, the IF statement at line 01560 determines whether there are any hundreds of thousands of dollars in the number. If there are, it STRINGs the appropriate words into the output field, MONEY-AMOUNT-IN-ENGLISH, and sets the POINTER to point to the first unused character in the output field. The phrase DELIMITED BY "." causes all the characters in the sending field, up to but not including the dot, to be sent to the output field.

In the paragraph TENS-OF-THOUSANDS, the IF statement at line 01640 determines whether there are any regular tens of thousands of dollars in the number. If there are, it STRINGs the appropriate word into MONEY-AMOUNT-IN-ENGLISH. The IF statement at line 01690 determines whether to STRING a hyphen or a SPACE after it. The IF statement at line 01770 handles the irregular tens of thousands.

Figure 17.7   (continued)

```
01830    THOUSANDS.
01840        IF TENS-OF-THOUSANDS-W NOT = 1
01850            IF THOUSANDS-W NOT = 0
01860                STRING UNITS-PLACE (THOUSANDS-W)     DELIMITED BY "."
01870                    INTO MONEY-AMOUNT-IN-ENGLISH
01880                    POINTER ENGLISH-FIELD-POINTER.
01890        IF HUNDREDS-OF-THOUSANDS-W NOT = 0 OR
01900            TENS-OF-THOUSANDS-W      NOT = 0 OR
01910            THOUSANDS-W              NOT = 0
01920                STRING "THOUSAND "                    DELIMITED BY SIZE
01930                    INTO MONEY-AMOUNT-IN-ENGLISH
01940                    POINTER ENGLISH-FIELD-POINTER.
01950
01960    HUNDREDS.
01970        IF HUNDREDS-W NOT = 0
01980            STRING UNITS-PLACE (HUNDREDS-W)          DELIMITED BY "."
01990                   "HUNDRED "                        DELIMITED BY SIZE
02000                INTO MONEY-AMOUNT-IN-ENGLISH
02010                POINTER ENGLISH-FIELD-POINTER.
02020
02030    TENS.
02040        IF TENS-W NOT = 0 AND NOT = 1
02050            STRING TENS-PLACE (TENS-W)               DELIMITED BY SPACE
02060                INTO MONEY-AMOUNT-IN-ENGLISH
02070                POINTER ENGLISH-FIELD-POINTER
02080            IF UNIT-DOLLARS-W NOT = 0
02090                STRING "-"                           DELIMITED BY SIZE
02100                    INTO MONEY-AMOUNT-IN-ENGLISH
02110                    POINTER ENGLISH-FIELD-POINTER
02120            ELSE
02130                STRING SPACE                         DELIMITED BY SIZE
02140                    INTO MONEY-AMOUNT-IN-ENGLISH
02150                    POINTER ENGLISH-FIELD-POINTER.
02160        IF TENS-W = 1
02170            STRING UNITS-PLACE (TEENS-W)             DELIMITED BY "."
02180                INTO MONEY-AMOUNT-IN-ENGLISH
02190                POINTER ENGLISH-FIELD-POINTER.
02200
02210    UNIT-DOLLARS.
02220        IF TENS-W NOT = 1
02230            IF UNIT-DOLLARS-W NOT = 0
02240                STRING UNITS-PLACE (UNIT-DOLLARS-W) DELIMITED BY "."
02250                    INTO MONEY-AMOUNT-IN-ENGLISH
02260                    POINTER ENGLISH-FIELD-POINTER.
02270
02280    CONSTANT-AND-CENTS.
02290        IF LESS-THAN-A-DOLLAR
02300            STRING "ONLY "                           DELIMITED BY SIZE
02310                INTO MONEY-AMOUNT-IN-ENGLISH
02320                POINTER ENGLISH-FIELD-POINTER
02330        ELSE
02340        IF ONE-DOLLAR
02350            STRING "DOLLAR AND "                     DELIMITED BY SIZE
02360                INTO MONEY-AMOUNT-IN-ENGLISH
02370                POINTER ENGLISH-FIELD-POINTER
02380        ELSE
02390            STRING "DOLLARS AND "                    DELIMITED BY SIZE
02400                INTO MONEY-AMOUNT-IN-ENGLISH
02410                POINTER ENGLISH-FIELD-POINTER.
02420        STRING WHOLE-CENTS-W
02430               "/XX"                                 DELIMITED BY SIZE
02440            INTO MONEY-AMOUNT-IN-ENGLISH
02450            POINTER ENGLISH-FIELD-POINTER.
```

Program P17-02 was run with the input data shown in Figure 17.8 and produced the output shown in Figure 17.9.

EXERCISE 2

Modify Program P17-02 so that it can handle nine-digit whole dollar amounts, up through $999,999,999.

Figure 17.8 Input to Program P17-02.

```
-------------------------------------------------------------------------------
         1         2         3         4         5         6         7        8
12345678901234567890123456789012345678901234567890123456789012345678901234567890
-------------------------------------------------------------------------------
00015890
90000000
08701706
77777777
00000005
00111919
02000000
00000000
00000110
00000099
00000199
00000200
00000100
```

Figure 17.9 Output from Program P17-02.

```
            MONEY

$      158.90   ONE HUNDRED FIFTY-EIGHT DOLLARS AND 90/XX

$900,000.00   NINE HUNDRED THOUSAND DOLLARS AND 00/XX

$ 87,017.06   EIGHTY-SEVEN THOUSAND SEVENTEEN DOLLARS AND 06/XX

$777,777.77   SEVEN HUNDRED SEVENTY-SEVEN THOUSAND SEVEN HUNDRED SEVENTY-SEVEN DOLLARS AND 77/XX

$        .05   ONLY 05/XX

$    1,119.19   ONE THOUSAND ONE HUNDRED NINETEEN DOLLARS AND 19/XX

$ 20,000.00   TWENTY THOUSAND DOLLARS AND 00/XX

$        .00   ONLY 00/XX

$       1.10   ONE DOLLAR AND 10/XX

$        .99   ONLY 99/XX

$       1.99   ONE DOLLAR AND 99/XX

$       2.00   TWO DOLLARS AND 00/XX

$       1.00   ONE DOLLAR AND 00/XX
```

The UNSTRING Statement

The **UNSTRING** statement can be used to scan a large sending field and break it down into pieces. The UNSTRING statement assigns each piece to a separate receiving field. The scan of the sending field can be based either on one or more delimiters or on size. If based on delimiters, the characters in the sending field are examined from left to right until a delimiter is found. Then, the characters in the sending field up to but not including the delimiter are MOVEd to a receiving field according to the rules of the MOVE statement. A delimiter may be any alphanumeric value or any integer of USAGE DISPLAY. An optional **COUNT** field may be provided, and COBOL will place into the COUNT field the number of characters that were examined before a delimiter was found.

A single UNSTRING statement can have as many receiving fields as desired, and each receiving field may have a COUNT field associated with it. After the first receiving field has had data MOVEd to it, the UNSTRING statement resumes scanning the sending field looking for the next appearance of a delimiter. It then MOVEs to the second receiving field all that portion of the sending field between the first and second appearances of delimiters, and places into the second COUNT field (if one is specified) the number of characters examined between delimiters. If there are no characters between delimiters, then spaces or zeros are moved to the receiving field depending on how the receiving field is defined. The delimiters themselves can optionally be MOVEd to separate receiving fields or not MOVEd. The scan continues until all characters in the sending field have been examined or until all the receiving fields have had data MOVEd to them, whichever comes first.

Receiving fields are listed in an UNSTRING statement in the order in which they are to receive pieces of the sending field. The optional **TALLYING** phrase causes the UNSTRING statement to count how many receiving fields have data MOVEd to them during execution of the statement.

An UNSTRING statement can also break down a large field into pieces of specific sizes, without any consideration of delimiters. There may be as many receiving fields as desired, and they may be of any sizes desired. The UNSTRING statement scans the sending field from left to right and MOVEs to the first receiving field exactly the number of characters that will fit into it. Then the UNSTRING statement continues the scan and MOVEs to the second receiving field exactly the number of characters that will fit into it. The scan continues until all characters in the sending field have been scanned or all of the receiving fields have had data MOVEd to them, whichever comes first. COUNT fields may not be used when an UNSTRING statement is operating on the basis of field sizes. A single UNSTRING statement can operate on the basis of delimiters or sizes, but not both.

An optional OVERFLOW phrase may be used to handle cases where there are more characters in the sending field than can fit into all the receiving fields. An optional POINTER may be used to keep track of which character in the sending field is next to be scanned.

Using the UNSTRING Statement

Program P17-03 shows how a large field may be broken down into smaller fields on the basis of delimiters contained in the large field. Program P17-03 accepts 80-character input records of the kind shown in Figure 17.10. These are selections from poems, written in "prose" format as they might be found in a book review, with slashes between the lines and quotation marks around the whole selection. Notice that some selections extend to more than one input record, but each individual line of poetry is completely contained in one record. A single line of poetry does not **span** records. Program P17-03 reads the selections and prints them in "poetry" format as shown in Figure 17.11. Notice that the program can handle lines up to 37 characters long. If an input record contains a line longer than that, the program prints a message LINE LONGER THAN 37 CHARACTERS.

Hierarchy Diagram for Program P17-03

A hierarchy diagram for Program P17-03 is shown in Figure 17.12. The diagram shows how to handle a situation where the input consists of several independent sets of data, as we have here. At the first level of subfunctions, "Initialization" and "Termination" refer to the usual program initialization and termination such as OPENing and closing files, the priming READ, and initializing and terminating the report. "Process all poems" executes until there are no more input data.

At the next level of subfunctions, we must process each poem as a separate set of data. "Initialize for poem" and "Terminate poem" carry out needed functions, which you will see when we look at the program. "Process one poem" executes until the end of a poem is recognized by its closing quotation marks.

Figure 17.10 Input to Program P17-03.

```
------------------------------------------------------------------------------
         1         2         3         4         5         6         7         8
12345678901234567890123456789012345678901234567890123456789012345678901234567890
------------------------------------------------------------------------------
"SOME PEOPLE/WILL DO ANYTHING/IN ORDER TO SAY/THEY'VE DONE IT."
"LIFE IS FUNNY/THAT WAY.../THERE'S A PIPER/'ROUND EVERY/CORNER/WAITING/
TO BE PAID."
"HOW MANY POETS DOES ONE SMALL PLANET NEED?/WHO KNOWS?/WHO IS ASKING?/
IS ANYONE ANSWERING?"
```

Figure 17.11 Output format for Program P17-03.

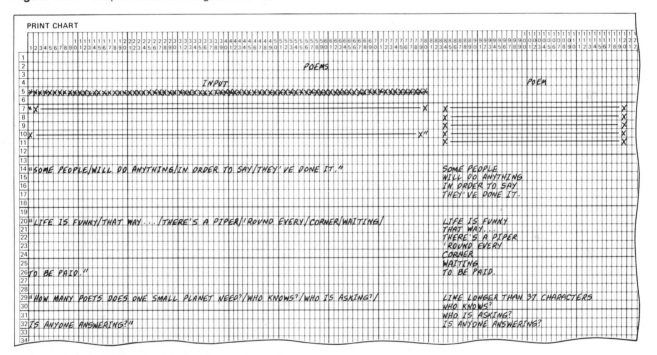

At the next level of subfunctions, we must process each of the input records that makes up a poem. Each input record may contain several lines of poetry. "Process one input record" extracts and prints lines of poetry from the input record, and continues to execute until it encounters the end of the record.

Figure 17.12   Hierarchy diagram for Program P17-03.

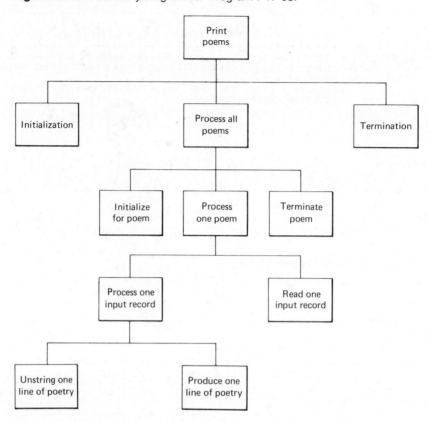

Program P17-03

Program P17-03 is shown in Figure 17.13. In the Working Storage Section are the fields we need to control the repetitive execution of the several loops in this program. MORE-INPUT, line 00360, starts out with VALUE "Y", and the main loop runs UNTIL MORE-INPUT becomes "N".

The field LINE-OF-POETRY, line 00370, is used to assign each line of a poem as it is extracted from an input record. When all the lines of poetry have been extracted from an input record and nothing remains in the input record except perhaps trailing blanks, the program knows that all the lines of poetry have been processed and that a new input record should be read. The program is arranged so that even if there are no trailing blanks in the input record, the end of the record will be detected correctly. You will soon see how.

The field POEMS-LINES, line 00450, is used to store each input record as it comes in from the input file. The field LINE-TERMINATOR, line 00460, is used to indicate whether any particular line of poetry terminates with a slash or with quotation marks. If with quotation marks, the program knows that a complete poem has been processed. Together, POEMS-LINES and LINE-TERMINATOR form an 81-character field that insures that the end of each input record will be detected even if the poetry goes right up through position 80.

POEMS-LINES-SAVE, line 00470, is part of the coding needed to effect a control break on POEMS-LINES. No totals are taken in this program, and the control break is needed only so that we can get group indication of POEMS-LINES. This means that each different value assigned to POEMS-LINES prints only once, as shown on the print chart in Figure 17.11.

Figure 17.13 Program P17-03.

```
CB1 RELEASE 2.4                           IBM OS/VS COBOL  JULY  1, 1982


                    22.57.13        APR 12,1988


00010  IDENTIFICATION DIVISION.
00020  PROGRAM-ID.  P17-03.
00030 *
00040 *    THIS PROGRAM READS POEMS IN "PROSE" FORMAT, WITH
00050 *    EACH PAIR OF LINES OF POETRY SEPARATED BY A SLASH,
00060 *    AND PRINTS EACH POEM IN "POETRY" FORMAT.
00070 *
00080 ***************************************************************
00090
00100  ENVIRONMENT DIVISION.
00110  CONFIGURATION SECTION.
00120  SOURCE-COMPUTER.  IBM-370.
00130  OBJECT-COMPUTER.  IBM-370.
00140
00150  INPUT-OUTPUT SECTION.
00160  FILE-CONTROL.
00170      SELECT POEMS-FILE-IN  ASSIGN TO INFILE.
00180      SELECT POEMS-FILE-OUT ASSIGN TO PRINTER.
00190
00200 ***************************************************************
00210
00220  DATA DIVISION.
00230  FILE SECTION.
00240  FD  POEMS-FILE-IN
00250      RECORD CONTAINS 80 CHARACTERS
00260      LABEL RECORDS ARE OMITTED.
00270
00280  01  POEMS-RECORD-IN                      PIC X(80).
00290
00300  FD  POEMS-FILE-OUT
00310      LABEL RECORDS ARE OMITTED.
00320
00330  01  POEMS-RECORD-OUT                     PIC X(120).
00340
00350  WORKING-STORAGE SECTION.
00360  01  MORE-INPUT        VALUE "Y"          PIC X.
00370  01  LINE-OF-POETRY                       PIC X(37).
00380  01  LINE-TOO-LONG                        PIC X(30)
00390      VALUE "LINE LONGER THAN 37 CHARACTERS".
00400  01  LINE-LIMIT        VALUE 37           PIC S99 COMP SYNC.
00410  01  CHARACTER-COUNTER                    PIC S99 COMP SYNC.
00420  01  CHARACTER-POINTER                    PIC S99 COMP SYNC.
00430
00440  01  POEMS-RECORD-W.
00450      05  POEMS-LINES                      PIC X(80).
00460      05  LINE-TERMINATOR                  PIC X.
00470  01  POEMS-LINES-SAVE                     PIC X(80).
00480
00490  01  REPORT-HEADING-1.
00500      05  FILLER           VALUE SPACES    PIC X(55).
00510      05  FILLER           VALUE "POEMS"   PIC X(5).
00520
00530  01  REPORT-HEADING-2.
00540      05  FILLER           VALUE SPACES    PIC X(35).
00550      05  FILLER           VALUE "INPUT"   PIC X(65).
00560      05  FILLER           VALUE "POEM"    PIC X(4).
00570
00580  01  REPORT-HEADING-3.
00590      05  FILLER           VALUE ALL "*"   PIC X(80).
00600
```

(continued)

The definition of the print line is shown in lines 00610 through 00630. POEMS-LINE-OUT contains the 80-character input record and three blanks. LINE-OF-POETRY-OUT contains a single line of poetry. Since a single input record will usually contain several lines of poetry, the program is designed to print the input record only with the first line of poetry and to print blanks in the POEMS-LINE-OUT field for all the subsequent lines of poetry in that input record, as shown in Figure 17.11.

The Procedure Division is not difficult to follow if the hierarchy diagram of Figure 17.12 is kept near at hand. In the main control paragraph PRINT-POEMS, the PERFORM statement at line 00740 executes UNTIL there are no more data. In PROCESS-ALL-POEMS the PERFORM statement at line 00800 processes each poem UNTIL the end of the poem is recognized by its QUOTE. And in PROCESS-ONE-POEM, the PERFORM statement at line 00850 processes a single input record UNTIL nothing remains of the input record except perhaps trailing SPACES.

Figure 17.13   (continued)

```
00610   01   PRINT-LINE.
00620        05   POEMS-LINE-OUT                      PIC X(83).
00630        05   LINE-OF-POETRY-OUT                  PIC X(37). ✓
00640
00650   01   NO-INPUT-DATA.
00660        05   FILLER           VALUE SPACES       PIC X(9).
00670        05   FILLER           VALUE "NO INPUT DATA" PIC X(13).
00680
00690   ******************************************************************
00700
00710   PROCEDURE DIVISION.
00720   PRINT-POEMS.
00730        PERFORM INITIALIZATION.
00740        PERFORM PROCESS-ALL-POEMS UNTIL MORE-INPUT IS EQUAL TO "N".
00750        PERFORM TERMINATION.
00760        STOP RUN.
00770
00780   PROCESS-ALL-POEMS.
00790        PERFORM INITIALIZE-FOR-POEM.
00800        PERFORM PROCESS-ONE-POEM UNTIL LINE-TERMINATOR = QUOTE.
00810        PERFORM TERMINATE-POEM.
00820
00830   PROCESS-ONE-POEM.
00840        MOVE HIGH-VALUES TO LINE-OF-POETRY.
00850        PERFORM PROCESS-ONE-INPUT-RECORD UNTIL
00860             LINE-OF-POETRY = SPACES.
00870        MOVE 1 TO CHARACTER-POINTER.
00880        PERFORM READ-ONE-INPUT-RECORD.
00890
00900   INITIALIZATION.
00910        OPEN INPUT  POEMS-FILE-IN
00920             OUTPUT POEMS-FILE-OUT.
00930        WRITE POEMS-RECORD-OUT FROM REPORT-HEADING-1 AFTER PAGE.
00940        WRITE POEMS-RECORD-OUT FROM REPORT-HEADING-2 AFTER 2.
00950        WRITE POEMS-RECORD-OUT FROM REPORT-HEADING-3.
00960        MOVE SPACES TO POEMS-RECORD-OUT.
00970        WRITE POEMS-RECORD-OUT.
00980        PERFORM READ-ONE-INPUT-RECORD.
00990        MOVE POEMS-LINES TO POEMS-LINES-SAVE, POEMS-LINE-OUT.
01000        IF MORE-INPUT IS EQUAL TO "N"
01010             WRITE POEMS-RECORD-OUT FROM NO-INPUT-DATA.
01020
01030   INITIALIZE-FOR-POEM.
01040        MOVE SPACES TO LINE-TERMINATOR.
01050        MOVE 2 TO CHARACTER-POINTER.
01060
01070   TERMINATION.
01080        CLOSE POEMS-FILE-IN
01090              POEMS-FILE-OUT.
01100
```

```
01110    PROCESS-ONE-INPUT-RECORD.
01120        PERFORM UNSTRING-ONE-LINE-OF-POETRY.
01130        IF LINE-OF-POETRY NOT = SPACES
01140            PERFORM PRODUCE-ONE-LINE-OF-POETRY.
01150
01160    UNSTRING-ONE-LINE-OF-POETRY.
01170        UNSTRING POEMS-RECORD-W
01180            DELIMITED BY "/" OR QUOTE
01190            INTO LINE-OF-POETRY
01200                DELIMITER LINE-TERMINATOR
01210                COUNT     CHARACTER-COUNTER
01220            POINTER CHARACTER-POINTER.
01230
01240    PRODUCE-ONE-LINE-OF-POETRY.
01250        IF CHARACTER-COUNTER GREATER THAN LINE-LIMIT
01260            MOVE LINE-TOO-LONG TO LINE-OF-POETRY.
01270        IF POEMS-LINES NOT = POEMS-LINES-SAVE
01280            MOVE POEMS-LINES TO POEMS-LINE-OUT, POEMS-LINES-SAVE.
01290        PERFORM PRINT-THE-LINE.
01300
01310    PRINT-THE-LINE.
01320        MOVE LINE-OF-POETRY TO LINE-OF-POETRY-OUT.
01330        WRITE POEMS-RECORD-OUT FROM PRINT-LINE.
01340        MOVE SPACES TO PRINT-LINE.
01350
01360    TERMINATE-POEM.
01370        MOVE SPACES TO POEMS-RECORD-OUT.
01380        WRITE POEMS-RECORD-OUT AFTER 2.
01390
01400    READ-ONE-INPUT-RECORD.
01410        READ POEMS-FILE-IN INTO POEMS-LINES
01420            AT END
01430                MOVE "N" TO MORE-INPUT.
```

The three PERFORM . . . UNTIL statements, lines 00740, 00800, and 00850, demonstrate a very important principle. The PERFORM . . . UNTIL statement makes its condition test before PERFORMing the named paragraph. This means that if you enter a PERFORM . . . UNTIL statement with the condition already satisfied, the named paragraph will not be executed even once. In this program we make sure that we enter each PERFORM . . . UNTIL with the condition not satisfied, so that the named paragraph will be PERFORMed. The PERFORM . . . UNTIL statement at line 00740 is entered with MORE-INPUT equal to "Y". The PERFORM . . . UNTIL statement at line 00800 is entered with LINE-TERMINATOR not equal to QUOTE, for the paragraph INITIALIZE-FOR-POEM sets LINE-TERMINATOR to SPACES. And the PERFORM . . . UNTIL statement at line 00850 is entered with LINE-OF-POETRY not equal to SPACES, for the MOVE statement at line 00840 sets LINE-OF-POETRY to HIGH-VALUES.

At line 00990 is part of the coding needed to get group indication of the input record, POEMS-LINES. POEMS-LINES is MOVEd both to POEMS-LINES-SAVE and the output print field, POEMS-LINE-OUT. Later, the program will test for a change in value of POEMS-LINE-SAVE and control the printing of POEMS-LINE-OUT appropriately. You will soon see how.

In the paragraph INITIALIZE-FOR-POEM, line 01030, the POINTER is set to 2 so that the first UNSTRING for the poem will begin with character position 2, ignoring the opening quotation marks. Scans of the second and subsequent records for each poem begin in character position 1.

The UNSTRING statement, at line 01170, shows many of the features of UNSTRING. The word following UNSTRING is the sending field. The DELIMITED BY clause, line 01180, lists all of the delimiters to be searched for, separated by OR. The INTO phrase names one receiving field.

Optional phrases follow, at lines 01200 through 01220. The **DELIMITER** phrase tells COBOL to MOVE, to the field named, each delimiter as it is found. In this case, our delimiters will be MOVEd to LINE-TERMINATOR. Remember that if two delimiters are found right next to each other in the sending field, SPACES will be MOVEd to LINE-OF-POETRY.

The COUNT phrase tells COBOL to MOVE, to the field named, a count of the number of characters scanned in the sending field (excluding the number of characters in the delimiter).

If there were more than one receiving field, each receiving field could have its own DELIMITER field and/or COUNT field.

The POINTER phrase names the field that is used to keep track of the scan in the sending field. After execution of the UNSTRING, the field CHARACTER-POINTER points one character position to the right of the last character scanned.

The remainder of the coding needed to get group indication of POEMS-LINES is shown in lines 01270, 01280, and 01340. POEMS-LINE-OUT gets data MOVEd to it only when its value changes, in the IF statement at line 01270. And at line 01340, POEMS-LINE-OUT is blanked (along with the rest of the output print area), so that it will not print except when it has data MOVEd to it in line 01280.

Program P17-03 was run with the input data shown in Figure 17.10 and produced the output shown in Figure 17.14.

Figure 17.14   Output from Program P17-03.

```
                                              POEMS

                           INPUT                                                    POEM
********************************************************************************
"SOME PEOPLE/WILL DO ANYTHING/IN ORDER TO SAY/THEY'VE DONE IT."        SOME PEOPLE
                                                                       WILL DO ANYTHING
                                                                       IN ORDER TO SAY
                                                                       THEY'VE DONE IT.


"LIFE IS FUNNY/THAT WAY.../THERE'S A PIPER/'ROUND EVERY/CORNER/WAITING/   LIFE IS FUNNY
                                                                         THAT WAY...
                                                                         THERE'S A PIPER
                                                                         'ROUND EVERY
                                                                         CORNER
                                                                         WAITING
TO BE PAID."                                                             TO BE PAID.

"HOW MANY POETS DOES ONE SMALL PLANET NEED?/WHO KNOWS?/WHO IS ASKING?/   LINE LONGER THAN 37 CHARACTERS
                                                                         WHO KNOWS?
                                                                         WHO IS ASKING?
IS ANYONE ANSWERING?"                                                   IS ANYONE ANSWERING?
```

EXERCISE 3

In certain computer systems, the names of data sets consist of one or more components separated by periods. Examples of such names are:

a. `DATA`
b. `DATA.PAYROLL`
c. `VSAM.DATA.SET`

Each component may be from 1 to 8 characters long.

Write a program to read input data records each containing the name of one data set starting in column 1. For each record read, have your program print the data set name and also print each component on a separate line, as shown in the output format in Figure 17.E3. If any component is longer than 8 characters, have your program print a message COMPONENT LONGER THAN 8 CHARACTERS.

Figure 17.E3 Output format for Exercise 3.

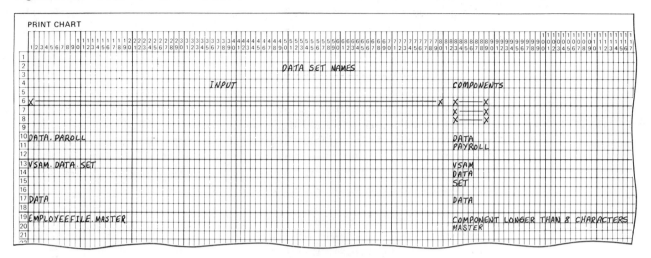

The Format of the UNSTRING Statement

The format of the UNSTRING statement is:

```
UNSTRING identifier-1

    [DELIMITED BY [ALL] {identifier-2}
                        {literal-1   }

        [, OR [ALL] {identifier-3} ] ... ]
                    {literal-2   }
    INTO identifier-4
            [, DELIMITER IN identifier-5]
            [, COUNT IN identifier-6]
        [, identifier-7
            [, DELIMITER IN identifier-8]
            [, COUNT IN identifier-9] ] ...
    [WITH POINTER identifier-10]
    [TALLYING IN identifier-11]
    [; ON OVERFLOW imperative-statement]
```

This format is difficult to read, because it has many optional words and phrases, and confusing nesting of optional phrases. The format shows that the word UNSTRING is required and that it must be followed by identifier-1, the name of the sending field. The DELIMITED BY clause is shown as optional. If it is omitted, the UNSTRING statement operates on the basis of the sizes of the receiving fields, as described earlier in this chapter. If DELIMITED BY is used, there can be only one such clause in the statement.

A DELIMITED BY clause must contain at least one identifier or literal, and it may contain as many as desired, separated by the word OR. These are shown in the format as identifier-2, literal-1, identifier-3, and literal-2. Any identifier or literal in a DELIMITED BY clause may be preceded by the optional word ALL. If ALL is used, then the UNSTRING statement treats consecutive appearances of the delimiter in the sending field as one appearance of that delimiter.

There must be exactly one INTO clause in an UNSTRING statement. It must contain at least one receiving field, and it may contain as many as desired. The receiving fields are shown as identifier-4 and identifier-7. Each receiving field may have associated with it an optional DELIMITER phrase and/or an optional COUNT phrase.

Using STRING and UNSTRING Together

We now develop a program to show how STRING and UNSTRING can be used together in one program to edit English prose. Program P17-04 examines English words, phrases, and sentences and replaces all occurrences of the word MAN with the word PERSON and all occurrences of the word MEN with PERSONS. Although the goal of such a program may seem admirable, the results are perhaps not exactly what one would expect or want. Typical input such as

```
MANY DISTINCTLY HUMAN ACTIVITIES EMANATED FROM ERAS
    AS DISTANT AS CAVEMAN DAYS.
MEN AND WOMEN ENGAGED IN MENDING, MANUFACTURING, AND
    MENTAL MANIPULATIONS.
```

and

```
THE MAN-EATING TIGER MANAGED ANYWAY TO MANGLE
    THE WOMAN'S MANDIBLE.
```

would produce output of the kind shown in Figure 17.15.

Figure 17.15   Output format for Program P17-04.

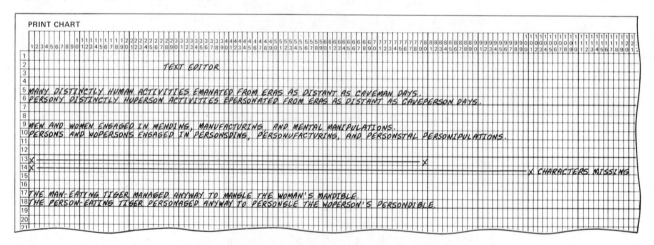

Each selection to be edited is keyed in a single input record starting in position 1. If the edited text occupies more than 120 print positions, Program P17-04 inserts the words CHARACTERS MISSING at the right end of the edited print line.

A hierarchy diagram of the main loop of Program P17-04 is shown in Figure 17.16. For each input record, the program will "Unstring entire line." The program will thus break the entire line into separate pieces. Each appearance of either of the delimiters MAN or MEN will get stored into a separate field, as will each of the segments of the line between appearances of delimiters and after the last delimiter. Then, in "Delimit line segment" each of the segments of the line in its separate field will have a HIGH-VALUE inserted at its right end. You will see why this is needed when we look at the program.

Figure 17.16 Hierarchy diagram for main loop of Program P17-04.

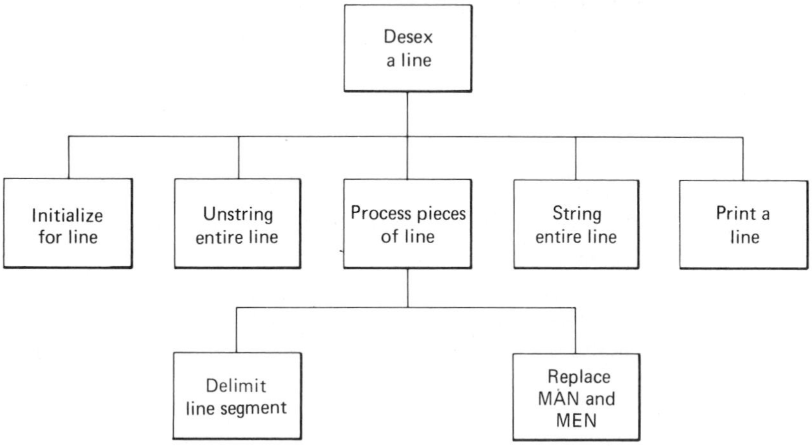

"Replace MAN and MEN" examines each of the separate fields containing the words MAN or MEN, and replaces each MAN with PERSON and each MEN with PERSONS in its own field. "String entire line" then puts back together all the line segments and all the fields containing PERSON and PERSONS.

Program P17-04 is shown in Figure 17.17. The field TEXT-RECORD-IN, line 00280, serves as the sending field for the UNSTRING operation. The input record

Figure 17.17 Program P17-04.

```
CB1 RELEASE 2.4                          IBM OS/VS COBOL   JULY  1, 1982


                    23.14.50        APR 12,1988


00010  IDENTIFICATION DIVISION.
00020  PROGRAM-ID.  P17-04.
00030 *
00040 *    THIS PROGRAM EDITS ENGLISH TEXT, REPLACING ALL
00050 *    APPEARANCES OF MAN WITH PERSON AND ALL APPEARANCES
00060 *    OF MEN WITH PERSONS.
00070 *
00080 ***********************************************************************
00090
00100  ENVIRONMENT DIVISION.
00110  CONFIGURATION SECTION.
00120  SOURCE-COMPUTER.  IBM-370.
00130  OBJECT-COMPUTER.  IBM-370.
00140
00150  INPUT-OUTPUT SECTION.
00160  FILE-CONTROL.
00170      SELECT TEXT-FILE-OUT  ASSIGN TO PRINTER.
00180      SELECT TEXT-FILE-IN   ASSIGN TO INFILE.
00190
00200 ***********************************************************************
00210
00220  DATA DIVISION.
00230  FILE SECTION.
00240  FD  TEXT-FILE-IN
00250      RECORD CONTAINS 80 CHARACTERS
00260      LABEL RECORDS ARE OMITTED.
00270
00280  01  TEXT-RECORD-IN                       PIC X(80).
00290
```

(continued)

in TEXT-RECORD-IN is broken down, and its pieces, namely its delimiters and its segments between delimiters, are placed into fields in working storage. The EDITED-LINE, line 00370, is where the edited pieces are later strung together for printing.

LINE-BREAKDOWN, line 00380, provides working storage space for all the possible line segments and delimiters that might be found in an input record. A line segment can be as long as 80 characters if the line contains no appearances of MAN or MEN. If instead there are lots of very short segments and lots of appearances of MAN or MEN, then there can be as many as 27 segments (and 26 appearances of MAN or MEN). Twenty-six appearances of MAN and/or MEN would occupy 78 columns of the input record, and most of the line segments would be of zero length. The field SEGMENT-LENGTH, line 00410, is used by the UNSTRING operation to record the number of characters in each LINE-SEGMENT.

Figure 17.17 (continued)

```
00300  FD  TEXT-FILE-OUT
00310      LABEL RECORDS ARE OMITTED.
00320
00330  01  TEXT-RECORD-OUT                          PIC X(120).
00340
00350  WORKING-STORAGE SECTION.
00360  01  MORE-INPUT                VALUE "Y"       PIC X(3).
00370  01  EDITED-LINE                               PIC X(120).
00380  01  LINE-BREAKDOWN.
00390      05  SEGMENT-DATA OCCURS 27 TIMES INDEXED BY SEGMENT-NUMBER.
00400          10  LINE-SEGMENT                      PIC X(81).
00410          10  SEGMENT-LENGTH    COMP SYNC       PIC S99.
00420          10  DELIMITER-W                       PIC X(7).
00430
00440  01  SIZES-AND-NUMBERS              COMP.
00450      05  SIZE-OF-INPUT-RECORD      VALUE 80    PIC S99.
00460      05  SIZE-OF-EDITED-LINE       VALUE 120   PIC S999.
00470      05  NUMBER-OF-SEGMENTS                    PIC S99.
00480
00490  01  POINTERS                       COMP.
00500      05  INPUT-RECORD-POINTER                  PIC S99.
00510      05  EDITED-LINE-POINTER                   PIC S999.
00520
00530  01  REPORT-HEADING.
00540      05  FILLER        VALUE SPACES            PIC X(27).
00550      05  FILLER        VALUE "TEXT EDITOR"     PIC X(11).
00560
00570  01  TEXT-LINE-OUT                             PIC X(80).
00580  01  EDITED-LINE-OUT                           PIC X(120).
00590
00600  01  NO-INPUT-DATA.
00610      05  FILLER        VALUE SPACES            PIC X(9).
00620      05  FILLER        VALUE "NO INPUT DATA"   PIC X(13).
00630
00640  **************************************************************************
00650
00660  PROCEDURE DIVISION.
00670  CONTROL-PARAGRAPH.
00680      PERFORM INITIALIZATION.
00690      PERFORM DESEX-A-LINE UNTIL MORE-INPUT = "N".
00700      PERFORM TERMINATION.
00710      STOP RUN.
00720
00730  INITIALIZATION.
00740      OPEN INPUT  TEXT-FILE-IN
00750           OUTPUT TEXT-FILE-OUT.
00760      READ TEXT-FILE-IN
00770          AT END
00780              MOVE "N" TO MORE-INPUT.
00790      WRITE TEXT-RECORD-OUT FROM REPORT-HEADING AFTER PAGE.
00800      IF MORE-INPUT = "N"
00810          WRITE TEXT-RECORD-OUT FROM NO-INPUT-DATA.
00820
```

```
00830   DESEX-A-LINE.
00840       PERFORM INITIALIZE-FOR-LINE.
00850       PERFORM UNSTRING-ENTIRE-LINE
00860           VARYING SEGMENT-NUMBER FROM 1 BY 1 UNTIL
00870               INPUT-RECORD-POINTER
00880                           GREATER THAN SIZE-OF-INPUT-RECORD.
00890       PERFORM PROCESS-PIECES-OF-LINE
00900           VARYING SEGMENT-NUMBER FROM 1 BY 1 UNTIL
00910               SEGMENT-NUMBER GREATER THAN NUMBER-OF-SEGMENTS.
00920       PERFORM STRING-ENTIRE-LINE
00930           VARYING SEGMENT-NUMBER FROM 1 BY 1 UNTIL
00940               SEGMENT-NUMBER GREATER THAN NUMBER-OF-SEGMENTS OR
00950               EDITED-LINE-POINTER
00960                           GREATER THAN SIZE-OF-EDITED-LINE.
00970       PERFORM PRINT-A-LINE.
00980       READ TEXT-FILE-IN
00990           AT END
01000               MOVE "N" TO MORE-INPUT.
01010
01020   INITIALIZE-FOR-LINE.
01030       MOVE SPACES TO EDITED-LINE.
01040       MOVE 0 TO NUMBER-OF-SEGMENTS.
01050       MOVE 1 TO INPUT-RECORD-POINTER
01060               EDITED-LINE-POINTER.
01070
01080   UNSTRING-ENTIRE-LINE.
01090       UNSTRING TEXT-RECORD-IN
01100           DELIMITED BY "MAN" OR "MEN"
01110               INTO LINE-SEGMENT (SEGMENT-NUMBER)
01120                   DELIMITER DELIMITER-W   (SEGMENT-NUMBER)
01130                   COUNT     SEGMENT-LENGTH (SEGMENT-NUMBER)
01140           POINTER INPUT-RECORD-POINTER
01150           TALLYING NUMBER-OF-SEGMENTS.
01160
01170   PROCESS-PIECES-OF-LINE.
01180       PERFORM DELIMIT-LINE-SEGMENT.
01190       PERFORM REPLACE-MAN-AND-MEN.
01200
01210   DELIMIT-LINE-SEGMENT.
01220       ADD 1 TO SEGMENT-LENGTH (SEGMENT-NUMBER).
01230       STRING HIGH-VALUE DELIMITED BY SIZE
01240           INTO LINE-SEGMENT (SEGMENT-NUMBER)
01250           POINTER SEGMENT-LENGTH (SEGMENT-NUMBER).
01260
```

(continued)

The Procedure Division, which starts at line 00660, follows the hierarchy diagram. The three PERFORM statements at lines 00850 through 00960 operate under control of several counters and indexes. Of these, three are initialized in INITIALIZE-FOR-LINE, line 01020, before each line of input is processed. There, NUMBER-OF-SEGMENTS is zeroed. Later, the UNSTRING statement will count line segments as it finds them. Also, the POINTERs for the sending and receiving fields are initialized to point to the left end of their respective fields.

The UNSTRING statement, line 01090, executes under control of the PERFORM statement at line 00850 UNTIL the entire input record has been scanned and unstrung. The indexing in lines 01110 through 01130 permit this one statement to find and store up to 27 line segments, their delimiters, and their lengths. The UNSTRING statement counts the NUMBER-OF-SEGMENTS by adding to the field named in the TALLYING phrase, line 01150, the number of receiving fields that have data MOVEd to them. The UNSTRING statement never zeros the TALLYING field; it only adds to its previous value.

In DELIMIT-LINE-SEGMENT, line 01210, each segment found gets a HIGH-VALUE strung immediately to its right. You will see why the HIGH-VALUE is needed when we look at the paragraph STRING-ENTIRE-LINE. In REPLACE-

Figure 17.17   (continued)

```
01270  REPLACE-MAN-AND-MEN.
01280      IF DELIMITER-W (SEGMENT-NUMBER) = "MAN"
01290          MOVE "PERSON" TO DELIMITER-W (SEGMENT-NUMBER)
01300      ELSE
01310      IF DELIMITER-W (SEGMENT-NUMBER) = "MEN"
01320          MOVE "PERSONS" TO DELIMITER-W (SEGMENT-NUMBER).
01330
01340  STRING-ENTIRE-LINE.
01350      STRING LINE-SEGMENT (SEGMENT-NUMBER) DELIMITED BY HIGH-VALUE
01360              DELIMITER-W  (SEGMENT-NUMBER) DELIMITED BY SPACE
01370          INTO EDITED-LINE
01380          POINTER EDITED-LINE-POINTER
01390          OVERFLOW
01400              MOVE 102 TO EDITED-LINE-POINTER
01410              STRING " CHARACTERS MISSING" DELIMITED BY SIZE
01420                  INTO EDITED-LINE
01430                  POINTER EDITED-LINE-POINTER.
01440
01450  PRINT-A-LINE.
01460      WRITE TEXT-RECORD-OUT FROM TEXT-RECORD-IN AFTER 3.
01470      WRITE TEXT-RECORD-OUT FROM EDITED-LINE.
01480
01490  TERMINATION.
01500      CLOSE TEXT-FILE-IN
01510          TEXT-FILE-OUT.
```

MAN-AND-MEN, line 01270, each appearance of MAN is replaced by PERSON, and each appearance of MEN by PERSONS. Both IF statements are needed, for a DELIMITER-W field might contain neither MAN nor MEN. If the UNSTRING statement reaches the end of the sending field without finding a delimiter, it places SPACES into the DELIMITER-W field.

STRING-ENTIRE-LINE, line 01340, puts all the pieces together. At this point, each LINE-SEGMENT has a HIGH-VALUE at its right end, and each DELIMITER-W field contains PERSON, PERSONS, or blanks. The OVERFLOW phrase executes if the sending fields strung together do not fit INTO the receiving field. If so, any characters that might have been strung INTO positions 102 through 120 of EDITED-LINE already are replaced by the words CHARACTERS MISSING preceded by a space.

Program P17-04 was run with the input data shown in Figure 17.18 and produced the output shown in Figure 17.19.

EXERCISE 4

Write a program to read free-form name data, rearrange the fields, and print the name with its first name first. The input name data begins in column 1 of each card and consists of a last name, a first name, an optional middle initial, and an optional tag such as Jr. or CPA. The name is in the following format:

a. Last name followed immediately by a comma and a space.
b. First name followed by a space, if there is a middle initial; first name followed by a space, if there is neither a tag nor a middle initial; first name followed by a comma and a space, if there is a tag but no middle initial.
c. Middle initial, if any, followed by a period. If there is also a tag, the period following the middle initial is followed by a comma and a space.
d. Tag, if any.

Examples of these possibilities are:

Input	Output
Popkin, Gary	Gary Popkin
Popkin, Gary S.	Gary S. Popkin
Popkin, Gary, CDP	Gary Popkin, CDP
Popkin, Gary S., CDP	Gary S. Popkin, CDP

In your own input data, make up names of different lengths to be sure your program works. Test your program with very short names and very long ones.

Figure 17.18   Input to Program P17-04.

```
-------------------------------------------------------------------------------
         1         2         3         4         5         6         7        8
12345678901234567890123456789012345678901234567890123456789012345678901234567890
-------------------------------------------------------------------------------
MANY DISTINCTLY HUMAN ACTIVITIES EMANATED FROM ERAS AS DISTANT AS CAVEMAN DAYS.
MEN AND WOMEN ENGAGED IN MENDING, MANUFACTURING, AND MENTAL MANIPULATIONS.
USE MANKIND, HUMANS, OR HUMANKIND INSTEAD OF MAN OR MEN IN WORDS LIKE SALESMEN.
THE MAN-EATING TIGER MANAGED ANYWAY TO MANGLE THE WOMAN'S MANDIBLE.
MAN MEN WOMAN WOMEN MAN WOMAN MAN MEN WOMAN WOMEN MAN MEN WOMAN WOMEN MAN MEN
MENMENMENMENMENMENMENMENMENMENMENMEN
```

Figure 17.19   Output from Program P17-04.

```
          TEXT EDITOR

MANY DISTINCTLY HUMAN ACTIVITIES EMANATED FROM ERAS AS DISTANT AS CAVEMAN DAYS.
PERSONY DISTINCTLY HUPERSON ACTIVITIES EPERSONATED FROM ERAS AS DISTANT AS CAVEPERSON DAYS.

MEN AND WOMEN ENGAGED IN MENDING, MANUFACTURING, AND MENTAL MANIPULATIONS.
PERSONS AND WOPERSONS ENGAGED IN PERSONSDING, PERSONUFACTURING, AND PERSONSTAL PERSONIPULATIONS.

USE MANKIND, HUMANS, OR HUMANKIND INSTEAD OF MAN OR MEN IN WORDS LIKE SALESMEN.
USE PERSONKIND, HUPERSONS, OR HUPERSONKIND INSTEAD OF PERSON OR PERSONS IN WORDS LIKE SALESPERSONS.

THE MAN-EATING TIGER MANAGED ANYWAY TO MANGLE THE WOMAN'S MANDIBLE.
THE PERSON-EATING TIGER PERSONAGED ANYWAY TO PERSONGLE THE WOPERSON'S PERSONDIBLE.

MAN MEN WOMAN WOMEN MAN WOMAN MAN MEN WOMAN WOMEN MAN MEN WOMAN WOMEN MAN MEN
PERSON PERSONS WOPERSON WOPERSONS PERSON WOPERSON PERSON PERSONS WOPERSON WOPERSONS PERSON PERSONS WO CHARACTERS MISSING

MENMENMENMENMENMENMENMENMENMENMENMEN
PERSONSPERSONSPERSONSPERSONSPERSONSPERSONSPERSONSPERSONSPERSONSPERSONSPERSONS              CHARACTERS MISSING
```

Using the INSPECT Verb

Program P17-04 has one slight defect that is not likely to be encountered in any practical use of the program. You can see in Figure 17.19 that under certain unusual conditions Program P17-04 finds that the edited line is too big to fit within the 120 character positions allowed, even though all of the characters beyond the 120th are only trailing blanks. Program P17-04 nonetheless inserts the message CHARACTERS MISSING, even though the only ones that are missing are blanks. One way to handle this matter involves the use of the **INSPECT** verb.

The INSPECT verb has a complicated format and a lot of capabilities. In general, the INSPECT verb examines a field from left to right looking for characters or groups of characters that are specified by the programmer. The INSPECT verb can be directed to look for ALL appearances of a character or group of characters, or only **LEADING** appearances (as with LEADING SPACES or LEADING ZEROS). The INSPECT verb can be directed to confine its search to only a particular portion of the field, BEFORE or AFTER the first appearance of some other character or group of characters.

Once the searched-for characters or groups of characters are found, the INSPECT verb can be directed to either count them, replace them with some other specified characters or groups of characters, or first count them and then replace them.

We will now modify Program P17-04 so that after each input record is read and before it is unstrung, it will have all of its trailing blanks replaced with HIGH-VALUES. Then the UNSTRING statement can break down the input record UNTIL it encounters the first HIGH-VALUE. In that way the trailing blanks will not be processed as a line segment and will cause no trouble.

Since the INSPECT verb can replace LEADING SPACES but not trailing ones, we will have to reverse the order of the characters in the input record before using INSPECT. That is, we will have to place column 80 into column 1, column 79 into column 2, column 78 into column 3, and so on, replace LEADING SPACES with HIGH-VALUES, and then put the record right end forward again for UN-STRINGing.

Program P17-05 is shown in Figure 17.20. Several changes have been made from Program P17-04. The input record has now been defined as 80 individual characters, at lines 00300 and 00310. This has been done so that the program can reverse the order of the characters in the record one at a time. An END-OF-LINE-

Figure 17.20 Program P17-05.

```
CB1 RELEASE 2.4                              IBM OS/VS COBOL   JULY  1, 1982


                        23.35.18        APR 12,1988


00010   IDENTIFICATION DIVISION.
00020   PROGRAM-ID.  P17-05.
00030 *
00040 *     THIS PROGRAM EDITS ENGLISH TEXT, REPLACING ALL
00050 *     APPEARANCES OF MAN WITH PERSON AND ALL APPEARANCES
00060 *     OF MEN WITH PERSONS.
00070 *     BEFORE EDITING AN INPUT RECORD, THE PROGRAM REPLACES
00080 *     TRAILING BLANKS WITH HIGH-VALUES.
00090 *
00100 *****************************************************************
00110
00120   ENVIRONMENT DIVISION.
00130   CONFIGURATION SECTION.
00140   SOURCE-COMPUTER.  IBM-370.
00150   OBJECT-COMPUTER.  IBM-370.
00160
00170   INPUT-OUTPUT SECTION.
00180   FILE-CONTROL.
00190       SELECT TEXT-FILE-OUT  ASSIGN TO PRINTER.
00200       SELECT TEXT-FILE-IN   ASSIGN TO INFILE.
00210
00220 *****************************************************************
00230
00240   DATA DIVISION.
00250   FILE SECTION.
00260   FD  TEXT-FILE-IN
00270       RECORD CONTAINS 80 CHARACTERS
00280       LABEL RECORDS ARE OMITTED.
```

```
00290
00300    01    TEXT-RECORD-IN.
00310          05    TEXT-CHARACTER-IN OCCURS 80 TIMES   PIC X.
00320
00330    FD    TEXT-FILE-OUT
00340          LABEL RECORDS ARE OMITTED.
00350
00360    01    TEXT-RECORD-OUT                           PIC X(120).
00370
00380    WORKING-STORAGE SECTION.
00390    01    MORE-INPUT              VALUE "Y"      PIC X(3).
00400    01    EDITED-LINE                            PIC X(120).
00410    01    END-OF-LINE-FLAG                       PIC X.
00420    01    LINE-BREAKDOWN.
00430          05    SEGMENT-DATA OCCURS 27 TIMES INDEXED BY SEGMENT-NUMBER.
00440                10   LINE-SEGMENT              PIC X(81).
00450                10   SEGMENT-LENGTH    COMP SYNC   PIC S99.
00460                10   DELIMITER-W               PIC X(7).
00470
00480    01    SIZES-AND-NUMBERS          COMP.
00490          05    SIZE-OF-INPUT-RECORD      VALUE 80      PIC S99.
00500          05    SIZE-OF-EDITED-LINE       VALUE 120     PIC S999.
00510          05    NUMBER-OF-SEGMENTS                      PIC S99.
00520
00530    01    POINTERS                   COMP.
00540          05    INPUT-RECORD-POINTER                   PIC S99.
00550          05    EDITED-LINE-POINTER                    PIC S999.
00560          05    INPUT-CHARACTER-SUBSCRIPT              PIC S99.
00570          05    REVERSED-CHARACTER-SUBSCRIPT           PIC S99.
00580
00590    01    REVERSED-INPUT-RECORD.
00600          05    REVERSED-CHARACTER OCCURS 80 TIMES         PIC X.
00610
00620    01    REPORT-HEADING.
00630          05    FILLER       VALUE SPACES         PIC X(27).
00640          05    FILLER       VALUE "TEXT EDITOR"  PIC X(11).
00650
00660    01    TEXT-LINE-OUT                           PIC X(80).
00670    01    EDITED-LINE-OUT                         PIC X(120).
00680
00690    01    NO-INPUT-DATA.
00700          05    FILLER       VALUE SPACES         PIC X(9).
00710          05    FILLER       VALUE "NO INPUT DATA"  PIC X(13).
00720
00730    **********************************************************************
00740
00750    PROCEDURE DIVISION.
00760    CONTROL-PARAGRAPH.
00770          PERFORM INITIALIZATION.
00780          PERFORM DESEX-A-LINE UNTIL MORE-INPUT = "N".
00790          PERFORM TERMINATION.
00800          STOP RUN.
00810
00820    INITIALIZATION.
00830          OPEN INPUT   TEXT-FILE-IN
00840               OUTPUT  TEXT-FILE-OUT.
00850          READ TEXT-FILE-IN
00860              AT END
00870                  MOVE "N" TO MORE-INPUT.
00880          WRITE TEXT-RECORD-OUT FROM REPORT-HEADING AFTER PAGE.
00890          IF MORE-INPUT = "N"
00900              WRITE TEXT-RECORD-OUT FROM NO-INPUT-DATA AFTER 3.
00910
```

(continued)

FLAG has been established, at line 00410, to detect the HIGH-VALUE that signals the end of an input record. A new 80-character area has been established in working storage, lines 00590 and 00600, for assigning the input record characters in reverse order.

Figure 17.20   (continued)

```
00920  DESEX-A-LINE.
00930      PERFORM INITIALIZE-FOR-LINE.
00940      PERFORM UNSTRING-ENTIRE-LINE
00950          VARYING SEGMENT-NUMBER FROM 1 BY 1 UNTIL
00960              INPUT-RECORD-POINTER GREATER THAN
00970                                  SIZE-OF-INPUT-RECORD OR
00980              END-OF-LINE-FLAG        = HIGH-VALUE.
00990      PERFORM PROCESS-PIECES-OF-LINE
01000          VARYING SEGMENT-NUMBER FROM 1 BY 1 UNTIL
01010              SEGMENT-NUMBER GREATER THAN NUMBER-OF-SEGMENTS.
01020      PERFORM STRING-ENTIRE-LINE
01030          VARYING SEGMENT-NUMBER FROM 1 BY 1 UNTIL
01040              SEGMENT-NUMBER GREATER THAN NUMBER-OF-SEGMENTS OR
01050              EDITED-LINE-POINTER
01060                                  GREATER THAN SIZE-OF-EDITED-LINE.
01070      PERFORM PRINT-A-LINE.
01080      READ TEXT-FILE-IN
01090          AT END
01100              MOVE "N" TO MORE-INPUT.
01110
01120  INITIALIZE-FOR-LINE.
01130      PERFORM REPLACE-TRAILING-BLANKS.
01140      MOVE SPACES TO EDITED-LINE
01150                     END-OF-LINE-FLAG.
01160      MOVE 0 TO NUMBER-OF-SEGMENTS.
01170      MOVE 1 TO INPUT-RECORD-POINTER
01180                EDITED-LINE-POINTER.
01190
01200  REPLACE-TRAILING-BLANKS.
01210      PERFORM REVERSE-RECORD
01220          VARYING INPUT-CHARACTER-SUBSCRIPT FROM 1 BY 1 UNTIL
01230              INPUT-CHARACTER-SUBSCRIPT GREATER THAN
01240                                  SIZE-OF-INPUT-RECORD.
01250      INSPECT REVERSED-INPUT-RECORD REPLACING
01260          LEADING SPACES BY HIGH-VALUES.
01270      PERFORM RESTORE-RECORD
01280          VARYING REVERSED-CHARACTER-SUBSCRIPT FROM 1 BY 1 UNTIL
01290              REVERSED-CHARACTER-SUBSCRIPT GREATER THAN
01300                                  SIZE-OF-INPUT-RECORD.
01310
01320  REVERSE-RECORD.
01330      COMPUTE REVERSED-CHARACTER-SUBSCRIPT =
01340          SIZE-OF-INPUT-RECORD - INPUT-CHARACTER-SUBSCRIPT.
01350      MOVE TEXT-CHARACTER-IN (INPUT-CHARACTER-SUBSCRIPT) TO
01360          REVERSED-CHARACTER (REVERSED-CHARACTER-SUBSCRIPT).
01370
01380  RESTORE-RECORD.
01390      COMPUTE INPUT-CHARACTER-SUBSCRIPT =
01400          SIZE-OF-INPUT-RECORD - REVERSED-CHARACTER-SUBSCRIPT.
01410      MOVE REVERSED-CHARACTER (REVERSED-CHARACTER-SUBSCRIPT) TO
01420          TEXT-CHARACTER-IN (INPUT-CHARACTER-SUBSCRIPT).
01430
01440  UNSTRING-ENTIRE-LINE.
01450      UNSTRING TEXT-RECORD-IN
01460          DELIMITED BY "MAN" OR "MEN" OR HIGH-VALUE
01470              INTO LINE-SEGMENT (SEGMENT-NUMBER)
01480                  DELIMITER DELIMITER-W    (SEGMENT-NUMBER)
01490                  COUNT       SEGMENT-LENGTH (SEGMENT-NUMBER)
01500          POINTER INPUT-RECORD-POINTER
01510          TALLYING NUMBER-OF-SEGMENTS.
01520      MOVE DELIMITER-W (SEGMENT-NUMBER) TO END-OF-LINE-FLAG.
01530
01540  PROCESS-PIECES-OF-LINE.
01550      PERFORM DELIMIT-LINE-SEGMENT.
01560      PERFORM REPLACE-MAN-AND-MEN.
01570
01580  DELIMIT-LINE-SEGMENT.
01590      ADD 1 TO SEGMENT-LENGTH (SEGMENT-NUMBER).
01600      STRING HIGH-VALUE DELIMITED BY SIZE
01610          INTO LINE-SEGMENT (SEGMENT-NUMBER)
01620          POINTER SEGMENT-LENGTH (SEGMENT-NUMBER).
01630
```

```
01640    REPLACE-MAN-AND-MEN.
01650        IF DELIMITER-W (SEGMENT-NUMBER) = "MAN"
01660            MOVE "PERSON" TO DELIMITER-W (SEGMENT-NUMBER)
01670        ELSE
01680        IF DELIMITER-W (SEGMENT-NUMBER) = "MEN"
01690            MOVE "PERSONS" TO DELIMITER-W (SEGMENT-NUMBER).
01700
01710    STRING-ENTIRE-LINE.
01720        STRING LINE-SEGMENT (SEGMENT-NUMBER) DELIMITED BY HIGH-VALUE
01730              DELIMITER-W  (SEGMENT-NUMBER) DELIMITED BY SPACE
01740            INTO EDITED-LINE
01750            POINTER EDITED-LINE-POINTER
01760            OVERFLOW
01770                MOVE 102 TO EDITED-LINE-POINTER
01780                STRING " CHARACTERS MISSING" DELIMITED BY SIZE
01790                    INTO EDITED-LINE
01800                    POINTER EDITED-LINE-POINTER.
01810
01820    PRINT-A-LINE.
01830        INSPECT TEXT-RECORD-IN REPLACING
01840            ALL HIGH-VALUES BY SPACES.
01850        INSPECT EDITED-LINE REPLACING
01860            ALL HIGH-VALUES BY SPACES.
01890        WRITE TEXT-RECORD-OUT FROM TEXT-RECORD-IN AFTER 3.
01900        WRITE TEXT-RECORD-OUT FROM EDITED-LINE.
01910
01920    TERMINATION.
01930        CLOSE TEXT-FILE-IN
01940             TEXT-FILE-OUT.
```

In the Procedure Division, a new condition has been included in the PER-FORM statement at line 00940. Now, UNSTRING-ENTIRE-LINE ceases executing either when the input record has been entirely unstrung or when HIGH-VALUE is found, whichever happens first.

The new process of replacing trailing blanks in each input record with HIGH-VALUES has been inserted in the paragraph INITIALIZE-FOR-LINE. The PER-FORM statement at line 01130 carries it out.

There are three INSPECT statements in this program. The one at line 01250 replaces LEADING SPACES in the reversed input record with HIGH-VALUES. All the words in that statement are reserved words except REVERSED-INPUT-RECORD. The other INSPECT statements, at lines 01830 through 01860, replace with SPACES any HIGH-VALUES that may have been left in the print lines by earlier processing. All the words in those two statements are reserved words except TEXT-RECORD-IN and EDITED-LINE.

Program P17-05 was run with the same input data as Program P17-04. Program P17-05 produced the output shown in Figure 17.21.

Figure 17.21 Output from Program P17-05.

```
                    TEXT EDITOR

MANY DISTINCTLY HUMAN ACTIVITIES EMANATED FROM ERAS AS DISTANT AS CAVEMAN DAYS.
PERSONY DISTINCTLY HUPERSON ACTIVITIES EPERSONATED FROM ERAS AS DISTANT AS CAVEPERSON DAYS.


MEN AND WOMEN ENGAGED IN MENDING, MANUFACTURING, AND MENTAL MANIPULATIONS.
PERSONS AND WOPERSONS ENGAGED IN PERSONSDING, PERSONUFACTURING, AND PERSONSTAL PERSONIPULATIONS.


USE MANKIND, HUMANS, OR HUMANKIND INSTEAD OF MAN OR MEN IN WORDS LIKE SALESMEN.
USE PERSONKIND, HUPERSONS, OR HUPERSONKIND INSTEAD OF PERSON OR PERSONS IN WORDS LIKE SALESPERSONS.


THE MAN-EATING TIGER MANAGED ANYWAY TO MANGLE THE WOMAN'S MANDIBLE.
THE PERSON-EATING TIGER PERSONAGED ANYWAY TO PERSONGLE THE WOPERSON'S PERSONDIBLE.


MAN MEN WOMAN WOMEN MAN WOMAN MAN MEN WOMAN WOMEN MAN MEN WOMAN WOMEN MAN MEN
PERSON PERSONS WOPERSON WOPERSONS PERSON WOPERSON PERSON PERSONS WOPERSON WOPERSONS PERSON PERSONS WO CHARACTERS MISSING


MENMENMENMENMENMENMENMENMENMENMEN
PERSONSPERSONSPERSONSPERSONSPERSONSPERSONSPERSONSPERSONSPERSONSPERSONSPERSONS
```

The INSPECT Statement

The format of the INSPECT statement is:

```
INSPECT identifier-1
  [TALLYING  {, identifier-2
        ┌ ┌ALL    ┐  ┌identifier-3┐
   FOR{,│ │LEADING│  │literal-1   │
        │ └───────┘  └────────────┘
        │ CHARACTERS
        │                                              ┐
        │  ┌ ┌BEFORE┐           ┌identifier-4┐  ┐      │
        │  │ │AFTER │  INITIAL  │literal-2   │  │  ... │ ... ]
        └  └ └──────┘           └────────────┘  ┘      ┘
  [REPLACING
        ┌                                                  ┐
        │ CHARACTERS  BY    ┌identifier-6┐                 │
        │                   │literal-4   │                 │
        │                   └────────────┘                 │
        │   ┌ ┌BEFORE┐           ┌identifier-7┐  ┐         │
        │   │ │AFTER │  INITIAL  │literal-5   │  │         │
        │   └ └──────┘           └────────────┘  ┘        [│]
        │ ┌ALL    ┐  ┌ ┌identifier-5┐      ┌identifier-6┐ ┐│
        │{,│LEADING│  │ │literal-3   │  BY  │literal-4   │ │{│]
        │ │FIRST  │  │ └────────────┘      └────────────┘ ┘│
        │ └───────┘                                        │
        │   ┌ ┌BEFORE┐           ┌identifier-7┐            │
        │   │ │AFTER │  INITIAL  │literal-5   │  ]} ...} ...│
        └   └ └──────┘           └────────────┘            ┘
```

    An INSPECT statement must contain either a TALLYING option or a **REPLACING** option, or both. If both are specified, all TALLYING is done before any replacement is made.

    Identifier-1 is the INSPECTed item. It must be of USAGE DISPLAY. All other identifiers, except identifier-2 (the count field) must be elementary items of USAGE DISPLAY. Each literal must be nonnumeric. Any figurative constant may be used except ALL literal.

    The TALLYING option is used to count ALL the appearances or just the LEADING appearances of literal-1 or the contents of identifier-3 in the INSPECTed field, or all **CHARACTERS** in the INSPECTed field. Optionally, the counting can be restricted to that portion of the INSPECTed field BEFORE or AFTER the **INITIAL** appearance of identifier-4 or literal-2.

    An INSPECT statement may have no more than one TALLYING phrase. It may have as many count fields as desired, and each count field may serve to count as many different identifiers or literals as desired.

    The REPLACING option is used to replace all CHARACTERS in the INSPECTed field BY literal-4 or the contents of identifier-6; or to replace ALL appearances, just the LEADING appearances, or just the **FIRST** appearance of literal-3 or the contents of identifier-5 in the INSPECTed field BY literal-4 or the contents of identifier-6. Optionally, replacement can be limited to that portion of the INSPECTed field BEFORE or AFTER the INITIAL appearance of literal-5 or the contents of identifier-7 in the INSPECTed field.

EXERCISE 5

Do the following:

a. Write an INSPECT statement that will count all appearances of the character M in the field WORD-2 and place the count into the field COUNT-2.

b. Write an INSPECT statement that will replace all appearances of leading zeros with the character F after the first appearance of the character M in WORD-3.

c. Write an INSPECT statement that will replace all appearances of the character B with the character H before the first appearance of the character Y in the field WORD-4.

d. Write an INSPECT statement that will count the number of characters in the field WORD-5 after the first appearance of the character K and place the count into the field COUNT-5.

Summary

The STRING verb enables COBOL to attach two or more fields or parts of fields end to end to form one large field. A STRING statement must have at least one sending field and exactly one receiving field; it may have as many sending fields as desired. Any combination of whole fields and parts of fields may be used as sending fields in a single STRING statement. Parts of fields to be sent may be DELIMITED BY one or more characters selected by the programmer. The STRING statement may use an optional POINTER field to keep track of the next available unused character position in the receiving field. An optional OVERFLOW phrase may be used to handle situations where all the sending fields together are too big to fit into the receiving field.

The UNSTRING verb can be used to break down a large field into smaller pieces. An UNSTRING statement must have exactly one sending field and at least one receiving field; it may have as many receiving fields as desired. An UNSTRING statement may have one DELIMITED BY clause, which must contain one or more delimiters. If the DELIMITED BY clause is used, the sending field is broken into pieces based on the appearances of the delimiter(s) in the sending field. For each piece of the sending field that is placed into a receiving field, the UNSTRING statement can also store the associated DELIMITER and a COUNT of the size of the piece.

If the DELIMITED BY phrase is not used, the UNSTRING statement breaks down the sending field on the basis of the sizes of the receiving fields. The DELIMITER and COUNT phrases may not be used when the DELIMITED BY phrase is omitted.

The TALLYING phrase may be used to obtain a count of the number of receiving fields that have data MOVEd to them. The UNSTRING statement does not zero out the TALLYING field but instead adds to its previous contents. An optional POINTER field may be used to keep track of the next character to be scanned in the sending field. An optional OVERFLOW phrase can be used to handle situations where the sending field is too large to fit into all the receiving fields.

The INSPECT verb examines a field from left to right, looking for characters or groups of characters specified by the programmer, and counts and/or replaces them when found. An INSPECT statement can look for ALL appearances of the searched-for character or characters, or it can look only for LEADING appearances. An INSPECT statement can be directed to confine its search to a particular portion of the field, BEFORE or AFTER the first appearance of some character or group of characters.

Fill-in Exercises

1. A STRING statement has exactly one _____ field.

2. The _____ fields in a STRING statement can all use the same _____ clause, or they may use separate ones.

3. The OVERFLOW phrase in a STRING statement handles situations where all the _____ fields cannot fit into the _____ field.

4. The POINTER in a STRING statement keeps track of the next _____ in the _____ field.

5. An UNSTRING statement has exactly one _____ field.

6. The delimiters in the DELIMITED BY clause of an UNSTRING statement are separated by the word _____ .

7. The OVERFLOW phrase in an UNSTRING statement handles situations where the _____ field cannot fit into all the _____ fields.

8. The POINTER in an UNSTRING statement keeps track of the next _____ in the _____ field.

9. The TALLYING phrase in an UNSTRING statement counts the number of _____ fields that have data MOVEd to them.

10. The INSPECT statement examines fields from _____ to _____ .

11. The _____ and _____ statements can operate on the basis of delimiters or field sizes, but not both.

12. If an INSPECT statement contains both a TALLYING option and a REPLACING option, all _____ is done before any _____ is done.

13. If the DELIMITER IN option is used in an UNSTRING statement and no delimiter is found in the sending field, the field named in the DELIMITER IN phrase is filled with _____ or _____ .

14. A STRING statement must have at least one _____ field, and may have as many as desired.

15. An UNSTRING statement must have at least one _____ field, and may have as many as desired.

Review Exercises

1. Write a program to read four-digit numbers with two decimal places and print the amount in words. Typical input and output are shown in Figure 17.RE1.

2. Write a program to read and process input records, each record containing three unsigned integers separated from one another by one blank. The first integer starts in column 1 and the integers may be from 1 to 5 digits in length. For each record read, have your program UNSTRING and ADD the three integers, and print on one line the three integers and their sum.

3. Modify Program P17-05 so that only if a blank or period follows MAN will it be replaced by PERSON, and only if a blank or period follows MEN will it be replaced by PERSONS. The change improves the program somewhat but still leaves it far from perfect.

4. Do the following:
   a. Write an INSPECT statement that will replace all appearances of the character B with the character C after the first appearance of the character K.
   b. Write an INSPECT statement that will replace all appearances of Y by X, Z by B, and Q by W after the first appearance of the character S.
   c. Write an INSPECT statement that will replace all characters before the first appearance of the character B with the character C.

Project

Write a program to read name and address records in the format shown on page 352. There may be three, four, or five input records for a single name and address. The first input record for each name and address contains a Code 1 in position 1. Have your program strip the trailing blanks from each input record and STRING together and print the records for a single name and address separated by asterisks. For example, the three input records

```
1Gary S. Popkin
21921 President Street
3Brooklyn, NY 11221
```

should produce the following output:

```
Gary S. Popkin*1921 President Street*Brooklyn, NY 11221
```

Figure 17.RE1 Output format for Review Exercise 1.

Subprograms

Here are the key points you should learn from this chapter:

1. The several ways that subprograms are useful
2. How to write a subprogram in COBOL
3. How to link a subprogram to a calling program

Key words to recognize and learn:

subprogram	LINKAGE SECTION
calling program	EXIT PROGRAM
called program	CALL
call	calling sequence
main program	last-used state
link	CANCEL
run unit	

A **subprogram,** in any programming language, is a program that cannot be executed by itself but must execute under control of some other program. A program that controls the execution of a subprogram is referred to as a **calling program.** The subprogram itself is sometimes referred to as the **called program.** We say that the calling program **calls** the subprogram.

A subprogram may itself control the execution of some other subprogram. In that case, the higher-level subprogram becomes a calling program for a lower-level subprogram. The highest-level program, the one that operates on its own and under the control of no other, is called a **main program.** All the programs we have seen so far in this book are main programs. A hierarchy of programs is shown in Figure 18.1.

Figure 18.1 Hierarchy of calling programs and called programs.

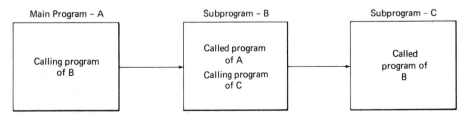

The Uses of Subprograms

There are about four main reasons why a computer installation might use subprograms written in COBOL. Different installations would find these four different reasons to have different degrees of importance.

First, a subprogram is portable. That is, it can be hooked on to, or **linked,** to whatever calling program needs it. To see how this feature can be useful, imagine a computer installation where many programmers are working on a large payroll system that contains many dozens of programs. Some of the programs might process only hourly-paid employees, some of the programs might process only employees paid semimonthly, and some might process all others. Several programs in the system might need to be able to compute employee withholding taxes. It would be very useful if a single routine could be written that would compute withholding taxes and that it be hooked on to each of the programs in the system that needed it. By writing the routine as a subprogram, exactly that result can be accomplished. In general, any procedure that is carried out by several programs should be written as a subprogram and made available to any program that needs it.

Another reason for using subprograms arises when a very large program is to be written. Often, such a program will be tested piece by piece. As each piece is found to work there is no need to test it further. Thus one piece of the program can be written as a main program and all the other pieces as subprograms. Each subprogram can be tested separately, without the need to recompile and retest other portions of the program that are known to work. When all the pieces of the program have been tested, they can be linked together and tested as a single **run unit.**

Later, if a modification needs to be made to this giant program, perhaps all the changes can be confined to just one or two of the subprograms in the run unit. Then it would be necessary to recompile and test only the subprograms that were changed. The remainder of the program, known to be working, would be left untouched.

A third reason for the use of subprograms is related to the second. Some programmers and managers think that breaking a big program into subprograms encourages good programming habits. They are probably right, though a programmer who is determined to make a mess of a program cannot be wholly stopped.

The final reason to use subprograms occurs when more than one language is needed to write a program. This can happen if a program written mainly in COBOL needs some coding in another language to carry out some processing that is either inconvenient or impossible in COBOL. Then a subprogram could be written in the other language and linked to a COBOL calling program. It can also happen that a program written mainly in some language other than COBOL would like to use some COBOL feature. Then a COBOL subprogram could be written and linked to a calling program in the other language.

EXERCISE 1

Try to think of other procedures such as the preceding withholding tax example, that would be useful in more than one program and that should be written as subprograms. What about some of the procedures in the COBOL programs you have written? Are any of them used in more than one program? If you were to write any of those procedures as a subprogram, do you think there might be students in other COBOL classes in your school who could use your subprogram in their programs? And what about students who are going to take this course next year. Could they use your subprogram? Could students who are studying COBOL at another college use it?

Passing Data Between Programs

A calling program and its subprograms are compiled separately. During their compilations, the programs have nothing to do with one another. They may use the same or different names for files, records, paragraphs, data items, anything, and the names in one program will not interfere with names in the other. When the programs are finally linked together to form a run unit, usually they must have some way of passing data between them. In the withholding tax example of the preceding section, a calling program would have to pass to its subprogram a worker's gross pay and perhaps some other data. After the subprogram computed the withholding tax, it would pass the results of its computation back to the calling program for further processing. The passing of data is accomplished not on the basis of the names that the data items have in the calling and called programs. You will see later how data are passed.

There can be situations where no data are passed between the calling program and the called program, and some where data are passed only one way — either from the calling program to the called program or from the called program to the calling program. It is this last case that we will see in our first example of a subprogram, Program P18-01.

Writing a Subprogram in COBOL

For this example, we will assume that a certain computer installation has many programs that need the time of day as one piece of data. Let's say that each of these programs prints the time of day as part of its output. Now, the COBOL statement "ACCEPT identifier FROM TIME" inserts the time of day into the field named as the identifier, but in a rather peculiar form, not a form that is suitable for printing directly onto an output report. So we can use a subprogram to ACCEPT the time of day, convert the TIME into printable form, and pass the printable time to any calling program that needs it.

The TIME, as provided by the ACCEPT statement, is an eight-digit field in the following form:

```
01  TIME-OF-DAY.
    05  HOUR              PIC 99.
    05  MINUTE            PIC 99.
    05  SECOND            PIC 99.
    05  100THS-OF-SECOND  PIC 99.
```

There is no punctuation in the field, and, to make matters worse, the HOUR field is given in 24-hour military time (0 hours to 23 hours). Thus 2:41 PM would be expressed in eight digits as 14410000. Let us say that we would like our subprogram to ACCEPT the time, convert the time to a printable format such as that shown in Table 18-1, and pass the whole printable field to a calling program. Seconds and hundredths of a second are to be ignored in printing the time.

Table 18-1
TIME as ACCEPTed into a COBOL program and in printable form.

Eight-digit Time	Printable Time
14410000	2:41 PM
02414567	2:41 AM
00101234	12:10 AM
00000000	12:00 AM
12000000	12:00 PM
12302345	12:30 PM
13450000	1:45 PM

You can see that converting the eight-digit time to printable form is not very easy. The program has to determine whether the time is AM or PM. That part is not too difficult, since all HOURs 0 through 11 are AM, and all HOURs 12 through 23 are PM. But then, if the time is PM, the program must adjust the HOUR figure to civilian time. Also, if the HOUR is 00, the program must print it as 12 AM (12 midnight). If the coding for this procedure had to appear in every program that prints the time, there would be a lot of unnecessary duplicate code.

Let us write this procedure as a subprogram so that it can be used by any calling program that needs it. Program P18-01A will be a calling program that we will write later to use the subprogram. Program P18-01B, which is shown in Figure 18.2, is the subprogram.

In the Environment Division, line 00100, there is no INPUT-OUTPUT SECTION. That is because this program uses no input or output files. It only ACCEPTs the TIME, prepares it for printing, and hands it to the calling program. The calling program can then do anything it likes with the field that it has been handed. The

Figure 18.2   Program P18-01B.

```
CB1 RELEASE 2.4                            IBM OS/VS COBOL   JULY  1, 1982


                      6.37.16         APR 13,1988


00010   IDENTIFICATION DIVISION.
00020   PROGRAM-ID.  P1801B.
00030 *
00040 *    THIS SUBPROGRAM ACCEPTS THE TIME OF DAY IN 8-DIGIT
00050 *    FORM AND CONVERTS IT TO HOURS AND MINUTES, AM OR PM,
00060 *    IGNORING SECONDS AND HUNDREDTHS OF A SECOND.
00070 *
00080 *******************************************************************
00090
00100   ENVIRONMENT DIVISION.
00110   CONFIGURATION SECTION.
00120   SOURCE-COMPUTER.  IBM-370.
00130   OBJECT-COMPUTER.  IBM-370.
00140
00150 *******************************************************************
00160
00170   DATA DIVISION.
00180   WORKING-STORAGE SECTION.
00190   01   TIME-OF-DAY-W.
00200        05   HOUR              PIC 99.
00210             88  AM       VALUES 0   THRU 11.
00220             88  PM       VALUES 12 THRU 23.
00230        05   MINUTE            PIC 99.
00240        05   FILLER            PIC 9(4).
00250
00260   LINKAGE SECTION.
00270   01   TIME-OF-DAY-L.
00280        05   HOUR              PIC Z9.
00290        05   COLON-L           PIC X.
00300        05   MINUTE            PIC 99.
00310        05   AM-OR-PM          PIC X(3).
00320
00330 *******************************************************************
00340
00350   PROCEDURE DIVISION USING TIME-OF-DAY-L.
00360   CONTROL-PARAGRAPH.
00370        ACCEPT TIME-OF-DAY-W FROM TIME.
00380        PERFORM SET-AM-OR-PM.
00390        PERFORM FIX-HOUR.
00400        MOVE CORR TIME-OF-DAY-W TO TIME-OF-DAY-L.
00410        MOVE ":" TO COLON-L.
00420        PERFORM EXECUTION-COMPLETE.
00430
```

(continued)

calling program will probably print it. The calling program will thus contain the definition of the output file.

In general, a subprogram can do anything that a main program can do. It can OPEN and CLOSE files, perform input and output operations, and have all of the same sections that a main program has. It just happens that this particular subprogram has no input or output operations to perform.

The Working Storage Section, line 00180, contains space for the TIME to be assigned to by the ACCEPT statement. TIME-OF-DAY-W, line 00190, is defined as eight digits long. Since we will not be using seconds or hundredths of a second in this program, the last four digits have been made FILLER.

The Linkage Section

The Data Division of this subprogram contains no File Section, for there are no files in this subprogram. There is a new section at line 00260, however, the **LINKAGE SECTION.** A Linkage Section may appear only in a subprogram. The Linkage Section may appear in the Data Division along with any of the other sections in that division. If used, the Linkage Section must appear after the Working Storage Section and before the Report Section.

The Linkage Section must contain the definitions of all data fields that are passed in either direction between the calling program and the called program. If no data are passed, the Linkage Section can be omitted. In this case, we want only to pass a printable time-of-day field to the calling program. This field is defined as TIME-OF-DAY-L, at line 00270. It consists of two characters for the HOUR, one character for a colon, two characters for the MINUTE, and three characters for a space and the letters AM or PM. This is the format of the field as it will be passed to the calling program, ready for printing by the calling program.

Any entries that are legal in the definitions of input and output records in the File Section may be used in the Linkage Section. This means that any PICTURE, OCCURS, REDEFINES, COMP, SYNC, and level-88 entries, among others, may be used. Especially important is the fact that the VALUE clause must not be used in the Linkage Section unless it is used in connection with a level-88 entry, as in the File Section.

Procedure Division USING

The Procedure Division header, line 00350, contains a USING phrase. A USING phrase must appear in the Procedure Division header of a called program whenever data are to be passed in either direction between the calling program and the called program. The USING phrase must name all of the data fields that are to be passed, or else name group-level items that include all the data fields that are to be passed. Here we list only TIME-OF-DAY-L in the USING phrase. TIME-OF-DAY-L is a group-level name that includes all the elementary fields that are to be passed to the calling program.

The remainder of the Procedure Division looks unusual because there is no initialization to be done and no repetitive loop to be PERFORMed. Instead, the TIME is ACCEPTed into TIME-OF-DAY-W and processed into printable form in TIME-OF-DAY-L.

Figure 18.2   (continued)

```
00440   EXECUTION-COMPLETE.
00450      EXIT PROGRAM.
00460
00470   SET-AM-OR-PM.
00480      IF AM
00490         MOVE " AM" TO AM-OR-PM
00500      ELSE
00510         MOVE " PM" TO AM-OR-PM.
00520
00530   FIX-HOUR.
00540      IF PM
00550         SUBTRACT 12 FROM HOUR OF TIME-OF-DAY-W.
00560      IF HOUR OF TIME-OF-DAY-W IS EQUAL TO 0
00570         MOVE 12 TO HOUR OF TIME-OF-DAY-W.
```

The **EXIT PROGRAM** statement at line 00450 terminates execution of this subprogram. Execution of a subprogram may be terminated with an EXIT PROGRAM statement or a STOP RUN statement. An EXIT PROGRAM statement returns control to the calling program and permits further processing. A STOP RUN statement, as usual, terminates the run unit. An EXIT PROGRAM statement must be the only statement in the paragraph in which it appears. Thus the EXIT PROGRAM statement in this subprogram is in its own paragraph, which here is EXECUTION-COMPLETE. The PERFORM statement in line 00420 is not strictly needed, because the flow of execution in COBOL programs proceeds from one paragraph to the next in the absence of any procedure branching statements such as PERFORM, STOP RUN, GO TO, or EXIT PROGRAM. The PERFORM statement was included here only for consistency of programming style.

Writing a Calling Program

Now that we have a subprogram that can provide the time of day to any calling program, let us write a calling program to use the subprogram. The calling program can be as complicated as we like. It can do any kind of processing, and when it needs the time of day, it can call upon the subprogram to provide it. Since right now we are mainly interested in seeing how the subprogram works, we can make our calling program very simple. The simplest possible calling program would be one that just has the subprogram hand the time of day to it, and then prints it. But to check that the subprogram is converting the time correctly, we will have our calling program do two things. It will call upon the subprogram to provide the time of day in printable form, and it will also ACCEPT the time of day itself and print the time in eight-digit form. Then we will be able to see whether the subprogram is doing the time conversion correctly. Program P18-01A, the calling program, will produce its output in the format shown in Figure 18.3.

Figure 18.3   Output format for Program P18-01A.

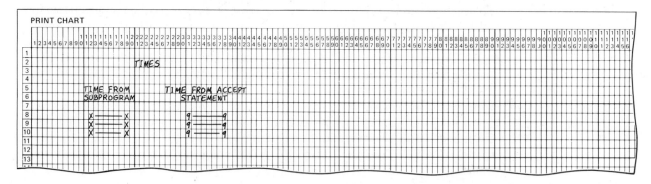

Program P18-01A is shown in Figure 18.4. PRINTABLE-TIME, line 00300, is the field that gets handed to Program P18-01A by the subprogram. In the print line, PRINTABLE-TIME-OUT, line 00480 gets the printable time MOVEd to it from PRINTABLE-TIME, and the field TIME-OF-DAY-OUT, line 00500, is used by Program P18-01A to ACCEPT the TIME into. Notice that we could choose the names of these fields in the main program without regard to what names were used in the subprogram. The field that is passed from the subprogram to the main program is called PRINTABLE-TIME in the main program and TIME-OF-DAY-L in the subprogram. This shows that the names in the main programs and subprograms are unrelated.

Figure 18.4 Program P18-01A.

```
CB1 RELEASE 2.4                              IBM OS/VS COBOL   JULY  1, 1982


                        6.37.15         APR 13,1988


00010   IDENTIFICATION DIVISION.
00020   PROGRAM-ID.  P1801A.
00030 *
00040 *     THIS MAIN PROGRAM OBTAINS THE TIME OF DAY IN PRINTABLE
00050 *     FORM FROM SUBPROGRAM P1801B AND PRINTS IT.  IT ALSO OBTAINS
00060 *     THE 8-DIGIT TIME VIA AN ACCEPT STATEMENT AND PRINTS IT.
00070 *
00080 ***************************************************************
00090
00100   ENVIRONMENT DIVISION.
00110   CONFIGURATION SECTION.
00120   SOURCE-COMPUTER.  IBM-370.
00130   OBJECT-COMPUTER.  IBM-370.
00140
00150   INPUT-OUTPUT SECTION.
00160   FILE-CONTROL.
00170       SELECT TIME-FILE-OUT ASSIGN TO PRINTER.
00180
00190 ***************************************************************
00200
00210   DATA DIVISION.
00220   FILE SECTION.
00230   FD  TIME-FILE-OUT
00240       LABEL RECORDS ARE OMITTED.
00250
00260   01  TIME-RECORD-OUT           PIC X(42).
00270
00280   WORKING-STORAGE SECTION.
00290   01  BLANK-LINE                PIC X       VALUE SPACE.
00300   01  PRINTABLE-TIME            PIC X(8).
00310
00320   01  REPORT-HEADING-1.
00330       05  FILLER                PIC X(20) VALUE SPACES.
00340       05  FILLER                PIC X(50) VALUE "TIMES".
00350
00360   01  REPORT-HEADING-2.
00370       05  FILLER                PIC X(10) VALUE SPACES.
00380       05  FILLER                PIC X(16) VALUE "TIME FROM".
00390       05  FILLER                PIC X(16) VALUE "TIME FROM ACCEPT".
00400
00410   01  REPORT-HEADING-3.
00420       05  FILLER                PIC X(10) VALUE SPACES.
00430       05  FILLER                PIC X(19) VALUE "SUBPROGRAM".
00440       05  FILLER                PIC X(9)  VALUE "STATEMENT".
00450
00460   01  DETAIL-LINE.
00470       05  FILLER                PIC X(11) VALUE SPACES.
00480       05  PRINTABLE-TIME-OUT    PIC X(8).
00490       05  FILLER                PIC X(11) VALUE SPACES.
00500       05  TIME-OF-DAY-OUT       PIC 9(8).
00510
00520 ***************************************************************
00530
```

(continued)

Figure 18.4   (continued)

```
00540    PROCEDURE DIVISION.
00550    CONTROL-PARAGRAPH.
00560        PERFORM INITIALIZATION.
00570        PERFORM PRINT-TIME 35 TIMES.
00580        PERFORM TERMINATION.
00590        STOP RUN.
00600
00610    INITIALIZATION.
00620        OPEN OUTPUT TIME-FILE-OUT.
00630        WRITE TIME-RECORD-OUT FROM REPORT-HEADING-1 AFTER PAGE.
00640        WRITE TIME-RECORD-OUT FROM REPORT-HEADING-2 AFTER 3.
00650        WRITE TIME-RECORD-OUT FROM REPORT-HEADING-3.
00660        WRITE TIME-RECORD-OUT FROM BLANK-LINE.
00670
00680    PRINT-TIME.
00690        ACCEPT TIME-OF-DAY-OUT FROM TIME.
00700        CALL "P1801B" USING PRINTABLE-TIME.
00710        MOVE PRINTABLE-TIME TO PRINTABLE-TIME-OUT.
00720        WRITE TIME-RECORD-OUT FROM DETAIL-LINE.
00730
00740    TERMINATION.
00750        CLOSE TIME-FILE-OUT.
```

In the Procedure Division, line 00540, we execute the main loop, PRINT-TIME, enough TIMES to see what it is doing. PRINT-TIME, line 00680, ACCEPTs the TIME into TIME-OF-DAY-OUT and also calls upon the subprogram to provide the time in printable form. The **CALL** statement at line 00700 transfers control to the subprogram.

Following the word CALL you may have the PROGRAM-ID of the subprogram, in quotation marks. Then a USING phrase must follow, if any data are to be passed in either direction between the calling program and the called program. The USING phrase must contain the names of all the data fields that are to be passed or else name group-level items that include all the data fields that are to be passed. When there is only one item in the USING phrase of the CALL statement, as in this case, it must be defined as being the same length as the field named in the USING phrase of the Procedure Division header in the called program. Here, both are eight-character fields. The items named in the USING phrase of a CALL statement or a Procedure Division header must all be at the 01 level.

Execution of an EXIT PROGRAM statement in a subprogram returns control to the statement in the calling program immediately following the CALL. In our case, the EXIT PROGRAM statement in the subprogram returns control to the MOVE statement at line 00710. Execution proceeds normally in the calling program.

Program P18-01B was linked to Program P18-01A one morning and run as a single run unit. The output shown in Figure 18.5 was produced. This is hardly an adequate test of the subprogram. The program would have to be run morning, noon, and night (and at midnight) for a more thorough check. The output does show the speed of execution of the program, though. At least 35 lines of output were produced inside of 0.01 second.

Figure 18.5 Output produced by a run unit consisting of Programs P18-01A and P18-01B.

```
              TIMES

TIME FROM          TIME FROM ACCEPT
SUBPROGRAM            STATEMENT

  6:37 AM            06371965
  6:37 AM            06371965
  6:37 AM            06371965
  6:37 AM            06371965
  6:37 AM            06371965
  6:37 AM            06371965
  6:37 AM            06371965
  6:37 AM            06371965
  6:37 AM            06371965
  6:37 AM            06371965
  6:37 AM            06371965
  6:37 AM            06371965
  6:37 AM            06371965
  6:37 AM            06371965
  6:37 AM            06371965
  6:37 AM            06371965
  6:37 AM            06371965
  6:37 AM            06371965
  6:37 AM            06371965
  6:37 AM            06371965
  6:37 AM            06371965
  6:37 AM            06371965
  6:37 AM            06371965
  6:37 AM            06371965
  6:37 AM            06371965
  6:37 AM            06371965
  6:37 AM            06371965
  6:37 AM            06371965
  6:37 AM            06371965
  6:37 AM            06371965
  6:37 AM            06371965
  6:37 AM            06371965
  6:37 AM            06371965
```

The CALL Statement

The format of the CALL statement is

```
CALL  {identifier-1}
      {literal-1   }
      [USING data-name-1 [, data-name-2] ... ]
      [; ON OVERFLOW imperative-statement]
```

The subprogram being CALLed may be referred to by way of a literal, as we do in the examples in this chapter, or by an identifier. If an identifier is used, it must contain the name of the subprogram being CALLed.

The format shows that the USING phrase is optional. We know that it is needed only when data are to be passed between the calling program and the called program. A USING phrase must contain at least one data name and may contain as many as desired. The data names may be qualified if they name items in the File Section. In Program P18-01 the USING phrase contains only one data name. In Program P18-02 you will see how more than one data name is used.

EXERCISE 2

Write a subprogram to ACCEPT the TIME and convert it into printable form as shown in Table 18-E2. Notice that seconds and hundredths of a second are included in the printable time.

Table 18-E2
TIME as ACCEPTed into a COBOL program and in printable form, with seconds and hundredths of a second.

Eight-digit Time	Printable Time
14410000	2:41:00.00 PM
02414567	2:41:45.67 AM
00101234	12:10:12.34 AM
00000000	12:00:00.00 AM
12000000	12:00:00.00 PM
12302345	12:30:23.45 PM
13450000	1:45:00.00 PM

Then write a calling program to use your subprogram. Have your calling program print the time as given to it by the subprogram, and also print the time in eight-digit form.

Passing Data in Both Directions

We will now write a subprogram that gets data passed to it by its calling program and hands results back to the calling program. Subprogram P18-02B will be similar to subprogram P18-01B, but will have the ability to hand the time of day to the calling program either in military form or standard form. Table 18-2 shows how program P18-02B can pass the time to its calling program.

Table 18-2
TIME as ACCEPTed into a COBOL program and in two printable forms.

Eight-digit Time	Time in Standard Form	Time in Military Form
14410000	2:41 PM	1441
02414567	2:41 AM	0241
00101234	12:10 AM	0010
00000000	12:00 AM	0000
12000000	12:00 PM	1200
12302345	12:30 PM	1230
13450000	1:45 PM	1345

Main program P18-02A will CALL subprogram P18-02B in much the same way that Program P18-01A CALLed Program P18-01B. But now when P18-02A CALLs P18-02B, the calling program will have to tell the called program whether it wants the printable time in standard form or military form. For that purpose a one-character field is set up in the calling program to signal the called program. If the one-character field contains an S when the subprogram is CALLed, that tells the subprogram that the printable time is wanted in standard form. If the field contains an M, then military form is wanted.

In order to test the subprogram to see whether it can produce printable time in both standard form and military form, we will have the main program call upon the subprogram for times in both forms. Our main program now will ACCEPT the time into itself, CALL the subprogram to hand it the time in standard form, then CALL the subprogram again, this time asking for the time in military form, and then print all three. The output format for Program P18-02 is shown in Figure 18.6.

Figure 18.6 Output format for Program P18-02.

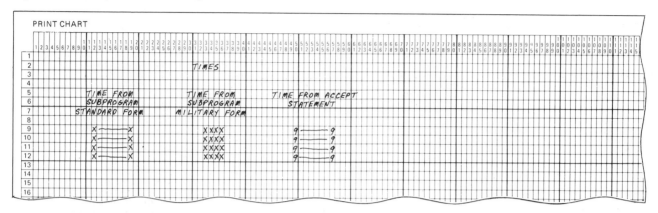

Main program P18-02A is shown in Figure 18.7. There are now two fields into which the program can be handed the time in printable form. STANDARD-FORM-TIME, line 00300, is used to obtain from the subprogram the time in standard form, and MILITARY-FORM-TIME, line 00310, is used to obtain from the subprogram the time in military form. STANDARD-FORM-INDICATOR and MILITARY-FORM-INDICATOR, lines 00320 and 00330, are used to tell the subprogram which form is wanted. When the subprogram is CALLed, one or another of these indicators will be passed to the subprogram. The subprogram will then pass back to the calling program (we hope) printable time in the form requested.

Figure 18.7 Program P18-02A.

```
CB1 RELEASE 2.4                                IBM OS/VS COBOL   JULY  1, 1982


                        23.32.30          APR 13,1988

00010   IDENTIFICATION DIVISION.
00020   PROGRAM-ID.  P1802A.
00030
00040 *    THIS MAIN PROGRAM OBTAINS THE TIME OF DAY IN STANDARD
00050 *    FORM AND IN MILITARY FORM FROM SUBPROGRAM P1802B
00060 *    AND PRINTS BOTH.  IT ALSO OBTAINS
00070 *    THE 8-DIGIT TIME VIA AN ACCEPT STATEMENT AND PRINTS IT.
00080 *
00090 ******************************************************************
00100
00110   ENVIRONMENT DIVISION.
00120   CONFIGURATION SECTION.
00130   SOURCE-COMPUTER.  IBM-370.
00140   OBJECT-COMPUTER.  IBM-370.
00150
00160   INPUT-OUTPUT SECTION.
00170   FILE-CONTROL.
00180       SELECT TIME-FILE-OUT ASSIGN TO PRINTER.
00190
00200 ******************************************************************
00210
00220   DATA DIVISION.
00230   FILE SECTION.
00240   FD   TIME-FILE-OUT
00250        LABEL RECORDS ARE OMITTED.
00260
```

(continued)

Figure 18.7 (continued)

```
00270  01  TIME-RECORD-OUT          PIC X(61).
00280
00290  WORKING-STORAGE SECTION.
00300  01  STANDARD-FORM-TIME       PIC X(8).
00310  01  MILITARY-FORM-TIME       PIC X(8).
00320  01  STANDARD-FORM-INDICATOR  PIC X           VALUE "S".
00330  01  MILITARY-FORM-INDICATOR  PIC X           VALUE "M".
00340  01  BLANK-LINE               PIC X           VALUE SPACE.
00350
00360  01  REPORT-HEADING-1.
00370      05  FILLER               PIC X(30)       VALUE SPACES.
00380      05  FILLER               PIC X(5)        VALUE "TIMES".
00390
00400  01  REPORT-HEADING-2.
00410      05  FILLER               PIC X(10)       VALUE SPACES.
00420      05  FILLER               PIC X(19)       VALUE "TIME FROM".
00430      05  FILLER               PIC X(16)       VALUE "TIME FROM".
00440      05  FILLER               PIC X(16)
00450                               VALUE "TIME FROM ACCEPT".
00460
00470  01  REPORT-HEADING-3.
00480      05  FILLER               PIC X(10)       VALUE SPACES.
00490      05  FILLER               PIC X(19)       VALUE "SUBPROGRAM".
00500      05  FILLER               PIC X(19)       VALUE "SUBPROGRAM".
00510      05  FILLER               PIC X(9)        VALUE "STATEMENT".
00520
00530  01  REPORT-HEADING-4.
00540      05  FILLER               PIC X(8)        VALUE SPACES.
00550      05  FILLER               PIC X(19)
00560                               VALUE "STANDARD FORM".
00570      05  FILLER               PIC X(13)
00580                               VALUE "MILITARY FORM".
00590
00600  01  DETAIL-LINE.
00610      05  FILLER               PIC X(11)       VALUE SPACES.
00620      05  STANDARD-FORM-TIME-O PIC X(8)B(12).
00630      05  MILITARY-FORM-TIME-O PIC X(5)B(13).
00640      05  TIME-OF-DAY-O        PIC 9(8).
00650
00660  **********************************************************************
00670
00680  PROCEDURE DIVISION.
00690  CONTROL-PARAGRAPH.
00700      PERFORM INITIALIZATION.
00710      PERFORM PRINT-TIME 35 TIMES.
00720      PERFORM TERMINATION.
00730      STOP RUN.
00740
00750  INITIALIZATION.
00760      OPEN OUTPUT TIME-FILE-OUT.
00770      WRITE TIME-RECORD-OUT FROM REPORT-HEADING-1 AFTER PAGE.
00780      WRITE TIME-RECORD-OUT FROM REPORT-HEADING-2 AFTER 3.
00790      WRITE TIME-RECORD-OUT FROM REPORT-HEADING-3.
00800      WRITE TIME-RECORD-OUT FROM REPORT-HEADING-4.
00810      WRITE TIME-RECORD-OUT FROM BLANK-LINE.
00820
00830  PRINT-TIME.
00840      ACCEPT TIME-OF-DAY-O FROM TIME.
00850      CALL "P1802B" USING STANDARD-FORM-INDICATOR,
00860                          STANDARD-FORM-TIME.
00870      CALL "P1802B" USING MILITARY-FORM-INDICATOR,
00880                          MILITARY-FORM-TIME.
00890      MOVE STANDARD-FORM-TIME TO STANDARD-FORM-TIME-O.
00900      MOVE MILITARY-FORM-TIME TO MILITARY-FORM-TIME-O.
00910      WRITE TIME-RECORD-OUT FROM DETAIL-LINE.
00920
00930  TERMINATION.
00940      CLOSE TIME-FILE-OUT.
```

The CALL statements at lines 00850 through 00880 show USING phrases containing more than one data name. Whenever a USING phrase contains more than one data name, the data names must be listed in a certain order. The order in which the data names must be listed is made up by the programmer and is called the **calling sequence.** Whenever the subprogram is CALLed, the data names must be listed in the same order in the USING phrase. Here we have established that the indicator field must be first in the calling sequence, and the field that is to contain the printable time must be second. That is, the main program will use the first data name in the calling sequence to tell the subprogram what form it wants the time in, and the subprogram will place the printable time into the field named as the second data name in the calling sequence.

Notice that in the two CALL statements to the subprogram, the names of the first and second data names are different. This is one of the important features of subprograms. The calling program can use any names it likes, regardless of what names are used in the subprogram.

Subprogram P18-02B is shown in Figure 18.8. The LINKAGE SECTION, line 00270, must now contain both TIME-OF-DAY-L as before and the INDICATOR field, since two fields are now passed between the calling program and the called program. The fields may appear in the LINKAGE SECTION in any order. This LINKAGE SECTION shows that the REDEFINES clause and level-88 entries may be used in the usual way.

The USING phrase in the Procedure Division header now must of course contain the names of both of the fields being passed. And most importantly, the

Figure 18.8 Program P18-02B.

```
CB1 RELEASE 2.4                          IBM OS/VS COBOL   JULY  1, 1982


                        23.32.32         APR 13,1988

00010   IDENTIFICATION DIVISION.
00020   PROGRAM-ID.  P1802B.
00030 *
00040 *    THIS SUBPROGRAM ACCEPTS THE TIME OF DAY IN 8-DIGIT
00050 *    FORM AND CONVERTS IT TO HOURS AND MINUTES
00060 *    IN STANDARD FORM OR MILITARY FORM
00070 *    IGNORING SECONDS AND HUNDREDTHS OF A SECOND.
00080 *
00090 ****************************************************************
00100
00110   ENVIRONMENT DIVISION.
00120   CONFIGURATION SECTION.
00130   SOURCE-COMPUTER.   IBM-370.
00140   OBJECT-COMPUTER.   IBM-370.
00150
00160 ****************************************************************
00170
00180   DATA DIVISION.
00190   WORKING-STORAGE SECTION.
00200   01  TIME-OF-DAY-W.
00210       05  HOUR-W              PIC 99.
00220           88  AM        VALUES 0   THRU 11.
00230           88  PM        VALUES 12 THRU 23.
00240       05  MINUTE-W            PIC 99.
00250       05  FILLER              PIC 9(4).
00260
00270   LINKAGE SECTION.
00280   01  TIME-OF-DAY-L.
00290       05  HOUR-M              PIC B99.
00300       05  STANDARD-HOUR REDEFINES HOUR-M.
00310           10  HOUR-S          PIC Z9.
00320           10  COLON-L         PIC X.
00330       05  MINUTE-L            PIC 99.
00340       05  AM-OR-PM            PIC X(3).
00350
00360   01  INDICATOR               PIC X.
00370       88  MILITARY-FORM-REQUESTED      VALUE "M".
00380       88  STANDARD-FORM-REQUESTED      VALUE "S".
00390
00400 ****************************************************************
```

(continued)

Figure 18.8   (continued)

```
00410
00420    PROCEDURE DIVISION USING INDICATOR, TIME-OF-DAY-L.
00430
00440    CONTROL-PARAGRAPH.
00450        ACCEPT TIME-OF-DAY-W FROM TIME.
00460        PERFORM SET-AM-OR-PM.
00470        IF STANDARD-FORM-REQUESTED
00480            MOVE ":" TO COLON-L
00490            PERFORM FIX-HOUR.
00500        PERFORM MOVE-TIME-OF-DAY.
00510        PERFORM EXECUTION-COMPLETE.
00520
00530    EXECUTION-COMPLETE.
00540        EXIT PROGRAM.
00550
00560    SET-AM-OR-PM.
00570        IF STANDARD-FORM-REQUESTED
00580            IF AM
00590                MOVE " AM" TO AM-OR-PM
00600            ELSE
00610                MOVE " PM" TO AM-OR-PM
00620        ELSE
00630            MOVE SPACES TO AM-OR-PM.
00640
00650    FIX-HOUR.
00660        IF PM
00670            SUBTRACT 12 FROM HOUR-W.
00680        IF HOUR-W IS EQUAL TO 0
00690            MOVE 12 TO HOUR-W.
00700
00710    MOVE-TIME-OF-DAY.
00720        IF MILITARY-FORM-REQUESTED
00730            MOVE HOUR-W TO HOUR-M
00740        ELSE
00750            MOVE HOUR-W TO HOUR-S.
00760        MOVE MINUTE-W TO MINUTE-L.
```

names of the fields must be in the same order in this USING phrase as they are in the USING phrase in the calling program. Once the calling sequence is established, it must be adhered to in every USING phrase in the CALL statements and the Procedure Division header. It is the calling sequence, the order in which the data names are written, that permits the calling program and the called program to use any names they like for the data fields that are passed between them.

When USING phrases contain more than one data name, the lengths of corresponding data names must be the same. That is, the length of the first data name in the USING phrase of the CALL statement must be the same as the length of the first data name in the USING phrase of the Procedure Division header. Here they are both one character in length. The length of the second data name in the USING phrase of the CALL statement must be the same as the length of the second data name in the USING phrase of the Procedure Division header. Here they are both eight characters long.

Program P18-02A was linked to Program P18-02B one night and run as a single run unit. The output shown in Figure 18.9 was produced.

Figure 18.9 Output from Program P18-02.

```
                                   TIMES


        TIME FROM            TIME FROM            TIME FROM ACCEPT
        SUBPROGRAM           SUBPROGRAM              STATEMENT
      STANDARD FORM        MILITARY FORM

         11:32 PM              2332                 23323665
         11:32 PM              2332                 23323665
         11:32 PM              2332                 23323665
         11:32 PM              2332                 23323665
         11:32 PM              2332                 23323665
         11:32 PM              2332                 23323665
         11:32 PM              2332                 23323665
         11:32 PM              2332                 23323665
         11:32 PM              2332                 23323665
         11:32 PM              2332                 23323665
         11:32 PM              2332                 23323665
         11:32 PM              2332                 23323666
         11:32 PM              2332                 23323666
         11:32 PM              2332                 23323666
         11:32 PM              2332                 23323666
         11:32 PM              2332                 23323666
         11:32 PM              2332                 23323666
         11:32 PM              2332                 23323666
         11:32 PM              2332                 23323666
         11:32 PM              2332                 23323666
         11:32 PM              2332                 23323666
         11:32 PM              2332                 23323666
         11:32 PM              2332                 23323666
         11:32 PM              2332                 23323666
         11:32 PM              2332                 23323666
         11:32 PM              2332                 23323666
         11:32 PM              2332                 23323666
         11:32 PM              2332                 23323666
         11:32 PM              2332                 23323666
         11:32 PM              2332                 23323666
         11:32 PM              2332                 23323667
         11:32 PM              2332                 23323667
         11:32 PM              2332                 23323667
         11:32 PM              2332                 23323667
```

EXERCISE 3

Rewrite your solution for Exercise 3, Chapter 12, page 392, as a main program and a subprogram. Put all the validity checking in the subprogram. Have the main program pass the input record to the subprogram for validity checking. Have the subprogram check the record and return a flag to the main program to say if the record is error-free. If there is an error in the record, have your subprogram stop checking the record when it finds the first error and return to the main program a flag saying that an error has been found, and also return an error message that the main program can print.

Define all possible error messages in working storage in the subprogram. When an error is found, have your program MOVE the appropriate message to the Linkage Section to be passed to the main program.

The Use of the CANCEL Statement

When a subprogram is CALLed more than once from a calling program, or when a single copy of a subprogram in storage is CALLed from more than one calling program, the subprogram is ordinarily in its **last-used state** each time it is CALLed. That is, if the subprogram has any fields in its File Section or Working Storage Section that are changed by the subprogram, those changes stay there and are present the next time the subprogram is CALLed.

For example, if a subprogram has an accumulator field in working storage defined with VALUE 0, and the subprogram ADDs to the accumulator in the course of execution, the sum stays in the accumulator after the subprogram has finished executing. The next time the subprogram is CALLed, the accumulator starts out not with zero, but with the old total.

It is possible to get a fresh copy of a subprogram, if one is needed, by using a **CANCEL** statement. A CANCEL statement is given in the calling program and has the effect of wiping out all traces of previous uses of the subprogram. The next CALL to the subprogram begins execution with a fresh copy. In the programs in this chapter, we had no need of the CANCEL statement because neither of our subprograms changed the contents of their Working Storage Section, nor did they have any File Section to change.

The CANCEL statement can be used only when certain compiler options are in effect. The particular options needed are different for different COBOL systems. Check your own COBOL literature for details.

The format of the CANCEL statement is

```
CANCEL {literal-1  }  [, literal-2   ] ...
       {identifier-1}  [, identifier-2]
```

The format shows that when a CANCEL statement is used, at least one subprogram must be CANCELed, and you may cancel as many as desired. The subprogram(s) can be referred to by way of literals, as we have done in the examples in this chapter, or by identifiers. If identifiers are used, they must contain the names of the subprograms to be CANCELed.

Summary

Subprograms can be used when two or more programs need identical computational procedures, when a very large program is to be divided into smaller units for efficiency, when a program is to be written in more than one language, or to encourage good programming practices.

A subprogram operates under control of a calling program, which CALLs the subprogram when needed. A subprogram may in turn be the calling program of another subprogram. A subprogram terminates execution with an EXIT PROGRAM statement or a STOP RUN statement. An EXIT PROGRAM statement must be the only statement in the paragraph in which it appears. A program that executes without being CALLed is a main program.

Data may be passed between the calling program and the called program by way of a USING phrase in the CALL statement of the calling program and a USING phrase in the Procedure Division header of the called program. Both USING phrases must list all the data fields that are to be passed in either direction, or else name group-level items that include all data fields to be passed. The data fields must be listed in the same order in all USING phrases. Items in corresponding positions in all USING phrases must be the same length. The order in which the data fields are listed is called the calling sequence. If no data are passed, the USING phrases may be omitted.

In the called program, all data fields that are passed in either direction must be defined in the Linkage Section. If no data are passed, the Linkage Section may be omitted. If used, the Linkage Section must appear after the Working Storage Section and before the Report Section.

The CANCEL statement may be used to wipe out a previous use of a subprogram so that a later CALL statement can obtain a fresh copy of the subprogram.

Fill-in Exercises

1. A program that requests execution of a subprogram is called a(n) _____ program.

2. A program that is not a subprogram to any other is called a(n) _____ program.

3. The statement that is used to begin execution of a subprogram is the _____ statement.

4. Statements that can be used to terminate execution of a subprogram are _____ and _____ .

5. All data fields that are passed between the calling program and the called program must be defined in the _____ Section of the _____ program.

6. A USING phrase appears in the _____ header of the _____ program if there are any data to be passed.

7. A USING phrase appears in the _____ statement in the _____ program if there are any data to be passed.

8. Data are passed between a calling program and a subprogram not on the basis of the _____ of the data fields.

9. The order in which data fields must be named in USING phrases is called the _____ _____ .

10. Any clauses that may be used in a _____ Section may be used in a Linkage Section.

11. A subprogram that executes under control of a calling program is called a _____ program.

12. When a subprogram completes executing, it is left in its _____ - _____ state.

13. When there is only one item in the USING phrase of a CALL statement, it must be the same _____ as the item in the USING phrase of the _____ _____ header in the called program.

14. A main program linked with all of the subprograms it needs for execution is called a _____ _____ .

15. Some programmers and managers think that breaking a large program into subprograms encourages _____ _____ _____ .

Review Exercises

1. Write a main program that CALLs two different subprograms (with separate CALL statements). Have the programs pass no data.

   Have your main program call one of the subprograms every 0.01 second, and call the second subprogram every 0.02 second. Have each subprogram print the time that it was called, in any form you desire, on a separate output file. Have your main program OPEN both output files in its initialization routine, and CLOSE both output files in its termination routine. Do not let your program run for more than one-tenth of a second.

2. Modify your solution for Review Exercise 1 so that each output file is OPENed by the program that uses it. Define a flag in each subprogram to say whether its output file has already been OPENed. Start the flag with VALUE 0. When the subprogram is CALLed the first time, have it OPEN its output file and set the flag to indicate that the file is now OPEN. The file then remains OPEN and must not be OPENed again on subsequent CALLs to the subprogram. Remember that a flag in working storage remains unchanged between CALLs.

   Why can the subprograms not CLOSE their output files? Why must the output files be CLOSEd by the main program?

3. Write a subprogram that reverses the order of the characters in an 80-character record and returns the reversed record to the calling program. Use only one data field to pass the data in both directions; that is, have the calling program hand an 80-character record to the subprogram, and have the subprogram hand the reversed 80-character record back to the main program in the same 80-character field. For each record have the main program print on one line the original record and the record with its characters reversed.

Project

Rewrite your solution to the Project in Chapter 10, page 331, as a calling program and a subprogram. Have the calling program read each input record and pass the Gross Pay to the subprogram. Include the tax tables in the subprogram, and have the subprogram compute the tax and pass it to the calling program. Have the calling program print output in the same format as in the Project in Chapter 10.

The Debugging Feature

Here are the key points you should learn from this chapter:

1. Why the debugging feature is useful
2. When to use the debugging feature
3. What debugging facilities are available
4. How to program using the debugging feature

Key words to recognize and learn:

debugging   ALL REFERENCES
debugging line   explicit reference
debugging section   ALL PROCEDURES
WITH DEBUGGING MODE   object-time switch
computer-name   USE FOR DEBUGGING
DEBUG-ITEM   USE DEBUGGING
monitor

Different COBOL systems provide different kinds of aids for **debugging,** that is, for testing and correcting programs. In this chapter we will discuss some general approaches to debugging, and show in some sample programs how the approaches are implemented using the ANSI standard debugging feature. The ANSI debugging feature is available on many large modern COBOL systems. If your system does not support this feature, you may be able to adapt the general approaches given in this chapter to the debugging aids available on your system.

The ANSI standard provides two types of debugging aids — **debugging lines** and **debugging sections.** Since debugging lines are the easier to understand and code, we will do those first.

Debugging Lines

When you are developing a new program or modifying an existing one, you will sometimes want to have the program produce some output that is to be used only for debugging. That is, you may want your program to produce, in addition to the output that it was designed to produce, extra output that will help you to find and correct errors in the program. Then, when the program is working correctly, you will want the program to cease producing the extra output. Debugging lines give you a way to control the production of the debug output.

To use this feature, you write into your program all the lines of code that you want for debugging, and put a D in position 7 of each line to indicate to COBOL that the lines are being used for debugging purposes only and are not meant to be part of the normal running of the program. Debugging lines may be written only after the OBJECT-COMPUTER paragraph and may be written in the Environment, Data, and Procedure Divisions. If a single debugging statement takes more than one line, each line must have a D in position 7. You cannot use the continuation indicator in debugging lines. But the continuation indicator is rarely used, and anything you can do by using a continuation indicator can be done with other (less convenient) coding techniques anyway. The continuation indicator is discussed fully in Chapter 5.

Then, when you run your program in the ordinary way that we have been doing so far, COBOL will ignore the debugging lines. The lines will appear in your program listing where you wrote them but they will not be executed. To get COBOL to execute the debugging lines you must insert the **WITH DEBUGGING MODE** clause into the SOURCE-COMPUTER paragraph in the Environment Division.

The format of the SOURCE-COMPUTER paragraph is:

```
SOURCE-COMPUTER.  computer-name [WITH DEBUGGING MODE].
```

In all our programs so far, we have used only **computer-name.** Now, if we have a program that contains debugging lines we can use the WITH DEBUGGING MODE clause to tell COBOL that we want the debugging lines executed. Then, when the program is working correctly we can remove the WITH DEBUGGING MODE clause and COBOL will ignore the debugging lines. Notice that only the words DEBUGGING and MODE are required in the WITH DEBUGGING MODE clause.

The main advantage of using debugging lines is that the lines can stay in the program permanently, and be activated and deactivated by proper use of the WITH DEBUGGING MODE clause. So if some change is to be made to the program in the future, the same debugging that was used originally can easily be reactivated again.

This advantage has a disadvantage. If, when the program is to be changed in the future, some different debugging is wanted instead, all the old debugging lines will have to be laboriously removed by the most junior programmer in the installation, probably you.

The use of debugging lines has another drawback: If the debugging lines are not removed from the program after debugging is completed, the program becomes difficult to read. Position 7 of the line is not where your eye normally falls when you are reading COBOL code, and the Ds there will be easy to overlook. Extra lines in the Environment and Data Divisions don't do much harm, but extra lines in the Procedure Division can make the program very confusing indeed.

These disadvantages can be overcome through the use of debugging sections, which will be discussed later. But first let's look at a program that contains debugging lines.

A Program with Debugging Lines

We will use Program P09-01 to show how debugging lines can be added to a program for use during program development and testing Review Program P09-01 before going on. The input format for Program P09-01 is given on page 250; the output format in Figure 9.1; Program P09-01 is shown in Figure 9.2; the input data, Figure 9.3; and the output in Figure 9.4. For Program P19-01, we will add debugging lines to Program P09-01 to enable us to check on the calculation of COMMISSION-FOR-SALESPERSON to see that it is working as we expect it to. COMMISSION-FOR-SALESPERSON is calculated at line 01530 in Program P09-01.

Program P19-01 will produce two reports. One will contain the original output of Program P09-01, and the other will contain just debug output.[1] The debug output will have the format shown in Figure 19.1.

Figure 19.1 Output format for debug output of Program P19-01.

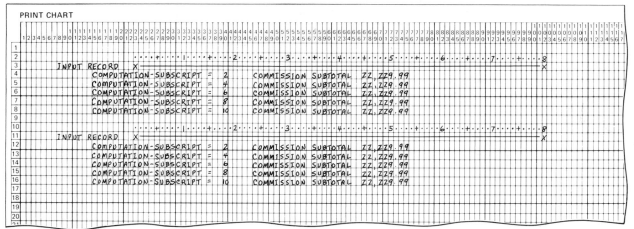

The Debug Output

Program P19-01 will print seven lines of debug output for each salesperson. One of the lines of debug output is labeled INPUT RECORD. Whenever you are doing debugging, you should print out each input record in the exact form in which it was read, with no editing and no reformatting. That way you can see whether you have all your input data in the correct positions. Also, if there are any IF statements in your program that test the input data, you can see which way the IF statements should come out. In general, when you have your input record before your eyes, you can know what the program is supposed to do and can check that it is doing it.

Immediately above the line called INPUT RECORD is a line of 80 dots, + signs, and numbers to make it easy for us to find any particular position of the input record. Immediately following the line called INPUT RECORD are five lines that should show us how COMMISSION-FOR-SALESPERSON is computed from that input record.

---

[1]The two reports will print one after the other on the same printer if the printer is not under direct control of your program. If only one printer under direct control of your program is available, the report lines will be interleaved in an unpredictable manner.

COMMISSION-FOR-SALESPERSON is calculated in the paragraph COM-MISSION-CALCULATION, which executes under control of the PERFORM . . . VARYING statement at line 01220 in Program P09-01. The paragraph COMMISSION-CALCULATION uses the field COMPUTATION-SUBSCRIPT as a subscript in its COMPUTE statements. In the normal execution of Program P09-01, COMMISSION-CALCULATION executes 10 times for each input record, with COMPUTATION-SUBSCRIPT set to 1, 2, 3, and so on to 10. Program P19-01 prints one line of debug output the second, fourth, sixth, eighth, and tenth times that COMMISSION-CALCULATION executes for each input record. Each line shows the value of COMPUTATION-SUBSCRIPT and the value of the field COM-MISSION-FOR-SALESPERSON. Remember that COMMISSION-FOR-SALESPERSON is zeroed for each input record and is used to accumulate the commission amounts as they are computed for a single salesperson from the 10 Sale Amounts.

Programming for Debug Output

Program P19-01 is shown in Figure 19.2. To produce the debug output we use the WITH DEBUGGING MODE clause in the SOURCE-COMPUTER paragraph, and some debugging lines in the Working Storage Section and in the Procedure Division. In working storage we define the GUIDE-LINE that is to be printed im-

Figure 19.2   Program P19-01.

```
CB1 RELEASE 2.4                                 IBM OS/VS COBOL   JULY  1, 1982


                        15.09.14        APR 14,1988


00010   IDENTIFICATION DIVISION.
00020   PROGRAM-ID.  P19-01.
00030  *AUTHOR.  DEBORAH ANN SENIOR.
00040  *
00050  *    THIS PROGRAM PRODUCES A SALESPERSON COMMISSION
00060  *    REPORT SHOWING TEN COMMISSION AMOUNTS
00070  *    AND THE TOTAL FOR EACH SALESPERSON.
00080  *
00090  *
00100  ******************************************************************
00110
00120   ENVIRONMENT DIVISION.
00130   CONFIGURATION SECTION.
00140   SOURCE-COMPUTER.  IBM-370 WITH DEBUGGING MODE.
00150   OBJECT-COMPUTER.  IBM-370.
00160
00170   INPUT-OUTPUT SECTION.
00180   FILE-CONTROL.
00190       SELECT SALES-FILE-IN               ASSIGN TO INFILE.
00200       SELECT COMMISSION-REPORT-FILE-OUT  ASSIGN TO PRINTER.
00210
00220  ******************************************************************
00230
00240   DATA DIVISION.
00250   FILE SECTION.
00260   FD  SALES-FILE-IN
00270       LABEL RECORDS ARE OMITTED
00280       RECORD CONTAINS 80 CHARACTERS.
00290
00300   01  SALES-RECORD-IN.
00310       05  SALESPERSON-NUMBER-IN    PIC X(7).
00320       05  SALE-AMOUNT-IN           PIC 9(4)V99     OCCURS 10 TIMES.
00330       05  FILLER                   PIC X(13).
```

```
00340
00350   FD    COMMISSION-REPORT-FILE-OUT
00360         LABEL RECORDS ARE OMITTED.
00370
00380   01    REPORT-LINE                      PIC X(119).
00390
00400   WORKING-STORAGE SECTION.
00410   01    MORE-INPUT                 PIC X          VALUE "Y".
00420   01    COMMISSION-RATE-1          PIC V99        VALUE .05.
00430   01    COMMISSION-RATE-2          PIC V99        VALUE .10.
00440   01    BRACKET-MAXIMUM            PIC 999V99     VALUE 100.00.
00450   01    NUMBER-OF-SALES            PIC S99        VALUE 10
00460                                    COMP           SYNC.
00470   01    GRAND-TOTAL-COMMISSIONS-W  PIC S9(6)V99   VALUE 0.
00480   01    COMMISSIONS.
00490         05   COMMISSION-AMOUNT-W    PIC S9(4)V99 OCCURS 10 TIMES.
00500   01    COMMISSION-FOR-SALESPERSON  PIC S9(5)V99.
00510   01    COMPUTATION-SUBSCRIPT      PIC S99        COMP SYNC.
00520   01    LINE-SPACING   VALUE 1     PIC S9         COMP, SYNC.
005205  01    GUIDE-LINE                 PIC X(102)
005210        VALUE "            ....+....1....+....2....+....3..
005215-        ..+....4....+....5....+....6....+....7....+....8".
005220  01    COMMISSION-FOR-SALESPERSON-E            PIC ZZ,ZZ9.99.
00530
00540   01    PAGE-HEADING-1.
00550         05   FILLER  PIC X(51)       VALUE SPACES.
00560         05   FILLER  PIC X(17)       VALUE "COMMISSION REPORT".
00570
00580   01    PAGE-HEADING-2.
00590         05   FILLER  PIC X(39)       VALUE "SALES-".
00600         05   FILLER  PIC X(73)
00610              VALUE "C O M M I S S I O N S   O N   S A L E S".
00620         05   FILLER  PIC X(5)        VALUE "TOTAL".
00630
00640   01    PAGE-HEADING-3.
00650         05   FILLER  PIC X(10)       VALUE "PERSON".
00660         05   FILLER  PIC X(10)       VALUE "SALE 1".
00670         05   FILLER  PIC X(10)       VALUE "SALE 2".
00680         05   FILLER  PIC X(10)       VALUE "SALE 3".
00690         05   FILLER  PIC X(10)       VALUE "SALE 4".
00700         05   FILLER  PIC X(10)       VALUE "SALE 5".
00710         05   FILLER  PIC X(10)       VALUE "SALE 6".
00720         05   FILLER  PIC X(10)       VALUE "SALE 7".
00730         05   FILLER  PIC X(10)       VALUE "SALE 8".
00740         05   FILLER  PIC X(10)       VALUE "SALE 9".
00750         05   FILLER  PIC X(11)       VALUE "SALE 10".
00760         05   FILLER  PIC X(7)        VALUE "COMMIS-".
00770
00780   01    PAGE-HEADING-4.
00790         05   FILLER  PIC X(112)      VALUE "NUMBER".
00800         05   FILLER  PIC X(4)        VALUE "SION".
00810
00820   01    DETAIL-LINE.
00830         05   SALESPERSON-NUMBER-OUT  PIC X(9).
00840         05   COMMISSION-AMOUNT-OUT   PIC Z,ZZ9.99BB
00850                                      OCCURS 10 TIMES.
00860         05   COMMISSION-FOR-SALESPERSON-OUT
00870                                      PIC BZZ,ZZ9.99.
```

(continued)

mediately before each input record, at lines 005205 through 005215. We also define COMMISSION-FOR-SALESPERSON-E, at line 005220, for editing COMMISSION-FOR-SALESPERSON for printing. You will see why we need COMMISSION-FOR-SALESPERSON-E when we look at the Procedure Division.

In the Procedure Division we need statements that will print each input record and the GUIDE-LINE above it. When you are doing debugging, one way to make sure you print each and every input record is to find the paragraph that contains the nonpriming READ statement or a nonpriming PERFORM of a READ statement. Then print the input record at the very beginning of that paragraph.

We will use DISPLAY statements to print all our debug output. Although DISPLAY has severe limitations which make it unsuitable for printing normal report output, it has two important advantages when used in debugging, as you will see.

Figure 19.2   (continued)

```
00880
00890   01  NO-INPUT-DATA.
00900       05   FILLER                    PIC X(53) VALUE SPACES.
00910       05   FILLER                    PIC X(13) VALUE "NO INPUT DATA".
00920
00930   01. TOTAL-LINE.
00940       05   FILLER                    PIC X(68) VALUE SPACES.
00950       05   FILLER                    PIC X(41)
00960       VALUE "TOTAL COMMISSION FOR ALL SALESPERSONS".
00970       05   GRAND-TOTAL-COMMISSIONS PIC ZZZ,ZZ9.99.
00980
00990   ****************************************************************
01000
01010   PROCEDURE DIVISION.
01020   CONTROL-PARAGRAPH.
01030       PERFORM INITIALIZATION.
01040       PERFORM MAIN-PROCESS UNTIL MORE-INPUT IS EQUAL TO "N".
01050       PERFORM TERMINATION.
01060       STOP RUN.
01070
01080   INITIALIZATION.
01090       OPEN INPUT  SALES-FILE-IN,
01100            OUTPUT COMMISSION-REPORT-FILE-OUT.
01110       WRITE REPORT-LINE FROM PAGE-HEADING-1 AFTER PAGE.
01120       WRITE REPORT-LINE FROM PAGE-HEADING-2 AFTER 4.
01130       WRITE REPORT-LINE FROM PAGE-HEADING-3.
01140       WRITE REPORT-LINE FROM PAGE-HEADING-4.
01150       MOVE 2 TO LINE-SPACING.
01160       PERFORM READ-A-RECORD.
01170       IF MORE-INPUT IS EQUAL TO "N"
01180            WRITE REPORT-LINE FROM NO-INPUT-DATA AFTER 2.
01190
01200   MAIN-PROCESS.
012005D     DISPLAY SPACE.
012010D     DISPLAY GUIDE-LINE.
012015D     DISPLAY "        INPUT RECORD    ", SALES-RECORD-IN.
01210       MOVE ZERO TO COMMISSION-FOR-SALESPERSON.
01220       PERFORM COMMISSION-CALCULATION
01230            VARYING COMPUTATION-SUBSCRIPT FROM 1 BY 1 UNTIL
01240            COMPUTATION-SUBSCRIPT IS GREATER THAN NUMBER-OF-SALES.
01250       PERFORM PRODUCE-THE-REPORT.
01260       PERFORM READ-A-RECORD.
01270
01280   TERMINATION.
01290       PERFORM PRODUCE-FINAL-TOTAL-LINE.
01300       CLOSE SALES-FILE-IN,
01310            COMMISSION-REPORT-FILE-OUT.
01320
01330   READ-A-RECORD.
01340       READ SALES-FILE-IN
01350            AT END
01360                 MOVE "N" TO MORE-INPUT.
01370
01380   COMMISSION-CALCULATION.
01390       IF SALE-AMOUNT-IN (COMPUTATION-SUBSCRIPT) IS NOT GREATER THAN
01400            BRACKET-MAXIMUM
01410            COMPUTE
01420            COMMISSION-AMOUNT-W (COMPUTATION-SUBSCRIPT) ROUNDED
01430            COMMISSION-AMOUNT-OUT (COMPUTATION-SUBSCRIPT) ROUNDED
01440            = SALE-AMOUNT-IN (COMPUTATION-SUBSCRIPT) *
01450            COMMISSION-RATE-1
01460       ELSE
01470            COMPUTE
01480            COMMISSION-AMOUNT-W (COMPUTATION-SUBSCRIPT) ROUNDED
01490            COMMISSION-AMOUNT-OUT (COMPUTATION-SUBSCRIPT) ROUNDED
01500            = BRACKET-MAXIMUM * COMMISSION-RATE-1 +
01510            (SALE-AMOUNT-IN (COMPUTATION-SUBSCRIPT) -
01520            BRACKET-MAXIMUM) * COMMISSION-RATE-2.
01530       ADD COMMISSION-AMOUNT-W (COMPUTATION-SUBSCRIPT) TO
01540            COMMISSION-FOR-SALESPERSON.
015405D     IF COMPUTATION-SUBSCRIPT IS EQUAL TO 2 OR 4 OR 6 OR 8 OR 10
015410D          MOVE COMMISSION-FOR-SALESPERSON TO
015415D          COMMISSION-FOR-SALESPERSON-E
015420D          DISPLAY "            COMPUTATION-SUBSCRIPT = "
015425D               COMPUTATION-SUBSCRIPT
015430D               "   COMMISSION SUBTOTAL = "
015435D               COMMISSION-FOR-SALESPERSON-E.
```

```
01550
01560    PRODUCE-THE-REPORT.
01570        MOVE SALESPERSON-NUMBER-IN TO SALESPERSON-NUMBER-OUT.
01580        MOVE COMMISSION-FOR-SALESPERSON TO
01590            COMMISSION-FOR-SALESPERSON-OUT.
01600        ADD COMMISSION-FOR-SALESPERSON TO GRAND-TOTAL-COMMISSIONS-W.
01610        WRITE REPORT-LINE FROM DETAIL-LINE AFTER LINE-SPACING.
01620        MOVE 1 TO LINE-SPACING.
01630
01640    PRODUCE-FINAL-TOTAL-LINE.
01650        MOVE GRAND-TOTAL-COMMISSIONS-W TO GRAND-TOTAL-COMMISSIONS.
01660        WRITE REPORT-LINE FROM TOTAL-LINE AFTER 4.
```

The three DISPLAY statements at lines 012005, 012010, and 012015 print first a line of blanks, then the GUIDE-LINE, and finally the line labeled INPUT RECORD. Each DISPLAY statement starts printing on a new line. Remember that, if necessary, you can use a DISPLAY statement before you have OPENed your print file and after you have CLOSEd it.

One of the limitations of the DISPLAY statement is that it automatically single-spaces before printing. No other kind of spacing or skipping is available. That is why we need a DISPLAY statement to print a line of blanks; there is no other way to double-space when using DISPLAY. Another difficulty with DISPLAY is that it does not provide convenient line-formatting capability; you certainly have nothing like the convenience or precision of output-record field definitions when using DISPLAY.

We now need a statement that will print the values of COMPUTATION-SUBSCRIPT and the commission subtotals. The statement would have to be in the paragraph COMMISSION-CALCULATION, and the IF statement at line 015405 is it. The IF statement tests to see whether this particular execution of COMMISSION-CALCULATION is one that is supposed to cause a line of debug output to print, and then DISPLAYs a debug line if it is.

The statement at line 015420 shows another limitation of the DISPLAY verb. DISPLAY does not allow you to do output editing directly. The ANSI standard says nothing about editing in connection with the DISPLAY verb. In the COBOL system used to run the programs in this book, DISPLAY edits all numeric output as it thinks best. DISPLAY can be counted on to do a reasonable job of editing a numeric field (but not an excellent one) only if the field is defined as COMPUTATIONAL. If the field is not COMPUTATIONAL, DISPLAY will sometimes make a mess of editing it. That is why we first MOVE COMMISSION-FOR-SALESPERSON to COMMISSION-FOR-SALESPERSON-E before DISPLAYing it. You will see how DISPLAY edits COMPUTATION-SUBSCRIPT when we look at the output.

Program P19-01 was run using the same input as Program P09-01, and produced the normal report output shown in Figure 19.3 and the debug output shown in Figure 19.4. For each line of normal print output, you can find the seven lines of debug output. Notice how the DISPLAY verb edited COMPUTATION-SUBSCRIPT.

Now the WITH DEBUGGING MODE clause can be removed from Program P19-01, and the debugging lines will be ignored. The program would then produce just the normal report output.

Figure 19.3   Normal output from Program P19-01.

COMMISSION REPORT

| SALES-
PERSON
NUMBER | SALE 1 | SALE 2 | SALE 3 | C O M M I S S I O N S   O N   S A L E S | | | | | | | TOTAL
COMMIS-
SION |
				SALE 4	SALE 5	SALE 6	SALE 7	SALE 8	SALE 9	SALE 10	
0001289	495.75	0.63	795.10	43.71	176.49	0.30	6.00	2.40	5.50	82.59	1,608.47
0942386	5.00	195.00	46.93	4.78	1.40	15.00	7.50	36.23	3.00	31.15	345.99
3684420	15.00	7.17	3.75	5.00	0.00	0.00	0.00	0.00	0.00	0.00	30.92
5236714	4.21	2.26	67.37	3.43	24.52	0.00	0.00	0.00	0.00	0.00	101.79
6612364	0.50	17.36	0.94	94.50	3.26	19.51	5.37	4.50	12.36	55.29	213.59
7747119	2.60	11.50	114.50	3.68	39.90	7.50	3.44	0.71	5.00	0.00	188.83

TOTAL COMMISSION FOR ALL SALESPERSONS   2,489.59

Figure 19.4   Debug output from Program P19-01.

```
              ....+....1....+....2....+....3....+....4....+....5....+....6....+....7....+....8
INPUT RECORD  00012895007500012568001000487121814920006000110000048000105000087593
      COMPUTATION-SUBSCRIPT = 02      COMMISSION SUBTOTAL =      496.38
      COMPUTATION-SUBSCRIPT = 04      COMMISSION SUBTOTAL =    1,335.19
      COMPUTATION-SUBSCRIPT = 06      COMMISSION SUBTOTAL =    1,511.98
      COMPUTATION-SUBSCRIPT = 08      COMMISSION SUBTOTAL =    1,520.38
      COMPUTATION-SUBSCRIPT = 10      COMMISSION SUBTOTAL =    1,608.47

              ....+....1....+....2....+....3....+....4....+....5....+....6....+....7....+....8
INPUT RECORD  09423860100002000000519270095500027950200000125000412250060000036150
      COMPUTATION-SUBSCRIPT = 02      COMMISSION SUBTOTAL =      200.00
      COMPUTATION-SUBSCRIPT = 04      COMMISSION SUBTOTAL =      251.71
      COMPUTATION-SUBSCRIPT = 06      COMMISSION SUBTOTAL =      268.11
      COMPUTATION-SUBSCRIPT = 08      COMMISSION SUBTOTAL =      311.84
      COMPUTATION-SUBSCRIPT = 10      COMMISSION SUBTOTAL =      345.99

              ....+....1....+....2....+....3....+....4....+....5....+....6....+....7....+....8
INPUT RECORD  36844200200000121650074950100000000000000000000000000000000000000000
      COMPUTATION-SUBSCRIPT = 02      COMMISSION SUBTOTAL =       22.17
      COMPUTATION-SUBSCRIPT = 04      COMMISSION SUBTOTAL =       30.92
      COMPUTATION-SUBSCRIPT = 06      COMMISSION SUBTOTAL =       30.92
      COMPUTATION-SUBSCRIPT = 08      COMMISSION SUBTOTAL =       30.92
      COMPUTATION-SUBSCRIPT = 10      COMMISSION SUBTOTAL =       30.92

              ....+....1....+....2....+....3....+....4....+....5....+....6....+....7....+....8
INPUT RECORD  52367140084120045190723680068500295180000000000000000000000000000000
      COMPUTATION-SUBSCRIPT = 02      COMMISSION SUBTOTAL =        6.47
      COMPUTATION-SUBSCRIPT = 04      COMMISSION SUBTOTAL =       77.27
      COMPUTATION-SUBSCRIPT = 06      COMMISSION SUBTOTAL =      101.79
      COMPUTATION-SUBSCRIPT = 08      COMMISSION SUBTOTAL =      101.79
      COMPUTATION-SUBSCRIPT = 10      COMMISSION SUBTOTAL =      101.79

              ....+....1....+....2....+....3....+....4....+....5....+....6....+....7....+....8
INPUT RECORD  66123640010000223580018730995000065150245120103680089950173600060287
      COMPUTATION-SUBSCRIPT = 02      COMMISSION SUBTOTAL =       17.86
      COMPUTATION-SUBSCRIPT = 04      COMMISSION SUBTOTAL =      113.30
      COMPUTATION-SUBSCRIPT = 06      COMMISSION SUBTOTAL =      136.07
      COMPUTATION-SUBSCRIPT = 08      COMMISSION SUBTOTAL =      145.94
      COMPUTATION-SUBSCRIPT = 10      COMMISSION SUBTOTAL =      213.59

              ....+....1....+....2....+....3....+....4....+....5....+....6....+....7....+....8
INPUT RECORD  77471190052000165001195000073500448950125000068750014250099990000000
      COMPUTATION-SUBSCRIPT = 02      COMMISSION SUBTOTAL =       14.10
      COMPUTATION-SUBSCRIPT = 04      COMMISSION SUBTOTAL =      132.28
      COMPUTATION-SUBSCRIPT = 06      COMMISSION SUBTOTAL =      179.68
      COMPUTATION-SUBSCRIPT = 08      COMMISSION SUBTOTAL =      183.83
      COMPUTATION-SUBSCRIPT = 10      COMMISSION SUBTOTAL =      188.83
```

EXERCISE 1

Add debugging lines to your solution to Exercise 3, Chapter 9, page 258, so that the program produces a debug output report as well as the normal output. On the debug output report have your program print each input record and an 80-position guide line. Also for each input record, have your program print the number of hours worked on Tuesday and on Friday. If the number of hours worked is greater than 8 on either of those days, have your program print also the effective hours. Have your program produce its debug output in the format shown in Figure 19.E1.

Figure 19.E1 Debug output format for Exercise 1.

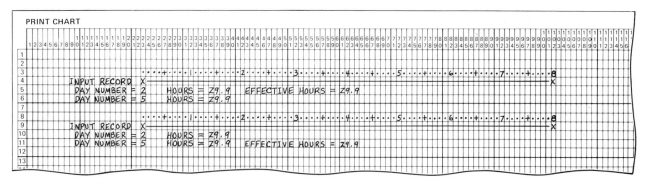

Debugging Sections

It was mentioned earlier that debugging lines in the Procedure Division of a program can make the program difficult to read once the debugging lines have been deactivated. Debugging sections, on the other hand, allow the programmer to group all the debugging code in the Procedure Division into one place, where it can easily be ignored by a reader of the program. Also, debugging sections provide some additional capabilities not conveniently available with debugging lines. In Program P19-02 we will show, by using two debugging sections, how the debugging code in the Procedure Division of a program can be grouped all together and out of the way.

Debugging sections and debugging lines may be used together in the same program. When both are used, it is possible to have:

a. The sections and the lines activated
b. The sections and the lines deactivated
c. The sections deactivated and the lines activated

It is not possible to have debugging sections activated while debugging lines are deactivated. It is not necessary to have a D in position 7 in debugging sections, although including the D may save some computer time when both the sections and lines are deactivated.

The Special Register DEBUG-ITEM

Whenever you set up one or more debugging sections in a program, COBOL automatically establishes a special storage area called **DEBUG-ITEM.** No matter how many debugging sections you have in a program, only one DEBUG-ITEM is established. COBOL assigns data to the fields in DEBUG-ITEM when your debugging sections are executed, and you may use the contents of those fields as you wish. We will discuss later what kind of data COBOL assigns to the fields in DEBUG-ITEM.

You must not define the field DEBUG-ITEM in your working storage or anywhere. COBOL defines it automatically. DEBUG-ITEM does not appear in your program listing, but it is there for you to use. The ANSI definition of DEBUG-ITEM is as follows:

```
01   DEBUG-ITEM,
     02   DEBUG-LINE      PICTURE IS X(6),
     02   FILLER          PICTURE IS X   VALUE SPACE,
     02   DEBUG-NAME      PICTURE IS X(30),
     02   FILLER          PICTURE IS X   VALUE SPACE,
     02   DEBUG-SUB-1     PICTURE IS S9999 SIGN IS LEADING SEPARATE CHARACTER,
     02   FILLER          PICTURE IS X   VALUE SPACE,
     02   DEBUG-SUB-2     PICTURE IS S9999 SIGN IS LEADING SEPARATE CHARACTER,
     02   FILLER          PICTURE IS X   VALUE SPACE,
     02   DEBUG-SUB-3     PICTURE IS S9999 SIGN IS LEADING SEPARATE CHARACTER,
     02   FILLER          PICTURE IS X   VALUE SPACE,
     02   DEBUG-CONTENTS PICTURE IS X(n),
```

The long form of the preceding PICTURE clauses, PICTURE IS, means exactly the same as the shorter forms, PICTURE and PIC.

COBOL adjusts the size of DEBUG-CONTENTS each time it assigns something to it, so that the data fit. The name DEBUG-ITEM and the names of all its elementary fields are reserved words. Notice that DEBUG-ITEM is defined so that you can just print the whole thing out on one line if you like. We will instead print out just the elementary fields as we need them.

DEBUG-ITEM and the fields subordinate to it may be referred to only in debugging sections. This is the other reason for using DISPLAY instead of, let's say, GENERATE, to print debug output. DEBUG-ITEM and its subordinate fields may not be used as SOURCE fields.

Execution of Debugging Sections

Debugging sections may be set up to **monitor** one or more files defined in the File Section, one or more paragraphs or sections in the Procedure Division, and/or one or more fields. The next several pages explain what it means to monitor a field, file, paragraph, or section. A single debugging section may monitor any combination of files, fields, paragraphs, or sections. Whenever you set up a debugging section in a program, you must tell COBOL which file(s), field(s), paragraph(s), and/or section(s) the debugging section is monitoring.

Monitoring a File

When a debugging section is used to monitor a file, COBOL executes the debugging section after it executes any statement that refers to the file name as it appears in the FD entry, except when a READ statement detects an end-of-file or an invalid key. Here's what COBOL does when it comes to a statement that names a file that is being monitored:

1. It executes the statement.
2. If a READ statement detects an end-of-file or invalid key, COBOL skips steps 3 and 4 below.
3. COBOL assigns data to the fields in DEBUG-ITEM as follows:
    a. To the field DEBUG-LINE, it assigns the sequence number (positions 1 through 6) of the statement just executed.
    b. To the field DEBUG-NAME, it assigns the file name.
    c. To DEBUG-SUB-1, DEBUG-SUB-2, DEBUG-SUB-3, it assigns spaces.
    d. To DEBUG-CONTENTS, it assigns the contents of the input record if the statement executed was a READ, and assigns spaces if the statement executed was any other.

4. It executes the debugging section that is monitoring the file.
5. It goes on to the next statement in the program.

A file name defined with an SD entry may not be monitored.

Monitoring a Field

When a debugging section is used to monitor a field, we have a choice. We can tell COBOL to execute the debugging section only when the program comes to statements that explicitly refer to the field and change its contents, or we can use the **ALL REFERENCES** option to tell COBOL to execute the debugging section when the program comes to ALL statements that explicitly refer to the field. An **explicit reference** to a field is one in which the name of the field actually appears in the statement. Statements like MOVE CORRESPONDING, ADD CORRESPONDING, SUBTRACT CORRESPONDING, READ, GENERATE, and group level MOVEs, which may act upon a field but not name it, do not cause execution of a debugging section that is monitoring that field.

Any field defined anywhere in the Data Division may be monitored, except that in the Report Section only fields defined as sum counters may be monitored. Here's what COBOL does when it comes to a statement that names a field that is being monitored:

1. It executes the statement.
2. It assigns data to the fields in DEBUG-ITEM as follows:
   a. To DEBUG-LINE, it assigns the sequence number of the statement.
   b. To DEBUG-NAME, it assigns the name of the field being monitored. If the field being monitored is subscripted or indexed, only the data name of the field is assigned to DEBUG-NAME; no subscripts or indexes are assigned to DEBUG-NAME. If the field is qualified, COBOL assigns to DEBUG-NAME as much of the field name as will fit into DEBUG-NAME's 30 character positions, with the qualifiers separated by IN or OF, depending on the COBOL system being used.
   c. If the field being monitored is subscripted or indexed, numbers representing the values of the subscripts or indexes are assigned to DEBUG-SUB-1, DEBUG-SUB-2, and/or DEBUG-SUB-3, as needed. Unneeded fields are assigned spaces.
   d. To DEBUG-CONTENTS, COBOL assigns the value of the field being monitored. COBOL MOVEs data to DEBUG-CONTENTS from the field being monitored as though the field being monitored were defined with a PICTURE of Xs. This means that under certain conditions DEBUG-CONTENTS will not be printable. The conditions under which DEBUG-CONTENTS is nonprintable are different for different COBOL systems.
3. It executes the debugging section that is monitoring the field.
4. It goes on to the next statement in the program.

If a field being monitored is named in a clause or phrase that is not executed, or is named as a qualifier, or is named in a statement in a debugging section, or is named as the object of a SEARCH or SEARCH ALL statement, steps 2 and 3 above are not executed. (Names appearing elsewhere in a SEARCH or SEARCH ALL statement can be monitored in the usual way, however.) If a field being monitored is named in the VARYING clause of a PERFORM statement, or in any of the AFTER or UNTIL clauses of a PERFORM statement, steps 2 through 4 above are executed each time after the field is initialized, changed, or evaluated, whether or not the ALL REFERENCES option is specified.

If a field being monitored is explicitly referred to in a WRITE or REWRITE statement (and in some COBOL systems a RELEASE statement also), the record being written is assigned to DEBUG-CONTENTS even though the record may no longer be available in the output area in the File Section. This holds true whether the field being monitored is the object of the verb or appears after the word FROM in the WRITE, REWRITE, or RELEASE statement, and whether or not the ALL REFERENCES option is specified.

Monitoring a Paragraph or Section

A debugging section may be set up to monitor the execution of one or more paragraphs or sections, or to monitor **ALL PROCEDURES.** Here's what COBOL does when it comes to a paragraph or section being monitored:

1.   It assigns data to the fields in DEBUG-ITEM as follows:
    a.   To DEBUG-NAME, COBOL assigns the name of the paragraph or section being monitored.
    b.   To DEBUG-SUB-1, DEBUG-SUB-2, and DEBUG-SUB-3, it assigns spaces.
    c.   To DEBUG-CONTENTS, it assigns the words PERFORM LOOP if the paragraph or section being monitored is being executed under control of a PERFORM statement, or it assigns the words USE PROCEDURE if the paragraph or section being monitored is among the DECLARATIVES, or it assigns the words START PROGRAM if the first nondeclarative paragraph or section in the program is being monitored and this is the first execution of that paragraph or section, or it assigns the words SORT INPUT, SORT OUTPUT, or MERGE OUTPUT if the section being monitored is an INPUT PROCEDURE of a SORT or an OUTPUT PROCEDURE of a SORT or a MERGE, or it assigns spaces if a GO TO statement transfers control to the paragraph or section being monitored.
    d.   To DEBUG-LINE, COBOL assigns a sequence number that depends on the words that were assigned to DEBUG-CONTENTS in (c). If the words PERFORM LOOP were assigned to DEBUG-CONTENTS, COBOL assigns to DEBUG-LINE the sequence number of the PERFORM statement. If the words USE PROCEDURE were assigned to DEBUG-CONTENTS, COBOL assigns to DEBUG-LINE the sequence number of the statement that caused the declarative procedure to be executed. If the words START PROGRAM were assigned to DEBUG-CONTENTS, COBOL assigns to DEBUG-LINE the sequence number of the first nondeclarative paragraph or section in the program. If the words SORT INPUT, SORT OUTPUT, or MERGE OUTPUT were assigned to DEBUG-CONTENTS, COBOL assigns to DEBUG-LINE the sequence number of the SORT or MERGE statement. And if spaces were assigned to DEBUG-CONTENTS, COBOL assigns to DEBUG-LINE the sequence number of the GO TO statement.
2.   COBOL executes the debugging section that is monitoring this paragraph or section.

3. It executes the paragraph or section being monitored.
4. It goes on to the next statement in the program.

You may not monitor a paragraph that is part of a debugging section, nor may you monitor a debugging section. You may monitor a USE BEFORE REPORTING or USE AFTER ERROR PROCEDURE section, or a paragraph that is part of such a section.

Using Debugging Sections

For Program P19-02 we will once again modify Program P09-01. Let's say that in Program P19-02 we would like to monitor the big IF statement at line 01390 in Program P09-01 to see if the correct path is being executed. The IF statement contains one COMPUTE statement in each path, so we can set up a debugging section to tell us which of the two COMPUTE statements is being executed. We can call the section MONITOR-THE-BIG-IF-STATEMENT SECTION. Since the field COMMISSION-RATE-IN is named in both COMPUTE statements and nowhere else in the Procedure Division, we can tell COBOL that the debugging section is monitoring COMMISSION-RATE-IN. We will monitor the IF statement only when COMPUTATION-SUBSCRIPT is equal to 2, 4, 6, 8, or 10.

And, of course, we would like to print out each input record just after it has been read, as usual. We will do this by setting up a debugging section to monitor the input file. We will call the section MONITOR-INPUT-FILE SECTION and will tell COBOL that the section is monitoring the file SALES-FILE-IN.

Program P19-02 produces debug output in the format shown in Figure 19.5. As in Program P19-01, we have seven lines of debug output for each input record. The line labeled INPUT RECORD of course will show each input record after it has been read. But now the line also contains a field called SEQ NO. This field will be used to show the sequence number of the statement that triggers the execution of the debugging section MONITOR-INPUT-FILE. The five lines following the line labeled INPUT RECORD will show the results of monitoring the IF statement. For values of COMPUTATION-SUBSCRIPT equal to 2, 4, 6, 8, and 10, we will see the sequence number of the COMPUTE statement that executes and the value of SALE-AMOUNT-IN. Then we can check that the correct path of the IF statement is being taken for different values of SALE-AMOUNT-IN.

Figure 19.5 Output format for debug output of Program P19-02.

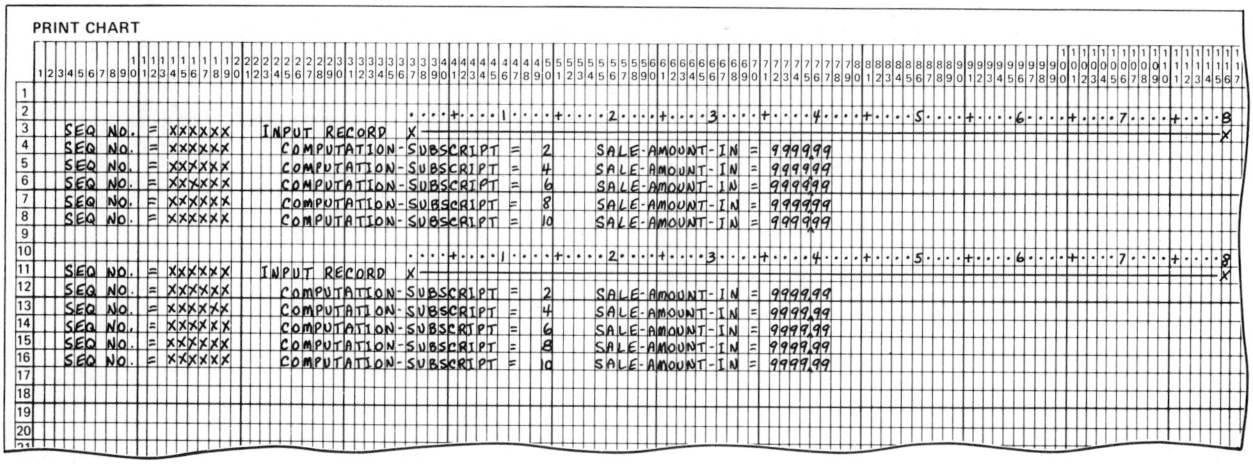

A Program with Debugging Sections

Program P19-02 is shown in Figure 19.6. The WITH DEBUGGING MODE clause must be included to indicate to COBOL that debugging sections (and of course debugging lines) are to be executed. But in addition, COBOL requires that something called an **object-time switch** be on in order for the debugging sections to be executed. Each COBOL system has its own object-time switch outside of the COBOL language.[2] If the object-time switch is off, the debugging sections are deactivated, but the debugging lines, if any, will execute. If the WITH DEBUGGING MODE clause is removed, both the sections and the lines are deactivated and the object-time switch has no effect.

The Procedure Division begins at line 010100. Debugging sections are always written into the Procedure Division as DECLARATIVES. A debugging section consists of a section header followed by a USE sentence, followed by one or more paragraphs. The USE sentence in a debugging section must contain the reserved words **USE FOR DEBUGGING** or **USE DEBUGGING,** followed by the name(s) of the file(s), field(s), paragraph(s), or section(s) being monitored by this debugging section. Our MONITOR-INPUT-FILE SECTION, line 010106, is being used to monitor only SALES-FILE-IN. The complete format of the USE FOR DEBUGGING sentence will be given shortly.

Figure 19.6 Program P19-02.

```
CB1 RELEASE 2.4                              IBM OS/VS COBOL  JULY  1, 1982


                        19.15.09        APR 14,1988


000100 IDENTIFICATION DIVISION.
000200 PROGRAM-ID.  P19-02.
000300*AUTHOR. DEBORAH ANN SENIOR.
000400*
000500*    THIS PROGRAM PRODUCES A SALESPERSON COMMISSION
000600*    REPORT SHOWING TEN COMMISSION AMOUNTS
000700*    AND THE TOTAL FOR EACH SALESPERSON.
000800*
000900*
001000*********************************************************************
001100
001200 ENVIRONMENT DIVISION.
001300 CONFIGURATION SECTION.
001400 SOURCE-COMPUTER.  IBM-370 WITH DEBUGGING MODE.
001500 OBJECT-COMPUTER.  IBM-370.
001600
001700 INPUT-OUTPUT SECTION.
001800 FILE-CONTROL.
001900     SELECT SALES-FILE-IN              ASSIGN TO INFILE.
002000     SELECT COMMISSION-REPORT-FILE-OUT  ASSIGN TO PRINTER.
002100
002200*********************************************************************
002300
002400 DATA DIVISION.
002500 FILE SECTION.
002600 FD  SALES-FILE-IN
002700     LABEL RECORDS ARE OMITTED
002800     RECORD CONTAINS 80 CHARACTERS.
002900
003000 01  SALES-RECORD-IN.
003100     05  SALESPERSON-NUMBER-IN   PIC X(7).
003200     05  SALE-AMOUNT-IN          PIC 9(4)V99    OCCURS 10 TIMES.
003300     05  FILLER                  PIC X(13).
003400
```

---

[2]In IBM OS/VS COBOL, the object-time switch is the operand PARM.GO='/DEBUG' or PARM.GO='/NODEBUG' in the EXEC statement. In NCR VRX COBOL, the object-time switch is the operand OPTS=00000001 or OPTS=00000000 in the JOB statement.

```
003500 FD   COMMISSION-REPORT-FILE-OUT
003600      LABEL RECORDS ARE OMITTED.
003700
003800 01   REPORT-LINE                  PIC X(119).
003900
004000 WORKING-STORAGE SECTION.
004100 01  MORE-INPUT                     PIC X           VALUE "Y".
004200 01  COMMISSION-RATE-1              PIC V99         VALUE .05.
004300 01  COMMISSION-RATE-2              PIC V99         VALUE .10.
004400 01  BRACKET-MAXIMUM                PIC 999V99      VALUE 100.00.
004500 01  NUMBER-OF-SALES                PIC S99         VALUE 10
004600                                    COMP            SYNC.
004700 01  GRAND-TOTAL-COMMISSIONS-W      PIC S9(6)V99    VALUE 0.
004800 01  COMMISSIONS.
004900     05  COMMISSION-AMOUNT-W        PIC S9(4)V99 OCCURS 10 TIMES.
005000 01  COMMISSION-FOR-SALESPERSON     PIC S9(5)V99.
005100 01  COMPUTATION-SUBSCRIPT          PIC S99         COMP SYNC.
005200 01  LINE-SPACING     VALUE 1       PIC S9          COMP SYNC.
005205 01  GUIDE-LINE                     PIC X(116)
005210     VALUE "                                        ....+....1....+...
005215-        ".2....+....3....+....4....+....5....+....6....+....7..
005220-        "..+....8".
005300
005400 01  PAGE-HEADING-1.
005500     05  FILLER  PIC X(51)          VALUE SPACES.
005600     05  FILLER  PIC X(17)          VALUE "COMMISSION REPORT".
005700
005800 01  PAGE-HEADING-2.
005900     05  FILLER  PIC X(39)          VALUE "SALES-".
006000     05  FILLER  PIC X(73)
006100         VALUE "C O M M I S S I O N S   O N   S A L E S".
006200     05  FILLER  PIC X(5)           VALUE "TOTAL".
006300
006400 01  PAGE-HEADING-3.
006500     05  FILLER  PIC X(10)          VALUE "PERSON".
006600     05  FILLER  PIC X(10)          VALUE "SALE 1".
006700     05  FILLER  PIC X(10)          VALUE "SALE 2".
006800     05  FILLER  PIC X(10)          VALUE "SALE 3".
006900     05  FILLER  PIC X(10)          VALUE "SALE 4".
007000     05  FILLER  PIC X(10)          VALUE "SALE 5".
007100     05  FILLER  PIC X(10)          VALUE "SALE 6".
007200     05  FILLER  PIC X(10)          VALUE "SALE 7".
007300     05  FILLER  PIC X(10)          VALUE "SALE 8".
007400     05  FILLER  PIC X(10)          VALUE "SALE 9".
007500     05  FILLER  PIC X(11)          VALUE "SALE 10".
007600     05  FILLER  PIC X(7)           VALUE "COMMIS-".
007700
007800 01  PAGE-HEADING-4.
007900     05  FILLER  PIC X(112)         VALUE "NUMBER".
008000     05  FILLER  PIC X(4)           VALUE "SION".
008100
008200 01  DETAIL-LINE.
008300     05  SALESPERSON-NUMBER-OUT  PIC X(9).
008400     05  COMMISSION-AMOUNT-OUT   PIC Z,ZZ9.99BB
008500                                 OCCURS 10 TIMES.
008600     05  COMMISSION-FOR-SALESPERSON-OUT
008700                                 PIC BZZ,ZZ9.99.
008800
008900 01  NO-INPUT-DATA.
009000     05  FILLER                     PIC X(53) VALUE SPACES.
009100     05  FILLER                     PIC X(13) VALUE "NO INPUT DATA".
009200
009300 01  TOTAL-LINE.
009400     05  FILLER                     PIC X(68) VALUE SPACES.
009500     05  FILLER                     PIC X(41)
009600     VALUE "TOTAL COMMISSION FOR ALL SALESPERSONS".
009700     05  GRAND-TOTAL-COMMISSIONS PIC ZZZ,ZZ9.99.
009800
009900***********************************************************************
010000
010100 PROCEDURE DIVISION.
```

(continued)

Figure 19.6 (continued)

```
010102
010104 DECLARATIVES.
010106 MONITOR-INPUT-FILE SECTION.
010108     USE FOR DEBUGGING SALES-FILE-IN.
010110 PRINT-INPUT-RECORD.
010112     DISPLAY SPACES.
010114     DISPLAY GUIDE-LINE.
010116     DISPLAY "   SEQ NO. = ", DEBUG-LINE
010118             "   INPUT RECORD  ", DEBUG-CONTENTS.
010120
010122 MONITOR-THE-BIG-IF-STATEMENT SECTION.
010124     USE FOR DEBUGGING ALL COMMISSION-RATE-1.
010126 PRINT-DEBUG-LINE.
010128     IF COMPUTATION-SUBSCRIPT IS EQUAL TO 2 OR 4 OR 6 OR 8 OR 10
010130         DISPLAY "   SEQ NO. = ", DEBUG-LINE
010132                 "    COMPUTATION-SUBSCRIPT = "
010134                 COMPUTATION-SUBSCRIPT
010136                 "   SALE-AMOUNT-IN = "
010138                 SALE-AMOUNT-IN (COMPUTATION-SUBSCRIPT).
010140 END DECLARATIVES.
010142
010144 NONDECLARATIVE SECTION.
010200 CONTROL-PARAGRAPH.
010300     PERFORM INITIALIZATION.
010400     PERFORM MAIN-PROCESS UNTIL MORE-INPUT IS EQUAL TO "N".
010500     PERFORM TERMINATION.
010600     STOP RUN.
010700
010800 INITIALIZATION.
010900     OPEN INPUT  SALES-FILE-IN,
011000          OUTPUT COMMISSION-REPORT-FILE-OUT.
011100     WRITE REPORT-LINE FROM PAGE-HEADING-1 AFTER PAGE.
011200     WRITE REPORT-LINE FROM PAGE-HEADING-2 AFTER 4.
011300     WRITE REPORT-LINE FROM PAGE-HEADING-3.
011400     WRITE REPORT-LINE FROM PAGE-HEADING-4.
011500     MOVE 2 TO LINE-SPACING.
011600     PERFORM READ-A-RECORD.
011700     IF MORE-INPUT IS EQUAL TO "N"
011800         WRITE REPORT-LINE FROM NO-INPUT-DATA AFTER 2.
011900
012000 MAIN-PROCESS.
012100     MOVE ZERO TO COMMISSION-FOR-SALESPERSON.
012200     PERFORM COMMISSION-CALCULATION
012300         VARYING COMPUTATION-SUBSCRIPT FROM 1 BY 1 UNTIL
012400         COMPUTATION-SUBSCRIPT IS GREATER THAN NUMBER-OF-SALES.
012500     PERFORM PRODUCE-THE-REPORT.
012600     PERFORM READ-A-RECORD.
012700
012800 TERMINATION.
012900     PERFORM PRODUCE-FINAL-TOTAL-LINE.
013000     CLOSE SALES-FILE-IN,
013100           COMMISSION-REPORT-FILE-OUT.
013200
013300 READ-A-RECORD.
013400     READ SALES-FILE-IN
013500         AT END
013600             MOVE "N" TO MORE-INPUT.
013700
013800 COMMISSION-CALCULATION.
013900     IF SALE-AMOUNT-IN (COMPUTATION-SUBSCRIPT) IS NOT GREATER THAN
014000         BRACKET-MAXIMUM
014100         COMPUTE
014200         COMMISSION-AMOUNT-W (COMPUTATION-SUBSCRIPT) ROUNDED
014300         COMMISSION-AMOUNT-OUT (COMPUTATION-SUBSCRIPT) ROUNDED
014400         = SALE-AMOUNT-IN (COMPUTATION-SUBSCRIPT) *
014500             COMMISSION-RATE-1
014600     ELSE
014700         COMPUTE
014800         COMMISSION-AMOUNT-W (COMPUTATION-SUBSCRIPT) ROUNDED
014900         COMMISSION-AMOUNT-OUT (COMPUTATION-SUBSCRIPT) ROUNDED
015000         = BRACKET-MAXIMUM * COMMISSION-RATE-1 +
015100             (SALE-AMOUNT-IN (COMPUTATION-SUBSCRIPT) -
015200             BRACKET-MAXIMUM) * COMMISSION-RATE-2.
015300     ADD COMMISSION-AMOUNT-W (COMPUTATION-SUBSCRIPT) TO
015400         COMMISSION-FOR-SALESPERSON.
015500
```

```
015600 PRODUCE-THE-REPORT.
015700     MOVE SALESPERSON-NUMBER-IN TO SALESPERSON-NUMBER-OUT.
015800     MOVE COMMISSION-FOR-SALESPERSON TO
015900         COMMISSION-FOR-SALESPERSON-OUT.
016000     ADD COMMISSION-FOR-SALESPERSON TO GRAND-TOTAL-COMMISSIONS-W.
016100     WRITE REPORT-LINE FROM DETAIL-LINE AFTER LINE-SPACING.
016200     MOVE 1 TO LINE-SPACING.
016300
016400 PRODUCE-FINAL-TOTAL-LINE.
016500     MOVE GRAND-TOTAL-COMMISSIONS-W TO GRAND-TOTAL-COMMISSIONS.
016600     WRITE REPORT-LINE FROM TOTAL-LINE AFTER 4.
```

Immediately following the USE sentence there must be zero, one, or more paragraphs containing the executable steps of the debugging section. The end of a debugging section is indicated by the beginning of another section or the words END DECLARATIVES.

USE FOR DEBUGGING sections, USE BEFORE REPORTING sections, and USE AFTER ERROR PROCEDURE sections may all appear together in the same program. If they do, all the USE FOR DEBUGGING sections must come before any of the others, immediately following the DECLARATIVES header. The USE BEFORE REPORTING sections and USE AFTER ERROR PROCEDURE sections may appear in any order.

The next debugging section, MONITOR-THE-BIG-IF-STATEMENT, begins at line 010122. Here the USE sentence says that this section is monitoring ALL statements that name the field COMMISSION-RATE-1. Remember that if ALL were omitted, this debugging section would monitor only statements that name and change COMMISSION-RATE-1.

In this program, the debugging procedures are simple enough that each fits into one paragraph. When more than one paragraph is required in a debugging section, remember the rule: PERFORM statements in a debugging section may refer only to paragraphs that are among the DECLARATIVES. The PERFORMed paragraph need not be in the same section as the PERFORM statement.

Output from Debugging Sections

Program P19-02 was run with its object-time switch on, using the same input data as Program P19-01. It produced the debug output shown in Figure 19.7, as well as normal report output (not shown). The empty INPUT RECORD lines at the beginning and end of the debug output arise from the statements that OPEN and CLOSE the file SALES-FILE-IN. Since we have a section that we USE FOR DEBUGGING SALES-FILE-IN, the section is executed for all statements that name the file. You can tell from the SEQ NO. fields that indeed the OPEN and CLOSE statements caused the empty lines.

By examining the SEQ NO. fields in the other lines of debug output, you can check that the correct path of the IF statement is being executed for each SALE-AMOUNT-IN.

EXERCISE 2

Find proof in the debug output in Figure 19.7 that the correct path of the IF statement at line 013900 in Program P19-02 is executed for values of SALE-AMOUNT-IN greater than $100.00, less than $100.00, and exactly $100.00.

Figure 19.7   Debut output from Program P19-02.

```
                                  ....+....1....+....2....+....3....+....4....+....5....+....6....+....7....+....8
          SEQ NO. = 010900    INPUT RECORD


                                  ....+....1....+....2....+....3....+....4....+....5....+....6....+....7....+....8
          SEQ NO. = 013400    INPUT RECORD   0001289500750001256800100048712181492000600011000004800010500087593
          SEQ NO. = 014100    COMPUTATION-SUBSCRIPT = 02       SALE-AMOUNT-IN = 001256
          SEQ NO. = 014700    COMPUTATION-SUBSCRIPT = 04       SALE-AMOUNT-IN = 048712
          SEQ NO. = 014100    COMPUTATION-SUBSCRIPT = 06       SALE-AMOUNT-IN = 000600
          SEQ NO. = 014100    COMPUTATION-SUBSCRIPT = 08       SALE-AMOUNT-IN = 004800
          SEQ NO. = 014700    COMPUTATION-SUBSCRIPT = 10       SALE-AMOUNT-IN = 087593


                                  ....+....1....+....2....+....3....+....4....+....5....+....6....+....7....+....8
          SEQ NO. = 013400    INPUT RECORD   0942386010000200000051927009550002795020000012500041225006000036150
          SEQ NO. = 014700    COMPUTATION-SUBSCRIPT = 02       SALE-AMOUNT-IN = 200000
          SEQ NO. = 014100    COMPUTATION-SUBSCRIPT = 04       SALE-AMOUNT-IN = 009550
          SEQ NO. = 014700    COMPUTATION-SUBSCRIPT = 06       SALE-AMOUNT-IN = 020000
          SEQ NO. = 014700    COMPUTATION-SUBSCRIPT = 08       SALE-AMOUNT-IN = 041225
          SEQ NO. = 014700    COMPUTATION-SUBSCRIPT = 10       SALE-AMOUNT-IN = 036150


                                  ....+....1....+....2....+....3....+....4....+....5....+....6....+....7....+....8
          SEQ NO. = 013400    INPUT RECORD   3684420020000012165007495010000000000000000000000000000000000000000
          SEQ NO. = 014700    COMPUTATION-SUBSCRIPT = 02       SALE-AMOUNT-IN = 012165
          SEQ NO. = 014100    COMPUTATION-SUBSCRIPT = 04       SALE-AMOUNT-IN = 010000
          SEQ NO. = 014100    COMPUTATION-SUBSCRIPT = 06       SALE-AMOUNT-IN = 000000
          SEQ NO. = 014100    COMPUTATION-SUBSCRIPT = 08       SALE-AMOUNT-IN = 000000
          SEQ NO. = 014100    COMPUTATION-SUBSCRIPT = 10       SALE-AMOUNT-IN = 000000


                                  ....+....1....+....2....+....3....+....4....+....5....+....6....+....7....+....8
          SEQ NO. = 013400    INPUT RECORD   5236714008412004519072368006850029518000000000000000000000000000000
          SEQ NO. = 014100    COMPUTATION-SUBSCRIPT = 02       SALE-AMOUNT-IN = 004519
          SEQ NO. = 014100    COMPUTATION-SUBSCRIPT = 04       SALE-AMOUNT-IN = 006850
          SEQ NO. = 014100    COMPUTATION-SUBSCRIPT = 06       SALE-AMOUNT-IN = 000000
          SEQ NO. = 014100    COMPUTATION-SUBSCRIPT = 08       SALE-AMOUNT-IN = 000000
          SEQ NO. = 014100    COMPUTATION-SUBSCRIPT = 10       SALE-AMOUNT-IN = 000000


                                  ....+....1....+....2....+....3....+....4....+....5....+....6....+....7....+....8
          SEQ NO. = 013400    INPUT RECORD   6612364001000022358001873099500006515024512010368008995017360060287
          SEQ NO. = 014700    COMPUTATION-SUBSCRIPT = 02       SALE-AMOUNT-IN = 022358
          SEQ NO. = 014700    COMPUTATION-SUBSCRIPT = 04       SALE-AMOUNT-IN = 099500
          SEQ NO. = 014700    COMPUTATION-SUBSCRIPT = 06       SALE-AMOUNT-IN = 024512
          SEQ NO. = 014100    COMPUTATION-SUBSCRIPT = 08       SALE-AMOUNT-IN = 008995
          SEQ NO. = 014700    COMPUTATION-SUBSCRIPT = 10       SALE-AMOUNT-IN = 060287


                                  ....+....1....+....2....+....3....+....4....+....5....+....6....+....7....+....8
          SEQ NO. = 013400    INPUT RECORD   7747119005200016500119500007350044895012500006875001425009999000000
          SEQ NO. = 014700    COMPUTATION-SUBSCRIPT = 02       SALE-AMOUNT-IN = 016500
          SEQ NO. = 014100    COMPUTATION-SUBSCRIPT = 04       SALE-AMOUNT-IN = 007350
          SEQ NO. = 014700    COMPUTATION-SUBSCRIPT = 06       SALE-AMOUNT-IN = 012500
          SEQ NO. = 014100    COMPUTATION-SUBSCRIPT = 08       SALE-AMOUNT-IN = 001425
          SEQ NO. = 014100    COMPUTATION-SUBSCRIPT = 10       SALE-AMOUNT-IN = 000000


                                  ....+....1....+....2....+....3....+....4....+....5....+....6....+....7....+....8
          SEQ NO. = 013000    INPUT RECORD
```

The USE FOR DEBUGGING Sentence

The format of the USE FOR DEBUGGING sentence is

```
USE FOR DEBUGGING
              ⎧ cd-name-1                         ⎫
              ⎪ [ALL REFERENCES OF] identifier-1  ⎪
         ON  ⎨  file-name-1                        ⎬
              ⎪ procedure-name-1                  ⎪
              ⎩ ALL PROCEDURES                     ⎭

              ⎡ cd-name-2                         ⎤
              ⎢ [ALL REFERENCES OF] identifier-2  ⎥
              ⎢ file-name-2                        ⎥  ...
              ⎢ procedure-name-2                  ⎥
              ⎣ ALL PROCEDURES                     ⎦
```

If a field being monitored is named more than once in a single statement, the debugging section for that field is executed only once.[3] Within an imperative statement, each occurrence of an imperative verb is considered to begin a new statement for debugging purposes. Tables 19-1 and 19-2 show all the imperative verbs defined in the 1974 and 1985 ANSI standards, respectively. Some COBOL systems may make additions to or deletions from these lists.

Table 19-1

The 1974 ANSI standard list of imperative verbs.

ACCEPT	GENERATE	SEND
ADD (1)	GO	SET
ALTER	INITIATE	SORT
CALL (3)	INSPECT	START (2)
CANCEL	MERGE	STOP
CLOSE	MOVE	STRING (3)
COMPUTE (1)	MULTIPLY (1)	SUBTRACT (1)
DELETE (2)	OPEN	SUPPRESS
DISABLE	PERFORM	TERMINATE
DISPLAY	READ (5)	UNSTRING (3)
DIVIDE (1)	RECEIVE (4)	WRITE (6)
ENABLE	RELEASE	
EXIT	REWRITE (2)	

(1) Without the optional SIZE ERROR phrase.
(2) Without the optional INVALID KEY phrase.
(3) Without the optional ON OVERFLOW phrase.
(4) Without the optional NO DATA phrase.
(5) Without the optional AT END phrase or INVALID KEY phrase.
(6) Without the optional INVALID KEY phrase or END-OF-PAGE phrase.

Table 19-2

The 1985 ANSI standard list of imperative verbs.

ACCEPT	GENERATE	REWRITE (2)
ADD (1)	GO TO	SEND
ALTER	INITIALIZE	SET
CALL (7)	INITIATE	SORT
CANCEL	INSPECT	START (2)
CLOSE	MERGE	STOP
COMPUTE (1)	MOVE	STRING
CONTINUE	MULTIPLY (1)	SUBTRACT (1)
DELETE(2)	OPEN	SUPPRESS
DISABLE	PERFORM	TERMINATE
DISPLAY	PURGE	UNSTRING(3)
DIVIDE (1)	READ (5)	WRITE (6)
ENABLE	RECEIVE (4)	
EXIT	RELEASE	

(1) Without the optional ON SIZE ERROR and NOT ON SIZE ERROR phrases.
(2) Without the optional INVALID KEY and NOT INVALID KEY phrases.
(3) Without the optional ON OVERFLOW and NOT ON OVERFLOW phrases.
(4) Without the optional NO DATA and WITH DATA phrases.
(5) Without the optional AT END, NOT AT END, INVALID KEY, and NOT INVALID KEY phrases.
(6) Without the optional INVALID KEY, NOT INVALID KEY, END-OF-PAGE, and NOT END-OF-PAGE phrases.
(7) Without the optional ON OVERFLOW, ON EXCEPTION, and NOT ON EXCEPTION phrases.

[3]In some COBOL systems, if a subscripted or indexed field is named more than once in a statement, the debugging section monitoring that field is executed once for each appearance of the field name.

When a subscripted or indexed field is being monitored, its name must be entered in the USE FOR DEBUGGING sentence without any subscripts or indexes.

Statements appearing outside debugging sections must not refer to paragraphs or sections defined within debugging sections.

Although a single debugging section may refer to any number of files, fields, paragraphs, and/or sections, there may be at most only one debugging section for any one file, field, paragraph, or section. That means that if there is some debugging section monitoring ALL PROCEDURES, no debugging section may monitor a specific paragraph.

EXERCISE 3

Modify your solution to Exercise 1 to use debugging sections instead of debugging lines.

Use the Debugging Feature

You can now use the debugging feature in any or all of the programming assignments in this book, even when the assignment does not call for it. Use the debugging feature as you see fit to help you test your programs, or as your instructor requires.

As a COBOL programmer in the working world, use of the debugging feature will enable you to avoid having to use some of the more cumbersome and difficult debugging aids commonly available.

Summary

As an aid in testing programs, debugging lines and/or debugging sections may be used to cause a program to produce debug output. Debugging lines may be activated and deactivated by use of the WITH DEBUGGING MODE clause, and debugging sections may be activated and deactivated by use of the object-time switch.

Debugging lines may appear anywhere after the OBJECT-COMPUTER paragraph, and may be written in the Environment, Data, and Procedure Divisions. Debugging lines must have a D in position 7.

The best verb to use for producing debug output is DISPLAY. Although DISPLAY has severe limitations that make it unsuitable for producing normal report output, it has two advantages that make it very useful for producing debug output. The advantages are that you may DISPLAY data on the high-speed printer before the printer file is OPENed and after it is CLOSEd, and that you may refer to the fields in DEBUG-ITEM conveniently within the DECLARATIVES.

A debugging section may be set up to monitor one or more files, fields, paragraphs, or sections. The USE FOR DEBUGGING sentence indicates which files, fields, paragraphs, and/or sections are being monitored by a particular debugging section. Any one file, field, paragraph, or section may be monitored by not more than one debugging section. When COBOL executes a debugging section it assigns data to the fields in DEBUG-ITEM to provide information about the conditions causing execution of the debugging section.

Fill-in Exercises

1. Debugging lines may appear anywhere after the _____ paragraph.

2. The clause that activates and deactivates debugging lines is the _____ _____ _____ clause.

3. Whenever your program produces debug output, it should always print each _input_ record soon after it has been read.

4. Three limitations of the DISPLAY verb are _inflexible editing_, _inconvenient line formatting_, and _"verticle" paper control_.

5. The field in DEBUG-ITEM to which COBOL assigns the name of the file, field, paragraph, or section being monitored is _debug name_

6. The field in DEBUG-ITEM to which COBOL assigns a line sequence number is _debug line_

7. The field in DEBUG-ITEM to which COBOL assigns the value of a field being monitored is _debug contents_

8. The field in DEBUG-ITEM to which COBOL assigns the words PERFORM LOOP is _debug contents_

9. The _use for Debugging_ sentence names the files, fields, paragraphs, and/or sections that are being monitored by a particular debugging section.

10. The _all procedures_ option may be used to indicate that a debugging section is monitoring all paragraphs and all sections in a program (except debugging sections, which cannot be monitored).

11. Debugging lines contain the letter _D_ in position _7_ .

12. The phrase that activates and deactivates debugging lines is part of the _object computer_ paragraph.

13. The switch that activates and deactivates debugging sections is called a(n) _object time_ switch.

14. Fields in DEBUG-ITEM can be referred to only within _debugging sections_

15. COBOL assigns the values of subscripts of fields being monitored to _debug sub-1_ _debug sub-2_, and _debug sub-3_ ∴ only 3 demensional table available

Review Exercises

1. For this exercise assume that FIELD-1 is the name of a field in working storage in some program and that PARAGRAPH-1 is the name of a paragraph in that program.
    Tell whether each of the following is a legal USE FOR DEBUGGING sentence:
   a. USE FOR DEBUGGING PARAGRAPH-1, FIELD-1.
   b. USE FOR DEBUGGING PARAGRAPH-1, ALL FIELD-1.
   c. USE FOR DEBUGGING ALL PARAGRAPH-1, FIELD-1.
   d. USE FOR DEBUGGING ALL PROCEDURES, PARAGRAPH-1.
   e. USE FOR DEBUGGING ALL PROCEDURES, FIELD-1.

2. Using the names of the field and paragraph in Review Exercise 1, write a USE FOR DEBUGGING sentence that will monitor all statements that refer to FIELD-1 and all the paragraphs and sections in the program.

3. This Review Exercise refers to Program P09-03, Figure 9.10, page 267. Describe the debug output that would be produced if the following statement were added to Program P09-03 at the line sequence numbers indicated:

```
012705D          DISPLAY  "STATE-CODE-IN = ",
012710D                   STATE-CODE-IN,
012715D                   "STATE-CODE-INDEX = ",
012720D                   STATE-CODE-INDEX,
012725D                   "STATE-NAME-INDEX = ",
012730D                   STATE-NAME-INDEX,
012735D                   "NAME OF STATE = ",
012740D                   STATE-NAME (STATE-NAME-INDEX)
```

4. Write a debugging section that will produce the same debug output as the debugging lines in Review Exercise 3. Be careful in selecting the name to specify in your USE FOR DEBUGGING sentence. Remember that a word that appears immediately after the word SEARCH does not trigger execution of a debugging section.
5. Modify Program P08-04 to monitor the COLUMN-HEADINGS-PARA-GRAPH. Include in each line of debug output a line sequence number and the value of the field MORE-INPUT. Run your program with the original input to Program P08-04. Notice in your output the line sequence numbers that trigger execution of your debugging section.

Project

Modify your solution to the Project in Chapter 10, to monitor the SEARCH through the tax table. Write a USE FOR DEBUGGING section so that it prints one line of debug output each time the Gross Pay field is compared to a field in the tax table as the tax table is being SEARCHed. Have each line of debug output contain the following fields:

a. The line sequence number of the SEARCH statement
b. The value of Gross Pay
c. The value of the table index
d. The field in the tax table against which the Gross Pay is being compared.

Have your program print identifying information with each field of debug output so it can be identified easily.

American National Standard List of COBOL Reserved Words — 1974

This list of reserved words is the 1974 ANSI standard. Your own COBOL system may make additions to or deletions from this list. Check your COBOL manual.

ACCEPT	CLOSE	DEBUG-SUB-3	EXIT
ACCESS	COBOL	DEBUGGING	EXTEND
ADD	CODE	DECIMAL-POINT	
ADVANCING	CODE-SET	DECLARATIVES	FD
AFTER	COLLATING	DELETE	FILE
ALL	COLUMN	DELIMITED	FILE-CONTROL
ALPHABETIC	COMMA	DELIMITER	FILLER
ALSO	COMMUNICATION	DEPENDING	FINAL
ALTER	COMP	DESCENDING	FIRST
ALTERNATE	COMPUTATIONAL	DESTINATION	FOOTING
AND	COMPUTE	DETAIL	FOR
ARE	CONFIGURATION	DISABLE	FROM
AREA	CONTAINS	DISPLAY	
AREAS	CONTROL	DIVIDE	GENERATE
ASCENDING	CONTROLS	DIVISION	GIVING
ASSIGN	COPY	DOWN	GO
AT	CORR	DUPLICATES	GREATER
AUTHOR	CORRESPONDING	DYNAMIC	GROUP
	COUNT		
BEFORE	CURRENCY	EGI	HEADING
BLANK		ELSE	HIGH-VALUE
BLOCK	DATA	EMI	HIGH-VALUES
BOTTOM	DATE	ENABLE	
BY	DATE-COMPILED	END	I-O
	DATE-WRITTEN	END-OF-PAGE	I-O-CONTROL
CALL	DAY	ENTER	IDENTIFICATION
CANCEL	DE	ENVIRONMENT	IF
CD	DEBUG-CONTENTS	EOP	IN
CF	DEBUG-ITEM	EQUAL	INDEX
CH	DEBUG-LINE	ERROR	INDEXED
CHARACTER	DEBUG-NAME	ESI	INDICATE
CHARACTERS	DEBUG-SUB-1	EVERY	INITIAL
CLOCK-UNITS	DEBUG-SUB-2	EXCEPTION	INITIATE

INPUT	OF	REPORTS	SYNC
INPUT-OUTPUT	OFF	RERUN	SYNCHRONIZED
INSPECT	OMITTED	RESERVE	
INSTALLATION	ON	RESET	TABLE
INTO	OPEN	RETURN	TALLYING
INVALID	OPTIONAL	REVERSED	TAPE
IS	OR	REWIND	TERMINAL
	ORGANIZATION	REWRITE	TERMINATE
JUST	OUTPUT	RF	TEXT
JUSTIFIED	OVERFLOW	RH	THAN
		RIGHT	THROUGH
KEY	PAGE	ROUNDED	THRU
	PAGE-COUNTER	RUN	TIME
LABEL	PERFORM		TIMES
LAST	PF	SAME	TO
LEADING	PH	SD	TOP
LEFT	PIC	SEARCH	TRAILING
LENGTH	PICTURE	SECTION	TYPE
LESS	PLUS	SECURITY	
LIMIT	POINTER	SEGMENT	UNIT
LIMITS	POSITION	SEGMENT-LIMIT	UNSTRING
LINAGE	POSITIVE	SELECT	UNTIL
LINAGE-COUNTER	PRINTING	SEND	UP
LINE	PROCEDURE	SENTENCE	UPON
LINE-COUNTER	PROCEDURES	SEPARATE	USAGE
LINES	PROCEED	SEQUENCE	USE
LINKAGE	PROGRAM	SEQUENTIAL	USING
LOCK	PROGRAM-ID	SET	
LOW-VALUE		SIGN	VALUE
LOW-VALUES	QUEUE	SIZE	VALUES
	QUOTE	SORT	VARYING
MEMORY	QUOTES	SORT-MERGE	
MERGE		SOURCE	WHEN
MESSAGE	RANDOM	SOURCE-COMPUTER	WITH
MODE	RD	SPACE	WORDS
MODULES	READ	SPACES	WORKING-STORAGE
MOVE	RECEIVE	SPECIAL-NAMES	WRITE
MULTIPLE	RECORD	STANDARD	
MULTIPLY	RECORDS	STANDARD-1	ZERO
	REDEFINES	START	ZEROES
	REEL	STATUS	ZEROS
NATIVE	REFERENCES	STOP	
NEGATIVE	RELATIVE	STRING	+
NEXT	RELEASE	SUB-QUEUE-1	−
NO	REMAINDER	SUB-QUEUE-2	*
NOT	REMOVAL	SUB-QUEUE-3	/
NUMBER	RENAMES	SUBTRACT	**
NUMERIC	REPLACING	SUM	>
	REPORT	SUPPRESS	<
OBJECT-COMPUTER	REPORTING	SYMBOLIC	=
OCCURS			

Additional Reserved Words in the 1985 ANSI Standard

This appendix contains reserved words which are not part of the 1974 ANSI standard that were added in the 1985 ANSI standard.

ALPHABET	END-SUBTRACT
ALPHABETIC-LOWER	END-UNSTRING
ALPHABETIC-UPPER	END-WRITE
ALPHANUMERIC	EVALUATE
ALPHANUMERIC-EDITED	EXTERNAL
ANY	
	FALSE
BINARY	
	GLOBAL
CLASS	
CONTENT	INITIALIZE
CONTINUE	
CONVERTING	NUMERIC-EDITED
DAY-OF-WEEK	ORDER
	OTHER
END-ADD	
END-CALL	PACKED-DECIMAL
END-COMPUTE	PADDING
END-DELETE	PURGE
END-DIVIDE	
END-EVALUATE	REFERENCE
END-IF	REPLACE
END-MULTIPLY	
END-PERFORM	STANDARD-2
END-READ	
END-RECEIVE	THEN
END-RETURN	TRUE
END-REWRITE	
END-SEARCH	> =
END-START	< =
END-STRING	

Complete ANSI Reference Summary — 1974

This appendix contains complete 1974 ANSI standard formats of all elements of the COBOL language.

General Format for Identification Division

IDENTIFICATION DIVISION.

PROGRAM-ID. program-name.

[AUTHOR. [comment-entry] ...]

[INSTALLATION. [comment-entry] ...]

[DATE-WRITTEN. [comment-entry] ...]

[DATE-COMPILED. [comment-entry] ...]

[SECURITY. [comment-entry] ...]

General Format for Environment Division

ENVIRONMENT DIVISION.

CONFIGURATION SECTION.

SOURCE-COMPUTER.   computer-name [WITH DEBUGGING MODE] .

OBJECT-COMPUTER.   computer-name

$$
\left[, \text{ MEMORY SIZE integer } \left\{ \begin{array}{l} \underline{\text{WORDS}} \\ \underline{\text{CHARACTERS}} \\ \underline{\text{MODULES}} \end{array} \right\} \right]
$$

[, PROGRAM COLLATING SEQUENCE IS alphabet-name]

[, SEGMENT-LIMIT IS segment-number] .

$$
\left[\text{SPECIAL-NAMES.} \quad \left[, \text{ implementor-name} \right. \right.
$$

$$
\left\{ \begin{array}{l} \text{IS mnemonic-name } [, \underline{\text{ON}} \text{ STATUS } \underline{\text{IS}} \text{ condition-name-1 } [, \underline{\text{OFF}} \text{ STATUS } \underline{\text{IS}} \text{ condition-name-2}]] \\ \text{IS mnemonic-name } [, \underline{\text{OFF}} \text{ STATUS } \underline{\text{IS}} \text{ condition-name-2 } [, \underline{\text{ON}} \text{ STATUS } \underline{\text{IS}} \text{ condition-name-1}]] \\ \underline{\text{ON}} \text{ STATUS } \underline{\text{IS}} \text{ condition-name-1 } [, \underline{\text{OFF}} \text{ STATUS } \underline{\text{IS}} \text{ condition-name-2}] \\ \underline{\text{OFF}} \text{ STATUS } \underline{\text{IS}} \text{ condition-name-2 } [, \underline{\text{ON}} \text{ STATUS } \underline{\text{IS}} \text{ condition-name-1}] \end{array} \right\} \quad \ldots
$$

$$
\left[, \text{ alphabet-name IS} \left\{ \begin{array}{l} \underline{\text{STANDARD-1}} \\ \underline{\text{NATIVE}} \\ \text{implementor-name} \\ \text{literal-1} \left[\begin{array}{l} \left\{ \begin{array}{l} \underline{\text{THROUGH}} \\ \underline{\text{THRU}} \end{array} \right\} \text{literal-2} \\ \underline{\text{ALSO}} \text{ literal-3 } [, \underline{\text{ALSO}} \text{ literal-4}]\ldots \end{array} \right] \\ \qquad \left[\text{literal-5} \left[\begin{array}{l} \left\{ \begin{array}{l} \underline{\text{THROUGH}} \\ \underline{\text{THRU}} \end{array} \right\} \text{literal-6} \\ \underline{\text{ALSO}} \text{ literal-7 } [, \underline{\text{ALSO}} \text{ literal-8}]\ldots \end{array} \right] \right] \ldots \end{array} \right\} \right] \ldots
$$

[, CURRENCY SIGN IS literal-9]

[, DECIMAL-POINT IS COMMA] .]

```
[INPUT-OUTPUT SECTION.

 FILE-CONTROL.

    {file-control-entry} ...

[I-O-CONTROL.

    [; RERUN [ON {file-name-1        }]
                 {implementor-name}

                 ⎧ {[END OF] {REEL}} OF file-name-2 ⎫
        EVERY    ⎨ {          {UNIT}}              ⎬  ...
                 ⎪ {integer-1 RECORDS}            ⎪
                 ⎪ integer-2 CLOCK-UNITS          ⎪
                 ⎩ condition-name                 ⎭

    [; SAME ⎡RECORD    ⎤ AREA FOR file-name-3 {, file-name-4} ...] ...
            ⎢SORT      ⎥
            ⎣SORT-MERGE⎦

    [; MULTIPLE FILE TAPE CONTAINS file-name-5 [POSITION integer-3]

        [, file-name-6 [POSITION integer-4]] ... ] ...   . ]
```

General Format for File Control Entry

Format 1:

```
SELECT [OPTIONAL] file-name

    ASSIGN TO implementor-name-1 [, implementor-name-2] ...

    [; RESERVE integer-1 [AREA  ]]
                         [AREAS ]

    [; ORGANIZATION IS SEQUENTIAL]

    [; ACCESS MODE IS SEQUENTIAL]

    [; FILE STATUS IS data-name-1] .
```

Format 2:

```
SELECT file-name

    ASSIGN TO implementor-name-1 [, implementor-name-2] ...

    [; RESERVE integer-1 [AREA  ]]
                         [AREAS ]

    ; ORGANIZATION IS RELATIVE

    [                    ┌ SEQUENTIAL  [, RELATIVE KEY IS data-name-1] ┐ ]
    [; ACCESS MODE IS    {                                            } ]
    [                    │ {RANDOM }   , RELATIVE KEY IS data-name-1   │ ]
    [                    └ {DYNAMIC}                                   ┘ ]

    [; FILE STATUS IS data-name-2] .
```

Format 3:

```
SELECT file-name

    ASSIGN TO implementor-name-1  [, implementor-name-2] ...

  [; RESERVE integer-1  ⎡AREA ⎤ ]
                        ⎣AREAS⎦

   ; ORGANIZATION IS INDEXED

  ⎡                    ⎧SEQUENTIAL⎫ ⎤
  ⎢; ACCESS MODE IS    ⎨RANDOM    ⎬ ⎥
  ⎣                    ⎩DYNAMIC   ⎭ ⎦

   ; RECORD KEY IS data-name-1

  [; ALTERNATE RECORD KEY IS data-name-2  [WITH DUPLICATES]] ...

  [; FILE STATUS IS data-name-3] .
```

Format 4:

```
SELECT file-name ASSIGN TO implementor-name-1  [, implementor-name-2] ...
```

General Format for Data Division

DATA DIVISION.

[FILE SECTION.

[FD file-name

       [; BLOCK CONTAINS [integer-1 TO] integer-2 $\begin{Bmatrix} \text{RECORDS} \\ \text{CHARACTERS} \end{Bmatrix}$]

       [; RECORD CONTAINS [integer-3 TO] integer-4 CHARACTERS]

       ; LABEL $\begin{Bmatrix} \text{RECORD IS} \\ \text{RECORDS ARE} \end{Bmatrix}$ $\begin{Bmatrix} \text{STANDARD} \\ \text{OMITTED} \end{Bmatrix}$

       [; VALUE OF implementor-name-1 IS $\begin{Bmatrix} \text{data-name-1} \\ \text{literal-1} \end{Bmatrix}$

           [, implementor-name-2 IS $\begin{Bmatrix} \text{data-name-2} \\ \text{literal-2} \end{Bmatrix}$] ...]

       [; DATA $\begin{Bmatrix} \text{RECORD IS} \\ \text{RECORDS ARE} \end{Bmatrix}$ data-name-3 [, data-name-4] ...]

       [; LINAGE IS $\begin{Bmatrix} \text{data-name-5} \\ \text{integer-5} \end{Bmatrix}$ LINES [, WITH FOOTING AT $\begin{Bmatrix} \text{data-name-6} \\ \text{integer-6} \end{Bmatrix}$]

           [, LINES AT TOP $\begin{Bmatrix} \text{data-name-7} \\ \text{integer-7} \end{Bmatrix}$] [, LINES AT BOTTOM $\begin{Bmatrix} \text{data-name-8} \\ \text{integer-8} \end{Bmatrix}$]]

       [; CODE-SET IS alphabet-name]

       [; $\begin{Bmatrix} \text{REPORT IS} \\ \text{REPORTS ARE} \end{Bmatrix}$ report-name-1 [, report-name-2] ...] .

[record-description-entry] ...] ...

[SD file-name

       [; RECORD CONTAINS [integer-1 TO] integer-2 CHARACTERS]

       [; DATA $\begin{Bmatrix} \text{RECORD IS} \\ \text{RECORDS ARE} \end{Bmatrix}$ data-name-1 [, data-name-2] ...] .

{record-description-entry} ...] ...]

[WORKING-STORAGE SECTION.

$\begin{bmatrix} \text{77-level-description-entry} \\ \text{record-description-entry} \end{bmatrix}$ ...

$\left[\underline{\text{LINKAGE}} \text{ } \underline{\text{SECTION}}.\right.$

$\left[\begin{matrix} \text{77-level-description-entry} \\ \text{record-description-entry} \end{matrix}\right] \text{ ... } \Big]$

$\left[\underline{\text{COMMUNICATION}} \text{ } \underline{\text{SECTION}}.\right.$

$\left[\text{communication-description-entry}\right.$

$\left[\text{record-description-entry}\right] \text{ ... } \Big] \text{ ... } \Big]$

$\left[\underline{\text{REPORT}} \text{ } \underline{\text{SECTION}}.\right.$

$\left[\underline{\text{RD}} \text{ report-name}\right.$

　　$\left[; \underline{\text{CODE}} \text{ literal-1}\right]$

　　$\left[; \left\{\begin{matrix} \underline{\text{CONTROL}} \text{ IS} \\ \underline{\text{CONTROLS}} \text{ ARE} \end{matrix}\right\} \left\{\begin{matrix} \text{data-name-1 } \left[, \text{ data-name-2}\right] \text{ ...} \\ \underline{\text{FINAL}} \text{ } \left[, \text{ data-name-1 } \left[, \text{ data-name-2}\right] \text{ ...}\right] \end{matrix}\right\}\right]$

　　$\left[; \underline{\text{PAGE}} \left[\begin{matrix} \text{LIMIT IS} \\ \text{LIMITS ARE} \end{matrix}\right] \text{ integer-1 } \left[\begin{matrix} \text{LINE} \\ \text{LINES} \end{matrix}\right] \text{ } \left[, \underline{\text{HEADING}} \text{ integer-2}\right]\right.$

　　　　$\left[, \underline{\text{FIRST}} \text{ } \underline{\text{DETAIL}} \text{ integer-3}\right] \text{ } \left[, \underline{\text{LAST}} \text{ } \underline{\text{DETAIL}} \text{ integer-4}\right]$

　　　　$\left.\left[, \underline{\text{FOOTING}} \text{ integer-5}\right] \text{ }\right].$

$\left\{\text{report-group-description-entry}\right\} \text{ ... } \Big] \text{ ... } \Big]$

General Format for Data Description Entry

Format 1:

$$\text{level-number } \left\{ \begin{array}{l} \text{data-name-1} \\ \underline{\text{FILLER}} \end{array} \right\}$$

$$\left[; \ \underline{\text{REDEFINES}} \text{ data-name-2} \right]$$

$$\left[; \ \left\{ \begin{array}{l} \underline{\text{PICTURE}} \\ \underline{\text{PIC}} \end{array} \right\} \text{ IS character-string} \right]$$

$$\left[; \ \left[\underline{\text{USAGE}} \text{ IS} \right] \ \left\{ \begin{array}{l} \underline{\text{COMPUTATIONAL}} \\ \underline{\text{COMP}} \\ \underline{\text{DISPLAY}} \\ \underline{\text{INDEX}} \end{array} \right\} \right]$$

$$\left[; \ \left[\underline{\text{SIGN}} \text{ IS} \right] \ \left\{ \begin{array}{l} \underline{\text{LEADING}} \\ \underline{\text{TRAILING}} \end{array} \right\} \ \left[\underline{\text{SEPARATE}} \text{ CHARACTER} \right] \right]$$

$$\left[; \ \underline{\text{OCCURS}} \ \left\{ \begin{array}{l} \text{integer-1 } \underline{\text{TO}} \text{ integer-2 TIMES } \underline{\text{DEPENDING}} \text{ ON data-name-3} \\ \text{integer-2 TIMES} \end{array} \right\} \right.$$

$$\left[\left\{ \begin{array}{l} \underline{\text{ASCENDING}} \\ \underline{\text{DESCENDING}} \end{array} \right\} \text{ KEY IS data-name-4 } \left[, \text{ data-name-5} \right] \ \ldots \right] \ \ldots$$

$$\left. \left[\underline{\text{INDEXED}} \text{ BY index-name-1 } \left[, \text{ index-name-2} \right] \ \ldots \right] \right]$$

$$\left[; \ \left\{ \begin{array}{l} \underline{\text{SYNCHRONIZED}} \\ \underline{\text{SYNC}} \end{array} \right\} \ \left[\begin{array}{l} \underline{\text{LEFT}} \\ \underline{\text{RIGHT}} \end{array} \right] \right]$$

$$\left[; \ \left\{ \begin{array}{l} \underline{\text{JUSTIFIED}} \\ \underline{\text{JUST}} \end{array} \right\} \text{ RIGHT} \right]$$

$$\left[; \ \underline{\text{BLANK}} \text{ WHEN } \underline{\text{ZERO}} \right]$$

$$\left[; \ \underline{\text{VALUE}} \text{ IS literal} \right] \ .$$

Format 2:

$$66 \text{ data-name-1; } \underline{\text{RENAMES}} \text{ data-name-2 } \left[\left\{ \begin{array}{l} \underline{\text{THROUGH}} \\ \underline{\text{THRU}} \end{array} \right\} \text{ data-name-3} \right] \ .$$

Format 3:

$$88 \text{ condition-name; } \left\{ \begin{array}{l} \underline{\text{VALUE}} \text{ IS} \\ \underline{\text{VALUES}} \text{ ARE} \end{array} \right\} \text{ literal-1 } \left[\left\{ \begin{array}{l} \underline{\text{THROUGH}} \\ \underline{\text{THRU}} \end{array} \right\} \text{ literal-2} \right.$$

$$\left. \left[, \text{ literal-3 } \left[\left\{ \begin{array}{l} \underline{\text{THROUGH}} \\ \underline{\text{THRU}} \end{array} \right\} \text{ literal-4} \right] \right] \ldots \right] \ .$$

General Format for Communication Description Entry

Format 1:

CD   cd-name;

FOR [INITIAL] INPUT

$$\left[\begin{array}{l}[; \text{SYMBOLIC } \underline{\text{QUEUE}} \text{ IS data-name-1}] \\ \quad [; \text{SYMBOLIC } \underline{\text{SUB-QUEUE-1}} \text{ IS data-name-2}] \\ \quad [; \text{SYMBOLIC } \underline{\text{SUB-QUEUE-2}} \text{ IS data-name-3}] \\ \quad [; \text{SYMBOLIC } \underline{\text{SUB-QUEUE-3}} \text{ IS data-name-4}] \\ \quad [; \underline{\text{MESSAGE}} \underline{\text{DATE}} \text{ IS data-name-5}] \\ \quad [; \underline{\text{MESSAGE}} \underline{\text{TIME}} \text{ IS data-name-6}] \\ \quad [; \text{SYMBOLIC } \underline{\text{SOURCE}} \text{ IS data-name-7}] \\ \quad [; \underline{\text{TEXT}} \underline{\text{LENGTH}} \text{ IS data-name-8}] \\ \quad [; \underline{\text{END}} \underline{\text{KEY}} \text{ IS data-name-9}] \\ \quad [; \underline{\text{STATUS}} \underline{\text{KEY}} \text{ IS data-name-10}] \\ \quad [; \text{MESSAGE } \underline{\text{COUNT}} \text{ IS data-name-11}] \\ [\text{data-name-1, data-name-2, ..., data-name-11}] \end{array}\right]$$

Format 2:

CD   cd-name; FOR <u>OUTPUT</u>

[; <u>DESTINATION</u> <u>COUNT</u> IS data-name-1]

[; <u>TEXT</u> <u>LENGTH</u> IS data-name-2]

[; <u>STATUS</u> <u>KEY</u> IS data-name-3]

[; <u>DESTINATION</u> <u>TABLE</u> <u>OCCURS</u> integer-2 TIMES

      [; <u>INDEXED</u> BY index-name-1 [, index-name-2]...]]

[; <u>ERROR</u> <u>KEY</u> IS data-name-4]

[; SYMBOLIC <u>DESTINATION</u> IS data-name-5]   .

General Format for Report Group Description Entry

Format 1:

```
01  [data-name-1]

    [; LINE NUMBER IS  {integer-1 [ON NEXT PAGE]}  ]
    [                  {PLUS integer-2            }  ]

    [; NEXT GROUP IS  {integer-3       } ]
    [                 {PLUS integer-4  } ]
    [                 {NEXT PAGE       } ]

                      ⎧ {REPORT HEADING }                     ⎫
                      ⎪ {RH             }                     ⎪
                      ⎪ {PAGE HEADING   }                     ⎪
                      ⎪ {PH             }                     ⎪
                      ⎪ {CONTROL HEADING} {data-name-2}       ⎪
    ; TYPE IS         ⎨ {CH             } {FINAL      }        ⎬
                      ⎪ {DETAIL }                             ⎪
                      ⎪ {DE     }                             ⎪
                      ⎪ {CONTROL FOOTING} {data-name-3}       ⎪
                      ⎪ {CF             } {FINAL      }        ⎪
                      ⎪ {PAGE FOOTING   }                     ⎪
                      ⎪ {PF             }                     ⎪
                      ⎩ {REPORT FOOTING }                     ⎭
                        {RF             }

    [; [USAGE IS] DISPLAY ] .
```

Format 2:

```
level-number  [data-name-1]

    [; LINE NUMBER IS  {integer-1 [ON NEXT PAGE]}  ]
    [                  {PLUS integer-2            }  ]

    [; [USAGE IS] DISPLAY ] .
```

Format 3:

```
level-number  [data-name-1]

    [; BLANK WHEN ZERO]

    [; GROUP INDICATE]

    [;  { JUSTIFIED }  RIGHT]
        { JUST     }

    [; LINE NUMBER IS  { integer-1 [ON NEXT PAGE]} ]
                       { PLUS integer-2            }

    [; COLUMN NUMBER IS integer-3]

     ;  { PICTURE }  IS character-string
        { PIC     }

    (  ; SOURCE IS identifier-1                                    )
    (                                                              )
    (  ; VALUE IS literal                                          )
    (                                                              )
    {  ; SUM identifier-2  [, identifier-3] ...                    }
    (                                                              )
    (      [UPON data-name-2  [, data-name-3] ...]} ...            )
    (                                                              )
    (      [RESET ON  { data-name-4 }]                             )
    (                 { FINAL       }                              )

    [;  [USAGE IS]  DISPLAY] .
```

General Format for Procedure Division

Format 1:

PROCEDURE DIVISION [USING data-name-1 [, data-name-2] ...] .

[DECLARATIVES.

{section-name SECTION [segment-number] . declarative-sentence

[paragraph-name. [sentence] ...] ...} ...

END DECLARATIVES.]

{section-name SECTION [segment-number] .

[paragraph-name. [sentence] ...] ...} ...

Format 2:

PROCEDURE DIVISION [USING data-name-1 [, data-name-2] ...] .

{paragraph-name. [sentence] ...} ...

General Format for Verbs

ACCEPT identifier [FROM mnemonic-name]

ACCEPT identifier FROM { DATE / DAY / TIME }

ACCEPT cd-name MESSAGE COUNT

ADD {identifier-1 / literal-1} [, identifier-2 / , literal-2] ... TO identifier-m [ROUNDED]

  [, identifier-n [ROUNDED]] ... [; ON SIZE ERROR imperative-statement]

ADD {identifier-1 / literal-1} , {identifier-2 / literal-2} [, identifier-3 / , literal-3] ...

  GIVING identifier-m [ROUNDED] [, identifier-n [ROUNDED]] ...

  [; ON SIZE ERROR imperative-statement]

ADD {CORRESPONDING / CORR} identifier-1 TO identifier-2 [ROUNDED]

  [; ON SIZE ERROR imperative-statement]

ALTER procedure-name-1 TO [PROCEED TO] procedure-name-2

  [, procedure-name-3 TO [PROCEED TO] procedure-name-4] ...

CALL {identifier-1 / literal-1} [USING data-name-1 [, data-name-2] ...]

  [; ON OVERFLOW imperative-statement]

CANCEL {identifier-1 / literal-1} [, identifier-2 / , literal-2] ...

CLOSE file-name-1 [{REEL / UNIT} [WITH NO REWIND / FOR REMOVAL] / WITH {NO REWIND / LOCK}]

  [, file-name-2 [{REEL / UNIT} [WITH NO REWIND / FOR REMOVAL] / WITH {NO REWIND / LOCK}]] ...

CLOSE file-name-1 [WITH LOCK] [, file-name-2 [WITH LOCK]] ...

COMPUTE identifier-1 [ROUNDED] [, identifier-2 [ROUNDED]] ...

   = arithmetic-expression [; ON SIZE ERROR imperative-statement]

DELETE file-name RECORD [; INVALID KEY imperative-statement]

DISABLE $\left\{ \begin{array}{l} \text{INPUT} \\ \text{OUTPUT} \end{array} \right.$ [TERMINAL]$\}$ cd-name WITH KEY $\left\{ \begin{array}{l} \text{identifier-1} \\ \text{literal-1} \end{array} \right\}$

DISPLAY $\left\{ \begin{array}{l} \text{identifier-1} \\ \text{literal-1} \end{array} \right\}$ $\left[\begin{array}{l} \text{, identifier-2} \\ \text{, literal-2} \end{array} \right]$ ... [UPON mnemonic-name]

DIVIDE $\left\{ \begin{array}{l} \text{identifier-1} \\ \text{literal-1} \end{array} \right\}$ INTO identifier-2 [ROUNDED]

   [, identifier-3 [ROUNDED]] ... [; ON SIZE ERROR imperative-statement]

DIVIDE $\left\{ \begin{array}{l} \text{identifier-1} \\ \text{literal-1} \end{array} \right\}$ INTO $\left\{ \begin{array}{l} \text{identifier-2} \\ \text{literal-2} \end{array} \right\}$ GIVING identifier-3 [ROUNDED]

   [, identifier-4 [ROUNDED]] ... [; ON SIZE ERROR imperative-statement]

DIVIDE $\left\{ \begin{array}{l} \text{identifier-1} \\ \text{literal-1} \end{array} \right\}$ BY $\left\{ \begin{array}{l} \text{identifier-2} \\ \text{literal-2} \end{array} \right\}$ GIVING identifier-3 [ROUNDED]

   [, identifier-4 [ROUNDED]] ... [; ON SIZE ERROR imperative-statement]

DIVIDE $\left\{ \begin{array}{l} \text{identifier-1} \\ \text{literal-1} \end{array} \right\}$ INTO $\left\{ \begin{array}{l} \text{identifier-2} \\ \text{literal-2} \end{array} \right\}$ GIVING identifier-3 [ROUNDED]

   REMAINDER identifier-4 [; ON SIZE ERROR imperative-statement]

DIVIDE $\left\{ \begin{array}{l} \text{identifier-1} \\ \text{literal-1} \end{array} \right\}$ BY $\left\{ \begin{array}{l} \text{identifier-2} \\ \text{literal-2} \end{array} \right\}$ GIVING identifier-3 [ROUNDED]

   REMAINDER identifier-4 [; ON SIZE ERROR imperative-statement]

ENABLE $\left\{ \begin{array}{l} \text{INPUT} \\ \text{OUTPUT} \end{array} \right.$ [TERMINAL]$\}$ cd-name WITH KEY $\left\{ \begin{array}{l} \text{identifier-1} \\ \text{literal-1} \end{array} \right\}$

ENTER language-name [routine-name] .

EXIT [PROGRAM] .

GENERATE $\left\{ \begin{array}{l} \text{data-name} \\ \text{report-name} \end{array} \right\}$

GO TO [procedure-name-1]

GO TO procedure-name-1 [, procedure-name-2] ... , procedure-name-n

    DEPENDING ON identifier

IF condition; $\left\{ \begin{array}{l} \text{statement-1} \\ \underline{\text{NEXT SENTENCE}} \end{array} \right\}$ $\left\{ \begin{array}{l} \text{; } \underline{\text{ELSE}} \text{ statement-2} \\ \text{; } \underline{\text{ELSE NEXT SENTENCE}} \end{array} \right\}$

INITIATE report-name-1 [, report-name-2] ...

INSPECT identifier-1 TALLYING

$$\left\{ \text{, identifier-2 } \underline{\text{FOR}} \left\{ \text{, } \left\{ \begin{array}{l} \underline{\text{ALL}} \\ \underline{\text{LEADING}} \\ \underline{\text{CHARACTERS}} \end{array} \right\} \left\{ \begin{array}{l} \text{identifier-3} \\ \text{literal-1} \end{array} \right\} \left[\left\{ \begin{array}{l} \underline{\text{BEFORE}} \\ \underline{\text{AFTER}} \end{array} \right\} \text{INITIAL} \left\{ \begin{array}{l} \text{identifier-4} \\ \text{literal-2} \end{array} \right\} \right] \right\} ... \right\} ...$$

INSPECT identifier-1 REPLACING

$$\left\{ \begin{array}{l} \underline{\text{CHARACTERS}} \underline{\text{BY}} \left\{ \begin{array}{l} \text{identifier-6} \\ \text{literal-4} \end{array} \right\} \left[\left\{ \begin{array}{l} \underline{\text{BEFORE}} \\ \underline{\text{AFTER}} \end{array} \right\} \text{INITIAL} \left\{ \begin{array}{l} \text{identifier-7} \\ \text{literal-5} \end{array} \right\} \right] \\ \left\{ \begin{array}{l} \underline{\text{ALL}} \\ \underline{\text{LEADING}} \\ \underline{\text{FIRST}} \end{array} \right\} \left\{ \text{, } \left\{ \begin{array}{l} \text{identifier-5} \\ \text{literal-3} \end{array} \right\} \underline{\text{BY}} \left\{ \begin{array}{l} \text{identifier-6} \\ \text{literal-4} \end{array} \right\} \left[\left\{ \begin{array}{l} \underline{\text{BEFORE}} \\ \underline{\text{AFTER}} \end{array} \right\} \text{INITIAL} \left\{ \begin{array}{l} \text{identifier-7} \\ \text{literal-5} \end{array} \right\} \right] \right\} ... \end{array} \right\} ...$$

INSPECT identifier-1 TALLYING

$$\left\{ \text{, identifier-2 } \underline{\text{FOR}} \left\{ \text{, } \left\{ \begin{array}{l} \underline{\text{ALL}} \\ \underline{\text{LEADING}} \\ \underline{\text{CHARACTERS}} \end{array} \right\} \left\{ \begin{array}{l} \text{identifier-3} \\ \text{literal-1} \end{array} \right\} \left[\left\{ \begin{array}{l} \underline{\text{BEFORE}} \\ \underline{\text{AFTER}} \end{array} \right\} \text{INITIAL} \left\{ \begin{array}{l} \text{identifier-4} \\ \text{literal-2} \end{array} \right\} \right] \right\} ... \right\} ...$$

REPLACING

$$\left\{ \begin{array}{l} \underline{\text{CHARACTERS}} \underline{\text{BY}} \left\{ \begin{array}{l} \text{identifier-6} \\ \text{literal-4} \end{array} \right\} \left[\left\{ \begin{array}{l} \underline{\text{BEFORE}} \\ \underline{\text{AFTER}} \end{array} \right\} \text{INITIAL} \left\{ \begin{array}{l} \text{identifier-7} \\ \text{literal-5} \end{array} \right\} \right] \\ \left\{ \begin{array}{l} \underline{\text{ALL}} \\ \underline{\text{LEADING}} \\ \underline{\text{FIRST}} \end{array} \right\} \left\{ \text{, } \left\{ \begin{array}{l} \text{identifier-5} \\ \text{literal-3} \end{array} \right\} \underline{\text{BY}} \left\{ \begin{array}{l} \text{identifier-6} \\ \text{literal-4} \end{array} \right\} \left[\left\{ \begin{array}{l} \underline{\text{BEFORE}} \\ \underline{\text{AFTER}} \end{array} \right\} \text{INITIAL} \left\{ \begin{array}{l} \text{identifier-7} \\ \text{literal-5} \end{array} \right\} \right] \right\} ... \end{array} \right\} ...$$

$$\underline{\text{MERGE}} \text{ file-name-1 ON } \begin{Bmatrix} \underline{\text{ASCENDING}} \\ \underline{\text{DESCENDING}} \end{Bmatrix} \text{KEY data-name-1 } [\text{, data-name-2}] \dots$$

$$\left[\text{ON } \begin{Bmatrix} \underline{\text{ASCENDING}} \\ \underline{\text{DESCENDING}} \end{Bmatrix} \text{KEY data-name-3 } [\text{, data-name-4}] \dots \right] \dots$$

$$[\text{COLLATING } \underline{\text{SEQUENCE}} \text{ IS alphabet-name}]$$

$$\underline{\text{USING}} \text{ file-name-2, file-name-3 } [\text{, file-name-4}] \dots$$

$$\begin{Bmatrix} \underline{\text{OUTPUT}} \underline{\text{PROCEDURE}} \text{ IS section-name-1 } \left[\begin{Bmatrix} \underline{\text{THROUGH}} \\ \underline{\text{THRU}} \end{Bmatrix} \text{ section-name-2} \right] \\ \underline{\text{GIVING}} \text{ file-name-5} \end{Bmatrix}$$

$$\underline{\text{MOVE}} \begin{Bmatrix} \text{identifier-1} \\ \text{literal} \end{Bmatrix} \underline{\text{TO}} \text{ identifier-2 } [\text{, identifier-3}] \dots$$

$$\underline{\text{MOVE}} \begin{Bmatrix} \underline{\text{CORRESPONDING}} \\ \underline{\text{CORR}} \end{Bmatrix} \text{identifier-1 } \underline{\text{TO}} \text{ identifier-2}$$

$$\underline{\text{MULTIPLY}} \begin{Bmatrix} \text{identifier-1} \\ \text{literal-1} \end{Bmatrix} \underline{\text{BY}} \text{ identifier-2 } [\underline{\text{ROUNDED}}]$$

$$[\text{, identifier-3 } [\underline{\text{ROUNDED}}]] \dots [\text{; ON } \underline{\text{SIZE}} \underline{\text{ERROR}} \text{ imperative-statement}]$$

$$\underline{\text{MULTIPLY}} \begin{Bmatrix} \text{identifier-1} \\ \text{literal-1} \end{Bmatrix} \underline{\text{BY}} \begin{Bmatrix} \text{identifier-2} \\ \text{literal-2} \end{Bmatrix} \underline{\text{GIVING}} \text{ identifier-3 } [\underline{\text{ROUNDED}}]$$

$$[\text{, identifier-4 } [\underline{\text{ROUNDED}}]] \dots [\text{; ON } \underline{\text{SIZE}} \underline{\text{ERROR}} \text{ imperative-statement}]$$

$$\underline{\text{OPEN}} \begin{Bmatrix} \underline{\text{INPUT}} \text{ file-name-1 } \left[\begin{matrix} \underline{\text{REVERSED}} \\ \text{WITH } \underline{\text{NO}} \text{ REWIND} \end{matrix} \right] \left[\text{, file-name-2 } \left[\begin{matrix} \underline{\text{REVERSED}} \\ \text{WITH } \underline{\text{NO}} \text{ REWIND} \end{matrix} \right] \right] \dots \\ \underline{\text{OUTPUT}} \text{ file-name-3 } [\text{WITH } \underline{\text{NO}} \text{ REWIND}] [\text{, file-name-4 } [\text{WITH } \underline{\text{NO}} \text{ REWIND}]] \dots \\ \underline{\text{I-O}} \text{ file-name-5 } [\text{, file-name-6}] \dots \\ \underline{\text{EXTEND}} \text{ file-name-7 } [\text{, file-name-8}] \dots \end{Bmatrix} \dots$$

$$\underline{\text{OPEN}} \begin{Bmatrix} \underline{\text{INPUT}} \text{ file-name-1 } [\text{, file-name-2}] \dots \\ \underline{\text{OUTPUT}} \text{ file-name-3 } [\text{, file-name-4}] \dots \\ \underline{\text{I-O}} \text{ file-name-5 } [\text{, file-name-6}] \dots \end{Bmatrix} \dots$$

$$\underline{\text{PERFORM}} \text{ procedure-name-1 } \left[\begin{Bmatrix} \underline{\text{THROUGH}} \\ \underline{\text{THRU}} \end{Bmatrix} \text{ procedure-name-2} \right]$$

$$\underline{\text{PERFORM}} \text{ procedure-name-1 } \left[\begin{Bmatrix} \underline{\text{THROUGH}} \\ \underline{\text{THRU}} \end{Bmatrix} \text{ procedure-name-2} \right] \begin{Bmatrix} \text{identifier-1} \\ \text{integer-1} \end{Bmatrix} \underline{\text{TIMES}}$$

$$\underline{\text{PERFORM}} \text{ procedure-name-1 } \left[\begin{Bmatrix} \underline{\text{THROUGH}} \\ \underline{\text{THRU}} \end{Bmatrix} \text{ procedure-name-2} \right] \underline{\text{UNTIL}} \text{ condition-1}$$

$$\underline{PERFORM}\ procedure\text{-}name\text{-}1\ \left[\begin{Bmatrix} \underline{THROUGH} \\ \underline{THRU} \end{Bmatrix} procedure\text{-}name\text{-}2\right]$$

$$\underline{VARYING}\ \begin{Bmatrix} identifier\text{-}2 \\ index\text{-}name\text{-}1 \end{Bmatrix}\ \underline{FROM}\ \begin{Bmatrix} identifier\text{-}3 \\ index\text{-}name\text{-}2 \\ literal\text{-}1 \end{Bmatrix}$$

$$\underline{BY}\ \begin{Bmatrix} identifier\text{-}4 \\ literal\text{-}3 \end{Bmatrix}\ \underline{UNTIL}\ condition\text{-}1$$

$$\left[\underline{AFTER}\ \begin{Bmatrix} identifier\text{-}5 \\ index\text{-}name\text{-}3 \end{Bmatrix}\ \underline{FROM}\ \begin{Bmatrix} identifier\text{-}6 \\ index\text{-}name\text{-}4 \\ literal\text{-}3 \end{Bmatrix}\right.$$

$$\underline{BY}\ \begin{Bmatrix} identifier\text{-}7 \\ literal\text{-}4 \end{Bmatrix}\ \underline{UNTIL}\ condition\text{-}2$$

$$\left[\underline{AFTER}\ \begin{Bmatrix} identifier\text{-}8 \\ index\text{-}name\text{-}5 \end{Bmatrix}\ \underline{FROM}\ \begin{Bmatrix} identifier\text{-}9 \\ index\text{-}name\text{-}6 \\ literal\text{-}5 \end{Bmatrix}\right.$$

$$\left.\left.\underline{BY}\ \begin{Bmatrix} identifier\text{-}10 \\ literal\text{-}6 \end{Bmatrix}\ \underline{UNTIL}\ condition\text{-}3\right]\right]$$

$$\underline{READ}\ file\text{-}name\ RECORD\ \left[\underline{INTO}\ identifier\right]\ \left[; AT\ \underline{END}\ imperative\text{-}statement\right]$$

$$\underline{READ}\ file\text{-}name\ \left[\underline{NEXT}\right]\ RECORD\ \left[\underline{INTO}\ identifier\right]$$

$$\left[; AT\ \underline{END}\ imperative\text{-}statement\right]$$

$$\underline{READ}\ file\text{-}name\ RECORD\ \left[\underline{INTO}\ identifier\right]\ \left[; \underline{INVALID}\ KEY\ imperative\text{-}statement\right]$$

$$\underline{READ}\ file\text{-}name\ RECORD\ \left[\underline{INTO}\ identifier\right]$$

$$\left[; \underline{KEY}\ IS\ data\text{-}name\right]$$

$$\left[; \underline{INVALID}\ KEY\ imperative\text{-}statement\right]$$

$$\underline{RECEIVE}\ cd\text{-}name\ \begin{Bmatrix} MESSAGE \\ \underline{SEGMENT} \end{Bmatrix}\ \underline{INTO}\ identifier\text{-}1\ \left[; \underline{NO}\ \underline{DATA}\ imperative\text{-}statement\right]$$

$$\underline{RELEASE}\ record\text{-}name\ \left[\underline{FROM}\ identifier\right]$$

$$\underline{RETURN}\ file\text{-}name\ RECORD\ \left[\underline{INTO}\ identifier\right]\ ; AT\ \underline{END}\ imperative\text{-}statement$$

$$\underline{REWRITE}\ record\text{-}name\ \left[\underline{FROM}\ identifier\right]$$

$$\underline{REWRITE}\ record\text{-}name\ \left[\underline{FROM}\ identifier\right]\ \left[; \underline{INVALID}\ KEY\ imperative\text{-}statement\right]$$

SEARCH identifier-1 $\left[\text{VARYING} \begin{Bmatrix} \text{identifier-2} \\ \text{index-name-1} \end{Bmatrix} \right]$ [; AT END imperative-statement-1]

; WHEN condition-1 $\begin{Bmatrix} \text{imperative-statement-2} \\ \text{NEXT SENTENCE} \end{Bmatrix}$

$\left[\text{; WHEN condition-2} \begin{Bmatrix} \text{imperative-statement-3} \\ \text{NEXT SENTENCE} \end{Bmatrix} \right]$ ...

SEARCH ALL identifier-1 [; AT END imperative-statement-1]

; WHEN $\begin{Bmatrix} \text{data-name-1} \begin{Bmatrix} \text{IS EQUAL TO} \\ \text{IS =} \end{Bmatrix} \begin{Bmatrix} \text{identifier-3} \\ \text{literal-1} \\ \text{arithmetic-expression-1} \end{Bmatrix} \\ \text{condition-name-1} \end{Bmatrix}$

$\left[\text{AND} \begin{Bmatrix} \text{data-name-2} \begin{Bmatrix} \text{IS EQUAL TO} \\ \text{IS =} \end{Bmatrix} \begin{Bmatrix} \text{identifier-4} \\ \text{literal-2} \\ \text{arithmetic-expression-2} \end{Bmatrix} \\ \text{condition-name-2} \end{Bmatrix} \right]$ ...

$\begin{Bmatrix} \text{imperative-statement-2} \\ \text{NEXT SENTENCE} \end{Bmatrix}$

SEND cd-name FROM identifier-1

SEND cd-name [FROM identifier-1] $\begin{Bmatrix} \text{WITH identifier-2} \\ \text{WITH ESI} \\ \text{WITH EMI} \\ \text{WITH EGI} \end{Bmatrix}$

$\left[\begin{Bmatrix} \text{BEFORE} \\ \text{AFTER} \end{Bmatrix} \text{ADVANCING} \begin{Bmatrix} \begin{Bmatrix} \text{identifier-3} \\ \text{integer} \end{Bmatrix} \begin{bmatrix} \text{LINE} \\ \text{LINES} \end{bmatrix} \\ \begin{Bmatrix} \text{mnemonic-name} \\ \text{PAGE} \end{Bmatrix} \end{Bmatrix} \right]$

SET $\begin{Bmatrix} \text{identifier-1} & [\text{, identifier-2}] & ... \\ \text{index-name-1} & [\text{, index-name-2}] & ... \end{Bmatrix}$ TO $\begin{Bmatrix} \text{identifier-3} \\ \text{index-name-3} \\ \text{integer-1} \end{Bmatrix}$

SET index-name-4 [, index-name-5] ... $\begin{Bmatrix} \text{UP BY} \\ \text{DOWN BY} \end{Bmatrix} \begin{Bmatrix} \text{identifier-4} \\ \text{integer-2} \end{Bmatrix}$

SORT file-name-1 ON $\left\{\begin{array}{l} \underline{ASCENDING} \\ \underline{DESCENDING} \end{array}\right\}$ KEY data-name-1 $\left[, \text{data-name-2} \right]$ ...

$\left[ON \left\{\begin{array}{l} \underline{ASCENDING} \\ \underline{DESCENDING} \end{array}\right\} \text{KEY data-name-3} \left[, \text{data-name-4} \right] ... \right]$ ...

$\left[\underline{COLLATING} \ \underline{SEQUENCE} \ IS \ alphabet\text{-}name \right]$

$\left\{\begin{array}{l} \underline{INPUT} \ \underline{PROCEDURE} \ IS \ section\text{-}name\text{-}1 \left[\left\{\begin{array}{l} \underline{THROUGH} \\ \underline{THRU} \end{array}\right\} \ section\text{-}name\text{-}2 \right] \\ \underline{USING} \ file\text{-}name\text{-}2 \ \left[, \ file\text{-}name\text{-}3 \right] ... \end{array}\right\}$

$\left\{\begin{array}{l} \underline{OUTPUT} \ \underline{PROCEDURE} \ IS \ section\text{-}name\text{-}3 \left[\left\{\begin{array}{l} \underline{THROUGH} \\ \underline{THRU} \end{array}\right\} \ section\text{-}name\text{-}4 \right] \\ \underline{GIVING} \ file\text{-}name\text{-}4 \end{array}\right\}$

START file-name $\left[KEY \left\{\begin{array}{l} IS \ \underline{EQUAL} \ TO \\ IS \ = \\ IS \ \underline{GREATER} \ THAN \\ IS \ > \\ IS \ \underline{NOT} \ \underline{LESS} \ THAN \\ IS \ \underline{NOT} \ < \end{array}\right\} data\text{-}name \right]$

$\left[; \ \underline{INVALID} \ KEY \ imperative\text{-}statement \right]$

STOP $\left\{\begin{array}{l} \underline{RUN} \\ literal \end{array}\right\}$

STRING $\left\{\begin{array}{l} identifier\text{-}1 \\ literal\text{-}1 \end{array}\right\} \left[, \ identifier\text{-}2 \\ , \ literal\text{-}2 \right]$ ... $\underline{DELIMITED}$ BY $\left\{\begin{array}{l} identifier\text{-}3 \\ literal\text{-}3 \\ \underline{SIZE} \end{array}\right\}$

$\left[, \left\{\begin{array}{l} identifier\text{-}4 \\ literal\text{-}4 \end{array}\right\} \left[, \ identifier\text{-}5 \\ , \ literal\text{-}5 \right] ... \underline{DELIMITED} \ BY \left\{\begin{array}{l} identifier\text{-}6 \\ literal\text{-}6 \\ \underline{SIZE} \end{array}\right\} \right]$ ...

$\underline{INTO}$ identifier-7 $\left[WITH \ \underline{POINTER} \ identifier\text{-}8 \right]$

$\left[; \ ON \ \underline{OVERFLOW} \ imperative\text{-}statement \right]$

SUBTRACT $\left\{\begin{array}{l} identifier\text{-}1 \\ literal\text{-}1 \end{array}\right\} \left[, \ identifier\text{-}2 \\ , \ literal\text{-}2 \right]$ ... $\underline{FROM}$ identifier-m $\left[\underline{ROUNDED} \right]$

$\left[, \ identifier\text{-}n \ \left[\underline{ROUNDED} \right] \right]$ ... $\left[; \ ON \ \underline{SIZE} \ \underline{ERROR} \ imperative\text{-}statement \right]$

SUBTRACT $\begin{Bmatrix} \text{identifier-1} \\ \text{literal-1} \end{Bmatrix}$ $\begin{bmatrix} \text{, identifier-2} \\ \text{, literal-2} \end{bmatrix}$ ... FROM $\begin{Bmatrix} \text{identifier-m} \\ \text{literal-m} \end{Bmatrix}$

   GIVING identifier-n [ROUNDED] [, identifier-o [ROUNDED]] ...

   [; ON SIZE ERROR imperative-statement]

SUBTRACT $\begin{Bmatrix} \underline{\text{CORRESPONDING}} \\ \underline{\text{CORR}} \end{Bmatrix}$ identifier-1 FROM identifier-2 [ROUNDED]

   [; ON SIZE ERROR imperative-statement]

SUPPRESS PRINTING

TERMINATE report-name-1 [, report-name-2] ...

UNSTRING identifier-1

   $\begin{bmatrix} \text{DELIMITED BY } [\underline{\text{ALL}}] \begin{Bmatrix} \text{identifier-2} \\ \text{literal-1} \end{Bmatrix} \begin{bmatrix} \text{, } \underline{\text{OR}} \; [\underline{\text{ALL}}] \begin{Bmatrix} \text{identifier-3} \\ \text{literal-2} \end{Bmatrix} \end{bmatrix} ... \end{bmatrix}$

   INTO identifier-4 [, DELIMITER IN identifier-5] [, COUNT IN identifier-6]

      [, identifier-7 [, DELIMITER IN identifier-8] [, COUNT IN identifier-9]] ...

   [WITH POINTER identifier-10] [TALLYING IN identifier-11]

   [; ON OVERFLOW imperative-statement]

USE AFTER STANDARD $\begin{Bmatrix} \underline{\text{EXCEPTION}} \\ \underline{\text{ERROR}} \end{Bmatrix}$ PROCEDURE ON $\begin{Bmatrix} \text{file-name-1 } [\text{, file-name-2}] ... \\ \underline{\text{INPUT}} \\ \underline{\text{OUTPUT}} \\ \underline{\text{I-O}} \\ \underline{\text{EXTEND}} \end{Bmatrix}$.

USE AFTER STANDARD $\begin{Bmatrix} \underline{\text{EXCEPTION}} \\ \underline{\text{ERROR}} \end{Bmatrix}$ PROCEDURE ON $\begin{Bmatrix} \text{file-name-1 } [\text{, file-name-2}] ... \\ \underline{\text{INPUT}} \\ \underline{\text{OUTPUT}} \\ \underline{\text{I-O}} \end{Bmatrix}$.

USE BEFORE REPORTING identifier.

USE FOR DEBUGGING ON $\left\{\begin{array}{l} \text{cd-name-1} \\ [\underline{\text{ALL}} \text{ REFERENCES OF}] \text{ identifier-1} \\ \text{file-name-1} \\ \text{procedure-name-1} \\ \underline{\text{ALL}} \underline{\text{PROCEDURES}} \end{array}\right\}$

$\left[, \left\{\begin{array}{l} \text{cd-name-2} \\ [\underline{\text{ALL}} \text{ REFERENCES OF}] \text{ identifier-2} \\ \text{file-name-2} \\ \text{procedure-name-2} \\ \underline{\text{ALL}} \underline{\text{PROCEDURES}} \end{array}\right\} \cdots \right]$.

$\underline{\text{WRITE}}$ record-name $\left[\underline{\text{FROM}} \text{ identifier-1} \right]$

$\left[\left\{\begin{array}{l} \underline{\text{BEFORE}} \\ \underline{\text{AFTER}} \end{array}\right\} \text{ADVANCING} \left\{\begin{array}{l} \left\{\begin{array}{l} \text{identifier-2} \\ \text{integer} \end{array}\right\} \left[\begin{array}{l} \text{LINE} \\ \text{LINES} \end{array}\right] \\ \left\{\begin{array}{l} \text{mnemonic-name} \\ \underline{\text{PAGE}} \end{array}\right\} \end{array}\right\} \right]$

$\left[\text{ ; } \underline{\text{AT}} \left\{\begin{array}{l} \text{END-OF-PAGE} \\ \underline{\text{EOP}} \end{array}\right\} \text{ imperative-statement} \right]$

$\underline{\text{WRITE}}$ record-name $\left[\underline{\text{FROM}} \text{ identifier} \right]$ $\left[\text{ ; } \underline{\text{INVALID}} \text{ KEY imperative-statement} \right]$

General Format for Conditions

Relation Condition

$$
\left\{ \begin{array}{l} \text{identifier-1} \\ \text{literal-1} \\ \text{arithmetic-expression-1} \\ \text{index-name-1} \end{array} \right\}
\left\{ \begin{array}{l} \text{IS } [\underline{\text{NOT}}] \ \underline{\text{GREATER}} \ \text{THAN} \\ \text{IS } [\underline{\text{NOT}}] \ \underline{\text{LESS}} \ \text{THAN} \\ \text{IS } [\underline{\text{NOT}}] \ \underline{\text{EQUAL}} \ \text{TO} \\ \text{IS } [\underline{\text{NOT}}] \ > \\ \text{IS } [\underline{\text{NOT}}] \ < \\ \text{IS } [\underline{\text{NOT}}] \ = \end{array} \right\}
\left\{ \begin{array}{l} \text{identifier-2} \\ \text{literal-2} \\ \text{arithmetic-expression-2} \\ \text{index-name-2} \end{array} \right\}
$$

Class Condition

$$
\text{identifier IS } [\underline{\text{NOT}}] \ \left\{ \begin{array}{l} \underline{\text{NUMERIC}} \\ \underline{\text{ALPHABETIC}} \end{array} \right\}
$$

Sign Condition

$$
\text{arithmetic-expression IS } [\underline{\text{NOT}}] \ \left\{ \begin{array}{l} \underline{\text{POSITIVE}} \\ \underline{\text{NEGATIVE}} \\ \underline{\text{ZERO}} \end{array} \right\}
$$

Condition-Name Condition

```
condition-name
```

Switch-Status Condition

```
condition-name
```

Negated Simple Condition

$\underline{\text{NOT}}$ simple-condition

Combined Condition

$$
\text{condition} \ \left\{ \left\{ \begin{array}{l} \underline{\text{AND}} \\ \underline{\text{OR}} \end{array} \right\} \ \text{condition} \right\} \ \ldots
$$

Abbreviated Combined Relation Condition

$$
\text{relation-condition} \ \left\{ \left\{ \begin{array}{l} \underline{\text{AND}} \\ \underline{\text{OR}} \end{array} \right\} [\underline{\text{NOT}}] \ [\text{relational-operator}] \ \text{object} \right\} \ \ldots
$$

Miscellaneous Formats

Qualification

$$\begin{Bmatrix} \text{data-name-1} \\ \text{condition-name} \end{Bmatrix} \quad \left[\begin{Bmatrix} \underline{\text{OF}} \\ \underline{\text{IN}} \end{Bmatrix} \text{data-name-2} \right] \dots$$

$$\text{paragraph-name} \quad \left[\begin{Bmatrix} \underline{\text{OF}} \\ \underline{\text{IN}} \end{Bmatrix} \text{section-name} \right]$$

$$\text{text-name} \quad \left[\begin{Bmatrix} \underline{\text{OF}} \\ \underline{\text{IN}} \end{Bmatrix} \text{library-name} \right]$$

Subscripting

$$\begin{Bmatrix} \text{data-name} \\ \text{condition-name} \end{Bmatrix} \quad (\text{subscript-1} \ [, \text{subscript-2} \ [, \text{subscript-3}]])$$

Indexing

$$\begin{Bmatrix} \text{data-name} \\ \text{condition-name} \end{Bmatrix} \quad \left(\begin{Bmatrix} \text{index-name-1} \ [\{\pm\} \text{literal-2}] \\ \text{literal-1} \end{Bmatrix} \right.$$

$$\left[, \begin{Bmatrix} \text{index-name-2} \ [\{\pm\} \text{literal-4}] \\ \text{literal-3} \end{Bmatrix} \left[, \begin{Bmatrix} \text{index-name-3} \ [\{\pm\} \text{literal-6}] \\ \text{literal-5} \end{Bmatrix} \right] \right])$$

Identifier: Format 1

$$\text{data-name-1} \left[\begin{Bmatrix} \underline{\text{OF}} \\ \underline{\text{IN}} \end{Bmatrix} \text{data-name-2} \right] \dots \left[(\text{subscript-1} \ [, \text{subscript-2} \right.$$

$$[, \text{subscript-3}]])]$$

Identifier: Format 2

$$\text{data-name-1} \left[\begin{Bmatrix} \underline{\text{OF}} \\ \underline{\text{IN}} \end{Bmatrix} \text{data-name-2} \right] \dots \left[\left(\begin{Bmatrix} \text{index-name-1} \ [\{\pm\} \text{literal-2}] \\ \text{literal-1} \end{Bmatrix} \right. \right.$$

$$\left[, \begin{Bmatrix} \text{index-name-2} \ [\{\pm\} \text{literal-4}] \\ \text{literal-3} \end{Bmatrix} \left[, \begin{Bmatrix} \text{index-name-3} \ [\{\pm\} \text{literal-6}] \\ \text{literal-5} \end{Bmatrix} \right] \right])$$

General Format for Copy Statement

$$\underline{\text{COPY}}\ \text{text-name}\ \left[\left\{\begin{array}{c}\underline{\text{OF}}\\\underline{\text{IN}}\end{array}\right\}\ \text{library-name}\right]$$

$$\left[\ \underline{\text{REPLACING}}\ \left\{,\ \left\{\begin{array}{l}==\text{pseudo-text-1}==\\\text{identifier-1}\\\text{literal-1}\\\text{word-1}\end{array}\right\}\ \underline{\text{BY}}\ \left\{\begin{array}{l}==\text{pseudo-text-2}==\\\text{identifier-2}\\\text{literal-2}\\\text{word-2}\end{array}\right\}\right\}\ \dots\right]$$

Complete ANSI Reference Summary — 1985

This appendix contains complete 1985 ANSI standard formats of all elements of the COBOL language. The appearance of the italic letter *S*, *I*, *R*, or *W* to the left of the format for the verbs CLOSE, OPEN, READ, and WRITE indicates that the format is used with sequential files, indexed files, relative files, or in Report Writer, respectively.

General Format for Identification Division

```
IDENTIFICATION DIVISION.

PROGRAM-ID.  program-name  [ IS  { | COMMON  | }  PROGRAM ] .
                                  | INITIAL | 

[AUTHOR.  [comment-entry] ... ]

[INSTALLATION.  [comment-entry] ... ]

[DATE-WRITTEN.  [comment-entry] ... ]

[DATE-COMPILED.  [comment-entry] ... ]

[SECURITY.  [comment-entry] ... ]
```

General Format for Environment Division

[ENVIRONMENT DIVISION.

[CONFIGURATION SECTION.

[SOURCE-COMPUTER. [computer-name [WITH DEBUGGING MODE].]]

[OBJECT-COMPUTER. [computer-name

$$\left[\text{MEMORY SIZE integer-1} \begin{Bmatrix} \underline{\text{WORDS}} \\ \underline{\text{CHARACTERS}} \\ \underline{\text{MODULES}} \end{Bmatrix} \right]$$

    [PROGRAM COLLATING SEQUENCE IS alphabet-name-1]

    [SEGMENT-LIMIT IS segment-number].]]

[SPECIAL-NAMES. [[implementor-name-1

$$\begin{Bmatrix} \text{IS mnemonic-name-1 [\underline{ON} STATUS IS condition-name-1 [\underline{OFF} STATUS IS condition-name-2]]} \\ \text{IS mnemonic-name-2 [\underline{OFF} STATUS IS condition-name-2 [\underline{ON} STATUS IS condition-name-1]]} \\ \underline{\text{ON}} \text{ STATUS IS condition-name-1 [\underline{OFF} STATUS IS condition-name-2]} \\ \underline{\text{OFF}} \text{ STATUS IS condition-name-2 [\underline{ON} STATUS IS condition-name-1]} \end{Bmatrix} \right] \dots$$

    [ALPHABET alphabet-name-1 IS

$$\begin{Bmatrix} \underline{\text{STANDARD-1}} \\ \underline{\text{STANDARD-2}} \\ \underline{\text{NATIVE}} \\ \text{implementor-name-2} \\ \begin{Bmatrix} \text{literal-1} \left[\begin{Bmatrix} \underline{\text{THROUGH}} \\ \underline{\text{THRU}} \end{Bmatrix} \text{literal-2} \right] \{ \underline{\text{ALSO}} \text{ literal-3} \} \dots \end{Bmatrix} \dots \end{Bmatrix} \right] \dots$$

$$\left[\underline{\text{SYMBOLIC}} \text{ CHARACTERS} \left\{ \{ \{ \text{symbolic-character-1} \} \dots \begin{Bmatrix} \text{IS} \\ \text{ARE} \end{Bmatrix} \{ \text{integer-1} \} \dots \right\} \dots \right.$$

        $[\underline{\text{IN}} \text{ alphabet-name-2}] \Big\} \Big] \dots$

$$\left[\underline{\text{CLASS}} \text{ class-name-1 IS} \begin{Bmatrix} \text{literal-4} \left[\begin{Bmatrix} \underline{\text{THROUGH}} \\ \underline{\text{THRU}} \end{Bmatrix} \text{literal-5} \right] \end{Bmatrix} \dots \right] \dots$$

    [CURRENCY SIGN IS literal-6]

    [DECIMAL-POINT IS COMMA].]]]

[INPUT-OUTPUT SECTION.

 FILE-CONTROL.

    {file-control-entry} ...

[I-O-CONTROL.

$$
\left[\left[\underline{\text{RERUN}}\ \left[\underline{\text{ON}}\ \begin{Bmatrix} \text{file-name-1} \\ \text{implementor-name-1} \end{Bmatrix}\right]\ \text{EVERY}\ \begin{Bmatrix} \begin{Bmatrix} [\underline{\text{END}}\ \text{OF}]\ \begin{Bmatrix} \underline{\text{REEL}} \\ \underline{\text{UNIT}} \end{Bmatrix} \\ \text{integer-1}\ \underline{\text{RECORDS}} \end{Bmatrix}\ \text{OF file-name-2} \\ \text{integer-2}\ \underline{\text{CLOCK-UNITS}} \\ \text{condition-name-1} \end{Bmatrix}\right] \cdots
$$

$$
\left[\underline{\text{SAME}}\ \begin{bmatrix} \underline{\text{RECORD}} \\ \underline{\text{SORT}} \\ \underline{\text{SORT-MERGE}} \end{bmatrix}\ \text{AREA FOR file-name-3}\ \{\text{file-name-4}\} \cdots \right] \cdots
$$

[MULTIPLE FILE TAPE CONTAINS {file-name-5 [POSITION integer-3]} ...] ... .]]]]

General Format for File Control Entry

Sequential File:

```
SELECT [OPTIONAL] file-name-1

    ASSIGN TO  {implementor-name-1}  ...
               {literal-1          }

    [RESERVE integer-1  [AREA ]]
                        [AREAS]

    [[ORGANIZATION IS] SEQUENTIAL]

    [PADDING CHARACTER IS  {data-name-1}]
                           {literal-2  }

    [RECORD DELIMITER IS  {STANDARD-1          }]
                          {implementor-name-2  }

    [ACCESS MODE IS SEQUENTIAL]

    [FILE STATUS IS data-name-2].
```

Relative File:

```
SELECT [OPTIONAL] file-name-1

    ASSIGN TO  {implementor-name-1}  ...
               {literal-1          }

    [RESERVE integer-1  [AREA ]]
                        [AREAS]

    [ORGANIZATION IS] RELATIVE

    [                  {SEQUENTIAL [RELATIVE KEY IS data-name-1]  }]
    [ACCESS MODE IS    {                                          }]
    [                  {{RANDOM } RELATIVE KEY IS data-name-1      }]
    [                  {{DYNAMIC}                                  }]

    [FILE STATUS IS data-name-2].
```

Indexed File:

SELECT [OPTIONAL] file-name-1

    ASSIGN TO $\begin{Bmatrix} \text{implementor-name-1} \\ \text{literal-1} \end{Bmatrix}$ ...

    $\left[\underline{\text{RESERVE}} \text{ integer-1} \begin{bmatrix} \text{AREA} \\ \text{AREAS} \end{bmatrix} \right]$

    [ORGANIZATION IS] INDEXED

    $\left[\underline{\text{ACCESS}} \text{ MODE IS } \begin{Bmatrix} \underline{\text{SEQUENTIAL}} \\ \underline{\text{RANDOM}} \\ \underline{\text{DYNAMIC}} \end{Bmatrix} \right]$

    RECORD KEY IS data-name-1

    [ALTERNATE RECORD KEY IS data-name-2 [WITH DUPLICATES]] ...

    [FILE STATUS IS data-name-3].

Sort or Merge File:

SELECT file-name-1 ASSIGN TO $\begin{Bmatrix} \text{implementor-name-1} \\ \text{literal-1} \end{Bmatrix}$ ... .

Report File:

```
SELECT [OPTIONAL] file-name-1

    ASSIGN TO  {implementor-name-1}  ...
               {literal-1          }

    [RESERVE integer-1  [AREA ]]
                        [AREAS]

    [[ORGANIZATION IS]  SEQUENTIAL]]

    [PADDING CHARACTER IS  {data-name-1}]
                           {literal-2  }

    [RECORD DELIMITER IS  {STANDARD-1          }]
                          {implementor-name-2  }

    [ACCESS MODE IS SEQUENTIAL]

    [FILE STATUS IS data-name-2].
```

General Format for Data Division

[DATA DIVISION.

[FILE SECTION.

$$\left[\begin{array}{l}\text{file-description-entry \{record-description-entry\} } \dots \\ \text{sort-merge-file-description-entry \{record-description-entry\} } \dots \\ \text{report-file-description-entry}\end{array}\right] \dots \Bigg]$$

[WORKING-STORAGE SECTION.

$$\left[\begin{array}{l}\text{77-level-description-entry} \\ \text{record-description-entry}\end{array}\right] \dots$$

[LINKAGE SECTION.

$$\left[\begin{array}{l}\text{77-level-description-entry} \\ \text{record-description-entry}\end{array}\right] \dots$$

[COMMUNICATION SECTION.

[communication-description-entry [record-description-entry] ...] ...]

[REPORT SECTION.

[report-description-entry {report-group-description-entry} ...] ...]]

General Format for File Description Entry

Sequential File:

```
FD  file-name-1

    [IS EXTERNAL]

    [IS GLOBAL]

    [BLOCK CONTAINS [integer-1 TO] integer-2 {RECORDS   }]
                                            {CHARACTERS}

    [RECORD {CONTAINS integer-3 CHARACTERS                                          }]
           {IS VARYING IN SIZE [[FROM integer-4] [TO integer-5] CHARACTERS]        }
           {       [DEPENDING ON data-name-1]                                       }
           {CONTAINS integer-6 TO integer-7 CHARACTERS                              }

    [LABEL {RECORD IS  } {STANDARD}]
          {RECORDS ARE} {OMITTED }

    [VALUE OF {implementor-name-1 IS {data-name-2}} ...]
                                    {literal-1  }

    [DATA {RECORD IS  } {data-name-3} ...]
         {RECORDS ARE}

    [LINAGE IS {data-name-4} LINES [WITH FOOTING AT {data-name-5}]
              {integer-8  }                        {integer-9  }

        [LINES AT TOP {data-name-6}] [LINES AT BOTTOM {data-name-7 }]]
                      {integer-10 }                   {integer-11 }

    [CODE-SET IS alphabet-name-1].
```

Relative File:

FD   file-name-1

    [IS EXTERNAL]

    [IS GLOBAL]

$$\left[\underline{\text{BLOCK}} \text{ CONTAINS } [\text{integer-1 } \underline{\text{TO}}] \text{ integer-2 } \left\{ \begin{matrix} \underline{\text{RECORDS}} \\ \text{CHARACTERS} \end{matrix} \right\} \right]$$

$$\left[\underline{\text{RECORD}} \left\{ \begin{matrix} \text{CONTAINS integer-3 CHARACTERS} \\ \text{IS } \underline{\text{VARYING}} \text{ IN SIZE } [[\text{FROM integer-4}] \text{ } [\underline{\text{TO}} \text{ integer-5}] \text{ CHARACTERS}] \\ [\underline{\text{DEPENDING}} \text{ ON data-name-1}] \\ \text{CONTAINS integer-6 } \underline{\text{TO}} \text{ integer-7 CHARACTERS} \end{matrix} \right\} \right]$$

$$\left[\underline{\text{LABEL}} \left\{ \begin{matrix} \underline{\text{RECORD}} \text{ IS} \\ \underline{\text{RECORDS}} \text{ ARE} \end{matrix} \right\} \left\{ \begin{matrix} \underline{\text{STANDARD}} \\ \underline{\text{OMITTED}} \end{matrix} \right\} \right]$$

$$\left[\underline{\text{VALUE}} \text{ } \underline{\text{OF}} \left\{ \text{implementor-name-1 IS } \left\{ \begin{matrix} \text{data-name-2} \\ \text{literal-1} \end{matrix} \right\} \right\} \text{ ... } \right]$$

$$\left[\underline{\text{DATA}} \left\{ \begin{matrix} \underline{\text{RECORD}} \text{ IS} \\ \underline{\text{RECORDS}} \text{ ARE} \end{matrix} \right\} \text{ \{data-name-3\} ... } \right].$$

Indexed File:

<u>FD</u> file-name-1

    [IS <u>EXTERNAL</u>]

    [IS <u>GLOBAL</u>]

$$\left[\underline{BLOCK}\ CONTAINS\ [integer\text{-}1\ \underline{TO}]\ \ integer\text{-}2\ \begin{Bmatrix} \underline{RECORDS} \\ CHARACTERS \end{Bmatrix} \right]$$

$$\left[\underline{RECORD} \begin{Bmatrix} CONTAINS\ integer\text{-}3\ CHARACTERS \\ IS\ \underline{VARYING}\ IN\ SIZE\ [[FROM\ integer\text{-}4]\ [\underline{TO}\ integer\text{-}5]\ CHARACTERS] \\ [\underline{DEPENDING}\ ON\ data\text{-}name\text{-}1] \\ CONTAINS\ integer\text{-}6\ \underline{TO}\ integer\text{-}7\ CHARACTERS \end{Bmatrix} \right]$$

$$\left[\underline{LABEL} \begin{Bmatrix} \underline{RECORD}\ IS \\ \underline{RECORDS}\ ARE \end{Bmatrix} \begin{Bmatrix} \underline{STANDARD} \\ \underline{OMITTED} \end{Bmatrix} \right]$$

$$\left[\underline{VALUE}\ \underline{OF}\ \begin{Bmatrix} implementor\text{-}name\text{-}1\ IS\ \begin{Bmatrix} data\text{-}name\text{-}2 \\ literal\text{-}1 \end{Bmatrix} \end{Bmatrix} \dots \right]$$

$$\left[\underline{DATA} \begin{Bmatrix} \underline{RECORD}\ IS \\ \underline{RECORDS}\ ARE \end{Bmatrix} \{data\text{-}name\text{-}3\} \dots \right].$$

Sort-Merge File:

```
SD   file-name-1
```

$$
\left[\underline{RECORD} \; \left\{ \begin{array}{l} \text{CONTAINS integer-1 CHARACTERS} \\ \text{IS } \underline{VARYING} \text{ IN SIZE } [[\text{FROM integer-2}] \; [\underline{TO} \text{ integer-3}] \text{ CHARACTERS}] \\ \qquad [\underline{DEPENDING} \text{ ON data-name-1}] \\ \text{CONTAINS integer-4 } \underline{TO} \text{ integer-5 CHARACTERS} \end{array} \right\} \right]
$$

$$
\left[\underline{DATA} \; \left\{ \begin{array}{l} \underline{RECORD} \text{ IS} \\ \underline{RECORDS} \text{ ARE} \end{array} \right\} \; \{\text{data-name-2}\} \; \ldots \right] \; .
$$

Report File:

```
FD   file-name-1
```

[IS EXTERNAL]

[IS GLOBAL]

$$
\left[\underline{BLOCK} \text{ CONTAINS } [\text{integer-1 } \underline{TO}] \quad \text{integer-2 } \left\{ \begin{array}{l} \underline{RECORDS} \\ \underline{CHARACTERS} \end{array} \right\} \right]
$$

$$
\left[\underline{RECORD} \quad \left\{ \begin{array}{l} \text{CONTAINS integer-3 CHARACTERS} \\ \text{CONTAINS integer-4 } \underline{TO} \text{ integer-5 CHARACTERS} \end{array} \right\} \right]
$$

$$
\left[\underline{LABEL} \; \left\{ \begin{array}{l} \underline{RECORD} \text{ IS} \\ \underline{RECORDS} \text{ ARE} \end{array} \right\} \; \left\{ \begin{array}{l} \underline{STANDARD} \\ \underline{OMITTED} \end{array} \right\} \right]
$$

$$
\left[\underline{VALUE} \; \underline{OF} \; \left\{ \text{implementor-name-1 IS } \left\{ \begin{array}{l} \text{data-name-1} \\ \text{literal-1} \end{array} \right\} \right\} \; \ldots \right]
$$

[CODE-SET IS alphabet-name-1]

$$
\left\{ \begin{array}{l} \underline{REPORT} \text{ IS} \\ \underline{REPORTS} \text{ ARE} \end{array} \right\} \; \{\text{report-name-1}\} \; \ldots \qquad .
$$

General Format for Data Description Entry

Format 1:

```
level-number  ⎡data-name-1⎤
              ⎣FILLER     ⎦

    [REDEFINES data-name-2]

    [IS EXTERNAL]

    [IS GLOBAL]

    ⎡⎧PICTURE⎫                      ⎤
    ⎢⎨PIC    ⎬ IS character-string  ⎥
    ⎣⎩       ⎭                      ⎦

    ⎡            ⎧BINARY         ⎫⎤
    ⎢            ⎪COMPUTATIONAL  ⎪⎥
    ⎢            ⎪COMP           ⎪⎥
    ⎢[USAGE IS]  ⎨DISPLAY        ⎬⎥
    ⎢            ⎪INDEX          ⎪⎥
    ⎣            ⎩PACKED-DECIMAL ⎭⎦

    ⎡         ⎧LEADING ⎫                      ⎤
    ⎢[SIGN IS]⎨TRAILING⎬ [SEPARATE CHARACTER] ⎥
    ⎣         ⎩        ⎭                      ⎦

    ⎡OCCURS integer-2 TIMES                                            ⎤
    ⎢                                                                  ⎥
    ⎢     ⎡⎧ASCENDING ⎫                        ⎤                       ⎥
    ⎢     ⎢⎨DESCENDING⎬ KEY IS  {data-name-3} ...⎥ ...                  ⎥
    ⎢     ⎣⎩          ⎭                        ⎦                       ⎥
    ⎢                                                                  ⎥
    ⎢          [INDEXED BY  {index-name-1} ... ]                       ⎥
    ⎢                                                                  ⎥
    ⎢OCCURS integer-1 TO integer-2 TIMES DEPENDING ON data-name-4      ⎥
    ⎢                                                                  ⎥
    ⎢     ⎡⎧ASCENDING ⎫                        ⎤                       ⎥
    ⎢     ⎢⎨DESCENDING⎬ KEY IS  {data-name-3} ...⎥ ...                  ⎥
    ⎢     ⎣⎩          ⎭                        ⎦                       ⎥
    ⎢                                                                  ⎥
    ⎣          [INDEXED BY  {index-name-1} ... ]                       ⎦

    ⎡⎧SYNCHRONIZED⎫ ⎡LEFT ⎤⎤
    ⎢⎨SYNC        ⎬ ⎣RIGHT⎦⎥
    ⎣⎩            ⎭       ⎦

    ⎡⎧JUSTIFIED⎫       ⎤
    ⎢⎨JUST     ⎬ RIGHT ⎥
    ⎣⎩         ⎭       ⎦

    [BLANK WHEN ZERO]

    [VALUE IS literal-1].
```

Format 2:

$$66 \; \text{data-name-1} \; \underline{\text{RENAMES}} \; \text{data-name-2} \; \left[\left\{ \begin{array}{l} \underline{\text{THROUGH}} \\ \underline{\text{THRU}} \end{array} \right\} \; \text{data-name-3} \right] \; .$$

Format 3:

$$88 \; \text{condition-name-1} \; \left\{ \begin{array}{l} \underline{\text{VALUE}} \; \text{IS} \\ \underline{\text{VALUES}} \; \text{ARE} \end{array} \right\} \; \left\{ \text{literal-1} \; \left[\left\{ \begin{array}{l} \underline{\text{THROUGH}} \\ \underline{\text{THRU}} \end{array} \right\} \; \text{literal-2} \right] \right\} \; ... \; .$$

General Format for Communication Description Entry

Format 1:

<u>CD</u> cd-name-1

```
                                    ┌                                        ┐
                                    [[SYMBOLIC QUEUE IS data-name-1]
                                         [SYMBOLIC SUB-QUEUE-1 IS data-name-2]
                                         [SYMBOLIC SUB-QUEUE-2 IS data-name-3]
                                         [SYMBOLIC SUB-QUEUE-3 IS data-name-4]
                                         [MESSAGE DATE IS data-name-5]
                                         [MESSAGE TIME IS data-name-6]
                                         [SYMBOLIC SOURCE IS data-name-7]
        FOR   [INITIAL]   INPUT        [TEXT LENGTH IS data-name-8]
                                         [END KEY IS data-name-9]
                                         [STATUS KEY IS data-name-10]
                                         [MESSAGE COUNT IS data-name-11]]
                                    [data-name-1, data-name-2, data-name-3,
                                         data-name-4, data-name-5, data-name-6,
                                         data-name-7, data-name-8, data-name-9,
                                         data-name-10, data-name-11]
                                    └                                        ┘
```

Format 2:

<u>CD</u>   cd-name-1 FOR <u>OUTPUT</u>

    [<u>DESTINATION</u> <u>COUNT</u> IS data-name-1]

    [<u>TEXT</u> <u>LENGTH</u> IS data-name-2]

    [<u>STATUS</u> <u>KEY</u> IS data-name-3]

    [<u>DESTINATION</u> <u>TABLE</u> <u>OCCURS</u> integer-1 TIMES

        [<u>INDEXED</u> BY {index-name-1} ...]]

    [<u>ERROR</u> <u>KEY</u> IS data-name-4]

    [SYMBOLIC <u>DESTINATION</u> IS data-name-5].

Format 3:

<u>CD</u>   cd-name-1

$$
\text{FOR} \quad [\underline{\text{INITIAL}}] \quad \underline{\text{I-O}}
\begin{bmatrix}
[[\underline{\text{MESSAGE}}\ \underline{\text{DATE}}\ \text{IS data-name-1}] \\
\quad [\underline{\text{MESSAGE}}\ \underline{\text{TIME}}\ \text{IS data-name-2}] \\
\quad [\text{SYMBOLIC}\ \underline{\text{TERMINAL}}\ \text{IS data-name-3}] \\
\quad [\underline{\text{TEXT}}\ \underline{\text{LENGTH}}\ \text{IS data-name-4}] \\
\quad [\underline{\text{END}}\ \underline{\text{KEY}}\ \text{IS data-name-5}] \\
\quad [\underline{\text{STATUS}}\ \underline{\text{KEY}}\ \text{IS data-name-6}]] \\
[\text{data-name-1, data-name-2, data-name-3,} \\
\quad \text{data-name-4, data-name-5, data-name-6}]
\end{bmatrix}
$$

General Format for Report Description Entry

RD   report-name-1

    [IS GLOBAL]

    [CODE literal-1]

$$
\left[\begin{matrix} \text{CONTROL IS} \\ \text{CONTROLS ARE} \end{matrix} \right\} \quad \left\{ \begin{matrix} \{\text{data-name-1}\} \dots \\ \text{FINAL [data-name-1] } \dots \end{matrix} \right\} \right]
$$

$$
\left[\text{PAGE} \left[\begin{matrix} \text{LIMIT IS} \\ \text{LIMITS ARE} \end{matrix} \right] \text{integer-1} \left[\begin{matrix} \text{LINE} \\ \text{LINES} \end{matrix} \right] \quad [\text{HEADING integer-2}] \right.
$$

        [FIRST DETAIL integer-3]   [LAST DETAIL integer-4]

$$
\left. [\text{FOOTING integer-5}] \right] .
$$

General Format for Report Group Description Entry

Format 1:

```
01  [data-name-1]

    ┌                    ┌                           ┐ ┐
    │ LINE NUMBER IS     │ integer-1  [ON NEXT PAGE] │ │
    │                    │ PLUS integer-2            │ │
    └                    └                           ┘ ┘

    ┌                    ┌                ┐ ┐
    │ NEXT GROUP IS      │ integer-3      │ │
    │                    │ PLUS integer-4 │ │
    │                    │ NEXT PAGE      │ │
    └                    └                ┘ ┘

                        ┌                                        ┐
                        │ ┌ REPORT HEADING ┐                     │
                        │ │ RH             │                     │
                        │ └                ┘                     │
                        │ ┌ PAGE HEADING ┐                       │
                        │ │ PH           │                       │
                        │ └              ┘                       │
                        │ ┌ CONTROL HEADING ┐  ┌ data-name-2 ┐   │
                        │ │ CH              │  │ FINAL       │   │
                        │ └                 ┘  └             ┘   │
    TYPE IS        {    │ ┌ DETAIL ┐                             │
                        │ │ DE     │                             │
                        │ └        ┘                             │
                        │ ┌ CONTROL FOOTING ┐  ┌ data-name-3 ┐   │
                        │ │ CF              │  │ FINAL       │   │
                        │ └                 ┘  └             ┘   │
                        │ ┌ PAGE FOOTING ┐                       │
                        │ │ PF           │                       │
                        │ └              ┘                       │
                        │ ┌ REPORT FOOTING ┐                     │
                        │ │ RF             │                     │
                        │ └                ┘                     │
                        └                                        ┘

    [[USAGE IS]  DISPLAY].
```

Format 2:

```
level-number  [data-name-1]
```

$$\left[\text{\underline{LINE}} \text{ NUMBER IS } \left\{ \begin{array}{l} \text{integer-1 } [\text{ON \underline{NEXT} \underline{PAGE}}] \\ \text{\underline{PLUS} Integer-2} \end{array} \right\} \right]$$

```
[[USAGE IS]  DISPLAY].
```

Format 3:

```
level-number  [data-name-1]
```

$$\left\{ \begin{array}{l} \text{\underline{PICTURE}} \\ \text{\underline{PIC}} \end{array} \right\} \text{ IS character-string}$$

```
[[USAGE IS]  DISPLAY]
```

$$\left[[\text{\underline{SIGN} IS}] \left\{ \begin{array}{l} \text{\underline{LEADING}} \\ \text{\underline{TRAILING}} \end{array} \right\} \text{\underline{SEPARATE} CHARACTER} \right]$$

$$\left[\left\{ \begin{array}{l} \text{\underline{JUSTIFIED}} \\ \text{\underline{JUST}} \end{array} \right\} \text{ RIGHT} \right]$$

```
[BLANK WHEN ZERO]
```

$$\left[\text{\underline{LINE}} \text{ NUMBER IS } \left\{ \begin{array}{l} \text{integer-1 } [\text{ON \underline{NEXT} \underline{PAGE}}] \\ \text{\underline{PLUS} integer-2} \end{array} \right\} \right]$$

```
[COLUMN NUMBER IS integer-3]
```

$$\left\{ \begin{array}{l} \text{\underline{SOURCE} IS identifier-1} \\ \\ \text{\underline{VALUE} IS literal-1} \\ \\ \{\text{\underline{SUM}} \ \{\text{identifier-2}\} \ ... \ [\text{\underline{UPON}} \ \{\text{data-name-2}\} \ ... \ ]\} \ ... \\ \quad \left[\text{\underline{RESET} ON } \left\{ \begin{array}{l} \text{data-name-3} \\ \text{\underline{FINAL}} \end{array} \right\} \right] \end{array} \right\}$$

```
[GROUP INDICATE].
```

General Format for Procedure Division

Format 1:

```
[PROCEDURE DIVISION  [USING  {data-name-1} ... ].

[DECLARATIVES.

{section-name SECTION [segment-number].

    USE statement.

[paragraph-name.

    [sentence] ... ] ... } ...

 END DECLARATIVES.]

{section-name SECTION [segment-number].

[paragraph-name.

    [sentence] ... ] ... } ... ]
```

Format 2:

```
[PROCEDURE DIVISION  [USING  {data-name-1} ... ].

{paragraph-name.

    [sentence] ... } ... ]
```

General Format for COBOL Verbs

ACCEPT identifier-1 [FROM mnemonic-name-1]

ACCEPT identifier-2 FROM $\begin{Bmatrix} \text{DATE} \\ \text{DAY} \\ \text{DAY-OF-WEEK} \\ \text{TIME} \end{Bmatrix}$

ACCEPT cd-name-1 MESSAGE COUNT

ADD $\begin{Bmatrix} \text{identifier-1} \\ \text{literal-1} \end{Bmatrix}$ ...   TO {identifier-2 [ROUNDED]} ...

  [ON SIZE ERROR imperative-statement-1]

  [NOT ON SIZE ERROR imperative-statement-2]

  [END-ADD]

ADD $\begin{Bmatrix} \text{identifier-1} \\ \text{literal-1} \end{Bmatrix}$ ...   TO $\begin{Bmatrix} \text{identifier-2} \\ \text{literal-2} \end{Bmatrix}$

  GIVING {identifier-3 [ROUNDED]} ...

  [ON SIZE ERROR imperative-statement-1]

  [NOT ON SIZE ERROR imperative-statement-2]

  [END-ADD]

ADD $\begin{Bmatrix} \text{CORRESPONDING} \\ \text{CORR} \end{Bmatrix}$ identifier-1 TO identifier-2 [ROUNDED]

  [ON SIZE ERROR imperative-statement-1]

  [NOT ON SIZE ERROR imperative-statement-2]

  [END-ADD]

ALTER {procedure-name-1 TO [PROCEED TO] procedure-name-2} ...

CALL $\begin{Bmatrix} \text{identifier-1} \\ \text{literal-1} \end{Bmatrix}$ $\left[\text{USING} \begin{Bmatrix} \text{[BY REFERENCE] \{identifier-2\} ...} \\ \text{BY CONTENT \{identifier-2\} ...} \end{Bmatrix} ... \right]$

  [ON OVERFLOW imperative-statement-1]

  [END-CALL]

CALL $\begin{Bmatrix} \text{identifier-1} \\ \text{literal-1} \end{Bmatrix}$ $\left[\underline{\text{USING}} \begin{Bmatrix} [\text{BY } \underline{\text{REFERENCE}}] & \{\text{identifier-2}\} \ldots \\ \text{BY } \underline{\text{CONTENT}} & \{\text{identifier-2}\} \ldots \end{Bmatrix} \ldots \right]$

    [ON <u>EXCEPTION</u> imperative-statement-1]

    [<u>NOT</u> ON <u>EXCEPTION</u> imperative-statement-2]

    [<u>END-CALL</u>]

<u>CANCEL</u> $\begin{Bmatrix} \text{identifier-1} \\ \text{literal-1} \end{Bmatrix}$ ...

SW <u>CLOSE</u> $\begin{Bmatrix} \text{file-name-1} \left[\begin{array}{l} \begin{Bmatrix} \underline{\text{REEL}} \\ \underline{\text{UNIT}} \end{Bmatrix} [\text{FOR } \underline{\text{REMOVAL}}] \\ \text{WITH} \begin{Bmatrix} \underline{\text{NO}} \ \underline{\text{REWIND}} \\ \underline{\text{LOCK}} \end{Bmatrix} \end{array} \right] \end{Bmatrix}$ ...

RI <u>CLOSE</u> {file-name-1 [WITH <u>LOCK</u>]} ...

<u>COMPUTE</u> {identifier-1 [<u>ROUNDED</u>]} ... = arithmetic-expression-1

    [ON <u>SIZE</u> <u>ERROR</u> imperative-statement-1]

    [<u>NOT</u> ON <u>SIZE</u> <u>ERROR</u> imperative-statement-2]

    [<u>END-COMPUTE</u>]

<u>CONTINUE</u>

<u>DELETE</u> file-name-1 RECORD

    [<u>INVALID</u> KEY imperative-statement-1]

    [<u>NOT</u> <u>INVALID</u> KEY imperative-statement-2]

    [<u>END-DELETE</u>]

<u>DISABLE</u> $\begin{Bmatrix} \underline{\text{INPUT}} \ [\underline{\text{TERMINAL}}] \\ \underline{\text{I-O}} \ \underline{\text{TERMINAL}} \\ \underline{\text{OUTPUT}} \end{Bmatrix}$ cd-name-1 $\left[\text{WITH } \underline{\text{KEY}} \begin{Bmatrix} \text{identifier-1} \\ \text{literal-1} \end{Bmatrix} \right]$

DISPLAY $\begin{Bmatrix} \text{identifier-1} \\ \text{literal-1} \end{Bmatrix}$ ...   [<u>UPON</u> mnemonic-name-1]   [WITH <u>NO</u> <u>ADVANCING</u>]

<u>DIVIDE</u> $\begin{Bmatrix} \text{identifier-1} \\ \text{literal-1} \end{Bmatrix}$ <u>INTO</u> {identifier-2 [<u>ROUNDED</u>]} ...

[ON <u>SIZE</u> <u>ERROR</u> imperative-statement-1]

[<u>NOT</u> ON <u>SIZE</u> <u>ERROR</u> imperative-statement-2]

[<u>END-DIVIDE</u>]

<u>DIVIDE</u> $\begin{Bmatrix} \text{identifier-1} \\ \text{literal-1} \end{Bmatrix}$ <u>INTO</u> $\begin{Bmatrix} \text{identifier-2} \\ \text{literal-2} \end{Bmatrix}$

<u>GIVING</u> {identifier-3 [<u>ROUNDED</u>]} ...

[ON <u>SIZE</u> <u>ERROR</u> imperative-statement-1]

[<u>NOT</u> ON <u>SIZE</u> <u>ERROR</u> imperative-statement-2]

[<u>END-DIVIDE</u>]

<u>DIVIDE</u> $\begin{Bmatrix} \text{identifier-1} \\ \text{literal-1} \end{Bmatrix}$ <u>BY</u> $\begin{Bmatrix} \text{identifier-2} \\ \text{literal-2} \end{Bmatrix}$

<u>GIVING</u> {identifier-3 [<u>ROUNDED</u>]} ...

[ON <u>SIZE</u> <u>ERROR</u> imperative-statement-1]

[<u>NOT</u> ON <u>SIZE</u> <u>ERROR</u> imperative-statement-2]

[<u>END-DIVIDE</u>]

<u>DIVIDE</u> $\begin{Bmatrix} \text{identifier-1} \\ \text{literal-1} \end{Bmatrix}$ <u>INTO</u> $\begin{Bmatrix} \text{identifier-2} \\ \text{literal-2} \end{Bmatrix}$ <u>GIVING</u> identifier-3 [<u>ROUNDED</u>]

<u>REMAINDER</u> identifier-4

[ON <u>SIZE</u> <u>ERROR</u> imperative-statement-1]

[<u>NOT</u> ON <u>SIZE</u> <u>ERROR</u> imperative-statement-2]

[<u>END-DIVIDE</u>]

DIVIDE {identifier-1} BY {identifier-2} GIVING identifier-3 [ROUNDED]
       {literal-1   }   {literal-2   }

    REMAINDER identifier-4

    [ON SIZE ERROR imperative-statement-1]

    [NOT ON SIZE ERROR imperative-statement-2]

    [END-DIVIDE]

ENABLE {INPUT [TERMINAL]} cd-name-1 [WITH KEY {identifier-1}]
       {I-O TERMINAL   }   {literal-1   }
       {OUTPUT   }

ENTER language-name-1 [routine-name-1].

EVALUATE {identifier-1 } [ALSO {identifier-2 }] ...
         {literal-1   }   {literal-2   }
         {expression-1 }   {expression-2 }
         {TRUE   }   {TRUE   }
         {FALSE   }   {FALSE   }

    {{WHEN

        {ANY   }
        {condition-1   }
        {TRUE   }
        {FALSE   }
        {   {identifier-3   } {THROUGH} {identifier-4   }   }
        {[NOT] {literal-3   } {THRU   } {literal-4   }   }
        {   {arithmetic-expression-1 }   {arithmetic-expression-2}   }

    [ALSO

        {ANY   }
        {condition-2   }
        {TRUE   }
        {FALSE   }
        {   {identifier-5   } {THROUGH} {identifier-6   }   } ... } ...
        {[NOT] {literal-5   } {THRU   } {literal-6   }   }
        {   {arithmetic-expression-3 }   {arithmetic-expression-4}   }

    imperative-statement-1} ...

    [WHEN OTHER imperative-statement-2]

    [END-EVALUATE]

<u>EXIT</u>

<u>EXIT</u> <u>PROGRAM</u>

<u>GENERATE</u> $\left\{\begin{array}{l}\text{data-name-1}\\\text{report-name-1}\end{array}\right\}$

<u>GO</u> TO [procedure-name-1]

<u>GO</u> TO {procedure-name-1} ...   <u>DEPENDING</u> ON identifier-1

<u>IF</u> condition-1 THEN $\left\{\begin{array}{l}\text{\{statement-1\} ...}\\\underline{\text{NEXT}}\ \underline{\text{SENTENCE}}\end{array}\right\}$ $\left\{\begin{array}{l}\underline{\text{ELSE}}\ \text{\{statement-2\} ...}\ [\underline{\text{END-IF}}]\\\underline{\text{ELSE}}\ \underline{\text{NEXT}}\ \underline{\text{SENTENCE}}\\\underline{\text{END-IF}}\end{array}\right\}$

<u>INITIALIZE</u> {identifier-1} ...

$$\left[\ \underline{\text{REPLACING}}\ \left\{\left\{\begin{array}{l}\underline{\text{ALPHABETIC}}\\\underline{\text{ALPHANUMERIC}}\\\underline{\text{NUMERIC}}\\\underline{\text{ALPHANUMERIC-EDITED}}\\\underline{\text{NUMERIC-EDITED}}\end{array}\right\}\ \text{DATA}\ \underline{\text{BY}}\ \left\{\begin{array}{l}\text{identifier-2}\\\text{literal-1}\end{array}\right\}\right\}\ ...\ \right]$$

<u>INITIATE</u> {report-name-1} ...

<u>INSPECT</u> identifier-1 <u>TALLYING</u>

$$\left\{\text{identifier-2}\ \underline{\text{FOR}}\ \left\{\begin{array}{l}\underline{\text{CHARACTERS}}\ \left[\left\{\begin{array}{l}\underline{\text{BEFORE}}\\\underline{\text{AFTER}}\end{array}\right\}\ \text{INITIAL}\ \left\{\begin{array}{l}\text{identifier-4}\\\text{literal-2}\end{array}\right\}\right]\ ...\\\left\{\begin{array}{l}\underline{\text{ALL}}\\\underline{\text{LEADING}}\end{array}\right\}\ \left\{\begin{array}{l}\text{identifier-3}\\\text{literal-1}\end{array}\right\}\ \left[\left\{\begin{array}{l}\underline{\text{BEFORE}}\\\underline{\text{AFTER}}\end{array}\right\}\ \text{INITIAL}\ \left\{\begin{array}{l}\text{identifier-4}\\\text{literal-2}\end{array}\right\}\right]\ ...\ \end{array}\right\}\ ...\ \right\}\ ...$$

<u>INSPECT</u> identifier-1 <u>REPLACING</u>

$$\left\{\begin{array}{l}\underline{\text{CHARACTERS}}\ \underline{\text{BY}}\ \left\{\begin{array}{l}\text{identifier-5}\\\text{literal-3}\end{array}\right\}\ \left[\left\{\begin{array}{l}\underline{\text{BEFORE}}\\\underline{\text{AFTER}}\end{array}\right\}\ \text{INITIAL}\ \left\{\begin{array}{l}\text{identifier-4}\\\text{literal-2}\end{array}\right\}\right]\ ...\\\left\{\begin{array}{l}\underline{\text{ALL}}\\\underline{\text{LEADING}}\\\underline{\text{FIRST}}\end{array}\right\}\ \left\{\left\{\begin{array}{l}\text{identifier-3}\\\text{literal-1}\end{array}\right\}\ \underline{\text{BY}}\ \left\{\begin{array}{l}\text{identifier-5}\\\text{literal-3}\end{array}\right\}\ \left[\left\{\begin{array}{l}\underline{\text{BEFORE}}\\\underline{\text{AFTER}}\end{array}\right\}\ \text{INITIAL}\ \left\{\begin{array}{l}\text{identifier-4}\\\text{literal-2}\end{array}\right\}\right]\ ...\ \right\}\ ...\end{array}\right\}\ ...$$

INSPECT identifier-1 TALLYING

$$\left\{ identifier\text{-}2 \ \underline{FOR} \ \left\{ \begin{array}{l} \underline{CHARACTERS} \ \left[\left\{ \begin{array}{l} \underline{BEFORE} \\ \underline{AFTER} \end{array} \right\} INITIAL \left\{ \begin{array}{l} identifier\text{-}4 \\ literal\text{-}2 \end{array} \right\} \right] \cdots \\ \left\{ \begin{array}{l} \underline{ALL} \\ \underline{LEADING} \end{array} \right\} \left\{ \begin{array}{l} identifier\text{-}3 \\ literal\text{-}1 \end{array} \right\} \left[\left\{ \begin{array}{l} \underline{BEFORE} \\ \underline{AFTER} \end{array} \right\} INITIAL \left\{ \begin{array}{l} identifier\text{-}4 \\ literal\text{-}2 \end{array} \right\} \right] \cdots \right\} \cdots \right\} \cdots \right\} \cdots$$

REPLACING

$$\left\{ \begin{array}{l} \underline{CHARACTERS} \ \underline{BY} \left\{ \begin{array}{l} identifier\text{-}5 \\ literal\text{-}3 \end{array} \right\} \left[\left\{ \begin{array}{l} \underline{BEFORE} \\ \underline{AFTER} \end{array} \right\} INITIAL \left\{ \begin{array}{l} identifier\text{-}4 \\ literal\text{-}2 \end{array} \right\} \right] \cdots \\ \left\{ \begin{array}{l} \underline{ALL} \\ \underline{LEADING} \\ \underline{FIRST} \end{array} \right\} \left\{ \begin{array}{l} identifier\text{-}3 \\ literal\text{-}1 \end{array} \right\} \underline{BY} \left\{ \begin{array}{l} identifier\text{-}5 \\ literal\text{-}3 \end{array} \right\} \left[\left\{ \begin{array}{l} \underline{BEFORE} \\ \underline{AFTER} \end{array} \right\} INITIAL \left\{ \begin{array}{l} identifier\text{-}4 \\ literal\text{-}2 \end{array} \right\} \right] \cdots \right\} \cdots \right\} \cdots$$

INSPECT identifier-1 CONVERTING $\left\{ \begin{array}{l} identifier\text{-}6 \\ literal\text{-}4 \end{array} \right\}$ TO $\left\{ \begin{array}{l} identifier\text{-}7 \\ literal\text{-}5 \end{array} \right\}$

$$\left[\left\{ \begin{array}{l} \underline{BEFORE} \\ \underline{AFTER} \end{array} \right\} INITIAL \left\{ \begin{array}{l} identifier\text{-}4 \\ literal\text{-}2 \end{array} \right\} \right] \cdots$$

MERGE file-name-1 $\left\{ ON \left\{ \begin{array}{l} \underline{ASCENDING} \\ \underline{DESCENDING} \end{array} \right\} KEY \ \{data\text{-}name\text{-}1\} \cdots \right\} \cdots$

[COLLATING SEQUENCE IS alphabet-name-1]

USING file-name-2 {file-name-3} ...

$$\left\{ \begin{array}{l} \underline{OUTPUT} \ \underline{PROCEDURE} \ IS \ procedure\text{-}name\text{-}1 \ \left[\left\{ \begin{array}{l} \underline{THROUGH} \\ \underline{THRU} \end{array} \right\} procedure\text{-}name\text{-}2 \right] \\ \underline{GIVING} \ \{file\text{-}name\text{-}4\} \cdots \end{array} \right\}$$

MOVE $\left\{ \begin{array}{l} identifier\text{-}1 \\ literal\text{-}1 \end{array} \right\}$ TO {identifier-2} ...

MOVE $\left\{ \begin{array}{l} \underline{CORRESPONDING} \\ \underline{CORR} \end{array} \right\}$ identifier-1 TO identifier-2

MULTIPLY $\left\{ \begin{array}{l} identifier\text{-}1 \\ literal\text{-}1 \end{array} \right\}$ BY {identifier-2 [ROUNDED]} ...

[ON SIZE ERROR imperative-statement-1]

[NOT ON SIZE ERROR imperative-statement-2]

[END-MULTIPLY]

$$\underline{\text{MULTIPLY}} \quad \begin{Bmatrix} \text{identifier-1} \\ \text{literal-1} \end{Bmatrix} \quad \underline{\text{BY}} \quad \begin{Bmatrix} \text{identifier-2} \\ \text{literal-2} \end{Bmatrix}$$

$$\underline{\text{GIVING}} \ \{\text{identifier-3} \ [\underline{\text{ROUNDED}}]\} \ \dots$$

[ON $\underline{\text{SIZE}}$ $\underline{\text{ERROR}}$ imperative-statement-1]

[$\underline{\text{NOT}}$ ON $\underline{\text{SIZE}}$ $\underline{\text{ERROR}}$ imperative-statement-2]

[$\underline{\text{END-MULTIPLY}}$]

$$S \ \underline{\text{OPEN}} \quad \begin{Bmatrix} \underline{\text{INPUT}} \quad \begin{Bmatrix} \text{file-name-1} \quad \begin{bmatrix} \underline{\text{REVERSED}} \\ \text{WITH } \underline{\text{NO}} \ \underline{\text{REWIND}} \end{bmatrix} \end{Bmatrix} \dots \\ \underline{\text{OUTPUT}} \ \{\text{file-name-2} \quad [\text{WITH } \underline{\text{NO}} \ \underline{\text{REWIND}}]\} \ \dots \\ \underline{\text{I-O}} \ \{\text{file-name-3}\} \ \dots \\ \underline{\text{EXTEND}} \ \{\text{file-name-4}\} \ \dots \end{Bmatrix} \dots$$

$$RI \ \underline{\text{OPEN}} \quad \begin{Bmatrix} \underline{\text{INPUT}} \ \{\text{file-name-1}\} \ \dots \\ \underline{\text{OUTPUT}} \ \{\text{file-name-2}\} \ \dots \\ \underline{\text{I-O}} \ \{\text{file-name-3}\} \ \dots \\ \underline{\text{EXTEND}} \ \{\text{file-name-4}\} \ \dots \end{Bmatrix} \dots$$

$$W \ \underline{\text{OPEN}} \quad \begin{Bmatrix} \underline{\text{OUTPUT}} \ \{\text{file-name-1} \ [\text{WITH } \underline{\text{NO}} \ \underline{\text{REWIND}}]\} \ \dots \\ \underline{\text{EXTEND}} \ \{\text{file-name-2}\} \ \dots \end{Bmatrix} \dots$$

$$\underline{\text{PERFORM}} \quad \begin{bmatrix} \text{procedure-name-1} \quad \begin{bmatrix} \begin{Bmatrix} \underline{\text{THROUGH}} \\ \underline{\text{THRU}} \end{Bmatrix} \ \text{procedure-name-2} \end{bmatrix} \end{bmatrix}$$

[imperative-statement-1 $\underline{\text{END-PERFORM}}$]

$$\underline{\text{PERFORM}} \quad \begin{bmatrix} \text{procedure-name-1} \quad \begin{bmatrix} \begin{Bmatrix} \underline{\text{THROUGH}} \\ \underline{\text{THRU}} \end{Bmatrix} \ \text{procedure-name-2} \end{bmatrix} \end{bmatrix}$$

$$\begin{Bmatrix} \text{identifier-1} \\ \text{integer-1} \end{Bmatrix} \quad \underline{\text{TIMES}} \quad [\text{imperative-statement-1} \ \underline{\text{END-PERFORM}}]$$

$$\underline{\text{PERFORM}} \quad \begin{bmatrix} \text{procedure-name-1} \quad \begin{bmatrix} \begin{Bmatrix} \underline{\text{THROUGH}} \\ \underline{\text{THRU}} \end{Bmatrix} \ \text{procedure-name-2} \end{bmatrix} \end{bmatrix}$$

$$\begin{bmatrix} \text{WITH } \underline{\text{TEST}} \quad \begin{Bmatrix} \underline{\text{BEFORE}} \\ \underline{\text{AFTER}} \end{Bmatrix} \end{bmatrix} \quad \underline{\text{UNTIL}} \ \text{condition-1}$$

[imperative-statement-1 $\underline{\text{END-PERFORM}}$]

PERFORM $\left[\text{procedure-name-1} \left[\left\{\begin{matrix}\underline{\text{THROUGH}}\\ \underline{\text{THRU}}\end{matrix}\right\} \text{procedure-name-2}\right]\right]$

$\left[\text{WITH } \underline{\text{TEST}} \left\{\begin{matrix}\underline{\text{BEFORE}}\\ \underline{\text{AFTER}}\end{matrix}\right\}\right]$

$\underline{\text{VARYING}} \left\{\begin{matrix}\text{identifier-2}\\ \text{index-name-1}\end{matrix}\right\} \underline{\text{FROM}} \left\{\begin{matrix}\text{identifier-3}\\ \text{index-name-2}\\ \text{literal-1}\end{matrix}\right\}$

$\underline{\text{BY}} \left\{\begin{matrix}\text{identifier-4}\\ \text{literal-2}\end{matrix}\right\} \underline{\text{UNTIL}} \text{ condition-1}$

$\left[\underline{\text{AFTER}} \left\{\begin{matrix}\text{identifier-5}\\ \text{literal-3}\end{matrix}\right\} \underline{\text{FROM}} \left\{\begin{matrix}\text{identifier-6}\\ \text{index-name-4}\\ \text{literal-3}\end{matrix}\right\}\right.$

$\left.\underline{\text{BY}} \left\{\begin{matrix}\text{identifier-7}\\ \text{literal-4}\end{matrix}\right\} \underline{\text{UNTIL}} \text{ condition-2}\right]$ ...

[imperative-statement-1 END-PERFORM]

PURGE cd-name-1

SRI READ file-name-1 [NEXT] RECORD [INTO identifier-1]

    [AT END imperative-statement-1]

    [NOT AT END imperative-statement-2]

    [END-READ]

R READ file-name-1 RECORD [INTO identifier-1]

    [INVALID KEY imperative-statement-3]

    [NOT INVALID KEY imperative-statement-4]

    [END-READ]

I READ file-name-1 RECORD [INTO identifier-1]

    [KEY IS data-name-1]

    [INVALID KEY imperative-statement-3]

    [NOT INVALID KEY imperative-statement-4]

    [END-READ]

RECEIVE cd-name-1 $\left\{ \begin{array}{l} \text{MESSAGE} \\ \text{SEGMENT} \end{array} \right\}$ INTO identifier-1

    [NO DATA imperative-statement-1]

    [WITH DATA imperative-statement-2]

    [END-RECEIVE]

RELEASE record-name-1 [FROM identifier-1]

RETURN file-name-1 RECORD [INTO identifier-1]

    AT END imperative-statement-1

    [NOT AT END imperative-statement-2]

    [END-RETURN]

S REWRITE record-name-1 [FROM identifier-1]

RI REWRITE record-name-1 [FROM identifier-1]

    [INVALID KEY imperative-statement-1]

    [NOT INVALID KEY imperative-statement-2]

    [END-REWRITE]

```
SEARCH identifier-1  ⎡ VARYING  ⎧identifier-2 ⎫ ⎤
                     ⎣          ⎩index-name-1 ⎭ ⎦

   [AT END imperative-statement-1]

   ⎧ WHEN condition-1 ⎧imperative-statement-2⎫ ⎫ ...
   ⎩                  ⎩NEXT SENTENCE         ⎭ ⎭

   [END-SEARCH]


SEARCH ALL identifier-1  [AT END imperative-statement-1]

        ⎧           ⎧IS EQUAL TO⎫ ⎧identifier-3             ⎫ ⎫
   WHEN ⎨data-name-1 ⎩IS =       ⎭ ⎨literal-1                ⎬ ⎬
        ⎩condition-name-1         ⎩arithmetic-expression-1  ⎭ ⎭

        ⎡     ⎧           ⎧IS EQUAL TO⎫ ⎧identifier-4             ⎫ ⎫ ⎤
        ⎢ AND ⎨data-name-2 ⎩IS =       ⎭ ⎨literal-2                ⎬ ⎬ ⎥ ...
        ⎣     ⎩condition-name-2         ⎩arithmetic-expression-2  ⎭ ⎭ ⎦

   ⎧imperative-statement-2⎫
   ⎨NEXT SENTENCE         ⎬
   ⎩                      ⎭

   [END-SEARCH]


SEND cd-name-1 FROM identifier-1


                                   ⎧WITH identifier-2⎫
SEND cd-name-1  [FROM identifier-1] ⎨WITH ESI         ⎬
                                   ⎨WITH EMI         ⎬
                                   ⎩WITH EGI         ⎭

   ⎡ ⎧BEFORE⎫            ⎧⎧identifier-3⎫ ⎡LINE ⎤⎫ ⎤
   ⎢ ⎨AFTER ⎬  ADVANCING ⎨⎩integer-1   ⎭ ⎣LINES⎦⎬ ⎥
   ⎣ ⎩      ⎭            ⎩⎧mnemonic-name-1⎫     ⎭ ⎦
                          ⎩PAGE           ⎭

   [REPLACING LINE]


SET ⎧index-name-1⎫ ... TO ⎧index-name-2⎫
    ⎩identifier-1 ⎭        ⎨identifier-2 ⎬
                          ⎩integer-1    ⎭
```

$$\underline{SET} \quad \{index\text{-}name\text{-}3\} \ \dots \ \begin{Bmatrix} \underline{UP}\ \underline{BY} \\ \underline{DOWN}\ \underline{BY} \end{Bmatrix} \begin{Bmatrix} identifier\text{-}3 \\ integer\text{-}2 \end{Bmatrix}$$

$$\underline{SET} \quad \begin{Bmatrix} \{mnemonic\text{-}name\text{-}1\} \ \dots \ \underline{TO} \ \begin{Bmatrix} \underline{ON} \\ \underline{OFF} \end{Bmatrix} \end{Bmatrix} \ \dots$$

$$\underline{SET} \quad \{condition\text{-}name\text{-}1\} \ \dots \ \underline{TO}\ \underline{TRUE}$$

$$\underline{SORT} \ file\text{-}name\text{-}1 \ \begin{Bmatrix} \underline{ON} \ \begin{Bmatrix} \underline{ASCENDING} \\ \underline{DESCENDING} \end{Bmatrix} \ KEY \ \{data\text{-}name\text{-}1\} \ \dots \end{Bmatrix} \ \dots$$

[WITH $\underline{DUPLICATES}$ IN ORDER]

[COLLATING $\underline{SEQUENCE}$ IS alphabet-name-1]

$$\begin{Bmatrix} \underline{INPUT}\ \underline{PROCEDURE}\ IS\ procedure\text{-}name\text{-}1 \ \begin{bmatrix} \begin{Bmatrix} \underline{THROUGH} \\ \underline{THRU} \end{Bmatrix} \ procedure\text{-}name\text{-}2 \end{bmatrix} \\ \underline{USING} \ \{file\text{-}name\text{-}2\} \ \dots \end{Bmatrix}$$

$$\begin{Bmatrix} \underline{OUTPUT}\ \underline{PROCEDURE}\ IS\ procedure\text{-}name\text{-}3 \ \begin{bmatrix} \begin{Bmatrix} \underline{THROUGH} \\ \underline{THRU} \end{Bmatrix} \ procedure\text{-}name\text{-}4 \end{bmatrix} \\ \underline{GIVING} \ \{file\text{-}name\text{-}3\} \ \dots \end{Bmatrix}$$

$$\underline{START} \ file\text{-}name\text{-}1 \ \begin{bmatrix} KEY \ \begin{Bmatrix} IS\ \underline{EQUAL}\ TO \\ IS\ = \\ IS\ \underline{GREATER}\ THAN \\ IS\ > \\ IS\ \underline{NOT}\ \underline{LESS}\ THAN \\ IS\ \underline{NOT}\ < \\ IS\ \underline{GREATER}\ THAN\ \underline{OR}\ \underline{EQUAL}\ TO \\ IS\ >= \end{Bmatrix} \ data\text{-}name\text{-}1 \end{bmatrix}$$

[$\underline{INVALID}$ KEY imperative-statement-1]

[$\underline{NOT}\ \underline{INVALID}$ KEY imperative-statement-2]

[$\underline{END\text{-}START}$]

$$\underline{STOP} \quad \begin{Bmatrix} \underline{RUN} \\ literal\text{-}1 \end{Bmatrix}$$

STRING $\left\{ \begin{matrix} \text{identifier-1} \\ \text{literal-1} \end{matrix} \right\}$ ... DELIMITED BY $\left\{ \begin{matrix} \text{identifier-2} \\ \text{literal-2} \\ \underline{\text{SIZE}} \end{matrix} \right\}$ ...

    INTO identifier-3

    [WITH POINTER identifier-4]

    [ON OVERFLOW imperative-statement-1]

    [NOT ON OVERFLOW imperative-statement-2]

    [END-STRING]

SUBTRACT $\left\{ \begin{matrix} \text{identifier-1} \\ \text{literal-1} \end{matrix} \right\}$ ... FROM {identifier-3 [ROUNDED]} ...

    [ON SIZE ERROR imperative-statement-1]

    [NOT ON SIZE ERROR imperative-statement-2]

    [END-SUBTRACT]

SUBTRACT $\left\{ \begin{matrix} \text{identifier-1} \\ \text{literal-1} \end{matrix} \right\}$ ... FROM $\left\{ \begin{matrix} \text{identifier-2} \\ \text{literal-2} \end{matrix} \right\}$

    GIVING {identifier-3 [ROUNDED]} ...

    [ON SIZE ERROR imperative-statement-1]

    [NOT ON SIZE ERROR imperative-statement-2]

    [END-SUBTRACT]

SUBTRACT $\left\{ \begin{matrix} \underline{\text{CORRESPONDING}} \\ \underline{\text{CORR}} \end{matrix} \right\}$ identifier-1 FROM identifier-2 [ROUNDED]

    [ON SIZE ERROR imperative-statement-1]

    [NOT ON SIZE ERROR imperative-statement-2]

    [END-SUBTRACT]

SUPPRESS PRINTING

TERMINATE {report-name-1} ...

UNSTRING identifier-1

$$\left[\underline{\text{DELIMITED}} \text{ BY } [\underline{\text{ALL}}] \begin{Bmatrix} \text{identifier-2} \\ \text{literal-1} \end{Bmatrix} \left[\underline{\text{OR}} [\underline{\text{ALL}}] \begin{Bmatrix} \text{identifier-3} \\ \text{literal-2} \end{Bmatrix} \right] \dots \right]$$

INTO {identifier-4 [DELIMITER IN identifier-5] [COUNT IN identifier-6]} ...

[WITH POINTER identifier-7]

[TALLYING IN identifier-8]

[ON OVERFLOW imperative-statement-1]

[NOT ON OVERFLOW imperative-statement-2]

[END-UNSTRING]

SRI USE [GLOBAL] AFTER STANDARD $\begin{Bmatrix} \text{EXCEPTION} \\ \text{ERROR} \end{Bmatrix}$ PROCEDURE ON $\begin{Bmatrix} \{\text{file-name-1}\} \dots \\ \text{INPUT} \\ \text{OUTPUT} \\ \text{I-O} \\ \text{EXTEND} \end{Bmatrix}$

W USE AFTER STANDARD $\begin{Bmatrix} \text{EXCEPTION} \\ \text{ERROR} \end{Bmatrix}$ PROCEDURE ON $\begin{Bmatrix} \{\text{file-name-1}\} \dots \\ \text{OUTPUT} \\ \text{EXTEND} \end{Bmatrix}$

USE [GLOBAL] BEFORE REPORTING identifier-1

USE FOR DEBUGGING ON $\begin{Bmatrix} \text{cd-name-1} \\ [\underline{\text{ALL}} \text{ REFERENCES OF}] \text{ identifier-1} \\ \text{file-name-1} \\ \text{procedure-name-1} \\ \underline{\text{ALL}} \text{ PROCEDURES} \end{Bmatrix} \dots$

S <u>WRITE</u> record-name-1   [<u>FROM</u> identifier-1]

$$\left[\left\{\genfrac{}{}{0pt}{}{\underline{BEFORE}}{\underline{AFTER}}\right\} \text{ADVANCING} \left\{\genfrac{}{}{0pt}{}{\left\{\genfrac{}{}{0pt}{}{\text{identifier-2}}{\text{integer-1}}\right\}\left[\genfrac{}{}{0pt}{}{\text{LINE}}{\text{LINES}}\right]}{\left\{\genfrac{}{}{0pt}{}{\text{mnemonic-name-1}}{\underline{PAGE}}\right\}}\right\}\right]$$

$$\left[\text{AT} \left\{\genfrac{}{}{0pt}{}{\underline{END\text{-}OF\text{-}PAGE}}{\underline{EOP}}\right\} \text{imperative-statement-1}\right].$$

$$\left[\underline{NOT} \text{ AT} \left\{\genfrac{}{}{0pt}{}{\underline{END\text{-}OF\text{-}PAGE}}{\underline{EOP}}\right\} \text{imperative-statement-2}\right]$$

[<u>END-WRITE</u>]

RI <u>WRITE</u> record-name-1   [<u>FROM</u> identifier-1]

[<u>INVALID</u> KEY imperative-statement-1]

[<u>NOT</u> <u>INVALID</u> KEY imperative-statement-2]

[<u>END-WRITE</u>]

General Format for Copy and Replace Statements

<u>COPY</u> text-name-1 $\left[\begin{Bmatrix}\underline{OF}\\ \underline{IN}\end{Bmatrix}\text{library-name-1}\right]$

$$\left[\underline{\text{REPLACING}}\ \begin{Bmatrix}\begin{Bmatrix}\text{==pseudo-text-1==}\\ \text{identifier-1}\\ \text{literal-1}\\ \text{word-1}\end{Bmatrix}\underline{\text{BY}}\begin{Bmatrix}\text{==pseudo-text-2==}\\ \text{identifier-2}\\ \text{literal-2}\\ \text{word-2}\end{Bmatrix}\end{Bmatrix}\ \ldots\right]$$

<u>REPLACE</u>   {==pseudo-text-1==   <u>BY</u>   ==pseudo-text-2==} ...

<u>REPLACE</u> <u>OFF</u>

General Format for Conditions

Relation Condition:

```
                           ⎧ IS [NOT] GREATER THAN           ⎫
                           ⎪ IS [NOT] >                      ⎪
                           ⎪ IS [NOT] LESS THAN              ⎪
⎧ identifier-1           ⎫ ⎪ IS [NOT] <                      ⎪ ⎧ identifier-2           ⎫
⎪ literal-1              ⎪ ⎪ IS [NOT] EQUAL TO               ⎪ ⎪ literal-2              ⎪
⎨ arithmetic-expression-1⎬ ⎨ IS [NOT] =                      ⎬ ⎨ arithmetic-expression-2⎬
⎩ index-name-1           ⎭ ⎪ IS GREATER THAN OR EQUAL TO     ⎪ ⎩ index-name-2           ⎭
                           ⎪ IS >=                           ⎪
                           ⎪ IS LESS THAN OR EQUAL TO        ⎪
                           ⎩ IS <=                           ⎭
```

Class Condition:

```
                        ⎧ NUMERIC          ⎫
                        ⎪ ALPHABETIC       ⎪
identifier-1 IS [NOT]   ⎨ ALPHABETIC-LOWER ⎬
                        ⎪ ALPHABETIC-UPPER ⎪
                        ⎩ class-name-1     ⎭
```

Condition-Name Condition:

```
condition-name-1
```

Switch-Status Condition:

```
condition-name-1
```

Sign Condition:

```
                                 ⎧ POSITIVE ⎫
arithmetic-expression-1 IS [NOT] ⎨ NEGATIVE ⎬
                                 ⎩ ZERO     ⎭
```

Negated Condition:

```
NOT condition-1
```

Combined Condition:

$$\text{condition-1} \quad \left\{ \left\{ \begin{matrix} \underline{\text{AND}} \\ \underline{\text{OR}} \end{matrix} \right\} \quad \text{condition-2} \right\} \; \dots$$

Abbreviated Combined Relation condition:

$$\text{relation-condition} \quad \left\{ \left\{ \begin{matrix} \underline{\text{AND}} \\ \underline{\text{OR}} \end{matrix} \right\} \quad [\underline{\text{NOT}}] \quad [\text{relational-operator}] \quad \text{object} \right\} \; \dots$$

General Format for Qualification

Format 1:

$$
\left\{ \begin{array}{l} \text{data-name-1} \\ \text{condition-name-1} \end{array} \right\}
\left\{ \begin{array}{l} \left\{ \left\{ \begin{array}{l} \underline{\text{IN}} \\ \underline{\text{OF}} \end{array} \right\} \text{data-name-2} \right\} \quad \cdots \quad \left[\left\{ \begin{array}{l} \underline{\text{IN}} \\ \underline{\text{OF}} \end{array} \right\} \left\{ \begin{array}{l} \text{file-name-1} \\ \text{cd-name-1} \end{array} \right\} \right] \\ \left\{ \begin{array}{l} \underline{\text{IN}} \\ \underline{\text{OF}} \end{array} \right\} \left\{ \begin{array}{l} \text{file-name-1} \\ \text{cd-name-1} \end{array} \right\} \end{array} \right\}
$$

Format 2:

$$
\text{paragraph-name-1} \quad \left\{ \begin{array}{l} \underline{\text{IN}} \\ \underline{\text{OF}} \end{array} \right\} \quad \text{section-name-1}
$$

Format 3:

$$
\text{text-name-1} \quad \left\{ \begin{array}{l} \underline{\text{IN}} \\ \underline{\text{OF}} \end{array} \right\} \quad \text{library-name-1}
$$

Format 4:

$$
\underline{\text{LINAGE-COUNTER}} \quad \left\{ \begin{array}{l} \underline{\text{IN}} \\ \underline{\text{OF}} \end{array} \right\} \quad \text{file-name-2}
$$

Format 5:

$$
\left\{ \begin{array}{l} \underline{\text{PAGE-COUNTER}} \\ \underline{\text{LINE-COUNTER}} \end{array} \right\} \quad \left\{ \begin{array}{l} \underline{\text{IN}} \\ \underline{\text{OF}} \end{array} \right\} \quad \text{report-name-1}
$$

Format 6:

$$
\text{data-name-3} \left\{ \begin{array}{l} \left\{ \begin{array}{l} \underline{\text{IN}} \\ \underline{\text{OF}} \end{array} \right\} \text{data-name-4} \left[\left\{ \begin{array}{l} \underline{\text{IN}} \\ \underline{\text{OF}} \end{array} \right\} \text{report-name-2} \right] \\ \left\{ \begin{array}{l} \underline{\text{IN}} \\ \underline{\text{OF}} \end{array} \right\} \text{report-name-2} \end{array} \right\}
$$

Miscellaneous Formats

Subscripting:

$$
\begin{Bmatrix} \text{condition-name-1} \\ \text{data-name-1} \end{Bmatrix} \quad \left(\begin{Bmatrix} \text{integer-1} \\ \text{data-name-2 } [\{\pm\} \text{ integer-2}] \\ \text{index-name-1 } [\{\pm\} \text{ integer-3}] \end{Bmatrix} \quad \dots \right)
$$

Reference Modification:

```
data-name-1 (leftmost-character-position: [length])
```

Identifier:

$$
\text{data-name-1} \quad \left[\begin{Bmatrix} \underline{\text{IN}} \\ \underline{\text{OF}} \end{Bmatrix} \text{ data-name-2} \right] \quad \dots \quad \left[\begin{Bmatrix} \underline{\text{IN}} \\ \underline{\text{OF}} \end{Bmatrix} \begin{Bmatrix} \text{cd-name-1} \\ \text{file-name-1} \\ \text{report-name-1} \end{Bmatrix} \right]
$$

$$
[(\{\text{subscript}\} \dots)] \quad [(\text{leftmost-character-position: [length]})]
$$

General Format for Nested Source Programs

IDENTIFICATION DIVISION.

PROGRAM-ID. program-name-1 [IS INITIAL PROGRAM].

[ENVIRONMENT DIVISION. environment-division-content]

[DATA DIVISION. data-division-content]

[PROCEDURE DIVISION. procedure-division-content]

[[nested-source-program] ...

END PROGRAM program-name-1.]

General Format for Nested-Source-Program

IDENTIFICATION DIVISION.

PROGRAM-ID. program-name-2 $\left[IS \left\{ \begin{vmatrix} \underline{COMMON} \\ \underline{INITIAL} \end{vmatrix} \right\} PROGRAM \right]$.

[ENVIRONMENT DIVISION. environment-division-content]

[DATA DIVISION. data-division-content]

[PROCEDURE DIVISION. procedure-division-content]

[nested-source-program] ...

END PROGRAM program-name-2.

General Format for a Sequence of Source Programs

```
{IDENTIFICATION DIVISION.

 PROGRAM-ID.  program-name-3  [IS INITIAL PROGRAM].

[ENVIRONMENT DIVISION.  environment-division-content]

[DATA DIVISION.  data-division-content]

[PROCEDURE DIVISION.  procedure-division-content]

[nested-source-program] ...

 END PROGRAM program-name-3.} ...

 IDENTIFICATION DIVISION.

 PROGRAM-ID.  program-name-4  [IS INITIAL PROGRAM].

[ENVIRONMENT DIVISION.  environment-division-content]

[DATA DIVISION.  data-division-content]

[PROCEDURE DIVISION.  procedure-division-content]

[[nested-source-program] ...

 END PROGRAM program-name-4.]
```

Permissible Input-Output Operations

The input and output statements permitted on any file depend on the ORGANIZATION, ACCESS MODE, and OPEN mode of the file. Permissible statements are indicated by the presence of an X in the following tables:

Table E-1
Permissible statements on files with ORGANIZATION SEQUENTIAL.

Statement	Open Mode			
	Input	*Output*	*I-O*	*Extend*
READ	X		X	
WRITE		X		X
REWRITE			X	

Table E-2
Permissible statements on files with ORGANIZATION INDEXED or ORGANIZA-TION RELATIVE. The EXTEND mode is included in the 1985 ANSI standard for indexed files and relative files and is not available in the 1974 standard for indexed files or relative files. Some CO-BOL systems which support the 1974 standard permit the EXTEND mode to be used with indexed files.

File Access Mode	Statement	Open Mode			
		Input	*Output*	*I-O*	*Extend*
Sequential	READ	X		X	
	WRITE		X		X
	REWRITE			X	
	START	X		X	
	DELETE			X	
Random	READ	X		X	
	WRITE		X	X	
	REWRITE			X	
	START				
	DELETE			X	
Dynamic	READ	X		X	
	WRITE		X	X	
	REWRITE			X	
	START	X		X	
	DELETE			X	

Input Data
for Selected
Programming
Exercises

Figure F.1 Input data for Review Exercise 5, Chapter 2.

```
            1         2         3         4         5         6         7         8
12345678901234567890123456789012345678901234567890123456789012345678901234567890
--------------------------------------------------------------------------------
00102001BASE MOUNT FOR FAN      203
00102002BLADE                   129
10100012MOTOR                   320
20100013SWITCH PANEL            529
30212301SHAFT                   010
```

Figure F.2 Input data for Review Exercise 5, Chapter 3.

```
            1         2         3         4         5         6         7         8
12345678901234567890123456789012345678901234567890123456789012345678901234567890
--------------------------------------------------------------------------------
00854991212008008008008008080
26536232202308403719902300
10338171624023900000080082
```

Figure F.3 Input data for Review Exercise 2, Chapter 4.

```
            1         2         3         4         5         6         7         8
12345678901234567890123456789012345678901234567890123456789012345678901234567890
--------------------------------------------------------------------------------
00854991212008008008008008080
26536232202308403719902300
10338171624023900000080082
45678212308309208107910110
82357921508008008008008008080
94553275608008008008007907
12357651207906500000080000
69127666406900009810200009
13765179208008008008008008080
96814535208007907800008008080
56893655108010010400000089
89656531710210010010000000
51368765308709004809208008080
63558478208012308000012309
47545285308000008000008000
45177896500008000008000008080
563789512080080080080080080
14586897708009009090080000
41587956908008008008008008080
89475614423900000000000000
417895689000000000000000240
584789531080080080080081000
```

Figure F.4   Input data for Review Exercise 3, Chapter 5.

```
--------------------------------------------------------------------------------
         1         2         3         4         5         6         7         8
1234567890123456789012345678901234567890123456789012345678901234567890123456789 0
--------------------------------------------------------------------------------
003682528V00950000
117260098Z01500000
265348425W01999999
229650287X02000000
009516254702235000
128659821
032002658401500000
038565462502000000
106562249203000000
756123422Z00500000
```

Figure F.5   Input data for Review Exercise 2, Chapter 6.

```
--------------------------------------------------------------------------------
         1         2         3         4         5         6         7         8
1234567890123456789012345678901234567890123456789012345678901234567890123456789 0
--------------------------------------------------------------------------------
-02005    0003034
 02005    0000000
 02005    9876201
-02005    0000006
-02005    8923551
 02005    3485910
 04502    9999999
-04502    0008399
-04502    4567212
-12121    7549900
-12121    0000002
-12121    0000000
 12121    2341111
 12121    0006667
-12121    6666222
 19596    9292929
-19596    1254720
-19596    2348764
-19596    0000020
 19596    0000239
 19596    0021345
-20023    9999999
-20023    8765499
-20023    8686868
 20023    8888880
 20023    8855332
 20023    5678923
-23456    0000211
-23456    0000453
-23456    0001200
 23456    0000012
 23456    0001800
 23456    0000054
-30721    0000101
 30721    0009912
-30721    0009844
-40101    0034287
 40101    0021245
-40101    6000201
 40101    0006700
-40101    3234323
 40101    9002341
-67689    0001114
 67689    0101010
-67689    0003335
 67689    0220330
-67689    0304020
 67689    1000000
-72332    0000004
 72332    0004444
-72332    0044444
 72332    0000444
-72332    0000044
 72332    0404040
```

Figure F.6   Input data for Review Exercise 5, Chapter 7.

```
         1         2         3         4         5         6         7         8
12345678901234567890123456789012345678901234567890123456789012345678901234567890
--------------------------------------------------------------------------------
34ABA 06543X843961V
78121H1000003874523
00000ACDEFGHIJKLMNO
1475852234210100000
4554150459218654216
9#121H1908705508973
91A00A0874900238400
99121H1908704508973
8242361714213999999
7331560439604000000
64876D    0100004
6745650953560000025
55252E054320043#0066
46701F2100505436528
374  31732990727982
00322A0000014999999
28421B069232500000
14756A0899430705924
89  6 9"94211764297
78932ZA932416763207
569$2 0094325923965
15008B0707630680429
05))6L0*92357009215
0344240350004000001
19123G1703670537654
```

Figure F.7   Input data for Review Exercise 6, Chapter 8.

```
         1         2         3         4         5         6         7         8
12345678901234567890123456789012345678901234567890123456789012345678901234567890
--------------------------------------------------------------------------------
ABC1234   365-09    900000010
CVNMR-D   2.CHJK    000009345
09G8239   6-7YT7    800001050
23879-J   JKSDF7    056000000
WQWEIOU   N-AFDH    990101010
ADJKGLE   512TYN    980200000
AKLJKNU   7-6DFE    XYXYXYXYX
ADGH784   1AN-07    050025000
9675473   S-1287    006700029
```

Figure F.8 Input data for Review Exercise 4, Chapter 9.

```
--------------------------------------------------------------------------------
          1         2         3         4         5         6         7         8
12345678901234567890123456789012345678901234567890123456789012345678901234567890
--------------------------------------------------------------------------------
0011
0021
0031
0041
0051
0061
0071
0081
1783
0153
0223
0017
0027
0037
0047
0057
0067
0087
0097
0016
0026
0076
0086
0096
0077
0015
0025
0035
0045
0055
0065
0075
0085
0095
0012
0022
0032
0042
0052
0062
0072
0082
0092
```

Figure F.9 Input data for Review Exercise 2, Chapter 10.

```
--------------------------------------------------------------------------------
          1         2         3         4         5         6         7         8
12345678901234567890123456789012345678901234567890123456789012345678901234567890
--------------------------------------------------------------------------------
024563200186400357906486204567000000012 3758
064352606456300000013684500364209781405 6897
011378000379800341600386903686100076400 1235
049764300067403448903495100036400007910 2803
053469800345870000000346900079600045705 6045
036475800674100000000003460147860065910 00000
024833200183400387903483204837000000025 1565
064382303483300000013384800334209781445 3893
011378000379800341300383903383100073403 3459
049734300037403448903498100033400007957 3513
053439800348870000000343900079300048700 0053
033478800374100000000034301478300389157 6585
025369800000000315790357510007840345690 12856
```

Figure F.10   Input data for Review Exercise 3, Chapter 11.

```
-------------------------------------------------------------------------------
          1         2         3         4         5         6         7        8
12345678901234567890123456789012345678901234567890123456789012345678901234567890
-------------------------------------------------------------------------------
45124N351
51302E285
65421N421
98741N438
19850E159
48932N375
26418N374
96127N376
10127E400
04575N400
45225N399
42598N401
00456E401
86156N401
```

Figure F.11   Input data for Review Exercise 2, Chapter 12.

```
-------------------------------------------------------------------------------
          1         2         3         4         5         6         7        8
12345678901234567890123456789012345678901234567890123456789012345678901234567890
-------------------------------------------------------------------------------
1001050000MILLER L   22 WEST 23RD STREET        COLUMBIA SC  29210  AD77
1001120002LANE R     1633 BROADWAY              E BRUNSWICK NJ 08816DP68
Y         CAPUANO M 1 BISCAYNE TOWER            MIAMI FL  33168       AC65
1001260007BUDD J     875 AVENUE OF THE AMERICAS NEW YORK NY  10014  DDZZ
1001330010LERNER P   432 PARK AVENUE SOUTH      TUCKAHOE NY  10707   OD
1001050000MILLER L   22 WEST 23RD STREET        COLUMBIA SC  29210  AD77
1001400000FALLON B   60 EAST 42 STREET          CHICAGO IL  60609    ET56
1000980000HALEY J    1300 NEWARK TURNPIKE       AMBLER PA  19002     EM73
1001050000           165 NAGLE AVENUE           FLEMINGTON NJ  08822NU80
7001610000RYAN R     45 FAIRVIEW AVENUE         SOMERVILLE NJ  08876SG78
1001680001HEDERMAN K17 FORT GEORGE HILL         PITTSBURGH PA  15237MK59
1001750000KEATING M 223 ELWOOD STREET           DOWNRS GRVE IL 60515DP81
2001820000LANIGAN B 84 VERMILYEA AVENUE         BROOKLYN NY  11211      81
1002030000MITCHELL J587A WEST 207TH STREET      YONKERS NY  10710    HT79
1002100002PARKS J    3 HAVEN PLAZA              NEW ROCHLLE NY 10804CT75
1002170000CALDERON C252 BROOME STREET           PRESIDIO CA  91127   DD55
1002240001WILLIAMS J94 MADISON AVENUE           SN FRANCSCO CA 94131AD59
1000350001LEHMAN J J689 COLUMBUS AVENUE         WESTFIELD CN  07090  NU60
1000490001GREENE J   40 CRANE AVENUE            LOUISVILLE KY  40206AC65
1000560000SLATER E                                                  DP
9                    27 HALLADAY STREET         KEY BSCAYNE FL 33149GA
1000700005LEE P J    67-35 YELLOWSTONE BLVD                p V         67
1000770000MINSKY J   1188 FIRST AVENUE          FREEHOLD NJ  07728   LA53
1000840015DAPRINO J 205 WEST END AVENUE         PITTSBURGH PA  15237LT78
1000980005CULHANE G 509 LAKE STREET             CHICAGO IL  60614    HT70
1002660000LANG M     68 BOWERY                  STATN ISLND NY 10306DL81
1002730002CACACI V   148 DELANCEY STREET        SAN DIEGO CA  92109  DH73
1002940015BURKE J    31 SAINT MARKS PLACE       ARLINGTON VA  02174  DL74
7003010FG1POWERS P P575 LEXINGTON AVENUE        ELMHURST NY  11313
1003080020GARCIA J   262 PARK WEST AVENUE       HARTSDALE NY  10530  EA79
9003150002MICELI G   8532 HAMILTON PARKWAY      NEW HAVEN CN  06575  HT75
3003220000                                      MILFORD NJ  08848    PM72
1003290000VOLPONE G 420 AVENUE L                                    MT80
1003368378CALI S     162 PRESIDENT STREET       CITY ISLAND NY 10464CT49
5002310005WILLIAM B 21 NEW YORK AVENUE          NEW MILFORD NJ 07646DP50
1002380000PARKER K   551 LORIMER STREET                            AC55
0002450000            23 SHERIDAN AVENUE                            MK57
1002520000GALLI G    406 DAHILL ROAD            MANHASSET NY  11030  EM51
1002590000           9219 RIDGE BLVD            WINOOSKI VT  05404   ET69
1000070010BUCCI R    1764 GERRITSEN AVENUE      S NYACK NY  10960    DD67
1000140000DAVIS R    195 ADAMS STREET           S ORANGE NJ  07079   GA66
1000210004MONTI L    381 MARLBOROUGH ROAD       ALEXANDRIA VA  22314SG77
1000280070SMITH M    66 BAY 22ND STREET         OAKLAND CA  94612    HT47
4003430010SESSA J    15 3RD PLACE               SCARSDALE NY  10583  MK68
1003500025SHAW R     47 LANCASTER AVENUE        NEW PALTZ NY  12561  DH73
```

Figure F.12   Input data for Review Exercise 4, Chapter 13.

```
----------------------------------------------------------------------------
          1         2         3         4         5         6         7         8
12345678901234567890123456789012345678901234567890123456789012345678901234567890
----------------------------------------------------------------------------
2001120002MAME R L
30021000027 HAVEN PLAZA
2001260007
1003920000WASH'TON I3 HAVEN PLAZA                  ARLINGTON VA   02174 DL66
30008432457 HAVEN PLAZA
4000070010MANHASSET NY  11030
4001750000S NYACK NY  10960
1004200015RICE J    49 LANCASTER AVENUE            ALEXANDRIA VA   22314HT58
1004200015PRICE J   49 LANCASTER AVE.              ALEXANDRIA VA   22314AD58
2004200015PRICE J
300420001551 LANCASTER AVENUE
5000490001SG
5002520000
6000700005%)
600014000079
7001050000
7001750000
3000770000111 EIGHTH AVENUE
7000770000
1013457892          53 LANCASTER AVENUE           ALEXANDRIA VA   223140D69
```

Figure F.13   Input data for Review Exercise 1, Chapter 14.

```
----------------------------------------------------------------------------
          1         2         3         4         5         6         7         8
12345678901234567890123456789012345678901234567890123456789012345678901234567890
----------------------------------------------------------------------------
1001050000MILLER L   22 WEST 23RD STREET           COLUMBIA SC   29210   AD78
1001120002LANE R     1633 BROADWAY                 E BRUNSWICK NJ 08816DP48
Y         CAPUANO M 1 BISCAYNE TOWER               MIAMI FL   33168      AC80
1001260007BUDD J     875 AVENUE OF THE AMERICAS    NEW YORK NY   10014   DD76
1001330010LERNER P   432 PARK AVENUE SOUTH         TUCKAHOE NY   10707  0D65
1001400000FALLON B   60 EAST 42 STREET             CHICAGO IL   60609    ET76
1000980000HALEY J    1300 NEWARK TURNPIKE          AMBLER PA   19002     EM79
1001050000            165 NAGLE AVENUE             FLEMINGTON NJ  08822NU66
7001610000RYAN R     45 FAIRVIEW AVENUE            SOMERVILLE NJ  08876SG53
1001680001HEDERMAN K17 FORT GEORGE HILL            PITTSBURGH PA  15237MK((
1001050000MILLER L   22 WEST 23RD STREET           COLUMBIA SC   29210   AD78
1001750000KEATING M  223 ELWOOD STREET             DOWNRS GRVE IL 60515DP71
2001820000LANIGAN B  84 VERMILYEA AVENUE           BROOKLYN NY   11211    72
1002030000MITCHELL J587A WEST 207TH STREET         YONKERS NY   10710    HT64
1002100002PARKS J    3 HAVEN PLAZA                 NEW ROCHLLE NY 10804CT81
1002170000CALDERON C252 BROOME STREET              PRESIDIO CA   91127   DD62
1002240001WILLIAMS J94 MADISON AVENUE              SN FRANCSCO CA 94131AD49
1000350001LEHMAN J J689 COLUMBUS AVENUE            WESTFIELD CN   07090 NU52
1000490001GREENE J   40 CRANE AVENUE               LOUISVILLE KY   40206AC65
1000560000SLATER E                                                      DPoo
9                   27 HALLADAY STREET             KEY BSCAYNE FL 33149GA73
1000700005LEE P J    67-35 YELLOWSTONE BLVD                              70
1000770000MINSKY J   1188 FIRST AVENUE             FREEHOLD NJ   07728  LA55
1000840015DAPRINO J  205 WEST END AVENUE           PITTSBURGH PA  15237LT77
1000980005CULHANE G  509 LAKE STREET               CHICAGO IL   60614   HT74
1002660000LANG M     68 BOWERY                     STATN ISLND NY 10306DL80
1002730002CACACI V   148 DELANCEY STREET           SAN DIEGO CA   92109 DH81
1002940015BURKE J    31 SAINT MARKS PLACE          ARLINGTON VA   02174 DL78
7003010FG1POWERS P P575 LEXINGTON AVENUE           ELMHURST NY   11313    73
1003080020GARCIA J   262 PARK WEST AVENUE          HARTSDALE NY   10530 EA79
9003150002MICELI G   8532 HAMILTON PARKWAY         NEW HAVEN CN   06575 HT74
3003220000                                         MILFORD NJ   08848   PM49
1003290000VOLPONE G  420 AVENUE L                                       MTZZ
1003368378CALI S     162 PRESIDENT STREET          CITY ISLAND NY 10464CT62
5002310005WILLIAM B  21 NEW YORK AVENUE            NEW MILFORD NJ 07646DP65
1002380000PARKER K   551 LORIMER STREET                                 AC73
0002450000            23 SHERIDAN AVENUE                                MK79
1002520000GALLI G    406 DAHILL ROAD               MANHASSET NY   11030 EM82
1002590000            9219 RIDGE BLVD              WINOOSKI VT   05404   ET82
1000070010BUCCI R    1764 GERRITSEN AVENUE         S NYACK NY   10960    DD77
1000140000DAVIS R    195 ADAMS STREET              S ORANGE NJ   07079  GA75
1000210004MONTI L    381 MARLBOROUGH ROAD          ALEXANDRIA VA  22314SG76
1000280070SMITH M    66 BAY 22ND STREET            OAKLAND CA   94612   HT67
4003430010SESSA J    15 3RD PLACE                  SCARSDALE NY   10583 MK64
1003500025SHAW R     47 LANCASTER AVENUE           NEW PALTZ NY   12561 DH60
```

Figure F.14 Input data for Review Exercise 2, Chapter 14.

```
         1         2         3         4         5         6         7         8
12345678901234567890123456789012345678901234567890123456789012345678901234567890
--------------------------------------------------------------------------------
2001120002MAME R L
30021000027 HAVEN PLAZA
2001260007
1003920000WASH'TON I3 HAVEN PLAZA                   ARLINGTON VA  02174 DL66
30008432457 HAVEN PLAZA
4000070010MANHASSET NY  11030
4001750000S NYACK NY  10960
1004200015RICE J    49 LANCASTER AVENUE             ALEXANDRIA VA  22314HT58
2004200015PRICE J
300420001551 LANCASTER AVENUE
5000490001SG
5002520000
6000700005%)
600014000079
7001050000
7001750000
3000770000111 EIGHTH AVENUE
7000770000
1013457892          53 LANCASTER AVENUE             ALEXANDRIA VA  223140D69
1002030000MITCHELL J587A WEST 207TH STREET           YONKERS NY  10710    HT64
```

Figure F.15 Input data for Review Exercise 2, Chapter 15.

```
         1         2         3         4         5         6         7         8
12345678901234567890123456789012345678901234567890123456789012345678901234567890
--------------------------------------------------------------------------------
1001050000MILLER L  22 WEST 23RD STREET             COLUMBIA SC  29210  AD78
1001120002LANE R    1633 BROADWAY                   E BRUNSWICK NJ 08816DP48
Y         CAPUANO M 1 BISCAYNE TOWER                MIAMI FL  33168    AC80
1001260007BUDD J    875 AVENUE OF THE AMERICAS      NEW YORK NY  10014  DD76
1001330010LERNER P  432 PARK AVENUE SOUTH           TUCKAHOE NY  10707  OD65
1001400000FALLON B  60 EAST 42 STREET               CHICAGO IL  60609   ET76
1000980000HALEY J   1300 NEWARK TURNPIKE            AMBLER PA  19002    EM79
1001050000          165 NAGLE AVENUE               FLEMINGTON NJ  08822NU66
7001610000RYAN R    45 FAIRVIEW AVENUE              SOMERVILLE NJ  08876SG53
1001680001HEDERMAN K17 FORT GEORGE HILL             PITTSBURGH PA  15237MK((
1001750000KEATING M 223 ELWOOD STREET               DOWNRS GRVE IL 60515DP71
2001820000LANIGAN B 84 VERMILYEA AVENUE             BROOKLYN NY  11211     72
1002030000MITCHELL J587A WEST 207TH STREET          YONKERS NY  10710   HT64
1002100002PARKS J   3 HAVEN PLAZA                   NEW ROCHLLE NY 10804CT81
1002170000CALDERON C252 BROOME STREET               PRESIDIO CA  91127  DD62
1002240001WILLIAMS J94 MADISON AVENUE               SN FRANCSCO CA 94131AD49
1000350001LEHMAN J  J689 COLUMBUS AVENUE            WESTFIELD CN  07090 NU52
1000490001GREENE J  40 CRANE AVENUE                 LOUISVILLE KY  40206AC65
1000560000SLATER E                                                     DP00
9                   27 HALLADAY STREET             KEY BSCAYNE FL 33149GA73
1000700005LEE P J   67-35 YELLOWSTONE BLVD                                70
1000770000MINSKY J  1188 FIRST AVENUE               FREEHOLD NJ  07728  LA55
1000840015DAPRINO J 205 WEST END AVENUE             PITTSBURGH PA  15237LT77
1000980005CULHANE G 509 LAKE STREET                 CHICAGO IL  60614   HT74
1002660000LANG M    68 BOWERY                       STATN ISLND NY 10306DL80
1002730002CACACI V  148 DELANCEY STREET             SAN DIEGO CA  92109 DH81
1002940015BURKE J   31 SAINT MARKS PLACE            ARLINGTON VA  02174 DL78
7003010FG1POWERS P P575 LEXINGTON AVENUE            ELMHURST NY  11313     73
1003080020GARCIA J  262 PARK WEST AVENUE            HARTSDALE NY  10530 EA79
9003150002MICELI G  8532 HAMILTON PARKWAY           NEW HAVEN CN  06575 HT74
3003220000                                          MILFORD NJ  08848   PM49
1003290000VOLPONE G 420 AVENUE L                                        MTZZ
1003368378CALI S    162 PRESIDENT STREET            CITY ISLAND NY 10464CT62
5002310005WILLIAM B 21 NEW YORK AVENUE              NEW MILFORD NJ 07646DP65
1002380000PARKER K  551 LORIMER STREET                                  AC73
0002450000          23 SHERIDAN AVENUE                                  MK79
1002520000GALLI G   406 DAHILL ROAD                 MANHASSET NY  11030 EM82
1002590000          9219 RIDGE BLVD                 WINOOSKI VT  05404  ET82
1000070010BUCCI R   1764 GERRITSEN AVENUE           S NYACK NY  10960   DD77
1000140000DAVIS R   195 ADAMS STREET                S ORANGE NJ  07079  GA75
1000210004MONTI L   381 MARLBOROUGH ROAD            ALEXANDRIA VA  22314SG76
1000280070SMITH M   66 BAY 22ND STREET              OAKLAND CA  94612   HT67
4003430010SESSA J   15 3RD PLACE                    SCARSDALE NY  10583 MK64
1003500025SHAW R    47 LANCASTER AVENUE             NEW PALTZ NY  12561 DH60
```

Figure F.16   Input data for Review Exercise 3, Chapter 15.

```
-----------------------------------------------------------------------------
          1         2         3         4         5         6         7         8
12345678901234567890123456789012345678901234567890123456789012345678901234567890
-----------------------------------------------------------------------------
2001120002MAME R L
30021000027 HAVEN PLAZA
2001260007
1003920000WASH'TON I3 HAVEN PLAZA                ARLINGTON VA  02174 DL66
30008432457 HAVEN PLAZA
4000070010MANHASSET NY  11030
4001750000S NYACK NY  10960
1004200015RICE J    49 LANCASTER AVENUE          ALEXANDRIA VA  22314HT58
2004200015PRICE J
300420001551 LANCASTER AVENUE
5000490001SG
5002520000
6000700005%)
600014000079
7001050000
7001750000
3000770000111 EIGHTH AVENUE
7000770000
1013457892         53 LANCASTER AVENUE          ALEXANDRIA VA  223140D69
1002030000MITCHELL J587A WEST 207TH STREET       YONKERS NY  10710   HT64
```

Figure F.17   Input data for Review Exercise 2, Chapter 17.

```
-----------------------------------------------------------------------------
          1         2         3         4         5         6         7         8  ⚫
12345678901234567890123456789012345678901234567890123456789012345678901234567890
-----------------------------------------------------------------------------
2 3 4
12 12 12
99999 99999 99999
0 0 0
```

Figure F.18   Input data for Review Exercise 3, Chapter 18.

```
-----------------------------------------------------------------------------
          1         2         3         4         5         6         7         8
12345678901234567890123456789012345678901234567890123456789012345678901234567890
-----------------------------------------------------------------------------
          A PALINDROME READS THE SAME WAY BACKWARDS AS FORWARDS.
                    ABLE WAS I ERE I SAW ELBA.
          A MAN, A PLAN, A CANAL - PANAMA.
```

Figure F.19   Input data for Review Exercise 5, Chapter 19.

```
-------------------------------------------- --------------------------------------
         1         2         3         4         5         6         7         8
12345678901234567890123456789012345678901234567890123456789012345678901234567890
-----------------------------------------------------------------------------------
010101003001123456
010101007002000224
010101039004843920
010101046005844848
010101053006001234
010101060006949493
010101067007400003
010102074212545499
010102081012000033
010102088013584958
010102095015039390
010103003234030303
020011007567999999
020011011454045600
020011023345833333
020222027345434343
020222031567990330
020222035001003421
020266039903453987
020266043854585830
030193059932585854
030193063419394949
040045067333000000
040045071323595950
040403048399392147
040403054392000000
040412060111999999
046012013538000000
046012017521069078
046012021504138156
046012025487207234
046012029470276312
046028033453345390
046028037436414468
046028041419483546
```

Glossaries

1974 ANSI Standard Glossary

Abbreviated Combined Relation Condition. The combined condition that results from the explicit omission of a common subject or a common subject and common relational operator in a consecutive sequence of relation conditions.

Access Mode. The manner in which records are to be operated upon within a file.

Actual Decimal Point. The physical representation, using either of the decimal point characters period (.) or comma (,), of the decimal point position in a data item.

Alphabet-Name. A user-defined word, in the SPECIAL-NAMES paragraph of the Environment Division, that assigns a name to a specific character set and/or collating sequence.

Alphabetic Character. A character that belongs to the following set of letters: A, B, C, D, E, F, G, H, I, J, K, L, M, N, O, P, Q, R, S, T, U, V, W, X, Y, Z, and the space.

Alphanumeric Character. Any character in the computer's character set.

Alternate Record Key. A key, other than the prime record key, whose contents identify a record within an indexed file.

Arithmetic Expression. An arithmetic expression can be an identifier of a numeric elementary item, a numeric literal, such identifiers and literals separated by arithmetic operators, two arithmetic expressions separated by an arithmetic operator, or an arithmetic expression enclosed in parentheses.

Arithmetic Operator. A single character, or a fixed two-character combination, that belongs to the following set:

Character	Meaning
+	Addition
−	Subtraction
*	Multiplication
/	Division
**	Exponentiation

Ascending Key. A key upon the values of which data is ordered starting with the lowest value of key up to the highest value of key in accordance with the rules for comparing data items.

Assumed Decimal Point. A decimal point position which does not involve the existence of an actual character in a data item. The assumed decimal point has logical meaning but no physical representation.

At End Condition. A condition caused:

1. During the execution of a READ statement for a sequentially accessed file
2. During the execution of a RETURN statement, when no next logical record exists for the associated sort or merge file
3. During the execution of a SEARCH statement, when the search operation terminates without satisfying the condition specified in any of the associated WHEN phrases

Block. A physical unit of data that is normally composed of one or more logical records. For mass storage files, a block may contain a portion of a logical record. The size of a block has no direct relationship to the size of the file within which the block is contained or to the size of the logical record(s) that are either continued within the block or that overlap the block. The term is synonymous with physical record.

Body Group. Generic name for a report group of TYPE DETAIL, CONTROL HEADING, or CONTROL FOOTING.

Called Program. A program which is the object of a CALL statement combined at object time with the calling program to produce a run unit.

Calling Program. A program which executes a CALL to another program.

Cd-Name. A user-defined word that names an MCS interface area described in a communication description entry within the Communication Section of the Data Division.

Character. The basic indivisible unit of the language.

Character Position. A character position is the amount of physical storage required to store a single standard data format character whose usage is DISPLAY. Further characteristics of the physical storage are defined by the implementor.

Character-String. A sequence of contiguous characters which form a COBOL word, a literal, a PICTURE character-string, or a comment-entry.

Class Condition. The proposition, for which a truth value can be determined, that the content of an item is wholly alphabetic or is wholly numeric.

Clause. A clause is an ordered set of consecutive COBOL character-strings whose purpose is to specify an attribute of an entry.

COBOL Character Set. The complete COBOL character set consists of the 51 characters listed below:

Character	Meaning
0, 1, . . . , 9	Digit
A, B, . . . , Z	Letter
	Space (blank)
+	Plus sign
−	Minus sign (hyphen)
*	Asterisk
/	Stroke (virgule, slash)
=	Equal sign
$	Currency sign
,	Comma (decimal point)
;	Semicolon
.	Period (decimal point)
"	Quotation mark
(	Left parenthesis
)	Right parenthesis
>	Greater than symbol
<	Less than symbol

COBOL Word. (See Word)

Collating Sequence. The sequence in which the characters that are acceptable in a computer are ordered for purposes of sorting, merging, and comparing.

Column. A character position within a print line. The columns are numbered from 1, by 1, starting at the leftmost character position of the print line and extending to the rightmost position of the print line.

Combined Condition. A condition that is the result of connecting two or more conditions with the 'AND' or the 'OR' logical operator.

Comment-Entry. An entry in the Identification Division that may be any combination of characters from the computer character set.

Comment Line. A source program line represented by an asterisk in the indicator area of the line and any characters from the computer's character set in area A and area B of that line. The comment line serves only for documentation in a program. A special form of comment line represented by a stroke (/) in the indicator area of the line and any characters from the computer's character set in area A and area B of that line causes page ejection prior to printing the comment.

Communication Description Entry. An entry in the Communication Section of the Data Division that is composed of the level indicator CD, followed by a cd-name, and then followed by a set of clauses as required. It describes the interface between the message control system (MCS) and the COBOL program.

Communication Device. A mechanism (hardware or hardware/software) capable of sending data to a queue and/or receiving data from a queue. This mechanism may be a computer or a peripheral device. One or more programs containing communication description entries and residing within the same computer define one or more of these mechanisms.

Communication Section. The section of the Data Division that describes the interface areas between the MCS and the program, composed of one or more CD description entries.

Compile Time. The time at which a COBOL source program is translated, by a COBOL compiler, to a COBOL object program.

Compiler Directing Statement. A statement, beginning with a compiler directing verb, that causes the compiler to take a specific action during compilation.

Complex Condition. A condition in which one or more logical operators act upon one or more conditions. (See Negated Simple Condition, Combined Condition, Negated Combined Condition.)

Computer-Name. A system-name that identifies the computer upon which the program is to be compiled or run.

Condition. A status of a program at execution time for which a truth value can be determined. Where the term 'condition' (condition-1, condition-2, . . .) appears in these language specifications in or in reference to 'condition' (condition-1, condition-2, . . .) of a general format, it is a conditional expression consisting of either a simple condition optionally parenthesized, or a combined condition consisting of the syntactically correct combination of simple conditions, logical operators, and parentheses, for which a truth value can be determined.

Condition-Name. A user-defined word assigned to a specific value, set of values, or range of values, within the complete set of values that a conditional variable may possess; or the user-defined word assigned to a status of an implementor-defined switch or device.

Condition-Name Condition. The proposition, for which a truth value can be determined, that the value of a conditional variable is a member of the set of values attributed to a condition-name associated with the conditional variable.

Conditional Expression. A simple condition or a complex condition specified in an IF, PERFORM, or SEARCH statement. (See Simple Condition and Complex Condition.)

Conditional Statement. A conditional statement specifies that the truth value of a condition is to be determined and that the subsequent action of the object program is dependent on this truth value.

Conditional Variable. A data item one or more values of which has a condition-name assigned to it.

Configuration Section.   A section of the Environment Division that describes overall specifications of source and object computers.

Connective.   A reserved word that is used to:

1.   Associate a data-name, paragraph-name, condition-name, or text-name with its qualifier.
2.   Link two or more operands written in a series.
3.   Form conditions (logical connectives). (See Logical Operator)

Contiguous Items.   Items that are described by consecutive entries in the Data Division and that bear a definite hierarchic relationship to each other.

Control Break.   A change in the value of a data item that is referenced in the CONTROL clause. More generally, a change in the value of a data item that is used to control the hierarchical structure of a report.

Control Break Level.   The relative position within a control hierarchy at which the most major control break occurred.

Control Data Item.   A data item, a change in whose contents may produce a control break.

Control Data-Name.   A data-name that appears in a CONTROL clause and refers to a control data item.

Control Footing.   A report group that is presented at the end of the control group of which it is a member.

Control Group.   A set of body groups that is presented for a given value of a control data item or of FINAL. Each control group may begin with a CONTROL HEADING, end with a CONTROL FOOTING, and contain DETAIL report groups.

Control Heading.   A report group that is presented at the beginning of the control group of which it is a member.

Control Hierarchy.   A designated sequence of report subdivisions defined by the positional order of FINAL and the data-names within a CONTROL clause.

Counter.   A data item used for storing numbers or number representations in a manner that permits these numbers to be increased or decreased by the value of another number, or to be changed or reset to zero or to an arbitrary positive or negative value.

Currency Sign.   The character '$' of the COBOL character set.

Currency Symbol.   The character defined by the CURRENCY SIGN clause in the SPECIAL-NAMES paragraph. If no CURRENCY SIGN clause is present in a COBOL source program, the currency symbol is identical to the currency sign.

Current Record.   The record which is available in the record area associated with the file.

Current Record Pointer.   A conceptual entity that is used in the selection of the next record.

Data Clause.   A clause that appears in a data description entry in the Data Division and provides information describing a particular attribute of a data item.

Data Description Entry.   An entry in the Data Division that is composed of a level-number followed by a data-name, if required, and then followed by a set of data clauses, as required.

Data Item.   A character or a set of contiguous characters (excluding, in either case, literals) defined as a unit of data by the COBOL program.

Data-Name.   A user-defined word that names a data item described in a data description entry in the Data Division. When used in the general formats, 'data-name' represents a word which can neither be subscripted, indexed, nor qualified unless specifically permitted by the rules for that format.

Debugging Line. A debugging line is any line with 'D' in the indicator area of the line.

Debugging Section. A debugging section is a section that contains a USE FOR DEBUGGING statement.

Declaratives. A set of one or more special purpose sections, written at the beginning of the Procedure Division, the first of which is preceded by the key word DECLARATIVES and the last of which is followed by the key words END DE-CLARATIVES. A declarative is composed of a section header, followed by a USE compiler directing sentence, followed by a set of zero, one, or more associated paragraphs.

Declarative-Sentence. A compiler-directing sentence consisting of a single USE statement terminated by the separator period.

Delimiter. A character or a sequence of contiguous characters that identifies the end of a string of characters and separates that string of characters from the following string of characters. A delimiter is not part of the string of characters that it delimits.

Descending Key. A key upon the values of which data is ordered starting with the highest value of key down to the lowest value of key, in accordance with the rules for comparing data items.

Destination. The symbolic identification of the receiver of a transmission from a queue.

Digit Position. A digit position is the amount of physical storage required to store a single digit. This amount may vary depending on the usage of the data item describing the digit position. Further characteristics of the physical storage are defined by the implementor.

Division. A set of zero, one, or more sections or paragraphs, called the division body, that is formed and combined in accordance with a specific set of rules. There are four (4) divisions in a COBOL program: Identification, Environment, Data, and Procedure.

Division Header. A combination of words followed by a period and a space that indicates the beginning of a division. The division headers are:

```
IDENTIFICATION DIVISION.
ENVIRONMENT DIVISION.
DATA DIVISION.
PROCEDURE DIVISION [USING data-name-1 [data-name-2] ... ].
```

Dynamic Access. An access mode in which specific logical records can be obtained from or placed into a mass storage file in a nonsequential manner (see Random Access) and obtained from a file in a sequential manner (see Sequential Access), during the scope of the same OPEN statement.

Editing Character.   A single character or fixed two-character combination belonging to the following set:

Character	Meaning
B	Space
0	Zero
+	Plus
−	Minus
CR	Credit
DB	Debit
Z	Zero suppress
*	Check protect
$	Currency sign
,	Comma (decimal point)
.	Period (decimal point)
/	Stroke (virgule, slash)

Elementary Item.   A data item that is described as not being further logically subdivided.

End of Procedure Division.   The physical position in a COBOL source program after which no further procedures appear.

Entry.   Any descriptive set of consecutive clauses terminated by a period and written in the Identification Division, Environment Division, or Data Division of a COBOL source program.

Environment Clause.   A clause that appears as part of an Environment Division entry.

Execution Time.   (See Object Time)

Extend Mode.   The state of a file after execution of an OPEN statement, with the EXTEND phrase specified, for that file and before the execution of a CLOSE statement for that file.

Figurative Constant.   A compiler generated value referenced through the use of certain reserved words.

File.   A collection of records.

File Clause.   A clause that appears as part of any of the following Data Division entries:

File description (FD)
Sort-merge file description (SD)
Communication description (CD)

FILE-CONTROL.   The name of an Environment Division paragraph in which the data files for a given source program are declared.

File Description Entry.   An entry in the File Section of the Data Division that is composed of the level indicator FD, followed by a file-name, and then followed by a set of file clauses as required.

File-Name.   A user-defined word that names a file described in a file description entry or a sort-merge file description entry within the File Section of the Data Division.

File Organization.   The permanent logical file structure established at the time that a file is created.

File Section.   The section of the Data Division that contains file description entries and sort-merge file description entries together with their associated record descriptions.

Format.   A specific arrangement of a set of data.

Group Item.   A named contiguous set of elementary or group items.

High Order End.   The leftmost character of a string of characters.

I-O-CONTROL.   The name of an Environment Division paragraph in which object program requirements for specific input-output techniques, rerun points, sharing of same areas by several data files, and multiple file storage on a single input-output device are specified.

I-O Mode.   The state of a file after execution of an OPEN statement, with the I-O phrase specified, for that file and before the execution of a CLOSE statement for that file.

Identifier.   A data-name, followed as required, by the syntactically correct combination of qualifiers, subscripts, and indices necessary to make unique reference to a data item.

Imperative Statement.   A statement that begins with an imperative verb and specifies an unconditional action to be taken. An imperative statement may consist of a sequence of imperative statements.

Implementor-Name.   A system-name that refers to a particular feature available on that implementor's computing system.

Index.   A computer storage position or register, the contents of which represent the identification of a particular element in a table.

Index Data Item.   A data item in which the value associated with an index-name can be stored in a form specified by the implementor.

Index-Name.   A user-defined word that names an index associated with a specific table.

Indexed Data-Name.   An identifier that is composed of a data-name, followed by one or more index-names enclosed in parentheses.

Indexed File.   A file with indexed organization.

Indexed Organization.   The permanent logical file structure in which each record is identified by the value of one or more keys within that record.

Input File.   A file that is opened in the input mode.

Input Mode.   The state of a file after execution of an OPEN statement, with the INPUT phrase specified, for that file and before the execution of a CLOSE statement for that file.

Input-Output File.   A file that is opened in the I-O mode.

Input-Output Section.   The section of the Environment Division that names the files and the external media required by an object program and which provides information required for transmission and handling of data during execution of the object program.

Input Procedure.   A set of statements that is executed each time a record is released to the sort file.

Integer.   A numeric literal or a numeric data item that does not include any character positions to the right of the assumed decimal point. Where the term 'integer' appears in general formats, integer must not be a numeric data item, and must not be signed, nor zero unless explicitly allowed by the rules of that format.

Invalid Key Condition.   A condition, at object time, caused when a specific value of the key associated with an indexed or relative file is determined to be invalid.

Key.   A data item which identifies the location of a record, or a set of data items which serve to identify the ordering of data.

Key of Reference.   The key, either prime or alternate, currently being used to access records within an indexed file.

Key Word.   A reserved word whose presence is required when the format in which the word appears is used in a source program.

Language-Name.   A system-name that specifies a particular programming language.

Level Indicator.   Two alphabetic characters that identify a specific type of file or a position in a hierarchy.

Level-Number.   A user-defined word which indicates the position of a data item in the hierarchical structure of a logical record or which indicates special properties of a data description entry. A level-number is expressed as a one or two digit number. Level-numbers in the range 1 through 49 indicate the position of a data item in the hierarchical structure of a logical record. Level-numbers in the range 1 through 9 may be written either as a single digit or as a zero followed by a significant digit. Level-numbers 66, 77, and 88 identify special properties of a data description entry.

Library-Name.   A user-defined word that names a COBOL library that is to be used by the compiler for a given source program compilation.

Library-Text.   A sequence of character-strings and/or separators in a COBOL Library.

Line.   (See Report Line)

Line Number.   An integer that denotes the vertical position of a report line on a page.

Linkage Section.   The section in the Data Division of the called program that describes data items available from the calling program. These data items may be referred to by both the calling and called program.

Literal.   A character-string whose value is implied by the ordered set of characters comprising the string.

Logical Operator.   One of the reserved words AND, OR, or NOT. In the formation of a condition, both or either of AND and OR can be used as logical connectives. NOT can be used for logical negation.

Logical Record.   The most inclusive data item. The level-number for a record is 01. (See Report Writer Logical Record)

Low Order End.   The rightmost character of a string of characters.

Mass Storage.   A storage medium on which data may be organized and maintained in both a sequential and nonsequential manner.

Mass Storage Control System (MSCS).   An input-output control system that directs, or controls, the processing of mass storage files.

Mass Storage File.   A collection of records that is assigned to a mass storage medium.

MCS.   (See Message Control System)

Merge File.   A collection of records to be merged by a MERGE statement. The merge file is created and can be used only by the merge function.

Message.   Data associated with an end of message indicator or an end of group indicator. (See Message Indicators)

Message Control System (MCS).   A communication control system that supports the processing of messages.

Message Count.   The count of the number of complete messages that exist in the designated queue of messages.

Message Indicators.   EGI (end of group indicator), EMI (end of message indicator), and ESI (end of segment indicator) are conceptual indications that serve to notify the MCS that a specific condition exists (end of group, end of message, end of segment).

Within the hierarchy of EGI, EMI, and ESI, an EGI is conceptually equivalent to an ESI, EMI, and EGI. An EMI is conceptually equivalent to an ESI and EMI.

Thus, a segment may be terminated by an ESI, EMI, or EGI. A message may be terminated by an EMI or EGI.

Message Segment. Data that forms a logical subdivision of a message normally associated with an end of segment indicator. (See Message Indicators)

Mnemonic-Name. A user-defined word that is associated in the Environment Division with a specified implementor-name.

MSCS. (See Mass Storage Control System)

Native Character Set. The implementor-defined character set associated with the computer specified in the OBJECT-COMPUTER paragraph.

Native Collating Sequence. The implementor-defined collating sequence associated with the computer specified in the OBJECT-COMPUTER paragraph.

Negated Combined Condition. The 'NOT' logical operator immediately followed by a parenthesized combined condition.

Negated Simple Condition. The 'NOT' logical operator immediately followed by a simple condition.

Next Executable Sentence. The next sentence to which control will be transferred after execution of the current statement is complete.

Next Executable Statement. The next statement to which control will be transferred after execution of the current statement is complete.

Next Record. The record which logically follows the current record of a file.

Noncontiguous Items. Elementary data items, in the Working-Storage and Linkage Sections, which bear no hierarchic relationship to other data items.

Nonnumeric Item. A data item whose description permits its contents to be composed of any combination of characters taken from the computer's character set. Certain categories of nonnumeric items may be formed from more restricted character sets.

Nonnumeric Literal. A character-string bounded by quotation marks. The string of characters may include any character in the computer's character set. To represent a single quotation mark character within a nonnumeric literal, two contiguous quotation marks must be used.

Numeric Character. A character that belongs to the following set of digits: 0, 1, 2, 3, 4, 5, 6, 7, 8, 9.

Numeric Item. A data item whose description restricts its contents to a value represented by characters chosen from the digits '0' through '9'; if signed, the item may also contain a '+', '−', or other representation of an operational sign.

Numeric Literal. A literal composed of one or more numeric characters that also may contain either a decimal point, or an algebraic sign, or both. The decimal point must not be the rightmost character. The algebraic sign, if present, must be the leftmost character.

OBJECT-COMPUTER. The name of an Environment Division paragraph in which the computer environment, within which the object program is executed, is described.

Object of Entry. A set of operands and reserved words, within a Data Division entry, that immediately follows the subject of the entry.

Object Program. A set or group of executable machine language instructions and other material designed to interact with data to provide problem solutions. In this context, an object program is generally the machine language result of the operation of a COBOL compiler on a source program. Where there is no danger of ambiguity, the word "program" alone may be used in place of the phrase "object program."

Object Time. The time at which an object program is executed.

Open Mode. The state of a file after execution of an OPEN statement for that file and before the execution of a CLOSE statement for that file. The particular open mode is specified in the OPEN statement as either INPUT, OUTPUT, I-O, or EXTEND.

Operand.   Whereas the general definition of operand is "that component which is operated upon," for the purposes of this publication, any lowercase word (or words) that appears in a statement or entry format may be considered to be an operand and, as such, is an implied reference to the data indicated by the operand.

Operational Sign.   An algebraic sign, associated with a numeric data item or a numeric literal, to indicate whether its value is positive or negative.

Optional Word.   A reserved word that is included in a specific format only to improve the readability of the language and whose presence is optional to the user when the format in which the word appears is used in a source program.

Output File.   A file that is opened in either the output mode or extend mode.

Output Mode.   The state of a file after execution of an OPEN statement, with the OUTPUT or EXTEND phrase specified, for that file and before the execution of a CLOSE statement for that file.

Output Procedure.   A set of statements to which control is given during execution of a SORT statement after the sort function is completed, or during execution of a MERGE statement after the merge function has selected the next record in merged order.

Page.   A vertical division of a report representing a physical separation of report data, the separation being based on internal reporting requirements and/or external characteristics of the reporting medium.

Page Body.   That part of the logical page in which lines can be written and/or spaced.

Page Footing.   A report group that is presented at the end of a report page as determined by the Report Writer Control System.

Page Heading.   A report group that is presented at the beginning of a report page as determined by the Report Writer Control System.

Paragraph.   In the Procedure Division, a paragraph-name followed by a period and a space and by zero, one, or more sentences. In the Identification and Environment Divisions, a paragraph header followed by zero, one, or more entries.

Paragraph Header.   A reserved word, followed by a period and a space that indicates the beginning of a paragraph in the Identification and Environment Divisions. The permissible paragraph headers are:

In the Identification Division:

```
PROGRAM-ID.
AUTHOR.
INSTALLATION.
DATE-WRITTEN.
DATE-COMPILED.
SECURITY.
```

In the Environment Division:

```
SOURCE-COMPUTER.
OBJECT-COMPUTER.
SPECIAL-NAMES.
FILE-CONTROL.
I-O-CONTROL.
```

Paragraph-Name.   A user-defined word that identifies and begins a paragraph in the Procedure Division.

Phrase.   A phrase is an ordered set of one or more consecutive COBOL character-strings that form a portion of a COBOL procedural statement or of a COBOL clause.

Physical Record.   (See Block)

Prime Record Key.   A key whose contents uniquely identify a record within an indexed file.

Printable Group.   A report group that contains at least one print line.

Printable Item.   A data item, the extent and contents of which are specified by an elementary report entry. This elementary report entry contains a COLUMN NUMBER clause, a PICTURE clause, and a SOURCE, SUM, or VALUE clause.

Procedure.   A paragraph or group of logically successive paragraphs, or a section or group of logically successive sections, within the Procedure Division.

Procedure-Name.   A user-defined word which is used to name a paragraph or section in the Procedure Division. It consists of a paragraph-name (which may be qualified), or a section-name.

Program-Name.   A user-defined word that identifies a COBOL source program.

Pseudo-Text.   A sequence of character-strings and/or separators bounded by, but not including, pseudo-text delimiters.

Pseudo-Text Delimiter.   Two contiguous equal sign (=) characters used to delimit pseudo-text.

Punctuation Character.   A character that belongs to the following set:

Character	Meaning
,	Comma
;	Semicolon
.	Period
"	Quotation mark
(	Left parenthesis
)	Right parenthesis
	Space
=	Equal sign

Qualified Data-Name.   An identifier that is composed of a data-name followed by one or more sets of either of the connectives OF and IN followed by a data-name qualifier.

Qualifier.

1.   A data-name which is used in a reference together with another data name at a lower level in the same hierarchy.
2.   A section-name which is used in a reference together with a paragraph-name specified in that section.
3.   A library-name which is used in a reference together with a text-name associated with that library.

Queue.   A logical collection of messages awaiting transmission or processing.

Queue Name.   A symbolic name that indicates to the MCS the logical path by which a message or a portion of a completed message may be accessible in a queue.

Random Access.   An access mode in which the program-specified value of a key data item identifies the logical record that is obtained from, deleted from or placed into a relative or indexed file.

Record. (See Logical Record)

Record Area. A storage area allocated for the purpose of processing the record described in a record description entry in the File Section.

Record Description. (See Record Description Entry)

Record Description Entry. The total set of data description entries associated with a particular record.

Record Key. A key, either the prime record key or an alternate record key, whose contents identify a record within an indexed file.

Record-Name. A user-defined word that names a record described in a record description entry in the Data Division.

Reference Format. A format that provides a standard method for describing COBOL source programs.

Relation. (See Relational Operator)

Relation Character. A character that belongs to the following set:

Character	Meaning
>	Greater than
<	Less than
=	Equal to

Relation Condition. The proposition, for which a truth value can be determined, that the value of an arithmetic expression or data item has a specific relationship to the value of another arithmetic expression or data item. (See Relational Operator)

Relational Operator. A reserved word, a relation character, a group of consecutive reserved words, or a group of consecutive reserved words and relation characters used in the construction of a relation condition. The permissible operators and their meaning are:

Relational Operator	Meaning
IS [NOT] GREATER THAN IS [NOT] >	Greater than or not greater than
IS [NOT] LESS THAN IS [NOT] <	Less than or not less than
IS [NOT] EQUAL TO IS [NOT] =	Equal to or not equal to

Relative File. A file with relative organization.

Relative Key. A key whose contents identify a logical record in a relative file.

Relative Organization. The permanent logical file structure in which each record is uniquely identified by an integer value greater than zero, which specifies the record's logical ordinal position in the file.

Report Clause. A clause, in the Report Section of the Data Division, that appears in a report description entry or a report group description entry.

Report Description Entry. An entry in the Report Section of the Data Division that is composed of the level indicator RD, followed by a report name, followed by a set of report clauses as required.

Report File. An output file whose file description entry contains a REPORT clause. The contents of a report file consist of records that are written under control of the Report Writer Control System.

Report Footing. A report group that is presented only at the end of a report.

Report Group. In the Report Section of the Data Division, an 01 level-number entry and its subordinate entries.

Report Group Description Entry. An entry in the Report Section of the Data Division that is composed of the level-number 01, an optional data-name, a TYPE clause, and an optional set of report clauses.

Report Heading. A report group that is presented only at the beginning of a report.

Report Line. A division of a page representing one row of horizontal character positions. Each character position of a report line is aligned vertically beneath the corresponding character position of the report line above it. Report lines are numbered from 1, by 1, starting at the top of the page.

Report-Name. A user-defined word that names a report described in a report description entry within the Report Section of the Data Division.

Report Section. The section of the Data Division that contains one or more report description entries and their associated report group description entries.

Report Writer Control System (RWCS). An object time control system, provided by the implementor, that accomplishes the construction of reports.

Report Writer Logical Record. A record that consists of the Report Writer print line and associated control information necessary for its selection and vertical positioning.

Reserved Word. A COBOL word specified in the list of words which may be used in COBOL source programs, but which must not appear in the programs as user-defined words or system-names.

Routine-Name. A user-defined word that identifies a procedure written in a language other than COBOL.

Run Unit. A set of one or more object programs which function, at object time, as a unit to provide problem solutions.

RWCS. (See Report Writer Control System)

Section. A set of zero, one, or more paragraphs or entries, called a section body, the first of which is preceded by a section header. Each section consists of the section header and the related section body.

Section Header. A combination of words followed by a period and a space that indicates the beginning of a section in the Environment, Data, and Procedure Divisions.

In the Environment and Data Divisions, a section header is composed of reserved words followed by a period and a space. The permissible section headers are:

```
CONFIGURATION SECTION.
INPUT-OUTPUT SECTION.
```

In the Data Division:

```
FILE SECTION.
WORKING-STORAGE SECTION.
LINKAGE SECTION.
COMMUNICATION SECTION.
REPORT SECTION.
```

In the Procedure Division, a section header is composed of a section-name, followed by the reserved word SECTION, followed by a segment-number (optional), followed by a period and a space.

Section-Name. A user-defined word which names a section in the Procedure Division.

Segment-Number. A user-defined word which classifies sections in the Procedure Division for purposes of segmentation. Segment-numbers may contain only the characters '0', '1', . . . , '9'. A segment-number may be expressed either as a one or two digit number.

Sentence. A sequence of one or more statements, the last of which is terminated by a period followed by a space.

Separator. A punctuation character used to delimit character-strings.

Sequential Access. An access mode in which logical records are obtained from or placed into a file in a consecutive predecessor-to-successor logical record sequence determined by the order of records in the file.

Sequential File. A file with sequential organization.

Sequential Organization. The permanent logical file structure in which a record is identified by a predecessor-successor relationship established when the record is placed into the file.

Sign Condition. The proposition, for which a truth value can be determined, that the algebraic value of a data item or an arithmetic expression is either less than, greater than, or equal to zero.

Simple Condition. Any single condition chosen from the set:

> relation condition
> class condition
> condition-name condition
> switch-status condition
> sign condition
> (simple-condition)

Sort File. A collection of records to be sorted by a SORT statement. The sort file is created and can be used by the sort function only.

Sort-Merge File Description Entry. An entry in the File Section of the Data Division that is composed of the level indicator SD, followed by a file-name, and then followed by a set of file clauses as required.

Source. The symbolic identification of the originator of a transmission to a queue.

SOURCE-COMPUTER. The name of an Environment Division paragraph in which the computer environment, within which the source program is compiled, is described.

Source Item. An identifier designated by a SOURCE clause that provides the value of a printable item.

Source Program. Although it is recognized that a source program may be represented by other forms and symbols, in this document it always refers to a syntactically correct set of COBOL statements beginning with an Identification Division and ending with the end of the Procedure Division. In contexts where there is no danger of ambiguity, the word "program" alone may be used in place of the phrase "source program."

Special Character. A character that belongs to the following set:

Character	Meaning
+	Plus sign
–	Minus sign (hyphen)
*	Asterisk
/	Stroke (virgule, slash)
=	Equal sign
$	Currency sign
,	Comma (decimal point)
;	Semicolon
.	Period (decimal point)
"	Quotation mark
(	Left parenthesis
)	Right parenthesis
>	Greater than symbol
<	Less than symbol

Special-Character Word. A reserved word which is an arithmetic operator or a relation character.

SPECIAL-NAMES. The name of an Environment Division paragraph in which implementor-names are related to user specified mnemonic-names.

Special Registers. Compiler generated storage areas whose primary use is to store information produced in conjunction with the use of specific COBOL features.

Standard Data Format. The concept used in describing the characteristics of data in a COBOL Data Division under which the characteristics or properties of the data are expressed in a form oriented to the appearance of the data on a printed page of infinite length and breadth, rather than a form oriented to the manner in which the data is stored internally in the computer, or on a particular external medium.

Statement. A syntactically valid combination of words and symbols written in the Procedure Division beginning with a verb.

Sub-Queue. A logical hierarchical division of a queue.

Subject of Entry. An operand or reserved word that appears immediately following the level indicator or the level-number in a Data Division entry.

Subprogram. (See Called Program)

Subscript. An integer whose value identifies a particular element in a table.

Subscripted Data-Name. An identifier that is composed of a data-name followed by one or more subscripts enclosed in parentheses.

Sum Counter. A signed numeric data item established by a SUM clause in the Report Section of the Data Division. The sum counter is used by the Report Writer Control System to contain the result of designated summing operations that take place during production of a report.

Switch-Status Condition. The proposition, for which a truth value can be determined, that an implementor-defined switch, capable of being set to an 'on' or 'off' status, has been set to a specific status.

System-Name. A COBOL word which is used to communicate with the operating environment.

Table.   A set of logically consecutive items of data that are defined in the Data Division by means of the OCCURS clause.

Table Element.   A data item that belongs to the set of repeated items comprising a table.

Terminal.   The originator of a transmission to a queue, or the receiver of a transmission from a queue.

Text-Name.   A user-defined word which identifies library text.

Text-Word.   Any character-string or separator, except space, in a COBOL library or in pseudo-text.

Truth Value.   The representation of the result of the evaluation of a condition in terms of one of two values:

True
False

Unary Operator.   A plus $(+)$ or a minus $(-)$ sign, which precedes a variable or a left parenthesis in an arithmetic expression and which has the effect of multiplying the expression by $+1$ or -1, respectively.

Unit.   A module of mass storage the dimensions of which are determined by each implementor.

User-Defined Word.   A COBOL word that must be supplied by the user to satisfy the format of a clause or statement.

Variable.   A data item whose value may be changed by execution of the object program. A variable used in an arithmetic expression must be a numeric elementary item.

Verb.   A word that expresses an action to be taken by a COBOL compiler or object program.

Word.   A character-string of not more than 30 characters which forms a user-defined word, a system-name, or a reserved word.

Working-Storage Section.   The section of the Data Division that describes working storage data items, composed either of noncontiguous items or of working storage records or of both.

77-Level-Description-Entry.   A data description entry that describes a noncontiguous data item with the level-number 77.

1985 ANSI Standard Glossary

Abbreviated Combined Relation Condition. The combined condition that results from the explicit omission of a common subject or a common subject and common relational operator in a consecutive sequence of relation conditions.

Access Mode. The manner in which records are to be operated upon within a file.

Actual Decimal Point. The physical representation, using the decimal point characters period (.) or comma (,), of the decimal point position in a data item.

Alphabet-Name. A user-defined word, in the SPECIAL-NAMES paragraph of the Environment Division, that assigns a name to a specific character set and/or collating sequence.

Alphabetic Character. A letter or a space character.

Alphanumeric Character. Any character in the computer's character set.

Alternate Record Key. A key, other than the prime record key, whose contents identify a record within an indexed file.

Arithmetic Expression. An identifier of a numeric elementary item, a numeric literal, such identifiers and literals separated by arithmetic operators, two arithmetic expressions separated by an arithmetic operator, or an arithmetic expression enclosed in parentheses.

Arithmetic Operation. The process caused by the execution of an arithmetic statement, or the evaluation of an arithmetic expression, that results in a mathematically correct solution to the arguments presented.

Arithmetic Operator. A single character or fixed two-character combination which belongs to the following set:

Character	Meaning
+	addition
−	subtraction
*	multiplication
/	division
**	exponentiation

Arithmetic Statement. A statement that causes an arithmetic operation to be executed. The arithmetic statements are the ADD, COMPUTE, DIVIDE, MULTIPLY, and SUBTRACT statements.

Ascending Key. A key upon the values of which data is ordered starting with the lowest value of key up to the highest value of key in accordance with the rules for comparing data items.

Assumed Decimal Point. A decimal point position which does not involve the existence of an actual character in a data item. The assumed decimal point has logical meaning with no physical representation.

At End Condition.   A condition caused:

1. During the execution of a READ statement for a sequentially accessed file, when no next logical record exists in the file, or when the number of significant digits in the relative record number is larger than the size of the relative key data item, or when an optional input file is not present.
2. During the execution of a RETURN statement, when no next logical record exists for the associated sort or merge file.
3. During the execution of a SEARCH statement, when the search operation terminates without satisfying the condition specified in any of the associated WHEN phrases.

Block.   A physical unit of data that is normally composed of one or more logical records. For mass storage files, a block may contain a portion of a logical record. The size of a block has no direct relationship to the size of the file within which the block is contained or to the size of the logical record(s) that are either contained within the block or that overlap the block. The term is synonymous with physical record.

Body Group.   Generic name for a report group of TYPE DETAIL, CONTROL HEADING, or CONTROL FOOTING.

Bottom Margin.   An empty area which follows the page body.

Called Program.   A program which is the object of a CALL statement combined at object time with the calling program to produce a run unit.

Calling Program.   A program which executes a CALL to another program.

Cd-Name.   A user-defined word that names an MCS interface area described in a communication description entry within the Communication Section of the Data Division

Character.   The basic indivisible unit of the language.

Character Position.   A character position is the amount of physical storage required to store a single standard data format character whose usage is DISPLAY. Further characteristics of the physical storage are defined by the implementor.

Character-String.   A sequence of contiguous characters which form a CO-BOL word, a literal, a PICTURE character-string, or a comment-entry.

Class Condition.   The proposition, for which a truth value can be determined, that the content of an item is wholly alphabetic or is wholly numeric or consists exclusively of those characters listed in the definition of a class-name.

Class-Name.   A user-defined word defined in the SPECIAL-NAMES paragraph of the Environment Division that assigns a name to the proposition for which a truth value can be defined, that the content of a data item consists exclusively of those characters listed in the definition of the class-name.

Clause.   A clause is an ordered set of consecutive COBOL character-strings whose purpose is to specify an attribute of an entry.

COBOL Character Set.   The complete COBOL character set consists of the characters listed below.

Character	Meaning
0, 1, . . . , 9	digit
A, B, . . . , Z	uppercase letter
a, b, . . . , z	lowercase letter
	space
+	plus sign
−	minus sign (hyphen)
*	asterisk
/	slant (solidus)
=	equal sign
$	currency sign (represented as ¤ in the International Reference Version of International Standard ISO 646-1973)
,	comma (decimal point)
;	semicolon
.	period (decimal point, full stop)
"	quotation mark
(	left parenthesis
)	right parenthesis
>	greater than symbol
<	less than symbol
:	colon

NOTE 1:   In the cases where an implementation does not provide all of the COBOL character set to be graphically represented, substitute graphics may be specified by the implementor to replace the characters not represented. The COBOL character set graphics are a subset of American National Standard X3.4-1977, Code for Information Interchange. With the exception of '$', they are also a subset of the graphics defined for the International Reference Version of International Standard ISO 646-1973, 7-Bit Coded Character Set for Information Processing Interchange.

NOTE 2:   When the computer character set includes lowercase letters, they may be used in character-strings. Except when used in nonnumeric literals and some PICTURE symbols, each lowercase letter is equivalent to the corresponding uppercase letter.

COBOL Word.   A character-string of not more than 30 characters which forms a user-defined word, a system-name, or a reserved word.

Collating Sequence.   The sequence in which the characters that are acceptable to a computer are ordered for purposes of sorting, merging, comparing, and for processing indexed files sequentially.

Column.   A character position within a print line. The columns are numbered from 1, by 1, starting at the leftmost character position of the print line and extending to the rightmost position of the print line.

Combined Condition.   A condition that is the result of connecting two or more conditions with the 'AND' or the 'OR' logical operator.

Comment-Entry.   An entry in the Identification Division that may be any combination of characters from the computer's character set.

Comment Line.   A source program line represented by an asterisk (*) in the indicator area of the line and any characters from the computer's character set in area A and area B of that line. The comment line serves only for documentation in a program. A special form of comment line represented by a slant (/) in the indicator area of the line and any characters from the computer's character set in area A and area B of that line causes page ejection prior to printing the comment.

Common Program. A program which, despite being directly contained within another program, may be called from any program directly or indirectly contained in that other program.

Communication Description Entry. An entry in the Communication Section of the Data Division that is composed of the level indicator CD, followed by a cd-name, and then followed by a set of clauses as required. It describes the interface between the message control system (MCS) and the COBOL program.

Communication Device. A mechanism (hardware or hardware/software) capable of sending data to a queue and/or receiving data from a queue. This mechanism may be a computer or a peripheral device. One or more programs containing communication description entries and residing within the same computer define one or more of these mechanisms.

Communication Section. The section of the Data Division that describes the interface areas between the message control system (MCS) and the program, composed of one or more communication description areas.

Compile Time. The time at which a COBOL source program is translated, by a COBOL compiler, to a COBOL object program.

Compiler Directing Statement. A statement, beginning with a compiler directing verb, that causes the compiler to take a specific action during compilation. The compiler directing statements are the COPY, ENTER, REPLACE, and USE statements.

Complex Condition. A condition in which one or more logical operators act upon one or more conditions.

Computer-Name. A system-name that identifies the computer upon which the program is to be compiled or run.

Condition. A status of a program at execution time for which a truth value can be determined. Where the term 'condition' (condition-1, condition-2, . . .) appears in these language specifications in or in reference to 'condition' (condition-1, condition-2, . . .) of a general format, it is a conditional expression consisting of either a simple condition optionally parenthesized, or a combined condition consisting of the syntactically correct combination of simple conditions, logical operators, and parentheses, for which a truth value can be determined.

Condition-Name. A user-defined word that assigns a name to a subset of values that a conditional variable may assume; or a user-defined word assigned to a status of an implementor-defined switch or device. When 'condition-name' is used in the general formats, it represents a unique data item reference consisting of a syntactically correct combination of a condition-name, together with qualifiers and subscripts, as required for uniqueness of reference.

Condition-Name Condition. The proposition, for which a truth value can be determined, that the value of a conditional variable is a member of the set of values attributed to a condition-name associated with the conditional variable.

Conditional Expression. A simple condition or a complex condition specified in an EVALUATE, IF, PERFORM, or SEARCH statement.

Conditional Phrase. A conditional phrase specifies the action to be taken upon determination of the truth value of a condition resulting from the execution of a conditional statement.

Conditional Statement. A conditional statement specifies that the truth value of a condition is to be determined and that the subsequent action of the object program is dependent on this truth value.

Conditional Variable. A data item one or more values of which has a condition-name assigned to it.

Configuration Section. A section of the Environment Division that describes overall specifications of source and object programs.

Contiguous Items. Items that are described by consecutive entries in the Data Division, and that bear a definite hierarchical relationship to each other.

Control Break. A change in the value of a data item that is referenced in the CONTROL clause. More generally, a change in the value of a data item that is used to control the hierarchical structure of a report.

Control Break Level. The relative position within a control hierarchy at which the most major control break occurred.

Control Data Item. A data item, a change in whose content may produce a control break.

Control Data-Name. A data-name that appears in a CONTROL clause and refers to a control data item.

Control Footing. A report group that is presented at the end of the control group of which it is a member.

Control Group. A set of body groups that is presented for a given value of a control data item or of FINAL. Each control group may begin with a control heading, end with a control footing, and contain detail report groups.

Control Heading. A report group that is presented at the beginning of the control group of which it is a member.

Control Hierarchy. A designated sequence of report subdivisions defined by the positional order of FINAL and the data-names within a CONTROL clause.

Counter. A data item used for storing numbers or number representations in a manner that permits these numbers to be increased or decreased by the value of another number, or to be changed or reset to zero or to an arbitrary positive or negative value.

Currency Sign. The character '$' of the COBOL character set.

Currency Symbol. The character defined by the CURRENCY SIGN clause in the SPECIAL-NAMES paragraph. If no CURRENCY SIGN clause is present in a COBOL source program, the currency symbol is identical to the currency sign.

Current Record. In file processing, the record which is available in the record area associated with a file.

Current Volume Pointer. A conceptual entity that points to the current volume of a sequential file.

Data Clause. A clause, appearing in a data description entry in the Data Division of a COBOL program, that provides information describing a particular attribute of a data item.

Data Description Entry. An entry, in the Data Division of a COBOL program, that is composed of a level-number followed by a data-name, if required, and then followed by a set of data clauses, as required.

Data Item. A unit of data (excluding literals) defined by the COBOL program.

Data-Name. A user-defined word that names a data item described in a data description entry. When used in the general formats, 'data-name' represents a word which must not be reference-modified, subscripted, or qualified unless specifically permitted by the rules of the format.

Debugging Line. A debugging line is any line with a 'D' in the indicator area of the line.

Debugging Section. A debugging section is a section that contains a USE FOR DEBUGGING statement.

Declarative Sentence. A compiler directing sentence consisting of a single USE statement terminated by the separator period.

Declaratives. A set of one or more special purpose sections, written at the beginning of the Procedure Division, the first of which is preceded by the key word DECLARATIVES and the last of which is followed by the key words END DECLARATIVES. A declarative is composed of a section header, followed by a USE compiler directing sentence, followed by a set of zero, one, or more associated paragraphs.

De-Edit. The logical removal of all editing characters from a numeric edited data item in order to determine that item's unedited numeric value.

Delimited Scope Statement. Any statement which includes its explicit scope terminator.

Delimiter. A character or a sequence of contiguous characters that identifies the end of a string of characters and separates that string of characters from the following string of characters. A delimiter is not part of the string of characters that it delimits.

Descending Key. A key upon the values of which data is ordered starting with the highest value of key down to the lowest value of key, in accordance with the rules for comparing data items.

Destination. The symbolic identification of the receiver of a transmission from a queue.

Digit Position. A digit position is the amount of physical storage required to store a single digit. This amount may vary depending on the usage specified in the data description entry that defines the data item. If the data description entry specifies that usage is DISPLAY, then a digit position is synonymous with a character position. Further characteristics of the physical storage are defined by the implementor.

Division. A collection of zero, one, or more sections or paragraphs, called the division body, that is formed and combined in accordance with a specific set of rules. Each division consists of the division header and the related division body. There are four divisions in a COBOL program: Identification, Environment, Data, and Procedure.

Division Header. A combination of words, followed by a separator period, that indicates the beginning of a division. The division headers in a COBOL program are:

```
IDENTIFICATION DIVISION.
ENVIRONMENT DIVISION.
DATA DIVISION.
PROCEDURE DIVISION [USING (data-name-1) ... ].
```

Dynamic Access. An access mode in which specific logical records can be obtained from or placed into a mass storage file in a nonsequential manner and obtained from a file in a sequential manner during the scope of the same OPEN statement.

Editing Character. A single character or a fixed two-character combination belonging to the following set:

Character	Meaning
B	space
0	zero
+	plus
−	minus
CR	credit
DB	debit
Z	zero suppress
*	check protect
$	currency sign
,	comma (decimal point)
.	period (decimal point)
/	slant (solidus)

Elementary Item. A data item that is described as not being further logically subdivided.

End of Procedure Division. The physical position of a COBOL source program after which no further procedures appear.

End Program Header. A combination of words, followed by a separator period, that indicates the end of a COBOL source program. The end program header is:

```
END PROGRAM program-name.
```

Entry. Any descriptive set of consecutive clauses terminated by a separator period and written in the Identification Division, Environment Division, or Data Division of a COBOL program.

Environment Clause. A clause that appears as part of an Environment Division entry.

Execution Time. The time at which an object program is executed. The term is synonymous with object time.

Explicit Scope Terminator. A reserved word that terminates the scope of a particular Procedure Division statement.

Expression. An arithmetic or conditional expression.

Extend Mode. The state of a file after execution of an OPEN statement, with the EXTEND phrase specified, for that file and before the execution of a CLOSE statement without the REEL or UNIT phrase for that file.

External Data. The data described in a program as external data items and external file connectors.

External Data Item. A data item which is described as part of an external record in one or more programs of a run unit and which itself may be referenced from any program in which it is described.

External Data Record. A logical record which is described in one or more programs of a run unit and whose constituent data items may be referenced from any program in which they are described.

External File Connector. A file connector which is accessible to one or more object programs in the run unit.

External Switch. A hardware or software device, defined and named by the implementor, which is used to indicate that one of two alternate states exists.

Figurative Constant. A compiler generated value referenced through the use of certain reserved words.

File. A collection of logical records.

File Attribute Conflict Condition. An unsuccessful attempt has been made to execute an input-output operation on a file and the file attributes, as specified for that file in the program, do not match the fixed attributes for that file.

File Clause. A clause that appears as part of any of the following Data Division entries: file description entry (FD entry) and sort-merge file description entry (SD entry).

File Connector. A storage area which contains information about a file and is used as the linkage between a file-name and a physical file and between a file-name and its associated record area.

FILE-CONTROL. The name of an Environment Division paragraph in which the data files for a given source program are declared.

File Control Entry. A SELECT clause and all its subordinate clauses which declare the relevant physical attributes of a file.

File Description Entry. An entry in the File Section of the Data Division that is composed of the level indicator FD, followed by a file-name, and then followed by a set of file clauses as required.

File-Name. A user-defined word that names a file connector described in a file description entry or a sort-merge file description entry within the File Section of the Data Division.

File Organization. The permanent logical file structure established at the time that a file is created.

File Position Indicator. A conceptual entity that contains the value of the current key within the key of reference for an indexed file, or the record number of the current record for a sequential file, or the relative record number of the current record for a relative file, or indicates that no next logical record exists, or that the number of significant digits in the relative record number is larger than the size of the relative key data item, or that an optional input file is not present, or that the at end condition already exists, or that no valid next record has been established.

File Section. The section of the Data Division that contains file description entries and sort-merge file description entries together with their associated record descriptions.

Fixed File Attributes. Information about a file which is established when a file is created and cannot subsequently be changed during the existence of the file. These attributes include the organization of the file (sequential, relative, or indexed), the prime record key, the alternate record keys, the code set, the minimum and maximum record size, the record type (fixed or variable), the collating sequence of the keys for indexed files, the blocking factor, the padding character, and the record delimiter.

Fixed Length Record. A record associated with a file whose file description or sort-merge description entry requires that all records contain the same number of character positions.

Footing Area. The position of the page body adjacent to the bottom margin.

Format. A specific arrangement of a set of data.

Global Name. A name which is declared in only one program but which may be referenced from that program and from any program contained within that program. Condition-names, data-names, file-names, record-names, report-names, and some special registers may be global names.

Group Item. A data item that is composed of subordinate data items.

High Order End. The leftmost character of a string of characters.

I-O-CONTROL. The name of an Environment Division paragraph in which object program requirements for rerun points, sharing of same areas by several data files, and multiple file storage on a single input-output device are specified.

I-O-CONTROL Entry. An entry in the I-O-CONTROL paragraph of the Environment Division which contains clauses which provide information required for the transmission and handling of data on named files during the execution of a program.

I-O Mode. The state of a file after execution of an OPEN statement, with the I-O phrase specified, for that file and before the execution of a CLOSE statement without the REEL or UNIT phrase for that file.

I-O Status. A conceptual entity which contains the two-character value indicating the resulting status of an input-output operation. This value is made available to the program through the use of the FILE STATUS clause in the file control entry for the file.

Identifier. A syntactically correct combination of a data-name, with its qualifiers, subscripts, and reference modifiers, as required for uniqueness of reference, that names a data item. The rules for 'identifier' associated with the general formats may, however, specifically prohibit qualification, subscripting, or reference modification.

Imperative Statement. A statement that either begins with an imperative verb and specifies an unconditional action to be taken or is a conditional statement that is delimited by its explicit scope terminator (delimited scope statement). An imperative statement may consist of a sequence of imperative statements.

Implementor-Name. A system-name that refers to a particular feature available on that implementor's computing system.

Implicit Scope Terminator. A separator period which terminates the scope of any preceding unterminated statement, or a phrase of a statement which by its occurrence indicates the end of the scope of any statement contained within the preceding phrase.

Index. A computer storage area or register, the content of which represents the identification of a particular element in a table.

Index Data Item. A data item in which the values associated with an index-name can be stored in a form specified by the implementor.

Index-Name. A user-defined word that names an index associated with a specific table.

Indexed File. A file with indexed organization.

Indexed Organization. The permanent logical file structure in which each record is identified by the value of one or more keys within that record.

Initial Program. A program that is placed into an initial state every time the program is called in a run unit.

Initial State. The state of a program when it is first called in a run unit.

Input File. A file that is opened in the input mode.

Input Mode. The state of a file after execution of an OPEN statement, with the INPUT phrase specified, for that file and before the execution of a CLOSE statement without the REEL or UNIT phrase for that file.

Input-Output File. A file that is opened in the I-O mode.

Input-Output Section. The section of the Environment Division that names the files and the external media required by an object program and which provides information required for transmission and handling of data during execution of the object program.

Input-Output Statement. A statement that causes files to be processed by performing operations upon individual records or upon the file as a unit. The input-output statements are: ACCEPT (with the identifier phrase), CLOSE, DELETE, DISABLE, DISPLAY, ENABLE, OPEN, PURGE, READ, RECEIVE, REWRITE, SEND, SET (with the TO ON or TO OFF phrase), START, and WRITE.

Input Procedure. A set of statements, to which control is given during the execution of a SORT statement, for the purpose of controlling the release of specified records to be sorted.

Integer.   A numeric literal or a numeric data item that does not include any digit position to the right of the assumed decimal point. When the term 'integer' appears in general formats, integer must not be a numeric data item, and must not be signed, nor zero unless explicitly allowed by the rules of that format.

Internal Data.   The data described in a program excluding all external data items and external file connectors. Items described in the Linkage Section of a program are treated as internal data.

Internal Data Item.   A data item which is described in one program in a run unit. An internal data item may have a global name.

Internal File Connector.   A file connector which is accessible to only one object program in the run unit.

Intra-Record Data Structure.   The entire collection of groups and elementary data items from a logical record which is defined by a contiguous subset of the data description entries which describe that record. These data description entries include all entries whose level-number is greater than the level-number of the first data description entry describing the intra-record data structure.

Invalid Key Condition.   A condition, at object time, caused when a specific value of the key associated with an indexed or relative file is determined to be invalid.

Key.   A data item which identifies the location of a record, or a set of data items which serve to identify the ordering of data.

Key of Reference.   The key, either prime or alternate, currently being used to access records within an indexed file.

Key Word.   A reserved word whose presence is required when the format in which the word appears is used in a source program.

Language-Name.   A system-name that specifies a particular programming language.

Letter.   A character belonging to one of the following two sets: (1) uppercase letters: A, B, C, D, E, F, G, H, I, J, K, L, M, N, O, P, Q, R, S, T, U, V, W, X, Y, Z; (2) lowercase letters: a, b, c, d, e, f, g, h, i, j, k, l, m, n, o, p, q, r, s, t, u, v, w, x, y, z.

Level Indicator.   Two alphabetic characters that identify a specific type of file or a position in a hierarchy. The level indicators in the Data Division are: CD, FD, RD, and SD.

Level-Number.   A user-defined word, expressed as a one- or two-digit number, which indicates the hierarchical position of a data item or the special properties of a data description entry. Level-numbers in the range 1 through 49 indicate the position of a data item in the hierarchical structure of a logical record. Level-numbers in the range 1 through 9 may be written either as a single digit or as a zero followed by a significant digit. Level-numbers 66, 77, and 88 identify special properties of a data description entry.

Library-Name.   A user-defined word that names a COBOL library that is to be used by the compiler for a given source program compilation.

Library Text.   A sequence of text words, comment lines, the separator space, or the separator pseudo-text delimiter in a COBOL library.

LINAGE-COUNTER.   A special register whose value points to the current position within the page body.

Line.   A division of a page representing one row of horizontal character positions. Each character position of a report line is aligned vertically beneath the corresponding character position of the report line above it. Report lines are numbered from 1, by 1, starting at the top of the page. The term is synonymous with report line.

Line Number.   An integer that denotes the vertical position of a report line on a page.

Linkage Section. The section in the Data Division of the called program that describes data items available from the calling program. These data items may be referred to by both the calling and the called program.

Literal. A character-string whose value is implied by the ordered set of characters comprising the string.

Logical Operator. One of the reserved words AND, OR, or NOT. In the formation of a condition, either AND, or OR, or both, can be used as logical connectives. NOT can be used for logical negation.

Logical Page. A conceptual entity consisting of the top margin, the page body, and the bottom margin.

Logical Record. The most inclusive data item. The level-number for a record is 01. A record may be either an elementary item or a group item. The term is synonymous with record.

Low Order End. The rightmost character of a string of characters.

Mass Storage. A storage medium in which data may be organized and maintained in both a sequential and nonsequential manner.

Mass Storage Control System (MSCS). An input-output control system that directs, or controls, the processing of mass storage files.

Mass Storage File. A collection of records that is assigned to a mass storage medium.

MCS. Message control system; a communication control system that supports the processing of messages.

Merge File. A collection of records to be merged by a MERGE statement. The merge file is created and can be used only by the merge function.

Message. Data associated with an end of message indicator or an end of group indicator.

Message Control System (MCS). A communication control system that supports the processing of messages.

Message Count. The count of the number of complete messages that exist in the designated queue of messages.

Message Indicators. EGI (end of group indicator), EMI (end of message indicator), and ESI (end of segment indicator) are conceptual indications that serve to notify the message control system that a specific condition exists (end of group, end of message, or end of segment). Within the hierarchy of EGI, EMI, and ESI, an EGI is conceptually equivalent to an ESI, EMI, and EGI. An EMI is conceptually equivalent to an ESI and EMI. Thus, a segment may be terminated by an ESI, EMI, or EGI. A message may be terminated by an EMI or EGI.

Message Segment. Data that forms a logical subdivision of a message, normally associated with an end of segment indicator.

Mnemonic-Name. A user-defined word that is associated in the Environment Division with a specific implementor-name.

MSCS. Mass storage control system; an input-output control system that directs, or controls, the processing of mass storage files.

Native Character Set. The implementor-defined character set associated with the computer specified in the OBJECT-COMPUTER paragraph.

Native Collating Sequence. The implementor-defined collating sequence associated with the computer specified in the OBJECT-COMPUTER paragraph.

Negated Combined Condition. The 'NOT' logical operator immediately followed by a parenthesized combined condition.

Negated Simple Condition. The 'NOT' logical operator immediately followed by a simple condition.

Next Executable Sentence. The next sentence to which control will be transferred after execution of the current statement is complete.

Next Executable Statement. The next statement to which control will be transferred after execution of the current statement is complete.

Next Record.   The record which logically follows the current record of a file.

Noncontiguous Item.   Elementary data items, in the Working-Storage and Linkage Sections, which bear no hierarchic relationship to other data items.

Nonnumeric Item.   A data item whose description permits its content to be composed of any combination of characters taken from the computer's character set. Certain categories of nonnumeric items may be formed from more restricted character sets.

Nonnumeric Literal.   A literal bounded by quotation marks. The string of characters may include any character in the computer's character set.

Numeric Character.   A character that belongs to the following set of digits: 0, 1, 2, 3, 4, 5, 6, 7, 8, 9.

Numeric Item.   A data item whose description restricts its content to a value represented by characters chosen from the digits '0' through '9'; if signed, the item may also contain a '+', '−', or other representation of an operational sign.

Numeric Literal.   A literal composed of one or more numeric characters that may contain either a decimal point, or an algebraic sign, or both. The decimal point must not be the rightmost character. The algebraic sign, if present, must be the leftmost character.

OBJECT-COMPUTER.   The name of an Environment Division paragraph in which the computer environment, within which the object program is executed, is described.

Object Computer Entry.   An entry in the OBJECT-COMPUTER paragraph of the Environment Division which contains clauses which describe the computer environment in which the object program is to be executed.

Object of Entry.   A set of operands and reserved words, within a Data Division entry of a COBOL program, that immediately follows the subject of the entry.

Object Program.   A set or group of executable machine language instructions and other material designed to interact with data to provide problem solutions. In this context, an object program is generally the machine language result of the operation of a COBOL compiler on a source program. Where there is no danger of ambiguity, the word 'program' alone may be used in place of the phrase 'object program.'

Object Time.   The time at which an object program is executed. The term is synonymous with execution time.

Obsolete Element.   A COBOL language element in Standard COBOL that is to be deleted from the next revision of Standard COBOL.

Open Mode.   The state of a file after execution of an OPEN statement for that file and before the execution of a CLOSE statement without the REEL or UNIT phrase for that file. The particular open mode is specified in the OPEN statement as either INPUT, OUTPUT, I-O, or EXTEND.

Operand.   Whereas the general definition of operand is 'that component which is operated upon,' for the purposes of this document, any lowercase word (or words) that appears in a statement or entry format may be considered to be an operand and, as such, is an implied reference to the data indicated by the operand.

Operational Sign.   An algebraic sign, associated with a numeric data item or a numeric literal, to indicate whether its value is positive or negative.

Optional File.   A file which is declared as being not necessarily present each time the object program is executed. The object program causes an interrogation for the presence or absence of the file.

Optional Word.   A reserved word that is included in a specific format only to improve the readability of the language and whose presence is optional to the user when the format in which the word appears is used in a source program.

Output File.   A file that is opened in either the output mode or extend mode.

Output Mode. The state of a file after execution of an OPEN statement, with the OUTPUT or EXTEND phrase specified, for that file and before the execution of a CLOSE statement without the REEL or UNIT phrase for that file.

Output Procedure. A set of statements to which control is given during execution of a SORT statement after the sort function is completed, or during execution of a MERGE statement after the merge function reaches a point at which it can select the next record in merged order when requested.

Padding Character. An alphanumeric character used to fill the unused character positions in a physical record.

Page. A vertical division of a report representing a physical separation of report data, the separation being based on internal reporting requirements and/or external characteristics of the reporting medium.

Page Body. That part of the logical page in which lines can be written and/or spaced.

Page Footing. A report group that is presented at the end of a report page as determined by the report writer control system.

Page Heading. A report group that is presented at the beginning of a report page as determined by the report writer control system.

Paragraph. In the Procedure Division, a paragraph-name followed by a separator period and by zero, one, or more sentences. In the Identification and Environment Divisions, a paragraph header followed by zero, one, or more entries.

Paragraph Header. A reserved word, followed by the separator period, that indicates the beginning of a paragraph in the Identification and Environment Divisions. The permissible paragraph headers in the Identification Division are:

```
PROGRAM-ID.
AUTHOR.
INSTALLATION.
DATE-WRITTEN.
DATE-COMPILED.
SECURITY.
```

The permissible paragraph headers in the Environment Division are:

```
SOURCE-COMPUTER.
OBJECT-COMPUTER.
SPECIAL-NAMES.
FILE-CONTROL.
I-O-CONTROL.
```

Paragraph-Name. A user-defined word that identifies and begins a paragraph in the Procedure Division.

Phrase. A phrase is an ordered set of one or more consecutive COBOL character-strings that form a portion of a COBOL procedural statement or of a COBOL clause.

Physical Page. A device dependent concept defined by the implementor.

Physical Record. The term is synonymous with block.

Prime Record Key. A key whose contents uniquely identify a record within an indexed file.

Printable Group. A report group that contains at least one print line.

Printable Item. A data item, the extent and contents of which are specified by an elementary report entry. This elementary report entry contains a COLUMN NUMBER clause, a PICTURE clause, and a SOURCE, SUM, or VALUE clause.

Procedure. A paragraph or group of logically successive paragraphs, or a section or group of logically successive sections, within the Procedure Division.

Procedure Branching Statement. A statement that causes the explicit transfer of control to a statement other than the next executable statement in the sequence in which the statements are written in the source program. The procedure branching statements are: ALTER, CALL, EXIT, EXIT PROGRAM, GO TO, MERGE (with the OUTPUT PROCEDURE phrase), PERFORM and SORT (with the INPUT PROCEDURE or OUTPUT PROCEDURE phrase).

Procedure-Name. A user-defined word which is used to name a paragraph or section in the Procedure Division. It consists of a paragraph-name (which may be qualified), or a section-name.

Program Identification Entry. An entry in the PROGRAM-ID paragraph of the Identification Division which contains clauses that specify the program-name and assign selected program attributes to the program.

Program-Name. In the Identification Division and the end program header, a user-defined word that identifies a COBOL source program.

Pseudo-Text. A sequence of text words, comment lines, or the separator space in a source program or COBOL library bounded by, but not including, pseudo-text delimiters.

Pseudo-Text Delimiter. Two contiguous equal sign (=) characters used to delimit pseudo-text.

Punctuation Character. A character that belongs to the following set:

Character	Meaning
,	comma
;	semicolon
:	colon
.	period (full stop)
"	quotation mark
(	left parenthesis
)	right parenthesis
	space
=	equal sign

Qualified Data-Name. An identifier that is composed of a data-name followed by one or more sets of either of the connectives OF or IN, followed by a data-name qualifier.

Qualifier.

1. A data-name or a name associated with a level indicator which is used in a reference either together with another data-name which is the name of an item that is subordinate to the qualifier or together with a condition-name.
2. A section-name which is used in a reference together with a paragraph-name specified in that section.
3. A library-name which is used in a reference together with a text-name associated with that library.

Queue. A logical collection of messages awaiting transmission or processing.

Queue Name. A symbolic name that indicates to the message control system the logical path by which a message or a portion of a completed message may be accessible in a queue.

Random Access. An access mode in which the program-specified value of a key data item identifies the logical record that is obtained from, deleted from, or placed into a relative or indexed file.

Record. The most inclusive data item. The level-number for a record is 01. A record may be either an elementary item or a group item. The term is synonymous with logical record.

Record Area. A storage area allocated for the purpose of processing the record described in a record description entry in the File Section of the Data Division. In the File Section, the current number of character positions in the record area is determined by the explicit or implicit RECORD clause.

Record Description. The total set of data description entries associated with a particular record. The term is synonymous with record description entry.

Record Description Entry. The total set of data description entries associated with a particular record. The term is synonymous with record description.

Record Key. A key whose contents identify a record within an indexed file. Within an indexed file, a record key is either the prime record key or an alternate record key.

Record-Name. A user-defined word that names a record described in a record description entry in the Data Division of a COBOL program.

Record Number. The ordinal number of a record in the file whose organization is sequential.

Reel. A discrete portion of a storage medium, the dimensions of which are determined by each implementor, that contains part of a file, all of a file, or any number of files. The term is synonymous with unit and volume.

Reference Format. A format that provides a standard method for describing COBOL source programs.

Reference Modifier. The leftmost-character-position and length used to establish and reference a data item.

Relation. The term is synonymous with relational operator.

Relation Character. A character that belongs to the following set:

Character	Meaning
>	greater than
<	less than
=	equal to

Relation Condition. The proposition, for which a truth value can be determined, that the value of an arithmetic expression, data item, nonnumeric literal, or index-name has a specific relationship to the value of another arithmetic expression, data item, nonnumeric literal, or index-name.

Relational Operator. A reserved word, a relation character, a group of consecutive reserved words, or a group of consecutive reserved words and relation characters used in the construction of a relation condition. The permissible operators and their meanings are:

Relational Operator	*Meaning*
IS [NOT] GREATER THAN IS [NOT] >	Greater than or not greater than
IS [NOT] LESS THAN IS [NOT] <	Less than or not less than
IS [NOT] EQUAL TO IS [NOT] =	Equal to or not equal to
IS GREATER THAN OR EQUAL TO IS >=	Greater than or equal to
IS LESS THAN OR EQUAL TO IS <=	Less than or equal to

Relative File. A file with relative organization.

Relative Key. A key whose contents identify a logical record in a relative file.

Relative Organization. The permanent logical file structure in which each record is uniquely identified by an integer value greater than zero, which specifies the record's logical ordinal position in the file.

Relative Record Number. The ordinal number of a record in a file whose organization is relative. This number is treated as a numeric literal which is an integer.

Report Clause. A clause, in the Report Section of the Data Division, that appears in a report description entry or a report group description entry.

Report Description Entry. An entry in the Report Section of the Data Division that is composed of the level indicator RD, followed by the report-name, followed by a set of report clauses as required.

Report File. An output file whose file description entry contains a REPORT clause. The contents of a report file consist of records that are written under control of the report writer control system.

Report Footing. A report group that is presented only at the end of a report.

Report Group. In the Report Section of the Data Division, an 01 level-number entry and its subordinate entries.

Report Group Description Entry. An entry in the Report Section of the Data Division that is composed of the level-number 01, an optional data-name, a TYPE clause, and an optional set of report clauses.

Report Heading. A report group that is presented only at the beginning of a report.

Report Line. A division of a page representing one row of horizontal character positions. Each character position of a report line is aligned vertically beneath the corresponding character position of the report line above it. Report lines are numbered from 1, by 1, starting at the top of the page.

Report-Name. A user-defined word that names a report described in a report description entry within the Report Section of the Data Division.

Report Section. The section of the Data Division that contains zero, one, or more report description entries and their associated report group description entries.

Report Writer Control System (RWCS). An object time control system, provided by the implementor, that accomplishes the construction of reports.

Report Writer Logical Record. A record that consists of the report writer print line and associated control information necessary for its selection and vertical positioning.

Reserved Word. A COBOL word specified in the list of words which may be used in a COBOL source program, but which must not appear in the program as user-defined words or system-names.

Resource. A facility or service, controlled by the operating system, that can be used by an executing program.

Resultant Identifier. A user-defined data item that is to contain the result of an arithmetic operation.

Routine-Name. A user-defined word that identifies a procedure written in a language other than COBOL.

Run Unit. One or more object programs which interact with one another and which function, at object time, as an entity to provide problem solutions.

RWCS. Report writer control system; an object time control system, provided by the implementor, that accomplishes the construction of reports.

Section. A set of zero, one, or more paragraphs or entries, called a section body, the first of which is preceded by a section header. Each section consists of the section header and the related section body.

Section Header. A combination of words followed by a separator period that indicates the beginning of a section in the Environment, Data, and Procedure Division. In the Environment and Data Divisions, a section header is composed of reserved words followed by a separator period. The permissible section headers in the Environment Division are:

```
CONFIGURATION SECTION.
INPUT-OUTPUT SECTION.
```

The permissible section headers in the Data Division are:

```
FILE SECTION.
WORKING-STORAGE SECTION.
LINKAGE SECTION.
COMMUNICATION SECTION.
REPORT SECTION.
```

In the Procedure Division, a section header is composed of a section-name, followed by the reserved word SECTION, followed by a segment-number (optional), followed by a separator period.

Section-Name. A user-defined word that names a section in the Procedure Division.

Segment-Number. A user-defined word which classifies sections in the Procedure Division for purposes of segmentation. Segment-numbers may contain only the characters '0', '1', . . . , '9'. A segment-number may be expressed either as a one- or two-digit number.

Sentence. A sequence of one or more statements, the last of which is terminated by a separator period.

Separately Compiled Program.   A program which, together with its contained programs, is compiled separately from all other programs.

Separator.   A charactor or two contiguous characters used to delimit character-strings.

Sequential Access.   An access mode in which logical records are obtained from or placed into a file in a consecutive predecessor-to-successor logical record sequence determined by the order of records in the file.

Sequential File.   A file with sequential organization.

Sequential Organization.   The permanent logical file structure in which a record is identified by a predecessor-successor relationship established when the record is placed into the file.

Sign Condition.   The proposition, for which a truth value can be determined, that the algebraic value of a data item or an arithmetic expression is either less than, greater than, or equal to zero.

Simple Condition.   Any single condition chosen from the set:

relation condition
class condition
condition-name condition
switch-status condition
sign condition
(simple-condition)

Sort File.   A collection of records to be sorted by a SORT statement. The sort file is created and can be used by the sort function only.

Sort-Merge File Description Entry.   An entry in the File Section of the Data Division that is composed of the level indicator SD, followed by a file-name, and then followed by a set of file clauses as required.

Source.   The symbolic identification of the originator of a transmission to a queue.

SOURCE-COMPUTER.   The name of an Environment Division paragraph in which the computer environment, within which the source program is compiled, is described.

Source Computer Entry.   An entry in the SOURCE-COMPUTER paragraph of the Environment Division which contains clauses which describe the computer environment in which the source program is to be compiled.

Source Item.   An identifier designated by a SOURCE clause that provides the value of a printable item.

Source Program.   Although it is recognized that a source program may be represented by other forms and symbols, in this document it always refers to a syntactically correct set of COBOL statements. A COBOL source program commences with the Identification Division, a COPY statement, or a REPLACE statement. A COBOL source program is terminated by the end program header, if specified, or by the absence of additional source program lines.

Special Character. A character that belongs to the following set:

Character	Meaning
+	plus sign
−	minus sign
*	asterisk
/	slant (solidus)
=	equal sign
$	currency sign
,	comma (decimal point)
;	semicolon
.	period (decimal point, full stop)
"	quotation mark
(	left parenthesis
)	right parenthesis
>	greater than symbol
<	less than symbol
:	colon

Special Character Word. A reserved word which is an arithmetic operator or a relation character.

SPECIAL-NAMES. The name of an Environment Division paragraph in which implementor-names are related to user-specified mnemonic-names.

Special Names Entry. An entry in the SPECIAL-NAMES paragraph of the Environment Division which provides means for specifying the currency sign; choosing the decimal point; specifying symbolic characters; relating implementor-names to user-specified mnemonic-names; relating alphabet-names to character sets or collating sequences; and relating class-names to sets of characters.

Special Registers. Certain compiler-generated storage areas whose primary use is to store information produced in conjunction with the use of specific COBOL features.

Standard Data Format. The concept used in describing data in a COBOL Data Division under which the characteristics or properties of the data are expressed in a form oriented to the appearance of the data on a printed page of infinite length and breadth, rather than a form oriented to the manner in which the data is stored internally in the computer or on a particular medium.

Statement. A syntactically valid combination of words, literals, and separators, beginning with a verb, written in a COBOL source program.

Sub-Queue. A logical hierarchical division of a queue.

Subject of Entry. An operand or reserved word that appears immediately following the level indicator or the level-number in a Data Division entry.

Subprogram. A program which is the object of a CALL statement combined at object time with the calling program to produce a run unit. The term is synonymous with called program.

Subscript. An occurrence number represented by either an integer, a data-name optionally followed by an integer with the operator + or −, or an index-name optionally followed by an integer with the operator + or −, which identifies a particular element in a table.

Subscripted Data-Name. An identifier that is composed of a data-name followed by one or more subscripts enclosed in parentheses.

Sum Counter. A signed numeric data item established by a SUM clause in the Report Section of the Data Division. The sum counter is used by the Report Writer Control System to contain the result of designated summing operations that take place during production of a report.

Switch-Status Condition. The proposition, for which a truth value can be determined, that an implementor-defined switch, capable of being set to an 'on' or 'off' status, has been set to a specific status.

Symbolic-Character. A user-defined word that specifies a user-defined figurative constant.

System-Name. A COBOL word which is used to communicate with the operating environment.

Table. A set of logically consecutive items of data that are defined in the Data Division of a COBOL program by means of the OCCURS clause.

Table Element. A data item that belongs to the set of repeated items comprising a table.

Terminal. The originator of a transmission to a queue, or the receiver of a transmission from a queue.

Text-Name. A user-defined word which identifies library text.

Text Word. A character or a sequence of contiguous characters between margin A and margin R in a COBOL library, source program, or in pseudo-text, which is:

1. A separator, except for: space; a pseudo-text delimiter; and the opening and closing delimiters for nonnumeric literals. The right parenthesis and left parenthesis characters, regardless of context within the library, source program, or pseudo-text, are always considered text words.
2. A literal including, in the case of nonnumeric literals, the opening quotation mark and the closing quotation mark which bound the literal.
3. Any other sequence of contiguous COBOL characters except comment lines and the word 'COPY,' bounded by separators, which is neither a separator nor a literal.

Top Margin. An empty area which precedes the page body.

Truth Value. The representation of the result of the evaluation of a condition in terms of one of two values:

true
false.

Unary Operator. A plus $(+)$ or a minus $(-)$ sign, which precedes a variable or a left parenthesis in an arithmetic expression and which has the effect of multiplying the expression by $+1$ or -1 respectively.

Unit. A discrete portion of a storage medium, the dimensions of which are determined by each implementor, that contains part of a file, all of a file, or any number of files. The term is synonymous with reel and volume.

Unsuccessful Execution. The attempted execution of a statement that does not result in the execution of all the operations specified by that statement. The unsuccessful execution of a statement does not affect any data referenced by that statement, but may affect status indicators.

User-Defined Word. A COBOL word that must be supplied by the user to satisfy the format of a clause or statement.

Variable. A data item whose value may be changed by execution of the object program. A variable used in an arithmetic-expression must be a numeric elementary item.

Variable Length Record. A record associated with a file whose file description or sort-merge description entry permits records to contain a varying number of character positions.

Variable Occurrence Data Item. A variable occurrence data item is a table element which is repeated a variable number of times. Such an item must contain an OCCURS DEPENDING ON clause in its data description entry, or be subordinate to such an item.

Verb. A word that expresses an action to be taken by a COBOL compiler or object program.

Volume. A discrete portion of a storage medium, the dimensions of which are determined by each implementor, that contains part of a file, all of a file, or any number of files. The term is synonymous with reel and unit.

Word. A character-string of not more than 30 characters which forms a user-defined word, a system-name, or a reserved word.

Working-Storage Section. The section of the Data Division that describes working storage data items, composed of either noncontiguous items or working storage records, or of both.

77-Level-Description-Entry. A data description entry that describes a non-contiguous data item with the level-number 77.

Index